Blue Book of
Acoustic Guitars™
8

by Zachary R. Fjestad
Edited by S.P. Fjestad

$24.95
Publisher's Softcover
Suggested List Price

Publisher's Limited
Edition Hardcover
Suggested List Price - $44.95

8th Edition Blue Book of Acoustic Guitars™

Publisher's Note: This book is the result of nonstop and continual guitar research obtained by attending guitar shows, receiving contributing editor's updates, communicating with guitar dealers and collectors throughout the country each year, and staying on top of trends as they occur. This book represents an analysis of prices and information on current manufacture, recently manufactured, and vintage/collectible guitars.

Although every reasonable effort has been made to compile an accurate and reliable guide, guitar prices may vary significantly depending on such factors as the locality of the sale, the number of sales we were able to consider, famous musician endorsement of certain makes/models, regional economic conditions, and other critical factors.

Accordingly, no representation can be made that the guitars listed may be bought or sold at prices indicated, nor shall the editor or publisher be responsible for any error made in compiling and recording such prices.

Blue Book Publications, Inc.
8009 34th Avenue South, Suite 175
Minneapolis, MN 55425 U.S.A.
Phone: 800-877-4867 (USA and Canada orders only)
Phone: 952-854-5229
Fax: 952-853-1486
Email: guitars@bluebookinc.com
Web site: http://www.bluebookinc.com

Published and printed in the United States of America
ISBN No. 1-886768-33-1
Library of Congress ISSN Number: Pending

Distributed in part by Music Sales Corporation and Omnibus Press
Order # BP10048
257 Park Avenue South, New York, NY 10010 USA
Phone: 212.254.2100; Fax: 212.254.2013
Email: 71360.3514@compuserve.com

8th Edition *Blue Book of Acoustic Guitars* Credits

Production Manager & Art Director - Clint Schmidt
Cover Layout & Design - Tom Heller
Copyeditor - Heather Mohr
Executive Assistant Editor - Cassandra Faulkner
Cover Photography & Design - Clint Schmidt, Tom Heller, & S.P. Fjestad
Printer - Bang Printing, Brainerd, MN

This publication was published and printed in the United States of America.

CONTENTS

Many of you have probably purchased products from Blue Book Publications, Inc. over the years, and it may be helpful for you to know more about the company operation and what we are currently publishing, both in books and software. We are also the leaders in online informational services in various fields of collectibles, including guns and pool cues. As this edition goes to press, the following titles, products, and services are currently available. All pricing is in U.S. dollars, and does not include any shipping charges. Many of these softcover editions are also available in hardcover deluxe editions. Please check our web site for more information, including the most current availablility, pricing, and S/H charges on all titles.

8th Edition *Blue Book of Electric Guitars* by Zachary R. Fjestad, edited by S.P. Fjestad - $29.95
8th Edition *Blue Book of Acoustic Guitars* by Zachary R. Fjestad, edited by S.P. Fjestad - $24.95
2nd Edition *Blue Book of Guitar Amplifiers* by Zachary R. Fjestad, edited by S.P. Fjestad - $24.95
8th Editions *Blue Book of Guitars* CD-ROM (includes information from both books) with inventory program - $19.95

The Nethercutt Collection - The Cars of San Sylmar by Dennis Adler (deluxe hardcover with slipcase) - $65.00

24th Edition *Blue Book of Gun Values* by S.P. Fjestad (also available on CD-ROM) - $39.95
3rd Edition *Blue Book of Airguns* by John Allen & Dr. Robert Beeman, edited by S.P. Fjestad - $24.95
3rd Edition *Blue Book of Modern Black Powder Values* by John Allen - $24.95
Colt Black Powder Reproductions & Replicas by Dennis Adler - $14.95
Parker Gun Identification & Serialization compiled by Charlie Price & S.P. Fjestad - $34.95

3rd Edition *Blue Book of Pool Cues* by Martyne S. Bachmen & Brad Simpson (to be published Spring, 2004)

Online Guitar, Gun, and Pool Cue Services: www.bluebookinc.com

If you would like to order or get more information about any of the above publications/products, simply contact us at:

Blue Book Publications, Inc.
8009 34th Avenue South, Suite 175
Minneapolis, MN 55425 USA
www.bluebookinc.com
800-877-4867 (toll free domestic)
952-854-5229 (non-domestic) • Fax: 952-853-1486

Since our phone system has been updated to auto-attendant technology, please follow the prompts and use the following extension numbers when contacting our staff:

Ext. No.: 10 - Beth Marthaler	bethm@bluebookinc.com	Ext. No.: 17 - Zachary Fjestad	zachf@bluebookinc.com
Ext. No.: 11 - Katie Sandin	katies@bluebookinc.com	Ext. No.: 18 - Tom Stock	toms@bluebookinc.com
Ext. No.: 12 - John Andraschko	johnand@bluebookinc.com	Ext. No.: 19 - Cassandra Faulkner	cassandraf@bluebookinc.com
Ext. No.: 13 - S.P. Fjestad	stevef@bluebookinc.com	Ext. No.: 22 - Heather Mohr	heatherm@bluebookinc.com
Ext. No.: 15 - Clint Schmidt	clints@bluebookinc.com	Ext. No.: 27 - Shipping	
Ext. No.: 16 - John Allen	johna@bluebookinc.com		

Office hours are: 8:30 a.m. - 5:00 p.m. CST, Monday - Friday.
Orders Only: 800-877-4867, Phone No.: 952-854-5229
Additionally, an automated message service is also available for both ordering and leaving messages.
Fax No.: 952-853-1486 (available 24 hours a day)
Email: guitars@bluebookinc.com (checked several times daily)
Web site: http://www.bluebookinc.com

We would like to thank all of you for your business in the past – you are the reason(s) we are successful. Our goal remains the same, to give you the best products, the most accurate and up-to-date information for the money, and the highest level of customer service available in today's marketplace. If something's right, tell the world over time. If something's wrong, please tell us immediately.

ACKNOWLEDGMENTS

Whenever possible, the *Blue Book of Acoustic Guitars* has listed proper reference sources within a section (see Guitar Reference & Periodicals pages for complete listings). These books are invaluable resources for gaining additional knowledge within separate fields and cover the wide variety of today's guitar marketplace.

CONTRIBUTING EDITORS

The editor and publisher extends a special thanks to those Contributing Editors listed below who took their valuable time to make important revisions, corrections, and additions – all making this a better publication. We couldn't have done it without them.

Fred Oster
Dave Hull
Dr. Tom Van Hoose
Michael Jones - Michael Jones
Vintage Guitars
Walter Carter
Dave Rogers, Eddy Thurston, and the
rest of the crew at Dave's Guitar Shop

Jim Fisch
Jay Pilzer
Gurney Brown
Robert & Carol Hartman
Rick Wilkiewicz
Jack Wadsworth - Ft. Worth, TX
Keith Smart
 - Zematis Guitar Owners Club

Dave Hinson - Killer Vintage
Jay Wolfe - Wolfe Guitars
Henry Lowenstein
Doug Tulloch
Scott Sanders
Jim Speros
Kwinn Kastrosky
David Newell

John Beeson - The Music Shoppe
Rick Powell - Mars Music
Larry Briggs
Walter Murray - Frankenstein
Fretworks
R. Steven Graves
Stan Jay - Mandolin Bros.

FACTORY SUPPORT & ASSISTANCE

The following factory people really went out of their way (as if they're not busy enough already) to either give us or track down the information we requested. A special thanks to all of you for your unselfishness – there's no greater gift than someone's time.

Lon Werner & Dick Boak
 - Martin Guitar Company
Robert & Cindy Benedetto
 - Benedetto Archtop Guitars
Paul Jernigan - Fender
Ren Ferguson, Vic Russelavage, Sam

Catalona, Thom Fowle, David Rohrer,
Rick Gembar, Cindy Bowker, David
Schenk - Gibson
Will Jones - Epiphone
Ray Memmel
 - Brian Moore Custom Guitars

Injae Park - Crafter
Tom Wayne & David Brown - Yamaha
Steve Helgeson - Moonstone
Andy Robinson - Taylor
Jim Donahue - Ibanez
Ziggy - Tacoma Guitars

Tommy Thomasson - Rickenbacker
International Corp.
Chuck Phillips - St. Louis Music
Frank Rindone - Hamer
Tom Anderson & Laurie Berg
 - Tom Anderson Guitarworks

ADVISORY BOARD

In addition to the above listed contributing editors and factory support and assistance personnel, the Advisory Board members listed below are generally people who let us pick their sometimes tortured and demented brains. We highly value their range of attitudes and opinions (no shortage there). Very little 9-5 mentality here! These elite, card-carrying members pretty much span the humanitarian gamut in guitar intelligence (guitarded?). Occasionally, you might even see some cocktails exchanged among various members of this group, sometimes disguised as rogues lurking in the dark shadows, boisterously discussing their next move on the ever-changing guitar chessboard! Thanks to the following, you really helped us out!

Chris F. Martin IV
 - C.F. Martin & Co.
Robert and Cindy (they work
weekends!) Benedetto
 - Benedetto Archtop Guitars
John and Rhonda Kinnemire
 - JK Lutherie
Trent Salter - Musician's Hotline
Charles H. Chapman
Rick Powell - Guitar Center
Rick Turner
Don & Jeff Lace - Lace Music
Products
Texas Amigos
 - John Brinkmann, Dave Crocker,

& Eugene Robertson
Joe Lamond & Larry Linkin
 - NAMM
Willie G. Moseley
Paul Day
George Gruhn - Gruhn's Guitars
Jimmy "the Wilbur" & Ryan "Lil'
Wilbur" Triggs - Triggs Guitars
Mark Pollock & Jimmy Wallace
 - Dallas Guitar Show
Marco Nobili
 - Guitar Club magazine, Italy
Ray Matusa, Lawrence and James
Acunto
 - 20th Century Guitar magazine

Greg Rich
Norm Harris - Norman's Rare Guitars
Paul Riario
 - Guitar World magazine
Tom "Murphdog" Murphy
 - Guitar Preservation
Dave Amato
 - lead guitarist, REO Speedwagon
Seymour Duncan
 - Seymour Duncan Pickups
Lisa Sharken
 - Guitar Shop magazine
Jeff "Skunk" Baxter - Steely Dan
Ray Kennedy
Chad Speck - Encore Music

Pete Wagener
 - LaVonne Wagener Music
Nate Westgor
 - Willie's American Guitars
The Podium - Minneapolis, MN
Ari Latella - Toys From the Attic
Rock and Roll Hall of Fame
Museum, Cleveland, OH
Steven A. Wilson
 - Music Sales Corp.

PHOTO ACKNOWLEDGEMENTS

The following people/companies provided instruments and advice for this edition's Photo Grading System (pages 33-48). Thanks again!

Dave Rogers - Dave's Guitar Shop
John Beeson - The Music Shoppe
Willie's American Guitars

Dale Hanson
George McGuire
Glenn Wetterland

Clint Schmidt
Zachary Fjestad

And thanks to all the dealers, collectors, and individuals who have been nice enough to let the digital "drive by catch & release" photo crew from Blue Book Publications, Inc. photograph their guitar(s) that have been included in the A-Z sections. We haven't lost/damaged an instrument yet!

Blue Book Publications would also like to send out a special thanks to John Beeson and Erick Johnson from The Music Shoppe for substantial help to our photos in the book. Without Erick, Clint and Zach would still be putting stuff away in Terre Haute! We would also like to thank the good folk in LaCrosse at Dave's Guitar Shop for letting us set up shop. Thanks again guys!

ACKNOWLEDGMENTS

GUITAR GROUPIE GASTRONOMICAL GUIDEBOOK

Yeeha cowboys! Traveling around the world meeting thousands of guitar perverts annually is no easy task. After the shows close, we like to head out to the cool spots, and then the real work begins. Here are a few of our favorite places that haven't kicked us out (yet). Tell 'em that we sent ya!

Jimmy Kelly's - Nashville, TN (a must, especially B-days!)

The Angry Dog Restaurant & Blue Cat Blues - Deep Ellum, TX (happiness guaranteed with the Angry Chicken sandwich)

Axel's River Grille - Mendota, MN (the walleye is a must, plus guitar slingers allowed on patio)

Cigar Box - Kansas City, KS (Wilbur's favorite, next to the titty bar - don't miss Frank or the chicken caesar salad!)

Tootsie's on Broadway - Nashville, TN (way too much fun)

Vienna, Austria (the wiener schnitzel - anywhere!)

Kincaid's - Ft. Worth, TX (best low rent burger in the U.S.?)

Bobby Van's on Park Ave. - NYC (America's greatest steak, bring buck$)

Gene & Georgetti's on Franklin - Chicago, IL (they need a good salad to be #1)

The Biker Bar north of Malibu on Hwy. 1 (greasy food, anything can/does happen)

Mike's Butcher Shop - St. Paul, MN (it's the meat, stupid)

McDonald's - 79th & Nicollet Bloomington, MN (you could say we are regulars)

ABOUT THE COVER

This edition's cover features a National Reso-Phonic Style 4 Tricone from National Reso-Phonic Guitars, located in San Luis Obispo, California.

A fine tribute to the early models manufactured during the 1920s, the National Style 4 features highly elaborate chrysanthemum engraving, ebony fingerboard, diamond pearl inlays, nickel-plated brass body, mahogany neck, ivoroid headstock overlay and heelcap, and vintage three-on-a-plate tuners on slotted headstock.

The original Style 4 was introduced in 1928, with a retail price of $195. If you are lucky enough to have one, it is quite rare and highly sought after. National's top-of-the-line model, the Style 4 was used only on Hawaiian and Spanish Tricone guitars. The original advertising of the day claimed purchases of the Style 4 by "royal families worldwide." Most original Style 4 Tricones date from 1928-1932, with sales falling off after that. Later models had a Plexiglas pickguard.

The original elaborate chrysanthemum pattern was reportedly designed by vaudeville guitar player George Beauchamp. John Dopyera started the National Stringed Instrument Co. in the mid 1920s in Los Angeles, California, which produced the first National resonator guitars. George Beauchamp was his partner. Beauchamp is also credited with resonator guitar innovation. National's mechanically amplified heyday came to an end in the mid 1930s when the electric guitar became the choice for many musicians.

One of the early artists to use the Style 4 Tricone was Tampa Red, the first black blues player to make a record with a National guitar. Tampa later became perhaps the most recorded bottleneck guitarist of the 1930s-40s and was one of the first Southern black players to establish a recording career in Chicago. Tampa Red's Style 4 was gold plated, hence the nickname "The Man with the Gold Guitar." He recorded with another Style 4 artist, Georgia Tom (Dorsey), who later became a well-known gospel composer and performer. Their first tune, "It's Tight Like That," recorded on the Vocalion label, became a huge hit, netted the duo an unheard of $2,400 royalty.

During the late 1980s, the National style resonator guitar came to life again when Don Young and McGregor Gaines formed the National Reso-Phonic Guitars company. National instruments are used by slide players and fingerpickers in many musical genres: Hawaiian, blues, country, bluegrass, folk, and world music.

Many of today's performing and recording artists appreciate the style, tone, and feel of National's resonator instruments. National also supports two non-profit organizations dedicated to assisting forgotten blues and folk musicians. One is the Music Maker Relief Foundation, which helps the true pioneers of Southern musical traditions with food, shelter, medical care, and other assistance – visit www.musicmaker.org. The other is BluesAid, created to help the aging population of blues artists with healthcare and memorial expenses. Since many of these influential blues men and women did not receive royalties for their music and have not fared well financially, BluesAid is dedicated to helping them receive much needed medical and other assistance (P.O. Box 237, Helena, AR, 72342, or email at: jpillow@ipa.net.)

The *Blue Book of Acoustic Guitars* encourages you to support these non-profit organizations and others like them to help keep the music you love alive, and to pay proper tribute and respect to those artists who first brought this music to life. ■

Guitar courtesy of Willie's American Guitars. Information courtesy National Reso-Phonics Guitars and *The History & Artistry of National Resonator Instruments* by Bob Brozman. Special thanks to Marie Gaines from National Reso-Phonics Guitars.

FOREWORD

Sesame Street's most famous music supporter, Elmo, with Editor & Publisher S.P. Fjestad at the recent Nashville NAMM Show.

For those of you who think that not a lot can change in two years, (the last time this acoustic foreword was published), New York City now has 20 acres of vacant space due to 9/11, our economy is trying to pull out of a recession, and the ongoing conflicts in both Afghanistan and Iraq have affected all of us immensely. It's a different world now, and we're all still adjusting.

This newest 8th Edition *Blue Book of Acoustic Guitars* continues to set the standard for the amount of acoustic guitar information and pricing in a single publication. Our all new digital color Photo Grading System™ (PGS) remains the standard for determining the proper grading of instruments. Many B&W photos have also been added within the text, while the important Trademark Index has been thoroughly updated. Now with almost 600 pages, the 8th Edition *Blue Book of Acoustic Guitars* continues to give you more volume using the same power.

The biggest news for the 8th editions is that my nephew, Zachary, has taken over as author of both books – no small job. I guess it's probably the result of him attending trade shows with me since he was 13. His first trade show was the American Booksellers Association Book Expo in Chicago, and the labor union wouldn't let him in for exhibitor set up because he was too young! A lot has happened since then, and it's really nice to have someone in house that can maintain these huge databases adequately. Both 8th editions have been thoroughly updated and revised. Setting corrections alone took almost 4 days, and once again, these reference books will become the standard of the guitar industry for up-to-date information and pricing.

New Acoustic Guitar Marketplace Overview

As a general overview, better quality new guitars from a major trademark/manufacturer will hold their value considerably better than an equally priced product from a little known company in the secondary marketplace. Many domestic companies continue to seek manufacturing alternatives in the Pacific Rim countries, with the most popular being Japan, China, South Korea, Indonesia, and Malaysia. Since many of these overseas companies now have years/decades of manufacturing experience, the quality of their instrument is perhaps the best it's ever been. And the quality comes at a price point that is very attractive for the potential buyer. Only the decreasing value of the dollar has hurt the competitive price points on these recent imports.

Because of the overall large demand factor, Gibsons, Martins, and Taylors will always have secondary marketplace appeal due to both trademark notoriety and a high level of quality. You can't charge extra for something that you don't have yet - a reputation!

How about all the new luthiers and companies that manufacture a much lower quantity of instruments annually? Who are these guitars sold to? Not to dealers – except maybe occasionally at a smaller 10%-15% discount. They're mostly sold to individuals, who typically custom order them at little or no discount. There are no MAPs (minimum advertised prices). So what's the gig here? Obviously, this is a much different economic scenario than the big dogs. These smaller manufacturers/companies are selling directly to consumers – most do not have a dealer base, and the majority of their sales are custom orders. Buying a custom order acoustic archtop from Mark Campellone is typically going to be a lot more expensive than one from a luthier most people don't recognize. However, with so many custom luthiers making instruments these days, there seems to be a glut of these newer, custom-made instruments, and the demand for the top end of this marketplace certainly hasn't increased over the past several years.

So how's the vintage marketplace doing overall?

As one of our contributing editors aptly put it, "With the popularity of Ebay, now everyone thinks they're a dealer." Good original Martins, Gibsons, D'Angelicos, and even the newer D'Aquistos, in addition to other recognized vintage acoustic instruments are still doing well in holding and/or increasing their value. As an example, a pre-war D-28 herringbone in Excellent condition has gone up over $15,000 in the past several years. Know what you're doing and who you're doing it with, as there are a lot of ways you can end up with expensive kindling if you don't do your homework these days.

In closing, we hope that you will appreciate and use the information contained within these pages. The sister publication, the 8th Edition *Blue Book of Electric Guitars*, contains similar information on electric instruments. Together, they are over 1,500 pages and weigh over 7 lbs.! No other two books provide as much guitar information and up-to-date pricing. As in the past, thanks for supporting this project, and we will continue to earn your patronage in future editions.

Sincerely,

S.P. Fjestad
Editor & Publisher
Blue Book of Acoustic Guitars

INTRODUCTION

Author Zachary R. Fjestad smiling happily with his favorite Sesame Street character Rosita.

played and used primarily as an investment (if they don't end up in Japan). The good news is that prices appear to be reaching somewhat of a plateau.

Acoustic guitars have never been so plentiful for anyone who wants to play the guitar. A beginner can find a decent guitar for under $200 and the high-end Martins and Taylors have never been so good. It also seems that everyone has an acoustic guitar these days. At almost any bonfire you go to, someone brings their cheap guitar to entertain their guests. If you look at Martin's serialization you can see that their numbers have jumped in the past five years. Their serialization is strictly numerical and with big gaps in numbers, it means they are producing a lot of guitars.

The *Blue Book of Acoustic Guitars* is going to be an annual publication from here on out so the customer can get the newest information each year. We also have all this information online as a subscription and as downloads. We update our information quarterly, so when there is a surge or change in a certain model we can update the information almost instantaneously.

Welcome to the Eighth Edition of the *Blue Book Acoustic Guitars*. You are currently reading the most up-to-date book on the pricing and information about guitars. I cannot even begin to describe the amount of work that was put into this book. This is good news for you – the customer, as this has the most information that any *Blue Book of Acoustic Guitars* has ever had!

There are several new changes in the book. We have a brand-new Photo Grading System™ to help determine condition of your guitar. We have also added several new pictures in the black and white including models that have never been shown before. We have also tried to make the book as user-friendly as possible. By dividing every model in its respective category, finding your model has never been easier. Also, check out the P.S. on the last page of the book for something fun to do.

It has been two years since the seventh editions were released and needless to say, a lot has changed in two years. The seventh edition was off the printer no less than a week before the tragedy of 9/11 occurred in New York, Washington D.C., and Pennsylvania. This event changed everything for everyone including the guitar market. Attendance fell at all guitar shows, but the big bucks were being spent on the pricy stuff. Early Martins and Gibsons are hot as ever, but it seems that the low end stuff keeps getting more affordable, which is good news for the player. Let's face it, the high end 'Bursts will never be

There is no way I could have completed this project without the help of several people. My first project was the *Blue Book of Guitar Amplifiers* and at only 304 pages, it seemed like nothing compared to 944 in the electric and 592 in the acoustic. I have to thank the entire staff at Blue Book for their constant support and willing to help at any time. The Trademark Index would not have been done without Katie and Beth and all the proofing done by Heather (it's amazing the amount of stuff she can catch!) For all the work that Clint has done on this book, he should almost get credit on the cover. If not for him, I would still be trying to figure out that stupid camera! I also cannot forget to mention our numerous trips to McDonalds. I can't forget the one man who gave me the opportunity to do this. My uncle Steve had always had faith in me and maybe one of these days I'll impress him with what I've done! Thanks again to anyone who I forgot to mention. Now after this is done I'll go out and indulge in some of my first "legal" drinks!

Sincerely,

Zachary R. Fjestad
Zachary R. Fjestad
Author
Blue Book of Acoustic Guitars

HOW TO USE THIS BOOK

This new Eighth Edition *Blue Book of Acoustic Guitars™*, when used properly, will provide you with more up-to-date acoustic guitar information and pricing than any other single source. Now with almost 600 pages of specific guitar models and pricing, this publication continues to be more of a complete informational source than strictly a "hold-your-hand" pricing guide. In theory, you should be able to identify the trademark/name off the guitar's headstock (where applicable), and find out the country of origin, date(s) produced, and other company/model-related facts for that guitar. **Many smaller, out-of-production trademarks and/or companies which are only infrequently encountered in the secondary marketplace are intentionally not priced in this text, as it is pretty hard to pin a tail on a donkey that is nowhere in sight.** Unfortunately, the less information known about a trademark is typically another way of asking the seller, "Would you take any less? After all, nobody seems to know anything about it." In other words, don't confuse rarity with desirability when it comes to these informational "blackholes." As in the past, if you own a current Eighth Edition of the *Blue Book of Acoustic Guitars™* and still have questions, we will try to assist you in identifying/pricing your guitar(s). Please refer to page 23 for this service.

The prices listed in the Eighth Edition *Blue Book of Acoustic Guitars™* are based on average national retail prices for both currently manufactured and vintage instruments. This is NOT a wholesale pricing guide – prices reflect the numbers you typically see on a guitar's price tag. More importantly, do not expect to walk into a music store, guitar, or pawn shop, and think that the proprietor should pay you the retail price listed in this text. Dealer offers on most models could be 20%-50% less than the values listed, depending upon desirability, locality, and profitability.

In other words, if you want to receive 100% of the price (retail value), then you have to do 100% of the work (become the retailer, which also includes assuming 100% of the risk). Business is business, and making regular bank deposits usually means turning a profit every once in a while.

Currently manufactured guitars are typically listed with the manufacturer's suggested retail (MSR), a 100% price (may reflect market place discounting), and in most cases, prices for both Excellent and Average condition factors are included. Please consult the revised digital color **Photo Grading System™** (pages 33-48) to learn more about the condition of your guitar(s). The *Blue Book of Acoustic Guitars™* will continue using selected photos to illustrate real world condition factors and/or problems. Guitar porno, it isn't. Since condition is the overriding factor in price evaluation, study these photos carefully. As the saying goes, one picture can be worth a thousand words.

For your convenience, an explanation of factors that can affect condition and pricing, guitar grading systems, how to convert them, and descriptions of individual condition factors appear on pages 31-32 to assist you in learning more about guitar grading systems and individual condition factors. Please read these pages carefully, as the values in this publication are based on the grading/condition factors listed. This will be especially helpful when evaluating older vintage instruments. **Remember, the price is wrong if the condition factor isn't right.**

All values within this text assume original condition. The grading lines within the Eighth Edition reflect the 100%, Excellent and Average condition factors only. From the vintage marketplace or (especially) a collector's point of view, any repairs, alterations, modifications, "enhancements," "improvements," "professionally modified to a more desirable configuration," or any other non-factory changes usually detract from an instrument's value. Please refer to page 31 regarding an explanation to finishes, repairs, alterations/modifications, and other elements which have to be factored in before determining the correct condition. Depending on the seriousness of the modification/alteration, you may have to lower the condition factor when re-computing prices for these alterations. Determining values for damaged and/or previously repaired instruments will usually depend on the parts and labor costs necessary to return them to playable and/or original specifications.

You may note that the Eighth Edition contains many new black-and-white photos of individual models/variations to assist you with more visual identification. **Remember, the photos will not necessarily be on the same page as the model listings and description.**

The Eighth Edition *Blue Book of Acoustic Guitars™* provides many company histories, notes on influential luthiers and designers, and other bits of knowledge as a supplement to the make/model format. Hopefully, this information will be shared to alleviate those "grey areas" of the unknown, and shed light on many new luthiers who have emerged within the past several decades, and produce excellent quality instruments.

We have designed an easy-to-use (and consistent) text format throughout this publication to assist you in finding specific information within the shortest amount of time, and there is a lot of information!

HOW TO USE THIS BOOK

1. Trademark, manufacturer, brand name, company, luthier or importer are listed in upper case, and in bold face type. They will appear alphabetically as follows:

COLLINGS, MARTIN, YAMAHA

2. Trademark, manufacturer, or other company/luthier information and production dates (if possible) are listed directly beneath the trademark heading:

    Instruments currently built in New Hartford, Connecticut since 1967. Distribution is handled by Kaman Music Corporation of Bloomfield, Connecticut.

3. A company overview, model information recap, and/or other relatively useful pieces of information may follow within a smaller block of text:

    In 1973, luthier George Lowden began designing and manufacturing hand built guitars in Ireland. Demand outgrew the one-person effort and the production of some models was farmed out to luthiers in Japan in 1981. However, full production was returned to Ireland in 1985.

4. When a proper model-by-model listing is not available (due to space considerations), a small paragraph may follow with the company history and related production data. These paragraphs may also include current retail prices. The following example is from Espanola:

    The wide range of Espanola acoustic guitars are designed and priced with the entry level or student guitarist in mind. Suggested new retail prices range from $200 up to $400 on the Korean-produced acoustic guitar models; $450 on the resonator-style models; $125 to $300 on four Paracho, Mexico classicals; and $350 to $550 on 4-string acoustic bass guitars.

5. The next major classification under a heading name may include a category name which appears in upper-case, is flush left, and inside a darkly shaded, approximately 3 1/2 inch box. A category name refers mostly to a guitar's primary configuration:

    ACOUSTIC

    ACOUSTIC ELECTRIC

6. A sub-classification of a category name (upper and lower-case description inside a lighter shaded box) usually indicates a grouping or series which has to be further defined under the category name:

    Hummingbird Series

    Thinline Series

7. A category note may follow either a category or subcategory heading, and contains information specific to that category. An example would be:

    All Breedlove Premier Line instruments have ivoroid or black plastic binding, top and back purflings, and abalone rosettes. Bridges, fingerboards, and peghead veneers are made of ebony.

8. Model names appear flush left, are bolded in upper case, and appear in alpha-numerical (normally) sequence which are grouped under the various subheadings:

CREMONA, PERFORMER, DOVE IN FLIGHT (ACDFACGH1), J-250, D-50 KOA, DUOLIAN, JANIS IAN MODEL

    Parentheses after a model or submodel name refers to either a previous model name or the factory family code/number to assist in proper identification. In some cases, it may include both.

9. Variations within a model appear as sub-models, are indented, italicized, and appear in both upper and lower case type:

    H-12 Hybrid, ATX Bass, Artist CS, Emperor Cutaway (New York Mfg.), HD-28 VS, Hollywood Tenor

    Model sub-variations appear in the text under the description/pricing of the main model(s).

10. Model/sub-model descriptions and related information appear directly under the model/sub-model names, and appear as follows:

    - single round cutaway dreadnought style, spruce top, round soundhole, black pickguard, 3-stripe bound body/rosette, mahogany back/sides/neck, 21-fret rosewood fingerboard with pearl dot inlay, rosewood bridge with white and black dot pins, 6-on-one-side chrome tuners, acoustic pickup, volume/tone control, available in Natural finish, Mfg. 1987-1994.

HOW TO USE THIS BOOK

Model/submodel descriptions are where most of the critical information regarding that model/submodel is located. Typically, these descriptions list configuration first, type of wood(s) second, fretboard description, special features, bridge/tuner specifications, finishes, and on acoustic electric instruments, will also list electronics. If possible, years of production are listed last. In many cases, this allows the last MSR and dates of manufacture to be known. Whenever possible, black and white photos have been provided on the right-hand pages, even though they may not appear on the same page as the model name/description.

11. Pricing. A pricing line will typically be located directly underneath the model description. You will notice that this Eighth Edition *Blue Book of Acoustic Guitars™* continues to feature a similar price line format throughout. Typically, it includes the Mfg.'s Sug. Retail (MSR) on currently manufactured instruments, a 100% price (this may reflect industry discounting, if any), and, if applicable, a single price for both Excellent and Average condition factors. When the following price line is encountered,

GRADING		100%	EXCELLENT	AVERAGE
MSR	$699	$495	$350	$250

it automatically indicates the guitar is currently manufactured and the manufacturer's suggested retail price (MSR) is shown left of the 100% column. **The 100% price on a new instrument is what a consumer can typically expect to pay for that instrument, and may reflect a discount off the manufacturer's suggested retail (MSR) price. The values for the remaining Excellent and Average condition factors represent actual retail selling prices for used instruments in these two conditions.**

An **"N/A"** instead of a price means that a firm market price is **Not Available** for that particular instrument and/or condition factor.

Musical instruments, like other consumer goods, may be discounted to promote consumer spending. Discounting is generally used as a sales tool within the music industry and includes many music/guitar establishments, chain stores, mail-order companies, Ebay, and other retailers to help sell merchandise. Discounted prices depend on the manufacturers and dealers (if any). Some companies/ dealers may not discount at all, but offer quality service and support/advice after your purchase. With the advent of manufacturer MAPs (minimum advertised prices), discounting seems to become more manageable than it was in the 90s. 25%-35% seems to be the rule for most manufacturer's MAPs.

The 100% condition factor (mint), when encountered in a currently manufactured guitar, assumes the guitar has not been previously sold at retail and includes a factory warranty. A currently manufactured new instrument must include EVERY-THING the factory originally provided with the instrument – including the case (if originally included), warranty card, instruction manual (if any), hang tags (if any), etc. Because of this, a slightly used instrument that appears new no longer qualifies for 100%, and may be worth 50%-90% of its current MSR, depending on the overall desirability factor. Simply refer to the correct condition column of the instrument in question and refer to the price listed directly underneath.

Several different price lines have been used to indicate out of production models. Typically, a recently discontinued model (less than 10 years old) will appear with 3 prices – 100%, Excellent, and Average (see first price line below.) On vintage guitars and instruments that have been discontinued for over 10 years, the 100% price is not listed, since it is unlikely to find an instrument in the 100% condition factor that is this old. On instruments that are 10 years or older, and still remain in 100% (mint) original condition, premiums of 10%-35% apply, depending on the desirability of the make/model.

A price line with 2 values listed (as the first two examples below demonstrate) indicates a discontinued, out of production model with values shown for Excellent and Average condition factors only. 100% prices have intentionally not been listed, since the longer an instrument has been discontinued, the less likely you will find it in 100% condition. Obviously, "MSR" will not appear in the left margin, but a model note may appear below the price line indicating the last manufacturer's suggested retail price. Also, an N/A (Not Available) may appear in place of values for instruments that are not commonly encountered in higher condition factor(s). Some instruments that are only 10 years old and have never been taken out of the case (unplayed), may not be 100% (new), as the finish may have slightly cracked, tarnished, faded, or deteriorated. 100% is new – no excuses, period.

GRADING		100%	EXCELLENT	AVERAGE
			$2,500	$1,500
		N/A	$17,500	$12,250
		$1,200	$900	$525

HOW TO USE THIS BOOK

On discontinued models that are less than 10 years old, the 100% price is typically included (see above price line), since this condition factor is more common on these recently manufactured instruments. On popular, non-custom, factory discontinued models within the past several years, 100% values (new condition) will typically be no higher than 70% of the last MSR. 100% pricing on desirable, low production discontinued models from well-known luthiers and/or small companies will normally be priced closer to the last Manufacturer's Suggested Retail Price (MSR) for that model.

The following price line indicates that this model has been in production for a short time only, and used guitars simply do not exist yet. Also, the 100% price is not listed, as this type of guitar is typically of limited production and/or special order, and dealer/consumer discounts usually do not apply.

MSR $499

12.   While the current Manufacturer's Suggested Retail (MSR) price is included on current models whenever possible, the last MSR on discontinued models may appear in smaller typeface to the right directly underneath the price line:

Last MSR was $4,995.

13.   Manufacturer's notes, related model information, and available options may appear after the model/submodel listings, are in a different font, and are important, as they contain both model changes and other useful information.

From 1934-1938, Varitone tailpiece replaced previous part/design. In 1936, upper bouts were widened. In 1937, Grover Imperial tuners became an option. In 1938, Kluson Sealfast tuners replaced original part/design. In 1939, Natural finish became an option. In 1941, engraved heel cap and rosewood bridge with pearl inlay were discontinued. Current production instruments (1939 Super 400 in Natural or Cremona Brown) are part of the Historic Collection Series, found at the end of this section.

14.   Extra cost features/special orders and other value added/subtracted items (add-ons for currently manufactured guitars reflect company suggested retails), are placed directly under individual price lines, and appear bolder than other descriptive typeface:

Add 35% for Natural finish.
Subtract approx. 50% if professionally refinished.

On many acoustic guitars that are less than 15 years old, these Add/Subtract items will be the last factory retail price for that option.

15.   A grading line will appear at the top of each page where applicable. This grading line is once again standard for the

GRADING	100%	EXCELLENT	AVERAGE

Blue Book of Acoustic Guitars™, and reflects the 100% value (this price could represent any industry discounting). Next to 100%, left to right, are the standard Excellent and Average condition factors. These two condition factors will hopefully eliminate some of the "grading graffiti" on these types of instruments, where a single percentage or abbreviation doesn't do them justice.

To find a particular acoustic guitar in this book, first identify the name of the manufacturer, luthier, trademark, importer, brand name, or in some cases – headstock logo. Refer to this listing within the correct alphabetical section. Next, locate the correct category name (Acoustic, Acoustic Electric). Models will be grouped either alphanumerically (i.e., AW600, AW700, AW800, etc.), or alphabetically (i.e., Buddy Holly Model, Elvis King of Rock Model, Hank Williams Jr. Model, etc.), or in some cases, chronological sequence, starting with the oldest model to the newest.

Once you find the correct model or sub-model under its respective heading or subheading, determine the acoustic guitar's original condition factor (see the Photo Grading System™ on pages 33-48), and simply find the corresponding condition column (Excellent or Average) to ascertain the correct price. Special/limited editions usually appear last under a manufacturer's heading. In order to save time when looking up a particular model(s), you may want to look first at our expanded Index on pages 577-591. Also, a greatly updated Trademark Index is located on pages 557-576 – it is the only up-to-date and comprehensive listing of current acoustic manufacturers and luthiers in print – use both of them, they can be very helpful!

Additional sections in this publication that will be of special interest are the Serialization Charts (pages 537-550), Anatomy of an Acoustic Guitar (page 16), Glossary (pages 26-30), and Strings/Luthier Organizations (page 555). When using the Serialization Charts, make sure your model is listed and find the serial number within the yearly range listings. However, do not date your instrument on serial number information alone! Double check parts/finish variations in the text accompanying the model, or reference the coding on your instrument's potentiometers (tone and volume knobs), if applicable on an acoustic electric model.

JERRY'S SCRAPBOOK

Amy Ray of The Indigo Girls - July 17, 2002

Emily Saliers of The Indigo Girls - July 17, 2002

Rick Springfield - Dec. 5, 2001

David Crosby of C.S.N. - May 31, 2003

Dan Fogelberg - June 29, 2002

Kevin Cronin of R.E.O. Speedwagon - May 10, 2003

Graham Nash of C.S.N. - May 31, 2003

Dave Pack of Ambrosia - July 15, 1997

Dewey Bunnell of America - June 23, 2001

Gerry Beckley of America - June 23, 2001

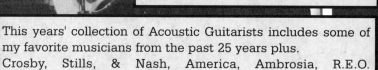

Stephen Stills of C.S.N. - May 31, 2003

This years' collection of Acoustic Guitarists includes some of my favorite musicians from the past 25 years plus.

Crosby, Stills, & Nash, America, Ambrosia, R.E.O. Speedwagon, Rick Springfield, and Dan Fogelberg have been putting out great music for over a quarter century!

Kevin Cronin and R.E.O. Speedwagon have been one of my favorite groups since 1980. I have seen them more than ten times during that span.

I was lucky enough to meet Kevin backstage after their concert in 1995. This photo is one year before he cut off the long curly hair! The concert photo is from my most recent R.E.O. concert in May of 2003 with Kevin sporting a shorter, blond hairstyle. After 30 years on the road R.E.O. Speedwagon still rocks and they perform their trademark ballads better than ever!

Jerry Adler and Kevin Cronin of R.E.O. Speedwagon - April 22, 1995

ANATOMY OF AN ACOUSTIC GUITAR

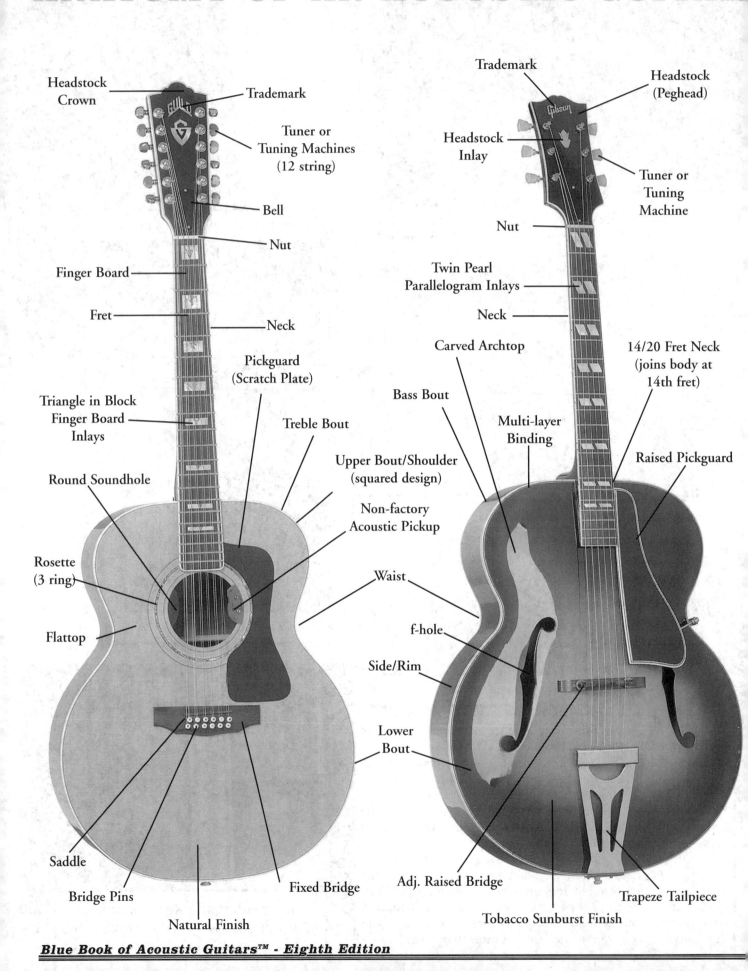

Headstock Crown

Trademark

Tuner or Tuning Machines (12 string)

Bell

Nut

Finger Board

Fret

Neck

Pickguard (Scratch Plate)

Treble Bout

Upper Bout/Shoulder (squared design)

Non-factory Acoustic Pickup

Triangle in Block Finger Board Inlays

Round Soundhole

Rosette (3 ring)

Flattop

Saddle

Bridge Pins

Fixed Bridge

Natural Finish

Trademark

Headstock (Peghead)

Headstock Inlay

Tuner or Tuning Machine

Nut

Twin Pearl Parallelogram Inlays

Neck

Carved Archtop

Bass Bout

Multi-layer Binding

14/20 Fret Neck (joins body at 14th fret)

Raised Pickguard

Waist

f-hole

Side/Rim

Lower Bout

Adj. Raised Bridge

Trapeze Tailpiece

Tobacco Sunburst Finish

A TRIBUTE TO DOC WATSON

by Dan Miller
Edited by Steve Carr
and Cassandra Faulkner

INTRODUCTION

Over the past fifty years, the guitar has had a very powerful influence on American music. Predominantly a rhythm instrument at the turn of the century, the guitar began to step out of the rhythm section in the 1930-40s and has maintained a dominant presence in every form of music from rock, to folk, country, bluegrass, blues, and oldtime. While Elvis, the Beatles, Bob Dylan, and other pop icons of the 1950-60s certainly played a large role in bolstering the guitar's popularity, the man who has had the deepest, most enduring, and most profound influence on the way the acoustic flattop guitar is played as a lead instrument in folk, old-time, and bluegrass music today is Arthel "Doc" Watson.

To those of us who have spent hundreds of hours slowing down Doc Watson records in order to learn the tastefully selected notes that he plays and emulate the clear, crisp tone he pulls out of his instrument, Doc is a legend. However, Doc's influence extends far beyond the small niche of guitar players who try to faithfully reproduce his guitar breaks because Doc Watson is not just a guitar player and singer - he is an American hero. To be recognized as a "national treasure" by President Jimmy Carter, honored with the National Medal of the Arts by President Bill Clinton, and given an honorary doctorate degree from the University of North Carolina calls for being more than a fine musician and entertainer. Doc Watson received these accolades not just for his talent, but for the honor, integrity, humility, grace, and dignity which he has displayed throughout his long and distinguished career. While there are many, many great guitar players and singers; there is only one Doc Watson.

Fans love Doc Watson's smooth baritone voice, sharp wit and intellect, easy-going manner, good nature, country charm, and wonderful story-telling abilities almost as much as his guitar playing and singing. One fan commented, "I would pay to go hear Doc Watson read names out of the phone book!" Many other of Doc's admirers agree, saying that no matter how big the performance hall, Doc makes you feel as if you are sitting with him in your own living room. He is comfortable, relaxed, laid-back, and plays, sings, and speaks from the heart. He appears to be enjoying the show as much as you are, and he probably is. The tie that binds is his obvious life long love of music.

THE EARLY YEARS

The sixth of nine children, Arthel Lane "Doc" Watson was born in Stoney Fork, Watauga County, North Carolina on March 3rd, 1923, to Annie Greene and General Dixon Watson. When he was born, he had a defect in the vessels that carry blood to the eyes. He later developed an eye infection which caused him to completely loose his vision before his first birthday. He was raised, and still resides, in Deep Gap, North Carolina.

The Watson family lineage can be traced back to Tom Watson, a Scots pioneer who homesteaded 3,000 acres in North Carolina around 1790. North Carolina homesteaders, like Watson, brought folk song and music to their new world and as it changed and evolved, passing from one generation to the next, it bound families, neighbors, and communities together through the best and the worst of times. In the introduction to the book "The Songs of Doc Watson," folklorist Ralph Rinzler wrote, "Western North Carolina has long been recognized as one of the richest repositories of folk song and lore in the southeastern United States." In the liner notes to The Doc Watson Family Tradition, A.L. Lloyd writes, "The northwest corner of North Carolina is still probably the busiest nook in the United States for domestic music, singing, fiddling, banjo-picking, and it's no accident that when Cecil Sharp was collecting songs and ballads in the Appalachians (in 1916) it was precisely this small area that yielded the greatest harvest." Western North Carolina song and lore are contained in some of Doc Watson's earliest memories.

Doc's mother would frequently sing old-time songs and ballads while doing chores during the day and she sung her children to sleep at night. In the evenings the family read from the Bible and sung hymns from the *Christian Harmony*, a shape-note book published in 1866. Doc's father, a farmer and day-laborer, also led the singing at the local Baptist church.

Doc has said that his earliest memories of music reach back to his days as a young child being held in his mother's arms at the Mt. Paron Church and listening to the harmony and shape-note singing. The first songs he remembers hearing are "The Lone Pilgrim" and "There is a Fountain." Singing led to an interest in making music and Doc says that he began "playing with anything around the house that made a musical sound." At about the age of six, Doc began to learn to play the harmonica and from that time was given a new one every year in his Christmas stocking. Doc's first stringed instrument, not to include a steel wire he had strung across the woodshed's sliding door to provide bass accompaniment to his harmonica playing, was a banjo his father built for him when he was

Gallagher G-70 courtesy Dave's Guitar Shop

eleven years old. His father taught him the rudiments of playing a fretless banjo, the rest Doc learned by trial and error.

Doc's new banjo had a fretless maple neck and friction tuning pegs. His father had first tried to make the head out of a ground hog hide, however, it didn't have good tone. When his grandmother's sixteen year old cat passed on, Doc's father used the cat's skin to make the banjo head. In an interview conducted by Frets magazine in 1979 Doc recalls, "That made one of the best banjo heads you ever seen and it stayed on that thing, I guess, as long as I picked it." Doc says that his father "got the notion" for using the cat skin from a Sears Roebuck advertisement of the Joe Rodgers banjo head made of cat skin. The first banjo tune Doc remembers his father playing for him was "Rambling Hobo."

Looking back at Doc's professional music career, it might be said that little banjo his father built for him was the most important thing the elder Watson could have done for his blind son. However, when asked, Doc will say that the most valuable thing his father did for him was put him at the end of a cross-cut saw when he was fourteen years old. In the same *Frets* magazine article (March 1979), Doc reflects on the occasion by saying, "He put me to work and that made me feel useful. A lot of blind people weren't ever put to work." In *Bluegrass Unlimited* (August 1984) Doc once again remembers that important moment, "He made me know that just because I was blind, certainly didn't mean I was helpless."

The confidence Doc's father instilled in him at this young age, by putting him at the end of a crosscut saw, taught him not to be afraid to do anything. Over the years, among other things, he has re-wired his house, built a two room utility building, and he has even been known to climb up on the roof to adjust the TV antenna. Regarding the utility building Doc built completely by himself with a handsaw and mitre box, Doc's current partner, Jack Lawrence states, "I went there and looked at it and I was amazed. There was no way I could have built anything that looked that good. I was curious and I got a carpenter's square and started checking things and that whole building was only a half inch out of square. He is the

most amazing man I have ever met in my life in that regard. He is not afraid to tackle most things in life. There is no stopping him when he has his mind set on something."

Doc's earliest musical influences came from his family, church, and neighbors (Carltons, Greers, Younces), however, by the time he was about seven years old his family had acquired a used wind-up Victrola and a stack of records from his mother's brother, Jerome Greene, and Doc was exposed to early county artists such as the Carter Family, Jimmie Rodgers, the Carolina Tar Heels, and Gid Tanner and the Skillet Lickers. His musical horizons were to broaden again when, at the age of ten, he entered the Governor Morehead School for the Blind in Raleigh, North Carolina.

In Raleigh, Doc was exposed to classical music and big band jazz, and he also was able to listen to guitar players such as Nick Lucas and Django Reinhardt. When asked about his reaction to hearing the great gypsy jazz guitar player, Doc said, "I couldn't figure out what the devil he was doing he went so fast on most of it, but I loved it." It was while he was away at school that he also began to learn how to play the guitar.

LEARNING TO PLAY THE GUITAR

One year at school, when Doc was about thirteen, a school friend, Paul Montgomery, had shown him how to play a few chords (G, C, and D) on the guitar. A short time later, when Doc was back at home, he was "messing around" with a guitar that his brother Linny had borrowed from a neighbor, Spencer Miller. One morning his father heard him trying to play the guitar and, not knowing that Doc had already learned a few chords, told him that if he could learn to play one song on the guitar by the time he got home from work that evening, he would take him down to Rhodes and Day's in North Wilkesboro that Saturday, combine his money with whatever Doc had in his piggy bank, and help Doc buy a guitar. Since Doc already knew a few chords, it didn't take him long to learn how to accompany himself while singing a simple song. The song Doc learned to play that day was the Carter Family's "When The Roses Bloom In Dixieland." That Saturday his father, true to his word, helped Doc buy a twelve dollar Stella guitar.

Not long after Doc got his first guitar, he and his brother Linny began learning how to play many of the old time mountain tunes that they had heard growing up, as well as some of the new songs they heard on the Grand Ole Opry. His early performances amounted to playing locally for family and friends. He also began to play music with another local boy named Paul Greer. When asked about his switch from playing the banjo to the guitar in an interview conducted by *Dirty Linen Magazine* (June/July 1995), Doc said, "The banjo was something I really liked, but when the guitar came along, to me that was my first love in music." Doc initially learned to just "strum and play" the guitar, using a thumb pick, in order to accompany his singing. His first attempts to play a bit of lead were in the old Carter Family "thumb lead" style. After he had learned to play the Carter style with a thumb pick, Doc says, "I began to listen to Jimmie Rodgers recordings seriously and I figured, 'Hey, he must be doing that with one of them straight picks.' So I got me one and began to work at it. Then I began to learn the Jimmie Rodgers licks on the guitar. Then all at once I began to figure out, 'Hey, I could play that Carter stuff a lot better with a flatpick.'"

When Doc was seventeen, his Stella guitar was replaced with a Silvertone from Sears that Doc paid for by working "at the end of a crosscut saw." He and his youngest brother David, cut wood for the tannery. Using the money they had earned, Doc bought a guitar and David bought a new suit of clothes. The guitar came with a book that contained various songs that you could learn to play with a flatpick. It had photos of Nick Lucas illustrating how to hold a pick and David showed Doc how the photographs in the book demonstrated the way to hold a flatpick. To this day, he still holds his pick as it was illustrated in that book.

Doc's first Martin guitar was a D-28 that he acquired from a music store in Boone, North Carolina, in about 1940. The store owner, Mr. Richard Green, allowed Doc to make payments on the guitar and gave him a year to pay it off. In order to pay for the guitar, Doc began to play music in the streets. When the weather permitted, Doc would play for tips at a cab stand in Lenoire, North Carolina, sometimes making as much as $50 a day. He had the guitar completely paid off in four or five months.

The street performing led to Doc being invited to play at some amateur contests and fiddlers' conventions. It was at one of these local shows that Arthel received the nickname "Doc." He was playing with his friend Paul Greer at a remote control radio show being broadcast from a furniture store in Lenoire. The radio announcer decided that "Arthel" was too long a name to announce on the radio and suggested they think of another name to call him. A young woman in the audience yelled out, "Call him 'Doc'" - the name stuck and has been with him ever since. When *Dirty Linen Magazine* (June/July 1995) asked Doc how he felt about his nickname, he replied, "I didn't pay much attention to it. If it hadn't happened . . . they probably would have called me Art for short, which is common, you know."

When Doc was around eighteen years old, he traveled "way over across the mountain" to meet with an old-time fiddler named Gaither Carlton. While he was there he was introduced to Gaither's daughter, Rosa Lee. Since Rosa Lee was eight years younger than Doc, he didn't think much of the meeting at the

time. However, six years later Gaither moved his family just a half mile down the road from Doc. Doc says, "I went out to their house and Rosa Lee and a neighbor girl were unpacking dishes. She turned around and said, 'Hello, I haven't seen you in a long time.' Somebody might as well have hit me with a brick. I lost it. I thought, 'Where have I been all these years! There she is!' It was like that, and it still is." Doc and Rosa Lee were married in 1947. Two years later, in 1949, their son

Eddy Merle (named after Eddy Arnold and Merle Travis) was born, followed by their daughter, Nancy Ellen, in 1951.

THE BIRTH OF "FLATPICKING"

After his marriage, Doc began tuning pianos in order to feed his family. It wasn't until 1953, when Doc got a job playing electric lead guitar in Jack Williams' country and western swing band, Jack Williams and the Country Gentlemen, that Doc began making money as a professional musician. It was during his eight year stay with Williams that he began to develop his ability to flatpick fiddle tunes on the guitar.

Doc was first inspired to learn how to play fiddle tunes on the guitar after he became frustrated trying to learn how to play the fiddle. He had obtained a fiddle when he was 18 years old, and says, "I used to try to fiddle. I had a fiddle for about eighteen months and my bowing hand weren't worth a stink. I stopped one day and said, 'Heck, I'm going to sell this thing. I can't fiddle.'" Although the fiddle itself frustrated him, Doc liked the bounce and rhythm of the fiddle music, so he worked to "put some of those tunes on the guitar."

Gallagher G-70 courtesy Dave's Guitar Shop

Williams' band did not have a fiddle player about 90% of the time, however, the dance halls that hired the band would usually want them to do a square dance set. Jack Williams, who had heard Doc fooling around with a few fiddle tunes on the guitar, suggested that Doc learn how to play lead on some fiddle tunes on his electric guitar. Doc said to himself, "If Grady Martin and Hank Garland can do it, so can I." (Garland and Martin had played some fiddle tunes on the electric guitar with Red Foley.) Doc began to learn how to play tunes like "Black Mountain Rag," "Old Joe Clark," "Sugarfoot Rag," and "Billy In The Lowground."

When Doc began playing with Williams he still owned his Martin D-28. He tried to play the Martin with a pickup installed for a while, but eventually traded it in for a 1953 Les Paul Standard. Later, when the folk revival began, Doc transferred the licks and techniques for playing fiddle tunes on the electric guitar over to the acoustic guitar. Doc recalls, "The technical practice on the electric guitar helped me greatly in learning those fiddle tunes. It was harder to do on the flattop when I went back to it, but the basics had already been learned."

THE FOLK BOOM

During his time with Williams' band Doc had kept his hand in old-time music by playing with his family and friends, which included Clarence "Tom" Ashley, one of the original members of the Carolina Tar Heels. In 1960, as the "folk boom" was blossoming, two musicologists, Ralph Rinzler and Eugene Earle, traveled to North Carolina to record Ashley. Ashley had gathered together some of the best local musicians, Doc being among them, for Rinzler to record. During that trip Rinzler recorded what was later to be released as "Old Time Music at Clarence Ashley's, Volume 1" (Folkways, FA2355).

...Doc eventually began to perform as a solo act, playing mostly coffee houses...

Rinzler, who was impressed with Doc's banjo and guitar playing abilities, went over to the Watson home several days later and recorded Doc playing with Gaither Carlton and several of Doc's other family members. At the session, Doc and Gaither expressed that they could not believe that people from the Northern cities were interested in their music, which had gone out of style after World War II. Ralph let them listen to a Folkways recording of early "hillbilly" music and Gaither said, "Sounds like old times."

One problem Doc had when Rinzler first came to record him at Tom Ashley's was that he did not own an acoustic guitar. He suggested to Rinzler that he could play his Les Paul with the volume turned down low. Not crazy about the idea of having an electric guitar on these recordings, Rinzler convinced Doc that it would be best to have an acoustic guitar and so Doc borrowed a Martin D-18 from his friend Joe Cox. Doc says, "That was a fine old D-18. I wish I owned it." Doc recollects that it was either a 1942 or 1943 model D-18. In 1961 Doc, Gaither, Tom Ashley, Fred Price, and his neighbor Clint Howard traveled to New York to perform a concert sponsored by Friends of Old Time Music. Doc's guitar breaks were enthusiastically received.

The word about this talented group of musicians spread and they were invited to perform at a number of colleges, folk festivals and clubs. With Rinzler's encouragement, Doc eventually began to perform as a solo act, playing mostly coffee houses like Gerde's Folk Club and the Gaslight in New York City while "trying to get a start in the business." His early career was boosted when he was invited to perform at the Newport Folk Festival in 1963 and 1964.

Rinzler also paired Doc with Bill Monroe together for a number of shows. Doc and Bill traded licks on hot fiddle tunes and recreated that old Monroe Brothers sound with their duet singing. Recordings from these shows, which were desirable bootleg items for years, were released by Smithsonian Folkways in 1993 as "Bill Monroe and Doc Watson: Live Duet Recordings 1963-1980." In the very early days of his solo career, Doc traveled by himself on a bus when he wasn't accompanied by Ralph Rinzler. Later, when Rinzler became involved in work that didn't allow him to travel, Doc's life traveling to shows by himself got real tough. However, in 1964, Doc's life on the road improved considerably when his son Merle joined him as his picking partner.

DOC AND MERLE

Doc has said that when Merle was young he had shown no interest in playing the guitar. However, when he was about 15 years old, Merle had his mother show him a few chords while Doc was away on a road trip. From there, Merle's playing took off like a rocket. After Doc returned from his road trip, road weary and almost ready to quit, he heard his son play the guitar for the first time and said, "Son, you're going to California with me." Amazingly, the first time Merle went on stage with his father he had only been playing the guitar for three months.

The first show Merle performed with his father was the Berkeley Folk Festival in 1964. The first album Merle played on was "Doc Watson & Son," recorded (in November 1964) just eight months after he had begun to learn how to pick the guitar. For the first two years Merle played rhythm and just went out with his dad on weekends and during the summers. When he graduated from high school, he began working with Doc full time. In an article printed in *Bluegrass Unlimited* magazine (November 1997), Doc is quoted as saying, "There's no way that I could have done the hard part of the dues paying days without Merle's driving and help on the road and taking care of business. Most people don't realize what it come to. He was doing the hard driving and things I could not do as far as the business." With Merle on the road with him and Manny Greenhill, of Folklore Productions, booking gigs, Doc's career began to take off.

Although Merle Watson had been listening to his father play the guitar all his life, he did not copy his father's guitar style. He had his own interests, his own influences, and his own style. Merle loved the blues and one of his first influences was Mississippi John Hurt. He also learned some blues scales from a black bluesman named Jerry Ricks. Merle took what he heard and made it his own. In 1973, inspired by the playing of Duane Allman, Merle began learning how to play the slide.

Doc feels that Merle was the most talented picker in the family. In an article printed in *Acoustic Guitar Magazine* (March/April 1993) Doc says, "What impressed me the most about Merle's guitar playing was the tasteful style that he had developed and his ability to learn very quickly." Doc has a number of interesting stories about Merle's ability to play a beautiful solo on a complex tune shortly after learning the melody.

While Doc and Merle remained the Watson family musicians who had been in the focus of the public's eye, Doc's wife Rosa Lee, who was responsible for teaching Merle his first guitar chords, is also a fine singer and his daughter Nancy plays the hammered dulcimer. When asked about his wife's music, Doc said, "I still think she has the prettiest singing voice I have ever heard. Simple, country, down to earth." Merle's son, Richard, is also a very fine guitar player and has been performing with his grandfather at shows close to home for the past several years.

LANDMARK RECORDINGS

The album that inspired thousands of folk and bluegrass guitarists to lock themselves in their rooms with their turntables slowed down to 16 rpm was recorded in February 1964 on the Vanguard label and simply titled "Doc Watson." This album was followed by seven more Vanguard releases:

• Doc Watson & Son (1965)
• Southbound (1966)
• Home Again (1967)
• Good Deal (1968)
• Doc Watson On Stage (1970)
• Ballads From Deep Gap (1971)
• Old Timey Concert (1977)

Selected songs from these projects, along with Doc's performances at the 1963 and 1964 Newport Folk Festivals, can be heard on the 4 CD Vanguard Doc Watson compilation called "The Vanguard Years" (1995).

For those of us who were not fortunate enough, or old enough, to be playing the guitar when Doc Watson recorded his first Vanguard release, our ears were first graced with the sound of Doc's voice and guitar on the "Will The Circle Be

Unbroken" album (1972). When Doc was invited to participate in this recording with the Nitty Gritty Dirt Band and other country and bluegrass legends such as Mother Maybelle Carter, Merle Travis, Roy Acuff, Earl Scruggs, and Jimmy Martin, he almost refused at first because his son Merle was not invited to be involved. In an interview printed in *Bluegrass Unlimited* in November of 1997, Doc explains, "Merle got me off in the corner and said, 'Dad, it did hurt my feelings, but do it. It will get us in audiences that have never heard us before.' He had a head on his shoulders, buddy. Let me tell you that. He said, 'Do it.' He said, 'I believe you ought to. It will help us out in the long run even if they didn't invite me.' Now that was being a man."

The exposure Doc received as a result of participating on the "Will The Circle Be Unbroken" LP did exactly what Merle had predicted it would do. Doc and Merle's career, which had been in a slight slump, picked up considerably. For a year or two Doc and Merle put together the Frosty Morn Band with Bob Hill, T. Michael Coleman, and Joe Smothers. After that group disbanded Doc and Merle began playing as a trio, with T. Michael Coleman on bass, in 1974. The trio toured the globe during the late seventies and early eighties, recorded nearly fifteen albums between 1973 and 1985, and brought Doc and Merle's unique blend of old time mountain music, folk, swing, bluegrass, traditional country, gospel, and blues to millions of new fans. Over the past three decades Doc Watson has won Grammy Awards for the following projects:

Year	Album	Grammy Award
1973	Then and Now*	Best Ethnic or Traditional Recording (album)
	Poppy LA022-F	
1974	Two Days in November*	Best Ethnic or Traditional Recording (album)
	Poppy LA210-G	
1979	Live and Pickin'	Best Country Instrumental Performance (song)
	United Artists LA943-H	"Big Sandy/Leather Britches" medley
1986	Riding the Midnight Train	Best Traditional Folk Recording (album)
	Sugar Hill 3752	
1990	On Praying Ground	Best Traditional Folk Recording (album)
	Sugar Hill 3779	
2002	Legacy	Best Traditional Folk Album w/David Holt
*both of these albums were reissued by Sugar Hill in 1994		

LIFE WITHOUT MERLE

In October of 1985, tragedy struck the Watson family when Merle was killed in a tractor accident at the age of 36. Doc Watson not only lost his son and partner, he lost, as Doc says, "the best friend I ever had in this world."

After Merle's passing, Doc found it difficult to go back out and play music, however, in an interview conducted by *Acoustic Musician* magazine (August 1997), Doc tells the following story, "The night before the funeral I had decided to quit, just give up playing. Well that night I had this dream. Now, usually I do have some light perception, but in this dream it was so dark I could hardly stand it. It was like I was in quicksand up to my waist and I felt I wasn't gonna make it out alive. Then suddenly this big old strong hand reached back and grabbed me by the hand and I heard this voice saying, 'Come on Dad, you can make it. Keep going.' Then I woke up. I think the good Lord was telling me it was all right to continue with my music. It's been a struggle, but I still have the love for the music."

About a year prior to Merle's death, he had become road weary and was not going out to perform with his father on many of the road trips. Merle's friend Jack Lawrence had been filling in for him and since Merle's passing, Jack has been Doc's consistent partner on the road.

Regarding Merle's death, Jack recalls, "We were supposed to go out on a two week trip the day after Merle died. I did not know what was going to happen and of course Doc didn't either. A couple of days after the funeral, Doc called me and said, 'I only cancelled the first week of that trip. Are you ready to go out and work? So we went back out on the road and that is how Doc dealt with it. He said, 'Merle would have not wanted me to just lay down and quit on this.' He is a very strong-willed man."

MERLEFEST

Doc, Jack, and T. Michael Coleman continued to play together until Coleman left to play with the Seldom Scene in October of 1987. Since he left, Doc and Jack have continued, to this day, to perform together as a duo. Although Doc does not tour as much as he used to, one event that he has hosted every April since 1988 in honor of his late son is the Merle Watson Memorial Festival, better known as "Merlefest." Held on the campus of Wilkes Community College, the event was initiated by Doc's close friend Bill Young and the director of development at Wilkes Community College, B. Townes. Young and Townes wanted to raise money to construct a memorial garden in honor of Merle by putting on a benefit concert. They approached Doc with the idea and Doc's daughter, Nancy, suggested that they also invite other artists, who where close to Merle, to perform.

At the first Merlefest event, the performers played on the back of two flatbed trucks to a crowd of about 4,000. The festival has become one of the largest traditional music events on the East coast. Today the performances include a wide range of musical styles including: folk, country, bluegrass, blues, Cajun,

Celtic, oldtime, gospel, and acoustic jazz.

One of the highlights of Merlefest for any avid guitarist is the opportunity to see Doc perform with his grandson, Merle's son, Richard. While Richard does not actively tour with his grandfather, he does occasionally play dates that are close to home and he can always be found at Merlefest. Of seeing Richard play a set with Doc in 1994, a correspondent from *Mother Earth News* (February/March 1995) writes: "Like Merle he was quiet, almost shy on stage. Like Merle, he sat on his grandfather's right hand. Doc, especially, notices the similarities. 'We sit here and practice and it's like looking at Richard and thinking, 'Son, you favor Merle' because Richard loved Merle's music and it comes out through his fingers.' "

THE DOC WATSON GUITAR STYLE

Doc's guitar style was certainly founded in the music that influenced him in his youth. In an interview conducted by *Acoustic Guitar* magazine (March/April 1993) Doc says, "I guess I liked every guitar player that I listened to, but there's some at the top of the list, like Chet, Merle, Smitty, Hank Garland . . . I like George Benson pretty much. And my son, Merle, of course. He was the best slide player I ever heard in my life."

Doc is quoted in an interview conducted by Ron Stanford in August of 1970 and printed, in part, in the introduction to the Oak Publications book, "The Songs of Doc Watson," as saying, "When I play a song, be it on the guitar or banjo, I live that song, whether it is a happy song or a sad song. Music, as a whole, expresses many things to me-everything from beautiful scenery to the tragedies and joys of life. . . . Whether I'm playing for myself or for an enthusiastic audience, I can get the same emotions I had when I found that Dad had seen to it that Santa Claus brought exactly what I wanted for Christmas. A true entertainer, I think, doesn't ever lose that feeling."

Later, in an interview printed in *Frets* magazine (March 1987), Doc says, "There are so many players that play for show; and then there are some that play for the love. Man, you sure can tell the difference when you sit down and listen to them." Playing for the love of music is what has sustained Doc Watson through the ups and downs of a professional career that has spanned nearly 50 years.

Dan Miller
Editor and Publisher
Flatpicking Guitar Magazine

The good thing about publishing a book on an annual basis is that you will find out what you don't know yearly. Each new edition should be an improvement on the last. Even though you can't do it all in one, 10, or even 20 editions, accumulating the new research is an ongoing process, with the results being published in each new edition.

The *Blue Book of Acoustic Guitars*™ has been the result of non-stop and continual guitar research obtained by getting the information needed from both manufacturers and luthiers (including visiting their production facilities whenever we get the opportunity). Also of major importance is speaking directly with acknowledged experts (both published and unpublished), reading books, catalogs, and company promo materials, gathering critical and up-to-date manufacturer/luthier information obtained from the NAMM Shows and the makers themselves, and observing and analyzing market trends by following major vintage dealer and collector pricing and trends.

We also have a great batch of contributing editors and advisory board members that pump out a lot of good information annually – including vintage pricing updates. Going to a lot of guitar/trade shows, in addition to visiting a variety of music stores, guitar shops, pawn shops, second-hand stores also hone our chops.

If you feel that you can contribute in any way to the materials published herein, you are encouraged to submit hard copy regarding your potential additions, revisions, corrections, or any other pertinent information that you feel would enhance the benefits this book provides to its readers. Unfortunately, we are unable to take your information over the phone (this protects both of us)! Earn your way into the ranks of the truly twisted, join the motley crew of contributing editors, and see that your information can make a difference! We thank you in advance for taking the time to make this a better publication.

All materials sent in for possible inclusion into upcoming editions of the *Blue Book of Acoustic Guitars*™ should be either mailed, faxed, or emailed to us at the address listed below:

Blue Book Publications, Inc.
Attn: Guitar Contributions
8009 34th Avenue South, Ste. 175
Minneapolis, MN 55425 USA
Fax: 952-853-1486
Email: guitars@bluebookinc.com
Web: http://www.bluebookinc.com
If you're emailing us an image, please make sure it is in TIF or JPEG format. Poor quality images cannot be used for publication.

CORRESPONDENCE INQUIRIES

Can't find your guitar in the book? No one's ever seen/heard of this make/model? Color/feature not listed? What's this thing worth? When was it manufactured? These are the most common type of questions we get when conducting research. This type of researching is a big job, and to do it properly, you must have a good working knowledge of instruments and their values, an up-to-date reference library, the right contacts (huge), keep going to guitar/trade shows, and actually read the guitar mags. We have helped out hundreds of people in the past, and hope to maintain this service in the future as well.

As with any ongoing publication, certain makes and models will not be included within the scope of the text. As expanded research uncovers model variations and new companies, the book's body of text will always have some unlisted instruments. Not believing in ivory towers and one-way traffic, this editor/publisher offers a mechanism for the consumer to get further information about makes/models not listed in these pages. For those reasons, we are offering correspondence inquiries to help you obtain additional information on items not listed, or even questions you may have regarding values and other related information.

Answering your correspondence (including letters, faxes, and email) under normal circumstances takes us between 10-14 working days. On hard to research items, more time is necessary. To make sure we can assist you with any correspondence, please include good quality photos of the specimen in question, any information available about that particular specimen – including manufacturer/trademark, model, body style, color/finish, unusual or other discernible features (if any) that will assist us with identifying your guitar(s). If you're emailing us an image, please make sure it is in TIF or JPEG format. Poor quality images cannot be properly used for determining value. The charge for this comprehensive research program is $20.00 per instrument. In addition to payment, be sure to include both your address and phone number, giving us an option of how to contact you for best service. To keep up with this constant onslaught of correspondence, we have a large network of both dealers and collectors who can assist us (if necessary) to answer most of your questions within this time frame.

Remember, the charge for this research service is $20.00 per guitar and payment must accompany your correspondence, and will be answered in a FIFO system (first in first out). Thank you for your patience. Sometimes proper research can't be hurried.

You may also want to check our web site for additional guitar information, including the Photo Grading System™ for ascertaining guitar condition factors. Good information never sleeps!

All correspondence regarding information and appraisals (not potential contributions or buying/selling guitars) should be directed to:

Blue Book Publications, Inc.
Attn: Guitar Research
8009 34th Avenue South, Ste. 175
Minneapolis, MN 55425 USA
Toll-free (U.S. & Canada): 800-877-4867 (voicemail only)
Fax: 952-853-1486
Email: guitars@bluebookinc.com
Web: http://www.bluebookinc.com
SORRY - No order or request for research paid by credit card will be processed without a credit card expiration date.

BUYING, SELLING, or TRADING

Interested in buying or selling a particular guitar(s)? Not sure about Ebay, or perhaps another risky alternative? Doe consigning scare you? Or maybe you're just hesitating because you're not sure what a fair market price is? To be sure tha you are getting a fair price/getting what you paid for, a buy/sell referral contact will be made, typically based on your inter est(s) and geographical location. This referral service is designed to help all those people who are worried or scared abou purchasing a potentially "bad guitar" or getting "ripped off" when selling. There is no charge for this referral service – w are simply connecting you with the best person(s) possible within your interest(s), making sure that you get a fair dea This sort of matchmaking (no easy task) can make a world of difference on potentially buying or selling a guitar. Pleas contact the *Blue Book of Acoustic Guitars*™ with your request(s) (email or fax preferred). If selling or trading, please ma or email (TIF or JPEG format) us a good quality image(s). On buy requests, please as specific as possible. All replies ar treated strictly confidentially, and should be directed to:

Blue Book Publications, Inc.
Attn: Guitars B/S/T
8009 34th Ave. S., Ste. 175
Minneapolis, MN 55425 USA
Email: guitars@bluebookinc.com
Web: http://www.bluebookinc.com
Fax: 952-853-1486
Toll-free (U.S. & Canada): 800-877-4867
Non-domestic: 952-854-5229

COMMON GUITAR ABBREVIATIONS

These abbreviations listed below may be found as prefixes and suffixes with a company's model names, and may indi cate a special quality about that particular designation. This list should be viewed as being a guide only; abbreviation specifically relating to individual trademarks (i.e., Fender, Gibson, Martin) are listed separately within their sections.

A	-Ash	F	Spanish -Fretless or Florentine		Not Available	S	-Spanish, Solid Body, Special or Super
AE	-Acoustic Electric			NAMM	-National Association of Musical Merchants		
B	-Bass, Brazilian Rosewood, or Blue (finish)	FB	-Fingerboard	NOS	-New Old Stock	SB, S/B	-Sunburst
		H	-Herringbone	OEM	-Original Equipment Manufacture	Ser. No.	-Serial Number
BLK, BK,		HB	-Humbucker			SG	-Solid Guitar
BL	-Black (finish)	HC	-Hard Case			SGL	-Single
B & S	-Back & Sides (not BS, that's the sales pitch!)	HDWR	-Hardware	OH	-Original Hardshell	SJ	-Super Jumbo
		HS	-Headstock	OHSC	-Original Hardshell Case	SN	-Serial Number
		J	-Jumbo	OM	-Orchestra Model	STD	-Standard
C	-Cutaway	K	-Koa	OSC	-Original Soft Case	SWD	-Smartwood
CH	-Channel	L, LH	-Left-Handed	OTRA	-On The Road Again	T	-Tremolo or Thinline
C.I.T.E.S.	-Convention for International Trade of Endangered Species (July 1,1975)	LE	-Limited Edition	PG	-Pickguard	TOB	-Tobacco
		M	-Mahogany or Maple	PU (P.U.)	-Pickup	TREM	-Tremolo
		MFG.	-Manufactured	R	-Reverse (headstock) Red (finish), or Rosewood	TV	-TV Color Finish
		MENG	-MENG!			V	-V shaped Neck, Venetian, Vibrato or Vintage Series
D	-Dreadnought or Double	MOP	-Mother-Of-Pearl				
		MPL	-Maple	REFIN	-Refinished	VIB	-Vibrato
DC	-Double Cutaway	MSR	-Manufacturer's Suggested Retail	REFRET	-Refretted	W/	-With
E	-Electric			REPRO	-Reproduction	W/O	-Without
EQ	-Equalizer	N, NAT	-Natural	RSH	-Round Soundhole	WOB	-Wood Out Binding
ES	-Electric (Electro)	N/A	-Not Applicable/				

KNOW YOUR WOODS!

Throughout the text of this book, readers may notice the different woods used in the construction of guitars and basses. In addition to wood types, we have also listed wood trade names as well (i.e., SmartWood, Certified Wood, Plywood, Wildwood, etc.). The following table is presented to help understand the names, family references, and many other common names that describe the woods used in guitar building. Without these woods, guitar building would be on a much lower plateau.

WOOD VARIETIES (SOFT & HARDWOOD) TRADENAMES, & RELATED INFORMATION

Common Name	Latin Name	Family	Other Names/Information
American Woods			
Alder	–	–	–
Ash	–	–	–
Cedar, Western Red	–	–	Typically harvested in California & Washington
Certified Wood	–	–	Term used by Smartwood Certified Forestry designating that the wood comes only from a certified forest.
Cherry	–	–	–
Deadwood	–	–	Stage following old wood, indigenous to a small area in South Dakota north of Rapid City.
Lyptus			Genetically grown eucalyptus hybrid (not SmartWood)
Madrone	Arbutus Menziessi	Ericaceae	–
Maple (generic)	Acer Macrophyllum	Aceraceae	–
Big Leaf Maple			–
Bird's-Eye Maple	–	–	Bird's-Eye, "dot-top," denoted by dark, small circular patterns, somewhat resembling bird's eyes.
Flame Maple	–	–	Flametop, denoted by discernible lines showing the dark and light contrast of the grain. Can be either wide or narrow.
Quilt Maple	–	–	Quilted, denoted by swirly, puffy, cloud-like patterns.
Red Birch			SmartWood
Rock Maple	Acer Saccharum	Aceraceae	Hard Maple, White Maple
	Good quality rock maple is straight grained, and almost white.		
Oak	—	—	Red or White Oak (mostly acoustic production)
Plywood	Cheapus Waytoomuchus	American Big Business	—
	Utilized in more recently mfg. instruments, allowing good overall tonal wood characteristics at a price point.		
SmartWood	Politicus Correctus	Treehuggers	Certified Wood
	The term SmartWood represents an organization called SmartWood Certified Forestry, run by the Rainforest Alliance, and governed by the Forest Stewardship Council. The SmartWood Certified Forestry program ensures that SmartWood is harvested only from certified managed forests that have been independently evaluated, ensuring that they meet internationally recognized environmental and socioeconomic standards.		
Spruce	—	—	Many variations
	The 3 main variations of American spruce are Sitka spruce, grown in the coastal region between Northern California & Alaska, Engelmann spruce is indigenous to the Rocky Mountain Range, including New Mexico, Idaho, and Montana, and Adirondack spruce, which comes from the Adirondack region in the eastern U.S. Other variations do exist.		
Sycamore	Acer Pseudoplatanus	Aceraceae	—
Tonewood (universal term)			Generic term referring to any wood selected in the manufacturing process for tonal quality and performance. Tonewoods usually include maple, mahogany, rosewood, ebony, spruce, koa, cedar, walnut, etc.
Walnut	Juglans Hindsii	Juglancaceae	California Walnut, Claro Walnut
Wildwood			Refers to Fender trademark for process utilizing German beech trees injected with dyes that have been cut into veneers and laminated to the top of the instrument, circa 1967–1970.
South and Central American Woods			
Bocate	Cordia spp.	—	Mexican Rosewood
Brazilian Rosewood	Harvest Interuptus	Mucho Centavos	
	Brazilian rosewood was mostly discontinued after 1968, the last legal year of importation. Current legal mfg. requires C.I.T.E.S. certification beginning 1992. Since this now very controlled hardwood has achieved almost cult-like status, prices for instruments utilizing Brazilian rosewood (mostly back & sides) have skyrocketed - both on new and vintage instruments.		
Cocobola	Dalbergia Retusa	Leguminosae	Granadillo
Imbuia	—	—	—
	Indigenous in southern Brazil		
Mahogany	Swietinia Macrophylla	Meliaceae	—
Nato	—	—	—
	Utility Grade Mahogany, not as high grade as African or Indian mahogany.		
Purpleheart	Peltogne spp.	Leguminosae	Amaranth, Violetwood, Morado, Saka, Koroboreli, Tananeo, Pau Roxo
Tulipwood	Dalbergia Fructescens	Leguminosae	Jacaranda Rosa, Pinkwood, Pau Rosa
African Woods			
Bubinga	Guibouria Demusi	Leguminosae	African Rosewood
Cocobola	Microberlinia	Leguminosae	Zebrano, Zingana, Brazzavillensis, Allene, Ele, Amouk
Ebony	Diospryus Crassiflora	Ebenaceae	Gabon Ebony
	(African ebony is generally categorized by the country of orgin, i.e., Madagascar, etc.)		
Mahogany	—	—	—
South America			
Ovangkol	—	—	—
Pink Ivory	—	—	—
Sapele	—	—	—
Wenge	Millettia Laurentii	Leguminosae	Panga Panga
Zebrawood	—	—	—
European Woods			
Spruce	—	—	typically German Spruce
Indian Woods			
Ebony	Diospryus Ebenaceae	Ebenaceae	—
Macassar Ebony	Diospryus Celebica	Ebenaceae	Striped Ebony
Indian Rosewood	Dalbergia Latifoloa	Leguminosae	Bombay Rosewood, Sissoo, Biti, Ervadi, Kalaruk
	(most currently manufactured guitars using rosewood are made from Indian rosewood - C.I.T.E.S. approval not needed)		
Vermillion	Pterocarpu Dalbergoides	Leguminosae	Paduak, Andaman Rosewood
Pacific Region Woods			
Koa	Acacia Koa	—	Australian Silky Oak
Lacewood	Carwellia Sublimis	Protaceae	Phillipine Mahogany, widely acclaimed for its tonal characteristics.
Mahogany	—	—	

(Wood information courtesy Mica Wickersham, Alembic, & S.P. Fjestad)

GLOSSARY

This glossary is divided into 4 sections: General Glossary, Hardware: Bridges, Pegs, Tailpieces, and Tuners, Pickups/Electronics, and Book Terminology. If you are looking for something and can't find it in one section, please check the others. You may also want to refer to Anatomy of An Acoustic Guitar (page 16) for visual identification on many of the terms listed below. For wood terminology, please see the Know Your Woods section.

GENERAL GLOSSARY

Abalone - Shellfish material used in instrument ornamentation.

Acoustic - Generic term used for hollow bodied instruments that rely on the body to produce the amplified sound of the instrument, rather than electronic amplification.

Acoustic Electric - A thin hollow bodied instrument that relies on a pickup to further amplify its sound.

Action - Everybody wants a piece of it. It is also the height the strings are off of the fingerboard, stretched between the nut and bridge.

Arch/Arched Top - The top of an instrument that has been carved or pressed to have a "rounded" top.

Avoidire - Blonde mahogany.

Back Plate - Refers to the cover plate on the back of an instrument allowing access into the body cavity for repair/alterations.

Bass Bout - Upper left hand part of body (left side of lower fingerboard on right-hand guitars).

Bell - Truss Rod cover located directly above nut. Most are bell shaped, and may have model/make information on the outside.

Belly - Refers to the inside of the soundboard.

Binding (bound) - Trim that goes along the outer edge of the body, neck or headstock. It is made out of many different materials, natural and synthetic.

Body - The main bulk of the instrument, usually. It is where the bridge, tailpiece and pickguard are located. On acoustics, the soundhole, or holes, are located on the body top, usually, and the sound is amplified inside it. On electrics, it is where the pickups are routed into and the electronics housing is stored. It is what the player cradles.

Bolt On/Bolt On Neck - Construction technique that involves attaching the neck to the body by means of bolts or screws. Bolt-on necks are generally built and finished separately from the guitar body, and parts are assembled together later.

Bookmatched – Refers to the process where a single block of wood is cut in half lengthwise. Both pieces are then "bookmatched" – glued so that the grain of the 2 pieces matches. Very popular on instruments with maple backs and a lot of flame.

Bound - See BINDING.

Bout/Bouts - Also see BASS BOUT, LOWER BOUT, and TREBLE BOUT. The rounded, generally, side/sides on the top and bottom of an instrument's body.

Bracing - The splayed pattern of supportive wooden struts that strengthen the top and back of a guitar and effect tone; "scalloped" braces are those that have been shaved or carved to lighten the guitar and/or to allow for tone-producing flexibility, especially on the top of the guitar; also "strutting."

Bridge - Component that rests on the top of the instrument and transfers vibrations from string to body. It is usually attached by glue or screws but is also held in place by string tension, the same as a violin.

Carved Top - See ARCHTOP.

Cello Tail Adjuster - The Cello tail adjuster is a 1/8" diameter black nylon-type material that attaches to the tailpiece and loops around an endpin jack (or ebony endpin). Nylon, of course, replaced the real (if unstable) gut material several years ago. This tail adjuster is used on virtually every cello tailpiece in the world and figures prominently in a number of archtop guitar designs.

Cutaway - An area that has been cut away on the treble bout, or both bouts, to allow access to the higher frets. See FLORENTINE and VENETIAN.

Ding - Small mark or dent on a guitar. Also the noise you swear you hear when your guitar hits another object, thus causing the mark.

Dovetail - Woodworking procedure allowing one piece to be precisely fit with another. This is a standard procedure used on set neck instruments. Also see MORTISE.

Dreadnought - A generic term used to describe steel string guitar configuration consisting of a boxy body and solid headstock.

Ebonized - A process by which the wood has been stained dark to appear to be ebony; alternatively, also referring to something black in color (such as bridge adjuster wheels) made to blend in with ebony fittings on an archtop guitar.

Ebonol - A synthetic material that is used as replacement for wood (generally as a fingerboard).

Electric - A generic term referencing the fact that the instrument relies on pickups to amplify its sound.

F-Hole - Stylized "f" shaped soundhole that is carved into the top of various instruments, most commonly acoustic. It usually comes in pairs.

Fingerboard - Older designation for fretboard. See Fretboard.

Finish - The outer coat of an instrument. The sealant of the wood. The protector of the instrument. Finishes include Gloss, Satin, Nitrocellulose, Matte, Spar, Polyurethane, Tongue Oil, etc.

Flamenco - Refers to a classically designed Spanish guitar with modifications made for the Flamenco music for which it became famous. Traditional flamenco guitars typically feature a slightly smaller body than a classical guitar, thinner rims made from Spanish cyprus, wooden pegs, and low action fingerboard with high tension strings. Flamenco music and instruments initially centered around Andalucia, a region in Spain, and was well established by the end of the 1800s.

FlatTop - Term used to describe an acoustic steel stringed instrument whose top is flat.

Florentine - Sharp point on the treble forward horn of a body cutaway. See also VENETIAN.

Fret - A strip of metal that is embedded at specific intervals into the fingerboard.

Fretboard - The area on front of the neck where the string(s) is pressed against to create the desired note (frequency). Another way of saying fingerboard and specifying that it has frets embed-

GLOSSARY

ded into it. Fretboards are usually made from extreme hardwoods, including ebony, rosewood, and maple.

Fretless Fingerboard - Commonly found on bass instruments, this fingerboard is smooth, with no frets.

Golpeador - Protective (generally clear) plate added to top of flamenco guitars for tapping.

Graphite - Used in various forms of instrument construction because of its rigidity and weight, this type of synthetic material may be used in the body, neck, nut, saddle, etc

Hardware - Generic term for the bridge, tailpiece, tuners or vibrato system.

Headless - This means the instrument has no headstock.

Headstock - Top portion of the neck assembly where the tuning machines are located. Headstock design is a field unto itself, and many makes/models can be instantly identified by simply looking at an instrument's headstock design/configuration. Additional information about the instrument, such as serialization (typically on back side or top), model number, and/or distinctive logo/trademark may also be part of the headstock.

Heel - On the backside of an instrument, the heel is located at the base of the lower neck where the neck meets the body. May be bound, inlaid, or carved as well.

Inlay - Decoration or identifying marks on an instrument that are inlaid into one of the surface areas. They are made of a number of materials, though abalone, pearl and wood are the most common.

Lining - Typically made from small wooden strips, this lining is traditionally "kerfed" (sawed frequently, but not through, allowing bending), and is glued around the inside of the body, both on the top and back. Both the top and back of the instrument are precisely glued to these body linings.

Locking Tuners - These tuners are manufactured with a locking mechanism built right into them, thus preventing string slippage.

Logo - An identifying feature on an instrument: it could be a symbol or a name; and it could appear as a decal, an inlay, or painted on (and it could be missing).

Lower Bout(s) - Refers to the lower part of an instrument's contour(s). A lower bout measurement is the maximum distance between an instrument's 2 lower bouts.

Maccaferri Design - Refers to unusual flattop design featuring wide oval soundhole, long/thin bridge, and distinctive body cutaway. This configuration was originally built by the French Selmer company during the early 1930s, and was the design used exclusively by noted guitarist Django Reinhardt.

Mortise - Wood construction procedure where one piece of wood is carefully fitted to join another. Also see DOVETAIL.

Mother-of-Pearl (MOP) - A shellfish (oyster/clam) material used for inlay.

Nato - A lower grade or quality of mahogany, sometimes referred to as "lumberyard" mahogany.

Neck - The area that the strings of the instrument are stretched along, the headstock sits at the top, and the body lies at the bottom.

Neck Angle/Pitch - The angle at which the neck joins the body (more common on set neck instruments). Different neck angles can affect both tone & volume, especially on acoustic guitars.

Octave - In Western Notation, every 12 frets on a stringed instrument is an octave in the musical scale of things.

Pearl - Short for mother-of-pearl, the inside shell from a shellfish. See MOTHER-OF-PEARL.

Pearloid - A synthetic material made of plastic and pearl dust.

Peghead - See HEADSTOCK. Originally used to describe the pegs/tuners extruding from the guitar head.

Phenolic - A synthetic material that is used as fingerboard wood replacement.

Pickguard - A piece of material used to protect the instrument's top or finish from gouges that are caused by the pick or your fingers.

Pickup - An electronic device utilizing magnetic induction to transform string vibrations into electronic signals needed for sound amplification. Pickups can either be high (most popular) or low (less output) impedance.

Position Marker - Usually, some form of decorative inlay which is inlaid into the neck to help the player identify fret position.

"Pre-CBS" - Collector's terminology that refers to the CBS purchase of Fender Instruments in 1965. A "Pre-CBS" instrument is one built by Leo Fender's original company.

Purfling - Decorative trim that is found running along the inside of the binding.

Relief - The upward slope of the fingerboard that keeps the strings off the frets.

Resonator - A metal device located in some instruments that is the means of their amplification. Resonator instruments transfer the vibrations of their strings through the bridge to a round metal dish or cone which acts as a resonator within the guitar. Because of this, they are typically louder than conventional acoustic instruments. Preferred by slide guitarists.

Reverse Headstock - On this instrument the headstock has been flipped over from the normal configuration and the tuners are all on the highest note side of the instrument (tuners are all located on one side).

Rims/Ribs - Also referred to as Sides – refers to the sides of an instrument, typically between 1½ -5 inches deep.

Rosette - A decorative design that is inlaid around the soundhole. A 3 ring rosette (see page 13) refers to 3 decorative rings inlaid around the soundhole, with varying widths.

Saddle - A natural or synthetic component generally attached to the bridge on which the strings rest, enabling the strings to resonate properly through the bridge and instrument top, and to assist in intonation. On many currently manufactured acoustic electric instruments, the area between the bottom of the saddle and bridge is where the acoustic pickup (Fishman, L.R. Baggs, etc.) is installed. Usually stepped or slanted.

Scale Length - The area between the nut and bridge over which the strings of the instrument are stretched.

Scalloped - This is what the area on the fingerboard between the frets is called when it has been scooped out, creating a dip between the frets.

Scratch Plate - Slang for Pickguard. See PICKGUARD.

Semi-Acoustic - Term used to describe a shallow bodied instrument that is constructed with a solid piece of wood running the length of the center of the body.

Sides - also referred to as Rims – refers to the sides of an instrument, typically between 1½ -5 inches deep.

Slotted Headstock - A headstock design usually associated with classical acoustic guitars, featuring 2 internal "slotted" areas where the strings are guided and the tuning machines spindles are placed horizontally.

Soundboard - The top of an acoustic guitar. This top (typically spruce for its tonal quality), resonates from the vibrations coming down from the saddle and bridge. It, in turn, vibrates the rims and backside. This amplified sound typically escapes through a round hole(s) or f-holes.

Soundhole - A hole found in the top of acoustic instruments (mostly), that allows the sound to be projected from the body.

Strings - Typically made from gut (older), nylon, steel, or bronze. Metal strings may or may not be coated also. They range in a variety of sizes, both in diameter and length. The weight of the string is what determines the range of frequencies it will cover.

Sunburst (Sunburst Finish) - Typically, either a 2 or 3 color finish that is applied around the outside of the body (may include rims, back, and neck also), leaving the inside a lighter, unstained natural color.

Thinline - Original Gibson terminology referring to a hollowbodied instrument that has a shallow depth of body.

Through Body (Thru Body; Neck Through) - Type of construction that consists of the neck wood extending through the entire length of the instrument and the pieces of wood that make up the body being attached to the sides of the neck wood (called wings).

Tone Bars - Traditional single strip bracing (one for treble, and one for bass) attached to the inside of an archtop to assist with an instrument's harmonics.

Top Block - Wood component that is attached to the inside part of the neck where it joins the body. This "locks" the neck in place with the body.

Treble Bout - Upper right-hand part of body (right side of lower fingerboard on right hand guitars).

Tremolo - An increase or decrease in the frequency of a tone. Tremolo in relation to guitars usually refers to a tremolo unit, or tremolo effects. Please refer to individual listings.

Truss Bar - A square or T-shaped bar fit into the back of the neck, typically non-adjustable.

Truss Rod - Refers to a metal truss rod fitted into the back of an instrument's neck, adding stability, and allowing for a neck adjustment in the case of a warped/curved neck. Gibson invented this solution for neck adjusting in the mid 1920s.

Venetian - Rounded point on the treble forward horn of a body cutaway. See also FLORENTINE.

Vibrato - The act of physically lengthening or shortening the medium (in this case, it will be strings) to produce a fluctuation in frequency. The pitch altering mechanism on your guitar is a vibrato, not a tremolo!

Volute (also Neck Volute) - Additional protruding wood used as a strengthening support where an angled-back headstock is spliced to the end of the neck. This carved (or shaped) piece of the neck is also referred to as a "handstop."

Warpage - Generally refers to a neck that becomes bowed or warped, making playability difficult/impossible. On necks with truss rods, the neck may be adjusted to become straight again. On instruments with set necks, often times the neck must be taken off and repaired, or needs to be replaced.

Wings - The body pieces attached to the sides of a through body neck blank, thus forming a complete body.

X Bracing - A traditional method of internal top bracing which resembles an X pattern.

Zero Fret - The zero fret is a length of fret wire fitted into a fret slot which is cut at the exact location as that of a conventional nut. The fingerboard is generally cut off 1/8" longer than usual, at which point the nut is fitted. When used in conjunction with the zero fret, the nut serves as a string guide. The fret wire used on the zero fret is usually slightly larger than that used on the fingerboard itself – the slightly higher zero fret establishes the open string's height above the fingerboard.

HARDWARE: BRIDGES, PEGS, TAILPIECES AND TUNERS

Acoustic Bridge - The bridge on an acoustic instrument is usually glued to the top and though pins are usually used there are still numerous ways of holding the strings taut.

Banjo Tuners - Tuners that are perpendicular to the headstock and pass through it, as opposed to being mounted on the side of the headstock, (like classic style headstock tuners).

Bigsby Vibrato - A vibrato system that involves a roller bar with little pegs that run in a perpendicular line, around which you hook the string balls. One end of the bar has an arm coming off of it, a spring is located under the arm, and the entire apparatus is connected to a trapeze tailpiece. The bridge is separate from the vibrato system. This vibrato was designed by Paul Bigsby.

Bridge - Component that connects the strings to the body of the instrument. Bridge materials may be wood, metal, alloy, synthetic, or even a combination. It is usually attached to the top of an instrument's body by glue or screws but can also be held in place by string tension, the same as a violin. Bridge placement is determined by the instrument's scale length.

Bridge Pins - Pins or dowels used to secure string to bridge. These pins usually utilize friction to seat properly, and are typically made from hard wood, synthetic materials (ivoroid is popular), or ivory. Also referred to as Pegs.

Double Locking Vibrato - A vibrato system that locks the strings into place by tightening down screws on each string, thus stopping the string's ability to slip. There is also a clamp at the top of the fingerboard that holds the strings from the tuners. These more modern designs were formulated separately by Floyd Rose and the Kahler company. As guitarist Billy Gibbons (ZZ Top) is fond of saying, the locking vibratos give you the ability to "turn

GLOSSARY

Steel into Rubber, and have 'er bounce back on a dime." See VIBRATO.

Fixed Bridge - Body hardware component that typically contains the saddles, bridge, and tailpiece in one integrated unit, and is usually mounted utilizing screws/studs.

Friction Pegs - Wooden dowels that rely on the friction created between itself and the wood of the hole it is put in to keep the tension of the strings constant.

Headless - Term meaning that the instrument's headstock is missing. The top of the neck is capped with a piece of hardware that acts like a regular tailpiece on the instrument body.

Locking Tuners - These tuners are manufactured with a locking mechanism built into them, thus preventing string slippage.

Nut - Device located at the top of the fingerboard (opposite from the bridge) that determines the action and spacing of the strings.

Pegs - See FRICTION PEGS. Can refer to either the small pegs used to secure the strings in the bridge or older tuners used on some vintage instruments (hence the term peghead).

Pins - Pegs that are used to anchor the strings in place on the bridge.

Roller Bridge - This is a Gretsch trademark feature. It is an adjustable metal bridge that sits on a wooden base, the saddles of this unit sit on a threaded bar and are easily moved back and forth to allow personal string spacing.

Saddle/Saddles - A part of the bridge that holds the string/strings in place, helps transfer vibrations to the instrument body and helps in setting the action.

Set-In Neck - Guitar construction that involves attaching the neck to the body by gluing a joint (such as a dovetail). Set necks cannot be adjusted by shims, as their angle of attachment to the body is pre-set in the design.

Single Locking Vibrato - A vibrato system that locks the strings on the unit to keep them from going out of tune during heavy arm use. This style of vibrato does not employ a clamping system at the top of the fingerboard.

Standard Vibrato - Usually associated with the Fender Stratocaster, this unit has the saddles on top and an arm off to one side. The arm allows you to bend the strings, making the frequencies (notes) rise or drop. All of this sits on a metal plate that rocks back and forth. Strings may have an area to attach to on top or they may pass through the body and have holding cups on the back side. A block of metal, usually called the Inertia Block, is generally located under the saddles to allow for increased sustain. The block travels through the instrument's body and has springs attached to it to create the tension necessary to keep the strings in tune. See VIBRATO.

Steinberger Bridge - A bridge designed by Ned Steinberger, it combines the instrument bridge and tuners all in one unit. It is used with headless instruments.

Stop Tailpiece - Machined metal part attached to lower body by screws, which is usually slotted to hold the string balls. Generally used with a tune-o-matic bridge.

Strap button - Typically refers to oversized metal buttons on the outside of an instrument allowing the player to attach a strap to the instrument.

Strings Through Body (Anchoring) - A tailpiece that involves the strings passing through an instrument's body and the string balls are held in place by recessed cups on the back side.

Stud Tailpiece - See STOP TAILPIECE.

Tailpiece - The device that holds and typically positions (along with a possible bridge) the strings at the lower body. It may be all in one unit that contains the saddle/saddles also, or stands alone. Electric tailpieces are mostly metal construction, although metal, wood, alloy, synthetic or other materials have also been used.

Tied Bridge - Style of bridge usually associated with "classical" style instruments that have the strings secured by tying them around the bridge.

Trapeze Tailpiece - A type of tailpiece that is hinged, has one end attached to the bottom bout of the instrument and the other end has grooves in it to hold the string balls.

Tremolo Unit - Refers to a mechanical device typically incorporated into the bridge of an instrument utilizing a tremolo (whammy) bar to produce changes in frequencies.

Tuner(s)/Tuning Machine(s) - Mechanical device that is used to stretch the strings to the right tension for adjustable tuning. These are typically located on the headstock.

Tunable Stop Tailpiece - A tailpiece that rests on a pair of posts and has small fine tuning machines mounted on top of it.

Tune-o-matic Bridge - A bridge that is attached to the instrument's top by two metal posts and has adjustable saddles on the topside.

Wrapover Bridge - A self contained bridge/tailpiece bar device that is attached to the body, with the strings wrapping over the bar.

Wrapunder Bridge - The same as above except the strings wrap under the bar.

PICKUPS/ELECTRONICS

The following terms are usually associated with acoustic electric guitars and basses. Please refer to the 8th Edition *Blue Book of Electric Guitars* for a more complete listing under this category.

Active Electronics - A form of electronic circuitry that involves some power source, usually a 9-volt battery. Most of the time the circuit is an amplification circuit, though it may also be onboard effects circuitry.

Alnico Pickup - A pickup utilizing an alloy magnet consisting of Aluminum, Nickel, and Cobalt.

Amplify/Amplification - To increase, in this case to increase the volume of the instrument.

Floating pickup - A magnetic pickup that is suspended over (versus being built into) the top of the guitar, just below the fingerboard. This enables the guitar to be used acoustically or electrically. Examples include the Benedetto pickup, the DeArmond #1100G, or the Gibson Johnny Smith pickup.

"Jazz" Pickup - A pickup, suspended (floating) or built-in on an archtop guitar that gives the instrument a traditional, mainstream jazz sound.

Onboard - Usually referencing effects, it means built into the instrument.

GLOSSARY

Parametric Equalizer - An equalizer that allows you to specifically choose which range of frequencies you wish to affect.

Passive Electronics - Electronic circuitry that has no power supply. Usually it consists of filter circuitry.

Pickup - An electronic device utilizing magnetic induction to transform string vibrations into electronic signals needed for sound amplification. Pickups can either be high (most popular) or low (less output) impedance. Pickups on most acoustic electric instruments are of the ribbon type, and are placed where the bottom of the saddle and bridge join. Often times, an onboard equalizer is utilized in conjunction with these acoustic pickups, allowing the player to control the tone and volume. Popular brands include Fishman, L.R. Baggs, Rio Grande, etc.

Piezo (Piezoelectric) - A crystalline substance that induces an electrical current caused by pressure or vibrations.

Pot - Short for "potentiometer."

Potentiometer - A variable resistor that is typically used to make tone and volume adjustments on an instrument.

Preamp - An electronic circuit that amplifies the signal from the pickup/s and preps it for the amplifier.

Soundhole - An opening in the instrument's top (usually), that allows the amplified sound out of the body cavity.

Transducer/Transducer Pickup - A device that converts energy from one form to another, in this instance it is the vibrations caused by the strings, moving along the wood and being converted into electrical energy for amplification.

BOOK TERMINOLOGY

This glossary section should help you understand the jargon used in the model descriptions of the instruments in this text.

3-per-side - Three tuners on each side of the headstock on a six string instrument.

3/2-per-side - This is in reference to a 5-string instrument with three tuners on one side of the headstock and two tuners on the other.

335 Style - refers to an instrument that has a semi-hollowbody cutaway body style similar to that of the Gibson 335.

4-on-one-side - Four tuners on one side of the headstock on a 4-string instrument.

4-per-side - Four tuners on each side of the headstock an eight-string instrument.

4/1-per-side - On an instrument with five strings this would mean four tuners are on one side of the headstock, and one is on the other.

4/2-per-side - Four tuners on one side and two on the other side of a headstock.

4/3-per-side - This instrument has seven strings with four of the tuners located on one side of the headstock and three on the other side.

5-on-one-side - All the tuners on one side of the headstock on a 5-string instrument.

6-on-one-side - All six tuners on one side of the headstock on a 6-string instrument.

6-per-side - Six tuners on each side of the headstock on a twelve string instrument.

6/1-per-side - A seven string instrument with six tuners on one side and one on the other.

7-on-one-side - A term referring to a seven-string instrument with all the tuners on the headstock are on one side.

14/20-Fret - Term in which the first number describes the fret at which the neck joins the body and the second number is the total number of frets on the fingerboard.

Classical Style - This term refers to a gut or nylon string instruments fashioned after the original guitar design. Used predominately in classical music, this design features a 12/19 fretboard, round soundhole, slotted (or open) headstock, and a tied-end bridge.

Contoured Body - A body design that features some carved sections that fit easier to the player's body.

Dreadnought Style - This term refers to steel string instruments that are fashioned after the traditional build of a Martin instrument, a boxy type instrument with squared top and bottom bouts, approximately 14 inches across the top bouts, 16 inches across the bottom bouts, there is not much of a waist and the depth of instrument is about 4-5 inches.

Dual Cutaway - Guitar design with two forward horns, both extending forward an equal amount (See OFFSET DOUBLE CUTAWAY, SINGLE CUTAWAY).

Flamenco Style - The Flamenco style guitar is similar to the Classical style, save for the addition of the (generally clear) 'tap plate.' by the bridge.

Jazz Style - A body shape similar to the traditional jazz archtop or semi-hollowbody design, or affiliated parts of such models.

Les Paul (LP) Body Style - Typically refers to original Gibson Les Paul style body.

Offset Double Cutaway - Guitar design with two forward horns, the top (bass side) horn more prominent of the two (See DUAL CUTAWAY, SINGLE CUTAWAY).

Point Fingerboard - A fingerboard that has a "V-ed" section on it at the body end of the fingerboard.

Point(y) Headstock - Tip of the headstock narrows (i.e. Charvel/Jackson or Kramer models).

Single Cutaway - Guitar design with a single curve into the body, allowing the player access to the upper frets of the fretboard (See DUAL CUTAWAY, OFFSET DOUBLE CUTAWAY).

Sleek - A more modern body style, perhaps having longer forward horns, more contoured body, or a certain aerodynamic flair (!).

Through Body (Neck-Through Construction) - Type of construction that consists of the neck wood extending through the entire length of the instrument and the pieces of wood that make up the body being attached to the sides of the neck wood.

Tune-o-matic Stop Tailpiece - This unit is a combination bridge/tailpiece that has adjustable (tune-o-matic) saddles mounted on a wrap around tailpiece.

Volume/Tone Control - When encountered, refers to an instrument which has a volume and/or tone control. A numerical prefix (2 or 3) preceding the term indicates the amount of volume/tone controls.

UNDERSTANDING CONDITION FACTORS

Rating the condition factor of a guitar is, at best, still subjective, while at worst, totally misrepresentative. We've attempted to give a few examples of things that may affect the pricing and desirability of vintage acoustic guitars, but it's almost impossible to accurately ascertain the correct condition factor (especially true on older instruments) without knowing what to look for – which means having the instrument in your hands (or someone else's whose checked out). Even then, three different experienced sources will probably come up with slightly different grades, not to mention different values based on different reasons. Listed below are major factors to consider when determining both the condition and value of any used acoustic instruments. Also, please study the PGS digital color photographs carefully on pages 33-48 to learn more about the factors described below.

Finish (read that original finish) - Original finish in good shape is, of course, the most desirable, and is the Holy Grail for collectors when hooked up with a major trademark and desirable model. A light professional overspray will negatively affect the value of a guitar somewhat. Professionally refinished instruments are typically worth 50% of the value of an original, and a poor refin is below than that. An exception might be a case where there's only one or two examples of a highly desirable item, and condition may take a back seat to rarity.

Major repairs - Many older guitars have had repairs, of course. A well-done neck reset won't affect the overall value that much. Replaced bridges will have an affect, but the better the work, the better the resale value. A replaced neck, fingerboard, part of a side, top or back will cause the price to drop noticeably. Again, if it's an especially rare item, the rarity factor might negate the major repair(s).

Modifications - Any non-factory modification on an original guitar is going to hurt the value. Deciding to refinish the top of your pre-war D-45 Martin for example, will cost you the price of refinishing, plus another $15,000-$35,000 for non-originality! Less visible but still important are altered bracing, shaved necks, and repaired/replaced/shaved bridges. Think really really hard before you make any of these changes on vintage guitars. On current acoustic instruments, playing modifications may add to an instrument's value on occasion. Remember, you won't get a second chance to make it original.

Replacement Tuners and other non-original parts - Many older guitars have been fitted with new tuners at some point. These days, there are good replacement tuners available that fit the original holes, etc. There are also sleeves that will make an oversized hole into the correct size for original style tuners. Even a good, appropriate replacement set will have a negative affect on value, even though it constitutes a playing improvement over what was available when the instrument was manufactured.

Cracks - Acoustic instruments are overall more susceptible to cracking than electric guitars. This is because the bodies are typically not solid, and the thinner wood may crack due to humidity and/or temperature variations. Many older pre-WWII acoustic guitars have a cracked top. The seriousness of the crack and/or how professional it has been repaired make all the difference in determining both playability and value. Unfortunately, unattended cracks tend to get bigger and usually do not go back together perfectly. Any crack will affect value, but a small, professionally well repaired crack will take much less of a bite out of the price than a large gaping crack that wouldn't go together properly.

Frets - A good analogy for frets would be found in the vintage car market: you rarely find a vintage car with original tires. Guitars were made to be played and frets do wear out. A good professional fret job using factory spec parts should not affect the value of your instrument. Again, this question won't come up with a mint, unplayed guitar.

Cosmetics - The cleaner an instrument, the more it's worth. Don't ever underestimate the value of eye appeal. A mint, unplayed, original condition guitar with tags will always bring more than the prices for "excellent" condition. On the other hand, an instrument with most of the finish worn off from years of use, but is unaltered with no problems is still more desirable than an instrument with higher condition but with a cracked top, replaced bridge, shaved neck, etc.

General Guitar Maintenance & Tips - Airplanes are meant to be flown, cars are meant to driven, and guitars are meant to be played. Since instrument construction is typically wood, and wood expands/contracts like many other natural materials, don't allow instruments to go from one extreme temp/humidity factor to another (i.e., don't ship your Stromberg Master 400 from Ft. Meyers, FL to Thief River Falls, MN in Jan.). Try to maintain a stable temp. and humidity level. Also, use good quality, professional products to clean, polish, and maintain (Virtuoso is recommended) your instrument (investment). Remember, maintaining a fine guitar requires some common sense and TLC.

Guitars, even vintage ones, are meant to be played. Enjoy yours, take proper care of it, play it once in awhile, and don't let temperature and/or humidity factors get to extremes.

Explanation & Converting Guitar Grading Systems

Since the 8th Edition *Blue Book of Acoustic Guitars*™ continues to use the descriptive grading system of Average & Excellent factors to describe condition, please study the digital color acoustic guitar condition photos on the following pages carefully to help understand and identify each acoustic guitar's unique condition factor. These photos, with condition factors, serve as a guideline, not an absolute. Remember, if the condition factor isn't right, the price is wrong!

The conversion chart listed below has been provided to help you convert to the **Photo Grading System**™ and several others. All percentage descriptions and/or possible conversions made thereof, are based on original condition – alterations, repairs, cracking, refinishing work, and any other non-original alterations that have changed the condition of an instrument must be listed additionally and typically subtracted from the values based on condition throughout this text (please refer to page 31 for an explanation of these critical factors affecting both condition and price).

Acoustic Guitar Condition Factors with Explanations

100% - New - New with all factory materials, including warranty card, owner's manual, case, and other items that were originally included by the manufacturer. On currently manufactured instruments, the 100% price refers to an instrument not previously sold at retail. Even if a new instrument has been played only twice and traded in a week later, it no longer qualifies at 100%. On out-of-production instruments (including dealer "new, old stock," or NOS), the longer a guitar has been discontinued, the less likely you will find it in 100% condition. Some instruments that are less than 20 years old and have never been taken out-of-the-case (unplayed) may not be 100% (new), as the finish may have slightly cracked, tarnished, faded, or deteriorated. **Remember, there are no excuses in 100% condition.**

Both Excellent & Average condition factors can be sub-divided slightly, depending on wear factors, within the range of conditions. Obviously, an Average acoustic with a lot of body wear is less desirable than an Average acoustic with little body wear - and should be priced accordingly.

Excellent (90%-98%, 9.0 to 9.8, or Excellent to Mint) - Though this Excellent range is none too broad, the intent is to capture a description that indicates a very clean, (barely) used guitar. The sort of guitar that looks almost new (a few light scratches only), but may not have the original manufacturer's warranty card. Should include original case on newer instruments.

Average (60%-85%, 6.0 to 8.5, or Good to Very Good) - The Average guitar condition factor indicates an acoustic guitar that has been in a player's hands and has worn due to player use (hopefully, no abuse). Average condition instruments have average dents, small chips, and light dings on the body, and/or scratches on the top and back. Also, fret wear should typically be visible and there may also be some minor problems/defects. No excuses as a player, however. May or may not have case.

ADDITIONAL PGS/DESCRIPTIVE/NUMERICAL CONDITION FACTORS

95% - 98%, Excellent Plus, 9.5 to 9.8 - Only very slightly used and/or played very little, may have minor "case" wear or light dings on exterior finish only, without finish checking, very close to new condition, also refers to a currently manufactured instrument that has previously sold at retail, even though it may not have been played. May have a slight scratch - otherwise as new.

90%, Excellent, approx. 9.0 - Light exterior finish wear with a few minor dings, no paint chips down to the wood, normal nicks and scratches, light observable neck wear in most cases.

80%, Very Good+ (VG+), Above Average, approx. 7.5 to 8.5 - More exterior finish wear (20% of the original finish is gone) that may include minor chips that extend down to the wood, body wear, but nothing real serious, nice shape overall, with mostly honest player wear.

70%, Very Good (VG), Average, approx. 6.5 to 7.5 - More serious exterior finish wear that could include some major gauges and nicks, player arm wear, and/or fret deterioration.

60%, Good (G), Sub-average, approx. 5.5 to 6.5 - Noticeable wear on most areas – normally this consists of some major belt buckle wear and finish deterioration, may include cracking, possible repairs or alterations. When this condition factor is encountered, normally an instrument should have all logos intact, original pickups, minor headstock damage, and perhaps a few non-serious alterations, with or without original case.

40%, Fair (F), Below Average, approx. 3.5 to 5.0 - Major features are still discernible, major parts missing, probably either refinished or repaired, structurally sound, though many times encountered with non-factory alterations.

20%, Poor (P), approx. 2.0 to 3.0 - Ending a life sentence of hard labor, must still be playable, most of the licks have left, family members should be notified immediately, normally not worthy unless the ad also mentions pre-war D-45. May have to double as kindling if in a tight spot on a cold night.

2001 Taylor Model 815L - ser. no. 0605148, Natural Gloss finish, 100% condition (new). This new Taylor features a solid Sitka spruce top, abalone rosette, pearl progressive diamond fretboard inlays, Indian rosewood back and sides, and a mahogany neck. Many acoustic players feel that the quality of today's major trademark instruments has never been better. 100% new condition on currently manufactured acoustic/acoustic electric instruments assumes not previously sold at retail, and there should be no visible wear anywhere on the instrument, unless it is a store demo model. Pictured with the hanging tags, this fine flattop is hopefully destined to find a new home shortly. Courtesy Dave Rogers/Dave's Guitar Shop.

2002 Larrivee OM-10 - ser. no. 45992, Excellent Plus (near mint) 98% condition. One of Canada's better flattop manufacturers, Jean Larrivee has been building excellent quality instruments in Vancouver, British Columbia since 1968.   In 98% condition, this instrument is just starting to be broken in, and the next lucky owner is going to pay a lot less than original retail. Good acoustic instruments such as this one actually get better with age, if they are maintained properly. East Indian rosewood back/sides, mahogany neck, abalone rosette/binding, ebony fretboard and pearl flower inlays are all hallmarks of this model. Courtesy Dave Rogers/Dave's Guitar Shop.

2001 Tacoma Model CB-10E3 Acoustic Electric Bass - ser. no. D-3075080, Excellent Plus 95% condition. This bass instrument's condition is similar to the Larrivee – played lightly and in excellent plus condition. Most newer bass guitars are not that collectible, and once the player value has been established, don't pay a penny more. Unique teardrop-shaped soundhole on the upper treble bout, thin neck and on-board electronics make this a powerful instrument – maybe its biggest benefit is the weight saving, less than half of a regular solid body bass guitar. Acoustic basses have never been more popular, especially with all the advances in acoustic pickup technology. Courtesy Dave Rogers/Dave's Guitar Shop.

1999 Ovation Elite Special - ser. no. 553189, Sunburst finish, Excellent Plus, approx. 95% condition. With 15 soundholes, a fiberglass back, five piece mahogany/maple neck and rosewood fretboard, this Ovation acoustic electric instrument has only been played a little. Ovation originally debuted its radical new instrument design at the 1967 NAMM Show, and early endorsees included Glen Campbell, Charlie Byrd, and Josh White. Light fret wear and a very few minor dents and dings are the only things wrong with this guitar. Ovation has released many models based on its fiberglass back design, including the Collector's Series, which was introduced in 1982, and changes each year. Courtesy John Beeson/The Music Shoppe.

1957 Martin Model 000-28 - ser. no. 155392, Natural finish, Excellent, approx. 90% condition. 1957 was an interesting year. The Soviets launched their Sputnik satellite, smoking was linked to cancer, and Chevrolet introduced its stylish Bel Air. While nothing fancy, this vintage Martin has a solid Spruce top, very desirable Brazilian rosewood back and sides (discontinued in 1969), cedar neck and ebony fingerboard and bridge. Also observe that there's no cracking on the top below the bridge, an important consideration on older acoustic instruments, especially if they were manufactured before WWII. Older Martins in this type of original condition are always desirable (and expensive!) Courtesy Dave Rogers/Dave's Guitar Shop.

1956 Gibson Country Western Jumbo - FON# W2771 31, Natural finish, Above Average, Very Good Plus, 80-90% condition. This older Gibson acoustic flattop was very similar to the SJ (Southern Jumbo model), introduced in WWII during 1942, except that it has a tortoise colored pickguard, not black. On major trademark acoustic guitars that are this old, it's always nice to see this amount of original finish on undarkened/unstained top wood, with no cracks or repairs. This Country Western Jumbo Model is 100% original, and is very collectible, especially since it was manufactured during the first year of this model's production – which usually commands a premium over later manufacture. Courtesy Dave Rogers/Dave's Guitar Shop.

1990 Ovation Pinnacle Model 3862 - ser. no. 407585, Blue Burst finish, Above Average, Very Good Plus, 80% condition. Note the wear around edge and binding – on Ovation instruments; it is difficult to determine condition from looking at the back of the guitar, since it is a fiberglass bowl that is very resistant to scratches, nicks, belt buckle wear, etc. Pay attention to fretwear, potential cracks in the top, and always check the action, making sure that it's not too high. If the bridge and/or saddle has been shaved as low as it can go, and the action is still way off the strings, the neck might have to be reset to insure playability. Courtesy Dave Rogers/Dave's Guitar Shop.

Late 1960s Fender Villager 12-String - ser. no. 255900, Mahogany finish, Average, Very Good, approx. 70-80% condition. Any older 12-string instrument should be initially evaluated by making sure the top has not cracked from the double tension of holding down 12 strings. Careful observation reveals a previously repaired crack extending diagonally down the bridge to where the two-piece top joins on the bottom. Inset image also reveals cracking on the top rim between four bolt back plate and neck. Once playability has been negatively affected by these types of cracking problems, the price usually goes down dramatically. The Fender Villager was the 12-string variation of the Malibu Model, originally introduced in 1965. Courtesy John Beeson/The Music Shoppe.

1965 Gibson LG-0 - ser. no. 301385, Light Mahogany finish, Average, Very Good, approx. 70% condition. If you like older, mahogany Gibson flattops, this LG-0 might interest you. With a mahogany top, back, sides, and neck, the only thing that is not mahogany on this instrument is the rosewood bridge and fingerboard. While the top of the instrument looks better than 70%, the inset image clearly shows a lot of wear on the back, especially on the rims. Originally retailing for approximately $85, the LG-0 was Gibson's entry level flattop acoustic guitar, with a 14¼ in. wide body and a 24¾ in. scale. Courtesy John Beeson/The Music Shoppe.

1955 Martin 0-15 - ser. no. 143239, Natural finish, Average, Very Good, 70% condition. This small Martin was made the same year Disneyland opened in Anaheim – 1955. A powerful, lightweight instrument, this model features a mahogany top, back, sides, and neck. Observe that the entire finish of the guitar (mostly Mahogany) is somewhat faded and worn after almost a half a century of playing and proper maintenance. Maybe the best thing about this instrument is that it is original, and there is nothing wrong with it – no major cracks, replacement parts, or older unprofessional repairs. The 14/20-fret rosewood fingerboard and bridge are also standard features on this model. Courtesy Dale Hanson.

Late 1930s Gibson L-30 - no ser. no., Dark Mahogany Sunburst finish, Sub-average, Good, approx. 60-70% condition. This instrument was made during the post-Depression – pre-WWII era, a very good period of production for most American guitar companies. The guitar had clearly replaced the banjo and mandolin by this time, and electrified instruments were soon to become en vogue. This specimen, with spruce top and unbound f-holes, maple back/sides, mahogany neck, and raised tortoise colored pickguard, has a hairline crack on the right side of the trapeze tailpiece, in addition to normal nicks, dings, scratches, and light oxidation on the nickel plated hardware. Courtesy John Beeson/The Music Shoppe.

Circa 1954 Gretsch Synchromatic 100 - ser. no. 8623, Sunburst finish, Sub-average, Good, approx. 60% condition. Note this instrument has a larger body than the Gibson on the previous page, even though both instruments are similarly appointed, with this Synchromatic having a unique bridge design and stepped trapeze tailpiece. Insert shows wear on back, in addition to where the top binding has partially come off. Yet, most players and collectors would rather have this type of original instrument with a few minor problems than either a refinished guitar or one that's no longer original. Courtesy John Beeson/The Music Shoppe.

Circa 1930s National Style 1 Tricone - ser. no. 1717, Sub-average, Good, approx. 60% condition. Most metal guitar aficionados will immediately recognize this instrument as a non-engraved Hawaiian style by noticing the square neck. This type of action requires a slide to play, and explains why a traditional round neck, Spanish configuration is worth twice as much as this Hawaiian style. Note how the back of this one-piece German silver body instrument is designed to also become the neck, with the headstock being held on with a single screw. As you can see, metal wears completely differently than wood, and metal oxidation becomes the major factor when determining this type of instrument's condition. Courtesy Dave Rogers/Dave's Guitar Shop.

Circa 1930s Lap Guitar - no ser. no., Below Average, Fair, Sunburst finish, approx. 50-60% condition. Maybe the most observable problem with this Depression era guitar is that the Oahu body is cracked in several places – most noticeably below the bridge and on the back. Unfortunately the cracking finally led to warping, and you can see where attempts to repair the cracks and sand down the warping have worn the finish off. This configuration of lap guitar is no longer as popular, and without playability, this type of instrument retains little value. Also note the square wooden neck with large heel and slotted headstock. Courtesy John Beeson/The Music Shoppe.

Circa mid 1960s Vox Rio Grande Eddy Arnold Model - ser. no. 901148, Natural finish, Below Average, Fair, approx. 50% or less condition. This Vox flattop model was actually built in Italy by EKO beginning in 1964, and explains the stylish pickguard and unique rosette, bearing a strong resemblance to the EKO models manufactured concurrently. Observe major cracks on both the sides and back, reducing the price of this instrument to player value only, with pricing usually in the $100-$150 range. In many cases, today's good quality, inexpensive Pacific Rim acoustic imports have negatively affected the values of this type of older, below average condition player guitar. Courtesy John Beeson/The Music Shoppe.

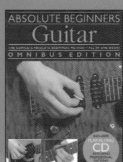

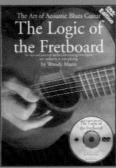

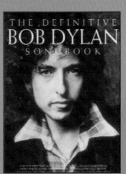

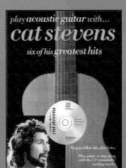

Section A

A
See chapter on House Brands.

This trademark has been identified as a House Brand of the Alden department store chain. One of the models shares similarities with the Harmony-built Stratotone of the 1960s, while a previously identified model dates back to the 1950s, (Source: Willie G. Moseley, *Stellas & Stratocasters*).

A.C.E. GUITARS
Instruments currently built in Somersworth, New Hampshire by the Poly-Tech Company.

Custom-made guitars built to order and some traditional styles as well. Current mfg. includes steel and nylon string acoustic guitars with onboard preamp and under-saddle transducer pickup. There is also a slim-body classical model with a high performance preamp and individual string output controls and bridge saddle transducer which is described as having Total Tonal Control. Archtop guitars are also built. Prices range from $1,200-$1,500 for classical and steel acoustic electrics. The slim hollow-body classical electric sells for $2,200-$2,800 depending on features. Archtops range from $1,400-$2,400. Hardshell case included with each guitar. For further information regarding specifications and pricing, contact A.C.E. Guitars directly (see Trademark Index).

ABILENE
Instruments currently produced in Korea by Samick. Distributed in the U.S. by Samick.

The Abilene trademark is distributed in the U.S. by Advantage Worldwide. The Abilene trademark is offered on a range of acoustic, acoustic/electric, and solid body electric guitars and practice amplifiers. The guitars are built by Samick of Korea. In recent years, Abilene has expanded its line immensely.

ACOUSTIC

There are a full range of acoustic models, ranging from the classical to dreadnought guitars. Recently there have been resonator and folk guitars added to the line. All guitars have model designations. The first letter (A) stands for Abilne, the second letter indicates dreadnought (w), classical (c), folk (f), or jumbo (j). The following numbers indicate the size and configuration. There may also be numbers following that indicate the finish color and if it has a satin or a gloss finish. Numbers typically start around 15 and contain many variations. Prices on these guitars are usually very reasonable and new models can typically be purchased between $50-$200.

ACADEMY
Instruments currently built in Korea. Distributed by Lark in the Morning of Mendocino, California.

Academy offers nice quality steel string guitars, 4-, 5-, and 6-string banjos, and chord harps.

ADAMAS
Instruments currently manufactured. Distributed by Kaman Music of Bloomfield, Connecticut.

Adamas guitars have been produced since 1975. Charlie Kaman, a innovator of the helicopter, took the carbon fiber material used in aviation and applied it to guitars. The top of this guitar is carbon fiber and is remarkably thin. They also have a round back to give a smooth sound. These guitars are close to Ovation in their style and layout.

ACOUSTIC

There are two different lines offered by Adamas, including the SMT and CVT lines. The SMT line has the **W597**, which is a 6-string multi-soundhole ($2,419), the **W598**, which is the same as the W597 except in 12-string configuration (MSR $2,569), and the **W591**, that has a center soundhole and six strings. The CVT line includes the **1597**, which is a multi-soundhole 6-string (MSR $2,139), the **1598**, a multi-soundhole 12-string (MSR $2,149), and the **6591**, a center soundhole 6 string. Recently, they added two Melissa Etheridge models.

ADLER CUSTOM GUITARS
Instruments currently produced in the Southern California.

Adler Guitars was started about four years ago by Michael Adler in an effort to bring genuinely custom instruments to those who couldn't previously afford them. All models are sold direct from the builder's southern California shop to the customer's specifications. Custom scale lengths, hardware, pickups, and preamps are all available at no extra cost. Custom body shapes and inlays are also available, contact Adler directly for more information (see Trademark Index).

ACOUSTIC

Adler currently produces only electric bass guitars, but they are working on releasing a California Acoustic Guitar. Look for more information in upcoming editions.

ADMIRA
Instruments currently handcrafted in Spain.

Admira guitars are all classical models with women model names. Models include Sofia, Elena, Alicia, Eva, Rosa, and Crisitina. Each model has different kinds of woods available, and Fishman electronics are available on all models.

AIRCRAFT
Current trademark of instruments built in Japan.

Guitars carrying the Aircraft logo are actually manufactured by the Morris company, which also builds instruments for such brand names as their own Morris trademark, as well as the Hurricane logo.

ALDEN
Instruments currently produced in Korea.

Alden currently produces a number of acoustic guitars as well as other products. The acoustic guitars are mostly dreadnoughts with spruce tops. For more information refer to the web site (see Trademark Index).

ALEX
See Domino. Instruments previously manufactured in Japan circa mid to late 1960s. Distributed by Maurice Lipsky Music Company, Inc. of New York, New York.

Alex acoustic guitar models featured laminated mahogany tops, backs, and sides, as well as internal fan bracing. The Alex acoustic was offered with standard size (retail list was $29.95), concert size (retail list was $34.50), grand concert (retail list was $37.50), or in a 12-string configuration (retail list was $80.00), (Domino catalog courtesy John Kinnemeyer, JK Lutherie).

ALHAMBRA
Instruments currently built in Spain. Distributed by Manufacturas Alhambra, S.L., of Alicante, Spain.

The first Alhambra guitar was manufactured in 1965 in Spain. Alhambra classical guitars are medium to very high quality Spanish instruments. These guitars epitomize the sound and beauty of a traditional Spanish guitar. Currently, models start out with the 2C at $540.00. Models then typcially average around $1,500.00. The more elaborate the wood is, the more the guitar is worth. rosewood is worth more than mahogany, and Brazillian rosewood comands a premium over all. Models are constructed with either solid cedar, red cedar, or solid spruce tops, and cypress, Brazilian rosewood, laminated rosewood,or laminated sycamore sides. Alhambra is also building a number of steel string guitars.

ALLAN
Instruments currently produced in China.

Allan guitars are all designed and supervised by Mr. Yulong Guo. Guo is a master guitar maker in China who has been building guitars for almost 20 years. Allan produces mainly classical acoustic nylon string guitars. The series include the C, AC, and HC models. Allan is working on releasing the AF Series, which is going to be a regular acoustic guitar. Allan also produces a line of violins and accordians.

ALLEN GUITARS
Instruments currently built in Colfax, California. Distributed by Randy Allen Guitars.

Luthier Randy Allen builds high quality acoustic instruments in several models; Dreadnought, OM, S-J, and Resonator guitars. All acoustic guitar models have options ranging from a cutaway body configuration, abalone edging, varied fingerboard inlays, and wood bindings. Allen imports and supplies exotic woods and abalone inlay materials to manufacturers. He also produces cast tailpieces for mandolin and resophonic guitar. Randy Allen guitars have been produced since 1982.

Standard features on the acoustic guitar models include East Indian rosewood or Honduran Mahogany back and sides, a Sitka spruce top; bound Ebony fingerboards and bridges. Basic models include the **Dreadnought** ($4,140), **Small Jumbo** ($4,537), the **Parlor** ($4,537), the **OM** ($4,537), the **Resophonic RN** ($3,875) and the **Resophonic SN** ($2,837).

In 1996, Allen debuted a new series of resophonic guitars. The **Allen Resonator** guitar models are equipped with high quality hardware, and a spun resonator cone. The chrome plate cover-plate is held in position with machine screws (as opposed to wood screws, which may strip out over time). The top, back, and sides are maple (a spruce top is available on request). All instruments include a custom case. For further information, contact luthier Randy Allen directly (see Trademark Index).

ALLEN, RICHARD C.
Instruments currently built in El Monte, California.

Luthier R.C. Allen has been playing guitar since his high school days in the late 1940s. Allen has been playing, collecting, repairing, and building guitars for a great number of years. After working sixteen years as a warehouseman for a paper company, Allen began doing repair work for West Coast guitar wholesaler/distributors like C. Bruno and Pacific Music. In 1972, Allen began building guitars full time.

Allen's designs focus on hollowbody and semi-hollowbody guitars. While he has built some electric, the design was semi-hollow (similar to the Rickenbacker idea) with a flattop/back and f-holes. Currently, Allen focuses on jazz-style archtops. Now in his 50th year of building guitars, he is building 15", 16", 17", and 18" wide guitars. He is also building a series of commemorative guitars honoring country singer Hank Thompson.

ALMANSA
Please refer to Guitarras Almansa in the G section of this text.

ALMCRANTZ

Instruments previously built in America in the late 1800s.

An Almcrantz acoustic guitar bearing a label reading "July 1895" was featured in the first edition of Tom Wheeler's reference book *American Guitars* (HarperCollins Publishers, New York). Research is continuing on the company history, and further information will be updated in future editions of the *Blue Book of Acoustic Guitars*.

ALOHA

Instruments built in San Antonio, Texas and Chicago, Illinois. Distributed by the Aloha Publishing and Musical Instrument Company of Chicago, Illinois.

The Aloha company was founded in 1935 by J.M. Raleigh. True to the nature of a House Brand distributor, Raleigh's company distributed both Aloha instruments and amplifiers and Raleigh brand instruments through his Chicago office. Acoustic guitars were supplied by Harmony, and initial amplifiers and guitars were supplied by the Alamo company of San Antonio, Texas. By the mid 1950s, Aloha was producing its own amps, but continued using Alamo products, (Source: Michael Wright, *Vintage Guitar Magazine*).

ALOSA

See Sandner.

ALVAREZ

Current trademark manufactured in either Japan and Korea. Distributed by St. Louis Music of St. Louis, Missouri.

The St. Louis Music Supply Company was originally founded in 1922 by Bernard Kornblum as a violin shop. In 1957, Gene Kornblum (Bernard's son) joined the family business.

The Alvarez trademark was established in 1965, and the company was the earliest of Asian producers to feature laminate-body guitars with solid wood tops. Initially, Alvarez guitars were built in Japan during the late 1960s, and distributed through St. Louis Music.

St. Louis Music also distributed the Electra and Westone brands of solid body electric. St. Louis Music currently manufactures Crate and Ampeg amplifiers in the U.S., while Alvarez instruments are designed in St. Louis and produced overseas.

**Alvarez 5004 Rosewwod
courtesy Alvarez**

GENERAL INFORMATION

All Alvarez acoustic steel string guitars (except models 5212, 5214 and 5216) have a stylized double A shell logo inlay and rosewood veneer on their pegheads. Regent series models are the entry level to the Alvarez line, and generally feature laminated tops, backs, and sides. Artist series models feature more exotic woods, and have shell and pearl inlay work. Professional series models have solid tops. The acoustic/electric Fusion series models currently feature the Alvarez System 500 bridge pickup/on-board EQ.

Alvarez numbered their guitars with a four digit designation up until 1998. In 1999 they started using a two letter and two number system. Each series can be identified by this system. The first letters are for the series and style i.e.: AD stands for Artist Dreadnought. The following two numbers are the rank in the series. The higher the number the higher quality wood and such.

Almost all Alvarez acoustic guitars are available with an electronic option. This addition retails for $300 for the System 500 MK II and $400 for the System 600T. As a rule an additional 20% can be added to instruments that feature this as an option and not standard equipment. Another 10% can be added with the original case that is an option and not standard equipment.

ACOUSTIC: ARTIST SERIES (DISC. MODELS, 4-DIGIT MODELS)

The Professional Series are split up into prior 1999 models with the four digit models, and post 1999 with two letter and two number model designations

5002 MAHOGANY CLASSIC - classical style, laminated spruce top, round soundhole, bound body, wooden inlay rosette, mahogany back/sides, nato neck, 12/19-fret rosewood fingerboard, rosewood bridge, rosewood veneer on peghead, 3-per-side gold tuners, available in Natural finish, disc. 1998.

$300	**$225**	**$125**

Last MSR was $410.

5004 ARTIST rosewood (rosewood CLASSIC) - similar to 5002, except has rosewood back/sides, available in Natural finish, disc. 1998.

$435	**$285**	**$195**

Last MSR was $579.

5014 ARTIST FOLK (MOUNTAIN FOLK) - folk style, laminated spruce top, round soundhole, multi-layer black/white body binding, black/white ring inlay rosette, tortoise pickguard, mahogany back/sides/neck, 14/20-fret rosewood fingerboard with pearl dot inlay, stylized bird wings inlay at 12th fret, rosewood bridge with white black dot pins, blackface peghead with pearl logo inlay, 3-per-side chrome die cast tuners, available in Sunburst finish, mfg. 1995-98.

                        $350 $235 $155
                       Last MSR was $479.

5019 MIDNIGHT SPECIAL - dreadnought style, laminated spruce top, round soundhole, multi-layer black/white body binding, abalone shell rosette, black pickguard, mahogany back/sides, nato neck, 14/20-fret rosewood fingerboard with pearl dot inlay, stylized bird wings inlay at 12th fret, rosewood bridge with white pearl dot pins, 3-per-side chrome tuners, available in Black finish, disc. 1998.

                        $475 $300 $200
                       Last MSR was $629.

5019 AV - similar to the 5019 except has electronics with a bridge pickup system, mfg. 1994 only.

                        $650 $400 $265
                       Last MSR was $825.

5020 MOUNTAIN DELUXE (MOUNTAIN) - dreadnought style, laminated spruce top, round soundhole, multi-layer black/white body binding, synthetic shell rosette, black pickguard, mahogany back/sides/neck, 14/20-fret rosewood fingerboard with pearl dot inlay/stylized bird wings inlay at 12th fret, rosewood bridge with black pearl dot pins, rosewood veneer on peghead, 3-per-side chrome tuners, available in Natural or Sunburst finishes, mfg. 1991-95, reintroduced 1997-98.

                        $375 $245 $160
                       Last MSR was $499.

5020 M - similar to 5020 Mountain, except has laminated mahogany top, disc. 1995.

                        $295 $215 $125
                       Last MSR was $400.

5020 SB Mountain Deluxe Sunburst - similar to 5020 Mountain, available in Sunburst finish, disc. 1998.

                        $375 $245 $160
                       Last MSR was $499.

5020 C Mountain Deluxe - similar to the 5020 Mountain except has a single cutaway and standard System 500 electronics with bridge pickup system, disc. 1998.

                        $675 $435 $295
                       Last MSR was $879.

5021 - similar to 5020, except has a 12-string configuration, 6-per-side tuners, disc. 1993.

                        $325 $225 $150
                       Last MSR was $425.

5040 KOA - dreadnought style, laminated koa top, round soundhole, 3-stripe bound body and rosette, brown pickguard, koa back/sides, nato neck, 14/20-fret rosewood fingerboard with pearl dot inlay, stylized bird wings inlay at 12th fret, rosewood bridge with black pearl dot pins, koa veneer on peghead, 3-per-side chrome tuners, available in Natural finish, disc. 1998.

                        $375 $245 $160
                       Last MSR was $500.

5043 BURGUNDY (BURGUNDY ARTIST) - dreadnought style, laminated oak top, round soundhole, multi bound body, abalone rosette, oak back/sides, mahogany neck, 20-fret rosewood fingerboard with pearl cross inlay, rosewood bridge with black white dot pins, oak peghead veneer with pearl logo inlay, 3-per-side diecast tuners, available in Burgundy Stain finish, mfg. 1994-98.

                        $475 $300 $215
                       Last MSR was $629.

5055 BLUESMAN - jumbo style, laminated spruce top, 2 f-holes, multi-bound body, mahogany back/sides/neck, 14/20-fret bound rosewood fingerboard with pearl dot inlay, stylized bird wings inlay at 12th fret, rosewood bridge with white black dot pins, blackface peghead with pearl logo inlay, 3-per-side chrome die cast tuners, available in Sunburst finish, mfg. 1995-98.

                        $450 $285 $175
                       Last MSR was $599.

5072 JUMBO (ARTIST JUMBO) - jumbo style, laminated spruce top, round soundhole, tortoise pickguard, abalone bound body/rosette, mahogany back/sides, 14/20-fret rosewood fingerboard with pearl dot inlay, stylized bird wings inlay at 12th fret, rosewood bridge with white black dot pins, rosewood peghead veneer with pearl logo inlay, 3-per-side diecast tuners, available in Natural finish, mfg. 1994-98.

                        $465 $300 $200
                       Last MSR was $619.

5072 C BK - similar to the 5072 except has a single cutaway, standard 3-band EQ System 500 electronics with piezo bridge pickup, available in Black finish, mfg. 1995-98.

                        $740 $495 $325
                       Last MSR was $979.

GRADING	100%	EXCELLENT	AVERAGE

5088 C (FUSION DELUXE) - dreadnought style, single rounded cutaway, laminated spruce top, round soundhole, tortoise pickguard, 3-stripe bound body/rosette, mahogany back/sides/neck, 20-fret rosewood fingerboard with pearl dot inlay, pearl curlicue inlay at 12th fret, rosewood bridge with black white dot pins, pearl logo peghead inlay, 3-per-side diecast tuners, piezo bridge pickups, 3-band EQ, System 500 electronics, available in Natural finish, mfg. 1994-98.

$695 $450 $300
Last MSR was $929.

5088 C BK (Fusion Deluxe) - similar to 5088C, except has black pickguard, abalone flake rosette, white black dot bridge pins, vailable in Black finish, mfg. 1994-98.

$755 $500 $335
Last MSR was $999.

This model was also available in a White finish with no pickguard (Model 5088 C WH). The White finish was disc. in 1996.

5088/12 12-String - similar to 5088 C, except has 12-string configuration, 6-per-side tuners, mfg. 1994 only.

$850 $625 $425
Last MSR was $850.

5220 C - single cutaway dreadnought style, spruce top, round soundhole, 3-stripe bound body and rosette, black pickguard, mahogany back/sides, nato neck, 20-fret rosewood fingerboard with pearl dot inlay, rosewood bridge with black pearl dot pins, 3-per-side chrome tuners, available in Natural finish, disc. 1995.

$250 $175 $115
Last MSR was $350.

5224 - dreadnought style, solid spruce top, round soundhole, 5-stripe bound body/rosette, mahogany back/sides, nato neck, 14/20-fret rosewood fingerboard with dot inlay, rosewood bridge with white pearl dot pins, 3-per-side chrome tuners, available in Natural finish, disc. 1988.

$325 $240 $125
Last MSR was $450.

5225 rosewood - similar to the 5224, except features rosewood back/sides, available in Natural finish, mfg. 1981-1992.

$335 $250 $125
Last MSR was $459.

5227 rosewood SPECIAL - similar to the 5225, except has laminated spruce top, disc. 1985.

$250 $175 $115
Last MSR was $349.

5237 CURLY MAPLE - dreadnought style, laminated spruce top, round soundhole, 5-stripe bound body/rosette, curly maple back/sides, nato neck, 14/20-fret rosewood fingerboard with pearl dot inlay/stylized bird wings inlay at 12th fret, rosewood bridge with white pearl dot pins, 3-per-side chrome tuners, available in Sunburst finish, disc. 1995.

$340 $250 $155
Last MSR was $475.

Alvarez 5055 Bluesman
courtesy Alvarez

ACOUSTIC: ARTIST (AC, AD, AF, & AJ) SERIES (RECENT MFG.)

AC 40 S - classical style, rounded body, spruce top, round soundhole, multi-layer black body binding, wood mosaic rosette, rosewood back/sides, mahogany neck, 12/19-fret rosewood fingerboard, rosewood bridge, 3-per-side gold tuners with plastic buttons, available in Natural gloss finish, mfg. 1998-2001.

$415 $295 $200
Last MSR was $579.

AC 40SC - similar to the AC 40S except has a single cutaway and a standard piezo bridge pickups with 3-band EQ System 500 electronics, mfg. 1998-2001.

$575 $380 $260
Last MSR was $799.

AC 60 S - grand concert classical style, rounded body, solid cedar top, round soundhole, multi-layer black body binding, wood mosaic rosette, mahogany back/sides, mahogany neck, 12/19-fret Indian-rosewood fingerboard, rosewood bridge, 3-per-side gold tuners with plastic buttons, optional system 600T electronics, available in Natural gloss finish, mfg. 2002-current.

MSR $389 $275 $200 $135

Alvarez 5072 C BK
courtesy Alvarez

AC 60SC - similar to the AC 60S except has a single cutaway and a standard piezo bridge pickups with System 600T electronics, mfg. 2002-current.

| MSR | $599 | $425 | $310 | $225 |

AD 60S - dreadnought body style, spruce top, mahogany sides and back, White Pearl soundhole rosette, ivory/black multi body binding, rosewood fingerboard, rosewood bridge, chrome die-cast tuners, optional electronics, available in Natural finish, current mfg.

| MSR | $379 | $275 | $200 | $125 |

Also available in black finish (Model AD 60SBK), retail $399.

AD 60SC - similar to AD 60S, except in a single cutaway body style, standard System 500 MK II electronics, available in Natural finish, current mfg.

| MSR | $529 | $375 | $275 | $200 |

Also available in black finish (Model AD 60SCBK).

AD 60S-12 - similar to the AD 60S except in 12-string configuration, optional electronics, mfg. 2001-current.

| MSR | $429 | $300 | $225 | $150 |

AD 60 K - dreadnought style, koa top, round soundhole, black pickguard, ivory body, white pearl rosette, koa back/sides, mahogany neck, 14/20-fret bound rosewood fingerboard with stylized Alvarez slash inlay at 12th fret, rosewood bridge with white pearl dot pins, 3-per-side chrome tuners, available in Natural gloss finish, mfg. 1998-current.

| MSR | $459 | $325 | $235 | $160 |

AD 60 CK - similar to AD60K except with a single cutaway dreadnought body, available in Natural finish, current mfg.

| MSR | $599 | $450 | $300 | $225 |

AD 65 BLUESMAN - vintage dreadnought body style, spruce top, mahogany sides and back, ivory/black multi body binding, rosewood fingerboard and bridge, chrome die-cast tuners, f-holes, available in Sunburst finish, disc. 2001.

| | | $485 | $320 | $210 |

Last MSR was $649.

AD 65CE - cutaway Arch Top, F-holes, spruce top, maple back and sides, ivory/black multi-ply binding, rosewood fingerboard, diagonal inlay on 12th fret, rosewood bridge, vintage nickel hardware, trapeze bridge, single coil Alnico and Piezo pickup, three control knobs, available in Natural and Sunburst finish (AD 65CESB), mfg. 2001 only.

| | | $700 | $550 | $425 |

Last MSR was $999.

AD 70S - dreadnought style, solid spruce top, rosewood back and sides, round soundhole with white pearl rosette, tortise pickguard, 14/20 rosewood fingerboard with 12th fret diagonal inlay, rosewood bridge, 3-per-side chrome tuners, optional System 500 MK II electronics, available in Natural finish, mfg. 2001-current.

| MSR | $429 | $300 | $225 | $150 |

AD 80S - dreadnought style, solid spruce top, Indian rosewood back and sides, round soundhole with white pearl rosette, tortise pickguard, 14/20 rosewood fingerboard with 12th fret diagonal inlay, rosewood bridge, 3-per-side chrome tuners, optional System 600T electronics, available in Natural or Sunburst finishes, new 2003.

| MSR | $599 | $450 | $300 | $225 |

AD 90SCK - dreadnought single cutaway style, solid spruce top, Figured Dao back and sides, round soundhole with white pearl rosette, tortise pickguard, 14/20 rosewood fingerboard with 12th fret diagonal inlay, rosewood bridge, 3-per-side chrome tuners, System 600T electronics, available in Natural finish, new 2003.

| MSR | $879 | $625 | $450 | $275 |

AF 60 CK - similar to AD60CK except with a cutaway folk body, available in Natural finish, current mfg.

| MSR | $599 | $450 | $300 | $225 |

AF 60 S - folk grand concert style, solid spruce top, mahogany back and sides, round soundhole with white pearl rosette, black pickguard, 14/20 rosewood fingerboard with 12th fret diagonal inlay, rosewood bridge, 3-per-side nickle die-cast tuners, optional System 600T electronics, available in Natural finish, mfg. 2002-current.

| MSR | $399 | $280 | $200 | $130 |

AJ 60-12 ARTIST MAPLE JUMBO 12-STRING - dreadnought style, koa top, round soundhole, black pickguard, ivory body, white pearl rosette, koa back/sides, mahogany neck, 14/20-fret bound rosewood fingerboard with stylized Alvarez slash inlay at 12th fret, rosewood bridge with white pearl dot pins, 3-per-side chrome tuners, available in Natural gloss finish, mfg. 1998-99.

| | | $450 | $300 | $195 |

Last MSR was $599.

AJ 60 S - jumbo body, maple back and sides, solid spruce top, rosewood fingerboard with 12th fret diagonal position marker, white pearl rosette, white/black multi-ply body binding, gold die cast tuners, rosewood bridge, available in Blonde finish, current mfg.

| MSR | $549 | $415 | $225 | $175 |

AJ 60 S 12 - similar to AJ60S but in a 12-string configuration, available in Blonde finish, current mfg.

| MSR | $599 | $450 | $300 | $225 |

GRADING		100%	EXCELLENT	AVERAGE

AJ 60 SC - similar to AJ60S except has a single cutaway jumbo body, available in Blonde finish, current mfg.

MSR	$699		$525	$350	$275

AJ 60 SC 12 - similar to AJ60SC except in a 12-string configuration, available in Blonde finish, current mfg.

MSR	$799		$600	$400	$325

ACOUSTIC: FUSION SERIES

FD 60 - cutaway thin dreadnought body, maple back and sides, quilted maple top, rosewood fingerboard with 12th fret diagonal position marker, pearl rosette, ivory/black body binding, gold die cast tuners, rosewood bridge, Alvarez System 600 T electronics, available in Tobacco Sunburst, Cherry Sunburst, Trans. Amber, Trans. Blue, Trans. Red, Trans. Purple, or Trans. Black finishes, current mfg.

MSR	$849		$599	$450	$285

Prior to 2001, the Fusion FD-60 featured Standard System 500 II electronics.

5008 C CLASSIC - classical style, single rounded cutaway, laminated spruce top, round soundhole, bound body, wooden inlay rosette, mahogany back/sides/neck, 19-fret rosewood fingerboard, rosewood wraparound bridge, rosewood peghead veneer with pearl logo inlay, 3-per-side gold tuners with plastic buttons, piezo bridge pickups, 3-band EQ, available in Natural finish, mfg. 1994 only.

**Alvarez 5220 C EQ VS
courtesy Alvarez**

		$675	$485	$295

Last MSR was $900.

5080 N FUSION DELUXE THINLINE (NATURAL) - dreadnought style, thinline rounded cutaway body, spruce top, round soundhole, multi-layer black/white body binding, abalone shell rosette, mahogany back/sides/neck, 20-fret rosewood fingerboard with pearl dot inlay/stylized bird wings inlay at 12th fret, rosewood bridge with black pearl dot pins, abalone logo peghead inlay, 3-per-side chrome tuners, piezo bridge pickups, volume/tone controls, System 500 electronics, available in Natural gloss finish, disc. 1998.

		$585	$375	$265

Last MSR was $799.

5081 N FUSION DELUXE THINLINE (BLUE) - similar to 5080 N, except has flamed maple top, maple back/sides, available in Trans. Blue gloss finish, disc. 1998.

		$600	$395	$265

Last MSR was $819.

5082 N - similar to 5080 N, except has laminated curly maple top, curly maple back and sides, available in Trans. Violin finish, disc. 1995.

		$600	$400	$250

Last MSR was $800.

5083 N FUSION DELUXE THINLINE (SUNBURST) - similar to 5080 N, except has flame maple top, maple back/sides, available in Trans. Red gloss finish, disc. 1998.

		$600	$395	$265

Last MSR was $819.

In 1996, Sunburst finish replaced Trans. Red finish.

5084 N - similar to 5080 N, available in Black gloss finish, mfg. 1994-96.

		$575	$375	$235

Last MSR was $750.

5220 C EQ FUSION STANDARD (5220 C EQ CH, 5220 C EQ VS) - dreadnought style, single rounded cutaway body, spruce top, round soundhole, 3-stripe bound body and rosette, black pickguard, mahogany back/sides, nato neck, 20-fret rosewood fingerboard with pearl dot inlay, rosewood bridge with black pearl dot pins, 3-per-side chrome tuners, bridge pickup system, 3-band EQ, available in Natural finish, disc. 1998.

		$525	$340	$225

Last MSR was $699.

Add $50 for Cherry (Model 5220 C EQ CH FUSION STANDARD) or Sunburst (Model 5220 C EQ VS FUSION STANDARD) finishes.

This model was similar to the Model 5220 C, with electronics.

ACOUSTIC: MASTERWORKS SERIES

MC 80 - classical style, solid cedar top, solid mahogany back and sides, round soundhole with mosaic rosette, rosewood fingerboard, green abalone inlays, die-cast gold 3-per-side tuners, rosewood bridge with white pins, multi-layer white/black binding, optional electronics, Natural finish, new 2003.

	MSR	$799		$575	$400	$285

MC 90 - similar to the MC 80, except has solid Indian rosewood back and sides, new 2003.

	MSR	$849		$595	$425	$275

MC 90C - similar to the MC 90, except has a single cutaway and standard System 600T electronics, new 2003.

	MSR	$1,049		$750	$525	$350

MD 80 - dreadnought style, solid spruce top, mahogany back and sides, round soundhole with black and white circles, 14/20 rosewood fingerboard, green abalone inlays, die-cast nickel 3-per-side tuners, rosewood bridge with white pins, multi-layer white/black binding, optional electronics, Natural finish, mfg. 2001-current.

	MSR	$799		$575	$400	$285

MD 80-12 - similar to the MD 80 except in 12-string configuration, mfg. 2002-current.

	MSR	$899		$630	$450	$325

MD 85 - similar to the MD 80, except has solid ovangkol back and sides, new 2003.

	MSR	$849		$595	$425	$275

MD 90 - similar to the MD 80 except has rosewood back and sides, mfg. 2001-current.

	MSR	$999		$700	$525	$400

MD 95 - similar to the MD 90 except has gold hardware, new 2003.

	MSR	$1,199		$850	$600	$450

MF 80 - folk style, solid spruce top, mahogany back and sides, round soundhole with black and white circles, 14/20 rosewood fingerboard, green abalone inlays, die-cast nickel 3-per-side tuners, rosewood bridge with white pins, multi-layer white/black binding, optional electronics, Natural finish, mfg. 2001-02.

		$575	$400	$295

Last MSR was $799.

MF 80C - similar to the MF 80 except has single cutaway and standard System 600T electronics, mfg. 2002-current.

	MSR	$999		$700	$525	$435

MF 90 - similar to the MF 80 except has rosewood back and sides, mfg. 2001-current.

	MSR	$999		$700	$525	$435

MJ 80 - jumbo style, solid Canadian spruce top, mahogany back and sides, round soundhole with black and white circles, 14/20 Indian rosewood fingerboard, 12th fret abalone inlay, die-cast nickel 3-per-side tuners, rosewood bridge with white pins, multi-layer white/black binding, optional System 600T electronics, Natural finish, mfg. 2002 only.

		$595	$435	$325

Last MSR was $849.

SLM 80 - dreadnought style, solid grade AAA Canadian spruce top, solid Indian rosewood back and sides, round soundhole with black and white circles, 14/20 Indian rosewood fingerboard, Tree-of-Life abalone inlay, gold vintage style 3-per-side tuners, rosewood bridge with white pins, multi-layer white/black binding, Natural finish, mfg. 2002 only.

		$1,275	$950	$675

Last MSR was $1,799.

This guitar is to commemorate the 80th anniversary of St. Louis Music. SLM is the parent company of the Alvarez guitar company.

ACOUSTIC: PROFESSIONAL SERIES (DISC. MODELS 4-DIGIT MODELS)

The Professional Series are split up into prior 1999 models with the four digit models, and post 1999 with two letter and two number model designations.

5009 PROFESSIONAL rosewood CLASSIC - classical style, solid spruce top, round soundhole, bound body, wooden inlay rosette, rosewood back/sides, nato neck, 19-fret rosewood fingerboard, rosewood bridge, rosewood veneer on peghead, 3-per-side gold tuners, available in Natural finish, disc. 1998.

		$500	$340	$225

Last MSR was $679.

5022 HERRINGBONE PROFESSIONAL (GLENBROOKE) - dreadnought style, solid spruce top, round soundhole, tortoise pickguard, herringbone bound body/rosette, rosewood back/sides, mahogany neck, 14/20-fret rosewood fingerboard with pearl dot inlay, stylized bird wings inlay at 12th fret, rosewood bridge with white pearl dot pins, rosewood peghead veneer with pearl logo inlay, 3-per-side chrome tuners, available in Natural finish, disc. 1998.

		$485	$325	$215

Last MSR was $649.

GRADING	100%	EXCELLENT	AVERAGE

5028 MAHOGANY PRO - dreadnought style, solid spruce top, round soundhole, tortoise pickguard, black/white multi-layer bound body, black/white inlay rosette, mahogany back/sides/neck, 14/20-fret rosewood fingerboard with pearl dot inlay/stylized bird wings inlay at 12th fret, rosewood bridge w/white pearl dot pins, 3-per-side chrome tuners, available in Natural satin finish, disc. 1998.

	$375	$245	$165

Last MSR was $499.

5030 TIMBERLINE SATIN - dreadnought style, solid spruce top, round soundhole, tortoise pickguard, black/white multi-layer bound body, abalone shell inlay rosette, mahogany back/sides/neck, 14/20-fret rosewood fingerboard with stylized diamond inlay at 12th fret, rosewood bridge with white pearl dot pins, 3-per-side chrome tuners, available in Natural satin finish, disc. 1998.

	$465	$300	$200

Last MSR was $619.

5031 TIMBERLINE - similar to the 5030 Timberline Satin, except has Natural gloss finish, disc. 1998.

	$485	$325	$215

Last MSR was $649.

5032 TIMBER RIDGE - dreadnought style, solid spruce top, round soundhole, tortoise pickguard, wood body binding, wood inlay rosette, mahogany back/sides/neck, 14/20-fret rosewood fingerboard with pearl dot inlay, stylized bird wings inlay at 12th fret, rosewood bridge with white pearl dot pins, rosewood peghead veneer with pearl logo inlay, 3-per-side chrome tuners, available in Natural finish, mfg. 1994-98.

	$475	$375	$215

Last MSR was $640.

**Alvarez MD-80
courtesy Dave Rogers
Dave's Guitar Shop**

5037 WILDWOOD 12-STRING - dreadnought style, solid cedar top, round soundhole, 5-stripe bound body/rosette, mahogany back/sides, nato neck, 14/20-fret rosewood fingerboard with pearl dot inlay, 12th fret has stylized bird wings inlay, rosewood bridge with white black dot pins, rosewood veneer on peghead, 6-per-side gold tuners with amber buttons, available in Natural finish, disc. 1998.

	$625	$395	$265

Last MSR was $819.

In 1995, solid spruce top replaces original part/design.

5045 MOUNTAIN - dreadnought style, solid spruce top, round soundhole, wood body binding, wood inlay rosette, mahogany back/sides/neck, 14/20-fret rosewood fingerboard with pearl dot inlay, stylized bird wings inlay at 12th fret, rosewood bridge with white pearl dot pins, peghead logo decal, 3-per-side chrome tuners, available in Vintage satin finish, disc. 1995.

	$375	$265	$160

Last MSR was $500.

5045 G Graphite Pro (5045 G Mountain) - similar to 5045, except has wood herringbone body binding, graphite bridge, mfg. 1996-98.

	$450	$295	$200

Last MSR was $599.

5054 (GOLDEN CHORUS) - dreadnought style, solid spruce top, round soundhole, herringbone bound body and rosette, tortoise pickguard, rosewood back/sides, nato neck, 14/20-fret rosewood fingerboard with pearl dot inlay, 12th fret has stylized bird wings inlay, rosewood bridge with white pearl dot pins, rosewood veneer on peghead, 6-per-side chrome tuners, available in Natural finish, disc. 1994.

	$450	$300	$185

Last MSR was $600.

5062 WILDWOOD (WILDWOOD NATURAL) - dreadnought style, solid spruce top, round soundhole, 5-stripe bound body/rosette, mahogany back/sides, nato neck, 14/20-fret rosewood fingerboard with pearl dot inlay, 12th fret has stylized bird wings inlay, rosewood bridge with white black dot pins, 3-per-side chrome tuners, available in Natural finish, disc. 1998.

	$495	$325	$215

Last MSRl was $649.

5063 Wildwood Special - similar to 5062, except has gold tuners with amber buttons, available in Natural finish, disc. 1993.

	$325	$215	$115

Last MSR was $430.

**Alvarez 5022 Glenbrooke
courtesy Alvarez**

5086 WILDWOOD - single cutaway dreadnought style, solid spruce top, round soundhole, 5-stripe bound body/rosette, mahogany back/sides, nato neck, 14/20-fret rosewood fingerboard with pearl dot inlay, 12th fret has stylized bird wings inlay, rosewood bridge with white black dot pins, 3-per-side gold tuners with amber buttons, and bi-phonic pickup system and controls, available in Natural finish, disc. 1995.

$775 $500 $275
Last MSR was $950.

This model was similar to the model 5062, with electronics.

5202 MAHOGANY - classical style, solid spruce top, round soundhole, bound body, wooden inlay rosette, African mahogany back/sides, nato neck, 19-fret rosewood fingerboard, rosewood bridge, rosewood veneer on peghead, 3-per-side gold tuners, available in Natural finish, disc. 1997.

$395 $275 $165
Last MSR was $525.

5224 MAHOGANY - dreadnought style, solid spruce top, round soundhole, 3-stripe bound body/rosette, black pickguard, mahogany back/sides, nato neck, 14/20-fret rosewood fingerboard with pearl dot inlay, rosewood bridge with black dot pins, rosewood veneer on peghead, 3-per-side chrome tuners, available in Natural finish, disc. 1995.

$350 $240 $140
Last MSR was $450.

5225 - similar to 5224, except has tiger rosewood back/sides, bound fingerboard, bound peghead, disc. 1994.

$350 $250 $150
Last MSR was $460.

6010 ELEGANCE SIGNATURE - dreadnought style, solid spruce top, round soundhole, multi-layer bound body, abalone rosette, mahogany back/sides/neck, 14/20-fret bound rosewood fingerboard with pearl double A inlay at 12th fret, rosewood bridge with white pearl dot pins, bound peghead with rosewood veneer/pearl logo inlay, 3-per-side gold die cast tuners, available in Natural finish, mfg. 1995-97.

$575 $425 $260
Last MSR was $775.

6015 ELEGANCE ROSE - similar to the 6010, except features a solid mahogany back, multi-layer maple/rosewood body binding, tortoise pickguard, 14/20-fret rosewood fingerboard with pearl rose inlay at 12th fret, rosewood bridge with black pearl dot pins, available in Natural semi-gloss finish, mfg. 1995-98.

$715 $500 $335
Last MSR was $999.

6020 C ELEGANCE CUTAWAY - similar to the 6010, except features florentine cutaway body, Honduran mahogany back/sides, abalone shell body binding, 14/20-fret bound rosewood fingerboard with pearl inlay at 12th fret, rosewood bridge with black pearl dot pins, ornate pearl headstock inlay, available in Natural gloss finish, disc. 1998.

$875 $700 $475
Last MSR was $1,399.

ACOUSTIC: PROFESSIONAL (PD, PF, & PC) SERIES (RECENT MFG.)

PC 50S - classical style, solid spruce top, rosewood sides and back, rosewood neck with 12/19 fretboard, rosewood bridge, rosette wood mosiac soundhole, open-style gold tuners, optional Standard System 600T electronics, Natural finish, mfg. 1998-2002.

$635 $450 $295
Last MSR was $899.

PC 50SC - similar to the PC-50S except has a single cutaway and standard electronics with Piezo bridge pickup, mfg. 1998-2002.

$775 $550 $415
Last MSR was $1,099.

PD 80 S - dreadnought body, mahogany back and sides, solid spruce top, rosewood fingerboard with 12th fret diagonal position marker, abalone soundhole rosette, ivory/herringbone body binding, chrome die cast tuners, rosewood bridge, optional System 500 electronics, available in Natural finish, current mfg.

MSR $649 $460 $335 $225

PD 80 SC - similar to PD80S except has a single cutaway dreadnought style body, available in Natural finish, current mfg.

MSR $799 $570 $425 $275

PD 80 S 12 - similar to PD80S except in a 12-string configuration, available in Natural finish, disc 2002.

$575 $425 $275
Last MSR was $759.

PD 90 S - dreadnought body, rosewood back and sides, solid spruce top, scalloped bracing, rosewood fingerboard with 12th fret diagonal position marker, abalone soundhole rosette, ivory/herringbone body binding, chrome die cast tuners, rosewood bridge, optional System 500 electronics, available in Natural finish, current mfg.

MSR $749 $550 $395 $250

GRADING	100%	EXCELLENT	AVERAGE

PD 100 S - dreadnought style, solid spruce top, round soundhole, abalone/ivory body binding, abalone rosette, black pickguard, rosewood back/sides, mahogany neck, 14/20-fret bound rosewood fingerboard with fancy pearl leaves/vine inlay, bound peghead, rosewood bridge with black abalone dot pins, 3-per-side gold tuners, available in Natural gloss finish, current mfg.

MSR	$999		$700	$500	$350

PF 90 S - similar to the PD90S except has a folk body, available in Natural finish, current mfg.

			$565	$425	$275

Last MSR was $749.

PF 90 SC - similar to PF90S except has a single cutaway folk body, available in Natural finish, current mfg.

MSR	$929		$675	$475	$300

ACOUSTIC: REGENT SERIES (DISC. 4-DIGIT MODELS)

The Regent series is divided into models made prior to 1999, which feature four digit models, and models after 1999 that have two letters and two numbers.

5003 ARTIST MAHOGANY - classical style, laminated spruce top, round soundhole, multi-layer black body, wood mosaic rosette, mahogany back/sides/neck, 12/19-fret rosewood fingerboard, rosewood bridge, slotted headstock, 3-per-side tuners with plastic buttons, available in Antique Natural gloss finish, disc. 1998.

	$285	$185	$125

Last MSR was $379.

5201 REGENT CLASSIC (5201 CLASSIC) - classical style, laminated spruce top, round soundhole, black body binding, wood mosaic rosette, mahogany back/sides/neck, 12/19-fret rosewood fingerboard, rosewood bridge, 3-per-side tuners with plastic buttons, available in Vintage Stain finish, mfg. 1994-95, 1997-98.

	$150	$95	$65

Last MSR was $199.

Add $100 for Model 5201 VP (retail list $299).

5208 N - dreadnought style, laminated spruce top, round soundhole, bound body, 3-stripe rosette, black pickguard, mahogany back/sides/neck, 14/20-fret rosewood fingerboard with pearl dot inlay, rosewood bridge with black pins, 3-per-side chrome tuners, available in Natural finish, mfg. 1995-97.

	$175	$135	$85

Last MSR was $250.

5208 M - similar to 5208 N, except has laminated mahogany top, mfg. 1995-97.

	$165	$120	$70

Last MSR was $225.

5209 REGENT - dreadnought style, laminated spruce top, round soundhole, single layer black body binding, black/white ring rosette, tortoise pickguard, mahogany back/sides/neck, 14/20-fret rosewood fingerboard with dot inlay, rosewood bridge with black pins, 3-per-side chrome tuners, available in Natural gloss finish, disc. 1998.

	$165	$100	$75

Last MSR was $219.

Add $90 for Model 5209 VP (retail list $309).

5210 SATIN - dreadnought style, laminated spruce top, round soundhole, bound body, 3-stripe rosette, tortoise pickguard, mahogany back/sides/neck, 14/20-fret rosewood fingerboard with pearl dot inlay, rosewood bridge with white pins, 3-per-side chrome tuners, available in Natural satin finish, mfg. 1994-97.

	$250	$175	$100

Last MSR was $335.

5212 REGENT SPECIAL - dreadnought style, laminated spruce top, round soundhole, multi-layer black/white body binding, 3-stripe rosette, tortoise pickguard, mahogany back/sides/neck, 14/20-fret rosewood fingerboard with dot inlay, rosewood bridge with white pins, 3-per-side chrome tuners, available in Natural gloss and Sunburst finishes, disc 1997.

	$200	$140	$95

Last MSR was $279.

In 1996, Sunburst finish was discontinued.

5212 BK - similar to the 5212 Regent Special, except has black pickguard, available in Black finish, disc. 1997.

	$275	$195	$120

Last MSR was $380.

Alvarez 5208 N
courtesy Alvarez

GRADING   **100%**   **EXCELLENT**   **AVERAGE**

5214 REGENT DELUXE - dreadnought style, spruce top, round soundhole, multi-layer black/white body binding, black/white ring rosette, black pickguard, mahogany back/sides/neck, 14/20-fret rosewood fingerboard with dot inlay, rosewood bridge with black pins, 3-per-side chrome tuners, available in Natural gloss finish, disc. 1998.

	$300	$195	$130

Last MSR was $399.

5214 12 Regent Deluxe 12-String - similar to 5214, except has 12-string configuration, 6-per-side tuners, disc. 1998.

	$435	$285	$195

Last MSR was $579.

5216 FOLK - similar to 5212, except has parlor style folk body configuration, disc. 1997.

	$215	$140	$85

Last MSR was $265.

ACOUSTIC: REGENT (RD, RC, & RF) SERIES (RECENT MFG.)

RC 10 - classical style, spruce top, mahogany back and sides, round soundhole, wood mosiac soundhole, single black binding, 12/19 fret rosewood fretboard, rosewood bridge, acrylic dot inlays, open tuners, Natural satin finish, mfg. 2001-current.

MSR	$199	$140	$100	$65

RD 8 - dreadnought style, spruce top, mahogany back and sides, round soundhole, black/white soundhole rings, black pickguard, multi-layer black binding, 14/20 fret rosewood fretboard, rosewood bridge, acrylic dot inlays, covered 3-per-side tuners, Natural gloss finish, case included, mfg. 2001-current.

MSR	$269	$190	$140	$85

RD 8C - similar to the RD 8 except is a single cutaway and has standard electronics with a 2-band EQ, mfg. 2002-current.

MSR	$389	$275	$180	$135

RD 10 - dreadnought style, spruce top, mahogany back and sides, round soundhole, black/white soundhole rings, single black binding, 14/20 fret rosewood fretboard, rosewood bridge, acrylic dot inlays, chrome covered tuners, Natural finish, mfg. 2001-current.

MSR	$219	$155	$110	$75

RD10VP - similar to the RD 10 except comes with a gig-bag, strings, winder, strap, picks, tuner, and polish, mfg. 2001 only.

	$225	$150	$95

Last MSR was $319.

RC 20 C - classical style, single cutaway, spruce top, mahogany back and sides, round soundhole, wood mosiac soundhole, single black binding, 12/19 fret rosewood fretboard, rosewood bridge, acrylic dot inlays, open tuners, 3-per-side tuners, 3-band equalizer, Natural satin finish, mfg. 2001-current.

MSR	$439	$310	$215	$130

RD 20 S - dreadnought style, laminated spruce top, round soundhole, multi-layer black/white body binding, 3-stripe rosette, tortoise pickguard, mahogany back/sides/neck, 14/20-fret rosewood fingerboard with dot inlay, rosewood bridge with white pins, 3-per-side chrome tuners, available in Natural, Black, or Sunburst finishes, current mfg.

MSR	$299	$200	$140	$95

RD20VP - similar to the RD 20 except comes with a gig-bag, strings, winder, strap, picks, tuner, and polish, mfg. 2001 only.

	$260	$175	$115

Last MSR was $369.

RD 20 SL - similar to the RD 20, except is in left-hand configuration, mfg. 1998-current.

MSR	$339	$260	$165	$115

RD 20S-12 12-String - similar to the RD 20, except has 12-string configuration, 6-per-side tuners, available in Natural gloss finish, mfg. 1998-current.

MSR	$389	$275	$195	$135

RD 20 SC - similar to the RD 20, except has single cutaway, 3-band EQ standarad, available in Natural, Black, or Sunburst finishes, mfg. 1998-current.

MSR	$439	$250	$165	$115

RF 8 - folk style, spruce top, mahogany back and sides, round soundhole, black/white soundhole rings, black pickguard, multi-layer black binding, 14/20 fret rosewood fretboard, rosewood bridge, acrylic dot inlays, covered 3-per-side tuners, Natural gloss finish, case included, mfg. 2001-current.

MSR	$269	$190	$140	$85

RF10 - folk style, spruce top, mahogany back and sides, round soundhole, black/white soundhole rings, black pickguard, multi-layer black binding, 14/20 fret rosewood fretboard, rosewood bridge, acrylic dot inlays, covered 3-per-side tuners, Natural gloss finish, case included, new 2003.

MSR	$219	$155	$110	$65

GRADING	100%	EXCELLENT	AVERAGE

RF 20 - folk style, spruce top, mahogany back and sides, round soundhole, black/white soundhole rings, multi-layer black/white binding, 14/20 fret rosewood fretboard, rosewood bridge, acrylic dot inlays, chrome tuners, 3-per-side tuners, optional electronics, Natural finish, mfg. 2001 only.

	$199	$140	$90

Last MSR was $279.

RF 20SC - similar to the RF 20 except has a single cutaway and standard electronics, mfg. 2001-current.

MSR	$439	$310	$225	$135

RD 30S - dreadnought style, spruce top, round soundhole, multi-layer black/white body binding, black/white ring rosette, black pickguard, mahogany back/sides/neck, 14/20-fret rosewood fingerboard with dot inlay, rosewood bridge with black pins, 3-per-side chrome tuners, optional electronics, available in Natural or Sunburst (SB) finishes, mfg. 1998-2001.

	$270	$185	$125

Last MSR was $379.

RD 30 L - similar to the RD 30 BK, except in left-handed configuration, available in Natural gloss finish, mfg. 1998-99, 2001.

	$300	$195	$130

Last MSR was $399.

RD 30SC - similar to the RD 30S except has a single cutaway with standard System MK II electronics, mfg 2001 only.

	$390	$275	$180

Last MSR was $549.

RD 50 Regent Deluxe rosewood - similar to the RD 30 BK, except has rosewood back/sides, available in Natural gloss finish, mfg. 1998-99.

	$325	$225	$150

Last MSR was $449.

RC 30S - classical style, spruce top, mahogany back and sides, wood mosiac rosette soundhole, 12/19 rosewood figerboard, black multi-layer binding, rosewood bridge, optional System 500 MK II electronics, Natural finish, mfg. 2001 only.

	$300	$195	$135

Last MSR was $399.

RF 30 - similar to RD 30 BK, except in folk body configuration, available in Natural gloss finish, mfg. 1998-2001.

	$285	$185	$125

Last MSR was $379.

**Alvarez RD 8
courtesy Dave Rogers
Dave's Guitar Shop**

SILVER ANNIVERSARY & WILLOW RIDGE ACOUSTIC SERIES

2551 rosewood - dreadnought style, solid spruce top, round soundhole, 5-stripe bound body, abalone rosette, rosewood back/sides, mahogany neck, 14/20-fret rosewood fingerboard with pearl diamond inlay, rosewood bridge with white black dot pins, rosewood veneer on bound peghead with Silver Anniversary inlay, 3-per-side chrome tuners, available in Natural finish, disc. 1997.

	$495	$375	$225

Last MSR was $650.

2551/12 12-String - similar to 2551 rosewood, except has 12-string configuration, 6-on-a-side tuners, disc. 1995.

	$595	$425	$250

Last MSR was $800.

2552 - dreadnought style, spruce top, round soundhole, 5-stripe bound body, abalone rosette, mahogany back/sides/neck, 14/20-fret rosewood fingerboard with pearl dot inlay, rosewood bridge with black white dot pins, rosewood veneer on peghead, 3-per-side chrome tuners, available in Natural finish, disc. 1993.

	$300	$225	$125

Last MSR was $400.

2555 JUMBO - jumbo style, florentine cutaway, laminated spruce top, round soundhole, 5-stripe bound body, abalone flake rosette, mahogany back/sides/neck, 21-fret rosewood fingerboard with abalone offset bar inlay, rosewood bridge with black white pins, rosewood veneer on bound peghead with Silver Anniversary inlay, 3-per-side chrome tuners, available in Natural or Sunburst finishes, disc. 1995.

	$750	$550	$325

Last MSR was $1,050.

This model was available with an Alvarez Bi-Phonic pickup system. In 1995, Natural finish was disc.

GRADING	100%	EXCELLENT	AVERAGE

2555 BK (Folk) - similar to the 2555, except has folk body configuration, single florentine cutaway, abalone body binding, abalone rosette, available in Gloss Black finish, mfg. 1994 only.

	$700	$450	$300

Last MSR was $900.

2531 - single round cutaway classical style, spruce top, round soundhole, wooden inlay rosette, bound body, mahogany back/sides/neck, 19-fret rosewood fingerboard, rosewood wraparound bridge, 3-per-side chrome tuners with plastic buttons, piezo bridge pickups, 3-band EQ, available in Natural finish, mfg. 1994 only.

	$750	$525	$325

Last MSR was $1,050.

2532 - single round cutaway dreadnought style, spruce top, black pickguard, 3-stripe bound body/rosette, maple back/sides, mahogany neck, 22-fret rosewood fingerboard with pearl dot inlay, rosewood bridge with white black dot pins, 3-per-side diecast tuners, piezo bridge pickups, 3-band EQ, available in Natural finish, disc. 1995.

	$750	$550	$325

Last MSR was $1,050.

2533 - similar to 2532, except has mahogany back/sides, available in Natural finish, disc. 1995.

	$750	$525	$325

Last MSR was $1,050.

ACOUSTIC ELECTRIC BASS

4070 ACOUSTIC BASS - single round jumbo style, laminated spruce top, round soundhole, 3-stripe bound body/rosette, mahogany back/sides/neck, 23-fret rosewood fingerboard, rosewood bridge with white black dot pins, bound rosewood peghead with pearl logo inlay, 2-per-side diecast tuners, piezo bridge pickups, 3-band EQ, available in Natural gloss finish, mfg. 1994-98.

	$875	$575	$385

Last MSR was $1,149.

Add $50 for Black finish (Model 4070 BK).
In 1996, Black finish was disc.

RB 30C - cutaway Jumbo Bass body, spruce top, mahogany back and sides, 17/23 fret rosewood fingerboard with acrylic dot inlay, round rosette soundhole with black and white rings, white/black multi-layer binding, chrome die-cast tuners, rosewood bridge, standard 4-band EQ System 500 MK II, Natural finish, mfg. 2000-current.

MSR	$789		$575	$400	$275

ALVAREZ YAIRI
Instruments built in Japan from 1966 to date. Current mfg is based in Kani, Japan. Distributed by in the U.S. by St. Louis Music of St. Louis, Missouri.

These handcrafted guitars are built by craftsmen under the direction of luthier/designer Kazuo Yairi. Yairi, who learned to construct violins and guitars from his father, started his own company to produce handmade guitars in larger quantities.

Alvarez Yairi acoustics were imported to the U.S. starting in 1966, and were exclusively distributed by St. Louis Music. Alvarez Yairi instruments are now a division of Alvarez and St. Louis Music. These quality acoustic guitars are designed by both luthier Yairi in Japan and the designers at St. Louis Music. Instruments are both adjusted at the Alvarez Yairi factory in Japan, and re-inspected after shipping at St. Louis Music before delivery to dealers.

ACOUSTIC: MISC. MODELS

All Alvarez Yairi acoustic steel string guitars have abalone or pearl peghead logo inlay. All Alvarez Yairi models may be purchased with Alvarez Natural Response or System 500 pickups.

Add $110 for installed BP Natural Response pickup (without volume/tone control). Add $135 for installed BT Natural Response pickup (with volume/tone control). Add $300 for installed System 500 pickup.

FY 40 CAROLINA FOLK - dreadnought clinched waist style, solid Canadian spruce top, round soundhole, ivoroid/wood bound top and back, 3-stripe rosette, mahogany back/sides/neck, 14/20-fret rosewood fingerboard with snowflake inlay, rosewood bridge, rosewood headstock veneer, 3-per-side chrome tuners, available in Natural finish, mfg. circa mid 1970s.

	$650	$450	$300

YB 1 BARITONE - jumbo style, solid spruce top, round soundhole, 5-stripe body binding, shell rosette, rosewood back/sides, mahogany neck, 14/20-fret ebony fingerboard, ebony bridge with white abalone dot pins, 3-per-side gold tuners, piezo bridge pickup, volume/tone controls, System 500 electronics, available in Natural gloss finish, current mfg.

MSR	$1,999		$1,500	$950	$650

JY 10 NASHVILLE JUMBO - jumbo style, solid spruce top, round soundhole, tortoise pickguard, ivoroid bound body, abalone purfling/rosette, maple back/sides, mahogany neck, 14/20-fret rosewood fingerboard with pearl dot inlay, 12th fret pearl curlicue inlay, ebony bridge with white black dot pins, ebony veneered bound peghead, 3-per-side gold tuners, available in Sunburst finish, mfg. 1994-98.

	$950	$775	$450

Last MSR was $1,400.

ACOUSTIC: CLASSICAL SERIES

All classical guitars have rosewood veneer on their pegheads. All of these models have a CY prefix. Check the Masterwork series for the CY-200 since it is part of the Masterworks.

CY 110 MAHOGANY CLASSIC - classical style, solid cedar top, round soundhole, black multiply body binding, wooden mosaic rosette, Honduran mahogany back/sides, mahogany neck, 12/19-fret rosewood fingerboard, rosewood bridge, slotted headstock, 3-per-side gold tuners with pearloid buttons, available in Natural semi-satin finish, disc 2002.

	$935	$650	$425

Last MSR was $1,249.

CY 116 BURLED (CY116 LA GRANJA) - classical style, solid cedar top, round soundhole, maple body binding, wooden mosaic rosette, burled mahogany back/sides, mahogany neck, 12/19-fret ebony fingerboard, rosewood bridge, rosewood veneer headstock, slotted headstock, 3-per-side gold tuners with pearloid buttons, available in Antique gloss finish, mfg. 1975-current.

MSR	$1,349	$1,000	$700	$500

CY 118 JACARANDA - similar to CY 116, except has jacaranda back/sides, wood multi-layer body binding, current mfg.

MSR	$1,449	$1,025	$750	$550

CY 125 EL LORCA - classical style, solid cedar top, round soundhole, wooden inlay rosette and stripe on headstock, three stripe bound body, rosewood sides, rosewood bookmatched back, mahogany neck, 12/19-fret ebony fingerboard, rosewood bridge and headstock veneer, 3-per-side gold tuners with pearloid buttons, available in Natural finish, mfg. circa mid 1970s.

	N/A	$600	$400

CY 127 CE CUTAWAY CLASSIC - shallow depth classical style body, rounded cutaway, solid cedar top, round soundhole, multi-layer wood body binding, wood mosaic rosette, rosewood back/sides, mahogany neck, 12/19-fret ebony fingerboard, rosewood bridge, slotted headstock, 3-per-side gold tuners with pearloid buttons, Alvarez Natural Response pickup system and volume/tone control, available in Natural gloss finish, mfg. 1991-current.

MSR	$1,649	$1,200	$875	$550

CY 128 CE - similar to the CY 127 CE except has a deeper body, and gloss finish, mfg. 2001-current.

MSR	$1,649	$1,200	$875	$550

CY 130 CONQUISTADOR - classical style, cedar top, round soundhole, wooden inlay rosette, 3-stripe bound body, rosewood sides, 2-piece rosewood back, mahogany neck/headstock, 12/19-fret ebony fingerboard, carved headstock design, rosewood bridge, 3-per-side gold tuners with pearloid buttons, available in Natural finish, mfg. circa mid 1970s.

	N/A	$700	$450

CY 132 C CONQUISTADOR CUTAWAY - similar to the CY 130 Conquistador, except has single stepped down cutaway, mfg. circa mid 1970s.

	N/A	$650	$375

CY 135 CONCERT MASTER - classical style, Canadian cedar top, round soundhole, wooden inlay bound body and rosette, jacaranda sides, jacaranda bookmatched back, mahogany neck/headstock, 12/19-fret ebony fingerboard, ebony bridge, 3-per-side gold tuners with pearloid buttons, available in Natural finish, mfg. circa mid 1970s.

	N/A	$750	$450

CY 140 CONCERT MASTER (CY 140 GRAND CONCERT MASTER) - classical style, solid cedar top, round soundhole, multi-layer wood body binding, wood mosaic rosette, jacaranda back/sides, mahogany neck, 12/19-fret ebony fingerboard, rosewood bridge, slotted headstock, 3-per-side gold tuners with pearl buttons, available in Antique Natural gloss finish, mfg. circa mid 1970s-current.

MSR	$1,749	$1,300	$925	$600

YC 1 CUSTOM CUTAWAY (NYLON STRING) - sloped rounded cutaway body, solid spruce top, round soundhole, multi-layer tortoise body binding, turquoise rosette, rosewood back/sides, mahogany neck, 12/20-fret ebony fingerboard with turquoise inlay, rosewood bridge, slotted headstock, 3-per-side gold tuners with pearloid buttons, piezo bridge pickup, volume/tone controls, System 500 electronics, available in Natural gloss finish, disc. 1998.

	$1,425	$900	$625

Last MSR was $1,899.

**Alvarez 4070 Wildwood Bass
courtesy Alvarez**

**Alvarez Yairi CY 118 Jacaranda
courtesy Alvarez Yairi**

GRADING	100%	EXCELLENT	AVERAGE

YC 2 CUSTOM CUTAWAY (STEEL STRING) - similar to the YC 1, except features graphite bridge, solid headstock, 3-per-side gold tuners, available in Natural gloss finish, disc. 1998.

	$1,425	$900	$625

Last MSR was $1,899.

ACOUSTIC: DREADNOUGHT SERIES (DY PREFIX)

Alvarez Yairi has produced several dreadnoughts over the years. Early models were just known as DY Models, but today they are broken up into series including the Traditional, Fusion, Innovative (Disc.), and Signature models.

DY 50 N - dreadnought style, cedar top, round soundhole, 3-stripe bound body, abalone rosette, tortoise pickguard, jacaranda back/sides, mahogany neck, 14/20-fret bound rosewood fingerboard with abalone diamond inlay, rosewood bridge with white pearl dot pins, rosewood veneer on bound peghead, 3-per-side gold tuners, available in Natural finish, mfg. 1991-95.

	$875	$650	$395

Last MSR was $1,275.

DY 50 NEQ - dreadnought style, cedar top, round soundhole, 3-stripe bound body, abalone rosette, tortoise pickguard, jacaranda back/sides, mahogany neck, 14/20-fret bound rosewood fingerboard with abalone diamond inlay, rosewood bridge with white pearl dot pins, rosewood veneer on bound peghead, 3-per-side gold tuners, piezo bridge pickup, 3-band EQ, available in Natural finish, mfg. 1994 only.

	$995	$725	$500

Last MSR was $1,575.

DY 51 BLUE RIDGE - dreadnought style, solid cedar top, round soundhole, ivoroid bound body, herringbone rosette, burled mahogany back/sides, nato mahogany neck, 14/20-fret ebony fingerboard with snowflake inlay, ebony bridge, burled mahogany headstock veneer, mother-of-pearl headstock inlay, 3-per-side chrome tuners, available in Natural finish, mfg. circa mid 1970s.

	N/A	$650	$400

DY 52 SILVER LARK - dreadnought style, solid Canadian spruce top, round soundhole, white maple bound body, herringbone rosette, walnut pickguard, walnut back/sides, mahogany neck, 14/20-fret ebony fingerboard with snowflake inlay, ebony bridge, MOP headstock inlay, walnut veneer on peghead, 3-per-side chrome tuners, available in Natural finish, mfg. circa mid 1970s.

	N/A	$750	$450

This model had a solid oboncol wood pickguard (adhesive-backed for optional installation) available.

DY 53 SILVER HARP - dreadnought style, solid Canadian spruce top, round soundhole, white maple bound body, herringbone rosette, burled mahogany back/sides, nato mahogany neck, 14/20-fret ebony fingerboard with snowflake inlay, ebony bridge, mother-of-pearl headstock inlay, 3-per-side chrome tuners, available in Natural satin finish, mfg. circa mid 1970s.

	N/A	$750	$450

This model had a solid oboncol wood pickguard (adhesive-backed for optional installation) available.

DY 53 N - jumbo style, spruce top, round soundhole, 5-stripe bound body and rosette, tortoise pickguard, rosewood back/sides, mahogany neck, 14/20-fret bound rosewood fingerboard with pearl block inlay, rosewood bridge with white pearl dot pins, rosewood veneer on bound peghead, 3-per-side chrome tuners, available in Natural finish, mfg. 1991-95.

	$775	$575	$350

Last MSR was $1,100.

In 1994, coral rosewood back/sides replaced original part/design.

DY 54 SILVER FAWN - dreadnought style, solid Canadian spruce top, round soundhole, maple bound body, turquoise/wood rosette, oboncol back/sides, nato mahogany neck, 14/20-fret black ebony fingerboard with snowflake inlay, ebony bridge, rosewood inlay on lower body bout, MOP headstock inlay, 3-per-side chrome tuners, available in Natural finish, mfg. circa mid 1970s.

	N/A	$650	$350

This model had a solid oboncol wood pickguard (adhesive-backed for optional installation) available.

DY 57 WINCHESTER DREADNOUGHT - dreadnought style, solid Canadian spruce top, round soundhole, ivoroid/wood marquetry bound body, herringbone rosette, mahogany back/sides, nato mahogany neck, 14/20-fret ebony fingerboard with dot inlay, ebony bridge, 3-per-side chrome tuners, available in Natural finish, mfg. circa mid 1970s.

	N/A	$650	$350

DY 58 DREADNOUGHT NINE - dreadnought style, solid Canadian spruce top, round soundhole, ivoroid bound body, wood inlay rosette, mahogany back/sides/neck, 14/20-fret ebony fingerboard with pearl dot inlay, ebony bridge, mahogany headstock veneer, tortoiseshell pickguard, 3 + 6-per-side chrome tuners, available in Natural finish, mfg. circa mid 1970s.

	N/A	$700	$450

This nine-stringed guitar combines three single bass-side strings with three pairs of treble strings. This model will also function as a six string acoustic.

DY 68 RAMBLING TWELVE - dreadnought style, solid Canadian spruce top, round soundhole, wood inlay bound body, wood inlay rosette, mahogany back/sides/neck, 14/20-fret ebony fingerboard with pearl dot inlay, ebony bridge, mahogany headstock veneer, abalone logo inlay on headstock, tortoiseshell pickguard, 6-per-side chrome tuners, abalone inlays on bridge pins, available in Natural finish, mfg. circa mid 1970s.

	N/A	$700	$450

GRADING	100%	EXCELLENT	AVERAGE

DY 75 - dreadnought style, spruce top, round soundhole, wooden inlay bound body/rosette, tortoise pickguard, rosewood back/sides, mahogany neck, 14/20-fret rosewood fingerboard with pearl dot inlay, Direct Coupled rosewood bridge, rosewood veneer on bound peghead, 3-per-side chrome tuners, available in Natural finish, mfg. 1991-95.

	$950	$700	$425

Last MSR was $1,300.

The original design circa mid 1970s featured a bound ebony fingerboard with abalone dot inlays and ebony bridge (DY75 Lexington Dreadnought).

DY 76 HERRINGBONE TWELVE - dreadnought style, solid Canadian spruce top, round soundhole, ivoroid bound body, 3-stripe wood rosette, rosewood back/sides/neck, 14/20-fret ebony fingerboard with snowflake inlay, ebony bridge, rosewood headstock veneer, abalone logo inlay on headstock, tortoise shell pickguard, 6-per-side chrome tuners, abalone inlays on bridge pins, available in Natural finish, mfg. circa mid 1970s.

	N/A	$650	$425

DY 77 N - dreadnought style, solid spruce top, round soundhole, herringbone bound body/rosette, tortoise pickguard, rosewood back/sides, mahogany neck, 14/20-fret ebony fingerboard with abalone diamond inlay, rosewood Direct Coupled bridge, rosewood veneer on bound peghead, 3-per-side chrome tuners, available in Natural finish, mfg. 1991-95.

	$825	$625	$375

Last MSR was $1,200.

DY 77 NEQ - dreadnought style, solid spruce top, round soundhole, herringbone bound body/rosette, tortoise pickguard, rosewood back/sides, mahogany neck, 14/20-fret ebony fingerboard with abalone diamond inlay, rosewood Direct Coupled bridge, rosewood veneer on bound peghead, 3-per-side chrome tuners, piezo bridge pickup, 3-band EQ, available in Natural finish, mfg. 1994 only.

	$1,050	$725	$500

Last MSR was $1,500.

DY 78 HERRINGBONE TRI-BACK - dreadnought style, Canadian spruce top, round soundhole, herringbone bound body, herringbone rosette, burled thuya pickguard, rosewood sides, three piece rosewood/mahogany/rosewood back, mahogany neck, 14/20-fret ebony fingerboard with pearl snowflake inlay, ebony bridge, burled thuya veneer on peghead, 3-per-side chrome tuners, available in Natural finish, mfg. circa mid 1970s.

	N/A	$800	$500

DY 85 STANDARD abalone - dreadnought style, Canadian spruce top, round soundhole, abalone and celluloid bound body and soundhole, black pickguard, burled mahogany sides, three piece burled mahogany/rosewood/burled mahogany back, nato mahogany neck, 14/20-fret ebony fingerboard with abalone inlay, ebony bridge, internal lacquering, 3-per-side gold Grover tuners, available in Natural finish, mfg. circa mid 1970s.

	N/A	$825	$500

DY 87 JUMBO DOUBLE NECK - dreadnought style, solid Canadian spruce top, shared oval soundhole, celluloid bound body, wood inlay rosette, mahogany back/sides, mahogany necks, 14/20-fret ebony fingerboard with snowflake inlay, double ebony bridge, black headstocks, 3-per-side headstock (6-string), 6-per-side headstock (12-string), chrome tuners, available in Natural finish, mfg. circa mid 1970s.

	N/A	$825	$500

DY 87 - dreadnought style, rounded cutaway body, curly maple top, round soundhole, 5-stripe bound body and rosette, maple back/sides, mahogany neck, 21-fret ebony fingerboard with pearl dot inlay, 12th fret has pearl snowflake inlay, ebony bridge with white abalone dot pins, 3-per-side chrome tuners, bridge pickup, 3-band EQ, available in Trans. Black finish, mfg. 1991-95.

	$975	$725	$475

Last MSR was $1,450.

DY 87/12 - similar to DY 87, except has 12 strings, 6-per-side tuners, available in Violin Sunburst finish, mfg. 1991-95.

	$1,025	$750	$525

Last MSR was $1,575.

DY 90 - dreadnought style, solid spruce top, round soundhole, abalone bound body and rosette, black pickguard with Alvarez Yairi logo in abalone, rosewood back/sides, mahogany neck, 14/20-fret bound ebony fingerboard with abalone diamond inlay, abalone bound ebony bridge with black pearl dot pins, rosewood peghead veneer with abalone logo inlay, 3-per-side gold tuners, available in Natural finish, mfg. circa mid 1970s-1995.

                              $950   **$750**   **$475**
                              Last MSR was $1,475.

     The original design featured a jacaranda three-piece back, jacaranda sides, Canadian spruce top, and internal lacquering as well as the abalone appointments (DY90 Super abalone).

DY 92 LUTE BACK - dreadnought style, spruce top, round soundhole, herringbone bound body and rosette, 33-piece mahogany/rosewood/maple lute style rounded back, 14/20-fret bound ebony fingerboard with pearl dot inlay, ebony bridge with black pearl dot pins, 3-per-side gold tuners, available in Natural finish, mfg. circa 1975-1993.

                             $1,875   **$1,475**   **$900**
                              Last MSR was $2,775.

     The DY 92 was produced in limited quantities.

DY 96 abalone SUPREME - dreadnought style, Canadian spruce top, round soundhole, abalone bound body and rosette, book-matched jacaranda back with inlaid middle strip of marquetry, jacaranda sides, abalone bound jacaranda pickguard, 14/20-fret abalone bound ebony fingerboard with abalone diamond shaped inlays, ebony bridge with abalone inlay, 3-per-side gold tuners, abalone bound headstock, available in Natural finish, mfg. circa mid 1970s.

                             N/A   **$1,000**   **$650**

ACOUSTIC: DREADNOUGHT INNOVATIVE SERIES (DY52, DY70, DY71, DY80)

DY 52 CANYON CREEK - dreadnought style, solid spruce top, round soundhole, 3-stripe body binding, shell rosette, tortoise pickguard, rosewood back/sides, mahogany neck, 14/20-fret rosewood fingerboard with pearl dot inlay/12th fret pearl snowflake inlay, Direct Coupled ebony bridge with black pearl dot pins, rosewood veneer on peghead, 3-per-side chrome tuners, available in Natural gloss finish, mfg. 1991-98.

                             $950   **$650**   **$425**
                              Last MSR was $1,249.

     In 1994, coral rosewood back/sides replaced original part/design.

DY 70 MAPLE GRAPHITE - dreadnought style, solid spruce top, round soundhole, tortoise shell bound body/rosette, flamed maple back/sides, mahogany neck, 14/20-fret rosewood fingerboard with pearl dot inlay/12th fret pearl curlicue inlay, graphite bridge with black abalone dot pins, graphite peghead veneer with pearl logo inlay, 3-per-side chrome tuners, available in Natural gloss finish, mfg. 1994-98.

                             $825   **$570**   **$385**
                              Last MSR was $1,099.

DY 71 KOA GRAPHITE - similar to DY 70, except has tortoise pickguard, tortoise shell/ivory body binding, koa back/sides, graphite bridge/bridge plate, disc. 1998.

                             $875   **$575**   **$390**
                              Last MSR was $1,149.

DY 80 CANYON CREEK 12-STRING - similar to the DY 52, except has 12-string configuration, 6-per-side chrome tuners, available in Natural gloss finish, mfg. 1991-98.

                             $975   **$650**   **$435**
                              Last MSR was $1,299.

FUSION SERIES

     The DY 88 Express Pro was renamed the Fusion Series in 1998.

DY 88 BK ADVANCED (DY 88 EXPRESS PRO) - dreadnought style, rounded cutaway Closed Chamber body, spruce top, abalone/ivory body binding, mahogany back/sides/neck, 23-fret ebony fingerboard with pearl dot inlay/pearl snowflake inlay on 12th fret, ebony bridge with white abalone dot pins, 3-per-side gold tuners, Hexaphonic piezo bridge pickup, System 500 electronics, available in Gloss Black, Transparent Blue, Sunburst, or Pearl White finish, mfg. 1991-2001.

                             $1,465   **$950**   **$650**
                              Last MSR was $1,949.

     In 1998, a spruce top and mahogany back and sides replaced the original curly maple top and maple back and sides.

DY 88 BK 12 Advanced (DY 88/12 Express Pro) - similar to DY 88 BK, except has 12-string configuration, 6-per-side gold tuners, available in Gloss Black finish, mfg. 1991-2001.

                             $1,500   **$1,020**   **$650**
                              Last MSR was $1,999.

DY 88K - similar to DY 88 BK, except has koa top, back and sides, mfg. 1998-2001.

                             $1,575   **$1,050**   **$750**
                              Last MSR was $2,099.

GRADING	100%	EXCELLENT	AVERAGE

SY 88 BK Advanced - similar to DY 88 BK, except features a thinline body, small Closed Chamber body, ivory body binding, available in Gloss Black finish, mfg. 1998-2001.

	$1,200	$825	$550

Last MSR was $1,599.

ACOUSTIC: MASTERWORKS SERIES

The Masterworks Series represents the Top-of-the-Line in Yairi production.

CY 95 - classical body style, solid spruce top with scalloped bracing, solid Indian rosewood sides and back, abalone shell soundhole rosette, maple body binding, ebony fingerboard and ebony direct coupled bridge, gold die-cast tuners, available in Vintage Natural Lacquer finish, current mfg.

MSR	$1,999	$1,500	$1,000	$700

CY 95CE - similar to the CY 95, except has a cutaway and Alvarez NR electronics, current mfg.

MSR	$2,399	$1,750	$1,250	$750

CY 200 - classical grand concert body, solid cedar top, solid Indian rosewood back and sides, round soundhole, wood multi-layer binding, 12/20 ebony fingerboard, ebony bridge, 6-on-a-side, gold plated tuning machines, available in Vintage Natural Lacquer, mfg 2001-current.

MSR	$3,299	$2,550	$1,700	$1,200

Both of the CY 200 and CY 200S are part of the Masterworks series.

CY 200S - similar to the CY 200 except has a solid spruce top for a lighter color, mfg. 2001 only.

	$2,550	$1,700	$1,200

Last MSR was $3,299.

DY 94 - dreadnought body style, sloped shoulder, solid spruce top with scalloped bracing, solid mahogany sides and back, abalone shell soundhole rosette, maple body binding, ebony fingerboard and ebony direct coupled bridge, gold die-cast tuners, available in Vintage Natural Lacquer finish, current mfg.

MSR	$1,799	$1,350	$950	$650

DY 95 - dreadnought body style, sloped shoulder, solid spruce top with scalloped bracing, solid Indian rosewood sides and back, abalone shell soundhole rosette, maple body binding, ebony fingerboard and ebony direct coupled bridge, gold die-cast tuners, available in Vintage Natural Lacquer finish, current mfg.

MSR	$1,999	$1,500	$1,000	$700

DY 100 - dreadnought body style, solid spruce top with scalloped braces, solid mahogany sides and back, abalone shell soundhole rosette, maple body binding, Indian rosewood fingerboard, rosewood direct coupled bridge, gold die-cast tuners, available in Vintage Natural Lacquer finish, disc 2002.

	$2,575	$1,725	$1,125

Last MSR was $3,299.

DY 200 - dreadnought body style, solid spruce top with scalloped bracing, solid Indian rosewood sides and back, abalone shell soundhole rosette, maple body binding, ebony fingerboard and ebony direct coupled bridge, gold die-cast tuners, available in Vintage Natural Lacquer finish, current mfg.

MSR	$3,399	$2,600	$1,750	$1,125

DY 500 - dreadnought body style, solid spruce top with scalloped bracing, solid Indian rosewood sides and back, abalone shell soundhole rosette, maple/abalone body binding, 14/20 ebony fingerboard and ebony direct coupled bridge, gold die-cast tuners, available in Natural Lacquer finish, mfg. 2001-current.

MSR	$4,999	$3,750	$2,900	$2,200

FY 94 - OM body style folk, solid spruce top, solid Mahogany sides and back, abalone shell soundhole rosette, maple body binding, rosewood fingerboard and direct coupled bridge, gold die-cast tuners, available in Vintage Natural Lacquer finish, current mfg.

MSR	$1,799	$1,350	$950	$650

FY 95 - OM body style folk, solid spruce top, solid Indian rosewood sides and back, abalone shell soundhole rosette, maple body binding, ebony fingerboard and ebony direct coupled bridge, gold die-cast tuners, available in Vintage Natural Lacquer finish, current mfg.

MSR	$1,999	$1,500	$1,000	$700

FY 95C - similar to the FY 95, except has a single cutaway, new 2003.

MSR	$2,399	$1,750	$1,250	$750

Alvarez Yairi DY 52
Canyon Creek
courtesy Alvarez Yairi

GRADING		100%	EXCELLENT	AVERAGE

FY 200 - orchestra body style, solid spruce top with scalloped braces, solid Indian rosewood sides and back, abalone shell soundhole rosette, maple body binding, ebony fingerboard and ebony direct coupled bridge, gold die-cast tuners, available in Vintage Natural Lacquer finish, current mfg.

MSR	$3,399		$2,550	$1,795	$1,150

Both the FY 200 and FY 200C are part of the Masterwork series.

FY 200C - similar to the FY 200 except has a single cutaway body, disc 2002.

			$2,800	$1,900	$1,250

Last MSR was $3,699.

ACOUSTIC: SIGNATURE SERIES

All Signature models have Kazuo Yairi's signature on them.

AY 20 SIGNATURE - concert style, solid cedar top, round soundhole, wood bound body, abalone rosette, walnut back/sides, mahogany neck, 14/20-fret rosewood fingerboard, 12th fret abalone diamond/slash inlay, rosewood bridge with black abalone dot pins, walnut peghead veneer with abalone logo inlay, 3-per-side gold tuners, available in Natural finish, mfg. 1994-98.

	$975	$700	$450

Last MSR was $1,250.

DY 61 SIGNATURE - dreadnought style, solid cedar top, round soundhole, maple/wood body binding, abalone shell rosette, burled mahogany back/sides, mahogany neck, 14/20-fret ebony fingerboard/12th fret pearl diamond/abalone slash inlay, rosewood bridge with black abalone dot pins, burl mahogany veneer on peghead with abalone/wooden strip inlays, abalone logo peghead inlay, 3-per-side gold tuners with amber buttons, available in Natural semi-satin finish, mfg. 1991-98.

	$1,124	$750	$500

Last MSR was $1,499.

In 1994, burled mahogany back/sides replaced original part/design.

DY 69 - similar to DY 61, except has spruce top, tortoise pickguard, wooden inlay rosette, burled mahogany back/sides, upper belly bridge with white abalone dot pins, mfg. 1994 only.

	$875	$625	$450

Last MSR was $1,350.

DY 72 12-STRING - similar to DY 61, except has 12 strings and rosewood veneer on peghead, disc. 1997.

	$875	$665	$400

Last MSR was $1,275.

YM 1 YAIRI MASTER MAHOGANY - dreadnought style, solid cedar top, multi-layer wood body binding, abalone shell rosette, solid mahogany back/sides, mahogany neck, 14/20-fret rosewood fingerboard, 12th fret abalone stripe/pearl cross inlay, rosewood bridge with black pearl dot pins, ebony veneered peghead with pearl logo inlay, 3-per-side gold die cast tuners, available in Natural semi-satin finish, mfg. 1995-98.

	$1,100	$725	$475

Last MSR was $1,399.

YM 2 YAIRI MASTER OVANGKOL - similar to the YM 1, except features solid spruce top, solid ovankol back/sides, disc. 1998.

	$1,150	$750	$500

Last MSR was $1,499.

AYL 1 LUTHIER CUTAWAY - dreadnought style, rounded cutaway body, solid spruce top, round soundhole, synthetic tortoise body binding, abalone shell rosette, mahogany back/sides/neck, 14/20-fret rosewood fingerboard/12th fret pearl diamond/abalone slash inlay, rosewood bridge with black abalone dot pins, 3-per-side gold tuners, piezo bridge pickup, volume/tone controls, System 500 electronics, available in Natural semi-gloss finish, disc. 1998.

	$1,150	$750	$525

Last MSR was $1,549.

ACOUSTIC: TONEWOOD SERIES

DY 84 - dreadnought style, Indian rosewood back and sides, solid spruce top, scalloped braces, ebony fingerboard, 12th fret diagonal fingerboard inlay, abalone shell rosette, ivory multi-layer binding, chrome die cast tuners, ebony direct coupled bridge, optional System 500 electronics, available in Natural Gloss finish, current mfg.

MSR	$1,549		$1,100	$750	$525

DY 84BR - similar to DY 84 except has Brazillian rosewood back and sides, available in Natural Gloss finish, current mfg.

MSR	$1,999		$1,550	$1,050	$700

DY 84C - similar to DY 84 except with a single cutaway dreadnought style body and standard system 600 T electronics, available in Natural Gloss finish, current mfg.

MSR	$1,949		$1,475	$975	$650

DY 84K - similar to DY 84 except has Koa back and sides, available in Natural Gloss finish, current mfg.

MSR	$1,549		$1,100	$750	$525

GRADING	100%	EXCELLENT	AVERAGE

DY 84M - similar to DY 84 except has flamed maple back and sides, available in Vintage Natural Lacquer finish, disc 2002.

	$1,100	$750	$525

Last MSR was $1,549.

DY 84W - similar to DY 84 except has walnut back and sides, available in Vintage Natural Lacquer finish, disc 2002.

	$1,100	$750	$525

Last MSR was $1,549.

DY 91 - dreadnought style, solid spruce top, round soundhole, abalone bound body and rosette, flamed koa back/sides, black pickguard with Alvarez Yairi logo in abalone, mahogany neck, 14/20-fret bound ebony fingerboard with abalone diamond inlay, abalone bound ebony bridge with black pearl dot pins, koa peghead veneer with abalone logo inlay, 3-per-side gold tuners, available in Natural gloss finish, mfg. 1994-current.

MSR	$1,899	$1,425	$975	$625

FY 84 - orchestra style body, solid spruce top, Indian rosewood back and sides, round soundhole with abalone shell, 14/20 ebony fingerboard with pearl dot/cat eye inlays, ebony direct coupled bridge, ivory multi-layer binding, 3-per-side chrome die-cast tuners, optional system 600T electronics, available in Natural gloss finish, mfg. 2001 only.

	$1,100	$850	$575

Last MSR was $1,549.

FY 91 - folk style, solid spruce top, round soundhole, abalone bound body and rosette, koa back/sides, black pickguard with Alvarez Yairi logo in abalone, mahogany neck, 14/20-fret bound ebony fingerboard with abalone diamond inlay, abalone bound ebony bridge with black pearl dot pins, koa peghead veneer w/abalone logo inlay, 3-per-side gold tuners, available in Natural gloss finish, new 2003.

MSR	$1,899	$1,425	$975	$625

JY 84 - jumbo style body, solid spruce top, coral rosewood back and sides, 14/20 ebony fingerboard, round soundhole, ebony bridge, ivory multi-layer binding, snowflake/cat's-eye fingerboard inlay, 3-per-side gold tuners, optional System 600T electronics, Natural gloss finish, mfg. 2002-current.

MSR	$1,599	$1,200	$850	$600

JY 84C - similar to the JY 84 except has a single cutaway and standard System 600T electronics, mfg. 2002-current.

MSR	$1,999	$1,500	$1,050	$750

JY 84-12 - similar to the JY 84 except is in 12-string configuration, mfg. 2002-current.

MSR	$1,899	$1,450	$975	$700

Alvarez Yairi DC 1 Virtuoso
courtesy Alvarez Yairi

ACOUSTIC: TRADITIONAL SERIES

CY 62 CE - single cutaway classical body, round soundhole with abalone shell, solid cedar top, burl mahogany back and sides, 14/20 rosewood fingerboard with snowflake/cat's-eye inlays, 3-per-side die cast tuning machines, maple and natural wood binding, rosewood direct coupled bridge, Standard System 600T electronics, available in Natural finish, new 2003.

MSR	$1,949	$1,475	$1,150	$750

DY 38 WOOD RIDGE - dreadnought style, solid spruce top, round soundhole, 3-stripe body binding, 5-stripe rosette, black pickguard, mahogany back/sides/neck, 14/20-fret rosewood fingerboard with pearl dot inlay/12th fret has pearl snowflake inlay, rosewood bridge with black white dot pins, 3-per-side chrome tuners, available in Natural gloss finish, mfg. 1991-current.

MSR	$1,099	$825	$600	$400

In 1996, flamed maple back/sides replaced mahogany back/sides.

DY 38 C CUTAWAY - dreadnought style, sloped rounded cutaway body, solid spruce top, round soundhole, 3-stripe body binding, 5-stripe rosette, black pickguard, flamed maple back/sides, mahogany neck, 14/20-fret rosewood fingerboard with pearl dot inlay/12th fret has pearl snowflake inlay, rosewood bridge with black white dot pins, 3-per-side chrome tuners, available in Natural gloss finish, mfg. 1991-98.

	$950	$625	$425

Last MSR was $1,249.

DY 40 - dreadnought body, mahogany back and sides, solid spruce top, scalloped bracing, ebony fingerboard, 12th fret diagonal position marker, abalone shell rosette, ivory multi-layer body binding, chrome die cast tuners, ebony direct coupled bridge, optional System 500 electronics, available in Natural Gloss, Black, or Sunburst finish, current mfg.

MSR	$1,349	$999	$675	$450

GRADING		100%	EXCELLENT	AVERAGE

DY 40C - similar to DY 40 except has a single cutaway dreadnought body, available in Natural Gloss or Black finish, current mfg.

MSR	$1,789		$1,350	$925	$600

DY 40-12 - similar to DY 40 except in a 12-string configuration, available in Natural Gloss finish, current mfg.

MSR	$1,549		$1,175	$800	$525

DY 45 WOOD RIDGE - dreadnought style, solid spruce top, round soundhole, 3-stripe body binding, 5-stripe rosette, black pickguard, mahogany back/sides/neck, 14/20-fret rosewood fingerboard with pearl dot inlay, 12th fret has pearl snowflake inlay, ebony bridge with black white dot pins, 3-per-side chrome tuners, available in Dark Satin Antique finish, mfg. 1975-1998.

		$675	$465	$300

Last MSR was $899.

In 1996, Sunburst Mahogany finish replaced Dark Satin Antique finish.

DY 45 AV - dreadnought style, solid spruce top, round soundhole, 3-stripe bound body, 5-stripe rosette, black pickguard, mahogany back/sides/neck, 14/20-fret rosewood fingerboard with pearl dot inlay, 12th fret has pearl snowflake inlay, ebony bridge with black white dot pins, 3-per-side chrome tuners, piezo bridge pickup, 3-band EQ, available in Dark Satin Antique finish, mfg. 1994 only.

		$775	$575	$350

Last MSR was $1,075.

This model is similar to DY 45, with electronics.

DY 46 DREADNOUGHT - similar to the DY 45 Vintage Dreadnought, except had gloss finish, mfg. circa mid 1970s.

		N/A	$650	$400

DY 62 C - single cutaway dreadnought body, round soundhole with abalone shell, solid cedar top, burl mahogany back and sides, 14/20 rosewood fingerboard with snowflake/cat's eye inlays, 3-per-side die cast tuning machines, maple and natural wood binding, rosewood direct coupled bridge, Standard System 600T electronics, available in Natural finish, mfg. 2001-current.

MSR	$1,949		$1,475	$1,150	$750

DY 74 WELLINGTON - dreadnought style, solid spruce top, round soundhole, 5-stripe bound body and rosette, tortoise pickguard, rosewood back/sides, mahogany neck, 14/20-fret ebony fingerboard with varying pearl inlay, ebony bridge with white pearl dot pins, rosewood veneer on peghead, 3-per-side chrome tuners, available in Natural gloss finish, mfg. circa 1975-1998.

		$975	$615	$425

Last MSR was $1,219.

The original design circa mid 1970s featured an ebony fingerboard and bridge, and jacaranda veneer peghead (DY74 Wellington rosewood).

DY 74 C (DY74 C Wellington Cutaway) - similar to DY 74, except has single rounded cutaway, mfg. circa 1975-1998.

		$1,000	$650	$435

Last MSR was $1,319.

DY 74 S Wellington Sunburst - similar to DY 74 Wellington rosewood, except has Brown Sunburst finish, mfg. circa mid 1970s.

		$775	$550	$325

DY 74 CEQ (DY 74 CEQ1) - dreadnought style, rounded cutaway body, solid spruce top, round soundhole, 5-stripe body binding/rosette, tortoise pickguard, rosewood back/sides, mahogany neck, 14/20-fret ebony fingerboard with varying pearl inlay, ebony bridge with white pearl dot pins, rosewood veneer on peghead, 3-per-side chrome tuners, piezo bridge pickups, 3-band EQ/System 500 electronics, available in Natural gloss finish, mfg. 1995-98.

		$1,100	$725	$495

Last MSR was $1,449.

FY 40 - orchestra style body, solid spruce top, mahogany back and sides, 14/20 rosewood fingerboard with 12th fret diagonal inlay, rosewood direct coupled bridge, ivory multi-layer binding, 3-per-side chrome die-cast tuners, optional system 600T electronics, available in Natural gloss finish, mfg. 2001-current.

MSR	$1,349		$1,025	$800	$550

ACOUSTIC: VIRTUOSO SERIES

DC 1 VIRTUOSO 12-STRING - rounded shoulder dreadnought style, solid spruce top, round soundhole, ivoroid bound body, herringbone purfling/rosette, Indian rosewood back/sides, mahogany neck, 12/19-fret ebony fingerboard with pearl cross/ellipse inlay, ebony bridge with white pearl dot pins, tortoise pickguard, ebony veneered peghead with pearl logo inlay, 6-per-side chrome die cast tuners, available in Natural gloss finish, mfg. 1995-99.

		$1,200	$825	$550

Last MSR was $1,599.

GY 1 - dreadnought style, rounded cutaway body, solid spruce top, round soundhole, 5-stripe bound body and rosette, tortoise pickguard, rosewood back/sides, mahogany neck, 20-fret bound ebony fingerboard with varied abalone inlay, rosewood bridge with white abalone dot pins, rosewood veneer on bound peghead with pearl tulip inlay, 3-per-side gold tuners, bridge pickup, 3-band EQ, available in Natural finish, mfg. 1991-96.

		$1,250	$850	$525

Last MSR was $1,700.

This model was co-designed with Jerry Garcia.

GRADING	100%	EXCELLENT	AVERAGE

GY 2 (VIRTUOSO DELUXE) - single round cutaway jumbo style, solid spruce top, round sound-hole, tortoise pickguard, ivoroid bound body, abalone purfling/rosette, lace wood back/sides, mahogany neck, 20-fret bound ebony fingerboard with pearl dot inlay, 12th fret pearl curlicue inlay, abalone bound ebony bridge, rosewood veneered peghead with pearl logo inlay, 3-per-side gold die cast tuners, available in Natural finish, mfg. 1995-97.

	$1,500	$1,000	$625
		Last MSR was $2,000.	

This instrument was co-designed with Jerry Garcia.

WY 1 - jumbo style, rounded cutaway body, solid cedar top, round soundhole, multi-layer wood body binding, abalone shell rosette, rosewood back/sides, mahogany neck, 14/20-fret ebony fingerboard/12th fret has pearl diamond/abalone slash inlay, Direct Coupled ebony bridge with black abalone dot pins, rosewood veneer on peghead with abalone and wooden strip inlays, 3-per-side gold tuners, piezo bridge pickup, 3-band EQ/System 500 electronics, available in Natural, Black, Trans. Purple, Trans. Red, or Sunburst finish, mfg. 1991-current.

MSR	$1,999	$1,500	$1,000	$650

In 1994, folk style body replaced original part/design. This model was co-designed with Bob Weir. The models finished in Trans. Purple and Red have Fiddleback Maple wood.

WY 112 12-String - similar to WY 1 Virtuoso (folk style body), except has 12-string configuration, 6-per-side tuners, available in Natural Semi-Satin finish, mfg. 1996-2001.

	$1,550	$1,050	$675
		Last MSR was $2,149.	

WY 1 K Koa - similar to WY 1 Virtuoso (folk style body), except features koa top/back/sides, abalone rosette, abalone body binding, fingerboard dot inlay, snowflake bridge inlay, available in Natural Gloss finish, mfg. 1998-current.

MSR	$1,999	$1,500	$1,000	$650

WY 1 RR - similar to WY 1 Virtuoso (folk style body), except features a thin cutaway body with solid spruce top, mahogany back and sides, has Roland GK2 electronics, available in Satin Graphite finish, mfg. 1998-current.

MSR	$2,299	$1,650	$1,150	$750

WY 80 LIMITED EDITION ANNIVERSARY - folk style single cutaway body, solid cedar top, round soundhole, multi-layer maple/abalone body binding, abalone shell rosette, Brazilian rosewood back/sides, mahogany neck, 14/20-fret ebony fingerboard, Tree-of-Life inlay, Direct Coupled ebony bridge w/black abalone dot pins, rosewood veneer on peghead w/abalone and wooden strip inlays, 3-per-side gold tuners, piezo bridge pickup, Standard System 600T electronics, available in Natural finish, mfg. 2002 only.

	$2,250	$1,600	N/A
		Last MSR was $2,999.	

Alvarez Yairi GY 2 Virtuoso
courtesy Alvarez Yairi

AMADA

Instruments previously produced in Luby, Czech Republic. Currently produced in China. Distributed by Geneva International Corporation of Wheeling, Illinois.

Amada classical guitars and mandolins (as well as Lidl orchestra instruments) are made by Strunal Manufacture of Luby. These guitars are available in five fractional sizes for the younger entry level student. Amada believes that fitting the right size guitar to the physical size of the student aids in the learning curve, as opposed to younger students struggling with a full sized guitar.

The fractional scale runs from 1/4, 1/2, 3/4, 7/8, up to full size. The scale lengths range from 17" (1/4 size), to 20 1/4" (1/2 size), 24" (3/4 size), 24 1/2" (7/8 size), up to 25 1/2" (Full size). Corresponding metric measurements run from 440 mm to 650 mm. Models are offered in oak or mahogany back and sides, and are available in a Natural high gloss or matte finish.

ACOUSTIC: A SERIES

All the models in Amada's Classical Nylon string series have a spruce top, round soundhole, classical style slotted headstock, 3-per-side tuners, and tied bridge.

A144 (4/4 SIZE) - spruce top, mahogany back and sides, nato neck with rosewood fingerboard, 25 ¾" scale, rosewood bridge, available in Natural Gloss finish, disc 2000.

	$120	$85	$50
		Last MSR was $179.	

A134 (3/4 SIZE) - similar to A144, except in 23 1/2" scale, disc 2000.

	$105	$75	$40
		Last MSR was $159.	

Alvarez Yairi WY 1 Virtuoso
courtesy Alvarez Yairi

GRADING	100%	EXCELLENT	AVERAGE

A112 (1/2 SIZE) - similar to A144, except has 22 1/4" scale, disc 2000.

	$90	$70	$35

Last MSR was $139.

A114 (1/4 SIZE) - similar to A144, except has 17 1/2" scale, disc 2000.

	$80	$65	$30

Last MSR was $129.

ACOUSTIC: 4000 SERIES

MODEL 4635 (4/4 SIZE) - spruce top, 25 1/2" scale, oak back/sides, rosewood fingerboard, rosewood bridge, available in Natural high gloss finish, disc. 1998.

	$175	$120	$70

Last MSR was $240.

Model 4635 PM (4/4 Size) - similar to the Model 4635, available in Natural Matte finish, disc. 1998.

	$165	$115	$65

Last MSR ws $232.

MODEL 4655 (4/4 SIZE) - spruce top, 25 1/2" scale, mahogany back/sides, rosewood fingerboard, rosewood bridge, available in Natural high gloss finish, disc. 1998.

	$175	$120	$70

Last MSR was $240.

Model 4655 PM (4/4 Size) - similar to the Model 4655, available in Natural Matte finish, disc. 1998.

	$165	$115	$65

Last MSR was $232.

MODEL 4735 (4/4 SIZE) - solid cedar top, 25 1/2" scale, oak back/sides, rosewood fingerboard, rosewood bridge, available in Natural high gloss finish, disc. 1998.

	$240	$175	$105

Last MSR was $342.

Model 4735 PM (4/4 Size) - similar to the Model 4735, available in Natural Matte finish, disc. 1998.

	$235	$165	$95

Last MSR was $332.

MODEL 4755 (4/4 SIZE) - solid cedar top, 25 1/2" scale, mahogany back/sides, rosewood fingerboard, rosewood bridge, available in Natural high gloss finish, disc. 1998.

	$240	$175	$105

Last MSR was $342.

Model 4755 PM (4/4 Size) - similar to the Model 4755, available in Natural Matte finish, disc. 1998.

	$235	$165	$95

Last MSR was $332.

ACOUSTIC: 5000 SERIES

MODEL 5432 (7/8 SIZE) - spruce top, 24 1/2" scale, oak back/sides, rosewood fingerboard, rosewood bridge, available in Natural high gloss finish, disc. 1998.

	$135	$100	$60

Last MSR was $198.

Model 5432 PM (7/8 Size) - similar to the Model 5432, available in Natural matte finish, disc. 1998.

	$125	$95	$55

Last MSR was $190.

MODEL 5433 (1/2 SIZE) - spruce top, 21" scale, oak back/sides, rosewood fingerboard, rosewood bridge, available in Natural high gloss finish, disc. 1998.

	$125	$95	$55

Last MSR was $190.

Model 5433 PM (1/2 Size) - similar to the Model 5433, available in Natural matte finish, disc. 1998.

	$125	$90	$50

Last MSR was $182.

MODEL 5434 (1/4 SIZE) - spruce top, 17" scale, oak back/sides, rosewood fingerboard, rosewood bridge, available in Natural high gloss finish, disc. 1998.

	$125	$90	$50

Last MSR was $184.

MODEL 5437 (3/4 SIZE) - spruce top, 22 1/2" scale, oak back/sides, rosewood fingerboard, rosewood bridge, available in Natural high gloss finish, disc. 1998.

	$125	$95	$55

Last MSR was $192.

GRADING	100%	EXCELLENT	AVERAGE

Model 5437 PM (3/4 Size) - similar to the Model 5437, available in Natural matte finish, disc. 1998.

	$125	$90	$50

Last MSR was $184.

MODEL 5452 (7/8 SIZE) - spruce top, 24 1/2" scale, mahogany back/sides, rosewood fingerboard, rosewood bridge, available in Natural high gloss finish, disc. 1998.

	$135	$100	$60

Last MSR was $198.

Model 5452 PM (7/8 Size) - similar to the Model 5452, available in Natural matte finish, disc. 1998.

	$125	$95	$55

Last MSR was $190.

MODEL 5453 (1/2 SIZE) - spruce top, 21" scale, mahogany back/sides, rosewood fingerboard, rosewood bridge, available in Natural high gloss finish, disc. 1998.

	$125	$95	$55

Last MSR was $190.

Model 5453 PM (1/2 Size) - similar to the Model 5453, available in Natural matte finish, disc. 1998.

	$125	$90	$50

Last MSR was $182.

MODEL 5457 PM (3/4 SIZE) - spruce top, 22 1/2" scale, mahogany back/sides, rosewood fingerboard, rosewood bridge, available in Natural matte finish, disc. 1998.

	$125	$90	$50

Last MSR was $184.

MODEL 5732 (7/8 SIZE) - solid cedar top, 24 1/2" scale, oak back/sides, rosewood fingerboard, rosewood bridge, available in Natural high gloss finish, disc. 1998.

	$240	$175	$105

Last MSR was $342.

MODEL 5737 (3/4 SIZE) - solid cedar top, 22 1/2" scale, oak back/sides, rosewood fingerboard, rosewood bridge, available in Natural high gloss finish, disc. 1998.

	$240	$175	$105

Last MSR was $342.

MODEL 5752 (7/8 SIZE) - solid cedar top, 24 1/2" scale, mahogany back/sides, rosewood fingerboard, rosewood bridge, available in Natural high gloss finish, disc. 1998.

	$240	$175	$105

Last MSR was $342.

MODEL 5757 (3/4 SIZE) - solid cedar top, 22 1/2" scale, mahogany back/sides, rosewood fingerboard, rosewood bridge, available in Natural high gloss finish, disc. 1998.

	$240	$175	$105

Last MSR was $342.

ACOUSTIC: 8000 SERIES

MODEL 8010 (4/4 SIZE) - solid spruce top, 25 1/2" scale, beechwood back/sides, available in Natural high gloss finish, disc. 2000.

	$125	$90	$50

Last MSR was $179.

MODEL 8011 (3/4 SIZE) - solid spruce top, 24" scale, beechwood back/sides, available in Natural high gloss finish, disc. 2000.

	$110	$80	$45

Last MSR was $159.

MODEL 8012 (1/2 SIZE) - solid spruce top, 20 1/4" scale, beechwood back/sides, available in Natural high gloss finish, disc. 2000.

	$99	$70	$40

Last MSR was $139.

ACOUSTIC STEEL STRING GUITARS

MODEL 8253 (4/4 SIZE) - solid beechwood top, 25 1/2" scale, beechwood back/sides, available in Natural matte finish, disc. 2000.

	$95	$65	$35

Last MSR was $129.

MODEL 8251 (3/4 SIZE) - solid beechwood top, 24" scale, beechwood back/sides, available in Natural matte finish, disc. 2000.

| | $70 | $50 | $25 |

Last MSR was $99.

MODEL 8252 (1/2 SIZE) - solid beechwood top, 20 1/2" scale, beechwood back/sides, available in Natural matte finish, disc. 2000.

| | $60 | $45 | $25 |

Last MSR was $89.

AMALIO BURGUET

Instruments currently produced in Spain. Distributed by Saga Musical Instruments of San Francisco, California.

Amalio Burguet acoustics are offered in the classical and flamenco configurations. Handmade in Spain, these guitars feature a solid cedar or solid spruce top, mahogany neck, rosewood or ebony fingerboard, rosewood bridge, an inlaid marquetry rosette, clear high gloss finish, gold-plated tuners, and a slotted 3-per-side headstock. Models feature rosewood, walnut, mahogany, cypress, or sycamore back and sides. For more information contact Saga directly (see Trademark Index).

AMERICAN ACOUSTECH

Instruments currently produced in Rochester, New York.

American Acoustech is currently producing guitar models.

AMERICAN ARCHTOP

Instruments currently built in Stroudsburg, Pennsylvania beginning 1996.

Dale Unger is currently handcrafting archtop guitars designed by Robert Benedetto. Unger, a former apprentice to Benedetto for four years, grew up in the Nazareth, Pennsylvania area, and recalls building *Martin-style flattop acoustics during the 1970s!* His twenty-plus years building guitars part-time was a great background for the four years working and studying with Benedetto.

ACOUSTIC

All of Unger's archtops are available in a 16" or 17" wide body, and a depth of 2 5/8" or 3". Bodies have a single cutaway, and feature solid maple sides and matching maple neck. The 21-fret fingerboard, bridge, finger rest, and tailpiece are all made of solid ebony. Scale length is 25". Models feature black Schaller tuning machines, Natural or Blonde finishes, and are available with or without binding. Unger also offers the option of floating or built-in Benedetto pickups.

Add $50 for tone control on a suspended pickup. Add $50 for ebony tuning buttons. Add $150 for built-in humbucker pickup with volume and tone controls. Add $250 for name inlaid on tailpiece. Add $300 for Violin finish.

The **American Dream** model with laminated maple top and back is available in 6- or 7-string configurations, with the retail price of $3,450. This model is also offered with a laminated German spruce top and European flamed maple back for $3,950.

The **American Legend** features voiced top and back plates of solid German spruce (top) and flamed European maple (back). Suggested list price is $5,950. The new **American Collector Series** model lists at $8,000 (contact Unger for specifications).

Unger's top-of-the-line **The American** (suggested list price is $16,000) has special design inlays and hand-carved voiced top and back plates of hand-select finest aged woods and materials.

AMIGO

Instruments currently manufactured in Europe. Distributed by Midco International of Effingham, Illinois.

Amigo acoustic guitars are designed and priced with students and entry level players in mind.

ACOUSTIC

The Amigo line of classical guitars features two 1/2 scale guitars. The **AM 10** steel string ($79.95) and the **AM 15** nylon string ($79.95) models both feature spruce tops and maple backs and sides. The **AM 10** has a Sunburst finish; the **AM 15** features a solid spruce top.

Amigo offers two 3/4 scale guitars. The **AM 20** steel string ($109) and the **AM 30** nylon string ($109) models again both feature spruce tops and maple backs and sides. The **AM 20** has a Sunburst finish; the **AM 30** has a natural solid spruce top.

There are two full sized acoustics in the Amigo line: the **AM 40** classical ($149) has a natural-amber laminate top, and beech back and sides. The **AM 50** classical ($169) has a solid spruce top and maple back and sides. The **AM 100** Dreadnought ($169) has a spruce top and mahogany back and sides. The **AM 200S** Dreadnought ($209) has mahogany back and sides and a solid spruce top.

ANDERSEN STRINGED INSTRUMENTS

Instruments currently built in Seattle, Washington beginning 1978. Instruments are available through luthier Steven Andersen, and Pioneer Music (Portland, Oregon).

Luthier Steven Andersen built his first guitar in 1973, and has earned his living solely as a guitar maker since 1978. Andersen specializes in custom building to meet the player's needs. Working alone, Andersen builds two or three instruments at a time, generally completing sixteen to eighteen a year. Andersen guitars have been sold across the U.S., as well as in a dozen countries around the world. Although Steven Andersen doesn't actively pursue the endorsements of famous musicians, he has been fortunate in having a number of well-known players purchase his instruments (Steve Miller, Bill Frisell, and mandolinist Sam Bush).

Andersen currently features six different archtop guitar models, and one flattop acoustic model. The Concert model flattop guitar ($3,500) is offered with numerous top/sides/back tone wood options. In addition to his guitar models, Andersen also builds A-Style mandolins ($3,000), A-Style mandolas ($3,300), and mandocellos ($4,000).

ACOUSTIC ARCHTOP

Andersen archtop guitars all share certain specifications. The body depth is three inches, and the scale lengths available are either 24.9" or 25.4". The soundboard is crafted of either Engelmann or Sitka spruce. The back, sides, and neck are highly figured maple; and the pickguard, bridge, fretboard and peghead face are ebony. The instrument's tailpiece is a graphite composite with an ebony veneer. The archtops are finished in Amber Blonde or Clear Blonde. Andersen does offer several options on various models, as well as suggestions for floating pickups. The base price also includes a standard hardshell case.

While work backlog is around twenty months, a delivery date will be confirmed when an order is placed. For those who prefer to purchase a guitar without the wait, Andersen occasionally has completed guitars available for sale (call for information). Prior to 2001, left-handed ($200) and 7-string models ($600) were available.

Add $500 for Sunburst or Violin finishes. Add $500 for Adirondack Spruce top. Add $1,000 to $4,000 for Brazilian rosewood.

The **Emerald City** ($9,500) and **Metropolitan** ($9,000) are the most ornate members of the Andersen family of archtop guitars. The designs are reminiscent of the Art Deco style popular in the 1930s and 1940s. Construction details include hand engraved mother-of-pearl inlays, ivoroid binding around the body, f-holes, neck and peghead; and the most highly figured maple for the back, sides, and neck. The Emerald City is available in either a 17" or 18" body width, and the Metropolitan is only available in a 17" body width. The Metropolitan was designed in collaboration with vintage guitar enthusiasts John G. Stewart and K.C. Wait.

The **Emerald City Reserve** ($12,000) is a limited edition model built with rare woods reserved especially for this model. Wood combinations include a European spruce top and European maple back, or an Adirondack spruce top with a 90-year-old one-piece American maple back. Further model specifications will be supplied by Andersen.

The **Model 16** ($7,000), **Model 17** ($7,000), and the **Model 18** ($7,000) are elegant in their simplicity. The Model 16 has a 16" body, the Model 17 has a 17" body width, and the Model 18 has an 18" body width. By using a minimal amount of inlay and decoration, Andersen is able to build a guitar whose design and materials are first class, yet at a price somewhat less than the more ornate instruments. Body, f-holes, neck and peghead are bound in ivoroid.

The **Oval Hole Archtop** model ($6,500) is designed as an archtop with a warmer sound than a traditional model. Andersen feels that the oval soundhole allows the guitar to sustain more than an f-hole top. The overall design of this model is intended to make the guitar as lightweight and resonant as possible.

Andersen's newest model is the **Model 14** Archtop guitar ($6,200). The Model 14 is designed as an option for guitarist who travel on airplanes. Due to space consideration, and the tightening of regulations regarding "carry-on" luggage, Andersen devised an archtop guitar that is full sized where it needs to be, and reduced where the designs allows. Thus, the scale length (25.4"), neck size and shape, and bridge/soundboard design retain their usual size. The body and peghead size then are reduced: the body width is 14", and the depth is 2" (or 2.5"). Pickup choices range from Armstrong, Bartolini, or EMG. Andersen collaborated with guitarist Bill Frisell on this new electrified archtop model.

**American Archtop
American Dream Maple
courtesy Dale Unger**

ANGELICA
Instruments previously built in Japan from circa 1967 to 1975.

The Angelica trademark is a brandname used by UK importers Boosey & Hawkes on these entry level guitars and basses based on classic American designs. Some of the original designs produced for Angelica are actually better in quality, (Source: Tony Bacon and Paul Day, *The Guru's Guitar Guide*).

Angelica instruments were not distributed to the U.S. market. Some models may be encountered on the Eastern Seaboard, but the average price for these guitars ranges around $100 to $150.

ANGELO
Instruments currently produced in Thailand. Distributed by T. Angelo Industrial Co., Ltd., of Bangkok, Thailand.

Don't let the Thailand address fool you – the T. Angelo Industrial company is building credible acoustic and electric guitar models based on classic American designs. The prices are in the entry to intermediate players range, with acoustic retailing between $185 to $260, acoustic/electrics ranging from $499 to $595. The A'50 and A'60 Vintage Strat-ish models fall between $450 to $545. Hot-rodded modern designs with locking tremolo systems run a bit higher ($540 to $675).

ANGUS
Instruments currently built in Laguna Beach, California since the mid 1970s.

Luthier Mark Angus built his first guitar over two decades ago, and combines his many years as a player and craftsman to deliver an exceptionally versatile instrument. The Carl Uerheyen (L.A. studio musician) Studio Signature Model is now available.

ACOUSTIC

Angus guitars are handcrafted instruments consisting of Honduran mahogany necks, Englemann, Sitka or European spruce bodies, Indian rosewood back and sides, and an ebony fretboard. These custom guitars come in many shapes and sizes, including one model with a seven-piece back of maple and rosewood. Prices run between $2,500 and $4,500 per instrument on the average.

ANTARES

Instruments currently manufactured in Korea. Distributed in the U.S. market by Vega Musical Instruments (VMI) Industries of Brea, California.

Antares guitars are designed for entry level musicians and guitar students. Designs range from a 6-string classical model, to six-string steel string models of various finishes and even a twelve-string model. Advertised prices start at $100 and up. VMI also supplies student level 10 and 20 watt guitar amplifiers under the "Animal" trademark.

ANTONIO APARICIO GUITARS

Instruments currently produced in Valencia, Spain.

Antonio Aparicio has been a guitar maker for over 35 years and been partners in several guitar comapanies. He is now making guitars with his name on them in a new workshop. All guitars currently produced are classical models and there are three current lines, the Craftman, the Stage, and the Standard series. All models are finished with a traditional finish, and built from the best woods around the world.

APOLLONIO GUITARS

Instruments currently built in Rockport, Maine.

Luthier Nick Appollonio, a musician interested in Celtic music, estimates that he has built about 600 stringed instruments such as lutes, louds, mandolins, mandocellos, and guitars. Prices vary on the commissioned works.

APPLAUSE

Instruments currently manufactured in Korea since 1980. Distributed by the Kaman Music Corporation of Bloomfield, Connecticut. Applause guitars were originally produced in New Hartford, Connecticut from 1975 to 1979.

The Applause instruments were originally designed to be the entry level version of the Ovation guitars. In 1975, the new line of guitars was first offered to Ovation dealers as the "Ovation Medallion." A year later, models under the Applause trademark were offered to Kaman distributors. The Medallion name ran into some trademark claim problems, and was changed to Matrix. Matrix "Applauses" carried a list price of $249. In 1983, The Ovation Celebrity (also Korean, with U.S. produced synthetic backs) was introduced, again serving as an entry point to Ovation guitars.

Applause instruments feature the same guitar design and synthetic "bowl back" that the American-built Ovations possess. While engineered and manufactured with the same attention to quality, production of these models overseas is Kaman's key to offering good quality guitars for players on a budget.

Applause guitars are offered in acoustic and acoustic/electric models. The acoustic/electrics offer similar under-the-saddle piezoelectric systems with volume and tone controls as the Ovation guitars. Models encoded with an "AA" are Applause Acoustics, while an "AE" denotes an Applause Electric. The "AN" code indicates an Applause Nylon string model.

ACOUSTIC: GENERAL INFORMATION

All Applause instruments feature a solid walnut bridge, Sitka spruce top (some models may be laminated tops), Ping tuning machines, a steel reinforced truss rod, and solid mahogany neck, mother-of-pearl inlay dots.

All models are available in a Natural finish; some models may also be Black, White, Brownburst, "Barnboard" (enhanced grain), and Purpleburst. On Model designations there is a number after the model that indicates the finish (-4 is Natural).

ACOUSTIC: MINI-APPLAUSE MODELS (AA10-AA13)

AA 10 VOYAGER - travel size body, spruce top, mini-bowl, 12/19 fret fingerboard with pearl dot inlay, 3-per-side tuners, available in Natural finish, current mfg.

	MSR	$286		$175	$125	$90

AA 12 - 1/2 size single round cutaway, 3-stripe bound body/rosette, mini bowl, 20-fret bound fingerboard with pearl dot inlay, 3-per-side tuners, available in Natural finish, current mfg.

	MSR	$286		$175	$115	$80

AA 13 - similar to AA 12, except has 3/4 size body, current mfg.

	MSR	$286		$175	$115	$80

Add $35 for electronics.

ACOUSTIC: SUMMIT SERIES (AA21 & AE28)

AA 21 - Lyrachord deep bowl body, round soundhole, binding, 14/20 rosewood fingerboard with pearl dot inlay, 3-per-side tuners, available in Natural or Black finishes, mfg. 2000-current.

	MSR	$330		$225	$145	$100

AA 28 - Lyrachord single cutaway super shallow bowl body, round soundhole, binding, 14/20 rosewood fingerboard with pearl dot inlay, 3-per-side tuners, DJ-2 electronics, available in Natural, Black, Ruby Red, or Honey Burst finishes, mfg. 2000-current.

	MSR	$430		$275	$195	$125

GRADING		100%	EXCELLENT	AVERAGE

ACOUSTIC: AA & AE SERIES

AA 31 - dreadnought style, black pickguard, 5-stripe bound body/rosette, deep bowl, 14/20-fret fingerboard with pearl dot inlay, body matching peghead, 3-per-side tuners, available in Barnboard, Brownburst and Natural finishes, current mfg.

MSR	$310		$250	$145	$100

AE 32 - dreadnought style, black pickguard, 5-stripe bound body/rosette, deep bowl, 14/20-fret bound fingerboard with pearl diamond inlay, 3-per-side tuners, available in Natural finish, current mfg.

MSR	$390		$315	$175	$125

AA 33 - classic style, bound body, decal rosette, deep bowl, 12/19-fret fingerboard, wraparound walnut bridge, 3-per-side gold tuners, available in Natural finish, current mfg.

MSR	$310		$250	$145	$100

AE 34 - single round cutaway classic style, bound body, decal rosette, shallow bowl, 12/19-fret fingerboard, wraparound walnut bridge, 3-per-side gold tuners, available in Natural finish, current mfg.

MSR	$430		$350	$195	$140

AA 35 - dreadnought style, black pickguard, 5-stripe bound body/rosette, deep bowl, 14/20-fret fingerboard with pearl dot inlay, 6-per-side tuners, optional electronics, available in Black or Natural finishes, current mfg.

MSR	$390		$315	$175	$125

Add $50 for electronics.

AE 36 - dreadnought style, black pickguard, 5-stripe bound body/rosette, deep bowl, 14/20-fret bound fingerboard with pearl diamond inlay, 3-per-side tuners, available in Barnboard, Brownburst, Natural and White finishes, current mfg.

MSR	$410		$325	$165	$135

AE 38 - dreadnought style, black pickguard, 5-stripe bound body/rosette, shallow bowl, 14/20-fret bound fingerboard with pearl diamond inlay, 3-per-side tuners, available in Barnboard, Black, Brownburst, Natural, Purpleburst and White finishes, current mfg.

MSR	$450		$360	$195	$145

ACOUSTIC ELECTRIC BASS

AE 40 - single round cutaway dreadnought style, Sitka spruce top, round soundhole, 5-stripe bound body/rosette, deep bowl, mahogany neck, 19-fret walnut fingerboard with pearl dot inlay, strings through walnut bridge, logo decal on peghead, 2-per-side chrome tuners, available in Black or Natural finishes, current mfg.

MSR	$600		$400	$250	$185

AE 40F - similar to AE 40, except features a fretless neck, disc.

			$375	$225	$160

Last MSR was $515.

**Applause AE 32
courtesy Dave Rogers
Dave's Guitar Shop**

ARBITER

Instruments previously built in Japan during the mid 1960s to late 1970s.

The ARBITER trademark is the brand of a UK importer. Original models are of entry level quality, later models are good quality copy designs and some original designs, (Source: Tony Bacon and Paul Day, *The Guru's Guitar Guide*).

ARBOR

Instruments currently manufactured in Asia. Distributed in the U.S. by Midco International of Effingham, Illinois.

Arbor guitars are aimed at the entry level student to the intermediate player. The Midco International company has been importing and distributing both acoustic and solid body guitars to the U.S. market for a good number of years, and now offers a five-year warranty on their acoustic guitar line.

Model coding carries an *A* for an acoustic model. The double digits after the prefix (such as A 30) indicates a regular acoustic, and triple digits following the prefix (like A 700) for acoustic/electric models.

ACOUSTIC

Unless specified otherwise, Acoustic models feature a dreadnought body size, mahogany neck, sides and back, rosewood fingerboard with dot position markers, rosewood bridge, 3+3 headstock, and chromed tuning machines.

A 12 - spruce top, 12-string configuration, black pickguard, available in Natural finish, current mfg.

MSR	$300		$225	$135	$95

**Applause Aa 35
courtesy Applause**

GRADING		100%	EXCELLENT	AVERAGE

A 19 - spruce top, black multiple binding on top and back, available in Natural finish, mfg. 1997-current.

MSR	$230	$175	$110	$80

A 20 - spruce top, mahogany back and sides, black pickguard, available in Natural finish, current mfg.

MSR	$260	$195	$120	$85

This model is also available in a left-handed configuration (A 20L) for the same retail price.

A 29 - spruce top, mahogany back and sides, bound fingerboard, white multiple binding on top and back, center marquetry stripe on back, available in Natural finish, mfg. 1997-current.

MSR	$260	$195	$120	$85

A 30 - spruce top, mahogany back and sides, black pickguard, available in gloss Black finish, current mfg.

MSR	$270	$225	$130	$90

This model is also available in a white finish as model A 45.

A 39 C - concert size classical body, spruce top, mahogany back and sides, multiple binding on top and back, center marquetry stripe on back, chrome butterfly button tuning machines, available in Natural finish, mfg. 1997-current.

MSR	$230	$175	$110	$80

A 40 - spruce top, mahogany back and sides, black pickguard, available in Tobacco Burst finish, current mfg.

MSR	$270	$225	$130	$90

A 60 - jumbo body, spruce top, ovankol back and sides, black pickguard, available in Natural finish, current mfg.

MSR	$460	$350	$225	$150

ACOUSTIC: ARBOR BY WASHBURN SERIES

AW 1 N - concert size body, spruce top, mahogany back and sides, rosewood fingerboard and bridge, available in Natural finish, Disc.

		$225	$130	$90

Last MSR was $270.

AW 2 N - dreadnought body, select spruce top, mahogany back and sides, rosewood fingerboard and bridge, available in Natural finish, disc.

		$225	$135	$95

Last MSR was $300.

AW 3 - dreadnought body, select spruce top, mahogany back and sides, rosewood fingerboard and bridge, die cast tuning machines, available in Natural finish, disc.

		$275	$175	$125

Last MSR was $350.

AW 5 S - dreadnought body, solid spruce top, scalloped spruce bracing, mahogany back and sides, rosewood fingerboard and bridge, Grover tuning machines, available in Natural finish, disc.

		$350	$225	$150

Last MSR was $480.

AW 6 S - dreadnought body, solid spruce top, scalloped spruce bracing, ovankol back and sides, rosewood fingerboard and bridge, Grover tuning machines, available in Natural finish, disc.

		$395	$250	$175

Last MSR was $520.

ACOUSTIC ELECTRIC

All acoustic/electric models have a single rounded cutaway, chromed tuning machines, rosewood fingerboards and bridges, and piezo pickups.

A 20 E - dreadnought non-cutaway body, spruce top, mahogany back and sides, black pickguard, 1 volume/1 tone controls, available in Natural finish, current mfg.

MSR	$300	$225	$135	$100

A 600 - spruce top, nato back and sides, hardwood fingerboard with white dot position markers, hardwood bridge, piezo pickup, black pickguard, 1 volume/1 tone controls, available in Natural finish, current mfg.

MSR	$340	$250	$150	$100

Add $10 for Tobaccoburst (A 600TB) or Wine Red (A 600WR).

A 800 CS - slim dreadnought body, curly maple top, mahogany back and sides, rosewood fingerboard with white dot and diamond position markers, rosewood bridge, gold hardware, piezo pickup, 4-band EQ preamp, volume slider, available in Cherry Burst finish, current mfg.

MSR	$520	$395	$250	$175

This model is also available in a Trans. Black finish (A 800TBK).

GRADING	100%	EXCELLENT	AVERAGE

ACOUSTIC ELECTRIC: ARBOR BY WASHBURN SERIES

AW 2 CE - dreadnought body with single cutaway, select spruce top, mahogany back and sides, rosewood fingerboard and bridge, active electronic pickup system, available in Natural finish, disc.

	$325	$200	$150
		Last MSR was $430.	

This model is also available in a Gloss Black finish (Model 2 CEB).

AW 3 CE - dreadnought body with single cutaway, select spruce top, mahogany back and sides, rosewood fingerboard and bridge, die cast tuning machines, active electronic pickup system, available in Natural finish, disc.

	$375	$225	$150
		Last MSR was $500.	

ACOUSTIC ELECTRIC BASS

A 100 - spruce top, mahogany back and sides, multiple binding, piezo pickup, 2-per-side headstock, 1 volume/1 tone controls, available in Natural finish, current mfg.

MSR	$500	$375	$225	$150

ARCH KRAFT

Instruments previously built by the Kay Musical Instrument Company of Chicago, Illinois during the early 1930s.

These entry level acoustic flattop and archtop guitars were built by Kay (one of the three U.S. jobber guitar companies), and distributed through various outlets. Arch Kraft developed a tilt-neck adjustment for the Venetian Kay Kraft models around the 1920s. Arch Kraft produced guitars between the 1920s and the 1960s. Used models in excellent condition can be priced between $150-$300, (Source: Michael Wright, *Vintage Guitar Magazine*).

ARIA/ARIA PRO II

Instruments currently produced in Japan beginning 1957. Current models are produced in the U.S., Japan, Korea, China, Indonesia, and Spain. Distributed in the U.S. market by Aria USA/NHF of Pennsauken, New Jersey.

Aria is the trademark of the Arai Company of Japan, which began producing guitars in 1957. Prior to 1975, the trademark was either Aria, or Aria Diamond. Original designs in the 1960s gave way to a greater emphasis on replicas of American designs in the late 1970s. Ironically, the recognition of these well-produced replicas led to success in later years as the company returned to producing original designs. The Aria trademark has always reflected high production quality, and currently there has been more emphasis on stylish designs (such as the Fullerton guitar series, or in bass designs such as the AVB-SB).

The Aria company has produced instruments under their Aria/Aria Diamond/Aria Pro II trademark for a number of years. They have also built instruments distributed under the Univox and Cameo labels as well. Aria also offers the Ariana line of acoustic steel-string and nylon-string models.

ACOUSTIC: MISC.

1 FA 50 BS - all mahogany construction, non-cutaway design with arched top, f-holes, vintage style tuners, Brown Sunburst finish, disc.

	$410	$265	$175
		Last MSR was $549.	

ACOUSTIC: AF SERIES

1 AF 20 - grand concert folk style, spruce top, round soundhole, black pickguard, bound body, 5-stripe rosette, whitewood back/sides hardwood neck, 14/20-fret rosewood fingerboard with pearl dot inlay, rosewood bridge with black pins, 3-per-side chrome tuners, available in Natural, Brown Sunburst, or Cherry Sunburst finish, current mfg.

MSR	$170	$120	$90	$65

This model is also available as a 3/4 sized body (retail $150) and a 1/2 sized body (retail $140).

1 AF 75 (AW-75 F) - grand concert folk style, spruce top, round soundhole, black pickguard, bound body, 5-stripe rosette, mahogany back/sides/neck, 14/20-fret rosewood fingerboard with pearl dot inlay, rosewood bridge with black pins, 3-per-side nickel tuners, available in Natural finish, current mfg.

MSR	$390	$290	$190	$135

GRADING		100%	EXCELLENT	AVERAGE

1 AF 530 - grand concert folk style, solid spruce top, round soundhole, black pickguard, bound body, 5-stripe rosette, maple back/sides, mahogany neck, 14/20-fret rosewood fingerboard with pearl dot inlay, rosewood bridge with black pins, 3-per-side deluxe tuners, available in Natural finish, mfg. 1998-current.

	MSR	$600		$450	$295	$200

ACOUSTIC: AK SERIES

AK Series guitars are currently produced in Korea.

1 AK 20 - classic style, spruce top, round soundhole, bound body, wooden inlay rosette, white wood back/sides hardwood neck, 12/19-fret ebonized maple fingerboard/bridge, 3-per-side chrome tuners, available in Natural finish, current mfg.

	MSR	$130		$99	$70	$50

1 AK 20 3/4 - similar to the AK 20 excpet has 3/4 size body, current mfg.

	MSR	$100		$80	$55	$35

1 AK 20 1/2 - similar to the AK 20 excpet has 1/2 size body, current mfg.

	MSR	$90		$70	$50	$30

3 AK 30CE - classic style, spruce top, round soundhole, bound body, wooden inlay rosette, mahogany back/sides/neck, 12/19-fret rosewood fingerboard/bridge, 3-per-side chrome tuners, PZP-5 Piezo pickup w/four band EQ, available in Natural finish, current mfg.

	MSR	$250		$190	$135	$90

This model was available as a regular classic with no cutaway and no electronics in 2001.

1 AK 50 - classic style, spruce top, round soundhole, bound body, wooden inlay rosette, mahogany back/sides/neck, 12/19-fret rosewood fingerboard/bridge, 3-per-side chrome tuners, available in Natural finish, current mfg.

	MSR	$200		$150	$105	$70

AK 70 - classic style, mahogany top, round soundhole, bound body, wooden inlay rosette, mahogany back/sides/neck, 12/19-fret rosewood fingerboard/bridge, 3-per-side nickel tuners, available in Natural finish, mfg. 1991-93.

				N/A	$100	$65
					Last MSR was $200.	

1 AK 75 - classic style, spruce top, round soundhole, bound body, wooden inlay rosette, mahogany back/sides/neck, 12/19-fret rosewood fingerboard/bridge, 3-per-side nickel tuners, available in Natural finish, mfg. 1991-99.

				$285	$190	$125
					Last MSR was $379.	

AK 100 - similar to AK 75, except has different rosette and rosewood veneer on peghead. Disc. 1993.

				N/A	$120	$80
					Last MSR was $240.	

AK 200 3/4 - similar to AK 75, except is three-quarter body size. Disc. 1993.

				N/A	$120	$80
					Last MSR was $240.	

AK 200 - similar to AK 75, except has different rosette and rosewood veneer on peghead. Disc. 1993.

				N/A	$120	$80
					Last MSR was $240.	

1 AK 210 - classic style, select cedar top, round soundhole, bound body, wooden inlay rosette, mahogany back/sides/neck, 12/19-fret rosewood fingerboard/bridge, 3-per-side chrome tuners, available in Natural finish. Mfg. 1994 to date.

	MSR	$399		$300	$195	$130

AK 310 - similar to AK 210, except has gold tuners, mfg. 1994-96.

				N/A	$219	$125
					Last MSR was $439.	

1 AK 80 - classic style, spruce top, round soundhole, bound body, wooden inlay rosette, mahogany back/sides/neck, 12/19-fret rosewood fingerboard/bridge, 3-per-side chrome tuners, available in Natural finish, current mfg.

	MSR	$250		$195	$125	$80

This model was available as the 3 AK 80CE, which had a cutaway and electronics, last MSR was $480.

1 AK 320 - classic style, solid cedar top, round soundhole, multiple bound body, wooden inlay rosette, mahogany back/sides/neck, 12/19-fret rosewood fingerboard/bridge, 3-per-side chrome tuners, available in Natural finish, mfg. 1997-current.

	MSR	$549		$415	$270	$180

AK 600 - classic style, solid spruce top, round soundhole, 5-stripe bound body, wooden inlay rosette, rosewood back/sides, mahogany neck, 12/19-fret rosewood fingerboard/bridge, rosewood veneer on peghead, 3-per-side gold tuners, available in Natural finish, mfg. 1991-96.

				N/A	$190	$120
					Last MSR was $400.	

GRADING	100%	EXCELLENT	AVERAGE

AK 900 - similar to AK 600, except has solid cedar top, mfg. 1991-96.

	N/A	$225	$150

Last MSR was $559.

1 AK 920 - classic style, solid cedar top, round soundhole, bound body, wooden inlay rosette, rosewood back/sides, mahogany neck, 12/19-fret rosewood fingerboard/bridge, rosewood veneer on peghead, 3-per-side gold tuners, available in Natural finish, mfg. 1997-current.

MSR	$659	$495	$325	$215

AK 1000 - classic style, spruce top, round soundhole, bound body, wooden inlay rosette, mahogany back/sides/neck, 12/19-fret rosewood fingerboard/bridge, rosewood peghead veneer, 3-per-side nickel tuners, available in Natural finish, mfg. 1991-93.

	N/A	$350	$230

Last MSR was $700.

ACOUSTIC: AW SERIES

1 AW 20 - dreadnought style, spruce top, round soundhole, black pickguard, bound body, 5-stripe rosette, whitewood back/sides hardwood neck, 14/20-fret rosewood fingerboard with white dot inlay, rosewood bridge, 3-per-side chrome tuners, available in Natural, Brown Sunburst, Blue Shade, Red Shade, Green Shade, or Black finish, current mfg.

MSR	$170	$120	$90	$65

3 AW 20CE - similar to the 1 AW 20 except has a single cutaway, pickup and 4-band EQ electronics, current mfg.

MSR	$270	$190	$140	$95

1 AW 50 - dreadnought style, spruce top, round soundhole, black pickguard, bound body, 5-stripe rosette, mahogany back/sides/neck, 14/20-fret rosewood fingerboard with white dot inlay, rosewood bridge, 3-per-side chrome tuners, available in Natural, Brown Sunburst, Blue Shade, Red Shade, or Black finish, current mfg.

MSR	$240	$170	$125	$85

1 AW 73 N - dreadnought style, spruce top, round soundhole, black pickguard, bound body, 5-stripe rosette, mahogany back/sides/neck, 14/20-fret rosewood fingerboard with white dot inlay, rosewood bridge, 3-per-side nickel tuners, available in Natural gloss finish, mfg. 1996-99.

	$200	$100	$85

Last MSR was $299.

1 AW 73 C - similar to the 1 AW 73 N, except has single cutaway, available in Black, Blue Sunburst, Natural, or Red Sunburst, mfg. 1996-99.

	$270	$170	$135

Last MSR was $369.

AW 70 - dreadnought style, mahogany top, round soundhole, black pickguard, bound body, 5-stripe rosette, mahogany back/sides/neck, 14/20-fret rosewood fingerboard with pearl dot inlay, rosewood bridge with black pins, 3-per-side nickel tuners, available in Walnut finish, mfg. 1991-93.

	N/A	$100	$65

Last MSR was $200.

1 AW 75 - dreadnought style, spruce top, round soundhole, black pickguard, bound body, 5-stripe rosette, mahogany back/sides/neck, 14/20-fret rosewood fingerboard with pearl dot inlay, rosewood bridge with black pins, 3-per-side chrome tuners, available in Black, Black Sunburst, Blue Sunburst, Brown Sunburst, Natural, Red Sunburst, or White finishes, current mfg.

MSR	$300	$225	$150	$95

1 AW 75 L - similar to the 1 AW 75, except in left-handed configuration, available in Natural gloss finish only, mfg. 1995-current.

MSR	$400	$280	$180	$135

1 AW 75 T - similar to the 1 AW 75, except in 12-string configuration, available in Natural gloss finish only, mfg. 1995-current.

MSR	$330	$250	$165	$105

AW 100 - dreadnought style, spruce top, round soundhole, black pickguard, bound body, 3-stripe rosette, black pickguard, mahogany back/sides/neck, 14/20-fret rosewood fingerboard with pearl dot inlay, rosewood bridge with black white dot pins, 3-per-side chrome tuners, available in Natural finish, disc. 1991.

	N/A	$140	$90

Last MSR was $275.

GRADING	100%	EXCELLENT	AVERAGE

AW 100 C - similar to AW-100, except has single round cutaway, disc. 1991.

	N/A	$150	$100

Last MSR was $300.

1 AW 110 N - dreadnought style, cedar top, round soundhole, black pickguard, bound body, 3-stripe rosette, black pickguard, mahogany back/sides/neck, 14/20-fret rosewood fingerboard with pearl dot inlay, rosewood bridge with black white dot pins, 3-per-side chrome tuners, available in Natural semi-gloss finish, mfg. 1991-99.

	$280	$180	$135

Last MSR was $399.

1 AW 110 C - similar to 1 AW 110 N, except has single rounded cutaway, mfg. 1991-2002.

	$350	$230	$160

Last MSR was $469.

AW 110 CT - similar to 1 AW 110 C, except in a 12-string configuration, disc 1991.

	N/A	$175	$115

Last MSR was $350.

1 AW 110 LN - similar to 1 AW 110 N, except in left-handed configuration, mfg. 1996-99.

	$340	$220	$150

Last MSR was $449.

1 AW 110 T - similar to 1 AW 110 N, except in a 12-string configuration, mfg. 1996-99.

	$360	$240	$160

Last MSR was $479.

1 AW 130 S - dreadnought style, solid spruce top, round soundhole, mahogany back/sides/neck, 14/20-fret rosewood fingerboard with white dot inlay, rosewood bridge, 3-per-side chrome diecast tuners, available in Natural satin finish, mfg. 1997-2002.

	$275	$185	$125

Last MSR was $350.

Available in Natural gloss finish for an additional $20 (1 AW 130).

1 AW 200 - dreadnought style, spruce top, round soundhole, bound body, 3-stripe rosette, black pickguard, ovankol back/sides/neck, 14/20-fret rosewood fingerboard with pearl dot inlay, rosewood bridge with white black dot pins, 3-per-side chrome diecast tuners, available in Antique Violin, Brown Sunburst, Black, or Natural finishes, mfg. 1991-2002.

	$365	$235	$160

Last MSR was $479.

In 1993, Brown Sunburst finish was disc. In 1996, Antique Violin finish was disc.

1 AW 200 C - similar to 1 AW 200, except has single round cutaway, available in Black and Natural finishes, mfg. 1991-2002.

	$375	$240	$160

Last MSR was $499.

AW 200 F - similar to 1 AW 200, except has folk style body, disc. 1993.

	N/A	$130	$90

Last MSR was $379.

1 AW 200 L - similar to 1 AW 200, except in left-handed configuration, available in Natural gloss finish only, mfg. 1997-2002.

	$395	$265	$175

Last MSR was $529.

1 AW 200 T - similar to AW-200, except has 12-strings, 6-per-side tuners, mfg. 1991-2002.

	$435	$285	$190

Last MSR was $579.

AW 250 - dreadnought style, figured maple top, round soundhole, black pickguard, 3-stripe bound body/rosette, flamed maple back/sides, mahogany neck, 14/20-fret rosewood fingerboard with pearl dot inlay, rosewood bridge with white black dot pins, 3-per-side chrome diecast tuners, available in Black Sunburst or Vintage Sunburst finishes, mfg. 1994-96.

	N/A	$225	$150

Last MSR was $450.

1 AW 300 N - dreadnought style, spruce top, round soundhole, black pickguard, 3-stripe bound body/rosette, rosewood back/sides, mahogany neck, 14/20-fret rosewood fingerboard with pearl dot inlay, rosewood bridge with white black dot pins, 3-per-side gold tuners, available in Black Sunburst or Natural finishes, mfg. 1997-2002.

	$495	$320	$220

Last MSR was $659.

In 1998, the Black Sunburst finish was disc.

1 AW 310 N - dreadnought style, cedar top, round soundhole, herringbone bound body/rosette, tortoiseshell pickguard, ovankol back/sides, mahogany neck, 14/20-fret rosewood fingerboard with pearl dot inlay, rosewood bridge with white black dot pins, 3-per-side gold tuners, available in Natural semi-gloss finish, mfg. 1991-92, 1996-99.

	$495	$320	$220

Last MSR was $659.

In 1997, rosewood back and sides replaced original part/design.

GRADING	100%	EXCELLENT	AVERAGE

AW 310 C - similar to 1 AW 310, except has single round cutaway and ovankol back/sides, mfg. 1991-92.

	N/A	$200	$130

Last MSR was $400.

AW 310 T - similar to AW 310, except has 12-strings, mfg. 1991-96.

	N/A	$185	$115

Last MSR was $400.

AW 320 T - similar to AW 310, except has 12-strings, gold hardware, mfg. 1991-96.

	N/A	$225	$150

Last MSR was $450.

AW 410 - jumbo style, cedar top, round soundhole, herringbone bound body/rosette, black pickguard, ovankol back/sides, mahogany neck, 14/20-fret rosewood fingerboard with pearl dot inlay, rosewood bridge with white black dot pins, 3-per-side chrome diecast tuners, available in Natural finish, mfg. 1991-92.

	N/A	$180	$120

Last MSR was $360.

1 AW 420 N - dreadnought style, solid cedar top, round soundhole, black pickguard, 3-stripe bound body, mahogany back/sides, mahogany neck, 14/20-fret bound rosewood fingerboard with pearl dot inlay, rosewood bridge with black pins, 3-per-side chrome diecast tuners, available in Natural gloss finish, mfg. 1997-2002.

$500	$325	$225

Last MSR was $669.

AW 600 - dreadnought style, spruce top, round soundhole, black pickguard, 3-stripe bound body/rosette, rosewood back/sides, mahogany neck, 14/20-fret bound rosewood fingerboard with pearl dot inlay, rosewood bridge with white black dot pins, rosewood veneer on bound peghead, 3-per-side chrome diecast tuners, available in Natural finish, disc. 1996.

	N/A	$240	$120

Last MSR was $479.

In 1994, gold tuners replaced original parts/design. This model was also available with mahogany back/sides.

AW 620 - dreadnought style, solid cedar top, round soundhole, tortoise shell pickguard, 3-stripe bound body, rosewood back/sides, mahogany neck, 14/20-fret bound rosewood fingerboard with pearl dot inlay, rosewood bridge with white black dot pins, 3-per-side gold tuners, available in Natural satin finish, disc. 1994.

	N/A	$250	$125

Last MSR was $500.

1 AW 630 - dreadnought style, solid spruce top, round soundhole, tortoiseshell pickguard, 3-stripe bound body, ovankol back/sides, mahogany neck, 14/20-fret bound rosewood fingerboard with pearl dot inlay, rosewood bridge with white black dot pins, 3-per-side gold tuners, available in Black or Natural gloss finishes, mfg. 1996-2002.

$425	$290	$200

Last MSR was $550.

AW 650 - similar to AW 600, except has solid spruce top, mahogany back/sides, gold tuners, mfg. 1994-96.

	N/A	$225	$150

Last MSR was $450.

AW-700 - dreadnought style, solid spruce top, round soundhole, black pickguard, 3-stripe bound body/rosette, rosewood back/sides, mahogany neck, 14/20-fret rosewood fingerboard with pearl diamond inlay, rosewood bridge with white black dot pins, rosewood veneer peghead, 3-per-side gold diecast tuners, available in Natural finish, mfg. 1991 only.

	N/A	$195	$125

Last MSR was $390.

AW 800 - dreadnought style, solid spruce top, round soundhole, tortoise shell pickguard, herringbone bound body/rosette, rosewood back/sides, mahogany neck, 14/20-fret rosewood fingerboard with pearl diamond inlay, rosewood bridge with white black dot pins, rosewood veneer on peghead, 3-per-side gold diecast tuners, available in Natural finish, disc. 1996.

	N/A	$240	$155

Last MSR was $559.

AW 800 T - similar to AW 800, except has 12 strings, 6-per-side tuners, disc. 1996.

	N/A	$275	$180

Last MSR was $599.

1 AW 830 N - dreadnought style, solid spruce top, round soundhole, tortoise shell pickguard, herringbone bound body/rosette, rosewood back/sides, mahogany neck, 14/20-fret rosewood fingerboard with pearl diamond inlay, rosewood bridge with white black dot pins, 3-per-side gold diecast tuners, available in Natural gloss finish, mfg. 1996-2000.

| | $525 | $350 | $235 |

Last MSR was $699.

1 AW 830 T - similar to 1 AW 830, except has 12 strings, 6-per-side tuners, mfg. 1996-current.

| | $560 | $370 | $250 |

Last MSR was $749.

1 AW 920 N - dreadnought style, solid cedar top, round soundhole, tortoise shell pickguard, abalone bound body/rosette, rosewood back/sides, mahogany neck, 14/20-fret rosewood fingerboard with pearl diamond inlay, rosewood bridge with white black dot pins, 3-per-side gold tuners, available in Natural finish, mfg. 1996-99.

| | $870 | $565 | $380 |

Last MSR was $1,159.

1 AW 930 N - dreadnought style, solid spruce top, round soundhole, tortoise shell pickguard, abalone bound body/rosette, rosewood back/sides, mahogany neck, 14/20-fret rosewood fingerboard with pearl diamond inlay, rosewood bridge with white black dot pins, 3-per-side gold tuners, available in Natural finish, mfg. 1996-2000.

| | $900 | $590 | $395 |

Last MSR was $1,199.

1 AW 930 T - similar to 1 AW 930, except has 12 strings, 6-per-side tuners, mfg. 1996-2000.

| | $975 | $640 | $430 |

Last MSR was $1,299.

ACOUSTIC: LW SERIES

LJ 8 - jumbo style, cedar top, round soundhole, 3-stripe bound body/rosette, black pickguard, bubinga back/sides, mahogany neck, 14/20-fret rosewood fingerboard with pearl dot inlay, ebonized maple bridge with white black dot pins, 3-per-side chrome diecast tuners, available in Natural finish, mfg. 1994-96.

| | N/A | $265 | $175 |

Last MSR was $530.

LW 8 - similar to LJ 8, except has dreadnought style, spruce top, ovankol back/sides, available in Natural finish, mfg. 1994-96.

| | N/A | $265 | $175 |

Last MSR was $530.

LW 10 - dreadnought style, spruce top, round soundhole, 3-stripe bound body/rosette, black pickguard, mahogany back/sides/neck, 14/20-fret rosewood fingerboard with pearl dot inlay, ebonized maple bridge with white black dot pins, 3-per-side chrome diecast tuners, available in Black, Natural, Tobacco Brown, or Wine Red finishes, mfg. 1991-92.

| | N/A | $280 | $190 |

Last MSR was $560.

LW 10 T - similar to the LW 10, except in a 12-string configuration, mfg. 1991-92.

| | N/A | $295 | $195 |

Last MSR was $575.

LW-12 - dreadnought style, cedar top, round soundhole, herringbone bound body/rosette, tortoise pickguard, walnut back/sides, mahogany neck, 14/20-fret rosewood fingerboard with pearl dot inlay, ebonized maple bridge with white black dot pins, rosewood veneer on peghead, 3-per-side chrome diecast tuners, available in Black or Natural finishes, disc. 1992.

| | N/A | $270 | $180 |

Last MSR was $540.

LW 12 T - similar to the LW 12, except in a 12-string configuration, mfg. 1991-92.

| | N/A | $305 | $200 |

Last MSR was $575.

LW 14 - dreadnought style, sycamore top, round soundhole, herringbone bound body/rosette, black pickguard, walnut back/sides, mahogany neck, 14/20-fret rosewood fingerboard with pearl dot inlay, ebonized maple bridge with white black dot pins, sycamore veneer on peghead, 3-per-side chrome diecast tuners, available in Tobacco Sunburst finish, disc. 1993.

| | N/A | $285 | $190 |

Last MSR was $575.

LW 18 - dreadnought style, spruce top, round soundhole, 5-stripe bound body/rosette, rosewood back/sides, mahogany neck, 14/20-fret rosewood fingerboard with pearl dot inlay, ebonized maple bridge with white black dot pins, rosewood veneer on peghead, 3-per-side chrome diecast tuners, available in Natural finish, disc. 1993.

| | N/A | $300 | $195 |

Last MSR was $600.

LW 18 T - similar to LW-18, except has 12 strings, 6-per-side tuners, disc. 1993.

| | N/A | $320 | $210 |

Last MSR was $640.

GRADING	100%	EXCELLENT	AVERAGE

ACOUSTIC: SW SERIES

SW 8 - dreadnought style, solid cedar top, round soundhole, tortoise shell bound body/rosette/pickguard, mahogany back/sides/neck, 14/20-fret rosewood fingerboard with pearl dot inlay, ebonized maple bridge with white black dot pins, rosewood veneer on peghead, 3-per-side chrome diecast tuners, available in Natural finish, disc. 1993.

	N/A	$320	$210

Last MSR was $640.

SW 8 C - similar to SW 8, except has single round cutaway, disc. 1993.

	N/A	$360	$240

Last MSR was $715.

SW 8 CT - similar to SW 8, except has single round cutaway, 12 strings, 6-per-side tuners, disc. 1993.

	N/A	$375	$245

Last MSR was $750.

SW 8 T - similar to SW 8, except has 12 strings, 6-per-side tuners, disc. 1993.

	N/A	$335	$220

Last MSR was $670.

ACOUSTIC: CONCERT CLASSIC SERIES

Instruments are made in Spain to Shiro Arai's specs. All instruments in this series have classical style body, round sound-hole, wood inlay rosette, mahogany neck, 12/19-fret fingerboard, tied rosewood bridge, rosewood veneered slotted peghead, 3-per-side tuners with pearloid buttons, available in Natural finish.

1 AC 25 - solid cedar top, African sapelli back/sides, rosewood fingerboard, nickel hardware, mfg. 1995-current.

MSR	$450	$315	$225	$130

3 AC 25CE - similar to 1 AC 25, except has single cutaway and Fishman Matrix electronics, current mfg.

MSR	$795	$560	$400	$250

1 AC 35 - solid cedar top, African sapelli back/sides, rosewood fingerboard, gold hardware, mfg. 1995-current.

MSR	$550	$395	$275	$175

3 AC 35CE - similar to 1 AC 35, except has single cutaway and Fishman Matrix electronics, current mfg.

MSR	$995	$695	$500	$300

AC 35 A - similar to AC 35, except has alto (530mm scale) style, solid spruce top, single flat cutaway, disc. 1997.

	$350	$250	$135

Last MSR was $495.

1 AC 50 - solid cedar top, rosewood back/sides/fingerboard, gold hardware, mfg. 1995-current.

MSR	$795	$560	$400	$250

This model was also available with a spruce top (Model AC 50 S). Model AC 50 S was disc. in 1997.

3 AC 50CE - similar to 1 AC 50, except has single cutaway and Fishman Matrix electronics, current mfg.

MSR	$1,295	$900	$650	$375

AC 50 A - similar to AC 50, except has alto (530mm scale) style, single flat cutaway, disc 1997, reintroduced 2001-current.

MSR	$695	$525	$395	$225

This model had an optional solid spruce top.

AC 75 CB - contra bass (750mm scale) style, solid cedar top, African sapelli back/sides, rosewood fingerboard, gold hardware, disc. 1997, reintroduced 2001-current.

MSR	$1,250	$875	$625	$425

Last MSR was $1,095.

AC 75 B - similar to AC 75 CB, except has bass (700mm scale) style, disc. 1997.

MSR	$1,250	$875	$625	$425

Last MSR was $1,095.

1 AC 80 - solid spruce top, rosewood back/sides, ebony fingerboard, gold hardware, mfg. 1995-current

MSR	$1,250	$875	$625	$425

3 AC 80CE - similar to 1 AC 80, except has single cutaway and Fishman Matrix electronics, current mfg.

MSR	$1,750	$1,225	$875	$550

GRADING		100%	EXCELLENT	AVERAGE

AC 85 A - single flat cutaway alto (530mm scale) style, solid spruce top, rosewood back/sides, ebony fingerboard, gold hardware, disc. 1997, reintroduced 2001-current.

MSR	$1,350		$950	$675	$450

AC 90 CB - contra bass (750mm scale) style, solid spruce top, rosewood back/sides, ebony fingerboard, gold hardware, disc.

			N/A	$630	$415
				Last MSR was $1,255.	

AC 90 B - similar to AC 90 CB, except has bass (700mm scale) style, disc.

			N/A	$630	$415
				Last MSR was $1,255.	

1 AC 150 - handcrafted, traditional Spanish construction, solid spruce or solid red cedar top, solid rosewood sides and back, ebony fingerboard, rosewood bridge, gold hardware, wood purfling, new 2003.

MSR	$1,895		$1,350	$950	$600

1 AC 200 - handcrafted, traditional Spanish construction, solid spruce top, solid rosewood sides and back, ebony fingerboard, rosewood bridge, gold hardware, wood purfling, current mfg.

MSR	$2,295		$1,700	$1,250	$850

1 AC 300 - handcrafted, traditional Spanish construction, solid spruce top, solid rosewood sides and back, ebony fingerboard, rosewood bridge, gold hardware, wood purfling, mfg. 2001-current.

MSR	$3,250		$2,275	$1,750	$1,100

ACOUSTIC: FLAMENCO SERIES

3 AC 65FCE - Flamenco guitar, single cutaway, solid spruce top, sycamore back and sides, rosewood fingerboard, 75mm body depth, mfg. 2001 only.

		$675	$475	$325
			Last MSR was $875.	

1 AC 70F - Flamenco guitar, traditional Spanish construction, solid spruce top, sycamore back and sides, rosewood fingerboard, 650mm scale, mfg. 2000-current.

MSR	$750		$525	$375	$250

3 AC 70FCE - similar to the 1 AC 70F except has a single cutaway with onboard pickup and Fishman PRO electronics, mfg. 2001-current.

MSR	$1,250		$875	$625	$450

1 AC 100F - Flamenco guitar, traditional Spanish construction, solid spruce top, solid cyprus back and sides, ebony fingerboard, 650mm scale, mfg. 2000-current.

MSR	$1,095		$775	$550	$375

1 AC 150F - Flamenco guitar, traditional Spanish construction, solid spruce top, solid cyprus back and sides, ebony fingerboard, 650mm scale, mfg. 2001-current.

MSR	$1,950		$1,450	$1,050	$700

ACOUSTIC: PEPE SERIES

The Pepe Series models are made in Spain. All instruments in this series have classical style body, solid cedar top, round soundhole, wood inlay rosette, African sapelli back/sides, mahogany neck, 12/19-fret rosewood fingerboard, tied rosewood bridge, rosewood veneered slotted peghead, 3-per-side gold tuners with pearloid buttons, available in Natural finish, mfg. 1995-current.

PS 48 - 480mm scale.

MSR	$450		$315	$225	$150

PS 53 - 530mm scale.

MSR	$450		$315	$225	$150

PS 58 - 580mm scale.

MSR	$450		$315	$225	$150

ACOUSTIC: SANDPIPER SERIES

ASP-75 - folk style body, spruce top, solid mahogany back and sides, mahogany neck, 14/21 rosewood fingerboard, round soundhole, rosewood bridge, 3-per-side chrome tuners, available in Black or Natural finishes, current mfg.

MSR	$295		$210	$150	$95

ASP-130 - folk style body, solid spruce top, solid mahogany back and sides, mahogany neck, 14/21 rosewood fingerboard, round soundhole, rosewood bridge, 3-per-side chrome tuners, available in Natural finish, current mfg.

MSR	$450		$325	$235	$150

ASP-130T - similar to the ASP-130 except is in 12-string configuration, current mfg.

MSR	$495		$350	$250	$175

GRADING		100%	EXCELLENT	AVERAGE

ASP-330 - folk style body, solid Engleman spruce top, rosewood back and sides, mahogany neck, 14/21 rosewood fingerboard, round soundhole, rosewood bridge, 3-per-side chrome tuners, available in Natural finish, current mfg.

MSR	$550		$395	$275	$200

ASP-930 - folk style body, solid spruce top, solid mahogany back and sides, mahogany neck, 14/21 rosewood fingerboard, round soundhole, rosewood bridge, 3-per-side gold tuners, available in Natural finish, current mfg.

MSR	$650		$475	$325	$225

ACOUSTIC ELECTRIC: MISC. MODELS

3 AW 73 CE - dreadnought style, single cutaway, spruce top, round soundhole, black pickguard, bound body, 5-stripe rosette, mahogany back/sides/neck, 14/20-fret rosewood fingerboard with white dot inlay, rosewood bridge, 3-per-side nickel tuners, piezo pickups, volume/tone controls, available in Black or Natural finishes, mfg. 1996-99.

Aria Pro II 3 CE-42 N
courtesy Aria Pro III

	$340	$225	$150
		Last MSR was $449.	

3 AW 200 E - dreadnought style, spruce top, round soundhole, bound body, 3-stripe rosette, black pickguard, ovankol back/sides/neck, 14/20-fret rosewood fingerboard with pearl dot inlay, rosewood bridge with white black dot pins, 3-per-side chrome diecast tuners, piezo pickup, and 3-band EQ, available in Black or Natural finishes, mfg. 1991-2000.

	$435	$285	$190
		Last MSR was $579.	

3 AW 200 CE - similar to 3 AW 200 E, except has single round cutaway, piezo pickup, 3-band EQ, mfg. 1991-2000.

	$490	$320	$215
		Last MSR was $649.	

3 AW 200 CTE - similar to AW-200 CE, except has 12 strings, 6-per-side tuners, piezo pickup, 3-band EQ, available in Natural finish only, disc 2000.

	$525	$340	$230
		Last MSR was $699.	

AW 310 CE - dreadnought style, single round cutaway, cedar top, round soundhole, herringbone bound body/rosette, ovankol back/sides, mahogany neck, 14/20-fret rosewood fingerboard with pearl dot inlay, rosewood bridge with white black dot pins, 3-per-side chrome diecast tuners, piezo pickup, 3-band EQ, available in Natural finish, mfg. 1991-92.

	N/A	$235	$155
		Last MSR was $470.	

CES 50 - single round cutaway classic style, spruce top, bound body, wooden inlay rosette, mahogany body/neck, 22-fret extended rosewood fingerboard, rosewood bridge, 3-per-side gold tuners, piezo pickups, volume/tone control, available in Black, Natural, or White finishes, mfg. 1992-94.

	N/A	$300	$195
		Last MSR was $600.	

This model is a solid body with a routed out soundhole and installed plastic dish for resonance.

3 CE 40 N - deep nylon string single round cutaway classical style, spruce top, round soundhole, mahogany neck, bound body, rosewood back/sides/neck, 19-fret rosewood fingerboard/bridge, 3-per-side gold tuners, Fishman Matrix pickup with 4-band EQ, available in Natural finish, mfg. 1996-99.

	$560	$370	$250
		Last MSR was $749.	

The 3 CE 40 N has a body depth of 100 mm (3.9 inches).

3 CE 42 N - similar to the 3 CE 40 N, except has a shallow body depth, mfg. 1996-99.

	$560	$370	$250
		Last MSR was $749.	

The 3 CE 42 N has a body depth of 75 mm (2.9 inches).

3 MBA 09 - single cutaway design, molded back, spruce top, volume and tone controls, chrome hardware, PZP - 3 pickup, available in See-Through Blue, See-Through Black, or Black finishes, disc 2000.

	$240	$160	$110
		Last MSR was $319.	

GRADING	100%	EXCELLENT	AVERAGE

3 MBA 11 - single cutaway design, molded back, spruce top, mahogany neck with rosewood fingerboard, chrome plated hardware, PZP-5 pickup and 3-band EQ, available in natural, Black, See-Through Blue, and 3-Tone Sunburst finishes, disc 2000.

	$275	$180	$120
	Last MSR was $369.		

3 MBA 21 - single cutaway design, molded back, spruce top, mahogany neck with rosewood fingerboard, chrome plated hardware. Fishman OEM/MAT pickup and Fishman 4-band EQ, available in Natural, Black, See-Through Blue, or 3-Tone Sunburst finishes, disc 2000.

	$400	$260	$170
	Last MSR was $529.		

3 MBA 31 FM - single cutaway design, molded back, Flamed Maple top, mahogany neck with rosewood fingerboard, gold plated hardware, Fishman OEM/MAT pickup and Fishman 4-band EQ, available in See-Through Blue, See-Through Red, See-Through Black, and Amber Natural finishes, disc 2000.

	$435	$280	$180
	Last MSR was $579.		

CE 60 - single round cutaway classic style, spruce top, round soundhole, bound body, wooden inlay rosette, mahogany back/sides/neck, 19-fret rosewood fingerboard/bridge, rosewood veneer on peghead, 3-per-side gold tuners, piezo pickups with 3-band EQ, available in Natural finish, mfg. 1991-94.

	N/A	$350	$230
	Last MSR was $700.		

CE 60 S - similar to CE 60, except has 22-fret extended fingerboard with pearl dot inlay, steel strings with white black dot bridge pins, disc. 1994.

	N/A	$350	$230
	Last MSR was $700.		

CE 60/14 - similar to CE 60, except has 22-fret extended fingerboard, disc. 1994.

	N/A	$350	$230
	Last MSR was $700.		

FEA 10 - single round cutaway dreadnought style, cedar top, round soundhole, bound body, wooden inlay rosette, mahogany back/sides/neck, 22-fret rosewood fingerboard with pearl dot inlay, rosewood bridge with black pearl dot pins, 3-per-side diecast tuners, piezo pickup, 3-band EQ, available in Natural or Walnut finishes, mfg. 1992-95.

	N/A	$440	$275
	Last MSR was $900.		

FEA 15 - similar to FEA 10, except has spruce top, available in Brown Sunburst, Natural, or Trans. Black finishes, disc. 1993.

	N/A	$475	$315
	Last MSR was $950.		

FEA 16 N - single round cutaway dreadnought style, figured sycamore top, round soundhole, bound body, wooden inlay rosette, mahogany back/sides/neck, 22-fret rosewood fingerboard with pearl dot inlay, rosewood bridge with black pearl dot pins, 3-per-side diecast tuners, piezo pickup, 3-band EQ, available in Natural finish, mfg. 1994 only.

	N/A	$525	$345
	Last MSR was $1,050.		

FEA 20 - single round cutaway dreadnought style, sycamore top, round soundhole, bound body, abalone designed rosette, sycamore back/sides, mahogany neck, 22-fret bound rosewood fingerboard with pearl dot inlay, rosewood bridge with black pearl dot pins, 3-per-side gold diecast tuners, piezo pickup, 3-band EQ, available in See-Through Black or See-Through Blue finishes, mfg. 1991-96.

	N/A	$605	$380
	Last MSR was $1,300.		

ACOUSTIC ELECTRIC: AMB SERIES

AMB-35 - Fiber Capsule backed single cutaway body, round soundhole with elaborate design, flamed maple top, ABS fiber back and sides, mahogany neck, 14/20 fret rosewood fingerboard with diamond inlays, 3-per-side chrome tuners, rosewood bridge, PZP-3 pickup, volume and tone controls, available in Brown Sunburst, Blue Shade, Red Shade, Green Shade, Black Shade, or Natural finishes, current mfg.

MSR	$295	$210	$150	$95

AMB-50 - similar to the AMB-35 except has an active 4-band EQ-7545, current mfg.

MSR	$395	$285	$200	$125

AMB-70 - Fiber Capsule backed single cutaway body, round soundhole with elaborate design, quilted maple top, ABS fiber back and sides, mahogany neck, 14/20 fret rosewood fingerboard with pearl dot inlays, 3-per-side gold tuners, rosewood bridge, Fishman Sonicore pickup, Fishman SC Deluxe 4 band EQ, available in Brown Sunburst, Blue Shade, Red Shade, Green Shade, Black Shade, or Natural finishes, current mfg.

MSR	$495	$350	$250	$175

GRADING	100%	EXCELLENT	AVERAGE

ACOUSTIC ELECTRIC: ELECORD SERIES

Elecord series guitars feature Fishman Matrix pickups and electronics, and a single rounded cutaway.

3 FET 01 - single rounded cutaway large body, spruce top, oval soundhole, bound body, soundhole rosette, daowood back/sides, mahogany neck, 22-fret bound rosewood fingerboard with pearl snow-flake inlay, rosewood bridge with white black dot pins, bound peghead, 3-per-side gold tuners, Fishman Matrix pickup, 4-band EQ, available in Blue Shade, Black and Natural finishes, mfg. 1996-99.

$590 $390 $265

Last MSR was $789.

In 1997, Blue Shade finish was disc.

3 FET 02 - single rounded cutaway small body, spruce top, oval soundhole, bound body, soundhole rosette, daowood back/sides, mahogany neck, 22-fret bound rosewood fingerboard with pearl snow-flake inlay, rosewood bridge with white black dot pins, bound peghead, 3-per-side gold tuners, Fishman Matrix pickup, 4-band EQ, available in Blue Shade, Black, Natural, or Vintage sunburst finishes, mfg. 1996-99.

$590 $390 $265

Last MSR was $789.

In 1997, Blue Shade and Vintage sunburst finishes were disc.; See-Through Blue and Violin Sunburst finishes were introduced.

3 FET 03 - similar to the 3 FET 02, except has a silky oak top/back/sides, available in Amber, See-Through Black, or Blue Shade finishes, mfg. 1996-99.

$645 $425 $285

Last MSR was $859.

In 1997, See-Through Black and Blue Shade finishes were disc.

**Aria Pro II 3 FET 01
courtesy Aria Pro II**

FET 85 - single sharp cutaway jumbo style, arched spruce top, oval soundhole, 5-stripe bound body/rosette, chestnut back/sides, mahogany neck, 21-fret bound rosewood fingerboard with pearl diamond inlay, rosewood bridge with black pearl dot pins and pearl diamond inlay, bound peghead with chestnut veneer, 3-per-side gold diecast tuners, piezo pickup, 3-band EQ, available in Amber Natural or Antique Sunburst finishes, mfg. 1991-92.

N/A $700 $460

Last MSR was $1,400.

This model had an optional rosewood back/sides.

FET 100 - cutaway jumbo style, arched chestnut/spruce laminated top, oval soundhole, 3-stripe bound body and rosette, chestnut arched back/sides, maple neck, 21-fret bound ebony fingerboard with abalone/pearl split block inlay, rosewood bridge with white pearl dot pins and pearl diamond inlay, bound peghead, 3-per-side gold diecast tuners, piezo pickup, 3-band EQ, available in Amber Natural, Blue Shade, or Red Shade finishes, mfg. 1991-92.

N/A $750 $495

Last MSR was $1,500.

FET 500 (FET SPL) - round cutaway jumbo style, spruce top, oval soundhole, 5-stripe bound body and rosette, mahogany arched back/sides/neck, 21-fret rosewood bound fingerboard with pearl dot inlay, rosewood bridge with white pearl dot pins, bound peghead, 3-per-side diecast tuners, piezo pickup, volume/tone control, available in Antique Sunburst, Black Sunburst, or Trans. Red finishes, mfg. 1991-92, reintroduced 2003.

MSR $750 $525 $375 $250

FET 600 (FET DLX) - cutaway jumbo style, arched sycamore top, oval soundhole, 5-stripe bound body and rosette, sycamore arched back/sides, mahogany neck, 21-fret bound rosewood fingerboard with pearl diamond inlay, rosewood bridge with white pearl dot pins, bound peghead, 3-per-side diecast tuners, piezo pickup, 3-band EQ, available in Amber Natural or Antique Sunburst finishes, mfg. 1991-92, reintroduced 2003.

N/A $375 $225

Last MSR was $765.

FET 600/12 - similar to the FET 600, except in a 12 string configuration, mfg. 1991-92.

N/A $380 $250

Last MSR was $765.

3 FET-STD - Elecord small body with spruce top and mahogany back and sides, mahogany neck with rosewood fingerboard, chrome plated hardware, 22 frets, Fishman System-1 pickup, volume control and 2-band EQ, available in black, See-Through Blue, See-Through Red, or Brown Sunburst, current mfg.

MSR $495 $350 $250 $175

**Aria Pro II 3 FET 02
courtesy Aria Pro II**

GRADING		100%	EXCELLENT	AVERAGE

3 FET-STD-T - similar to the 3 FET-STD except is in twelve string configuration, current mfg.

MSR	$595	$425	$295	$185

3 FET-SPT - same as 3 FET-STD, except has a Piezo PZP-CG pickup and AEQ-5 4-band EQ, current mfg.

MSR	$260	$185	$130	$75

3 FET-DLX - Elecord small body with Flamed Maple top, mahogany back, sides, and neck, rosewood fingerboard, 22-frets, chrome plated hardware. Fishman System 1 pickup, volume control and 2-band EQ, available in See-Through Blue or See-Through Red finishes, current mfg.

MSR	$595	$425	$300	$200

3 CE-STD - classical body with spruce top and mahogany back and sides, mahogany neck with rosewood fingerboard, gold hardware, 22 frets, Fishman Matrix pickup, volume control and 4-band EQ, available in Natural finish, current mfg.

MSR	$495	$350	$250	$175

ACOUSTIC ELECTRIC: SANDPIPER SERIES

The Sandpiper Series was introduced in 1998. Models feature solid spruce tops, arched backs, fine ornamentation, and Fishman electronics.

3 SP-1 SANDPIPER (SP-CST) - folk style, single rounded cutaway body, solid spruce top, round soundhole, pearl rosette, pearl/ivory body binding, rosewood back/sides, mahogany neck, 21-fret rosewood ebony with pearl inlay, rosewood bridge with black pins, 3-per-side gold tuners, Fishman Matrix Pro pickup, volume/brilliance/3-band EQ, phase switch, available in Natural finish, mfg. 1998-99, 2001-current.

MSR	$2,500	$1,875	$1,300	$910

3 SP-2 Sandpiper - similar to the 3 SP-1, except features inset soundhole mosaic, rosewood fingerboard, PZP-6 piezo pickup, volume/mid contour/3-band EQ, PR-500 electronics, available in Natural finish, mfg. 1998-99.

		$1,500	$1,050	$735

Last MSR was $1,999.

3 SP-3 Sandpiper - similar to the 3 SP-1, except features rosewood fingerboard, Fishman pickup, volume/mid contour/3-band EQ, available in Natural finish, mfg. 1998-99.

		$1,350	$945	$660

Last MSR was $1,779.

3 SP-4 SANDPIPER - similar to the 3 SP-1, except features Pau Ferro back/sides, rosewood fingerboard, Fishman pickup, volume/mid contour/3-band EQ, available in Blue Sunburst, Natural, and Sunburst finishes. Mfg. 1998 to 1999, 2001-current.

MSR	$1,460	$1,025	$775	$525

SP STD SANDPIPER - folk style, single rounded cutaway body, solid spruce top, round soundhole, pearl rosette, pearl/ivory body binding, mahogany back/sides/neck, 21-fret rosewood fingerboard with pearl inlay, rosewood bridge with black pins, 3-per-side gold tuners, Fishman Sonicore pickup, 4-band EQ, phase switch, available in Natural finish, current mfg.

MSR	$650	$475	$325	$225

SP STD-T Sandpiper - similar to the SP STD except is in 12-string configuration, current mfg.

MSR	$750	$525	$375	$250

ACOUSTIC ELECTRIC BASS

AMB-50B - single rounded cutaway body, spruce top, round soundhole, bound body, ABS fiber back/sides, mahogany neck, 22-fret bound rosewood fingerboard with pearl dot inlay, rosewood bridge, bound peghead, 2-per-side chrome tuners, PZP-3 Piezo, AEQ-41 Active 4-band EQ, available in Black Shade, Blue Shade, Red Shade Brown Sunburst, or Natural finishes, mfg. 1996-current.

MSR	$395	$275	$200	$125

FEB-SPL - single rounded cutaway body, spruce top, oval soundhole, bound body, mahogany back/sides, maple neck, 24-fret bound rosewood fingerboard with pearl dot inlay, string through rosewood bridge, bound peghead, 2-per-side chrome tuners, Fishman Sonicore pickup, 4-band EQ, available in Black, Black Shade, or Natural finishes, mfg. 1996-2002.

		$595	$415	$275

Last MSR was $790.

4 FEB DLX - single round cutaway dreadnought style, arched flame maple top, f-holes, multi bound body, figured maple back/sides/neck, 21-fret rosewood fingerboard with pearl snowflake inlay, string-through rosewood bridge, flame maple peghead veneer with pearl flower/logo inlay, 2-per-side gold tuners, piezo bridge pickup, 4-band EQ, available in Brown Sunburst, Natural, or Violin Sunburst finishes, mfg. 1994-97 & 1999.

		$645	$450	$315

Last MSR was $859.

4 FEB STD - similar to FEB DLX, except has spruce top, mahogany back/sides, chrome tuners, mfg. 1994-96.

		$625	$425	$280

Last MSR was $900.

ACOUSTIC ELECTRIC BASS: SANDPIPER SERIES

4 SPB 04 SANDPIPER BASS 4-STRING - single rounded cutaway body, solid spruce top, round soundhole, ivory body binding, ivory rosette, rosewood back/sides, maple neck, 24-fret ebony fingerboard with pearl inlay, rosewood bridge with black pins, 2-per-side gold tuners, Fishman pickup, volume/3-band EQ, available in Natural finish, mfg. 1998-2002.

                         $1,650   **$1,150**   **$800**
                                Last MSR was $2,200.

4 SPB 05 Sandpiper Bass 5-String - similar to the 4 SPB 04, except has 5-string configuration, 3/2-per-side tuners, available in Natural finish, mfg. 1998-2000.

                         $1,875   **$1,300**   **$925**
                                Last MSR was $2,500.

4 SPB 05 FL Sandpiper Bass 5-String Fretless - similar to the 4 SPB 05 5-String, except has fretless fingerboard, available in Natural finish, mfg. 1998-2000.

                         $1,875   **$1,300**   **$925**
                                Last MSR was $2,500.

4 SPB 06 Sandpiper Bass 6-String - similar to the 4 SPB 04, except has 6-string configuration, 3-per-side tuners, available in Natural finish, mfg. 1998-2000.

                         $1,950   **$1,365**   **$955**
                                Last MSR was $2,600.

ARIANA

Instruments currently built in Asia. Distributed in the U.S. market by Aria USA/NHF of Pennsauken, New Jersey.

Ariana is one of the trademarks of the Aria Company of Japan, which began producing guitars in 1957. Aria offers the Ariana line of acoustic steel-string and nylon-string models for beginner to intermediate guitar students as a quality instrument at affordable prices.

ARIRANG

Instruments previously built in Korea during the early 1980s.

This trademark consists of entry level copies of American designs, and some original designs, (Source: Tony Bacon and Paul Day, *The Guru's Guitar Guide*).

ARISTONE

See Framus & Besson. Instruments previously built in West Germany during the late 1950s through the early 1960s.

While Aristone was the brandname for a UK importer, these guitars were made by and identical to certain Framus models. Research also indicates that the trademark Besson was utilized as well, (Source: Tony Bacon and Paul Day, *The Guru's Guitar Guide*).

ARITA

Instruments previously manufactured in Japan.

Arita instruments were distributed in the U.S. market by the Newark Musical Merchandise Company of Newark, New Jersey, (Source: Michael Wright, *Guitar Stories,* Volume One).

ARMY & NAVY SPECIAL

See chapter on House Brands.

This trademark has been identified as a Gibson built budget line available only at military post exchanges (PXs) towards the end of World War I (1918). They will have a label different from the standard Gibson label of the time, yet still be credited to the Gibson Mandolin – Guitar Co. of Kalamazoo, Mich., USA. As a Gibson-built budget line instrument, these guitars do not possess an adjustable truss rod in the neck, (Source: Walter Carter, *Gibson: 100 Years of an American Icon*).

ART & LUTHERIE

Instruments currently produced in La Patrie, Canada. Distributed by La Si Do, Inc. of St. Laurent (Quebec), Canada.

Art & Lutherie models are an affordable line of acoustic guitars by La Si Do that complements their higher end models from Godin and Simon & Patrick. Lead by Guitare Luthier Daniel Gervais, Art & Lutherie produces guitars built with Canadian tonewoods such as wild cherry, maple, and walnut (gives those trees from the Rain Forest a little breathing room!)

In 2000 Art & Lutherie underwent a model number change where all models were changed to a five number designation from a four number. All efforts have been made to update these changes.

GRADING | | **100%** | **EXCELLENT** | **AVERAGE**

ART & LUTHERIE COLORED MODELS

ART & LUTHERIE NO. 14620 (8568) - 3 ply wild cherry laminated top, wild cherry back/sides, round soundhole, big leaf maple neck, walnut fingerboard with a white dot inlay, solid headstock, 3-per-side chrome tuners, black pickguard, and walnut bridge with white bridgepins, available in Almond Brown (**Model 8568**), Antique Burst (**Model 14644, 8582**), Sunrise (**Model 15931**), Black (**Model 14668, 8605**), Chestnut Brown (**Model 14682, 8629**), Trans. Blue (**Model 14729, 9190**), or Trans. Red (**Model 14705, 9176**) satin lacquer finish, current mfg.

| MSR | $219 | | $160 | $100 | $75 |

Add $75 for EPM EQ electronic pickup (available in all models with different number designations).

ART & LUTHERIE CUTAWAY - similar to the Art & Lutherie model, except features a single sloped shoulder cutaway body, available in Almond Brown CW (**Model 14743, 9213**), Antique Burst CW (**Model 14767, 9237**), Black CW (**Model 14781, 9251**), Chestnut Brown CW (**Model 14804, 9275**), Trans. Blue CW (**Model 14842, 9312**), or Trans. Red CW (**Model 14828, 9299**) satin lacquer finish, current mfg.

| MSR | $279 | | $200 | $150 | $100 |

Add $75 for EPM EQ electronic pickup (available in all models with different number designations).

ART & LUTHERIE CEDAR TOP NO. 14866 (0180) - similar to the Art & Lutherie model, except features a solid cedar top, available in Natural semi-gloss lacquer finish, current mfg.

| MSR | $299 | | $225 | $175 | $125 |

Add $75 for EPM EQ electronic pickup.

ART & LUTHERIE SPRUCE TOP NO. 13043 - similar to the Art & Lutherie model, except features a solid spruce top, available in Natural semi-gloss lacquer finish, mfg. 2000-current.

| MSR | $329 | | $250 | $195 | $140 |

Add $75 for EPM EQ electronic pickup (Model 13050).

ART & LUTHERIE AMI MODELS

Drawing inspiration from those turn-of-the-century parlor guitars, Art & Lutherie also offers the **Ami** model. This model has full scale fingerboard yet scaled down body size designed with children in mind.

AMI NYLON STRING No. 14583 (8704) - 3 ply laminated wild cherry top, wild cherry back/sides, round soundhole, maple neck, walnut fingerboard, classical style tied walnut bridge, slotted headstock, 3-per-side tuners, available in Almond Brown lacquer finish, mfg. 1998-current.

| MSR | $199 | | $150 | $100 | $65 |

Add $75 for EPM EQ electronic pickup (Model 14590, previously 11230).

Ami Nylon String Cedar Top No. 14606 (11155) - similar to the Ami Nylon String model, except features a solid cedar top, available in Natural lacquer finish, mfg. 1998-current.

| MSR | $209 | | $160 | $110 | $70 |

Add $75 for EPM EQ electronic pickup (Model 14613, previously 11162).

AMI STEEL STRING - similar to the Ami Nylon String, except features a solid headstock, walnut bridge with white bridgepins, chrome tuners, available in Almond Brown (**Model 14460, 8643**), Antique Burst (**Model 14507, 8667**), Black (**Model 14569, 9404**), Chestnut Brown (**Model 14484, 8681**), Trans. Blue (**Model 14545, 9152**), or Trans. Red (**Model 14521, 9138**) lacquer finishes, mfg. 1998-current.

| MSR | $199 | | $150 | $100 | $65 |

Add $75 for EPM EQ electronic pickup (available in all models with different number designations).

ARTESANO

Current trademark distributed by Juan Orozco Corporation of Maunabo, Puerto Rico.

Artesano acoustics are currently available in the U.S. market. For further information regarding models and pricing, please contact the Juan Orozco Corporation directly (see Trademark Index).

ARTISAN

Instruments previously produced in Japan.

Artisan instruments were distributed in the U.S. market by the Barth-Feinberg company of New York, (Source: Michael Wright, *Guitar Stories*, Volume One).

ARTISAN (CURRENT MFG.)

Instruments currently manufactured by Eikosha Musical Instrument Co., Inc. of Nagoya, Japan. Distributed in the U.S. by V.J. Rendano of Boardman, OH.

Artisan acoustic instruments include archtops, flattops, classical, a mini-series, and acoustic electric models. Please contact the distributor directly for more current model lineup and availability.

ARTISTA

Instruments currently built in Spain. Distributed by Musicorp, a division of MBT of Charleston, South Carolina.

These reasonably priced handmade guitars are designed for the beginning classical guitar student. The Artista line features three models: the Granada ($275) has an Oregon Pine top, sapelle (mahogany) body, and a jacaranda fingerboard; the Morena ($350) has the same Oregon Pine top combined with a Mongoy (Brazilian jacaranda) body, and mahogany neck; and the Segovia ($525) features a solid cedar top, rosewood back and sides, and a rosewood fingerboard.

ASAMA

Instruments previously built in Japan during the early 1980s.

Guitars with this trademark are generally medium to good quality copies of American design as well as some original designs, (Source: Tony Bacon and Paul Day, *The Guru's Guitar Guide*).

ASHLAND

Instruments currently manufactured in Asia. Distributed by VMI Industries of Brea, California.

Ashland instruments are manufactured for the entry level or beginning guitarist. Ashland offers three dreadnought style guitars with a spruce top and mahogany back and sides. Prices start at $249 (AD 26), to $269 (AD 36), up to $299 (AD 39). A fourth model, the AE 16 ($279) is an acoustic/electric that features a fingerboard-mounted pickup with adjustable pole pieces.

ASPEN

Instruments previously produced in Korea between 1987 to 1991. Distributed by International Music Corporation (IMC) of Fort Worth, Texas.

Aspen was a trademark used by the International Music Corporation on a number of imported acoustic guitars and banjos. The A series featured laminated tops/bodies, and had a retail price range between $200 up to $570. Aspen's high end Aspen Luthier (or AL) series had solid wood tops, and a retail new price range between $790 to $1,500.

Aspen A-Series guitars carry a used price around $100, depending on condition; the AL-Series rates a bit higher around $300 to $400.

ASPRI CREATIVE ACOUSTICS

Current trademark distributed by Aspri Creative Acoustics of Montreal, Canada.

Further information is still being researched for future editions of the *Blue Book of Acoustic Guitars*.

ASTURIAS

Instruments currently built on the island of Kyushu, Japan. Distribution in the U.S. market by J.T.G. of Nashville, located in Nashville, Tennessee.

The Asturias Workshops in southern Japan employ seventeen people who have worked at Asturias most of their lives or have a family connection. Guided by chief luthier Wataru Tsuji, these luthiers take great care with their production methods to ensure a quality guitar.

ATHELETE

Instruments previously built in New York, New York.

Luthier Fumi Nozawa created high quality 4, 5, or 6-string acoustic basses, as well as acoustic guitars for several years.

ATLAS

See chapter on House Brands.

This trademark has been identified as a House Brand of the RCA Victor Records Stores, (Source: Willie G. Moseley, *Stellas & Stratocasters*).

AUDITION

See chapter on House Brands.

This trademark has been identified by researcher Willie G. Moseley as a House Brand of the F.W. Woolworth (Woolco) department stores.

Further information from authors Tony Bacon and Paul Day indicate that guitars with this trademark originated in Japan (later Korea) during the 1960s and 1970s, (Source: Tony Bacon and Paul Day, *The Guru's Guitar Guide*).

AUSTIN

Instruments currently built in Korea and China. Distributed by St. Louis Music of St. Louis, Missouri.

Asian-produced Austin instruments are good quality entry or student level acoustic and electric guitars.

ACOUSTIC

The **AU 339 N 39 Guitar** (list $120) is a classical model with a spruce top, agathis back and sides, Nato/mahogany neck, and hardwood fingerboard; the full sized **AU 560 Concert Classic** (list $209) has a laminated spruce top, mahogany back/sides/neck, rosewood bridge and fingerboard, and inlaid marquetry soundhole rosette.

The student series are entry level guitars that include the **AU132** and **AU134** models which are of folk and classical designs. These models start at $54.95 retail. The step up line from these are the Intermediate models that are the **AU33X** models. There are a few more variations of these that include the **AU 341 S Dreadnought** (list $150), which has a spruce top, mahogany back and sides, and rosewood fingerboard. Prices on these retail from $90-$150.

The Deluxe series includes the Ozark models, the **AU502** (Concert Folk, list $209), and the **AU560** (Concert Classic, list $209). The **AU 506 Ozark** features a rosewood bridge, chrome tuners, and a gloss finish (list $229). The **AU 506** is an option in a Gloss Black finish for $239. The 12-string **AU 518 Osage** dreadnought has a laminated spruce top, mahogany back and sides, hardwood bridge and fingerboard, chrome tuners, 5-ply body binding, and a pearl inlaid logo (disc. $289).

For folk style guitars, Austin offers two models. The **AU 339 S** model (list $120) has a spruce top, agathis back and sides, and a Nato/mahogany neck with hardwood fingerboard. The **AU 502 Meramac Folk** (list $209) has a spruce top and mahogany back and sides, along with a maple neck and rosewood fingerboard and bridge.

ACOUSTIC ELECTRIC

The **AU 520 Table Rock** (list $329) has a cutaway dreadnought body with laminated spruce top, mahogany back/sides/neck, diecast tuners, pearl inlaid logo, bridge pickup with volume and 3-band EQ controls, and a Natural Gloss finish. The AU 520 is an option in a Gloss Black finish for $339.

The Branson series was introduced recently. These feature "000" sized bodies, spruce tops, mahogany back/sides/neck, and a bridge pickup with volume control and four band EQ. These models are designated the **AU510** and are available in natural, Blue Burst, Purple Burst, Tobacco Sunburst, and Wine Red. These guitars retail for $329 for all colors.

AVALON

Instruments currently produced in North Ireland. Distributed in the U.S.A. by the Lowden Guitar Co. in Fort Worth, Texas.

The Avalon company was launched in 2002 as a new brand of acoustic guitars by the Lowden Guitar Company. This guitar line was established to make guitars that are of the Lowden quality but keep the price range lower. Lowden guitars typically sell in the $3,000-$5,000 range. The Avalon guitars start at a retail price of under $2,000, with none going over $2,600. The Avalon line of guitars were available in stores as of April 2002. There are dreadnought, auditorium, and concert models available.

AVON

Instruments previously built in Japan during the early to late 1970s.

The Avon trademark is the brand name of a UK importer. Avons are generally low to medium quality copies of American designs, (Source: Tony Bacon and Paul Day, *The Guru's Guitar Guide*).

AXELSON

Instruments currently built in Duluth, Minnesota.

Luthier Randy Axelson has been providing top-notch guitar repair, restoration, and custom guitar building on a regular basis. For information, pricing, and availability contact luthier Axelson directly (see Trademark Index).

AXEMAN

Instruments previously built in Japan during the late 1970s.

The Axeman trademark is the brand name of a UK importer. The guitars are generally medium quality copies of American designs, (Source: Tony Bacon and Paul Day, *The Guru's Guitar Guide*).

AXL

Instruments currently built overseas, and distributed by The Music Link.

The Axl trademark was introduced in 2001 as a line of electric and acoustic guitars as well as a line of amplifiers. These instruments are produced with modern equipment and the best available material to create a quality line of guitars at affordable prices. For more information on Axl refer to The Music Link's web site.

ACOUSTIC

Currently, Axl offers the Songwriter and Studio series acoustic guitars. All of these guitars are dreadnoughts in style. The Songwriter Series is offered as the AG-700, which has a Canadian sitka spruce top and mahogany back and sides. This retails for $199. The AG-710 is the same as the AG-700 except has Indian rosewood back and sides and retails for $239. The Studio series is the same as the Songwriter series except features a solid Sitka spruce top. The AG-705 has mahogany back and sides like the AG-700 and retails for $229. The AG-715 has Indian rosewood back and sides and lists for $279. Essentially, there are four models that are the same with wood differences separating them.

AXTECH

Instruments currently built in Korea.

Axtech instruments are generally entry level to medium quality solid body and acoustic guitars based on Classic American designs.

AYERS

Instruments currently produced in Taiwan.

Ayers currently produces a wide variety of acoustic guitars from folk guitars to dreadnoughts. For more information refer to their web site (see Trademark Index).

Section B

B & J

See chapter on House Brands.

This was a New York City distributor during the 1920s. B&J stands for Buegeleisen and Jacobson. Other companies built guitars for them including Martin. Also distributed guitars under the name S.S. Stewart after 1915, (Source: Willie G. Moseley, *Stellas & Stratocasters*).

B.C. RICH

Instruments currently built in Hesperia, California (American Handmade series) and Asia (NJ, Platinum and Bronze series). Distributed by B.C. Rich Guitars International, Inc. of San Bernadino, California and B.C. Rich Guitars USA.

Import models (NJ, Platinum, and Bronze Series) distributed by Davitt & Hanser Music of Cincinnati, Ohio.

Luthier Bernardo Chavez Rico used to build classical and flamenco guitars at Bernardo's Valencian Guitar Shop, the family's business in Los Angeles. During the mid 1960s folk music boom (and boom in guitar sales), a distributor suggested a name change – and B.C. Rich guitars was born. Between 1966 and 1968, Rico continued to build acoustic guitars, then changed to solid body electrics. The company began producing custom guitars based on Fender and Gibson designs, but Rico wanted to produce designs that represented his tastes and ideals. The Seagull solid body (first produced in 1971) was sleek, curvy, and made for rock 'n roll. Possessing a fast neck, hot-rodded circuitry and pickups, and a unique body profile was (and still is) an eye-catching design.

In 1974, Neal Mosher joined the company. Mosher also had a hand in some of the guitars designed, and further explored other designs with models like the Mockingbird, Eagle, Ironbird, and the provocatively-named Bich. The first 6-tuners-on-a-side headstocks began to appear in 1981. In the mid 1980s, B.C. Rich moved from Los Angeles to El Monte, California.

The company began to import models in the U.S. Production Series, Korean-produced kits that were assembled in the U.S. between 1984 to 1986. In 1984, the Japanese-built N.J. Series line of B.C. Rich designs were introduced, and were built by the Terada company for two years. Production of the N.J. series was moved to Korea in 1986 (models were built in the Cort factory).

In 1988, Rico licensed the Korean-built lower priced Platinum and entry level Rave Series to the Class Axe company, and later licensed the B.C. Rich name and designs in 1989. Class Axe moved production of the U.S.-built guitars to a facility in Warren, New Jersey, and stepped up importation of the N.J. (named after Nagoya, Japan – not New Jersey), Platinum, and Rave Series models.

Unfortunately, the lower priced series soon began to show a marked drop in quality. In 1994, Rico came back out of semi-retirement, retook control over his trademark, and began to rebuild the company. Rico became partners with Bill Shapiro, and the two divided up areas of responsibility. Rico once more began building acoustic and high end electrics at his Hesperia facilities; and Shapiro began maintaining quality control over the imported N.J., Platinum, and U.S. series in San Bernadino. In 1998, Davitt & Hanser Music of Cincinnati, Ohio began distributing the import models (NJ, Platinum, and Bronze Series). Additional model commentary courtesy Bernie Rich, President/Founder of B.C. Rich International, May 1997.

GRADING	100%	EXCELLENT	AVERAGE

ACOUSTIC: SIGNATURE SERIES

The Signature Series acoustics are handcrafted in the U.S.

Add $100 for 6-on-a-side headstock (acoustic models). Add $150 for an installed Fishman Matrix 4-band EQ.

B20-D - dreadnought style, solid spruce top, round soundhole, white body binding, solid mahogany back/sides, mahogany neck, 21-fret rosewood fingerboard with white dot inlay, rosewood bridge, white pearl dot bridge pins, 3-per-side chrome tuners, available in Stained High Gloss finish, disc.

$910	$600	$420

Last MSR was $1,299.

This model is also available with a solid Black finish with white body binding or solid White finish with black body binding.

B20-C Cutaway - similar to B20-D, except has single rounded cutaway, available in Natural High Gloss finish, disc.

$980	$645	$445

Last MSR was $1,399.

This model is also available with a solid Black finish with white body binding or solid White finish with black body binding.

B

GRADING	100%	EXCELLENT	AVERAGE

B20-C DS Cutaway - similar to the B20-D, except has a solid red cedar top, single rounded cutaway, diamond shaped soundhole with abalone and rosewood inlays, disc.

	$1,050	$690	$480

Last MSR was $1,499.

This model is also available with a solid black finish with white body binding or solid white finish with black body binding.

B30-D - dreadnought sized flattop body, select spruce top, round soundhole, rosewood bound body, abalone rosette, solid quilted maple back/sides, mahogany neck, 21-fret rosewood fingerboard with abalone diamond inlay, rosewood bridge, white pearl dot bridge pins, 3-per-side chrome tuners, available in Natural, Trans. Blue, Trans. Emerald Green, Trans. Pagan Gold, or Trans. Red finishes, disc.

	$1,050	$690	$480

Last MSR was $1,499.

B30-C - similar to B30-D, except has a single rounded cutaway, disc.

	$1,050	$690	$480

Last MSR was $1,499.

B35-D - dreadnought style, select spruce top, round soundhole, white body binding, solid rosewood back/sides, mahogany neck, 14/21-fret bound ebony fingerboard with abalone cloud inlay, ebony bridge with pearl cloud inlay, white pearl dot bridge pins, peghead with abalone logo inlay, 3-per-side chrome tuners, available in Natural finish, mfg. 1995-disc.

	$1,190	$785	$545

Last MSR was $1,699.

B35-C - similar to B35-D, except has a single rounded cutaway, disc.

	$1,190	$785	$545

Last MSR was $1,699.

B41-C DIAMOND - single round cutaway flat top body, select spruce top, diamond shaped soundhole, abalone purfling/rosette, rosewood back/sides, mahogany neck, 21-fret bound ebony fingerboard with abalone cloud inlay, ebony bridge with pearl cloud inlay, white pearl dot bridge pins, bound rosewood veneered peghead with abalone logo inlay, 3-per-side Grover Imperial gold tuners, available in Natural finish, mfg. 1995-disc.

	$2,025	$1,325	$890

Last MSR was $2,699.

B41-D - similar to B41-C, except has non cutaway dreadnought style body, 14/21-fret rosewood fingerboard, available in Natural finish, mfg. 1995-96.

	N/A	$1,325	$800

Last MSR was $2,495.

ACOUSTIC: ELITE SERIES

Elite Series acoustic guitars are imported to the U.S. market.

BR40D - dreadnought style, solid spruce top, round soundhole, mahogany back/sides, mahogany neck, 21-fret rosewood fingerboard with white dot inlay, rosewood bridge, white pearl dot bridge pins, 3-per-side chrome tuners, available in Natural or Sunburst high gloss finishes, disc.

	$335	$225	$155

Last MSR was $479.

BR60D - dreadnought style, solid cedar top, round soundhole, mahogany back/sides, abalone body binding, mahogany neck, 21-fret rosewood fingerboard with pearl eagle inlay, rosewood bridge, white pearl dot bridge pins, 3-per-side gold plated die cast tuners, available in Natural satin finish, disc.

	$480	$320	$220

Last MSR was $689.

Add $200 for factory installed Fishman Matrix 4-band EQ system/bridge transducer.

BR65DE - dreadnought style, solid spruce top, round soundhole, mahogany back/sides, white body binding, mahogany neck, 21-fret bound rosewood fingerboard with white dot inlay, rosewood bridge, white pearl dot bridge pins, 3-per-side chrome tuners, Fishman Matrix EQ system, available in Gloss Black finish, disc.

	$630	$415	$290

Last MSR was $899.

BR65DCE - similar to the BR65DE, except has single rounded cutaway, current mfg.

	$630	$415	$290

Last MSR was $899.

BR70D - dreadnought style, solid spruce top, round soundhole, rosewood back/sides, abalone/white body binding, abalone rosette, mahogany neck, 21-fret bound rosewood fingerboard with cats eye position markers, rosewood bridge, white pearl dot bridge pins, bound headstock, 3-per-side tuners, available in Natural Gloss finish, current mfg.

	$455	$300	$210

Last MSR was $649.

Add $200 for factory installed Fishman Matrix 4-band EQ system/bridge transducer.

BD DEY

Instruments previously built in the Czech Republic. Distributed by BD Dey Musical Instruments of the Czech Republic.

The Czech Republic is the popular place for companies looking for an alternative to Asian guitar production. Various areas in the Czech Republic have a reputation for excellent instrument craftsmanship, evolving from the earlier days of violin and viola production. B D Dey offered 5 different electric guitar models, and a 6 - and 12-string jumbo acoustic guitar model.

ACOUSTIC

The **Rieger-Kloss** jumbo guitar model featured a solid spruce top, mahogany veneer back and sides, maple neck, 14/20-fret ebony fingerboard with pearl dot inlays, ebony bridge, 3 (or 6, depending on the configuration) per side chrome tuners, plastic pickguard. The acoustics were available in Natural and Sunburst finishes; both configurations also available with a piezo pickup and on board equalizer.

BACON & DAY

See Vega.

BACORN CUSTOM GUITARS

Instruments currently built in Nichols, NY.

Roger Bacorn manufacturers both acoustic and electric custom instruments, built per individual work order. Almost any configuration/type is possible. He specializes in instruments using older vintage aesthetics, with modern construction innovations such as X-bracing, and spring fitted braces on both archtops and mandolins. Each instrument has a hand rubbed lacquer finish.

BALDWIN

Instruments previously produced in England by Burns; later models were shipped by components and assembled in Booneville, Arkansas. Baldwin guitars and basses were produced between 1965 to 1970. Distribution of instruments was handled by the Baldwin Piano Company of Cinncinati, Ohio.

In 1962, as Leo Fender's health was faltering, he discussed the idea of selling the Fender Electric Instruments company to Don Randall (head of Fender Sales). While Randall toyed with the idea even as late as the summer of 1963, they eventually concluded to sell to a third party who had money. Negotiations began with the Baldwin Piano Company in April of 1964, who offered $5 million (minus Fender's liabilities). When talks bogged down over acoustic guitar and electric piano operations, Randall met with representatives of the Columbia Broadcasting System (CBS). An agreement with CBS was signed in October, 1964, for $13 million that took effect in January of 1965.

Baldwin, outbid by CBS but still looking to diversify its product lines, then bought the Burns manufacturing facilities from Jim Burns (regarded as "the British Leo Fender") in September, 1965. U.S. distributed models bore the Baldwin trademark. During Baldwin's first year of ownership, only the logos were changed on the imported guitars. In 1966, the Burns-style scroll headstock was redesigned; and in 1967 the *700* series was debuted. The Baldwin company then began assembling the imported Burns parts in Booneville, Arkansas.

Baldwin acquired the Gretsch trademark when Fred Gretsch, Jr. sold the company in 1967. As part of a business consolidation, the New York Gretsch operation was moved to the Arkansas facility in 1970. Baldwin then concentrated their corporate interests in the Gretsch product line, discontinuing further Baldwin/Burns models. However, it is interesting to note that many Burns-style features (like the bridge vibrato) began to turn up on Gretsch models after 1967. For further Baldwin/Gretsch history, see Gretsch, (Source: Paul Day, *The Burns Book*; and Michael Wright, *Vintage Guitar Magazine*).

**Baldwin Virginio
courtesy Dave Rogers
Dave's Guitar Shop**

BARBERO

Instruments previously built in Spain.

This brand name belonged to Marcelo Barbero (1904-1955), considered one of the great flamenco guitar makers, (Source: Tony Bacon, *The Ultimate Guitar Book*).

BARNEY, CARL

Instruments currently built in Southbury, Connecticut beginning 1968.

Luthier Carl Barney started building classical guitars in 1968, and built his first archtop guitar in 1972. Two years later, Barney built a guitar for jazz legend Sal Salvador – and began a long friendship and collaboration with Salvador (Barney later created the Sal Salvador Artist model for Salvador in 1980).

All guitars are handcrafted by Barney in his workshop. Since the mid 1970s, Barney has been searching and stockpiling fine instrument woods. In 1976, Barney purchased a good-sized quantity of Gabon ebony, as well as Brazilian and Indian rosewood. Barney currently uses figured woods for all models, and has a supply of figured maple for special commissions. Barney began using Adirondack (American Red) spruce for guitar tops since 1993, which is whiter in appearance than Sitka spruce that is also available.

Since mid 1996, Barney has built over eighty archtop guitars. Although archtops have been Barney's focus since 1974, he has also built over 100 classical, flat-top acoustics, and solid body electrics since the mid 1970s. Prices quoted are for base models; for further information please contact luthier Barney directly (see Trademark Index).

B

ACOUSTIC

Add $100 for 18" body width.

Barney offers three versions of his **Jazzmaker Series** archtop guitars. The **Jazzmaker I** features a hand carved top and back, figured maple back and sides, 4-line top binding, 1-line back/fingerboard/headstock binding, small fingerboard markers, unbound f-holes, ebony tailpiece and pickguard, and is available in 16" and 17" body widths. The retail price in a Sunburst finish is $3,700; Natural finish is $3,900.

The **Jazzmaker II** is the standard custom model. This model has a hand carved top and back, highly figured maple back and sides, 7-line top binding, 4-line back/fingerboard/headstock binding, block fingerboard markers, bound f-holes, inlaid and engraved headstock, ebony bridge and tailpiece and pickguard, and is available in 16" and 17" body widths. The retail price in a Sunburst finish is $4,300; Natural finish is $4,500.

The **Jazzmaker Deluxe** is similar to the Jazzmaker II, except has exceptionally figured maple back and sides; 7-line binding on top, back, and headstock; split block fingerboard inlay; 4-line binding on fingerboard and f-holes; inlaid ebony heel cap, inlaid ebony veneer on the back of headstock. The retail price in a Sunburst finish is $4,700; Natural finish is $4,900.

The **OV Jazz Model** is an oval soundhole guitar similar to the 1960s Howard Robert Epiphone model. Retail prices start at $2,600 for the basic model, and increase up to $3,400 to the deluxe version based on the amount of detail and inlay work.

The current **Sal Salvador Artist** model is based on the third model Barney built for Salvador, and is the second Artist model design (the first design was created in 1981). The model has an Adirondack spruce top, flamed maple back and sides, abalone/pearl split block fingerboard inlay/headstock/heel cap. The ebony tailpiece and pickguard also have decorative inlays. This model is available with a built-in pickup, or with a floating pickup. The body width is 16", and the body depth 2 3/4" depth. The Salvadore Artist model is available with a Natural top/tinted back and sides, Natural, and 4 color Sunburst finishes. Retail list price is $5,000, and includes a hard shell case.

In addition to the archtop models, Barney also offers flattop top steel strings models (list $2,000), classicals ($2,300), and even solid body electric designs ($1,500).

BARON (U.S. MFG.)
See chapter on House Brands.

This trademark has been identified as a House Brand of the RCA Victor Records Store; furthermore, KAY exported guitars bearing this trademark to the Thibouville-Lamy company of France, (Source: Willie G. Moseley, *Stellas & Stratocasters*).

BARRINGTON
Instruments previously produced in Japan during the late 1980s. Distribution in the U.S. market was handled by Barrington Guitars of Barrington, Illinois.

Barrington Guitars offered both solid body electric guitars and basses during the late 1980s, as well as acoustic and acoustic/electric models. The guitar models were produced in Japan by Terada. The company now specializes in brass instruments as the L.A. Sax Company of Barrington, Illinois.

Barrington offered both acoustic and acoustic/electric Barrington Gruhn signature series models as well. The acoustics were similar to a design prototype produced in collaboration between George Gruhn and Collings guitars in 1988; and the Barrington models carried a new retail list price between $1,225 and $1,325 (a Fishman transducer pickup was optional equipment on the four models). The **AT-1** and **AT-2** f-hole archtops listed new at $1,650.

BARTOLINI, BILL
Instruments previously built in 1960s. Bartolini now produces a line of high quality guitar pickups in Livermore, California.

Luthier Bill Bartolini used to build classical guitars in California during the 1960s. Bartolini estimates that perhaps only a dozen guitars were built. Research on resonances produced during this time formed the basis for his pickup designs, and his clear, high quality pickups are standard features on numerous luthiers' creations, (Information courtesy Bill Bartolini).

BAUER
See S.S. Stewart.

George Bauer, a noted guitar builder in Philadelphia during the late 1800s, entered into a partnership with banjo producer S.S. Stewart. The two produced guitars under the Stewart & Bauer trademark. After Stewart passed away, Bauer continued to release instruments under the Stewart & Bauer label, and also under the Monogram trademark, (Source: Tom Wheeler, American Guitars).

BAY STATE
Instruments previously manufactured in Boston, Massachusetts from 1865 to circa early 1900s.

The Oliver Ditson Company, Inc. was formed in 1835 by music publisher Oliver Ditson (1811-1888). Ditson was a primary force in music merchandising, distribution, and retail sales on the East Coast. He also helped establish two musical instrument manufacturers: The John Church Company of Cincinnati, Ohio, and Lyon & Healy (Washburn) in Chicago, Illinois.

In 1865 Ditson established a manufacturing branch of his company under the supervision of John Haynes, called the John C. Haynes Company. This branch built guitars for a number of trademarks, such as **Bay State**, **Tilton**, and **Haynes Excelsior**, (Source: Tom Wheeler, *American Guitars*).

BEAR CREEK GUITARS
Instruments currently built in Kula, Hawaii.

Bear Creek Guitars builds fine handmade Hawaiian steel guitars in the "Weissenborn" tradition. The instruments are styled after the classic steel guitars of the 1920s but with beautiful craftsmanship and more attention to details than the originals. The price range for the four styles available runs from $1,495 to $6,500. Bear Creek instruments are played and recommended by noted musician/author Bob Brozman. They were previously located in Monterey, California. For more information refer to their web site (see Trademark Index).

B

BELTONA

Instruments currently built in Whangarei, New Zealand.

Beltona produces custom-made resonator instruments, all out of metal construction. Beltona manufactures all of their own parts. All guitars are made to customer specifications, as well as the custom engraving.

The Beltona Shop produces a limited number of instruments per year. Current models include a triple resonator guitar, a single resonator guitar (either 12 - or 14-fret), and an electro resonator model, as well as mandolin and ukulele models. For further information regarding prices and specifications, please contact Beltona directly (see Trademark Index).

BENEDETTO, ROBERT

Instruments currently built in Riverview, Florida beginning 2001, and in Nashville, TN, by the Guild Custom Shop (select models only) beginning in mid -2000, through a licensing agreement. Previously manufactured in East Stroudsburg, PA.

Master Luthier Robert Benedetto has been handcrafting fine archtop guitars since 1968. Benedetto was born in New York in 1946. Both his father and grandfather were master cabinetmakers, and Benedetto's uncles were musicians. While growing up in New Jersey, Benedetto began playing the guitar professionally at age thirteen. Being near the New York/New Jersey jazz music scene, Benedetto had numerous opportunities to perform repair and restoration work on other classic archtops. Benedetto built his first archtop in 1968, and his pre-eminence in the field is evidenced by his having made archtop guitars longer than any living builders and has a growing list of endorsers. Current endorsers range from Jimmy Bruno and Kenny Burrell to Earl Klugh and Andy Summers.

Benedetto moved to Homosassa, Florida in 1976. Three years later, he relocated to Clearwater, Florida. A veteran innovator, Benedetto began concentrating on the acoustic properties of the guitar designs, and started a movement to strip away unnecessary adornment (inlays, bindings) in 1982. While continuing his regular work on archtop building, Benedetto also built violins between 1983-1987. Violinist extraordinaire Stephane Grappelli purchased one of his violins in 1993. Benedetto even built a small number of electric solid body guitars and basses (which debuted at the 1987 NAMM show) in addition to his regular archtop production schedule. After 10 years in East Stroudsburg, PA, Benedetto relocated back to Florida during 2000.

His endorsers span three generations of jazz guitarists. Not since John D'Angelico has anyone made as many archtop guitars nor had as many well-known players endorsing and recording with his guitars. Closer scrutiny reveals nuances found only from a maker of his stature. His minimalist delicate inlay motif has become a trademark as have his novel use of black, rather than gold, tuning machines, black bridge height adjustment wheels, and an ebony nut (versus bone), all of which harmonize with the ebony fittings throughout the guitar. He is the originator of the solid ebony tailpiece, uniquely fastened to the guitar with cello tail adjustor. Likewise, he was the first to use exotic and natural wood veneers on the headstock and pioneered the use of violin-pigments to shade his guitars. His Honey Blonde finish is now widely used within the guitar industry. Benedetto is also well-known for refining the 7-string archtop and is that unique model's most prolific maker.

Benedetto is the Archtop Guitar Construction Editor and "Guitar Maintenance" columnist for *Just Jazz Guitar* magazine, and is the author of *Making an Archtop Guitar* (Centerstream Publishing, 1994). He released his 9 1/2 hour instructional video, Archtop Guitar Design & Construction, in 1996. His forthcoming biography is being written by eminent jazz guitar historian Adrian Ingram.

His Benedetto pickups were licensed in late 1999 to be sold exclusively by Seymour Duncan pickups. In March 1999, Benedetto licensed his standard models to Fender Musical Instrument Corporation to be made at the Guild custom shop in Nashville, TN, beginning in 2000.

As of spring 2001, Benedetto has built over 750 musical instruments. While the majority (466) are archtop guitars, he has produced 157 electric solid body guitars, 52 electric basses, 48 violins, 5 violas, 2 mandolins and 1 cello. Benedetto currently schedules his production to 6 archtop guitar instruments per year, as well as a few violins, (Biographical information courtesy Cindy Benedetto).

Carl Barney Jazzmaker II
courtesy Carl Barney

ACOUSTIC ARCHTOP

Robert Benedetto's custom archtop guitars are individually handcrafted in the USA. Prices include hardshell case and Benedetto suspended jazz pickup. As of March 1, 1999, he no longer makes standard models. Used prices have been intentionally omitted, since each Benedetto instrument must be appraised individually to ensure accurate value. All current instruments are custom order only, one-of-a-kind, and individually handmade with prices ranging from 60,000.

Effective March 1, 1999, Benedetto has licensed his name to Fender Musical Instruments Corporation for his standard models to be made by Guild at the Guild custom shop in Corona, CA. Initially, the first 3 Benedetto models listed below will be offered by Guild. Additionally, Benedetto will personally work with and instruct Guild's custom shop guitar makers as to the exact specifications of his new model designs.

The Frank Vignola model is slated for production by 2004. This Django-esque Benedetto guitar, designed by acoustic jazz master Frank Vignola, will feature an arched top and back. Look for more information for further editions.

The Benedetto E-6/E-7 solid ebony archtop tailpiece is available for $150 from www.stewmac.com

MANHATTAN (NO. 395-9600) - neo-classically designed full-bodied archtop with European spruce top and European flamed maple back/sides, ebony finger rest, gold Schaller tuners, mfg. by Benedetto until 1999, and by the Guild custom shop beginning in 2000-current.

MSR   **$15,000**

Benedetto Manhattan
courtesy Tom Zan Hoose

B

FRATELLO (NO. 395-9500) - traditional full-bodied archtop with European spruce top and European flamed maple back/sides, ebony pickguard, gold Schaller tuners, mfg. by Benedetto until 1999, and by the Guild custom shop beginning in 2000-current.

    MSR   **$14,000**

LA VENEZIA (NO. 395-9800) - purely acoustic full-bodied archtop with European woods, serpentine headstock, no bindings or inlays, black Schaller tuners, mfg. by Benedetto until 1999, and by the Guild custom shop beginning in 2000-current.

    MSR   **$17,500**

    The La Venezia was inspired by a unique guitar built for Chuck Wayne in 1982, and features an intermingling of design ideas from violin and archtop building.

THE 7-STRING - 7 string configuration, carved select aged spruce tops, carved flamed maple back with matching sides, black/white binding, 3-piece flamed maple neck, Neo-classical fingerboard, narrow Chuck Wayne-style finger rest, gold Schaller tuners with solid ebony buttons, current mfg.

    MSR   **$17,500**

AMERICANA - 18" body width, carved select aged spruce tops, non-cutaway body, carved select flamed maple back with matching sides, black/white binding, 3-piece flamed maple neck, large flared headstock, Neo-classical (no inlays) fingerboard, narrow Chuck Wayne-style finger rest, gold Schaller tuners with solid ebony buttons, disc. 1999.

Last MSR was $35,000.

    Both the Americana and Limelite models offer a tribute to the early days of archtop building and big bands.

LIMELITE - carved select aged spruce tops, carved flamed maple back with matching sides, 3-piece flamed maple neck, large flared headstock, split fingerboard inlay, traditionally-shaped bound pickguard, intricate inlay work on the pickguard/tailpiece, gold Schaller tuners with solid ebony buttons, disc. 1999.

Last MSR was $45,000.

CREMONA - hand carved/graduated/tuned European cello wood top and back, matching sides, fine line binding, flamed maple neck, large flared burl-veneered headstock with elegant mother-of-pearl/abalone inlay, gold Schaller tuners with gold (or solid ebony or mother-of-pearl) buttons, disc. 1999.

Last MSR was $60,000.

    The Cremona was Benedetto's first standard model. Options included headstock-matching inlay on tailpiece and pickguard, and split block mother-of-pearl fingerboard inlay.

ACOUSTIC ARCHTOP: RENAISSANCE SERIES

Renaissance Series instruments are very custom, one-of-a-kind archtop guitars. While the features may vary, the most distinct similarity between them are the clustered sound openings (unique to Benedetto) which range in design and location from one instrument to another. To date, only two instruments have been constructed – the Il Fiorentino, and the Il Palissandro. List price on these models is $50,000. All Renaissance series instruments will have their own name.

The Il Palissandro model has a 16" width, non-cutaway body, and features a European spruce top, Indian rosewood back and sides, one-piece Honduran mahogany neck, ebony fingerboard/bridge/tailpiece/endpin, rosewood binding/natural wood purfling, a classical-style tapered neck heel, serpentine-style headstock with flamed curly maple and rosewood border/flamed curly maple truss rod cover, no finger rest and no pickup.

BENTLY
Instruments currently manufactured in Asia.

Bently instruments are entry level to medium quality solid body guitars and basses that feature designs based on classic American favorites.

BESSON
See Framus & Aristone. Instruments previously built in West Germany during the late 1950s through the early 1960s.

While Besson was the brand name for a UK importer, these guitars were made by and identical to certain Framus models. Research also indicates that the trademark Aristone was utilized as well, (Source: Tony Bacon and Paul Day, *The Guru's Guitar Guide*)

BEVERLY
See chapter on House Brands.

This trademark has been identified as a House Brand of Selmer U.K. in England, (Source: Willie G. Moseley, *Stellas & Stratocasters*).

BI LEVEL GUITARS
See La Jolla Luthiers.

BIG HEART
Instruments currently built in the U.S. beginning 1998. Distributed by the Big Heart Slide Company of Placentia, California.

In 1998, the Big Heart Slide Company debuted their own guitar model, the **Big Heart BrassTop**. The Big Heart Slide Company is well-known for their various aluminum, porcelain, and glass slides; the guitar model is an electric hollow body guitar set up for the slide technique, and features a full brass top. Retail prices range from $750 to $1,200. For further information and specifications, contact the Big Heart Slide Company directly (see Trademark Index).

BLACK HILLS
See chapter on House Brands.

This trademark has been identified as a House Brand of the Wall Drug stores, (Source: Willie G. Moseley, *Stellas & Stratocasters*).

BLACKSHEAR, TOM

Instruments currently built in San Antonio, Texas.

Luthier Tom Blackshear builds high quality Classical guitar models. For further information, please contact luthier Blackshear directly (see Trademark Index).

BLAIR GUITARS LTD.

Instruments currently built in Ellington, Connecticut.

Designer Douglas Blair has over twenty years experience in the music field, and has been building his own guitars since his teens. Blair has recorded 3 independent EP/LPs, and toured with acts like W.A.S.P. and Run 21. Throughout his professional playing career, Blair found himself constantly switching between his electric guitar and an Ovation acoustic on a stand for live performances. In 1990, Blair conceived of the **Mutant Twin** guitar model as a way to solve the problem, which combined a solid body half with an "acoustic" half (with hollow tuned sound chamber and Fishman preamp). Prototypes were developed with the aid of Ovation R & D designer Don Johnson in 1990, and the guitar debuted in Boston in 1991. Blair Guitars Ltd. debuted at the 1994 NAMM winter show.

In 1997, Blair's design was licensed to Guild (FMIC) as the new Slash signature **Crossroads** custom design double neck guitar. This model is available in Black or Crimson Transparent finishes (Guild retail list $4,000).

ACOUSTIC

Blair recently introduced the **ASIA Acoustic 12**, a "Dual Format 12-string model with 6 pairs of unison strings and nylon strings. This guitar has a cedar top, mahogany neck, mahogany/koa back and sides, Steinberger tuners, Fishman piezo bridge pickup, active volume/tone/controls, discrete outputs, and a 3-way format selector (list price $1,999).

BLUE LION

Instruments currently built in Santa Margarita, California beginning 1975.

The Blue Lion company of Robert and Janita Baker is more known for the dulcimers they produce, but they did build an estimated 6 to 8 acoustic guitars a year. The model is dubbed the B 1 Standard, and many custom options were featured.

The last list price recorded for the B 1 Standard was $1,650 (with case).

BLUERIDGE

Instruments currently produced in Asia. Distributed by Saga Musical Instruments of San Francisco, California.

Blueridge acoustics are dreadnought style guitars designed in part for the entry level to intermediate guitar player. These guitars feature a solid spruce top, mahogany neck, bound rosewood fingerboard with mother-of-pearl position dots, rosewood bridge, a concentric circle rosette, black pickguard, Natural Satin or Clear high gloss finish, chrome sealed tuners, and a solid 3-per-side headstock. Models feature rosewood or mahogany back and sides. Visit Saga's web site for more information (see Trademark Index).

BLUESOUTH

Instruments currently built in Muscle Shoals, Alabama.

Ronnie Knight began Bluesouth Guitars in 1991 with the idea of building stringed musical instruments which celebrate the musical heritage of the American South. Blues, jazz, country, rock, and spiritual music were all created in the southern American states. This small area from Texas to the Carolinas, from Kentucky to Florida, has been the hotbed of the world's musical culture in the twentieth century. Several small towns within the southeast have had a huge impact on today's popular music: Muscle Shoals, Alabama; Macon, Georgia; and Clarksdale, Mississippi.

The results of this project have been unique, light-bodied guitars with large, comfortable necks. Bluesouth contends that "fierce individualism" is the key ingredient in their guitar making operation. Starting in a small shop over a record store in early 1992, Bluesouth moved to a much larger industrial facility in the spring of 1995. To date, the company offers 7 models, including 2 electric basses. Bluesouth also builds its own cases and pickups in house, (Company history courtesy Ronnie Knight, April 17, 1996).

ACOUSTIC

Bluesouth guitars offers two acoustic models, an archtop model and a flattop model. The archtop **Storyville** model has a single cutaway body with hand carved European spruce top, European maple back and sides, 5-ply black/ivoroid body binding, hard maple neck, and ivoroid bound ebony fingerboard. The list price of $5,300 includes a case. The **Tutweiler** (list $2,195, case included) has a solid spruce top, mahogany back and sides, ivoroid body binding, mahogany neck, and rosewood fingerboard.

BOAZ ELKAYAM GUITARS

Instruments currently built in North Hollywood, California.

Boaz Elkayam hand builds commissioned guitars, customized prototypes, classical and flamenco style guitars, mandolins, and his Travel Guitar. Elkayam, the son of a violin builder, was taught building techniques of stringed instruments, and has performed restoration work on museum pieces.

Luthier Elkayam handcrafts his guitars using traditional lutherie techniques, and eschews the use of power tools. Elkayam prefers to build with top-of-the-line woods such as Brazilian and Indian rosewood, Macassar

Bendetto Limelite
courtesy John Bender

Bendetto La Cremona
courtesy Scott Chinery

and Gaboon ebony, Honduran mahogany, German and Canadian spruce, and Alaskan red cedar. Pieces are limited to a small yearly output. Refer to their web site for more information (see Trademark Index).

BOHMANN, JOSEPH

Instruments previously built in Chicago, Illinois from 1878 to the late 1920s.

Luthier Joseph H. Bohmann was born in Neumarkt (Bohemia), Czechoslavakia in 1848. He later emigrated to America, and then founded Bohmann's American Musical Industry in 1878. Bohmann's Perfect Artist violins won a number of international honors, and his American mandolin model was the top of the line in both the Montgomery Ward and Sears catalogs in 1894. By 1900, Bohmann was offering thirteen grades of guitars, (Source: Michael Wright, *Vintage Guitar Magazine*).

BOOM BASSES

See Ken Donnell.

BOUCHET

Instruments previously built in Paris, France from 1946 to possibly the late 1970s.

Luthier and painter Robert Bouchet (1898-1986) began building guitars in Paris in the mid 1940s. A keen guitarist, he produced very high quality guitars in small numbers, (Source: Tony Bacon, *The Ultimate Guitar Book*).

BOURGEOIS

Instruments currently produced in Lewiston, Maine.

Bourgeios guitars was created by Dana Bourgeois. Dana has been producing guitars for many years, was co-founder of Schoenberg guitars, was a consultant for the start-up to the Gibson Montana plant, was a product designer for PRS, and learned CAD drawing from Bob Taylor. In 2000 Dana joined forces with Patrick Theimer to form Pantheon guitars. Bourgeois guitars are available through Pantheon guitars now. They build their guitars in an 1840 Textile Mill in a southern Maine city. Bourgeois guitars are high quality acoustics that are bulit with several options and features in mind. Special inlays of diamonds and Brazilian rosewood are some of the features found on the guitars. For more information on Bourgeois, visist their web site or Pantheon's (see Trademark Index).

ACOUSTIC

Bourgeios' current line of guitars is known as the Professional Series. All models include 25.5" scale length, bone nut & saddle, ebony fretboard & bridge, high gloss body, satin neck finish, Ivoroid bridge & end pins, custom hardshell case, and a limited lifetime warranty. Bourgeois makes several different types of acoustics. In the dreadnought field they produce the Country Boy, Vintage, and D-150. The Country Boy Dreadnought starts at $2,795 and has a sitka top with mahogany back & sides. The Vintage is a step above at $3,295 with an Adirondack top with Indian rosewood back and sides. The D-150, which is the top end model of the entire guitar line, retails for $5,995. This model features an Adriondack top, Brazilian rosewood back and sides and elaborate binding and inlays.

For other models they have the Slope D that has an sitka top with mahogany back & sides and a slope D body style retailing for $3,195. For the OM series they have the Vintage OM that retails for $3,295, the regular OMC that goes for $3,595, the JOMC listing for $3,595, and the JOMC Deluxe that has a price tag of $4,995. They also have a line of Acoustic Archtops. The A-350 lists for $4,995 with a spruce top, and curly maple back and sides. They also have a model A-500. Bourgeois has also produced other models in the past years that carry different model designations. Signature models of Rick Scaggs and Martin Simpson have also been produced.

There is an extensive list of options available on all guitars. There is no charge for you southpaws out there that need a left-handed guitar. Different kinds of woods, bindings, inlays, and other features are available at a charge. For more information contact Bourgeois directly (see Trademark Index).

BOWN, RALPH S.

Instruments currently built in York, England.

This independent luthier is currently building high quality guitars.

BOZO

Trademark of instruments currently built in Lindenhurst, Illinois.

Master Luthier Bozidar Podunavac has been creating guitars for forty years. Bozo (pronounced Bo-Zho) was originally apprenticed to luthier Milutin Mladenovicin his native Yugoslavia. In 1959, Bozo and his wife Mirjana emigrated to the U.S., and were located in Chicago, Illinois. Bozo initially did repair work for various music stores, and later opened his own shop in 1965. His original guitars were designed after the Dreadnought body style, but changed to his own original Bell Western design in 1968.

The Podunavacs moved to Escondido (near San Diego), California in 1972, and to San Diego three years later. In 1978, Bozo opened a school of lutherie, which he ran for a number of years. The family later relocated to Florida, where the current guitar building is based today. Although Podunavac is currently retired, he was enticed back into making the guitars he loves by a prominent musical instrument dealer. Bozo was one of the luthiers contacted by esteemed collector Scott Chinery for a model in the Blue Guitars Collection. Bozo still constructs guitars on a limited basis. In the late 1970s, some guitars based on Bozo's designs were constructed in Japan. Research still continues on the nature and designation of these models.

ACOUSTIC

Known for both his flattop and archtop guitar designs, Bozo is currently building archtop models only. Instruments feature very ornate detailing and inlay work, as well as a large distinct headstock. The guitars feature hand-selected European woods, carved tops, elaborate abalone and herringbone inlays, and wood binding (no plastic or celluloid is used on his guitars). The Bell Western model ranges from $5,000-$11,000, the Bell Western XII from $5,500-$12,000, the Requinto from $5,000-$11,000 and Archtops from $8,000-$20,000.

BRADFORD

See chapter on House Brands.

This trademark has been identified as a House Brand of the W. T. Grant company, one of the old style Five and Dime retail stores. W. T. Grant offered the Bradford trademarked guitars during the mid 1960s. Many of the instruments have been identified as produced by Guyatone in Japan. Bradford models ranged from flattop acoustics to thinline hollowbody and solidbody electric guitars and basses, (Source: Michael Wright, *Vintage Guitar Magazine*).

BRADLEY

Instruments previously produced in Japan.

The American distributor for this trademark was Veneman Music of Bethesda, Maryland, (Source: Michael Wright, *Guitar Stories,* Vol. 1).

BREEDLOVE

Instruments currently built in Tumalo, Oregon beginning 1990. Distributed by the Breedlove Guitar Company of Tumalo, Oregon.

Larry Breedlove and Steve Henderson spent time refining their lutherie skills with Bob Taylor (Taylor Guitars). The two partners then moved up into the Pacific Northwest and founded the Breedlove Guitar Company in 1990. Henderson and Breedlove experimented with other tonewoods, and offer instruments built with high quality aged woods like walnut, myrtlewood, and red cedar as well as the traditional maple, spruce, rosewood, and mahogany.

Breedlove is also focusing on mandolin models. Breedlove mandolins feature solid flamed maple backs and sides, carved solid Sitka spruce tops, ebony bridge/fingerboard/peghead veneers, and Schaller tuners. All models are available in a classic Sunburst finish. The Cascade (retail list $2,395) is modeled after the CM guitar body design. The Columbia (list $2,395) is similar to the Cascade, except features an oval soundhole and X-shaped top bracing. The Oregon (list $1,995) is a tear drop shaped mandolin with parallel bracing, and the Olympic (list $1,995) is a similar tear drop shape with an oval soundhole and X-braced top.

**Bourgeois Martin Simpson
courtesy Fred Shed**

GENERAL INFORMATION

In 1997, Breedlove developed a new system that designates model description. This system consists of three parts: a letter (or letters) indicates the body shape:

C	**Concert**
CM	**Concert Asymmetrical**
RD	**Dreadnought**
MJ	**Jumbo**
EG	**Gerhard Jumbo**
SC	**S Series Concert**
SD	**S Series Dreadnought**
SJ	**S Series Jumbo**

The first number indicates body depth:

1	**Shallow (4 1/16" at tail)**
2	**Deep (4 9/16" at tail)**

The second number indicates body cutaway style:

0	**Non-cutaway**
2	**Sharp (pointed horn) cutaway**
5	**Soft (rounded horn) cutaway**

An optional 'X' following the model designation indicates traditional 'X-bracing.'

Breedlove is offering the Extraordinary Experience. This is a once-in-a-lifetime experience where you sign up to tour the Breedlove Guitar Workshop and scenic Oregon area. During this time you spend time with a consultant who will learn about your playing style and they end up building a guitar for you. It is an experience where you tout the workshop and they build a guitar for you while you are touring. Contact Breedlove for more information.

Breedlove guitars feature an asymmetrical peghead, 25 1/2" scale, and an ebony pinless bridge. Breedlove offers several different abalone and mother-of-pearl fingerboard inlay patterns. Wood options for the back and sides include walnut, maple, myrtlewood (add $100), rosewood (add $200), koa (add $600), striped ebony ($Call), and Brazilian rosewood ($Call). Different solid wood options for guitar's top Englemann spruce (add $150), Adirondack spruce (add $350), Redwood (add $175), and bear claw Sitka spruce (add $175). Various other options such as different appointments, abalone rosettes, fingerboard inlay patterns, and electronic packages are also available at additional costs (Contact Breedlove for price quotations).

Add $225 for Fishman Matrix Natural pickup system. Add $230 for L.R. Baggs Ribbon RTS pickup system. Add $400 for L.R. Baggs Dual Source pickup system. Add $350 for 12-string configuration. Add $350 for left-handed configuration.

ACOUSTIC: PREMIER LINE STANDARD SERIES

All Breedlove Premier Line instruments have ivoroid or black plastic binding, top and back purflings, and abalone rosettes. Bridges, fingerboards, and peghead veneers are made of ebony. The following suggested retail list prices are for guitars with Sitka spruce tops and mahogany back and sides (price includes a case).

Add $495 for Classic Appointments (choice of bloodwood, koa, maple, walnut, or rosewood body/fingerboard and headstock binding, top/side/ back purfling, and a V-shaped tailstrip.)

**Bourgeois Slope D
courtesy Sandy Njoes**

B

C 10 - concert style shallow body, extensive purfling on body/neck/fingerboard, 14/20-fret bound ebony fingerboard with pearl dot inlay, ebony pinless bridge, bound peghead, ebony peghead veneer, 3-per-side gold Schaller tuners, available in satin finish, body length - 19 7/8 inches, body width - 15 3/8 inches, body depth - 4 1/16 inches, current mfg.

MSR $3,099

C 12 - concert style shallow body with sharp cutaway, similar construction details as the C 10, current mfg.

MSR $3,399

C 15 - concert style shallow body with soft cutaway, similar construction details as the C 10, current mfg.

MSR $3,399

C 20 - concert style deep body, extensive purfling on body/neck/fingerboard, 14/20-fret bound ebony fingerboard with pearl dot inlay, ebony pinless bridge, bound peghead, ebony peghead veneer, 3-per-side gold Schaller tuners, available in satin finish, body length - 19 7/8 inches, body width - 15 3/8 inches, body depth - 4 9/16 inches, current mfg.

MSR $3,099

C 22 - concert style deep body with sharp cutaway. Similar construction details as the C 20, current mfg.

MSR $3,399

C 25 (C 5) - concert style deep body with soft cutaway. Similar construction details as the C 20, current mfg.

MSR $3,399

CM CLASSIC - concert style asymmetrical (similar to the C 20, except longer and wider) body, extensive purfling on body/neck/fingerboard, 14/20-fret bound ebony fingerboard with pearl dot inlay, ebony pinless bridge, bound peghead, ebony peghead veneer, 3-per-side gold Schaller tuners, available in satin finish, body length - 21 1/8 inches, body width - 16 1/8 inches, body depth - 4 5/16 inches, current mfg.

MSR $5,499

EG 15 (ED GERHARD CUSTOM) - jumbo style shallow body with soft cutaway, choice of tone wood on top/back/sides, extensive purfling on body/neck/fingerboard, 14/20-fret bound ebony fingerboard with pearl dot inlay, ebony pinless bridge, bound peghead, ebony peghead veneer, 3-per-side gold Schaller tuners, available in satin finish, disc.

N/A $2,475 $1,595

Last MSR was $3,295.

MJ 20 - jumbo style deep body, extensive purfling on body/neck/fingerboard, 14/20-fret bound ebony fingerboard with pearl dot inlay, ebony pinless bridge, bound peghead, ebony peghead veneer, 3-per-side gold Schaller tuners, available in satin finish, body length - 21 inches, body width - 17 inches, body depth - 4 9/16 inches, current mfg.

MSR $2,695

MJ 22 - jumbo style deep body with sharp cutaway. Similar construction details as the MJ 20, current mfg.

MSR $3,095

RD 20 X - dreadnought style deep body, extensive purfling on body/neck/fingerboard, 14/20-fret bound ebony fingerboard with pearl dot inlay, ebony pinless bridge, bound peghead, ebony peghead veneer, 3-per-side gold Schaller tuners, available in Natural satin finish, body length - 20 1/8 inches, body width - 16 1/8 inches, body depth - 4 9/16 inches, current mfg.

MSR $2,595

RD 22 X - jumbo style deep body with sharp cutaway. Similar construction details as the RD 20 X, current mfg.

MSR $2,995

ACOUSTIC: SPECIAL EDITION SERIES

DESCHUTES (C2 DESCHUTES) - concert style deep body with sharp cutaway, figured mahogany back/sides, herringbone purfling, striped ebony rosette/peghead veneer, 14/20-fret bound ebony fingerboard with mother-of-pearl trout and trout fly inlays, ivoroid neck binding, ebony pinless bridge, bound peghead, 3-per-side gold Schaller tuners, available in satin finish, disc.

N/A $2,395 $1,550

Last MSR was $3,195.

This model was dedicated to the Deschutes River and the sport of fly fishing.

ED GERHARD SIGNATURE - jumbo style shallow body with soft cutaway, Sitka spruce top, rosewood back/sides, koa binding, wood rosette, 14/20-fret bound ebony fingerboard with pearl dot inlay, ebony pinless bridge, bound peghead, ebony peghead veneer, 3-per-side gold mini tuners with oversized buttons, available in satin finish, current mfg.

MSR $3,399

NORTHWEST (C5 NORTHWEST) - concert style deep body with soft cutaway, myrtlewood back/sides, maple neck, walnut binding, 14/20-fret bound ebony fingerboard with hand-engraved abalone and mother-of-pearl reproductions of North West Indian totems (whale and fish motifs), ebony pinless bridge, bound peghead, ebony peghead veneer, 3-per-side gold Schaller tuners, available in satin finish, current mfg.

MSR $4,499

CLASSIC 12 - deep bodied jumbo 12-string featuring sharp cutaway, select striped ebony back and sides, Sitka spruce top, ivoroid binding, abalone rosette, current mfg.

MSR $4,799

ACOUSTIC: S SERIES

The S Series guitars may not be as ornate as the regular line but are built with the same materials at the Breedlove facility with the same attention to detail. The primary difference is in the appointments, less purflings, a simpler bridge, abalone rosette, and a rosewood peghead veneer. The following suggested retail list prices are for guitars with Sitka spruce tops and Walnut back and sides (price includes a case).

Add $100 for western red cedar top. Add $100 for myrtlewood back and sides. Add $200 for rosewood back and sides.

SC 20 - concert style deep body, Sitka spruce top, walnut back/sides, round soundhole, top purfling, one piece wood rosette, ebony fingerboard/pinless bridge, rosewood peghead veneer, 3-per-side asymmetrical headstock with gold Grover tuners, available in satin finish, body length - 19 7/8 inches, body width - 15 3/8 inches, body depth - 4 9/16 inches, current mfg.

    MSR   **$2,399**

SC 25 - concert style deep body with soft cutaway, similar construction details as the SC 20, current mfg.

    MSR   **$2,699**

SD 20X - dreadnought style deep body, round soundhole, walnut back/sides, top purfling, one piece wood rosette, ebony fingerboard/pinless bridge, rosewood peghead veneer, 3-per-side asymmetrical headstock with gold Grover tuners, available in satin finish, body length - 20 1/8 inches, body width - 16 1/8 inches, body depth - 4 9/16 inches, current mfg.

    MSR   **$2,399**

SC 25 - dreadnought style deep body with soft cutaway, similar construction details as the SC 20, current mfg.

    MSR   **$2,699**

SJ 10 - jumbo style shallow body, round soundhole, walnut back/sides, top purfling, one piece wood rosette, ebony fingerboard/pinless bridge, rosewood peghead veneer, 3-per-side asymmetrical headstock with gold Grover tuners, available in satin finish, disc.

    Last MSR was $2,095.

SJ 15 - jumbo style shallow body with soft cutaway, similar construction details as the SJ 10, disc.

    Last MSR was $2,395.

SJ 20 - jumbo style deep body, similar construction details as the SJ 10, current mfg.

    MSR   **$2,499**

The SJ 20 model was offered in a 12-string configuration as a separate model up to 1998. Retail list price for Walnut back/sides was $1,995; Rosewood back/sides were $2,145. Models featured similar construction details as the SJ 20, with 6 per side tuners.

SJ 25 - jumbo style deep body with soft cutaway. Similar construction details as the SJ 10, current mfg.

    MSR   **$2,799**

ACOUSTIC: NYLON SERIES

SN20 - western red cedar top, East Indian rosewood back and sides, mahogany neck, ebony fingerboard, slotted peghead, gold Schaller tuners, ebony bridge and peghead veneer, 12 frets, 25 1/2" scale, current mfg.

    MSR   **$2,399**

SN25 - similar to Model SN20, except has a single soft cutaway, current mfg.

    MSR   **$2,699**

NL20 - similar to Model NS20, except has 14-fret neck, disc.

    Last MSR was $2,995.

NL25 - similar to Model NL20, except has single soft cutaway, disc.

    Last MSR was $2,995.

BRIDWELL WORKSHOP
Instruments currently produced in Palatine, Illinois.

The Bridwell Workshop is currently building high quality guitars. For further information, please contact the Bridwell Workshop directly (see Trademark Index).

BRILEY, CLINT
See chapter on House Brands. Instruments previously built in Florida.

This company was founded by Clint Briley in 1989, motivated by his experience of making new parts for his vintage National Duolian Resonator guitar. Briley, a machinist, has a background in die making. With assistance from local luthier/repairman (and friend) Charlie Jirousek, Briley hand built necks and steel bodies as he established his company. While this trademark has been identified as a House Brand, the distributor is still unknown, (Sources: Hal Hammer & Willie G. Moseley, *Stellas & Stratocasters*).

Briley offered two models that feature his own spun resonator cones and parts. The Cutaway Steel Body (last MSR - $1,500) has a mahogany neck and rosewood fingerboard, and meets the metal body at the twelfth fret. The Econo-Steel (last MSR - $800) has no cutaway on its steel body.

BRUKO

Instruments currently built in Germany. Distributed by Lark in the Morning of Mendocino, California.

Bruko Instruments consists of solid wood ukuleles and half-size miniature guitars.

C. BRUNO & SON

See chapter on House Brands.

C. Bruno & Son was originally formed in Macon, Georgia in 1834. The company has been in the music distribution business since then. C. Bruno & Son guitars were built by another manufacturer, and distributed by the company. C. Bruno & Son distributors is currently part of Kaman Music Corporation.

In 1838, Charles Bruno and C.F. Martin entered into a partnership to produce and distribute acoustic guitars. These specific guitars are labeled with both names, and were produced in New York. In 1839, Martin moved the company to Nazareth, Pennsylvania and dissolved the partnership. C.F. Martin did not provide the guitars that bear the "Bruno" or "C. Bruno & Sons" logos on the peghead, (Source: Mike Longworth, *Martin Guitars*).

BURTON, CYNDY

Instruments currently built in Portland, Oregon.

Luthier Cyndy Burton builds high quality acoustic guitars.

BUSCARINO, JOHN

Instruments currently built in Largo, Florida. Distributed by the Buscarino Guitar Company of Largo, Florida.

Luthier John Buscarino apprenticed with Master acoustic guitar builder Augustino LoPrinzi for over a year in 1978, and with Bob Benedetto of archtop lutherie fame from 1979 to 1981. Later that year, Buscarino formed **Nova U.S.A.**, which built high quality solid body electrics, and acoustic/electric instruments. In 1990, Buscarino changed the company name to **Buscarino Guitars** to reflect the change to building acoustic instruments. Buscarino continues to produce limited production custom guitars, and is currently focusing on archtop guitar building.

ACOUSTIC ARCHTOP

Buscarino archtop guitars are offered with a variety of options such as custom finishes, Tree-of-Life inlay, neck or tailpiece inlays. There is no charge for a suspended pickup. Contact luthier Buscarino for pricing information.

Add $100 for a built-in humbucker pickup. Add $100 for bound fingerboard. Add $650 for AAA highly figured wood. Add $800 for a 7-string configuration. Add $800 for an 18" body width. Add $800 for wood binding. Add $800 for left-handed configuration. Add $1,200 for European cello woods. Add $1,500 for the Poly-Drive MIDI system.

ARTISAN (16" OR 17") - carved single-A aged spruce top, carved single-A flamed maple back with matching sides, Venetian cutaway, black/white body binding, 3-piece flamed maple neck, 25" scale, 22-fret ebony fingerboard, ebony pickguard/tailpiece/truss rod cover, 3-per-side gold M6 Schaller tuners with solid ebony buttons, available in Natural high gloss lacquer finish, current mfg.

> **MSR** **$4,200**

> **Add $300 for Honey Blonde, Vintage Natural finishes. Add $300 for solid white binding on f-holes. Add $500 for a Sunburst finish.**
> Price includes a 3-ply case.

MONARCH (16" OR 17") - carved double-A aged spruce top, carved double-A flamed maple back with matching sides, Venetian cutaway, bound f-holes, black/white body binding, 3-piece flamed maple neck, 25" scale, 22-fret ebony fingerboard, ebony pickguard/tailpiece/truss rod cover, 3-per-side gold M6 Schaller tuners with solid ebony buttons, available in Honey Blonde, Natural, Traditional Sunburst, or Vintage Natural high gloss lacquer finishes, current mfg.

> **MSR** **$6,000**

> **Add $300 for a Sunburst finish.**
> Price includes a double arched 5-ply case. Buscarino's Monarch archtop is produced through associative efforts with Master Luthier Bob Benedetto.

VIRTUOSO (16" OR 17") - carved master grade aged spruce top, carved master grade flamed maple back with matching sides, Venetian cutaway, bound f-holes, fine line black/white body binding, 3-piece flamed maple neck, 25" scale, 22-fret ebony fingerboard with block inlay, ebony pickguard/tailpiece/truss rod cover, bound pickguard, 3-per-side gold M6 Schaller tuners with solid ebony buttons, available in Honey Blonde, Natural, Traditional Sunburst, or Vintage Natural high gloss lacquer finishes. Current mfg.

> **MSR** **$10,000**

> **Add $300 for a Sunburst finish.**
> Price includes a double arched 5-ply case.

ACOUSTIC

The Cabaret model is available with optional lattice bracing or flying braces, Gilbert tuners, or internal (or external) electronics (call for price quote).

Add $350 for wood binding. Add $350 for RMC Diffu pickup system. Add $500 for RMC Poly-Drive II Outside MIDI electronics. Add $800 for the 7-string configuration. Add $1,000 for RMC Poly-Drive IV built-in electronics.

CABARET - Englemann spruce (or Sitka spruce or Western cedar) top, flame maple (or mahogany or Indian rosewood or Bolivian rosewood) carved back with matching sides, rounded cutaway, round soundhole, black plastic binding with multiple purflings, Honduran mahogany neck, 25 1/2" scale, ebony fingerboard, ebony bridge with abalone inlay, slotted headstock, 3-per-side Schaller Deluxe tuners with ebony buttons, available in Natural high gloss lacquer finish, body width 13 7/8", body depth 3 1/2", current mfg.

> **MSR** **$3,000**

> Price includes a custom double arched 5-ply case with crushed velvet lining.

Grand Cabaret - similar construction as Cabaret offered in a larger body style, body width 14 3/8", body depth 3 3/4".

> **MSR** **$3,300**

> Price includes a custom double arched 5-ply case with crushed velvet lining.

Section C

CA GUITARS
Instruments currently produced.

CA Guitars stands for Composite Acoustic Guitars and are guitars that are made out of composite and graphite materials instead of wood. This material is stronger and is able to withstand extreme conditions where a regular wood guitar would not. They currently offer the Legacy and Alternate Tuning series for guitars and an acoustic bass line as well. For more information refer to their web site (see Trademark Index).

C. B. ALYN GUITARWORKS
Instruments currently built in Pacific Palisades, California.

The Rosebud models are high quality, solid top (no soundholes) acoustic guitars with a piezo pickup system. Retail list ranges from $1,299 (basic) to $1,449 (RB70 Artist).

CADENZA
Instruments currently produced in Korea. Distributed by the Kimex Company of Seoul, Korea.

Cadenza features a wide range of steel-string, classical, and bass acoustic guitars.

CALVIN CRAMER
Instruments previously built in Markneukirchen, Germany. Distributed in the U.S. by Musima North America of Tampa, Florida.

Calvin Cramer concert guitars debuted in the United States, Canada, and South American markets in 1996. The guitars were built by Musima, Germany's largest acoustic guitar manufacturer. The company headquarters in Markneukirchen, Germany are near the Czech border. In 1991, Musima was purchased by industry veteran Helmet Stumpf following the German re-unification.

M. CAMPELLONE GUITARS
Instruments currently built in Greenville, Rhode Island.

Luthier Mark Campellone originally began building solid body guitars in the late 1970s, and turned his attention to archtops around 1987. All of his models are constructed of solid wood, and feature carved tops and backs.

Campellone's 17" width guitars are offered in two versions. The Full-sized 17" has a 21" body length, while the Short 17" has a body length of 20 1/2" and a more compact feel to the instrument.

Campellone Special
courtesy Mark Campellone

ACOUSTIC

Campellone currently offers three models of solid wood carved acoustics: each model is available in a 16", 17", or 18" Venetian cutaway body, body depth of 2 7/8" to 3 3/8"; with fingerboard scales of 24.5", 25", or 25.5", nut width of 1 11/16" or 1 3/4", with an optional floating pickup system. All three models have genuine shell inlays, and gold plated hardware. Finishes include Natural, Tinted Blonde, and a variety of Transparent Sunbursts.

Add $200 for floating pickup system. Add $250 for the 18" body.

SPECIAL SERIES - hand graduated select spruce top, hand graduated back of choicest figured maple with matching rims, multi-bound top, back, fingerboard, peghead, f-holes, and tortoise shell style pickguard, figured maple neck, ebony fingerboard with five-piece keystone position markers of mother-of-pearl and abalone, ebony bridge, Special Series peghead inlay, rear peghead inlay, bridge bass inlay, shell truss rod cover, Special series tailpiece, and custom case.

    MSR   **$6,750**

DELUXE SERIES - hand graduated select spruce top, hand graduated back of highly figured maple with matching rims, multi-bound top, back, fingerboard, peghead, and tortoise shell style pickguard, bound f-holes, figured maple neck, ebony fingerboard with three-piece keystone position markers, ebony bridge, Deluxe Series peghead inlay, and Deluxe series tailpiece.

    MSR   **$4,950**

STANDARD SERIES - hand graduated spruce top, hand graduated figured maple back with matching rims, multi-bound top, single-bound back, fingerboard, peghead, and tortoiseshell style pickguard, maple neck, rosewood fingerboard, bridge, and tailpiece applique.

    MSR   **$3,750**

CAPITAL
See chapter on House Brands.

This Gibson-built budget line of guitars has been identified as a House Brand of the J.W. Jenkins Company of Kansas City. While built to the same standards as other Gibson guitars, they lack the one true Gibson touch:

Campellone Deluxe
courtesy Mark Campellone

an adjustable truss rod. House Brand Gibsons were available to musical instrument distributors in the late 1930s and early 1940s, (Source: Walter Carter, *Gibson Guitars: 100 Years of an American Icon*).

CARELLI

Instruments previously built in Chicago, Illinois circa mid 1930s.

Carelli archtop guitars were produced in the 1930s by the Harmony Guitar company. Harmony, well-known for producing an estimated 57 "different" brands throughout its history, was the largest jobber production house in the history of guitar production. The Carelli trademark, or distributing company is yet unidentified.

ACOUSTIC ARCHTOP

The Carelli Artist E that was documented at the 19th Annual Dallas Vintage Guitar show has a number of features similar to Harmony's **Cremona** models. Harmony began producing the Cremona series circa 1934, and these models featured carved solid tops and laminated curly maple backs. The Carelli Artist E bears the same distinct features as the Cremona model *#7*. It is estimated that the model shown in the picture is a mid (1935 or 1936) 1930s vintage, (Source: Jim Fisch, author (with L.B. Fred) of Epiphone: *The House of Stathopoulo*; and Gary Sullivan, owner).

CARSON ROBISON

See chapter on House Brands.

Carson J. Robison was a popular country singer and songwriter in the 1930s who endorsed a Recording King flattop model. Recording King was the House Brand for Montgomery Ward, and Gibson built the high end models for the line (cheaper models were built by someone else). Early models had only a white paint stencil of "Carson J. Robison" on the peghead (hence this listing) but later models had the Recording King Logo as well, (Source: Walter Carter, *Gibson Guitars: 100 Years of an American Icon*).

CARVIN

Instruments currently produced in Escondido, California beginning 1969. Previous production was located in Covina, California from 1949 to 1969. Carvin instruments are sold through direct catalog sales, as well as through their four factory stores in California: Corvina, Hollywood, San Diego, and Santa Ana.

In 1946, Lowell Kiesel founded Kiesel Electronics in Los Angeles, California. Three years later, the Kiesel family settled in Covina, California and began the original catalog business of manufacturing and distributing lap steel guitars, small tube amps and pickups. The Carvin trademark was derived from Kiesel's two oldest sons, Carson and Gavin. Guitars were originally offered in kit form, or by parts since 1949; Carvin began building complete guitars in 1964. By 1978, the glued set-neck design replaced the bolt-on necks. The majority of the current guitar and bass models currently feature a neck-through design.

Carvin has always been a mail-order only company, and offers the players a wide range of options on the individual models. Even though they can't be tried out before they're bought, Carvin offers a 10-day money back guarantee. Because Carvin sells factory direct, they are not stocked in music stores; by requesting a catalog the careful shopper will also find a difference between the new list price and the actual sales price. Carvin offers a full range of guitar and bass replacement parts in their full line catalog. The Carvin company also offers mixing boards, power amplifiers, powered mixers, P.A. speakers, monitor speakers, guitar combo amps/heads/cabinets, and bass amps/cabinets as well.

For current information regarding the Carvin line of electric guitars and basses, please refer to the *Blue Book of Electric Guitars*.

CUSTOM INFORMATION

Almost every Carvin guitar is available with an extensive list of options. Options include different types of woods, binding, inlays, hardware and finishes. Each option has a different price that alters the value of the guitar. For each option, depending on how elaborate it is, add 10%. For more information on the options and Carvin guitars refer to the company directly to get a catalog (see Trademark Index.)

ACOUSTIC ELECTRIC

AC175 - single cutaway hollowed-out mahogany body, spruce top, round soundhole, through-body mahogany neck, 24-fret ebony fingerboard with pearl dot inlay, ebony bridge with black pins, blackface peghead with screened logo, 3-per-side gold tuners, transducer bridge Fishman pickup, volume/treble/bass controls, active electronics, available in Classic White, Ferrari Red, Jet Black, Natural, Pearl Blue, Pearl Red and Pearl White finishes, mfg. 1994-current.

MSR	$1,399	$769	$575	$475

AC275 - similar to the AC175, except the mahogany body in 1 1/2" wider, and features a F60 acoustic transducer with volume/treble/ bass controls and active electronics, mfg. 1996-current.

MSR	$1,499	$819	$625	$490

AC275-12 - similar to the AC275, except in 12-string configuration and 6 per side headstock, mfg. 1997-current.

MSR	$1,799	$889	$650	$525

CC275 - similar to the AC275 except is the Craig Chaquico model, which features a flamed maple top, MOP inlayed eagle headstock & fingerboard, body binding gold hardware, "Craig Chaquico" on truss-rod cover, current mfg.

MSR	$1,999	$979	$725	$600

CC275-12 - similar to the CC275, except in 12-string configuration and 6 per side headstock, mfg. 2002-current.

MSR	$1,799	$1,049	$750	$650

GRADING		100%	EXCELLENT	AVERAGE

C

AC375 - single rounded cutaway hollowed-out mahogany body, round soundhole, through body neck, 21-fret ebony fingerboard with pearl dot inlay, ebony bridge with black pins, natural peghead with 3-per-side tuners, Fishman Acoustic Matrix pickup, active electronics, gold hardware, available in Natural or custom color finishes, mfg. 2000-current.

MSR	$1,699	$899	$700	$550

CL450 CLASSICAL - single rounded cutaway hollowed-out mahogany body, AAA cedar top, round soundhole, through body neck, 21-fret ebony fingerboard with pearl dot inlay, ebony bridge with black pins, matching finish peghead with 3-per-side banjo-style tuners, Fishman Acoustic Matrix pickup, active electronics, gold hardware, available in Natural or custom color finishes, mfg. 2000-current.

MSR	$1,799	$949	$725	$550

ACOUSTIC ELECTRIC BASS

All acoustic bass models have a 34" scale, and are available in these standard colors: Classic White, Ferrari Red, Jet Black, Pearl Blue, Pearl Red, Pearl White, and a Tung Oil finish. Translucent finishes are optional

AC40 - offset double cutaway semi-hollow mahogany body, AAA Englemann spruce top, through-body mahogany neck, 24-fret ebony fingerboard with pearl dot inlay, fixed acoustic-style bridge, 4-on-a-side tuners, Carvin F40 acoustic bridge transducer, master volume control, bass/treble tone controls, current mfg.

MSR	$1,499	$799	$550	$425

This model has an optional fretless fingerboard (AC40F).

AC50 - similar to the AC40, except in a 5-string configuration, 3/2 per side tuners, current mfg.

MSR	$1,669	$849	$625	$475

This model has an optional fretless fingerboard (AC50F).

ACOUSTIC: COBALT SERIES

C250 - dreadnought body, AA solid spruce top, mahogany back & sides, tortise shell pickguard, 14/20 fret fingerboard, binding, 3-per-side tuners, chrome hardware, available in Natural finish, mfg. 2001-current.

MSR	$799	$399	$300	$175

Add $25 for solid cedar top (C250S).
Also available as a left-handed model (C-250LH).

C350 - dreadnought body, AA solid mahogany top/back/sides, tortise shell pickguard, 14/20 fret fingerboard, binding, 3-per-side tuners, chrome hardware, available in Natural finish, mfg. 2001-current.

MSR	$869	$439	$325	$190

C550 - dreadnought body, AA solid spruce top rosewood back/sides, tortise shell pickguard, 14/20 fret fingerboard, binding, 3-per-side tuners, chrome hardware, available in Natural finish, mfg. 2001-current.

MSR	$1,049	$539	$425	$250

C650 - dreadnought body, AA solid spruce top rosewood back/sides, tortise shell pickguard, 14/20 fret fingerboard, binding, 3-per-side tuners, chrome hardware, Fishman Matrix pickup and electronics, available in Natural finish, mfg. 2001-current.

MSR	$1,299	$659	$495	$325

C750 - dreadnought single cutaway body, AA solid spruce top, mahogany back/sides, tortise shell pickguard, 14/20 fret fingerboard, binding, 3-per-side tuners, chrome hardware, Fishman Matrix pickup and electronics, available in Natural finish, mfg. 2001-current.

MSR	$1,149	$589	$450	$285

C780 - Jumbo single cutaway body, AA solid spruce top, mahogany back/sides, tortise shell pickguard, 14/20 fret fingerboard, binding, 3-per-side tuners, chrome hardware, Fishman Matrix pickup and electronics, available in Natural finish, mfg. 2001-current.

MSR	$1,199	$599	$460	$295

C850 - dreadnought single cutaway body, AA solid spruce top, rosewood back/sides, tortise shell pickguard, 14/20 fret fingerboard, binding, 3-per-side tuners, chrome hardware, Fishman Matrix pickup and electronics, available in Natural finish, mfg. 2001-current.

MSR	$1,299	$669	$495	$325

This model is also available in a left-handed configuration.

Carelli Artist
courtesy Gary Sullivan

Carvin AC275
courtesy Carvin

C

C980 - jumbo single cutaway body, AA solid spruce top, rosewood back/sides, tortise shell pickguard, 14/20 fret fingerboard, elaborate binding and inlays, 3-per-side tuners, gold hardware, Fishman Matrix pickup and electronics, available in Natural finish, mfg. 2001-current.

MSR	$1,599		$799	$600	$475

C980-12 - similar to the C980, except in 12-string configuration, 6-per-side tuners, new 2003.

MSR	N/A		$869	$650	$500

CATALINA

See chapter on House Brands.

This trademark has been identified as a House Brand of the Abercrombie & Fitch company, (Source: Willie G. Moseley, *Stellas & Stratocasters*).

CATALUNA

Instruments currently built in Taiwan, Republic of China. Distributed by Reliance International Corporation of Taiwan, Republic of China.

Reliance International's Cataluna instruments are entry level to medium quality acoustic guitars. The Apex series features 4 traditional style Dreadnought style acoustics, and two classical acoustics. Apex series instruments feature spruce tops, Nato backs/sides/necks, and rosewood fingerboards.

CELEBRITY

Instruments previously built in Korea, and distributed by the Kaman Music Corporation of Bloomfield, Connecticut during the late 1980s.

The Celebrity line of bowl back guitars was introduced in 1983 as a Korean-built entry level introduction to the American-built Ovation line. Celebrity models offer similar design features, and a variety of options as their overseas production saves money on their retail price. The Celebrity trademark was also applied to a number of solid body electrics based on popular American designs.

CFOX

Current trademark manufactured by Charles Fox Guitars. Instruments are currently built in Healdsburg, California since 1997.

Charles Fox Guitars debuted at the 1998 NAMM industry show in January, and introduced the newest line of high quality handcrafted acoustic guitar models. While the company is new, the luthier and designer is not – Charles Fox has a worldwide reputation as a luthier, educator, and consultant in the field of guitar building. The CFox guitar line is the product of Fox's 30 years experience as an artist, craftsman, and teacher.

Charles Fox (b. 1943) did his undergraduate work at the Art Institute of Chicago and completed his postgraduate work at Northwestern University in 1966. Fox began building his own guitars in 1968, and since then has worked both as a custom guitar builder and as the head of his own guitar production shop. In the late 1970s and early 1980s, Fox's GRD Guitars (see GRD) were among the first instruments to define the market for high end electric guitars.

In 1973, Fox founded the first school for guitar builders in North America, the Guitar Research and Design Center. In recent years Fox has founded and directed the American School of Lutherie in Healdsburg, California; and has been a founder and educational coordinator of the Healdsburg Guitar Festival.

ACOUSTIC

All 4 of the CFox models are available in 3 different quality series. Left-handed configurations are available at no extra charge. For custom inlay work or Brazilian rosewood back/sides, please contact Charles Fox Guitars directly (see Trademark Index).

Add $100 for Engelmann Spruce soundboard. Add $150 for Western Red Cedar soundboard. Add $175 for extended fretboard. Add $250 for German Spruce soundboard. Add $350 for cocobola back and sides. Add $400 for figured maple back and sides. Add $400 for wood binding. Add $500 for wood binding, cutaway configuration. Add $500 for koa back and sides. Add $500 for standard cutaway. Add $700 for abalone trim. Add $750 for compound cutaway.

C CONCERT (NAPA SERIES) - solid AAA Sitka spruce top, carbon-graphite reinforced Honduran mahogany neck, 25 1/2" scale, Honduran mahogany back/sides, black top binding, round soundhole with rosette, 14/21-fret ebony fingerboard, ebony peghead overlay with mother-of-pearl logo, ebony bridge with ebony bridgepins, ebony end pin, 3-per-side nickel Grover tuners, available in Natural finish, Total Length 39 3/4", Body Width 14 13/16" (lower bout), Body Thickness 3 1/4" (heel) to 4" (end), mfg. 1998-current.

MSR	$2,800

C Concert (Sonoma Series) - similar to the C Concert (Napa Series), except features Indian rosewood back/sides, grained ivoroid top binding, grained ivoroid neck/headstock binding, abalone rosette, ebony bridgepins with abalone dots, 3-per-side chrome Schaller tuners, available in Natural finish, mfg. 1998-current.

MSR	$3,200

C Concert (Frisco Series) - similar to the C Concert (Napa Series), except features master grade Sitka spruce top, Indian rosewood back/ sides, ebony end graft, grained ivoroid body binding, grained ivoroid neck/headstock binding, abalone rosette, ebony bridgepins with

C

abalone dots, 3-per-side gold Schaller tuners with ebony buttons, available in Natural finish, mfg. 1998-current.

> MSR $3,700

D DREADNOUGHT (NAPA SERIES) - solid AAA Sitka spruce top, carbon-graphite reinforced Honduran mahogany neck, 25.5" scale, Honduran mahogany back/sides, black top binding, round soundhole with rosette, 14/21-fret ebony fingerboard, ebony peghead overlay with mother-of-pearl logo, ebony bridge with ebony bridgepins, ebony end pin, 3-per-side nickel Grover tuners, available in Natural finish, total length 40 7/8", body width 15 5/8" (lower bout), body thickness 3 7/8" (heel) to 4 7/8" (end), mfg. 1998-current.

> MSR $2,800

D Dreadnought (Sonoma Series) - similar to the D Dreadnought (Napa Series), except features Indian rosewood back/sides, grained ivoroid top binding, grained ivoroid neck/headstock binding, abalone rosette, ebony bridgepins with abalone dots, 3-per-side chrome Schaller tuners, available in Natural finish, mfg. 1998-current.

> MSR $3,200

D Dreadnought (Frisco Series) - similar to the D Dreadnought (Napa Series), except features master grade Sitka spruce top, Indian rosewood back/sides, ebony end graft, grained ivoroid body binding, grained ivoroid neck/headstock binding, abalone rosette, ebony bridgepins with abalone dots, 3-per-side gold Schaller tuners with ebony buttons, available in Natural finish, mfg. 1998-current.

> MSR $3,700

H HYBRID (NAPA SERIES) - solid AAA Sitka spruce top, carbon-graphite reinforced Honduran mahogany neck, 25 1/2" scale, Honduran mahogany back/sides, black top binding, round soundhole with rosette, 14/21-fret ebony fingerboard, ebony peghead overlay with mother-of-pearl logo, ebony bridge with ebony bridgepins, ebony end pin, 3-per-side nickel Grover tuners, available in Natural finish, total length 40 5/8", body width 14 7/8" (lower bout), body thickness 3 1/4" (heel) to 4" (end), mfg. 1998-current.

> MSR $2,800

H Hybrid (Sonoma Series) - similar to the H Hybrid (Napa Series), except features Indian rosewood back/sides, grained ivoroid top binding, grained ivoroid neck/headstock binding, abalone rosette, ebony bridgepins with abalone dots, 3-per-side chrome Schaller tuners, available in Natural finish, mfg. 1998-current.

> MSR $3,200

H Hybrid (Frisco Series) - similar to the H Hybrid (Napa Series), except features master grade Sitka spruce top, Indian rosewood back/sides, ebony end graft, grained ivoroid body binding, grained ivoroid neck/headstock binding, abalone rosette, ebony bridgepins with abalone dots, 3-per-side gold Schaller tuners with ebony buttons, available in Natural finish, mfg. 1998-current.

> MSR $3,700

H-12 HYBRID (NAPA SERIES) - solid AAA Sitka spruce top, carbon-graphite reinforced Honduran mahogany neck, 25 1/2" scale, Honduran mahogany back/sides, black top binding, round soundhole with rosette, 12/19-fret ebony fingerboard, ebony peghead overlay with mother-of-pearl logo, ebony bridge with ebony bridgepins, ebony end pin, 3-per-side nickel Grover tuners, available in Natural finish, total length 39 1/8", body width 14 7/8" (lower bout), body thickness 3 1/4" (heel) to 4" (end), mfg. 1998-current.

> MSR $2,800

H-12 Hybrid (Sonoma Series) - similar to the H-12 Hybrid (Napa Series), except features Indian rosewood back/sides, grained ivoroid top binding, grained ivoroid neck/headstock binding, abalone rosette, ebony bridgepins with abalone dots, 3-per-side chrome Schaller tuners, available in Natural finish, mfg. 1998-current.

> MSR $3,200

H-12 Hybrid (Frisco Series) - similar to the H-12 Hybrid (Napa Series), except features master grade Sitka spruce top, Indian rosewood back/sides, ebony end graft, grained ivoroid body binding, grained ivoroid neck/headstock binding, abalone rosette, ebony bridgepins with abalone dots, 3-per-side gold Schaller tuners with ebony buttons, available in Natural finish, mfg. 1998-current.

> MSR $3,700

SJ SMALL JUMBO (NAPA SERIES) - solid AAA Sitka spruce top, carbon-graphite reinforced Honduran mahogany neck, 25 1/2" scale, Honduran mahogany back/sides, black top binding, round soundhole with rosette, 14/21-fret ebony fingerboard, ebony peghead overlay with mother-of-pearl logo, ebony bridge with ebony bridgepins, ebony end pin, 3-per-side nickel Grover tuners, available in Natural finish, total length 41 7/8", body width 16 1/4" (lower bout), body thickness 3 1/2" (heel) to 4 1/4" (end), mfg. 1998-current.

> MSR $2,800

C

SJ Small Jumbo (Sonoma Series) - similar to the SJ Small Jumbo (Napa Series), except features Indian rosewood back/sides, grained ivoroid top binding, grained ivoroid neck/headstock binding, abalone rosette, ebony bridgepins with abalone dots, 3-per-side chrome Schaller tuners, available in Natural finish, mfg. 1998-current.

MSR   **$3,200**

SJ Small Jumbo (Frisco Series) - similar to the SJ Small Jumbo (Napa Series), except features master grade Sitka spruce top, Indian rosewood back/sides, ebony end graft, grained ivoroid body binding, grained ivoroid neck/headstock binding, abalone rosette, ebony bridgepins with abalone dots, 3-per-side gold Schaller tuners with ebony buttons, available in Natural finish, mfg. 1998-current.

MSR   **$3,700**

CHAPIN

Instruments currently built in San Jose, California.

Handcrafted Chapin guitars feature carefully thought out designs that provide ergonomic comfort and a wide palette of tones. All Chapin guitars are handcrafted by luthiers Bill Chapin and Fred Campbell; all guitars feature the Campbell/Chapin locking dovetail set-in neck joint.

The Chapin Insight guitar inspection camera features a small-bodied camera on a flexible mount that allows the luthier/repairman an inside view of the acoustic guitar to help solve internal problems. This low-light camera features 3.6 mm lens for ultra close crack inspection, and has an RCA output that feeds directly into a VCR or camcorder for video documentation. The Insight (list $349) operates on a 9-volt battery – so it is mobile as well. The importance to collectors? Now there is a tool for proper guitar authentication: the internal signatures and dates of an acoustic (or semi-hollow body) guitar can be read in seconds – and right at the guitar show, if necessary! For current information on Chapin's electric models, please refer to the *Blue Book of Electric Guitars*.

ACOUSTIC ELECTRIC

All of Chapin's models are available with additional options such as choice of wood(s), pickups, or hardware (call for price quote). Retail prices listed below reflect the base price.

Chapin's acoustic electric **Eagle** (list $1,850) is available in nylon or steel string configuration. It features semi-solid body design with tuned acoustic chambers, spruce (or maple) top, rosewood acoustic-style bridge or electric-style bridge with piezo pickups (steel string model only), and Gilbert or Sperzel tuners. The **Eagle Custom** model has a figured redwood or master-grade spruce top, interchangeable ebony soundports, figured wood binding, violin-style purfling, acoustic transducer, and Gilbert tuners with abalone inlay (retail list is $3,475).

CHARVEL

Trademark previously manufactured in Korea until 1999. The Charvel trademark was established in 1978 by the Charvel Manufacturing Company. Previously distributed until 1999 by Jackson/Charvel Guitar Company (Akai Musical Instruments) of Fort Worth, Texas. Previously produced in the U.S. between 1978-1985; later, (post-1985) production was based in the U.S., Japan, and Korea.

In the late 1970s, Wayne Charvel's Guitar Repair shop in Azusa, California acquired a reputation for making custom high quality bodies and necks. Grover Jackson began working at the shop in 1977, and a year later bought out Charvel and moved the company to San Dimas. Jackson debuted the Charvel custom guitars at the 1979 NAMM show, and the first catalog depicting the bolt-neck beauties and custom options arrived in 1981.

The standard models from Charvel Manufacturing carried a list price between $880 to $955, and the amount of custom options was staggering. In 1983, the Charvel company began offering neck-through models under the Jackson trademark.

Grover Jackson licensed the Charvel trademark to the International Music Corporation (IMC) in 1985; the company was sold to them a year later. In late 1986, production facilities were moved to Ontario, California. Distribution eventually switched from Charvel/Jackson to the Jackson/Charvel Guitar company, currently a branch of the Akai Musical Instruments company. As the years went by and the Charvel line expanded, its upper end models were phased out and moved into the Jackson line (which had been the Charvel/Jackson Company's line of custom-made instruments) and were gaining more popularity. For example, the **Charvel Avenger** (mfg. 1991 to 1992), became the **Jackson Rhoads EX Pro** (mfg. 1992 to date). For further details, see the Jackson guitars section in this edition.

In 1988, Charvel sent a crew of luthiers to Japan for a year or so to cross-train the Japanese builders on building methods for custom built guitars. The resulting custom instruments had a retail list price between $1,000 to $1,300. U.S. custom-built guitars have a four digit serial number, the Japanese custom built models have a six digit serial number. Numbers may be prefaced with a "C," which may stand for custom made (this point has not been completely verified).

By the early 1990s, the only Charvel models left were entry level Strat-style electrics and Dreadnought and jumbo-style (full bodied and cutaways) acoustic guitars. In the late 1990s, even the electrics were phased out in favor of the acoustic and acoustic/electric models. During 1999, instruments with the Charvel trademark had ceased production, and Wayne Charvel began building a new line of instruments utilizing the Wayne Guitars trademark, (Early Charvel history courtesy Baker Rorick, Guitar Shop magazine; additional information courtesy Roland Lozier, Lozier Piano & Music).

ACOUSTIC/ACOUSTIC ELECTRIC

125S - dreadnought style, solid spruce top, round soundhole, 7-stripe bound body/rosette, mahogany back/sides/neck, 14/20-fret bound rosewood fingerboard with abalone dot inlay, rosewood bridge with white black pins, rosewood veneered peghead with pearl logo inlay, 3-per-side chrome tuners, available in Natural or Tobacco Sunburst finishes, mfg. 1994-96.

               N/A   **$325**   **$200**
               Last MSR was $595.

GRADING	100%	EXCELLENT	AVERAGE

125SE - similar to 125S, except has transducer bridge pickup, 3-band EQ, available in Natural or Tobacco Sunburst finishes, mfg. 1994-96.

N/A	$375	$250

Last MSR was $695.

150SC - single round cutaway dreadnought style, solid spruce top, round soundhole, 7-stripe bound body/rosette, rosewood back/sides, mahogany neck, 14/20-fret bound rosewood fingerboard with abalone dot inlay, rosewood bridge with white black pins, rosewood veneered peghead with pearl logo inlay, 3-per-side chrome tuners, available in Natural or Tobacco Sunburst finishes, mfg. 1994-96.

N/A	$325	$200

Last MSR was $595.

150SEC - similar to 150SC, except has transducer bridge pickup, 3-band EQ, available in Natural or Tobacco Sunburst finishes, mfg. 1994-96.

N/A	$375	$250

Last MSR was $695.

325SL - double offset cutaway asymmetrical style, spruce top, offset wedge soundhole, bound body and soundhole, nato back/sides/neck, 22-fret rosewood fingerboard with offset abalone dot inlay, rosewood bridge with white pearl dot pins, rosewood veneer with abalone Charvel logo, 3-per-side chrome tuners, transducer bridge pickup, 3-band EQ, active electronics, available in Black, Bright Red and Turquoise finishes, mfg. 1992-94.

N/A	$275	$175

Last MSR was $500.

325SLX - similar to 325SL, except has figured maple top, rosewood back/sides, bound fingerboard with shark fin inlay, bound peghead, active electronics with built-in chorus, available in Cherry Sunburst, Tobacco Sunburst, or Trans. Red finishes.

N/A	$350	$225

Last MSR was $600.

Charvel 125 S
courtesy Charvel

525 - single round cutaway dreadnought style, spruce top, round soundhole, 5-stripe bound body and rosette, mahogany arched back/sides/neck, 22-fret bound rosewood fingerboard with pearl dot inlay, rosewood bridge with white black dot pins, bound peghead with abalone Charvel logo inlay, 3-per-side chrome tuners, available in Cherry Sunburst, Metallic Black, Natural, or Tobacco Sunburst, disc. 1994.

N/A	$225	$150

Last MSR was $400.

525D - similar to 525, except has transducer bridge pickup with 3-band EQ, available in Metallic Black, Natural or Tobacco Sunburst finishes, disc. 1994.

N/A	$225	$150

Last MSR was $500.

550 - dreadnought style, spruce top, round soundhole, black pickguard, 3-stripe bound body/rosette, mahogany back/sides/neck, 25.6" scale, 14/20-fret rosewood fingerboard with pearl dot inlay, rosewood bridge with black white dot pins, rosewood veneered peghead with pearl logo inlay, 3-per-side chrome tuners, available in Mahogany or Natural finishes, mfg. 1994-2000.

$200	$135	$95

Last MSR was $275.

Add $20 for single round cutaway (Model 550C), available in Natural finish only.

550E - similar to 550, except has transducer bridge pickup, 3-band EQ, available in Natural finish, mfg. 1994-2000.

$325	$200	$125

Last MSR was $450.

Add $25 for single round cutaway (Model 550CE), available in Natural finish only.

625 - single round cutaway jumbo style, spruce top, round soundhole, 5-stripe bound body and rosette, nato back/sides, mahogany neck, 25.6" scale, 20-fret rosewood fingerboard with abalone dot inlay, rosewood bridge with white black dot pins, rosewood veneer on peghead with abalone Charvel logo inlay, 3-per-side gold tuners, available in Cherry Sunburst, Metallic Black, Natural, and Tobacco Sunburst finishes, mfg. 1992-2000.

$250	$175	$100

Last MSR was $365.

In 1997, abalone inlay was changed to faux abalone.

Charvel 550
courtesy Charvel

GRADING		100%	EXCELLENT	AVERAGE

625C - similar to 625, except has abalone bound body/rosette, rosewood back/sides, 24-fret bound extended fingerboard, abalone dot pins, bound peghead, transducer bridge pickup, 3-band EQ, active electronics, mfg. 1992-2000.

		$450	$325	$225

Last MSR was $645.

625C-12 - similar to 625, except has 12-string configuration, abalone bound body/rosette, rosewood back/sides, 24-fret bound extended fingerboard, abalone dot pins, bound peghead, 6-per-side tuners, transducer bridge pickup, 3-band EQ, active electronics, available in Metallic Black, Natural, or Tobacco Sunburst finishes, mfg. 1994-2000.

		$525	$350	$250

Last MSR was $795.

625D - similar to 625, except has transducer bridge pickup, 3-band EQ, active electronics, disc.

		$350	$235	$150

Last MSR was $475.

625F - similar to 625, except has figured maple top, available in Tobacco Sunburst, Transparent Black and Trans. Red, mfg. 1994-95.

		$475	$325	$225

Last MSR was $650.

725 - jumbo style, solid spruce top, round soundhole, 7-stripe bound body/rosette, mahogany back/sides/neck, 14/20-fret rosewood fingerboard with pearl offset dot inlay, rosewood bridge with white black pins, rosewood veneered peghead with pearl logo inlay, 3-per-side chrome tuners, available in Natural finish, mfg. 1994-96.

		N/A	$275	$175

Last MSR was $495.

725E - similar to 725, except has transducer bridge pickup, 3-band EQ, available in Natural finish, mfg. 1994-96.

		N/A	$325	$200

Last MSR was $595.

750E - jumbo style, solid spruce top, round soundhole, 7-stripe bound body/rosette, figured maple back/sides, mahogany neck, 14/20-fret rosewood fingerboard with pearl offset dot inlay, rosewood bridge with white black pins, figured maple veneered peghead with pearl logo inlay, 3-per-side gold tuners, available in Natural finish. Mfg. 1994 to 1996.

		N/A	$375	$225

Last MSR was $695.

ATX - single cutaway hollow mahogany body, bound maple top, maple neck, 24-fret rosewood fingerboard with offset pearl dot inlay, strings through rosewood bridge, six on side one chrome tuners, Fishman transducer bridge pickup, volume/3-band EQ controls, available in Black, Deep Metallic Blue, Dark Metallic Red, or Deep Metallic Violet finishes, mfg. 1993-96.

		N/A	$475	$300

Last MSR was $895.

ATX Trans - similar to ATX, except has figured maple top, available in Tobacco Sunburst, Trans. Black, or Trans. Violet finishes, disc. 1996.

		N/A	$550	$325

Last MSR was $995.

CM-100 - dreadnought style, cedar top, round soundhole, multibound body, 3-stripe rosette, figured mahogany back/sides, mahogany neck, 14/20-fret bound rosewood fingerboard with pearl dot inlay, ebony bridge with white black dot pins, bound rosewood veneered peghead with pearl logo inlay, 3-per-side chrome tuners, available in Natural finish, mfg. 1994 only.

		N/A	$450	$300

Last MSR was $895.

CM-400 LIMITED EDITION - jumbo style, solid spruce top, round soundhole, maple bound/abalone purfling body, abalone rosette, jacaranda back/sides, mahogany neck, 14/20-fret ebony fingerboard with pearl cloud inlay, ebony bridge with black abalone dot pins, abalone bound rosewood veneered peghead with abalone logo inlay, 3-per-side gold tuners, available in Natural finish, mfg. 1994 only.

		N/A	$1,950	$1,250

Last MSR was $3,995.

ACOUSTIC ELECTRIC BASS

425 SL - offset double rounded cutaway asymmetrical style, spruce top, offset wedge soundhole, bound body and soundhole, nato back/sides/neck, 22-fret rosewood fingerboard with offset abalone inlay, rosewood bridge with abalone dot inlay, abalone Charvel logo peghead inlay, 2 per side chrome tuners, transducer bridge pickup, 3-band EQ, active electronics, available in Bright Red, Metallic Black, or Turquoise finishes, mfg. 1992-94.

		N/A	$275	$175

Last MSR was $550.

425SLX - similar to 425SL, except has figured maple top, rosewood back/sides, bound fingerboard/peghead, active electronics with built-in chorus, available in Cherry Sunburst, Tobacco Sunburst, or Trans. Red finishes, mfg. 1992-94.

		N/A	$325	$200

Last MSR was $650.

ATX BASS - single cutaway hollow mahogany body, bound maple top, maple neck, 22-fret rosewood fingerboard with offset pearl dot inlay, strings through rosewood bridge, 4-on-a-side chrome tuners, volume/3-band EQ controls, available in Black, Deep Metallic Blue, or Deep Metallic Violet finishes, mfg. 1993-96.

	N/A	$500	$300

Last MSR was $995.

ATX Bass Trans - similar to ATX Bass, except has figured maple top, available in Tobacco Sunburst, Trans. Black, or Trans. Violet finishes, disc.

	N/A	$550	$350

Last MSR was $1,095.

CHARVETTE

Instruments previously produced in Korea from 1989 to 1994. Charvette, an entry level line to Charvel, was distributed by the International Music Corporation of Ft. Worth, Texas.

The Charvette trademark was distributed by the Charvel/Jackson company as a good quality entry level guitar based on their original Jackson USA superstrat designs. Where the Charvel and Jackson models may sport Jackson pickups, Charvettes invariably had Charvel pickups to support a company/product unity.

ACOUSTIC ELECTRIC

500 - single round cutaway flattop style, maple top, plectrum shape soundhole, one stripe bound body/rosette, bolt-on maple neck, 22-fret rosewood fingerboard with pearl dot inlay, rosewood bridge with black pins, 6-on-a-side tuners, black hardware, 6 piezo bridge pickups, volume/treble/bass controls, active electronics, available in Ferrari Red, Midnite Black, or Snow White finish, mfg. 1991-92.

	N/A	$250	$125

Last MSR was $495.

CHATWORTH

Instruments currently built in England.

Luthier Andy Smith is currently building high quality guitars.

Charvel 625 C
courtesy Charvel

CHRIS

See chapter on House Brands.

This trademark has been identified as a separate budget line of guitars from the Jackson-Guldan company of Columbus, Ohio, (Source: Willie G. Moseley, *Stellas & Stratocasters*).

CHRIS LARKIN CUSTOM GUITARS

Instruments currently built in Ireland beginning 1977.

Since 1977, Chris Larkin Custom Guitars have been based at Castlegregory, County Kerry, on the west coast of Ireland. Chris Larkin works alone hand building a range of original designs to custom order to a very high level of quality from the finest available materials. The range is wide ("it stops me from becoming bored!") including acoustic, electric, archtop, and semi-acoustic guitars; acoustic, electric, semi-acoustic, and upright stick basses; and archtop mandolins. One-off designs are also built and Chris admits to having made some very high spec copies when offered enough money, (Company information courtesy Chris Larkin, Chris Larkin Custom Guitars).

As each instrument is handmade to order, the customer has a wide choice of woods, colors, fret type, fingerboard radius, neck profile, and dimensions within the design to enable the finished instrument to better suit the player. All Larkin instruments from 1980 on have a shamrock as the headstock inlay. Sales are worldwide through distributors in some areas, or direct from the maker.

SERIALIZATION

Since 1982, a simple six digit system has been used. The first two digits indicate the year, the next two the month, and the final two the sequence in that month. For example, 970103 was the third instrument in January 1997. Before 1982 the numbers are a bit chaotic! Chris Larkin has full documentation for almost every instrument that he has ever built, so he can supply a history from the serial number in most cases.

ACOUSTIC

ASAP acoustic flattop models are lightly built for performances with an emphasis on balanced tone. This model is available in various configurations such as a nylon string, a 12-string, an acoustic bass model, and a jumbo. Prices run from $2,400 up to $2,890. All models feature a Highlander pickup and preamp system, and gold tuners.

ASAS archtop guitars are available in two acoustic models and one semi-acoustic (both acoustic models feature fingerboard mounted custom made humbuckers). All models are built from European spruce and highly figured maple, and have multiple binding on body, neck, headstock, and scratchplate. The archtops are available with a Florentine cutaway ($3,785) and Venetian cutaway ($4,000). The ASA semi-hollow (list $3,440) has a cedar sustain block running from neck to tail, 2 Schaller G50 humbuckers, and a stop tailpiece. Prices are currently listed on their web site, but they are in Euro's. You need to use a conversion system to figure out your respective price.

Charvel 725 E
courtesy Charvel

CIMARRON GUITARS

Instruments currently built in Ridgeway, Colorado beginning 1978.

In addition to the handcrafted acoustic models, luthier John Walsh produces electric semi-acoustic guitars as well.

Early in his career, it was estimated that Walsh produced 24 acoustic guitars a year. The acoustic guitar models featured Sitka spruce tops, maple or mahogany necks, and ebony fingerboards on standard models to custom configurations. The thinline Model One has bent wood sides, Rio Grande pickups, Sperzel tuners, and numerous custom options. Contact Walsh for retail prices (see Trademark Index).

CITATION

Instruments previously produced in Japan.

The U.S. distributor of Citation guitars was the Grossman company of Cleveland, Ohio, (Source: Michael Wright, *Guitar Stories,* Volume One).

CITRON, HARVEY

Instruments currently built in Woodstock, New York beginning 1983.

Luthier Harvey Citron has been building high quality, innovative, solid body guitars since the early 1970s. Citron, a noted guitarist and singer, co-founded the Veillette-Citron company in 1975. During the partnership's eight years, they were well-known for the quality of their handcrafted electric guitars, basses, and baritone guitars. Citron also designed the **X-92 Breakaway** model for Guild and was a regular contributing writer for several guitar magazines.

Citron instruments are available direct from Harvey Citron, or through a limited number of dealers. Citron maintains a current price list and descriptions of his models at his web site. His **Basic Guitar Set-Up and Repair** instructional video is available from Homespun Tapes; Citron's cleverly designed **Guitar Stand** has a list price of $399.

ACOUSTIC ELECTRIC

All acoustic electric models are available with or without a headstock at no additional charge.

Add $450 for MIDI capability (acoustic electric models).

AEG - offset double cutaway body, 25 1/2" scale, 6-on-a-side headstock, magnetic pickup/piezo bridge transducers, active electronics, volume/blend/tone controls, current mfg.

> **MSR**   **$3,600**

AEG-3 - similar to the AEG except has 3 mag. pickups, current mfg.

> **MSR**   **$3,800**

ACOUSTIC ELECTRIC BASS

All acoustic electric bass models are available with or without a headstock or a fretless fingerboard at no additional charge.

A 5 - offset double cutaway body, 35" scale, 5-string configuration, 5-on-a-side headstock, magnetic pickup/piezo bridge transducers, on-board electronics, volume/blend/tone controls, mfg. 1998-2001.

> **Last MSR was $2,799.**

AE4 - offset double cutaway body, 34" scale, bolt-on neck, 4-on-a-side headstock, magnetic pickup/piezo bridge transducers, active electronics, volume/blend/tone controls located on upper bass horn, current mfg.

> **MSR**   **$3,800**

AE5 - similar to the AE4, except has 35" scale and 5-string configuration, current mfg.

> **MSR**   **$4,100**

COLLINGS GUITARS

Instruments currently built in Austin, Texas beginning 1986. Distributed by Collings Guitars, Inc. of Austin, Texas.

Luthier Bill Collings was born in Michigan, and raised in Ohio. In 1973, Collings moved from Ohio to Houston, Texas, and originally did guitar repair work. Colling's first flattop guitars date from this period. In 1980, Collings relocated his workshop to Austin, Texas. In addition to his flattop guitars, he also began building archtop guitars. Collings Guitars was founded in 1986. Today, the company maintains tight quality control over their production, and consumer demand remains high, (Company information courtesy Collings Guitars).

LABEL IDENTIFICATION

1975-1979: Models do not have a label; instead, there is a signature in ink on the inside back strip.

1979-1984: Light brown oval label with brown ink marked *Bill Collings, Luthier* and illustrated with logs floating in a river.

1984-1989: Darker brown oval label with brown ink marked *Bill Collings, Luthier* and illustrated with logs and guitars floating in a river.

1989 to date: Light brown oval label with black ink marked *Collings, Austin, Texas.*

ARCHTOP SERIALIZATION

Before 1991: Archtops before 1991 had their own separate serialization.

1991 to date: Archtops are now numbered with a two part serial number. The first number indicates the archtop as part of the general company serialization, and the second number indicates the ranking in the archtop series list.

GRADING **100%** **EXCELLENT** **AVERAGE**

FLATTOP SERIALIZATION

1975-1987: Guitars do not posses a serial number. Most are marked with a handwritten date on the underside of the top. Some guitars from 1987 may have a serial number.

1988 to date: Guitars began a consecutive numbering series that began with number 175. The serial number is stamped on the neck block.

GENERAL INFORMATION & OPTIONS

Collings guitars are offered with a number of options, such as abalone top border inlays, custom inlays, tuning machines, wood binding, and body wood, including Brazilian rosewood (please call for prices and availability). Each custom feature that is on a Collins needs to be assessed separately. All models are available with these following options:

Add $100 for Engelmann spruce top. Add $175 for abalone rosette. Add $350 for koa top. Add $250 for left-handed configuration. Add $250 for German spruce top. Add $400 for sunburst top. Add $550 for maple body and neck. Add $600 for rounded single cutaway ($675 on Herringbone Model). Add $1,350 for koa back and sides. Add $150 for headstock binding. Add $150 for fingerboard binding.

ACOUSTIC: ARCHTOP SERIES

In addition to their well-known flattop acoustic models, the Collings handcrafted **Archtop** model is offered in a 17" wide body ($14,500) and an 18" wide body ($15,500). Prior to 1997, a 16" wide body was offered (original retail list was $10,000), but has since been discontinued.

ACOUSTIC: BABY SERIES

BABY - 3/4 size dreadnought style, spruce top, ivoroid binding, herringbone purfling, round soundhole, ivoroid/wood stripe rosette, tortoise style pickguard, East Indian rosewood back/sides, mahogany neck, 24 1/8" scale, 14/20-fret bound ebony fingerboard with pearl diamond/square inlay, ebony bridge with white black dot pins, rosewood veneer on bound peghead with mother-of-pearl logo inlay, 3-per-side nickel Waverly tuners, available in Natural finish, total length 36 1/2", body length 17 1/8", body width 12 1/2", body thickness 3 15/16", mfg. 1997-current.

MSR	**$3,050**		
	$2,750	**$1,995**	**$1,475**

ACOUSTIC: C SERIES

C-10 - folk style, spruce top, round soundhole, tortoise style pickguard, ivoroid bound body/rosette, mahogany back/sides/neck, 25 1/2" scale, 14/20-fret bound ebony fingerboard, ebony bridge with white black dot pins, rosewood veneer on bound peghead with mother-of-pearl logo, 3-per-side gold Kluson tuners, available in Natural finish, total length 39 1/2", body length 19 1/4", body width 14.75", body thickness 4 1/4", current mfg.

MSR	**$2,850**		
	$2,575	**$1,875**	**$1,425**

In 1992, this model was also available in Blonde, Blue, Midnight Black, and Red finishes with a pearloid pickguard and pearloid headstock veneer. In 1995, nickel Schaller mini-tuners replaced original part/design.

C-10 Deluxe - similar to C-10, except has East Indian rosewood back/sides, pearl dot fingerboard inlay, ebony peghead veneer with pearl logo inlay, gold Schaller mini tuners, available in Natural finish, current mfg.

MSR	**$3,300**		
	$2,975	**$2,150**	**$1,700**

In 1995, nickel Schaller mini-tuners replaced original part/design.

C-100 - similar to C-10, except has larger body dimensions, body length 20 1/8", body width 16", body thickness 4 1/2", disc. 1995.

	N/A	**$1,700**	**$1,100**
		Last MSR was $2,225.	

C-100 Deluxe - similar to C-10 Deluxe, except has larger body dimensions, body length 20 1/8", body width 16", body thickness 4 1/2", disc. 1995.

	N/A	**$1,900**	**$1,250**
		Last MSR was $2,725.	

CJ COLLINGS JUMBO - folk style, spruce top, round soundhole, tortoise style pickguard, double black/white strip purfling, black/white strip rosette, East Indian back/sides, mahogany neck, 25 1/2" scale, 14/20-fret ivoroid bound ebony fingerboard with pearl dot markers, ebony bridge with white black dot pins, ebony veneer on ivoroid bound peghead with mother-of-pearl logo, 3-per-side nickel Waverly tuners, available in Natural finish, total length 40 1/4", body length 20 1/8", body width 16", body thickness 4 7/8", mfg. 1995-current.

MSR	**$3,450**		
	$3,100	**$2,275**	**$1,750**

C

GRADING	100%	EXCELLENT	AVERAGE

ACOUSTIC: D SERIES

D-1 - dreadnought style, spruce top, round soundhole, tortoise pickguard, 3-stripe bound body/rosette, mahogany back/sides/neck, 25.5" scale, 14/20-fret bound ebony fingerboard, ebony bridge with white black dot pins, rosewood veneer on bound peghead with pearl logo inlay, 3-per-side chrome Gotoh tuners, available in Natural finish, total length 40 1/4", body length 20", body width 15 5/8", body thickness 4 7/8", current mfg.

MSR	$2,900		$2,600	$1,900	$1,500

In 1995, nickel Waverly tuners replaced original part/design.

D-2 - similar to D-1, except has Indian rosewood back/sides, pearl diamond/square peghead inlay, disc. 1995.

			N/A	$1,700	$1,050

Last MSR was $2,300.

D-2H - dreadnought style, spruce top, ivoroid binding, herringbone purfling, round soundhole, ivoroid/wood stripe rosette, tortoise style pickguard, East Indian rosewood back/sides, mahogany neck, 14/20-fret bound ebony fingerboard with pearl diamond/square inlay, ebony bridge with white black dot pins, rosewood veneer on bound peghead with mother-of-pearl logo inlay, 3-per-side nickel Waverly tuners, available in Natural finish, current mfg.

MSR	$3,050		$2,750	$1,995	$1,500

D-3 - similar to D-2H, except has abalone purfling/rosette, no fingerboard inlays, and gold Waverly tuners, current mfg.

MSR	$3,700		$3,350	$2,425	$1,875

DS-2H 12-FRET - dreadnought style, spruce top, ivoroid binding, herringbone purfling, round soundhole, ivoroid/wood stripe rosette, tortoise style pickguard, East Indian rosewood back/sides, mahogany neck, 25 1/2" scale, 12/20-fret bound ebony fingerboard with pearl diamond/square inlay, ebony bridge with white black dot pins, rosewood veneer on bound slotted peghead with mother-of-pearl logo inlay, 3-per-side nickel Waverly tuners, available in Natural finish, total length 40 1/8", body length 20 7/8", body width 15 5/8", body thickness 4 1/8", mfg. 1995-current.

MSR	$3,450		$3,100	$2,250	$1,750

ACOUSTIC: OM SERIES

OM-1 - grand concert style, spruce top, round soundhole, tortoise pickguard, 3-stripe bound body/rosette, mahogany back/sides/neck, 25 1/2" scale, 14/20-fret bound ebony fingerboard with pearl dot markers, ebony bridge with white black dot pins, rosewood veneer on bound peghead with mother-of-pearl logo inlay, 3-per-side chrome Gotoh tuners, available in Natural finish, total length 39 1/2", body length 19 1/4", body width 15", body thickness 4 1/8", current mfg.

MSR	$2,900		$2,625	$1,900	$1,475

In 1995, nickel Waverly tuners replaced original part/design.

OM-2 - similar to OM-1, except has Indian rosewood back/sides, pearl diamond/square peghead inlay, disc. 1995.

			N/A	$1,650	$1,050

Last MSR was $2,300.

OM-2H - grand concert style, spruce top, ivoroid binding, herringbone purfling, round soundhole, ivoroid/wood stripe rosette, tortoise style pickguard, East Indian rosewood back/sides, mahogany neck, 14/20-fret bound ebony fingerboard with pearl diamond/square inlay, ebony bridge with white black dot pins, rosewood veneer on bound peghead with mother-of-pearl logo inlay, 3-per-side nickel Waverly tuners, available in Natural finish, current mfg.

MSR	$3,050		$2,750	$1,995	$1,500

OM-3 - similar to OM-2H, except has abalone purfling/rosette, no fingerboard inlays, and gold Waverly tuners, current mfg.

MSR	$3,700		$3,350	$2,425	$1,875

OOO-2H 12-FRET - orchestra style, spruce top, ivoroid binding, herringbone purfling, round soundhole, ivoroid/wood stripe rosette, tortoise style pickguard, East Indian rosewood back/sides, mahogany neck, 25 1/2" scale, 12/20-fret bound ebony fingerboard with pearl diamond/square inlay, ebony pyramid bridge with white black dot pins, rosewood veneer on bound slotted peghead with mother-of-pearl logo inlay, 3-per-side nickel Waverly slot-head tuners, available in Natural finish, total length 39 1/2", body length 20 1/4", body width 15", body thickness 4 1/8", mfg. 1994-current.

MSR	$3,450		$3,100	$2,275	$1,750

OO-2H 12-FRET - similar to the 000-2H except is smaller including, a total length of 38", body length 19 3/8", body width 19 3/8", and a body thickness 4", current mfg.

MSR	$3,450		$3,100	$2,275	$1,750

ACOUSTIC: SJ (SMALL JUMBO) SERIES

SJ SMALL JUMBO - small jumbo style, spruce top, round soundhole, tortoise pickguard, double black/ivoroid strip purfling, black/white wood and nitrate strip rosette, maple back/sides/neck, 25 1/2" scale, 14/20-fret bound ebony fingerboard with modern pearl diamond inlay, ebony bridge with white black dot pins, ebony veneer on bound peghead with pearl diamond and logo inlay, 3-per-side gold Schaller mini tuners, available in Natural finish, total length 40 1/4", body length 20 1/8", body width 16", body thickness 4 1/2", current mfg.

MSR	$3,700		$3,350	$2,400	$1,925

COLLOPY
Instruments currently built in San Francisco, California.

Luthier Rich Collopy has been building and performing repairs on guitars for the past 25 years. In the last year, Collopy opened a retail musical instrument shop in addition to his repairs and building. For further information concerning specifications and pricing, please contact luthier directly (see Trademark Index).

COMINS GUITARS
Instruments currently built in Willow Grove, Pennsylvania beginning 1991.

Bill Comins has been a guitar player since the age of six. While attending Temple University, Comins majored in Jazz Guitar Performance as well as performing professionally and teaching.

Following his background in building and repairing stringed instruments, Comins maintained his own repair/ custom shop in addition to working in a violin repair shop for 4 years after college. In 1991, Comins met with Master Luthier Bob Benedetto. Benedetto's shared knowledge inspired Comins to develop his own archtop guitar design. Comin's archtop guitar design is based in part on his professional guitar playing background, and has devised a guitar that is comfortable to play. Comins currently offers 4 different archtop models.

Realizing that other players may have tastes that vary from his, Comins offers a number of following options to his standard models like the choice of tone woods, cutaway or non-cutaway design, 16", 17", or 18" lower bout, choice of an oval soundhole or f-holes, parallel or X-bracing, and a 7-string configuration.

ACOUSTIC ARCHTOP

**Comins Chester Avenue
courtesy Scott Chinery**

The following is standard on all Comins Archtop guitars: Handcarved solid Sitka or Engelmann spruce tops, handcarved solid maple back and matching sides, a 16" or 17" lower bout, 3 1/8" body depth, violin style floating ebony tail piece, adjustable ebony bridge, choice of f-holes or an oval soundhole, 25" scale; and a 22-fret ebony fingerboard. List prices include a 3-ply hardshell case.

There is no charge for other scale lengths (24 3/4", 25 1/2", etc.), an oval sound hole, non-cutaway body, or other body depths. Wood binding may run between $300 to $600; other options are available on request. Contact luthier Comins directly (see Trademark Index).

Add $250 for fancy split block pearl fingerboard inlay. Add $300 for 18" lower bout.

Add $700 for 7-string configuration.

The **Chester Avenue** model (list $7,200) features a select Sitka or Englemann spruce top that is hand carved from solid woods, and nicely figured maple back and sides. The bound ebony fingerboard has 22-frets; ebony is also featured in the adjustable bridge and violin style floating tail piece. The **Chester Avenue** is available in Sunburst or Honey blonde finishes, and features multi-laminated bindings and purfling around the top, bottom, peghead, f-holes, and raised pickguard. The gold Schaller mini tuning machines have ebony buttons, and the model comes equipped with a Benedetto Suspended pickup with volume control.

In 1996, Comins introduced the **Classic** model archtop. Its design is similar to the Chester Avenue, but features a 3-piece laminated figured neck, bound f-holes/unbound ebony pickguard, and has slightly less ornate appointments. The **Classic** carries a suggested retail of $6,200.

The **Concert** model ($5,500) is another archtop with a hand carved top and back and three-piece maple neck. The body, neck, and headstock are bound, while the chambered f-holes and Chuck Wayne-style raised pickguard are not. The Concert model is available only in a Sunburst finish.

The violin-style finish and straight forward appointments of the **Parlor** archtop are reminiscent of a violin. This model also features the 3-piece laminated neck, no raised pickguard, and mini tuning machines in a black finish with ebony buttons. The **Parlor** (list $4,750) is available with an oval soundhole or classically-styled f-holes. The Parlor also has optional violin-style purfling around the top and back (add $250).

CONCERTONE
See chapter on House Brands.

This trademark has been identified as a House Brand of Montgomery Wards. Instruments were built by either Kay or Harmony, (Source: Michael Wright, *Guitar Stories*, Volume One).

CONDE HERMANOS
Instruments currently produced in Madrid, Spain. Distributed by Luthier Music Corporation of New York City, New York.

Conde Hermanos offers a wide range of Classical, Concert-grade Classical, Flamenco, and Concert-grade Flamenco acoustic guitars built in Madrid, Spain. These models are constructed with the medium level to professional classical guitarist in mind.

ACOUSTIC: AC/EC CLASSICAL SERIES

AC Series Concert Classical guitars feature German Spruce or Canadian red cedar tops, Indian rosewood back and sides, cedar neck, and an ebony fingerboard. Prices (in U.S.) range from $3,100 (**Model AC 22**), to $4,310 (**Model AC 23**); the **Model AC 23 R** has Brazilian rosewood (Jacaranda) back and sides (retail U.S. $5,361). The 8-string **Model AC 23 R.8** also features Brazilian rosewood (Jacaranda) back and sides (retail U.S. $CALL) and is available in a 10-string configuration. The top of the line **Felipe V** has a retail price of $9,271.

The **EC** Studio classical guitars, like the Concert classicals, have German Spruce or Canadian red cedar tops, Indian rosewood back and sides, cedar neck, and an ebony fingerboard. U.S. retail prices range from $1,226 (**Model EC 1**), to $1,607 (**Model EC 2**), to $2,271 (**Model EC 3**).

ACOUSTIC: AF/EG FLAMENCO SERIES

Conde Hermano's **AF Series** Concert Flamenco guitars have German spruce tops, Indian rosewood back and sides, cedar neck, and an ebony fingerboard. These flamenco models are equipped with a transparent tapping plate ("Golpeador transparente") and choice of machine head or wooden peg tuners. Prices (in U.S.) range from $3,097 (**Model AF 24**), to $4,310 (**Model AF 25**); the **Model AF 25 R** has Brazilian rosewood (Jacaranda) back and sides (retail U.S. $5,362). The top of the line **Felipe V Flamenco** has a retail price of $9,271. Other models include the **Model A 26** ($4,310), **Model A 27** ($2,555), and **Model A 28** ($1,987).

The **EF** Studio Flamenco guitars feature Spanish cypress back and sides, German Spruce or Canadian red cedar tops, cedar neck, and an ebony fingerboard. Flamenco models are equipped with a transparent tapping plate and choice of machine head or wooden peg tuners. U.S. retail prices range from $1,226 (**Model EF 4**), to $1,394 (**Model EF 5**). The **Model EF 5 N** features Indian rosewood back and sides (retail U.S. $1,607).

CONN
Instruments previously built in Japan circa 1968 to 1978.

The U.S. distributor for Conn brand name instruments was Conn/Continental Music Company of Chicago, Illinois. The Conn trademark is perhaps more recognizable on their brass band instruments. Conn offered both classical models and 6 - and 12-string acoustic steel-string models, built by Aria and Company in Japan. Many models of student level to intermediate quality, and some feature a bolt-on neck instead of the usual standard, (Source: Michael Wright, *Guitar Stories*, Volume One).

CONQUEROR
Instruments previously produced in Japan circa 1970s (estimated).

ACOUSTIC

The Conqueror label is found on classical-style acoustic guitars.

These models have a spruce top, round soundhole, geometric rosette (black, red, green, yellow pattern), nato back and sides, one piece nato neck ("steel reinforced"), 12/19-fret laminated fingerboard (perhaps bubinga), nato bridge. The slotted headstock has three per side ivory-colored plastic tuners. The soundboard is stained redwood color, the back/sides/neck stained mahogany. They have a distinctive coat of arms and armor plastic ornament on the headstock, with the word "Conqueror" in Old English typeface. A similar crest can be found on the interior paper label inside the body, and a *Made in Japan* label on the back of the headstock. Conqueror acoustics in average condition are valued around $50-$100, (Source: Walter Murray, *Frankenstein Fretworks*).

CONRAD
Instruments previously produced in Japan circa 1972 to 1978.

The Conrad trademark was a brand name used by U.S. importers David Wexler and Company of Chicago, Illinois. The Conrad product line consisted of 6 - and 12-string acoustic guitars, thinline hollowbody electrics, solid body electric guitars and basses, mandolins, and banjos. Conrad instruments were produced by Kasuga International (Kasuga and Tokai USA, Inc.), and featured good quality designs specifically based on popular American designs, (Source: Michael Wright, *Guitar Stories*, Volume One).

CONTESSA
Instruments previously built in Italy between 1966 to early 1970s. Distributed in the U.S. by M. Hohner, Inc. of Hicksville, New York.

The Contessa trademark covered a wide range of medium quality guitars and solid state amplifiers. The HG series (for Hohner Guitars?) featured acoustic ("Folk, Classical, and Country & Western") and original design solid body electrics, (Source: Tony Bacon and Paul Day, *The Guru's Guitar Guide*).

ACOUSTIC

HG 01 - dreadnought style, spruce top, round soundhole, mahogany back/sides, 18-fret rosewood fingerboard with white dot inlay, rosewood bridge with white pins, black pickguard, 3-per-side Contessa tuners with plastic buttons, available in Natural finish, length 38.5", body width 14 1/2", mfg. circa early 1970s.

	N/A	$75	$35

Last MSR was $79.95.

HG 06 J - dreadnought style, spruce top, round soundhole, mahogany back/sides, 20-fret rosewood fingerboard with white dot inlay, rosewood bridge with white black-dot pins, black pickguard (half covers soundhole rosette), 3-per-side Contessa tuners, available in Natural finish, Length 40 1/4", Body Width 14 1/2", mfg. circa early 1970s.

	N/A	$90	$50

Last MSR was $99.95.

HG 12 J - dreadnought style, spruce top, round soundhole, mahogany back/sides, 21-fret rosewood fingerboard, rosewood bridge, black pickguard, 3-per-side Contessa tuners, available in Natural finish, length 42 1/2", body width 14 1/4", mfg. circa early 1970s.

	N/A	$95	$50

Last MSR was $139.95.

CONTINENTAL
See also CONN. Instruments previously produced in Japan.

As well as distributing the Conn guitars, the Continental Music Company of Chicago, Illinois also distributed their own brand name guitars under the Continental logo in the U.S., (Source: Michael Wright, *Guitar Stories*, Volume One).

COOG INSTRUMENTS
Instruments currently built in Santa Cruz, California.

Luthier Ronald Cook runs Coog Instruments as a hobby/semi-business. Cook's primary focus is on handcrafted folk instruments such as guitars and dulcimers, but has also constructed various electric guitars, hurdy-gurdies, and harpsichords through the years. Cook also performs repair work on antique or vintage stringed instruments.

Cook's building and repairs are conducted in his spare time; thus, the lead time on a custom guitar or dulcimer order is a bit longer than running down to your local "guitar club mega-gigantic store" and buying one off the wall. If patience and a custom built folk instrument is what you're into, then please call luthier Cook directly (see Trademark Index).

CORDOBA
Instruments currently produced in Spain. Distributed exclusively in the U.S. by Guitar Salon International of Santa Monica, California.

The Cordoba line of classical guitars is designed for the characteristics of a handmade guitar, but priced for the serious student. Prices range from $579 up to $2,739.

ACOUSTIC

30 R - classical style, solid cedar top, round soundhole, laminated mahogany back/sides, mahogany neck, 650 mm scale, 12/19-fret rosewood fingerboard, rosewood tied bridge, slotted headstock, 3-per-side nickel plated tuners, available in Natural finish, current mfg.

MSR	$579

40 R - similar to the 30 R, except features laminated rosewood back/sides, maple purfling, gold plated tuners, available in Natural finish, current mfg.

MSR	$759

50 R - similar to the 30 R, except features laminated rosewood back/sides, ebony-reinforced Honduran cedar neck, ebony fingerboard, gold plated tuners, available in Natural finish, current mfg.

50 EC - similar to the 50 R, except features a single rounded cutaway body, slightly narrower fingerboard, Fishman transducer, available in Natural finish, current mfg.

MSR	$1,679

60 R - similar to the 50 R, except features rosewood back/sides, maple purfling, available in Natural finish, current mfg.

MSR	$1,239

70 R - similar to the 60 R, except features German spruce top, ebony-reinforced Spanish cedar neck, detailed headstock/purfling/rosette, available in Natural finish, current mfg.

MSR	$1,239

70 F Flamenco - similar to the 70 R, except features solid cypress back/sides, translucent tap plate, available in Natural finish, current mfg.

MSR	$1,459

90 - similar to the 70 R, except features quartersawn German spruce (or cedar) top, solid Indian rosewood back/sides, available in Natural high gloss lacquer finish, current mfg.

MSR	$2,099

110 - similar to the 70 R, except features quartersawn German spruce (or cedar) top, solid Indian rosewood back/sides, detailed headstock/purfling/rosette, available in Natural high gloss lacquer finish, current mfg.

MSR	$2,739

CORT
Instruments currently produced in Inchon and Taejon, Korea; and Surabuya, Indonesia. Distributed in the U.S. by Cort Musical Instrument Company, Ltd. of Northbrook, Illinois.

Since 1960, Cort has been providing students, beginners and mid-level guitar players quality acoustic, semi-hollowbody, and solid body guitars and basses. All Cort instruments are produced in Asia in Cort company facilities, which were established in 1973. Cort is one of the few U.S. companies that owns their overseas production facilities. Cort also produces most of their own electronics (pickups, circuit boards, and other guitar parts); additional parts and custom pieces are available under the MightyMite trademark.

The Cort engineering and design center is located in Northbrook, Illinois. Wood is bought from the U.S. and Canada, and shipped to their production facilities in Korea. Cort instruments are then produced and assembled in the main Cort factories in Korea. After shipping the finished instruments back to the U.S., all instruments are checked in the Illinois facilities as part of quality control prior to shipping to the dealer.

C

In addition to their traditional designs, Cort also offers a large number of their own designs, as well as featured designs by other luthiers. Beginning in 1996, Cort began commissioning designs from noted luthier Jerry Auerswald; this lead to other designs from such noted U.S. luthiers as Jim Triggs, Bill Conklin, and Greg Curbow. Cort has also worked with guitarists Larry Coryell and Matt "Guitar" Murphy on their respective signature series models (the **LCS-1** and the **MGM-1**).

GENERAL INFORMATION

The Cort instruments listed below are listed alphabetically by series. Cort's left-handed models are generally a special order, and produced in limited quantities. There is an additional $30 charge for left-handed configuration models in the current production line-up.

Cort briefly offered specialty versions of their acoustic models: SJ-DLX (retail list $1,295); The SF-Classic (retail list $995), and the NAT-28 DLX (retail list $795) between 1996 to 1998.

ACOUSTIC: CLASSICAL MODELS

CEC-1 - classical single cutaway, solid cedar top, mahogany back/sides/neck, 14/22 fret fingerboard, nylon-string, 3-per-side banjo style tuners, soundhole inlay, Fishman Classic 4 & Sonicore pickup, available in Natural finish, mfg. 2001-current.

	MSR	$650	$465	$325	$215

ACOUSTIC: EARTH SERIES

EARTH 100 - dreadnought style, solid spruce top, round soundhole, tortoise pickguard, black body binding, 4-ring rosette, maple back/sides/neck, 14/20-fret rosewood fingerboard with dot inlay, rosewood bridge with white pins, 3-per-side chrome diecast tuners, available in Tone finish or Natural Tone finish, mfg. 1998-current.

	MSR	$270	$210	$135	$100

Earth 100 F - similar to Earth 100, except has Fishman Classic 4 electronics and Sonicore pickup, available in Tone finish, current mfg.

	MSR	$370	$270	$165	$130

EARTH 150 - similar to the Earth 100 except is available in Natural, Trans. Red, Trans. Blue, or Sunburst finishes, current mfg.

	MSR	$299	$225	$145	$105

Earth 150 F - similar to Earth 150, except has Fishman Classic 4 electronics and Sonicore pickup, available in Tone finish, disc 2003.

			$280	$175	$135

Last MSR was $390.

EARTH 190 - similar to the 150, Natural finish, current mfg.

	MSR	$280	$220	$145	$105

EARTH 200 - dreadnought style, solid spruce top, round soundhole, tortoise pickguard, herringbone bound body/rosette, mahogany back/sides/neck, 14/20-fret rosewood fingerboard with dot inlay, stylized inlay at 12th fret, rosewood bridge with white pins, 3-per-side chrome Grover tuners, available in Natural Satin finish, current mfg.

	MSR	$395	$275	$150	$105

Earth 200 LH - similar to the Earth 200, except in left-handed configuration, current mfg.

	MSR	$430	$295	$175	$125

Earth 200-12 - similar to the Earth 200, except in 12-string configuration, 6-per-side tuners, mfg. 1998-current.

	MSR	$499	$335	$225	$150

Earth 200 GC - similar to the Earth 200, except in a grand concert style body, and featuring a solid cedar top, no pickguard, mfg. 1996-current.

	MSR	$399	$325	$150	$100

EARTH 250 - similar to the Earth 200 except features a solid mahogany top and back, and mahogany sides and neck, gives a darker natural finish, disc. 2003.

			$350	$185	$125

Last MSR was $450.

EARTH 500 - similar to the Earth 200, except has gold Grover tuners, available in Natural Glossy finish, disc. 2000.

			$325	$225	$150

Last MSR was $469.

EARTH 600 - dreadnought style, solid spruce top, rosewood sides/back, mahogany neck, 14/20 rosewood fingerboard with pearl dot inlay, rosewood bridge, tortise pickguard, abalone soundhole rosette, 3-per-side tuners, chrome hardware, Natural finish, mfg. 2001-current.

	MSR	$550	$425	$275	$175

EARTH 900 - parlor style guitar, solid cedar top, solid mahogany back, mahogany neck, 12/19 fret rosewood fingerboard with abalone inlay, soundhole rosette, 3-per-side banjo-style tuners, availibile in Natural Satin finish, mfg. 1998-current.

	MSR	$595	$450	$275	$195

C

GRADING	100%	EXCELLENT	AVERAGE

EARTH 1000 - similar to the Earth 200, except has rosewood sides and back, abalone fingerboard/soundhole inlays, and gold Grover tuners, available in Natural Glossy finish, disc 1999.

	$425	$275	$195

Last MSR was $595.

EARTH 1200 - dreadnought style, solid spruce top, rosewood sides/back, mahogany neck, 14/20 rosewood fingerboard with abalone "Tree-Of-Life" inlay, rosewood bridge, tortoise pickguard, abalone soundhole rosette, 3-per-side Grover tuners, gold hardware, Natural finish, mfg. 1999-current.

MSR	$750	$575	$375	$250

EARTH CUSTOM - dreadnought style, master grade Engelmann solid spruce top, solid rosewood sides/back, mahogany neck, 14/20 ebony fingerboard with pearl dot inlay, ebony bridge, flamed maple wood binding on body, fretboard, and headstock, abalone soundhole rosette, Grover 3-per-side Super Rotomatic tuners, Fishman Prefix Plus & Matrix pickups, gold hardware, Natural finish, made in the Cort Custom Shop, mfg. 2002-current.

MSR	$1,195	$850	$625	$485

ACOUSTIC: NATURAL SERIES

NATURAL - dreadnought style, solid cedar top, round soundhole, maple bound body, wood design rosette, mahogany back/sides/neck, 14/20-fret rosewood fingerboard with double dot inlay at 12th fret, rosewood bridge with white pins, 3-per-side vintage chrome tuners, available in Natural Satin finish, mfg. 1996-99.

	$335	$225	$175

Last MSR was $479.

NATURAL DLX - similar to the Natural, except has solid rosewood back, rosewood sides, stylized inlay at 12th fret, vintage gold tuners, mfg. 1996-98.

	N/A	$425	$250

Last MSR was $795.

ACOUSTIC: NTL SERIES

NTL CUSTOM - body slightly larger than Earth Series guitars, Engelmann spruce AA grade top, solid indian rosewood sides and back, mahogany neck with ebony fingerboard, Grover Super Rotomatic gold tuners, 25 1/4" scale, figured maple bindings, bone nut and bone bridge saddle, produced in the Cort Custom Shop, case included, available in Natural finish, mfg. 1999-current.

MSR	$1,195	$825	$625	$395

NTL 50 - similar to NTL Custom, except has solid spruce A grade top, rosewood sides and back, rosewood fingerboard, available in Natural finish, mfg. 1999-2002.

	$395	$260	$185

Last MSR was $595.

NTL 20 - similar to NTL 50, except has solid spruce top, mahogany sides and back, Grover Super Rotomatic chrome tuners, available in Natural Satin finish, mfg. 1999-current.

MSR	$470	$335	$200	$135

ACOUSTIC: MR SERIES

MR710 F - dreadnought style, single cutaway body, spruce top, round soundhole, black body binding, 4-ring rosette, maple back/sides/neck, 14/20-fret rosewood fingerboard with offset dot inlay, rosewood bridge with white pins, 3-per-side chrome diecast tuners, Fishman acoustic pickup, Fishman Deluxe EQ with 3-band sliders and mid frequency sweep/volume controls, available in Natural Tone finish, mfg. 1998-current.

MSR	$430	$315	$195	$125

MR720 F - single cutaway dreadnought style, spruce top, round soundhole, tortoiseshell pickguard, multiple ivory body binding/rosette, mahogany back/sides/neck, 14/20-fret rosewood fingerboard with offset dot inlay, rosewood bridge with white pins, 3-per-side chrome Grover tuners, Fishman acoustic pickup, Fishman Deluxe EQ with 3-band sliders and mid frequency sweep/volume controls, available in Natural Glossy, Natural Satin, and See-Through Black finishes, disc. 1999.

	$395	$250	$175

Last MSR was $550.

C

GRADING	100%	EXCELLENT	AVERAGE

MR727F - dreadnought single cutaway, flamed maple top, maple sides/back, matching headstock, 14/20 fret rosewood fingerboard, 3-per-side tuners, rosewood bridge, multiple layer binding and soundhole rosette, Fishman Classic4 & Sonicore pickup, available in Antique Violin, Translucent Red, Translucent Blue, or Natural finishes, mfg. 2003 only.

	$390	$260	$175

Last MSR was $550.

MR730 FX (MR730 F) - similar to the MR720 F, except has a solid spruce top, Fishman Prefix EQ system, available in Natural Satin finish only, disc 2003.

	$450	$350	$195

Last MSR was $650.

MR740 FX - similar to MR730 FX, except has Grover gold tuning gears. Natural finish, mfg. 1999-2001, reintroduced 2003.

MSR	$769	$495	$350	$250

MR750 F (MR750 FX) - similar to the MR720 F, except has a bound flamed maple top, bound neck/headstock, Fishman Prefix EQ system, tortoise pickguard, gold Grover tuners, available in Amber Satin, See-Through Black, See-Through Blue, See-Through Red, and Tobacco Sunburst finishes, disc. 1999.

	$495	$325	$225

Last MSR was $695.

MR770 F - similar to MR750 F, except has a rounded profile back, disc. 1999.

	$495	$325	$225

Last MSR was $695.

MR780 FX - dreadnought single cutaway, flamed maple top, maple sides/back, matching headstock, 14/20 fret rosewood fingerboard with 12th fret inlay, 3-per-side tuners, rosewood bridge, multiple layer binding and soundhole rosette, Fishman Prefix Plus & Matrix pickup, chrome hardware, available in Antique Violin, Red Burst, Blue Burst, or Natural finishes, mfg. 1998-current.

MSR	$799	$575	$405	$275

MR-A - dreadnought single cutaway, spruce top, mahogany sides/back, maple or mahogany neck, 14/20 fret rosewood fingerboard with pearl dot inlay, 3-per-side tuners, rosewood bridge, black binding and soundhole rosette, tortise pickguard, CE-300 active EQ & Slim Jim pickup, chrome hardware, available in Sun Burst Satin, Black, or Natural Satin finishes, mfg. 2001-current.

MSR	$325	$240	$175	$125

MR CUSTOM - dreadnought single cutaway, master grade solid Engelmann spruce top, solid rosewood back and sides, mahogany neck, 14/20 ebony fingerboard with pearl dot inlay, ebony bridge, flamed maple wood binding on body, fretboard, and headstock, abalone soundhole rosette, Grover 3-per-side Super Rotomatic tuners, Fishman Prefix Plus & Matrix pickups, gold hardware, Natural finish, made in the Cort Custom Shop, mfg. 2002-current.

MSR	$1,495	$1,075	$850	$600

ACOUSTIC: RESONATOR SERIES

ADR6 - dreadnought style resonator guitar, spruce top, mahogany back/sides, mahogany rounded neck, multiple ivory body binding, a 14/20-fret rosewood fingerboard with white dot inlays, resonator cone/soundwell, two mesh soundholes, spider bridge, 3-on-a-side chrome diecast tuners, available in Natural Glossy or Tobacco Sunburst finishes, mfg. 1996-98.

	N/A	$375	$225

Last MSR was $699.

ADS6 - similar to the ADR6, except has square neck and chrome open tuning machines, mfg. 1996-98.

	N/A	$395	$225

Last MSR was $750.

ACOUSTIC: SF SERIES

SF models are not currently available in the USA.

SF1 (1F) - single cutaway body, spruce top, round soundhole, bound body, rosette, maple back/sides/neck, 14/20-fret rosewood fingerboard with offset dot inlay, rosewood bridge with white pins, 3-per-side chrome diecast tuners, Slim Jim pickup, Cort EQ with 3-band/volume sliders, available in Natural Satin finish, currently not available in the U.S.A.

	$315	$195	$110

Last MSR was $450.

Early models may have mahogany back/sides, and mahogany neck.

SF5 X (SF5) - similar to SF1, except has solid cedar top, mahogany back/sides/neck, gold Grover tuners, Fishman acoustic pickup, Fishman Prefix EQ with 3-band/contour/volume sliders, available in Natural Satin finish, mfg. 1996-97 (as SF5), 1998-2000, currently not available in the USA.

	$475	$300	$225

Last MSR was $650.

C

GRADING		100%	EXCELLENT	AVERAGE

SFA - folk single cutaway body, solid spruce top, mahogany or maple back/sides, mahogany neck, 14/20 fret rosewood fingerboard with pearl dot inlay, binding, abalone soundhole rosette, CE-300 active EQ & Slim Jim pickup, 3-per-side tuners, chrome hardware, available in Natural, Natural Satin, or Sunburst Satin finishes, currently not available in the USA.

MSR	$325		$240	$175	$125

ACOUSTIC: SJ SERIES

CJ3 (SJ3) - traditional jumbo body, solid spruce top, flamed maple sides/back, maple neck, 14/20 fret rosewood fingerboard with pearl dot inlay, multiple layer binding, abalone rosette soundhole, 3-per-side tuners, chrome hardware, available in Natural, Natural Satin, or 3-Tone Sunburst, mfg. 2001-02.

MSR	$499		$400	$250	$175

SJ3F - similar to the SJ3 except has Fishman Classic 4 & Sonicore pickups, not available in the USA.

MSR	$499		$350	$265	$175

CJ3-12 (SJ3-12) - similar to the SJ3 except is in 12 string configuration, not available in the USA.

MSR	$569		$400	$295	$190

CJ5X (SJ5 X) - similar to the SF1, except has a deeper body, solid spruce top, mahogany back/sides/neck, gold Grover tuners, Fishman acoustic pickup, Fishman Prefix EQ with 3-band/contour/volume sliders, available in Natural Satin finish, current mfg.

MSR	$650		$475	$300	$225

SJ7 X - similar to SJ5 X, except has quilted maple top, sides, and back, maple neck and rosewood fingerboard, available in Red Burst and Blue Burst, disc 2001.

			$550	$350	$250

Last MSR was $795.

CJ10X (SJ10 X) - similar to the SJ5, except has rosewood back and sides, abalone binding on body/soundhole, abalone position inlays, available in black or Natural Glossy finish, mfg. 1996-current.

MSR	$950		$675	$450	$325

CJ10 X12 (SJ10X) - similar to SJ10 X, except in a 12-string version. Natural finish, mfg. 1999-current.

MSR	$995		$700	$475	$345

ACOUSTIC: STANDARD SERIES

The Standard Series was introduced as a budget-line or entry level of Cort acoustic guitars. Most of these guitars are dreadnoughts but there is one folk model. Prices start as $179 and the most expensive model is the 12-string AD-870-12 for $270. For more information on the Standard series refer to the Cort web site.

ACOUSTIC: WESTERN (AJ) SERIES

AJ 850 - dreadnought style, spruce top, round soundhole, tortoise pickguard, black body/rosette binding, mahogany back/sides/neck, 14/20-fret rosewood fingerboard with dot inlay, rosewood bridge with white pins, 3-per-side chrome diecast tuners, available in Tone finish, disc. 1999.

			$195	$125	$90

Last MSR was $279.

AJ 860 - dreadnought style, spruce top, round soundhole, black pickguard, multiple black body/rosette binding, mahogany back/sides/neck, 14/20-fret rosewood fingerboard with dot inlay, rosewood bridge with white pins, 3-per-side chrome diecast tuners, available in Natural Satin finish, disc. 1999.

			$200	$125	$90

Last MSR was $299.

AJ 870 - similar to the AJ 860, except available in Natural Glossy or Tobacco Sunburst finishes, disc 1999.

			$250	$175	$125

Last MSR was $349.

AJ 870 BK - similar to the AJ 870, except in Black finish, disc. 1998.

			$275	$200	$125

Last MSR was $399.

AJ 870 C - similar to the AJ 870, except has a transducer pickup mounted in the bridge, disc. 1998.

			$280	$180	$130

Last MSR was $399.

AJ 870 12 - similar to the AJ 870, except in a 12-string configuration, 6-per-side tuners, available in Natural Glossy finish only, disc. 1998.

			$275	$175	$125

Last MSR was $389.

C

ACOUSTIC ELECTRIC BASS

MR720 BF - single cutaway dreadnought style, spruce top, round soundhole, multiple ivory body binding/rosette, maple back/sides, mahogany neck, 15/20-fret rosewood fingerboard with offset dot inlay, rosewood bridge with white pins, 2 per side chrome diecast tuners, Fishman acoustic pickup, Fishman Deluxe EQ with 3-band sliders and mid frequency sweep/volume controls, available in Natural Glossy and See-Through Black finishes, disc. 2000.

	$575	$375	$250

Last MSR was $795.

NTL B - classic design with solid spruce top and rosewood sides and back, mahogany neck with rosewood fingerboard, diecast gold tuning gears. Fishman Prefix EQ and Fishman sonicore pickup. 34" scale, available in Natural finish, mfg. 1999-2001.

	$625	$450	$325

Last MSR was $895.

NTL FBL - similar to NTL B, except fretless. Natural finish, mfg. 1999-2000.

	$625	$435	$300

Last MSR was $995.

SJB - single cutaway design with solid spruce top, maple sides, back, and neck. Rosewood fingerboard. 29 3/4" scale. Diecast gold tuning gears. Fishman Prefix EQ and Fishman sonicore pickup, available in Natural Satin finish, disc. 2000.

	$550	$385	$275

Last MSR was $795.

SJB3 - jumbo body bass, 4-string, solid spruce top, mahogany sides/back, mahogany neck, 30" scale, 15/20 rosewood fingerboard, natural headstock 2-per-side tuners, binding, abalone soundhole rosette, CE-300B active EQ, Slim Jim pickup, available in Natural Satin or Black finishes, mfg. 2002-current.

MSR	$399	$285	$210	$145

SJB CE - jumbo body single cutaway bass, 4-string, solid spruce top, mahogany sides/back, mahogany neck, 34" scale, 19/22 rosewood fingerboard, natural headstock 2-per-side tuners, binding, abalone soundhole rosette, Fishman Classic 4 & Sonicore pickup, available in Natural Satin finish, mfg. 2002-current.

MSR	$750	$525	$400	$275

CORTEZ

Instruments previously built in Japan circa 1969 to 1988. Distributed in the U.S. market by Westheimer Musical Industries of Chicago, Illinois.

Cortez acoustics were produced in Japan, and imported to the U.S. market as an affordable alternative in the acoustic guitar market. Westheimer's Cortez company and trademark could be viewed as a stepping stone towards his current Cort company (See Cort).

COSI

Instruments currently built in Les Plages, France. Distributed by Applications de technologies Nouvelles (ATN) International of Les Plages, France.

Designer J.C. Lagarde's CoSI (Composite String Instruments) brand of upright basses feature wood soundboards and graphite back and sides. The wood top maintains the proper response, while the graphite body maintains a stable equilibrium regardless of room temperature. CoSI instruments are recognized worldwide for their acoustic qualities, and are priced such that students and professionals can easily afford to have proper sound. For further information regarding CoSI instruments, please contact Applications de technologies Nouvelles International directly (see Trademark Index).

CRAFTER

Instruments currently built in Korea. Distributed in the U.S. by HSS (a Division of Hohner, Inc.), located in Richmond, Virginia.

Crafter guitars was founded by HyunKwon Park in April, 1972. He started business in his home, making guitars in a 20 square meter area with four employees. Early guitars were classical models that were distributed in Korea. Guitars at this time were branded Sungeum. In 1978, they moved to a bigger location in Yangju-gun. In 1986, his oldest son, Injae Park, joined forces and decided to change the name to something more user friendly. They came up with the name Crafter, which has been in use ever since. In 2000, they opened a new 7,000 square meter factory with a workforce of 140 people. They currently are distributing guitars in 40 different countries.

ACOUSTIC

C18 - classical style body, solid cedar top, rosewood back & sides, satin finish, new 2003.

MSR	$539	$375	$270	$195

D-6 - dreadnought style body, solid Sitka spruce top, mahogany back and sides, die-cast tuners, satin finish, current mfg.

MSR	$329	$235	$175	$125

D-7 - dreadnought style body, solid cedar top, mahogany back and sides, Mushroom chrome tuners, current mfg.

MSR	$369	$250	$190	$135

GRADING		100%	EXCELLENT	AVERAGE

D-8 - dreadnought style body, solid engelmann spruce top, mahogany back and sides, Mushroom chrome tuners, current mfg.

	MSR	$399		$275	$210	$145

D-18 - dreadnought style body, solid cedar top, rosewood back and sides, wood inlay, Grover tuners, current mfg.

	MSR	$519		$370	$265	$175

D-30 - dreadnought style body, solid engelmann spruce top, brown tiger maple back and sides, gold Grover tuners, current mfg.

	MSR	$765		$535	$375	$250

MD-35 - dreadnought body style, spruce top, mahogany back and sides, die-cast tuners, current mfg.

	MSR	$299		$210	$150	$100

MD-50 - dreadnought style body, spruce top, bubinga back and sides, die-cast tuners, current mfg.

	MSR	$339		$240	$180	$125

MD-60 - dreadnought body style, tiger maple top, ash back and sides, mahogany neck, rosewood fingerboard with dot position markers, rosewood bridge, disc.

				$250	$190	$135
				Last MSR was $369		

Crafter D-8 N
courtesy Crafter

MD-80-12 - dreadnought sytle body, 12-string configuration, solid Sitka spruce top, mahogany back and sides, chrome die-cast tuners, current mfg.

	MSR	$429		$300	$225	$150

MD-220-OS - dreadnought style body, quilted maple top, back and sides, abalone soundhole, gold die-cast tuners, current mfg.

	MSR	$529		$370	$275	$180

SD0038N - dreadnought body, Englemann solid spruce top, solid rosewood back and sides, new 2003.

	MSR	$1,059		$750	$525	$400

SGA008N - grand auditorium, Englemann solid spruce top, solid rosewood back & sides, new 2003.

	MSR	$1,059		$750	$525	$400

TD06-N - dreadnought style body, Englemann solid spruce top, mahogany solid back, wooden mosaic soundhold and abalone inlay, current mfg.

	MSR	$549		$385	$280	$190

T-035 - folk size body, Englemann solid spruce top, mahogany back and sides, new 2003.

	MSR	$419		$295	$225	$150

TA050 - concert style body, Englemann solid spruce top, mahogany back and sides, new 2003.

	MSR	$639		$450	$325	$215

ACOUSTIC ELECTRIC

All current acoustic electric models include the Shadow pickup and Timber Plus preamp system unless otherwise noted.

ATE70CEQ - arched top body, tiger maple top, maple back and sides, current mfg.

	MSR	$559		$390	$285	$195

ATE70CEQ-LH - similar to the ATE70CEQ except is in left-handed configuration, current mfg.

	MSR	$569		$395	$285	$195

ATE100CEQ - arched top body, tiger maple top, back, and sides, current mfg.

	MSR	$699		$490	$355	$235

CE24 - classical body, solid Englemann spruce top, rosewood back and sides, new 2003.

	MSR	$729		$510	$370	$245

CT120-12 - 12-String thin body, spruce top, sound chamber, basswood back and sides, current mfg.

	MSR	$599		$420	$305	$215

CTS150-N - thin body, solid Sitka top, CTS brace system, current mfg.

	MSR	$649		$460	$335	$230

CTS155C-BK - thin body classical, CTS brace system, current mfg.

	MSR	$649		$460	$335	$230

GAB24S - bass body, solid Sitka top, rosewood back and sides, current mfg.

	MSR	$819		$575	$425	$290

Crafter CTS155C-BK
courtesy Crafter

GRADING		100%	EXCELLENT	AVERAGE

GAE36 - grand auditorium body, Englemann solid spruce top, rosewood back & sides, gold Grover tuners, current mfg.

	MSR	$1,049		$735	$550	$345

ED155EQ-TB - dreadnought body, quilted maple top, bubinga back and sides, current mfg.

	MSR	$549		$385	$280	$195

ML-BUBINGA - Englemann solid spruce top, mahogany back and sides, current mfg.

	MSR	$799		$560	$410	$275

ML-ROSE - Englemann solid spruce top, rosewood back & sides, b-band pickup & preamp, current mfg.

	MSR	$899		$630	$460	$325

SE33 - Englemann solid spruce top, quilted maple back & sides, gold Grover tuners, EMF preamp, current mfg.

	MSR	$995		$695	$525	$325

SN285EQ - ultra slim classical body, spruce top, mahogany back and sides, current mfg.

	MSR	$479		$335	$250	$170

TC035 - folk cutaway body, Englemann spruce top, rosewood back and sides, current mfg.

	MSR	$549		$385	$280	$195

TGAE06-N - grand auditorium body, Englemann spruce top, mahogany back and sides, current mfg.

	MSR	$699		$490	$355	$235

ACOUSTIC ELECTRIC: FIBERGLASS BACK MODELS

FSG250 - spruce top, single cutaway, shadow pickup, PR-40 Passive Slide controls, available in Natural or Sunburst, current mfg.

	MSR	$429		$300	$225	$150

FA820-EQ - Ashwood top, single cutaway, shadow pickup, P4 Preamp, Dark Brown Sunburst, current mfg.

	MSR	$489		$345	$250	$165

FSG260EQ-BK - spruce top, single cutaway, shadow pickup, P4 Preamp, Black finish, current mfg.

	MSR	$499		$350	$255	$170

FX550 - ashwood top, single cutaway, shadow pickup, P4 Preamp, available in Trans. Blue or Trans. Red finishes, current mfg.

	MSR	$499		$350	$255	$170

FA900EQ-TR - quilted maple top, single cutaway, shadow pickup, P4 Preamp, available in Trans. Red finish, current mfg.

	MSR	$529		$370	$265	$175

ACOUSTIC ELECTRIC: MINI SERIES

The Crafter Mini Series debuted in 1997. The travel-style **Mini RF 30** had a fiberglass back, full scale mahogany neck and rosewood fingerboard, and a spruce top. The RF 30 was available in Natural, Blue Stain, and Black Stain finishes (last MSR was $299). The acoustic/electric **RF 40 E** has a similar construction, and includes a piezo bridge pickup with volume and tone controls. The RF 40 E (list $339) is available in Green Stain, Purple Stain, and Tobacco Sunburst finishes.

ACOUSTIC ELECTRIC: SUPER JUMBO SERIES

The **SJC 330 EQ** Super Jumbo had a spruce top, and was available in a Tobacco Sunburst finish (last MSR was $589); the **SJC 390 EQ** (last MSR was $679) had a similar construction design. The **SJ 270** Super Jumbo had a tiger maple top, mahogany back/sides/neck, rosewood fingerboard, and Tobacco Sunburst finish (last MSR was $499).

CRAFTERS OF TENNESSEE

Instruments currently built in Old Hickory, Tennessee.

Mark Taylor's company is currently offering a range of high quality acoustic guitars, banjos and resophonic guitars marketed under the Tennessee brand name. These instruments reflect a deep commitment to the players that seek the tone and vibe of the fabled "pre-war" instruments that are so often sought out by players and collectors alike. As the son of internationally acclaimed "flat picking reso man" and collector Tut Taylor, Mark Taylor's Crafters Of Tennessee also offers a premium signature line of Tut Taylor Resophonic Guitars.

ACOUSTIC

All **Tut Taylor Signature Model** resophonic guitars feature a solid peghead with an ebony overlay, bound ebony fingerboard with intricate abalone inlay, an old style sound well with parallelogram openings, an aluminum cast and machined spider, and improved design brass cover plate.

Square neck resophonic guitars include the Tut Taylor Tennessean which retails for $2,199, the Tut Taylor Virginian for $2,599, the Tut Taylor Vigrinian Deluxe for $2,799, the Tut Taylor Californian for $2,799, the Tut Taylor Californian Deluxe for $2,999, the Tut Taylor Carolina for $3,199 and the Tennessee Original for $1,700.

Round neck resophonic models include the Tennessee blues 10 1/2" which lists for $2,599 and the Tennessee Blues 9 1/2" model which retails for $2,349. Acoustic models include the Tennessee Studio which has a suggested list price of $2,199, the Tennessee Spruce Studio which sells for $2,399, the Tennessee FlatTop Rosewood at $2,999 and the Tennessee FlatTop Mahogany which lists at $2,599.

CRAFTSMAN

Instruments previously produced in Japan during the late 1970s through the mid 1980s.

Craftsman built entry level to medium quality copies of American designs, (Source: Tony Bacon and Paul Day, *The Guru's Guitar Guide*).

CRANDALL, TOM

Instruments previously built in Phoenix, Arizona, and in Iowa City, Iowa (circa 1990-2000).

Luthier Tom Crandall built a limited number of flattop and archtop acoustic guitars and also did repairs during the 1990s.

CRESTLINE

Instruments previously built in Japan circa mid to late 1970s. Distributed by the Grossman Music Corporation of Cleveland, Ohio.

These entry level to intermediate solid body guitars featured designs based on classic American favorites. Crestline offered a wide range of stringed instruments, including classical, folk, dreadnought, and 12-string acoustics; solid body electric guitars and basses; amplifiers; banjos, mandolins, and ukuleles. Considering the amount of instruments available, the Crestline trademark was probably used on guitars built by one of the bigger Japanese guitar producers and rebranded for the U.S. market. One model reviewed at a vintage guitar show was based on Gibson's Les Paul design, and had Grover tuners, 2 Japanese covered humbuckers, and decent wood.

CROMWELL

See chapter on House Brands.

While the distribution of this trademark was handled by midwestern mail order companies, Gibson built this line of budget guitars sometime in the mid 1930s to the early 1940s. While the guitars were built to roughly similar Gibson standards, they lack the adjustable truss rod in the neck that differentiates them from a true Gibson of the same period, (Source: Walter Carter, *Gibson Guitars: 100 Years of an American Icon*).

CUMBUS

Instruments currently built in Turkey. Distributed by Lark in the Morning of Mendocino, California.

These instruments are traditional stringed instruments of Turkey, and include the Cumbus 12-string fretless banjo, 12-string banjo guitar, Cumbus saz, Cumbus banjo mandolin, and others.

CUMPIANO, WILLIAM R.

Instruments currently built in Northampton, Massachusetts.

Luthier William Cumpiano trained under Michael Gurian in the early 1970s at the Michael Gurian Workshop, as well as working with Michael Millard in the mid 1970s. After training with Millard, Cumpiano opened his own lutherie shop.

For the past 25 years, William R. Cumpiano has been making guitars in the North American, European, and Latin American traditions, primarily on a commission basis. Over the years, he has achieved wide recognition in the field for his innovative designs and fine craftsmanship, as well as for having authored the principle textbook (*Guitarmaking: Tradition and Technology*) and for his numerous feature articles in guitar magazines, such as *Acoustic Guitar* and *Guitarmaker*. Cumpiano has supplied custom-made instruments to some of the finest and most prominent guitarists in the United States, (Biographical material courtesy of William R. Cumpiano, September 1997).

CURBOW

Instruments currently built in Morgantown, Georgia.

Luthier Greg Curbow offers a line of high quality stringed instruments that feature **Rockwood** necks. The Rockwood material is a composite of birch and phenolic based resins formed under pressure and heat, which produces a neck unaffected by changes in temperature and humidity. Curbow basses and guitars are handcrafted directly at the Curbow workshop in the North Georgia mountains.

For current information on Curbow electric guitars and basses, please refer to the *Blue Book of Electric Guitars*.

ACOUSTIC ELECTRIC BASS

ACOUSTIC ELECTRIC 4 - mahogany back and sides, quilted maple top, Rockwood neck, fretless Rockwood fingerboard, 2-per-side headstock, chrome hardware, fixed bridge, custom Bartolini piezo and magnetic pickup system, current mfg.

MSR $19,995

Price includes a hardshell case. This model is available in a 30" or 34" scale, and in 5-, 6-, and 7-string configurations.

CUSTOM KRAFT

See chapter on House Brands.

This trademark has been identified as a House Brand of St. Louis Music. The St. Louis Music Supply Company was founded in 1922 by Bernard Kornblum, originally as an importer of German violins. The St.

Crafter FA820-EQ
courtesy Crafter

Crafter FA900EQ-TR
courtesy Crafter

Louis, Missouri-based company has been a distributor, importer, and manufacturer of musical instruments over the past seventy-five years.

In the mid 1950s, St. Louis Music distributed amplifiers and guitars from other producers such as Alamo, Harmony, Kay, Magnatone, Rickenbacker, and Supro. By 1960, the focus was on Harmony, Kay, and Supro: all built "upstream" in Chicago, Illinois. 1960 was also the year that St. Louis Music began carrying Kay's **Thinline** single cutaway electric guitar.

Custom Kraft was launched in 1961 as St. Louis Music's own House Brand. The first series of semi-hollowbody Custom Kraft **Color Dynamic** Electric guitars were built by Kay, and appear to be Thinline models in Black, Red, and White. In 1963, a line of solid body double cutaway electrics built by Valco were added to the catalog under the Custom Kraft moniker, as well as Kay-built archtop and flattop acoustic.

In 1967, Valco purchased Kay, a deal that managed to sink both companies by 1968. St. Louis Music continued advertising both companies models through 1970, perhaps NOS supplies from their warehouse. St. Louis Music continued to offer Custom Kraft guitars into the early 1970s, but as their sources had dried up so did the trademark name. St. Louis Music's next trademark guitar line was Electra (then followed by Westone, and Alvarez).

Custom Kraft models are generally priced according to the weirdness/coolness factor, so don't be surprised to see the range of prices from $125 up to $400! The uncertainty indicates a buyer-directed market, so if you find one that you like, don't be afraid to haggle over the price. The earlier Kay and Valco built guitars date from the 1960s, while later models were probably built in Japan, (Source: Michael Wright, *Vintage Guitar Magazine*).

CYCLONE
Instruments previously produced in Japan.

Cyclone guitars were distributed in the U.S. market by Leban Imports of Baltimore, Maryland, (Source: Michael Wright, *Guitar Stories,* Volume One).

C is for Crafter Guitars. Injae Park, Crafter's President, is shown taking a break at the recent Summer NAMM Show in Nashville. Located in South Korea, Crafter Guitars manufactures over 40,000 instruments annually.

Section D

D

D.C. HILDER BUILDER
Instruments currently built in Guelph (Ontario), Canada.

D.C. Hilder's Garcia's Guitar model features seven laminated layers of hard wood, which are then hand carved for the top and back contouring. Specific models are unknown at this point.

D.J. ARGUS
Instruments previously built in New York, New York circa early 1990s. Distributed through Rudy's Music Shop of New York City, New York.

D.J. Argus archtops featured traditional D'Angelico stylings, solid spruce tops, laminated curly maple back and sides, engraved tailpieces, and Grover Imperial tuners. Research continues on the D.J. Argus archtop models for future editions of the *Blue Book of Acoustic Guitars*.

D'AGOSTINO
Instruments produced in Italy by the EKO company between 1978 and 1982. After 1982, instruments were produced in Japan (then later Korea). Instrument production was contracted to the EKO custom shop in Milwaukee, Wisconsin. Distributed by PMS Music of New York, New York.

Pat D'Agostino (ex-Gibson/Maestro effects) began his own instrument importing company in 1975. The D'Agostino Corporation of New Jersey began importing acoustic dreadnoughts, then introduced the Italian-built Benchmark Series of guitars in 1977. These models featured laminated neck-through designs, 2 humbuckers and a 3-per-side headstock. Production then moved to Korea in the early 1980s, although some better models were built in Japan during the 1990s. Pat, assisted by Steven D'Agostino and Mike Confortti, has always maintained a high quality control level and limited quantities, (Source: Michael Wright, *Vintage Guitar Magazine*).

**D'Angelico 17" Special
courtesy John Miller**

D'ANGELICO
Instruments previously built in New York City, New York between 1932 and 1964.

Master Luthier John D'Angelico (1905-1964) was born and raised in New York City, New York. In 1914, he apprenticed to his great uncle, and learned the luthier trade of building stringed instruments and repair. After 18 years of working on stringed instruments, he opened his own shop on Kenmare Street (D'Angelico was 27). D'Angelico guitars were entirely handcrafted by D'Angelico with assistance by shop employees such as Vincent DiSerio (assistant/apprentice from 1932 to 1959). In the early 1950s, D'Angelico's workshop had a bench and counter for guitar work, and a showcase with new United or Favilla guitars, used "trade-ins" and a few amplifiers from Nat Daniel's Danelectro or Everett Hull's Ampeg company. A very young James D'Aquisto became the second assistant to the shop in 1953.

In 1959, the building where D'Angelico worked and lived was condemned by the city due to an unsafe foundation. While scouting out new locations, D'Angelico and DiSerio had a serious argument over finances. DiSerio left and accepted work at the Favilla guitar plant. After a number of months went by, D'Angelico and D'Aquisto finally reopened the guitar shop at its new location. Unfortunately, D'Angelico's health began to take a turn for the worse. John D'Angelico passed away in his sleep in September of 1964, (Source: Paul William Schmidt, *Acquired of the Angels*).

D'ANGELICO HISTORY

The publisher wishes to express thanks to Mr. Jim Fisch, co-author of *Epiphone: The House of Stathopoulo,* and senior contributing editor for 20th Century Guitar, for the following D'Angelico information.

Although D'Angelico maintained a relative amount of consistency in his production, an overview of his instruments shows that the design of his guitars was representative of his evolution as a luthier, the demands of his customers and the external influences of other, commercial guitar manufacturers. Since he did very little in the way of advertising and publishing catalogs, his ledger books (Reprinted in Paul William Schmidt's *Acquired of the Angels* and Akira Tsumura's *American Guitars*) have become the bible for D'Angelico collectors. In spite of the fact that these are incomplete and often contain puzzling references known only to the maker or his clients, the bulk of his work –1,164 guitars – is represented and accurately dated. However, since some early examples lack any manufacturing dates, the subsequent list of models notes the first date entered for a particular model, but it is not necessarily the first appearance of the model on the consecutive serial number list or the first example to be produced. Reference will be made to earlier undated examples where necessary.

EARLY GUITARS 1932-34

The first documented date, for a D'Angelico guitar – 11/28/32 – corresponds to serial #1002. His early guitars were strongly influenced by Gibson's 16" L5 model. These examples have the distinctive, bound "snake head" headstock which features a script "D'Angelico" logo engraved upon a mother-of-pearl arch inlaid above a filigree, marquetry torch. The tuners were typically gold-plated, oval button Grovers. The necks, like those of the L5, consisted of two pieces of maple, bisected with a narrow strip of mahogany. The fingerboards were bound and constructed of ebony, inlaid with pearl blocks at frets 3, 5, 7, 9, 12, and 15. They terminated in a decorative, reverse pendant arch. The book matched, carved

**D'Angelico New Yorker
courtesy Dr. Tom Van Hoose**

spruce top was multiple bound, parallel braced and featured narrow f-holes. The bridge was of ebony, and the bound tortoise shell, celluloid pickguard was closely copied from that of the L5. Early tailpieces were simple, wire trapeze units, generally with a "reverse" string attachment. Later guitars bore the more substantial and decorative, gold-plated Grover "DeLuxe" tailpiece. The sides and book matched, carved back were of highly figured curly maple. The standard finish was a full Sunburst.

LATER GUITARS 1935-1964

By late 1935, John D'Angelico was developing three distinct models, the "Style A," "Style B," and "Excel." Following Gibson's then recent example, he increased the width of his new instruments to 17 inches – grand auditorium size. They were likewise priced, so as to be competitive with Gibson's comparable models, with the A, B and Excel – priced at $150.00, $200.00 and $275.00 respectively – roughly matching up with Gibson's L10, L12, and aforementioned L5.

The New Yorker was D'Angelico's 1936 entry into the 18" guitar market. With a $400.00 price tag, it was a competitor of Gibson's Super 400, Epiphone's Emperor, and Stromberg's Master 400. It - along with the Excel - is considered by connoisseurs to be amongst the finest vintage archtop guitars. Taking its name and aesthetics from the city of its manufacture, the recurrent skyscraper motifs which adorned it represented the epitome of Art Deco design applied to a guitar.

The 17" A-1 was introduced by 1938 as D'Angelico's least expensive model, and would have been comparably priced to Gibson's L7 and Epiphone's Triumph. It varied from the Style A, in that, like the L7 of the period, it was sunbursted only on the top, with the sides and back having a monochromatic mahogany finish. Also like certain L7s, it had only single bindings. The luthier, however, still paid close attention to the sound of this economy model, and they can sound every bit as good as his most costly guitars.

The features which were standard to all D'Angelico models were: Carved spruce tops, carved maple backs, maple sides and necks, ebony fingerboards and adjustable bridges, and later, the inlaid pearl, script "D'Angelico" logo on the headstock. It is important to note however, that any instrument could be customized according to a client's wishes. Hence, many deviations from standard specifications exist. These typically include body size, bracing, neck construction, fingerboard and headstock inlays, headstock shape, hardware, bindings, pickguard and finish. D'Angelico would commonly use the designation "Special" in his ledger books to identify many of these guitars. He also made a few guitars with round or oval soundholes, and at least one which measured 19" across the lower bout.

Customers would also bring their older instruments back to the maker for refinishing, updated hardware, rebinding and occasionally the installation of an adjustable truss rod (a standard feature by the late '40s) or new fingerboard, resulting in many instruments today having features from different periods, but all done by John D'Angelico, himself. One of the most common ailments of D'Angelico guitars is deterioration of the nitrocellulose bindings and pickguards. In order to preserve the integrity of the instrument, it is often necessary to have them completely replaced.

As previously stated, early D'Angelicos featured simple wire or Grover DeLuxe tailpieces, nickel or gold-plated according to the type of instrument. By 1936, tailpieces designed by John D'Angelico and fabricated by the Joseph Schaffner Co. began to appear on his instruments. The earliest was apparently designed for the newly introduced New Yorker, and was used on the Excel, as well. It was hinged, and featured a cutout reminiscent of the Chrysler Building's distinctive spire, although the initials "DA" can also be traced in its combination of curves and angles. The strings were threaded through a broad rectangular, horizontal retainer with the logo "D'Angelico, New York" engraved in script.

It was followed by the first of his "compensated" tailpieces (circa 1937). This consisted of a diagonally positioned, rhomboidal plate through which the strings passed. It was likewise engraved, and affixed to a non-hinged bracket whose face also employed a rectilinear skyscraper inspired motif. This was short-lived. An adaptation, with the diagonal rhomboid replaced by a more conventional horizontal plate, was used on some later acoustic instruments, and many electric guitars of the '50s.

By the late '30s, the compensated "stair step" tailpiece was standard issue on Excels and New Yorkers. This is the unit which most people associate with D'Angelico guitars. It harked back to the original Chrysler building motif, however that was now surmounted by a diagonally positioned, engraved "stair step" plate. This consisted of a series of graduated steps, the center six designed to accommodate a single string anchor apiece. The New Yorker's was a bit fancier than that of the Excel's. Eventually this unique design was utilized throughout the entire D.A. line.

As X-bracing became more popular towards the end of the 1930s, it became the preferred method of bracing the more expensive D'Angelico models, although later examples of parallel braced instruments are not uncommon, and most likely reflect a specific client's desires. Again, it is important to remember that deviations from the norm characterize this master's guitars.

In 1947, he introduced a cutaway option on his Excel and New Yorker models, setting a standard for modern jazz guitars which has seldom been equaled. After 1948, D'Angelico concentrated mainly on the manufacture of New Yorkers and Excels (the bulk of which were cutaway,) and electric models, which he continued to make up until his death.

ACOUSTIC MODELS/STYLES

Style A - Earliest ledger date: 3/10/36. 17" wide, generally parallel braced, carved spruce top, carved maple back and maple sides, f-holes not bound, 3-ply bound body (some early models single bound,) adjustable ebony bridge, rounded bound tortoiseshell celluloid pickguard (later models w/ bound stair step guard,) bound ebony fingerboard w/block position markers (some early models w/dots,) usually equipped with simpler trapeze and Grover DeLuxe tailpieces, bound 3-or 5-point headstock, early models having a block inlays bearing "D'Angelico" logo and model name (later models w/"Style A" engraved on inlaid shield design and inlaid "D'Angelico" script logo), button tuners, originally available only in full Dark Brown Sunburst, some later models in Blonde, all metal parts nickle-plated. Last ledger date: 9/14/45.

Style B - Earliest ledger date: 9/2/33. 17" wide, generally parallel braced, carved spruce top, carved maple back and maple sides, f-holes not bound, 3 - 5-ply bindings on top, adjustable ebony bridge, rounded bound tortoise shell celluloid pickguard (later models w/bound double stair step pickguard), bound ebony fingerboard w/block position markers and pendant arch, early models w/simpler trapeze or Grover DeLuxe tailpieces, later models w/stair step tailpiece, triple-bound broken arch pediment headstock (w/decorative finial) w/"Style B" in banner, oval pearl marquetry inlay (later models w/engraved "Style B" on inlaid pearl shield) and inlaid "D'Angelico" script logo, button tuners (later examples w/Grover Imperials), originally available only in full reddish brown Sunburst, some later models in Blonde, all metal parts gold-plated. Last ledger date: 2/17/48.

Excel - Earliest ledger date: 3/16/36, some earlier undated entries. 17" wide, generally X-braced, carved spruce top, carved maple back and maple sides, 1-3-ply bound f-holes, 7-ply binding on top, adjustable ebony bridge, engraved 3-5-ply bound double or triple stair step tortoise shell celluloid pickguard, triple bound ebony fingerboard w/engraved block position markers and pendant arch, early models with w/simpler trapeze or Grover DeLuxe tailpieces, (later models see preceding explanation), 3-5-ply bound broken arch pediment headstock (w/decorative finial - some later w/center dip headstock), w/script "Excel" logo inlaid in shield (some early examples labeled "Exel") and pearl "D'Angelico" script logo (pearl or aluminum skyscraper truss rod cover by the late '40s), scalloped Grover tuners (later examples w/Grover Imperials), originally available only in full reddish Brown Sunburst, Blonde option by late '30s, all metal parts gold-plated.

Excel Cutaway - Earliest ledger date: 05/09/47. Appointments as above (see New Yorker Special).

New Yorker - Earliest ledger date: 9/26/36. 18" wide, generally X-braced, carved spruce top, carved maple back and maple sides, 7+ ply binding on top, 5-ply bound f-holes, inlaid ebony bridge, engraved 7-ply bound tortoise shell celluloid triple stairstep pickguard, 3-ply bound ebony fingerboard w/diagonally segmented pearl block position markers and pendant arch, (tailpieces see preceding explanation), center dip headstock w/7-ply binding (some later models w/broken arch pediment headstock and decorative finial), inlaid pearl script "D'Angelico" logo, "New Yorker" skyscraper logo (pearl or aluminum skyscraper truss rod cover by the late '40s), Grover Imperial tuners (some w/Kluson "Seal-Fast" models), originally available in full reddish brown sunburst, blonde option by late '30s, all metal parts gold-plated.

New Yorker Cutaway - Earliest ledger date: 9/18/48. Appointments as above.

New Yorker Special - Earliest ledger date: 11/26/47. Listed as "small NY Cutaway," also later referred to as "Excel New Yorker" or "Excel Cutaway Johnnie (sic) Smith" model. Smith's personal guitar (01/05/55) was listed as an "Excel 1000." All names were applied interchangeably to 17" Excel Cutaways w/ New Yorker appointments.

Mel Bay (Special) - Earliest ledger date: 05/07/49. A variation of the New Yorker, headstock inlaid with the guitarist's name. Sold through Gravois Music, St. Louis, Mo.

A-1 - Earliest ledger date: 5/2/38. 17" wide, parallel braced, carved spruce top, carved maple back and maple sides, single bound top, f-holes not bound, adjustable ebony bridge, rounded single bound tortoiseshell celluloid pickguard (later examples w/double stairstep pickguard), single bound ebony fingerboard w/block position markers (some models w/ dots), usually equipped w/simpler trapeze or Grover DeLuxe tailpiece (some later models w/hinged "A-1" tailpiece - flat plate trapeze w/diagonal cross bar and arched string retainer), single bound arched headstock bearing "D'Angelico" pearl script logo and engraved diagonal pearl block w/"A-1" name, button tuners, sunburst top only, all metal parts nickel plated. Last ledger date: 11/20/43.

D'ANGELICO PRICING

The following values represent current price ranges, depending on the model, configuration, and overall condition. Most D'Angelicos are in better than average condition.

> **Style A** - $7,500-$10,000
> **Style B** - $9,000-$12,500
> **Excel** - $15,000-$25,000
> **Excel Cutaway** - $25,000-$35,000
> **New Yorker** - $25,000-$35,000
> **New Yorker Cutaway** - $45,000-$70,000
> **A-1** - $7,000-$9000

Because each guitar was normally custom built per individual specifications, there is very little standardized pricing structure within the variations. The price range of a D'Angelico guitar can be under $10,000 for a repaired, player's grade instrument; the high range has exceeded $100,000 – specifically depending on the condition, rarity, and even previous owner premium in some cases. It is highly recommended that several professional appraisals be secured before buying/ selling/trading any D'Angelico guitar.

With the rise of the "archtop renaissance" in the 1990s, a number of current luthiers are offering very high quality archtops in the same price range as the player's grade D'Angelicos (various models that have had professional repair). As a result, the player's grade D'Angelico market is fairly soft these days while challenged by the instruments of such builders as Triggs, Mortoro, De Cava, and a number of others.

D'ANGELICO BY VESTAX
Instruments currently built in Japan. Distributed by D'Angleico Guitars of America in Westfield, New Jersey.

In 1988 Mr. Jerry Berberine signed a deal with Mr. Hidesato Shino to re-launch the D'Angelico line of guitars that were to be made in Japan. These new instruments are built with the same quality that the vintage models were, and if any improvments can be made, are. Since 1997, more models have been introduced and they are now available in the U.S. market. Refer to the web site for more information (see Trademark Index).

ACOUSTIC

D'Angelico now has full jumbo sized acoustics available. The Round Body series have rounded tops and backs. The NYA-2R is the round 16" body model with a solid spruce top with maple back/sides/neck, 21-fret fingerboard with pearl zigzag position inlays, black New Yorker style pickguard, and is available in Natural Yellow, V-Blue, Natural, or Transparent Sunburst finish. The NYA-2 is similar to the NYA-2R except is a flat top and back. It also features elaborate binding.

Currently, D'Angelico offers only one archtop that is fully acoustic. This model is the New York Large Body Tear Drop (NYL-1). This model is based off the original. For other acoustic models made by Vestax refer to the Vestax section.

D'ANGELICO II
Instruments currently built in the U.S. Distributed by Archtop Enterprises, Inc. of Merrick, New York.

The D'Angelico II company is currently producing high quality reproductions of John D'Angelico's New Yorker and Excel models. Models share similar construction features such as spruce tops, figured maple back and sides, Ebony fingerboard with mother-of-pearl inlays, and gold-plated Grover tuners and tailpiece. All guitars are individually handcrafted and hand engraved.

The 18" New Yorker is offered in cutaway ($12,000) and non-cutaway ($11,750) versions, and in a Sunburst or Antique Natural finish. The Excel cutaway model ($11,500), Style B non-cutaway ($9,500), and Jazz Classic ($7,250) share a 17" body (measured across the lower bout). A smaller single pickup electric model

**D'Angelico New Yorker
courtesy Killer Vintage**

**D'Angelico Style B
courtesy Jay Wolfe**

D

called the Jazz Artist ($4,650) has a 16" body. Finally, a semi-hollowbody electric archtop called the Fusion ($3,750) is offered in Antique Natural, New Yorker Sunburst, or Flaming Red nitrocellulose lacquer finish.

D'ANGELICO REPLICA
Instruments currently built in Grass Valley, California beginning 1994. Distributed by The Working Musician of Arcadia, California.

Frank W. Green, author of the book, *D'Angelico, What's in a Name*, is currently offering a replica of the D'Angelico Excel (**Deluxe LB-175**). The D'Angelico replicas are officially sanctioned by the current name owner.

Green's book, offered by Centerstream Publishing, details the D'Angelico guitars from the point of view of the players and owners. The book contains a number of personal stories that bring to life the D'Angelico mystique, (Centerstream Publishing, P.O. Box 17878, Anaheim Hills CA 92807, phone or fax 714.779.9390).

ACOUSTIC ARCHTOP

Green is offering the Excel Deluxe LB-175, an instrument with a 17 1/2" lower bout, hand carved Engelmann spruce top, western curly maple back and sides, a curly maple neck, bound ebony fingerboard with 'split block' inlays, Grover tuners, and gold plated stairstep tailpiece. Retail list prices range between $10,000 to $18,000. An 18 1/2" **New Yorker** has a retail price between $12,000 to $20,000. The top of the line instruments allow for personalizing and custom features as long as they fall within the parameters of what the master would do.

D'AQUISTO
Instruments previously built in Huntington, New York, and Greenport, New York, between 1965 to 1995. D'Aquisto are currently being produced again as "re-issues" of the old world craftsmanship.

Master Luthier James L. D'Aquisto (1935-1995) met John D'Angelico around 1953. At the early age of 17, D'Aquisto became D'Angelico's apprentice, and by 1959 was handling the decorative procedures and other lutherie jobs. When D'Angelico had a falling out with another member of the shop during the move of the business, D'Aquisto began doing actual building and shaping work. This lutherie work continued until the time of D'Angelico's death in 1964. The loss of D'Angelico in 1964 not only affected D'Aquisto personally, but professionally. Although he took over the business and shop with the encouragement of D'Angelico's brother, business under his own trademark started slowly. D'Aquisto continued to work in D'Angelico's shop repairing instruments at the last address – 37 Kenmare Street, New York City, New York. Finally, one year after D'Angelico's death, D'Aquisto summoned the nerve to build a guitar with the D'Aquisto inlay on the headpiece.

In 1965, D'Aquisto moved his shop to Huntington, New York, and sold his first instrument, styled after a D'Angelico New Yorker. Most of D'Aquisto's traditional design instruments are styled after John D'Angelico's Excel and New Yorker, with D'Aquisto adding refinements and improvements. D'Aquisto set up a deal with the Swedish-based Hagstrom company to produce guitars based on his designs in 1968, and the Ampeg company was one of the U.S. distributors. In 1973, D'Aquisto relocated his business once again, this time setting up shop in Farmingdale, New York. He produced his first flattop guitar in 1975, and his first solid body electric one year later. The Fender Musical Instrument Corporation produced a number of D'Aquisto-designed guitars beginning in the 1980s, and two models in the Designer series (D'Aquisto Ultra and Deluxe) are still in production today at the Fender USA Custom shop.

In the late 1980s, D'Aquisto again moved his shop to Greenport, New York, and continued to produce instruments from that location. In 1987, D'Aquisto broke away from archtop design tradition when he debuted the Avant Garde. The Excel and New Yorker style models were discontinued in 1991, as D'Aquisto concentrated on creating more forward-looking and advanced archtops. In 1994, models such as the Solo with four soundholes (only nine built), and Centura models were introduced. James L. D'Aquisto passed away in April, 1995, (Source: Paul William Schmidt, *Acquired of the Angels*).

James D'Aquisto built several hundred instruments, from archtops to flattops to solid body electrics. D'Aquisto prices have gone up considerably in the past several years, and as a result, instruments have to be evaluated individually to ascertain the current market desirability and price. Generally, prices start in the $20,000 range, with the model, configuration (very important), and special order embellishments adding considerably to the base price. Deluxe New Yorkers are currently in the $40,000-$65,000 range. Remember, many of D'Aquisto's finer archtops sold for $15,000+ when new! Like D'Angelico, most of D'Aquisto's instruments were made to order and varied in dimensions and details. When buying/selling/appraising a D'Aquisto, it is the recommendation of the *Blue Book of Acoustic Guitars* that two or three professional appraisals be obtained.

Since D'Aquisto's death in 1995, a line of D'Aquisto reproductions are now available. These models use the old design, with new technology to produce some decent guitars. Little is know about the new guitars.

DAIMARU
Instruments previously produced in Japan.

Daimaru guitars were distributed in the U.S. by the Daimaru New York Corporation of New York, New York, (Source: Michael Wright, *Guitar Stories*, Volume One).

DAION
Instruments previously built in Nagoya, Japan circa late 1970s through the mid 1980s by Terada Guitars. Some guitars may also carry the trademark of Joodee or Yamaki. Distributed by MCI, Inc. of Waco, Texas.

Originally, these Japanese-produced high quality guitars were based on popular U.S. designs in the 1970s, but turned to original designs in the 1980s. The Daion logo was applied to a range of acoustic, semi-hollowbody, and solid body guitars and basses. Some Daion headstocks also feature a stylized lyre.

ACOUSTIC: HERITAGE SERIES

The Heritage series was Daion's top of the line for acoustic models. The following models were produced circa late 1970s to the early 1980s. To date, reliable market prices for this model series are not available.

GRADING	100%	EXCELLENT	AVERAGE

78 DAION HERITAGE - dreadnought style, solid cedar top with hand-stained mahogany finish, hardwood neck, round soundhole, maple binding, mahogany sides/2-piece back, 14/20-fret rosewood fingerboard with brass dot inlay, rosewood bridge with brass saddle, brass nut, rosewood string pins, 3-per-side gold plated sealed tuning machines, available in Natural finish.

78/12 Daion Heritage - similar to the 78 Daion Heritage, except in a 12-string configuration, slotted headstock, 6-per-side tuners.

79 DAION HERITAGE - similar to the 78 Daion Heritage, except has spruce or solid cedar top and brass binding, available in gloss Black finish.

80 DAION HERITAGE - dreadnought style, solid spruce top with hand-stained ovancol facing, nato neck, oval soundhole, maple binding, ovangkol back/sides, 14/20-fret maple bound rosewood fingerboard with brass dot inlay, tortoise pickguard, rosewood bridge with brass saddle, brass nut, maple bound headstock with carved Daion design inlay, rosewood string pins, 3-per-side gold plated sealed tuning machines, available in Natural finish.

ACOUSTIC: MAPLEWOOD SERIES

The Maplewood Series debuted in 1980. The dreadnought-styled MS-100 had a spruce top, maple back/sides/neck/fingerboard, brown dot inlays, sealed tuners, 3-on-a-side headstock, and a Natural Blonde finish. The MS-101 was similar, but featured a hand-rubbed Tan finish. A 12-string configuration with slotted headstock and 6-on-a-side plate tuners was called the MS-100/12. Reliable market prices for these models are not available.

ACOUSTIC: MARK SERIES

The Mark Series was offered circa late 1970s to the early 1980s. Truss rod access was at the body end of the neck, through the soundhole.

MARK I - dreadnought style, solid cedar top, hardwood neck, round soundhole, black binding, mahogany sides/back, 14/20-fret rosewood fingerboard with white dot inlay, rosewood bridge, rosewood pickguard, 3-per-side chrome sealed tuning machines, available in Natural finish.

	N/A	$250	$125

Last MSR was $255.

Mark I/12 - similar to the Mark I, except has a 12-string configuration, slotted headstock, 6-on-a-side tuners.

	N/A	$225	$100

Last MSR was $289.50.

MARK II - dreadnought style, solid cedar top, hardwood neck, round soundhole, white binding, redwood sides/2-piece back, 14/20-fret rosewood fingerboard with white dot inlay, rosewood bridge, rosewood pickguard, 3-per-side chrome sealed tuning machines, available in Natural finish.

	N/A	$250	$125

Last MSR was $299.50.

Mark II/12 - similar to the Mark II, except has a 12-string configuration, slotted headstock, 6-on-a-side tuners.

	N/A	$225	$100

Last MSR was $315.

MARK III - dreadnought style, spruce top, maple neck, round soundhole, white binding, maple sides/2-piece back, 14/20-fret maple fingerboard with brown dot inlay, maple bridge, rosewood pickguard, 3-per-side chrome sealed tuning machines, available in Natural finish.

	N/A	$275	$125

Last MSR was $340.

Mark III/12 - similar to the Mark III, except has a 12-string configuration, slotted headstock, 6-on-a-side tuners.

	N/A	$250	$125

Last MSR was $380.

MARK IV - dreadnought style, solid cedar top, hardwood neck, round soundhole, black binding, 5-layer maple/rosewood soundhole purfling, rosewood sides/2-piece back, 14/20-fret rosewood fingerboard with offset slash inlay, bone nut, rosewood bridge with bone saddle, rosewood pickguard, 3-per-side chrome rotomatic tuners, available in Natural finish.

	N/A	$275	$125

Last MSR was $395.

D'Aquisto Centura courtesy Scott Chinery

Mark IV/12 - similar to the Mark IV, except has a 12-string configuration, slotted headstock, 6-on-a-side tuners.

	N/A	$250	$125

Last MSR was $425.

MARK V - dreadnought style, solid cedar top, hardwood neck, round soundhole, herringbone binding/soundhole purfling, rosewood sides/2-piece back, 14/20-fret rosewood fingerboard with offset white dot inlay, bone nut, rosewood smile-shaped bridge with bone saddle, rosewood pickguard, 3-per-side chrome sealed tuners, available in Natural finish.

	N/A	$300	$150

Last MSR was $479.

Mark V/12 - similar to the Mark V, except has a 12-string configuration, slotted headstock, 6-on-a-side tuners.

	N/A	$275	$150

Last MSR was $495.

DAISY ROCK

Instruments currently produced overseas. Daisy Rock guitars are distributed by Alfred Publishing.

Daisy Rock was founded by Tish Ciravolo in October, 2000. Tish created Daisy rock to make guitars that appealed to girls specifically. In a male-dominated rock 'n roll world, guitars that were sculpted to the female, just didn't exist. Being the mother of two girls and playing guitar for many years, she was inspired to create this company. Guitars feature slimer necks for smaller hands, more light-weight and smaller bodies, and they also have visual features appealing towards women. Early in existance, Daisy Rock was a division of Schecter Guitar Research. Daisy Rock is now teamed up with Alfred Publishing, who distributes the line exclusively. Hard shell cases and custom guitars are also available. For more information on Daisy Rock and Alfred Publishing, refer to the web site (see Trademark Index).

ACOUSTIC

The Daisy Acoustic is available as the increasingly popular Guitar Pack Set. This includes a gig-bag, strap, picks, polishing cloth, string winder, and Girl's Guitar Method book and enhanced CD.

DAISY ACOUSTIC - composite oval back with spruce top body, 24 2/4" scale, mahogany set-neck, 20-fret rosewood fingerboard with pearloid daisy inlay, body binding, matching color headstock with 3-per-side tuners, chrome hardware, available in Powder Pink, Sky Blue, or Sunny Yellow finishes, mfg. 2000-current.

MSR	$279	$225	$150	$75

Add $20 for left-handed configuration.

Every guitar comes with a gig-bag as well as two full pages filled with removable butterfly and daisy decals.

PIXIE ACOUSTIC/ELECTRIC - composite oval back with flamed maple top body, 25 1/4" scale, mahogany set-neck, 20-fret rosewood fingerboard with pearloid daisy inlay, body binding, matching color headstock with 3-per-side tuners, chrome hardware, Daisy Custom piezo pickup and electronics, available in Blueberry Burst, or Plum Purple Burst finishes, new 2003.

MSR	$399	$300	$200	$125

Add $20 for left-handed configuration.

DAKOTA

Instruments previously built in Asia. Previously distributed by Sound Trek Distributors of Tampa, Florida.

Dakota Guitars' acoustic models are constructed with traditional 'old world' craftsmanship augmented by high tech computer designs. Dakota models are named after America's rare wildlife, and are quite recognizable by their abalone bound headstock which features a white pearl "Snow-covered mountain top" inlay. While Dakota Guitars has announced that the current models are being built in limited quantities, they have not yet disclosed how limited those quantities are. Currently there is no information available on the Dakota or Sound-Trek manufactures.

ACOUSTIC

Dakota Guitars' models are built with solid bone nuts and saddles, Sperzel U.S.A. tuners, abalone and white pearl inlays, and solid Engelmann spruce or tiger maple tops. Retail list prices include a case.

BH1 BIG HORN - grand concert style, solid Englemann spruce top, round soundhole, abalone binding, Indian rosewood back/sides, 14/20-fret fingerboard with inlay, bone nut, bridge with bone saddle, 3-per-side tuners, available in Natural finish, disc. mfg.

Last MSR was $899.

B1 BUCK - dreadnought style, solid Englemann spruce top, round soundhole, abalone binding, Indian rosewood back/sides, 14/20-fret fingerboard with inlay, bone nut, bridge with bone saddle, 3-per-side tuners, available in Natural finish, disc. mfg.

Last MSR was $915.

W1 WOLF - dreadnought style, tiger maple top, round soundhole, tiger maple back/sides, 14/20-fret fingerboard with inlay, bone nut, bridge with bone saddle, 3-per-side tuners, available in Gloss See-Through Black finish with matching headstock, disc. mfg.

Last MSR was $749.

ACOUSTIC ELECTRIC

Dakota Guitars' acoustic/electric models feature a Max-Q 1 preamp system built in.

C1 COUGAR - dreadnought style, single rounded cutaway, solid Englemann spruce top, round soundhole, abalone and wood rosette, Indian rosewood back/sides, 14/20-fret fingerboard with inlay, bone nut, bridge with bone saddle, 3-per-side tuners, Max-Q 1 Deluxe pickup, available in Natural finish, disc mfg.

Last MSR was $949.

E1 EAGLE - grand concert style, single rounded cutaway, solid Englemann spruce top, round soundhole, abalone binding, Indian rosewood back/sides, 14/20-fret fingerboard with inlay, bone nut, bridge with bone saddle, 3-per-side tuners, Max-Q 1 Deluxe pickup, available in Natural finish, disc mfg.

Last MSR was $1,049.

G1 GRIZZLY - dreadnought style, single rounded cutaway, solid Englemann spruce top, round soundhole, abalone binding, Indian rosewood back/sides, 14/20-fret fingerboard with inlay, bone nut, bridge with bone saddle, 3-per-side tuners, Max-Q 1 Deluxe pickup, available in Natural finish, disc mfg.

Last MSR was $1,065.

DALACK, TED
Instruments currently built in Gainesville, Georgia.

Luthier Ted Dalack has been handcrafting custom flattop steel string acoustic guitars for a number of years. Prices on Dalack's custom-built instruments range from $3,000 to $5,000. Dalack also offers repairs, restorations, and custom services on all fretted instruments. Dalack's shop is an authorized factory service repair shop for Martin and Taylor. For further information regarding custom built instruments or repairs, contact Ted Dalack directly (see Trademark Index).

DALLAS
Instruments previously built in England, West Germany, and Japan during the early to mid 1960s. Some guitars may also carry the trademark of Tuxedo.

The Dallas and Tuxedo trademarks are the brand names used by a UK importer/distributor. Early solid body guitars were supplied by either Fenton-weill or Vox in Britain, with entry level German and Japanese original design guitars imported in, (Source: Tony Bacon and Paul Day, *The Guru's Guitar Guide*).

DANA BOURGEOIS GUITARS
See Bourgeois

DAVID DAILY GUITARS
Instruments currently built in the U.S. Distributed by Kirkpatrick Guitar Studio of Baltimore, Maryland.

Luthier David Daily has been building high quality classical model guitars since 1976. These guitars are classical guitars with either Indian rosewood ($5,000) or Brazilian rosewood ($6,000-$7,000) and have either spruce or cedar tops. Other options are available and the current waiting list is over two years. For further information regarding model specifications and pricing, please contact the Kirkpatrick Guitar Studio directly (see Trademark Index).

DAVIS, J. THOMAS
Instruments currently built in Columbus, Ohio.

J. Thomas Davis began building guitars in a basement workshop while working on a music degree in 1975. The shop was moved to a storefront in Grandview Heights, OH in 1977 and relocated to the present location in Columbus, OH in 1993. The shop now employs four people dedicated to the service of fretted instruments (both electric and acoustic) while Tom spends his time building individual hand-made instruments. Tom individually designs and builds acoustic guitars one instrument at a time. He performs all of the work on his handmade guitars himself. Each instrument is built for a specific customer; each designed with a specific set of goals in mind.

In general, the materials selected, as well as the shape and size of the body, are contingent upon the sound characteristics desired by the customer. Prices are dependent upon the various materials used to as well as the specific work that is required to accomplish the customer's objectives. General prices: Steel string flattop guitars ($4,000-$6,000), Twelve string guitars ($4,500-$6,500), Classical guitars ($4,500-$8,000), Archtop guitars ($7,000-$10,000), and Harp guitars that are no longer available ($7,000-$9,000). Carved top Irish citterns and flat-top Irish bouzoukis are also available. The Waiting list is currently 12 – 16 months. For further information about repair work or custom guitar pricing, please contact luthier J. Thomas Davis directly (see Trademark Index).

DAVIS, WILLIAM
Instruments currently built in Boxford, Maine.

William Davis' hand built guitars are available through his Boxford, Maine lutherie. For up-to-date information concerning models and pricing, please contact luthier William Davis directly (see Trademark Index).

DAWAI

Instruments currently produced in Indonesia.

Dawai makes a number of acoustic guitars in their production facilities overseas. Models are the Primrose and the Rasquedo. These designs are basic folk and dreadnought models that are available in a number of colors. Most of these guitars are entry level guitars at entry level prices, but no distributors are in the U.S. currently.

DE CAVA

Instruments currently built in Stratford, Connecticut.

Born and raised in Stratford, Connecticut, luthier James R. De Cava began playing guitar and banjo as a teenager. De Cava began performing repairs on his guitars simply because there were few repair people around at the time. While spending time meeting others with similar interests, De Cava came into contact with Paul Morrisey and Bob Flesher at Liberty Banjo Co. De Cava worked for them between 1975 to the early 1980s cutting and inlaying mother-of-pearl with intricate designs. Through the years De Cava has built many different stringed instruments (banjos, mandolins, flattop and solid body guitars). De Cava now focuses on archtop guitar building.

De Cava briefly offered the Classic model ($5,720), which featured a flame or quilted maple top, fancy scroll position markers on the fingerboard, a pearl nut, an engraved pearl truss rod cover, and hand-engraved inlay pieces on the peghead (front and back)/pickguard/tailpiece/heel. An 18" body width was available at no extra charge.

GENERAL INFORMATION

All De Cava archtop guitars share similar features such as a solid hand-carved Sitka or Adirondack spruce top, carved maple back with matching sides, ebony fingerboard, hinged ebony tailpiece, an adjustable bridge, ebony pickguard, ebony peghead overlays, and bound f-holes. De Cava offers his models in either a 16" or 17" body width, with parallel or X-bracing. Prices include a hard shell case. Banjos, Ukuleles, Mandolin, and Classical guitars are also available.

Add $125 (and up) for special fingerboard inlays. Add $200 for Blonde finish. Add $200 (and up) for floating or built-in pick-up.

ACOUSTIC: ARCHTOP SERIES

De Cava's **Stratford** (list $5,200) is his traditional style guitar model, and features three layer body binding/single layer bound peghead and fingerboard, gold plated trim and tuners, pearl peghead logo, ebony truss rod cover, and gold and ebony tailpiece, available in a traditional Sunburst finish. This is also available in a seven-string model at no extra cost.

The **Stylist** model, discontinued, (last MSR was $7,450) was the deluxe model, with the highly figured maple back and sides, multi-layer bindings on the body/neck/peghead, 5-piece laminated figured maple neck, hand cut and engraved pearl pattern throughout the guitar, hand engraved pearl truss rod cover, and gold plated Schaller tuners with ebony buttons. The **Stylist** was available in either 16", 17", or 18" body widths; and Antique, Natural, or Sunburst finishes. A 7-string configuration was available at no extra charge.

ACOUSTIC: SIGNATURE SERIES

De Cava has a new model, the **Signature Blues**. The Signature Blues model was designed in conjunction with blues guitarist Debbie Davis. The Signature models are lightweight, contemporary hand-carved hollow body archtops with all the sleek contours of a solid body. Signature Series models have a 15 1/4" body width, 2 1/4" body depth, either a single neck pickup (Jazz model) or double pickups (Blues model), tune-o-matic style bridge/ebony tailpiece, and Neo-Classic fingerboard. The retail price of $4,700 includes a durable gig bag. The Signature models are available with optional customer's signature inlaid in pearl, and fingerboard inlays. This model is available in 7-string for $5,100 and a 8 or 9-string for $5,700.

The **Mark Elf Custom Classic** is a guitar designed by and for Mark Elf. It has Grover Imperial tuners, one-piece neck, multi-bound body, neck and peghead, split-block fingerboard inlays, Adirondack spruce and other select woods used throughout, 17" body width, floating pickup, jack, voume and tone controls mounted on the pickguard. Sug. Retail is $7,200. The **Auditorium Model** begins at $2,750. It has Indian rosewood back and sides, Adirondack red spruce top, ebony fingerboard and bridge, gold plated tuners, other wood options.

DEAN

Instruments currently produced in Plant City, Florida (Custom Shop and all the USA series) and Korea (all of the American Spirit series). Distributed by Armadillo Enterprises of Clearwater, Florida.

Previously, Dean guitars with the set-neck design were built in Evanston, Illinois from 1977 to 1986. In 1985, Dean began production of some models in Japan and Korea. Dean production from 1986 to 1993 was based in Asia.

The original Evanston, Illinois-based company was founded by Dean Zelinsky in 1977, after graduating from high school in 1976. Zelinsky, fond of classic Gibson designs, began building high quality electric solid body instruments and eventually started developing his own designs. Originally, there were three models: The **V** (similar to the Flying V), The **Z** (Explorer body shape), and the **ML** (sort of a cross between the V and an Explorer – and named after the initials of Matt Lynn, Zelinsky's best friend growing up). As the company's guitars gained popularity, production facilities were moved to Chicago in 1980.

Zelinsky originally got into the guitar building business to fill a void he felt the larger companies had: a high quality, set neck, eye-catching stage guitar. Though new designs continued to be developed, manufacturing of these instruments was shifted more and more to overseas builders. In 1986, Dean closed the USA Shop, leaving all construction to be completed overseas. The U.S. market had shifted towards the then-popular bolt neck super-strat design, and Zelinsky's personal taste leaned in the opposite direction.

Zelinsky sold Dean Guitars in 1990 to Oscar Medros, founder and owner of Tropical Music (based in Miami, Florida). The Dean Guitars facility in Plant City, Florida is currently run by Tracy Hoeft and Jon Hill, and new guitars are distributed to markets in the U.S., Japan, Korea, and Europe.

Zelinsky has estimated that between 6,000 and 7,000 (possibly 8,000) guitars were built in the U.S. between 1977 and 1986.

It has been estimated by various Dean collectors that the Japanese Dean models were built by the ESP Guitar company in Japan (circa 1986 to 1989).

In 1998, the Dean Guitar company introduced the Dean Stack in the Box (retail new $44.95), a stereo headphone amp that can be hooked up to home stereos; and the Dean Mean 16 (list $109.95), a 16 watt solid state amp with overdrive.

GRADING	100%	EXCELLENT	AVERAGE

ACOUSTIC ELECTRIC BASS

PERFORMER BASS CE (MODEL DGA-PBCE) - jumbo style, single rounded cutaway body, spruce top, round soundhole, multi-ply body binding, mahogany back/sides, 20-fret fingerboard with white dot inlay, triangular Dean rosewood bridge, 2-per-side Grover tuners, chrome hardware, piezo bridge pickup, 4-band EQ, available in Satin Natural finish, mfg. 1998-current.

MSR	$419		$315	$150	$95

Performer Bass CE Fretless - similar to the Performer Bass CE except in Fretless configuration, mfg. 2002-current.

MSR	$489		$395	$200	$135

PERFORMER PLUS BASS - jumbo style, single rounded cutaway body, spruce top, round soundhole, multi-ply body binding, mahogany back/sides, 22-fret fingerboard with white dot inlay, triangular Dean rosewood bridge, 2-per-side Grover tuners, chrome hardware, Shadow P7 pickup, 4-band EQ, available in Transparent Black or Satin Natural finish, mfg. 1998-current.

MSR	$589		$475	$255	$170

Performer Plus 5 Bass - similar to the Performer Plus bass except in 5-string configuration, mfg. 1998-current.

MSR	$689		$550	$295	$185

EXOTICA RADIANT BASS - single rounded cutaway, Sitka spruce top, flame maple top, mahogany neck, 15/22 fret rosewood fingerboard with radiant sun inlays, 2-per-side chrome Grover tuners, Shadow pickups, multi-ply binding, abalone soundhole inlay, available in Gloss Natural finish, mfg. 2000-current.

MSR	$699		$560	$305	$190

**Dean Artist CSE
courtesy Armadillo Enterprises**

ACOUSTIC: ARTIST SERIES

ARTIST CE - single cutaway thin body, solid Englemann spruce top, mahogany back/sides/neck, 14/22 fret rosewood fingerboard with pearl dot inlay, multi-ply binding, Abalone sound hole inlay, Grover 3-per-side tuners, Shadow P7 Electronics, available in Gloss Natural finish, mfg. 1999-current.

MSR	$469		$375	$250	$150

ARTIST CS (MODEL DGA-ACS) - jumbo style, single rounded cutaway medium thin body, solid spruce top, round soundhole, body binding, mahogany back/sides, 14/20-fret fingerboard with white dot inlay, triangular Dean rosewood bridge, 3-per-side Grover tuners, chrome hardware, available in Classic Black and Gloss Natural finishes, mfg. 1998-2000.

			$299	$145	$95

Last MSR was $399.

ARTIST CSE (MODEL DGA-ACSE) - jumbo style, single rounded cutaway medium thin body, solid spruce top, round soundhole, abalone binding, Dean "Wing" design rosette, solid rosewood sides, rosewood back, 14/24-fret extended fingerboard with block inlays, triangular Dean rosewood bridge, 3-per-side Grover tuners, gold hardware, piezo bridge pickup, Shadow 5-band EQ, available in Classic Black, Gloss Amber, and Gloss Natural finishes, mfg. 1998-current.

MSR	$699		$525	$325	$195

ACOUSTIC: CONCERT SERIES (CLASSICAL)

CONCERT - classical style body, cedar top, mahogany back/sides/neck, 12/18 fret rosewood fingerboard, 3-per-side open-gear tuners, multi-ply binding, abalone sound hole inlay, available in Gloss Natural finish, mfg. 1999-current.

MSR	$239		$195	$125	$70

Concert CE - similar to the Concert except has a single rounded cutaway and Dean electronics, mfg. 1999-current.

MSR	$369		$295	$205	$120

CONCERT C (MODEL DGA-CC) - classical style, single rounded cutaway body, select cedar top, round soundhole, multi-ply body binding, mahogany back/sides, 12/19-fret fingerboard, slotted headstock, tied bridge, 3-per-side tuning machines, available in Gloss Natural finish, mfg. 1998-2000.

			$185	$85	$50

Last MSR was $249.

**Dean Concert C
courtesy Armadillo Enterprises**

GRADING	100%	EXCELLENT	AVERAGE

CONCERT CRSE (CONCERT 24) - single rounded cutaway classical body, solid spruce top, rosewood back and sides, mahogany neck, 12/18-fret rosewood fingerboard, 3-per-side open-gear gold tuners, multi-ply binding, abalone soundhole inlay, Shadow P7 Electronics, available in Gloss Natural finish, mfg. 1999-current.

	MSR	$619		$495	$300	$175

ACOUSTIC: CONTOUR SERIES

CONTOUR - single cutaway hollow mahogany body, solid spruce top, set mahogany neck, 25 1/4" scale, multi-ply binding, extended rosewood fingerboard with dot position markers, 23 frets, Shadow P7 preamp, Grover tuners, chrome hardware, Abalone soundhole inlay, available in Metallic Blue (Calypso), Metallic Red (Del Feugo), Classic Black (Onyx) or Metallic White (Tundra), mfg 2001-02.

			$449	$225	$125

Last MSR was $599.

Each color specifies a different model. In another words there are four different model names, one for each color.

ACOUSTIC: "D" SERIES

D-1 - dreadnought style, laminated spruce top, round soundhole, maple neck, rosewood fingerboard with dot inlays, mahogany back/sides, enclosed chrome tuning machines, available in Natural finish, mfg. 1991-92.

			N/A	$125	$85

Last MSR was $199.

ACOUSTIC: EXOTICA SERIES

There are other new Exotica models introduced in 2003 that don't have any prices yet. These include an Exotica 9/11 which features custom New York inlays. The Extoica FM is also available in left-hand configuration.

EXOTICA FM - single cutaway hollow flame maple body, flame maple top, mahogany set neck with rosewood fingerboard, dot position markers, 25 1/4" scale, Abalone soundhole inlay, multi-ply binding, Dean Electronics, 21 frets, Grover tuners, chrome hardware, available in Trans. Black, Trans. Blue, Trans. Green, Trans. Red, or Gloss Natural finishes, mfg. 1999-current.

	MSR	$439		$329	$150	$95

EXOTICA ANDES - similar to the Exotica FM except features East Andes rosewood top/back/sides, available in Gloss Natural finish, mfg. 2001-current.

	MSR	$489		$350	$165	$95

Last MSR was $469.

EXOTICA BB - similar to Exotica FM, except has solid spruce top, bubinga back and sides, available in Gloss Natural finish, mfg. 1999-current.

	MSR	$489		$350	$165	$95

EXOTICA DAO - similar to Exotica FM, except has dao top/back/sides, available in Gloss Natural finish, mfg. 2001-current.

	MSR	$489		$350	$165	$100

EXOTICA FREEDOM - similar to Exotica FM, except has custom Statue of Liberty inlay on fingerboard, available in Transparent Black finish, new 2003.

	MSR	$629		$510	$300	$150

EXOTICA RADIANT - similar to Exotica FM, except has solid Englemann spruce top, rosewood back/sides, radiant sun inlays, available in Gloss Natural finish, mfg. 2001-current.

	MSR	$829		$665	$375	$225

EXOTICA QSE - similar to Exotica BB, except has Shadow P7 electronics, solid Engelmann Spruce top, quilt maple back and sides, AB multi-ply binding, available in Gloss Natural, Quilt Blue and Quilt Red finishes, mfg. 1999-current.

	MSR	$629		$505	$235	$145

EXOTICA RSE - similar to Exotica QSE, except has rosewood back and sides, rosewood EX fingerboard, hexagon position markers, available in Gloss Natural finish, mfg. 1999-current.

	MSR	$749		$599	$275	$185

ACOUSTIC: EXOTIGLASS SERIES

EXOTIGLASS - single rounded cutaway body, flame maple top, fiberglass composite back and sides, mahogany neck, 14/20-fret rosewood fingerboard with pearl dot inlay, 3-per-side chrome tuners, multi-ply binding, abalone soundhole inlay, Dean Electronics, available in Gloss Natural finish, mfg. 2000-current.

	MSR	$369		$295	$200	$130

Add $25 for Translucent Brownbust, Blue, or Red finishes.

GRADING	100%	EXCELLENT	AVERAGE

D

ACOUSTIC: MASTERS SERIES

Masters Series acoustics are produced in Czechoslovakia.

MASTERS SD (MODEL DGA-MSD) - dreadnought style, solid cedar top, round soundhole, wood body binding, mahogany back/sides, 14/20-fret fingerboard with white dot inlay, triangular Dean rosewood bridge, 3-per-side Schaller tuners, chrome hardware, available in Satin Natural finish, mfg. 1998-2000.

	$335	$160	$95

Last MSR was $449.

MASTERS SS (MODEL DGA-MSS) - similar to the Masters SD, except features a solid spruce top, mahogany neck, available in Gloss Natural finish, mfg. 1998-2000.

	$375	$175	$110

Last MSR was $449.

MASTERS SR (MODEL DGA-MSR) - similar to the Masters SD, except features a solid spruce top, rosewood back/sides, mahogany neck, available in Gloss Natural finish, mfg. 1998-2000.

	$425	$195	$125

Last MSR was $569.

MASTERS SE (MODEL DGA-MSE) - dreadnought style, solid spruce top, round soundhole, wood body binding, mahogany back/sides, mahogany neck, 14/20-fret fingerboard with white dot inlay, triangular Dean rosewood bridge, 3-per-side Schaller tuners, chrome hardware, piezo bridge pickup, Shadow 5-band EQ, available in Gloss Natural finish, mfg. 1998-2000.

	$449	$215	$125

Last MSR was $599.

ACOUSTIC: NTA (NEW TECHNOLOGY ACOUSTICS) SERIES

**Dean Exotica FM
courtest Dave Rogers
Dave's Guitar Shop**

NOUVEAU CM - offset double cutaway hollow mahogany body, solid Engelmann spruce top, 25 1/4" scale, mahogany set neck, 22 frets, rosewood fingerboard with dot position markers, Dean electronics, Grover tuners, chrome hardware, abalone sound hole inlay, available in Gloss Natural finish, mfg. 2001-02.

	$395	$195	$125

Last MSR was $529.

Nouveau CR - similar to Noveau CM, except has gold hardware, Shadow P7 electronics, rosewood back and sides, AB multi-ply binding, available in Gloss Natural finish, mfg. 2001-02.

	$525	$250	$150

Last MSR was $699.

FRANA TM - similar to Nouveau CM, except has 80mm body, available in Gloss Natural finish, mfg. 2001-02.

	$375	$175	$95

Last MSR was $499.

Frana TR - similar to Frana TM, except has gold hardware, Shadow P7 electronics, rosewood back and sides, AB multi-ply binding, available in Gloss Natural finish, mfg. 2001-02.

	$525	$250	$150

Last MSR was $699.

Frana R - similar to Frana TR, except has solid spruce top, available in Gloss Natural finish, mfg. 2001-02.

	$499	$240	$140

Last MSR was $669.

ACOUSTIC: PERFORMER SERIES

PERFORMER E - jumbo style, single rounded cutaway body, select spruce top, round soundhole, body binding, mahogany back/sides, 14/20-fret fingerboard with white dot inlay, triangular Dean rosewood bridge, 3-per-side die cast tuners, chrome hardware, piezo bridge pickup, volume/tone controls, available in Classic Black and Gloss Natural finishes, mfg. 1998-current.

MSR	$319		$239	$125	$75

Perfomer EA - similar to the Performer E except has no electronics, available in Brownburst or Vintage Sunburst finishes, new 2003.

MSR	$259		$210	$105	$60

D

GRADING		100%	EXCELLENT	AVERAGE

Performer DSE (Model DGA-PDSE) - similar to the Performer E, except features a solid spruce top, solid rosewood sides, rosewood back, abalone binding, 14/24 fret extended fingerboard with block inlays, Dean "Wing" design rosette, 3-per-side Grover tuners, gold hardware, Shadow 5-band EQ, available in Classic Black and Gloss Natural finishes, mfg. 1998-current.

MSR	$599	$449	$215	$150

Performer QSE - similar to Performer DSE, except has chrome hardware, quilt maple back and sides, dot position markers, available in Gloss Natural and Gloss Amber finishes, mfg. 1998-current.

MSR	$559	$419	$195	$125

PERFORMER SE (MODEL DGA-PSE) - similar to the Performer E, except features a solid spruce top, abalone binding, extended fingerboard, 3-per-side Grover tuners, Shadow 5-band EQ, available in Classic Black and Gloss Natural finishes, mfg. 1998-2002.

$395	$195	$125

Last MSR was $529.

Add $40 for left-handed configuration (Model DGA-PSE-L), available in Gloss Natural finish only.

Performer SE-7 - similar to Performer SE, except in a 7-string configuration, available in Gloss Natural finish, mfg. 1998-2002.

$465	$225	$125

Last MSR was $619.

Performer SE-12 - similar to Performer SE, except in a 12-string configuration, available in Gloss Natural and Classic Black finishes, mfg. 1998-current.

MSR	$639	$479	$225	$135

ACOUSTIC: RESONATOR SERIES

RESONATOR C (MODEL DGA-RC) - single rounded cutaway body, metal resonator plate, multi-ply body binding, mahogany back/sides, biscuit bridge, chrome hardware, 3-per-side tuning machines, available in Black Satin and Natural Mahogany finishes, mfg. 1998-2000.

$299	$150	$85

Last MSR was $399.

RESONATOR SP (MODEL DGA-RSP) - dreadnought style, metal resonator plate, multi-ply body binding, mahogany back/sides, mahogany neck, spider bridge, chrome hardware, 3-per-side tuning machines, available in Cherry Sunburst and Natural Mahogany finishes, mfg. 1998-current.

MSR	$399	$299	$145	$85

Resonator SPS - similar to the Resonator SP except features mahogony back/top/sides, mfg. 1998-current.

MSR	$499	$399	$195	$135

RESONATOR CE (MODEL DGA-RCE) - single rounded Dean cutaway body, metal resonator plate, multi-ply body binding, mahogany back/sides, biscuit bridge, chrome hardware, 3-per-side tuning machines, chrome lipstick pickup, volume/tone controls, available in Natural Mahogany of Black Satin finishes, mfg. 1998-current.

MSR	$529	$395	$190	$115

RESONATOR GCE (MODEL DGA-RGCE) - single rounded Dean cutaway body, metal resonator plate, multi-ply body binding, mahogany back/sides, biscuit bridge, gold hardware, 3-per-side tuning machines, humbucker pickup, volume/tone controls, available in Black Satin finish, mfg. 1998-current.

MSR	$629	$475	$225	$135

RESONATOR CHROME G/S - chrome steel resonator body, mahogany neck, 15/19 rosewood fingerboard with dot inlay, 3-per-side chrome tuners, biscuit bridge, mfg. 2001-current.

MSR	$699	$560	$295	$180

Add $35 for Chrome G version.

Resonator Chrome Engraved - similar to the Resonator Chrome except features an engraved chrome body, mfg. 2001-current.

MSR	$899	$725	$425	$275

ACOUSTIC: STAGE SERIES

STAGE ACOUSTIC (MODEL DGK-SA) - offset double cutaway hollow basswood body, round soundhole, body binding, set-in neck, 22-fret rosewood fingerboard with dot inlay, rosewood bridge, chrome hardware, small offset V-shaped headstock, 3-per-side tuners, available in Classic Black, Cherry Sunburst, Trans. Blue, or Trans. Purple finishes, mfg. 1998-2000.

$350	$225	$150

Last MSR was $499.

STAGE ACOUSTIC DELUXE (MODEL DGK-SD) - similar to the Stage Acoustic, except features a flame maple top, gold hardware, Shadow piezo bridge, volume/tone controls, available in Flame Black, Flame Cherry Sunburst, Flame Gloss Natural, and Flame Red finishes, mfg. 1998-2000.

$425	$275	$195

Last MSR was $599.

Add $20 for left-handed configuration (Model DGK-SD-L), available in Flame Gloss Natural finish only.

GRADING	100%	EXCELLENT	AVERAGE

ACOUSTIC: STUDIO SERIES

STUDIO S - classic body style, solid spruce top, mahogany back/sides/neck, 14/20-fret rosewood fingerboard with dot inlay, multi-ply binding, abalone soundhole inlay, 3-per-side Grover chrome tuners, availabe in Gloss Natural or Vintage Sunburst finishes, mfg. 2001-current.

MSR	$319	$260	$170	$110

STUDIO S DELUXE - similar to the Studio S except has an extended fingerboard to 23 frets and abalone body binding, available in Gloss Natural finish, mfg. 2001-current.

MSR	$419	$340	$195	$125

Dean Performance SE
courtest Armadillo Enterprises

ACOUSTIC: SWEETWOOD SERIES

The Sweetwood series was introduced in 2003. These are a higher end line of acoustic guitars having the highest price tag of any new Dean acoustic guitars. Models include two dreadnoughts, a classical, and a cutaway jumbo style. Look for more information in further editions of the *Blue Book of Acoustic Guitars*.

TRADITION SERIES

The **AcousticPack (Model DGP-AP)** is an all-in-one starter system that includes a Tradition One acoustic guitar in Gloss Natural, a guitar strap, Dean picks, and a guitar tuner. This complete package retails for $269.

In 2003, the Daytona series was introduced. These are the entry line level acoustics in the entire Dean line. The acoustic retails for $229 and the Acoustic/Electric version is $289. More research is underway for these models. Other Tradition series models that have been introduce include the Noir, Tucson, and the Phantom. More information will appear in upcoming editions of the *Blue Book of Acoustic Guitars*.

TRADITION ONE (MODEL DGA-T1) - dreadnought style, select spruce top, round soundhole, body binding, mahogany back/sides, 14/20-fret fingerboard with white dot inlay, triangular Dean rosewood bridge, 3-per-side die cast tuners, available in Gloss Natural finish, mfg. 1998-current.

MSR	$249	$175	$85	$50

Add $20 for left-handed configuration (Model DGA-T-L), available in Gloss Natural finish only. Left-hand model discontinued in 2000.

TRADITION S - dreadnought style, solid spruce top, round soundhole, body binding, mahogany back/sides, 14/20-fret fingerboard with white dot inlay, triangular Dean rosewood bridge, 3-per-side Grover tuners, available in Gloss Natural, Classic Black, Satin Natural, Trans. Red, or vintage Sunburst finishes, mfg. 1998-current.

MSR	$319	$240	$115	$65

Add $40 for left-hand configuration.

Tradition SE - similar to the Tradition S except features a piezo bridge pickup and Shadow 5-band EQ, available in Gloss Natural finish, mfg. 1998-2000.

		$325	$150	$95

Last MSR was $429.

Tradition C SE - similar to the Tradition S except features a single cutaway with Dean electronics, available in Gloss Natural finish, mfg. 2001-current.

MSR	$449	$350	$225	$95

Tradition S12 - similar to the Tradition S except in 12-string configuration, available in Gloss Natural finish, mfg. 1999-current.

MSR	$419	$325	$175	$95

TRADITION TQS12 - dreadnought style 12-string body, solid spruce top, quilted maple back and sides, mahogany neck, 14/20 rosewood fingerboard with dot inlay, 6-per-side gold Grover tuners, multi-ply binding, abalone soundhole inlay, available in Gloss Natural finish, mfg. 2001-current.

MSR	$569	$460	$240	$150

TRADITION D24 - dreadnought style body, solid Englemann spruce top, quilted rosewood back and sides, mahogany neck, 14/20 rosewood fingerboard with abalone tree of life inlay, 3-per-side gold Grover tuners, multi-ply binding, abalone soundhole inlay, available in Gloss Natural finish, mfg. 2001-current.

MSR	$589	$475	$250	$155

Dean Tradition S
courtest Armadillo Enterprises

DEAR

Instruments currently produced in Asia. Distributed by L.A. Guitar Works of Reseda, California.

Dear guitars are medium quality acoustic guitars that feature a wood top mated to a shallow fiberglass back. The Dear design is similar to the design pioneered by Ovation, except instead of a rounded bowl back the Dear design is squared. At the given list price point, it is estimated that the Dear guitar tops are laminated, not solid.

ACOUSTIC ELECTRIC

The three Dear acoustic/electric models have a cutaway body, on board preamp and bridge-mounted pickup system. The **DAC-480E** has a round soundhole, spruce top, and a retail price of $299. The **DAC-485E** features similar construction, with a highly flamed maple top (list $319). Instead of a round soundhole, the **DAC-500E** has a pair of f-holes.

In addition to the acoustic/electrics, Dear also offers two classical style/synthetic back models. The EL 1500 (list $439) has a cedar top and matte finish; the EL 2000 has a spruce top (list $459).

DECCA

Instruments previously produced in Japan.

The Decca trademark is a brand name used by U.S. importers Decca Records, (Source: Michael Wright, *Guitar Stories,* Volume One).

DEERING

Current banjo manufacturer located in Lemon Grove since 1975. Guitars were previously built from 1989-1991.

In 1975, Greg and Janet Deering began producing the quality banjos for which the company is known for. While continuing to offer innovative banjo designs, the Deerings also offer several models from entry level to professional play.

Deering offers a banjo model that is tuned and played like a guitar. The **MB-6** is designed for the guitar player who doesn't have to learn banjo to play banjo. The MB-6 is also available in a 12-string configuration.

In the late 1980s, Deering offered 4 different solid body guitar models in 2 variations that carried a retail price between $1,498-$2,850. The guitar models were also offered with some custom options, but were only produced for little over one year.

DELL'ARTE INSTRUMENTS, INC.

Instruments currently built in Santee, CA.

Dell'Arte and Finegold quality acoustic guitars and mandolins are hand built by John Kinnard, Luthier. His standard models include: Anouman ($2,400 retail), Sweet Chorus ($1,800 retail), Dark Eyes ($2,400 retail), Minor Swing ($1,800 retail), Swing 42 Standard ($2,200 retail), Swing 42 Deluxe ($2,400 retail), Finegold OM (3 variations priced $1,400-$2,200 retail), and Jazz Arch Top ($2,900 retail). They also have some recent models including the Angelo Debarre Signature, the Leadbelly 12-String, the Jimmy Roseberg, the Studio Dreadnought, and the Studio OM. In 2001, Dell'Arte strings were introduced. Please contact the company directly for current information and pricing (see Trademark Index).

DELMUNDO

Instruments currently produced in Boulder, CO.

Delmundo guitars are produced under the direction of Bob Alexander.

DEY

See BD Dey.

DIASONIC

Instruments previously produced in Japan, circa unknown.

It is estimated that Diasonic instruments were constructed in the 1970s, as their headstock design skirts infringe on Gibson's standard design.

The Diasonic folk style acoustic has a spruce top, geometric pattern rosette, nato back and sides, 14/20-fret rosewood fingerboard with rectangular pearloid inlay, 3-per-side chrome tuners, adjustable saddle, white bridge pins, and tortoise pickguard. Diasonic instruments in average condition command about $100, (Source: Walter Murray, *Frankenstein Fretworks*).

DILLON

Instruments currently built in Bloomsburg, Pennsylvania.

John Dillon started building guitars in New Mexico in 1975. Dillon now produces guitars in Pennsylvania. Dillon Guitars offers quality custom-built instruments. For pricing and options refer to the web site. For further information, contact Dillon Guitars directly (see Trademark Index).

DINOSAUR

Instruments and other products currently produced in China. Distributed by Eleca International Inc. in Walnut, California.

Dinosaur makes a wide variety of products including guitars, amplifiers, and other accessories in the music industry. They are built in China and sold throughout the United States. Among the products that they produce include combo packs that have a guitar, amp, and other accessories for the starting guitar player. For more information refer to the distributors web site (see Trademark Index).

ACOUSTIC

Dinosaur's guitars are mainly basic acoustic models such as the dreadnought, the folk-style, and the classical. Some models are offered with electronics and have cutaways. These guitars are offered at a competitive price.

DITSON

Instruments previously manufactured in Boston, Massachusetts from 1865 to the early 1900s.

The Oliver Ditson Company, Inc. was formed in 1835 by music publisher Oliver Ditson (1811-1888). Ditson was a primary force in music merchandising, distribution, and retail sales on the East Coast. He also helped establish two musical instrument manufacturers: The John Church Company of Cincinnati, Ohio, and Lyon & Healy (Washburn) in Chicago, Illinois.

In 1865 Ditson established a manufacturing branch of his company under the supervision of John Haynes, called the John C. Haynes Company. This branch built guitars for a number of trademarks, such as Bay State, Tilton, and Haynes Excelsior, (Source: Tom Wheeler, *American Guitars*).

DOBRO

Current trademark of instruments currently built by Original Acoustic Instruments (OAI), located in Nashville, TN. Original Acoustic Instruments is a division of the Gibson Guitar Corporation. Previously manufactured by Original Musical Instruments Company, located in Huntington Beach, California. In 1997, production was moved to Nashville, Tennessee. Distributed by the Gibson Guitar Corporation of Nashville, Tennessee.

The original Dobro company was formed in 1928 in Los Angeles, California.

The Dopyera family emigrated from the Austro-Hungary area to Southern Califonia in 1908. In the early 1920s, John and Rudy Dopyera began producing banjos in Southern California. They were approached by guitarist George Beauchamp to help solve his volume (or lack thereof) problem with other instruments in the vaudeville orchestra. In the course of their conversation, the idea of placing aluminum resonators in a guitar body for amplification purposes was developed. John Dopyera and his four brothers (plus some associates, like George Beauchamp) formed National in 1925. The initial partnership between Dopyera and Beauchamp lasted for about two years, and then John Dopyera left National to form the Dobro company. The Dobro name was chosen as a contraction of the Dopyera Brothers (and it also means *good* in Slavic languages).

The Dobro and National companies were later remerged by Louis Dopyera in 1931 or 1932. The company moved to Chicago, Illinois in 1936, and a year later granted Regal the rights to manufacture Dobros. The revised company changed its name to Valco in 1943, and worked on war materials during World War II. In 1959, Valco transferred the Dobro name and tools to Emil Dopyera. Between 1966 and 1967, the Dobro trademark was sold to Semie Moseley, of Mosrite fame. Moseley constructed the first Dobros out of parts from Emil's California plant, and later built his own necks and bodies. Moseley also built Mobros, a Mosrite-inspired Dobro design. After Mosrite collapsed, the name was still held by Moseley; so in the late 1960s, Emil's company produced resonator guitars under the tradename of Hound Dog and Dopera (note the missing 'y') Originals. When the Dobro name finally became available again, Emil and new associates founded the Original Musical Instruments Company, Inc. (OMI) in 1970. OMI has been producing Dobros ever since.

In 1985, Chester and Mary Lizak purchased OMI from Gabriela and Ron Lazar; and eight years later in 1993, OMI was purchased by the Gibson Guitar Corporation, and production continued to be centered in California. The production of Dobro instruments was moved to Nashville, Tennessee in the Spring of 1997. Early company history courtesy Bob Brozman, The History and Artistry of National Resonator Instruments.

ACOUSTIC: CALIFORNIA MADE MODELS 1929-1939

Not only do Dobro guitars not have the model number, models were often inconsistent. To determine your model of Dobro, you have to read through the model descriptions in order to match it up with the correct number. Woods and other pieces are known to be inconsistent as well. There is also overlapping models where a California model was made and at the same time a Regal model was introduced with the same number designation.

MODEL 36 - magnolia body, mahogany round neck, macawood fingerboard, silver painted hardware, available in Black finish, mfg. 1932-34.

| | N/A | $1,900 | $1,400 |

MODEL 37 - mahogany body, round neck, bound body and bound 12-fret fingerboard with dot inlay, Light-red finish, mfg. 1932-34.

| | N/A | $2,000 | $1,500 |

MODEL 45 - wood body of unknown woods, square or round-neck, silver metal parts and other painted parts, Dark Walnut finish, mfg. 1929-1934.

| | N/A | $1,900 | $1,400 |

Certain pieces may be painted a mahogany color and serial numbers of this variation run between 1200-1300.

MODEL 55/56 - hardwood body, round or square neck, binding on the 12-fret fingerboard only, chrome plated hardware, Walnut finish, mfg. 1929-1934.

| | N/A | $1,900 | $1,400 |

In 1932 the Model 55 was renamed the Model 56 and featured a birch body, mahogany neck, a bound red bean fingerboard, and nickel hardware. This model was also referred to as the Standard.

GRADING	100%	EXCELLENT	AVERAGE

MODEL 65/66 - wood body with sandblasted French scroll design on the entire body, binding on fingerboard, mfg. 1929-1933.

	N/A	$2,800	$2,200

In 1932, the Model 66 replaced the Model 65 with a birch body, mahogany neck, and chrome-plated hardware. Some models were available with a sandblasted design on the headstock as well. In 1932 the Model 66 was also available as the 66B with body binding.

Model 60 - similar to the Model 66 except features a large D on the back and a bound red bean fingerboard, mfg. 1933-36.

	N/A	$2,800	$2,200

MODEL 85/86 - mahogany body, engraved coverplate, handrest with fleur-de-lis engraving, triple bound body, mahogany neck, bound fingerboard, available in round or square neck, mfg. 1929-1934.

	N/A	$3,000	$2,400

This model was also known as the Professional. In 1932 it was renamed from the Model 85 to the Model 86 and features a rosewood fingerboard, chrome plated hardware, engraved tuners, and has a 2-tone red/brown finish.

MODEL 125 (DE LUXE) - 5-ply black walnut body with matching burl, handrest engraved with "Dobro Deluxe," triple bound body, black walnut round or square neck, ebony fingerboard, celluloid inlay logo, nickel plated hardware, available in Natural finish, mfg. 1929-1934.

	N/A	$3,200	$2,500

ACOUSTIC: REGAL ERA INSTRUMENTS

REGAL MODEL 27 - birch, mahogany, or maple body, round or square neck with 12 or 14 frets, holes at the end of the fingerboard, available in 2-tone walnut finish, mfg. 1933-1942.

	N/A	$1,500	$1,100

This model was produced in California. In 1939, 3-segment f-holes were added to specifications of the Model 25.

REGAL MODEL 37 - mahogany body, round or square neck with 12 or 14 frets, bound body, available in Sunburst finish, mfg. 1933-1937.

	N/A	$1,800	$1,250

Some models were produced with bound fingerboards, and this model was also available as a California.

REGAL MODEL 45 - spruce top, mahogany back and sides, 4-ply top binding, single-ply back binding, ebony fingerboard, round or square neck, mfg. 1933-37.

	N/A	$2,000	$1,400

REGAL MODEL 46/47 - aluminum body dobro lite or luma lite body, 14 fret round neck joint, slotted headstock, silver finish with gold highlights, mfg. 1935-1942.

	N/A	$1,200	$750

In 1937, the finish was changed to a mahogany or maple grain paint. In 1939, the model was changed to the number 47.

REGAL MODEL 55 - spruce top, mahogany back and sides, arched back, bound body, round or square neck, chrome hardware with inlays, mfg. 1933-34.

	N/A	$2,000	$1,400

REGAL MODEL 62/65 - brass body with nickel plating, Spanish dancer etching on the back, solid headstock, mfg. 1935-1942.

	N/A	$1,200	$750

By 1937 the rosewood fingerboard was documented. In 1939 the Model 62 was changed to the 65.

ANGELUS - birch body, round or square neck, 3-segment F-holes, 12 large round holes in the coverplate, simulated binding by paint, slotted peghead, Walnut, Natural, or Sunburst finish, mfg. 1933-36.

	N/A	$900	$650

ACOUSTIC: 1960S ERA MFG.

There are other models produced during this time and more research is underway for upcoming editions.

ACOUSTIC: ACOUSTIC SERIES

MAHOGANY TROUBADOUR (DWTRUMH) - available in Natural finish, mfg. 1996-2000.

$1,200	$780	$510

Last MSR was $1,499.

SPRUCE TOP TROUBADOUR (DWTRUSP) - similar to the Mahogany Troubadour, except has a spruce top, mfg. 1996-2000.

$1,360	$885	$580

Last MSR was $1,699.

ACOUSTIC: ARTIST SIGNATURE SERIES

The Artist Signature models are limited edition models that are signed up on the headstock by the Artist involved with the specialty design (Dobro also offers the same design in an unsigned/un-numbered edition as well).

GRADING	100%	EXCELLENT	AVERAGE

D

JERRY DOUGLAS LTD (DWJDS LTD) - hollow style with internal soundposts and tone bars, bound mahogany top/back/sides, 2 screened/3 smaller uncovered soundholes, single cone resonator with squared sound holes, 25" scale, mahogany neck, 12/19-fret bound rosewood fingerboard with pearl dot inlay (dots begin at 5th fret), spider bridge/trapeze tailpiece, solid peghead with logo decal/signature, chrome hardware, 3-per-side tuners, available in Natural finish, mfg. 1996-current.

MSR	$3,738		$2,995	$1,950	$1,200

Jerry Douglas (DWJDS) - similar to the Jerry Douglas Ltd., except has no signature on peghead, mfg. 1996-current.

MSR	$2,738		$2,195	$1,525	$950

JOSH GRAVES LTD (DWJOSH LTD) - hollow style, bound wood body, 2 screened soundholes, single cone resonator, 25" scale, 12/19-fret rosewood fingerboard with pearl dot inlay, spider bridge/trapeze tailpiece, solid peghead with logo decal/signature, chrome hardware, 3-per-side tuners, available in Sunburst finish, mfg. 1996-current.

MSR	$3,738		$2,995	$1,950	$1,200

This model is based on Graves' own 1928 Model 37.

Josh Graves (DWJOSH) - similar to the Josh Graves Ltd., except has no signature on peghead, mfg. 1996-current.

MSR	$2,738		$2,195	$1,525	$950

PETE BROTHER OSWALD KIRBY LTD (DWOS LTD) - hollow style, bound wood body, 2 screened soundholes, single cone resonator with parallelogram soundwell holes, 12/19-fret rosewood fingerboard with pearl dot inlay (position markers begin at 5th fret), 'V'-shaped roundneck, metal high-nut adaptor, spider bridge/trapeze tailpiece, slotted peghead with logo decal/signature, chrome hardware, 3-per-side tuners, available in Sunburst finish, mfg. 1996-current.

MSR	$3,738		$2,995	$1,950	$1,200

This model is based on Kirby's own 1928 Model 27.

Pete Brother Oswald Kirby (DWOS) - similar to the Pete Brother Oswald Kirby Ltd., except has no signature on peghead, mfg. 1996-current.

MSR	$2,738		$2,195	$1,525	$950

AL PERKINS LTD (DW PERKINS LTD) - hollow style, bound figured maple top/back/sides, 2 f-holes, single cone resonator with engraved pointsettia palmplate, 12/19-fret bound rosewood fingerboard with pearl dot inlay (dots begin at 5th fret), spider bridge/trapeze tailpiece, solid peghead with logo decal/signature, gold hardware, 3-per-side tuners, available in Trans. Black finish, mfg. 1996-current.

MSR	$3,738		$2,995	$1,950	$1,200

Al Perkins (DW Perkins) - similar to the Al Perkins Ltd., except has no signature on peghead, mfg. 1996-current.

MSR	$2,738		$2,195	$1,525	$950

TOM SWATZELL LTD (DWTS LTD) - hollow style, bound wood body, 2 screened/3 smaller uncovered soundholes, single cone resonator with engraved diamond palmplate/coverplate, 12/19-fret bound ebony fingerboard with abalone diamond inlay (position markers begin at 5th fret), spider bridge/trapeze tailpiece, slotted peghead with logo decal/signature, chrome hardware, 3-per-side tuners, available in Sunburst finish, mfg. 1996-current.

MSR	$3,738		$2,995	$1,950	$1,200

Tom Swatzell (DWTS) - Similar to the Tom Swatzell Ltd., except has no signature on peghead, mfg. 1996-current.

MSR	$2,738		$2,195	$1,525	$950

Dobro Model 66
courtesy Gibson
Guitar Company

ACOUSTIC: BOTTLENECK SERIES

Bottleneck Series instruments are specifically designed for bottleneck-style guitar playing, and feature a flat 14/19-fret fingerboard, biscuit bridge, and a single 9 1/2" resonator cone.

CHROME-PLATED 90 (DM90) - hollow style, chrome plated bell brass body, 2 f-holes, single cone resonator, maple neck, 14/19 fret rosewood fingerboard with white dot inlay, biscuit bridge/trapeze tailpiece, chrome hardware, solid peghead, 3-per-side tuners, available in Chrome finish, disc. 2000.

	N/A	$1,000	$700

Last MSR was $1,799.

D

GRADING	100%	EXCELLENT	AVERAGE

90 DELUXE (DM90 DLX) - similar to the Chrome-Plated 90, except features a bound ebony fingerboard with pearl diamond inlays, sand-blasted Palm Tree scene on front and back, disc. 2000.

	N/A	$1,250	$825

Last MSR was $2,099.

STEEL BODY 90 (DS90) - similar to the Chrome-Plated 90, except has a steel body, available in Amberburst or Darkburst finishes, mfg. 1996-2000.

	$1,200	$780	$510

Last MSR was $1,499.

HULA BLUES (DWHB) - hollow style, maple top, 2 f-holes, single cone resonator, maple back/sides/neck, 12/19-fret rosewood fingerboard with pearl dot inlay, spider bridge/trapeze tailpiece, chrome hardware, slotted peghead, 3-per-side tuners, available in Brown/Cream or Green/Cream screened Hawaiian scenes (front and back) finishes, disc. 2000.

	N/A	$750	$450

Last MSR was $1,099.

ACOUSTIC: DM33 (THE METAL BODY) SERIES

33 Series instruments have round necks, 2 f-holes (instead of mesh-covered soundholes) biscuit bridge, and a 10 1/2" inverted resonator cone.

DM33 - hollow style, chrome plated bell brass body, 2 f-holes, single cone resonator, maple neck, 14/19-fret rosewood fingerboard with white dot inlay, biscuit bridge/trapeze tailpiece, chrome hardware, 3-per-side tuners, available in California Girl, Dobro D, Gator, Hawaiian (palm trees), Sand-blasted Flower, or Sailboat finishes on back, current mfg.

MSR	$2,472	$1,980	$1,375	$850

In 1996 the Sand-blasted Flower finish was discontinued and all the other finishes were introduced.

DM33 POWDERCOAT (DS33) - similar to the DM33 except features a black, silver, bronze or gray powder coat (black and gray disc. 2002), current mfg.

MSR	$2,142	$1,725	$1,250	$750

DM20 (DECO) - similar to the DM33 except features the "Deco" engraving, current mfg.

MSR	$3,165	$2,545	$1,750	$1,100

DM36 (ROSE) - similar to the DM33 except features the "Rose" engraving, current mfg.

MSR	$2,748	$2,199	$1,500	$950

DM75 (LILY OF THE VALLEY) - similar to the DM33 except features the "Lily of the Valley" engraving, current mfg.

MSR	$3,649	$2,925	$1,900	$1,250

DM1000 (DOBRO SHIELD) - similar to the DM33 except features the "Dobro Shield" engraving, current mfg.

MSR	$4,218	$3,375	$2,175	$1,425

DM3000 (CHRYSANTHEMUM) - similar to the DM33 except features the "Crysanthemum" engraving, current mfg.

MSR	$4,828	$3,875	$2,425	$1,600

33 DELUXE MESA (MODEL DM33 DLX M) - similar to the Chrome Plated 33, except has mesa style sand-blasted design on back, mfg. 1996-2000.

	$1,680	$1,090	$715

Last MSR was $2,099.

STEEL 33 (MODEL DS33) - similar to the Chrome Plated 33, except has steel body, available in Amberburst and Darkburst finishes, mfg. 1996-2000.

	$1,200	$780	$500

Last MSR was $1,499.

WOOD 33 (MODEL DW33) - similar to the Chrome Plated 33, except has 3-ply laminated maple body, available in Natural finish, mfg. 1996-2000.

	$1,040	$670	$440

Last MSR was $1,299.

ACOUSTIC: ROUNDNECK SERIES

The 60 Roundneck Series, like their Squareneck counterparts, have a 12/19 fingerboard, 3-ply laminated wood bodies, 10 1/2" resonator, and a original-style spider bridge. The Roundneck series has a rounded (Spanish) neck.

DW60 (F-60) - hollow style, 3-ply laminated maple top/back/sides, 2 screened/3 smaller uncovered soundholes, single cone resonator, maple neck, 12/19-fret rosewood fingerboard with white dot inlay, spider bridge/trapeze tailpiece, solid peghead with logo decal, chrome hardware, 3-per-side tuners, available in Amber, Natural, and Sunburst finishes, disc. 2000.

	$995	$700	$500

Last MSR was $1,399.

DWF60RDB - similar to 60 Classic, available in Darkburst finish, current mfg.

MSR	$1,926	$1,545	$1,050	$650

D

CLASSIC 60 AMBER - similar to 60 Classic, except has bound body, available in Amber finish, disc. 1996.

	N/A	$610	$370

Last MSR was $1,149.

This model was also available with a square neck (Model DW60 A S).

CLASSIC 60 MAHOGANY (MAHOGANY CLASSIC MODEL DW60 MN) - similar to 60 Classic, except has mahogany body, 2 screened/3 clear soundholes, bound body/fingerboard/peghead, pearl diamond/dot fingerboard inlay, available in Natural finish, disc. 1996.

	N/A	$660	$400

Last MSR was $1,249.

This model was also available with a square neck (Model DW60 MN S).

CLASSIC 60 NATURAL (NATURAL CLASSIC MODEL DW60 N) - similar to 60 Classic, except has bound body, available in Natural finish, disc. 1996.

	N/A	$610	$370

Last MSR was $1,149.

This model was also available with a square neck (Model DW60 N S).

CLASSIC 60 SUNBURST (MODEL DW60 S) - similar to 60 Classic, except has bound body, available in 3-Tone Sunburst finish, disc. 1996.

	N/A	$640	$385

Last MSR was $1,199.

This model was also available with a square neck (Model DW60 S S).

CLASSIC 60 WALNUT (WALNUT CLASSIC MODEL DW60 WN) - hollow style, walnut top, 2 screened/3 clear soundholes, single cone resonator, walnut back/sides, maple neck, 14/19 fret bound ebony fingerboard with pearl vine inlay, spider bridge/trapeze tailpiece, chrome hardware, slotted peghead w/logo decal, 3-per-side tuners w/plastic buttons, available in Natural finish, disc. 1996.

	N/A	$700	$425

Last MSR was $1,299.

This model was also available with a square neck (Model DW60 WN S).

Dobro Woody Body
courtesy Gibson
Guitar Company

DW90 - figured maple body, 2 F-Holes, Spider-style resonator, poinsetta cover plate, single body binding, 14/19 fret flat fingerboard with dot inlay, 3-per-side tuners, nickel plated hardware, available in Vintage Sunburst, Trans. Red, Trans. Blue, Tran. Green, Trans. Black, or Natural finishes, deluxe hardshell case included, current mfg.

MSR	$2,099	$1,680	$1,125	$700

DW90C - similar to the DW90 except has a single cutaway, only one f-hole, current mfg.

MSR	$2,215	$1,775	$1,175	$725

Wood Body 90 Deluxe (DW90 DLX) - similar to the DW90, except features a bound peghead, bound ebony fingerboard with pearl diamond inlay, mfg. 1996-2000.

	N/A	$1,000	$700

Last MSR was $1,799.

Wood Body 90 Soft Cutaway (DWSFT) - similar to the DW90, except has single rounded cutaway, slotted headstock, multiple soundholes in 2 diamond-shaped groups, available in Natural or Darkburst finishes, disc. 2000.

	$850	$550	$545

Last MSR was $1,599.

DOBROLEKTRIC - figured maple single cutaway body, single upper body F-Hole, single body binding, biscuit style resonator, poinsettia cover plate, two pickups (nickel bridge transducer and black P-90 neck), 3 knobs, available in Vintage Sunburst finish, slimline deluxe hardshell case included, current mfg.

MSR	$2,142	$1,720	$1,150	$725

The Dobrolektric was also available in Blackburst and Wine Red finishes for a short time.

HOUND DOG - laminated and figure maple body, open sound well constrution, 2 F-holes, no body binding, round neck, spider style resonator, fan cover plate, Fishman resonator pickup, nickel plated hardware, available in hand-rubbed brown finish, gig-bag included, new 2003.

MSR	$999	$800	$525	$350

MISSISSIPPI VOODOO - single cutaway mahogany body with figured maple top, "lizard" shaped f-hole, no resonator, poinsettia cover plate, gold plated hardware, VooDoo Magic Pickups, 3 knobs, available in Heritage Cherry Sunburst, Sunrise, or Vintage Brown finishes, current mfg.

MSR	$2,250	$1,800	$1,200	$750

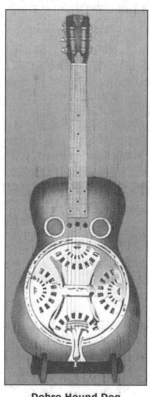

Dobro Hound Dog
courtesy Gibson
Guitar Company

D

GRADING	100%	EXCELLENT	AVERAGE

ZEPHYR SUNBURST (DW60 ZSC) - single sharp cutaway hollow style, maple top, multiple soundholes, single cone resonator, bound body, maple back/sides/neck, 19-fret ebony fingerboard with abalone seagull inlay, spider bridge/trapeze tailpiece, chrome hardware, slotted peghead, 3-per-side tuners with plastic buttons, available in Sunburst finish, disc. 1995.

	N/A	$740	$445
		Last MSR was $1,399.	

F60 CLASSIC (F-HOLE CLASSIC, DWF60) - hollow style, laminated maple top, 2 f-holes, single cone resonator, maple back/sides/neck, 12/19-fret rosewood fingerboard with pearl dot inlay, spider bridge/trapeze tailpiece, slotted peghead with logo decal, chrome hardware, 3-per-side tuners with plastic buttons, available in Blackburst, Tobacco Burst, or Vintage Burst finishes, disc. 2000.

	$880	$575	$375
		Last MSR was $1,099.	

ACOUSTIC: SPECIAL EDITION SERIES

Special Edition models were offered with round (Spanish) or square (Hawaiian) necks (square neck models were designated with an *S* after the model code).

CURLY MAPLE SPECIAL (DWS60 C) - hollow style, curly maple back/sides, single cone resonator, maple neck, 12/19-fret rosewood fingerboard with white dot inlay, spider bridge/trapeze tailpiece, solid peghead with logo decal, chrome hardware, 3-per-side tuners, available in Natural, disc. 1995.

	N/A	$955	$575
		Last MSR was $1,799.	

Koa Special (DWS60 K) - similar to the Curly Maple Special, except has koa back and sides, disc. 1995.

	N/A	$1,480	$895
		Last MSR was $2,799.	

Mahogany Special (DWS60 M) - similar to the Curly Maple Special, except has mahogany back and sides, disc. 1995.

	N/A	$850	$530
		Last MSR was $1,599.	

Rosewood Special (DWS60 R) - similar to the Curly Maple Special, except has rosewood back and sides, disc. 1995.

	N/A	$1,060	$640
		Last MSR was $1,999.	

ACOUSTIC: SQUARENECK SERIES

The 60 Squareneck Series is constructed similar to the Roundneck models, except have a squared (Hawaiian) neck for lap steel-style playing, high nut, and 2 mesh-covered soundholes.

27 DELUXE (DW27 DLX) - hollow style, laminated figured maple top/back/sides, 2 smaller screened soundholes, single cone resonator with parallelogram sound holes, maple neck, 12/19-fret rosewood fingerboard with elaborate pearl inlay, spider bridge/trapeze tailpiece, solid peghead with logo decal, chrome hardware, 3-per-side tuners, available in Vintage Burst, mfg. 1996-current.

MSR	$2,760	$2,210	$1,500	$950

F-60 SQUARENECK (DW60) - hollow style, laminated maple top/back/sides, 2 screened/3 smaller uncovered soundholes, single cone resonator with squared sound holes, maple neck, 12/19-fret rosewood fingerboard with pearl dot inlay, spider bridge/trapeze tailpiece, solid peghead with logo decal, chrome hardware, 3-per-side tuners, available in Amberburst, Natural, or Sunburst finishes, disc 2000.

	$1,200	$850	$525
		Last MSR was $1,399.	

60 Squareneck Darkburst (DW60 SDB) - similar to 60 Squareneck, available in Darkburst finish, mfg. 2000-current.

MSR	$1,926	$1,545	$1,025	$650

60-D CLASSIC SQUARENECK (DW60SVSB) - hollow style, laminated maple top, 2 f-holes, single cone resonator, maple back/sides/neck, 12/19-fret rosewood fingerboard with pearl dot inlay, spider bridge/trapeze tailpiece, slotted peghead with logo decal, chrome hardware, 3-per-side tuners with plastic buttons, available in Blackburst (disc.), Tobacco Burst (disc.), or Vintage Sunburst finishes, current mfg.

MSR	$2,012	$1,610	$1,075	$675

Model 63 (Dobro 8-String DW63) - similar to the F60 Squareneck, except has 8-string configuration, 2 screened/3 smaller uncovered soundholes, 4-per-side slotted headstock, redesigned bridge, available in Natural or Sunburst finishes, mfg. 1996-2000.

	$1,120	$730	$475
		Last MSR was $1,399.	

HOUND DOG - laminated and figure maple body, open sound well constrution, 2 f-holes, no body binding, square neck, spider style resonator, fan cover plate, Fishman resonator pickup, nickel plated hardware, avialable in hand-rubbed Brown finish, gig-bag included, new 2003.

MSR	$999	$800	$525	$350

ACOUSTIC BASS

Resonator-equipped Acoustic bass models debuted in 1995. Both models listed are available with an optional fretless fingerboard.

D

GRADING	100%	EXCELLENT	AVERAGE

MODEL D DELUXE (DBASS) - hollow style, bound laminated maple top/back/sides, 2 screened/3 smaller uncovered soundholes, single cone resonator, maple neck, 18/24-fret rosewood fingerboard with white dot inlay, spider bridge/trapeze tailpiece, solid peghead with logo decal, chrome hardware, 2-per-side tuners, available in Darkburst finish, mfg. 1995-2000.

	N/A	$1,100	$650
		Last MSR was $1,899.	

Model D Deluxe Natural (DBASS N) - similar to the Model D Deluxe in construction, available in Natural finish, mfg. 1995-2000.

	N/A	$1,150	$675
		Last MSR was $1,999.	

MODEL F (FBASS) - similar to the Model D, except has 2 f-holes, available in Black Burst, Tobacco Burst, or Vintage Burst finishes, mfg. 1996-2000.

	N/A	$850	$500
		Last MSR was $1,499.	

The Model F bass is not available in a fretless configuration. The Model F Deluxe versions are, however.

Model F Deluxe (FBASS DLX) - similar to the Model F in construction, available in Dark Burst finish, mfg. 1996-2000.

	N/A	$1,150	$675
		Last MSR was $1,899.	

Model F Deluxe Natural (FBASS DLX N) - similar to the Model F in construction, available in Natural finish, mfg. 1996-2000.

	N/A	$1,225	$725
		Last MSR was $1,999.	

MODEL F DELUXE 5 STRING (DBASS DLX 5) - similar to the Model F, except has a 5-string configuration, available in Dark Burst finish, mfg. 1996-2000.

	N/A	$1,300	$775
		Last MSR was $2,099.	

Model F Deluxe 5 String Natural (DBASS DLX N 5) - similar to the Model F Deluxe 5 string in construction, available in Natural finish, mfg. 1996-2000.

	N/A	$1,375	$825
		Last MSR was $2,199.	

DOLCE
See chapter on House Brands.

This trademark has been identified as the House Brand used by such stores as Marshall Fields, Macy's, and Gimbles, (Source: Willie G. Moseley, *Stellas & Stratocasters*).

DOMINO
Instruments previously manufactured in Japan circa mid to late 1960s. Distributed by Maurice Lipsky Music Company, Inc., of New York, New York.

These Japanese-produced guitars and basses were imported to the U.S. market by the Maurice Lipsky company of New York, New York (Domino was a division of The Orpheum Manufacturing Company). Domino offered a wide range of Vox - and Fender-derived solid body models, and Gibson-esque 335 semi-hollow (or perhaps completely hollow) models. In 1967, the Domino design focus spotlighted copies of Fender's Jazzmaster/ Jaguar and Mustang models renamed the Spartan and the Olympic. You just know that these guitars are the product of the 1960s, as the Domino catalog claimed that their guitars had "Lightning Fast Action - Psychedelic Sounds - Elegant Mod Styling." As they say on late night commercials, "Now how much will you pay? But Wait!"

The entire Domino product line featured Japanese hardware and pickups. Domino's Thunder-Matic line of drums featured 6-ply shells, and internal adjustable mufflers, (Source: Michael Wright, *Guitar Stories*, Volume One; Domino catalog courtesy John Kinnemeyer, JK Lutherie).

ACOUSTIC

Here's some more "Features built into Every Domino:" 1) Mallory 'Full Range' adjustable pickups. 2) Mark Steel "Lightning Fast" Speed Scale Jazz Neck - the shorter distances between frets permits easier fingering and, naturally faster handling. 3) Mark Steel 3 ounce tremolo/micrometric roller bridge, 6 coats of gloss lacquer. 4) extra value(!) $400 worth of dramatic sound, features, superb styling, handling - yet Domino prices started as low as $22.50; compare and you'll agree!

Domino guitars may look cool from a distance, but up close they're a tough tone nut to crack. Prices in the vintage market range from $75 to $175 (in excellent condition) as many players bypass the wacky 1960s models to look for a newer model entry level guitar. For further information regarding Domino electric guitars, please refer to the *Blue Book of Electric Guitars*.

The Mark V Nylon model was a classical-style acoustic with laminated top/back/sides, round soundhole, a slotted headstock, tied bridge, and featured 3-per-side tuners (retail list was $90).

DONNELL, KEN
Instruments previously built in Chico, California during the late 1980s to the early 1990s. Distributed by Donnell Enterprises of Chico, California.

Luthier Ken Donnell offered an acoustic bass that was optionally augmented with a magnetic pickup in the soundhole or an internal Donnell Mini-Flex microphone system. Currently, Boom basses are not in production while Donnell focuses on the development of the Donnell Mini-Flex microphone system.

This internal mini-microphone installs inside the acoustic guitar with no modifications to the guitar itself. The mic and gooseneck clip to an interior brace near the soundhole, and the cable runs along the bass side of the fingerboard to the output jack. Other models are installed through the endblock of the guitar in place of the strap button. The Mini-Clip series is offered in a number of different models (featuring different low impedance microphones). For further product information, contact Donnell Enterprises.

Boom basses have a cedar soundboard, mahogany back, sides, and neck, and rosewood fingerboards and bridges. The tuning machines are chrome Schallers. The basses have a 32" scale (45 1/2" overall), and a six inch depth. The neck joined the non-cutaway body at the 14th fret, and had 19 frets overall. The original suggested list price (direct from the company) was $1,600.

DORADO
Instruments previously produced in Japan circa early 1970s. Distributed in the U.S. by the Baldwin Piano and Organ Company of Cincinnati, Ohio.

The Dorado trademark was briefly used by Baldwin (during its Gretsch ownership) on a product line of Japanese-built acoustics and electric guitars and basses. Dorado instruments are of decent quality, but are often found at slightly inflated asking prices due to the attachment of the Gretsch name. Remember, these are 1970s Japanese guitars imported in by Gretsch during their phase of Baldwin ownership! Dorados are sometimes rightly priced between $125 to $175; but many times they are tagged at prices double that. Of course, what a guitar is tagged at and what it sells at (cash talks, baby!) are always two different animals, (Source: Walter Murray, Frankenstein Fretworks; and Michael Wright, *Vintage Guitar Magazine*).

DREAM GUITARS & APPAREL INC.
Instruments and Western apparel currently made in Glendale, California.

Dream Guitars currently is operating under Paul Heumiller and Martin Simpson. They currently offer custom instruments and perform other services as well. Dream guitars has produced limited editions of Art Guitars, including The Roy Rogers & Dale Evans creations featuring the artwork of Greg Rich (former manager of Gibson's Custom Shop in Nashville, Tennessee), and the construction talent of Crafters of Tennessee. For more information, please contact the company directly (see Trademark Index).

DUNN, MICHAEL GUITARS
Instruments currently built in Vancouver (British Columbia), Canada.

Michael Dunn apprenticed for three years under maestros Jose Orti and Jose Ferrer at George Bowden's workshop in Palma De Mallorca, Spain during the mid 1960s. As a guitarist, Dunn was fascinated by Django Reinhardt's acoustic style of jazz. Dunn's interest in the Maccaferri guitar design, along with his background of the Spanish guitar-building tradition, is the basis for his modern interpretation of Maccaferri-styled models. Dunn also offers two classical style models, a flamenco style acoustic, and a Weissenborn-style acoustic Hawaiian guitar.

Dunn uses spruce or cedar for the tuned soundboard, and an ebony fingerboard on top of a Honduran mahogany neck. Models have a brass tailpiece, and are finished with a French polish process. A slotted peghead is optional. The **Mystery Pacific** model (list price $3,000) was developed from the original design patented by Mario Maccaferri in 1930. The Mystery Pacific is fitted with an internal soundbox and reflector, and possesses the D-shaped soundhole, cedar soundboard, and rosewood back and sides. The **Stardust** (list $2,500) has an oval soundhole, and features Paduak or a similar medium density tropical hardwood for the back and sides. The scale length of the **Belleville** is 670 mm, as compared to the Stardust's 640 mm scale. Construction of the longer-scaled Belleville (list $2,500) is similar to the Stardust model.

In addition to the three Maccaferri-derived models, Dunn also builds a 660 mm scale Classical guitar (list $3,000); a 1939 Hauser-type Classical (650 mm scale length) guitar for $3,000; a Flamenco model (list $2,500); and a Weissenborn-style acoustic Hawaiian guitar model (list $2,500). Check the Michael Dunn web site for other models and options that have been updated (see Trademark Index).

DUPONT, GUITARES MAURICE
Please refer to the G section in this text.

DURANGO (CURRENT MFG.)
Instruments currently produced in Asia. Distributed by Saga Musical Instruments of San Francisco, California.

Durango full-sized classical acoustics are designed in part for the entry level guitar student, and features laminated spruce tops, birch back and sides, black body binding, a matte finish, chrome hardware, and 3-per-side slotted headstocks. For further information regarding models and pricing, contact Saga Musical Instruments directly (see Trademark Index).

DURANGO (PREVIOUS MFG.)
Instrument production and dates of production unknown. Distributed by Sayre Woods Music & Band Instrument Company of Madison Township, New Jersey.

Guitarist/Blue Book reader Kenneth Heller offers this yet unspecified Durango trademark for your inspection. The inside label reads "Distributed by Sayre Woods Music & Band Instrument Company of Madison Township, New Jersey"; model "# SAY 622"; serial "#-283" (or perhaps G000315). Other readers with information concerning the Durango trademark are invited to write to the *Blue Book of Guitars* for future inclusions, (Information courtesy Kenneth Heller).

W.J. DYER & BRO.
See LARSON BROTHERS (1900-1944).

From the 1880s to the 1930s, the Dyer store in St. Paul was *the* place for musical merchandise for the midwest in the areas northwest of Chicago. They sold about anything music related on the market at that time. The Larson brothers of Maurer & Co., Chicago were commissioned to build a line of Symphony harp-guitars and Symphony harp-mandolin orchestra pieces along with the J.F. Stetson brand of guitars. They started building these great instruments circa 1905.

The original design of these harp-style instruments came from that of Chris Knutsen who had been building that style since 1898. The early Larsons showed a resemblance to the Knutsen ideas but evolved to a final design by 1912. The harp-guitars are labeled **Style #4** through **#8** whereas the higher the number, the better the grade of material and intricacy of the trim. The Style #4 is very plain with dot inlays in the fingerboard and no binding on the back. The Style #8 has a pearl trimmed top, fancy peghead inlay and the beautiful tree-of-life fingerboard. This Tree-Of-Life pattern is also used on the fanciest Maurers and Prairie States having the 12-fret-to-the-body necks.

The harp-mandolin series includes a harp-mandola and harp-mando-cello also in different degrees of ornamentation. Some of the Stetson guitars are Larson-made, but others were possibly made by Harmony, Lyon & Healy, or others. If the Stetson trademark is burned into the inside back strip, it is probably a Larson.

For more information regarding other Larson-made brands, see Maurer, Prairie State, Euphonon, Wm. C. Stahl, and The Larson Brothers. For more detailed information regarding all Larson brands, see The Larsons' Creations, G Carl Hartman, Centerstream Publishing, P.O. Box 17878, Anaheim Hills CA 92807, phone/fax (714) 779-9390.

D

NOTES

_____

_____

_____

_____

_____

_____

_____

_____

_____

D is for the Dallas Guitar Show. DGS show co-promoters Mark Pollock (left, with largest still working cell phone) and Jimmy Wallace are caught burning up air time at the recent Arlington Guitar Show.

Section E

ECCLESHALL

Instruments currently built in England since the early 1970s.

Luthier Christopher J. Eccleshall is known for the high quality guitars that he produces. Eccleshall also builds violins, mandolins, and banjos. Some of his original designs carry such model designations like **Excalibur, EQ**, and **Craftsman**. Luthier Eccleshall was also the first UK maker to have Japanese-built solid body guitars. Eccleshall also is an authorized repairer of Gibson, Guild, and Martin, (Source: Tony Bacon and Paul Day, *The Guru's Guitar Guide*).

EHLERS, ROB

Instruments currently built in Oregon since 1985.

Luthier Rob Ehlers has been building high quality acoustic steel string guitars in his workshop over the last ten years. Because of current backlog, Rob Ehlers is not taking any orders currently for guitars. Inventory is limited to what was on hand as of January 28, 2002. For more information about Rob Ehlers, contact Buffalo Brothers as they are an authorized dealer.

EHLERS & BURNS

See Ehlers. Instruments previously custom built in Oregon from 1974 to 1984. The E & B (Ehlers & Burns) trademark was used by luthiers Rob Ehlers and Bruce Burns during a ten year period. Most instruments produced then were custom ordered. After 1984, Bruce Burns was no longer involved in the construction of the instruments.

EICHELBAUM CUSTOM GUITARS

Instruments currently built in Santa Barbara, California.

Eichelbaum Custom Guitars is offering three different styles (the Grand Auditorium, Grand Parlor, and Grand Concert) of handcrafted acoustic guitars. These models are also available with a number of custom options, thus personalizing the guitar to the owner. Models are constructed with Master-grade woods: Sitka spruce tops, Indian rosewood back and sides, Honduran mahogany necks, and ebony fingerboards/bridges/binding (with maple or Koa)/endpins. The **Sierra Orchestra Model**, the **Sierra Jumbo Model**, and the **Sierra Cutaway Model** are all custom-made instruments, and are priced per quotation, deluxe case included. Base price on all models is $5,300. For further information regarding the specifications, custom options, and pricing please contact Eichelbaum Custom Guitars directly (see Trademark Index).

EISELE

Instruments currently built in Kailua, Hawaii.

Donn H. Eisele began playing guitar about thirty years ago, and started collecting in the past ten years. In 1989, Eisele began building guitars as a hobby; he decided to pursue it full time in early 1995. To find the date of the guitar get a mirror and look at the underside of the top of the guitar.

ACOUSTIC

Eisele offers a range of both flattop and archtop acoustic guitars. All models have a wide range of custom features available, and both prices include a hardshell case.

Eisele's flattop guitars include such standard features as mahogany back and sides, one piece or laminated mahogany neck, Sitka spruce or Western red cedar top, ebony or rosewood fingerboard with dot inlays, ebony or rosewood bridge, single body binding (white, ivoroid, or tortoises), chrome Schaller tuners, and a nitrocellulose lacquer finish. The Standard list price begins at $2,500. The **F-00** has a 15" body similar to a Gibson L-00, while the **F-OM's** 15" body resembles a Martin OM. The **F-100** is the 16" version of the F-00, and the **F-J** model is a 16" jumbo shaped like a Gibson J-185. The 17" **F - SJ** jumbo resembles a Gibson J-200.

Eisele's Archtop guitar is featured in a 16" or 17" body, and the Standard has a list price beginning at $4,750. The Archtop includes such standard features as hand carved back of big leaf maple with matching sides, 1 piece or laminated figured maple neck, hand carved Englemann or Sitka spruce top, ebony fingerboard/finger rest/bridge/tailpiece, black/white/black body purfling, ivoroid fingerboard binding, gold Schaller tuners, and a nitrocellulose lacquer finish.

EKO

Trademark of instruments currently built the Czech Republic, Asia, Spain (classical), and Italy. EKO is now part of the E Group, which is split into EKO (Italian distributor of musical instruments), Esound (Italian distributor of musical instruments), Etek (professional audio producer and world wide musical instruments distributor), and Res (service society). Instruments were formerly built in Italy from the early 1960s through 1987. Distribution in the U.S. market by the LoDuca Bros. of Milwaukee, Wisconsin.

The LoDuca Bros. musical distribution company was formed in 1941 by brothers Tom and Guy LoDuca. Capitalizing on money made through their accordion-based vaudevillian act, lessons, and accordion repair, the

**Eisele F-100 Acoustic
courtesy Donn Eisele**

LoDucas began importing and selling Italian accordions. Throughout the 1940s and 1950s, the LoDucas built up a musical distributorship with accordions and sheet music. By the late 1950s, they were handling Magnatone amplifiers and guitars.

In 1961, the LoDucas teamed up with Italy-based Oliviero Pigini & Company to import guitars. Pigini, one of the LoDuca's accordion manufacturers, had formed the EKO company in anticipation of the boom in the guitar market. The LoDucas acted as technical designers and gave input on EKO designs (as well as being the exclusive U.S. dealers), and EKO built guitars for their dealers. Some of the sparkle finishes were no doubt inspired by the accordions produced in the past. In fact, the various on/off switches and tone settings are down right reminiscent of accordion voice settings! The plastic covered-guitars lasted through to the mid 1960s, when more conventional finishes were offered. EKO also built a number of guitars for Vox, Goya, and Thomas companies.

By 1967 EKO had established dealers in 57 countries around the world. During the late 1960s and early 1970s the guitar market began to get soft, and many guitar builders began to go out of business. EKO continued on, but cut back the number of models offered. In the late 1970s, EKO introduced a custom shop branch that built neck-through designed guitars for other trademarks. Once such company was D'Agostino, and EKO produced the **Bench Mark** models from 1978 to 1982.

The EKO company kept producing models until 1985. By the mid 1980s, the LoDuca Bros. company had begun concentrating on guitar case production, and stopped importing the final Alembic-styled set-neck guitars that were being produced. The original EKO company's holdings were liquidated in 1987.

Currently, the EKO trademark has again been revived in Italy, and appears on entry level solid body guitars built in various countries. The revived company is offering a wide range of acoustic, classical, and solid body electric guitars and amplifiers – all with contemporary market designs, (Eko history source: Michael Wright, *Guitar Stories,* Volume One).

ACOUSTIC

The current Eko product line has a wide range of classical (**Conservatorio** and **Studio** series), classical models with EQ and piezo bridges (**Classic EQ**), jumbo-style acoustic/electrics (**Electro-Acoustic** series), and Dreadnought models (**Acoustic** series). The current acoustic models all have different, re-styled headstocks from the earlier Eko Italian-production models. Most EKO models in average original condition are priced in the $150-$350 price range, depending on condition, originality, and overall appeal.

EL CID
Instruments currently produced in Asia. Distributed by the L.A. Guitar Works of Reseda, California.

El Cid classical guitars are offered in **King** and **Queen** designated models that have slotted headstocks, solid spruce or cedar tops, and rosewood or lacewood back/sides. List price for either model is $799 (with hardshell case).

EL DEGAS
Instruments previously produced in Japan.

The El Degas trademark was a brand name used by U.S. importers Buegeleisen & Jacobson of New York, New York, (Source: Michael Wright, *Guitar Stories,* Volume One).

ELECA
Instruments currently produced in China. Distributed by Eleca International Inc. of Walnut, California.

Eleca instruments are produced in China and distributed throughout the United States. They produce a variety of electric and acoustic guitars. Most acoustic guitars are based off of popular American designs, such as the dreadnoughts, classicals, and folk guitars. Most of their products are offered at a competitive price. For more information please refer to the web site (see Trademark Index).

ELGER
Instruments previously produced in Ardmore, Pennsylvania from 1959 to 1965. Elger began importing instruments produced in Japan during the early 1960s.

Elger instruments were distributed in the U.S. by the Elger Company of Ardmore, Pennsylvania. The roots of the Elger company were founded in 1954 by Harry Rosenbloom when he opened Medley Music in Bryn Mawr, Pennsylvania. In 1959, Rosenbloom decided to produce his own acoustic guitars as the Elger Company (named after his children, Ellen and Gerson). Rosenbloom soon turned from U.S. production to Japanese when the Elger company became partners with Hoshino Gakki Gen, and introduced the Ibanez trademark to the U.S. market. Elger did maintain the Pennsylvania facilities to check incoming shipments and correct any flaws prior to shipping merchandise out to their dealers. For further company history, see Ibanez, (Source: Michael Wright, *Guitar Stories,* Volume One).

ELLIOT, JEFFREY R.
Instruments currently built in Portland, Oregon.

Luthier Jeffrey R. Elliot began professionally building guitars in 1966. Elliot builds between six to eight classical or steel string guitars on a yearly basis. A variety of woods are available for the top and body; inlay work and designs are custom ordered. Please contact Jeffrey Elliot directly (see Trademark Index).

EMERALD
Instruments currently built in Donegal, Ireland.

Emerald Guitars were launched at the 2003 NAMM show. These guitars are a result of four years of intensive research and development to create a guitar that is built out of carbon-fiber. The bodies and neck are constructed out of carbon-fiber and have elaborate designs and colors. For more information on Emerald, please refer to their web site (see Trademark Index).

ACOUSTIC

Currently, Emerald has two different series of guitars the **Artisan** and the **Opus**. The Opus series features the carbon-fiber body, Graphtech nut, saddle, and bridge pins, and a Fishman Classic 4 or LR Boggs IRT electronic system. The **Opus X10** is a folk style and retails for $1,450, the **X20** is a dreadnought style and also retails for $1,450. The **X30** is a super jumbo and lists for $1,595. The Artisan series has everything the Opus does along with elaborate inlays and LR Boggs I-Beam, RT Blender, or Fishman Prefix Pro electronics system. The models are numbered just like the Opus. The **X10** and **X20** retail for $2,350, and the **X30** goes for $2,495. You can upgrade to a 12-string for $250. All guitars are single cutaways and feature the cool emerald color.

EMPERADOR

Instruments previously built in Japan by the Kasuga company circa 1966 to 1992. Distributed by Westheimer Musical Instruments of Chicago, Illinois.

The Emperador trademark was a brand name used in the U.S. market by the Westheimer Musical Instruments of Chicago, Illinois. The Emperador trademark was the Westheimer company's entry level line to their Cort products line through the years. Emperador models are usually shorter-scaled entry level instruments, and the trademark can be found on both jazz-style thinline acoustic/electric archtops and solid body electric guitars and basses.

ENCORE

Instruments currently produced in Asia. Distributed by John Hornby Skewes & Co., Ltd. of Garforth (Leeds), England.

The Encore trademark is the brand name of UK importer John Hornby Skewes & Co., Ltd. The company was founded in 1965 by the namesake, Mr. John Hornby Skewes. The Encore line consists of solidly built guitars and basses that feature designs based on popular American favorites. Encore instruments are of medium to good quality, and their model E83 bass was named "Most Popular U.K. Bass Guitar" in 1992, 1993, 1994, and 1995. In addition to the Encore line, the John Hornby Skewes company distributes the Vintage instruments line (see Vintage).

ACOUSTIC

The current Encore line of acoustic guitars is well represented by over 10 models. In addition to the steel string acoustics, there are currently 6 classical models (three full size, two 3/4 scale, and one 1/2 scale), and construction ranges from a beech laminate top to solid spruce, with either a maple laminate or beech laminate back and sides. Typically, these instruments are priced in the $100-$175 range. Please contact the distributor directly for more information regarding model lineup and availability.

**EKO Ranger 12 Acoustic
1967 EKO Catalog**

ENSENADA

Instruments previously produced in Japan, circa 1970s. Distributed by Strum & Drum of Chicago, Illinois.

The Ensenada trademark was a brand name of U.S. importers Strum & Drum of Chicago, Illinois. Strum and Drum were later owners of the National trademark, acquired when Valco's holdings were auctioned off. Ensenada instruments were distributed between roughly 1973 to 1974, (Source: Michael Wright, *Guitar Stories,* Volume One).

EPI

Trademark of instruments currently produced in China or Indonesia. Distributed by Epiphone (Gibson Musical Instruments) of Nashville, Tennessee.

Epi stringed instruments are the entry level line to the current Epiphone range of guitars and basses.

ACOUSTIC

ED-100 (MODEL ED10) - available in Natural Matte finish, disc.

	$145	$100	$70
		Last MSR was $209.	

EC-100 (MODEL EC10) - available in Natural Matte finish, disc.

	$145	$100	$70
		Last MSR was $189.	

EPIPHONE

Current trademark of instruments produced in Korea beginning 1983. Epiphone is a division of and distributed by Gibson Musical Instruments of Nashville, Tennessee. The original Epiphone company was based in New York, New York from 1904 to 1953; and later in Philadelphia, Pennsylvania from 1954 to 1957. When Epiphone was purchased by Gibson, production moved to Kalamazoo, Michigan from 1958 to 1969; then to Japan from 1970 to 1983. Some specialty models were built in Nashville, Tennessee in 1982 to 1983, also from 1989 to 1994.

According to family history, Anastasios Stathopoulo (b. 1863) began constructing musical instruments in his home town of Sparta, Greece in 1873. He moved to the U.S. with his family is 1903, settling in New York City, where he produced a full range of stringed instruments bearing his own name up until the time of his death in 1915. The company, which soon became known as "The House of Statopoulo," continued under the direction and ownership of his wife, Marianthe (b. 1875) and eldest son, Epaminondas (Epi [b. 1893]).

Following Marianthe's death in 1923, The House of Statopoulo was incorporated with Epi as president and majority shareholder, his sister Alkminie (Minnie [1897-1984]) as treasurer, and brother Orpheus (Orphie [1899-1973]) as secretary. They immediately announced "The new policy of business" would be "the production of banjos, tenor banjos, banjo mandolins, banjo guitars, and banjo ukuleles under the registered trademark of Epiphone." The name Epiphone was a combination of Epi's nickname with the Greek word for sound, phone. Their elegant Recording line of tenor banjos was considered to be amongst the finest ever made. These were joined in the late 1920s by a full line of Recording model guitars. In 1928, the company's name was changed to The Epiphone Banjo Co. The Masterbilt series of guitars was introduced in 1931 and marked Epiphone's entrance into the production of modern, carved, f-hole archtop guitars, based on violin construction principles. Indeed, at the time of their introduction, the Masterbilt guitar line was the most complete selection of f-hole guitars available from any instrument maker in the world. Complementary Spanish and Hawaiian flattop models and carved-top mandolins were likewise included under the Masterbilt aegis. Soon, Epiphone advertisements would claim that it was "The World's Largest Producer of First Grade Fretted Instruments." Whether this was an accurate boast or not, it set the stage for a two decade rivalry between Epiphone and its largest competitor, Gibson.

By 1935, the company was now known simply as Epiphone, Inc., and was producing its Electar brand of electric Hawaiian and Spanish guitars, as well as amplifiers which were designed by electronics pioneer and Danelectro founder, Nat Daniels (1912-1994). That same year marked the introduction of the flagship 18 3/8" Emperor model archtop guitar and signaled the re-design and enlargement of the company's entire Masterbilt archtop line.

Notable Epiphone innovations in this era included the first patented electronic pickup with individual pole pieces and the distinctive Frequensator tailpiece. Both were designed by salesman and acknowledged jack-of-all-trades, Herb Sunshine (1906-1988), and in production by 1937. In 1940, the company also introduced a full line of well respected bass violins produced under the watchful eye of the youngest of the Stathopoulo brothers, Frixo (1905-1957) who had joined the firm in the early 1930s.

During this period, Epiphone's growing product line was considered second to none, and could boast such endorsers as George Van Eps (with the Ray Noble Orchestra), Carmen Mastren (with Tommy Dorsey), Allan Reuss (with Benny Goodman's band), and many, many more.

Epi Stathopoulo died from leukemia in 1943 at the age of 49, and this, combined with the many hardships incurred during World War II, set the company on a downward spiral. Orphie Stathopoulo, who took over as president, was unable to recapture the momentum of the prewar years, and constant friction between he and his brother Frixo (now vice-president) began to pull the company apart at the seams.

In 1951, simmering labor problems resulted in a strike which shut down the New York plant for several months. During this time, Orphie sold a stake in the business to the large distribution company, Continental Music. Continental moved production to Philadelphia, and most instruments manufactured from 1952 to 1957 were made there. It is doubtful, however, if much was produced in the final two years, as Epiphone was rapidly being overtaken by new entrants into the guitar market, notably Fender and Guild, the later of which had ironically been started by many former Epiphone employees under the leadership of Alfred Dronge and former Epiphone executive, George Mann.

It had become increasingly apparent that Epiphone was no longer capable of developing the new products necessary to capture the imagination of the guitar-buying public and its financial viability had come to an end. Following Frixo's sudden death in 1957, Orphie, by now the company's sole owner, approached Gibson president Ted McCarty, who had previously expressed interest in buying Epiphone's bass violin production. A deal was signed and trucks were dispatched from Kalamazoo to New York and Philadelphia to make the move. Records during this time period indicate that the out-of-work ex-Epiphone workers in New Berlin, New York "celebrated" by hosting a bonfire behind the plant with any available lumber (both finished and unfinished!). When the vans returned to the Gibson warehouse in Michigan, McCarty realized (much to his surprise) that not only had he received the bass making operation, but all the jigs, fixtures, and machinery necessary for making guitars, plus much of the work in progress. For the sum of $20,000, Gibson had acquired its once mighty rival (including what would become the most profitable trademark) lock, stock, and barrel.

It was decided that Epiphone would be re-established as a first rate guitar manufacturer, so that Gibson's parent company, CMI (Chicago Musical Instruments), could offer a product comparable in every way to Gibson. This was done primarily as a way of offering music stores which, due to existing contractual obligations in a particular sales area, were not allowed to carry the exclusive Gibson line. The Epiphone brand could now be offered to competing retailers who were also carrying many of the other well-known brands which were distributed by the giant CMI. Though Epiphone was set up as an autonomous company, in a separate part of the Gibson complex, parallel product lines were soon established, and Gibson was (in effect) competing with itself.

After Epiphone was moved to Kalamazoo, instruments were built in the U.S. through 1969. In 1970, production was moved overseas. Instruments were originally built in Japan (1970-1983), but during the early 1980s, Japanese production costs became pricey due to the changing ratio of the dollar/yen.

Since 1984, the majority of guitars have been produced in Korea. However, there have been a number of models like the Spirit, Special, USA Pro, and USA Coronet that were produced in Nashville, Tennessee. These models are the exception to the rule. Epiphone currently offers a very wide range of acoustic, semi-hollow, and solid body electric guitars.

In 1998, Epiphone offered the new **EZ-Bender**, a detachable "B" string bender that can be installed on any guitar equipped with a stop bar tailpiece. The EZ-Bender can be installed with no modifications whatsoever to the guitar.

Source: N.Y. Epiphone information by L.B. Fred and Jim Fisch, *Epiphone: The House of Stathopoulo*, additional Epiphone history courtesy Walter Carter, *Epiphone: The Complete History*.

EPIPHONE OWNED PRODUCTION

Epiphone guitars have been produced in a wide range of places. The following list gives a rough approximation to production facilities by year. For information regarding archtop models with built-in pickups, please refer to the Epiphone Electric Archtop section in the *Blue Book of Electric Guitars*.

Guitars produced from the late 1920s up to the time of Gibson's purchase of the company are known by collectors as "New York Epiphones."

New York, NY	Late 1920s to 1952
Philadelphia, PA	1952 to 1957

GIBSON OWNED PRODUCTION

Kalamazoo, MI	1958 to 1969
Japan	1970 to 1983
Taiwan	1979 to 1981
Nashville, TN	1982 to 1983 (Spirit, Special, U.S. Map)
Korea	1983 to date

GRADING		100%	EXCELLENT	AVERAGE
Japan	1988 to 1989 (Spotlights, Thinlines)			
Nashville, TN	1989 to 1994 (USA Pro)			
Nashville, TN	1991 to 1994 (USA Coronet)			
China	1997 to date			
Indonesia	1997 to date			

ACOUSTIC: RECORDING MODELS

Recording Model archtop guitars feature an asymmetrical body with angled cutaway on treble bout. Some models had flattops, others an arched top (see descriptions below). Recording Model guitars are relatively rare in the vintage guitar market. These models were introduced during the 1920s, and Discontinued around 1931.

RECORDING MODEL A - graduated spruce top, maple or mahogany back/sides, single black body binding, 25" scale, rosewood fingerboard with dot inlay, 3-per-side tuners, pin bridge or trapeze tailpiece, available in Natural or Natural with shaded top finishes.

	N/A	$2,000	$1,200

RECORDING MODEL B - similar to Recording Model A, except features bound rosewood fingerboard with paired diamond inlay.

	N/A	$2,500	$1,500

RECORDING MODEL C - similar to Recording Model A, except features carved spruce top, bound ebony fingerboard with paired diamond inlay, single white body binding, available in Shaded Top finish.

	N/A	$3,500	$2,000

Some models may have rosewood fingerboards with block inlay; some may have a black pickguard.

RECORDING MODEL D - similar to Recording Model A, except features carved spruce top, bound ebony fingerboard with pearloid block inlay, single white body binding, black pickguard, available in Shaded Top finish.

	N/A	$4,000	$2,750

Epiphone Broadway
courtesy Cam Water

RECORDING MODEL E - similar to Recording Model A, except features carved spruce top, laminated curly maple body, 3-ply white body binding, bound ebony fingerboard with celluloid blocks with floral engraving, black pickguard, gold plated tuners, available in Shaded top finish.

	N/A	$5,000	$3,250

ACOUSTIC ARCHTOP

All high-end professional model Epiphone tenor guitars should be considered rarities, and bring a price comparable to their 6-string counterparts.

BEVERLY - flat spruce top, 2 segmented f-holes, raised black pickguard, mahogany arched back, mahogany sides/neck, 14/20-fret rosewood fingerboard with pearl dot inlay, adjustable rosewood bridge/trapeze tailpiece, blackface peghead, 3-per-side tuners, available in Brown finish, 13" body width, mfg. 1931-37.

	N/A	$500	$350

For historical interest, this instrument originally sold for $35.

BLACKSTONE - carved spruce top, f-holes, raised black pickguard, bound body, maple back/sides, 14/20-fret bound rosewood fingerboard with pearl dot inlay, adjustable rosewood bridge/trapeze tailpiece, bound blackface peghead with pearl logo inlay, 3-per-side plate mounted tuners, available in Ebony or Sunburst finish, 14 3/4" body width, mfg. 1931-1951.

1931-1932	N/A	$950	$600
1933-1935	N/A	$700	$375
1936-1951	N/A	$850	$500

The Ebony finish was briefly available from 1931 to 1932. In 1931, engraved pearloid peghead overlay with pearl Masterbilt banner peghead inlay was added. In 1934, 15 1/2" body width, mahogany back/sides, redesigned unbound peghead with redesigned inlay replaced original part/designs. In 1936, parallelogram fingerboard inlay replaced original part/design, auditorium style body, maple back/sides, diamond/script logo peghead inlay replaced original part/designs. In 1939, center dip style peghead replaced original part/design. In 1941, Blonde finish became an option.

Blackstone Tenor - similar to the Blackstone, except in 4-string tenor configuration, mfg. 1931-1949.

1931-1932	N/A	$850	$550
1933-1935	N/A	$600	$350
1936-1951	N/A	$750	$500

Epiphone De Luxe Masterbilt
courtesy Dave Hull

BROADWAY - carved spruce top, f-holes, raised black pickguard, multi bound body, walnut back/sides, mahogany neck, 14/20-fret bound ebony fingerboard with pearl diamond inlay, adjustable ebony bridge/trapeze tailpiece, blackface peghead with pearl Masterbilt banner/logo inlay, 3-per-side nickel tuners, available in Sunburst finish, 16 3/8" body width, mfg. 1931-1957.

1931-1934	N/A	$1,800	$900
1935-1957	N/A	$2,000	$1,400

In 1934, bound pickguard, block fingerboard inlay, vine/block logo peghead inlay, gold hardware replaced original part/designs; carved back added to design. In 1937, 17 3/8" body width, redesigned pickguard/tailpiece/logo replaced original part/designs, bound peghead replaced original part/design. In 1939, maple back/sides, Frequensator tailpiece, redesigned peghead replaced original part/designs.

In 1941, Blonde finish was an option. In 1944, pearl flower peghead inlay replaced original part/design. In 1949, Broadway Regent (cutaway body) was introduced. (For historical interest, this instrument originally sold for $175.)

Bretton Tenor - tenor version of the Broadway model, 15 1/2" body width, mfg. 1931-36.

	N/A	$1,200	$600

This tenor model was originally called the Bretton from its introduction in 1931 to 1936. The name was changed to Broadway Tenor in 1937.

Broadway Tenor - similar to the Blackstone, except in 4-string tenor configuration, mfg. 1937-1949.

	N/A	$2,200	$1,400

Broadway Regent - similar to the Blackstone, except features a single rounded cutaway body, mfg. 1949-1957.

	N/A	$3,000	$2,000

BYRON - carved spruce top, mahogany back/sides, single body binding, mahogany neck, 20-fret rosewood fingerboard with dot inlay, f-holes, 3-per-side tuners with plastic buttons, nickel hardware, tortoiseshell pickguard, trapeze tailpiece, available in Sunburst Top finish, 15 3/8" body width, mfg. 1949-1955.

	N/A	$650	$375

DE LUXE - carved spruce top, 2 f-holes, multi bound body, black/white diagonal purfling on top, figured maple back/sides, 5-piece carved figured maple neck, 14/20-fret bound rosewood fingerboard with pearl slotted diamond inlay, adjustable rosewood bridge/trapeze tailpiece, bound blackface peghead with pearl Masterbilt banner inlay, 3-per-side gold die cast tuners, available in Sunburst finish, 16 3/8" body width, mfg. 1931-1957, 1959.

1931-1936	N/A	$4,000	$2,250
1937-1957	N/A	$4,500	$2,500
1959	N/A	$5,000	$3,000

In 1934, floral fingerboard inlay, vine/logo peghead inlay replaced original part/designs, raised white pickguard was added. In late 1935, (grand auditorium style) 17 3/8" body width, redesigned black pickguard, bound f-holes, resigned tailpiece replaced original part/designs, cloud fingerboard inlay, script peghead logo replaced original part/designs. In 1937, Frequensator tailpiece replaced original part/design. In 1939, Natural finish was an option. In 1949, De Luxe Regent (cutaway body) was introduced. Under Gibson ownership, this model was re-introduced in 1958/1959. In 1959, 70 instruments were produced in Gibson's Kalamazoo plant.By 1965, the model was available by special order; and discontinued in 1970.

Empire (De Luxe Tenor) - tenor version of the De Luxe model, 15 1/2" body width, mfg. 1931-35.

	N/A	$3,500	$2,000

De Luxe Regent - similar to the De Luxe, except has a single round cutaway body, mfg. 1949-1958.

	N/A	$5,000	$3,500

Some models may feature the flower peghead inlay.

DEVON - carved spruce top, mahogany back/sides, single bound body, mahogany neck, 20-fret rosewood fingerboard with oval inlay, f-holes, 3-per-side tuners, nickel hardware, bound tortoise shell logo with 'E' logo, Frequensator tailpiece, available in Sunburst top or Natural finishes, 17 3/8" body width, mfg. 1949-1957.

	N/A	$1,100	$650

EMPEROR (MFG. 1935-1957) - carved spruce top, multi bound f-holes, raised bound tortoise pickguard, multi bound body, maple back/sides/neck, carved back, 14/20-fret bound ebony fingerboard with pearl split block inlay, adjustable ebony bridge/logo engraved trapeze tailpiece, bound peghead with pearl vine/logo inlay, 3-per-side gold tuners, available in Cremona Brown Sunburst finish, 18 1/2" body width, mfg. 1935-1957.

1935-1936	N/A	$5,500	$3,500
1937-1957	N/A	$5,200	$3,200

In 1937, Frequensator tailpiece replaced original part/designs. In 1939, pearl block/abalone triangle fingerboard, redesigned peghead replaced original part/designs; Natural finish was an option. By the mid 1940s, rosewood fingerboard replaced original part/design. In 1948, Emperor Regent (cutaway body) was introduced. A limited number of cutaway Emperors bearing the label Soloist Emperor were produced in 1948 as well. For historical interest, this instrument originally sold for $400.

Emperor (Mfg. 1958-1970) - reintroduced by Gibson in 1958, available by special order only in 1963, Disc. 1970.

	N/A	$7,000	$4,500

Emperor Cutaway (New York Mfg.) - similar to Emperor, except has single round cutaway, mfg. 1948-1955.

	N/A	$7,000	$4,500

GRADING	100%	EXCELLENT	AVERAGE

HOWARD ROBERTS CUSTOM - similar to ES-175, arched spruce top, maple back/sides, 25 1/2" scale, 16 1/4" lower bout, 7-piece laminated neck, Tree-of-Life headstock inlay, single Johnny Smith pickup attached to the fingerboard, ebony bridge base, tune-o-matic bridge, ES-175 bail fern tailpiece, oval sound hole, nickel hardware, 1 tone and 1 volume control, available in Black, Sunburst, or Brown finishes, mfg. 1964-67.

	N/A	$3,000	$1,750

Last MSR was $825.

OLYMPIC - carved spruce or poplar top, mahogany back/sides, single body binding, mahogany neck, segmented f-holes, 20-fret rosewood fingerboard with dot inlay, small black pickguard, 3-per-side tuners with plastic buttons, available in Golden Brown and Brown with Sunburst top, 13" body width, mfg. 1931-1949.

	N/A	$600	$325

In 1939, large tortoise shell pickguard replaced original part/design.

Olympic Tenor - tenor version of the Olympic model, mfg. 1937-1949.

	N/A	$550	$300

RITZ - carved spruce top, maple back/sides, tortoise shell body binding, cello style f-holes, cherrywood neck, 20-fret rosewood fingerboard with dot inlay, trapeze tailpiece, available in Natural opaque finish only, 15 1/4" body width, mfg. 1941-49.

	N/A	$750	$400

Ritz Tenor - tenor version of the Ritz model, mfg. 1941-49.

	N/A	$600	$375

ROYAL - carved spruce top, mahogany back and sides, single body binding, segmented f-holes, 2-piece mahogany neck, 20-fret rosewood fingerboard with dot inlay, black pickguard, trapeze tailpiece, available in Brown with Sunburst top finish, 15 1/2" body width, mfg. 1931-35.

	N/A	$750	$400

In 1933, American walnut back/sides replaced original part/design.

Epiphone Emperor
Blue Book Publications, Inc.

SPARTAN - carved spruce top, round soundhole, raised black pickguard, one stripe rosette, bound body, maple back/sides, mahogany neck, 14/20-fret bound rosewood fingerboard with pearl dot inlay, adjustable rosewood bridge/nickel trapeze tailpiece, bound peghead with pearl wedge/logo inlay, 3-per-side nickel tuners, available in Sunburst finish, 16 3/8" body width, mfg. 1934-1949.

1934-1935	N/A	$1,200	$700
1936-1949	N/A	$950	$600

In 1936, carved back added to design; f-holes, walnut back/sides, block fingerboard inlay, column/logo peghead inlay replaced original part/designs. In 1939, center dip peghead replaced original part/design. In 1941, white mahogany back/sides replaced original part/design, Blonde finish was an option. For historical interest, this instrument originally sold for $100.

Regent Tenor - similar to the Spartan, except has a bound body, mahogany back/sides, trapeze tailpiece, 15 1/2" body width, mfg. 1934-36.

	N/A	$850	$500

This model originally was the companion tenor model to the Spartan guitar. Discontinued in favor of the Spartan Tenor, introduced in 1937.

Spartan Tenor - similar to the Regent Tenor, 15 1/2" body width, mfg. 1937-1949.

	N/A	$850	$500

The Regent tenor guitar was the original companion to the Spartan guitar. The Regent was Discontinued in 1936 in favor of the Spartan Tenor.

TUDOR - carved spruce top, curly maple back/sides, carved back, 3-ply body binding, 5-ply maple/mahogany neck, segmented f-holes, bound black pickguard, gold hardware, trapeze tailpiece, available in Brown with Sunburst top, 16 3/8" body width, mfg. 1932-36.

	N/A	$3,000	$1,800

TRIUMPH (MFG. 1931-1957) - 15 1/2" body width, carved spruce top, f-holes, raised black pickguard, bound body, walnut back/sides, mahogany neck, 14/20-fret bound rosewood fingerboard with pearl diamond inlay, adjustable rosewood bridge/trapeze tailpiece, bound peghead with pearl Masterbilt banner/logo inlay, 3-per-side nickel tuners, available in Sunburst finish, mfg. 1931-1957.

1931-1932	N/A	$950	$500
1933-1935	N/A	$1,250	$750
1936-1957	N/A	$2,000	$1,000

In 1933, the body was redesigned to 16 3/8" across the lower bout. In 1934, maple back/sides, unbound peghead with pearl fleur-de-lis/logo inlay replaced original part/designs; carved back added to design. In 1935, redesigned script peghead logo replaced original part/design. In 1936, the body was redesigned to

Epiphone Ritz
Courtesy Clay Leighton

E

17 3/8" across the lower bout. In 1937, bound pickguard, Frequensator tailpiece replaced original part/designs, bound peghead replaced original part/design. In 1939, Frequensator tailpiece replaced original part/design. In 1941, redesigned peghead replaced original part/design, Blonde finish was optional. In 1949, redesigned pickguard with stylized E, column peghead inlay replaced original part/designs. In 1949, the Triumph Regent (cutaway body) was introduced. For historical interest, this instrument originally sold for $125.

Triumph (Mfg. 1958-1970) - reintroduced by Gibson in 1958, available by special order only in 1963, disc. 1970.

	N/A	$1,000	$650

Triumph Regent - similar to Triumph, except has single round cutaway, mfg. 1949-1958.

	N/A	$2,500	$1,400

Hollywood Tenor - tenor version of the Triumph, mfg. 1931-36.

	N/A	$1,200	$600

This model was originally called the Hollywood from its introduction in 1934 to 1936. The name was changed to Triumph Tenor in 1937.

Triumph Tenor - similar to the Hollywood Tenor, mfg. 1937-1957.

	N/A	$1,800	$950

ZENITH - carved spruce top, f-holes, raised black pickguard, bound body, maple back/sides, mahogany neck, 14/20-fret rosewood fingerboard with pearl dot inlay, adjustable rosewood bridge/trapeze tailpiece, blackface peghead, 3-per-side single unit nickel tuners with plastic buttons, available in Sunburst finish, 13 5/8" body width, mfg. 1931-1957.

	N/A	$850	$500

In 1934, (grand concert style) 14 3/8" body width, walnut back/sides replaced original part/designs, pearl wedge/logo peghead inlay added. In 1936, 16 3/8" body width introduced. In 1937, diamond/script logo peghead inlay replaced original part/design. Tenor and Plectrum version of the Zenith are available. In 1942, redesigned peghead replaced original part/design. In 1954, pearl oval peghead inlay replaced original part/design, Blonde finish was optional. This instrument originally sold for $50.

Melody Tenor - tenor version of the Zenith, walnut back/side, 13 1/4" body width, mfg. 1931-36.

	N/A	$850	$450

This model was originally called the Melody from its introduction in 1931 to 1936. The name was changed to Zenith Tenor in 1937.

Zenith Tenor - similar to the Melody tenor, 13 1/4" body width, mfg. 1937-1957.

	N/A	$850	$450

ACOUSTIC: GENERAL INFORMATION

In 1998, Epiphone began offering guitar and accessory packages for that "one stop shopping" experience for entry level guitars. Actually, the notion of a guitar package plus strings, a tuner, a gigbag, and a How-To video makes perfect sense for the first time guitar student.

The **C-10 Gig Rig** package (list $331) includes a C-10 nylon string acoustic guitar, Qwik-Tune quartz tuner, black gigbag, strap, picks, and a 30 minute Guitar Essentials Hal Leonard video tape. The **C-5 Player Pack** has a 3/4 sized classical guitar for $199. The **PR-100 Gig Rig** (list $329) is similar, but substitutes a PR-100 steel string guitar. The **AJ-10** is also available in a player pack for $329.

ACOUSTIC: AJ (ADVANCED JUMBO) SERIES

AJ-10 (MODEL EAJ1) - similar to AJ-15, except in dreadnought style, available in Ebony, Natural, or Vintage Sunburst finishes, mfg 1999-current.

MSR	$232	$149	$100	$75

AJ-15 (MODEL EAA1) - sloped shoulder jumbo style, select spruce top, round soundhole, black pickguard, bound body, stripe rosette, mahogany back/sides/neck, 14/20-fret fingerboard with pearl dot inlay, rosewood bridge with black bridgepins, 3-per-side chrome tuners, available in Ebony, Natural, or Vintage Sunburst finishes, mfg. 1998-current.

MSR	$299	$199	$140	$100

AJ-15L (Model EAA2) - similar to AJ-15, except in left-handed configuration, available in Natural finish, mfg. 1998-2000, 2002-current.

MSR	$332	$225	$155	$110

AJ-1512 (Model EAA3) - similar to AJ-15, except in a 12-string configuration, 6-per-side tuners, available in Natural finish, mfg. 1998-2000.

	$245	$165	$115

Last MSR $349.

AJ-18S (MODEL EAA4) - similar to AJ-15, except has a solid spruce top, single rounded cutaway body, no pickguard, diamond fingerboard inlay/block inlay at 12th fret, gold hardware, available in Ebony, Natural, or Vintage Sunburst finishes, mfg. 1998-current.

MSR	$382	$270	$185	$130

AJ-18SL (Model EAA5) - similar to AJ-18S, except in a left-handed configuration, available in Natural finish, mfg. 1998-2001.

	$290	$195	$135

Last MSR was $414.

AJ-1812S (Model EAA6) - similar to AJ-18S, except in a 12-string configuration, 6-per-side tuners, available in Natural finish, mfg. 1998-2000, 2002-current.

MSR	$449	$275	$200	$145

GRADING	100%	EXCELLENT	AVERAGE

AJ-1812SL (Model EAA7) - similar to AJ-18S, except in a left-handed 12-string configuration, 6-per-side tuners, available in Natural finish, mfg. 1998-2000.

	$315	$215	$150

Last MSR was $454.

AJ-28S (MODEL EAT1) - similar to AJ-15, except has a solid spruce top, bound body/fingerboard/headstock, diamond fingerboard inlay/block inlay at 12th fret, rosewood headstock veneer, available in Ebony, Natural, or Vintage Sunburst finishes, mfg. 1998-2002.

	$399	$285	$200

Last MSR was $569.

AJ-2812S (Model EA28) - similar to AJ-28S except in a 12-string model, 6-per-side tuners, chrome hardware, available in Natural Satin finish, disc. 2000.

	$475	$325	$250

Last MSR was $679.

AJ-35S (MODEL EAT2) - similar to AJ-15, except has a solid spruce top, triple-ply body binding, abalone rosette, dot fingerboard inlay/block inlay at 12th fret, rosewood headstock veneer, gold hardware, available in Ebony, Natural, or Vintage Sunburst finishes, mfg. 1998 to 2000.

	$475	$325	$225

Last MSR was $679.

AJ-45S (MODEL EAA8) - similar to AJ-15, except has a solid spruce top, 24¾ in. scale, bound body, blackface headstock with screened logo, tortoise shell pickguard, 3-per-side vintage-style tuners, available in Vintage Sunburst finish, mfg. 1998-2000, 2002.

	$455	$310	$220

Last MSR was $649.

The AJ-45S is based on Gibson's J-45 model.

ACOUSTIC: BARD SERIES

BARD - 12-string configuration, spruce top, mahogany back/sides, multiple-bound body, 24 3/4" scale, oval peghead inlay, mfg. 1962-1970.

	N/A	$700	$500

ACOUSTIC: BLUEGRASS SERIES

BISCUIT RESOPHONIC (MODEL EFB1) - resonator model with round neck, chrome hardware, 2 f-holes, available in Black, Brown, Heritage Cherry Sunburst, Red Brown Mahogany, or Translucent Blue finishes, current mfg.

MSR	$569	$399	$300	$225

SPIDER RESOPHONIC (MODEL EFSP) - similar to Biscuit Resophonic, except has square neck, 2 mesh-covered soundholes, slotted headstock, disc.

	$399	$300	$195

Last MSR was $569

MD-100 - metal resphonic guitar, chrome/brass body, round mahogany neck, rosewood fingerboard with dot inlay, 3-per-side tuners, chrome finish, new 2003.

MSR	$832	$499	$375	$250.

ACOUSTIC: CLASSICAL SERIES

ALHAMBRA - spruce top, curly maple back/sides, round soundhole, mahogany neck, 12/20-fret rosewood fingerboard, rosewood bridge, slotted headstock, 14 3/8" body width, mfg. 1938-1941.

	N/A	$1,000	$750

BARCELONE - maple back/sides, 25 1/2" scale, black body binding, gold hardware, pearloid tuner buttons, 14 1/4" body width, mfg. 1963-69.

	N/A	$525	$375

BARCELONA CE (MODEL EC7C) - single soft cutaway body, solid spruce top, mahogany body and neck, rosewood fingerboard, 25 1/2" scale, gold hardware, Piezo/Epi-Six pickup and preamp/EQ, available in Antique Natural finish, mfg. 1999-2000.

	$675	$460	$325

Last MSR was $899.

**Epiphone Zenith
courtesy Robert Aponte**

**Epiphone Biscuit
courtesy Gibson**

E

GRADING	100%	EXCELLENT	AVERAGE

CLASSICA (MODEL EC70) - top of the line traditional classical model, solid spruce top, rosewood body and fingerboard, mahogany neck, 25 1/2" scale, gold hardware, available in Antique Natural finish, mfg. 1999-2000.

	$485	$335	$235

Last MSR was $649.

C-5 (MODEL EC05) - 3/4 size classical size, similar to the C-10, available in Natural finish, new 2003.

MSR	$149	$105	$75	$50

C-10 (MODEL EC15) - classical style body, mahogany body and neck, spruce top, chrome hardware, available in Natural Satin finish, mfg. 1997-current.

MSR	$199	$150	$100	$70

C-25 (Model EC25) - classical style, available in Natural Satin finish, disc. 2000.

	$200	$135	$95

Last MSR was $269.

C-40 (Model EC40) - classical style, available in Natural gloss finish, current mfg.

MSR	$299	$210	$150	$100

CLASSIC - spruce top, mahogany back/sides, tortoise body binding, mfg. 1963-1970.

	N/A	$275	$175

CONCERT - maple back/sides, mutiple-body bindings, bound rosewood fingerboard (extends over soundhole), rosewood bridge, slotted peghead, gold hardware, available in Natural finish, 16 1/2" body width, mfg. 1938-1941.

	N/A	$1,400	$925

ESPANA - maple back/sides, black bound body, available in Walnut finish, mfg. 1962-69.

	N/A	$350	$250

GRANADA (MODEL EC60) - traditional classical body, Select Spruce top, mahogany back and sides, rosewood fingerboard, bound body, 25 1/2" scale, gold hardware, available in Antique Natural finish, mfg. 1999-2001.

	$295	$195	$130

Last MSR was $419.

ACOUSTIC: DOVE & HUMMINGBIRD SERIES

These models are based off of Gibson's Dove and Hummingbird, respectively.

DOVE (MODEL EADV) - double parallelogram fingerboard inlay, dove artwork on tortoise shell pickguard, moustache-style bridge with wing inlay, bound fingerboard, available in Cherry or Natural finish, mfg. 1998-2000.

MSR	$599	$450	$300	$210

HUMMINGBIRD (MODEL EAHB) - dreadnought style, bound body, double parallelogram block inlays, flowers/hummingbird artwork on tortoise shell pickguard, 3-per-side chrome vintage-style tuners, available in Heritage Cherry Sunburst finish, current mfg.

MSR	$599	$359	$275	$175

ACOUSTIC: EJ & ELVIS PRESLEY EJ SERIES

EJ-200 (MODEL EAJ2) - jumbo style, spruce top, round soundhole, tortoise pickguard with engraved flowers/pearl dot inlay, 3-stripe bound body/rosette, maple back/sides/neck, 14/20-fret bound pointed fingerboard with pearl crown inlay, rosewood mustache bridge with pearl block inlay, white black dot bridge pins, bound blackface peghead with pearl crown/logo inlay, 3-per-side gold tuners, available in Ebony, Natural, or Vintage Sunburst finishes, current mfg.

MSR	$665	$399	$290	$215

EJ-212 - similar to the EJ-200, except has 12-string configuration, 6-per-side tuners, available in Black, Natural, or Vintage Sunburst finishes, disc. 1999.

	$575	$425	$275

Last MSR was $819.

ELVIS PRESLEY EJ-200 (MODEL EAEP) - similar to the EJ-200, except has special fingerboard inlay, yellow Elvis graphic on lower bout, special graphic pickguard, available in Black finish, disc. 1999.

	$575	$375	$275

Last MSR was $799.

Elvis Presley EJ-200 CE (Model EEEP) - similar to the Elvis Presley EJ-200, except features single rounded cutaway, piezo bridge pickup, volume/tone controls, available in Black finish, disc. 1999.

	$695	$450	$325

Last MSR was $999.

GRADING	100%	EXCELLENT	AVERAGE

ACOUSTIC: EL, EL DORADO, EO-1, EXCELLENTE, & FOLKSTER SERIES

EL-00 - rounded cutaway mahogany body, solid spruce top, mahogany neck, 19-fret rosewood fingerboard with dot inlay, round soundhole, tortise pickguard with E logo, 3-per-side-tuners, E logo on truss rod cover, chrome hardware, available in Vintage Sunburst finish, based on Gibson's small OO size, mfg. 2001-current.

MSR	$631	$379	$295	$200

EL DORADO - squared shoulder dreadnought, spruce top, mahogany back and sides, multiple body binding, bound fingerboard with single parallelogram inlay, oval headstock inlay, available in Natural finish, mfg. 1963-1970.

		N/A	$1,500	$850

EO-1 - rounded cutaway, spruce top, round soundhole, 3-stripe bound body/rosette, mahogany back/sides/neck, 21-fret bound rosewood fingerboard with pearl dot inlay, rosewood bridge with white black dot pins, rosewood veneer on bound peghead with star/crescent inlay, 3-per-side chrome tuners, available in Natural finish, mfg. 1992-2000.

		N/A	$325	$200

Last MSR was $630.

EXCELLENTE - squared shoulder dreadnought style, spruce top, rosewood back/sides, multiple body binding, round soundhole, bound ebony fingerboard with cloud inlay, pearl and abalone peghead inlay, eagle inlay on pickguard, tune-o-matic bridge, gold hardware, available in Natural finish, mfg. 1963-1970.

		N/A	$5,300	$3,500

Excellente (Model EAEX) - contemporary re-issue, available in Natural and Vintage Sunburst finishes, disc. 2000.

	$875	$575	$390

Last MSR was $1,249.

FOLKSTER - 14 1/4" body width, spruce top, mahogany back/sides, rosewood fingerboard with dot inlay, 2 white pickguards, mfg. 1966-1970.

		N/A	$375	$225

**Epiphone Granada
courtesy Gibson**

ACOUSTIC ARCHTOP: ELITIST SERIES

ELITIST L-00 (JAPAN) - solid spruce top, solid mahogany back, mahogany sides, 1-piece mahogany set neck with rosewood fingerboard and 19 frets, 25½ inch scale, bone nut, rosewood bridge, nickel hardware, Grover tuners, available in Vintage Sunburst finish, new 2003.

ELITIST J-45 (JAPAN) - jumbo body style, solid spruce top, solid mahogany back, mahogany sides, 1-piece mahogany set neck with rosewood fingerboard, 20 frets, 24¾ inch scale, bone nut and saddle, rosewood bridge, nickel hardware, Grover tuners, available in Vintage Sunburst or Natural finishes, new 2003.

ELITIST '65 TEXAN (JAPAN) - solid spruce top, solid mahogany back, mahogany sides, 1-piece mahogany set neck with rosewood fingerboard and 20 frets, 25½ inch scale, bone nut, rosewood bridge, intonated, adjustable saddle, nickel hardware, Grover tuners, available in Natural or Vintage Sunburst finishes, new 2003.

ELITIST J-200 (JAPAN) - jumbo body style, solid spruce top, solid maple back and sides, 5-piece maple and rosewood set neck with Ebonized rosewood fingerboard. 25 ½ inch scale, bone nut and saddle, 24kt. gold plated hardware, Grover tuners with Imperial buttons, available in Vintage Sunburst or Natural finishes, new 2003.

ACOUSTIC: FT SERIES

Between 1980 to 1982, Epiphone offered a number of additional FT Series models. The **FT-120** (retail list $170) was offered in a Natural finish, while the **FT-130** (list $190) was featured in Brown Sunburst. All other models were available in a Natural finish. The **FT-140** had a retail list price of $200; the **FT-145**, list $220; **FT-150**, list $270; **FT-160**, list $250; **FT-165**, list $300. The **FT-165** was produced between 1980 to 1981. Most secondary prices on these early 1980s FT Series models range between $95 to $125.

FT DE LUXE - spruce top, maple back/sides, round soundhole, multiple body binding, maple neck, bound rosewood fingerboard with cloud inlay, tortoise pickguard, trapeze tailpiece, vine peghead inlay, gold hardware, available in Natural and Sunburst finishes, 16 1/2" body width, mfg. 1939-1942.

		N/A	$3,000	$2,000

This model is similar to the De Luxe Archtop, except in a flattop configuration.

**Epiphone EJ-200
courtesy Gibson**

FT De Luxe Cutaway - similar to the FT De Luxe, except features a single rounded cutaway body, flower peghead inlay, 17 3/8" body width, mfg. 1954-57.

	N/A	$3,500	$2,000

FT 27 - spruce top, mahogany back/sides, bound top, 14/20-fret rosewood fingerboard with dot inlay, Masterbilt peghead decal, rosewood bridge, available in Sunburst finish, 14 1/2" body width, mfg. 1935-1941.

	N/A	$550	$375

FT 30 (CABALLERO) - OO style, mahogany top, round soundhole, tortoise pickguard, mahogany back/sides/neck, 14/20-fret rosewood fingerboard with pearl dot inlay, rosewood bridge with white pins, 3-per-side tuners with plastic buttons, available in Natural finish, 14 1/2" body width, mfg. 1941-49.

1941-1949	N/A	$1,000	$500
1958-1970	N/A	$650	$350

The FT 30 was renamed the Caballero by Gibson in 1958. Mfg. 1958 to 1970. In 1958, tortoise pickguard with logo was introduced. In 1961, non logo pickguard replaced original part/design. In 1963, adjustable saddle replaced original part/design.

FT 37 - spruce top, quartered walnut back/sides, cherry neck, 20-fret rosewood fingerboard with dot inlay, tortoiseshell pickguard, rosewood bridge, 3-per-side tuners with plastic buttons, available in Yellow Sunburst top and Natural finishes, 15 1/2" body width, mfg. 1935-1941.

	N/A	$800	$525

FT 45 (CORTEZ) - OO style, spruce top, round soundhole, tortoise pickguard, white body binding, walnut back/sides, cherry neck, 20-fret rosewood fingerboard with pearl dot inlay, rosewood bridge with white pins, metal logo plate mounted on peghead, 3-per-side tuners, available in Natural or Sunburst finishes, 14 1/2" body width, mfg. 1941-49, 1958-1970.

1941-1949	N/A	$1,000	$600
1958-1970	N/A	$900	$450

The FT 45 was renamed the Cortez by Gibson in 1958, mfg. 1958 to 1970. In 1962, Natural finish with adjustable bridge became an option.

FT 50 - OO style, spruce top, round soundhole, mahogany back/sides, tortoise shell body binding, cherry neck, tortoise pickguard, 14/20-fret bound rosewood fingerboard with dot inlay, rosewood bridge, 3-per-side tuners with plastic buttons, available in Natural finish, 14 1/2" body width, mfg. 1941-49.

	N/A	$900	$550

FT 75 - spruce top, curly maple back/sides, multiple body binding, mahogany neck, 20-fret bound rosewood fingerboard with parallelogram inlay, rosewood bridge, 3-per-side open back tuners, available in Cherry Burst, Natural, or Sunburst finishes, 16 1/2" body width, mfg. 1935-1942.

	N/A	$1,400	$900

FT 79 (TEXAN) - dreadnought style, spruce top, walnut back/sides, cherry neck, 20-fret bound rosewood fingerboard with parallelogram inlay, rosewood bridge, 3-per-side open back tuners, available in Natural and Sunburst finish, 16 1/2" body width, mfg. 1941-1970.

1941-1957	N/A	$1,300	$700
1958-1970	N/A	$1,000	$500

In 1949, a new jumbo body style was introduced. In 1954, curly maple back/sides replaced original part/design. The FT 79 was renamed the Texan by Gibson in 1958, mfg. 1958-1970.

Texan (Model EATX) - contemporary model, available in Natural or Vintage Sunburst finishes, mfg. 1996-2002.

	$560	$380	$265

Last MSR was $799.

FT 110 (FRONTIER) - dreadnought style, spruce top, curly maple back/sides, 5-piece cherry neck, 20-fret bound rosewood fingerboard with slotted block inlay, rosewood bridge, 3-per-side open back tuners, available in Natural and Sunburst finish, 16 1/2" body width, mfg. 1941-1970.

1941-1956	N/A	$1,800	$1,000
1957-1970	N/A	$1,500	$800

In 1949, a new jumbo body style was introduced. The FT 110 was renamed the Frontier by Gibson in 1958, mfg. 1958-1970.

Frontier (Model EAFT) - contemporary re-issue, available in Natural and Vintage Sunburst finishes, disc.

	$630	$410	$295

Last MSR was $899.

Frontier Left-Handed (Model EAFTL) - similar to Frontier, except in left-handed configuration, available in Natural or Vintage Sunburst finishes, mfg. 1997-98.

	$775	$625	$400

Last MSR was $1,269.

FT 140 (KOREA MFG.) - spruce top, mahogany back/sides, bolt-on neck, zero fret, 20-fret rosewood fingerboard with pearl dot inlay, black pickguard, rosewood bridge with black buttons, 3-per-side chrome tuners, available in Natural finish, mfg. 1973-76.

	N/A	$175	$100

Last MSR was $145.

GRADING	100%	EXCELLENT	AVERAGE

ACOUSTIC: MADRID & NAVARRE SERIES

MADRID (MFG. 1931-1941) - spruce top, curly maple back/sides, tortoise body binding, 12/19-fret fingerboard, available in Natural finish, 16 1/2" body width, mfg. 1931-1941.

1931-1935	N/A	$2,200	$1,250
1936-1941	N/A	$2,000	$1,000

This model was originally introduced as an f-hole guitar, Hawaiian (or Spanish) style. In 1936, the Madrid was re-designated as a jumbo size, round soundhole, Hawaiian style only.

Madrid (Mfg. 1962-1970) - classical style, mahogany back/sides, tortoise body binding, available in Natural finish, mfg. 1962 - 1970.

	N/A	$500	$250

NAVARRE - Hawaiian style, spruce top, mahogany back/sides/neck, round soundhole, 20-fret bound rosewood fingerboard with dot inlay, tortoise shell pickguard, rosewood bridge, 3-per-side tuners with plastic buttons, available in Brown finish, 16 1/2" body width, mfg. 1931-1941.

	N/A	$1,500	$1,000

ACOUSTIC: PR SERIES

PR-100 (MODEL EA10) - dreadnought style, spruce top, round soundhole, black pickguard, stripe rosette, mahogany back/sides/neck, 14/20-fret rosewood fingerboard with dot inlay, rosewood bridge with black pins, 3-per-side chrome tuners, available in Ebony, Natural Gloss, Wine Red, or Vintage Sunburst finishes, mfg. 1997-current.

MSR	$249	$150	$105	$75

Also available with an ash top at no additional charge (Model PR-100A). Also was available in a single cutaway design for an additional $50 (Model PR-100C). Wine Red added in 2002.

PR-100-12 (Model EA12) - similar to the PR-100 except in 12 string configuration, available in Natural finish, current mfg.

MSR	$332	$199	$125	$95

PR-200 (MODEL EA20) - dreadnought style, spruce top, round soundhole, black pickguard, stripe rosette, bound body, mahogany back/sides/neck, 14/20-fret rosewood fingerboard with pearl dot inlay, rosewood bridge with white pins, 3-per-side chrome tuners, available in Natural Satin finish, mfg. 1992-current.

MSR	$299	$185	$140	$100

In 1998, Ebony, Natural Gloss, and Vintage Sunburst finishes were introduced (previously a $15 option).

PR-350 (MODEL EA35) - dreadnought style, spruce top, round soundhole, tortoise pickguard with stylized *E*, 3-stripe bound body/rosette, mahogany back/sides/neck, 14/20-fret rosewood fingerboard with pearl snowflake inlay, pearl crown/logo inlay, 3-per-side chrome tuners, available in Natural finish, mfg. 1992-2000.

	$225	$175	$125
	Last MSR was $369.		

In 1998, Ebony and Vintage Sunburst finishes were introduced (previously a $10 option).

PR-350 C (Model EA3C) - similar to the PR-350, except features a single cutaway body, available in Natural finish, disc. 1999.

	$250	$200	$150
	Last MSR was $409.		

In 1998, Ebony and Vintage Sunburst finishes were introduced (previously a $10 option).

PR-350 M (Model EM35) - similar to PR-350, except has mahogany top, mfg. 1994-98.

	N/A	$200	$125
	Last MSR was $379.		

PR-350 S (Model EAO5) - similar to PR-350, except has spruce top, mfg. 1992-current.

MSR	$382	$235	$180	$130

In 1998, Ebony and Vintage Sunburst finishes were introduced (previously a $10 option).

PR-350 SM (Model EO35) - similar to the PR-350, except has solid mahogany back and sides, Natural satin finish, new 2003.

MSR	$832	$499	$375	$275

PR-350 SO (Model EM35) - similar to the PR-350, except has solid ovangkol back and sides, Natural satin finish, new 2003.

MSR	$999	$599	$475	$350

PR-350 SR (Model ER35) - similar to the PR-350, except has solid rosewood back and sides, Natural satin finish, new 2003.

MSR	$999	$599	$475	$350

**Epiphone FT 45 (Cortez)
courtesy Rod & Hank's**

**Epiphone PR-100
courtesy Gibson**

GRADING		100%	EXCELLENT	AVERAGE

PR-350 S Left-Handed (Model EAOL) - similar to the PR-350 S, except in left-handed configuration, available in Natural finish, disc. 2000, 2002-current.

MSR	$415	$250	$195	$140

PR-350-12 (Model EA3T) - similar to the PR-350 S, except has 12-string configuration, available in Natural finish, current mfg.

MSR	$331	$199	$150	$100

PR-400 (MODEL EA40) - available in Natural finish, mfg. 1997-99.

		$325	$225	$150

Last MSR was $459.

PR-600 - small body style, mahogany back and sides, solid spruce top, rosewood fingerboard, binding, available in Natural or Antique Sunburst finishes, mfg. 1980-mid 1980s.

		N/A	$175	$100

PR-650 - available in natural or Antique Sunburst finishes, mfg. 1980-mid 1980s.

		N/A	$175	$100

PR-650-12 - similar to the PR-650 except in 12 string configuration, mfg. 1980-mid 1980s.

		N/A	$200	$125

PR-715 - available in Natural, Antique Sunburst, or Antique Cherry Sunburst finishes, mfg. 1981-mid 1980s.

		N/A	$225	$145

PR-715-12 - similar to the PR-715 except in 12 string configuration, mfg. 1980-mid 1980s.

		N/A	$250	$150

PR-720 S - dreadnought style, solid spruce top, round soundhole, tortoise shell pickguard, 3-stripe rosette, bound body, African ovankol back/sides, mahogany neck, 14/20-fret rosewood fingerboard with pearl diamond inlay, rosewood bridge with white pins, 3-per-side chrome tuners, available in Natural finish, mfg. 1992 only.

		N/A	$225	$135

PR-725 - mahogany back and sides, laminated top, dot inlays, available in Natural finish, mfg. early 1970s-mid 1980s.

		N/A	$250	$125

PR-725S - similar to the PR-725 except has solid spruce top, mfg. 1979-mid 1980s.

		N/A	$275	$145

PR-735 - dreadnought style, available in natural finish, mfg. 1979-mid 1980s.

		N/A	$280	$150

PR-735S - similar to the PR-735 except has solid spruce top, mfg. 1979-mid 1980s.

		N/A	$300	$175

PR-745 - rosewood back and sides, solid top, dot inlay, available in Natural finish, mfg. early 1970s-1979.

		N/A	$300	$175

PR-755S - dreadnought style, solid top, available in natural finish, mfg. 1979-mid 1980s.

		N/A	$350	$225

PR-765 - dreadnought style, rosewood back and sides, solid top, V Block inlay, vine peghead inlay, available in Natural finish, early 1970s-1979.

		N/A	$350	$225

PR-775 S - dreadnought style, solid spruce top, round soundhole, tortoise shell pickguard, abalone bound body/rosette, rosewood back/sides, mahogany neck, 14/20-fret bound rosewood fingerboard with abalone pearl block/triangle inlay, rosewood bridge with white black dot pins, rosewood veneer on bound peghead with crescent/star/logo inlay, 3-per-side chrome tuners, available in Natural finish, disc. 1996.

		N/A	$250	$175

Last MSR was $500.

PR-775-12 - similar to the PR-775 S, except in 12-string configuration.

		N/A	$250	$175

Last MSR was $500.

PR-800 S (MODEL EA80) - available in Natural finish, disc. 1998.

		N/A	$325	$200

Last MSR was $619.

ACOUSTIC: SJ (SUPER JUMBO) SERIES

SJ-15 (MODEL EAS1) - super jumbo acoustic, mahogany body with spruce top, mahogany neck, rosewood fingerboard with dot inlays, round soundhole, black pickguard, 3-per-side tuners, chrome hardware, available in Natural Satin finish, current mfg.

MSR	$365	$225	$175	$125

E

GRADING		100%	EXCELLENT	AVERAGE

SJ-18S (MODEL EAS2) - super jumbo, mahogany body and neck, rosewood fingerboard with split diamond inlays, 3-per-side tuners, solid spruce top, rosewood bridge, round soundhole, tortoise pickguard, gold hardware, available in Ebony, Natural Satin, or Vintage Sunburst finishes, mfg. 2000-current.

	MSR	$449	$275	$220	$150

ACOUSTIC: SQ SERIES (DON EVERLY & NEIL DIAMOND)

DON EVERLY SQ-180 (MODEL EAQ1) - star fingerboard inlay, soundhole-surrounding pickguard, available in Ebony finish, disc. 2000, reintroduced 2002-current.

	MSR	$519	$375	$250	$175

NEIL DIAMOND SQ-180 (MODEL EAND) - maple body, select spruce top, mahogany neck, rosewood fingerboard with diamond-shaped inlays, 24 3/4" scale, facsimile signature on headstock, gold hardware, available in Black Metallic finish, mfg. 1999-2000, reintroduced 2002.

			$420	$280	$185

Last MSR was $599.

Epiphone SJ-15
courtesy Gibson

ACOUSTIC: SERENADER & SEVILLE SERIES

SERENADER - 12-string configuration, 14 1/4" body width, mahogany back/sides, 25 1/2" scale, adjustable saddle, dot fingerboard inlay, available in Walnut finish, mfg. 1963-1970.

			N/A	$700	$400

SEVILLE (MFG. 1938-1941) - classical style, spruce top, round soundhole, mahogany back/sides, mahogany neck, 12/20-fret rosewood extended fingerboard, rosewood bridge, slotted headstock, available in Natural finish, 14 3/8" body width, mfg. 1938-1941.

			N/A	$600	$450

Seville (Mfg. 1961-1970) - classical style, mahogany back/sides, 25 1/2" scale, tortoise body binding, available in Natural finish, 14.25" body width, mfg. 1961-1970.

			N/A	$350	$250

The Seville model was offered with a ceramic pickup between 1961 to 1964 as the Seville Electric.

ACOUSTIC: SONGWRITER & TROUBADOUR SERIES

SONGWRITER (MODEL EABM, BLUESMASTER) - slope shouldered folk style, bound body, available in Ebony, Natural, or Vintage Sunburst finishes, disc. 1999.

			$475	$300	$225

Last MSR was $679.

TROUBADOUR - squared shoulder dreadnought style, spruce top, maple back/sides, multiple body binding, 12/19-fret rosewood fingerboard with slotted block inlay, 2 white pickguards, solid peghead, gold hardware, available in Walnut finish, mfg. 1963-1970.

			N/A	$400	$275

ACOUSTIC ELECTRIC: AJ SERIES

AJ-10CE (MODEL EE1C) - available in Natural finish, mfg. 2002-current.

	MSR	$299	$179	$135	$85

AJ-15 E (MODEL EEA1) - sloped shoulder jumbo style, solid sitka spruce top, round soundhole, black pickguard, bound body, stripe rosette, mahogany back/sides/neck, 14/20-fret fingerboard with pearl dot inlay, rosewood bridge with black bridgepins, 3-per-side chrome tuners, piezo pickup, Electar preamp system, available in Ebony, Natural or Vintage Sunburst finishes, mfg. 1998-current.

	MSR	$332	$199	$150	$95

AJ-18SCE (MODEL EEA2) - similar to AJ-15 E, except has single rounded cutaway body, no pickguard, diamond fingerboard inlay/block inlay at 12th fret, gold hardware, piezo pickup, Electar Epiphone 6 preamp system (equipped with Epiphonic-Six preamp/EQ as of 2001), available in Ebony, Natural, or Vintage Sunburst finishes, mfg. 1998-current.

	MSR	$549	$329	$250	$175

AJ-2812SE (MODEL EE28) - 12-string, jumbo body, mahogany body and neck, solid spruce top, rosewood fingerboard with dot inlays, 3-per-side tuners, sound soundhole, black pickguard, chrome hardware, piezo pickup with Epiphonic-Six preamp/EQ, disc 2002.

			$450	$375	$275

Last MSR was $749.

Epiphone AJ-18SCE
courtesy Gibson

GRADING	100%	EXCELLENT	AVERAGE

AJ-30 CE (MODEL EEA3) - similar to AJ-15 E, except has single rounded cutaway body, dot fingerboard inlay/block inlay at 12th fret, piezo pickup, Electar Epiphone 6 preamp system, available in Ebony, Natural, or Vintage Sunburst finishes, mfg. 1998-2000.

	$425	$350	$240
	Last MSR was $679.		

AJ-30CE (Model EE6C) - reintroduced model with piezo pickup and Epiphonic-Six Chorus, available in Ebony, Natural and Vintage Sunburst finishes, disc. 2002.

	$440	$375	$250
	Last MSR was $729.		

AJ-40 TLC (MODEL EE4C) - similar to AJ-15 E, except has single rounded cutaway body, no pickguard, bound body, dot fingerboard inlay/block inlay at 12th fret, gold hardware, piezo pickup, Electar Epiphonic 2000 preamp system (equipped with Epiphonic-Six preamp/EQ as of 2001), available in Ebony, Natural, or Vintage Sunburst finishes, mfg. 1998-2002.

	$425	$350	$245
	Last MSR was $699.		

AJ-45S E (MODEL EEA8) - similar to AJ-15 E, except has 24¾ in. scale, bound body, blackface headstock with screened logo, tortoise shell pickguard, 3-per-side vintage-style tuners, piezo pickup, Electar Epiphone 6 preamp system (equipped with Epiphonic-Six preamp/EQ as of 2001), available in Vintage Sunburst finish, based on Gibson's J-45 model, mfg. 1998-99.

	$475	$400	$275
	Last MSR was $779.		

ACOUSTIC ELECTRIC: C SERIES & CLASSICAL MODELS

C-70 CE (MODEL EOC7) - classic style, single rounded cutaway body, spruce top, round soundhole, bound body, wooden inlay rosette, rosewood back/sides, mahogany neck, 19-fret rosewood fingerboard, rosewood tied bridge, rosewood peghead veneer with circles/star design, 3-per-side chrome tuners with pearl buttons, piezo pickup, volume/3-band EQ, available in Natural finish, disc. 2000.

	$425	$325	$225
	Last MSR was $649.		

Selena C-70 CE (Model EESE) - similar to the C-70 CE, except features Selena signature graphic on body, available in Black finish, mfg. 1997 only.

	$539	$475	$295
	Last MSR was $899.		

VALENCIA CE (MODEL EC6C) - single smooth cutaway classical mahogany body, select spruce top, rosewood fretboard, nylon string, open style tuners, body binding, Epiphonic Six preamp, gold hardware, Antique Natural finish, mfg. 2002-current.

MSR	$699	$420	$295	$225

This model is the same as the Granada except features a cutaway and electronics.

Valencia CE Left-Handed (Model EC6CL) - similar to the Valencia CE except in left-handed configuration, mfg. 2002-current.

MSR	$724	$440	$310	$235

ACOUSTIC ELECTRIC: CABALLERO SERIES

CABALLERO (MODEL EECB) - contemporary re-issue, available in Natural finish, mfg. 1997-99.

	$800	$600	$425
	Last MSR was $1,299.		

ACOUSTIC ELECTRIC: CHET ATKINS SERIES

CHET ATKINS SST STUDIO (MODEL ECSS) - semi-solid thinline acoustic, mahogany set neck, maple top, rosewood fingerboard with dot inlays, 3-per-side tuners, Shadow piezo pickup, passive electronics, gold hardware, available in Ebony, Heritage Cherry Sunburst (Disc. 2000), or Natural finishes, current mfg.

MSR	$659	$399	$275	$190

Chet Atkins CEC (Model ECCE) - available in Antique Natural finish, mfg. 1995-99.

	$425	$250	$175
	Last MSR was $599.		

Chet Atkins CE (Model ECCE) - nylon string version of Chet Atkins SST, banjo style tuners, available in Natural finish, current mfg.

MSR	$659	$399	$275	$190

Chet Atkins Custom (Model ECSF) - available in Heritage Cherry Sunburst or Natural finishes.

	N/A	$375	$225
	Last MSR was $699.		

Chet Atkins Deluxe (Model ECBE) - available in Heritage Cherry Sunburst or Natural finishes.

	N/A	$400	$250
	Last MSR was $749.		

E

GRADING	100%	EXCELLENT	AVERAGE

ACOUSTIC ELECTRIC: DOVE SERIES

DOVE A/E (MODEL EEDV) - double parallelogram fingerboard inlay, dove artwork on tortoise shell pickguard, moustache-style bridge with wing inlay, bound fingerboard, piezo pickup, Electar preamp system, available in Cherry and Natural finish, based on Gibson's Dove acoustic guitar, mfg. 1998-99.

	$475	$315	$220

Last MSR was $679.

ACOUSTIC ELECTRIC: EJ, JOHN LENNON EJ-160E, & EO-2 SERIES

JOHN LENNON EJ-160 E (MODEL EEEJ) - dreadnought style, bound body/fingerboard, trapezoid fingerboard inlay, built-in pickup, volume/tone controls (on top), tortoise shell pickguard, screened 'John Lennon' signature on body, available in Natural or Vintage Cherry Sunburst finishes, mfg. 1997-current.

MSR	$899	$539	$450	$375

In 1998, Natural finish was disc.

EJ-200 CE (MODEL EEJ2) - similar to the EJ-200 (Model EAJ2), except features piezo bridge pickup, volume/tone controls, available in Black, Natural, or Vintage Sunburst finishes, current mfg.

MSR	$799	$479	$400	$325

EO-2 (MODEL EO2E) - rounded cutaway folk style, arched walnut top, oval soundhole, 3-stripe bound body/rosette, walnut back/sides, mahogany neck, 21-fret bound rosewood fingerboard with pearl dot inlay, rosewood bridge with white black dot pins, rosewood veneer on bound peghead with star/crescent inlay, 3-per-side chrome tuners, piezo pickup, volume/tone controls, available in Natural finish, mfg. 1992-97.

	N/A	$425	$250

Last MSR was $799.

This model has a wooden butterfly inlay between the soundhole and bridge.

Epiphone AJ-30 CE
courtesy Gibson

ACOUSTIC ELECTRIC: JEFF "SKUNK" BAXTER SIGNATURE SERIES

JEFF "SKUNK" BAXTER (MODEL EAJB) - available in Ebony, Red Brown Mahogany, Natural, or Vintage Sunburst finishes, current mfg.

MSR	$819	$575	$375	$275

Ebony and Vintage Sunburst were discontinued.

ACOUSTIC ELECTRIC: PR-E SERIES

PR-5 E (MODEL EEP5) - single sharp cutaway folk style, figured maple top, round soundhole, multi-bound body/rosette, mahogany back/sides/neck, 20-fret bound rosewood fingerboard with pearl diamond slot inlay, rosewood bridge with white black dot pins, blackface peghead with pearl crown/logo inlay, 3-per-side gold tuners, piezo bridge pickup, 4-band EQ, available in Black, Natural, or Vintage Sunburst finishes, mfg. 1992-current.

MSR	$582	$349	$275	$175

PR-5 E Artist (Model EEA5) - available in Heritage Cherry Sunburst, Vintage Sunburst or White (Disc. 1999) finishes.

	$575	$375	$250

Last MSR was $799.

PR-5 E Left-Handed (Model EEP5L) - similar to the PR-5 E, except in a left-handed configuration, available in Natural finish, current mfg.

MSR	$615	$369	$290	$185

PR-6 E (MODEL EEP6) - single rounded solid mahogany body, solid spruce top, mahogany neck, RW fingerboard with split diamond inlay, binding, Shadow Classic P-4 preamp (new 2003), available in Natrual, Heritage Cherry Sunburst, Trans. Amber, Trans. Red, Trans. Blue, Trans. Black, or Tobacco Sunburst finish, disc. 1998, reintroduced 2003.

MSR	$749	$449	$375	$250

Epiphone AJ-40 TLC
courtesy Gibson

GRADING		100%	EXCELLENT	AVERAGE

E

PR-6E Left-Handed (Model EEP6L) - similar to the PR-6E except in left-handed configuration, available in Natural or Trans. Amber finishes, new 2003.

MSR	$799	$479	$395	$260

PR-7 E (MODEL EEP7) - similar to the PR-5E except has a bird's-eye maple top, slim taper neck, and Epiphonic 2000, available in Heritage Cherry Sunburst, Natural, Orange Sunburst, Trans. Black, or Vintage Cherry Sunburst, disc 2002.

		$450	$325	$250

Last MSR was $749.

PR-200 E (MODEL EE20) - dreadnought style, spruce top, round soundhole, tortoise pickguard with stylized *E*, 3-stripe bound body/rosette, mahogany back/sides/neck, 14/20-fret rosewood fingerboard with pearl snowflake inlay, pearl crown/logo inlay, 3-per-side chrome tuners, available in Natural finish, mfg. 1992-2001.

		$199	$150	$105

Last MSR was $329.

PR-350 CE (MODEL EE3C) - single rounded cutaway dreadnought style mahogany body, select spruce top, mahogany neck, rosewood fingerboard with split diamond inlays, tortise pickguard with E logo, piezo pickup, Epiphonic-Six preamp, chrome hardware, body binding, available in Ebony, Natural, or Vintage Sunburst finishes, current mfg.

MSR	$479	$290	$235	$165

In 1998, Ebony and Vintage Sunburst finishes were introduced (previously a $10 option).

PR-350 E (Model EE35) - similar to the PR-350CE except with no cutaway, available in Natural finish, disc. 1998.

		$290	$235	$165

Last MSR was $459.

PR-350 12-string E (Model EE3T) - similar to PR-350 E, except in 12-string configuration, available in Natural finish, disc. 1998.

		$350	$275	$195

Last MSR was $529.

PR-350 ME (Model EME5) - similar to PR-350 E, except has mahogany top, piezo bridge pickup, mfg. 1993-98.

		$325	$275	$165

Last MSR was $499.

PR-775 SCE (MODEL EO77) - single rounded cutaway body, gold hardware, Electar preamp system, available in Antique Natural finish, mfg. 1997-99.

		$575	$375	$250

Last MSR was $799.

PR-795AE - acoustic electric Presentation guitar, available in Natural, Anitque Sunburst, or Antique Cherry Sunburst finishes, mfg. 1980-mid 1980s.

		N/A	$250	$150

PR-800 SE (MODEL EE80) - dreadnought style, gold hardware, Electar preamp system, available in Natural finish, disc. 1999.

		$525	$350	$250

Last MSR was $719.

ACOUSTIC ELECTRIC: SJ-E SERIES

SJ-18SCE - single rounded cutaway super jumbo mahogany body, solid spruce top, mahogany neck, rosewood fingerboard, split diamond inlays, Piezo pickup, Epiphonic Six preamp, body and neck binding, gold hardware, available in Natural or Vintage sunburst finishes, mfg. 2000-current.

MSR	$699	$420	$350	$260

ACOUSTIC ELECTRIC BASS

EL CAPITAN (MODEL EBEC) - jumbo style, maple body, set-in maple neck, 34" scale, rosewood fingerboard with dot inlay, piezo bridge pickup, Para-EQ preamp system, available in Ebony, Natural, or Vintage Sunburst finishes, disc. 2000.

		$675	$450	$325

Last MSR was $949.

El Capitan Cutaway (Model EBC4) - similar to El Capitan, except features a single rounded cutaway body, available in Ebony, Natural, or Vintage Sunburst finishes, current mfg.

MSR	$999	$599	$475	$350

El Capitan Cutaway Fretless (Model EBC4F) - similar to El Capitan, except features a single rounded cutaway body, fretless fingerboard, available in Ebony, Natural, or Vintage Sunburst finishes, disc. 1998.

		$675	$525	$350

Last MSR was $1,099.

El Capitan 5 String Cutaway (Model EBC5) - similar to El Capitan, except features a single rounded cutaway body, 5-string configuration, 3/2-per-side tuners, available in Ebony, Natural, or Vintage Sunburst finishes, disc. 2000.

	$675	$500	$375

Last MSR was $1,049.

El Capitan 5 String Cutaway Fretless (Model EBC5F) - similar to the El Capitan 5 String Cutaway, except features a fretless fingerboard, available in Ebony, Natural, or Vintage Sunburst finishes, disc. 2000.

	$675	$500	$375

Last MSR was $1,049.

EL SEGUNDO (MODEL EBS4) - jumbo mahogany body, laminated maple top, maple set neck, rosewood fingerboard with dot inlays, 2-per-side tuners, bound body, chrome hardware, Epiphonic-Six preamp with Shadow piezo pickup, available in Natural finish, current mfg.

MSR	$582	$349	$275	$180

Epiphone PR-7 E
courtesy Clint H Schmidt

E

ERNIE BALL'S EARTHWOOD
Instruments previously produced in San Luis Obispo, California in the early to mid 1970s.

After finding great success with prepackaged string sets and custom gauges, Ernie Ball founded the Earthwood company to produce a four-string acoustic bass guitar. George Fullerton built the prototype, as well as helping with other work before moving to Leo Fender's CLF Research company in 1974. Earthwood offered both the acoustic bass guitar and a lacquer finished solid body guitar with large sound chambers in 1972, but production was short lived (through February 1973). In April of 1975, bass guitar operations resumed on a limited basis for a number of years.

EROS
Instruments previously produced in Japan between the early 1970s through the early 1980s.

The EROS trademark is the brand name of a UK importer. These guitars were generally entry level copies of American designs, (Source: Tony Bacon and Paul Day, *The Guru's Guitar Guide*).

ESPANA
Instruments previously produced in Asia. Distributed in the U.S. by Espana Guitars (Buegeleisen & Jacobson) of New York, New York.

Espana trademark acoustic guitars were distributed by Buegeleisen & Jacobson of New York, New York under the "Espana Guitars" company name during the early 1970s. The New York distributors Buegeleisen & Jacobson also imported in Kent and Val Dez guitars during the same time period. That's why all three "companies" shared the same address: 5 Union Square, New York, New York, 10003!

These Espana acoustic models have been described as having "inlay" on the fingerboards and rosettes. This inlay may vary from model to model. All guitar models are equipped with a "stress channel" style truss rod.

ACOUSTIC: CLASSICAL MODELS

2000 - nylon string configuration, 25" scale, spruce top, round soundhole, mahogany back/sides, 18-fret rosewood fingerboard, 7-piece mahogany neck, rosewood bridge, 3-per-side tuners, available in Natural finish, mfg. circa early 1970s.

	N/A	$75	$40

Last MSR was $100.

2001 (3/4 Size) - similar to the 2000, except features a 22" scale, rosewood bridge with inlay, available in Natural finish, Length 35", Body Width 16 1/4", Body Thickness 3 3/4", mfg. circa early 1970s.

	N/A	$75	$40

Last MSR was $110.

2002 - nylon string configuration, 25" scale, spruce top, round soundhole, mahogany back/sides, marquetry on back, 18 fret rosewood fingerboard, 7-piece mahogany neck, rosewood bridge with inlay, 3-per-side tuners, available in Natural finish, Body Width 18 1/4", Body Thickness 4 1/4", mfg. circa early 1970s.

	N/A	$80	$45

Last MSR was $125.

2004 - nylon string configuration, 25 1/2" scale, spruce top, round soundhole, rosewood back/sides, 18-fret rosewood fingerboard, 7-piece mahogany neck, rosewood bridge, 3-per-side tuners, available in Natural finish, Body Width 18 7/8", Body Thickness 4 3/8", mfg. circa early 1970s.

	N/A	$100	$70

Last MSR was $165.

2006 - similar to the 2004, except has additional inlay, rosewood bridge with inlay, 3-per-side gold-plated tuners, available in Natural hand-rubbed finish, mfg. circa early 1970s.

	N/A	$125	$80

Last MSR was $250.

Epiphone EL Segundo
courtesy Gibson

GRADING	100%	EXCELLENT	AVERAGE

ACOUSTIC: DREADNOUGHT MODELS

2100 - dreadnought style, 25" scale, spruce top, round soundhole, mahogany back/sides, 21-fret rosewood fingerboard, 7-piece mahogany neck, rosewood bridge, 3-per-side tuners, Natural finish, length 18", body thickness 3 7/8", mfg. circa early 1970s.

	N/A	$75	$40

Last MSR was $100.

2102 - similar to the 2100, available in Natural finish, length 18 1/4", body thickness 4 1/4", mfg. circa early 1970s.

	N/A	$85	$45

Last MSR was $125.

2104 - similar to the 2100, except features round soundhole with inlay, rosewood back/sides, adjustable bridge, Natural finish, length 18 7/8", body thickness 4 3/8", mfg. circa early 1970s.

	N/A	$95	$55

Last MSR was $165.

2106 - dreadnought style, 25" scale, spruce top, round soundhole with inlay, rosewood back/sides, 21-fret rosewood fingerboard, 7-piece mahogany neck, rosewood bridge, 3-per-side tuners, Natural finish, length 20", body thickness 4 3/8", mfg. circa early 1970s.

	N/A	$100	$60

Last MSR was $175.

2108 12-STRING - similar to the 2106, except has 12-string configuration, 6-per-side tuners, 18-fret rosewood fingerboard, additional inlay, available in Natural finish, length 20", body thickness 4 3/8", mfg. circa early 1970s.

	N/A	$115	$65

Last MSR was $195.

2114 TENOR - dreadnought style, 23" scale, spruce top, round soundhole, mahogany back/sides, 20-fret rosewood fingerboard, 7-piece mahogany neck, adjustable rosewood bridge, 3-per-side tuners, available in Natural finish, length 18 1/4", body thickness 4 1/4", mfg. circa early 1970s.

	N/A	$80	$45

Last MSR was $125.

ESPANOLA
Instruments currently produced in Korea. Distributed by V.J. Rendano Music Company, Inc. of Youngstown, Ohio.

The wide range of Espanola acoustic guitars are designed and priced with the entry level or student guitarist in mind. Suggested new retail prices range from $200 up to $450 on the Korean-produced acoustic guitar models; $450 on the resonator-style models; $125 to $300 on four Paracho, Mexico classicals; and $350 to $550 on 4-string acoustic bass guitars.

ESPANOLA, GUITARRAS
Please refer to the G section in this text.

ESTEBAN, ANTONIO
Instruments currently produced in Spain.

Antonio Esteban classical guitars are currently available in the European market. **Models 10** and **30** are constructed with mahogany (bubinga on **Model 20**) bodies, Canadian cedar tops, and palisander fingerboards and bridges. The top of the line **Model 40** has a palisander body, and ebony fingerboard. Antonio Esteban also offers a Flamenco model (**Model 40 F**) with tap plates and a palisander fingerboard.

ESTESO
Guitars previously built in Spain.

The Esteso label indicated instruments built by Domingo Esteso (1882 - 1937). Originally trained at the Madrid workshop of Manuel Ramirez, Esteso later set up shop in the same town, and his instruments were widely praised, (Source: Tony Bacon, *The Ultimate Guitar Book*).

ESTEVE
Instruments currently built in Alboraya (Valencia), Spain. Distributed by Fernandez Music of Irvine, California.

Esteve guitars are built in an artisan workshop in Spain, and have solid tops as well as traditional Spanish integrated neck/body construction. There is a wide range of classical and flamenco guitars available, as well as requintos and special models (bass, contrabass, and an octave guitar).

ACOUSTIC

There are several models currently offered by Esteve. The classic models start at $450 and go up from there. The different variations range from different sizes to the different types of woods that are used. There are also **Deluxe Classical** models that retail upwards towards $3,000.

Flamenco models (with a clear tap plate) feature sycamore back and sides and double rosewood purfling (retail list $825). The **Deluxe Artisan Flamenco models** range from $1,350 (solid Mukali with ebony fingerboard) up to $2,600 (Indian rosewood body). Wooden tuning pegs (instead of metal) are an additional $100.

Esteve also offers some acoustic electric models as well as a variety of different sized guitars. For more information and to find that perfect model for you, refer to their web site (see Trademark Index).

EUPHANON COMPANY
See Walter Lipton.

EUPHONON
See Larson Brothers (1900-1944).

The Euphonon brand of guitars and mandolins was made by the Larson brothers of Maurer & Co. in Chicago from circa 1934 till the demise of the company in 1944. In 1934, there were a number of Euphonon guitars in different combinations of the old style 12-fret to the body necks, slotted pegheads, with elevated pickguards, or without pickguards. This was a transition year which probably saw the beginning of the 14-fret to the body sizes also. They all had the new purfling consisting of a series of B&W stripes side by side around the body edges, and soundhole that was to remain the style for the Euphonon brand except when the abalone trim was used on the top of the line guitars. By 1935, the larger bodies with narrower necks were the norm.

The Larsons made Euphonon guitars in two main types: the traditional round-hole and the dreadnought. The round-hole guitar sizes range from 15" student grade to 16", 17", 19", and a very rare 21" in the better and best grades. Many of the better and all of the best grades have laminated top braces and laminated necks. Euphonons have backs and sides made of oak, maple, mahogany, or rosewood.

Some of the fret markers used on the Euphonons and the larger Prairie State guitars are the same as the ones used on the earlier Maurers and Prairie States of the smaller body sizes. The fancier trimmed instruments often have engraved pearl fret markers along with a similar inlay on each end of the bridge. The Euphonon guitars are quite rare, of very high quality, and are sought by players and collectors.

For more information regarding other Larson-made brands, see Maurer, Prairie State, Wm. C. Stahl, W.J. Dyer, and The Larson Brothers.

For more detailed information regarding all Larson brands, see The Larsons' Creations, Guitars and Mandolins, by Robert Carl Hartman, Centerstream Publishing, P.O. Box 17878, Anaheim Hills CA 92807, phone/fax (714) 779-9390.

**Everett Milan L
courtesy Kent Everett**

EVERETT, KENT
Instruments currently built in Atlanta, Georgia.

Luthier Kent Everett has been crafting guitars since 1977. Everett had 18 years experience in performing guitar repairs during his early days custom building acoustics, and now focuses directly on guitar building only.

ACOUSTIC: AZALEA SERIES

The Azalea Series are the guitars that are currently being produced by Kent one by one. These are built one at a time on a custom order basis. The Azalea retails at $5,800. There is also an Everett Concierto, which is a classical model that reatils for $6,200.

ACOUSTIC: EMERALD SERIES

All models feature an AAA Sitka spruce top, mahogany neck, ebony peghead overlay/fingerboard/bridge, lacewood fingerboard binding and appointments, ivoroid or tortoise shell body binding, bone saddle, abalone inlays/rosette, tortoise shell (or black or clear or no) pickguard, small emerald at 12th fret, and a natural high gloss nitrocellulose finish. The following four models are offered in two different wood packages: mahogany back and sides, or rosewood back and sides. Prices include an arched top hardshell case. Disc.ontinued 1999. Last Suggested Retail for all body styles with rosewood back and sides was $2,328. Last Suggested Retail for all body styles with mahogany back and sides was $2,247.

MILAN SERICES - AAA Sitka Spruce top, 5-piece mahogany neck, ebony peghead overlay/fingerboard/bridge, lacewood fingerboard binding and appointments, ivoroid or highly figured wood bindings, bone saddle, abalone inlays/rosette, tortoise shell (or black or clear or no) pickguard, natural high gloss nitrocellulose finish, Schaller tuners, ebony buttons, wood bound soundhole. The 4 body styles are offered in two different wood packages; mahogany or rosewood back and sides, prices include an arched top hardshell case. A.C. model is an extra large body with a tight waist, L is a small body, Grand Concert shape, N is a dreadnought size, and the P is the same style as the N dreadnought but a smaller size, disc.

Last MSR was $4,200.

ACOUSTIC: ELITE SERIES

In 1996, Everett began offering three new high-end guitar packages. These premium Elan Instruments feature wood bindings, select shell inlays, ebony bound soundholes, and AAA-plus quality woods.

ELITE - figured Sitka top, ebony or ziricote with multiple black/white body binding, lacewood bound fingerboard extension, mother-of-pearl logo, 14kt gold line peghead trim, gold plated Waverly or Schaller (with ebony) tuners, special decorative inlay options, copper/white side position markers, paua shell rosette, mfg. 1996-disc.

Last MSR was $4,800.

ACOUSTIC: LAUREL SERIES

The Laurel guitar is built now by a "high-quality production." Less than 100 of these are produced every year.

**Everett Laurel O
courtesy Kent Everett**

E

GRADING	100%	EXCELLENT	AVERAGE

LAUREL - Indian rosewood back and sides, solid Sitka top, ebony fingerboard, bridge, tuner buttons, and bridgepins, flamed maple binding, heart abalone inlays, 3-per-side tuners, available as the O Model (Orchestra), A Model (Auditorium), or D Model (Dreadnought), current mfg.

MSR   **$2,100**

ACOUSTIC: SIERRA SERIES

SIERRA - figured Sitka top, mahogany or rosewood back/sides, vermillion with black/white body binding, lacewood bound fingerboard extension, mother-of-pearl logo, black or gold Grover mini-tuners with ebony buttons, silver/white side position markers, lacewood or koa rosette, mfg. 1996-disc.

Last MSR was $4,600.

ACOUSTIC: SILVER SERIES

SILVER - figured sitka top, vermillion with black/white body binding, lacewood or ziricote bound square fingerboard end, mother-of-pearl logo, sterling silver line peghead trim, nickel plated Waverly tuners, abalone fingerboard inlay, silver/white side position markers, paua shell rosette, mfg. 1996-2000.

Last MSR mahogany was $2,975. Last MSR rosewood was $3,045.

EVERGREEN MOUNTAIN INSTRUMENTS
Instruments currently built in Cove, Oregon.

Jerry Nolte has been producing handcrafted instruments since 1971. Nolte's guitars are available in 6-string, 12-string, tenor, and bass configurations. His acoustics feature cedar or spruce tops; 3-piece mahogany necks; rosewood fingerboard and bridge; back and sides of American black walnut, maple, koa, and cherry; and hand-rubbed violin varnish. The order process includes a $350 down payment, which is non-refundable. Base prices vary from very from model to model, but are generally in the $1,500 range plus options. For more information on Evergreen Mountain Instruments please refer to the web site (see Trademark Index).

EVERLY GUITARS
Instruments previously built in Portland, OR from 1982-2001.

The Ike Everly Model guitar was built by Robert Steinegger, who is currently on hiatus. The last retail price was $4,500.

E is for exceptional. Luthier Ed Schaefer is justifiably proud of one of his most recent 17 inch archtops.

Section F

FAIR LADY

Instruments previously produced in China. Distributed by Kwo Hsiao Company, Ltd., of Taipei, Taiwan.

The Kwo Hsiao Company, Ltd. offered a wide range of student level to intermediate grade acoustic guitar models. Models ranged from classical-style nylon strings, to dreadnought and jumbo style models (some with single rounded cutaways), and include models with built-in piezo bridge pickups and preamp systems. Models featured a spruce top, nato wood back and sides, rosewood fingerboard and bridge, and a solid headstock with 3-per-side chrome tuners. One example is the **Model FAW-688**, which features a double cutaway body design.

FASCINATOR

See chapter on House Brands.

This Gibson built budget line of guitars has been identified as a House Brand of the Tonk Bros. company of Chicago, Illinois. While built to the same standards as other Gibson guitars, they lack the one true 'Gibson' touch: an adjustable truss rod. House Brand Gibsons were available to musical instrument distributors in the late 1930s and early 1940s, (Source: Walter Carter, *Gibson Guitars: 100 Years of an American Icon*).

FAVILLA

Instruments previously built in New York City, New York between 1890 to 1973.

In 1888, brothers John and Joseph Favilla left their home country of Italy and moved to Manhattan in New York City. Two years later, they founded Favilla Brothers, which later became Favilla Guitars, Inc. The workshop moved to Brooklyn in 1929, and later back to Manhattan.

Frank Favilla (John's elder son) began running the facility in the late 1940s. The company moved to larger facilities in Brooklyn in 1959, and in 1965 moved to a 20,000 square-foot plant out in Long Island. The larger facilities employed between fifteen and twenty workers, and the staff produced about 3,000 acoustic guitars a year. Higher production costs were one of the factors that led to the plant closing in 1973.

In 1970, Tom Favilla (third generation) began importing guitars from Japan. Japanese Favillas had the company name in script; American-built Favillas will have the family crest on the headstock, (Source: Tom Wheeler, *American Guitars*).

FENDER

Instruments currently produced in Corona, California (U.S.), Mexico, Japan, Tianjin (China), and Korea. Distributed by the Fender Musical Instruments Corporation of Scottsdale, Arizona. The Fender trademark established circa 1948 in Fullerton, California.

Clarence Leonidas Fender was born in 1909, and raised in Fullerton, California. As a teenager he developed an interest in electronics, and soon was building and repairing radios for fellow classmates. After high school, Leo Fender held a bookkeeping position while he still did radio repair at home. After holding a series of jobs, Fender opened up a full scale radio repair shop in 1939. In addition to service work, the Fender Radio Service store soon became a general electronics retail outlet. However, the forerunner to the Fender Electric Instruments company was a smaller two-man operation that was originally started as the K & F company in 1945. Leo Fender began modestly building small amplifiers and electric lap steels with his partner, Clayton Orr Doc Kaufman. After K & F dissolved, Fender then formed the Fender Electric Instrument company in 1946, located on South Pomona Avenue in Fullerton, California. The company sales, though slow at first, began to expand as his amplifiers and lap steel began meeting acceptance among West Coast musicians. In 1950, Fender successfully developed the first production solid body electric guitar. Originally the Broadcaster, the name was quickly changed to the Telecaster after the Gretsch company objected to the infringement of their Broadkaster drum sets.

Soon Fender's inventive genius began designing new models through the early 1950s and early 1960s. The Fender Precision Bass guitar was unveiled in 1951. While there is some kind of an existing background for the development of an electric solid body guitar, the notion of a 34" scale instrument with a fretted neck that could replace an upright acoustic doublebass was completely new to the music industry. The Precision bass (so named because players could fret the note precisely) coupled with a Fender Bassman amplifier gave the bass player more sonic projection. Fender then followed with another design in 1954, the Stratocaster. The simplicity in design, added to the popular sounds and playability, makes this design the most copied world wide. Other popular models of guitars, basses, and amplifiers soon followed.

By 1964, Fender's line of products included electric guitars, basses, steel guitars, effects units, acoustic guitars, electric pianos, and a variety of accessories. Leo's faltering health was a factor in putting the company up for sale, and first offered it to Don Randall (the head of Fender Sales) for a million and a half dollars. Randall opened negotiations with the Baldwin Piano & Organ company, but when those negotiations fell through, offered it to the conglomerate CBS (who was looking to diversify the company holdings). Fender (FEIC) was purchased by CBS on January 5, 1965 (actually in December of 1964) for thirteen million dollars. Leo Fender was kept on as a special consultant for five years, and then left when then contract was up in 1970. Due to a ten year no compete clause, the next Leo Fender-designed guitars did not show up in the music industry until 1976 (Music Man).

While Fender was just another division of CBS, a number of key figures left the company. Forrest White, the production manager, left in 1967 after a dispute in producing solid state amplifiers. Don Randall left in 1969, disenchanted with corporate life. George Fullerton, one of the people involved with the Stratocaster design, left in 1970. Obviously, the quality in Fender products did not drop the day Leo Fender sold the company. Dale Hyatt, another veteran of the early Fender days, figured that the quality on the products stayed relatively stable until around 1968 (Hyatt left in 1972). But a number of cost-cutting strategies, and attempts to produce more products had a deteriorating effect. This reputation leads right to the classic phrase heard at vintage guitar shows, "Pre-CBS?"

In the early 1980s, the Fender guitar empire began to crumble. Many cost-cutting factors and management problems forced CBS to try various last ditch efforts to salvage the instrument line. In March of 1982, Fender (with CBS' blessing) negotiated with Kanda Shokai and Yamano Music to establish Fender Japan. After discussions with Tokai (who built a great Fender Strat replica, among other nice guitars), Kawai, and others, Fender finally chose Fuji Gen Gakki (based in Matsumoto, about 130 miles northwest of Tokyo). In 1983 the Squier series was built in Japan, earmarked for European distribution. The Squier trademark came from a string-making company in Michigan (V.C. Squier) that CBS had acquired in 1965.

In 1984 CBS decided to sell Fender. Offers came in from IMC (Hondo, Charvel/Jackson), and the Kaman Music Corporation (Ovation). Finally, CBS sold Fender to an investment group led by William Schultz in March for twelve and a half million dollars. This investment group formally became the Fender Musical Instruments Corporation (FMIC). As the sale did not include production facilities, USA guitar production ceased for most of 1985. It has been estimated that 80% of the guitars sold between late 1984 and mid 1986 were made in Japan. Soon after, a new factory was built in Corona, California, and USA production was restored in 1986 and continues to this day. FMIC expanded their company by purchasing Sunn amplifiers in 1987.

In 1990, the Fender (FMIC) company built an assembly facility in Mexico to offset rising costs of oriental production due to the weakening of the American dollar in the international market. Fender also experimented with production based in India from 1989 to 1990. The Fender (FMIC) company currently manufactures instruments in China, Japan, Korea, Mexico, and the U.S. In 1991, Fender relocated its headquarters from Corona, California to Scottsdale, Arizona. This is where they are to date. In 1992, the amplifier custom shop was opened.

As FMIC began to expand in the 1990s, they also started to buy into other interests. The Guild guitar company has been making high-quality instruments since 1952, but the company went up for the sale in the early '90s. Fender completed the sale in 1995 and began building instruments in the Custom Shop in Nashville, TN in 1996. Fender also picked up Manuel Rodriguez guitars for classical guitars handcrafted in Spain.

As reported in the March 1998 edition of MMR, Fender CEO Schultz sent out a letter to Fender dealers (dated January 9, 1998) which discussed the company establishing a limited number of Fender mail-order catalog dealers. Fender has announced specific guidelines as to what is allowed in mail-order catalog sales. Most importantly, Fender "announced a minimum advertised price (MAP) policy applicable to mail-order catalogs only," stated Schultz, "The MAP for mail-order catalogs is set at a maximum 30 percent off the Fender suggested retail price, and will be enforced unilaterally by Fender." What this does to the Fender retail price overall is basically lower the bar – but the impact on regular guitar stores has not been fully realized. While it's one thing to buy because of a discounted price through a catalog, it's a different situation to walk into a dealer's shop and be able to "test drive" a guitar before it is purchased. Retail music stores have to be aware that there is now an outside source (not under their control) that dictates minimum sales prices – the national catalogs. Of course, retail shops still control the maximum sale price applied to an instrument. Readers familiar to the *Blue Book of Electric Guitars* will note both the Manufacturer's suggested retail price and the appropriate discounted price (100% listing) under currently produced models.

In 1998, Fender opened up a new 177,000 square-foot manufacturing facility in Corona, California. This is a state-of-the-art facility that can pump out 350 guitars a day and produces 95% clean air that comes from the factory. In Summer 2002, Fender announced the purchase of the Gretsch guitar line. Gretsch has been making guitars and other instruments since the 1900s! The sale went into effect on January 1, 2003, (Source for earlier Fender history: Richard R. Smith, *Fender: The Sound Heard 'Round the World*).

PRODUCTION MODEL CODES

Current Fender instruments are identified by a part number that consists of a three digit location/facility code and a four digit model code (the two codes are separated by a hyphen). An example of this would be:

010 - 9200

(The 010-9200 part number is the California-built Stevie Ray Vaughn model.)

As Fender guitars are built in a number of locations worldwide, the three digit code will indicate where production took place (this does not indicate where the parts originated, however; just assembly of components). The first digit differentiates between Fender bridges and Floyd Rose tremolos:

0	**Fender Product, non-Floyd Rose**
1	**Floyd Rose Bridge**
3	**Guild Product**

The second/third digit combination designates the production location:

10	**U.S., Guitar (Corona)**
13	**Mexico, Guitar and Bass (Ensenada)**
19	**U.S., Bass (Corona)**
25	**Japan, Guitar and Bass**
26	**Korea**
27	**Japan, Guitar and Bass**
33	**Korea, Guitar and Bass**
33	**China, Guitar and Bass**
33	**Indonesia, Guitar and Bass**
50	**Guild Product, Acoustic and Electric (Rhode Island)**
94	**Spain, Acoustic Guitar (Classical)**

GRADING	100%	EXCELLENT	AVERAGE

The four digits on the other side of the hyphen continue defining the model. The fourth/fifth digit combination is the product designation. The sixth digit defines left-handedness, or key parts inherent to that product. The final seventh digit indicates which type of wood fingerboard. Any digits that follow the second hyphen (eighth/ninth/tenth) are color descriptions (01 = Blond, 02 = Lake Placid Blue, etc.). Happy Hunting!

For further information on Fender electric models, please refer to the *Blue Book of Electric Guitars*.

ACOUSTIC: GA & GC (GRAND AUDITORIUM & CONCERT SERIES)

Fender recently introduced Grand series guitars, which includes the Auditorium and Concert models. These guitars offer more styles than just the dreadnought they have produced for several years.

GA-43S NATURAL (NO. 095-4300) - custom designed body shape, solid AA Grade spruce top, solid mahogany back, rosewood fingerboard with dot position markers, 3-per-side tuners, available in Natural (-021) finish, mfg. 2001-current.

MSR	$665		$425	$300	$215

GA-45S NATURAL (NO. 095-4500) - similar to GA-43S, custom designed body shape, solid AA Grade spruce top, solid mahogany back, rosewood fingerboard with dot position markers, 3-per-side tuners, available in Natural (-021) finish, mfg. 2001-current.

MSR	$765		$475	$350	$265

Fender CG-11
courtesy Dave Rogers
Dave's Guitar Shop

GC-12 (NO. 095-1200) - economy version of the GC-23S, spruce top, Nato back, sides and neck, rosewood fingerboard with dot position markers, chrome plated covered tuners, 3-per-side tuners, available in Natural Gloss finish, mfg. 2000-current.

MSR	$280		$180	$140	$95

GC-23 S (NO. 095-2300) - grand concert style, solid spruce top, round soundhole, mahogany back/sides, 14/20-fret rosewood fingerboard, rosewood bridge, 3-per-side chrome die-cast tuners, available in Natural Gloss finish, mfg. 1997-current.

MSR	$466		$285	$225	$145

GC-42S (NO. 094-4200) - non-cutaway design, solid AA grade spruce top, solid mahogany back, rosewood fingerboard, die-cast silver tuning machines, abalone fret markers, 20 frets, tortise shell-style binding, available in Natural finish, mfg. 2001-current.

MSR	$665		$470	$350	$235

ACOUSTIC: CLASSICAL CG SERIES

The CG Series is Fender's classical guitars (with nylon strings). CG Series models were produced in Asia.

CG-5 (NO. 094-0500-021) - classical style, nato top/back/sides, round soundhole, nato neck, 12/18-fret rosewood fingerboard, slotted headstock, 3-per-side chrome tuners, available in Satin finish, mfg. 1995-98.

		N/A	$75	$45

Last MSR was $155.

CG-7 (NO. 094-0700-021) - similar to the CG-5, except features spruce top, meranti back/sides, 12/19-fret fingerboard, available in Gloss finish, mfg. 1995-current.

MSR	$190		$135	$90	$60

CG-11 (NO. 094-1100) - similar to CG-7, except has Nato back, sides, and neck, 20 frets, 25.3" scale, available in Natural finish, disc 2001.

		$225	$140	$98

Last MSR was $320.

CG-21 S (NO. 094-2405) - similar to CG-11, except has solid spruce top, rosewood back and sides, rosewood fingerboard, gold tuners, available in Natural finish, mfg. 1999-current.

MSR	$500		$325	$225	$160

ACOUSTIC: CLASSICAL MISC. MODELS

AVALON - folk style, spruce top, round soundhole, black pickguard, 3-stripe bound body/rosette, mahogany back/sides/neck, 14/20-fret bubinga fingerboard with pearl dot inlay, bubinga strings through bridge, 6-on-one-side die-cast tuners, available in Natural finish, mfg. 1987-1994.

		N/A	$225	$150

Last MSR was $301.

GRADING	100%	EXCELLENT	AVERAGE

2100 SX - single round cutaway classic style, solid cedar top, round soundhole, 5-stripe bound body, wood inlay rosette, ovankol back/sides, nato neck, 19-fret rosewood fingerboard, rosewood bridge, rosewood veneered peghead, 3-per-side gold tuners with pearloid buttons, available in Natural finish, mfg. 1994-95.

	N/A	$350	$225

Last MSR was $640.

ACOUSTIC: DREADNOUGHT AG SERIES

AG Series acoustics were discontinued in 1994, in favor of the DG Series. AG Series models were produced in Asia.

AG-10 - dreadnought style, spruce top, round soundhole, black pickguard, 5-stripe bound body/rosette, mahogany back/sides/neck, 14/20-fret rosewood fingerboard with pearl dot inlay, rosewood bridge with black white dot pins, 6-on-one-side chrome tuners, available in Natural finish, disc. 1994.

	N/A	$115	$70

Last MSR was $230.

AG-15 - similar to AG-10, except has High Gloss finish, disc. 1994.

	N/A	$120	$75

Last MSR was $250.

AG-20 - similar to AG-10, except has rosewood back/sides, disc. 1994.

	N/A	$125	$75

Last MSR was $280.

ACOUSTIC: DREADNOUGHT CALIFORNIA SERIES

The California series was discontinued in 1994. California Series models were produced in Asia.

CATALINA - dreadnought style, spruce top, round soundhole, black pickguard, 3-stripe bound body/rosette, mahogany back/sides/neck, 14/20-fret rosewood fingerboard with pearl dot inlay, rosewood bridge with white black dot pins, 6-on-one-side die-cast tuners, available in Black finish, mfg. 1987-1994.

	N/A	$180	$115

Last MSR was $370.

CONCORD - similar to Catalina, except has bubinga fingerboard/bridge, available in Natural finish, mfg. 1987-1994.

	N/A	$150	$90

Last MSR was $300.

LA BREA - single round cutaway dreadnought style, spruce top, round soundhole, black pickguard, 3-stripe bound body/rosette, mahogany back/sides/neck, 21-fret rosewood fingerboard with pearl dot inlay, rosewood bridge with white black dot pins, 6-on-one-side chrome tuners, acoustic pickup, volume/tone control, available in Natural finish, mfg. 1987-1994.

	N/A	$250	$145

Last MSR was $480.

Add 20% for figured maple top/back/sides.

MALIBU - dreadnought style, sycamore top, round soundhole, black pickguard, sycamore back/sides, mahogany neck, 14/20-fret rosewood fingerboard with pearl dot inlay, rosewood bridge with white black dot inlay, 6-on-one-side die-cast tuners, available in Dark Violin Sunburst finish, mfg. 1987-1994.

	N/A	$195	$120

Last MSR was $385.

MONTARA - single round cutaway dreadnought style, spruce top, oval soundhole, bound body, multi-ring rosette, mahogany back/sides/neck, convex back, 21-fret rosewood fingerboard with pearl dot inlay, rosewood bridge with white pins, 6-on-one-side die-cast tuners with pearl buttons, acoustic pickup, volume/treble/mid/bass controls, available in Natural finish, mfg. 1990-94.

	N/A	$350	$225

Last MSR was $650.

Add 20% for flame maple top/back/sides/neck.

NEWPORTER - dreadnought style, mahogany top, round soundhole, black pickguard, 3-stripe bound body/rosette, mahogany back/sides/neck, 14/20-fret rosewood fingerboard with pearl dot inlay, rosewood bridge with white black dot pins, 6-on-one-side die-cast tuners, Natural finish, disc. 1994.

	N/A	$175	$95

Last MSR was $325.

REDONDO - similar to the Newporter, except has spruce top, available in Natural finish, disc. 1994.

	N/A	$175	$110

Last MSR was $335.

SANTA MARIA - similar to the Newporter, except has spruce top, tortoise pickguard, available in Natural finish, mfg. 1989-1994.

	N/A	$195	$120

Last MSR was $360.

GRADING	100%	EXCELLENT	AVERAGE

SAN LUIS REY - dreadnought style, solid spruce top, round soundhole, black pickguard, rosewood back/sides, mahogany neck, 14/20-fret rosewood fingerboard with pearl snowflake inlay, 6-on-one-side chrome tuners, available in Natural finish, mfg. 1990-94.

	N/A	$225	$130

Last MSR was $445.

SAN MARINO - similar to the San Luis Rey, except has 3-stripe bound body/rosette, mahogany back/sides/neck, 14/20-fret rosewood fingerboard with pearl dot inlay, available in Natural finish, mfg. 1989-1994.

	N/A	$185	$115

Last MSR was $370.

SAN MIGUEL - single round cutaway dreadnought style, spruce top, round soundhole, black pickguard, 3-stripe bound body/rosette, mahogany back/sides/neck, 14/20-fret rosewood fingerboard with pearl dot inlay, rosewood bridge with white black dot pins, 6-on-one-side tuners, Natural finish, disc. 1994.

	N/A	$175	$110

Last MSR was $360.

This model had an optional left-handed configuration.

ACOUSTIC: DREADNOUGHT DG SERIES

The DG Series acoustics are steel-string dreadnought designs. The DG series was introduced in 1995, filling the same niche as the AG and Spring Hill series. DG Series models are produced in Asia. Fender had a **DG-3 ValuePak** (Model 095-0300-021) features a DG-3 acoustic, polish, polishing cloth, picks, strings, gig bag, and chord book for $319. The Value Pack now features the **DG-8** (No. 095-0801-021) for $350.

DG-3 VALUEPAK (NO. 095-0300-021) - dreadnought style, spruce top, round soundhole, black pickguard, nato back/sides, 14/20-fret rosewood fingerboard with white dot inlay, 6-on-one-side die-cast tuners, available in Natural finish, mfg. 1995-99.

	$225	$125	$85

Last MSR was $319.

DG-5 (NO. 095-0500-021) - dreadnought style, nato top/back/sides, round soundhole, 14/20-fret rosewood fingerboard, rosewood bridge, black plastic pickguard, 3-per-side chrome tuners, available in Satin finish, mfg. 1995-98.

	N/A	$90	$55

Last MSR was $175.

DG-6 (NO. 095-0600-021) - dreadnought style, Laminated Agathis top, back and sides, Nato neck with rosewood fingerboard, dot inlays, rosewood bridge, compensated Urea saddle, 25.3" scale, chrome tuners, black pickguard, available in Natural satin (- 021) finish, mfg. 1999-2000.

	$130	$75	$60

Last MSR was $190.

Add $40 for Candy Apple Red (-009) and Metallic Blue (-096) finishes, new 2001.
In 2001, this guitar was introduced as a Squire model. Refer to Squire for current mfg.

DG-7 (NO. 095-0700-021) - dreadnought style, spruce top, round soundhole, meranti back/sides, 14/20-fret rosewood fingerboard, rosewood bridge, pickguard, 3-per-side chrome tuners, available in High Gloss Natural finish, mfg. 1995-2000, 2003-current.

MSR	$233	$165	$110	$75

DG-8 VALUE PACK (NO. 095-0800) - dreadnought style, Napo top, back and sides, round soundhole, 14/20-fret rosewood fingerboard with white dot inlay, 3-on-a-side chrome tuners, also included is a gig bag, tuner, polish cloth, picks, DVD, chord book, stringwinder & an extra set of strings, available in Natural finish, mfg. 1995-current.

MSR	$350	$210	$150	$125

DG-9 (NO. 095-0900) - dreadnought style, select spruce top, round soundhole, mahogany back/sides, 14/20-fret rosewood fingerboard, rosewood bridge, black pickguard, 3-per-side chrome tuners, available in Satin finish, mfg. 1997-2002.

	$170	$100	$75

Last MSR was $266.

DG-10 (NO. 095-1000) - dreadnought style, select spruce top, round soundhole, mahogany back/sides, 14/20-fret rosewood fingerboard, rosewood bridge, black pickguard, 3-per-side chrome tuners, available in Satin finish, mfg. 1995-96, reintroduced 2003.

MSR	$266	$160	$125	$75

GRADING		100%	EXCELLENT	AVERAGE

DG-10 LH (No. 095-1020) - similar to the DG-10, except in a left-handed configuration, mfg. 1995-current.

MSR	$300	$180	$135	$85

DG-10-12 (No. 095-1012) - similar to the DG-10, except in a 12-string configuration, mfg. 1995-current.

MSR	$316	$190	$145	$95

DG-11 (NO. 095-1100) - dreadnought style, spruce top, round soundhole, nato back/sides, 14/20-fret rosewood fingerboard with dot inlay, rosewood bridge, black pickguard, 3-per-side chrome tuners, available in Black, Sunburst, or Natural Gloss finishes, mfg. 1998-current.

MSR	$283	$169	$125	$90

DG-14 S (NO. 095-1400) - dreadnought style, Solid Spruce top, maple back and sides, Nato neck, rosewood fingerboard, dot inlays, 20 frets, 25.3" scale. Minimum finish allows for better resonance. Natural Gloss Wood-Tone finish, current mfg.

MSR	$350	$210	$165	$120

DG-14 LH (No. 095-1420) - similar to the DG-10, except in a left-handed configuration, mfg. 1999-current.

MSR	$366	$220	$175	$125

DG-14S-12 (No. 095-1412) - similar to Model DG-14 S, only in a 12-string configuration, available in Natural Wood-Tone finish, mfg. 1999-current.

MSR	$383	$230	$180	$125

DG-15 (NO. 095-1500) - similar to the DG-10 model, available in Jet Black, Gloss Sunburst, or Natural finishes, mfg. 1995-98.

		$225	$175	$115

Last MSR was $359.

DG-16 (NO. 095-1600) - dreadnought style, spruce top, round soundhole, mahogany back/sides, 14/20-fret rosewood fingerboard with snowflake inlay, rosewood bridge, black pickguard, 3-per-side die-cast tuners, available in Black, Sunburst, or Natural gloss finishes, mfg. 1998-current.

MSR	$366	$220	$150	$100

DG-16 LH (No. 095-1620) - similar to the DG-10, except in a left-handed configuration, available in Natural or Black finishes, mfg. 1999-current.

MSR	$380	$230	$160	$105

DG-16-12 (No. 095-1612) - similar to Model DG-16, except in a 12-string configuration, available in Natural Gloss or Black finishes, current mfg.

MSR	$400	$240	$175	$125

DG-20 S (NO. 095-2000) - dreadnought style, solid spruce top, round soundhole, mahogany back/sides, 14/20-fret rosewood fingerboard, rosewood bridge, tortoise shell pickguard, 3-per-side chrome tuners, available in Natural Gloss finish, mfg. 1995-current.

MSR	$417	$250	$195	$140

DG-21 S (NO. 095-2100) - dreadnought style, solid spruce top, round soundhole, rosewood back/sides, 14/20-fret rosewood fingerboard, rosewood bridge, tortoise shell pickguard, 3-per-side gold die-cast tuners, available in Natural Gloss finish, mfg. 1995-current.

MSR	$500	$300	$250	$165

DG-22 S (NO. 095-2200) - dreadnought style, solid spruce top, round soundhole, figured maple back/sides, 14/20-fret rosewood fingerboard, rosewood bridge, tortoise shell pickguard, 3-per-side gold die-cast tuners, available in Cherry, Natural, Crimson Red Burst, Blue Burst, or Sunburst Gloss finishes, mfg. 1995-current.

MSR	$533	$325	$240	$170

Blue Burst (-036) and Crimson Red Burst (-028) finishes were added in 1999.

DG-24 (NO. 095-2400) - dreadnought style, wood bound mahogany top/back/sides, round soundhole, wood inlay rosette, 14/20-fret rosewood fingerboard, rosewood bridge, 3-per-side chrome die-cast tuners with pearloid buttons, available in Satin finish, mfg. 1997-current.

MSR	$500	$300	$250	$165

DG-25 S (NO. 095-2500) - dreadnought style, solid cedar top, mahogany back and sides, round soundhole, wood inlay rosette, 14/20-fret rosewood fingerboard, rosewood bridge, 3-per-side chrome die-cast tuners with pearloid buttons, available in Satin finish, mfg. 1997-current.

MSR	$584	$350	$275	$200

DG-31 S (NO. 095-3100-021) - dreadnought style, solid Englemann spruce top, round soundhole, mahogany back/sides, 14/20-fret rosewood fingerboard, rosewood bridge, 3-per-side chrome die-cast tuners, available in Natural Gloss finish, mfg. 1995-99.

		$350	$250	$175

Last MSR was $549.

GRADING	100%	EXCELLENT	AVERAGE

DG-31 S LH (No. 095-3120-021) - similar to the DG-31, except in a left-handed configuration, mfg. 1995-99.

	$360	$260	$185

Last MSR was $559.

DG-31-12 (No. 095-3112-021) - similar to the DG-31, except in a 12-string configuration, spruce top, 6-per-side tuners, available in Natural Gloss finish, mfg. 1995-99.

	$375	$250	$195

Last MSR was $529.

DG-41 S (NO. 095-4100-021) - dreadnought style, solid Englemann spruce top, round soundhole, rosewood back/sides, 14/20-fret rosewood fingerboard, rosewood bridge, tortoise sshell pickguard, 3-per-side gold die-cast tuners, available in Gloss finish, mfg. 1995-2000.

	$400	$275	$195

Last MSR was $599.

DG-41 S-12 (No. 095-4112-021) - similar to the DG-41, except in 12-string configuration, available in Natural Gloss finish, mfg. 1995-2000.

	$450	$325	$225

Last MSR was $689.

ACOUSTIC: DREADNOUGHT 1963-1970 MFG. SERIES

CONCERT (MFG. 1963-1970) - dreadnought style, 15 3/8" body width, spruce top, round soundhole, maple back/sides, bound top/back, bolt-on maple neck with neckplate, 25 1/2" scale, 20-fret rosewood fingerboard with pearl dot inlays, 6-on-one-side chrome tuners, rosewood bridge with white bridgepins, single ply pickguard, aluminum support rod (through body), available in Natural finish, mfg. 1963-1970.

	N/A	$675	$500

Fender Concert
courtesy C.W. Green

In 1966, mahogany, rosewood, vermillion, or zebrawood back and sides were an option. In 1968, Sunburst finish was an option.

KING - dreadnought style, 15 5/8" body width, spruce top, round soundhole, mahogany back/sides, multiple bound top/back, bolt-on maple neck with neckplate, 25 1/2" scale, 21-fret bound rosewood fingerboard with pearl dot inlays, 6-on-one-side chrome tuners, aluminum support rod (through body), available in Natural finish, mfg. 1963-1966.

	N/A	$900	$600

This model was optional with back and sides of Brazilian rosewood, Indian rosewood, vermillion, or zebrawood.

KINGMAN (KING) - similar to the King model, available in Natural or Sunburst finishes, mfg. 1966-1971.

	N/A	$850	$550

In 1968, maple, rosewood, or vermillion back and sides were optional; in addition to Black, Custom Colors, and Antigua finishes.

SHENANDOAH - similar to the Kingman, except features 12-string configuration, 6-per-side tuners, available in Natural, Black, Suburst, or Antigua finishes, mfg. 1965-1971.

Natural, Black, or Sunburst finishes	N/A	$800	$550
Antigua Finish	N/A	$1,150	$750

In 1967 Antigua finish was introduced. In 1968, Black and Sunburst finishes were introduced.

WILDWOOD ACOUSTIC - similar to the Kingman, except features beechwood back/sides, 3-ply pickguard, block fingerboard inlay, available in injected-dye colors (primary color of green, blue, and gold), mfg. 1966-1971.

	N/A	$750	$525

The Wildwood finish was the result of a seven year process in Germany where dye was injected into growing beech trees. Veneers for laminating were available after the beech trees were harvested.

MALIBU - dreadnought style, 14 7/8" body width, spruce top, round soundhole, mahogany back/sides, mahogany neck, one-ply bound top, 25 1/2" scale, 14/20-fret rosewood fingerboard with dot inlay, rosewood bridge, available in Black, Mahogany, or Sunburst finishes, mfg. 1965-1971.

	N/A	$600	$350

VILLAGER - similar to the Malibu, except features 12-string configuration, 6-per-side tuners, mfg. 1965 to 1971.

	N/A	$650	$375

In 1969, Sunburst finish was optional.

Fender Villager
courtesy John Beeson
The Music Shoppe

GRADING	100%	EXCELLENT	AVERAGE

NEWPORTER - dreadnought style, 14 3/8" body width, spruce top, round soundhole, mahogany back/sides, mahogany neck, one-ply bound top, 25 1/2" scale, 14/20-fret rosewood fingerboard with dot inlay, rosewood bridge, available in Mahogany finish, mfg. 1965-1971.

	N/A	$500	$325

In 1968, Mahogany top, 3-ply pickguard, and Black finish was optional.

REDONDO - similar to the Newporter, except features a spruce top, mfg. 1969-1971.

	N/A	$525	$325

PALOMINO - dreadnought style, 15 3/8" body width, spruce top, round soundhole, mahogany back/sides, mahogany neck, 3-ply bound top and back, 25 1/2" scale, 14/20-fret rosewood fingerboard with dot inlay, rosewood bridge, tuners with plastic buttons, available in Black Vermillion, Mahogany, or Sunburst finishes, mfg. 1968-1971.

	N/A	$550	$325

ACOUSTIC: DREADNOUGHT F, FC, FG, & GEMINI SERIES

F Series instruments were produced circa late 1970s through the early 1980s, and featured a flattop/Dreadnought design. Models ranged from the F-3 (retail price $149) up to the F-115 (retail price $895); the **F-200** series ranged in price from the F-200 (retail price $300) up to the F-360S-12 12-string (retail price $535). Used market prices depend on condition and demand; regular F series models range from $50 to $150 – F-200 series models range from $125 to $200.

FC Series instruments were produced circa late 1970s through the early 1980s, and featured a classical design, slotted headstock. Suggested list prices ranged from $165 (FC-10) up to $395 (FC-130S). Used market prices may range from $75 to $150, depending on demand and condition.

Fender also offered a **FG-210S**, a solid spruce top dreadnought with mahogany neck/back/sides with a rosewood fingerboard/bridge from 1990 to 1994. Suggested retail price was $360.

The **Gemini I and II** were offered between 1983 to 1994 (later models only during the 1990s) and had spruce tops and Nato or mahogany back/sides. Retail list prices ranged from $265 up to $315. Used market prices range around $125 to $150.

ACOUSTIC: DREADNOUGHT GD SERIES

See Acoustic Electric section for the GD-47SCE.

GD-47 S (NO. 095-4700) - non-cutaway, solid AA grade spruce top, rosewood back and sides, 3-per-side gold die-cast grover tuning keys, rosewood fingerboard, Nato neck, 20 abalone rosette frets, tortise style binding, available in Natural finish, mfg. 2002-current.

MSR	$765	$460	$375	$300

GD-47 S 12 (No. 095-4712) - similar to the GD-47 S except in 12-string configuration, mfg. 2002-current.

MSR	$800	$480	$400	$325

ACOUSTIC: DREADNOUGHT SPRINGHILL SERIES

Springhill Series models were produced in the USA.

LS-10 - dreadnought style, solid spruce top, round soundhole, tortoise pickguard, mahogany back/sides/neck, 14/20-fret bound rosewood fingerboard with pearl dot inlay, rosewood bridge with black pearl dot pins, ebony veneered peghead with pearl logo inlay, 3-per-side chrome tuners, available in Natural finish, mfg. 1994-95.

	N/A	$750	$500

Last MSR was $1,700.

LS-20 (NO. 095-4000) - similar to LS-10, except has rosewood back/sides, ebony fingerboard/bridge, gold tuners, mfg. 1994-95.

	N/A	$1,000	$650

Last MSR was $2,075.

Add $200 for Fishman electronics and left-handed configuration LS-20LH (Model 095-4020-320)

LS-30 - similar to LS-10, except has figured maple back/sides, ebony fingerboard/bridge, bound peghead, gold tuners, mfg. 1994-95.

	N/A	$900	$575

Last MSR was $2,000.

LS-40C - single sharp cutaway dreadnought style, solid spruce top, round soundhole, tortoise pickguard, mahogany back/sides/neck, 14/20-fret bound rosewood fingerboard with pearl dot inlay, rosewood bridge with black pearl dot pins, ebony veneered peghead with pearl logo inlay, 3-per-side chrome tuners, available in Natural finish, disc. 1994.

	N/A	$850	$575

Last MSR was $1,900.

LS-50C - similar to LS-40C, except has rosewood back/sides, ebony fingerboard/bridge, gold tuners, disc. 1994.

	N/A	$875	$625

Last MSR was $2,100.

LS-60C - similar to LS-40C, except has figured maple back/sides, ebony fingerboard/bridge, bound peghead, gold tuners, disc. 1994.

	N/A	$900	$650

Last MSR was $2,200.

GRADING			100%	EXCELLENT	AVERAGE

ACOUSTIC: DREADNOUGHT SX SERIES

600 SX - dreadnought style, spruce top, round soundhole, tortoise pickguard, 5-stripe bound body/rosette, nato back/sides/neck, 14/20-fret rosewood fingerboard with pearl dot inlay, rosewood bridge with white black dot pins, rosewood veneered peghead with pearl logo inlay, 3-per-side chrome tuners, available in Natural finish, mfg. 1994-95.

			N/A	$165	$100

Last MSR was $405.

800 SX - similar to 600 SX, except has rosewood back/sides, gold hardware, mfg. 1994-95.

			N/A	$195	$110

Last MSR was $460.

1000 SX - dreadnought style, solid spruce top, round soundhole, 3-stripe bound body/rosette, mahogany back/sides/neck, 14/20-fret rosewood fingerboard with pearl dot inlay, strings through rosewood bridge, bound rosewood veneered peghead with pearl logo inlay, 3-per-side chrome tuners, available in Natural finish, mfg. 1993-95.

			N/A	$275	$185

Last MSR was $645.

1100 SX - similar to 1000 SX, except has rosewood back/sides, ebony fingerboard/bridge, gold tuners, mfg. 1993-95.

			N/A	$350	$225

Last MSR was $780.

1200 SX - dreadnought style, solid spruce top, round soundhole, 3-stripe bound body/rosette, mahogany back/sides/neck, 14/20-fret rosewood fingerboard with pearl dot inlay, strings through rosewood bridge, bound rosewood veneered peghead with pearl logo inlay, 3-per-side chrome tuners, available in Natural finish, mfg. 1993-95.

			N/A	$400	$275

Last MSR was $965.

1300 SX - similar to 1200 SX, except has rosewood back/sides, ebony fingerboard with pearl snowflake inlay, ebony bridge, gold tuners, mfg. 1993-95.

			N/A	$500	$350

Last MSR was $1,175.

Fender FR-50 Resonator
courtesy Dave Rogers
Dave's Guitar Shop

ACOUSTIC: RESONATOR SERIES

FR-48 RESONATOR (NO. 095-4800) - steel body resonator, custom Fender f-holes, mahogany neck, 19-fret rosewood fingerboard with dot inlay, Micarta saddle bridge, chrome die-cast 3-per-side uners, available in chrome, new 2003.

MSR	$800		$480	$350	$225

FR-50 RESONATOR (NO. 095-5000) - spruce top, mahogany neck, back and sides, rosewood fingerboard with dot position markers, 25.3" scale, die-cast chrome tuners, chrome finished resonator, custom Fender f-holes, 3-per-side tuners, available in Sunburst or Black finishes, mfg. 2000-current.

MSR	$490		$299	$230	$160

ACOUSTIC: D'AQUISTO SERIES

D'AQUISTO MASTERBUILT ULTRA ACOUSTIC (U.S. MFG., NO. 010-2070) - Single round cutaway hollow figured maple body (17" width), arched bound spruce top, bound f-holes, set-in maple neck, raised bound ebony pickguard, 22-fret bound ebony fingerboard with pearl block inlay, adjustable ebony bridge/ebony trapeze tailpiece, bound peghead with pearl fan/logo inlay, 3-per-side gold tuners with ebony buttons, available in Antique Burst and Natural finish, mfg. 1994-2001.

			$10,500	$7,500	$5,500

Last MSR was $15,030.

Add $500 for pickguard mounted custom Kent Armstrong floating pickup (with volume and tone controls) as Model 010-2080 (Mfg. Sug. Retail $15,530).

GRADING	100%	EXCELLENT	AVERAGE

ACOUSTIC: TRAVEL SERIES

TRAVEL GUITAR TG-4 (NO. 095-0040-321) - travel size acoustic model, solid spruce top, Nato back, sides and neck, rosewood fingerboard with dot position markers, 3 per side chrome, covered tunes, comes with gig bag, available in Natural finish, mfg. 2000-current.

MSR	$280	$175	$135	$95

ACOUSTIC: SB SERIES

SB Series models were produced in Asia.

SB-15 (NO. 095-4515) - jumbo style, solid spruce top, round soundhole, tortoise pickguard, mahogany back/sides/neck, 14/20-fret bound rosewood fingerboard with pearl dot inlay, rosewood bridge with black pearl dot pins, ebony veneered peghead with pearl logo inlay, 3-per-side chrome tuners, available in Natural finish, mfg. 1994-95.

	N/A	$850	$575
		Last MSR was $1,925.	

SB-25 (NO. 095-4525) - similar to SB-15, except has rosewood back/sides, ebony fingerboard/bridge, gold tuners, mfg. 1994-95.

	N/A	$900	$650
		Last MSR was $2,125.	

SB-35 - similar to SB-15, except has figured maple back/sides, ebony fingerboard/bridge, bound peghead, gold tuners, mfg. 1994-95.

	N/A	$875	$625
		Last MSR was $2,100.	

SB-45C - single sharp cutaway jumbo style, solid spruce top, round soundhole, tortoise pickguard, mahogany back/sides/neck, 14/20-fret bound rosewood fingerboard with pearl dot inlay, rosewood bridge with black pearl dot pins, ebony veneered peghead with pearl logo inlay, 3-per-side chrome tuners, available in Natural finish, mfg. 1994-95.

	N/A	$800	$525
		Last MSR was $2,000.	

SB-55C - similar to SB-45C, except has rosewood back/sides, ebony fingerboard/bridge, gold tuners, mfg. 1994-95.

	N/A	$900	$650
		Last MSR was $2,200.	

SB-65C - similar to SB-45C, except has figured maple back/sides, ebony fingerboard/bridge, bound peghead, gold tuners, mfg. 1994-95.

	N/A	$925	$700
		Last MSR was $2,300.	

ACOUSTIC: SJ SERIES

SJ-64 S (NO. 095-6400) - super jumbo body, solid spruce top, rosewood back and sides, mahogany neck, bound neck and body, rosewood fingerboard with split block position markers, 20 frets, 25.6" scale, gold die-cast tuners, available in Natural Gloss finish, disc 2002.

	$450	$325	$225
		Last MSR was $700.	

SJ-65 S (NO. 095-6500) - super jumbo body, similar to SJ-64 S, except has flamed maple back and sides, maple neck, available in Natural Gloss finish, disc 2002.

	$475	$335	$230
		Last MSR was $720.	

ACOUSTIC: JUMBO SX SERIES

1500 SX - jumbo style, solid spruce top, round soundhole, black pickguard, rosewood back/sides, mahogany neck, 14/20-fret rosewood fingerboard with pearl block inlay, strings through rosewood bridge, bound rosewood veneered peghead with pearl logo inlay, 3-per-side gold tuners, available in Natural finish, mfg. 1993-95.

	N/A	$425	$295
		Last MSR was $965.	

1505 SX - similar to 1500 SX, except has sycamore back/sides, available in Sunburst Top finish, mfg. 1993-95.

	N/A	$475	$325
		Last MSR was $1,015.	

ACOUSTIC: MINI SERIES

MA-1 (NO. 094-0100-021) - 3/4 scale mini-acoustic, Laminated Agathis top, back, and sides, Nato neck with rosewood fingerboard, chrome, open-gear tuners, 18 frets, 23.3" scale, available in Natural finish, disc 2001.

	$90	$65	$45
		Last MSR was $150.	

In 2001 this model became part of the Squire line. See Squire for current mfg.

GRADING	100%	EXCELLENT	AVERAGE

MA-2 (NO. 094-0200-021) - similar to MA-1, except has laminated spruce top, 20 frets, chrome, covered tuners, rosewood bridge, Compensated Urea saddle, multi-ABS inlays on soundhole and body edge, black neck binding, available in Natural finish, mfg. 1999-2000.

		$130	**$85**	**$60**
			Last MSR was $189.	

ACOUSTIC ELECTRIC: GRAND ACOUSTIC (GA) SERIES

Fender Acoustic and Auditorium models have only recently appeared on the market.

GA-43 SCE NATURAL (NO. 095-4305) - solid AA Grade spruce top, solid mahogany back, single cutaway design, rosewood fingerboard with dot position markers, special bracing, 3-per-side tuners, Fender Fishman Classic 4 ACLR Pickup System, available in Natural finish, mfg. 2000-current.

MSR	**$865**	**$525**	**$425**	**$315**

GA-45 SCE NATURAL (NO. 095-4505) - solid AA Grade spruce top, solid mahogany back, single cutaway design, rosewood fingerboard with dot position markers, special bracing, 3-per-side tuners, Fender Fishman 4 ACLR Pickup System, available in Natural finish, mfg. 2001-current.

MSR	**$965**	**$580**	**$475**	**$340**

GA-45 SCE Left-Handed Model (No. 095-4525) - similar to the GA-45 SCE except in left-handed configuration, available in Natural finish, mfg. 2002-current.

MSR	**$995**	**$599**	**$500**	**$350**

ACOUSTIC ELECTRIC: CLASSICAL (CG) SERIES

CG-11 E (NO. 094-1101) - classical style, spruce top, nato back and sides, nato neck with rosewood fingerboard, 20 frets, 25.3" scale, chrome tuners, Fender Passive Piezo electronics, available in Natural finish, current mfg.

MSR	**$333**	**$200**	**$175**	**$125**

CG-24 SCE (NO. 094-2405) - classical body with cutaway, solid cedar top, ovankol back and sides, Nato neck, rosewood fingerboard, wood mosaic rosette, multi-ABS body binding, brown neck binding, 18 frets, 25.3" scale, gold tuners, Fender Piezo Transducer pickup with Onboard Active Preamp, 3-Band EQ plus Mid Sweep, available in Natural finish, mfg. 1999-current.

MSR	**$600**	**$360**	**$295**	**$215**

CG-25 SCE (NO. 094-2505) - classical style with cutaway design, solid cedar top, round soundhole, ovankol back/sides, nato neck, 12/19-fret rosewood fingerboard, slotted headstock, 3-per-side gold tuners, piezo transducer, active EQ, available in Gloss finish, mfg. 1995-99.

		$475	**$325**	**$225**
			Last MSR was $699.	

CG-35SCE (NO. 094-3505) - single cutaway design, solid cedar top, rosewood back and sides, mahogany neck, rosewood fingerboard with dot position markers, 25.6" scale, Piezo pickup with Fishman Classic 4 Preamp, available in Natural Gloss finish, mfg. 2000-01.

		$525	**$365**	**$250**
			Last MSR was $749.	

GN-45SCE (NO. 094-4505) - single cutaway design, solid AA grade spruce top, solid rosewood back, rosewood fingerboard, die-cast gold tuning machines, abalone fret markers, 20 frets, tortoise shell-style binding, Fender/Fishman exclusive ACLR preamp, Piezo pickup, available in Natural finish, mfg. 2001-current.

MSR	**$965**	**$580**	**$475**	**$340**

ACOUSTIC ELECTRIC: DREADNOUGHT AG SERIES

AG-25 - single round cutaway dreadnought style, spruce top, round soundhole, black pickguard, mahogany back/sides/neck, 20-fret rosewood fingerboard with pearl dot inlay, rosewood bridge with black white dot pins, 6-on-one-side chrome tuners, piezo bridge pickup, volume/tone slide control, available in Natural finish, disc. 1994.

		N/A	**$150**	**$95**
			Last MSR was $335.	

GRADING		100%	EXCELLENT	AVERAGE

ACOUSTIC ELECTRIC: DREADNOUGHT DG SERIES

DG-10 CE (NO. 095-1005) - dreadnought style with cutaway design, spruce top, round soundhole, mahogany back/sides, 14/20-fret rosewood fingerboard, rosewood bridge, black pickguard, 3-per-side chrome tuners, bridge transducer, volume/tone controls, Natural Satin finish, mfg. 1995-current.

MSR	$383	$230	$175	$125

DG-10 CE LH (No. 095-1025) - similar to the DG-10 CE, except features a left-handed configuration, mfg. 1998-current.

MSR	$400	$240	$185	$135

DG-11 E (NO. 095-1101) - dreadnought body, laminated spruce top, nato back, sides, and neck, rosewood fingerboard with dot inlays, 25.3" scale, rosewood bridge, Urea nut and saddle, chrome tuners, Piezo pickup with Passive volume and tone, black pickguard, Black Gloss finish, current mfg.

MSR	$333	$199	$150	$100

DG-14 SCE (NO. 095-1405) - single cutaway dreadnought laminated maple body, solid spruce top, nato neck, 20 fret rosewood fingerboard with dot inlays, rosewood bridge, tortise pickguard, 3-per-side chrome tuners, Fishman Classic 4 with ACLR electronics, available in Natural Gloss finish, new 2003.

MSR	$450	$270	$200	$140

DG-16E-12 (NO. 095-1613) - 12-string dreadnought, laminated spruce top, mahogany back, sides, and neck, Grade-A Rosewood fingerboard, snow-flake position markers, 25.3" scale, 20 frets, chrome die-cast tuners, rosewood bridge, Compensated Urea nut and saddle, black pickguard, Fender Piezo pickup with volume and 3-Band Active EQ, available in Natural or Black finishes, current mfg.

MSR	$466	$280	$215	$140

DG-20 CE (NO. 095-2005) - dreadnought style with cutaway design, solid spruce top, round soundhole, mahogany back/sides, 14/20-fret rosewood fingerboard, rosewood bridge, tortoise shell pickguard, 3-per-side chrome die-cast tuners, piezo pickup, onboard preamp, volume/3-band EQ/mid-sweep controls, available in Natural or Black finish, mfg. 1995-current.

MSR	$600	$360	$295	$215

Black finish was added in 1999 (Model 095-2005-006).

DG-22 CE (NO. 095-2205) - single cutaway dreadnought body, figured maple top/back/sides, round soundhole, 14/20-fret rosewood fingerboard, rosewood bridge, tortoise shell pickguard, 3-per-side gold die-cast tuners, Fishman Matrix pickup, onboard preamp, volume/3-band EQ/mid-sweep controls, available in Cherry, Natural, Blue Burst, Crimson Red Burst, or Sunburst finishes, mfg. 1995-current.

MSR	$730	$440	$375	$280

Crimson Red Burst (-028) and Blue Burst (-036) finishes were added in 1999.

DG-27 SCE (NO. 095-2705) - dreadnought style body with Florentine cutaway, solid spruce top, premium mahogany back and sides, mahogany neck, rosewood fingerboard with dot inlays, rosewood bridge, Compensated Urea saddle, 25.6" scale, chrome tuners, Piezo pickup, volume control and Active 3-band EQ, Mid Sweep, tortoise shell pickguard, available in Natural and Black finishes, disc 2002.

	$395	$290	$200

Last MSR was $650.

DG-31 SCE (NO. 095-3105) - dreadnought style with cutaway design, solid Englemann spruce top, round soundhole, mahogany back/sides, 14/20-fret rosewood fingerboard, rosewood bridge, tortoise shell pickguard, 3-per-side chrome die-cast tuners, Fishman Acoustic Matrix pickup, onboard preamp, volume/3-band EQ/mid-sweep controls, available in Black, Cherry Sunburst, or Natural Gloss finishes, mfg. 1995-99.

	$550	$375	$250

Last MSR was $799.

DG-41 SCE (NO. 095-4105) - dreadnought style with cutaway design, solid Englemann spruce top, round soundhole, rosewood back/sides, 14/20-fret rosewood fingerboard, rosewood bridge, tortoise shell pickguard, 3-per-side gold die-cast tuners, Fishman Acoustic Matrix Professional pickup, onboard preamp, volume/4-band EQ/phase reversal controls, available in Gloss finish, mfg. 1995-2000.

	$699	$450	$325

Last MSR was $999.

ACOUSTIC ELECTRIC: DREADNOUGHT GD SERIES

GD-47 SCE (NO. 094-4705) - solid AA Grade spruce top, solid rosewood back and sides, single cutaway design, rosewood fingerboard with dot position markers, 3-per-side tuners, Fender Fishman 4 ACLR Pickup System, available in Natural finish, mfg. 2002-current.

MSR	$965	$580	$475	$340

GRADING	100%	EXCELLENT	AVERAGE

ACOUSTIC ELECTRIC: DREADNOUGHT SX SERIES

1105 SXE - dreadnought style, solid spruce top, round soundhole, 3-stripe bound body/rosette, mahogany neck, rosewood back/sides, 14/20-fret ebony fingerboard with pearl dot inlay, strings through ebony bridge, bound rosewood veneered peghead with pearl logo inlay, 3-per-side gold tuners, piezo pickup, volume/treble/bass/mix controls, available in Natural finish, mfg. 1993-95.

	N/A	$375	$250

Last MSR was $880.

ACOUSTIC ELECTRIC: MINI-JUMBO (JG) SERIES

JG-12 CE-12 (NO. 095-1217) - mini-jumbo style with cutaway design, spruce top, round soundhole, mahogany back/sides, 14/20-fret rosewood fingerboard, rosewood bridge, 6-per-side chrome die-cast tuners, Fender piezo pickup, onboard preamp, volume/3-band EQ/mid-sweep controls, available in Satin finish, mfg. 1998-current.

MSR	$616	$370	$295	$225

JG-26 SCE (NO. 095-2605) - mini-jumbo style with cutaway design, solid cedar top, round soundhole, mahogany back/sides, 14/20-fret rosewood fingerboard, rosewood bridge, 3-per-side gold die-cast tuners with pearloid buttons, Fishman Acoustic Matrix pickup, onboard preamp, volume/3-band EQ/mid-sweep controls, available in Satin finish, mfg. 1997-current.

MSR	$715	$430	$350	$250

ACOUSTIC ELECTRIC: JUMBO SX SERIES

1600 SXE - jumbo style, solid spruce top, round soundhole, black pickguard, rosewood back/sides, mahogany neck, 14/20-fret rosewood fingerboard with pearl block inlay, strings through rosewood bridge, bound rosewood veneered peghead with pearl logo inlay, 3-per-side gold tuners, piezo pickup, volume/treble/bass/mix controls, available in Natural finish, mfg. 1993-95.

	N/A	$575	$350

Last MSR was $1,065.

ACOUSTIC ELECTRIC: ELECTRACOUSTIC SERIES

TELECOUSTIC STANDARD - single round cutaway style, spruce top, oval soundhole, basswood back/sides, maple neck, 22-fret rosewood fingerboard, rosewood bridge with white pins, 6-on-one-side chrome tuners with plastic buttons, piezo bridge pickup, volume/treble/bass slide controls, available in Antique Burst, Black, or Natural finishes, mfg. 1993-95.

	N/A	$500	$350

Last MSR was $960.

Telecoustic Custom - similar to Telecoustic Standard, except has bound solid spruce top, mahogany back/sides/neck, pau ferro fingerboard, pau ferro/ebony laminate bridge, Schaller tuners with pearl buttons, active electronics, available in Antique Burst and Natural finishes, mfg. 1993-95.

$1,150	$725	$550

Last MSR was $2,150.

Telecoustic Deluxe - similar to Telecoustic Standard, except has mahogany back/sides/neck, rosewood/ebony laminate bridge, pearl tuner buttons, mfg. 1993-95.

$625	$425	$295

Last MSR was $1,160.

STRATACOUSTIC (NO. 095-7400) - solid spruce top, double cutaway design, state of the art one-piece fiberglass body, bol-on neck with rosewood fingerboard, dot position markers, thinline body, trademark Stratocaster style headstock, Fender Fishman Classic 4 Preamp, die-cast tuners, available in Olympic White, and Black finishes, current mfg.

MSR	$450	$270	$225	$150

TELECOUSTIC (NO. 095-7500) - solid spruce top, single cutaway, state of the art one-piece fiberglass body, bolt-on neck with rosewood fingerboard, dot position markers, thinline body, trademark Telecaster headstock design, die-cast tuners, Fender Fishman Classic 4 Preamp, available in Inca Silver, Sunburst, Natural, and Candy Apple Red finishes, mfg. 2000-current.

MSR	$450	$270	$225	$150

Natural and Sunburst finishes were introduced in 2002.

GRADING		100%	EXCELLENT	AVERAGE

ACOUSTIC ELECTRIC BASS

BG-29 (NO. 095-2900-021) - slimline dreadnought style with cutaway design, maple top, round soundhole, maple back/sides, 14/20-fret rosewood fingerboard, rosewood bridge, 2-per-side chrome die-cast tuners, Fishman Acoustic Matrix pickup, onboard preamp, volume/3-band EQ/mid-sweep controls, available in Natural Gloss finish, gig-bag included, mfg. 1995-current.

	MSR	$800		$480	$375	$280

BG-29 Black (No. 095-2900-306) - similar to the BG-29 Black, except has spruce top, mahogany back/sides, available in Natural Satin finish, gig-bag included, mfg. 1997-current.

	MSR	$833		$499	$385	$290

BG-32 (NO. 095-3200) - non-cutaway design, spruce top, mahogany back and sides, rosewood fingerboard with dot position markers, chrome die cast tuners, 2-per-side tuners, Fishman Classic 4 Preamp and pickup, Natural Satin finish, mfg. 2000-current.

	MSR	$700		$420	$350	$265

GB-41 SCE (NO. 095-4105) - single cutaway solid mahogany body, solid AA spruce top, Maogany neck, 24-fret rosewood fingerboard with dot inlays, 2-per-side Hipshot chrome tuners, Fishman Classic 4 with ACLR pickup and electronics, available in Natural finish, new 2003.

	MSR	$965		$579	$475	$350

FERNANDES

Instruments currently produced in Tokyo, Japan beginning 1969. Distributed in the U.S. by Fernandes Guitars U.S.A. Inc., of Van Nuys, California.

In 1969, Fernandes Company Ltd. (based in Tokyo, Japan) was established to produce quality classical guitars at an affordable price. Over the next twenty years, Fernandes expanded the line and became one of the largest selling guitar manufacturers in the world. Fernandes is the number one selling guitar in Japan, and at times has held as much as 40% of the Japanese market.

In late 1992, Fernandes Company Ltd. began distributing their entire line of guitars to the U.S. market as Fernandes Guitars U.S.A., Inc. Fernandes Company Ltd. uses only the top facilities located in Japan, Taiwan, China, and Korea to produce their guitars. Once the factory is done manufacturing the guitars, they are shipped to the United States where they are inspected and set up again.

In 1998, Fernandes renamed their instruments. For example, the eye-catching H-80 art-deco-style guitar model became the **Vertigo Deluxe.** In addition to their **RetroRocket** and **Retrospect** series, Fernandes is concentrating on the newer additions to their line like the **P-Project, Native, Dragonfly,** and **Lexington** series. Fernandes also offers a line of practice amps (15 to 20 watts) for guitars and basses, (Company history courtesy Bryan Wresinski, Fernandes Guitars U.S.A.).

ACOUSTIC: PALISADE SERIES

PALISADE D30 - dreadnought body, spruce top with "X"-bracing, Sapele back and sides, nato set neck, 25 1/4" scale, rosewood fingerboard with dot position markers, 20 medium frets, chrome covered tuners, rosewood bridge, available in Black, Natural, or Dark Red finishes, current mfg.

	MSR	$249		$190	$145	$100

Palisade D30-12 - similar to Palisade D30, except in a 12-string configuration, available in Natural finish, mfg. 2000-current.

	MSR	$299		$225	$160	$110

PALISADE D34 - similar to Palisade D30, except as a single cutaway, available in Natural finish, disc 2001.

				$250	$175	$125

Last MSR was $339.

PALISADE D38 - similar to Palisade D30, except has mahogany back and sides, bound body and neck, Tortoise pickguard, available in Natural Gloss finish, current mfg.

	MSR	$359		$270	$200	$140

PALISADE CC50 - classical style body, rosewood sides/back, solid spruce top, nato neck, 20-fret rosewood fingerboard, rosewood bridge, 3-per-side open tuners, under-the-bridge saddles (no Chili Peppers), Piezo pickup, active preamp, 4-band EQ, available in Natural finish, current mfg.

	MSR	$575		$435	$325	$250

PALISADE DC50 - dreadnought body with single cutaway, spruce top with "X"-bracing, mahogany back and sides, nato set neck, 25.25" scale, piezo pickup under the bridge saddle, volume, bass, middle, treble, chrome die cast tuners, rosewood bridge, available in Natural or Black finishes, current mfg.

	MSR	$379		$285	$215	$150

ACOUSTIC: FAA & REYNA SERIES

FAA-400 ACOUSTIC/ELECTRIC - single rounded cutaway body, spruce top, molded back, set-in nato neck, 25 1/4" scale, multi-layer binding, 22-fret rosewood fingerboard, rosewood bridge, chrome hardware, 3-per-side tuners, bridge mounted piezo pickup, active preamp/3-band EQ, available in Natural finish, disc. 1998.

				N/A	$300	$175

Last MSR was $519.

GRADING	100%	EXCELLENT	AVERAGE

REYNA STANDARD - single cutaway hollowbody, select spruce top, molded back and sides, nato set neck, rosewood fingerboard with dot position markers, 22-frets, 3-per-side tuners, piezo pickup mounted under the bridge saddle, volume/tone controls, chrome tuners, rosewood bridge, bound body and neck, available in See-Through Black, Natural, or Cherry Sunburst, current mfg.

MSR	$329		$250	$175	$115

Reyna (FAA-500) - similar to the FAA-400, except features a bound flame maple top, bound neck, active preamp with volume/bass/mid/treble slider controls, available in 3-Tone Sunburst, Black Burst, Cherry Sunburst, or Natural finishes, disc.

$425 $275 $175

Last MSR was $549.

Early versions of the FAA-500 were also available in Antique Sunburst and Greyburst finishes.

**Flanders Archtop
courtesy Martin Flanders**

FERRINGTON, DANNY
Instruments currently built in Santa Monica, California since 1980.

Luthier Danny Ferrington was born and raised in Louisiana. Ferrington's father, Lloyd, was a cabinet maker who had previously played guitar and bass in a local country western combo. Ferrington's first experiences with woodworking were in his father's shop in Monroe, Louisiana.

Ferrington accepted an apprenticeship in 1975 at the Old Time Pickin' Parlour in Nashville, Tennessee. He spent the next five years working with noted acoustic guitar builder Randy Woods. Ferrington's first acoustic was built in 1977, and he continued to hone his craft.

In 1980, Ferrington moved to Los Angeles, California. Ferrington spent a number of years experimenting with different designs, and tones from instruments, and continued building custom guitars. Many of the features on the custom guitars are developed through discussions with the musician commissioning the piece. It is estimated that by 1992, Ferrington had constructed over one hundred custom instruments.

In the late 1980s, the Kramer guitar company was offering several models designed by Ferrington. After Kramer went under, the Ferrington Guitar Company of Long Branch, New Jersey (phone number was previously listed at 908.870.3800) offered essentially the same models (KFS-1, KFT-1, and KFB-1) with Ferrington on the headstock. These models featured a maple neck, rosewood fingerboard, acoustic body, 3-band EQ, and a thinline bridge transducer, (Source: Kate Geil, et al, the *Ferrington Guitars book*).

FINOCCHIO GUITARS WORKS
Instruments currently produced in Easton, Pennsylvania.

Luthier Frank Finocchio has been building guitars for over 20 years now. He specializes in acoustic, flattop, arch top, and classical instruments. Frank is also known as a teacher of restoring and building guitars. He teaches his workshop four times a year. Frank learned many of his traits from working at Martin Guitars. He was a major developer for the DXM guitar. Finocchio is also an authorized Martin repair site. For more information on either Finocchio's workshops or custom built guitars refer to the web site (see Trademark Index).

FITZPATRICK JAZZ GUITARS
Instruments currently built in Wickford, Rhode Island.

Luthier Charles Fitzpatrick builds acoustic, acoustic-electric, and semi-hollow body electric archtop guitars in 15", 16", 17", and 18" body widths. The **Jazz Box Select** features single cutaway body consisting of fancy quilted or flamed maple with matching rim and neck, solid carved top of North American spruce, fine line black and white body binding, mother-of-pearl block fingerboard inlays, gold tune-o-matic tailpiece, bound tortoise shell finger rest, and a suspended jazz pickup. List prices range from $3,270 (16"), $3,800 (17"), to $4,500 (18"). The list price includes a hardshell case, and Fitzpatrick offers a range of options and custom inlays.

FIVE STAR
See chapter on House Brands.

While this trademark has been identified as a House Brand, the retailer or distributor has not yet been identified. These smaller bodied acoustics have the logo and star position markers painted on, as opposed to the inlay work of a more expensive guitar, (Source: Willie G. Moseley, *Stellas & Stratocasters*).

FLANDERS CUSTOM GUITARS
Instruments currently built in New England since 1979. Distributed by Fretboard Corner of Lake Ronkonkoma, New York.

Building his first guitar in 1979, Martin Flanders has managed to walk the fine line between old world craftsmanship and modern vision. Flanders gained experience and respect for quality by restoring antique furniture in his father's shop. Living in New England (where select tone woods exist) has afforded Flanders the thrill of harvesting his own stock. Luthier Flanders' business strategy consists of marketing his custom-built guitars at a price customers would expect to pay for a 'production' instrument.

F

ACOUSTIC

Flanders currently offers five guitar models like the **Model 200** (a hybrid carved guitar with tone bars), **Model 300 Executive** single cutaway acoustic arch-top, to the stunning archtop like the **Soloist**. There is also a **Bostonian** model, where Bostonians would pronouce it the Flandas Bostonian. The base models are all available with many cusomization options to choose from. For more information contact Flanders directly (see Trademark Index).

FLEISHMAN
Instruments currently built in Boulder, Colorado.

Luthier Harry Fleishman has been designing and building high quality guitars and basses since 1975. In addition to the electric solid body models that Fleishman is known for, he also builds a small number of acoustic guitars on a yearly basis. Fleishman has also been a columnist for the *Guild of American Luthiers Newsletter*. Fleishman designed the Flash model for Hondo during the 1980s, a minimalist body reverse-tuned bass with a number of innovative design features. Harry is also the director of Luthier's School International.

ACOUSTIC

Harry Fleishman offers both bass and guitars. They are for the most part on custom orders. You can see what different types of instruments Fleishman has by visiting their web site (see Trademark Index).

FLETA
Instruments previously built in Barcelona, Spain from 1927 to 1977.

Luthier Ignacio Fleta (1897-1977) built classical guitars in Spain that reflected the influence of Antonio de Torres, but featured some of Fleta's design ideas as well. Fleta would varnish the inside of the guitar as well, with the intent of brightening the sound. Fleta also added an extra strut under the treble side of the top as a means of increasing volume, (Source: Tony Bacon, *The Ultimate Guitar Book*).

RUBEN FLORES GUITARS
Please refer to the R section in this text.

FOLEY GUITARS
Instruments currently built in Andover, New Jersey since 1988. Distributed by Foley Guitars, Inc. of Andover, New Jersey.

Luthier Ed Foley has been hand crafting high quality acoustic guitars since the late 1980s. Many of his guitars can be found with a large number of Nashville artists, as well as other recording professionals. Foley headstocks are quite distinct, for they feature the graphic of a cow's skull!

Foley only builds about 15 guitars a year. In addition to his custom bracing, Foley also used graphite to reinforce his contoured necks, and Groove Tubes "Flat Heads" embedded in the headstock for improved sustain.

ACOUSTIC

Ordering a Foley acoustic is exactly like ordering a custom built guitar. True to form, the price list runs three pages; the customer starts at the top of page one and makes the necessary choices as the list is run down. At the end of the choices for the model, the customer totals up all additional charges, and that's the retail price. All Foley guitars come with a hardshell case and John Pearse strings.

The base list price for a Foley acoustic is $1,950 (and that begins with the body size). A left-handed configuration is no extra charge; but a body cutaway adds $225 and the 12-string configuration is an additional $200. The basic model consists of a scalloped brace sitka spruce top, mahogany sides, 2 piece mahogany back, ivoroid or tortoise body binding, black and white rings rosette, dot fingerboard inlay, 24.9" or 25.4" scale, rosewood fingerboard and bridge, 3-per-side chrome Schaller tuners, and choice of black, tortoise, or no fingerboard.

Any other custom choice carries an additional cost, such as a choice of Engelmann spruce (or flame koa or Alpine or German spruce) top for $175 (each), Brazilian rosewood back and sides (add $1,450) or flame koa (or flame maple or birdseye maple or quilted maple) for $325 (each). The list of options is actually staggering; but the end result is a custom built guitar the way the customer wanted it. For additional information and pricing, please contact luthier Foley directly (see Trademark Index).

FOSTER
Instruments currently built in Covington, Louisiana.

Luthier Jimmy Foster offers repair and restoration work in addition to his current guitar designs, and has been working in the New Orleans area for over twenty five years. In addition to his standard models (listed below), Foster also offers custom orders available with choice of woods, inlays, and trim. For further information, contact luthier Foster directly (see Trademark Index). For the AT series refer to the Foster section in the *Blue Book of Electric Guitars*.

FLAT-TOP FT SERIES

The **FT1** flattop acoustic has a 17" body width, spruce top, body binding, mahogany back/sides/neck, 25.5" scale, ebony fingerboard/bridge/headstock overlay (last retail $2,450). A piezo bridge pickup is an option for an additional $175. This model is discontinued.

PRODIGY SERIES

Add $450 for 7-string configuration.

PRODIGY 1 - 17" cut-a-way body bound body, sitka spruce top, mahogany back and sides, ebony fingerboard, bridge, and headstock, 25 1/2" scale, 3 1/2" depth, disc. mfg.

Last MSR was $2,450.

PRODIGY 2 - similar to Prodigy 1, except has a carved mahogany back and even 3" body, disc. mfg.

Last MSR was $3,250.

FRAMUS

Instruments currently produced in Markneukirchen, Germany. Distributed by Warwick GmbH & Co. Music Equipment Kg of Markneukirchen, Germany. Instruments were previously produced in Germany from the late 1940s through the mid 1970s. In 1996, the trademark was re-introduced in Europe (no U.S. distributors listed to date).

When Frederick Wilfer returned to his home town of Walthersgrun at the end of World War II, he realized that the American-controlled Sudetenland area was soon to fall under control of the Russian forces. With the help of the Americans, Wilfer succeeded in resettling a number of violin makers from Schonbach to Franconia (later in the district of Erlangen). Between 1945 to 1947, Wilfer continued to find homes and employment for the Schonbach violin makers.

In 1946, Wilfer founded the Framus production company, the company name an acronym for Franconian Musical instruments. As the company established itself in 1946, Wilfer drew on the knowledge of his violin builder from Schonbach to produce a range of musical instruments including violins and cellos. The new Framus company expanded out of its first couple of production buildings, eventually building a new factory in Bubenreuth in 1955.

The first Framus electric guitars appeared in the 1950s. Due to the presence of American servicemen stationed there, the influence of rock-'n-roll surfaced earlier in Germany than other European countries. As a result, German guitar builders had a head start on answering the demand caused by the proliferation of pop groups during the 1960s. Furthermore, as the German production increased, they began exporting their guitars to other countries (including the U.S.). The Framus company stayed active in producing acoustic and electric guitars, and electric basses until the mid 1970s.

In the 1970s, increased competition and serious price undercutting from firms in the Asian market had a serious effect on established companies. Unfortunately, one aspect was to force a number of firms into bankruptcy – and Framus was one of those companies in 1975. However, Wilfer did have the opportunity to watch his son, Hans-Peter Wilfer, establish his own company in 1982 (see Warwick). Warwick's success allowed Hans-Peter to re-introduce the Framus trademark to the European musical market in 1996. In honor of his father Frederick, Hans-Peter chose to use the world-famous Framus trademark when he began offering guitar models in 1996, (Source: Hans Peter Wilfer, Warwick GmbH & Co. Music Equipment Kg; and Tony Bacon and Paul Day, *The Guru's Guitar Guide*).

ACOUSTIC & SERIALIZATION

In order to properly date the year of issue, most Framus guitars had a separate pair of digits after the main serial number. If the separate pair is present, the two numbers will indicate the year. Current Framus instruments, including the electric guitars and handwired tube guitar amps, are produced at the Warwick facility. Acoustic instruments are no longer produced by Framus. Currently, Framus instruments are available in England, Germany, Sweden, and Switzerland; worldwide distribution is in the planning stages.

The majority of Framus acoustic guitars were produced in the 1960s. Some of the models that were produced inlcude the Texan, King, Blueridge, Tenor, Hootenany, and the Camping King. Used prices for these instruments range anywhere between $300-$700 depending on the model.

FRANCISCAN

Instruments previously produced in Indonesia. Previously distributed in the U.S. by Kaman Musical Instruments of Bloomfield, Connecticut.

The Franciscan line offered a full line of beginner, student, and intermediate quality guitars, as well as mandolins. Most of the instruments in the line retailed between $75 up to $175. The last Franciscan model was produced in 1998. These guitars then became Castillas and all of those have since become Montana guitars, (Source: Walter Murray, *Frankenstein Fretworks*, Tim Campbell at Kaman Music).

ACOUSTIC

Models included the **CS-3**, which has a 3/4 size acoustic with a classical-style slotted headstock, 12/18-fret fingerboard, black pickguard, trapeze-style tailpiece, pearloid tuner buttons, and a 2-tone Sunburst finish (retail list $75). The **CS-19** (list $100) is a full sized acoustic folk guitar, with spruce top, round soundhole, black rosette, black body binding, nato back and sides, 14/20-fret laminated fretboard with pearl dot inlay, 3-per-side chrome tuners, and hardwood bridge with black bridge pins. The **CS-20 E** is similar in construction to the **CS-19**, except also has a transducer pickup (list $150).

FRANCONIA

Instruments previosuly built in Japan between 1980 and 1985.

The Franconia trademark was a brand name used by a UK importer. The guitars were generally entry level to mid quality copies of American designs, (Source: Tony Bacon and Paul Day, *The Guru's Guitar Guide*).

FRANKLIN GUITAR COMPANY

Instruments previously built in Seattle, Washington.

Luthier Nick Kukich began the Franklin Guitar Company in 1976. It is estimated that he has been building 36 guitars a year, offered in OM and jumbo body styles. Kukich's acoustic guitars feature Engelmann spruce tops, Indian (or Brazilian) rosewood and koa back/sides, mahogany necks, ebony fingerboards and bridges, and herringbone purfling. Options such as a left-hand configuration, cutaway body design, or inlay/ornamentation was available by customer's specifications. Nick quite producing guitars to apparent health reasons. Production of guitars stopped by the mid 1990s.

FRESHMAN
Instruments previously built in Japan during the mid 1960s.

As an inexpensive, entry level guitar, the Freshman trademark is quite apt: a Senior, it isn't. In fact, it's not even close to a Sophomore, (Source: Tony Bacon and Paul Day, *The Guru's Guitar Guide*).

FROGGY BOTTOM GUITARS
Instruments currently built in Newfane, Vermont since 1970. Instruments are available through Froggy Bottom Guitars as well as selected dealers.

Luthier Michael Millard initially began Froggy Bottom Guitars as a custom shop back in 1970, as a means to providing guitars crafted for the customers who commission them. Millard, a one-time guitar student of Reverend Gary Davis, responds to the customer's request for certain tone or feel. Although there is a standard for each of Millard's models, it is the customer who defines certain parameters that are incorporated in the player's special guitar.

Luthier Millard, who is assisted by his partner Andrew Mueller, also builds production models in their two-man shop. These guitars also share more in common with the specially commissioned models than the average production line acoustics. These luthiers are joined by Petria Mitchell, who creates the scrimshaw work on many of the Froggy Bottom heelcaps; and canine "neck carver" Bubba Le Bump.

The name "Froggy Bottom" is derived from the nickname given to land along the Mississippi Delta that is prone to flooding each year. The term was used by the sharecroppers who worked the land, and Millard seeks to capture the spirit of the place and its people in his custom guitar construction.

GUITAR IDENTIFICATION & CONSTRUCTION DETAILS

Froggy Bottom guitars are offered in four style options on the standard models. Each style adds features to the preceding listing, which defines the different levels of refinement.

Basic: The Basic style offers maple trim, a single herringbone rosette ring, 8-ply top purfling, mother-of-pearl peghead logo, a Brazilian rosewood bridge, and chrome Schaller tuners. This option is now discontinued.

Standard: The Standard options go one step up with an ebony bridge, abalone position markers, an abalone logo, 2 ring rosette, maple end inlay and heel cap, and back and side purfling.

Deluxe: Further options in the Deluxe category include an abalone rosette, curly maple neck heel trim, Gold Schaller tuners, a bound headstock, and a distinctive fretboard inlay.

Limited: The Limited style option offers an abalone back seam inlay and abalone top trim inlay to the preceding steps.

Custom: The Custom style is entirely different as it is typically a player's own choices on the guitar. When there have been some serious alterations to the body and ornamentation, it is classified as Custom.

All guitar models are offered in four standard back and sides materials such as mahogany, Indian rosewood, curly maple, and curly Hawaiian koa. Each series listed below will have a series of numbers described at the list price: the format follows the Basic/Standard/Deluxe/Limited model. For further information regarding specifications, pricing, and clarity, please contact Michael Millard and Andy Mueller at Froggy Bottom Guitars directly (see Trademark Index).

Froggy Bottom Guitars has numerous custom options available to the customer. There is no extra charge for nut width variations; all other options do have a price. For price quotes on wood options (like Brazilian rosewood back and sides) or abalone inlays (rosette, backstrip, or trim), please call Froggy Bottom Guitars.

Add $100 for Gold Schaller tuners. Add $150 for nickel finish Waverly G-98 tuners. Add $200 for Gold finish Waverly G-98 tuners. Add $150 for oversized soundhole. Add $160 for bound headstock (6-string models). Add $200 for left-handed configuration. Add $225 for engraved Mammoth Ivory heel cap. Add $500 (and up) for Florentine or Venetian cutaway body. Add $2,500 and up for Madagascar rosewood.

ACOUSTIC SMALL BODY GUITARS: 12-FRET MODELS

For each model in the small body model series there are a series of options. Prices are the same for the A-12, H-12, and Parlor models. Last price for the **Basic** series, only available in mahogany, was at $2,665. Prices for the **Standard** models are as follows, mahogany: $4,225, rosewood: $4,425, maple: $4,625, walnut: $5,125, and koa is $5,625. Here are the prices for the **Deluxe** models, mahogany: $4,925, rosewood: $5,125, maple: $5,325, walnut: $5,825, and koa is $6,325. The following are retail on the **Limited** models, mahogany: $6,025, rosewood: $6,225, maple: $6,425, walnut: $6,925, and koa is $7,425.

MODEL A (MODEL A-12) - concert (00) style, 25" scale, Adirondack spruce top, round soundhole, rosette, mahogany neck, 12/20-fret (Model A-12) or 14/20-fret (Model A) fingerboard, solid peghead, 3-per-side tuners, tortoise pickguard, available in Natural finish, body length 19 3/4", body width 14.5", body depth 4 1/4", current mfg.

MODEL H (MODEL H-12) - grand concert style, 25 1/4" scale, Engelmann spruce top, round soundhole, rosette, mahogany neck, 12/20-fret (Model H-12) or 14/20-fret (Model H) fingerboard, solid peghead, 3-per-side tuners, tortoise pickguard, available in Natural finish, body length 19.375", body width 15", body depth 4 1/4", current mfg.

PARLOR GUITAR (MODEL P-12) - 24 3/4" scale, Adirondack spruce top, round soundhole, rosette, mahogany neck, 12/20-fret fingerboard, slotted peghead, bar-style bridge, 3-per-side Waverly tuners, tortoise pickguard, available in Natural finish, body length 20", body width 13 3/8", body depth 4 1/4", current mfg.

ACOUSTIC: SMALL BODY GUITARS: 14-FRET MODELS

For each model in the small body there is a 14-fret model that corresponds to the 12-fret. The features are essentially the same except the neck is joined at the 14th fret instead of the 12th. Prices are the same for the A-14, H-14, and Parlor P-14 models. Prices for the **Standard** models are as follows, mahogany: $3,875, rosewood: $4,075, maple: $4,275, walnut: $4,775, and koa is $5,275. Here are the prices for the **Deluxe** models, mahogany: $4,575, rosewood: $4,775, maple: $4,975, walnut: $5,475, and koa is $5,975. The following are retail on the **Limited** models, mahogany: $5,675, rosewood: $5,875, maple: $6,075, walnut: $6,575, and koa is $7,075.

MODEL A (MODEL A-14) - concert (00) style, 25" scale, Adirondack spruce top, round soundhole, rosette, mahogany neck, 14/20-fret fingerboard, solid peghead, 3-per-side tuners, tortoise pickguard, available in Natural finish, body length 19 3/4", body width 14.5", body depth 4 1/4", current mfg.

MODEL H (MODEL H-14) - grand concert style, 25 1/4" scale, Engelmann spruce top, round soundhole, rosette, mahogany neck, 14/20-fret fingerboard, solid peghead, 3-per-side tuners, tortoise pickguard, available in Natural finish, body length 19 1/8", body width 15", body depth 4 1/4", current mfg.

PARLOR GUITAR (MODEL P-14) - 24 3/4" scale, Adirondack spruce top, round soundhole, rosette, mahogany neck, 14/20-fret fingerboard, slotted peghead, bar-style bridge, 3-per-side Waverly tuners, tortoise pickguard, available in Natural finish, body length 20", body width 13 3/8", body depth 4 1/4", current mfg.

ACOUSTIC: FULL SIZE MODELS

The **Model D** is based on the ever popular dreadnought body developed by the Martin company. While the traditional dreadnought guitar is both powerful and bass heavy, the Froggy Bottom adds clarity, especially up the neck. The **Model F** evolved out of conversions of Martin arch tops in the New York shop of Matt Umanov. Those early conversions demonstrated the virtues of reducing the body volume of larger instruments and clearly altered the course of contemporary flat-top guitar design.

Models D, F and F-12, and K share the same basic retail pricing system; only one pricing table is supplied for brevity. Last price for the **Basic** series, only available in mahogany, was at $2,460. Prices for the **Standard** models are as follows, mahogany: $4,075, rosewood: $4,275, maple: $4,475, walnut: $4,975, and koa is $5,475. Here are the prices for the **Deluxe** models, mahogany: $4,775, rosewood: $4,975, maple: $5,175, walnut: $5,675, and koa is $6,175. The following are retail on the **Limited** models, mahogany: $5,875, rosewood: $6,075, maple: $6,275, walnut: $6,775, and koa is $7,275.

MODEL D - dreadnought style, 25 1/4" scale, Sitka spruce top, round soundhole, rosette, mahogany neck, 14/20-fret fingerboard, solid peghead, 3-per-side tuners, pickguard, available in Natural finish, body length 20", body width 16", body depth 4 1/2", current mfg.

MODEL F - dreadnought style, 25 1/4" scale, Sitka spruce top, round soundhole, rosette, mahogany neck, 14/20-fret fingerboard, solid peghead, 3-per-side tuners, tortoise pickguard, available in Natural finish, body length 20 1/4", body width 16", body depth 4 1/8", current mfg.

Model F-12 - similar to the Model F except has a 12/20 fret fingerboard, and a body length of 21", current mfg.

MODEL K - tight waist/rounded profile body, 25 1/4" scale, Sitka spruce top, round soundhole, rosette, mahogany neck, 14/20-fret fingerboard, solid peghead, 3-per-side tuners, pickguard, available in Natural finish, body length 20", body width 16", body depth 4 1/4", current mfg.

ACOUSTIC: JUMBO MODELS

With the revival of interest in older 12-fret guitars (i.e. where the neck joins the body) such as the Martin original D, the **Model B** is designed as a 12-string with a long (26") scale for blues master Paul Geremia (this is THE guitar for those who love the old Stellas of Willie McTell and Leadbelly). The **Model G** is based on the beautiful Gibson L-5 profile. The **Model J** is the original "Froggy Bottom Special," Millard's earliest jumbo model (first built in 1972). Models B-12, G, and J share the same basic retail pricing system; only one pricing table is supplied.

Models D, F and F-12, and K share the same basic retail pricing system; only one pricing table is supplied for brevity. Last price for the **Basic** series, only available in mahogany, was at $2,775. Prices for the **Standard** models are as follows, mahogany: $4,375, rosewood: $4,575, maple: $4,775, walnut: $5,275, and koa is $5,775. Here are the prices for the **Deluxe** models, mahogany: $5,075, rosewood: $5,275, maple: $5,475, walnut: $5,975, and koa is $6,475. The following are retail on the **Limited** models, mahogany: $6,175, rosewood: $6,375, maple: $6,575, walnut: $7,075, and koa is $7,575.

MODEL B (MODEL B-12) - jumbo style, 26" scale, Sitka spruce top, round soundhole, rosette, mahogany neck, 12-string configuration, 12/20-fret fingerboard, solid peghead, 6-per-side tuners, pickguard, available in Natural finish, body length 21", body width 16 1/2", body depth 4 1/2", current mfg.

MODEL G - jumbo style, 25 1/4" scale, Sitka spruce top, round soundhole, rosette, mahogany neck, 14/20-fret fingerboard, solid peghead, 3-per-side tuners, pickguard, available in Natural finish, body length 20 7/8", body width 17", body depth 4 3/8", current mfg.

This model is optional as a 4-string bass guitar (34" scale).

MODEL J - tight waist jumbo style, 25 1/4" scale, Sitka spruce top, round soundhole, rosette, mahogany neck, 14/20-fret fingerboard, solid peghead, 3-per-side tuners, pickguard, available in Natural finish, body length 20 5/8", body width 17", body depth 4 1/8", current mfg.

FRONTIER

Instruments previously produced in Japan during the early 1980s.

Frontier guitars are decent to good quality original designs as well as copies of American designs. The puzzling one is the signature model of Norris Fant. Guitar collectors or Fan club members who wish to enlighten us on Mr. Fant are invited to write to the *Blue Book of Acoustic Guitars,* (Source: Tony Bacon and Paul Day, *The Guru's Guitar Guide*).

FYLDE

Instruments previously built in Penrith (Cumbria), England.

Luthier Roger Bucknall began building guitars at age nine (back in the late 1950s), and continued occasionally building until he was twenty-one. While he was running a folk club, Bucknall soon had a large number of orders for his designs. A friend offered to finance Bucknall's new endeavor, and Bucknall moved to the Fylde coast of Lancashire in 1973 to begin producing guitars. Rather than set up a one-man shop, Bucknall was determined to enter into full production.

Bucknall continued to expand the business through the 1970s, and by the end of the decade had a staff of around twelve people building twenty guitars a week. Bucknall estimates that half of the production was being sold to the U.S. market, the rest in Europe.

In the later half of 1979 to 1980, Bucknall suffered through personal family problems, coupled with a fading market and struggling finances. In 1980, the company went broke, and Fylde Instruments Ltd. was closed down.

Bucknall, with the help of another close friend, continued making about 100 guitars a year under the Fylde Guitars name. He also launched a business making snooker cues at this time.

Bucknall sold the snooker business in 1992 and re-invested in Fylde Guitars. Fylde produced around 400 instruments a year. With traditional wood supplies becoming scarce, Bucknall sought a source of renewable new materials for his guitars, and was committed to not purchasing any more rosewood or ebony unless the wood came from a substantial source.

In addition to the numerous guitar models, Fylde Guitars also offered a number of models from the Mandolin family, such as the Mandola, Cittern, Portuguese Mandola, "Octavious" Bouzouki, and the Mandolin.

ACOUSTIC

The clever folks at Fylde named many of the current guitar models after characters in Shakespeare plays (which, in the long run, is more entertaining than a simple model number). The **Ariel** model (list $1,542) has a slotted headstock, and a body design somewhere between a nylon and steel-string guitar design. The Ariel features a cedar top, mahogany back and sides, and a 12/19-fret ebony neck with a 629 mm scale length. The **Goodfellow** (list $1,351) is slightly larger than the Ariel, and has a 14/20-fret rosewood fingerboard.

If you combine a single cutaway with a Hot Club-era Selmer acoustic, the results may be a **Caliban** (list $2,375). The D - shaped soundhole and deep cutaway mark this model, constructed with a cedar top, Indian rosewood back and sides, and ebony fingerboard and bridge. The **Egyptian** (list $2,338) features a spruce top, an oval soundhole, and bridge/metal tailpiece with its deep cutaway and Indian rosewood back and sides. Both models feature a 24 fret fingerboard.

The **Falstaff** and **Oberon** models share similar construction such as spruce tops, Indian rosewood back and sides, and an ebony fingerboard and bridge (and a similar list price of $2,215 each). The Falstaff has a dreadnought body appearance and a 68 mm scale, while the Oberon leans toward a grand concert style and 629 mm scale.

Fylde's **Orsino** (list $1,351) acoustic is a dreadnought style guitar with a cedar top and mahogany back and sides. The **Othello (disc.)** (list $1,393) is very similar to the Orsino, except has a narrower fingerboard and wider frets. Both models feature rosewood fingerboards and bridges.

The deep-bodied jumbo-style **Magician** (list $2,091) features a cedar top, walnut back and sides, a 5-piece laminated neck, and an ebony fingerboard and bridge. The **Alchemist** lists for $2,030.

ACOUSTIC ELECTRIC

The **Model 42** was available with either mahogany (-M) or Indian rosewood (-R) back and sides, with a spruce top, and L.R. Baggs Duet amplification system. The M version has rosewood fingerboard and bridge, while the R version has a shaded spruce top and ebony fingerboard and bridge. The scale length is 648 mm. Retail prices ranged between $2,093 up to $2,513.

ACOUSTIC BASS

Fylde has two models of acoustic bass, the **King John** (860 mm scale) and the **Sir Toby** (762 mm scale). Both basses feature mahogany back and sides, a voiced cedar top, and rosewood fingerboard and bridge. The **King John** and **Sir Toby** (both discontinued models) retailed at $1,393 (each). The Magician acoustic bass listed for $2,301.

Section G

GRD (GUITAR RESEARCH AND DESIGN)

Instruments previously built in South Strafford, Vermont between 1978 to 1982. Distributed initially by United Marketing International of Grapevine, Texas; distribution was later retained by Guitar Research and Design.

GRD (Guitar Reseach and Design) was founded in 1978 by luthier/designer Charles Fox. The Guitar Reseach and Design company grew out of the School of Guitar Research and Design Center, which was founded by Fox in South Strafford, Vermont in 1973. The GRD Center was the first guitar building school in North America. The GRD company workforce consisted of graduates from the school.

GRD first advertised in *Guitar Player* magazine in the October 1978 issue, and were distributed by United Marketing International of Grapevine, Texas. This same issue also featured pictures of their Chicago NAMM booth on page 23, while page 24 showed a picture of then-GP columnist and vintage guitar expert George Gruhn holding one of their double cutaway models. The ads in the November and December 1978 issues of *Guitar Player* announced that they were available direct to the musician and to select professional sound shops around the country. A letter to customers during this time period who had requested the company's brochures announced that GRD had broken ties with their distributor.

George Gruhn's January 1979 *Guitar Player* column featured GRD instruments. Gruhn called them "one of the most interesting guitars I saw at the entire (NAMM) show...and are capable of producing almost any type of sound. The instruments are beautifully crafted, and while modernistic in design, they were tasteful, reserved, and elegant...it is a significant instrument that demonstrates the future potential in both electrical and physical design." The last mention of GRD was in the January 1981 issue of *Guitar Player* magazine, in which Jim Nollman stated that Charles Fox was designing him a 3/4-size guitar to use in playing slide guitar in Jim's attempt to communicate with whales. And you thought that slide guitar playing only perked up the ears of dogs in the neighborhood!

GRD closed its doors in 1982, and Fox moved to San Francisco to pursue other interests. Fox became a biofeedback therapist, yoga instructor, and professional gambler as he stayed out of the guitar business. However, the lure of teaching and the world of lutherie beckoned, and Fox started the American School of Lutherie in Healdsburg, California. In 1998, Fox also returned to guitar manufacturing as he founded the CFOX guitar company (see CFOX) which is currently building high quality acoustic guitars, (Source: Vincent Motel, GRD Historian).

DESIGN FEATURES

Guitar Reseach and Design was an innovative company during the late 1970s. Some of the company's ideas include the thin body acoustic guitar, brass nuts, hexaphonic pickups, and active electronics that featured onboard compression, distortion, and wireless broadcasters. GRD electric guitars utilized fade/mix controls (instead of the usual toggle switches) to blend the pickups' outputs; and featured coil tap (coil split) and phase switches. GRD electric guitars were also available with built-in 6-band graphic equalizers that offered 18 dB of cut or boost, and parametric equalizers with selectable frequency centers and cut or boost controls (these features are usually associated with P.A. mixing boards).

GRD hardware was manufactured in-house, and the pickups used on the electric models were specially wound and potted by DiMarzio. What appears to be binding on the solid body models is actually two laminated layers of maple sandwiching a layer of ebonized maple in the center. GRD instruments all feature the highly noticeable "Omega" headstock cutaway.

ACOUSTIC

The 1978 GRD brochure featured 6 acoustic models; but also mentioned 6- and 10-string classic guitars, baroque, flamenco, and smaller sized steel stringed instruments which were available on a custom basis. All braces are fully scalloped, tapered, and floated free of the linings. The phenolic fretboard is relieved over the soundboard. Upper linings are individual tentalones, back linings are solid bent rosewood. The nut and saddle are solid brass (interchangeable saddles of bone, phenolic, and epoxy graphite were available in special order. The body/neck connection was a Spanish-style foot and shelf neck/body joint.

GRD acoustics feature a solid rosewood back and sides, peghead overlay, back linings, center web, bindings, and trim. The standard soundboard was spruce; cedar was optional. GRD necks are Honduran mahogany with the head and arm spliced instead of being band sawn from one piece. Headstocks featured 3-per-side gold plated Schaller tuners.

On-board electronics featured a transducer pickup and tone control system that required no preamp – one pickup was mounted beneath the bridge, and the second was mounted beneath the fretboard. The on-board electronics featured volume, tone, and balance controls. The output jacks were flush mounted, and the guitars had Strap Lock fittings.

The model **F** and **F 1** were full sized acoustics with a jumbo-esque (tight waist) body style, 660 mm scale, 21-fret fingerboard. The **F 1** model has a single Florentine-style cutaway. The **T** and **T 1** acoustics were full sized models with a dreadnought-style body, 630 mm scale, 21-fret fingerboard. The **T 1** model has a single Florentine-style cutaway. The shallow body **S 1** and **S 2** models have a 645 mm scale, and a 21-fret fingerboard. The **S 1** has a single Florentine-style cutaway; the **S 2** is a double (dual) cutaway body.

Prices are still relatively unknown for used GRD models because so few of them are ciruclating in the market.

GAGLIANO

Instruments previously produced in Korea. Distributed by Avnet, Inc.

Gagliano acoustic guitars have the Gagliano trademark name in gold script on the headstock, while their internal label states "Meisel Music, a subsidiary of Avnet, Inc." Research continues on the Gagliano trademark.

One model observed, a Model 2060 may or may not be indicative of the entire product line: The different components are of various levels of quality and state of technology. For example, the neck is a decent quality nato, with an adjustable truss rod. This neck is about as good a quality as you could expect on this genre of instrument; on the other hand, the bridge is made of plastic and the soundboard is plywood, with a paper-like laminate to make it look like spruce. The internal bracing is also a mish-mash of technological styles, (Source: Walter Murray, Frankenstein Fretworks).

GALLAGHER GUITARS

Instruments currently built in Wartrace, Tennessee. Distributed by J.W. Gallagher & Sons of Wartrace, Tennessee.

The Gallagher family settled in Wartrace (about 60 miles southeast of Nashville) back in the late 1820s. John William Gallagher was born in 1915, and in 1939 established a furniture making business. Don Gallagher was born in 1947, and grew up among the tools and wood in the family's woodworking shop. The furniture business converted to guitar production later in the 1960s. Gallagher and his son Don produced 24 guitars in their first year.

In 1976, Don Gallagher took over management of the business, three years before the luthier community lost J.W. Gallagher in 1979. Don Gallagher continues to build acoustic guitars in the family tradition, (Source: Tom Wheeler, American Guitars).

Gallagher guitars have been built in very limited numbers. From the opening year of 1965 to 1990, only 2,064 guitars were made. According to the Gallagher catalog, early instruments had paper labels. The serial number on these labels indicate the year and month the guitar was made. Starting in 1970, the serialization began to reflect the number of guitars that had been built. This number, along with the model number, is stamped on the neck block inside every Gallagher guitar.

ACOUSTIC

All Gallagher guitars are meticulously handcrafted, using the finest woods available at the workshop. Hardshell cases are an extra charge, at $150 for a standard hardshell case or $575 for a Calton case, which is custom made for Gallagher instruments.

Add $300 for 12-string configuration. Add $250 for Sunburst finish. Add $250 for Fishman Acoustic Matrix system. Add $400 for single cutaway body design. Add $500 for a slotted headstock. Add $100 for a modified body. Add $150 for left-handed configuration.

The first Gallagher guitar model was built back in 1965, and was designated the **G-50** in honor of J.W. Gallagher's age at the time. The G-50 features mahogany back and sides, a spruce top, and a soundhole edged in black and white wood strips. The rosewood fingerboard has pearl dot inlays, and the guitar has a bound peghead and body that is finished in highly polished lacquer. Retail list price is $2,000. The **G-45** is similar to the G-50, except it does not have the bound headstock and the body binding is in black. List price is also $2,000.

The **G-70** has a two-piece top and a body of rosewood, and retails for $2,500. The bound ebony fingerboard is inlaid with mother-of-pearl diamonds and squares, and the top and the soundhole are bound in herringbone. The **G-65** features a book matched rosewood back, and rosewood sides. Black and white wood inlays surround the top and the soundhole, while the nut and saddle are constructed of bone. This model lists at $2,300.

In 1968 both Doc and Merle Watson began playing guitars crafted by J.W. and Don. Six years later, Doc Watson requested certain particular features in a guitar that was built for him. This model was the basis for the **Doc Watson Model**. In 1975, Merle received the first cutaway version of this model. The Doc Watson model has a spruce top, mahogany back and sides, and a bridge and fingerboard of ebony. The nut and saddles are constructed of bone, and the top and soundhole have herringbone inlays. List price is $2,400. There is also a **Doc Watson Signature** which retails for $2,800.

Steve Kaufman has a signature model that has a rosewood cutaway body, Engleman spruce top, Sunburst finish, abalone inlays, body binding, and a number of other features and the guitar retails for $4,200. The **75 Special** is the most elaborate and most expensive model in the Gallagher lineup. It includes a rosewood body, Sitka spruce top, elaborate inlays and bindings with other features and it retails for $6,000.

The **G-70M** is a modified version of the G-70 model, and features a bound fingerboard, herringbone trim around the top and soundhole, a longer body design, and the neck joins at the twelfth fret. The **G-45M** is the same size as the G-70M, but features mahogany back and sides, black/white trim around the top and soundhole, and the neck joins at the twelfth fret as well. Last retail on the G-70M was $2,400, while the G-45M was $2,060.

Model **GC-70** is similar in appointments to the G-70, except in the grand concert body size. The first GC-70 was built in 1968 for country artist Grandpa Jones. Rosewood back and sides, spruce top, bound ebony fingerboard, ebony bridge, and herringbone trim comprise this model at a price of $2,500. There is a **GC-Short Scale** which has a shorter scale body and retails for $2,500 as well.

The **71 Special** was introduced in 1970, and features a rosewood back and sides, spruce top, herringbone purfling and soundhole rosette, bound ebony fingerboard, ebony bridge, abalone snowflake inlays. List price is $3,000. The very first **72 Special** was built by Don Gallagher in late 1977. The body is rosewood, with a spruce top and mahogany neck. Both the bridge and fingerboard are ebony, and the nut and saddle are crafted of bone. The 72 Special carries a list price of $3,600.

A more defined waist is featured on the **Ragtime Special**, which is an auditorium size guitar. The model has mahogany back and sides, spruce top, black-bound body and peghead, ebony fingerboard and bridge. Retail list is $2,400. The **A-70** is similar to the GC-70 model, but has a 14-fret neck and retails for $2,500. The **GA-70** features a grand auditorium sized body with similar specs to the GC-70 and retails for $2,500. The GA is available as the GA Dogwood Design for a price of $3,000.

GALLAGHER, KEVIN

See Omega Instruments.

GALLOUP, BRYAN

Instruments currently built in Big Rapids, Michigan beginning 1992.

Luthier Bryan Galloup has been a guitar repairman on vintage guitars for the past 20 years. Galloup began building his own guitars in 1992, and went full time in guitar building in 1995.

Galloup's techniques of neck resets, fretting, bridge and bridge plate replacement were featured in the Guild of American Luthier's *American Luthier* publication; Galloup is also the repair and modification columnist for The Association of Stringed Instrument Artisans' quarterly magazine.

In addition to his acoustic guitar models, Galloup also runs the Bryan Galloup's School of Guitar Building and Repair, a fully equipped wood working shop that is designed to handle the most advanced repairs, restorations, and custom ordered acoustic and electric guitars. Students during the 8 week class are outfitted with their own workbench, hand tools, and supplies and receive a hands-on education in the lutherie arts. There is also a 24 week Masters course available.

ACOUSTIC

Galloup's acoustic guitar models include the **G-1 American Classic** (list $2,650), the **GD-1 Classic Deluxe** (list $3,800), **GS-2 Hutchinson** (list $2,975), and the **GE-3 Hired Hand** (list $2,495). For further information regarding model specifications and pricing, please contact luthier Bryan Galloup directly (see Trademark Index). Currently the models have different names: **G-1** is the **Big Mitten**, the **G-2 Northern Light**, and the **G-3 Solstice**.

GARRISON GUITARS
Instruments currently produced in St. John's, Newfoundland, Canada.

Chris Griffiths started his first company in 1993 at the age of 19, which was called Griffiths Guitar Works. They sold high end instruments only and did repair work. Towards the end of the 1990s the idea of Garrison guitars was in full swing and the Garrison guitar was released at the 2000 NAMM show. What separates this guitar from others is the Griffiths Active Bracing System. This system intergrates the binding, bridge plate, neck and bracing all into one glass fibre component. Guitars can be produced at a rate of 45 seconds apiece. For more information refer to their web site (see Trademark Index).

ACOUSTIC

Garrison produces mainly dreadnoughts that are available in various configurations, which include: left-hand configuration, 12-string, cutaways, and Fishman pickups. The **G-10** has a birch top and neck and prices start at $425. The **G-20** has a solid cedar top and starts at $469. The **G-30** features a solid Sitka spruce top and the price starts at $491. The **G-40** has an Englemann top and mahogany neck and the price starts at $833. The **G-50** is the top end instrument with rosewood back and sides as well as an Englemann top and the price is listed at $1,075 and above. There are also three new models the **G-25**, introduced in 2002, and the **G-35** and **G-41**, which were introduced in 2003.

GASSER, MARK
Instruments currently built in Cottonwood, Arizona. Distributed by GuitArts of Cottonwood, Arizona.

Luthier Mark Gasser has been hand crafting guitars for over eleven years. Gasser studied techniques originated by Bozo Podunavac. Finding that each wood creates its own unique tone, Gasser likes to experiment with non-traditional woods in crafting his guitars.

Gasser's guitars are made from exotic hardwoods, such as African paduak, Alaskan spruce and cedar, and Honduran mahogany. His fretboards are rosewood and ebony. Retail list prices start at $1,695.

GAY
Instruments previously built in Edmonton (Alberta), Canada between circa early-to-mid 1950s to the mid 1970s.

Luthier Frank Gay maintained his guitar building and repair services for more than two decades in Edmonton. A formidable jazz and classical guitarist, his flattop acoustics were the most recognizable instrument – and oddly enough, his biggest endorsers were country western artists (one notable player was Webb Pierce). Gay guitars are recognized by the exaggerated checkerboard rosette inlays, six on a side headstocks, and the occasional heart-shaped soundhole, (Source: Teisco Del Rey, *Guitar Player Magazine*).

GENEVA
Instruments previously produced in the Czech Republic from 1981 to 1999. Distributed by the Geneva International Corporation of Wheeling, Illinois.

Geneva acoustic guitars were produced in the Czech Republic from 1981-1999, and carry the same European traditions of quality workmanship. Geneva guitars feature a different bridge design that changes the pitch of the string crossing the bridge's saddle, adding to the transfer of vibrations from the strings to the top via the bridge.

ACOUSTIC: PRO DREADNOUGHT STYLE SERIES

D 1 P - dreadnought style, solid cedar top, round soundhole, laminated mahogany back/sides, mahogany neck, rosewood fingerboard with white dot inlay, rosewood bridge, 3-per-side Schaller tuners, available in Natural matte finish, disc. 1999.

N/A	$500	$350

Last MSR was $739.

Gallagher G-70
Blue Book Publications, Inc.

Gallagher 71 Special
courtesy Don Gallagher

GRADING	100%	EXCELLENT	AVERAGE

D 5 P - dreadnought style, solid spruce top, round soundhole, solid rosewood back/sides, mahogany neck, ebony fingerboard with abalone inlay, ebony bridge, 3-per-side gold tuners, available in Natural High Gloss finish, disc. 1999.

	N/A	$950	$700

Last MSR was $1,439.

D 61 - dreadnought style, solid cedar top, round soundhole, laminated mahogany back/sides, mahogany neck, rosewood fingerboard with white dot inlay, rosewood bridge, 3-per-side Schaller tuners, available in Natural Matte finish, disc. 1999.

	N/A	$450	$325

Last MSR was $659.

D 62 - dreadnought style, solid spruce top, round soundhole, solid rosewood back/sides, mahogany neck, rosewood fingerboard with white dot inlay, rosewood bridge, 3-per-side Schaller tuners, available in Natural High Gloss finish, disc. 1999.

D 63 - dreadnought style, solid spruce top, round soundhole, solid rosewood back/sides, mahogany neck, ebony fingerboard with abalone inlay, ebony bridge, 3-per-side gold tuners, available in Natural High Gloss finish, disc. 1999.

	N/A	$1,000	$750

Last MSR was $1,499.

JV 61 - jumbo style, single rounded cutaway, solid cedar top, round soundhole, laminated mahogany back/sides, mahogany neck, rosewood fingerboard with white dot inlay, rosewood bridge, 3-per-side Schaller tuners, available in Natural Matte finish, disc. 1999.

	N/A	$450	$300

Last MSR was $695.

ACOUSTIC: PRO ROUNDBACK STYLE SERIES

Z 122 12-STRING - roundback body design, 12-string configuration, solid spruce top, round soundhole, ebony fingerboard with abalone inlay, ebony bridge, 6-per-side tuners, available in Natural High Gloss finish, disc. 1999.

	N/A	$750	$500

Last MSR was $999.

Z V 62 6-STRING - roundback body design, solid spruce top, round soundhole, ebony fingerboard with abalone inlay, ebony bridge, 3-per-side tuners, available in Natural High Gloss finish, disc. 1999.

	N/A	$600	$450

Last MSR was $869.

ACOUSTIC: SELECT SERIES

The **GS-10** features a spruce top, round soundhole, rosewood back/sides, bound body, rosewood fingerboard with white diamond-shaped inlays, rosewood bridge, black teardrop-shaped pickguard, 3-per-side tuners, and is available in a high gloss finish. The **GS-20** is similar to the GS-10, except features a rounded cutaway body; the **GS-21** is similar to the GS-20 and has an on-board preamp (9-volt) with EQ controls. Series was discontinued in 1999.

GIANNINI
Instruments currently built in Brazil. Distributed by Music Industries Corporation of Floral Park, New York.

Giannini acoustics are offered in a wide range of entry level to professional quality instruments. Circa 1900 Tranquillo Giannini left Italy and migrated to San Paulo, Brazil where he began manufacturing guitars. The company eventually became one of the largest manufacturers of guitars in Brazil. In the early 1970s, Giannini was distributed in the U.S. by Giannini Guitars at 75 Frost Street, Westbury (New York 11590). If that address seems somewhat familiar, it was shared by Westbury Guitars, the Merson company, and currently Korg USA (Marshall, Parker, Korg, and Vox).

ACOUSTIC

CRA-65 - dreadnought style, yellow spruce top, round soundhole, Brazilian rosewood back/sides, 19-fret rosewood fingerboard and bridge, 3-per-side tuners, available in Natural finish, length 40", body width 15 1/4", body thickness 4", mfg. circa early 1970s.

Model has not traded sufficiently to quote prices.

Last MSR was $160.

CRA-125 - dreadnought style, spruce top, round soundhole, Brazilian rosewood back/sides, 20-fret rosewood fingerboard, rosewood bridge, 3-per-side tuners, available in Natural finish, length 43", body width 15 1/4", body thickness 4", mfg. circa early 1970s.

Model has not traded sufficiently to quote prices.

Last MSR was $175.

CRA 6N CRAVIOLA - nylon strings, spruce top, round soundhole, Brazilian rosewood back/sides, 19-fret rosewood fingerboard and bridge, 3-per-side tuners, available in Natural finish, length 40", body width 15 1/4", body thickness 4", mfg. circa early 1970s.

Model has not traded sufficiently to quote prices.

Last MSR was $150.

This model was also available in a 12-string configuration. The Craviola is the "kidney bean-shaped" body Giannini model that turns up occasionally in the secondary market. This model may also have a Merson company label.

GIBSON

Current trademark manufactured by the Gibson Guitar Corp., with plants in Bozeman, MT (beginning 1989), Nashville, TN (beginning 1974), and Memphis, TN (electrics only, beginning 2001). Most acoustic instruments (excluding banjos, Dobros, and mandolins) are currently produced by Gibson Montana Acoustic Guitars located in Bozeman, MT, a division of Gibson Guitar Corp., located in Nashville, TN. Gibson Acoustic Guitars have been produced in Bozeman, MT since 1989, and the Bozeman Custom Shop is also producing many of Gibson's best quality acoustic guitars. All Gibson instruments (including OAI) are distributed by the Gibson Guitar Corporation located in Nashville, TN.

**Gibson (Wards) Archtop
courtesy Dave Hull**

Gibson acoustic instruments were previously produced in Kalamazoo, MI from 1896 to 1984. The Gibson Mandolin-Guitar Manufacturing Company, Limited (which evolved into the Gibson Guitar Corporation) produced acoustic instruments in Kalamazoo, MI from 1902 to 1984. Gibson banjos, mandolins, and Dobros are currently manufactured by Original Acoustic Instruments (OAI), located in the Opryland Mall, in Nashville, TN.

Gibson solid body and semi-hollowbody electrics are currently produced in Nashville & Memphis, TN – please refer to the *Blue Book of Electric Guitars* for both up-to-date pricing and information.

Luthier Orville H. Gibson was born in Chateaugay, New York. In 1856 he moved west to Kalamazoo, Michigan. City records from 1896-1897 indicate a business address of 114 South Burdick for O.H. Gibson, Manufacturer, Musical Instruments. By 1899-1902, the city directories indicate a change to the Second Floor of 104 East Main.

The Gibson Mandolin-Guitar Manufacturing Company, Limited was established at 2:55 p.m. on October 11, 1902. The agreement was formed by John W. Adams (pres.), Samuel H. Van Horn (treasurer), Sylvo Reams (sec. and also production mgr.), Lewis Williams (later secretary and gen. mgr.), and Leroy Hornbeck. Orville Gibson was not one of the founding partners, but had a separate contract to be a consultant and trainer. Gibson was also the first to purchase 500 shares of the new company's stock. In 1915, Gibson and the company negotiated a new agreement in which Orville was to be paid a monthly salary for the rest of his life. Orville, who had some troubles with his health back in 1911, was treated in 1916 at the psychiatric center of St. Lawrence State hospital in Ogdensburg, New York. Orville Gibson died of endocarditis on August 21, 1918.

In 1906 the company moved to 116 East Exchange Place, and the name was changed to Gibson Mandolin Guitar Company. In 1917, production facilities were opened at Parsons Street (the first of a total of five buildings at that location). Chicago Musical Instruments (CMI) acquired controlling interest in Gibson, Inc. in 1944. Maurice H. Berlin (president of CMI) became general secretary and treasurer of Gibson. From this date, the Gibson Sales Department became located in Chicago while the Kalamazoo plant concentrated on production.

In 1935, Gibson began investigating into a prototype electric pickup. Musician Alvino Rey started research with engineers at the Lyon & Healy company (See Washburn) in Chicago, and a year later the research was moved in-house to Kalamazoo. In late 1935, Gibson debuted the hexagonal pickup on a lap steel model; this same pickup was applied to an archtop guitar and offered as the ES (Electric Spanish) 150 in 1936. The ES-150 was used by jazz guitarist Charlie Christian, and this model is still known as the "Charlie Christian" model.

After the release of Leo Fender's Broadcaster (later Telecaster) model, Gibson and guitarist Les Paul collaborated in the release of the solid body Gibson Les Paul in 1952. This model was refined with the introduction of the tune-o-matic bridge/stop tailpiece combination, and P.A.F. humbuckers through the 1950s. Under the direction of then Gibson president Ted McCarty, the Gibson company attempted to throw off the tag of being "stodgy" and old fashioned when they introduced the Flying V and Explorer models in the late 1950s. In this case, they pre-judged the public's tastes by about 10 years! As guitar players' tastes changed in the late 1950s, Gibson discontinued the single cutaway Les Paul model in favor of the double cutaway SG in 1960. As the popularity of the electric blues (as championed by Eric Clapton and Michael Bloomfield) grew during the 1960s, Gibson reissued the Les Paul in 1968.

Gibson acquired Epiphone in 1957, and production of Gibson-made Epiphones began in 1959, and lasted until 1969. In 1970, production moved to Japan (or, the Epiphone name was then applied to imported instruments).

In December of 1969, E.C.L. Industries, Inc. took control of CMI. Gibson, Inc. stayed under the control of CMI until 1974, when it became a subsidiary of Norlin Industries (Norlin is named after H. Norton Stevens, President of E.C.L. and Maurice H. Berlin, President of CMI). A new factory was opened in Nashville, Tennessee during 1969.

In 1980, Norlin decided to sell Gibson. Norlin also relocated some of the sales, marketing, administration, and finance personnel from Chicago to the Nashville plant. Most Gibson production took place in Nashville after 1980, and the Kalamazoo plant was utilized mostly for custom orders. In 1983, then-Gibson president Marty Locke informed plant manager Jim Deurloo that the Kalamazoo plant would close. Final production was June 1984, and the plant closed three months later. [On a side note: Rather than give up on the 65-year-old facilities, Jim Deurloo, Marv Lamb, and J.P. Moats started the Heritage Guitar Company in April of 1985. The company is located in the original 1917 building.]

**Gibson Advanced Super Jumbo
courtesy Killer Vintage**

In January of 1986, Henry Juszkiewicz (current CEO), David Berryman (current president), and Gary Zebrowski bought Gibson for five million dollars. Since the sale in 1986, the revived Gibson USA company has been at work to return to the level of quality the company had reached earlier. Expansion of the acoustic guitar production began in Bozeman, Montana during 1989.

Gibson's Historic Collection models were introduced in 1991, and during 1993, the Custom Shop moved into a separate production facility on Massman Drive. Custom Shop instruments built at Gibson's Custom Shops (both Nashville, TN and Bozeman, MT plants) began using their own Gibson Custom Art Historic logo on the back of the headstock in 1996. The Gibson Custom, Art, and Historic division is responsible for producing Historic Collection models, commemorative guitars, custom-ordered and special edition guitars.

In the tail end of 1996, both the Dobro production facilities in California and the Montana mandolin facilities were closed down. Current Dobro production was resumed in Nashville at the OAI facility in the Opryland Mall beginning 1997, and banjo & mandolin manufacture followed shortly.

In 1998, Gibson opened up a new dealer level for specialty guitars, both acoustic and electric. The Gibson Historic Collection Award Dealer models are only available through approximately 37 Award Level dealers, and feature specific year/model designated custom instruments at an upscale price.

Gibson started the new millennium in perhaps its best shape for a long time. With the Montana plant now producing consistently high quality acoustic instruments (perhaps their best ever), and the electric models being led by the extensive offerings from the Gibson Custom, Art, and Historic Division, this legendary American guitar company seems to be in great shape for the next century of guitar manufacturing.

During 2001, Gibson opened up a new production facility in Memphis, TN, primarily manufacturing ES-335 type electric instruments and variations. At the end of 2001, Gibson Guitar Corp. purchased Baldwin, longtime manufacturer of pianos and organs.

During 2002, Gibson purchased long time guitar retailer Valley Arts Guitars, and opened up a separate retail store in downtown Nashville.

Sources include: Gibson.com, Walter Carter, *Gibson Guitars: 100 Years of an American Icon*; and Tom Wheeler, *American Guitars*.

GIBSON ACOUSTIC IDENTIFYING FEATURES: HEADSTOCK LOGO

The most consistent and easily found feature that goes across all models of Gibson production is the logo, or lack of one, found on the peghead. The very earliest instruments made are generally found with a star inside a crescent design, or a blank peghead, and labels inside the body. This lasted until approximately 1902.

From 1902 to the late 1920s, "The Gibson," inlaid in pearl and placed at a slant, is found on the peghead. In the late 1920s, this style of logo was changed to having "The Gibson" read straight across the peghead as opposed to being slanted. Peghead lettering was done in silver stencil from the mid-late 1920s, then were white silk screened until 1942, when it changed to gold. Pearl logos were also different.

Flattop acoustics production began during 1926, and these instruments generally do not have "The" on the inlay, it just has "Gibson" in script writing. By circa 1931-32, this was the established peghead logo for Gibson. Just before WWII, Gibson began making the lettering on the logo thicker and this became standard on most pre-war instruments. Right after WWII, the styling of the logo remained but it became slanted once again.

In 1947, the logo that is still in use today made its debut. This logo has a block styling with the "G" having a tail, the "i" dot is touching the "G," the "b" and "o" are open and the "n" is connected at the bottom. The logo is still slanted. By 1951, the dot on the "i" was no longer connected to the "G." In 1967, the logo styling became even more squared (pentographed) with the "b" and "o" becoming closed and the "i" dot being removed.

In 1970, Gibson replaced the black tinted piece of wood that had been used on the peghead face with a black fiber that the logo and other peghead inlay were placed into. With the change in peghead facing came a slightly smaller logo lettering. In 1972, the "i" dot reappeared on the peghead logo. In 1981, the "n" is connected at the top of the "o." There are a few models through the years that do not follow this timeline, i.e.: reissues and limited editions, but most of the production instruments can be found with the above feature changes.

GIBSON ACOUSTIC IDENTIFYING FEATURES: TUNERS

The configuration of the Kluson tuners used on Gibson instruments can be used to date an instrument. Before 1959, all Kluson tuners with plastic buttons had a single ring around the stem end of the button. In 1960, this was changed to a double ring configuration. Early 1950s tuners have no writing in the center line. Mid-late 1950s production features Kluson deluxe tuners with single line marking. By the mid 1960s, a two-line marking states "Kluson Deluxe."

GIBSON ACOUSTIC IDENTIFYING FEATURES: PEGHEAD VOLUTE

"Made in USA" stamped into wood in back of peghead beginning 1969. Another dating feature of Gibsons is the use of a peghead volute found on instruments between 1970 and 1973. Also, in 1965 Gibson switched from 17 degrees to 14 degrees on the tilt of the peghead. Before 1950, peghead thickness varied, getting narrower towards the top of the peghead. After 1950, pegheads all became one uniform thickness, from bottom to top.

GIBSON COMMON ABBREVIATIONS

C - Cutaway	J - Jumbo	SG - Solid Guitar
D - Dreadnought or Double	LE - Limited Edition	SJ - Super Jumbo
E - Electric	MOP - Mother-of-Pearl	T - Tremolo or Thinline
ES - Electric (Electro) Spanish	S - Spanish, Solid Body, Special or Super	V - Venetian or Vibrato
GS - Gut String		

GIBSON ACOUSTIC FINISH CODES

Current Gibson finish codes with abbreviations include the following:

AC - Antique Cherry Back & Sides	EB - Ebony	VCS - Vintage Cherry Sunburst
AN - Antique Natural	HC - Heritage Cherry Sunburst	VS - Vintage Sunburst
AT - Antique Walnut Back & Sides	NAT - Natural	

GIBSON PRODUCTION MODELS CODES & SHIPMENT TOTALS

For ease in identifying current Gibson production guitar models in this section, the Gibson Family Code/SKU may follow the model's name in parenthesis (in some cases, only the alphabetical prefix is listed, as the individual finishes and/or colors will result in the rest of the code). This also is true when brackets[] are encountered within a family code.

For anyone who is interested in individual Gibson model production totals from 1937-1979 (including guitars, basses, artist models, custom models, mandolins, banjos, ukuleles, steel guitars, effects, and amps), it is recommended to look at *Gibson Shipment Totals 1937-1979* by Larry Meiners. Please refer to www.bluebookinc.com to order.

Gibson acoustic archtop models that include "floating" pickups or built-in acoustic/electric pickups are listed in the acoustic electric category at the end of the Gibson section.

ACOUSTIC: GENERAL INFORMATION

For organizational consideration, the category names and variations have been listed in alphabetical sequence. In the numbered series, models will start with the lowest number, and end with the highest. Named models will appear at the end of the categories whenever possible. The following categories appear in this order: B Series, Blue Ridge/Blues King Series, C Models, Centennial Series, CL Series, Dove Series, Everly Brothers Series, Folksinger/Gospel Series, Hall of Fame Models, Hummingbird Series, Jumbo/J and SJ Models, L Series, LG Series, Mark Series, Misc., Model O & U Series, Songbird Series, Songwriter Series, Super 300/Super 400 Series, Working Man & Working Musician Series. The current/recent Gibson Historic Collection models can be found after these categories.

While the thought of a Sunburst finished Les Paul brings many players (and collectors) a case of the warm fuzzies, Gibson acoustic guitar collectors are more partial to a Natural finish acoustic over a similar model finished in Sunburst. As a result, there is a premium for Natural finished Gibson acoustics.

Add 15%-30% for Natural finish, depending on the model (including rarity factor), configuration, and original condition. Add approx. 20%-25% for first year of manufacture on pre-WWII Mfg.

ACOUSTIC: B SERIES

Gibson B-25
courtesy Dale Hanson

B-15 - small body, spruce top, round soundhole, tortoise pickguard, 1-stripe rosette, bound top, mahogany back/sides/neck, 14/20-fret rosewood fingerboard with pearl dot inlay, rosewood bridge with white pins, 3-per-side tuners with plastic buttons, available in Natural finish, over 12,000 mfg. 1967-1971.

	N/A	$300	$175

B-20 - mahogany back/sides, 14 1/2 in. wide, black binding, standard peghead, approx. 500 mfg. 1971-72.

	N/A	$350	$200

B-25 - small body, spruce top, round soundhole, tortoise pickguard, 3-stripe bound body/rosette, mahogany back, laminated mahogany sides, mahogany neck, 14/20-fret rosewood fingerboard with pearl dot inlay, upper belly on laminated rosewood bridge with adjustable saddle and white pins, blackface peghead with decal logo, 3-per-side tuners with plastic buttons, available in Cherry Sunburst and Natural finishes, mfg. 1961-1977.

1961-1969	N/A	$775	$350
1970-1977	N/A	$450	$275

In 1965, a plastic special bridge replaced the laminated rosewood bridge. In 1968, wood bridge replaced previous part/design.

B-25 3/4 - similar to B-25, except is 3/4 size body, limited mfg. 1961-68.

	N/A	$850	$400

In 1966, Natural finish was discontinued.

B-25-12 - spruce top, round soundhole, tortoise pickguard, bound body/rosette, mahogany back/sides/neck, 14/20-fret rosewood fingerboard with pearl dot inlay, reverse belly rosewood bridge with white pins, blackface peghead with decal logo, 6-per-side tuners with plastic buttons, available in Cherry Sunburst and Natural finishes, mfg. 1962-1977.

1962-1969	N/A	$600	$400
1970-1977	N/A	$400	$250

In 1963, strings through bridge replaced original part/design, no bridge pins. In 1965, redesigned reverse bridge replaced previous part/design, trapeze tailpiece added. In 1970, standard bridge with white pins replaced previous part/design, no trapeze tailpiece, Cherry Sunburst finish was discontinued.

Gibson B-25-12
courtesy Jason Crisp

B-45-12 - slope shouldered large body, spruce top, round soundhole, tortoise pickguard, 2-stripe bound body/rosette, mahogany back/sides/neck, 14/20-fret rosewood fingerboard with pearl dot inlay, rosewood bridge with adjustable saddle, trapeze tailpiece, blackface peghead with pearl split diamond inlay/logo decal, 6-per-side nickel tuners with plastic buttons, available in Tobacco Sunburst, Natural and Cherry Sunburst finish, mfg. 1961-1979.

	100%	EXCELLENT	AVERAGE
1961-1969	N/A	$1,000	$600
1970-1979	N/A	$600	$350

In 1962, reverse belly bridge with pins, adjustable saddle replaced original part/design. In 1964, string through reverse belly bridge replaced previous part/design, Natural finish (Model B-45-12 N) became an option. In 1965, rectangular bridge/trapeze tailpiece replaced previous part/design. In 1970, redesigned pickguard, 12/20-fret fingerboard, standard bridge with pins, Tobacco Sunburst finish became an option.

ACOUSTIC: BLUE RIDGE/BLUES KING SERIES

BLUE RIDGE - slope shouldered body style, solid spruce top, round soundhole, black pickguard, 3-stripe bound body/rosette, laminated rosewood back/sides, mahogany neck, 14/20-fret rosewood fingerboard with pearl dot inlay, reverse belly rosewood bridge with black white dot pins, blackface peghead with screened logo, 3-per-side chrome tuners, available in Natural finish, approx. 5,000 mfg. 1968-1975.

	N/A	$600	$300

In 1969, standard bridge replaced original part/design. In 1973, low impedance pickup became an option – only one was shipped. Less than 20 left-hand instruments were mfg. 1971-75.

Blue Ridge 12 - similar to Blue Ridge, except has 12-strings, 6-per-side tuners, approx. 370 mfg. 1970-78.

	N/A	$500	$275

BLUES KING L-00 - parlor style, spruce top, round soundhole, tortoise pickguard, 3-stripe bound body/rosette, mahogany back/sides/neck, 14/20-fret rosewood fingerboard with pearl dot inlay, straight rosewood bridge with white pins, blackface peghead with pearl logo inlay, 3-per-side nickel tuners, available in Ebony (new 2003) Antique Ebony (disc.), Natural top/Antique Walnut back/sides (disc.), Antique Natural (new 2003), or Vintage Sunburst finishes, mfg. 1994-96, reintroduced 2003.

MSR	$1,944	$1,400	$925	$600

Add $194 for left-hand model.

Blues King Special - similar to Blues King L-00, except has Indian rosewood back/sides, bound ebony fingerboard with pearl block inlay, ebony belly bridge with white pins, bound blackface peghead with pearl vase/logo inlay, transducer pickup/preamp system, available in Antique Natural or Vintage Sunburst finishes, mfg. 1994-96.

	N/A	$1,625	$900

Last MSR was $2,500.

ACOUSTIC: C SERIES

The following models represent Classical instruments, and all models have dual slotted headstock. 14 1/4 in. wide by 19 in. long, by 4 1/2 in. deep, 25 1/2 in. scale.

C-L - student model, thin shouldered dreadnought shape, transducer pickup, abalone rosette, two-point tortoise shell celluloid pickguard, mahogany back, non-gloss finish, approx. 3,750 1969-1971.

	N/A	$400	$250

C-0 - spruce top, round soundhole, bound body, rosette decal, mahogany back/sides/neck, 12/19-fret rosewood fingerboard, rosewood wraparound bridge, slotted peghead with 3-per-side chrome tuners and plastic buttons, available in Natural finish, over 15,000 mfg. 1962-1971.

	N/A	$450	$300

C-1 - spruce top, round soundhole, bound body, 2-stripe rosette, mahogany back/sides/neck, 12/19-fret rosewood fingerboard, rosewood wraparound bridge, 3-per-side nickel tuners with plastic buttons, available in Natural finish, over 14,000 mfg. 1957-1971.

	N/A	$500	$350

In 1966, wooden inlay rosette, chrome tuners replaced original part/design.

C-1 E - similar to C-1, except has ceramic bridge pickup, approx. 675 mfg. 1960-68.

	N/A	$400	$200

C-1 S - similar to C-1, except has petite student size body, approx. 865 mfg. 1961-67.

	N/A	$250	$150

C-1 D Laredo - similar to C-1, except has rounded peghead, mfg. 1963-1970.

	N/A	$350	$200

C-2 - spruce top, round soundhole, bound body, 2-stripe rosette, maple back/side, mahogany neck, 12/19-fret rosewood fingerboard, rosewood wraparound bridge with pearl block inlay, 3-per-side nickel tuners with plastic buttons, available in Natural Top/Mahogany back/side finish, approx. 960 mfg. 1960-1970.

	N/A	$500	$250

In 1966, redesigned rosette, peghead replaced original part/design.

C-4 - similar to C-2, except has gold tuners, available in Natural top/rosewood back/sides finish, approx. 150 mfg. 1962-68.

	N/A	$500	$250

GRADING	100%	EXCELLENT	AVERAGE

C-6 RICHARD PICK CUSTOM - classic style, spruce top, round soundhole, tortoise bound body, wooden inlay rosette, Brazilian rosewood back/sides, mahogany neck, 12/19-fret ebony fingerboard, wraparound rosewood bridge, rosewood veneered peghead, 3-per-side gold tuners, available in Natural finish, approx. 450 mfg. 1958-1970.

| | N/A | $850 | $500 |

In 1966, pearl block bridge inlay was added.

C-8 GRAND CLASSIC - similar to C-6, except has different rosette pattern, narrow peghead, approx. 110 mfg. 1962-69.

| | N/A | $650 | $300 |

C-100 - mahogany back, ebony fingerboard, standard width slotted peghead, labeled "Master Style," satin non-gloss finish, approx. 430 mfg. 1970-71.

| | N/A | $500 | $350 |

C-200 - mahogany back and sides, similar to C-100 model, except has gloss finish, approx. 200 mfg. 1971-72.

| | N/A | $600 | $425 |

C-300 - mahogany back and sides, wood binding, wider rosette, rosewood fingerboard, narrow peghead with dip in center of top, approx. 65 mfg. 1971-72.

| | N/A | $850 | $625 |

C-400 GRAND - similar to C-500, except has chrome plated hardware, approx. 30 mfg. 1971-72.

| | N/A | $950 | $675 |

C-500 - rosewood back and sides, decorative Spanish purfling, abalone and ivory bridge inlays, laminated mahogany/ebony neck, ebony fingerboard, narrow peghead with dip in center of top, gold plated hardware, mfg. 1969-1970.

| | N/A | $1,250 | $850 |

C-800 - rosewood back and sides, mfg. 1969-1970.

| | N/A | $1,375 | $950 |

C-1000 - rosewood back and sides, mfg. 1969-1970.

| | N/A | $1,450 | $1,000 |

Gibson Dove
courtesy Gibson

FLAMENCO 2 - classical styling, spruce top, round soundhole, 2 white pickguards, tortoise bound body, wooden inlay rosette, cypress back/side, mahogany neck, 12/19-fret rosewood fingerboard, rosewood wraparound bridge with pearl block inlay, rosewood veneered peghead with logo decal, 3-per-side nickel tuners with plastic buttons, available in Natural Top/Mahogany back/side finish, approx. 300 mfg. 1963-68.

| | N/A | $475 | $275 |

ACOUSTIC: CENTENNIAL SERIES

During 1994, Gibson began offering the acoustic Centennial series models to celebrate Gibson's 100 year anniversary (1894 to 1994). There were 12 models in the program – and were released at the rate of one new model per month. No more than 101 instruments of each model were produced. Gibson's plan was to have 100 dealers that year, with each one committed to a package of 12 guitars. Those dealers received a custom-made oak & glass humidfied display cabinet at no charge to display each new model.

Models included the 1929 L-2 (Jan. 1994), 1933 Century (Feb. 1994), 1934 Gibson Jumbo (Mar. 1994), 1934 Roy Smeck Radio Grande (April 1994), 1938 Super Jumbo 200 (May 1994), 1939 Super Jumbo 100 (June 1994), 1940 Jumbo 55 (July 1994), 1948 SJ-200N Aug. 1994), 1950 CF-100E (Sept. 1994), 1951 J-185 (Oct. 1994), 1963 Hummingbird (Nov. 1994), and the J-200 Rose (Dec. 1994). More information, including original MSRs and current values, is being researched, and will be updated in future editions.

ACOUSTIC: CF SERIES

CF-100 - single sharp cutaway small body, spruce top, round soundhole, tortoise pickguard, bound body, 1-stripe rosette, mahogany back/sides/neck, 20-fret bound rosewood fingerboard with pearl trapezoid inlay, rosewood reverse bridge with pearl dot inlay, white bridge pins, blackface peghead with logo decal, 3-per-side nickel tuners, available in Golden Sunburst finish, approx. 1,675 mfg. 1950-59.

| | N/A | $2,450 | $1,650 |

In 1952, pearl crown/logo inlay replaced original part/design. In 1957, redesigned pickguard replaced original part/design.

CF-100 E - similar to CF-100, except has one single coil pickup, volume/tone control, approx. 1,250 mfg. 1951-59.

| | N/A | $2,750 | $1,850 |

Gibson Dove Artist
courtesy Gibson

GRADING	100%	EXCELLENT	AVERAGE

ACOUSTIC: CL SERIES

The Custom Acoustic Line Series was manufactured 1997-98. Most models featured the Gibson Advanced Bracing pattern and factory-installed transducer.

CL-20 STANDARD PLUS (CL20) - solid spruce top, round soundhole, black body binding, solid mahogany back/sides, 14/20-fret rosewood fingerboard with abalone snowflake inlay, moustache-style rosewood bridge with white bridgepins, 3-per-side gold tuners, batwing-shaped tortoise pickguard, available in Antique Natural finish, mfg. 1997-98.

	N/A	$1,000	$650

Last MSR was $1,499.

This model did not feature the installed transducer.

CL-30 DELUXE (CL30) - solid spruce top, round soundhole, multiple-ply body binding, solid African bubinga back/sides, 14/20-fret rosewood fingerboard with abalone floret inlay, rosewood headstock veneer, mother-of-pearl headstock logo/abalone floret inlay, moustache-style rosewood bridge with white bridgepins, 3-per-side gold tuners, batwing-shaped tortoise pickguard, available in Antique Natural gloss lacquer finish, mfg. 1997-98.

	N/A	$1,250	$800

Last MSR was $1,849.

CL-35 Deluxe Cutaway (CL35) - similar to the CL-30, except features a single Venetian cutaway body, available in Antique Natural gloss lacquer finish, mfg. 1997-98.

	N/A	$1,325	$850

Last MSR was $1,949.

CL-40 ARTIST (CL40) - Sitka spruce top, round soundhole, abalone rosette, multiple-ply body binding, solid rosewood back/sides, 14/20-fret ebony fingerboard with abalone angel wing inlay, mother-of-pearl headstock logo/abalone angel wing inlay, moustache-style ebony bridge with abalone dot bridgepins, 3-per-side gold tuners, batwing-shaped tortoise pickguard, available in Antique Natural Gloss Lacquer finish, mfg. 1997-98.

	N/A	$1,700	$1,050

Last MSR was $2,649.

CL-45 Artist Cutaway (CL45) - similar to the CL-40, except features a single Venetian cutaway body, available in Antique Natural Gloss Lacquer finish, mfg. 1997-98.

	N/A	$1,775	$1,100

Last MSR was $2,749.

CL-50 SUPREME (CL50) - solid Sitka spruce top, round soundhole, abalone rosette, abalone body binding, solid rosewood back/sides, 14/20-fret ebony fingerboard with abalone autumn leaf inlay, bound headstock, mother-of-pearl headstock logo/abalone autumn leaf inlay, moustache-style ebony bridge with abalone dot bridgepins, 3-per-side gold tuners, batwing-shaped tortoise pickguard, available in Antique Natural Gloss Lacquer finish, mfg. 1997-98.

	N/A	$2,850	$1,950

Last MSR was $4,999.

This model was available with a tree of life fingerboard inlay (with cost upcharge).

ACOUSTIC: DOVE SERIES

DOVE - slope shouldered body, spruce top, round soundhole, tortoise pickguard with dove inlay, 3-stripe bound body/rosette, figured maple back/sides, 14/20-fret bound rosewood fingerboard with pearl parallelogram inlay, enlarged rosewood bridge with black pearl dot pins, pearl dove inlay on bridge wings, blackface peghead with pearl plant/logo inlay, 3-per-side gold tuners with pearl buttons, available in Natural or Antique Cherry finish, mfg. 1962-1996.

1962-1968	N/A	$3,000	$2,000
1969-1989	N/A	$1,200	$750
1990-1996	N/A	$1,595	$800

Last MSR was $2,450.

In 1969, adjustable bridge replaced original part/design. In 1970, non-adjustable bridge replaced previous part/design. In 1975, ebony fingerboard replaced original part/design. In 1996, the '60s Dove model superseded the original Dove model (see listing below).

DOVE REISSUE - dreadnought body, solid Sitka spruce top, round soundhole, 3-ply bound body/rosette, flamed maple back/sides, maple neck, 14/20-fret bound rosewood fingerboard with pearl parallelogram inlay, rosewood dove-wing bridge with mother-of-pearl inlay, black white dot bridgepins, bound blackface peghead with abalone crown/logo inlay, 3-per-side gold tuners, tortoise pickguard with engraved dove inlay, available in Antique Cherry (Natural top and Cherry finish back/sides) Lacquer finish, current mfg.

MSR	$3,899	$2,550	$1,950	$1,300

DOVE ARTIST MODEL - solid Sitka spruce top, Indian rosewood back/sides, mahogany neck, ebony fingerboard/bridge, mother-of-pearl wing bridge and fretboard inlays, includes active tranducer pickup, available in Antique Natural finish, mfg. 1999-current.

MSR	$3,119	$2,200	$1,725	$1,050

Add $208 for cutaway body (Dove Artist Cutaway EC.)

GRADING	100%	EXCELLENT	AVERAGE

ELVIS DOVE (ARTIST MODEL) - features square shouldered body, solid spruce top, maple back/sides, rosewood fingerboard and bridge, mahogany neck, Elvis Presley signature engraved on truss rod cover, distinctive black pickguard, available in Black Lacquer finish, mfg. 2001-current.

MSR	$2,999	$2,125	$1,450	$975

This model is available in left-hand at no extra charge.

DOVE IN FLIGHT (ACDFACGH1) - dove dreadnought style, hand select solid spruce top, round soundhole, bound body, flamed maple back/sides, 3-piece maple neck, 14/20-fret bound ebony fingerboard with pearl parallelogram inlay, ebony dove-tail bridge with dove inlay, white bridgepins, blackface peghead with mother-of-pearl "3 Doves in Flight"/logo inlay, Custom Shop seal on back of headstock, 3-per-side gold tuners, tortoise pickguard with engraved dove inlay, available in Antique Cherry (Natural top and Cherry back and sides) Lacquer finish, mfg. 1997-98.

		$3,575	$2,750	$1,750

Last MSR was $5,499.

NEW DOVES IN FLIGHT CUSTOM - customer selected back/side wood, features 28 mother-of-pearl doves inlaid in fingerboard, pickguard, and bridge, ebony neck and fingerboard, abalone top trim and rosette, available in Antique Cherry finish, mfg. by MT Custom Shop beginning 1999.

MSR	$6,270	$4,375	$3,350	$2,050

ACOUSTIC: EVERLY BROTHERS SERIES

EVERLY BROTHERS - spruce top, round soundhole, 2 tortoise pickguards, 2-stripe bound body/rosette, maple back/sides, 1 piece mahogany neck, 14/20-fret rosewood fingerboard with pearl star inlay, reverse belly adjustable bridge with pearl dot inlay, blackface peghead with pearl star/logo inlay, 3-per-side gold tuners, available in Black, Cherry Sunburst, Natural top/Red back/sides, or Natural top/Walnut back/sides (rare, approx. 45 mfg. 1963 only) finishes, approx. 440 mfg. 1962-1971.

1962-1968	N/A	$7,000	$5,000
1969-1971	N/A	$2,500	$2,000

1963 Gibson Everly Bros courtesy Rod and Hank's Vintage Guitars

This model also known as Model J-180. In 1968, black pickguards, Natural Top/Walnut Back/Sides finish replaced original part/design.

The Everly J-180 (AC18) - jumbo style, spruce top, round soundhole, 2 black pickguards, multistripe bound body/rosette, figured maple back/sides/neck, 14/20-fret bound rosewood fingerboard with pearl star inlay, rosewood mustache bridge with pearl star inlay/white pins, multibound blackface peghead with pearl star/logo inlay, 3-per-side nickel tuners, available in Antique Ebony or Heritage Cherry Sunburst finishes, mfg. 1994-97.

	N/A	$1,300	$700

Last MSR was $2,000.

Everly Cutaway - similar to The Everly, except has single sharp cutaway, tortoise pickguards, gold tuners, transducer pickups/preamp system, available in Antique Ebony or Heritage Cherry Sunburst finishes, mfg. 1994-97.

	N/A	$1,495	$850

Last MSR was $2,300.

ACOUSTIC: FOLKSINGER & GOSPEL SERIES

F-25 (FOLKSINGER) - small body, spruce top, round soundhole, 2 white pickguards, 2-stripe bound body/rosette, mahogany back/sides/neck, 12/18-fret rosewood fingerboard with pearl dot inlay, rosewood reverse belly bridge with white pins/2 pearl dot inlay, blackface peghead with screened logo, 3-per-side nickel tuners with plastic buttons, available in Natural finish, approx. 3,350 mfg. 1963-1970.

	N/A	$600	$400

In 1969, redesigned body/peghead, standard bridge replaced original part/design, white pickguards were discontinued.

FJ-N (FOLKSINGER JUMBO) - jumbo body, spruce top, round soundhole, 2 white pickguards, 3-stripe bound body/rosette, mahogany back/sides/neck, 12/18-fret bound rosewood fingerboard with pearl trapezoid inlay, rosewood reverse bridge with white pins/2 pearl dot inlay, blackface peghead with pearl crown/logo inlay, 3-per-side nickel tuners with plastic buttons, available in Natural finish, approx. 650 mfg. 1963-68.

	N/A	$1,000	$700

Gibson Everly Bros courtesy FLy By Night

GRADING	100%	EXCELLENT	AVERAGE

GOSPEL - dreadnought body, spruce top, round soundhole, tortoise pickguard, 3-stripe bound body/rosette, laminated maple back/sides, maple neck, 14/20-fret ebony fingerboard with pearl dot inlay, ebony bridge with black pearl dot pins, blackface peghead with dove/logo decals, 3-per-side chrome tuners, available in Walnut (approx. 270 mfg.) or Natural (most common) finish, mfg. 1973-1980.

	N/A	$800	$500

GOSPEL - dreadnought style, spruce top, round soundhole, tortoise pickguard, multistripe bound body/rosette, mahogany back/sides/neck, 14/20-fret rosewood fingerboard with pearl dot inlay, rosewood bridge with white pins, blackface peghead with screened vase/logo, 3-per-side nickel tuners with pearloid buttons, available in Antique Natural or Natural top/Antique Walnut back/sides finishes, mfg. 1994-96.

	N/A	$695	$450

Last MSR was $1,050.

Gospel AV - similar to Gospel, except has transducer pickup/preamp system. Available in Antique Natural, Natural top/Antique Walnut back/sides or Vintage Sunburst finishes, mfg. 1994-96.

	N/A	$875	$500

Last MSR was $1,350.

ACOUSTIC: HALL OF FAME MODELS

Hall of Fame models celebrate a famous artist's association with a specific acoustic guitar. All Hall of Fame models are numbered, limited editions.

BUDDY HOLLY MODEL (ACBH) - J-45 style, solid Sitka spruce top, round soundhole, bound body, mahogany back/sides, 14/20-fret bound rosewood fingerboard with pearl dot inlay, rosewood bridge, black bridgepins, blackface peghead with abalone banner/logo inlay, 3-per-side nickel tuners, teardrop-shaped black pickguard, available in Vintage Sunburst lacquer finish, mfg. 1997-98.

	N/A	$2,850	$2,000

Last MSR was $4,999.

This model has a certificate of authenticity signed by Maria Elena Holly (Buddy Holly's widow).

ELVIS KING OF ROCK J-200 MODEL (ACEP) - J-200 style, solid Sitka spruce top, round soundhole, bound body, maple back/sides, 14/20-fret bound ebony fingerboard with 10 mother-of-pearl crown inlays, custom ebony bridge, white bridgepins, bound blackface peghead with mother-of-pearl crown/logo inlay, 3-per-side gold tuners, bound black pickguard with mother-of-pearl crown inlay, available in Ebony Lacquer finish, mfg. 1997-98, reintroduced 2002.

$3,000	$2,350	$1,850

Last MSR was $4,000.

This limited edition model was scheduled for 250 instruments. All models certified and endorsed by Graceland.

Elvis Presley Signature Model (Mfg. 1997-98, ACEP) - similar to the Elvis King of Rock model, except features a premium Sitka spruce top, flamed maple back/sides, Elvis Presley fingerboard inlay with two stars, custom engraved "Elvis" pickguard, bound blackface peghead with mother-of-pearl flowerpot/logo inlay, ebony moustache bridge with pearl inlay, available in Antique Natural Lacquer finish, mfg. 1997-98.

	N/A	$4,250	$3,000

Last MSR was $7,999.

The Elvis Presley Signature model was based on the custom J-200 used by Elvis during his 1969 concert at the International Hotel in Las Vegas. Built in cooperation with Graceland, this limited edition model is scheduled for 250 instruments. Models have a signed certificate of authenticity.

Elvis Presley Signature J-200 Model (New 2002, ACEP) - similar to earlier model, except has Elvis Presley name inlayed into truss rod cover, available in Antique Natural Lacquer finish, mfg. 2002 only.

$3,750	$2,650	$1,975

Last MSR was $5,000.

SJ HANK WILLIAMS JR. MODEL (ACJS) - super Jumbo (SJ) style, solid Sitka spruce top, round soundhole, multiple-ply bound body/rosette, mahogany back/sides, 14/20 bound rosewood fingerboard with pearl parallelogram inlay, rosewood bridge, black bridgepins, blackface peghead with pearl logo inlay, 3-per-side nickel Kluson-style tuners, teardrop-shaped black pickguard, available in Vintage Sunburst Lacquer finish, mfg. 1997-98.

	N/A	$2,850	$2,000

Last MSR was $4,999.

ACOUSTIC: HAWAIIAN, PLECTRUM, & TENOR GUITARS

HG (HAWAIIAN) - approx. 15 mfg. 1953 only.

	N/A	$5,000	$3,250

HG-0 (HAWAIIAN) - approx. 165 mfg. 1937-circa 1941.

	N/A	$3,500	$2,350

HG-00 (HAWAIIAN) - L-00 style body, 14 3/4 in. wide by 19 1/4 in. long, mahogany back/sides, bound top, high bone nut, 12/19-fret fingerboard, Natural finish, approx. 625 mfg. 1932-circa 1946.

	N/A	$2,750	$1,850

GRADING	100%	EXCELLENT	AVERAGE

HG-CENTURY (HAWAIIAN, CENTURY OF PROGRESS) - 14 3/4 in. long, approx. 30 mfg. 1937-38.

| | N/A | $2,750 | $1,850 |

HG-20 (HAWAIIAN) - dreadnought style body with 4 f-holes plus round soundhole, maple back/sides, limited mfg. 1929-1933.

| | N/A | $2,750 | $1,850 |

HG-22 (HAWAIIAN) - similar to HG-20, 14 in. wide body, very limited mfg. 1929-1932.

| | N/A | $3,000 | $2,000 |

HG-24 (HAWAIIAN) - dreadnought style body, Brazilian rosewood back/sides, with 4 f-holes plus round soundhole, limited mfg. 1929-1932.

| | N/A | $5,500 | $3,350 |

PLECTRUM MODELS - 4-string, spruce top, mahogany back/sides/neck, 14 3/4 in. by 19 1/4 in., 27 in. scale, 22-fret fingerboard, Sunburst finish. Gibson mfg. less than 10 of these instruments between 1937-1955. The 2 models were the PG-00 and the PG-1 (more common).
   Extreme rarity factor precludes accurate pricing on this model.

TG-0 TENOR - 4-string, most common Gibson tenor guitar, L-0 body style 1927-1933, LG-0 body style 1960-1974, mahogany body, light amber finish during L-0 production, Natural Mahogany finish 1960-1974, early mfg. 1927-1933, and over 2,500 mfg. 1960-1974.

| 1927-1933 MFG. | N/A | $1,325 | $775 |
| 1960-1974 MFG. | N/A | $750 | $450 |

TG-00 TENOR - 4-string, based on L-00 body style, 23 in. scale, approx. 250 mfg. 1937-circa 1941.

| | N/A | $1,100 | $600 |

TG-1 TENOR - 4-string, based on L-1 body style, mahogany back/sides, bound body, very rare, approx. 5 mfg. 1927-1937.
   Extreme rarity factor precludes accurate pricing on this model.

TG-2 TENOR - 4-string, ultra rare, only 2 mfg. 1939 - 1940.
   Extreme rarity factor precludes accurate pricing on this model.

TG-25 TENOR - 4-string, B-25 body style, mahogany back/sides, Sunburst or Natural finish, approx. 890 mfg. 1962-1973.

| | N/A | $850 | $500 |

TG-50 TENOR - 4-string, archtop tenor configuration based on the L-50, mahogany back/sides, available in Sunburst or Natural finish, approx. 50 mfg. 1948-1963.

| | N/A | $850 | $500 |

**Gibson H-20
courtesy Fuller's**

ACOUSTIC: HUMMINGBIRD SERIES

HUMMINGBIRD - dreadnought style, spruce top, round soundhole, tortoise pickguard with engraved floral/hummingbird pattern, 3-stripe bound body/rosette, mahogany back/sides/neck, 14/20-fret bound rosewood fingerboard with pearl parallelogram inlay, rosewood bridge with black pearl dot pins, blackface peghead with pearl plant/logo inlay, 3-per-side nickel tuners with pearl buttons, available in Vintage Cherry Sunburst (most common) or Natural finish, mfg. 1960-1996.

1960-1965	N/A	$3,500	$2,000
1965-1969	N/A	$2,500	$1,500
1970-1989	N/A	$1,100	$600
1990-1996	N/A	$1,250	$695

Last MSR was $2,299.

Between 1962-1963, some models were produced with maple back/sides. In 1966, adjustable saddle replaced original part/design. In 1970, non-adjustable saddle replaced previous part/design. In 1973, block fingerboard inlay replaced original part/design. In 1984, parallelogram fingerboard inlay replaced previous part/design. In 1996, the Early '60s Hummingbird model superseded the original Hummingbird model (see listing below).

HUMMINGBIRD REISSUE - dreadnought style, solid Sitka spruce top, round soundhole, bound body, mahogany back/sides, 24 3/4" scale, 14/20-fret bound rosewood fingerboard with mother-of-pearl parallelogram inlay, rosewood bridge, black bridgepins, blackface peghead with abalone crown/logo inlay, 3-per-side nickel tuners, tortoise shell pickguard with floral/hummingbird design, available in Heritage Cherry Sunburst Lacquer finish, current mfg.

| MSR | $3,199 | $2,250 | $1,575 | $1,125 |

Add $320 for left-hand model.

**Gibson Hummingbird
courtesy Gibson**

HUMMINGBIRD CUSTOM - custom shop variation featuring hummingbird inlays on the headstock, pickguard, and bridge, beginning 2003, hummingbird inlays are also on ebony fingerboard, customer selected back/side wood, including koa (standard beginning 2003), mahogany neck, abalone top trim, engraved gold tuners, available in Antique Natural (new 2003), Heritage Cherry, or Sunburst finish, mfg. by the MT Custom Shop beginning 1999.

MSR	$6,054	$4,250	$3,100	$2,200

HUMMINGBIRD SHERYL CROW ARTIST MODEL - solid Sitka spruce top, replica of a 1962 Country Western Model with antique lacquer finish and dark cherry stained sides, mahogany back/sides/neck, hummingbird pickguard w/o artwork, Sheryl Crow signed label, limited edition beginning 2000.

MSR	$3,134	$2,200	$1,550	$975

ACOUSTIC: JUMBO, J, & SJ MODELS

JUMBO - round soundhole, stripe bound body/rosette, mahogany back/sides/neck, 14/19-fret rosewood fingerboard with pearl dot inlay, rectangular rosewood bridge with white pins, blackface peghead with pearl logo inlay, 3-per-side nickel tuners, tortoise pickguard, available in Sunburst finish, mfg. 1934-36.

	N/A	$18,000	$12,000

In 1935, fingerboard binding was added.

ADVANCED JUMBO (MFG. 1936-1940) - similar to jumbo, 16 in. wide, 20 1/4 in. long, and 4 1/2 in. deep, rosewood back/sides, pearl diamond/arrow fingerboard inlay, white black dot bridge pins, pearl diamond/arrow peghead inlay, available in Sunburst finish, approx. 300 mfg. 1936-1940.

	N/A	$38,000	$25,000

ADVANCED JUMBO REISSUE (HLAJ - CURRENT, ACAJ-DISC.) - slope shouldered body, solid Sitka spruce top, round soundhole, bound body, Indian rosewood back/sides, 14/20-fret bound rosewood fingerboard with mother-of-pearl arrow inlay, rosewood bridge, white bridgepins, blackface peghead with abalone crown/logo inlay, 3-per-side nickel tuners, "flame" colored pickguard, available in Vintage Sunburst or Antique Walnut (new 2002) Lacquer finish, disc. 1998, reintroduced 2002.

MSR	$3,199	$2,275	$1,600	$1,150

ADVANCED JUMBO CUSTOM REISSUE - slope shouldered body, solid red spruce top, round soundhole, bound body, Brazilian rosewood back/sides, 14/20-fret bound rosewood fingerboard, 3-per-side nickel Waverly tuners. available in Vintage Sunburst finish, mfg. 2001-current.

MSR	$8,599	$5,500	$4,600	$2,950

JUMBO DELUXE - round shouldered dreadnought, 16 in. wide, mahogany back/sides, moustache shaped bridge with cutouts at bridge ends, height adj. saddle bearings, four semi-rectangular pearl inlays and two pearl dots on bridge, single bound top/back, unbound fingerboard, dot inlays, pearl logo, Sunburst finish, less than 5 mfg. 1938 only.

Extreme rarity precludes accurate pricing on this model.

ORIGINAL JUMBO - round shouldered body, solid Sitka (standard) or red (optional) spruce top, patterned after the original round shoulder model released in 1934, mahogany back/sides, Madagascar rosewood fingerboard, tapered headstock, 19 or 20 fret, 24 3/4 in. scale, 1930s Sunburst finish, Custom Historic Collection, new late 2003.

MSR	$3,027	$1,995	$1,475	$1,000

J-10 - Gibson shipping records indicate approx. 30 mfg. 1971-73.

Extreme rarity factor precludes accurate price evaluation on this model.

J-25 - slope shouldered body, laminated spruce top, round soundhole, tortoise pickguard, bound body/rosette, synthetic back/sides bowl, mahogany neck, 14/20-fret rosewood fingerboard with pearl dot inlay, rosewood bridge with white pins, blackface peghead with screened logo, 3-per-side nickel tuners with pearloid buttons, available in Natural finish, mfg. 1984-87.

	N/A	$550	$350

J-30 - dreadnought body, spruce top, round soundhole, tortoise pickguard, 3-stripe bound body/rosette, mahogany back/sides/neck, 14/20-fret rosewood fingerboard with pearl dot inlay, blackface peghead with pearl banner/logo inlay, rosewood bridge with black pins, 3-per-side nickel tuners with pearloid buttons, available in Antique Walnut or Vintage Sunburst finishes, mfg. 1985-1998.

	N/A	$850	$450

Last MSR was $1,400.

In 1994, reverse bridge with rosewood pins replaced original part/design.

J-30 Cutaway - similar to J-30, except has single round cutaway, reverse belly bridge with rosewood pins, transducer pickup/preamp system, available in Antique Walnut or Vintage Sunburst finishes, mfg. 1994-98.

	N/A	$1,150	$600

Last MSR was $1,750.

GRADING	100%	EXCELLENT	AVERAGE

JUMBO 35 (J-35) - spruce top, round soundhole, bound body, 1-ply stripe rosette, mahogany back/sides/neck, 14/19-fret rosewood fingerboard with pearl dot inlay, rosewood straight bridge with pearl dot inlay, white bridge pins, blackface peghead with screened logo, 3-per-side tuners with plastic buttons, "tiger stripe" pickguard, available in Natural (approx. 25 mfg. 1941 only) or Sunburst finish, approx. 2,500 mfg. 1936-1942.

	N/A	$7,000	$5,000

In 1939, Natural finish was also available. In 1941, both Natural and Sunburst finishes were available. Natural finish brings a slightly higher premium. 3-tone bar models bring slightly higher premium.

J-35 (1985-87 MFG.) - spruce top, round soundhole, tortoise pickguard, 3-stripe bound body/rosette, maple back/sides/neck, 14/20-fret rosewood fingerboard with pearl dot inlay, rosewood reverse bridge with white black dot pins, blackface peghead with screened logo, 3-per-side tuners with plastic buttons, available in Cherry Sunburst finish, mfg. 1985-87.

	N/A	$800	$450

J-35 1995 LIMITED EDITION - select solid Sitka spruce top, mahogany back/sides, ebony fingerboard and bridge, historic firestripe pickguard, advanced bracing pattern, vintage nickel tuners, 250 manufactured, mfg. 1995 only.

$1,150	$750	$450

There is also a J-35 Fuller, which is made for Fuller's Vintage Guitar located in Houston, TX. 2002 MSR - $2,402.

J-40 - spruce top, round soundhole, black pickguard, bound body, 3-stripe rosette, laminated mahogany back/sides, mahogany neck, 14/20-fret rosewood fingerboard with pearl dot inlay, rosewood strings through bridge, screened peghead logo, 3-per-side chrome tuners, available in Cherry Sunburst or Natural finish, mfg. 1971-1982.

	N/A	$600	$350

In 1973, 3-piece maple neck replaced original part/design. This model was available in Cherry Sunburst finish as an option.

**Gibson Jumbo
courtesy Dave Hull**

J-45 - slope shouldered body, spruce top, round soundhole, tortoise shell pickguard, 3-stripe bound body/rosette, mahogany back/sides/neck, 14/19 (pre-war) or 14/20-fret rosewood fingerboard with pearl dot inlay, rosewood bridge with black pins, 3-per-side nickel tuners with pearl buttons, available in Sunburst finish, mfg. 1942-1985.

1942	N/A	$4,500	$3,000
1943-1945	N/A	$3,500	$2,800
1946	N/A	$3,000	$2,500
1947-1954	N/A	$2,800	$2,200
1955-1959	N/A	$2,200	$1,500
1960-1964	N/A	$1,500	$1,000
1965-1968	N/A	$1,200	$800
1969-1985	N/A	$700	$450

During WWII, Gibson used whatever materials were handy. A mahogany top J-45 will bring about 15% less than above values, but a mahogany back with rosewood or maple sides will bring 15% higher values. Add 25% for maple back/sides. Add a significant premium for rosewood back and sides (rare).

This model was originally offered with a single stripe body binding. The banner peghead inlay was offered from 1942 to 1945. In 1942, multi-ply body binding was offered; In 1943, one stripe body binding replaced multi-ply body binding. In 1950, upper belly on bridge, 3-stripe body binding replaced original part/design. In 1955, redesigned pickguard replaced original part/design. In 1956, adjustable bridge became an option. The fixed bridge was discontinued in late 1961. In 1962, Cherry Sunburst finish was offered. In 1968, belly under bridge replaced previous part/design. In 1969, redesigned body/pickguard replaced previous part/design. In 1971, non-adjustable saddle became standard. In 1975, redesigned pickguard, 4-stripe top purfling, tortoise body binding replaced previous part/design. In 1981, 3-stripe top purfling replaced previous part/design.

J-45 Celebrity - similar to J-45, except has rosewood back/sides, abalone "The Gibson" and fern design peghead inlay, 5-ply bound headstock, ebony fingerboard and bridge, 7-ply front and back binding, gold hardware, mfg. 1985 only.

	N/A	$1,800	$1,200

Approximately 100 of these instruments were produced.

J-45 REISSUE - slope (round) shouldered dreadnought style, solid Sitka spruce top, round soundhole, white body binding, mahogany back/sides, 14/20-fret rosewood fingerboard with mother-of-pearl dot inlay, vintage-style rosewood reverse belly bridge, white bridgepins, blackface peghead with logo inlay, 3-per-side vintage-style nickel tuners, teardrop-shaped black pickguard. Available in various finishes, current finishes are Vintage Cherry Sunburst or Vintage Sunburst. New 1984, current mfg. is by MT Custom Shop.

MSR	$2,402	$1,675	$1,200	$775

**Gibson J-45
courtesy Cam Waters**

Add $81 for Antique Natural (Bubinga) finish (disc. 2002.)

Beginning in 1984, the J-45 Reissue was available in Ebony, Natural and Sunburst finishes. When the model was re-designated the Early J-45, the finish was changed to a Vintage Sunburst finish. Beginning 1999, model nomenclature was again changed back to the J-45, and a transducer pickup was added as standard equipment. Recent finishes include Antique Natural (Bubinga), Cherry, Ebony, Heritage Cherry Sunburst, Pre-War Vintage Sunburst, and Triburst.

J-45 Rosewood - similar to J-45, except has Indian rosewood back/sides, ebony fingerboard/bridge, gold hardware, and abalone fingerboard inlays, transducer pickup standard, available in Vintage Sunburst or Antique Natural finish, mfg. 1999-current.

	MSR	$3,124	$2,200	$1,550	$1,150

J-45 Dwight Yoakam Honky Tonk Deuce - similar to J-45 reissue, except has solid Indian rosewood back/sides and bridge, V profile mahogany neck with double paralellogram inlays and dice at the 12th fret, tortoise shell J-50 pickguard has mother-of-pearl dice inlays, available in Antique Natural or Vintage Sunburst finish. New 2003.

	MSR	$3,299	$2,350	$1,625	$1,075

J-45 Rosewood Custom - similar to J-45 Rosewood, except has abalone top trim and no transducer, mfg. 1999-current, mfg. by the MT Custom Shop.

	MSR	$4,060	$2,850	$2,150	$1,450

J-45 Custom Vine - similar to J-45 Rosewood Custom, except has customer selected maple and elaborate custom vine fretboard inlays, mfg. 1999-current, mfg. by the MT Custom Shop.

	MSR	$5,747	$4,025	$2,975	$1,995

SOUTHERN JUMBO - J-45 style body, solid spruce top, mahogany back/sides/neck, bound rosewood fingerboard and bridge, vintage styling. Available in Vintage Sunburst (disc.) or Triburst '47 (new 2002) finish, New 1999.

	MSR	$3,124	$2,200	$1,550	$1,050

J-50 - similar to J-45, except has Natural finish, mfg. 1947-1985.

			100%	EXCELLENT	AVERAGE
1946-1950			N/A	$2,800	$1,900
1951-1959			N/A	$2,000	$1,400
1960-1964			N/A	$1,500	$1,100
1965-1969			N/A	$1,200	$800
1970-1985			N/A	$750	$500

During 1956, an adjustable bridge became an option, and in 1961, the fixed bridge was discontinued.

J-50 REISSUE - spruce top, mahogany back/sides, traditional J-50 features, nickel hardware, available in Antique Natural finish, mfg. 1999-current.

	MSR	$2,298	$1,650	$1,175	$775

Also available in left-hand configuration beginning 2003, at no charge.

JUMBO 55 (J-55, 1939-1942 MFG.) - spruce top, round soundhole, tortoise pickguard, bound body, 1-stripe rosette, mahogany back/sides/neck, 14/20-fret bound coffeewood fingerboard with pearl dot inlay, coffeewood mustache bridge with pearl dot inlay, white bridge pins, blackface stairstep peghead with pearl logo inlay, 3-per-side tuners with amber buttons, available in Sunburst finish, approx. 325 mfg. 1939-1942.

			100%	EXCELLENT	AVERAGE
1939			N/A	$8,500	$6,000
1940-42			N/A	$6,500	$4,000

In 1940, standard peghead replaced original design. In 1941, rosewood fingerboard, wings shaped rosewood bridge with pearl dot inlay replaced original part/design.

J-55 (1972-1982 Mfg.) - slope shouldered body, spruce top, round soundhole, tortoise pickguard, bound body, 3-stripe rosette, laminated mahogany back/sides, maple neck, 14/20-fret rosewood fingerboard with pearl dot inlay, rosewood bridge with black white dot pins, blackface peghead with pearl logo inlay, 3-per-side chrome tuners, available in Natural finish, approx. 3,900 mfg. 1972-1982.

			N/A	$650	$300

J-60 - dreadnought body, spruce top, round soundhole, tortoise pickguard, 3-stripe bound body/rosette, rosewood back/sides, mahogany neck, 14/20-fret rosewood fingerboard with pearl dot inlay, rosewood bridge with black pins, 3-per-side nickel tuners with pearl buttons, available in Antique Natural or Vintage Sunburst finishes, disc. 1998.

			N/A	$1,100	$650

Last MSR was $1,999.

J-60 TRADITIONAL (CL60) - square shoulder dreadnought, solid Sitka spruce top, round soundhole, abalone body binding, solid rosewood back/sides, 14/20-fret ebony fingerboard with pearl dot inlay, bound headstock with mother-of-pearl script logo, ebony belly bridge with white bridgepins, 3-per-side gold tuners, teardrop-shaped tortoise pickguard, available in Antique Natural Gloss Lacquer finish, mfg. 1997-98.

			N/A	$1,200	$750

Last MSR was $2,099.

J-100/J-100 CUSTOM (1939-1975 MFG.) - mahogany neck/back/sides, cedar top, 17 in. wide, black teardrop pickguard, rosewood belly bridge, four-ply top binding with black outer layer, black bound back, 25 1/2 in. scale, dot inlays, crown peghead inlay, pearl logo, approx. 140 mfg. 1939-1941, and approx. 290 mfg. 1972-1975.

			N/A	$3,250	$2,500
1939-1941			N/A	$3,250	$2,500
1972-75			N/A	$1,325	$975

GRADING	100%	EXCELLENT	AVERAGE

G

Add 10%-15% for maple back/sides.

This model was renamed the J-100 Custom in 1970. Moustache bridge and stairstep peghead became optional in 1972.

J-100 (1985-1991 MFG.) - spruce top, round soundhole, black pickguard, 2-stripe bound body/rosette, maple back/sides/neck, 14/20-fret rosewood fingerboard with pearl dot inlay, rosewood bridge with black pins, 3-per-side nickel tuners with pearl buttons, available in Natural finish, mfg. 1985-1991.

	N/A	$1,000	$725

This model was available with a cedar top as an option.

J-100 XTRA - J-200 size super jumbo body, spruce top, round soundhole, black pickguard, 2-stripe bound body/rosette, maple (new 1999) or mahogany (disc. 1998) back/sides/neck, 14/20-fret rosewood fingerboard with pearl dot inlay, rosewood bridge with black pins, blackface peghead with pearl crown logo inlay, 3-per-side nickel (disc.) or gold tuners/hardware with pearloid buttons, available in Antique Natural (new 1999), Black Cherry (new 2003) Antique Walnut, or Vintage Sunburst (disc. 1998) finishes, current mfg.

MSR	$2,484	$1,750	$1,250	$850

Add $111 for Black Cherry finish (new 2003).

In 1994, tortoise pickguard, mustache bridge with rosewood (disc. 1998) or white (new 1999) pins replaced original part/design.

J-100 Xtra Cutaway - similar to J-100 Xtra, except has single round cutaway, tortoise pickguard, mustache bridge with rosewood pins, transducer pickup/preamp system, available in Antique Walnut and Vintage Sunburst finishes, mfg. 1994-98.

	N/A	$1,200	$650

Last MSR was $1,850.

J-150 - J-200 size super jumbo body, spruce top, figured maple back/sides/neck, rosewood fingerboard/bridge, engraved multi-color flower pattern pickguard, with transducer, mfg. 1999-current.

MSR	$3,230	$2,275	$1,600	$1,050

J-160 E - please refer to listings under the Acoustic Electric subheading later in this section.

J-180 - spruce top, round soundhole, 2 tortoise pickguards, 3-stripe bound body/rosette, maple back/sides, 1 piece mahogany neck, 14/20-fret rosewood fingerboard with pearl star inlay, reverse belly bridge with black white dot pins, blackface peghead with pearl star/logo inlay, 3-per-side nickel tuners with pearloid buttons, available in Black finish, mfg. 1986-1991.

	N/A	$1,000	$585

Gibson J-180
courtesy Gibson

J-180 - solid Sitka spruce top, round soundhole, white body binding, maple back/sides, 14/20-fret bound rosewood fingerboard with mother-of-pearl star inlays, rosewood bridge, white bridgepins, blackface peghead with abalone star/logo inlay, 3-per-side nickel tuners, "dual side" black pickguard, available in Ebony finish, current mfg.

MSR	$2,571	$1,700	$1,300	$825

J-180 Dwight Yoakam Y2K Artist Model - solid Sitka spruce top, J-180 body with double pickguards and J-200 features including a mustache bridge, crown inlays, and figured maple back/sides/neck, rosewood fingerboard/bridge, 25½ in. scale, Dwight Yoakam signed label, available in Antique Natural finish, limited edition 2000-2002.

	$2,000	$1,425	$975

Last MSR was $2,820.

J-180 EC - please refer to the Acoustic Electric subheading later in this text.

J-185 - spruce top, round soundhole, tortoise pickguard, 2-stripe bound body/rosette, figured maple back/sides, mahogany neck, 14/20-fret rosewood fingerboard with pearl parallelogram inlay, upper belly rosewood bridge with white pins, pearl cross bridge wings inlay, blackface peghead with pearl crown/logo inlay, 3-per-side nickel tuners, available in Cremona Brown Burst (most common) or Natural finishes, mfg. 1951-59.

	N/A	$7,000	$5,000

J-185 EC (Blues King) - please refer to listing under the Acoustic Electric subheading later in this section.

J-185 REISSUE - spruce top, maple back/sides, Maltese cross bridge wing inlays, pearl parallelogram fretboard inlays, available in Antique Natural or Vintage Sunburst finish. New 1999.

MSR	$2,571	$1,700	$1,300	$825

Add $257 for left-hand model.

Gibson J-185 EC
courtesy Gibson

GRADING		100%	EXCELLENT	AVERAGE

J-185 12-String - similar to J-185 Reissue, except has 12-strings and flamed maple back/sides, availabile in Antique Natural finish, limited production beginning 2000.

MSR	$3,149	$2,200	$1,550	$975

This model is available in left-hand at no extra charge.

J-200/SJ-200 - spruce top, round soundhole, black pickguard with engraved floral pattern, figured maple back/sides/neck, 14/20-fret bound rosewood fingerboard with pearl crown inlay, rosewood mustache bridge with pearl block inlay, black pearl dot pins, bound peghead with pearl plant/logo inlay, 3-per-side gold tuners with pearl buttons. Available in Antique Walnut, Natural, or Vintage Sunburst finishes, mfg. 1938-1942, and 1945-1996.

1938-1942 (Rosewood back/sides, approx. 100 mfg.)		N/A	$25,000+	
1945-1949 (Figured maple back/sides)		N/A	$9,000	$5,000
1951-1954		N/A	$6,000	$4,000
1955-1959		N/A	$4,500	$3,000
1960-1965		N/A	$3,000	$2,000
1966-1969		N/A	$1,800	$1,100
1970-1989		N/A	$1,500	$800
1990-1996		N/A	$1,750	$1,100

Last MSR was $2,700.

When this model was introduced in 1938, it was known as the Super Jumbo (SJ-200). Some prototypes made during late 1937 were labeled "Super Jumbo" and "L-5 Spec." In 1939, this model was renamed the Super Jumbo 200. In 1947, it was renamed in the company catalogs to the J-200. However, many instruments continued to be labeled SJ-200 well into the early 1950s. Pre-war instruments should be determined on a piece-by-piece basis as opposed to the usual market, as this model and many of Gibson's high end instruments were not manufactured during the war – thus, there simply aren't that many guitars available in the secondary marketplace.

When this model was originally released, it featured a single peghead binding. In 1948, Natural finish became an option. In 1960, adjustable saddle bridge became an option. In 1961, tune-o-matic bridge with pearl block inlay replaced original part/design. In 1969, adjustable saddle became standard. In 1971, ebony fingerboard replaced original part/design, non-adjustable bridge replaced previous part/design. In 1979, rosewood fingerboard replaced previous part/design. In 1985, mustache bridge with pearl block inlay replaced previous part/design, multi-bound peghead replaced original part/design. In 1994, Antique Ebony finish was introduced, pearl crown fingerboard inlay, gold hardware replaced previous part/design. In 1996, the '50s Super Jumbo 200 model superseded the J-200 model (see listing below).

J-200 12-String - similar to J-200, except has 12-strings, 6-per-side tuners, disc. 1998.

		N/A	$2,100	$1,250

Last MSR was $3,200.

J-200 Celebrity - similar to J-200, except has ornate scroll type fingerboard inlay, fern peghead inlay, mfg. 1985 only.

		N/A	$2,000	$1,500

J-200 Deluxe - spruce top, round soundhole, black pickguard with engraved floral pattern/abalone dot inlay, abalone bound body/rosette, figured maple back/sides/neck, 14/20-fret bound ebony fingerboard with abalone crown inlay, ebony mustache bridge with abalone block inlay/white abalone dot pins, bound blackface peghead with abalone crown/logo inlay, 3-per-side gold Grover Imperial tuners, available in Antique Natural or Vintage Sunburst finishes, mfg. 1994-96.

		N/A	$3,375	$2,075

Last MSR was $5,200.

This model has a rosewood back/sides/neck as an option.

J-200 Jr. - similar to J-200, except has smaller body, nickel tuners, disc. 1994.

		N/A	$1,250	$725

Last MSR was $1,800.

This model was also offered in a 12-string configuration (Model J-200 Jr. 12-String).

SJ-200 REISSUE - Sitka spruce top, round soundhole, abalone bound body/rosette, flame maple back/sides, maple neck, 14/20-fret bound Madagascar rosewood fingerboard with abalone crown inlays, Madagascar rosewood mustache bridge with abalone block inlay/white abalone dot pins, bound blackface peghead with abalone crown/logo inlay, 3-per-side gold tuners, black pickguard with engraved floral pattern/abalone dot inlay, available in Antique Natural or Vintage Sunburst finishes, current mfg.

MSR	$3,999	$2,800	$1,825	$1,425

Add $200 for Antique Natural finish. Add $400 for left-hand model.

SJ-200 Elite Custom - similar to SJ-200 Reissue, except has ebony fingerboard and bridge, gold Imperial tuners, and abalone rosette, mfg. 1999-current.

MSR	$5,433	$3,775	$2,900	$1,900

SJ-200 Pre-War Western Classic - Indian rosewood back/sides, maple neck with ebony bridge and fingerboard with mother-of-pearl block inlays, patterned after the 1937 Ray Whitley model, available in Vintage Sunburst finish, Custom Shop model, mfg. 1999-current.

MSR	$6,270	$4,375	$3,400	$2,250

SJ-200 Pre-War Western Classic Brazilian - similar to SJ-200 Pre-War Western Classic, except back/sides are Brazilian rosewood, Custom Shop model, new 2003.

MSR	$9,038	$5,875	$4,250	$3,000

GRADING		100%	EXCELLENT	AVERAGE

SJ-200 Artist Supreme - top-of-the-line Custom Shop model, Zircote back and sides, Sitka spruce top, multi-bound body with abalone at all joints, mother-of-pearl and abalone inlays on neck headstock and pickguard, ebony fretboard and bridge, A2 relief carved maple neck with contrasting color veneers, neck is sunbursted "V S," ebony multi-bound headstock overlayed with ebony, hand engraved tuners, designed by Ren Ferguson, new 2003.

MSR	$32,500	$21,150	$16,000	$12,000

RON WOOD SIGNATURE J-200 (ACRW) - J-200 style, hand select solid Sitka spruce top, round soundhole, bound body, flamed maple back/sides, flamed maple neck, 14/20-fret bound ebony fingerboard with abalone flame inlay, ebony moustache bridge with gold lip pearl inlay, white bridgepins, blackface peghead with mother-of-pearl "Ron Wood" signature/logo inlay, Custom Shop seal on back of headstock, 3-per-side gold tuners, dual hand-engraved pickguards with a flame design, available in Antique Natural Lacquer finish, mfg. 1997-98.

	N/A	$4,950	$3,250

Last MSR was $7,999.

This model was designed in conjunction with guitarist Ron Wood (Rolling Stones). Wood personally signed the first 100 labels for this limited edition model. This Special Custom model was designed by Gibson Master Luthier Ren Ferguson, is specially numbered, and has a certificate of authenticity.

MONTANA GOLD J-200 (ACMGANGH1) - J-200 style, hand select solid spruce top, round soundhole, bound body, flamed maple back/sides, flamed maple neck, 14/20-fret bound ebony fingerboard with pearl block inlay, ebony moustache bridge with pearl inlay, white bridgepins, blackface peghead with mother-of-pearl "Harvested Wheat"/logo inlay, Custom Shop seal on back of headstock, 3-per-side gold Imperial tuners, tortoise pickguard with engraved "Montana Gold"/Wheat inlay, available in Antique Natural Lacquer finish, mfg. 1997-98.

	N/A	$2,650	$1,850

Last MSR was $4,399.

This model's serial number is inside the guitar on the headblock. This Special Custom model was designed by Gibson Master Luthier Ren Ferguson, is specially numbered, and has a certificate of authenticity.

Montana Gold 200 Custom - J-200 super jumbo size body, solid Sitka spruce top, highly flamed maple back/sides/neck, ebony fingerboard, gold plated imperial tuners, special wheat inlays on pickguard and Montana Gold banner on both headstock and pickguard, available in Trans. Amber finish, Custom Shop model, mfg. 2001-2002.

	$3,775	$2,900	$1,900

Last MSR was $5,433.

Gibson J-200
courtesy Dave Rogers
Dave's Guitar Shop

SUPER 200 CUSTOM - J-200 super jumbo size body with Super 400 appointments, solid Sitka spruce top, figured maple back and sides, ebony bridge and fingerboard, mother-of-pearl split block inlays, Venetian cutaway pickguard with headstock style inlay, available in Antique Natural or Vintage Sunburst finish, Custom Shop model, mfg. 2001-current.

MSR	$6,270	$4,375	$3,350	$2,225

SJ-200 CUSTOM VINE - top-of-the-line custom SJ-200, featuring elaborate custom vine abalone fingerboard inlays, hand engraved pickguard, and abalone body trim, available in Antique Natural or Vintage Sunburst finish, custom shop model, new 1999.

MSR	$10,450	$7,350	$5,700	$3,750

J-250 R - spruce top, round soundhole, black pickguard with engraved floral pattern, rosewood back/sides, mahogany neck, 14/20-fret bound rosewood fingerboard with pearl crown inlay, rosewood mustache bridge with pearl block inlay, black pearl dot pins, bound peghead with pearl crown/logo inlay, 3-per-side gold tuners with pearl buttons, available in Natural finish, approx. 20 mfg. 1972-78.

	N/A	$850	$375

J-250 MONARCH CUSTOM - J-200 Super Jumbo body, top-of-the-line model with solid spruce top, Brazilian rosewood back/sides, ebony bridge and fingerboard, Monarch crown fretboard inlays, extensive and elaborate mother-of-pearl and abalone bindings/inlays, 25½ in. scale, available in Antique Natural or Vintage Sunburst finish, Custom Shop model, limited mfg. 2001-2002.

	$15,750	$9,000	$7,500

Last MSR was $22,594.

J-250 PRESENTATION - J-200 super jumbo body, top-of-the-line model with rare Schmetterling spruce top, select 3-piece figured maple back, ebony fingerboard and SJ200 bridge, ancient Siberian mammoth bone saddle, bridge pins, and endpin, custom carved "volute" headstock with ebony overlays, hand carved solid mother-of-pearl nut, cloud mother-of-pearl fingerboard inlay, fleur-de-lis and

Gibson J-250 Monarch
courtesy Dave Rogers
Dave's Guitar Shop

GRADING	100%	EXCELLENT	AVERAGE

scroll abalone and mother-of-pearl headstock inlays, multiple bound body, headstock, fingerboard, and rosette, handmade, bound caramel shell pickguard, MT Custom Shop Limited Edition, only 101 produced, mfg. 1995 only.

	$5,500	$4,000	$2,750

J-300 - similar to J-250 R, except has 12-strings, 6-per-side tuners, only 1 mfg. 1973.
   Extreme rarity precludes accurate pricing on this model.

J-1000 - rounded single cutaway body, spruce top, round soundhole, 3-stripe bound body/rosette, rosewood back/sides, mahogany neck, 20 bound rosewood pointed fingerboard with pearl diamond inlay, rosewood mustache bridge with black pearl dot pins, bound blackface peghead with pearl diamond/logo inlay, 3-per-side gold tuners, available in Natural finish, mfg. 1992 only.

	N/A	$1,400	$850

Last MSR was $1,999.

J-1500 - rounded single cutaway body, spruce top, round soundhole, 3-stripe bound body, abalone rosette, rosewood back/sides, mahogany neck, 20-fret bound ebony pointed fingerboard with abalone varied diamond inlay, ebony mustache bridge with white black dot pins, bound blackface peghead with abalone fleur-de-lis/logo inlay, 3-per-side gold tuners, available in Natural finish, mfg. 1992 only.

	N/A	$1,700	$1,100

Last MSR was $2,750.

J-2000/CUSTOM - single rounded cutaway body, spruce top, round soundhole, abalone bound body/rosette, rosewood back/sides, mahogany neck, 20-fret bound ebony point fingerboard with abalone leaf inlay, ebony bridge with white abalone dot pins, abalone leaf bridge wings inlay, bound peghead with leaf/logo inlay, 3-per-side gold tuners with pearl buttons, piezo bridge pickup, endpin pickup jack, available in Antique Natural or Vintage Sunburst finishes, disc. 1994.

	N/A	$2,500	$1,600

Last MSR was $4,010.

J-2000 CUSTOM CUTAWAY - single rounded cutaway body, solid spruce top, customer selected back and side wood, mahogany neck, abalone top trim, "autumn leaf" fretboard, and headstock inlays, hand carved gold tuners, available in Antique Natural or Vintage Sunburst finish, mfg. 1999-2002 by MT Custom Shop.

	$4,375	$3,375	$2,250

Last MSR was $6,270.

JG-0 - spruce top, round soundhole, bound body, 1-stripe rosette, mahogany back/sides/neck, 14/20-fret rosewood fingerboard with pearl dot inlay, rosewood bridge with white pins, logo peghead decal, 3-per-side tuners. Available in Natural finish, approx. 550 mfg. 1970-75.

	N/A	$500	$250

JG-12 - similar to JG-0, except has 12-strings, 6-per-side tuners, approx. 185 mfg. 1970 only.

	N/A	$450	$200

SJ (SOUTHERNER JUMBO) - spruce top, round soundhole, black pickguard, 2-stripe bound body/rosette, mahogany back/sides/neck, 14/20-fret bound rosewood fingerboard with pearl parallelogram inlays, rosewood bridge with white pins, blackface peghead with pearl banner logo inlay, 3-per-side nickel tuners, available in Sunburst finish, mfg. 1942-1978.

1942-1945	N/A	$4,500	$3,500
1946-1954	N/A	$3,500	$2,600
1955-1960	N/A	$2,700	$1,700
1961-1969	N/A	$1,500	$800
1970-1978	N/A	$700	$450

   During WWII, Gibson used whatever materials were handy. Add 15% for mahogany back and rosewood or maple sides, and 25% for maple back/sides. Add a 15%-25% for early striped pickguard, depending on condition.   Add a significant premium for rosewood back and sides (rare).
   Banner peghead inlay mfg. 1942-45, disc. 1946. A few early models are found with rosewood back/sides. In 1946, the banner inlay on the peghead was discontinued. In 1949, upper belly bridge replaced original part/design. In 1954, Natural finish became an option. In 1955, redesigned pickguard replaced original part/design. In 1956, the SJ in Natural finish was renamed the Country-Western Jumbo. In 1960, this new designation was again renamed the SJN (See SJN listing below). In mid to late 1962, adjustable saddle replaced original part/design; redesigned body/pickguard replaced previous part/design. In 1969, standard style bridge replaced previous part/design. In 1970, non-adjustable saddle replaced previous part/design. In 1974, 4-stripe body/2-stripe neck binding replaced original part/design.

SJN (SJN Country Western, Country-Western Jumbo) - similar to SJ (Southern Jumbo), except has tortoise pickguard, available in Natural finish, mfg. 1954-1978.

1954-1969	N/A	$2,000	$1,100
1970-1978	N/A	$700	$450

   In 1956, the SJ in Natural finish was renamed the Country-Western Jumbo. In 1960, this new designation was again renamed the SJN. In 1962, the SJN was again called the Country-Western.

SJ-45 DELUXE - spruce top, round soundhole, tortoise pickguard, abalone bound body, 3-stripe rosette, rosewood back/sides, mahogany neck, 14/20-fret bound rosewood fingerboard with pearl flower inlay, rosewood bridge with white pins, bound blackface peghead with pearl banner/logo inlay, 3-per-side gold tuners, available in Antique Natural or Special Vintage Sunburst finishes, mfg. 1994-98.

	N/A	$1,950	$1,000

Last MSR was $4,010.

GRADING	100%	EXCELLENT	AVERAGE

G

ACOUSTIC: L SERIES

There is a great deal of confusion about the difference between the small bodied L-0 and L-00 series guitars. The L-0 was introduced in 1926 in the "Robert Johnson" shape. By 1928, it was produced with a mahogany top, back and sides. The L-0 was redesigned circa 1930 as a Martin 00 shaped guitar. It had a spruce top, mahogany back and sides, and 12 frets were clear of the body. By 1932 the L-0 had 14 frets to the body, and by 1933, it had been discontinued in favor of the more popular L-00. The L-0 was reintroduced in 1937 as a black guitar with a tortoise shell celluloid pickguard and remained in the line until 1942.

The L-00 was introduced in 1932 with a spruce top, mahogany back and sides, Black finish and a white pickguard. By 1933, the L-00 was available in a Sunburst finish with a striped celluloid pickguard. The L-00 Series was discontinued in 1942.

In terms of L Series desirability, an early Robert Johnson style shaped instrument is less than the post-1930 design. A mahogany top is less valuable than spruce. Rosewood and maple sides with a mahogany back will add to the rarity and price, while a maple back and side will be even more desirable. Brazilian rosewood back and sides are the most desirable in this series. 12 frets to the body will be less desirable than 14, while the infrequently encountered 13 fret Nick Lucas will be somewhere in between.

STYLE L - arched spruce top, round soundhole, bound body, wood inlay rosette, maple back/sides/neck, 13/19-fret ebony fingerboard with pearl dot inlay, ebony bridge/trapeze tailpiece, blackface peghead, 3-per-side tuners, available in Orange Top finish, mfg. approx. 1902.

	N/A	$1,200	$900

Gibson SJ
courtesy Willie's
American Guitars

L-0 (1926-1933 MFG.) - spruce top, round soundhole, bound body, 2-stripe rosette, maple back/sides, mahogany neck, 12/19-fret ebonized fingerboard with pearl dot inlay, ebony pyramid bridge with black pins, blackface peghead with screened logo, 3-per-side tuners with plastic buttons, available in Amber Brown finish, mfg. 1926-1933.

1926-1929	N/A	$1,200	$700
1930-1933	N/A	$1,600	$1,200

A few of these instruments are found with black tuner buttons. In 1928, mahogany top/back/sides, bound soundhole, rosewood fingerboard, rosewood standard bridge with extra white pin replaced original part/design. In 1929, straight bridge with no extra pin replaced previous part/design. In 1932, 14/19-fret fingerboard replaced original part/design.

L-00 - spruce top, 14 3/4 in. wide, 19 1/4 in. long, round soundhole, tortoise or white pickguard, bound body, 2-stripe rosette, mahogany back/sides/neck, 14/19-fret rosewood fingerboard with pearl dot inlay, rosewood straight bridge with black white dot pins, blackface peghead with screened logo, 3-per-side tuners with plastic buttons, available in Ebony, Natural (rare), or Sunburst (most common) finishes, mfg. approx. 1930-1945.

Ebony finish, 12-fret	N/A	$1,800	$1,200
14-fret	N/A	$2,200	$1,800

Models with maple back/sides command a premium (up to 50% for flamed maple). Early versions of this model have 12/19-fret fingerboards. In 1934, Sunburst finish became available. In 1941, Natural finish became an option, Ebony finish was discontinued. In 1942, banner peghead logo found on a few instruments.

L-00 3/4 - similar to Model L-00, except has 3/4 size body, approx. 35 mfg. 1938-39 only.

	N/A	$3,750	$2,750

L-00 (1936 REISSUE) - spruce top, round soundhole, 2-stripe bound body/rosette, mahogany back/sides/neck, 14/19-fret bound rosewood fingerboard with pearl dot inlay, rosewood bridge with white pins, 3-per-side nickel tuners with plastic buttons. Patterned after Gibson's older 00 size body, available in Antique Walnut, Vintage Sunburst, or Ebony (new 1999) finishes, mfg. 1992-96, reissued 1999-2002.

$1,575	$1,200	$775

Last MSR was $2,391.

NICK LUCAS (GIBSON SPECIAL) - slightly arched spruce top, mahogany back/sides/neck, bound body, bound rosewood fingerboard with dot inlay, rosewood bridge, "The Gibson" headstock logo, special round Nick Lucas label, this model underwent redesign several times in its short production span, originally introduced as a mahogany/spruce "Robert Johnson" shaped guitar with at least a 4½ in. depth and 12 frets to the body, models can be found with 12, 13, and 14 fret-to-the-body fingerboards in mahogany, rosewood, and maple, available in Sunburst finish, original body width was 13 1/2 in., later mfg. was 14 3/4 in. wide, 19 1/4 in. long, 4 1/2 in. deep, mfg. circa 1928-1941. Limited mfg. (probably less than 250 instruments.)

1928-1930 (ROBERT JOHNSON STYLE)	N/A	$3,500	$2,500
1929-1941	N/A	$4,500	$3,500
Rosewood or Maple	N/A	$6,000	$5,000

Subtract 20%-30% for tailpiece.

Gibson L-00
courtesy Glenn Wetterland

In 1929, this model was redesigned in the L-00 body shape, retaining its deep body and 12-fret configuration. During 1930, most production featured rosewood back and sides, 13 frets to the body. During 1932, an adjustable bridge and tailpiece were listed as optional. In 1934, 14 frets to the body, mostly maple back and sides (mahogany on some), became standard. While this model was discontinued in 1938, the last production was shipped as late as 1941.

NICK LUCAS REISSUE CLASSIC (L-00 VARIANT) - solid spruce top, flame maple back/sides, rosewood fingerboard/bridge, patterned after the original Nick Lucas model, includes 1930s Nick Lucas label, available in Vintage Sunburst finish. New 1999.

| MSR | $2,989 | $1,950 | $1,475 | $1,000 |

Nick Lucas Elite (L-00 Variant) - similar to Nick Lucas Reissue, except has Ebony fingerboard, maple neck, abalone Lucas style fretboard inlays, top trim, and rosette, vintage gold hardware, available in Antique Natural or Vintage Sunburst, mfg. 1999-2002.

| | | $2,850 | $2,000 | $1,350 |

Last MSR was $4,040.

L-1 ARCHTOP - carved spruce top, bound round soundhole, raised tortoise pickguard, bound body, 2 rope pattern rosette, birch back/sides, maple neck, 13/19-fret ebony fingerboard with pearl dot inlay, ebony bridge/trapeze tailpiece, slotted peghead, 3-per-side tuners with plastic buttons, available in Orange Top/Mahogany finish, mfg. 1903-1925.

| | | N/A | $850 | $450 |

This model was also produced with maple back/sides. In 1918, Brown finish replaced original part/design. In 1920, 5-ring rosette replaced original part/design.

L-1 FlatTop - spruce top, round soundhole, bound body, 3-ring rosette, mahogany back/sides, maple neck, 12/19-fret ebony fingerboard with pearl dot inlay, ebony pyramid bridge with black pins, painted peghead logo, 3-per-side tuners with plastic buttons, mfg. 1926-1937.

| | | N/A | $2,800 | $1,800 |

This model was produced in the "Robert Johnson" body shape between 1926-28 – Sunburst finish became available in 1927. The body style changed to an L-0 shape circa 1929. By 1928, bound rosewood fingerboard, 3-stripe bound body/rosette, rosewood belly bridge with white pins, Brown Sunburst finish replaced original part/design, extra bridge pin was added. In 1929, straight bridge replaced original design, extra bridge pin was discontinued. In 1931, the body and bridge were redesigned, unbound fingerboard replaced previous part/design. In 1932, single bound body, 14/19-fret fingerboard replaced previous part/design. From 1932-33, a tortoise shell pickguard was added.

L-1 Reissue - spruce top, round soundhole, 2-stripe bound body/rosette, mahogany back/sides/neck, 14/19-fret bound rosewood fingerboard with pearl dot inlay, rosewood bridge with white pins, 3-per-side nickel tuners with plastic buttons, available in Vintage Cherry Sunburst finish, disc. 1998.

| | | N/A | $900 | $500 |

Last MSR was $1,400.

There is also a J-35 Fuller, which is made for Fuller's Vintage Guitar located in Houston, TX. 2002 MSR - $2,402.

L-1 ROBERT JOHNSON - patterned after Robert Johnson's original L-1, shallow L-1 body, Sitka spruce top, mahogany back/sides/neck, ebony fingerboard, 25 in. scale, 12/19-fret, ebony bridge, period hardware, Robert Johnson signature at bottom of fingerboard, New 2003.

| MSR | $2,919 | $1,975 | $1,500 | $1,000 |

L-2 ARCHTOP (1910 to 1923 MFG.) - carved spruce top, round soundhole, raised tortoise pickguard, bound body, 3-rope pattern rosette, birch back/sides, maple neck, 13/19-fret ebony fingerboard with pearl dot inlay, adjustable ebony bridge/trapeze tailpiece, snakehead peghead with pearl logo inlay, 3-per-side tuners with plastic buttons, available in Orange Top finish, mfg. 1910-1923.

| | | N/A | $1,000 | $600 |

L-2 Archtop (1924-26 Mfg.) - carved spruce top, round soundhole, raised tortoise pickguard, bound body, 2-ring rosette, maple back/sides, mahogany neck, 13/19-fret bound ebony fingerboard with pearl dot inlay, adjustable ebony bridge/trapeze tailpiece, snakehead peghead with pearl logo inlay, 3-per-side tuners with plastic buttons, available in Amber finish, mfg. 1924-26.

| | | N/A | $1,300 | $700 |

L-2 FlatTop - spruce top, round soundhole, 3-stripe body/rosette, bound body, rosewood back/sides, mahogany neck, 13/19-fret bound ebony fingerboard with pearl dot inlay, ebony pyramid bridge, blackface peghead with pearl logo inlay, 3-per-side tuners with plastic buttons, available in Natural or Sunburst finish, mfg. 1929-1934.

| **ROSEWOOD W/TAILPIECE** | N/A | $3,500 | $2,500 |
| **MAHOGANY** | N/A | $4,500 | $3,500 |

This model had a rosewood bridge 1929-1931. This model was also available with adjustable ebony bridge/trapeze tailpiece. In 1931, mahogany back/sides, 12/19-fret fingerboard replaced original part/design, gold sparkle inlay rosette/body, pearl flame peghead inlay were added. In 1932, rosewood back/sides, 13/19-fret fingerboard adjustable ebony bridge/trapeze tailpiece replaced previous part/design, raised pickguard was added, gold sparkle inlay no longer available. In 1933, top glued pickguard, ebony bridge with black pins replaced previous part/design. In 1934, 14/19-fret fingerboard replaced previous part/design.

L-3 - carved spruce top, bound round soundhole, raised tortoise pickguard, bound body, 3-ring wooden inlay rosette, birch back/sides, maple neck, 13/19-fret bound ebony fingerboard with pearl dot inlay, ebony bridge/trapeze tailpiece, blackface peghead with pearl logo inlay, 3-per-side tuners with plastic buttons, available in Orange Top/Mahogany finish, mfg. 1902-1933.

| | | N/A | $1,000 | $700 |

GRADING	100%	EXCELLENT	AVERAGE

L-4 - arched carved spruce top, oval soundhole, wooden inlay rosette, raised tortoise pickguard, bound soundhole/body, maple back/sides, mahogany neck, 12/20-fret bound ebony pointed fingerboard with pearl dot inlay, ebony bridge/trapeze tailpiece with black pins, bound blackface peghead with pearl logo inlay, 3-per-side tuners with buttons, available in Black finish, mfg. 1912-1956.

1912-1923	N/A	$2,000	$1,500
1924-1935	N/A	$1,750	$1,300
1936-1945	N/A	$1,800	$1,200
1946-1956	N/A	$1,600	$1,000

Add 20% for truss rod or snake head.

16 1/4 in. by 20 1/4 in. body. In 1914, 3 ring rosette, Mahogany finish replaced original part/design, Black and Orange finishes became an option. In 1918, Mahogany Sunburst finish replaced previous part/design. By 1920, rosette and peghead logo inlay were redesigned. In 1923, tailpiece pins were removed. In 1927, rosette was redesigned. In 1928, round soundhole 14/20-fret unbound fingerboard, unbound peghead replaced original part/design, 2-ring rosette, redesigned peghead logo replaced previous part/design. By 1933, bound fingerboard replaced previous part/design, pearl diamond peghead inlay was added. In 1935, f-holes, bound pickguard, redesigned fingerboard inlay, redesigned trapeze tailpiece, bound peghead with lily inlay replaced previous part/design. In 1937, unbound pickguard replaced previous part/design, round soundhole was an option. In 1940, Natural finish was an option. In 1941, unbound peghead replaced previous part/design. In 1946, bound pickguard, multi bound body replaced previous part/design. In 1947, laminated pickguard, parallelogram fingerboard inlay replaced previous part/design.

L-4 C - single pointed cutaway body, arched spruce top, f-holes, raised laminated pickguard, bound body, carved maple back/sides, mahogany neck, 19-fret bound rosewood fingerboard with pearl parallelogram inlay, adjustable rosewood bridge/trapeze tailpiece, blackface peghead with pearl flowerpot/logo inlay, 3-per-side tuners with plastic buttons, available in Natural or Sunburst finishes, mfg. 1949-1970.

1949-1962	N/A	$2,200	$1,600
1962-1971	N/A	$2,000	$1,400

L-5 - carved spruce top, f-holes, raised multi-bound pickguard, multi-bound body, carved figured maple back/sides, figured maple/ebony neck, 14/20-fret bound ebony pointed fingerboard with pearl dot inlay, adjustable ebony bridge/trapeze tailpiece, multi-bound blackface snakehead peghead with pearl flowerpot/logo inlay, 3-per-side silver plate tuners with pearl buttons, Master Model/Loyd Loar signature labels, available in Natural or Cremona Brown Sunburst finish, limited in mfg. 1922-1958.

	N/A	$35,000+	

Add 20% for Natural finish, originally offered beginning 1939.
Models signed by Lloyd Loar (1922 to 1924).

Loar Signature Label - discontinued in 1924.

1925-1928 (dot neck)	N/A	$15,000	$8,000
1929-1934	N/A	$8,000	$5,000

Advanced Body - offered in 1934 (17 in. body width).

1934-1948 (17 in. body)	N/A	$6,000	$4,500
1949-1958	N/A	$5,000	$3,500

Some early versions of this instrument have birch back/sides. In 1925, gold tuners replaced original part/design. In 1927, Master Model label was discontinued. In 1929, flat fingerboard with block inlay replaced original part/design, individual tuners replaced previous part/design. In 1935, The Advanced L-5's larger body (17 inches across lower bout by 21 in. long), binding, tailpiece, peghead replaced original part/design, redesigned fingerboard replaced previous part/design. In 1936, bound f-holes replaced original part/design. In 1937, gold tailpiece with silver insert, Grover Imperial tuners replaced previous part/design. In 1939, redesigned tailpiece replaced previous part/design, pearloid pickguard, Natural finish became an option. In 1948, 1 or 2 pickguard mounted pickups became an option.

Current production instruments (1934 L-5) are part of the Historic Collection Series, found at the end of this section.

L-5 P (Premiere)/L-5 C - single rounded cutaway body, arched spruce top, bound f-holes, raised multi-bound pearloid pickguard, multi-bound body, carved figured maple back/sides, figured maple neck, 14/20-fret multi-bound ebony pointed fingerboard with pearl block inlay, adjustable ebony bridge/gold trapeze tailpiece with silver insert, multi-bound blackface peghead with pearl flowerpot/logo inlay, 3-per-side gold tuners, available in Natural or Sunburst finishes, mfg. 1939-1989.

1939-1941	N/A	$14,000	$10,000
1942-1949	N/A	$9,000	$6,000
1950-1969	N/A	$8,500	$5,500
1970-1989	N/A	$6,000	$4,000

In 1948, renamed L-5 C, and 1 or 2 pickguard mounted pickups became an option.

L-5 CT - similar to L-5 C, except has thin body, shorter scale length, available in Red finish, approx. 35 mfg. 1959-1961.

	N/A	$12,000	$8,000

Also referred to as the George Gobel model with 2 humbucker pickups, 2 volume/tone controls, and a 3-position switch became options. George Gobel's personal guitar was non-electric.

Gibson L-1 flat-top
courtesy Rod & Hank's
Vintage Guitar

Gibson L-4
courtesy Jay Wolfe

GRADING	100%	EXCELLENT	AVERAGE

L-7 - arched spruce top, f-holes, raised bound black pickguard, bound body, carved maple back/sides, mahogany neck, 14/19-fret bound rosewood fingerboard with pearl multi-design inlay, adjustable rosewood bridge/trapeze tailpiece, bound blackface peghead with pearl fleur-de-lis/logo inlay, 3-per-side tuners with plastic buttons, available in Natural or Sunburst (most common) finish, approx. 1,200 mfg. 1933-1956.

1933-1934	N/A	$2,500	$1,800
1935-1948	N/A	$2,100	$1,600
1949-1956	N/A	$2,000	$1,500

Advanced Body (17" body width) offered. In 1934, Advanced body (17 in. wide by 21 in. long) fingerboard/peghead inlay, trapeze tailpiece replaced original part/design. In 1937, redesigned trapeze tailpiece replaced previous part/design. In 1939, Natural finish became available. In 1942, multi bound body, parallelogram fingerboard inlay, crown peghead inlay replaced previous part/design. In 1944, redesigned trapeze tailpiece replaced previous part/design. In 1948, laminated pickguard replaced previous part/design, 1 or 2 pickguard mounted pickups became options.

L-7 C - single rounded cutaway body, arched spruce top, f-holes, raised black laminated pickguard, bound body, carved maple back/sides, mahogany neck, 14/19-fret bound rosewood fingerboard with pearl parallelogram inlay, adjustable rosewood bridge/trapeze tailpiece, bound blackface peghead with pearl crown/logo inlay, 3-per-side tuners with plastic buttons, available in Natural or Sunburst (most common) finishes, mfg. 1948-1972.

1948-1968	N/A	$3,500	$2,200
1969-1972	N/A	$2,000	$1,500

Natural (Blonde) finish commands a higher premium.

This model had 1 or 2 pickguard mounted pickups as an option. In 1957, redesigned trapeze tailpiece replaced original part/design.

L-7 E Variations - please refer to the Acoustic Electric section for information and values on the L-7 E, L-7 ED, L-7 CE, L-7 CED, L-7 CEN, and L-7 CNED models.

L-10 - arched spruce top, f-holes, raised black pickguard, unique checkered white/back ivroid body on top of body, carved maple back/sides, mahogany neck, 14/19-fret bound ebony fingerboard with pearl dot inlay, adjustable ebony bridge/wrapover trapeze tailpiece, blackface peghead with pearl logo inlay, 3-per-side nickel tuners, available in Black finish, mfg. 1931-39.

1931-1934	N/A	$2,500	$1,800
1935-1939	N/A	$2,500	$1,800

Advanced Body (17" body width) offered. In 1934, Advanced Body (17 in. wide by 21 in. long), bound pickguard, checkered top binding, double triangle fingerboard inlay, redesigned trapeze tailpiece, bound peghead with pearl vase inlay, Red Mahogany finish replaced original part/design. In 1935, redesigned tailpiece, redesigned peghead inlay replaced previous part/design.

L-12 - arched spruce top, f-holes, raised bound black pickguard, bound body, carved maple back/sides, mahogany neck, 14/19-fret bound ebony fingerboard with pearl flowers inlay, adjustable ebony bridge/trapeze tailpiece, bound blackface peghead with pearl vase/logo inlay, 3-per-side gold tuners, available in Red Mahogany Sunburst finish, limited mfg. 1932-1955.

1932-1934	N/A	$2,500	$1,800
1935-1955	N/A	$2,500	$1,800

Advanced Body (17 in. body width by 21 in. long) offered. In 1934, multi-bound pickguard/top/peghead, parallelogram fingerboard inlay, diamond/star peghead inlay replaced original part/design. In 1937, redesigned tailpiece replaced previous part/design. In 1941, bound pickguard/peghead, crown peghead inlay replaced previous part/design.

L-12 P (Premiere) - similar to L-12, except has single round cutaway, approx. 90 mfg. 1947-1950.

	N/A	$4,500	$2,600

L-20 SPECIAL - spruce top, round soundhole, 2-stripe bound body/rosette, rosewood back/sides/neck, 14/19-fret bound rosewood fingerboard with pearl dot inlay, rosewood bridge with white pins, 3-per-side gold tuners with plastic buttons, piezo bridge pickup, endpin pickup jack, available in Antique Natural or Vintage Sunburst finishes, disc. 1998.

	N/A	$1,300	$800

Last MSR was $2,000.

L-30 - arched spruce top, f-holes, raised black pickguard, bound body, maple back/sides, mahogany neck, 14/19-fret ebony fingerboard with pearl dot inlay, adjustable ebony bridge/trapeze tailpiece, blackface peghead with screened logo, 3-per-side tuners with plastic buttons, available in Black finish, mfg. 1935-1943.

	N/A	$750	$500

In 1936, Dark Mahogany Sunburst finish replaced original part/design. In 1938, rosewood bridge replaced original part/design. 14 3/4 in. wide, 19 1/4 in. long.

L-37 - similar to L-30, except has Red Mahogany Sunburst finish, mfg. 1935-1941.

	N/A	$750	$500

In 1936, Brown Sunburst finish replaced original part/design.

L-47 - arched spruce top, f-holes, raised bound pickguard, tortoise bound body, maple back/sides, mahogany neck, 14/19-fret ebony fingerboard with pearl dot inlay, adjustable ebony bridge/trapeze tailpiece, blackface peghead with screened logo, 3-per-side tuners with plastic buttons, available in Natural or Sunburst finishes, mfg. 1940-43.

	N/A	$650	$400

GRADING	100%	EXCELLENT	AVERAGE

G

L-48 - arched mahogany top, f-holes, raised black pickguard, bound body, mahogany back/sides/neck, 14/19-fret rosewood fingerboard with pearl dot inlay, adjustable rosewood bridge/trapeze tailpiece, blackface peghead with screened logo, 3-per-side tuners, available in Cremona Brown Sunburst finish, mfg. 1946-1970.

| | N/A | $600 | $400 |

A few early instruments have spruce tops, trapezoid fingerboard inlay. In 1952, spruce top, maple back, mahogany sides replaced original part/design. In 1957, mahogany top replaced previous part/design, some instruments found with mahogany back also.

L-50 - arched spruce top, f-hole, black pickguard, bound body, maple back/sides, mahogany neck, 14/19-fret ebony fingerboard with trapezoid or pearl dot inlay, adjustable ebony bridge/trapeze tailpiece, blackface peghead with screened logo, 3-per-side tuners with plastic buttons, available in Dark Mahogany Sunburst finish, mfg. 1932-1970.

| **1932-1942** | N/A | $1,200 | $900 |
| **1943-1971** | N/A | $900 | $600 |

In 1934, redesigned body (16 1/4 in. body width, 20 1/4 in. long, arched back), raised pickguard, redesigned tailpiece replaced original part/design. In 1935, orchestra style body replaced previous part/design, arched back replaced original part/design. In 1936, redesigned tailpiece replaced previous part/design. In 1943, redesigned tailpiece replaced original part/design, 3-per-side plate mounted tuners replaced original part/design. In 1946, bound pickguard/fingerboard with pearl trapezoid inlay replaced original part/design, redesigned tailpiece, 3-per-side tuners with plastic buttons replaced previous part/design. In 1949, laminated pickguard replaced previous part/design.

L-75 - arched spruce top, f-holes, bound body, mahogany back/sides, mahogany neck, 14/19-fret pearloid fingerboard with pearl multi-design inlay in blocks of rosewood, adjustable rosewood bridge/trapeze tailpiece, pearloid veneered peghead, rosewood diamond peghead inlay with pearl logo, 3-per-side tuners with plastic buttons, available in Natural or Sunburst finish, mfg. 1932-39.

| | N/A | $900 | $650 |

In 1934, redesigned body/tailpiece, bound rosewood fingerboard with pearl dot inlay, blackface peghead with pearl vase logo inlay replaced original part/design. In 1935, carved back replaced original part/design, orchestra style body, redesigned peghead inlay replaced previous part/design, raised pickguard added. 16 1/4 in. by 20 1/4 in. body.

Gibson L-10
courtesy Dave Hull

L-130 - features Gibson's Advanced 00 body design, spruce top, bubinga back/sides, rosewood fingerboard/bridge, mahogany neck, abalone fingerboard inlays and rosette, active transducer, available in Antique Natural finish. New 1999.

| **MSR** | **$2,391** | $1,575 | $1,200 | $775 |

Add $239 for left hand model.

L-140 - similar to L-130, except has Indian rosewood back/sides, and ebony fingerboard/bridge. New 1999.

| **MSR** | **$3,109** | $2,200 | $1,525 | $1,025 |

L-150 CUSTOM - custom shop model with customer selected wood, without active transducer pickup, available in Antique Natural finish, mfg. 1999-2002.

| | $4,075 | $3,100 | $2,050 |

Last MSR was $5,748.

L-200 EMMYLOU HARRIS - custom shop model with newly designed body that's smaller and thinner than the SJ-200, new bracing, includes Schertler Bluestick transducer pickup system, SJ-200 features include flame maple back/sides, mother-of-pearl crest fingerboard inlays, moustache bridge, and engraved pickguard, available in Antique Natural or Vintage Sunburst finish, new 2002.

| **MSR** | **$3,299** | $2,350 | $1,625 | $1,075 |

L-CENTURY (CENTURY OF PROGRESS) - spruce top, 14 3/4 in. by 19 1/4 in., round soundhole, tortoise pickguard, bound body, 1-stripe rosette, curly maple back/sides, mahogany neck, 14/19-fret bound pearloid fingerboard, rosewood block with pearl diamonds fingerboard inlay, rosewood straight bridge with white pins, bound peghead with pearloid veneer, rosewood wedge with pearl slotted diamond/logo inlay, 3-per-side tuners with plastic buttons, available in Sunburst finish, mfg. 1933-1940.

| | N/A | $3,500 | $2,500 |

In 1938, 2 types of rosewood peghead veneer replaced original part/design; one featured pearl diamond inlay, the other was bound with pearl slotted diamond/logo inlay.

L-JR. - carved spruce top, round bound soundhole, birch back/sides, maple neck, 13/19-fret ebony fingerboard with pearl dot inlay, ebony bridge/trapeze tailpiece, tortoise plate with black pins on trapeze tailpiece, slotted peghead, 3-per-side tuners with plastic buttons, available in Brown finish, body width 13 1/2", mfg. 1919-1926.

| | N/A | $500 | $350 |

L-Jr. models with truss rod or factory black finish command a higher premium.
The L-Jr. model is a "budget" version of the L-1 archtop.

Gibson L-30
courtesy John Beeson
The Music Shoppe

GRADING	100%	EXCELLENT	AVERAGE

ACOUSTIC: LG SERIES

LG-0 - mahogany top, round soundhole, black pickguard, bound body, 1-stripe rosette, mahogany back/sides/neck, 14/20-fret rosewood fingerboard with pearl dot inlay, rosewood straight bridge with pearl dot inlay, white bridge pins, blackface peghead with screened logo, 3-per-side nickel tuners with plastic buttons, available in Natural finish, mfg. 1958-1974.

	N/A	$450	$300

In 1962, plastic screw-on bridge replaced original part/design. In 1963, redesigned tortoise pickguard replaced original part/design. In 1966, rosewood reverse bridge replaced previous part/design. In 1969, spruce top, standard bridge replaced previous part/design. In 1970, veneerless peghead replaced original part/design, black pickguard replaced previous part/design.

LG-1 - spruce top, round soundhole, tortoise pickguard, bound body, 1-stripe rosette, mahogany back/sides/neck, 14/19-fret rosewood fingerboard with pearl dot inlay, rosewood straight bridge with pearl dot inlay, black bridge pins, blackface peghead with screened logo, 3-per-side nickel tuners with plastic buttons, available in Sunburst finish, approx. 27,000 mfg. 1947-1968.

	N/A	$750	$500

In 1955, redesigned pickguard, 14/20-fret fingerboard replaced original part/design. In 1962, plastic screw-on bridge replaced original part/design.

LG-2 - red spruce top, round soundhole, tortoise shell pickguard, bound body, 1-stripe rosette, mahogany back/sides/neck, 14/19-fret rosewood fingerboard with pearl dot inlay, rosewood straight bridge with pearl dot inlay, black bridge pins, blackface peghead with screened logo, 3-per-side nickel tuners with plastic buttons, available in Cherry Sunburst or Golden Sunburst finishes, mfg. 1942-1962.

1942-1946	N/A	$1,800	$1,500
1947-1962	N/A	$1,350	$900

Add 20% for banner headstock and striped pickguard (produced 1942) variations, add 15% for mahogany back with maple or rosewood sides, 25% for maple sides and back. Add a significant premium for rosewood back and sides.

Subtract 15% for mahogany top.

During WWII, Gibson used whatever materials were available to construct instruments. Consequently, there are LG-2's found with mahogany tops, maple back/sides/neck, no truss rods and other little differences from other production models found before and after the war. In 1955, redesigned pickguard, 14/20-fret fingerboard replaced original part/design. In 1961, Cherry Sunburst finish replaced original part/design.

LG-2 3/4 - similar to LG-2, except has 3/4 size body, mfg. 1949-1968.

	N/A	$950	$650

ARLO GUTHRIE LG-2 3/4 - patterned after the LG-2 that Woody Guthrie gave to Arlo Guthrie in 1953, similar to LG-2 3/4, except has Sitka spruce top, 14/20-fret, mahognay neck/back/sides, available in Vintage Sunburst, new 2003.

MSR	$2,595	$1,700	$1,495	$1,150

LG-3 - spruce top, round soundhole, tortoise shell pickguard, 3-stripe bound body/rosette, mahogany back/sides/neck, 14/19-fret rosewood fingerboard with pearl dot inlay, rosewood straight bridge with pearl dot inlay, white bridge pins, blackface peghead with banner/logo decal, 3-per-side nickel tuners with plastic buttons, available in Natural finish, mfg. 1945-1963.

	N/A	$1,850	$1,350

Add 25% for pre-1955 mfg. with teardrop pickguard.

In 1955, teardrop pickguard was replaced by the longer Gibson style pickguard with a single point, 14/20-fret fingerboard replaced original part/design. In 1961, adjustable bridge replaced original part/design. In early 1962, reverse rosewood bridge with adjustable saddle replaced previous part/design. In late 1962, plastic screw-on bridge replaced previous part/design. The LG-3 has a "X-braced" top. In 1963, the LG-3 was renamed the B-25N.

LG-12 - mahogany back/sides, 12-string, large belly bridge with bridge pins, adj. saddle, 14 1/8 in. wide, long pickguard with point at upper bout (some models had teardrop pickguard), single black soundhole ring, single-bound top, unbound back, three-piece neck, 18-fret rosewood fingerboard, 24 3/4 in. scale, dot inlays, no peghead veneer, available in Natural top finish, light mahogany finish on back and sides, approx. 1,150 mfg. 1967-1973.

	N/A	$900	$550

This model does not appear in the Gibson shipping total records until 1970. Non-adj. saddle and teardrop pickguard were introduced in 1970.

ACOUSTIC: MARK SERIES

All of the following instruments have these features: sloped shouldered body, spruce top, round soundhole, removable pickguard, bound body, mahogany neck, 14/20-fret fingerboard, fan bridge, 3 different replaceable saddles, blackface snakehead peghead, 3-per-side tuners. Available in Natural and Sunburst finishes (unless otherwise noted). The Mark series were produced between 1975 and 1979.

MK-35 - spruce top, 2-stripe rosewood soundhole cap, mahogany back/sides, rosewood fingerboard with pearl dot inlay, nickel tuners, approx. 5,225 mfg.

	N/A	$550	$300

MK-35-12 - similar to MK-35, except has 12-strings, 6-per-side tuners, mfg. 1977 only.

	N/A	$600	$300

Only 12 of these instruments were produced.

MK-53 - spruce top, multi-bound body, 2-stripe rosewood soundhole cap, maple back/sides, rosewood fingerboard with pearl dot inlay, nickel tuners. Approx. 1,425 mfg.

	N/A	$650	$400

GRADING	100%	EXCELLENT	AVERAGE

MK-72 - spruce top, 3-stripe rosette, rosewood back/sides, 3-piece ebony/rosewood/ebony fingerboard with pearl dot inlay, nickel tuners. Approx. 1,225 mfg.

	N/A	$850	$550

MK-81 - spruce top, 3-stripe rosewood rosette cap, multi-bound body, rosewood back/sides, ebony fingerboard with block abalone inlays, gold tuners. Approx. 430 mfg.

	N/A	$900	$625

MK-99 - spruce top, round soundhole with 2-stripe rosewood soundhole cap, red stripe bound body, purple stained rosewood back/sides, purple stained maple neck, 14/20-fret red stripe bound ebony fingerboard with abalone bowtie inlay, ebony fan bridge with silver red dot pins, blackface red bound peghead, 3-per-side gold tuners, available in Natural finish, mfg. 1975-79.

Extreme rarity precludes accurate pricing on this model.
This model was handcrafted and signed by Richard Schneider while he was Gibson's Master Luthier. Less than 12 instruments are known to have been made.

ACOUSTIC: MISC.

CHICAGO 35 - slope shoulder dreadnought style, spruce top, round soundhole, tortoise pickguard, 3-stripe bound body/rosette, mahogany back/sides/neck, 14/19-fret rosewood fingerboard with pearl cross inlay, rosewood straight bridge with white pins, blackface peghead with screened logo, 3-per-side nickel tuners, transducer pickup/preamp system, available in Antique Natural or Special Vintage Sunburst finishes, mfg. 1994-96.

	N/A	$1,300	$750

Last MSR was $2,000.

Gibson LG-0
Blue Book Publications, Inc.

GS-1 - classic style, round soundhole, bound body, 3-stripe rosette, bound body, 2-stripe rosette, mahogany back/sides/neck, 12/19-fret rosewood fingerboard, rosewood tied bridge with pearl cross inlay, blackface peghead with screened logo, 3-per-side tuners with plastic buttons, available in Natural finish, approx. 140 mfg. 1950-56.

	N/A	$550	$375

This series has gut strings.

GS-2 - similar to GS-1, except has maple back/sides, approx. 175 mfg. 1954-1959.

	N/A	$600	$375

GS-5 (Custom Classic) - similar to GS-1, except has rosewood back/sides, approx. 85 mfg. 1954-1959.

	N/A	$750	$400

This model was originally designated the Custom Classic in 1954. In 1957, it was renamed the GS-5.

GS-35 - classical style, spruce top, round soundhole, bound body, 2-stripe rosette, mahogany back/sides/neck, 12/19-fret ebony fingerboard, rosewood tied bridge, solid blackface peghead with screened logo, 3-per-side tuners with plastic buttons, available in Natural finish, approx. 40 mfg. 1939-1941.

	N/A	$650	$300

This series has gut strings.

GS-85 - similar to GS-35, except has rosewood back/sides, pearl bridge inlay, approx. 25 mfg. 1939-1941.

	N/A	$850	$400

This series has gut strings.

HERITAGE - dreadnought body, round soundhole, tortoise pickguard, 2-stripe bound body/rosette, laminated rosewood back/sides, mahogany neck, 14/20-fret ebony fingerboard with pearl dot inlay, reverse ebony bridge with white pins, adjustable saddle, blackface peghead with logo decal, 3-per-side nickel tuners, available in Natural finish, mfg. 1965-1982.

1965-1969	N/A	$1,100	$700
1970-1982	N/A	$600	$450

Several Heritage Deluxe models were mfg. in 1968 only.
In 1968, standard bridge replaced original part/design. In 1969, black pickguard, pearl diamond/curlicue/logo peghead inlay replaced original part/design. In 1971, pearl block fingerboard inlay replaced original part/design, redesigned bridge with pearl curlicue inlay replaced previous part/design. In 1973, bound fingerboard replaced original part/design.

Heritage 12 - similar to Heritage, except has 12-strings, 6-per-side tuners, approx. 140 mfg. 1968-1970.

	N/A	$750	$500

Gibson LG-2
courtesy Rockohaulix

GRADING	100%	EXCELLENT	AVERAGE

JUBILEE - 3/4 size square shouldered body, spruce top, round soundhole, black pickguard, bound body/rosette, mahogany back/sides/neck, 14/20-fret rosewood fingerboard with pearl dot inlay, adjustable rosewood bridge, 3-per-side tuners, available in Natural finish, approx. 255 mfg. 1970-71.

	N/A	$700	$400

Jubilee 12-string - similar to Jubilee, except has 12-strings, 6-per-side tuners. Approx. 75 mfg. 1970-71.

	N/A	$500	$300

Jubilee Deluxe - similar to Jubilee, except has multi-wooden binding/purfling, rosewood back/sides. Approx. 165 mfg. 1970 only.

	N/A	$800	$600

ROY SMECK RADIO GRANDE - spruce top, 16 in. wide, 20 1/4 in. long, 4 1/2 in. deep, round soundhole, tortoise pickguard, bound body, 1-stripe rosette, rosewood back/sides, mahogany neck, 12/19-fret bound rosewood fingerboard with pearl varying diamond inlay, rosewood straight bridge with black pearl dot pins, blackface peghead with screened model name/logo, 3-per-side tuners with plastic buttons, available in Natural finish, less than 100 mfg. 1934-39.

	N/A	$6,000	$4,500

Roy Smeck Stage Deluxe - similar to Radio Grande, except has mahogany back/sides, pearl dot fingerboard inlay, white pearl dot bridge pins, available in Sunburst finish, mfg. 1934-1942.

	N/A	$3,000	$2,500

Two styles of this model were available; Standard and Hawaiian. The Standard model had the logo only screened on the peghead. The Hawaiian model featured inlaid ivoroid pieces instead of frets. The ivoroid pieces were usually replaced by frets, making the original ivoroid inlay configuration more desired by collectors. In 1935, bound fingerboard with varying pearl diamond inlay replaced original part/design.

ACOUSTIC: MODEL O & STYLE U HARP SERIES

MODEL O - arched spruce top, oval soundhole, bound body, wood inlay rosette, walnut back/sides, mahogany neck, 12/20-fret bound pointed rosewood fingerboard with pearl dot inlay, rosewood bridge/trapeze tailpiece with black pearl dot pins, bound blackface peghead with pearl logo inlay, friction tuners, available in Black Top finish, mfg. 1902-07.

	N/A	$5,000	$4,000

The Model O had features from both archtop and flat top construction. Some models have an 18" body width. This model was also available in a Presentation version, which is extremely rare (the last recorded sale of a Presentation model was for $15,000). In 1906, a slotted peghead was introduced.

STYLE O ARTIST - single sharp cutaway body, carved spruce top, scrolled upper bass bout, oval soundhole, raised tortoise pickguard, bound body, wood inlay rosette, maple back/sides, mahogany neck, 15/22-fret bound extended ebony fingerboard with pearl dot inlay, ebony bridge/trapeze tailpiece with black pearl dot pins, bound blackface peghead with pearl fleur-de-lis/logo inlay, 3-per-side diecast tuners, available in Amber, Black, Mahogany Stain, or Mahogany Sunburst finishes, mfg. 1908-1923.

	N/A	$4,000	$3,000

In 1914, Amber and Mahogany finishes replaced original finishes. In 1918, redesigned pickguard/peghead inlay replaced original part/design. Mahogany Sunburst finish replaced previous finish.

STYLE U HARP GUITAR - 6-string/9 or 10 bass string configuration, round soundhole, scroll on upper bass bout, maple back and sides, bound soundhole, mahogany bridge, ebony fingerboard with dot inlay, veneer peghead, available in Black Top/Dark Mahogany back/sides finish, body width 21", mfg. 1902-1939.

	N/A	$5,500	$3,250

Although this model stayed listed in Gibson catalogs until 1939, it's unlikely that models were manufactured after 1924.

ACOUSTIC: SONGBIRD SERIES

SONGBIRD - square shoulder body similar to the Hummingbird & Dove Series, solid spruce top, mahogany back/sides/neck, morado fingerboard/bridge, contoured 2 point pickguard, gloss finished top with satin back, available in Antique Walnut finish, mfg. 1999-2002.

$1,325	$950	$625
	Last MSR was $1,846.	

SONGBIRD DELUXE - similar to Songbird, except has Indian rosewood back/sides/fingerboard/bridge, abalone fingerboard inlays and rosette, includes active transducer pickup, available in Antique Natural finish, mfg. 1999-2002.

$1,675	$1,200	$825
	Last MSR was $2,399.	

Add $208 for cutaway body. (Songbird Deluxe Cutaway EC, disc. 2002).

SONGBIRD DELUXE KOA - similar to Songbird, except has koa back/sides, limited mfg. beginning 2003.

MSR	$3,027	$1,975	$1,500	$1,150

GRADING	100%	EXCELLENT	AVERAGE

ACOUSTIC: SONGWRITER SERIES

SONGWRITER - square shoulder body similar to the Hummingbird & Dove Series, solid Sitka spruce top, solid mahogany back/sides/neck, morado fingerboard with pearloid trapezoid inlays, gold Grover Kidney tuners and tortoise 3 point mini-hummingbird shape pickguard, available in Natural Gloss Top/Satin Back finish, new 2003.

MSR	$1,846	$1,325 $900	$600

SONGWRITER DELUXE - similar to Songwriter, except has solid rosewood back/sides, abalone double paralellogram fingerboard inlays and rosette, ebony fingerboard and bridge, includes Fishman active transducer pickup, available in Antique Natural finish. New 2003.

MSR	$2,399	$1,575 $1,200	$775

Add $208 for cutaway body.

Special Songwriter Deluxe Brazilian - features Brazilian rosewood back/sides. Antique Natural finish only, mfg. by Custom Shop, new 2003.

MSR	$3,892	$2,550 $1,950	$1,475

Custom Songwriter Deluxe 12-String Brazilian - similar to Special Songwriter Deluxe Brazilian, except is 12-string, new 2003.

MSR	$4,324	$2,825 $2,150	$1,675

ACOUSTIC: SUPER 300 & SUPER 400 SERIES: DISC.

For current Super 400 Series pricing, please refer to the individual listings under Gibson Historic Collection Acoustic Models section.

SUPER 300 - same dimensions as the Super 400, arched spruce top, f-holes, raised multi-ply black pickguard, figured maple back/sides, multiple bound body, 3-piece figured maple/mahogany neck, 14/20-fret bound Brazilian rosewood fingerboard with pearl parallelogram inlay, adjustable rosewood bridge/nickel trapeze tailpiece, multi-bound blackface peghead with pearl crown/logo inlay, 3-per-side nickel tuners, available in Golden Sunburst finish, approx. 200 mfg. 1948-1955.

	N/A	$3,500	$3,000

Super 300 C - similar to Super 300, except has a single rounded cutaway, very limited mfg. 1957-58.

	N/A	$5,000	$4,000

SUPER 400 - carved spruce top, bound f-holes, raised multi-bound tortoise shell pickguard, carved maple back/sides, multiple bound body, 3-piece figured maple neck, model name engraved into heel cap, 13/20-fret bound ebony fingerboard with point on bottom, pearl split block fingerboard inlay, adjustable rosewood bridge with pearl triangle wings inlay, gold trapeze tailpiece with engraved model name, multi-bound blackface peghead with pearl 5-piece split diamond/logo inlay, pearl 3-piece split diamond inlay on back of peghead, 3-per-side engraved gold tuners, available in Brown Sunburst or Natural finishes, 25 1/2 in. scale, body width 18 in., 21 3/4 in. long, 3 1/2 in. deep, mfg. 1934-1955.

1934-1939	N/A	$8,000	$5,000
1945-1955	N/A	$7,500	$5,000

From 1934 to 1938, Varitone tailpiece replaced previous part/design. In 1936, upper bouts were widened. In 1937, Grover Imperial tuners became an option. In 1938, Kluson Sealfast tuners replaced original part/design. In 1939, Natural finish became an option. In 1941, engraved heel cap and rosewood bridge with pearl inlay were discontinued. This model, like many of Gibson's high end instruments, was not manufactured during World War II. Current production instruments (1939 Super 400 in Natural or Cremona Brown) are part of the Historic Collection Series, found at the end of this section.

Super 400 Premier (Super 400 C) - similar to Super 400, except has a single rounded cutaway, multi-bound pearloid pickguard, unhinged Varitone tailpiece, available in Brown Sunburst (most common) or Natural finishes, limited mfg. 1939-1983, typically less than 25 were mfg. each year.

1939-1942	N/A	$18,000	$13,500
1944-1962	N/A	$14,000	$10,000
1963-1969	N/A	$10,000	$7,500
1970-1983	N/A	$10,000	$7,500

Some early models were produced with solid metal tuners. In 1942, no model name was indicated on heel cap. This model, like many of Gibson's high end instruments, was not manufactured during World War II. In 1948, this model was renamed the Super 400 C. In 1949, rosewood fingerboard replaced original part/design. In 1953, ebony fingerboard replaced previous part/design. By 1957, metal tuners replaced original part/design. Current production instruments (1939 Super 400 Premier in Natural or Cremona Brown) are part of the Historic Collection Series, found at the end of this section.

**Gibson Songbird
courtesy Gibson**

G

**Gibson Super 300
courtesy LaVonn
Wagner Music**

GRADING	100%	EXCELLENT	AVERAGE

ACOUSTIC: WORKING MAN/WORKING MUSICIANS SERIES

Working Musician and Working Man models are available in limited quantities.

WORKING MUSICIAN OO - features Gibson's new Advanced 00 body design, spruce top, mahogany back/sides/neck, morado fingerboard and bridge, gloss top with satin back and sides, available in Antique Walnut finish, mfg. 1999-2000.

	$975	$720	$500

Last MSR was $1,439.

BLUESBENDER (WM00) - small body, Sitka spruce top, round soundhole, mahogany back/sides, 3-per-side nickel tuners, available in Antique Walnut satin finish, mfg. 1998 only.

	N/A	$675	$450

Last MSR was $1,099.

SONGWRITER DREADNOUGHT (WM10) - dreadnought style, Sitka spruce top, round soundhole, mahogany back/sides, 3-per-side nickel tuners, available in Antique Walnut satin finish, mfg. 1998 only.

	N/A	$675	$450

Last MSR was $1,099.

WORKING MAN 45 (WM45) - soft round shouldered dreadnought style, Sitka spruce top, round soundhole, mahogany back/sides, 3-per-side nickel tuners, available in Antique Walnut satin finish, mfg. 1988-current.

MSR	$1,768	$1,250	$875	$575

WORKING MUSICIAN J-180 - solid spruce top, mahogany back/sides/neck, morado fingerboard/bridge, Antique Walnut finish with gloss top and satin back, mfg. 1999-2000.

	$1,200	$900	$525

Last MSR was $1,639.

GIBSON HISTORIC COLLECTION ACOUSTIC MODELS

The instruments in these series are reproductions of Gibson classics, manufactured by the Custom Shop in Nashville, TN. These guitars are manufactured to the exact specifications of their original release and in several cases, use the same tooling when available. The Gibson Historic Collection first debuted in 1991, and is now formally part of the Gibson Custom, Art, Historic Division.

Historic Collection instruments are produced in limited quantities. The few guitars that do show up in the secondary marketplace are usually in Excellent+ (95% - 98% condition).

CITATION (HSCTNAGH) - single rounded cutaway multi-bound body, carved spruce top, bound f-holes, raised multi-bound flamed maple pickguard, figured maple back/sides/neck, 20-fret multi-bound pointed fingerboard with pearl cloud inlay, adjustable ebony bridge with pearl fleur-de-lis inlay on wings, gold trapeze tailpiece with engraved model name, multi-bound ebony veneered peghead with abalone fleur-de-lis/logo inlay, abalone fleur-de-lis inlay on back of peghead, floating BJB pickup with volume control on pickboard, 3-per-side gold engraved tuners, available in Natural finish, current mfg.

MSR	$30,187	$20,500	$11,750	$9,600

Citation (HSCT( )GH) - with Faded Cherry Sunburst (FC) and Honeyburst (HB) finishes.

MSR	$24,941	$16,600	$9,800	$8,300

1934 L-5 NON-CUTAWAY (HSL5BRGH) - multi-bound body, carved spruce top, layered tortoise pickguard, bound f-holes, maple back/sides/neck, 20-fret bound pointed ebony fingerboard with pearl block inlay, ebony bridge with pearl inlay on wings, model name engraved trapeze tailpiece with chrome insert, multi-bound blackface peghead with pearl flame/logo inlay, 3-per-side gold tuners, available in Cremona Brown Sunburst finish, current mfg.

MSR	$5,891	$3,850	$2,325	$1,975

L-5 CT (HSLCTFCGH) - single rounded cutaway bound hollow thinline body, carved spruce top, bound f-holes, solid maple back/sides, 5-piece laminated maple neck, 20-fret bound pointed ebony fingerboard with pearl block inlay, ebony bridge/model name engraved trapeze tailpiece with chrome insert, multi-ply bound blackface peghead with pearl flowerpot/logo inlay, 3-per-side Schaller M-6 tuners, gold hardware, layered tortoise pickguard, available in Natural (NA), Vintage Sunburst (VS), or Faded Cherry (FC) finish, body width 17", mfg. 1998-current.

MSR	$7,829	$5,150	$3,200	$2,525

L-5 CT (HSLCTVSGH) - with Vintage Sunburst (VS) finish.

MSR	$10,448	$6,875	$4,225	$3,150

L-5 CT (HSLCTNAGH) - with Natural finish.

MSR	$13,065	$8,550	$5,300	$4,300

GRADING	100%	EXCELLENT	AVERAGE

1939 SUPER 400 (HSS4NAGH) - arched spruce top, bound f-holes, raised multi-bound mottled plastic pickguard, figured maple back/sides, multiple bound body, 3-piece figured maple/mahogany neck, model name engraved into heel cap, 14/20-fret bound ebony fingerboard with point on bottom, pearl split block fingerboard inlay, adjustable rosewood bridge with pearl triangle wings inlay, gold trapeze tailpiece with engraved model name, multi-bound blackface peghead with pearl 5-piece split diamond/logo inlay, pearl 3-piece split diamond inlay on back of peghead, 3-per-side gold Grover Imperial tuners, available in Natural or Cremona Brown Burst finish, disc. 1998.

$7,750 $5,000 $3,500
Last MSR was $14,719.

1939 Super 400 (HSS4BRGH) - with Cremona Brown Burst finish.

$7,500 $4,750 $3,250
Last MSR was $13,739.

1939 SUPER 400 PREMIER (HS4PNAGH) - single round cutaway body, arched spruce top, bound f-holes, raised multi-bound pearloid pickguard, figured maple back/sides, multiple bound body, 3-piece figured maple/mahogany neck, model name engraved into heel cap, 14/20-fret bound ebony fingerboard with point on bottom, pearl split block fingerboard inlay, adjustable rosewood bridge with pearl triangle wings inlay, gold unhinged PAF trapeze tailpiece with engraved model name, multi-bound blackface peghead with pearl 5-piece split diamond/logo inlay, pearl 3-piece split diamond inlay on back of peghead, 3-per-side gold Grover Imperial tuners, available in Natural or Cremond Brown Burst finish, disc. 1998.

$7,750 $5,000 $3,500
Last MSR was $14,719.

1939 Super 400 Premier (HS4PBRGH) - with Cremona Brown Burst finish.

$7,500 $4,750 $3,250
Last MSR was $13,739.

**Gibson Chet Akins
courtesy Mitch Mitchell**

ACOUSTIC ELECTRIC: GENERAL INFORMATION

The following Acoustic Electric category names appear in this order: Chet Atkins Series, J Series (numbered), L Series, Les Paul Series, and Misc. Even though many of Gibson's current acoustic models now have either transducer or active transducer pickups, only those acoustic electric models with the traditional Gibson E suffix or visible pickup with controls will appear in this section.

ACOUSTIC ELECTRIC: CHET ATKINS SERIES

This series is manufactured in Nashville, TN, and is part of Gibson USA.

CHET ATKINS CE (ARCE) - single rounded cutaway mahogany body with hollow sound chambers, solid spruce top, round soundhole with plastic bowl insert, 2-stripe bound body, wood inlay rosette, mahogany neck, 19-fret rosewood fingerboard, tied rosewood bridge, rosewood veneer on slotted peghead, 3-per-side gold tuners with pearl buttons, Gibson piezo bridge pickups, volume/tone control, active electronics, available in Alpine White (AW), Cedar (CD), Ebony (EB), or Wine Red (WR) finishes. Disc. 2002.

$1,285 $940 $575
Last MSR was $1,898.

In 1994, Alpine White and Ebony finishes were discontinued.

Chet Atkins CE-AN (ARCE) - similar to the Chet Atkins CE, except is available with Antique Natural finish with gold hardware. Disc. 2002.

$2,190 $1,600 $1,075
Last MSR was $3,248.

Chet Atkins True Cedar CE-AN (ARER) - similar to the Chet Atkins CE, except is available with True Cedar top (new 1999), Antique Natural finish with gold hardware. Disc. 2002.

$2,275 $1,650 $1,175
Last MSR was $3,398.

CHET ATKINS CEC (ARCC) - similar to Chet Atkins CE, except has 2" nut width. Available in Cedar (CD), or Wine Red (WR) finishes. Disc. 2002.

$1,375 $995 $615
Last MSR was $1,998.

Chet Atkins CEC-AN (ARCC) - similar to the Chet Atkins CEC, except is available with Antique Natural finish with gold hardware, current mfg.

$2,275 $1,650 $1,175
Last MSR was $3,398.

**Gibson Chet Akins CEC
courtesy Gibson**

Chet Atkins CEC-AN (ARCR) - similar to the Chet Atkins CEC, except available with True Cedar top (new 1999), Antique Natural finish with gold hardware. Disc. 2002.

	100%	EXCELLENT	AVERAGE
	$2,375	$1,775	$1,175

Last MSR was $3,548.

CHET ATKINS STUDIO CE (ARSE) - single rounded cutaway hollow mahogany body, bound body, solid spruce top, 3-piece mahogany neck, 24-fret ebony fingerboard with no inlay, 3-per-side tuners with plastic buttons, slotted headstock, gold hardware, bridge-mounted piezo pickup, volume/bass/treble controls, available in Antique Natural finish with gold hardware, mfg. 1993-99.

	$2,800	$1,825	$1,275

Last MSR was $3,999.

Chet Atkins Studio CEC (ARST) - similar to the Chet Atkins Studio CE, except has a solid cedar top, available in Antique Natural finish with gold hardware, disc. 1999.

	$2,850	$1,850	$1,300

Last MSR was $4,107.

CHET ATKINS SST (ARSS) - single round cutaway mahogany body with hollow sound chamber, 5-stripe bound solid spruce top with Chet Atkins' signature, mahogany neck, 21-fret ebony fingerboard with pearl star inlay, ebony bridge with black pearl dot pins, pearl star bridge wings inlay, blackface peghead with pearl star/logo inlay, 3-per-side gold tuners, transducer bridge pickup, volume/treble/bass controls, active electronics, available in Alpine White (AW), Ebony (EB), Heritage Cherry Sunburst (HS), or Wine Red (WR) finishes, mfg. 1987-current.

MSR	$2,398	$1,660	$1,150	$700

In 1994, Alpine White and Wine Red finishes were discontinued.

Chet Atkins SST-AN (ARSS-AN) - similar to Chet Atkins SST, except has spruce or True Cedar (new 1999) top, Antique Natural finish and gold hardware, current mfg.

MSR	$2,598	$1,775	$1,300	$925

Add $200 for true cedar top.

In 1994, Translucent Red finish was discontinued.

Chet Atkins SST Flame Top - similar to Chet Atkins SST, except has figured maple top. Available in Antique Natural, Heritage Cherry Sunburst, or Translucent Red finishes, disc. 1995.

	N/A	$925	$575

Last MSR was $2,179.

In 1994, Translucent Amber finish was introduced, Translucent Red finish was discontinued.

Chet Atkins SST 12 - similar to Chet Atkins SST, except has 12-string configuration, 6-per-side tuners, available in Ebony or Wine Red finishes, disc. 1994.

	N/A	$625	$425

Last MSR was $1,250.

Add $250 for Antique Natural finish.

Chet Atkins SST 12 Flame Top - similar to Chet Atkins SST, except has 12-string configuration, flame maple top, 6-per-side tuners, available in Antique Natural, Heritage Cherry Sunburst, or Translucent Red finishes, disc. 1994.

	N/A	$800	$525

Last MSR was $1,600.

ACOUSTIC ELECTRIC: CITATION & KALAMAZOO SERIES

CITATION - single round cutaway multi-bound body, carved spruce top, bound f-holes, raised multi-bound flamed maple pickguard, figured maple back/sides/neck, 20-fret multi-bound pointed fingerboard with pearl cloud inlay, adjustable ebony bridge with pearl fleur-de-lis inlay on wings, gold trapeze tailpiece with engraved model name, multi-bound ebony veneered peghead with abalone fleur-de-lis/logo inlay, abalone fleur-de-lis inlay on back of peghead, floating pickup with volume control on pickguard, 3-per-side gold engraved tuners, 17 in. wide, 20 1/2 in. long, 3 in. deep, available in Faded Cherry Sunburst, Honeyburst or Natural finishes. Very limited mfg. beginning 1969, currently produced by the Gibson Custom Shop.

	N/A	$14,000-$17,500	$8,750-$10,000

Less than 10 Citations were mfg. between 1969 - 1979. In 1982, Gibson produced 3 more (by customer request). Current production instruments are part of the Historic Collection Series (see Gibson Historic Collection Acoustic Models).

KALAMAZOO AWARD - top-of-the-line archtop mfg. in Kalamazoo, MI, circa 1978-1984, similar dimensions as the Citation, except is 4 inches deep, trapeze tailpiece has eagle inlay and pickguard has eagle landing in tree branch, floating pickup with volume control on pickguard, available in Natural or Sunburst finish. Less than 30 mfg. 1978-1984.

	N/A	$12,000-$15,000	$6,500-$8,500

The Kalamazoo Award model followed the Citation in production.

ACOUSTIC ELECTRIC: J SERIES

J-160 E - slope shouldered body, spruce top, round soundhole, tortoise pickguard, 2-stripe bound body/rosette, mahogany back/sides/neck, 15/19-fret bound rosewood fingerboard with pearl block/trapezoid inlay, rosewood bridge with white pins, adjustable saddle,

GRADING	100%	EXCELLENT	AVERAGE

blackface peghead with pearl crown/logo inlay, 3-per-side nickel tuners, single coil pickup, volume/tone control, available in Sunburst finish, over 4,400 mfg. 1954-1979.

1954-1959	N/A	$2,000	$1,275
1960-1964	N/A	$1,450	$1,100
1965-1968	N/A	$1,300	$900
1969-1979	N/A	$1,200	$950

J-160 E (REISSUE) - similar to J-160 E, except has regular saddle, available in Vintage Sunburst finish, mfg. 1991-96.

	N/A	$900	$595

Last MSR was $1,900.

J-160 E STANDARD - patterned after the original J-160 E, Vintage Sunburst finish, J-45 body style, solid spruce top and mahogany back/sides, rosewood bridge and fretboard, P-100 pickup with nickel Gotch and Keystone buttons, limited mfg. beginning 2003.

MSR	$3,050		$1,995	$1,525	$1,175

J-160 E JOHN LENNON LIMITED EDITION - slope/round shoulder, laminated spruce top with ladder bracing, mahogany back/sides/neck, rosewood fingerboard and bridge, 24¾ in. scale, P-90 single coil pickup between fretboard/soundhole, Lennon signature truss rod cover, available in Vintage Sunburst finish, limited mfg. 2000 only.

	$2,275	$1,750	$1,450

Last MSR was $3,500.

**Gibson Chet Akins SST
courtesy Gibson**

G

J-160 E JOHN LENNON PEACE MODEL - slope/round shoulder, solid Sitka spruce top, mahogany back/sides/neck, 15/20 rosewood fretboard with pearloid trapezoid inlays, P-100 stacked humbucker pickups, unsigned tortoise pickguard, Lennon signature truss rod cover, authentic replica strap, limited edition with certificate of authenticity. New 2003.

MSR	$3,674		$2,625	$1,825	$1,200

This model is patterned after John Lennon's original J-160 E guitar circa 1969, after he stripped away the psychedelic paint job he commissioned in 1967.

J-160 E JOHN LENNON COLLECTION SET - includes 3 separate J-160E variations – a Fab Four Model (Lennon Model 1), Magical Tour Model (Lennon Model 2), Bed-In Model (Lennon Model 3), only 47 sets are scheduled for production by the MT Custom Shop, limited mfg. 1999-2002.

	$39,500	$28,500	$16,500

Last MSR was $50,000.

J-160 E John Lennon Bed-In - available individually 2001-2002.

	$12,500	$8,750	$5,250

Last MSR was $18,020.

J-160 E John Lennon Magical Tour - available individually 2001-2002.

	$12,500	$8,750	$5,250

Last MSR was $18,020.

J-160 E John Lennon Fab Four - available individually 2001-2002.

	$12,500	$8,750	$5,250

Last MSR was $18,020.

J-180 EC - solid spruce top, figured maple back/sides/neck, rosewood fingerboard and bridge, mother-of-pearl starburst or dot fingerboard inlays and abalone rosette, with onboard controls, available in Antique Walnut, Vintage Sunburst, or Ebony finish, mfg. 1999-2002.

	$1,800	$1,275	$850

Last MSR was $2,571.

Subtract $427 for dot inlays and Ebony finish.

J-185 EC (BLUES KING ELECTRO) - solid spruce top, flame maple back/sides/neck, ebony fingerboard and bridge, parallelogram mother-of-pearl fingerboard inlays and abalone rosette, with onboard controls, available in Antique Natural or Vintage Sunburst finish, New 1999.

MSR	$3,343		$2,325	$1,675	$1,025

J-190 EC SUPER FUSION - solid spruce top, flame maple back/sides/neck, gold hardware, features Gibson's dual pickup system (single coil pickup and acoustic transducer), available in Antique Natural and Vintage Sunburst (new 2001) finish. New 1999.

MSR	$4,710		$3,300	$2,350	$1,550

**Gibson Chet Akins SST
courtesy Gibson**

GRADING	100%	EXCELLENT	AVERAGE

ACOUSTIC ELECTRIC: L SERIES

L-4 A CUTAWAY - jumbo cutaway body with solid Sitka spruce top, curly maple back/sides/neck, 14/20 rosewood fingerboard with mother-of-pearl trapezoid inlays, rosewood bridge, gold Grover tuners, Fishman Prefix Plus pickup, available in Antique Natural, Vintage Sunburst, Blue Jean, Chet Orange, Emerald, Antique Cherry, Ice Blue, Ebony, and Natural Gloss Top. New 2003.

	MSR	$2,376		$1,725	$1,200	$775

L-7 E/ED/NED - electric variation of the L-7, non-cutaway, L-7 E has one pickup, L-7 ED has two pickups, Sunburst (most common) or Natural (L-7 CNED) finish, limited mfg. 1948-1954.

			N/A	$2,750	$1,875

L-7 CE/CED/CEN - electric cutaway variation of the L-7E, available with either one (L-7CE) or two pickups (L-7 CED), Sunburst (most common) or Natural (L-7 CEN) finish, mfg. 1948-1954.

			N/A	$3,250	$2,300

LC-1 CASCADE - cedar top, thin line cutaway body, quilted maple back/sides, curly maple neck with Indian rosewood 14/20 fingerboard and mother-of-pearl dot inlays, abalone rosette and headstock crown, sculpted Indian rosewood bridge with Schertler Bluestick transducer pickup, volume control, available in Antique Nautral or Vintage Sunburst, includes hardshell case, new 2003.

	MSR	$2,486		$1,775	$1,225	$795

LC-2 SONOMA - similar design to LC-1 Cascade, except has solid cedar top and walnut sides/back, ebony fingerboard with abalone florette inlays, and bridge, new 2003.

	MSR	$3,189		$2,275	$1,675	$1,100

LC-3 CALDERA - similar design to LC-2 Sonoma, except has solid flame koa back/sides, autumn leaf abalone inlays in ebony fingerboard, new 2003.

	MSR	$4,194		$2,995	$1,925	$1,450

ACOUSTIC ELECTRIC: LES PAUL SERIES

LES PAUL JUMBO - slope shouldered body, single rounded cutaway, spruce top, round soundhole, tortoiseshell pickguard, 2-stripe bound body/rosette, bookmatched rosewood back/sides, mahogany neck, 19-fret rosewood fingerboard with pearl dot inlay, rosewood bridge with black and white dot pins, 3-per-side chrome tuners, low impedance single coil pickup, volume/treble/mid/bass controls, 2-position switch, available in Natural finish, approx. 140 mfg. 1969-1973.

			N/A	$1,495	$1,000

LES PAUL ACOUSTIC (CSLPA) - features LP style hollow mahogany body with carved figured maple top, unique bridge is carved directly into top, button type tailpiece with dark bridgepins, L.R. Baggs piezo pickup, tone and volume controls, traditional LP unbound rosewood fingerboard with trapezoid inlays, available in Tangerine Burst (TBG) or Translucent Black (TBK). Limited mfg. 2001-2002.

		$3,800	$2,500	$1,900

Last MSR was $5,680.

This model is produced by the Nashville Gibson Custom Shop, and is part of the Custom Collection.

LES PAUL ACOUSTIC PLAIN TOP - features LP style solid mahogany body with plain maple top, relief carved Pro Shop bridge, L.R. Baggs piezo pickup, tone and volume controls, traditional LP unbound rosewood fingerboard with trapezoid inlays, nickel hardware, available in Tangerine Burst (TBG) Washed Cherry (WC) or Trans Black (TB), new 2003.

	MSR	$3,856		$2,625	$1,950	$1,550

This model is produced by the Nashville Gibson Custom Shop, and is part of the Custom Collection.

ACOUSTIC ELECTRIC: MISC.

ACAPULCO GOLD KOA CUSTOM - advanced 00 body, solid koa top/back/sides, abalone rosette, mother-of-pearl floret fretboard inlays, equipped with Schertler Bluestick pickup system, supplied with certificate of authenticity, 24 mfg. July, 2003.

	MSR	$3,459		$2,250	$1,725	$1,400

ACOUSTIC FIREBIRD - patterned after the J-30, square shoulder dreadnought, Sitka spruce top, quilted Western maple back/sides, curly maple neck with ebony fingerboard with mother-of-pearl/abalone flame inlays, pickguard has engraved flames, 24 3/4 in. scale, 14/20-fret, active Fishman pickup, gold Grover tuners, Antique Cherry finish, limited mfg. 2002.

		$3,300	$2,450	$1,750

Last MSR was $4,701.

BOSSA NOVA - nylon string configuration, single round cutaway body, spruce top, round soundhole, 2-stripe bound body/rosette, rosewood back/sides, mahogany neck, 20-fret rosewood fingerboard, rosewood tied bridge, classical style slotted peghead, 3-per-side nickel tuners with plastic buttons, ceramic bridge pickup, available in Natural finish, 7 mfg. 1971-73.

			N/A	$750	$495

GRADING	100%	EXCELLENT	AVERAGE

G

EAS STANDARD - single round cutaway body, solid spruce top, round soundhole, tortoise pickguard, bound body, 2 multi-stripe rings rosette, maple back/sides/neck, 20-fret rosewood fingerboard with pearl dot inlay, rosewood reverse bridge with white pins, blackface peghead with screened logo, 3-per-side chrome tuners, bridge pickup, 3-band EQ, available in Antique Natural, Cherry and Vintage Sunburst finishes, mfg. 1992-94.

	N/A	$650	$425

Last MSR was $1,300.

EAS Deluxe - similar to EAS Standard, except has figured maple top, white pickguard, bound fingerboard with trapezoid inlay, pearl crown/logo peghead inlay, nickel tuners with plastic buttons, available in Vintage Cherry Sunburst finish, mfg. 1992-94.

	N/A	$750	$495

Last MSR was $1,500.

The Custom Acoustic Line Series was manufactured 1994-98. Models featured the Gibson Advanced Bracing pattern and included a factory-installed transducer with onboard controls.

EC-10 STANDARD (EC10) - single rounded cutaway jumbo style, solid spruce top, round soundhole, body binding, arched maple back, solid maple sides, 24 3/4" scale, 14/20-fret rosewood fingerboard with pearl dot inlay, moustache-style rosewood bridge with white bridgepins, 3-per-side nickel tuners, batwing-shaped tortoise pickguard, bridge transducer, volume/brilliance/3-band EQ controls, phase switch. Available in Cherry, Blue, or Ebony Lacquer finishes, mfg. 1997-98.

	N/A	$1,175	$725

Last MSR was $1,699.

Add $100 for Emerald Forest finish with gold hardware (Model EC-10 Emerald Forest).

EC-20 Starburst (EC20) - similar to the EC-10 Standard, except features multiple-ply body binding, mother-of-pearl starburst-design fingerboard inlay, 3-per-side gold tuners, volume/brilliance/treble contour/bass frequency/notch controls, phase switch, available in Antique Natural, Cherry, or Blue finishes, mfg. 1997-98.

	N/A	$1,500	$950

Last MSR was $2,149.

This model was available with abalone floret position markers as an option.

EC-30 BLUES KING ELECTRO (EC30) - single round cutaway jumbo style, solid spruce top, round soundhole, tortoise pickguard, multistripe bound body/rosette, flame maple back/sides, mahogany neck, 14/20-fret bound ebony fingerboard with pearl parallelogram inlay, ebony bridge with white pins, bound blackface peghead with pearl vase/logo inlay, 3-per-side gold tuners, transducer bridge pickup, volume/brilliance/treble contour/bass frequency/notch controls, phase switch, available in Antique Natural lacquer finish, mfg. 1994-98.

	N/A	$1,800	$1,200

Last MSR was $2,999.

**Gibson Les Paul Acoustic
courtesy Gibson**

Early EC-30 models may have rosewood fingerboards and bridges, nickel tuners. Available in Heritage Cherry Sunburst, Natural top/Antique Chocolate back/sides and Vintage Sunburst finishes.

MAUI WOWIE KOA CUSTOM - round shoulder J-45 style body, solid koa top/back/sides, abalone dot fretboard inlays, equipped with Schertler pickup system, includes custom shop label, decal insignia, and supplied with certificate of authenticity, 24 mfg. July, 2003.

MSR	$3,892		$2,550	$2,000	$1,525

GILBERT GUITARS, JOHN AND BILL

Instruments currently built outside San Francisco, California.

Luthier John Gilbert built his first classical guitar in 1965 as a hobby. By 1974, after performing repair work in addition to his guitar building, Gilbert was concentrating on building full time. In 1991, Gilbert was joined by his son Bill. Gilbert's classical guitars have been favored by a large number of professional players. The design features a responsive projection of volume and tone coloration that depends on the guitarist' playing. Between 1974 to 1991, John Gilbert built an estimated 140 guitars. Both Gilberts build between 6 to 10 guitars annually. Bill has produced 42 guitars now under his own name. For more information on Gilbert Guitars refer to the web site (see Trademark Index).

GILCHRIST, STEPHEN

Instruments currently built in Australia. Distributed by the Carmel Music Company of Carmel, California.

Australian luthier Stephen Gilchrist is known for his high quality mandolins, mandolas and mandocellos. Gilchrist began building instruments in 1976, and spent 1980 in the U.S. working in Nashville, Tennessee at Gruhn Guitars. After 1980, Gilchrist returned to Australia and continues to produce guitars and mandolins. For further information regarding current model specifications and pricing, contact the Carmel Music Company directly (see Trademark Index). Gilchrist has built a number of acoustic and electric guitars; most of

**Gibson Acoustic Firebird
courtesy Gibson**

the electric guitars were built between 1987 and 1988. Currently acoustic guitars and mandolins are offered. To make identification of these guitars a bit difficult, some models do not have the Gilchrist name anywhere on the instrument and none of them have a serial number.

GIRDIS, ROBERT
Instruments currently produced in Seattle, Washington.

1n 1978, luthier Robert Girdis began his studies in guitar construction at the Northwest School of Instrument Design in Seattle. After his first year of intensive studies apprenticeship, Girdis stayed on for a second year as a teaching assistant. In 1981 Girdis established his own workshop of Guemes Island (Washington), sharing a large workshop with a boat builder.

After a short time at work in an Anacortes boat yard, Girdis formed a collaboration with a local wildlife artist to make 50 realistic carved cedar duck decoys. Girdis also served as assistant to Guemes Island's artist/sculptor Phillip McCracken, working on several sculptures in progress in wood, stone, and bronze. Returning to his own shop, Girdis began fashioning commissioned guitars and dulcimers as well as performing instrument repair work. Dulcimer construction offered Girdis the chance to experiment with several different designs, and different exotic woods. Girdis then began to focus on building acoustic guitars, and accepting more commissions for steel string models.

Girdis has been featured in *Frets* Magazine, focusing on the artistic side of the craft. Girdis' guitars are noted for their big acoustic sound and attention to detail in the construction. The list price for Girdis' acoustic guitars start from $2,400. For further information regarding specifications and pricing, contact Robert Girdis directly (see Trademark Index).

GIVENS, ROBERT L.
Instruments previously built circa 1960-1993.

Luthier Robert L. Givens (1944-1993) began building guitars in 1960, and continued through until his untimely death in March of 1993. He built around 1,500 mandolins (about 700 of those for Tut Taylor's GTR company), around 200 guitars, and nearly 750 custom 5-string tenor banjo necks. According to Greg Boyd of the Stringed Instrument Division (Missoula, Montana), Givens built one mandolin a week except during his yearly two week vacation. Givens eschewed modern conveniences like telephones, and business was generally done face to face. Luthier Givens sometimes had one or two part time workers assisting him.

GLOBE
See Goodman, and chapter on House Brands.

This trademark has been identified as a House Brand of the Goodman Community Discount Center, circa 1958-1960, (Source: Willie G. Moseley, *Stellas & Stratocaster*s).

GODIN
Current trademark of instruments built in La Patrie and Princeville, Quebec, in Canada; and Berlin, New Hampshire since 1987. Distributed by La Si Do, Inc. of St. Laurent, Canada.

Robert Godin has been a mainstay in the guitar building industry since 1972, although the trademark and instruments bearing his name are relatively new. Godin got his first guitar at age seven and never looked back. By the time he was 15, he was working at La Tosca Musique in Montreal selling guitars and learning about minor repairs and set up work. Before long, Robert's passion for guitar playing was eclipsed by his fascination with the construction of the instruments themselves. In 1968 Godin set up a custom guitar shop in Montreal called Harmonilab. Harmonilab quickly became known for its excellent work and musicians were coming from as far away as Quebec City to have their guitars adjusted. Harmonilab was the first guitar shop in Quebec to use professional strobe tuners for intonating guitars.

Although Harmonilab's business was flourishing, Robert was full of ideas for the design and construction of acoustic guitars. So in 1972, the Norman Guitar Company was born. From the beginning the Norman guitars showed signs of the innovations that Godin would eventually bring to the guitar market. Perhaps the most significant item about the Norman history is that it represented the beginning of guitar building in the village of La Patrie, Quebec. La Patrie has since become an entire town of guitar builders – more on that later.

By 1978, Norman guitars had become quite successful in Canada and France, while at the same time the people in La Patrie were crafting replacement necks and bodies for the electric guitar market. Before long there was a lineup at the door of American guitar companies that wanted Godin's crew to supply all their necks and bodies.

In 1980 Godin introduced the Seagull guitar. With many innovations like a bolt-on neck (for consistent neck pitch), pointed headstock (straight string pull) and a handmade solid top, the Seagull was designed for an ease of play for the entry level to intermediate guitar player. Most striking was the Satin Lacquer finish. Godin borrowed the finishing idea that was used on fine violins, and applied it to the acoustic guitar. When the final version of the Seagull guitar went into production, Godin went about the business of finding a sales force to help introduce the Seagull into the U.S. market. Several independent U.S. sales agents jumped at the chance to get involved with this new guitar, and armed with samples off they went into the market. A couple of months passed, and not one guitar was sold. Rather than retreat back to Harmonilab, Godin decided that he would have to get out there himself and explain the Seagull guitar concept. So he bought himself an old Ford Econoline van and stuffed it full of about 85 guitars, and started driving through New England visiting guitar shops and introducing the Seagull guitar. Acceptance of this new guitar spread, and by 1985 La Si Do was incorporated and the factory in La Patrie expanded to meet the growing demand. Godin introduced the La Patrie brand of classical acoustic guitars in 1982. The La Patrie trademark was used to honor the town's tradition of luthiery that had developed during the first ten years since the inception of the Norman guitars trademark. In 1985, Godin also introduced the Simon & Patrick line (named after his two sons) for people interested in a more traditional instrument. Simon & Patrick guitars still maintained a number of Seagull innovations.

Since Godin's factory had been producing necks and bodies for various American guitar companies since 1978, he combined that knowledge with his background in acoustic guitar design for an entirely new product. The 'Acousticaster' was debuted in 1987, and represented the first design under the Godin name. The Acousticaster was designed to produce an acoustic sound from an instrument that was as easy to play as the player's favorite electric guitar. This was achieved through the help of a patented mechanical harp system inside the guitar. Over the past few years, the Godin name has become known for very high quality and innovative designs. Robert Godin is showing no signs of slowing down, having recently introduced the innovative models Multiac, LGX, and LGX-SA.

Today, La Si Do, Inc. employs close to 500 people in four factories located in La Patrie and Princeville, Quebec (Canada), and Berlin, New Hampshire. Models of the La Si Do guitar family are in demand all over the world, and Godin is still on the road teaching people about guitars.

In a final related note, the Ford Econoline van "died" with about 300,000 miles on it about 14 years ago, (Company History courtesy Robert Godin and Katherine Calder [Artist Relations], La Si Do, Inc., June 5, 1996).

PRODUCTION MODEL CODES

Godin is currently using a system similar to the original Gretsch system, in that the company is assigning both a model name and a four digit number that indicates the color finish specific to that guitar model. Thus, the four digit code will indicate which model and color from just one number. References in this text will list the four digit variances for color finish within the model designations.

ACOUSTIC ELECTRIC: A6 & ACS SERIES

**Godin A 12
courtesy Godin**

A 6 6-STRING ACOUSTIC/ELECTRIC (MODEL 7523) - single rounded cutaway semi-hollow chambered light maple body, solid cedar top, mahogany neck, 25 1/2" scale, 22-fret rosewood fingerboard with offset dot inlay, solid peghead with Godin logo, 3-per-side black tuners, rosewood bridge with white bridgepins, L.R. Baggs ribbon transducer, volume/3-band EQ slider controls, on-board preamp, available in Blue (7486), CognacBurst (7479), or Natural (7523) Semi-gloss finishes, current mfg.

| MSR | $795 | $650 | $425 | $275 |

    Add $100 for Black High Gloss finish (9435).

A 12 12-STRING ACOUSTIC/ELECTRIC (MODEL 9602) - similar to the A 6, except features a maple neck, 12-string configuration, 6-per-side headstock, available in Blue (10653), CognacBurst (10646), or Natural (9602) Semi-gloss finishes, mfg. 1997-current.

| MSR | $845 | $675 | $450 | $300 |

    Add $100 for Black High Gloss finish (9619).

ACS NYLON WITH SYNTH ACCESS "2-VOICE" (MODEL 7745) - nylon string configuration single rounded cutaway semi-hollow chambered light maple body, maple top, mahogany neck, 22-fret ebony fingerboard with offset dot inlay, multiple (5) small soundholes on upper bass bout, slotted peghead with "R. Godin" signature logo, 3-per-side gold tuners with pearloid buttons, rosewood tied bridge, 6 individual micro transducer bridge saddles, RMC hexaphonic multi sensors, volume/3-band EQ/synth volume slider controls, 2 synth (program up/down) push buttons, on board preamp, 13-pin connector for Roland GR series guitar synths, available in CognacBurst (9381) and Natural (7745) Semi-gloss finishes and Black Pearl (11872) and Blue (9428) High Gloss finish, current mfg.

| MSR | $995 | $795 | $525 | $350 |

    Add $100 for Blue High Gloss finish (Model 9428). Add $100 for Black Pearl high gloss finish (Model 11872).

ACOUSTIC ELECTRIC: ACOUSTICASTER SERIES

Early Acousticaster models have a black or creme colored controls plate in the bass horn bout.

ACOUSTICASTER 6 (MODEL 3518) - single cutaway semi-hollow maple body, solid spruce top, fan bracing with mechanical harp (18 tuned metal tines), rock maple neck, 25 1/2" scale, 22-fret maple or rosewood fingerboard with offset dot inlay, 6-on-one-side gold tuners, rosewood bridge with white bridgepins, L.R. Baggs bridge transducer, volume/active 3-band EQ, available in Black High Gloss finish (maple fingerboard: 3471; rosewood fingerboard: 3518), current mfg.

| MSR | $899 | $725 | $450 | $295 |

    This model was initially available in Aqua and White finishes.

Acousticaster 6 Left (Model 3532) - similar to Acousticaster 6, except features a left-handed configuration, rosewood fingerboard (only), available in Black High Gloss finish, current mfg.

| MSR | $1,039 | $850 | $550 | $350 |

    This model was initially available in Cherryburst, Cognacburst, or Natural finishes.

Acousticaster 6 Deluxe (Model 3594) - similar to Acousticaster 6, except has semi-hollow mahogany body, available in Natural High Gloss finish (maple fingerboard: 3563; rosewood fingerboard: 3594), current mfg.

| MSR | $969 | $775 | $500 | $325 |

    This model was initially available in Cherryburst, Cognacburst, or Natural finishes.

ACOUSTICASTER 12 - similar to Acousticaster, except has 12-strings, 6-per-side tuners, available Black or White finishes, disc. 1996.

| | N/A | $475 | $275 |

                Last MSR was $960.

GRADING	100%	EXCELLENT	AVERAGE

Acousticaster Deluxe 12 - Similar to Acousticaster, except has semi-hollow mahogany body, 12-strings, 6-per-side tuners, available in Cognacburst or Natural finishes, disc. 1996.

	N/A	$500	$300

Last MSR was $1,020.

ACOUSTIC ELECTRIC: MULTIAC SERIES

All MultiAc semi-acoustic models feature a dual-chambered mahogany body, solid spruce top, and mahogany neck. **Synth Access** models have an RMC hexaphonic multi-sensor, while the **Duet** models feature the L.R. Baggs Duet system.

MULTIAC NYLON STRING WITH SYNTH ACCESS (MODEL 4713) - nylon string configuration single cutaway two-chambered mahogany body, bound spruce top, mahogany neck, 25 1/2" scale, 22-fret ebony fingerboard with offset dot inlay, multiple (5) small soundholes on upper bass bout, slotted peghead with "R. Godin" signature logo, 3-per-side gold tuners with pearloid buttons, rosewood tied bridge, 6 individual micro transducer bridge saddles, RMC hexaphonic multi-sensors, volume/3-band EQ/synth volume slider controls, 2 synth (program up/down) push buttons, on-board preamp, 13-pin connector for Roland GR series guitar synths, available in Natural Semi-gloss finish, current mfg.

MSR	$1,375	$1,100	$725	$475

Add $100 for Natural high gloss finish (Model 4690).

MULTIAC GRAND CONCERT SA WITH SYNTH ACCESS "2-VOICE" - nylon string configuration single cutaway Grand Concert style guitar, two-chambered mahogany body with solid cedar top, mahogany neck and ebony fingerboard, width at nut 2", Custom RMC Polydrive electronics with a 13-pin connector for direct access to Roland GR Series and Axon AX100 guitar synths, available in semi-gloss or High Gloss Natural finish, current mfg.

MSR	$1,375	$1,025	$800	$600

Add $100 for High-gloss finish.

Multiac Grand Concert Duet - similar to Grand Concert With Synth Access except has rosewood fingerboard and a custom L.R. Baggs Duet System (Ribbon Transducer and Internal Microphone), available in Semi Gloss or High Gloss Natural finishes, new 2000.

MSR	$1,075	$805	$625	$450

Add $100 for High Gloss finish.

MULTIAC NYLON DUET (MODEL 7615) - similar to MultiAc Nylon String With Synth Access, except has rosewood fingerboard, L.R. Baggs Duet system (ribbon transducer and internal microphone), available in Natural semi-gloss finish, current mfg.

MSR	$1,075	$875	$550	$375

Add $100 for Natural High Gloss finish (Model 7608).

MultiAc Nylon Duet Custom Shop (Model 4836) - similar to MultiAc Nylon Duet, except has ebony fingerboard, abalone bound body/neck/headstock, abalone bridge inlay, available in Black (4836) and Natural (4843) High Gloss finish, mfg. 1998-99.

	$2,000	$1,500	$1,000

Last MSR was $2,745.

List price includes a hardshell case.

MULTIAC STEEL STRING WITH SYNTH ACCESS (MODEL 4812) - steel string configuration single cutaway two-chambered mahogany body, bound spruce top, mahogany neck, 25 1/2" scale, 22-fret ebony fingerboard with offset dot inlay, multiple (5) small soundholes on upper bass bout, slotted peghead with "R. Godin" signature logo, 3-per-side gold tuners with pearloid buttons, rosewood tied bridge, 6 individual micro transducer bridge saddles, RMC hexaphonic multi-sensors, volume/3-band EQ/synth volume slider controls, 2 synth (program up/down) push buttons, on-board preamp, 13-pin connector for Roland GR series guitar synths, available in Natural semi-gloss finish, current mfg.

MSR	$1,425	$1,150	$750	$525

Add $100 for Blue (Model 7905), CognacBurst (Model 7912), and Natural (Model 4775) high gloss finishes.

MultiAc Steel Duet (Model 7646) - similar to MultiAc Steel String With Synth Access, except has rosewood fingerboard, L.R. Baggs Duet system (ribbon transducer and internal microphone), available in Natural semi-gloss finish, current mfg.

MSR	$1,175	$950	$525	$400

Add $100 for Blue (Model 7899), CognacBurst (Model 7622), and Natural (Model 4639) high gloss finishes.

MultiAc Steel Duet Custom Shop (Model 4881) - similar to MultiAc Steel Duet, except has ebony fingerboard, abalone bound body/neck/head stock, abalone bridge inlay, available in Black (4881) or Natural (4898) high-gloss finish, mfg. 1998-current.

MSR	$2,845	$2,130	$1,600	$1,200

List price includes a hardshell case.

ACOUSTIC ELECTRIC BASS

A 4 SEMI-ACOUSTIC BASS (MODEL 10134) - single rounded cutaway semi-hollow chambered maple body, solid cedar top, maple neck, 34" scale, 22-fret rosewood fingerboard with offset dot inlay, blackface peghead with Godin logo, 4-on-a-side gold tuners, strings-through rosewood bridge, L.R. Baggs ribbon transducer, volume/3-band EQ slider controls, onboard preamp, available in CognacBurst (10141) or Natural (10134) Semi Gloss finishes, current mfg.

MSR	$895	$725	$475	$300

Add $100 for Black High Gloss finish (Model 10585).

GRADING		100%	EXCELLENT	AVERAGE

A 4 Semi-Acoustic Fretless Bass (Model 10158) - similar to the A 4 Semi-Acoustic Bass, except features a fretless ebony fingerboard, available in CognacBurst (10165) or Natural (10158) semi-gloss finishes, current mfg.

MSR	$995		$795	$525	$350

Add $100 for Black High Gloss finish (Model 10578).

A 5 SEMI-ACOUSTIC BASS (MODEL 10585) - similar to Model A 4, except in a 5-string configuration, available in high-gloss Black, semi-gloss Natural or Cognac Burst finishes, mfg. 2000-current.

MSR	$1,045		$785	$500	$350

Add $100 for high-gloss finish. Add $100 for fretless configuration.

ACOUSTIBASS - single cutaway routed out maple body, bound spruce top, thumb rest, bolt-on maple neck, fretless ebony fingerboard, strings-through ebony bridge, 4-on-one-side gold tuners, piezo bridge pickup, 4-band EQ, available in Aqua, Black or White finishes, disc. 1996.

		N/A	$525	$325

Last MSR was $1,060.

AcoustiBass Deluxe (Model 3754) - similar to AcoustiBass, except has routed out mahogany body, available in Cherryburst, Cognacburst and Natural finishes, disc. 1998.

		N/A	$675	$395

Last MSR was $1,159.

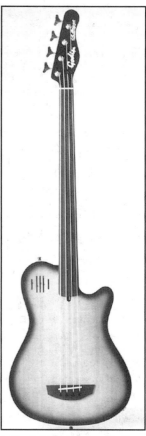

**Godin A 4 Semi-Acoustic Bass
courtesy Godin**

GOLDENTONE
Instruments previously produced in Japan during the 1960s.

The Goldentone trademark was used by U.S. importers Elger and its partner Hoshino Gakki Ten as one of the brand names used in their joint guitar producing venture. Hoshino in Japan was shipping Fuji Gen Gakki-built guitars marketed in the U.S. as Goldentone, Elger, and eventually Ibanez. These guitars featured original body designs in the early to mid 1960s, (Source: Michael Wright, *Guitar Stories,* Volume One).

GOLDEN WOOD
Instruments currently built in Gualala, California.

The Golden Wood company is currently offering handcrafted guitars. For further information regarding specifications and pricing, please contact the Golden Wood company directly (see Trademark Index).

GOODALL
Instruments currently built in Kailua-Kona, Hawaii. Distributed by James Goodall Guitars of Kailua-Kona, Hawaii.

Luthier James Goodall grew up in Lemon Grove, California. Apparently, there must be something in the water, for a number of high profile luthiers (such as Greg Deering, Geoff Stelling, and Larry and Kim Breedlove) have sprung from the same area. Prior to building his first acoustic guitar, Goodall's woodworking experience was limited to his surfboard building during high school (of course, having a father with wood carving knowledge certainly helps). After his initial success, Goodall began building guitars for friends — which lead to a backlog of orders by the mid 1970s. Goodall moved to full time guitar building in 1978.

In 1981, Goodall relocated his shop to Mendocino, California. From 1981 to 1989, he averaged around 40 guitars a year. In 1992, Goodall moved off the mainland to Kailua-Kona, Hawaii. His shop now has five employees, and ships 5 instruments a week. For further information regarding pricing and specifications, please contact Goodall Guitars directly (see Trademark Index).

ACOUSTIC: GENERAL INFORMATION

Goodall offers a wide range of custom options, including wood choices, fingerboard inlay, and body binding. For models constructed with birdseye maple, Macassar ebony, quilted mahogany, or Brazilian rosewood back and sides (all with Master Grade tops), please call James Goodall for a price request. Here are some of the most common options.

Add $55 for ebony buttons (for Schaller tuners). Add $95 for gold Schaller tuners. Add $125 for cedar or redwood top. Add $155 for Engelmann spruce top. Add $200 for Baritone. Add $295 for L.R. Baggs Ribbon transducer pickup. Add $200 for left-handed configuration. Add $520 for 12-string configuration. Add $595 for cutaway body configuration.

ACOUSTIC: CONCERT, JUMBO, PARLOR, & STANDARD SERIES

The following prices and descriptions apply to the following models: **Parlor** (14" bout, 25" scale), **Grand Concert** (15" bout), **Concert Jumbo** (15 7/8" bout), **Standard** (16" bout), and **Jumbo** (17" bout) Series. These guitars feature: Alaskan Sitka spruce top, round soundhole, abalone rosette, ebony binding, 14/20-fret ebony fingerboard with abalone dot inlays, ebony bridge with black white dot pins, 3-per-side chrome Schaller tuners, available in Natural finish (with satin finish neck), current mfg. Prices are: $3,200 for mahogany back & sides with rosewood or maple binding, $3,400 for E.I. Rosewood back & sides, with curly koa binding, $3,700 for curly koa back/sides with rosewood or curly maple binding, $3,700 for curly maple back & sides with rosewood or curly koa binding, and $3,600 for curly walnut back & sides with curly maple binding. Add $200 to the retail price for the Jumbo model.

ACOUSTIC: ROYAL HAWAIIAN SERIES

The **Royal Hawaiian** has curly top/back/sides, pearl rosette with island scene fb inlay, ebony fretboard and bridge, & peghead venner, gold Schaller tuners with ebony buttons, purpleheard wood bindings, 1.75" satin finish neck, 25.5" scale, and comes in Natural finish. The Royal Hawaiian is available as the Grand Concert, Concert Jumbo, or Standard for a retail price of $5,700 and as a Jumbo for $5,900.

ACOUSTIC: TRADITIONAL OM, DREADNOUGHT, & ALOHA SERIES

The **Traditional OM** and **Dreadnought** models feature: mahogany or E.I. rosewood back & sides, herringbone rosette and top purfling, chevron marketry backstrip, MOP notched square fretboard inlay, ebony peghead, tortise pickguard, nickel Waverly tuners with ivoroid knobs, 1.75" or 1 11/16" neck width, 25.5" scale, and maple binding. These guitars retail for $3,995 with a bear claw Sitka spruce top, and $4,300 for an Adirondack spruce top.

The Aloha model features a solid Sitka spruce top, koa or mahogany back & sides, pheasant wood fretboard & bridge, koa peghead veneer, pearl inlay with MOP dots, chrome Gotoh tuners, 25.5" scale, and black wood fiber binding. This guitar is available in Standard, Concert Jumbo, or Grand Concert sizes, retails for $2,845, and comes with a plush hard shell case in the price.

GOODMAN

See chapter on House Brands.

This trademark has been identified as a House Brand of the Goodman Community Discount Center, circa 1961-1964. Previously, the company used the trademark of Globe, (Source: Willie G. Moseley, *Stellas & Stratocasters*).

GOODMAN GUITARS

Instruments currently built in Brewster, New York.

Luthier Brad Goodman took to woodworking in his early childhood, and by the end of high school has completed several guitars and mandolins. Over the past twenty years, Goodman has continued to refine his guitar building skills by building lutes, mandolins, acoustic flattop and archtop guitars. Goodman is currently focusing on a series of archtop models.

Goodman archtops have similar construction features like AAA figured maple back and sides, Sitka spruce tops, 3-piece curly maple necks, ebony fingerboard/tailpiece/bridge/pickguard/peghead veneers. Instruments also feature multiple-layer binding, abalone side dots, gold Schaller tuners, and clear lacquer finishes. Prices range from $2,800 on his **Jazz Classical** (a classical guitar with an arched back) to his archtop models ($4,000).

GOYA

Instruments previously produced in Sweden circa 1900s to mid 1960s. Distributed by Hershman Musical Instrument Company of New York. Later Goya instruments were built in Korea from the early 1970s to 1996, and were distributed by The Martin Guitar Company, located in Nazareth, Pennsylvania.

The Goya trademark was originally used by the Hershman Musical Instrument Company of New York City, New York in the 1950s on models built by Sweden's Levin company (similar models were sold in Europe under the company's Levin trademark). Levin built high quality acoustic flattop, classical, and archtop guitars as well as mandolins. A large number of rebranded Goya instruments were imported to the U.S. market.

In the late 1950s, solid body electric guitars and basses built by Hagstrom (also a Swedish company) were rebranded Goya and distributed in the U.S. as well. In 1963 the company changed its name to the Goya Musical Instrument Corporation.

Goya was purchased by Avnet (see Guild) in 1966, and continued to import instruments such as the Rangemaster in 1967. By the late 1960s, electric solid body guitars and basses were then being built in Italy by the EKO company. Avnet then sold the Goya trademark to Kustom Electronics. It has been estimated that the later Goya instruments of the 1970s were built in Japan.

The C.F. Martin company later acquired the Levin company, and bought the rights to the Goya trademark from a company named Dude, Inc. in 1976. Martin imported a number of guitar, mandolin, and banjo string instruments from the 1970s through to 1996. While this trademark is currently discontinued, the rights to the name are still held by the Martin Guitar company.

The Goya company featured a number of innovations that most people are not aware of. Goya was the first classic guitar line to put the trademark name on the headstock, and also created the ball end classic guitar string. Levin-Era Goya models feature interior paper label with the Goya trademark in a cursive style, and designated "Made by A.B. Herman Carlson Levin - Gothenburg, Sweden." Model and serial number appear on the label, as well as on the neck block.

ACOUSTIC

G-1 - classic style, spruce ply top, round soundhole, bound body, rosette decal, mahogany stain ply back/sides, nato neck, 12/19-fret ebonized fingerboard, ebonized tied bridge, 3-per-side chrome tuners with white buttons, available in Natural finish, disc. 1996.

	N/A	$60	$35
		Last MSR was $115.	

G-2 - similar to the G-1, except has rosewood stain ply back/sides, 3-per-side chrome tuners with pearloid buttons, available in Natural finish, disc. 1996.

	N/A	$75	$50
		Last MSR was $155.	

G-3 - dreadnought style, spruce ply top, round soundhole, black pickguard, bound body, rosette decal, mahogany stain ply back/sides, nato neck, 14/20-fret ebonized fingerboard with pearl dot inlay, ebonized bridge with white pins, screened peghead logo, 3-per-side chrome diecast tuners, available in Natural finish, disc. 1996.

	N/A	$70	$45
		Last MSR was $135.	

GRADING	100%	EXCELLENT	AVERAGE

G-4 - similar to the G-3, except has rosewood stain ply back/sides, rosewood bridge with white pins, available in Natural finish, disc. 1996.

| | N/A | $80 | $55 |

Last MSR was $170.

G-120 - classic style, spruce top, round soundhole, bound body, wood inlay rosette, mahogany back/sides/neck, 12/18-fret rosewood fingerboard, rosewood tied bridge, 3-per-side chrome tuners, available in Natural finish, disc. 1996.

| | N/A | $130 | $80 |

Last MSR was $260.

G-125 - similar to the G-120, except has a 12/19-fret rosewood fingerboard, available in Natural finish, disc. 1996.

| | N/A | $145 | $95 |

Last MSR was $290.

G-145 - classic style, cedar top, round soundhole, bound body, wood inlay rosette, rosewood back/sides, mahogany neck, 12/19-fret rosewood fingerboard, rosewood tied bridge, 3-per-side gold tuners, available in Natural finish, disc. 1996.

| | N/A | $175 | $115 |

Last MSR was $350.

G-145 S - similar to G-145, except has solid cedar top, disc. 1996.

| | N/A | $275 | $175 |

Last MSR was $510.

G-215 - grand concert style, spruce top, round soundhole, black pickguard, 3-stripe bound body/rosette, mahogany back/sides/neck, 14/20-fret rosewood fingerboard with pearl dot inlay, rosewood bridge with white black dot pins, rosewood veneered peghead with screened logo, 3-per-side chrome tuners, available in Natural finish, disc. 1996.

| | N/A | $165 | $110 |

Last MSR was $330.

G-215 L - similar to the G-215, except in left-handed configuration, disc. 1996.

| | N/A | $175 | $120 |

Last MSR was $350.

G-230 S - similar to G-215, except has solid spruce top, tortoise pickguard, gold tuners, disc. 1996.

| | N/A | $200 | $130 |

Last MSR was $405.

G-300 - dreadnought style, spruce top, round soundhole, black pickguard, bound body, 3-stripe rosette, mahogany back/sides/neck, 14/20-fret rosewood fingerboard with pearl dot inlay, rosewood bridge with black white dot pins, screened peghead logo, 3-per-side diecast tuners, available in Natural or Sunburst finishes, disc. 1996.

| | N/A | $150 | $100 |

Last MSR was $300.

G-300 L - similar to the G-300, except in left-handed configuration, disc. 1996.

| | N/A | $160 | $110 |

Last MSR was $320.

G-312 - similar to the G-300, except has 3-stripe bound body/rosette, 3-per-side chrome tuners, available in Natural or Sunburst finish, disc. 1996.

| | N/A | $180 | $120 |

Last MSR was $360.

G-316 H - dreadnought style, spruce top, round soundhole, tortoise pickguard, herringbone bound body/rosette, rosewood back/sides, mahogany neck, 14/20-fret rosewood fingerboard with pearl dot inlay, rosewood bridge with white black dot pins, screened peghead logo, 3-per-side chrome tuners, available in Natural finish, disc. 1996.

| | N/A | $240 | $155 |

Last MSR was $480.

G-318 C - single round cutaway dreadnought style, spruce top, round soundhole, black pickguard, 3-stripe bound body/rosette, mahogany back/sides/neck, 14/20-fret rosewood fingerboard with pearl dot inlay, rosewood bridge with black white dot pins, screened peghead logo, 3-per-side chrome tuners, available in Natural finish, disc. 1996.

| | N/A | $185 | $120 |

Last MSR was $375.

Goya G-120
courtesy C.F. Martin Company

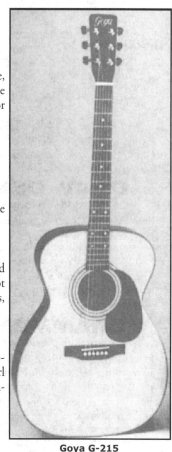

Goya G-215
courtesy C.F. Martin Company

GRADING	100%	EXCELLENT	AVERAGE

G-330 S - dreadnought style, solid spruce top, round soundhole, tortoise pickguard, multibound body/rosette, rosewood back/sides/neck, 14/20-fret bound ebonized rosewood fingerboard with pearl dot inlay, rosewood bridge with white black dot pins, bound peghead with pearl torch inlay, 3-per-side gold tuners, available in Natural finish, disc. 1996.

	N/A	$280	$185

Last MSR was $555.

G-335 S - similar to the G-330 S, except has herringbone bound body/rosette, rosewood back/sides, mahogany neck, 14/20-fret bound rosewood fingerboard with pearl snowflake/tree of life inlay, available in Natural finish, disc. 1996.

	N/A	$290	$190

Last MSR was $580.

G-415 - dreadnought style, spruce top, round soundhole, black pickguard, multibound body/rosette, mahogany back/sides/neck, 14/20-fret rosewood fingerboard with pearl dot inlay, rosewood bridge with black white dot pins, screened peghead logo, 6-per-side chrome tuners, available in Natural finish, disc. 1996.

	N/A	$195	$125

Last MSR was $390.

ACOUSTIC ELECTRIC

G-312 E - dreadnought style, spruce top, round soundhole, black pickguard, bound body, 3-stripe rosette, mahogany back/sides/neck, 14/20-fret rosewood fingerboard with pearl dot inlay, rosewood bridge with black white dot pins, screened peghead logo, 3-per-side diecast tuners, piezo bridge pickup, volume/tone controls, available in Natural finish, disc. 1996.

	N/A	$235	$155

Last MSR was $475.

G-318 CE - single round cutaway dreadnought style, spruce top, round soundhole, black pickguard, 3-stripe bound body/rosette, mahogany back/sides/neck, 14/20-fret rosewood fingerboard with pearl dot inlay, rosewood bridge with black white dot pins, screened peghead logo, 3-per-side chrome tuners, piezo bridge pickup, volume/tone control, available in Natural finish, disc. 1996.

	N/A	$260	$170

Last MSR was $515.

G-500 - single round cutaway hollow style, round soundhole, multibound body/rosette, mahogany back/sides/neck, 20-fret bound rosewood fingerboard with pearl dot inlay, rosewood bridge with white black dot pins, bound peghead with screened logo, 3-per-side chrome tuners, piezo bridge pickup, 3-band EQ, available in Black, Blueburst, or Natural finishes, disc. 1996.

	N/A	$300	$195

Last MSR was $600.

G-600 - single sharp cutaway Dreadnought body, spruce top, round soundhole, black pickguard, multibound body/rosette, mahogany back/sides/neck, 14/20-fret rosewood fingerboard with pearl dot inlay, rosewood bridge with black white dot pins, bound peghead with screened logo, 3-per-side chrome tuners, piezo bridge pickup, 3-band EQ, available in Black or Natural finishes, disc. 1996.

	N/A	$290	$190

Last MSR was $580.

GRACIA GUITARS
Instruments currently produced in Buenos Aires, Argentina.

Gracia guitaras was founded by Don Dionisio Garcia. They produce mainly nylon string classical guitars but have a few dreadnought styles as well. For more information contact the company via email (see Trademark Index).

GRAF, OSKAR
Instruments currently built in Clarendon, Ontario (Canada) since 1970.

Luthier Oskar Graf has been handcrafting classical and steel-string acoustic guitars for more than 30 years. In addition, Graf now offers acoustic bass guitars, solid body upright string basses, 8-and 10-string classical guitars as well as custom designs and restorations. Graf has built flamenco style guitars and lutes through the years, and estimates that he has produced maybe 350 guitars (mostly as commissioned pieces). Instruments feature cedar and spruce tops, and rosewood and koa backs and sides.

The average price of a steel string is $3,800 and classical is $4,600. Turnaround on a guitar from the date the guitar is ordered is about 18 months and a 20% down payment is required. Occasionally there are guitars in stock. For more information contact the luthier directly (see Trademark Index).

GRAMMER
Instruments previously built in Nashville, Tennessee circa early 1960s until 1971.

RG & G was founded in the Spring of 1965 in Nashville, Tennessee, by Grand Ole Opry performer Billy Grammer. The company was very active in the Nashville area, and many local performers used these acoustic guitars during the 1960s. The factory burned down in April, 1968 and was rebuilt in June, 1968. RG & G was reformed as Grammer Guitars in the fall of 1968.

The Grammer Guitar company was later sold to Ampeg (circa unknown, late 1960s), and the later models have an Ampeg "A" logo on the front of the headstock below the Grammer name. Grammer went out of business in 1971; the company's assets (but not the trademark name) was sold at a bankruptcy auction the same year, (Source: George Gruhn, *Vintage Guitar Magazine*, Walter Murray of *Frankenstein Fretworks*, and Tom Wheeler, *American Guitars*).

GRADING	100%	EXCELLENT	AVERAGE

G

ACOUSTIC

In general, Grammer guitars can be distinguished by their batwing-shaped headstock and typically feature a crown-shaped bridge, although some may have a moustache bridge. They feature solid spruce tops, and the fingerboard inlay has dot fretmarkers with double dots at frets 3, 7, and 17 and triple dots at 12 position. The pickguards and headstock overlays were layered black on white plastic. The pickguards were asymetrical and the headstock features the name "The Grammer Guitar." Most guitars were finished in Natural but there were some unusual colorations used such as a green-burst and a bright yellow clearcoat. Chrome Grover Roto-Matic tuners were standard on most models. Early models made under RG & G ownership have a paper label in the soundhole that reads RG & G on the label.

G-10 - features Brazilian rosewood back & sides.

| | $1,800 | $1,300 | $700 |

G-30 - features maple back & sides, and railroad track inlay on the fingerboard.

| | $1,500 | $1,000 | $500 |

G-40 - features figured maple back & sides.

| | $1,500 | $1,000 | $500 |

MERLE HAGGARD MODEL - features a slotted headstock with rear-facing tuners, Brazilian rosewood back and sides with a blonde center stripe on the back, spruce top, has Merle Haggard in white script writing on the headstock.

| | $1,700 | $1,200 | $650 |

**Goya G-500
courtesy C.F. Martin Company**

GRAND
Instruments currently produced in China.

Grand produces entry level dreadnoughts, classicals, and acoustic basses. There are various models and options offered. For more information contact the company via email (see Trademark Index).

GRANDE
Instruments previously built in Japan during the mid to late 1970s. Imported by Jerry O'Hagan of St. Louis Park, Minnesota.

Between 1975 and 1979, Jerry O'Hagan imported the Japanese-built Grande acoustic guitars to the U.S. market. O'Hagan later went on to produce the American-built solid body electric O'Hagan guitars (1979 to 1983, Source: Michael Wright, *Guitar Stories*, Volume One).

GRANT
Instruments previously produced in Japan from the 1970s through the 1980s.

The Grant trademark was the brand name of a UK importer, and the guitars were medium quality copies of American designs, (Source: Tony Bacon and Paul Day, *The Guru's Guitar Guide*).

GRANTSON
Instruments previously produced in Japan during the mid 1970s.

These entry level guitars featured designs based on popular American models, (Source: Tony Bacon and Paul Day, *The Guru's Guitar Guide*).

GRECO
Instruments previously produced in Japan during the 1960s.

Greco instruments were imported to the U.S. through Goya Guitars/Avnet. Avnet was the same major company that also acquired Guild in 1966, (Source: Michael Wright, *Guitar Stories*, Volume One).

GREEN MOUNTAIN GUITARS
Instruments currently built in Bradford, Vermont.

Green Mountain Guitars was started by Glen DeRusha, and is currently run by him and his family. Glen grew up in Cloquet, Minnesota and loved to play guitar and craft things out of wood. He worked for years building furniture and cabinets. Glen attended Roberto-Venn school of Luthiery in Phoenix, Arizona where he learned the skills and techniques for building guitars. He then repaired and restored guitars for some time when he was able to start building his own guitars. Green Mountain Guitars currently produce dreadnoughts, jumbos, and orchestra models. For more information visit their web site (see Trademark Index).

GREMLIN
Instruments currently built in Asia. Distributed in the U.S. market by Midco International of Effingham, Illinois.

Gremlin guitars are designed for the entry level or student guitarist.

**Grammer G-10
courtesy John Miller**

GRETSCH

Current trademark manufactured in the U.S. from the early 1900s-1981, and from 1995 to date (three current models). Japanese manufacture began in 1989. Distributed by the Fred Gretsch Company, located in Savannah, Georgia.

Gretsch instruments were originally produced in New York City, NY from the early 1900s to 1970. Production was moved to Booneville, Arkansas during 1970, and production continued until 1979. Gretsch (as owned by D. H. Baldwin Piano Company) ceased production (of guitars) in 1981. During 1985, the Gretsch trademark returned to the Gretsch family, and in 1989, production once again resumed in Japan.

Friedrich Gretsch was born in 1856, and emigrated to America when he was 16. In 1883 he founded a musical instrument shop in Brooklyn which prospered. The Fred Gretsch Company began manufacturing instruments in 1883 (while Friedrich maintained his proper name, he "Americanized" it for the company). Gretsch passed away unexpectedly (at age 39) during a trip to Germany in April 1895, and his son Fred (often referred to as Fred Gretsch, Jr. in company histories) took over the family business (at 15!). Gretsch Sr. expanded the business considerably by 1916. Beginning with percussion, ukuleles, and banjos, Gretsch introduced guitars in the early 1930s, developing a well respected line of archtop orchestra models. In 1926 the company acquired the rights to K. Zildjian Cymbals, and debuted the Gretsch tenor guitar. During the Christmas season of 1929, the production capacity was reported to be 100,000 instruments (stringed instruments and drums); and a new midwestern branch was opened in Chicago, Illinois. In March of 1940 Gretsch acquired the B & D trademark from the Bacon Banjo Corporation. Fred Gretsch, Sr. retired in 1942.

William Walter Gretsch assumed the presidency of the company until 1948, and then Fred Gretsch, Jr. took over the position. Gretsch, Jr. was the primary president during the great Gretsch heyday, and was ably assisted by such notables as Jimmy Webster and Charles "Duke" Kramer (Kramer was involved with the Gretsch company from 1935 to his retirement in 1980, and was even involved after his retirement!). During the 1950s, the majority of Gretsch's guitar line was focused on electric six-string Spanish instruments. With the endorsement of Chet Atkins and George Harrison, Gretsch electrics became very popular with both country and rock 'n roll musicians through the 1960s.

Outbid in their attempt to buy Fender in 1965, the D.H. Baldwin company bought Gretsch in 1967, and Gretsch, Jr. was made a director of Baldwin. Baldwin had previously acquired the manufacturing facilities of England's James Ormstron Burns (Burns Guitars) in September 1965, and Baldwin was assembling the imported Burns parts in Booneville, Arkansas. In a business consolidation, The New York Gretsch operation was moved down to the Arkansas facility in 1970. Production focused on Gretsch, and Burns guitars were basically discontinued.

In January of 1973 the Booneville plant suffered a serious fire. Baldwin made the decision to discontinue guitar building operations. Three months later, long-time manager Bill Hagner formed the Hagner Musical Instruments company and formed an agreement with Baldwin to build and sell Gretsch guitars to Baldwin from the Booneville facility. Baldwin would still retain the rights to the trademark. Another fire broke out in December of the same year, but the operation recovered. Baldwin stepped in and regained control of the operation in December of 1978, the same year that they bought the Kustom Amplifier company in Chanute, Kansas. Gretsch production was briefly moved to the Kansas facility, and by 1982 they moved again to Gallatin, Tennessee. 1981 was probably the last date of guitar production, but Gretsch drum products were continued at Tennessee. In 1983 the production had again returned to Arkansas.

Baldwin had experimented briefly with guitar production at their Mexican organ facilities, producing perhaps 100 Southern Belle guitars (basically renamed Country Gentlemans) between 1978 and 1979. When Gretsch production returned to Arkansas in 1983, the Baldwin company asked Charles Kramer to come out of retirement and help bring the business back (which he did). In 1984, Baldwin also sold off their rights to Kustom amps. In 1985 Kramer brokered a deal between Baldwin and Fred Gretsch, III that returned the trademark back to the family.

Kramer and Gretsch, III developed the specifications for the reissue models that are currently being built by the Terada company in Japan. The majority of Japanese-produced Gretsch models are brokered in the U.S. market; however, there has been some "grey market" Japan-only models that have been brought into the U.S. One such model, the White Penguin Reissue, was briefly offered through Gretsch to the U.S. market – it is estimated that perhaps a dozen or so were sold through dealers.

In 1995, three models were introduced that are currently built in the U.S: **Country Club 1955** (model G6196-1955), **Nashville 1955** (model G6120-1955), and the **White Falcon I - 1955** (model G6136-1955).

On January 1, 2003, Gretsch guitars was sold to Fender (FMIC) as the exclusive distributor, producer, developer, and marketer of Gretsch. Look for Fred Gretsch and Gretsch guitars in the Fender booth now at the NAMM shows! Fred is still consulting for Gretsch guitars, (Later company history courtesy Michael Wright, *Guitar Stories,* Volume One).

Charles *Duke* Kramer first joined the Gretsch company at their Chicago office in 1935. When Kramer first retired in 1980, he formed D & F Products. In late 1981, when Baldwin lost a lease on one of their small production plants, Kramer went out and bought any existing guitar parts (about three 42-foot semi-trailers worth!). While some were sold back to the revitalized Gretsch company in 1985, Kramer still makes the parts available through his D & F Products company. D & F Products can be reached at: 6735 Hidden Hills Drive, Cincinnati, Ohio 45230 (513.232.4972).

PRODUCTION MODEL CODES

The Gretsch company assigned a name and a four digit number to each guitar model. However, they would also assign a different, yet associated number to the same model in a different color or component assembly. This system helped expedite the ordering system, says Charles Duke Kramer, you could look at an invoice and know exactly which model and color from one number. References in this text, while still incomplete, will list variances in the model designations.

Current Gretsch models may have a G preface to the four digit code, and also letters at the end that designate different bridge configuration (like a Bigsby tremolo), or a cutaway body style. Many of the reissue models also have a hyphen and four digit year following the primary model number designation that indicate a certain vintage-style year.

For further information regarding Gretsch electric models, please refer to the *Blue Book of Electric Guitars.* Gretsch archtop models with built-in pickups can be found in the Gretsch Electric section of the Electric edition.

GRADING	100%	EXCELLENT	AVERAGE

ACOUSTIC ARCHTOP

MODEL 35 - carved spruce top, f-holes, raised bound black pickguard, bound body, maple back/sides, 3-piece maple/rosewood neck, 14/20-fret ebony fingerboard with pearloid dot inlay, ebony bridge/trapeze tailpiece, rosewood peghead veneer with pearl logo inlay, 3-per-side diecast tuners, available in Dark Red Sunburst finish, body width 16", mfg. 1933-1949.

	N/A	$650	$350

In 1936, adjustable maple bridge and black plastic peghead veneer replaced original parts/designs. By 1939, 3-stripe body binding, rosewood fingerboard, tortoise shell tuner buttons, nickel plated hardware, and Brown Sunburst finish became standard.

MODEL 50 - carved spruce top, f-holes, raised black pickguard, bound body, avoidire back, figured maple sides/neck, 14/20-fret bound ebony pointed end fingerboard with pearloid diamond inlay, adjustable maple bridge/trapeze tailpiece, black face peghead with pearl scroll inlay, 3-per-side nickel tuners with tortoise buttons, available in Brown Sunburst finish, body width 16", mfg. 1936-1949.

	N/A	$700	$400

This model also available with round soundhole (Model 50R), which was discontinued by 1940. By 1940, rosewood fingerboard with dot inlay replaced ebony fingerboard with diamond inlay.

MODEL 75 - arched spruce top, raised bound tortoise pickguard, f-holes, bound body, figured maple back/sides, 3-piece maple neck, 14/20-fret bound rosewood pointed end fingerboard with pearloid block inlay, adjustable rosewood stairstep bridge/nickel trapeze tailpiece, black face peghead with large floral/logo inlay, 3-per-side nickel tuners, available in Brown Sunburst finish, body width 16", mfg. 1939-1949.

	N/A	$750	$450

Early models had bound pegheads. By 1940, 3-stripe bound pickguard/body replaced original parts/designs, pickguard was also enlarged.

MODEL 100 - arched spruce top, raised bound tortoise pickguard, f-holes, 2-stripe bound body, curly maple back/sides, 3-piece curly maple/rosewood neck, 14/20-fret bound rosewood fingerboard with pearl block inlay, adjustable rosewood stairstep bridge/step tailpiece, bound blackface peghead with pearl floral/logo inlay, 3-per-side gold tuners, available in Natural or Sunburst finishes, body width 16", mfg. 1939-1955.

	N/A	$800	$475

MODEL 150 - carved spruce top, raised bound tortoise pickguard, f-holes, multibound body, curly maple back/sides, curly maple neck, 14/20-fret bound ebony fingerboard with pearl block inlay, adjustable ebony stairstep bridge/stop tailpiece, bound blackface peghead w/pearl "Artist"/logo inlay, 3-per-side gold tuners, available in Natural or Sunburst finishes, body width 16", mfg. 1935-39.

	N/A	$800	$500

MODEL 250 - arched spruce top, raised bound tortoise pickguard, bound cat's-eye soundholes, 3-stripe bound body, arched maple back/sides, 14/20-fret bound ebony fingerboard with pearl block inlay, adjustable stylized ebony bridge/trapeze tailpiece, bound blackface peghead with 2 pearl quarter notes/logo inlay, 3-per-side gold tuners with pearloid buttons, available in Sunburst finish, body width 16", mfg. 1936-39.

	N/A	$850	$500

CONSTELLATION (MODEL 6030) - single round cutaway body, arched spruce top, 2-stripe bound f-holes, raised bound tortoise pickguard, 2-stripe bound body, laminated maple back/sides, 3-piece maple/rosewood neck, 19-fret bound rosewood fingerboard with pearloid block inlay, adjustable rosewood stairstep bridge/gold trapeze tailpiece, bound black face peghead with pearl logo inlay, 3-per-side gold tuners, available in Natural (6031) or Sunburst (6030) finishes, mfg. 1951-1960.

	N/A	$1,750	$1,100

Originally released as the Synchromatic, it was later known as the Constellation. By 1955, hump top block fingerboard inlay and ebony bridge/G logo trapeze tailpiece replaced original parts/designs.

ELDORADO (SYNCHROMATIC 400, MODEL 6040) - single round cutaway body, arched spruce top, 2 f-holes, 3-stripe bound body, maple back/sides/neck, 21-fret bound ebony fingerboard with pearloid hump top block inlay, adjustable ebony stairstep bridge/gold G logo trapeze tailpiece, bound black face peghead with logo inlay, raised pickguard, 3-per-side gold tuners, available in Natural (6041) or Sunburst (6040) finishes, body width 18", mfg. 1955-1970.

	N/A	$2,000	$1,250

This model was introduced in 1955 as a custom order only. By 1968, Natural finish was discontinued.

G

Gretsch Eldorado
courtesy Fred Gretsch
Enterprises

Gretsch Synchromatic 200
courtesy Thoroughbred Music

GRADING		100%	EXCELLENT	AVERAGE

ELDORADO 18" CARVED TOP (MODEL G410) - similar to the Eldorado (Model 6040). Synchromatic Jazz Model, available in Sunburst (G410) or Natural (G410 M) finishes, body width 18", mfg. 1991-current.

	MSR	$5,700		$4,200	$1,950	$1,395

Add $300 for model in Natural finish (Model G410 M). Shaded finish added and Sunburst finish discontinued in 1999.

FLEETWOOD (MODEL 6038) - similar to Eldorado, except has smaller body, Synchromatic/logo on peghead, available in Natural (6039) or Sunburst (6038) finishes, body width 17", mfg. 1955-1968.

	N/A	$1,800	$1,200

In 1959, the thumbnail fingerboard inlays replaced block inlays.

ACOUSTIC ARCHTOP: SYNCROMATIC SERIES

Early Synchromatic models have bulb shaped pegheads. Fingerboard inlay listed as the standard, though models are also found with split block, thumb print and other inlay styles.

SYNCROMATIC 160 (MODEL 6028) - carved spruce top, raised bound tortoise pickguard, bound cat's-eye soundholes, tortoise bound body, carved curly maple back, curly maple sides, 5-piece maple neck, 14/20-fret bound rosewood fingerboard with pearl block inlay, adjustable stylized rosewood bridge/trapeze tailpiece, bound blackface peghead with pearl model name/logo inlay, 3-per-side chrome Grover tuners, available in Sunburst (6028) finish, body width 17", mfg. 1939-1951.

	N/A	$1,500	$800

In 1942, Natural finish (Model 6029) became available.

SYNCROMATIC 200 - carved spruce top, raised bound tortoise pickguard, bound cat's-eye soundholes, 2-stripe bound body, carved flame maple back, curly maple sides, 5-piece maple neck, 14/20-fret bound rosewood fingerboard with pearl hump block inlay, adjustable stylized rosewood bridge/trapeze tailpiece, bound blackface peghead with pearl model name/logo inlay, 3-per-side gold Grover tuners, available in Natural and Sunburst finishes, body width 17", mfg. 1939-1949.

	N/A	$1,750	$900

SYNCROMATIC 300 (MODEL 6036) - carved spruce top, raised bound tortoise pickguard, bound cats-eye soundholes, single bound body, carved flame maple back, curly maple sides, 5-piece maple/rosewood neck, 14/20-fret bound ebony fingerboard with pearl hump block inlay, adjustable stylized Brazilian rosewood bridge/trapeze tailpiece, bound blackface peghead w/pearl model name/logo inlay, 3-per-side gold Grover tuners, available in Natural (6037) or Sunburst (6036) finishes, body width 17", mfg. 1939-1959.

	N/A	$2,500	$1,500

SYNCROMATIC 400 (MODEL 6040) - carved spruce top, raised bound tortoise pickguard, multibound cats eye soundholes, multibound body with gold inner stripe, carved flame maple back, curly flame sides, 3-piece curly maple neck, 14/20-fret multibound ebony fingerboard with pearl hump block with gold stripe inlay, adjustable stylized ebony bridge/trapeze tailpiece, multibound blackface peghead with pearl cat's eye-stairstep/logo inlay, 3-per-side gold Grover Imperial tuners, available in Natural (6041) or Sunburst (6040) finishes, body width 18", mfg. 1939-1955.

	N/A	$6,000	$4,000

SYNCHROMATIC G400 (NO. 260-0100) - arched spruce top, raised bound tortoise pickguard, bound cat's-eye soundholes, 3-stripe bound body, arched maple back, maple sides/neck, 14/20-fret bound rosewood fingerboard with pearl split hump block inlay, adjustable stylized ebony bridge/step trapeze tailpiece, bound blackface peghead with pearl model name/logo inlay, 3-per-side gold tuners, available in Sunburst or Black finishes, mfg. 1991-current.

	MSR	$1,725		$1,400	$900	$600

Synchromatic G400 C (No. 260-0101) - similar to Synchromatic, except has single round cutaway, available in Sunburst finish, mfg. 1991-current.

	MSR	$1,975		$1,595	$1,050	$700

Blonde Maple Synchromatic G400 MC - similar to Synchromatic C, except has Blonde Maple finish, available in Natural finish, mfg. 1991-96.

	$1,495	$975	$675

Last MSR was $1,850.

Synchromatic G400 CV - similar to Synchromatic C, except has Filtertron pickup and Bigsby tremolo bridge, available in Sunburst finish, or Blonde finishes, mfg. 1994-current.

	MSR	$2,400		$1,800	$900	$775

Add $100 for Blonde finish.

17" SYNCHROMATIC LIMITED EDITION (MODEL G450) - similar to the Synchromatic, except features handcarved spruce top, floating Jazz pickup, available in Walnut Stain finish, body width 17", mfg. 1997-2002.

	$3,100	$1,550	$1,300

Last MSR was $4,000.

This Limited Edition model comes with a Certificate of Authenticity signed by Fred Gretsch.

GRADING		100%	EXCELLENT	AVERAGE

17" Maple Synchromatic Limited Edition (Model G450 M) - similar to the 17" Synchromatic Limited Edition, except features a carved maple top, body width 17", mfg. 1997-2002.

		$3,300	$1,650	$1,370

Last MSR was $4,300.

SYNCHROMATIC THINLINE G460 - similar to the Synchromatic, except features a laminated spruce top, available in Orange finish, mfg. 1997-current.

MSR	$1,525		$1,225	$800	$600

Maple Synchromatic G460 M - similar to the Orange Synchromatic, except features a laminated maple top, mfg. 1997-2002.

		$1,050	$700	$525

Last MSR was $1,295.

SYNCHROMATIC JUMBO 125F (MODEL 6021) - arched spruce top, triangle soundhole, tortoise shell pickguard, 2-stripe bound body/rosette, figured maple back/sides/neck, 14/21-fret bound rosewood fingerboard with pearloid block inlay, adjustable rosewood bridge/stop tailpiece mounted on triangular rosewood base, black face peghead with pearl logo inlay, 3-per-side diecast tuners, available in Natural top, Sunburst back/side finish, mfg. 1947-1954.

		N/A	$1,200	$700

Some models had tortoise binding all around, other models came with single body binding.

ACOUSTIC

BURL IVES (MODEL 6004) - spruce top, round soundhole, tortoise pickguard, 2-stripe bound body/rosette, mahogany back/sides/neck, 14/19-fret rosewood fingerboard with pearloid dot inlay, rosewood bridge with black pins, black peghead face with Burl Ives/logo, 3-per-side tuners with plastic buttons, available in Natural finish, mfg. 1952-55.

		N/A	$550	$350

FOLK (MODEL 6003) - spruce top, round soundhole, tortoise pickguard, 3-stripe bound body/rosette, mahogany back/sides/neck, 14/19-fret rosewood fingerboard with pearloid dot inlay, rosewood bridge with black pins, black peghead face with logo, 3-per-side tuners with plastic buttons, available in Natural finish, mfg. 1951-1975.

		N/A	$450	$275

In 1955, this model was named the Grand Concert (Model 6003) and had a slanted peghead logo. In 1959, renamed the Jimmy Rogers Model (endorsed by 1950s/1960s pop star Jimmie Rogers). In 1963, renamed Folk Singing Model. In 1965, renamed Folk Model. In 1967, straight across peghead logo was added, zero fret added. In 1969, Mahogany Top (Model 6004) and Sunburst finish (Model 6002) became optional.

ACOUSTIC: RANCHER SERIES

RANCHER - spruce top with stylized G brand, triangle soundhole, tortoise pickguard with engraved longhorn steer head, 3-stripe bound body/rosette, maple arched back/sides/neck, 14/21-fret bound rosewood fingerboard with pearloid block inlay, adjustable rosewood bridge/stop tailpiece mounted on triangular rosewood base, black face bound peghead with pearl steer head/logo inlay, 3-per-side gold tuners, available in Golden Red finish, mfg. 1954-1973.

1954-1959		N/A	$3,000	$2,100
1960-1964		N/A	$2,500	$1,400
1965-1969		N/A	$2,000	$1,100
1970-1973		N/A	$1,500	$750

G brand was on bass side of top, fingerboard inlay was inscribed with cows and cactus. By 1957, gold pickguard and hump top fingerboard inlay with no engraving replaced original parts/designs. In 1959, tan pickguard, thumbnail fingerboard inlay replaced original parts/designs. In 1961, no G brand on top, and horseshoe peghead inlay replaced original parts/designs.

Rancher (1st Reissue) - similar to Rancher, except has block fingerboard inlay with engraved cows and cacti, rosewood bridge with white pins, horseshoe peghead inlay, mfg. 1975-1980.

		N/A	$1,000	$600

In 1978, tri-saddle bridge with white pins replaced original parts/design.

RANCHER 2ND REISSUE MODEL G6022 (NO. 260-0202) - spruce top with G brand, bound triangle soundhole, tortoise pickguard with engraved steerhead, 3-stripe bound body, maple back/sides/neck, 14/21-fret bound rosewood fingerboard with western motif engraved pearl block inlays, rosewood bridge with black white dot pins, bound peghead with pearl steerhead/logo inlay, 3-per-side gold tuners, available in Orange Satin finish, mfg. 1991-current.

MSR	$1,775		$1,425	$1,050	$750

Gretsch Synchromatic G-400
courtesy Fred Gretsch
Enterprises

Gretsch Rancher
courtesy Fred Gretsch
Enterprises

G

GRADING	100%	EXCELLENT	AVERAGE

Rancher Double Neck Model G6022-6/12 - similar to the Rancher-2nd Reissue, except has 6-string and 12-string neck configurations, mfg. 1997-2002.

	$2,550	$1,700	$1,275
		Last MSR was $3,200.	

Rancher C Model G6022C (No. 260-0203) - similar to Rancher-2nd Reissue, except has single round cutaway, single coil pickup, volume/tone control, current mfg.

MSR	$1,825	$1,475	$1,100	$800

Rancher CV Model G6022CV - similar to Rancher-2nd Reissue, except has single round cutaway, no pickguard, adjust-a-matic metal bridge with rosewood base/Bigsby vibrato, single coil pickup, volume/tone control, disc. 1999.

	$1,400	$700	$575
		Last MSR was $1,750.	

1954 Rancher Reissue Model G6022-1954 - similar to Rancher-2nd Reissue, except features 1954 model specifications, mfg. 1997-2002.

	$1,325	$900	$650
		Last MSR was $1,650.	

RANCHER 12 MODEL G6022-12 (NO. 260-0204) - similar to Rancher-2nd Reissue, except has 12-string configuration, 6-per-side tuners, current mfg.

MSR	$1,775	$1,425	$1,050	$750

Rancher C 12 (Model G6022 C/12) - similar to Rancher-2nd Reissue, except has 12-strings, single round cutaway, 6-per-side tuners, single coil pickup, volume/tone control, disc.

	$1,275	$650	$525
		Last MSR was $1,600.	

RANCHER SWEET 16 MODEL G6012 (NO. 260-0200) - similar to the Rancher except is available in Natural, Purple, Candy Apple Red, Regal Blue, Tangerine, Black, Tobacco Burst, or Anniversary Green finishes, current mfg.

MSR	$1,875	$1,500	$1,150	$800

WHITE FALCON RANCHER MODEL G6022 CWFF (NO. 260-0101) - single round cutaway jumbo style, solid spruce top with "G" brand, tortoise pickguard, bound triangle soundhole, gold sparkle bound body, maple back/sides/neck, 21-fret gold sparkle bound rosewood fingerboard with western motif engraved pearl block inlays, rosewood bridge with black white dot pins, gold sparkle bound peghead with gold sparkle inlay, 3-per-side gold tuners, internal acoustic pickup, volume/3-band EQ controls, available in White finish, mfg. 1994-current.

MSR	$3,025	$2,450	$1,800	$1,300

White Falcon Rancher with Fishman Pickup (Model G6022 CWFF) - similar to the White Falcon Rancher, except features a Fishman transducer pickup, mfg. 1997-2002.

MSR	$2,800	$1,995	$1,500	$1,075
			Last MSR was $2,800.	

ACOUSTIC: SUN VALLEY SERIES & MISC. MODELS

SUN VALLEY (MODEL 6010) - spruce top, round soundhole, tortoise pickguard, 3-stripe bound body/rosette, mahogany back/sides/neck, 14/20-fret bound rosewood fingerboard with dot inlay, rosewood bridge with black pins, bound peghead, 3-per-side chrome tuners, available in Natural or Sunburst finishes, mfg. 1959-1977.

1959-1964	N/A	$750	$500
1965-1969	N/A	$600	$425
1970-1977	N/A	$450	$300

By 1973, Sunburst finish was optional.

Sun Valley Dreadnought Acoustic (Model G6010) - dreadnought style, solid spruce top, triangle soundhole, 3-stripe bound body, floral pattern rosette, rosewood back/sides, mahogany neck, 14/20-fret bound rosewood fingerboard with pearl diamond inlay, pearl scroll inlay at 12th fret, rosewood bridge with black pearl dot pins, pearl floral bridge wing inlay, bound blackface peghead with pearl floral/logo inlay, 3-per-side gold tuners, available in Natural finish, mfg. 1991-disc.

	$1,000	$500	$425
		Last MSR was $1,250.	

SYNCHROMATIC 300F - spruce top, triangle soundhole, raised pickguard, 3-stripe body/rosette, maple arched back/sides/neck, 14/21-fret bound rosewood fingerboard with pearloid slashed hump top block inlay, adjustable rosewood stairstep bridge/gold trapeze tailpiece, bound cloud peghead with silkscreened Synchromatic/logo, 3-per-side gold tuners, available in Natural top, dark back/side finish, mfg. 1947-1955.

	N/A	$1,750	$1,150

SYNCHROMATIC 400F - similar to Synchromatic 300F, except has larger body, available in Sunburst back/side finish.

	N/A	$2,750	$1,750

GRADING		100%	EXCELLENT	AVERAGE

WAYFARER JUMBO (MODEL 6008) - dreadnought style, spruce top, round soundhole, lucite pickguard with engraved sailboat/logos, 3-stripe bound body/rosette, red maple back/sides/neck, 14/21-fret bound rosewood fingerboard with pearl split block inlay, rosewood bridge with white pins, black face peghead with logo inlay, 3-per-side Grover chrome tuners, available in Natural finish, mfg. 1969-1972.

		N/A	$500	$325

ACOUSTIC: HISTORIC SERIES

DREADNOUGHT G3503 (NO. 270-1302/8) - 16" dreadnought acoustic 6-string, solid Sitka spruce top, rosewood back and sides, 25 1/2" scale, maple neck with rosewood fingerboard, neoclassical position markers, 3-per-side tuners, available in Aged Natural or Tobacco Sunburst finish, current mfg.

MSR	$640	$525	$395	$315

Subtract $200 for Satin Sunburst finish (Model G3520) and (Model G3523), both new 2001.

DREADNOUGHT 12-STRING G3523-12 (NO. 270-1307) - similar to the dreadnought except in 12-string configuration, 6-per-side tuners, available in Natural Satin finish, current mfg.

MSR	$460	$375	$295	$200

GRAND CONCERT G3303 (NO. 270-1201/3) - 15" grand concert acoustic 6-string, solid Sitka spruce and hardwood top, rosewood/hardwood sides and back, 25 1/2" scale, maple neck with rosewood fingerboard, neoclassical inlays, gold hardware, 3-per-side tuners, available in Aged Natural finish, current mfg.

MSR	$620	$495	$350	$275

Subtract $100 for single cutaway model with Deep Red Stain finish (Model G3366), or single cutaway model with maple top, back and sides (Model G3373).

HAWAIIAN G3100 (NO. 270-1101) - 16" auditorium acoustic 6-string, 24.75" scale, solid Sitka spruce top, mahogany back and sides, maple neck with rosewood fingerboard, neoclassical position markers, 3-per-side tuners, available in Tobacco Sunburst finish, current mfg.

MSR	$620	$495	$350	$275

Add $30 for Black finish (Model G3101). Add $150 for Deluxe Model with celluloid fingerboard and headstock and Vintage Sunburst finish (Model G3105).

RESONATOR G3170 (NO. 270-1601) - 14" body, 25.3" scale, laminated maple top, back and sides, maple neck with rosewood fingerboard, neoclassical position markers, chrome plated resonator, 3-per-side tuners, available in Tobacco Sunburst finish, current mfg.

MSR	$800	$650	$495	$350

SIERRA JUMBO G3738 (NO. 270-1502) - 17" Jumbo acoustic 6-string, maple top, back and sides, maple neck, 25 1/2" scale, 3-per-side tuners, mfg. 2001-current.

MSR	$700	$575	$450	$325

Sierra Jumbo G3713 (No. 270-1900) - similar to the Sierra Jumbo except has a solid Sitka spruce top, 16" wide bout, and mahogany neck, current mfg.

MSR	$900	$725	$575	$400

ACOUSTIC: SYNCHROMATIC SERIES

DREADNOUGHT G3553 (NO. 270-1802) - dreadnought style body, available in Natural, Black (G3551), Blue (G3557), or Red (G3559) finishes, current mfg.

MSR	$320	$260	$210	$140

STANDARD FOLK G1653 (NO. 270-1800) - folk style body, Neo-Classical "Thumbnail" Inlay position markers, bound fingerboard, triple bound body, aged B/W/B rosette, adjustable truss rod, available in Natural or Red (G1659) finishes, current mfg.

MSR	$280	$225	$175	$125

ACOUSTIC ELECTRIC: PROFESSIONAL & MISC.

CRIMSON FLYER G6020 - single round cutaway body, solid spruce top, triangle soundhole, multi bound body, floral pattern rosette, chestnut back/sides, 2 piece mahogany neck, 22-fret rosewood fingerboard with pearl dot inlay, pearl scroll inlay at 12th fret, rosewood bridge with black pearl pins, pearl floral bridge wing inlay, bound body matching peghead w/pearl logo inlay, 3-per-side gold tuners, active ceramic pickup, volume/tone control, available in Cherry Sunburst finish, mfg. 1991 - 96.

		$1,050	$675	$450

Last MSR was $1,350.

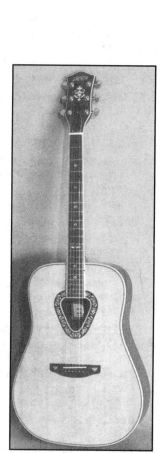

Gretsch White Falcon Rancher
courtesy Fred Gretsch
Enterprises

Gretsch Sun Valley
courtesy Fred Gretsch
Enterprises

GRADING	100%	EXCELLENT	AVERAGE

Crimson Flyer V G6020 V - similar to Crimson Flyer, except has rosewood/metal tune-o-matic bridge/Bigsby vibrato, disc.

	$1,325	$650	$550

Last MSR was $1,650.

NIGHTBIRD G6030 - single round cutaway body, solid spruce top, triangle soundhole, 3-stripe bound body, floral pattern rosette, maple back/sides, 2 piece mahogany neck, 21-fret bound rosewood fingerboard with pearl dot inlay, pearl scroll inlay at 12th fret, rosewood bridge with black pearl dot pins, pearl floral pattern bridge wing inlay, bound blackface peghead with pearl logo inlay, 3-per-side gold tuners, active ceramic pickup, volume/tone control, available in Ebony finish, disc.

	$960	$480	$395

Last MSR was $1,200.

Nightbird V (Model 6030 V) - similar to Nightbird, except has rosewood/metal tune-o-matic bridge/Bigsby vibrato tailpiece, disc.

	$995	$600	$495

Last MSR was $1,500.

SYNCHROMATIC G6040MCSS FILTERTRON (NO. 260-0107) - similar to the Synchromatic except has a vintage Filtertron pickup, available in Natural finish, current mfg.

MSR	$2,725	$2,195	$1,750	$1,250

ACOUSTIC ELECTRIC: HISTORIC SERIES

DREADNOUGHT G3603 (NO. 270-1303) - similar to Historic Series Dreadnought acoustic model except, has a Fishman Prefix pickup system with built-in preamp and tone circuit, available in Aged Natural finish, current mfg.

MSR	$880	$705	$525	$375

Add $15 for Black finish (Model G3601).

GRAND CONCERT G3400 (NO. 270-1202) - similar to Historic Series Grand Concert acoustic model except, has a Fishman Prefix pickup system with built-in preamp and tone circuit, available in Aged Natural finish, current mfg.

MSR	$860	$695	$515	$350

HAWAIIAN G3203 (NO. 270-1102) - similar to the Historic Series Hawaiian acoustic model except, has a Fishman Prefix pickup with built-in preamp & tone circuit, gold hardware, faux tortoise shell pickguard, available in Aged Natural finish, current mfg.

MSR	$880	$705	$525	$375

Add $15 for Black finish (Model G3201). Add $200 for Deluxe model with Vintage Sunburst finish (Model G3205).

RANCHER JR. G341X (NO. 270-1202) - similar to the Rancher design except has a smaller 15" wide body, has a Fishman Prefix pickup and preamp system, available in Orange Stain, Black, Tobacco Sunburst, Blue, Purple, or Red finishes, current mfg.

MSR	$900	$725	$575	$425

SIERRA JUMBO G3700 (NO. 270-1502) - 17" jumbo body, 25 1/2" scale, solid Sitka spruce top, mahogany back and sides, maple neck with rosewood fingerboard, neoclassical position markers, 3-per-side tuners, French soundhole, Fishman Prefix pickup with built-in preamp and tone circuit, available in Tobacco Sunburst, Black (G3701), or Natural (G3703) finish, current mfg.

MSR	$920	$750	$575	$425

Add $50 for Black finish (Model G3701).

Sierra Jumbo G3700-12 (No. 270-1504) - similar to the Sierra Jumbo except in 12-String configuration, 6-per-side tuners, current mfg.

MSR	$960	$775	$600	$450

SYNCHROMATIC JR. G3900 (NO. 251-0107) - 15" body, single cutaway archtop design, Laminated Maple top, back and sides, 24¾" scale, maple neck with rosewood fingerboard, 3-per-side tuners, neoclassical position markers, single neck-mounted jazz style pickup, available in Tobacco Sunburst, Metallic Gold, or Vintage Sunburst finish, current mfg.

MSR	$1,100	$895	$650	$450

Add $100 for Left-hand model (Model G3900LH), available in Tobacco Sunburst finish. Add $150 for Metallic Gold finish (Model G3967). Add $175 for Vintage Sunburst finish (Model G3905).

ACOUSTIC ELECTRIC BASS

ACOUSTIC FRETTED BASS G6175 (NO. 260-0900) - single round cutaway body, spruce top, triangle soundhole, 3-stripe bound body, floral pattern rosette, maple back/sides/neck, 23-fret bound rosewood fingerboard with pearl dot inlay, pearl scroll inlay at 12th fret, rosewood strings through bridge, bound blackface peghead with pearl logo inlay, 2-per-side gold tuners, active ceramic pickup, volume/tone control, available in Orange Stain finish, current mfg.

MSR	$1,725	$1,395	$950	$600

Acoustic Fretless Bass G6176 - similar to the Acoustic Fretted Bass, except has fretless fingerboard, current mfg.

MSR	$1,725	$1,395	$950	$600

ACOUSTIC FRETTED BASS WESTERN G6175W (NO. 260-0903) - similar to the G6175 except in Western style, available in Orange Stain finish, current mfg.

MSR	$1,975	$1,595	$1,100	$700

GREVEN GUITARS

Instruments currently built in Portland, OR. Previously built in Bloomington, IN.

Luthier John Greven has been building guitars for the past thirty-two years. While he has always been building good sounding acoustics, Greven is perhaps better known for the outstanding quality of his inlay work. Rather than waste words attempting to describe the quality of his guitars, simply contact John Greven directly (see Trademark Index) for specification and pricing information.

A number of years ago, Greven devised a faux tortoise shell material that can be used as pickguards or body binding without the problems encountered by the real material. This faux shell is available through the Luthier's Mercantile International of Healdsburg CA.

GRIMES, STEVEN

Instruments currently built in Kula, Hawaii.

Luthier Steven Grimes originally apprenticed with a violin maker and set up his own mandolin shop in Port Townsend, Washington in 1972. During that time period, Grimes also began handcrafting archtop guitars. In Grimes moved to Hawaii, and continues to produce guitars on a custom basis. Grimes estimates that he produces about 20 guitars a year (half of them are archtops). Customers have choices on size, woods used, color of finish, inlay work, electronic packages, and the neck profile.

ACOUSTIC

Grimes' models include the **Beamer**, a double soundhole flattop acoustic that is constructed with highly figured wood (list $3,400); the **Jazz Nouveau**, an archtop model with curly maple top/koa body and ebony fingerboard/bridge/pickguard/tailpiece (list $5,600); and the **Montreux**, an archtop model with European spruce top and figured German maple back and sides (list $8,800). Both archtop models are optionally available in a 7-string configuration, with custom inlay, or with a floating pickup. The **Beamer** acoustic is optional with custom electronics, a cutaway body, or custom inlays.

GRIMSHAW

Instruments previously produced in England from the 1950s through the late 1970s.

While this company is best known for its high quality archtop guitars, they also produced a notable semi-hollowbody design in the mid 1950s called the Short-Scale. In the early 1960s, Emil Grimshaw introduced the Meteor solid body guitar. The company then focused on both original and copies of American designs from the late 1960s on, (Source: Tony Bacon and Paul Day, *The Guru's Guitar Guide*).

GROSSMAN

See chapter on House Brands.

Before World War II, the majority of guitars were sold through mail-order distributors. The Grossman company distributed a number of guitars built for them with their trademark on the headstock, (Source: Tom Wheeler, American Guitars).

GROVES CUSTOM GUITARS

Instruments currently built in Tucson, Arizona.

Luthier Gordon S. Groves is currently offering handcrafted guitar models built to customers specifications. They also offer a repair shop. For further information regarding specifications and pricing, please contact luthier Groves directly (see Trademark Index).

GUDELSKY MUSICAL INSTRUMENTS

Instruments previously built in Vista, California from 1985 to 1996.

Luthier Harris Paul Gudelsky (1964-1996) had apprenticed to James D'Aquisto before starting Gudelsky Musical Instruments. Gudelsky's personal goal was to try to build a more modern version of the archtop guitar. Gudelsky offered a small line of instruments exclusively on a customer order basis that included hollowbody archtops (acoustic and electric/acoustic) ranged between $4,290 and $5,500; semi-hollowbodies ranged from $4,235 to $4,400; and set-neck solid bodies ranged from $2,450 to $3,500. Paul Gudelsky was found fatally shot at his Vista, California home in May, 1996.

GUGINO

Instruments previously built in Buffalo, New York between the 1930s and 1940s.

Luthier Carmino Gugino built instruments that featured high quality conventional building (the frets, finish, carving, etc.) combined with very unconventional design ideas. As detailed by Jay Scott, certain models feature necks that screw on to the body, or have asymmetrical bodies, or an archtop that has a detachable neck/body joint/bridge piece that is removable from the body, (Source: Teisco Del Rey, *Guitar Player* magazine).

GUILD

Currently manufactured in Westerly, Rhode Island beginning in 1969, and distributed by the Fender Musical Instrument Corporation (FMIC) of Scottsdale, Arizona. In 1997, Guild (FMIC) opened up a new Guild Custom Shop in Nashville, Tennessee. Guild was originally located in New York City between 1952-1956, and production was moved to Hoboken, New Jersey, from late 1956 to 1968.

Gretsch Rancher Jr. courtesy Fred Gretsch Enterprises

G

Gretsch Acoustic Fretted F courtesy Fred Gretsc' Enterprises

Contrary to the notions about a "guild of old world-style craftsmen" gathering to build these exceptional guitars, Guild was founded in 1952 by Alfred Dronge (who did hire great guitar builders). Dronge, a Jewish emigrant from Europe, grew up in New York City and took jobs working for various music stores on Park Row. Dronge became an accomplished musician who played both banjo and guitar, and loved jazz music. His experience in teaching music and performing in small orchestras led to the formation of the Sagman and Dronge music store.

After World War II, Dronge gave up the music store in favor of importing and distributing Italian accordions. The Sonola Accordion Company was successful enough to make Dronge a small fortune. It is with this reputation and finances that Dronge formed Guild Guitars, Inc. with ex-Ephiphone sales manager George Mann. Incidentally, the Guild name came from a third party who was involved with a guitar amplifier company that was going out of business. As the plant was closing down Dronge and Gene Detgen decided to keep the name. The Guild company was registered in 1952.

As the original New York-based Epiphone company was having problems with the local unions, they decided to move production down to Philadelphia. Dronge took advantage of this decision and attracted several of their ex-luthiers to his company. Some of the workers were of Italian ancestry, and felt more comfortable remaining in the Little Italy neighborhood rather than moving to Pennsylvania.

The company was originally located in a New York loft from 1952 through 1956. They expanded into a larger workshop in Hoboken, New Jersey, in late 1956. Finally, upon completion of new facilities, Guild moved to its current home in Westerly, Rhode Island, in 1969.

As pop music in the 1960s spurred on a demand for guitars, musical instrument companies expanded to meet the business growth. At the same time, large corporations began to diversify their holdings. Most people are aware of the CBS decision to buy Fender in 1965, or Baldwin Piano's purchase of the Burns trademark and manufacturing equipment in 1967. In 1966, electronic parts producer Avnet Inc. bought Guild Musical Instruments, and Alfred Dronge stayed on as president. Dronge also hired Jim Deurloo (of Gibson and later Heritage fame) as plant manager in December 1969. Deurloo's commitment to quality control resulted in better consistency of Guild products.

Tragedy occurred in 1972 as Alfred Dronge was killed in an aircraft crash. The relationships he built with the members of the company dissipated, and the driving force of twenty years since the inception was gone. However, Leon Tell (Guild's vice president from 1963 to 1973) became the company president in 1973 and maintained that position until 1983.

In mid August of 1986, Avnet sold Guild to a management/investment group from New England and Tennessee. Officers of the newly formed Guild Music Corporation included company President Jerre R. Haskew (previously Chief Executive Officer and President of the Commerce Union Bank of Chattanooga Tennessee), Executive Vice President of Plant and Operations George A. Hammerstrom, and Executive Vice President of Product Development and Artist Relations George Gruhn (Gruhn later left the company in early 1988).

Unfortunately, the remaining members of the investment group defaulted on bank obligations in November of 1988, leading to a court supervised financial restructuring. The Faas Corporation of New Berlin, Wisconsin (now U.S. Musical Corporation) bought Guild in January 1989. Solid body guitar production was discontinued in favor of acoustic and acoustic-electric production (a company strength) although some electric models were reissued in the mid 1990s.

Most recently, the Guild company was purchased by Fender Musical Instrument Corporation in 1995. A recent 1996 catalog shows an arrangement of acoustic and acoustic electric models, as well as some semi-hollowbody guitars and one solid body electric. Guild has introduced more solid body electrics lately; all current models are based on memorable Guild models from earlier years (such as the Starfire models). In 1997, Guild opened a new Custom Shop in Nashville, Tennessee,(Reference source for early Guild history: Hans Moust, *The Guild Guitar Book*; contemporary history courtesy Jay Pilzer; Guild model information courtesy Bill Acton, Guild Guitars).

GUILD IDENTIFYING FEATURES

According to noted authority and Guild enthusiast Jay Pilzer, there are identifying features on Guild instruments that can assist in determining their year of production. For information regarding archtop models with floating or built-in pickups, please refer to the *Blue Book of Electric Guitars.*

Knobs on Electrics: 1953-58 transparent barrel knobs; 1959-63 transparent yellowish top hat knobs with Guild logo in either chrome or gold; 1964-72 black top hat knobs, Guild logo, tone or vol; circa 1990-present black top hat with Guild logo, no numbers or tone/vol.

Electric Pickguards: Except for the Johnny Smith/Artist Award (which used the stairstep pickguard), Guild pickguards were rounded, following the shape of the guitar until 1963 when the stairstep became standard on archtop electrics.

Acoustic Pickguards: Most models have a distinct Guild shape in either tortoise or black with rounded edges that follow the line of guitar, except the F-20, M-20, and new *A* series which have teardrop pickguards.

Headstock Inlays: The earliest were simple Guild inverted *V* with triangular insert, with *G* logo below, later the triangular insert disappears, Chesterfield introduced on some models by 1957. In general the more elaborate the headstock, the higher price the instrument.

ACOUSTIC ARCHTOP

A-50 GRANADA - hollow non-cutaway style bound body, laminated arched spruce top, f-holes, raised black pickguard, mahogany back/sides/neck, 14/20-fret rosewood fingerboard with pearl dot inlay, adjustable rosewood bridge/trapeze tailpiece, blackface peghead with screened logo, 3-per-side nickel tuners, available in Sunburst finish, body width 16 1/4", mfg. 1952-1968.

	N/A	$850	$500

A-150 - hollow single round cutaway style bound body, carved solid spruce top, f-holes, raised black pickguard, laminated maple back and sides, 20-fret rosewood fingerboard with block inlay, 24 3/4" inch scale, adjustable rosewood bridge/trapeze tailpiece, blackface peghead with screened logo, 3-per-side nickel tuners, available in Sunburst finish, body width 17", mfg. 1953-1973.

	N/A	$1,500	$1,250

A-350 STRATFORD - single round cutaway hollow style, arched spruce top, raised black laminated pickguard, 2 bound f-holes, multibound body, maple back/sides/neck, 20-fret bound rosewood fingerboard with pearl block inlay, adjustable rosewood bridge/harp tailpiece, multibound blackface peghead with pearl shield/logo inlay, 3-per-side gold tuners, available in Sunburst finish, mfg. 1952-1972.

	N/A	$2,500	$1,900

GRADING	100%	EXCELLENT	AVERAGE

A-500 STUART - single round cutaway hollow style, bound arched solid spruce top, 2 bound f-holes, bound tortoise pickguard, maple back/sides/neck, 20-fret bound ebony fingerboard with pearl block/ abalone wedge inlay, adjustable ebony bridge, stylized trapeze tailpiece, bound peghead with pearl shield/logo inlay, 3-per-side gold Imperial tuners, available in Natural or Sunburst finishes, mfg. 1952-1966.

	N/A	$3,400	$2,500

ARTIST AWARD (MODEL 350-8300) - single rounded cutaway hollow body, bound hand-carved solid spruce top, 2 bound f-holes, bound tortoise pickguard, solid German figured maple back/sides, 5-piece maple neck, 20-fret bound ebony fingerboard with pearl block/abalone wedge inlay, adjustable ebony bridge, stylized trapeze tailpiece, bound peghead with pearl/abalone inscribed block/logo inlay, 3-per-side Imperial tuners, gold hardware, floating Guild single coil pickup, available in Antique Burst (837) and Blonde (801) finishes, mfg. 1954-1999.

This model was originally the Johnny Smith Model, but shortly after its debut Mr. Smith discontinued his association with Guild.

	100%	EXCELLENT	AVERAGE
1954-1959	N/A	$4,250	$2,900
1960-1969	N/A	$3,800	$2,700
1970-1979	N/A	$3,500	$2,500
1980-1989	N/A	$3,250	$2,200
1990-1996	N/A	$3,000	$2,000
1997-1999	$4,500	$3,000	$2,000

Last MSR was $6,399.

Guild Benedetto Johnny Smith Award - in late 1999, this model was redesigned by Robert Benedetto, with limited production beginning at the Westerly, RI plant. New features include recarved top and back, refined f-hole and pickguard design, changed bracing, and mother-of-pearl "Benedetto" logo inlay on the 19th fret, available in Antique Burst, Honey Blonde, or Opulent Brown, current mfg.

MSR $11,000

Guild Benedetto Johnny
Smith Award
courtesy Guild Guitars

BENEDETTO BRAND LA VENEZIA - select aged spruce hand graduated and tuned archtop, highly flamed European maple back/sides, ebony fingerrest and fretboard, 25 in. scale, available in Autumn Burst or Honey Blonde finish, mfg. 2000-current.

MSR $17,500

CA-100 CAPRI - single sharp cutaway hollow style, arched bound spruce top, raised bound black pickguard, 2 f-holes, maple back/sides/neck, 20-fret bound rosewood fingerboard with pearl block inlay, adjustable rosewood bridge/trapeze tailpiece, blackface peghead with pearl shield/logo inlay, 3-per-side chrome tuners, available in Sunburst finish, mfg. 1956-1972.

	N/A	$1,400	$1,000

In 1954, harp tailpiece replaced original parts/design.

ACOUSTIC: GENERAL INFORMATION

On many of the acoustic models a Fishman pickup and preamp is offered. In most cases the following applies:

Add $150 for Fishman Matrix/Transducer pickup. Add $225 for both Fisman Matrix/Transducer pickup and preamp system.

ACOUSTIC: A SERIES

A-25HR - concert size body, spruce top, mahogany back and sides, rosewood fingerboard with dot inlays, rosewood bridge, 3-per-side tuners, tortoise shell pickguard, available in Natural satin finish, disc. 1998.

	N/A	$525	$250

Last MSR was $999.

A-25HG - similar to the A-25HR, except has a high gloss finish, disc. 1995.

	N/A	$600	$450

Last MSR was $1,099.

A-50 - similar to the A-25HR, except has rosewood back and sides, abalone rosette, ebony fingerboard and bridge, disc. 1998.

	N/A	$850	$575

Last MSR was $1,499.

The A-50 steel string model is not to be confused with the earlier A-50 Archtop model.

ACOUSTIC: DREADNOUGHT SERIES

All models in this series have dreadnought style bodies.

Guild Benedetto Brand
La Venezia
courtesy Guild Guitars

GRADING	100%	EXCELLENT	AVERAGE

D-4 (NO. 350-0100) - solid spruce top, round soundhole, tortoise pickguard, 3-stripe bound body/rosette, arched mahogany back, solid mahogany sides/neck, 14/20-fret rosewood fingerboard with pearl dot inlay, rosewood bridge with white black dot pins, 3-per-side chrome tuners, available in Natural (021) hand rubbed satin finish, disc. 2002.

	$675	$425	$325

Last MSR was $799.

D-4 LH model available at no additional cost (Model 350 - 0120).

D-4 G (Model 350-0140, D-4 HG) - similar to D-4, available in Natural (021) high gloss finish, mfg. 1990-94, 1998-2002.

	$749	$485	$350

Last MSR was $999.

D-4 G LH model available at no additional cost (Model 350-0160).

D-4 12 12-String (Model 350-0900) - similar to D-4, except has 12-string configuration, 6-per-side tuners, available in Natural (721) hand rubbed satin finish, disc. 1999.

	$795	$525	$350

Last MSR was $1,049.

Add $130 for left-handed configuration model D-4 12 LH (Model 350-0920).

List Price includes hardshell case.

D-6 - similar to D-4, except has gold hardware, available in Natural finish, disc. 1995.

	N/A	$425	$250

Last MSR was $950.

D-6 HG - similar to D-4, except has gold hardware, available in Natural high gloss finish, disc. 1996.

	N/A	$525	$300

Last MSR was $1,100.

D-15 - mahogany top/back/sides/neck, round soundhole, tortoise pickguard, 3-stripe rosette, 14/20-fret rosewood fingerboard with pearl dot inlay, rosewood bridge with white black dot pins, 3-per-side chrome tuners, available in Black, Natural, or Wood grain Red finishes, mfg. 1987-1994.

	N/A	$525	$325

Last MSR was $850.

D-25 (NO. 350-0200) - solid spruce top, round soundhole, tortoise pickguard, black bound body, 3-stripe rosette, arched mahogany back, solid mahogany sides/neck, 14/20-fret rosewood fingerboard with pearl dot inlay, rosewood bridge with white black dot pins, 3-per-side chrome tuners, available in Black (706), Natural (721), and Antique (Sun)Burst (737) high gloss finishes, price includes hardshell case, mfg. 1979-2002.

1979-1989	N/A	$625	$375
1990-1993	N/A	$650	$375
1994-2002	$925	$650	$450

Last MSR was $1,249.

D-25 LH model available at no additional cost (Model 350-0220).

D-25 12 12-String (Model 350-1000) - similar to D-25 except has 12-string configuration, 6-per-side tuners, available in Black (706), Natural (721), and Antique (Sun)Burst (737) high gloss finishes, price includes hardshell case, disc. 1999.

	$950	$625	$425

Last MSR was $1,249.

D-25 M - similar to D-25, except has mahogany top, disc. 1995.

	N/A	$450	$325

D-25 CURRENT MFG. (NO. 380-0000) - solid mahogany top/back/sides, mahogany neck, rosewood fretboard, pearl dot inlays, available in Amber, Sapphire Blue Trans., Brown Sunburst, Red Trans., Seafoam Green, or Honey Blonde finishes, new 2003.

MSR	$1,200	$900	$700	$500

D-30 (NO. 350-1200) - solid spruce top, round soundhole, arched maple back, solid maple sides, mahogany neck, 14/20 rosewood fingerboard with pearl dot inlay, tortoise pickguard, 3-per-side chrome tuners, available in Black (706), Blonde (701), or Antique (Sun)Burst (737) high gloss finishes, price includes hardshell case, disc.

	$1,050	$795	$550

Last MSR was $1,399.

D-30 LH model available at no additional cost (Model 350-1220).

D-35 - solid spruce top, round soundhole, tortoise pickguard, bound body, 1-stripe rosette, mahogany back/sides/neck, 14/20-fret rosewood fingerboard with pearl dot inlay, rosewood bridge with white black dot pins, screened peghead logo, 3-per-side chrome tuners, available in Natural finish, disc.

	N/A	$800	$575

GRADING	100%	EXCELLENT	AVERAGE

D-40 (NO. 380-0100) - solid spruce top, round soundhole, tortoise pickguard, bound body, 3-stripe rosette, mahogany back/sides/neck, 14/20-fret rosewood fingerboard with pearl dot inlay, rosewood bridge with white black dot pins, pearl Chesterfield/logo peghead inlay, 3-per-side chrome tuners, available in Natural, Black, Antique Burst, or Red Trans. finishes, disc. 1991, reintroduced 2003.

	MSR	$1,700		$1,275	$950	$650

This model had an optional single sharp cutaway prior to 1991 (Model D-40C).

D-40 Richie Havens Signature (No. 380-0110) - similar to the D-40 except has a double pickguard setup and signature on truss rod cover, available in Black or Natural finishes, new 2003.

	MSR	$1,800		$1,350	$1,000	$700

D-44 - solid spruce top, round soundhole, tortoise pickguard, 5-stripe bound body/rosette, pearwood back/sides, mahogany neck, 14/20-fret ebony fingerboard with pearl dot inlay, ebony bridge with white black dot pins, pearl Chesterfield/logo peghead inlay, 3-per-side chrome tuners, available in Natural or Sunburst finishes, mfg. 1965-1979.

			N/A	$900	$600

In 1974, maple back/sides replaced original parts/design (Model D-44M).

D-46 - similar to the D-44, except has ash back and sides, available in Natural or Sunburst finishes, mfg. 1980-85.

			N/A	$950	$625

D-50 (NO. 380-0300) - solid spruce top, round soundhole, tortoise pickguard, 5-stripe bound body/rosette, rosewood back/sides, mahogany neck, 14/20-fret ebony fingerboard with pearl dot inlay, ebony bridge with white black dot pins, pearl Chesterfield/logo peghead inlay, 3-per-side chrome tuners, available in Natural or Antique Burst finishes, mfg. 1963-1994, reintroduced 2003.

	MSR	$1,900		$1,425	$1,050	$750

D-55 (NO. 350-0300/380-0500) - solid spruce top, round soundhole, tortoise pickguard, 3-stripe bound body, abalone rosette, bookmatched rosewood back, solid rosewood sides, 3-piece mahogany neck, 14/20-fret bound ebony fingerboard with pearl block/abalone wedge inlay, ebony bridge with white abalone dot pins, maple endpin wedge, bound peghead with pearl shield/logo inlay, 3-per-side gold tuners, available in Natural or Antique Burst lacquer finishes, case included in the price, mfg. 1968-current.

	MSR	$2,700		$2,025	$1,500	$975

D-55 LH model available at no additional cost (Model 350-0320).

DK-70 PEACOCK (LIMITED EDITION) - dreadnought style, koa body, ebony fingerboard with abalone cloud inlays, abalone Guild logo inlay on headstock, abalone peacock inlay on pickguard, available in Natural finish, mfg. 1995-96.

			N/A	$1,800	$1,100

Last MSR was $4,999.

The projected production run of this model was 50 pieces. It is estimated that only half were actually completed.

**Guild D-40
courtesy Guild Guitars**

ACOUSTIC: VINTAGE DREADNOUGHT SERIES

DV models feature shaved or hand scalloped top bracing.

DV-6 (NO. 350-0500) - solid spruce top, round soundhole, solid mahogany back/sides, shaved bracing, vintage herringbone rosette, 14/20-fret rosewood fingerboard with dot inlay, 3-per-side gold tuners, available in Natural (721) hand rubbed satin finish, price includes hardshell case, disc. 1999.

		$825	$600	$400

Last MSR was $1,099.

Add $130 for left-handed configuration model DV-6 LH (Model 350-0520).

DV-6 HG (No. 350-0600) - similar to the DV-6, available in Antique Burst (737) and Natural (721) high gloss lacquer finishes, price includes hardshell case, mfg. 1998-99.

		$1,050	$675	$450

Last MSR was $1,299.

Add $130 for left-handed configuration model DV-6 HG LH (Model 350-0620).

DV-52 (NO. 350-0700) - solid spruce top, round soundhole, hand-scalloped bracing, tortoise pickguard, 3-stripe bound body, abalone rosette, solid rosewood back/sides, mahogany neck, 14/20-fret ebony fingerboard with pearl dot inlay, ebony bridge with white black dot pins, pearl Chesterfield/logo peghead inlay, 3-per-side gold tuners, available in Natural (721) satin lacquer finishes, price includes hardshell case, disc.

		$1,275	$895	$625

Last MSR was $1,699.

DV-52 LH model available at no additional cost (Model 350-0720).

**Guild D-55
courtesy Guild Guitars**

GRADING	100%	EXCELLENT	AVERAGE

DV-52 HG (No. 350-0800) - similar to DV 52, except features shaved bracing, available in Antique Burst (737) and Natural (721) high gloss lacquer finishes, price includes hardshell case, mfg. 1990-94, 1998-disc.

	$1,225	**$825**	**$575**

Last MSR was $1,642.

DV-52 HG LH model available at no additional cost (Model 350-0820).

DV-62 - solid spruce top, round soundhole, tortoise pickguard, herringbone bound body/rosette, rosewood back/sides, mahogany neck, 14/20-fret ebony fingerboard with pearl dot inlay, ebony bridge with white black dot pins, pearl shield/logo peghead inlay, 3-per-side gold tuners, available in Natural or Sunburst finishes, mfg. 1994-95.

	N/A	**$1,100**	**$750**

Last MSR was $1,500.

DV-74 PUEBLO (LIMITED EDITION) - dreadnought style, solid spruce top, herringbone top binding, rosewood back and sides, ebony fingerboard with South Sea coral/onyx/turquoise/nickel silver Southwestern motif, South Sea coral/onyx/turquoise/nickel silver design on rosette, chrome silver hardware, Grover Imperial tuners, mfg. 1996 only.

	N/A	**$1,600**	**$1,200**

Last MSR was $2,499.

In 1996, Guild announced that only 50 of these guitars would be constructed. It is not known if the full production run was completed.

ACOUSTIC: F SERIES

Guild's F Series flattop models feature tight waisted bodies and 24 3/4" scale lengths.

F-20 TROUBADOR - solid spruce top, round soundhole, tortoise pickguard, bound body, single rosette, maple back/sides, mahogany neck, 14/20-fret rosewood fingerboard with pearl dot inlay, rosewood bridge with white pins, blackface peghead with screened logo, 3-per-side chrome tuners, available in Natural top/Mahogany Stain back/sides finish, body length 18", body width 13 1/3", body depth 4 1/4", mfg. 1956-1987.

1952-1956	N/A	$900	$550
1957-1973	N/A	$750	$500

In 1957, mahogany back/sides replaced original parts/designs.

M-20 - similar to F-20, except has mahogany top, mfg. 1958-1973.

	N/A	$525	$400

F-30 ARAGON - solid spruce top, round soundhole, black pickguard, bound body, single rosette, maple back/sides, mahogany neck, 14/20-fret rosewood fingerboard with pearl dot inlay, rosewood bridge with white pins, blackface peghead with screened logo, 3-per-side chrome tuners, available in Natural top/Mahogany Stain back/sides finish, body length 19 1/4", body width 15 1/2", body depth 4 1/4", mfg. 1952-1985.

1952-1956	N/A	$1,000	$700
1957-1985	N/A	$800	$550

F-30 R (Limited Edition) - similar to the F-30, except featured rosewood back and sides.

	N/A	$1,700	$1,350

Before being put into full production in 1998 (See Model 350-5500), the F-30 R was only available as a Limited Edition model.

M-30 - similar to F-30 Aragon, except has mahogany top, black pickguard, mfg. 1952-1985.

	N/A	$1,050	$725

F-30 HR (NO. 350-5300) - solid spruce top, round soundhole, solid mahogany back/sides, 24 3/4" scale, 14/20-fret rosewood fingerboard with dot inlay, 3-per-side chrome tuners, black pickguard, available in Natural (721) hand rubbed satin finish, price includes hardshell case, mfg. 1998-2000.

	$825	**$525**	**$375**

Last MSR was $1,100.

M-20 (NO. 350-5300) - solid mahogany top, round soundhole, solid mahogany back/sides, 24 3/4" scale, 14/20-fret rosewood fingerboard with pearl dot inlay, 3-per-side chrome tuners, tortoiseshell pickguard, available in Natural (721) hand rubbed satin finish, price includes hardshell case, mfg. 1998-disc.

	$825	**$575**	**$395**

Last MSR was $1,099.

M-20 LH model available at no extra cost (Model 350-5320).

F-30 HG (NO. 350-5400) - similar to the F-30 HR, available in Antique Burst (737), Black (706), and Natural (721) high gloss finishes, price includes hardshell case, mfg. 1998-2000.

	$975	**$700**	**$475**

Last MSR was $1,356.

F-30 HG LH model available at no additional cost (Model 350-5420).

GRADING	100%	EXCELLENT	AVERAGE

F-30 R (Model 350-5500) - similar to the F-30 HR, except features rosewood back/sides, 3-per-side gold tuners, available in Antique Burst (737) and Natural (721) high gloss finishes, price includes hardshell case, mfg. 1998-disc.

$1,195 $825 $575
Last MSR was $1,599.

F-30 R LH model available at no additional cost (Model 350-5520).

F-40 VALENCIA - solid spruce top, round soundhole, black pickguard, multibound body, 2-stripe rosette, maple back/sides, mahogany neck, 14/20-fret bound rosewood fingerboard with pearl block inlay, rosewood bridge with white pins, blackface peghead with pearl shield/logo inlay, 3-per-side chrome tuners, available in Natural or Sunburst finishes, body length 19 1/4", body width 16", body depth 4 1/4", mfg. 1952-1964.

N/A $950 $700

F-40 Reissue - has pearl Chesterfield/logo peghead inlay, mfg. 1973-circa 1985.

N/A $950 $625

F-42 - folk style, spruce top, mahogany back and sides, rosewood fingerboard with dot inlays, body width 16", mfg. circa late 1980s.

N/A $950 $650

F-44 - similar to the F-42, except has maple back and sides, multiple bindings, bound fingerboard, mfg. 1984-88.

N/A $1,200 $800

F-47 - similar to the F-50 model, except has mahogany construction, rosewood fingerboard with block inlays, and chrome tuners.

N/A $1,100 $800

F-48 - solid spruce top, round soundhole, black pickguard, multibound body, 3-stripe rosette, mahogany back/sides, mahogany neck, 14/20-fret bound rosewood fingerboard with pearl block inlay, rosewood bridge with white black dot pins, bound blackface peghead with pearl shield/logo inlay, 3-per-side gold tuners, available in Natural or Sunburst finishes, body length 21", body width 17", body depth 5", mfg. 1973-75.

N/A $1,050 $700

**Guild F-40 Valencia
courtesy Guild Guitars**

F-50 NAVARRE - solid spruce top, round soundhole, black pickguard, multibound body, 3-stripe rosette, figured maple back/sides, mahogany neck, 14/20-fret bound ebony fingerboard with pearl block/abalone wedge inlay, ebony bridge with white black dot pins, bound blackface peghead with pearl shield/logo inlay, 3-per-side gold tuners, available in Natural, Red Trans., or Sunburst finishes, body length 21", body width 17", body depth 5", mfg. 1953-circa 1990, reintroduced 2003.

1953-1960		N/A	$1,650	$1,250
1961-1974		N/A	$1,450	$1,075
1975-1990		N/A	$1,250	$950
MSR	$2,600	$1,950	$1,450	$1,100

F-50 R - similar to F-50, except has rosewood back/sides, mfg. 1953-circa 1990, reintroduced 2003.

1953-1960		N/A	$1,750	$1,300
1961-1974		N/A	$1,500	$1,100
1975-1990		N/A	$1,250	$975
MSR	$2,700	$2,025	$1,500	$1,100

F-64 - similar to the F-42, but has rosewood back and sides, bound ebony fingerboard, and bound headstock, mfg. circa late 1980s.

N/A $1,350 $925

F-112 - flattop body, solid spruce top, round soundhole, tortoise pickguard, tortoise bound body, single rosette, mahogany back/sides/neck, 14/20-fret rosewood fingerboard with pearl dot inlay, rosewood bridge with white pins, blackface peghead with screened logo, 6-per-side chrome tuners, available in Natural finish, body length - 19 1/4", body width 15 1/4", body depth 4 1/2", mfg. 1968-1982.

N/A $850 $550

F-212 - flattop body, solid spruce top, round soundhole, tortoise pickguard, multibound body, single rosette, mahogany back/sides/neck, 14/20-fret rosewood fingerboard with pearl dot inlay, rosewood bridge with white pins, blackface peghead with screened logo, 6-per-side chrome tuners, available in Natural finish, body length 20", body width 15 7/8", body depth 5", mfg. 1963-1985.

N/A $900 $750

**Guild F-50 Navarre
courtesy Guild Guitars**

GRADING	100%	EXCELLENT	AVERAGE

F-212 XL - similar to F-212, except has larger body, body length 21", body width 17", body depth 5", mfg. 1970-1985.

	N/A	$1,100	$800

F-312 - similar to F-212, except has multibound body, rosewood back/sides, ebony fingerboard, body length 21", body width 17", body depth 5", mfg. 1964-1974.

	N/A	$1,300	$850

F-412 (NO. 380-2500) - flattop body, solid spruce top, round soundhole, black pickguard, multibound body, 3-stripe rosette, maple back/sides, mahogany neck, 14/20-fret bound ebony fingerboard with pearl block inlay, ebony bridge with white pins, bound blackface peghead with pearl shield/logo inlay, 6-per-side gold tuners, available in Natural, Blonde, Antique Burst, or Red Trans. finishes, body length 21", body width 17", body depth 5", mfg. 1970-circa 1990, reintroduced 2002.

MSR	$2,650	$1,995	$1,500	$1,200

F-512 (NO. 380-2900) - flattop body, solid spruce top, round soundhole, black pickguard, wood bound body, multistripe purfling/rosette, rosewood back/sides, mahogany neck, 14/20-fret bound/purfled ebony fingerboard with pearl block/abalone wedge inlay, ebony bridge with white black dot pins, bound blackface peghead with pearl shield/logo inlay, 6-per-side gold tuners, available in Natural or Antique Burst finishes, body length 21", body width 17", body depth 5", mfg. 1970-circa 1990, reintroduced 2002.

MSR	$2,800	$2,100	$1,650	$1,300.

ACOUSTIC: G SERIES

G-37 - solid spruce top, round soundhole, tortoise pickguard, bound body, 3-stripe rosette, maple back/sides/neck, 14/20-fret rosewood fingerboard with pearl dot inlay, rosewood bridge with white black dot pins, pearl Chesterfield/logo peghead inlay, 3-per-side chrome tuners, available in Black, Natural and Sunburst finishes, mfg. circa 1973-1986.

	N/A	$850	$500

The G-37 is nearly the same guitar as the D-30, but features chrome tuners (which some D-30s have as well).

G-41 - oversized dreadnought style, solid spruce top, mahogany back and sides, rosewood fingerboard with dot inlay, 26 1/4 inch scale, body width 17", mfg. circa 1974-78.

	N/A	$950	$650

G-75 - 3/4 size dreadnought style, solid spruce top, rosewood back and sides, 25 1/2" scale, ebony fingerboard, body width 15", mfg. circa 1975-77.

	N/A	$950	$625

G-212 NT - dreadnought style, 12-string configuration, solid spruce top, round soundhole, tortoise pickguard, w/b/w bound body, 3-stripe rosette, mahogany back/sides/neck, double truss rods, 25 1/2" scale, 14/20-fret rosewood fingerboard, rosewood bridge with white black dot pins, pearl Chesterfield/logo peghead inlay, 6-per-side chrome Guild tuners, available in Natural finish, mfg. 1974 - 1989.

	N/A	$900	$625

Last MSR was $895.

The G-212 was advertised that it was "Built on a D-40 body," according to company literature.

G-312 NT - similar to the G-212 NT, except featured black pickguard, 7-ply white ivoroid binding, rosewood back/sides, 3-piece mahogany neck, ebony fingerboard, Schaller tuners, mfg. 1974-1987.

	N/A	$950	$650

Last MSR was $1,130.

The G-312 advertising announced that "Guild's D-50 body is available in a 12-stringed instrument."

GV-52 - bell-shaped flattop body, solid spruce top, round soundhole, tortoise pickguard, bound body, herringbone rosette, rosewood back/sides, mahogany neck, 14/20-fret ebony fingerboard with pearl dot inlay, ebony bridge with white black dot pins, blackface peghead with pearl Chesterfield/logo inlay, 3-per-side gold tuners, available in Natural finish, mfg. 1994-95.

	N/A	$1,050	$550

Last MSR was $1,150.

ACOUSTIC: GF SERIES

GF-25 - folk style, spruce top, arch mahogany back/sides.

	N/A	$850	$600

GF-30 - folk style, solid spruce top, arched maple back, and maple sides, rosewood fingerboard with dot inlays, 3-per-side headstock, chrome hardware, body width 16", mfg. circa late 1980s.

	N/A	$900	$600

GF-50 - similar to the F-64, except featured dot inlays on the ebony fingerboard, and ebony bridge, mfg. circa late 1980s.

	N/A	$1,250	$850

GF-60 - similar to the F-64 (the original model was renamed), mfg. circa late 1980s.

	N/A	$1,350	$950

GF-60 C - similar to the GF-60, except has single cutaway body.

	N/A	$1,450	$975

GRADING	100%	EXCELLENT	AVERAGE

STUDIO 24 - double cutaway body, spruce top, maple back and sides, redesigned neck joint that allows access to upper frets, mfg. circa late 1980s.

| | N/A | $2,500 | $1,800 |

Designed in conjunction with noted vintage guitar expert George Gruhn.

ACOUSTIC: J SERIES

All models in this series have jumbo style bodies, round soundholes and tortoise pickguards.

JF-4 - solid spruce top, bound body, 3-stripe rosette, mahogany back/sides/neck, 14/20-fret rosewood fingerboard with pearl dot inlay, rosewood bridge with white black dot pins, 3-per-side chrome tuners, available in Natural finish, disc. 1995.

| | N/A | $575 | $350 |

Last MSR was $880.

Add $200 for high gloss finish (Model JF4-HG).

JF-4 12 S - similar to JF-4, except has 12-string configuration, 6-per-side tuners, disc. 1994.

| | N/A | $700 | $450 |

Last MSR was $995.

JF-30 (NO. 350-2000/380-2000) - solid spruce top, arched maple back, solid curly maple sides, bound body, 3-stripe rosette, maple neck, 14/20-fret rosewood fingerboard with pearl dot inlay, rosewood bridge with white black dot pins, pearl Chesterfield/logo peghead inlay, 3-per-side gold tuners, available in Blonde, Black, or Antique Burst, Red Trans., high gloss finishes, price includes hardshell case, current mfg.

| MSR | $1,800 | $1,350 | $950 | $650 |

JF-30 LH model available at no additional cost (Model 350-2020).

JF-30-12 12-String (No. 350-2500/380-2100) - similar to JF-30, except has 12-string configuration, 6-per-side tuners, available in Blonde, Black, Red Trans., and Antique Burst, high gloss finishes, price includes hardshell case, current mfg.

| MSR | $1,900 | $1,275 | $895 | $570 |

JF-30 12 LH model available at no additional cost (Model 350-2520).

JF-55 (NO. 350-2100) - solid spruce top, scalloped bracing, 3-stripe bound body, abalone rosette, solid rosewood back/sides, mahogany neck, 14/20-fret bound ebony fingerboard with pearl block/abalone wedge inlay, ebony bridge with white abalone dot pins, maple endpin wedge, bound peghead with pearl shield/logo inlay, 3-per-side gold tuners, available in Antique Burst (837) or Natural (821) high gloss finishes, price includes hardshell case, disc.

| | $1,875 | $1,295 | $915 |

Last MSR was $2,499.

JF-55 LH model available at no additional cost (Model 350-2120).

JF-55-12 12-String (Model 350-2600) - similar to the JF-55, except has 12-string configuration, 6-per-side tuners, available in Natural (821) or Antique (Sun)Burst (837) high gloss finishes, price includes hardshell case, disc.

| | $1,950 | $1,365 | $950 |

Last MSR was $2,599.

JF-55 12 LH model available at no additional cost (Model 350-2620).

JF-65 (NO. 350-2900) - solid spruce top, 3-stripe bound body, abalone rosette, arched maple back, solid curly maple sides, maple neck, 14/20-fret bound ebony fingerboard with pearl block/abalone wedge inlay, ebony bridge with white abalone dot pins, maple endpin wedge, bound peghead with pearl shield/logo inlay, 3-per-side gold tuners, available in Blonde (801) or Antique (Sun)Burst (837) finishes, price includes hardshell case, disc.

| | $1,795 | $1,250 | $875 |

Last MSR was $2,399.

JF-65 LH model available at no additional cost (Model 350-2920).

JF-65 12 12-String (Model 350-2700) - similar to the JF-65, except has 12-string configuration, 6-per-side tuners, available in Blonde (801) and Antique (Sun)Burst (837) high gloss finishes, price includes hardshell case, disc.

| | $1,875 | $1,295 | $895 |

Last MSR was $2,499.

JF-65 12 LH model available at no additional cost (Model 350-2720).

**Guild JF-30
courtesy Guild Guitars**

G

**Guild JF-55-12
courtesy Dave Rogers
Dave's Guitar Shop**

GRADING	100%	EXCELLENT	AVERAGE

JV-52 - jumbo style, solid spruce top, round soundhole, tortoise pickguard, bound body, herringbone rosette, rosewood back/sides, mahogany neck, 14/20-fret ebony fingerboard with pearl dot inlay, ebony bridge with white black dot pins, blackface peghead with pearl Chesterfield/logo inlay, 3-per-side gold tuners, available in Natural finish, mfg. 1994-95.

	N/A	$1,000	$600

Last MSR was $1,250.

ACOUSTIC: MARK SERIES

Instruments in this series are classically styled.

MARK I - mahogany top, round soundhole, simple marquetry rosette, mahogany back/sides/neck, 12/19-fret rosewood fingerboard, tied rosewood bridge, 3-per-side nickel tuners, available in Natural finish, mfg. 1960-1973.

	N/A	$500	$325

MARK II - similar to Mark I, except has spruce top, bound body, mfg. 1960-1988.

	N/A	$550	$375

MARK III - similar to Mark I, except has spruce top, multibound body, floral rosette marquetry, mfg. 1960-1988.

	N/A	$650	$475

MARK IV - spruce top, round soundhole, multi-bound body, marquetry rosette, figured pearwood back/sides, mahogany neck, 12/19-fret ebony fingerboard, tied ebony bridge, 3-per-side chrome tuners w/pearloid buttons, available in Natural finish, mfg. 1960-1985.

	N/A	$700	$525

This model had optional figured maple back/sides.

MARK V - similar to Mark IV, except has ebony bound body, elaborate marquetry rosette, figured maple back/sides, gold tuners with engraved buttons, mfg. 1960-1988.

	N/A	$750	$600

This model had optional rosewood back/sides.

MARK VI - similar to Mark IV, except has ebony bound body, elaborate marquetry rosette, Brazilian rosewood back/sides, gold tuners with engraved buttons, mfg. 1966-68.

	N/A	$1,100	$700

ACOUSTIC: CUSTOM SHOP

In 1997, Guild opened a Custom Shop in Nashville, Tennessee. Guild Custom Shop models are built in limited quantities.

45TH ANNIVERSARY - solid spruce top, round soundhole, solid maple back/sides, multiple body binding, abalone purfling/rosette, 14/20-fret bound ebony fingerboard with abalone/pearl inlay, ebony bridge, bound peghead with abalone shield/logo inlay, 3-per-side gold tuners, available in Natural finish, mfg. 1997 only.

	N/A	$2,900	$2,200

Last MSR was $4,500.

Only 45 instruments were built. This 45th Anniversary model commemorates Guild's beginning in 1952.

D-100 - solid spruce top, scalloped bracing, round soundhole, black pickguard, maple bound body, abalone purfling/rosette, solid rosewood back/sides, 3-piece mahogany/maple neck, 14/20-fret maple bound ebony fingerboard with abalone crown inlay, ebony bridge with white abalone dot pins, maple endpin wedge, maple bound peghead with abalone shield/logo inlay, 3-per-side gold tuners, available in Natural or Sunburst finishes.

	N/A	$2,700	$1,950

Last MSR was $3,600.

D-100 C Dreadnought (No. 350-0400) - similar to D-100, except has handcarved heel, available in Antique Burst (837) and Natural (821) high gloss lacquer finishes, price includes hardshell case, disc.

$3,150	$2,400	$1,600

Last MSR was $3,999.

D-100 C LH model available at no additional cost (Model 350-0420).

JF-100 JUMBO - solid spruce top, scalloped bracing, maple bound body, abalone purfling, abalone rosette, solid rosewood back/sides, 3-piece mahogany neck with maple center strip, 14/20-fret maple bound ebony fingerboard with abalone crown inlay, ebony bridge with white abalone pins, maple endpin wedge, ebony endpin, maple bound peghead with abalone shield/logo inlay, 3-per-side tuners, available in Natural finish, disc. 1995.

	N/A	$2,400	$1,600

Last MSR was $3,700.

JF-100 12 Jumbo 12-String - similar to JF-100, except has 12-strings, 6-per-side tuners, disc. 1995.

	N/A	$2,200	$1,450

Last MSR was $4,000.

JF-100 C JUMBO (NO. 350-2200) - similar to JF-100, except has hand carved heel, available in Antique Burst or Natural high gloss lacquer finish, price includes hardshell case, mfg. 1994-2000.

$3,450	$2,500	$1,750

Last MSR was $4,299.

GRADING	100%	EXCELLENT	AVERAGE

JF-100 C 12 Jumbo 12-String (No. 350-2800) - similar to JF-100 C, except has 12-string configuration, 6-per-side tuners, available in Antique Burst or Natural high gloss lacquer finish, price includes a hardshell case, mfg. 1994-disc.

	$3,600	$2,500	$1,750
		Last MSR was $4,499.	

JF-100 C LH model available at no additional cost (Model 350-2820).

DECO DREADNOUGHT (NO. 395-0850) - solid AAA spruce top, scalloped bracings, round soundhole, abalone rosette, bookmatched rosewood back, solid rosewood sides, abalone top binding, 3-piece mahogany neck, abalone-bound black pickguard, 14/20-fret bound ebony fingerboard with abalone Deco inlay, ebony bridge, bound peghead with abalone shield/logo inlay, 3-per-side gold tuners, available in Natural high gloss lacquer finish, price includes hardshell case, mfg. 1997-2000.

	$3,000	$1,925	$1,335
		Last MSR was $3,799.	

FINESSE DREADNOUGHT (NO. 395-0805) - similar to the Deco, except has herringbone rosette, unbound peghead, unbound fingerboard with abalone dot inlay, tortoise shell pickguard, tortoise shell bound top, Fishman Matrix Natural II pickup, available in Natural high gloss lacquer finish, price includes hardshell case, mfg. 1997-99.

	$2,200	$1,560	$1,110
		Last MSR was $2,699.	

VALENCIA CONCERT (NO. 395-3550) - solid AAA spruce top, shaved bracings, round soundhole, abalone rosette, solid highly figured maple back/sides, abalone top binding, solid figured maple neck, black pickguard, 14/20-fret bound ebony fingerboard with abalone Deco inlay, ebony bridge, bound peghead with abalone shield/logo inlay, 3-per-side gold tuners, available in Black, Blonde, Antique Burst, or Torino Red (858) high gloss lacquer finish, price includes a hardshell case, mfg. 1998-current.

MSR	$4,300		$3,225	$2,250	$1,575

Valencia Cutaway (No. 395-3560) - similar to the Valencia Concert except has a custom Florentine Cutaway and Fishman Matrix pickup, current mfg.

MSR	$4,800		$3,600	$2,500	$1,700

Guild D40CE
courtesy Guild Guitars

ACOUSTIC ELECTRIC: CCE & D SERIES

CCE-100 - single round cutaway classic style, oval soundhole, bound body, wood inlay rosette, mahogany back/sides/neck, 24-fret rosewood fingerboard, rosewood bridge, 3-per-side chrome tuners, transducer pickup, 4-band EQ with preamp, available in Natural finish, mfg. 1994-95.

	N/A	$650	$400
		Last MSR was $1,200.	

CCE-100 HG - similar to CCE-100, except has gold hardware, available in Natural high gloss finish, disc. 1995.

	N/A	$700	$450
		Last MSR was $1,400.	

DCE-1 (NO. 350-1306) - single cutaway body, solid spruce top, round soundhole, black pickguard, bound body, 3-stripe rosette, mahogany back/sides/neck, 20-fret rosewood fingerboard with dot inlay, rosewood bridge with white black dot pins, 3-per-side gold tuners, transducer pickup, Fishman Acoustic Matrix system, available in Natural (021) hand rubbed satin finish, mfg. 1994-disc.

	$895	$650	$425
		Last MSR was $1,199.	

Left-handed configuration model DCE-1 LH (Model 350-1326) available at no extra cost.

DCE-1 HG (No. 350-1406) - similar to the DCE-1, available in Antique Burst (037), Black (006), and Cherry (038) high gloss finishes, mfg. 1996-disc.

	$1,050	$750	$475
		Last MSR was $1,399.	

Left-handed configuration model DCE-1 HG LH (Model 350-1426) available at no extra cost.

DCE-5 (NO. 350-1506) - similar to DCE-1, except has rosewood back/sides, ebony fingerboard, Fishman Prefix On-Board Blender system, available in Natural or Antique Burst high gloss finishes, price includes hardshell case, mfg. 1994-95 and 1999.

	$1,350	$950	$650
		Last MSR was $1,799.	

Left-handed configuration model D-55 LH (Model 350-1526) available at no extra charge.

Guild D50CE
courtesy Guild Guitars

GRADING	100%	EXCELLENT	AVERAGE

D40CE (NO. 380-3106) - dreadnought single cutaway, solid spruce top, solid mahogany back/sides/neck, rosewood fingerboard with dot inlays and Chesterfield logo, Fishman Prefix Pro Blend system, available in black, Natural, Antique Burst, or Red Trans., finishes, new 2003.

	MSR	$2,000		$1,500	$1,300	$850

D50CE (NO. 380-3306) - dreadnought single cutaway, solid spruce top, solid rosewood back/sides, mahogany neck, ebony fingerboard with dot inlays and Chesterfield logo, Fishman Prefix Pro Blend system, 3-per-side tuners, available in Natural or Antique Burst, finishes, new 2003.

	MSR	$2,200		$1,650	$1,275	$850

ACOUSTIC ELECTRIC: TRADITIONAL (F) SERIES

All models in this series have single rounded cutaway folk style body, oval soundhole, tortoise pickguard, 3-stripe bound body/rosette, transducer pickup, volume/4-band EQ preamp system with built in phase reversal, unless otherwise listed.

F-4 CE (NO. 350-3006) - solid spruce top, mahogany back/sides/neck, 14/20-fret rosewood fingerboard with pearl dot inlay, rosewood bridge with white black dot pins, 3-per-side chrome tuners, Fishman Acoustic Matrix system, available in Natural hand rubbed satin finish, price includes hardshell case, disc. 2000.

				$975	$700	$425

Last MSR was $1,284.

Left-handed configuration model F-4 CE LH (Model 350-3026) available at no extra cost.

Black and Vintage White high gloss finishes were available between 1994 and 1997.

F-4 CE HG (No. 350-3106) - similar to F-4 CE, available in Antique Burst, Black, Crimson Red Transparent, or Teal Green Trans. high gloss finishes, price includes hardshell case, mfg. 1998-2000.

				$1,100	$725	$515

Last MSR was $1,470.

Left-handed configuration model F-4 CE HG LH (Model 350-3126) available at no extra cost.

F-4 CE MH - similar to F-4 CE, except has mahogany top, available in Amber finish, disc. 1995.

				N/A	$550	$350

Last MSR was $1,050.

F-5 CE (NO. 350-3206) - solid spruce top, rosewood back/sides, mahogany neck, 14/20-fret rosewood fingerboard with pearl dot inlay, rosewood bridge with white black dot pins, 3-per-side chrome Grover tuners, Fishman Acoustic Matrix system, available in Black, Natural, or Antique Burst high gloss lacquer finishes, price includes hardshell case, disc. 2000.

				$1,175	$800	$575

Last MSR was $1,570.

Add $100 for deep body Model FF-5 CE (discontinued in 1998). Left-handed configuration model F-5 CE LH (Model 350-3226) available at no extra cost.

F-25 CE - solid spruce top, mahogany back/sides/neck, 24-fret rosewood fingerboard with pearl dot inlay, rosewood bridge with white black dot pins, 3-per-side chrome Grover tuners, volume control, concentric treble/bass control, active preamp, available in Black, Natural or Sunburst finishes, disc. 1992.

				N/A	$700	$450

Last MSR was $1,195.

F-30 CE - solid spruce top, flame maple back/sides, mahogany neck, 24-fret rosewood fingerboard with pearl dot inlay, rosewood bridge with white black dot pins, pearl Chesterfield/logo peghead inlay, 3-per-side gold Grover tuners, available in Black, Blonde, Natural, or Sunburst finishes, disc. 1995.

				N/A	$900	$550

Last MSR was $1,495.

F-45 CE - solid spruce top, mahogany back/sides/neck, rosewood fingerboard with pearl dot inlay, rosewood bridge with white black dot pins, pearl Chesterfield/logo peghead inlay, 3-per-side gold Grover tuners, available in Black, Blonde, Natural, or Sunburst finishes, mfg. 1983-1992.

				N/A	$1,000	$650

FS-46 CE - solid body with fake soundhole and new pickup under the saddle, mahogany body with spruce top, rosewood fingerboard, mfg. 1983-86.

				N/A	$700	$550

F-47 RCE - grand auditorium cutaway body, solid spruce top, rosewood back/sides, mahogany neck, rosewood fingerboard with pearloid block inlays, Chesterfield logo, Fishman Prefix Pro Blend system, available in Natural or Anitque Burst, current mfg.

	MSR	$2,400		$1,800	$1,350	$950

GRADING	100%	EXCELLENT	AVERAGE

F-47 MCE - similar to the F-47 RCE except has maple back/sides, available in Blonde, Black, Antique Burst, or Red Trans., current mfg.

MSR	$2,400	$1,800	$1,350	$950

F-65 CE (NO. 350-3306) - solid spruce top, abalone rosette, curly maple back/sides, mahogany neck, 14/20-fret bound ebony fingerboard with pearl block/abalone wedge inlay, ebony bridge with white abalone dot pins, bound peghead with pearl shield/logo inlay, 3-per-side gold Grover tuners, Fishman Prefix On-Board Blender system, available in Antique Burst, Black, Blonde, Crimson Red Trans., Sapphire Blue Trans., or Teal Green Trans. high gloss finishes, price includes hardshell case, disc.

$1,725 $1,300 $850

Last MSR was $2,299.

Left-handed configuration model F-65 CE LH (Model 350-3326) available at no extra cost.

Early versions of this model had optional figured maple top with Amber and Sunburst finishes. In 1994, transducer pickup, and preamp were introduced.

FS-48 DECEIVER - single cutaway body style, maple fingerboard, pointed headstock design, with piezo pickup and humbucker hidden between the soundhole and bridge, mfg. circa 1984.

Model has not traded sufficiently to quote pricing.

ACOUSTIC ELECTRIC: SPECIALIST (S-4) SERIES

The S-4 CE Specialist models were previously called the Songbird models. The S-4 CE has a body the size of a Bluesbird, and has a routed-out acoustic chamber in the mahogany body that is capped with an X-braced solid spruce top.

S-4 CE HR (NO. 350-6000) - Bluesbird-style solid mahogany body with (routed out) acoustic chamber, solid spruce top, round soundhole, tortoise pickguard, 3-stripe bound body/rosette, mahogany neck, 22-fret rosewood fingerboard with pearl dot inlay, rosewood bridge with white black dot pins, 3-per-side chrome tuners, transducer bridge pickup, volume/concentric treble/bass control, Fishman Acoustic Matrix preamp, available in Natural hand rubbed satin finish, price includes hardshell case, disc. 2000.

$965 $635 $450

Last MSR was $1,285.

S-4 CE HG (No. 350-6100) - similar S-4 CE HR, except has pearl Chesterfield/logo peghead inlay, gold tuners, available in Black or Natural high gloss finishes, price includes hardshell case, disc.

$1,125 $775 $550

Last MSR was $1,499.

Early Songbird models were also available in a White finish.

S-4 CE BG BARRY GIBB SIGNATURE (NO. 350-6100) - similar S-4 CE HG, available in Crimson Red Trans. or Sapphire Blue Trans. custom high gloss finishes, mfg. 1998-disc.

$1,175 $795 $550

Last MSR was $1,549.

This model was designed in conjunction with Barry Gibb (BeeGees). List price includes deluxe hardshell case. In 2000, Sapphire Blue Trans. finish was discontinued. In 2001, Metallic Blue finish was introduced.

ACOUSTIC & ACOUSTIC ELECTRIC BASS

B-30 - grand concert style, spruce top, round soundhole, tortoise pickguard, 3-stripe bound body/rosette, mahogany back/sides/neck, 14/20-fret rosewood fingerboard with pearl dot inlay, rosewood bridge with white pins, pearl Chesterfield/logo peghead inlay, 2-per-side chrome tuners, available in Natural or Sunburst finishes, mfg. 1987-1995.

N/A $1,100 $725

Last MSR was $1,400.

B-500 C - similar to B-30, except has single round cutaway, maple back/sides, transducer bridge pickup, volume/concentric treble/bass control, preamp, available in Natural or Sunburst finishes, disc. 1994.

N/A $1,200 $750

Last MSR was $1,695.

B-4 E (NO. 350-4006) - single rounded cutaway folk style, solid spruce top, oval soundhole, tortoise pickguard, 3-stripe bound body/rosette, arched mahogany back, mahogany sides/neck, 14/20-fret rosewood fingerboard with pearl dot inlay, rosewood bridge with white black dot pins, 2-per-side chrome tuners, transducer pickup, volume/4-band EQ control, Fishman Acoustic Matrix preamp, available in Natural hand rubbed satin finish, price includes harshell case, disc. 2000.

$1,025 $750 $500

Last MSR was $1,356.

Guild F-47 RCE
courtesy Guild Guitars

G

Guild F-47 MCE
courtesy Guild Guitars

Right-handed fretless (Model 350-4106), left-handed model (Model 350-4026), and left-handed fretless model (Model 350-4126) are available at no extra cost.

Early models were available with gold hardware.

B-4 E HG (No. 350-4206) - similar to B-4 E, except has multiple-ply body binding, available in Antique Burst, Black, Crimson Red Trans., or Teal Green Trans. high gloss finishes, price includes hardshell case, mfg. 1994-95, 1998-2000.

| | $1,125 | $745 | $525 |

Last MSR was $1,499.

Right-handed fretless (Model 350-4306), left-handed model (Model 350-4226), and left-handed fretless model (Model 350-4326) are available at no extra cost.

B-4 E MH - similar to B-4E, except has mahogany top, mfg. 1994-95.

| | $1,100 | $675 | $500 |

Last MSR was $1,150.

B-30 E (NO. 350-4406) - jumbo style, solid spruce top, round soundhole, tortoise pickguard, 3-stripe bound body/rosette, arched mahogany back, mahogany sides/neck, 14/20-fret rosewood fingerboard with pearl dot inlay, rosewood bridge with white pins, pearl Chesterfield/logo peghead inlay, 2-per-side chrome tuners, transducer bridge pickup, volume/concentric treble/bass control, Fishman Acoustic Matrix system, available in Natural or Antique Burst high gloss lacquer finishes, price includes hardshell case, disc.

| MSR | $1,999 | | $1,499 | $990 | $700 |

Last MSR was $1,999.

Right-handed fretless (Model 350-4506), left-handed model (Model 350-4426), and left-handed fretless model (Model 350-4526) are available at no extra cost.

B-30 E T - similar to B-30E, except has thinline body style, disc. 1992.

| | N/A | $850 | $575 |

Last MSR was $1,595.

GUITAR FARM
Instruments currently built in Sperryville, Virginia.

The Guitar Farm is currently offering handcrafted guitar models. For further information regarding specifications and pricing, contact The Guitar Farm directly (see Trademark Index).

GUITARES MAURICE DUPONT
Instruments currently built in France. Distributed by Paul Hostetter of Santa Cruz, California.

After spending a number of years repairing and restoring Selmer/Maccaferri guitars, luthier Maurice Dupont began building Selmer replicas that differ in the fact the Dupont features a one-piece neck with adjustable trussrod inside (Selmers had a three piece neck), and better construction materials. Dupont also hand builds his own classical, flamenco, steel-string, and archtop guitars. Both the **Excellence** and **Privilege** archtops are offered in 16" or 17" bodies, and with a Florentine or Venetian cutaway. For further information on either the Selmer-type guitars, or his other Dupont models, please contact Paul Hostetter in Santa Cruz, California, (Dupont history courtesy Paul Hostetter).

GUITARRAS ALMANSA S.A.
Guitarras Almansa guitars are handcrafted in Almansa, (Albacete) Spain, under the directorship of Pedro-Angel Lopez. Distributed in the USA by Ruben Flores, located in Seal Beach, California.

ACOUSTIC

Almansa Classical guitars are constructed to 650 (25.6"), 636, 580, and 544mm scales and, in various models for children, students and professional guitarists. Classical Models 401 through 436 are Studio models with solid cedar tops and laminated mahogany, bubinga, and rosewood back and sides. Conservatory models 457 through 461 are of solid cedar or spruce tops with solid Indian Rosewood back and sides. The Concert guitars are fully handcrafted with solid cedar or German Spruce tops, back and sides of Indian Rosewood or brazilian Rosewood of the finest quality. Many models of classical guitar are built in regular and thin body cutaways with pickups for students and professionals. Almansa also buids Flamenco guitars; models 447 and 449 as well as the Professional model. These have German Spruce tops and solid cypress back and sides. Studio Flamenco models 413 and 415 have solid spruce tops and sycamore back and sides. Also available are regular and thin body Flamenco Cutaway models with pickups. All feature clear pickguards.

MSR: Classical Models 401 ($490), 402 ($560), 403 ($630), 424 ($720), 434 ($790), 435 ($990), 436 ($1,290), 457 ($1,630), 459 ($2,140), 461 ($2890). Flamenco Models 413 ($690), 415 ($1,040), 447 ($1,420), 449 ($2,240), Professional ($4,200). Cadete Models are special order. Senorita Models are special order. Bandurrias: 403 ($630), 434 ($790), and 435 ($990). Lauds: 403 ($630), and 434 ($790). Professional Rosewood ($4,300), Professional Jacaranda ($5,400), Grand Professional Jacaranda (inquire).

GUITARRAS ESPANOLA
Instruments currently built in Paracho (Michoacan), Mexico.

Guitarras Espanola has been handcrafting classical guitars through three generations. The guitars are built of exotic Mexican woods in the artisan tradition workshop, and feature cedar tops, mahogany or walnut sides, as well as Siricote or Palo Escrito woods. For more information contact the company directly (see Trademark Index).

GURIAN, MICHAEL
Instruments previously built in New York City, New York between 1965 and 1982.

Luthier Michael Gurian built quality classical and steel string acoustic guitars, as well as being a major American wood supplier. He debuted his classical designs in 1965 and offered steel string designs four years later. In 1971, at the encouragement of vintage retailer Matt Umanov, Gurian designed a cutaway model that later became a regular part of the product line.

In the early 1970s, Gurian moved his production facilities to Hinsdale, New Hampshire. Gurian's four story mill building housed a large band saw (for slabbing logs), two resaws (cutting slabs to dimension), and various planers. During this time period, Gurian imported ebony, rosewood, mansonia, and spruce; his U.S. sources supplied walnut, maple, and other woods. Disaster struck in 1979, as a fire consumed their current stock of guitars as well as tooling and machinery. Gurian rebuilt by later that year and continued producing guitars until 1982.

Michael Gurian may have stopped offering guitars in 1982, but he still continues to be a major presence in the guitar building industry. Gurian serves as a consultant in guitar design, and his company offers guitar fittings (such as bridge pins) and supplies, custom built marquetry, and guitar-building tools based on his designs, (Source: The Alembic Report (*Guitar Player* magazine); and Tom Wheeler, *American Guitars*).

Michael Gurian S3R
courtesy Mitchell M. Walters

ACOUSTIC

Michael Gurian was perhaps one of the first smaller guitar producers to combine production techniques with hand crafted sensibilities. Guitars produced at the New Hampshire site were built in 3 distinct phases. In Phase One, the basic guitar parts (tops, backs, necks, fingerboards, etc.) were produced in large lots and inventoried. Gurian's factory did use carving lathes to "rough out" the neck blanks, and heated hydraulic presses to bend the guitar sides. During Phase Two, the company's luthiers would choose "kits" from the part supplies and construct the guitar individually. This allowed the luthiers control over individual guitar's construction and tuning. Finally, in Phase Three, the finished guitars were sent to the finishing technicians to spray the finish. This method would guarantee a similarity in the finishes from one guitar to the next.

The market is wide open on Gurian prices. The majority of guitars are probably in the hands of players and collectors, and as a result do not trade too often. It is estimated that the guitars are more plentiful on the east coast than the rest of the nation, given the location of the production facilities. Finally, as Gurian guitars have not been well notated previously, various dealers perhaps shyed away from dealing an "unknown quantity" when the opportunity arose. The *Blue Book of Acoustic Guitars* recommends playing a Gurian when they are encountered; let your fingers and ears do the preliminary investigation.

G

NOTES

G is for the Gibson Custom Shop located in Bozeman, MT. One of the more talented luthiers on the planet, Ren Ferguson, proudly shows off one of his more recent creations, the "Big-Five" Gibson Guitar, featuring inlays and engravings of an elephant, cape buffalo, rhino, lion, and leopard. 1,000 tickets were sold at $100 each, and the lucky winner will have a truly unique instrument.

Section H

WM. HALL & SON

Instruments previously built. Location and date of production currently unknown.

The *Blue Book of Acoustic Guitars* was contacted by Lester Groves in regards to an older acoustic guitar he currently owns. The label inside reads *Wm. Hall & Son - 239 Broadway NY*, and carries a serial number of 5138. This acoustic has a spruce top and rosewood sides. The *Blue Book of Acoustic Guitars* is still trying to figure out if the company is the distributor or the manufacturer! If any readers have any helpful information, please contact Blue Book Publications.

HANNAH

Instruments currently built in Vancouver, B.C., Canada.

Luthier Rod Hannah hand builds both Dreadnought and 000 12-Fret acoustic guitars in "short lot" sizes (approximately 4 instruments at a time). Hannah guitars are built with recording and performing musicians in mind. For information email Hannah guitars directly (see Trademark Index).

HARMONY

Instruments previously produced in the Chicago, Illinois area from the 1890s to 1975. Harmony, along with Kay, were the two major producers for instrument wholesalers for a number of years (see chapter on House Brands). When the U.S. manufacturing facilities were closed, the Harmony trademark was sold and later applied to Korean-built instruments from the mid 1970s to the late 1980s.

Harmony H6659
1973 Harmony Catalog

The Harmony Company of Chicago, Illinois was one of the largest American musical instrument manufacturers. Harmony has the historical distinction of being the largest "jobber" house in the nation, producing stringed instruments for a number of different wholesalers. Individual dealers or distributors could get stringed instruments with their own brand name on it (as long as they ordered a minimum of 100 pieces). At one time the amount of instruments being produced by Harmony made up the largest percentage of stringed instruments being manufactured in the U.S. market (archtops, flattops, electric Spanish, Hawaiian bodies, ukuleles, banjos, mandolins, violins and more).

Harmony was founded by Wilhelm J.F. Schultz in 1892. Schultz, a German immigrant and former foreman of Lyon & Healy's drum division, started his new company with four employees. By 1884, the number of employees had grown to forty, and Shultz continued to expand into larger and larger factories through 1904. Shultz built Harmony up to a 125 employee workforce (and a quarter of a million dollars in annual sales) by 1915.

In 1916, the Sears, Roebuck Company purchased Harmony, and seven years later the company had annual sales of 250,000 units. Max Adler, a Sears executive, appointed Jay Kraus as vice-president of Harmony in 1925. The following year Jay succeeded founder Wilhelm Schultz as president, and continued expanding production. In 1930, annual sales were reported to be 500,000 units, with 35 to 40 percent being sold to Sears (catalog sales). Harmony had no branch offices, territorial restrictions, or dealer reps – wholesalers purchased the musical instruments and aggressively sold to music stores.

Harmony bought several trademarks from the bankrupt Oscar Schmidt Company in 1939, and their Sovereign and Stella lines were Harmony's more popular guitars. In 1940, Krause bought Harmony by acquiring the controlling stock, and continued to expand the company's production to meet the market boom during the 1950s and 1960s. Mr. Kraus remained president until 1968, when he died of a heart attack. Charles Rubovits (who had been with Harmony since 1935) took over as president, and remained in that position for two years. Kraus' trust still maintained control over Harmony, and trust members attempted to form a conglomerate by purchasing Chicago-based distributor Targ & Dinner and a few other companies. Company (or more properly the conglomerate's) indebtedness led to a liquidation auction to satisfy creditors – although Harmony continued to turn in impressive annual sales figures right up until the company was dissolved in 1974 (or early 1975). The loss of Harmony in the mid 1970s, combined with the decline of Kay/Valco, Inc. in 1969 (or 1970) definitely left the door wide open for Asian products to gain a larger percentage of the entry or student level guitar market (for example, W.M.I. began using the Kay trademark on Teisco-built guitars as early as 1973; these guitars were sold through department store chains through the 1970s), (Harmony company history courtesy Tom Wheeler, *American Guitars*, Harmony model information courtesy John Kennemire of JK Lutherie, Ryland Fitchett of Rockohaulix, Ronald Rothman of Rothman's Guitars).

IDENTIFYING RE-BRANDED HARMONY TRADEMARKS

Harmony reportedly made 57 "different" brands throughout their productive years. Early models featured the Harmony trademark, or remained unlabeled for the numerous wholesalers. In 1928 Harmony introduced the **Roy Smeck Vita** series, and two years later the **Grand Concert** and **Hawaiian** models debuted. The **Vagabond** line was introduced in 1931, the **Cremona** series in 1934, and **Patrician** guitars later in 1938.

As Harmony was purchased by Sears, Roebuck in 1916, Harmony built a number of **Silvertone** models. Harmony continued to sell to Sears even after Kraus bought the company. Harmony bought a number of trademarks from the bankrupt Oscar Schmidt Company in 1939 (such as **La Scala, Stella, Sovereign**), as well as expanding their own brand names

Harmony Sing Cowboy
1973 Harmony Catalog

with **Valencia, Monterey, Harmony Deluxe, Johnny Marvin, Vogue**, and many (like Carelli from the mid 1930s) that are being researched today! Although the Kay company built most of the **Airline** guitars for the Montgomery Ward stores, Harmony would sometimes be subcontracted to build Airlines to meet the seasonal shopping rush. National (Valco) supplied resonator cones for some Harmony resonator models, and probably bought guitar parts from Harmony in return.

HARMONY PRODUCTION: 1961-1975

The Harmony company of 4600 South Kolin Avenue in Chicago, Illinois built a great deal of guitars. Harmony catalogs in the early 1960s proudly proclaimed "we've produced millions of instruments but we make them one at a time." Harmony guitars can be found practically anywhere: the guitar shop, the antique shop, the flea market, the Sunday garage sale right around the corner. Due to the vast numbers of Harmony guitars, and because the majority of them were entry level models, the vintage guitar market's response is a collective shrug of the shoulders as it moves on to the higher dollar American built Fenders and Gibsons, etc.

As a result, the secondary Harmony guitar market is rather hard to pin down. Outside of a few hardy souls like Willie Moseley, Ronald Rothman, Paul Day, and Tony Bacon, very little has been written about Harmony guitar **models** as a means to identify them. As a result, rather than use the exact model designations, most dealers tend to offer a "Harmony Acoustic," or a "'60s Harmony Archtop" through their ads or at guitar shows. It becomes difficult to track the asking prices of various models if the information regarding that model is not available.

The majority of Harmony guitars encountered today are generally part of the millions produced during the 1960s through the company's closing in 1975. As most of them were entry level models, condition (especially physical condition) becomes a bit more critical in pricing. A dead mint Harmony Rocket is worth the money because it's clean – a beat up, player's grade Rocket might not be worth a second look to the interested party. However, the market interest is the deciding factor in pricing – the intrinsic value of (for example) a laminated body Harmony archtop will be the deciding factor in the asking price to the public.

The *Blue Book of Acoustic Guitars* continues to seek out additional input on Harmony models, specifications, dates of production, and any serialization information. This year's section is the starting point for defining Harmony products. Additional information gathered on Harmony will be updated in future editions of the *Blue Book of Acoustic Guitars*.

HARMONY PRICING OVERVIEW

While Harmony did produce a wide range of acoustic archtop and archtop models with pickups, the majority of models were the entry level or student grade instruments. The average Harmony encountered at a guitar show or secondhand store is probably going to be one of the 1960s production models, and for a player's value, most of these will fall in the under $300 range. Prices are listed in models where specific data was available.

Given the interest in other brand name American-produced guitars, there is the faint beginnings of collector desirability on certain Harmony models. Certainly the pre-war arched (or carved) top acoustics, Rocket series (especially the **H-59 Rocket III** model), or any of the laminated arch tops in mint condition will begin to bring a higher premium. In this case, condition will be everything – the majority of Harmony guitars encountered **have been played** and are not in mint condition.

For example, the Harmony/Silvertone guitar models (offered by Sears) may range in price between $225 to $400, depending on configuration and condition. The Silvertone model with the black finish and single cutaway hollow body with the huge aluminum binding (pickguard and 2 humbuckers) may bring $400 if in clean condition.

HARMONY SERIES DESIGNATIONS

In addition to the Harmony trademark, Harmony models also carry the model (series) designation on the headstock, i.e. **Broadway, Monterey, Patrician, Sovereign**, etc. Some of the Sovereign models may further be designated as **Jet Set** variations as well. Keep in mind that there are model distinctions within the series.

For further information regarding Harmony electric guitars, please refer to the *Blue Book of Electric Guitars*. Archtop guitars with floating or built-in pickups can be found in the Harmony Electric section of the Electric edition.

ACOUSTIC: ARCHED TOP SERIES

The 1200 Series Arched Guitars were originally designated the Auditorium models; in 1969, they were renamed to Archtone models.

H 1213 ARCHTONE (H 1214 BLONDE, H 1215 BROWN MAHOGANY) - hollowbody with white striped edges, arched birch top/birch back/sides, 16" body width, 2 f-holes, 14/19-fret hard maple fingerboard with white dot inlay, 3-per-side tuners, chrome hardware, adjustable bridge/raised tailpiece, raised celluloid pickguard with stencilled Harmony logo, serial numbers inside body, available in Shaded Brown Sunburst (Model H 1213), Blonde Ivory Enamel with Grained effect (Model H 1214), or Gloss Brown Mahogany with Grained effect (Model H 1215) finishes, disc. circa 1972.

N/A	$200	$100

Last MSR was $49.95.

The hard maple fingerboard was "grained to resemble rosewood," according to the 1961 Harmony catalog.

HTG 1215 Archtone Tenor - similar to the H 1215 Archtone, except in Tenor (4-string) configuration, available in Gloss Brown Mahogany finish with Grained effect, disc. circa 1972.

N/A	$225	$100

Last MSR was $49.95.

H 954 BROADWAY (AUDITORIUM SIZE) - bound hollowbody, arched select hardwood top/hardwood back/sides, 2 f-holes, 20-fret ebonized maple fingerboard with white dot inlay, 3-per-side tuners, chrome hardware, adjustable bridge/raised tailpiece, raised celluloid pickguard with stencilled design, available in Mahogany Sunburst finish, length 40 3/4", body width 15 3/4", disc. circa 1972.

N/A	$325	$175

Last MSR was $74.50.

GRADING	100%	EXCELLENT	AVERAGE

H 1310 CUTAWAY - bound single cutaway body, arched spruce top/maple back, 2 segmented f-holes, 20-fret rosewood fingerboard with pearlette block inlay, pearlette inlaid logo on rosewood peg-head veneer, 3-per-side tuners, chrome hardware, adjustable bridge/raised tailpiece, raised black pick-guard, available in Shaded Brown finish, length 41", body width 16 1/2", disc. circa 1972.

	N/A	$475	$275

Last MSR was $149.50.

H 1311 Cutaway Blonde - similar to the H 1310, available in Blonde finish, disc. circa 1965.

	N/A	$500	$300

Last MSR was $105.

H 945 MASTER (AUDITORIUM SIZE) - celluloid bound hollow body, arched hardwood top/back, 2 f-holes, 20-fret ebonized maple fingerboard with white block inlay, 3-per-side tuners, chrome hardware, adjustable ebonized bridge/raised tailpiece, raised shell pickguard with stencilled Master logo, available in Sunburst lacquer finish, length 40", body width 15 3/4", disc. circa 1972.

	N/A	$275	$150

Last MSR was $59.95.

H 950 MONTEREY LEADER - celluloid bound hollow body, arched hardwood top/back, 2 f-holes, 20-fret ebonized maple fingerboard with white dot inlay, 3-per-side tuners, chrome hardware, adjustable ebonized bridge/raised tailpiece, raised black pickguard with stencilled M logo, available in Figured Red Sunburst finish, length 40", body width 15 3/4", disc. circa 1972.

	N/A	$375	$225

Last MSR was $69.95.

HTG 950 Monterey Tenor (TG 950) - similar to the H 950, except in Tenor (4-string) configuration, available in Figured Red Sunburst finish, disc. circa 1972.

	N/A	$395	$225

Last MSR was $69.50.

Harmony H 1215 Achtone
1973 Harmony Catalog

H 1325 MONTEREY (GRAND AUDITORIUM) - celluloid bound hollowbody, arched spruce top/hardwood back/sides, 2 f-holes, 20-fret bound fingerboard with white dot inlay, 3-per-side tuners, chrome hardware, adjustable bridge/raised tailpiece, raised shell pickguard with stencilled M logo, available in Shaded Brown finish, length 41", body width 16 1/4", disc. circa 1972.

	N/A	$425	$250

Last MSR was $79.50.

H 1456 MONTEREY (GRAND AUDITORIUM PROFESSIONAL) - celluloid bound hollowbody, arched select spruce top/maple back, 2 segmented f-holes, 20-fret celluloid bound rosewood fingerboard with pearlette block inlay, 3-per-side tuners, chrome hardware, adjustable bridge/raised tailpiece, raised brown pickguard with stencilled M logo, available in Sunburst finish, length 40 1/2", body width 16 1/2", disc. circa 1968.

	N/A	$450	$250

Last MSR was $85.

H 1457 Monterey Blonde - similar to the H 1456, except features raised white pickguard with stencilled M logo, available in Blonde finish, disc. circa 1965.

	N/A	$475	$275

Last MSR was $78.

H 956 W MONTCLAIR (GRAND AUDITORIUM PROFESSIONAL) - bound hollowbody, arched hardwood top/hardwood back/sides, 2 f-holes, 20-fret bound fingerboard with white dot inlay, 3-per-side tuners, chrome hardware, adjustable bridge/raised tailpiece, raised white pickguard, available in Black finish, length 40 1/2", body width 16 1/2", disc. circa 1965.

	N/A	$300	$150

Last MSR was $65.

H 956 Montclair - similar to the H 956 W, except features white block fingerboard inlay, available in Black finish, length 40 1/2", body width 16 1/2", mfg. 1966-67.

	N/A	$325	$150

Last MSR was $75.

H 1407 PATRICIAN (AUDITORIUM SIZE) - shell celluloid bound hollowbody, arched spruce top/mahogany back/sides, mahogany neck, 2 f-holes, 20-fret rosewood fingerboard with white dot inlay, 3-per-side tuners, chrome hardware, adjustable bridge/raised tailpiece, raised shell celluloid pickguard with stencilled P logo, available in Natural finish, length 40 3/4", body width 15 3/4", disc. circa 1972.

	N/A	$350	$175

Last MSR was $79.50.

Harmony H 945 Master
1973 Harmony Catalog

ACOUSTIC: CLASSICAL SERIES

Classic Series models are classical guitars with Harmony's "Fan-Rib" construction (a Spanish-style fan-braced top).

H 171 CLASSIC/FOLK - nylon string, 25 1/4" scale, spruce top, round soundhole, hardwood back/sides/neck, 12/19-fret ebonized maple fingerboard, slotted headstock, pinless bridge, 3-per-side Waverly tuners, available in Pumpkin finish, length 36", body width 13 1/8", mfg. 1969-circa 1971.

	N/A	$150	$75

Last MSR was $49.95.

The H 171 does not have the fan-rib bracing.

H 172 - nylon string, 25 1/4" scale, bound spruce top, fan ribbed, round soundhole with marquetry inlay, hardwood back/sides/neck, 12/19-fret ebonized maple fingerboard, rosewood pinless bridge, 3-per-side Waverly tuners, available in Pumpkin finish, length 38 1/2", body width 14 5/8", mfg. 1971-circa 1973.

	N/A	$250	$125

Last MSR was $79.95.

H 173 - nylon string, bound select spruce top, bound round soundhole, hardwood back/sides/neck, 12/19-fret ebonized maple fingerboard, ebonized maple tie bridge, 3-per-side tuners, squared slotted headstock, available in Natural finish, Length 38 1/2", Body Width 14 5/8", disc. 1971.

	N/A	$250	$125

Last MSR was $79.50.

H 174 - nylon string, bound seasoned spruce top, round soundhole with inlay, mahogany back/sides/neck, 12/19-fret fingerboard, rosewood tie bridge, 3-per-side tuners, rounded slotted headstock, available in Natural finish, length 38 1/2", body width 14 5/8", disc. circa 1968.

	N/A	$275	$135

Last MSR was $95.

H 175 - nylon string, 25 1/4" scale, black bound select spruce top, fan ribbed, round soundhole with wood marquetry inlay, mahogany neck, hard maple back/sides, 12/19-fret ebonized maple fingerboard, slotted headstock with wood marquetry inlay, pinless bridge with wood marquetry inlay, 3-per-side Waverly tuners, available in Natural finish, length 38 1/2", body width 14 5/8", mfg. 1967-circa 1973.

	N/A	$300	$150

Last MSR was $135.

H 177 - nylon string, 25 1/4" scale, bound seasoned spruce top, bound back, fan ribbed, round soundhole with marquetry inlay, mahogany back/sides/neck, 12/19-fret ebonized hard maple fingerboard, pinless rosewood bridge, slotted headstock, 3-per-side Waverly tuners, available in Pumpkin finish, length 38 1/2", body width 14 5/8", mfg. 1969-circa 1973.

	N/A	$275	$135

Last MSR was $99.50.

H 937 STUDENT GUITAR - nylon string, 24 1/4" scale, hardwood top, round soundhole, hardwood back/sides, 18-fret ebonized maple fingerboard, slotted headstock, pinless bridge, 3-per-side Waverly tuners, available in Natural finish, length 36", body width 13 1/8", mfg. 1969-circa 1971.

	N/A	$150	$75

Last MSR was $41.50.

ACOUSTIC: FLATTOP SERIES

H 150 STUDIO SPECIAL (3/4 SIZE) - dreadnought style, celluloid bound hardwood top, round soundhole, hardwood back/sides, 12/18-fret ebonized maple fingerboard, pinless bridge, white celluloid pickguard, 3-per-side tuners, available in Natural finish, length 34 1/4", body width 13 1/8", disc. 1971.

	N/A	$150	$75

Last MSR was $41.50.

H 151 BEST BEGINNERS (3/4 SIZE) - dreadnought style, bound hardwood top, celluloid edge binding, round soundhole, hardwood back/sides, 12/18-fret maple fingerboard, bolted-on pinless bridge, black celluloid batwing pickguard with vine design, solid blackface headstock, 3-per-side Waverly tuners, available in Shaded Brown finish, length 34 1/4", body width 13 1/8", body thickness 3 1/4", disc. 1971.

	N/A	$150	$75

Last MSR was $41.50.

Harmony designated the H 151 the "Best Beginners or 'Loaner' Guitar."

GRADING	100%	EXCELLENT	AVERAGE

H 159 JUMBO - dreadnought style, 25 1/4" scale, hardwood top, white striped edge/black pin line, white celluloid bindings, round soundhole with simulated marquetry inlay, hardwood back/sides, 20-fret ebonized maple fingerboard with white dot inlay, ebonized maple pin bridge with white bridgepins, black pickguard with small logo design, 3-per-side Waverly tuners, available in Natural Top/Dark Brown Rosewood body stain finish, length 40 3/4", body width 16", body thickness 4 1/4", mfg. circa 1969-1970.

N/A **$175** **$95**

Last MSR was $59.95.

H 162 GRAND CONCERT - dreadnought style, 24 1/4" scale, spruce top, round soundhole, mahogany back/sides, hardwood neck, 14/19-fret rosewood fingerboard with white dot inlay, adjustable truss rod, rosewood pin bridge, shell celluloid pickguard, 3-per-side tuners, available in Natural lacquer finish, length 39", body width 15 1/8", disc. 1970.

N/A **$225** **$125**

Last MSR was $64.50.

H 162 3/4 - similar to the H 162, except in smaller (3/4) size configuration, Length 32", body width 11 1/4", disc. 1970.

N/A **$200** **$125**

Last MSR was $64.50.

H 165 Grand Concert Mahogany - similar to the H 162, except features a mahogany top, Brazilian rosewood fingerboard, pinless bridge, disc. 1970.

It is unknown if Brazilian rosewood was actually used and because of this the secondhand market is still undefined.

Last MSR was $64.50.

H 162/1 FOLK (GRAND CONCERT SIZE) - dreadnought style, 24 1/4" scale, spruce top, round soundhole, mahogany back/sides, 19-fret rosewood fingerboard, adjustable truss rod, pinned bridge, black pickguard, 3-per-side Waverly tuners, available in Natural finish, length 39", body width 15 1/8", mfg. 1971-72.

N/A **$225** **$125**

Last MSR was $64.50.

H 162 3/4 - similar to the H 162/1, available in Natural finish, length 39", body width 15 1/8", mfg. 1971-72.

N/A **$200** **$125**

Last MSR was $64.50.

H 165/1 Folk Mahogany (Grand Concert Size) - similar to the H 162/1, except features a mahogany top and pinless bridge, length 39", body width 15 1/8", mfg. 1971-72.

N/A **$225** **$125**

Last MSR was $64.50.

H 166 FOLK - dreadnought style, 24 1/4" scale, spruce top, white body binding, round soundhole, hardwood back/sides/neck, 19-fret bound rosewood fingerboard with white dot inlay, pin bridge, 3-per-side Waverly tuners, black batwing-pickguard with small 'H' logo, white truss rod cover, available in Pumpkin Top/Dark Rosewood stain gloss finish, length 40", body width 15 1/8", disc. 1971.

N/A **$250** **$150**

Last MSR was $74.50.

H 167 FOLK - dreadnought style, spruce top, round soundhole, hardwood back/sides, 19-fret bound rosewood fingerboard with white dot inlay, rosewood pin bridge with white bridgepins, 6-on-a-side tuners, white truss rod cover, black 'batwing' pickguard with small 'H' logo, available in Natural finish, length 39", body width 15 1/8", mfg. circa 1969-1970.

N/A **$275** **$175**

Last MSR was $74.50.

H 168 Folk - similar to the H 167 Folk, available in Pumpkin Top/Dark Rosewood Body Color finish, length 39", body width 15 1/8", mfg. circa 1969-1970.

N/A **$275** **$175**

Last MSR was $74.50.

H 180 GRAND CONCERT - dreadnought style, bound selected spruce top, round soundhole, mahogany back/sides, 19-fret bound rosewood fingerboard with white dot inlay, adjustable saddle rosewood pin bridge with white bridgepins, black pickguard with design pattern, 6-on-a-side Waverly tuners, available in Antique Mahogany (Antique limed grain over Dark Rosewood stain) finish, length 39", body width 15 1/8", mfg. circa 1969-1970.

N/A **$325** **$200**

Last MSR was $104.50.

**Harmony H 1203
Grand Concert Special
1973 Harmony Catalog**

H

**Harmony H 1260 Jumbo
1973 Harmony Catalog**

GRADING	100%	EXCELLENT	AVERAGE

H 181 GRAND CONCERT - similar to the H 180, except features inlaid rings rosette, available in Pumpkin Top/Dark Rosewood stain finish, Length 39", Body Width 15 1/8", mfg. circa 1969-1970.

	N/A	$350	$225

Last MSR was $104.50.

H 182 GRAND CONCERT - dreadnought style, 24 1/4" scale, bound selected spruce top, round soundhole, mahogany back/sides/neck, 19-fret bound rosewood fingerboard with white dot inlay, bound blackface headstock with decorative design, adjustable pin bridge, teardrop-shaped black pickguard, 3-per-side Waverly tuners with white buttons, white truss rod cover, available in Pumpkin Top/Dark Rosewood body finish, length 40", body width 15 1/8", disc. 1971.

	N/A	$350	$225

Last MSR was $104.50.

ACOUSTIC: SOVEREIGN FLATTOP SERIES

HTG 1201 TENOR GUITAR - tenor (4-string) configuration, spruce top/mahogany back/sides, round soundhole, mahogany neck, celluloid edge binding, 14/20-fret fingerboard with white dot inlay, ebonised pin bridge, shell celluloid pickguard, 2 per side tuners, available in Natural finish, length 34", body width 13 1/8", disc. circa 1972.

	N/A	$300	$175

Last MSR was $82.50.

H 1203 GRAND CONCERT SPECIAL (WESTERN SPECIAL) - dreadnought style, 24.25" scale, select spruce top/mahogany back/sides, round soundhole, mahogany neck, 19-fret rosewood fingerboard with white dot inlay, adjustable truss rod, pinless rosewood bridge, 3-per-side Waverly tuners, available in Natural finish, length 40", body width 15 1/8", disc. circa 1972.

	N/A	$500	$250

Last MSR was $98.50.

The H 1203 model was originally designated the Western Special. In 1966, it was re-designated the Grand Concert Special.

H 1260 JUMBO - jumbo style, 25 1/4" scale, spruce top/mahogany back/sides, round soundhole, mahogany neck, shell edge binding, 19-fret rosewood fingerboard with white dot inlay, pinless bridge, teardrop-shaped pickguard, 3-per-side Waverly tuners, available in Natural finish, length 40 1/4", body width 16", body thickness 4 5/16", disc. circa 1972.

	N/A	$550	$275

Last MSR was $119.50.

H 1266 SOVEREIGN DELUXE JUMBO - dreadnought style, 25 1/4" scale, bound spruce top, round soundhole, mahogany back/sides, 14/19-fret rosewood fingerboard with white block inlays, adjustable mustache-style bridge with white pins, 2 black batwing pickguards (1 per side of soundhole), 3-per-side Waverly tuners, available in Sunburst finish, length 41 1/2", body width 16", body thickness 4 5/64", mfg. 1969-circa 1972.

	N/A	$550	$300

Last MSR was $169.50.

H 1265 Sovereign Deluxe Jumbo - similar to the H 1266, except features 2-piece black "State of Alaska"-shaped pickguard, available in Sunburst finish, length 41 1/2", body width 16", body thickness 4 5/64", mfg. 1967-68.

	N/A	$600	$350

Last MSR was $159.50.

The H 1265 was the forerunner to the H 1266 model (the H 1266 has a "more sensible" pickguard scheme).

H 164 "JET SET" SOVEREIGN FOLK GUITAR - dreadnought style, 24 1/4" scale, select spruce top, bound body, round soundhole with inlaid rings, hardwood back/sides/neck, 14/19-fret rosewood fingerboard with white dot inlay, rosewood pin bridge, white edged tear-drop shaped black pickguard with small 'H' design, 3-per-side Waverly tuners, available in Jet Black gloss finish, length 39", body width 15 1/8", mfg. circa 1971.

	N/A	$300	$150

Last MSR was $74.50.

H 1204 "JET SET" SOVEREIGN GRAND CONCERT - dreadnought style, 24 1/4" scale, rosewood top, round soundhole, hardwood back/sides, 19-fret rosewood fingerboard, adjustable truss rod, adjustable pin bridge, 3-per-side Waverly tuners, available in Natural finish, Length 40", body width 15 1/8", mfg. circa 1971.

	N/A	$375	$225

Last MSR was $99.50.

H 1264 "JET SET" SOVEREIGN JUMBO - dreadnought style, 25 1/4" scale, bound spruce top, round soundhole with wood marquetry inlay, hardwood back/sides, 14/19-fret rosewood fingerboard with white block inlays, adjustable mustache-style bridge with white pins, 2 black batwing pickguards (1 per side of soundhole), 3-per-side Waverly tuners, available in Jet Black gloss finish, length 41 1/2", body width 16", body thickness 4 5/64", mfg. 1971-circa 1972.

	N/A	$600	$325

Last MSR was $159.50.

GRADING	100%	EXCELLENT	AVERAGE

ACOUSTIC: 12-STRING SERIES

Many of Harmony's catalogs recommended that, "You do not tune a 12-string guitar as high as regular 6-string guitar pitch." As a result, the *Blue Book of Acoustic Guitars* offers a caution that current owners of these same models may want to tune down to avoid any structural problems (bridges separating or pulling off, top warpage, etc.).

H 1230 GRAND CONCERT 12-STRING - 25 1/4" scale, select spruce top, round soundhole, mahogany back/sides, bound body, mahogany neck, 12/18-fret tapered rosewood fingerboard with white dot position markers, solid headstock, dual-saddle rosewood bridge/chrome metal tailpiece, 6-per-side Waverly tuners, black batwing pickguard with silk-screened design, available in Pumpkin Top/Dark stain body finish, length 40 3/4", body width 15 1/8", mfg. circa 1969-circa 1971.

	N/A	$250	$125

Last MSR was $129.50.

H 1270 JUMBO 12-STRING - 25 1/4" scale, select spruce top, round soundhole, mahogany back/sides, bound body, 12/18-fret rosewood fingerboard with white dot position markers, slotted headstock, dual-saddle rosewood bridge/chrome metal tailpiece, 6-per-side Waverly tuners, teardrop-shaped black pickguard, available in Natural finish, length 40 1/2", body width 16", body thickness 4 5/16", mfg. 1963-circa 1972.

	N/A	$325	$150

Last MSR was $164.50.

ACOUSTIC ELECTRIC

H 55 SOVEREIGN DUAL PURPOSE - dreadnought style, 24 1/4" scale, spruce top, round soundhole, mahogany back/sides, 20-fret rosewood fingerboard with white dot inlay, pinless bridge, black teardrop-shaped pickguard, 3-per-side Waverly tuners, pickup (concealed under fingerboard), volume/tone controls, available in Natural finish, length 40", body width 15 1/8", body thickness 3.75", disc. 1971 (as H 55), 1972-75 (as H 655).

	N/A	$350	$200

Last MSR was $137.50.

This model is designated Harmony and Sovereign on the black peghead. In circa 1973, the H 55 model was redesignated the H 655.

Harmony H 1230
Grand Concert 12-String
1973 Harmony Catalog

HARPTONE

Harptone Manufacturing Corporation; Instruments previously built in Newark, New Jersey 1966 to mid 1970s.

The Harptone company was a commercial successor to the Felsberg Company (circa 1893). During the 1930s, Harptone was more known for musical instrument accessories, although a few guitars were built between 1924 and 1942.

The Harptone Manufacturing Corporation was located at 127 South 15th Street in Newark, New Jersey (07107) during the early to mid 1960s. Harptone's main guitar designer was Stan Koontz (who also designed Standel and his own signature guitars). Harptone's guitar product line consisted of mainly acoustic guitar models, including acoustic archtop models.

When Micro-Frets closed operations in Maryland in either 1974 or 1975, the company assets were purchased by David Sturgill. Sturgill, who served as the company president of Grammer Guitars for three years, let his sons John and Danny gain access to leftover Micro-Frets parts. In addition to those parts, they had also purchased the remains of New Jersey's Harptone guitar company. The two assembled a number of solid body guitars which were then sold under the Diamond-S trademark. Unfortunately, that business venture did not catch on, and dissolved sometime in 1976, (Company history courtesy Tom Wheeler, *American Guitars*).

Harptone instruments were built between 1966 to the mid -1970s. Research continues on the production dates per model, and as such none of the following models below will have an indicated date(s) of manufacture. Instruments can be dated by examining the components (pickups, hardware, tuners) and especially the potentiometers (where applicable). The *Blue Book of Acoustic Guitars* will continue to update further discoveries in future editions.

The secondary market (defined used sales prices) for Harptone guitar models are still undefined as very few models are being sold. Model pricing can be potentially determined by weighing the value of the components and and craftmanship versus desirability in the vintage guitar market. For further information regarding Harptone electric models, please refer to the *Blue Book of Electric Guitars*.

ACOUSTIC ARCHTOP

520 - 24 5/8" scale, maple top/back/sides, 21-fret rosewood fingerboard, adjustable metal bridge, 3-per-side Grover tuners, 2 D'Armond pickups, volume/tone controls, pickup selector switch, body width 16", body thickness 1 3/4".

Last MSR was $525.

Harmony H 55
Sovereign Dual Purpose
1973 Harmony Catalog

550 S - 24 5/8" scale, spruce top, maple back/sides, 21-fret ebony fingerboard, 3-per-side Grover tuners, adjustable metal bridge, 3-per-side Grover tuners, 2 D'Armond pickups, volume/tone controls, pickup selector switch, body width 16", body thickness 3".

Last MSR was $625.

811 - 24 5/8" scale, maple top/back/sides, 21-fret ebony fingerboard, adjustable metal bridge, 3-per-side Grover tuners, 2 D'Armond pickups, volume/tone controls, pickup selector switch, body width 17", body thickness 3 1/4".

Last MSR was $675.

910 - 24 5/8" scale, spruce top, maple back/sides, 21-fret ebony fingerboard, adjustable metal bridge, 3-per-side Grover tuners, gold-plated hardware, 2 D'Armond pickups, volume/tone controls, pickup selector switch, Body Width 17", Body Thickness 3 1/4".

Last MSR was $850.

1000 - 24 5/8" scale, spruce top, maple back/sides, 21-fret ebony fingerboard, adjustable wood bridge, 3-per-side Grover tuners, gold-plated hardware, 1 D'Armond pickups, volume/tone controls, body width 18", body thickness 3 1/4".

Last MSR was $1,295.

ACOUSTIC

E 6N (EAGLE) - dreadnought style, 24 5/8" scale, sitka spruce top, round soundhole, qrtd. mahogany back, mahogany sides, 20-fret rosewood fingerboard, double truss rod, pin bridge, 3-per-side Grover tuners, available in Natural finish, body width 15 5/8", body thickness 4 7/8".

Last MSR was $225.

E 12N 12-String (Eagle) - similar to the E 6N, except features mahogany back/sides, 12-string configuration, 6-per-side Grover tuners, available in Natural finish, body width 15 5/8", body thickness 4 7/8".

Last MSR was $249.95.

F 6NC (FOLK MASTER) - dreadnought style with single rounded cutaway, 24 5/8" scale, Sitka spruce top, round soundhole, flamed maple back/sides, 20-fret rosewood fingerboard, double truss rod, adjustable pin bridge, 3-per-side Grover tuners, available in Natural finish, body width 17", body thickness 4 7/8".

Last MSR was $329.95.

F 12NC 12-String (Folk Master) - similar to the F 6NC, except features maple back/sides, pin bridge, 12-string configuration, 6-per-side Grover tuners, available in Natural finish, body width 17", body thickness 4 7/8".

Last MSR was $329.95.

L 6N (LARK) - dreadnought style, 24 5/8" scale, Sitka spruce top, round soundhole, mahogany back/sides, 20-fret rosewood fingerboard, double truss rod, pin bridge, 3-per-side Grover tuners, available in Natural finish, body width 17", body thickness 4 7/8".

Last MSR was $269.95.

P 6N (PIONEER) - dreadnought style, 24 5/8" scale, Sitka spruce top, round soundhole, mahogany back/sides, 20-fret rosewood fingerboard, double truss rod, pin bridge, 3-per-side Grover tuners, available in Natural finish, body width 16", body thickness 4 7/8".

Last MSR was $225.

S 6NC (SULTAN) - dreadnought style with single rounded cutaway, 24 5/8" scale, sitka spruce top, round soundhole, flamed maple back/sides, 14/20-fret rosewood fingerboard with white dot inlay, double truss rod, teardrop-shaped black pickguard, adjustable bridge with white pins, unbound pincher headstock, 3-per-side Grover tuners, Natural finish, body width 16", body thickness 4 7/8".

Last MSR was $269.

S 12NC 12-String (Sultan) - similar to the S 6NC, except features maple back/sides, pin bridge, 12-string configuration, 6-per-side Grover tuners, available in Natural finish, body width 16", body thickness 4 7/8".

Last MSR was $295.

Z 6N (ZODIAC) - dreadnought style, 24 5/8" scale, Sitka spruce top, round soundhole, rosewood back/sides, 20-fret bound rosewood fingerboard, double truss rod, adjustable pin bridge, 3-per-side Grover tuners, available in Natural finish, body width 15 5/8", body thickness 4 7/8".

Last MSR was $350.

Z 12N 12-String (Zodiac) - similar to the Z 6N, except features a pin bridge, 12-string configuration, 6-per-side Grover tuners, available in Natural finish, body width 15 5/8", body thickness 4 7/8".

Last MSR was $375.

RENZI 100 - nylon string, 25 5/8" scale, Alpine spruce top, round soundhole, mahogany back/sides, 19-fret rosewood fingerboard, hand-engraved headstock, rosewood bridge, 3-per-side German tuners, available in Natural finish.

Last MSR was $250.

Renzi 200 - similar to the Renzi 100, except features maple back/sides, available in Natural finish.

Last MSR was $350.

HARRIS, RICHARD
Instruments currently built in Indianapolis, Indiana.

Luthier Richard Harris builds custom acoustic Tele-style guitars – the models are all acoustic, but are shaped with the single cutaway body like a Tele. For further information regarding his custom guitars, contact Richard Harris directly (see Trademark Index).

HAUSER, HERMAN

Instruments currently built in Reisbach, Germany. Instruments built in Munich, Germany since the early 1900s.

Luthier Hermann Hauser (1882-1952) built a variety of stringed instruments throughout his career. While earlier models did not share the same designs as the "Spanish school," Hauser soon adopted designs introduced by Antonio de Torres. In the late 1930s Maestro Andres Segovia moved from a Ramirez guitar to a Hauser built classical, which he played until 1970.

Hermann Hauser was succeeded by his son, Herman Hauser II, and a grandson, Herman Hauser III, who continues the family tradition of building fine acoustic guitars. In the same tradition of his father and grandfather, Hauser III builds perhaps 12 guitars a year utilizing fine aged German spruce and rosewood, (Source: Tony Bacon, *The Ultimate Guitar Book*).

HAWK

See Framus and Klira. Instruments previously built in West Germany during the early 1960s.

The Hawk trademark was a brandname used by a UK importer. Instruments imported into England were built by either Framus or Klira in Germany, and are identical to their respective builder's models, (Source: Tony Bacon and Paul Day, *The Guru's Guitar Guide*).

HAYNES

Instruments previously manufactured in Boston, Massachusetts from 1865 to the early 1900s.

The Oliver Ditson Company, Inc. was formed in 1835 by music publisher Oliver Ditson (1811-1888). Ditson was a primary force in music merchandising, distribution, and retail sales on the East Coast. He also helped establish two musical instrument manufacturers: The John Church Company of Cincinnati, Ohio, and Lyon & Healy (Washburn) in Chicago, Illinois.

In 1865, Ditson established a manufacturing branch of his company under the supervision of John Haynes, called the John C. Haynes Company. This branch built guitars for a number of trademarks, such as Bay State, Tilton, and Haynes Excelsior, (Source: Tom Wheeler, *American Guitars*).

HAYNIE, LES

Instruments currently built in Eureka Springs, Arkansas.

Les Haynie handcrafts custom guitars in his shop in Eureka Springs. For further information concerning models and pricing, please contact luthier Haynie directly (see Trademark Index).

HEIDEN, MICHAEL

Instruments currently built in Chilliwac (British Columbia), Canada. Distributed by Heiden Stringed Instruments of Chilliwac (British Columbia), Canada.

Luthier Micheal Heiden is currently handcrafting some very high quality acoustic guitar models and mandolins. For further information regarding model specifications, custom orders, and pricing, please contact luthier Heiden directly (see Trademark Index).

HENDERSON, WAYNE

Instruments currently built in Mouth of Wilson, Virgina.

Guitars currently built in Virginia. Wayne is also the host of the Wayne C. Henderson Music Festival and Guitar Competition that is held every third week in June.

HENDERSON, WILLIAM

Instruments currently built in the U.S. Distributed by Kirkpatrick Guitar Studios of Baltimore, Maryland.

Luthier William Henderson, a rapidly developing talent, is currently building high quality classical guitars.

HENRY GUITAR COMPANY

Instruments previously built in Atlanta, GA, 1997-2000, and in Asheville, NC 1994-97.

Luthier Jeff Henry studied under Nick Apollonio of Rockport, Maine before forming his own company. Henry offered five different handcrafted acoustic guitar models, as well as custom options. Henry guitars carry a stylized H on the headstock, as well as a full label inside the soundhole.

ACOUSTIC

Jeff Henry offered five different acoustic guitar models: the **ML**, his smallest instrument with lively response; **LJ**, a Little Jumbo that combines the balance of a ML with the power of a full body; the **Jumbo**, a full sized acoustic; the **D**, a dreadnought sized acoustic; and the **SD**, which is similar to the **D** except had sloped shoulders.

Henry guitars were offered with other custom options such as installed pickups, and additional wood choices on the soundboard, or back and sides. These are some of the option prices for the guitars:

Add $25 for an exotic wood pickguard. Add $75 for an exotic wood rosette. Add $200 for a cutaway body configuration. Add $200 for a 12-string configuration.

All five models were available in either the Standard or Deluxe package, and the prices included a hardshell case. The **Standard** package (last retail was $1,500) had a Sitka spruce or western red cedar soundboard, mahogany back and

GRADING	100%	EXCELLENT	AVERAGE

sides, a rosewood fingerboard and bridge, pearl dots inlay, ivoroid or tortoise shell body binding, a herringbone rosette, a tortoise shell pickguard, and Grover tuners. More upscale was the Deluxe package (last retail was $2,100). The **Deluxe** offers the same Sitka spruce or western red cedar soundboard, a mahogany back with a hardwood backstrip, mahogany sides, a bound ebony fingerboard, ebony bridge, abalone diamond inlays, abalone bridge inlay, rosewood or maple mitered body binding, an abalone rosette, a tortoise shell pickguard, and Schaller tuners.

HERITAGE GUITAR, INC.

Currently manufacture located in Kalamazoo, Michigan since 1985. The Lasar Music Corporation is the exclusive sales and marketing company for Heritage Guitars, Inc.

The Gibson guitar company was founded in Kalamazoo in 1902. The young company continued to expand, and built production facilities at 225 Parsons Street (the first of a total of five buildings at that location) in 1917. In 1974, Gibson was acquired by the Norlin corporation, which also opened facilities the same year in Nashville, Tennessee. However, financial troubles led Norlin to consider shutting down either the Kalamazoo or Nashville facilities in the early 1980s. Even though the Kalamazoo plant was Gibson's home since 1917, the decision was made in July of 1983 by Norlin to close the plant. The doors at 225 Parsons Street closed in the fall of 1984.

Heritage Guitar, Inc. opened in 1985 in the original Gibson building. Rather than uproot and move to Tennessee, Jim Deurloo, Marvin Lamb, and J.P. Moats elected to leave the Gibson company, and stay in Kalamazoo to start a new guitar company. Members of the original trio were later joined by Bill Paige and Mike Korpak (other long time Gibson workers). Korpack left the Heritage company in 1985.

Jim Deurloo began working at Gibson in 1958, and through his career was promoted from neck sander to pattern maker up to general foreman of the pattern shop, machine shop, and maintenance. Deurloo was the plant manager at Guild between 1969 to 1974, and had been involved with the opening and tooling up of the newer Nashville facility in 1974. During this time period, Deurloo was also the head of engineering, and was later promoted to assistant plant manager. In 1978, Deurloo was named plant manager at the Kalamazoo facility.

Marv Lamb was hired by Gibson in 1956 to do hand sanding and other jobs in the wood shop (Lamb was one of the workers on the '58 Korina Flying Vs and Explorers). He was promoted through a series of positions to general foreman of finishing and final assembly, and finally to plant superintendent in 1974 (a position he held until Gibson closed the plant in 1984).

J.P. Moats was hired by Gibson in 1957 for sanding and final cleaning. Through promotions, Moats became head of quality control as well as the supervisor of inspectors, and later the wood inspector. While inspecting wood for Gibson, Moats was also in charge of repairs and custom orders.

Bill Paige, a graduate of the business school at Western Michigan University joined Gibson in 1975 as a cost accountant and other capacities in the accounting department. Paige is currently the Heritage controller, and handles all non-guitar manufacturing functions.

All current owners of Heritage continue to design models, and produce various instruments in the production facilities. Heritage continues to develop new models along with their wide range of acoustic, hollow body, semi-hollow, and electric guitar models. Heritage is also one of the few *new* guitar companies with models that are stocked in vintage and collectible guitar stores worldwide.

Heritage also builds mandolins and a banjo model on a "Limited Availability" basis. The H-5 Mandolin (retail list $3,725) has a solid spruce top, scrolled body design, curly maple back/rim/one piece neck, ebony fingerboard, bound peghead with mother-of-pearl/abalone inlays, and gold hardware. Featuring a more traditional body style, the H-50 Mandolin (retail list $1,350) also has a solid spruce top, curly maple back/rim/ one piece neck, rosewood fingerboard, 4 on a plate tuners, and chrome hardware. The H-40 Mandolin (retail list $1,200) is similar to the H-50, except has a plain maple back/rim/neck. All three models are available in an Antique Sunburst finish.

The Kalamazoo Standard Banjo (retail list $2,700) has a bound curly maple resonator/neck, maple rim, bound ebony fingerboard with mother-of-pearl inlays, and chrome hardware, available in Honey Stain finish. Heritage offers a wide range of custom features. Unless specified, a hardshell case is optional with the guitar. Cases for the acoustics, jazz guitars, and basses run $160 while the cases for electric guitars are $150; cases for the Super Eagle model are $190.

ACOUSTIC

Heritage's acoustic instruments are available on a limited basis.

H-450 - dreadnought style, solid spruce top, round soundhole, 25 1/2" scale, white bound body, wooden inlay rosette, black pickguard, mahogany back/sides, maple neck, 14/20-fret rosewood fingerboard with mother-of-pearl dot inlay, rosewood bridge with white pins, 3-per-side chrome tuners, available in Antique Sunburst or Natural finishes on top; Walnut finish on back/sides/neck, disc. 1990.

N/A	$450	$275

Last MSR was $850.

H-480 - narrow waist rounded single cutaway style, solid spruce top, oval soundhole, 25 1/2" scale, white bound body/rosette, carved mahogany back, solid mahogany sides, mahogany neck, 14/21-fret rosewood fingerboard with mother-of-pearl dot inlay, rosewood bridge with white pins, 3-per-side chrome tuners, available in Antique Sunburst or Natural finishes on top; Walnut finish on back/ sides/neck, disc. 1990.

N/A	$450	$275

Last MSR was $850.

HFT-445 (H-445) - dreadnought style, solid spruce top, round soundhole, white bound body and wooden inlay rosette, black pickguard, mahogany back/sides, maple neck, 14/20-fret rosewood fingerboard with pearl dot inlay, rosewood bridge with white pins, 3-per-side chrome tuners, available in Antique Sunburst finish, mfg. 1987-2000.

$1,000	$700	$475

Last MSR was $1,400.

Add $50 for Natural finish.

HFT-475 - single sharp cutaway jumbo style, solid spruce top, round soundhole, 5-stripe bound body and rosette, black pickguard, mahogany back/sides/neck, 20-fret bound rosewood fingerboard with pearl block inlay, rosewood bridge with white pins, bound peghead, 3-per-side chrome tuners, available in Antique Sunburst finish, disc. 1999.

                             N/A   **$1,100**   **$700**
                                      Last MSR was $2,050.

Add $50 for Natural finish. Add $150 for DeArmond pickup.

HFT-485 - jumbo style, solid spruce top, round soundhole, 3-stripe bound body/rosette, rosewood pickguard, rosewood back/sides, mahogany neck, 14/21-fret bound rosewood fingerboard with pearl block inlay, rosewood bridge with white pins, bound peghead, 3-per-side chrome tuners, available in Antique Sunburst finish, disc. 1999.

                             N/A   **$1,200**   **$775**
                                      Last MSR was $2,300.

Add $50 for Natural finish. Add $150 for DeArmond pickup.

HERNANDEZ y AGUADO
Instruments previously built in Madrid, Spain during the 1960s.

Luthiers Manuel Hernandez and Victoriano Aguado combined guitar making skills to build world class classical guitars, (Source: Tony Bacon, *The Ultimate Guitar Book*).

HILL, DENNIS
Instruments currently built in Panama City, Florida. Distributed by Dennis Hill and Leitz Music, Inc. of Panama City, Florida.

Dennis Hill has a tradition of music in his life that reaches back to his father, who was a dance band musician. After a five year career in the U.S. Navy (Hill received his Honorable Discharge in 1969), Hill became the student to classical guitar teacher Ernesto Dijk. As Hill's interest in guitars grew, he met Augustino LoPrinzi in 1987. Hill finally became a sales representative for LoPrinzi's guitars, and studied guitarmaking at LoPrinzi'z shop. Hill spent days in the shop as LoPrinzi's shadow observing construction techniques and finishing methods. For the sake of efficiency, Hill and LoPrinzi agreed to reserve in depth question and answer sessions for breakfast/lunch meetings (Those encounters now highly regarded and much appreciated by Hill). All building was done after hours in Hill's art studio (Hill lived as a portrait artist and art teacher at that time). In 1992 Hill moved to Panama City and established his own shop.

Heritage H-445
courtesy Heritage Guitar

Hill currently builds classical, flamenco and archtop guitars and violins employing traditional Spanish and Italian construction styles. Woods include European or Englemann spruce tops: cedar, mahogany or maple necks; cypress, maple, mahogany or rosewood back and sides; ebony fingerboards, rosewood or maple binding and trim. The Classical and Flamenco models have a list price from $4,000. The Archtop guitar has a list price from $7,500. The Vioin has a list price from $4,500. For further information contact Leitz Music, Inc. directly (see Trademark Index), (Source: Hal Hammer).

HILL GUITAR COMPANY
See Also New World Guitar Company. Instruments currenly built in Felton, California. Distributed by the Hill Guitar Company of Ben Lomond, California.

Kenny Hill has been a professional classical guitarist for 25 years, and has performed extensively throughout the United States and Mexico. His ability and experience as a performer result in a special gift for making an instrument that is very playable and appealing to the player, as well as the audience.

He has been awarded two major grants from the California Arts Council. One of those grants was to establish a guitar building program inside Soledad State Prison. He continues to act as a guitar building consultant, there and in other prisons. He is also the founder and director of the New World Guitar Co., listed elsewhere in this directory. Mr. Hill is a regular contributor to several national magazines, including *Guitar, Soundboard*, and *American Lutherie*, (Biography courtesy Kenny Hill, September 1997).

Kenny Hill has built quality concert classical and flamenco guitars since 1975. He builds about 25 guitars per year in his shop in the mountains outside of Santa Cruz, California. His Kenneth Hill Signature Series instruments are handmade from the finest traditional materials, and sell for $3,600 to $5,000 (special terms are available to dealers). Hill guitars are characterized as having a clear and warm sound, with excellent balance and separation. The neck and action are among the most playable available anywhere.

ACOUSTIC

The (Classical) guitar models in the Old Master Series seek to emulate the instruments of important historical guitar builders. This project offers the guitarist a chance to own an instrument with the musicial and design characteristics that might otherwise be unavailable due to the scarity or cost of an original.

Heritage HFT-475
courtesy Heritage Guitar

BARCELONA MODEL - built in the style of Ignacio Fleta guitars, western red cedar top, Indian rosewood back/sides, 650 mm scale, ebony fingerboard, slotted headstock with 3-per-side Fustero tuners, current mfg.

    MSR   **$2,995**

LA CURVA - cutaway classical model, spruce or cedar top, rosewood or cypress back and sides, ebony fingerboard, Schaller tuners, available in Natural finish, current mfg.

    MSR   **$1,995**

LA TRIANA FLAMENCO - built in the style of Santos Hernandez guitars, Canadian spruce top, cypress back/sides, 650 mm scale, ebony fingerboard, slotted headstock with 3-per-side Schaller (or peg) tuners, current mfg.

    MSR   **$1,750**

LONDON MODEL (19TH CENTURY) - built in the style of Louis Panormo guitars, Canadian spruce top, rosewood back/sides, 635 mm scale, ebony fingerboard, slotted headstock with 3-per-side Sloane tuners, current mfg.

    MSR   **$1,995**

    This style of guitar is nicknamed "Cacahaute" (Peanut) because of its size and distinctive shape.

MADRID MODEL - built in the style of Jose Ramirez guitars, western red cedar top, Indian rosewood back/sides, 650 mm scale, ebony fingerboard, slotted headstock with 3-per-side Gotoh tuners, current mfg.

    MSR   **$1,995**

MUNICH MODEL - built in the style of Herman Hauser I guitars, Canadian spruce top, Indian rosewood back/sides, 640 or 650 mm scale, ebony fingerboard, slotted headstock with 3-per-side Schaller tuners, current mfg.

    MSR   **$1,995**

PALO ESCRITO - student model, cedar top, palo escrito back and sides, ebony or granadillo fingerboard, Spanish cedar neck, classical style headstock, Natural finish, new 2003.

PRODIGY (STUDENT MODEL) - spruce or cedar top, Mexican rosewood back/sides, 650 mm scale, granadillo fingerboard, slotted headstock with 3-per-side Gotoh tuners, disc.

                           Last MSR was $975.

RUCK MODEL - revolutionary new design classical model that produces more volume than previously obtained, two 30mm holes are present in the upper shoulders of the guitar and the fan bars have been modified to obtain this, current mfg.

    MSR   **$2,950**

HIRADE
See Takamine (Hirade Series).

HOFFMAN GUITARS
Instruments currently built in Minneapolis, Minnesota beginning 1971.

Luthier Charlie Hoffman and Hoffman Guitars offers both high quality handcrafted guitars and high quality instrument repair services. Hoffman Guitars is the factory authorized warranty service for Martin, Gibson, Guild, Fender, Taylor, and other manufacturers.

To date, Charlie Hoffman has built over 360 handcrafted guitars, which are played by such guitarists as Leo Kottke, Dakota Dave Hull, Ann Reed, and many others. Hoffman's web site offers a vast plethora of guitar and lutherie information as well.

ACOUSTIC

Given the nature of hand building custom guitars, the following information is more of a guide than an exact specification for the commissioned guitar.

The **Concert Model** was designed with a fingerpicking player in mind, and also works well with vocal accompaniment. This Concert Model is available with a cutaway body, or a 12-fret (body joins the neck at the 12th fret) configuration: body length 18.75", depth 4.5", lower bout 15.25".

Hoffman's **Dreadnought** model is built along the lines of the classic Martin Dreadnought shape, with a somewhat "stiff" top (to accentuate the treble) and a slightly deeper body. This model is also available with a cutaway body, or a 12-fret (body joins the neck at the 12th fret) configuration: body length 20", depth 5", lower bout 15.6".

The **Parlor** guitar is patterned after the numerous parlor guitars of the 1900s to the 1930s, and is standard with a 12-fret neck. It is optional in a slotted or solid headstock: body length 19", depth 4.125", lower bout 13.75".

Hoffman's three primary body shapes are all priced the same – by the nature of the body woods that determine the construction. African mahogany body woods retail at $3,000; East Indian body woods at $3,000; koa or flame maple body woods are $3,400 each. Given the nature of Brazilian rosewood or highly flamed koa, the customer must call for an estimate. Other custom features on Hoffman guitars include a custom neck width or contour (no charge), a cutaway body ($450), herringbone purfling ($50), abalone rosette ($150), abalone back center strip ($150), a slotted peghead with Waverly gears ($250),a Pyramid bridge ($150), or abalone top edging ($350), or a 12-string configuration ($350). For proper information regarding prices and specifications, contact Charlie Hoffman at Hoffman Guitars directly (see Trademark Index).

HOFNER
Instruments currently produced in Bubenreuth and Hagenau, Germany. Hofner instruments are distributed in the U.S. by Boosey & Hawkes Musical Instruments, Inc. of Libertyville, Illinois.

The Hofner instrument making company was originally founded by Karl Hofner in 1887. Originally located in Schonbach (in the area now called Czechoslovakia), Hofner produced fine stringed instruments such as violins, cellos, and doublebasses. Karl's two sons, Josef and Walter, joined the company in 1919 and 1921 (respectively), and expanded Hofner's market to North American and the Far East. Production of guitars began in 1925, in the area that was to become East Germany during the "Cold War" era. Following World War II, the Hofner family moved to West Germany and established a new factory in Bubenreuth in 1948. By 1950, new production facilities in Bubenreuth and Hanenau were staffed by over 300 Hofner employees.

The first Hofner electric archtop debuted in the 1950s. While various guitar models were available in Germany since 1949 (and earlier, if you take in the over 100 years of company history), Hofners were not officially exported to England until Selmer of London took over distributorship in 1958. Furthermore, Selmer's British models were specified for the U.K. only – and differ from those available in the German market.

The concept of a violin-shaped bass was developed by Walter Hofner (Karl's son) in 1956. Walter's idea to electrically amplify a bass was new for the company, but the hollow body model itself was based on family design traditions. The **500/1.** model made its debut at the Frankfurt Music Fair the same year. While most people may recognize that model as the Beatle Bass popularized by Paul McCartney, the Hofner company also produced a wide range of solid, semi-hollow, and archtop designs that were good quality instruments.

Until 1997, Hofner products were distributed by EMMC (Entertainment Music Marketing Corporation, which focused on distributing the 500/1 Reissue violin electric bass. In 1998, distribution for Hofner products in the U.S. market was changed to Boosey & Hawkes Musical Instruments, Inc. of Libertyville, Illinois. Boosey & Hawkes wasted no time in introducing three jazz-style semi-hollow guitar models, which includes a **New President** (Model HP-55) model guitar. Boosey & Hawkes is also distributing Thomastik guitar and bass strings along with the Hofner accessories, (Hofner history source: Gordon Giltrap and Neville Marten, *The Hofner Guitar – A History*; and Tony Bacon, *The Ultimate Guitar Book*, current Hofner product information courtesy Rob Olsen, Boosey & Hawkes Musical Instruments, Inc.).

Hoffman Parlor
courtesy Hoffman Guitars

MODEL DATING INFORMATION

Hofner began installing adjustable truss-rods in their guitar necks beginning in 1960. Any model prior to that year will not have a truss-rod cover.

Between the late 1950s and early 1970s, Hofner produced a number of semi-hollow or hollowbody electric guitars and basses that were in demand in England. English distribution was handled by **Selmer** of London, and specified models that were imported. In some cases, English models are certainly different from the domestic models offered in Germany.

There will always be interest in Hofners; either Paul McCartney's earlier association with the **Beatle Bass** or the thrill of a **Committee** or **Golden Hofner**.

From the late 1960s to the early 1980s, the company produced a number of guitar models based on popular American designs. In addition, Hofner also built a number of better quality original models such as **Alpha, Compact**, and **Razorwood** from the late 1970s to the mid 1980s. However, you have to *know 'em before you tag 'em*. The *Blue Book of Acoustic Guitars* recommends discussions with your favorite vintage dealers. Also, inquiries can be addressed to Boosey & Hawkes as to models nomenclature.

Hofner (and Boosey & Hawkes) is currently offering a wider range of models outside of the U.S. market. In fact, Hofner has 4 different series of acoustic guitars that are not represented below: the child-sized **Jugend-/Schulergitarren** (HS Series), classical-style **Konzertgitarren** (HF Series), enviroment-friendly **Green Line** (HGL Series), and the upscale **Meistergitarrren** (HM Series). Electric models include the **Jazzica Standard** and **Jazzica Special, Vice President**, and **New President**, as well as the **Nightingale Standard** and the **Nightingale Special**. Electric bass models are the same.

ACOUSTIC ARCHTOP MODELS

The models listed below have not been priced individually. In general, Hofner prices range as follows. Guitars produced between 1951-1964 (pre-Beatles era) are generally priced between $250-$450. Instruments produced from the mid-'60s through the mid-'80s will command slightly more, usually in the $650-$850 range. As with any maker, prices are based on configuration, originality factor and condition. Used clean big-body hollowbody guitars had been advertised nationally for $750 to $950, with the more ornate models carrying an asking price of $1,500 to $2,200.

MODEL 455 - archtop hollowbody, laminated maple top, back & sides, rosewood fingerboard with white celluloid inlays, 3-per-side tuners, black & white celluloid binding on top, back, & f-holes, redwhite celluloid inlays on headstock, white pickguard, lyre tailpiece, available in Cherry Red shaded finish, mfg. 1951-1968.

MODEL 455/S - similar to Model 455 except in a single cutaway design, mfg. 1961-1970.

> **Model 455/S/B** - similar to 455/S except in Blonde finish, mfg. 1963-67.

MODEL 4550 - similar to Model 455 except features a larger archtop body, laminated maple top, back & sides, bound top, back, fingerboard, & f-holes, rosewood fingerboard, celluloid band position markers, white pickguard, 3-per-side tuners, lyre tailpiece, Shaded Brown finish, also available in a single cutaway model (Model 4550/S), mfg. 1955-1966.

MODEL 456 - archtop hollowbody, flame maple back & sides, rosewood fingerboard, celluloid band position markers, bound top, back, fingerboard & f-holes, red, black, or white headstock, white pickguard, lyre tailpiece, 3-per-side tuners, available in Dark Brown Sunburst finish or Blonde (Model 456/b), mfg. 1951-1961.

> Subvariations include Model 456/S with single cutaway and 456/S/b, single cutaway with blonde finish, mfg. 1961-62.

MODEL 457 - archtop hollowbody, nicely flamed maple back & sides, spruce top, bound top, back, fingerboard & f-holes, headstock decorated with gold plated clef & staff, 3-per-side tuners, celluloid band position markers, available in Brown Sunburst or Blonde finishes, Model 457/b, mfg. 1954-1994.

> Subvariations include Model 457/S, single cutaway version and Model 457/S/b, single cutaway design with Blonde finish, mfg. 1961-1970.

Hoffman Custom
courtesy Dave Hull

GRADING	100%	EXCELLENT	AVERAGE

MODEL 458 - archtop hollowbody, laminated maple top and back, bound top, back, fingerboard & f-holes, celluloid band position markers, decorated headstock, 3-per-side tuners, white pickguard, lyre tailpiece, available in highly polished Black finish, mfg. 1954-1966.

Also available in single cutaway design, Model 458/S, mfg. 1961-66.

MODEL 461/S - archtop hollowbody, single cutaway design, bound top, back & f-holes, additional small oval soundhole in the traditional location, harp tailpiece, 3-per-side tuners, black & white celluloid decoration on the headstock with stylized arrow, split trapezoid position markers, unusually shaped f-holes, available in highly polished Black finish only, mfg. 1954-1964.

MODEL 462 - archtop hollowbody, flamed maple back & sides, selected spruce top, elliptical sound holes, 2-piece tailpiece, bound top, back, fingerboard & f-holes, headstock has gold plated clef & staff, celluloid band position markers (1 wide & 2 narrow), 3-per-side tuners, white pickguard, available in Light Brown Varnish finish, mfg. 1951 only.

Model 462/S - similar to Model 462 except in a single cutaway design, available in Light Brown Varnish finish, mfg. 1954-1970.

MODEL 463 - archtop hollowbody, sapeli mahogany back & sides, selected spruce top, bound mahogany fingerboard, split trapezoid position markers, wooden inlays & celluloid bindings on top & back, wooden inlays around f-holes, harp tailpiece, 3-per-side tuners, white pickguard, available in Shaded Brown finish, mfg. 1952-1994.

Also available in single cutaway design, Model 463/S, mfg. 1961-1970.

MODEL 464/S - archtop hollowbody, single cutaway design, spruce top, flame maple back & sides, bound top, back, fingerboard & f-holes, eliptical sound holes, one additional rhombic soundhole located in the traditional position, celluloid band position markers (2 wide & 2 narrow), lyre tailpiece, 3-per-side tuners, white pickguard, available in Dark Wine Red finish, mfg. 1954-1968.

MODEL 465 - archtop hollowbody, well selected fine spruce top, rosewood back & sides, ebony fingerboard, wood & celluloid bindings on top, back, fingerboard & f-holes, MOP headstock inlays (bell-flowers) and position markers (1 narrow rectangle flanked by 2 pentagons that resemble arrowheads), lucite pickguard, 3-per-side tuners, lyre tailpiece, Shaded Brown finish, mfg. 1951-1962.

Also available in a single cutaway design, Model 465/S, mfg. 1961-1970.

MODEL 470/S - archtop hollowbody, single cutaway design, selected spruce top, best quality flame maple back & sides, wooden flower inlays on back, ebony fingerboard & headstock, bound top, back, fingerboard & f-holes, 3-per-side tuners, MOP headstock inlays (lillies) and position markers (1 narrow rectangle flanked by 2 pentagons that resemble arrowheads), rosewood pickguard, available in high polish Blonde finish, mfg. 1961-1994.

MODEL 471 - archtop hollowbody, enlarged body, selected spruce top, flame maple back & sides, florentine cutaway, celluloid bound top & back, ebony fingerboard with split trapezoid MOP inlays, elaborate headstock inlays, 3-per-side tuners, harp tailpiece, Blonde finish, mfg. 1969-1977.

MODEL 477 - archtop hollowbody, spruce top, flame maple back & sides, florentine cutaway, 3 dot position markers, 3-per-side tuners, harp tailpiece, bound top, back, fingerboard & f-holes, black pickguard, available in high polish Yellow-red Shaded finish, mfg. 1969-1994.

HOHNER

Instruments currently produced in Korea, although earlier models from the 1970s were built in Japan. Currently distributed in the U.S. by HSS (a Division of Hohner, Inc.), located in Richmond, Virginia.

The Hohner company was founded in 1857, and is currently the world's largest manufacturer and distributor of harmonicas. Hohner offers a wide range of solidly constructed musical instruments. The company has stayed contemporary with the current market by licensing designs and parts from Ned Steinberger, Claim Guitars (Germany), and Wilkinson hardware.

In addition to their guitar models, Hohner also distributes Sonor drums, Sabian cymbals, and Hohner educational percussion instruments.

ACOUSTIC: MISC. MODELS

In 2002, Hohner released a series called the Americana Series. These are basic dreadnought guitars with basic specifications, but they have a graphic on the lower part of the body. They are available with a Mt Rushmore, American Bald Eagle, Golden Gate Bridge, or the Statue of Liberty graphic. Retail is $599 for all of these, but the secondary market has been developed yet.

HAG21 - single round cutaway classic style, solid maple body, spruce top, round soundhole, bound body, wooden inlay rosette, mahogany neck, 20-fret rosewood fingerboard with white dot inlay, rosewood bridge with white pins, 3-per-side chrome tuners, piezo bridge pickup, volume/tone control, available in Natural finish, mfg. 1990-92.

	N/A	$275	$150
		Last MSR was $500.	

HAG22 - similar to HAG21, except has dreadnought style body, available in Sunburst finish, disc. 1992.

	N/A	$275	$150
		Last MSR was $500.	

HAG250P - half-size body, nylon strings, available in Natural finish, current mfg.

MSR	$50	$30	$20	$10

HAG294 - small body, spruce top, round soundhole, bound body, 5-stripe rosette, black pickguard, mahogany back/sides/neck, 12/18-fret ebonized fingerboard with white dot inlay, ebonized bridge, 3-per-side diecast tuners, available in Natural finish, mfg. 1991-96.

	N/A	$65	$40
		Last MSR was $110.	

GRADING		100%	EXCELLENT	AVERAGE

HAG294C - similar to HAG294, except has classical body styling, disc. 1996.

		N/A	$65	$40

Last MSR was $110.

HF70 - 3/4 size, spruce top, round soundhole, bound body, black pickguard, mahogany back/sides/neck, 14/20-fret rosewood fingerboard with white dot inlay, rosewood bridge with white pins, 3-per-side covered tuners, available in Natural finish, disc 2001.

		$200	$130	$90

Last MSR was $269.

HF75 - concert size steel string body, solid Sitka spruce top, ovangkol back and sides, pearloid position markers and bridge inlays, 18 frets, gold open style tuners, available in Natural finish, current mfg.

MSR	$299	$215	$150	$105

HFX - cutaway body, Engleman solid spruce top, mahogany back and sides, 20-fret rosewood fingerboard, abalone position markers and soundhole inlay, Shadow Megatech 8 digital preamp with 20 factory presets and 20 user presets, onboard effects include reverb, Delay, tremolo, Chorus, Flanger, Compressor, Noise gate, and Phase reverb switch, available in Natural finish, disc 2001.

		$625	$450	$225

Last MSR was $849.

TWP600 - single cutaway dreadnought style, spruce top, triangular soundhole, bound body, 3-stripe rosette, mahogany back/sides/neck, 20-fret rosewood fingerboard with white dot inlay, rosewood bridge with white pins, 3-per-side chrome tuners, piezo bridge pickup, 3-band EQ system, available in Black, Blue Sunburst, Natural, or Pumpkin Burst finishes, mfg. 1992-96.

		N/A	$275	$175

Last MSR was $550.

Hohner HMW 400
courtesy Hohner

ACOUSTIC: HW MODELS

HW03 STUDENT MODEL - 3/4 size, spruce top, round soundhole, bound body, black pickguard, mahogany back/sides/neck, 14/20-fret fingerboard, nylon string tied bridge, 3-per-side open tuners, available in Natural finish, current mfg.

MSR	$109	$85	$55	$40

HW90 - dreadnought style, solid Sitka spruce top, ovangkol back and sides, gold die-cast tuners, tortise shell pickguard, O series dot inlays, available in Natural finish, current mfg.

MSR	$339	$240	$175	$125

Add $20 for left-handed configuration (HW90LH). Add $30 for 12-string configuration (HW90-12).

HW200 - auditorium-size body, mahogany back, sides and neck, spruce top, hardwood fingerboard, 18 frets, open tuners, adjustable tension rod, available in Natural finish, current mfg.

MSR	$105	$75	$50	$20

HW220 - dreadnought-size body, mahogany back, sides and neck, spruce top, hardwood fingerboard, 20 frets, open tuners, adjustable tension rod, available in Natural finish, current mfg.

MSR	$139	$100	$65	$35

HW300 (HW-300CM) - dreadnought style, mahogany top, round soundhole, single body binding, 5-stripe rosette, black pickguard, mahogany back/sides/neck, 14/20-fret rosewood fingerboard with white dot inlay, rosewood bridge with white pins, 3-per-side open tuners, available in Natural Satin finish, mfg. 1994-current.

MSR	$189	$150	$95	$65

Add $10 for Natural Gloss finish (Model HW300G). Add $20 for Gloss Sunburst finish (Model HW300G-SB). Add $35 for Trans. Black (HW300G-TBK), Trans. Blue (HW300G-TB), or Trans. Wine Red (HW300G-TWR).

HW300E - similar to the HW300 except has Shadow electronic, available in Amber, Gloss, or Sunburst finish, current mfg.

MSR	$249	$175	$125	$80

HW400 (HMW400) - dreadnought body, spruce top, round soundhole, bound body, 5-stripe rosette, black pickguard, mahogany back/sides/neck, 14/20-fret rosewood fingerboard with white dot inlay, rosewood bridge with white pins, 3-per-side covered tuners, available in Natural and Sunburst finishes, mfg. 1990-99.

		$200	$130	$90

Last MSR was $269.

Add $20 for left-handed configuration (Model HW400 LH). Add $60 for Black finish.

Hohner HMW 600
courtesy Hohner

GRADING	100%	EXCELLENT	AVERAGE

HW12 - similar to the HW400, except features ashwood back/sides, multiple body binding, bound neck/headstock, 12-string configuration, 6-per-side covered tuners, available in Natural finish, disc. 1999.

	$250	$175	$125
		Last MSR was $339.	

HW420 - dreadnought-size body, Siberian willow top, back and sides, mahogany neck, rosewood fibgerboard, 20 frets, die cast tuners, multi-ply binding, available in Natural, Trans. Black, Cherry Sunburst, Tobacco, Emerald Green, or Amber finishes, current mfg.

MSR	$269	$200	$125	$75

HW440 - dreadnought-size body with cutaway, mahogany back, side, top and neck, rosewood fingerboard, 20 frets, passive pickup with volume and tone control, die-cast tuners, available in Natural, Tobacco, Trans. Black, or Trans. Wine Red finishes, current mfg.

MSR	$299	$225	$150	$95

Add $10 for left-hand Model (Model HW440LH).

HMW600 - similar to HMW400, except has herringbone binding and rosette, enclosed chrome tuners, available in Black and Natural finishes, disc. 1996.

	N/A	$125	$85
		Last MSR was $290.	

HW640 - dreadnought-size body, maple back, sides and neck, solid Sitka spruce top, rosewood fingerboard, 20 frets, tortoise shell-style binding, satin finish, die-cast tuners, available in natural finish, current mfg.

MSR	$299	$225	$150	$95

Add $20 for left-hand model (Model HW640LH).

HW655 - dreadnought-size body, rosewood back and sides, solid Sitka spruce top, maple neck, rosewood fingerboard, 20 frets, tortoise shell-style binding, die cast tuners, available in Natural Gloss finish, current mfg.

MSR	$399	$299	$195	$110

HW660CEQ - dreadnought-size body with cutaway, maple back, sides and neck, solid Sitka spruce top, rosewood fingerboard, 20 frets, Shadow 4-band EQ with anti-feedback switch, Shadow pickup, die cast tuners, available in Natural finish, current mfg.

MSR	$599	$450	$300	$175

HW700S - dreadnought body, solid spruce top, round soundhole, bound body, black pickguard, mahogany back/sides/neck, 14/20-fret rosewood fingerboard with white dot inlay, rosewood bridge with white pins, 3-per-side deluxe tuners, available in Natural finish, disc. 1999.

	$295	$195	$150
		Last MSR was $389.	

HW720S - similar to HW700S, except features rosewood back and sides, available in Natural finish, disc. 1999.

	$350	$225	$150
		Last MSR was $469.	

HW750S - similar to HW700S, except features solid cedar top, ashwood back and sides, available in Natural finish, disc. 1999.

	$375	$250	$175
		Last MSR was $499.	

HMW1200 - similar to HMW400, except has 12-string configuration, 6-per-side tuner, disc. 1996.

	N/A	$150	$100
		Last MSR was $325.	

ACOUSTIC: HC MODELS

All models in this series have a round soundhole, bound body, wooden inlay rosette, 14/19-fret ebonized fingerboard, nylon strings, tied bridge, 3-per-side diecast tuners (unless otherwise noted).

HC03 STUDENT MODEL - 3/4 size body, available in Natural finish, current mfg.

MSR	$109	$80	$50	$35

HC06 - spruce top, mahogany back/sides, available in Natural finish, current mfg.

MSR	$139	$100	$70	$50

HC06E - similar to the HC06 except has Shadow electronics, current mfg.

MSR	$169	$125	$95	$65

HC09 - full-size body, mahogany neck, back and sides, spruce top, rosewood fingerboard, 18 frets, multi-ply binding, classical gold tuners, available in Natural finish, current mfg.

MSR	$189	$140	$95	$65

HC09E - similar to the HC09 except has Shadow electronics, current mfg.

MSR	$249	$175	$125	$85

HC15 - mahogany back/sides/top/neck, available in Natural Mahogany finish, disc. 1999.

	$140	$95	$65
		Last MSR was $189.	

GRADING		100%	EXCELLENT	AVERAGE

HC20 - spruce top, Philippine mahogany back/sides, available in Natural finish, disc. 1999.

		$200	$135	$90
			Last MSR was $269.	

HC30 - classical style, solid Sitka spruce top, ovangkol back and sides, gold tuners, available in Natural finish, current mfg.

MSR	$299		$215	$140	$95

HC35S - solid spruce top, rosewood back/sides, available in Natural finish, disc. 1999.

		$299	$200	$135
			Last MSR was $399.	

HMC10 - spruce top, mahogany back/sides/neck, available in Natural finish, mfg. 1991-96.

		N/A	$125	$70
			Last MSR was $220.	

HMC30 - similar to HMC10, except has rosewood back/sides.

		N/A	$150	$100
			Last MSR was $300.	

**Hohner HMC30
courtesy Hohner**

ACOUSTIC: EA & EC MODELS

EA55CEQ - single cutaway body, spruce top, oval soundhole, bound body, striped rosette, ashwood back/sides, mahogany neck, 22-fret rosewood fingerboard with white dot inlay, rosewood bridge, 2 per side chrome tuners, piezo bridge pickup, volume/4-band EQ controls, available in Natural or Trans. Red finishes, disc 2001.

	$375	$250	$150
		Last MSR was $499.	

EA12 - similar to EA55CEQ, except features a 12-string configuration, 6-per-side tuners, available in Trans. Black finish, disc. 1999.

	$425	$275	$195
		Last MSR was $569.	

EA60CEQ - similar to EA55CEQ, except features maple top, available in Trans. Blue or Trans. Black finishes, disc 2001.

	$395	$250	$175
		Last MSR was $525.	

EA65CEQ - medium body size, single cutaway, solid Sitka spruce top, ovangkol back and sides, gold die cast tuners, Shadow electronics, available in Natural finish, current mfg.

MSR	$429		$305	$225	$150

EA95CEQ "EL BACHATERO" - medium-size body with cutaway, mahogany neck and sides, arched mahogany back, spruce top, rosewood fingerboard with mother-of-pearl diamond position markers, 24 frets, Shadow 4-band EQ with anti-feedback switch, Shadow pickup, die cast tuners, 3-per-side tuners, available in Black, Natural, Trans. Red, or Trans. Blue finishes, current mfg.

MSR	$525		$395	$250	$175

EA100CEQ - similar to EA55CEQ, except features a flamed maple top, available in Natural finish, disc. 1999.

	$450	$295	$200
		Last MSR was $599.	

EA120CEQ - similar to EA55CEQ, except features a solid cedar top, available in Natural finish, disc 2001.

	$475	$300	$200
		Last MSR was $629.	

EA140CEQ - jumbo size body with cutaway, rosewood back and sides, solid cedar top, mahogany neck, rosewood fingerboard, 20 frets, Shadow 4-band EQ with anti-feedback switch, Shadow pickup, die cast tuners, 3-per-side tuners, available in Natural finish, disc 2001.

	$490	$310	$200
		Last MSR was $649.	

EC280CEQ (EC280EQ) - single cutaway classical style, spruce top, round soundhole, bound body, striped rosette, mahogany back/sides/neck, 19-fret rosewood fingerboard, rosewood bridge, slotted headstock, 3-per-side gold tuners, piezo bridge pickup, volume/4-band EQ controls, available in Natural finish, current mfg.

MSR	$499		$375	$250	$150

**Hohner EA60CEQ
courtesy Hohner**

GRADING	100%	EXCELLENT	AVERAGE

ACOUSTIC ELECTRIC BASS

EAB40 - single cutaway body, spruce top, oval soundhole, bound body, striped rosette, ashwood back/sides, mahogany neck, 22-fret rosewood fingerboard with white dot inlay, rosewood bridge, 2 per side chrome tuners, piezo bridge pickup, volume/4-band EQ controls, available in Natural finish, disc 2001.

	$475	$300	$200

Last MSR was $625.

Add $70 for maple top with Sunburst finish (Model EAB50).

EAB65 - medium sized body with single cutaway, solid Sitka spruce top, ovangkol back and sides, pearloid O series dot markers and bridge inlays, 20 fret fingerboard, Shadow electronics, gold die-cast tuners, available in Natural finish, mfg. 2002-current.

MSR	$569	$400	$295	$185

Add $20 for left-handed configuration.

TWP600B - single cutaway dreadnought style, spruce top, triangle soundhole, bound body, 3-stripe rosette, mahogany back/sides/neck, 20-fret rosewood fingerboard with white dot inlay, strings through rosewood bridge, 2 per side chrome tuners, piezo electric bridge pickup, 3-band EQ system, available in Black, Blue Sunburst, Natural, Pumpkin Burst, or Trans. Red finishes, mfg. 1992-96.

	N/A	$350	$215

Last MSR was $650.

HOLIDAY
See chapter on House Brands.

This trademark has been identified as a House Brand distributed by Montgomery Wards and Alden's department stores. Author/researcher Willie G. Moseley also reports seeing a catalog reprint showing Holiday instruments made by Harmony, Kay, **and** Danelectro. Additional information in regards to instruments with this trademark will be welcome, **especially** any Danelectro with a Holiday logo on the headstock. Future updates will be included in upcoming editions of the *Blue Book of Acoustic Guitars*, (Source: Willie G. Moseley, *Stellas & Stratocasters*).

HOLLENBECK, BILL
Instruments currently built in Lincoln, Illinois.

Luthier Bill Hollenbeck took a serious interest in guitars as a youth, and used to modify his own instruments in his attempt to improve them. Hollenbeck has a Master's Degree in Industrial Arts, and taught electronics to high school students for twenty-five years. During his teaching years, Hollenbeck met well-known midwestern luthier Bill Barker in 1970, and served as Barker's apprentice as he learned the art of guitar construction. In 1990, Hollenbeck left education to devote himself full-time to guitar building, restoration, and repair. Hollenbeck was featured at the Smithsonian Institute in 1996 and currently offers a range of guitar models. Prices range from $3,800 to $6,800 Call Hollenbeck directly for more information, (Source: Hal Hammer).

ACOUSTIC

Hollenbeck currently handcrafts archtop guitars with aged Sitka spruce tops, and back and sides from Bird's-eye, flame, or quilted maple. The truss rod, fingerboard, pickguard, bridge, saddle, and tailpiece are matching ebony or rosewood. Metal parts are polished brass and 24kt gold plated or nickled, and inlays are constructed with mother-of-pearl or abalone. Colors include blonde or lacquer shading. Scale lengths include 24 27/32" or 25 11/32". Models have 2 f-holes, and 3-per-side headstocks.

Some of the models include the Reminisce, which has an 16" body, The Simplicity, which has a 17" body, the Jazz Reflections, and that also has a 17" body, and the Time Traveler, which features the massive 18" body. There is also the Ebony-n-Blue, which was built for Scott Chinery and comes in a 18" body. The Fleur-de-lis is a guitar that features this type of flower all over the guitar and has a 17" sized body.

Prices include a hardshell case, and a floating pickup. An optional Fishman transducer can be mounted in the saddle if requested by the customer.

JIM NICHOLS SIGNATURE SERIES

The Jim Nichols Signature guitar features a semi-hollowbody, carved top and backs, and Seymour Duncan pickups. It has other options such as gold hardware and a vibrato tailpiece. It is available in two variations the A Series and the B Series. Contact Hollenbeck for more information on Jim Nichols.

HOLLISTER GUITARS
Instruments currently built in Dedham, Massachusetts.

Luthier Kent Hollister is currently offering high quality, custom built guitars such as the **Archtop** ($3,000), **Semi-hollow** ($1,900), **Carved Top Solid Body** ($1,500), and **The Plank** ($1,200). The Plank is an electric solid body with neck-through design. Hollister has also created the **Archtop Bass** ($2,800), which features a central soundhole (as opposed to f-holes). Just the thing to swing with the archtop guitarists! For further information contact luthier Kent Hollister directly (see Trademark Index).

HOLST, STEPHEN
Instruments currently built in Eugene, Oregon since 1984.

Luthier Stephen Holst began building guitars in 1984, and through inspiration and refinement developed the models currently offered. Holst draws on his familiarity of Pacific Northwest tonewoods in developing tonal qualities in his handcrafted instruments. Holst specifically works with the customer commissioning the instrument, tailoring the requests to the specific guitar. In addition, Holst has experimented in other designs such as nylon string, 7- and 12-string, and baritone archtops.

ACOUSTIC

Luthier Holst chooses aged spruce and maple for the tops and backs, and figured eastern hard rock maple for the neck. Fingerboards, bridges, finger rests, and tailpieces are constructed from ebony. The archtop guitars are finished in Natural Blonde or Sunburst, and feature gold Schaller M6 tuning machines. Both models in the archtop series are offered in a 16", 17", or 18" body width, and have a number of options available, many at no additional charge.

The Holst **K 100 Traditional** model is designed as a tribute to past glories in archtop construction. The K 100 models are appointed with multiple layers of fine-lined binding throughout the neck, body, f-holes, headstock, and finger rest. The K 100 has an additional option of engraved mother-of-pearl inlays on the fretboard, headstock, and tailpiece. The base list price is set at $4,000.

Holst's **K 200** series is a contemporary look at the evolution of the archtop design. The K 200 has a more modern feel in its simplicity in design, yet the same attention to building quality as the K 100. The K 200's understated elegance is captured in the all wood binding on the body, neck, and peghead. The f-holes are more contoured, the fingerboard and tailpiece are unadorned, and the finger rest is narrower in design. Base asking price begins at $3,500.

There is also a nylon string guitar available and a Jazz model K-250, which can be found in the *Blue Book of Electric Guitars*.

HONDO

Instruments currently produced in Korea. Distributed by MBT International of Charleston, South Carolina. Between 1974 to early 1980s some models were produced in Japan.

The Hondo guitar company was originally formed in 1969 when Jerry Freed and Tommy Moore of the International Music Corporation (IMC) of Fort Worth, Texas, combined with the recently formed Samick company. IMC's intent was to introduce modern manufacturing techniques and American quality standards to the Korean guitar manufacturing industry.

The Hondo concept was to offer an organized product line and solid entry level market instruments at a fair market price. The original Korean products were classical and steel-string acoustic guitars. In 1972, the first crudely built Hondo electrics were built. However, two years later the product line took a big leap forward in quality under the new Hondo II logo. Hondo also began limited production of guitars in Japan in 1974.

By 1975, Hondo had distributors in 70 countries worldwide, and had expanded to producing stringed instruments at the time. In 1976, over 22,000 of the Bi-Centennial banjos were sold. The company also made improvements to the finish quality on their products, introduced scalloped bracing on acoustics, and began using a higher quality brand of tuning machines.

Hondo was one of the first overseas guitar builders to feature American-built DiMarzio pickups on the import instruments beginning in 1978. By this year, a number of Hondo II models featured designs based on classic American favorites. In 1979, over 790,000 Hondo instruments were sold worldwide. All guitar production returned to Korea in 1983. At that point, the product line consisted of 485 different models!

In 1985, IMC acquired major interest in the Charvel/Jackson company, and began dedicating more time and interest in the higher end guitar market. The Hondo trademark went into mothballs around 1987. However, Jerry Freed started the Jerry Freed International company in 1989, and acquired the rights to the Hondo trademark in 1991 (the "Est. 1969" tagline was added to the Hondo logo at this time). Freed began distribution of a new line of Hondo guitars. In 1993, the revamped company was relocated to Stuart, Florida; additional models added to the line were produced in China and Taiwan.

The Hondo Guitar Company was purchased by the MBT International in 1995. MBT also owns and distributes J.B. Player instruments. The Hondo product line was revamped for improved quality while maintaining student-friendly prices.Hondo celebrated their 25th year of manufacturing electric guitars in 1997, (Source: Tom Malm, MBT International; and Michael Wright, *Guitar Stories,* Volume One).

Hondo guitars generally carried a new retail price range between $179 and $349 (up to $449). While their more unusually designed model may command a slghtly higher price, the average used price range is between $100-$325, depdning on configuration, original condition, and overall coolness in today's vintage marketplace.

ACOUSTIC

Hondo currently offers a wide range of dreadnought and classical style guitars. The five models in the **H18** (list $289) series feature select spruce tops, mahogany back/sides, 2-ply binding, chrome tuners, and a gloss finish; models like the **H124** (list $299) and **H125** (list $285) have nato back/sides, and single-ply binding. The Classical guitar models feature a variety of select spruce, nato, and agathis tops, backs, and sides.

Older models, like the 12-string **H-180** with a trapeze tailpiece, may be worth between $100 to $125 on the secondary market.

The Deluxe Series was first offered in 1982, and featured 11 classical and 22 steel string acoustic models.

The Professional Series was introduced in 1982, and had a number of classical and steel string models.

Standard Series guitars were also introduced in the early 1980s, and were Hondo's single or double pickup entry level guitars. The acoustic models were beginner's guitars as well. The Standard line did offer 11 banjo models of different add-ons, and 4 distinct mandolins.

HOOTENANNY

See chapter on House Brands.

This trademark has been identified as a "sub-brand" from the budget line of Chris guitars by the Jackson-Guldan company. However, another source suggests that the trademark was marketed by the Monroe Catalog House, (Source: Willie G. Moseley, *Stellas & Stratocasters*).

HOPF

Instruments previously built in Germany from the late 1950s through the mid 1980s.

The Hopf name was established back in 1669, and lasted through the mid 1980s. The company produced a wide range of good quality solid body, semi-hollow, and archtop guitars from the late 1950s on. While some of the designs do bear an American design influence, the liberal use of local woods (such as beech, sycamore, or European pine) and certain departures from conventional styling give them an individual identity, (Source: Tony Bacon, *The Ultimate Guitar Book*).

HOPF, DIETER

Instruments currently built in Germany. Distributed by Luthier Music Corporation, of New York City, New York.

Dieter Hopf guitars are currently available through the Luthier Music Corporation. Dieter has a web site for its guitars, but it is all in German (www.hopfguitars.com). For current information on pricing and specifications, contact the Luthier Music Corporation directly (see Trademark Index).

HOWARD (U.S. MFG.)

Instruments previously built in New York, New York circa 1930s.

The construction technique and overall appearance indicate the possibility that Epaminondas "Epi" Stathopoulos' Epiphone company built instruments under the Howard trademark for a dealer or distributor. Models that have appeared in the vintage guitar market have the Howard brand name and fleur-de-lis inlaid on the headstock. The dealer or distributor involved in the Howard trademark has yet to be identified, (Source: Paul Bechtoldt, *Vintage Guitar Magazine*, February 1996).

HOYER

Current production instruments are distributed internationally by Mario Pellarin Musikwaren of Cologne, Germany. Distributed in Germany by Fa. Mario Pellarin. Instruments previously built in West Germany from the late 1950s through the late 1980s.

The Hoyer company produced a wide range of good to high quality solid body, semi-hollow body, and archtop guitars, with some emphasis on the later during the 1960s. During the early 1970s, there was some production of solid bodied guitars with an emphasis on classic American designs.

The Hoyer trademark was re-introduced in the 1990s with the cheerful "A Legend is Back!" motto. Hoyer is currently offering a wide range of acoustic and electric guitars in Europe; a U.S. distributor has not yet been named. Further information on Hoyer instruments is available through the company; contact them directly (see Trademark Index), (Source: Tony Bacon and Paul Day, *The Guru's Guitar Guide*).

ACOUSTIC

Hoyer has several acoustic models (primarily dreadnought designs) and two resonator guitar models. Models fall under the **Select Top Series** (laminated bodies), **Solid Top Series** (solid wood top and laminated back and sides), and the **Electric Acoustic Series** (which has Fishman Matrix and Prefix systems).

The five Hoyer classical and flamenco acoustic models are currently built in Spain, and are offered in the **Solid Top Series** (laminated wood back and sides) or the **Solid Body Series** (Solid Body Series models still have a solid wood top).

Both the classical style **HC-150E** and **HC-200E** models have an L.R. Baggs RT preamp and ribbon pickup. Both have a solid cedar top, rosewood back and sides, and ebony fingerboards.

HUIPE, BENITO

Instruments currently built in Paracho, Mexico. Distributed by Casa Talamantes of Albuquerque, New Mexico.

Benito Huipe started making guitars in his hometown of Paracho (Michoacan) Mexico, but as a youth, he moved to Los Angeles, California, where he perfected his craft during his 22 years there. While he makes all types of guitars, he is particularly known for the high quality of his flamenco guitars. In 1994, he returned to live permanently in Paracho, and continues to produce guitars.

Huipe's basic flamenco guitar of cypress and either spruce or cedar sells for $1,250. Models are available through Casa Talamantes in New Mexico. For more information refer to the Casa Talamantes web site (see Trademark Index).

HUMPHREY, THOMAS

Instruments currrently produced in Gardiner, New York. Previous production was located in New York City, New York.

Luthier Thomas Humphrey has been building classical guitars for the past 30 years. In 1985, Humphrey startled the lutherie world when he introduced the **Millennium** models, which featured an innovative, tapered body design and elevated fingerboard. This innovation to the classical guitar represented some of the very few alterations to the fundamental design of the traditional Antonio Torres model. Though initially questioned, the new design has since been universally accepted by both players and other guitar makers.

Luthier Humphrey is known for producing primarily spruce top guitars and (almost exclusively) Brazilian rosewood back and sides. Humphrey produced guitars for the first 27 years in New York City; his workshop now is located in the countryside near the village of Gardiner, New York. Presently, his guitars are used in both recording and concert situations by many of the world's leading guitarists. Humphrey presently produces an estimated twenty-one guitars a year.

Though always changing and modifying the design as well as seeking new innovations, the current embodiment has become somewhat standardized due to a collaboration with the C.F. Martin Guitar company. The C.F. Martin company currently is producing three different models, (Biography courtesy Thomas Humphrey, October, 1997).

According to the Martin Guitar company's Sounding Board newsletter, "a survey of 100 of the world's top classical guitarists revealed that approximately 20% play a Humphrey Millennium."

ACOUSTIC

Humphrey's classical design features primarily spruce tops and (almost exclusively) Brazilian rosewood back and sides. The classical model design has a tapered body and elevated fingerboard. For further specifications and questions about pricing, contact luthier Humphrey directly (see Trademark Index).

In 1996, Humphrey contracted a standardized design of his design to the C.F. Martin Guitar company of Nazareth, Pennsylvania. The Martin-built versions of Humphrey's design, **Model C-TSH** (Standard Series) and **Model C-1R** (1 Series), were available in late 1996 (nearer to early 1997). The Martin version of the Humphrey design utilizes both spruce and cedar soundboards as well as rosewood and other back and side material in order to reach a wide range of price points. These guitars also have met with tremendous response from many different styles of guitarists.

In late 1997, the C.F. Martin company introduced the Sting Signature version of the Humphrey design (**Model C-MSH** Limited Edition).

HUSS & DALTON
Instruments currently produced in Staunton, Virgina.

Huss and Dalton is located in the heart of the Shenadoah Valley of Virgina, which is rich in the tradition of fine acoustic music. Huss and Dalton produce fine quality acoustic guitars as well as banjos. Models start at $2,650 and range up to $4,865. For information on the crew, options, information, and the company refer to the web site (see Trademark Index).

HUTTL
Instruments previously built in Germany from the 1950s to the 1970s.

The Huttl trademark may not be as well-known as other German guitar builders such as Framus, Hopf, or Klira. While their designs may be as original as the others, the quality of workmanship is still fairly rough in comparison. Research continues into the Huttl trademark.

HUVARD, ANTHONY J.
Instruments currently built in Sandston, Virginia.

Luthier Anthony J. Huvard builds a limited number of high quality guitars. Huvard also offers a very comprehensive web site called Luthiers Around The World, which offers information regarding independent luthiers and lutherie products. For additional information, please contact Anthony J. Huvard directly via email (see Trademark Index).

HYUNDAI
Instruments currently built in Korea. Distributed in the U.S. through Hyundai Guitars of West Nyack, New York.

Hyndai offers a range of medium quality guitars designed for beginning students that have designs based on popular American classics.

H

NOTES

H

H is for half-price! You'd expect nothing less for half a guitar.

Section I

IBANEZ

Instruments currently produced in Japan since the early 1960s, and some models produced in Korea since the 1980s. Ibanez guitars are distributed in the U.S. by Ibanez USA (Hoshino) in Bensalem, Pennsylvania. Other distribution offices include Quebec (for Canada), Sydney (for Australia), and Auckland (for New Zealand).

The Ibanez trademark originated from the Fuji plant in Matsumoto, Japan. In 1932, the Hoshino Gakki Ten, Inc. factory began producing instruments under the Ibanez trademark. The factory and offices were burned down during World War II, and were revived in 1950. By the mid 1960s, Hoshino was producing instruments under various trademarks such as Ibanez, Star, King's Stone, Jamboree, and Goldentone.

In the mid 1950s, Harry Rosenbloom opened the Medley Music store outside Philadelphia. As the Folk Music boom began in 1959, Rosenbloom decided to begin producing acoustic guitars and formed the Elger company (named after Rosenbloom's children, Ellen and Gerson). Elger acoustics were produced in Ardmore, Pennsylvania between 1959 and 1965.

In the 1960s, Rosenbloom travelled to Japan and found a number of companies that he contracted to produce the Elger acoustics. Later, he was contacted by Hoshino to form a closer business relationship. The first entry level solid body guitars featuring original designs first surfaced in the mid 1960s, some bearing the Elger trademark, and some bearing the Ibanez logo. One of the major keys to the perceived early Ibanez quality is due to Hoshino shipping the guitars to the Elger factory in Ardmore. The arriving guitars would be re-checked, and set up prior to shipping to the retailer. Many distributors at the time would just simply ship product to the retailer, and let surprises occur at the unboxing. By reviewing the guitars in a separate facility, Hoshino/Ibanez could catch any problems before the retailer – so the number of perceived flawed guitars was reduced at the retail/sales end. In England, Ibanez was imported by the Summerfield Brothers, and sometimes had either the CSL trademark or no trademark at all on the headstock. Other U.K. distributors used the Antoria brand name, and in Australia they were rebranded with a Jason logo.

**Ibanez AC10
courtesy Ibanez**

In the early 1970s, the level of quality rose as well as the level of indebtedness to classic American designs. It has been argued that Ibanez' reproductions of Stratocasters and Les Pauls may be equal to or better than the quality of Norlin era Gibsons or CBS era Fenders. While the *Blue Book of Acoustic Guitars* would rather stay neutral on this debate (we just list them, not rate them), it has been suggested by outside sources that next time *close your eyes and let your hands and ears be the judge*. In any event, the unauthorized reproductions eventually led to Fender's objections to Tokai's imports (the infamous *headstock sawing* rumour), and Norlin/Gibson taking Hoshino/Ibanez/Elger into court for patent infringement.

When Ibanez began having success basically reproducing Gibson guitars and selling them at a lower price on the market, Norlin (Gibson's owner at the time) sent off a cease-and-desist warning. Norlin's lawyers decided that the best way to proceed was to defend the decorative (the headstock) versus the functional (body design), and on June 28th, 1977 the case of Gibson vs. Elger Co. opened in Philadelphia Federal District Court. In early 1978, a resolution was agreed upon: Ibanez would stop reproducing Gibsons if Norlin would stop suing Ibanez. The case was officially closed on February 2, 1978.

The infringement lawsuit ironically might have been the kick in the pants that propelled Ibanez and other Japanese builders to get back into original designs. Ibanez stopped building Gibson exact reproductions, and moved on to other designs. By the early 1980s, certain guitar styles began appealing to other areas of the guitar market (notably the Hard Rock/Heavy Metal genre), and Ibanez's use of famous endorsers probably fueled the appeal. Ibanez's continuing program of original designs and artist involvement continued to work in the mid to late 1980s, and continues to support their position in the market today, (Source: Michael Wright, *Guitar Stories*, Volume One).

MODEL DATING IDENTIFICATION

In addition to the Ibanez company's model history, a serialization chart is provided in the back of the *Blue Book of Acoustic Guitars* to further aid the dating of older Ibanez guitars (not all potentiometer builders use the EIA source code, so overseas-built potentiometer codes on Japanese guitars may not help in the way of clues).

1959-1967: Elger Acoustics are built in Ardmore, Pennsylvania; and are distributed by Medley Music, Grossman Music (Cleveland), Targ and Dinner (Chicago), and the Roger Balmer Company on the west coast. Elger imported from Japan the Tama acoustics, Ibanez acoustics, and some Elger electrics.

1971-1977: The copy era begins for Ibanez (Faithful Reproductions) as solid body electrics based on Gibson, Fender, and Rickenbacker models (both bolt-ons and set-necks) arrive. These are followed by copies of Martin, Guild, Gibson, and Fender acoustics. Ibanez opens an office and warehouse outside of Philadelphia, Pennsylvania to maintain quality control on imported guitars in 1972.

1973: Ibanez's Artist series acoustics and electrics are debuted. In 1974, the Artist-style neck joint; later in 1976 an Artist Les Paul arrives. This sets the stage for the LP variant double cutaway Artist model in 1978.

1975: Ibanez began to use a meaningful numbering system as part of their warranty program. In general, the letter stands for the month (January = A, February = B, etc.) and the following two digits are the year.

**Ibanez AJ307 CE 7-String
courtesy Ibanez**

GRADING		100%	EXCELLENT	AVERAGE

1981-1987: In 1984, the Lonestar acoustics are introduced, and Ibanez responds to the MIDI challenge of Roland by unveiling the IMG-2010 MIDI guitar system.

1992-1993: The ATL acoustic/electric design is unveiled, and RT Series guitars debut in 1993.

This overview, while brief, will hopefully identify years, trends, and series. For further information and deeper clarification, please refer to Michael Wright's *Guitar Stories,* Volume One).

ACOUSTIC: ARTWOOD (AC, AG, AJ, & AW) SERIES

AC Series models specifications: body length 18 1/2", body width 14 3/4", body depth 4 1/2". AG Series models specifications: body length 19", body width 14 3/4", body depth 4". AW Series models specifications: body length 20", body width 15 3/4", body depth 4 3/4".

AC10 - grand concert body, solid Sitka spruce top, mahogany back/sides/neck, rosewood fingerboard with dot inlay, tortoise pickguard, Natural finish, current mfg.

MSR	$320		$225	$170	$115

AC50 LG - OM-style body, solid Sitka spruce top, round soundhole, tortoise shell pickguard, maple back/sides/neck, 14/20-fret rosewood fingerboard with pearl dot inlay, rosewood bridge with white black dot pins, Ibanez/'AW' logo on peghead, chrome hardware, 3-per-side die-cast tuners available in Natural Low Gloss finish, mfg. 1998-2002.

			$250	$160	$115

Last MSR was $340.

AC70 LG - similar to the AC50 LG, except features mahogany back/sides, available in Natural Low Gloss finish, mfg. 1997-99.

			$275	$195	$125

Last MSR was $399.

AC100 - OM-style body, solid Sitka spruce top, round soundhole, tortoise shell pickguard, bound body, mahogany back/sides/neck, 14/20-fret rosewood fingerboard with pearl dot inlay, rosewood bridge with white black dot pins, Ibanez/'AW' logo on peghead, chrome hardware, 3-per-side die - cast tuners, available in Natural Low Gloss finish, disc. 1998.

			N/A	$250	$150

Last MSR was $449.

AC300 - similar to the AC100, except features rosewood back/sides, bound fingerboard/peghead, abalone dot fingerboard inlay, Grover tuners, available in Natural Gloss finish, disc. 1999.

			$475	$295	$200

Last MSR was $599.

AC900 - similar to the AC100, except features solid Engelmann spruce top, rosewood back/sides, bound fingerboard/peghead, abalone snowflake fingerboard inlay, gold hardware, Grover tuners, available in Antique Stained Gloss finish, disc. 1999.

			$875	$550	$375

Last MSR was $1,099.

AG200 - tight waist/rounded lower bout body with single rounded cutaway, solid Engelmann spruce top, round soundhole, tortoise shell pickguard, bound body, mahogany back/sides/neck, 14/20-fret rosewood fingerboard with pearl diamond inlay, rosewood bridge with snowflake inlay, white black dot pins, Ibanez/'AW' logo on peghead, chrome hardware, 3-per-side Grover tuners, available in Natural Low Gloss finish, disc. 1998.

			$475	$395	$225

Last MSR was $669.

AG200E - similar to the AG200 execpt has a Slim Jim pickup, volume/3-band EQ controls, available in Natural Gloss finish, disc. 1999.

			$675	$400	$275

Last MSR was $829.

AG600E - similar to the AG200 E, except features Mexican abalone rosette/binding, bound fingerboard/peghead, snowflake inlay on bridge, Fishman pickup, volume/3-band EQ controls, available in Natural Gloss finish, disc. 1999.

			$799	$495	$325

Last MSR was $999.

AJ307 CE 7-STRING - 7-string configuration, tight waist/rounded lower bout body with single rounded cutaway, solid Sitka spruce top, round soundhole, tortoiseshell pickguard, bound body, rosewood back/sides/neck, 14/20-fret rosewood fingerboard with abalone dot inlay, rosewood bridge with white bridgepins, Ibanez/'AW' logo on peghead, gold hardware, 4/3-per-side Grover tuners, Fishman transducer, volume/3-band EQ controls, available in Natural Gloss finish, current mfg.

MSR	$1,100		$770	$540	$375

AW10 - dreadnought body, solid Sitka spruce top, mahogany back and sides, tortise pickguard, chrome hardware, Natural finish, mfg. 2000-current.

MSR	$320		$225	$165	$115

AW10CE - similar to the AW10 except has a single cutaway, Fishman Sonicore pickup and Ibanez AEQ-SS EQ, Natural finish, current mfg.

MSR	$480		$340	$240	$150

AW20 - dreadnought body, solid Sitka spruce top, maple back and sides, tortise pickguard, chrome hardware, available in Honey Gloss Sunburst or Gloss Burgandy Sunburst finishes, new 2003.

MSR	$370		$275	$185	$130

GRADING		100%	EXCELLENT	AVERAGE

AW20CE - Similar to the AW20 except has a single cutaway, Fishman Sonicore pickup and Ibanez AEQ-SS EQ, same finishes, current mfg.

MSR	$500		$350	$250	$150

AW70 - dreadnought style body, solid Sitka spruce top, round soundhole, tortoise shell pickguard, bound body, mahogany back/sides/neck, 14/20-fret rosewood fingerboard with pearl dot inlay, rosewood bridge with white black dot pins, Ibanez/'AW' logo on peghead, chrome hardware, 3-per-side die-cast tuners, available in Natural Low Gloss finish, mfg. 1997-99.

$299 $195 $125
Last MSR was $399.

**Ibanez AW10
courtesy Ibanez**

AW70 LG - dreadnought style, solid Sitka spruce top, round soundhole, tortoise shell pickguard, bound body, mahogany back/sides/neck, 14/20-fret rosewood fingerboard with pearl dot inlay, rosewood bridge with white black dot pins, Ibanez/'AW' logo on peghead, chrome hardware, 3-per-side die-cast tuners, Slim Jim pickup, volume/3-band EQ controls, available in Natural Low Gloss finish, mfg. 1998-99.

$275 $195 $125
Last MSR was $399.

AW70 CE LG Limited Edition - similar to the AW70 LG, except features a single rounded cutaway body, available in Natural Low Gloss finish, mfg. 1998-1999.

$425 $295 $195
Last MSR was $599.

AW100 - dreadnought style body, solid Sitka spruce top, round soundhole, tortoiseshell pickguard, bound body, mahogany back/sides/neck, 14/20-fret rosewood fingerboard with pearl dot inlay, rosewood bridge with white black dot pins, Ibanez/'AW' logo on peghead, chrome hardware, 3-per-side die-cast tuners, available in Natural gloss finish, current mfg.

MSR	$450		$315	$225	$150

AW100 CE-NT - dreadnought style body with single rounded cutaway, solid Sitka spruce top, round soundhole, tortoise shell pickguard, bound body, mahogany back/sides/neck, 14/20-fret rosewood fingerboard with pearl dot inlay, rosewood bridge with white black dot pins, Ibanez/'AW' logo on peghead, chrome hardware, 3-per-side die-cast tuners, Slim Jim pickup, volume/3-band EQ controls, available in Natural gloss finish, current mfg.

MSR	$700		$550	$325	$225

Add $50 for Black gloss finish (Model AW100 CE BK). Add $50 for left-handed configuration (AW100LCE NT).

AW112 NT - similar to AW100, except in 12-string configuration, 6-per-side tuners, available in Natural gloss finish, mfg. 1997-2000.

$425 $295 $195
Last MSR was $600.

AW200 - dreadnought body, solid Englemann spruce top, flamed maple back and sides, mahogany neck, rosewood fingerboard and bridge, dot inlay, 3-per-side tuners, matching headstock, available in Natural or Vintage Violin finishes, current mfg.

MSR	$580		$410	$290	$175

AW200CE - similar to the AW200 except has a Fishman Acoustic Matrix and Fishman prefix EQ, Natural finish, current mfg.

MSR	$850		$595	$425	$275

AW300 - similar to the AW100, except features rosewood back/sides, abalone dot inlay, gold Grover tuners, available in Natural gloss finish, disc 2000, reintroduced 2003.

MSR	$600		$475	$295	$175

AW300CE - similar to the AW300, except features rosewood back/sides, abalone dot inlay, gold Grover tuners, Fishman pickup, volume/3-band EQ controls, available in Natural gloss finish, current mfg.

MSR	$900		$695	$425	$295

AW400 - dreadnought body, solid Englemann spruce top, mahogany sides and solid mahogany back, mahogany neck, rosewood fingerboard, tortoise pickguard, Natural finish, gold hardware, disc 2002.

$420 $305 $175
Last MSR was $600.

AW400CE - similar to the AW400 except has a Fishman Acoustic Matrix and Fishman prefix EQ, Natural finish, current mfg.

$630 $450 $325
Last MSR was $900.

**Ibanez AW100
courtesy Ibanez**

GRADING		100%	EXCELLENT	AVERAGE

AW500 - similar to the AW100, except features solid Engelmann spruce top, rosewood back/sides, herringbone rosette/body binding, abalone snowflake inlay, gold Grover tuners, available in Natural Gloss finish, current mfg.

MSR	$650	$475	$350	$225

AW500CE - similar to the AW500, except features rosewood back/sides, abalone dot inlay, gold Grover tuners, Fishman pickup, volume/3-band EQ controls, available in Natural gloss finish, current mfg.

MSR	$950	$675	$475	$325

AW600 - similar to the AW100, except features solid Engelmann spruce top, rosewood back/sides, Mexican abalone rosette/body binding, abalone snowflake inlay, gold Grover tuners, available in Natural gloss finish, disc. 1998.

		$525	$425	$250
			Last MSR was $749.	

AW900 AN - similar to the AW100, except features solid Engelmann spruce top, rosewood back/sides, Mexican abalone rosette/body binding, abalone snowflake inlay, gold Grover tuners. Available in Antique Stained gloss finish, disc. 1999.

		$895	$550	$375
			Last MSR was $1,099.	

ACOUSTIC: CHARLESTON SERIES

CR80 - auditorium style, spruce top, bound f-holes, 3-layer black pickguard, nato back/sides, mahogany neck, 14/22-fret bound rosewood fingerboard with pearl dot inlay, rosewood bridge with white black dot pins, blackface peghead with screened logo, 3-per-side chrome tuners, available in Brown Sunburst and Cherry Sunburst finishes, mfg. 1994-96.

		N/A	$225	$150
			Last MSR was $500.	

CR100E - similar to CR80, except has thinner body, piezo bridge pickup, 4-band EQ, disc. 1996.

		N/A	$325	$200
			Last MSR was $700.	

ACOUSTIC: CLASSIC (GA) SERIES

GA5 - classical style, spruce top, round soundhole, wood inlay rosette, mahogany back/sides, mahogany neck, 12/19-fret rosewood fingerboard, rosewood tied bridge, 3-per-side chrome tuners, available in Natural Gloss finish, mfg. 1998-current.

MSR	$200	$140	$100	$70

GA5TCE - similar to the GA5 except has a single cutaway and a Piezo Transducer with a 3 band EQ, current mfg.

MSR	$400	$280	$210	$135

GA6 CE - classical style body with single rounded cutaway, spruce top, round soundhole, wood inlay rosette, mahogany back/sides, mahogany neck, 12/19-fret rosewood fingerboard, rosewood tied bridge, 3-per-side gold tuners, piezo pickup, volume/4-band EQ, available in Natural gloss finish, mfg. 1998-current.

MSR	$400	$275	$195	$125

GA7 - similar to the GA5, except features rosewood back/sides, gold tuners, available in Natural Gloss finish, mfg. 1998-2000.

		$160	$115	$80
			Last MSR was $229.	

GA10 - classical style, spruce top, round soundhole, bound body, wood inlay rosette, nato back/sides, mahogany neck, 12/19-fret rosewood fingerboard, rosewood tied bridge, rosewood peghead veneer, 3-per-side chrome tuners with pearloid buttons, available in Natural Gloss finish, mfg. 1994-96, 1998-99.

		$195	$120	$90
			Last MSR was $259.	

GA30 - similar to the GA10, except features mahogany back/sides, gold tuners, available in Natural gloss finish, mfg. 1998-99.

		$205	$135	$95
			Last MSR was $299.	

ACOUSTIC: DAYTRIPPER SERIES

DT5 - similar to the DT10 except has covered tuners, disc. 2000.

		$165	$135	$95
			Last MSR was $230.	

DTMA (10) - spruce top, mahogany back/sides, rosewood fingerboard with pearl dot inlay, rosewood bridge, chrome die cast tuners, available in Natural Gloss finish, mfg. 1998-current.

MSR	$270	$190	$135	$95

DT 10 CA - similar to the DT 10. Available in Natural Gloss finish, mfg. 1998-99.

		$225	$150	$100
			Last MSR was $329.	

GRADING		100%	EXCELLENT	AVERAGE

DTME - similar to the DTMA except has a Piezo transducer with 2-band EQ, available in Gloss Trans. Blue, mfg. 2000-current.

MSR	$380		$275	$175	$125

ACOUSTIC: MASA SERIES

GX90 BK - dreadnought size body with MASA 90 System (Magnetic Acoustic Solid-top Acoustic). Ibanez AP1 magnetic pickup located at neck/body joint, AEQ3M equalizer and EQ phase switch, solid Sitka Spruce top, mahogany neck, back, and sides, die-cast tuners, rosewood bridge and fretboard. Available in Black High Gloss finish, mfg. 1999-2000.

		$525	$365	$260

Last MSR was $699.

SX90 BK - similar to GX90 BK, except has single cutaway design and smaller body. 24 3/4" neck, modified triangle soundhole. Available in Black High Gloss finish, mfg. 1999-2000.

		$600	$425	$300

Last MSR was $799.

JX70 - similar to GX90 BK, except has sharp single cutaway original design and smaller body, available in Transparent Deep Blue or Transparent Blue Sunburst finishes, mfg. 2001-02.

		$350	$255	$150

Last MSR was $500.

ACOUSTIC: N SERIES

N600 - single cutaway classical style, cedar top, round soundhole, 5-stripe bound body, wooden inlay rosette, mahogany back/sides/neck, 21-fret rosewood fingerboard with pearl dot inlays, rosewood bridge with white black dot pins, 3-per-side chrome die-cast tuners, piezo pickup, volume/3-band EQ controls, available in Natural finish, mfg. 1992-94.

		N/A	$275	$175

Last MSR was $600.

Ibanez GA5
courtesy Ibanez

N601 N - similar to the N600, except features slotted peghead, gold hardware, 3-per-side open classic tuners, available in Natural finish, mfg. 1992-94.

		N/A	$300	$200

Last MSR was $680.

N700 D - single rounded cutaway dreadnought style, spruce top, round soundhole, 5-stripe bound body, wooden inlay rosette, ovankol back/sides, mahogany neck, 21-fret rosewood fingerboard with snowflake inlays, rosewood bridge with white black dot pins, 3-per-side gold die-cast tuners, piezo pickup, volume/3-band EQ controls, available in Natural finish, mfg. 1992-94.

		N/A	$325	$200

Last MSR was $700.

N800 - single cutaway jumbo style, flame maple top, round soundhole, abalone bound body and rosette, flame maple back/sides, mahogany neck, 21-fret bound rosewood fingerboard with abalone block inlays, rosewood bridge with black white dot pins, bound peghead, 3-per-side chrome die-cast tuners, piezo pickup, Matrix 4-band EQ, available in Trans. Blue or Trans. Violin finishes, mfg. 1992-94.

		N/A	$375	$250

Last MSR was $850.

N900 S - similar to N800, except has solid spruce top, gold diecast tuners, disc. 1994.

		N/A	$500	$325

Last MSR was $1,100.

ACOUSTIC: PERFORMANCE SERIES

PC5 NT - miniature jumbo style, spruce top, round soundhole, black body binding, 5-stripe rosette, nato back/sides/neck, 14/20-fret rosewood fingerboard with pearl dot inlay, rosewood bridge with white black dot pins, 3-per-side chrome covered tuners, Mini Jumbo models specifications: body length 19", body width 14 1/2", body depth 3 3/4", available in Natural low gloss finish, mfg. 1998-current.

MSR	$220		$160	$115	$85

Add $20 for limited edition Black gloss finish (Model PC5 BK). Add $20 for limited edition Tobacco Sunburst gloss finish (Model PC5 TS).

PC300CE-NT - similar to the PC-5, except has a sharp cutaway original design body and a Piezo transducer with 3 band EQ, current mfg.

MSR	$450		$315	$225	$150

Ibanez PC300CE-NT
courtesy Ibanez

PF GUITAR JAM PACK (IJP1) PACKAGE - dreadnought style, spruce top, round soundhole, black pickguard, 3-stripe rosette, nato back/sides, mahogany neck, 14/20-fret rosewood fingerboard with pearl dot inlay, rosewood bridge with black pins, 3-per-side covered tuners, available in Natural low gloss finish, current mfg.

MSR	$320	$225	$160	$115

The different Ibanez **Jam Pack** combinations include a PF guitar, gig bag, instructional video, electronic tuner, extra strings, strap, chord chart, picks, and a free subscription to *Plugged In* (the official Ibanez newsletter).

PF Guitar Jam Pack (IJP1 BK) Package - similar to the IJP1 Jam Pack, available in Black finish, mfg. 1997-current.

MSR	$340	$240	$170	$120

PF Guitar Jam Pack (IJP1 SM) Package - similar to the IJP1 Jam Pack, except features Grand Concert size acoustic, available in Natural finish, mfg. 1998-99.

$235	$165	$120

Last MSR was $330.

PF Guitar Jam Pack (IJP1 CL) Package - similar to the IJP1 Jam Pack, except features Classical acoustic, available in Natural finish, mfg. 1998-99.

$225	$160	$115

Last MSR was $319.

PF GUITAR JAM PACK (IJP1 DE AMP) PACKAGE - dreadnought style, spruce top, round soundhole, black pickguard, 3-stripe rosette, nato back/sides, mahogany neck, 14/20-fret rosewood fingerboard with pearl dot inlay, rosewood bridge with black pins, 3-per-side covered tuners, available in Natural low gloss finish, disc. 1999.

$395	$275	$190

Last MSR was $549.

The Jam Pack includes an acoustic/electric model PF guitar, 10 watt acoustic amp, gig bag, instructional video, electronic tuner, extra strings, strap, chord chart, picks, and a free subscription to Plugged In (the official Ibanez newsletter). Everything must be included to bring the full value.

PF3 - dreadnought style, spruce top, round soundhole, black pickguard, bound body, 3-stripe rosette, nato back/sides, mahogany neck, 14/20-fret rosewood fingerboard with pearl dot inlay, rosewood bridge with black white dot pins, 3-per-side chrome tuners. Available in Natural finish, mfg. 1994-97.

$155	$100	$70

Last MSR was $220.

PF5 NT - dreadnought style, spruce top, round soundhole, bound body, 5-stripe rosette, mahogany back/sides/neck, 14/20-fret rosewood fingerboard with pearl dot inlay, rosewood bridge with white black dot pins, 3-per-side chrome covered tuners, available in Natural gloss finish, mfg. 1992-current.

MSR	$260	$185	$115	$85

Add $20 for Black gloss finish (Model PF5 BK) or Gloss Marine Sunburst (Model PF5 MS). Add $40 for left-handed configuration (Model PF5 L NT).

In 1994, black pickguard was introduced.

PF5 S - similar to PF5, except features solid spruce top, pearl snowflake fingerboard inlay, mfg. 1994-96.

$275	$175	$115

Last MSR was $390.

PF512 - similar to PF5, except in 12-string configuration, 6-per-side tuners, black pickguard. Available in Natural low gloss finish, mfg. 1994-current.

MSR	$300	$210	$135	$95

PF5 CE NT - single rounded cutaway dreadnought style, spruce top, round soundhole, bound body, 5-stripe rosette, mahogany back/sides/neck, 14/20-fret rosewood fingerboard with pearl dot inlay, rosewood bridge with white black dot pins, 3-per-side chrome covered tuners, piezo bridge pickup, volume/3-band EQ, available in Natural gloss finish, mfg. 1994-current.

MSR	$400	$280	$205	$125

PF5 DE NT - similar to the PF5 CE NT, except has dreadnought body (no cutaway), passive volume/tone controls. Available in Natural gloss finish, mfg. 1998-2000.

$250	$150	$100

Last MSR was $340.

PF18 S CE - similar to the PF5 CE, except features solid spruce top, 3-per-side chrome diecast tuners, available in Natural gloss finish, mfg. 1994-96.

N/A	$300	$175

Last MSR was $600.

PF10 - dreadnought style, spruce top, round soundhole, bound body, 5-stripe rosette, mahogany back/sides/neck, 14/20-fret rosewood fingerboard with pearl dot inlay, rosewood bridge with black white dot pins, 3-per-side chrome die-cast tuners, available in Natural Gloss finish, mfg. 1991-99.

$225	$150	$100

Last MSR was $319.

GRADING			**100%**	**EXCELLENT**	**AVERAGE**

Add $20 for left-handed configuration (Model PF10 L). Add $60 for Black gloss finish (Model PF10 BK). When this option was discontinued in 1998, the list price for a PF10 BK was $399.

In 1994, black pickguard was introduced.

PF10 12 - similar to PF10, except in 12-string configuration, 6-per-side tuners, available in Natural Gloss finish, disc.

	$275	**$175**	**$125**
	Last MSR was $369.		

PF10 CE - similar to the PF5 CE, except features 3-per-side chrome die-cast tuners, available in Natural Gloss finish, mfg. 1992-98.

	$385	**$300**	**$175**
	Last MSR was $549.		

PF18 S - similar to the PF10, except features solid spruce top, available in Natural Gloss finish, mfg. 1992-98.

	$310	**$195**	**$120**
	Last MSR was $440.		

PF20 - similar to PF10, except features flame maple top, 3-per-side chrome enclosed tuners, available in Traditional Violin finish, mfg. 1991-96.

	$260	**$175**	**$110**
	Last MSR was $370.		

In 1994, black pickguard was introduced.

PF25 - similar to PF10, except features herringbone body binding, oak back/sides, 14/20-fret rosewood fingerboard with pearl snowflake inlay, available in Natural finish, mfg. 1994-96.

	$255	**$175**	**$110**
	Last MSR was $360.		

PF30 - similar to PF10, except features cedar top, 3-per-side chrome enclosed tuners, available in Natural finish, mfg. 1991-92.

	N/A	**$130**	**$85**
	Last MSR was $290.		

PF40 - similar to PF10, except features flame maple top, 3-per-side chrome diecast tuners. Available in Natural finish, mfg. 1991-96.

	$305	**$195**	**$125**
	Last MSR was $430.		

In 1994, black pickguard was introduced, spruce top, flame maple back/sides replaced original parts.

PF40 FM - similar to PF40, except has flame maple top, available in Natural or Trans. Blue finishes, mfg. 1994-96.

	$350	**$225**	**$150**
	Last MSR was $500.		

PF50 - dreadnought style, spruce top, round soundhole, herringbone bound body and rosette, rosewood back/sides, mahogany neck, 14/20-fret bound rosewood fingerboard with abalone dot inlay, rosewood bridge with black abalone dot pins, bound peghead, 3-per-side chrome diecast tuner, available in Natural finish, mfg. 1991-94.

	N/A	**$195**	**$125**
	Last MSR was $430.		

PF50 S - similar to PF50, except has solid spruce top, disc. 1994.

	N/A	**$250**	**$175**
	Last MSR was $550.		

PF50 12 - similar to PF50, except has 12-string configuration, 6-per-side tuners, disc. 1994.

	N/A	**$225**	**$150**
	Last MSR was $480.		

PF75 M - similar to PF50, except features flame maple back/sides, maple neck, 14/20-fret bound maple fingerboard with black dot inlays, rosewood bridge with white abalone dot pins, bound peghead with abalone Ibanez logo inlay, available in Natural finish, mfg. 1992-96.

	$385	**$250**	**$175**
	Last MSR was $550.		

PF8O V - similar to PF50, except features ovankol top, ovankol back/sides, available in Natural finish, mfg. 1994-98.

	$225	**$160**	**$100**
	Last MSR was $320.		

PF300NT - similar to the PF50, disc 2000.

	$235	**$165**	**$105**
	Last MSR was $330.		

Ibanez PF512
courtesy Ibanez

Ibanez PF5 CE NT
courtesy Ibanez

PF300CE-NT - similar to the PF300NT, execpt has a Piezo transducer with a 3 band EQ, disc. 2000.

	$315	$185	$125

Last MSR was $450.

ACOUSTIC: RAGTIME SERIES

R001 - parlor style, solid spruce top, round soundhole, wooden inlay binding and rosette, rosewood back/sides/neck, 14/20-fret rosewood fingerboard, rosewood bridge with white black dot pins, gold hardware, 3-per-side die-cast tuners, available in Natural finish, mfg. 1992-94.

	N/A	$305	$195

Last MSR was $600.

R300 - similar to the R001, except features cedar top, mahogany back/sides/neck, chrome hardware, available in Natural finish, mfg. 1992-94.

	N/A	$215	$120

Last MSR was $400.

R302 - similar to R001, except features 12-string configuration, 6-per-side tuners, cedar top, mahogany back/sides/neck, chrome hardware, available in Natural finish, disc. 1994.

	N/A	$225	$135

Last MSR was $450.

R350 - similar to R001, except features cedar top, ovankol back/sides, mahogany neck, chrome hardware, available in Natural finish, disc. 1994.

	N/A	$215	$125

Last MSR was $450.

ACOUSTIC: TALMAN SERIES

TCY10 - double cutaway unique body style, spruce top, mahogany back/sides/neck, 20-fret rosewood fingerboard with dot inlay, Ibanez Piezo pickup & 2 band EQ, 3-per-side tuners, chrome hardware, available in Trans. Blue Sunburst or Black finishes, mfg. 2000-current.

MSR	$300	$210	$150	$100

TCY15 - similar to the TCY10 except has black hardware and triangle inlays, available in Galaxy Violet or Galaxy Magenta, mfg. 2000-current.

MSR	$380	$275	$190	$125

ACOUSTIC: TULSA & VINTAGE SERIES

Ibanez' Vintage models feature tempered mahogany necks (thinner and flatter profile) and synthetic Ivorex nuts and saddles.

TU5 - grand concert style, round soundhole, bound body, 3-stripe rosette, nato back/sides, mahogany neck, 14/20-fret rosewood fingerboard with pearl dot inlay, rosewood bridge with black white dot pins, black pickguard, 3-per-side chrome tuners, available in Natural finish, mfg. 1994-96.

	N/A	$115	$75

Last MSR was $250.

VS100 NT - dreadnought style, spruce top, round soundhole, body binding, mahogany back/sides, tempered mahogany neck, 14/20-fret rosewood fingerboard with pearl dot inlay, rosewood bridge with white bridgepins, 3-per-side chrome die-cast tuners, tortoise pickguard, available in Natural gloss finish, mfg. 1998-2000.

	$260	$155	$105

Last MSR was $370.

Add $30 for Black gloss finish (Model V100 BK).

V100 CE NT - dreadnought style body with single rounded cutaway, spruce top, round soundhole, body binding, mahogany back/sides, tempered mahogany neck, 14/20-fret rosewood fingerboard with pearl dot inlay, rosewood bridge with white bridgepins, 3-per-side chrome die-cast tuners, tortoise pickguard, available in Natural gloss finish, piezo bridge pickup, EQ30 volume/3-band EQ, mfg. 1998-99.

	$385	$250	$165

Last MSR was $550.

ACOUSTIC ELECTRIC: AE & ATL SERIES

AE Series models specifications: body length 20", body width 15 3/4", body depth 3".

ATL10 - single cutaway hollow style, spruce top, oval soundhole, bound body, 3-stripe rosette, maple back/sides/neck, 22-fret rosewood fingerboard with pearl dot inlays, rosewood bridge with white pearl dot pins, 6-per-side black diecast tuners, piezo pickup, volume/3-band EQ controls, available in Black or Blue Night finishes, mfg. 1992-96.

	N/A	$265	$175

Last MSR was $550.

AE10 - single rounded cutaway dreadnought style, spruce top, bound body, 3-stripe rosette, mahogany back/sides, mahogany neck, 14/21-fret rosewood fingerboard with pearl dot inlay, rosewood bridge with white black dot pins, wood peghead with screened plant/logo, 3-per-side chrome die-cast tuners, piezo bridge pickup, AEQ-20 volume/tone/4-band EQ slider controls, available in Natural low gloss finish, current mfg.

	$325	$215	$150

Last MSR was $449.

AEG10 - similar to the AE10 except has a Fishman Sonicore pickup and Ibanez AEZ-SS electronics, available in Black, Gloss Tangerine, Trans. Red Sunburst, or Trans. Purple finishes, current mfg.

MSR	$420	$295	$220	$125

AE18 - similar to the AE10 (with the Ibanez AEQ system), available in Natural Gloss finish, disc. 1998.

	N/A	$300	$200

Last MSR was $599.

AE18 BK/TRS - similar to the AE18, available in Black Gloss or Trans. Red Sunburst finishes, mfg. 1998-current.

MSR	$600	$425	$295	$200

AE18 NT - similar to AE18, except has Fishman Sonicore electronics with 4-band EQ, available in Natural gloss finish, current mfg.

MSR	$549	$385	$265	$175

AE18 TBU - similar to the AE18, available in Trans. Blue Gloss finish, mfg. 1998-2000.

	$425	$295	$200

Last MSR was $599.

AEF18 NT/TVS - similar to the AE18, available in Natural or Trans. Violet Sunburst finishes, mfg. 2000-current.

MSR	$480	$340	$250	$150

Add $15 for Trans. Violet Sunburst finish.

AEF1812 - similar to the AE18, excet in 12-string configuration, mfg. 2000-current.

MSR	$700	$490	$350	$225

AE20 - similar to the AE10, except featured nato back/sides, 22-fret rosewood fingerboard with pearl dot inlay, available in Natural gloss finish, mfg. 1994-96.

	N/A	$325	$215

Last MSR was $700.

AE20 N - similar to AE20, except has classic style body/peghead, no fingerboard inlay, rosewood tied bridge, 3-per-side tuners with pearloid buttons, disc. 1996.

	N/A	$315	$215

Last MSR was $700.

AE25 (TB, TS) - single rounded cutaway dreadnought style, flame maple top, bound body, 3-stripe rosette, bound body, maple back/sides, mahogany neck, 21-fret bound rosewood fingerboard with abalone dot inlay, rosewood bridge with white black dot pins, black peghead with screened plant/logo, 3-per-side gold die-cast tuners, piezo bridge pickup, volume/tone/3-band EQ slider controls, available in Trans. Blue (TB) and Tobacco Sunburst (TS) finishes, disc. 1999.

	$550	$350	$225

Last MSR was $699.

In 1998, Transparent Blue finish was discontinued.

AE30 TP - similar to AE18, except has flame maple top, maple back and sides, abalone/pearl block fingerboard inlays, gold hardware, Fishman Sonicore pickup and Ibanez AEQ40 4-band EQ, available in Trans. Purple finish, mfg. 1999-2001.

	$490	$340	$230

Last MSR was $699.

**Ibanez AEF18 TVS
courtesy Ibanez**

**Ibanez AEB305
courtesy Ibanez**

GRADING		100%	EXCELLENT	AVERAGE

AE30MS/TVS - similar to the AE30 except is in Gloss Marine Sunburst, Gloss Trans. Cherry Sunburst, or Trans. Violet Sunburst finishes, mfg. 2000-current.

MSR	$640	$450	$325	$210

AE40 - single rounded cutaway dreadnought style, figured maple top, bound body, 3-stripe rosette, nato back/sides, mahogany neck, 22-fret bound rosewood fingerboard with abalone/pearl block inlay, rosewood bridge with white black dot pins, bound peghead with screened plant/logo, 3-per-side gold die-cast tuners with pearloid buttons, piezo bridge pickup, volume/tone/4-band EQ controls. Available in Honey Sunburst, Red Sunburst, and Transparent Blue finishes. Mfg. 1994 to 1996.

	N/A	$400	$275

Last MSR was $900.

AE60S - similar to the AE40, except features solid spruce top, ovankol back/sides, bound blackface peghead with screened plant/logo, available in Natural finish, mfg. 1994-96.

	N/A	$450	$300

Last MSR was $1,000.

ACOUSTIC ELECTRIC BASS

AEB30 - 4-string bass single cutaway AEF body, spruce top, mahogany back/sides/neck, rosewood fingerboard with dot ilnay, Ivorex saddle, Fishman Sonicore pickup and AEQ-SS electronics, Natural finish, current mfg.

MSR	$700	$490	$350	$225

AEB305 - similar to the AEB30 except in five-string configuration, current mfg.

MSR	$800	$560	$410	$260

AEB45 - 4-string bass single cutaway AEF body, spruce top, ovangkol back/sides mahogany neck, rosewood fingerboard with dot inlay, Shadow pickup and 4 band EQ, Natural finish, disc 2000.

	$490	$350	$225

Last MSR was $700.

ITHACA GUITAR WORKS
Instruments currently built in Ithaca, New York.

The Ithaca Guitar Works consists of both a retail music store and a custom guitar shop. Ithaca Guitar Works' shop offers repairs on stringed instruments as well as a nylon string acoustic guitar model. They are authorized dealers for many major brands. For more information refer to their web site (see Trademark Index).

ITHACA STRINGED INSTRUMENTS
Instruments currently built in Trumansburg, New York.

After a long association with Ithaca Guitar Works, luthiers Eric Aceto and Dan Hoffman established their own company in 1997. The company is now building the **Oneida** acoustic/electric guitar, scrolled acoustic instruments, **N.S. by Ithaca** electric violin, and the **Aceto/Violect** pickup system. The company also offers several other stringed instruments. The Oneida acoustic/electric (last MSR $3,500) was constructed with a spruce or cedar top, mahogany or walnut back and sides, and an ebony fingerboard and bridge.

1/3 of the blance is due when placing the order on a guitar. For further information, please contact Ithaca Stringed Instruments directly (see Trademark Index).

Section J

J.B. PLAYER

Instruments currently produced in Asia; specific model Classical guitars are built in Spain. Distributed by MBT International of Charleston, South Carolina.

MBT International, owner of J.B. Player, is the parent company to the Hondo Guitar Company, Musicorp, Engl USA, and MBT Lighting and Sound.

J.B. Player offers a wide range of entry to student level instruments in acoustic or electric solid body guitars and basses. Many higher quality models that are currently offered may appeal to working musicians, and feature such parts as Schaller hardware, Wilkinson bridges, and APC pickups. The current catalog illustrates the four different levels offered: the **JBP Artist, Standard, Professional,** and **Sledgehammer** series.

ACOUSTIC: ARTISTA CLASSICAL & RIDGEVILLE SERIES

J.B. Player offers four models of classical guitars, built in Spain. The Granada (list $299) has an Oregon pine top, and mahogany body. The Morena (list $385) has an Oregon pine top and rosewood body, while the Flamenco (list $399) has a sycamore body. The Segovia (list $579) features a solid cedar top and rosewood body.

J.B. Player's **Ridgeville** series offers three different model acoustic guitars. The **JBR-20** Dreadnought (list $229) has a spruce top, mahogany back and sides, and diecast tuners. The **JBR-30** Dreadnought (list $259) has a spruce top and ovankol back and sides. The **JBR-10 C** classical (list $199) has an agathis top, mahogany back and sides, and plank-style tuners. All models are available in a Natural finish

GRADING	100%	EXCELLENT	AVERAGE

J.B. Player JBA-2200
courtesy J.B. Player

ACOUSTIC: ARTIST SERIES

JBA-1010 - grand auditorium style, flame maple top, round soundhole, multiple-ply body binding, mahogany back/sides, nato neck, 14/20-fret rosewood fingerboard with dot inlay, rosewood bridge with white dot pins, 3-per-side diecast tuners, available in Sunburst finish, mfg. 1998-current.

MSR	$399		$275	$195	$135

JBA-1150 - auditorium style, solid cedar top, round soundhole, multiple-ply body binding, rosewood back/sides, mahogany neck, 14/20-fret rosewood fingerboard with dot inlay, rosewood bridge with white dot pins, blackface peghead, 3-per-side tuners, available in Natural finish, mfg. 1998-current.

MSR	$525		$375	$250	$175

JBA-1200 - dreadnought style, solid cedar top, black pickguard, round soundhole, mahogany back/sides/neck, 14/20-fret rosewood fingerboard with dot inlay, rosewood bridge with white dot pins, 3-per-side diecast tuners, available in Natural finish, current mfg.

MSR	$430		$325	$225	$150

> **Add $110 for 2 piece mahogany back and sides (Model JBA-1250). Add $290 for 2 piece ovankol back and sides (Model JBA-1275).**

JBA-1200-12 - similar to the JBA-1200, except features a 12-string configuration, 6-per-side tuners, available in Natural finish, disc. 1998.

	$335	$250	$125
	Last MSR was $475.		

JBA-1500 - similar to the JBA-2000, except features mahogany back and sides, no abalone rosette, black pickguard, disc. 1998.

	$275	$200	$125
	Last MSR was $395.		

JBA-1520 - similar to the JBA-2000, except features mahogany back and sides, abalone-style rosette, black pickguard, mfg. 1998-current

MSR	$299		$225	$150	$100

JBA-2000 - dreadnought style, solid spruce top, tortoise pickguard, round soundhole, 4-stripe bound body, abalone rosette, rosewood back/sides, mahogany neck, 14/20-fret bound rosewood fingerboard with abalone block inlay, rosewood bridge with white black dot pins, 3-per-side gold tuners, available in Natural finish, mfg. 1994-96.

	$380	$275	$175
	Last MSR was $540.		

JBA-2200 - similar to the JBA-2000, except features back and sides, herringbone rosette/body binding, bound fingerboard with pearl palm tree inlay, current mfg.

MSR	$620		$500	$325	$225

GRADING	100%	EXCELLENT	AVERAGE

ACOUSTIC: STANDARD SERIES

JB-95 COUNTRY JUMBO - jumbo style, maple top, round soundhole, 3-stripe bound body/rosette, mahogany back/sides, mahogany neck, 14/20-fret rosewood fingerboard with pearl dot inlay, rosewood bridge with black bridgepins, 3-per-side chrome tuners, available in Natural satin finish, mfg. 1998-current.

	MSR	$290		$200	$135	$95

JB-402 - dreadnought style, spruce top, round soundhole, black pickguard, bound body, 5-stripe rosette, nato back/sides/neck, 14/20-fret bound rosewood fingerboard with pearl dot inlay, rosewood bridge with white black dot pins, 3-per-side chrome diecast tuners, available in Natural finish, current mfg.

	MSR	$275		$200	$135	$95

JB-403 - similar to JB-402, except has multiple-ply body binding, available in Natural finish, mfg. 1991-94, 1998-current.

	MSR	$299		$210	$150	$100

JB-405-12 - dreadnought style, 12-string configuration, spruce top, round soundhole, black pickguard, stripe bound body/rosette, ash back/sides, bound mahogany neck, 14/20-fret bound rosewood fingerboard with pearl dot inlay, rosewood bridge with white black dot pins, 6-per-side chrome diecast tuners, available in Natural finish, current mfg.

	MSR	$335		$235	$150	$100

JB-407 - dreadnought style, ash top, round soundhole, black pickguard, bound body, 5-stripe rosette, ash back/sides, nato mahogany neck, 14/20-fret bound fingerboard with pearl dot inlay, rosewood bridge with white black dot pins, 3-per-side chrome diecast tuners. Available in Tobacco Sunburst finish, current mfg.

	MSR	$280		$200	$125	$85

This model was optional with an acoustic pickup, active volume/3-band EQ (JB-407 E). This option discontinued in 1998.

JB-408 - similar to the JB-407, except features mahogany neck, available in Trans. Blonde finish, mfg. 1998-current.

	MSR	$325		$225	$150	$100

JB-409 - dreadnought style, spruce top, round soundhole, black pickguard, bound body, 5-stripe rosette, mahogany back/sides/neck, 14/20-fret bound fingerboard with pearl dot inlay, rosewood bridge with white black dot pins, 3-per-side chrome diecast tuners, available in Black, Natural, or Tobacco Sunburst finish, mfg. 1998-current.

	MSR	$315		$210	$150	$100

JBL-409 - similar to the JB-409, except features a left-handed configuration, available in Black, Natural, or Tobacco Sunburst finish, mfg. 1998-current.

	MSR	$330		$225	$150	$100

JB-450 - dreadnought style, spruce top, round soundhole, black pickguard, imitation abalone bound body/rosette, ash back/sides, mahogany neck, 14/20-fret bound rosewood fingerboard with hexagon imitation abalone inlay, rosewood bridge with white black dot pins, 3-per-side chrome diecast tuners, available in Natural finish, current mfg.

	MSR	$315		$215	$150	$100

JB-502 - dreadnought style, spruce top, round soundhole, black pickguard, bound body, 5-ring rosette, mahogany finishes nato back/sides, nato neck, 14/20-fret rosewood fingerboard with pearl dot inlay, rosewood bridge with black bridgepins, 3-per-side chrome diecast tuners, available in Natural finish, mfg. 1998-current.

	MSR	$360		$250	$175	$115

JB-502-12 - similar to JB-502 except features a 12-string configuration, 6-per-side tuners, available in Natural finish, mfg. 1998-current.

	MSR	$395		$275	$175	$125

JB-505 - classical style, spruce top, round soundhole, herringbone bound body, wooden inlay rosette, ash back/sides, mahogany neck, 12/18-fret rosewood fingerboard, rosewood bridge, 3-per-side chrome tuners with nylon buttons, available in Natural finish, disc. 1994.

				$185	$130	$85

Last MSR was $260.

JB-506 - similar to JB-502 except features a blackface peghead, available in Violin (shaded Brown Sunburst) finish, mfg. 1998-current.

	MSR	$375		$275	$175	$125

JB-1000 - dreadnought style, spruce top, oval soundhole, black pickguard, 3-stripe bound body/rosette, mahogany back/sides/neck, 14/20-fret bound rosewood fingerboard with pearl dot inlay, rosewood bridge with white black dot pins, 3-per-side chrome tuners, available in Black or White (White finish model has black chrome tuners) finishes, disc. 1996.

				$230	$175	$115

Last MSR was $325.

Add $70 for flame maple top and jacaranda back/sides (available in Natural finish).

JB-5000 - classical style, spruce top, round soundhole, bound body, wooden inlay rosette, mahogany back/sides/neck, 12/18-fret rosewood fingerboard, rosewood bridge, 3-per-side gold tuners with pearloid buttons, available in Natural finish, disc. 1994.

				$245	$175	$100

Last MSR was $350.

GRADING	100%	EXCELLENT	AVERAGE

JB-8000 - similar to the JB-1000, except features round soundhole, bound body, 5-stripe rosette, rosewood back/sides, available in Natural finish, disc. 1994.

	$299	**$200**	**$125**

Last MSR was $425.

JB-9000 - similar to the JB-1000, except features round soundhole, bound body, 5-stripe rosette, available in Tobacco Sunburst finish, disc. 1996.

	$275	**$195**	**$125**

Last MSR was $395.

JB-9000-12 - similar to JB-9000, except has 12 strings, black white dot pins, 6-per-side tuners, available in Natural finish.

	$290	**$200**	**$135**

Last MSR was $410.

ACOUSTIC ELECTRIC: ARTIST SERIES

JB-300 E - single round cutaway dreadnought style, maple top, black pickguard, round soundhole, 3-stripe bound body/rosette, ash back/sides, mahogany neck, 20-fret bound rosewood fingerboard with pearl dot inlay, rosewood bridge with white black dot pins, bound blackface peghead with screened logo, 3-per-side chrome tuners, acoustic pickup, volume/presence/3-band EQ control, available in Brownburst, Cherryburst, Natural, or White finishes, mfg. 1994-current.

MSR	**$440**	**$325**	**$175**	**$125**

JBA-50 CEQ NYLON STRING - single rounded cutaway body, flame maple top, round soundhole, maple back/sides, mahogany neck, 12/19-fret rosewood fingerboard, rosewood tied bridge, slotted headstock, 3-per-side gold tuners with white buttons, piezo pickup, active electronics, available in Sunburst finish, mfg. 1998-current.

MSR	**$525**	**$375**	**$250**	**$175**

JBA-65 CEQ - single rounded cutaway folk-style body, flame maple top, round soundhole, ash back/sides, mahogany neck, 14/20-fret rosewood fingerboard with white diamond inlay, rosewood bridge with white bridgepins, 3-per-side gold tuners, piezo pickup, 3-band EQ, presence control, active electronics, pop-out battery compartment, available in Natural (JBA-65 NCEQ) or Tobacco Sunburst (JBA-65 CEQ) finishes, mfg. 1998-current.

MSR	**$599**	**$375**	**$250**	**$175**

JBA-97 CEQ - single rounded cutaway jumbo-style body, spruce top, round soundhole, mahogany back/sides/neck, 14/20-fret rosewood fingerboard with white dot inlay, rosewood bridge with white bridgepins, 3-per-side gold tuners, piezo pickup, 3-band EQ, presence control, active electronics, pop-out battery compartment, available in Natural satin finishes, mfg. 1998-current.

MSR	**$495**	**$350**	**$225**	**$150**

JBA-260 - single cutaway alder body with carved tone chambers, spruce top, f-hole, mahogany neck, 21-fret rosewood fingerboard with dot inlay, rosewood bridge with black pins, 6 on a side diecast tuners, piezo pickup, volume/tone controls, available in Natural finish, disc. 1998.

	$520	**$400**	**$250**

Last MSR was $740.

JBA-910 - single round cutaway body, solid cedar top, round soundhole, body binding, 3 ring rosette, mahogany back/sides/neck, 14/20-fret bound rosewood fingerboard with pearl dot inlay, rosewood bridge with black bridgepins, 3-per-side gold Schaller tuners with white pearloid buttons, piezo pickup, 3-band EQ, active electronics, 1/4" and XLR outputs, available in Natural finishes, current mfg.

MSR	**$775**	**$550**	**$375**	**$250**

KJ-330-PU - single rounded cutaway body, tiger maple top, oval soundhole, abalone bound body/rosette, tiger maple back/sides, mahogany neck, 20-fret bound rosewood fingerboard with pearl split block inlay, rosewood bridge with white black dot pins, 3-per-side gold tuners with amber buttons, acoustic pickup, 4-band EQ, active electronics, available in Brownburst or Natural finishes, mfg. 1994-current.

MSR	**$675**	**$500**	**$325**	**$225**

KJ-609-WPU - single round cutaway body, spruce top, round soundhole, 3-stripe bound body, abalone rosette, maple back/sides, mahogany neck, 14/20-fret rosewood fingerboard with pearl dot inlay, 12th fret pearl horns inlay, rosewood bridge with white black dot pins, 3-per-side chrome tuners, acoustic pickup, active 4-band EQ, active electronics, available in Natural finish, mfg. 1994-current.

MSR	**$660**	**$495**	**$325**	**$225**

GRADING	100%	EXCELLENT	AVERAGE

KJ-705-WPU - similar to the KJ-609-WPU, except features mahogany back/sides/neck, available in Tobacco Sunburst finish, disc. 1998.

	$510	$425	$250

Last MSR was $720.

ACOUSTIC ELECTRIC BASS

JBA-3000 EAB - single round cutaway folk-style, select spruce top, round soundhole, 3-stripe bound body/rosette, mahogany back/sides/neck, 22-fret bound rosewood fingerboard with pearl dot inlay, rosewood strings thru bridge, 2-per-side chrome tuners, acoustic pickup, active 3-band EQ, available in Natural finish, mfg. 1994-current.

MSR	$720	$500	$325	$225

JDS
Instruments currently built in Asia. Exclusively distributed by Wolf Imports of St. Louis, Missouri.

JDS Limited Edition instruments are medium quality acoustic and solid body electric guitars that feature designs based on popular American classics.

JHS
Instruments previously built in Japan during the late 1970s.

The JHS trademark was the initials of the UK importer John Hornby Skewes, who founded his import company in 1965 (See Encore). The generally good quality instruments featured both original designs and those based on classic American designs. The line focused primarily on solid body guitars, much like the Encore line today, (Source: Tony Bacon and Paul Day, *The Guru's Guitar Guide*).

JTG OF NASHVILLE
Instruments currently built in Japan and Mexico. Distributed by JTG of Nashville located in Nashville, Tennessee.

The JTG of Nashville company is currently importing quality Japanese and Mexican acoustic guitars. For further information regarding JTG of Nashville's acoustic models, please contact JTG directly (see Trademark Index).

JACKSON, DOUGLAS R.
Instruments currently built and distributed by Douglas R. Jackckson Guitar Shop in Destin, Florida.

Luthier Douglas R. Jackson handcrafts his own acoustic and electric guitars, which are built on commission. On occasion, Jackson may build a model on speculation, but that is not the norm. All models are marketed through his guitar shop.

Jackson attended a guitar building school in the Spring of 1977. While enrolled, he was hired by the school to teach and perform repairs. Jackson taught two classes in the 1977 school year, and helped build over 150 instruments (plus his own personal guitars and repairs). Jackson then went to work for a vintage guitar dealer on and off for three years, while he studied just about anything he could get his hands on. During this research phase, Jackson continued to build three or four guitars a year (in addition to his shop repairs).

In 1986, Jackson moved from Arizona to his present location in Destin, Florida (the Pensacola/Fort Walton Beach area). Jackson currently owns and operates a 1,500 square foot building that houses his guitar shop and manufacturing equipment, (Biography courtesty Douglas R. Jackson).

Jackson estimates that he has built close to 150 instruments consisting of acoustic and electric 6 - and 12-string guitars, electric basses and mandolins, resonator guitars, ukuleles, and dulcimers.

ACOUSTIC

The majority of Jackson's acoustic guitars have been the dreadnought style, with his own scalloped bracing pattern. These dreadnought models feature herringbone trim on the front, back, back center strip, and soundhole; ebony fingerboards, bridges, and peghead laminates; curly maple binding, mother-of-pearl inlay; and spruce tops. The backs and sides are constructed out of either mahogany, Indian rosewood, curly koa, curly claro walnut, or curly maple (although other woods have been used through the years). Jackson now regularly makes a body size the same as a resonator or "classical in a steel-string."

Acoustic prices start at $3,000 for a plain mahogany body and go up according to the woods and appointments used. A used one in good condition may sell for $1,000 to $2,000, depending on how fancy a model it is.

JAIME JULIA
Distributed by Manufacturas Alhambra S.L. of Muro del Alcoy, Spain.

Jaime Julia brand nylon string classical guitars are distributed by Manufacturas Alhambra S.L. of Muro del Alcoy, Spain. Suggested retail in the US is $4,261. For information regarding model specifications and pricing, please contact Jaime Julia directly (see Trademark Index).

JAMBOREE
Instruments produced in Japan.

The Jamboree trademark was a brandname used by U.S. importers Elger/Hoshino of Ardmore, Pennsylvania. Jamboree, along with others like Goldentone, King's Stone, and Elger were all used on Japanese guitars imported to the U.S. Elger/Hoshino evolved into Hoshino USA, the distributor of Ibanez guitars, (Source: Michael Wright, *Guitar Stories*, Volume One).

JAMMER
Instruments produced in Asia. Distributed by VMI Industries (Vega Musical Instruments) of Brea, California.

Jammer instruments are designed with the entry level and student guitarist in mind.

GRADING		100%	EXCELLENT	AVERAGE

JASMINE

Instruments currently produced in Asia. Distributed by Kaman Music Corporation of Bloomfield, Connecticut.

The Jasmine trademark is a division of Takamine. Jasmine guitars can be viewed as an entry level step into the Takamine product line. Jasmine guitars may not be as ornate, and may feature different construction methods than Takamine models.

ACOUSTIC: C CLASSICAL SERIES

C-22 - classical style, agathis top, round soundhole, hardwood back/sides, nato neck, 12/19-fret rosewood fingerboard, rosewood tied bridge, 3-per-side chrome tuners with pearloid buttons, available in Natural finish, current mfg.

MSR	$249	$175	$115	$85

C-23 - classic style, spruce top, round soundhole, bound body, wood inlay rosette, mahogany back/sides, nato neck, 12/19-fret rosewood fingerboard, rosewood tied bridge, 3-per-side chrome tuners with pearloid buttons, available in Natural finish, mfg. 1994-current.

MSR	$289	$200	$135	$95

C-26 - classic style, spruce top, round soundhole, 3-stripe bound body, wood inlay rosette, mahogany back/sides, nato neck, 12/19-fret rosewood fingerboard/bridge, 3-per-side gold tuners with pearloid buttons, available in Natural finish, disc. 1994.

	N/A	$150	$90

Last MSR was $280.

C-27 - classic style, cedar top, round soundhole, bound body, wood inlay rosette, mahogany back/sides, nato neck, 12/19-fret rosewood fingerboard, rosewood tied bridge, 3-per-side chrome tuners with pearloid buttons, available in Natural finish, mfg. 1994-98.

	N/A	$100	$65

Last MSR was $200.

C-28 - classic style, spruce top, round soundhole, 3-stripe bound body, wood inlay rosette, rosewood back/sides, nato neck, 12/19-fret rosewood fingerboard, tied rosewood bridge, 3-per-side gold tuners with pearloid buttons, available in Natural finish, disc. 1992.

	N/A	$175	$115

Last MSR was $350.

C-36 S - classic style, solid spruce top, round soundhole, 3-stripe bound body, wood inlay rosette, rosewood back/sides, nato neck, 12/19-fret rosewood fingerboard, tied rosewood bridge with marquetry inlay, 3-per-side gold tuners with pearloid buttons, available in Natural finish, mfg. 1994-98.

	N/A	$225	$135

Last MSR was $520.

C-48 M - single round cutaway classic style, figured maple top, round soundhole, 3-stripe bound body, wood inlay rosette, figured maple back/sides, nato neck, 12/19-fret rosewood fingerboard, tied rosewood bridge, figured maple veneered peghead, 3-per-side gold tuners with pearloid buttons, available in Natural finish, mfg. 1994-98.

	N/A	$225	$135

Last MSR was $500.

RQ-28 - requinto style, spruce top, round soundhole, bound body, wood inlay rosette, rosewood back/sides, nato neck, 12/19-fret extended rosewood fingerboard, tied rosewood bridge with marquetry inlay, 3-per-side gold tuners with pearloid buttons, available in Natural finish, mfg. 1994-98.

	N/A	$195	$125

Last MSR was $420.

ACOUSTIC: S DREADNOUGHT SERIES

S-31 - dreadnought style, spruce top, round soundhole, black pickguard, 3-stripe bound body/rosette, nato back/sides/neck, 14/20-fret rosewood fingerboard with pearl dot inlay, rosewood bridge with white pins, 3-per-side chrome tuners, available in Black finish, mfg. 1994-current.

MSR	$389	$275	$125	$95

S-32 - dreadnought style, spruce top, round soundhole, black pickguard, 3-stripe bound body/rosette, nato back/sides/neck, 14/20-fret rosewood fingerboard with pearl dot inlay, rosewood bridge with white pins, 3-per-side chrome diecast tuners, available in Natural gloss finish, current mfg.

MSR	$269	$195	$125	$90

J.B. Player JBA-3000 EAB
courtesy J.B. Player

J

Jasmine C-36 S
courtesy Kaman Music Corp.

S-312 12-String - similar to the S-32, except features a 12-string configuration, 6-per-side tuners, 5-stripe bound body/rosette, available in Natural gloss finish, current mfg.

		100%	EXCELLENT	AVERAGE
MSR	$319	$225	$150	$100

S-33 - dreadnought style, spruce top, round soundhole, black pickguard, stripe bound body/rosette, mahogany back/sides, nato neck, 14/20-fret rosewood fingerboard with pearl dot inlay, rosewood bridge with white black dot pins, 3-per-side chrome diecast tuners, available in Natural finish, disc. 1998.

	N/A	$200	$95

Last MSR was $380.

S-34C - dreadnought style single cutaway mahogany body, laminated spruce top, mahogany neck, 14/21-fret rosewood fingerboard with dot inlay, 3-per-side-tuners, rosewood bridge, chrome hardware, available in Natural finish, mfg. 2001-current.

MSR	$250	$130	$95	$65

S-35 - dreadnought style nato bound body, spruce top, mahogany neck, 14/20-fret rosewood fingerboard with dot inlay, 3-per-side-tuners, rosewood bridge, black pickguard, chrome hardware, available in Natural finish, mfg. 2001-current.

MSR	$200	$100	$75	$50

S-37 - dreadnought style, spruce top, round soundhole, black pickguard, bound body, 3-stripe rosette, nato back/sides/neck, 14/20-fret rosewood fingerboard with pearl dot inlay, rosewood bridge with white pins, 3-per-side diecast tuners, available in Natural finish, mfg. 1994-98.

	N/A	$125	$80

Last MSR was $250.

S-38 - dreadnought style, solid spruce top, round soundhole, black pickguard, 3-stripe bound body/rosette, mahogany back/sides, nato neck, 14/20-fret bound rosewood fingerboard with pearl dot inlay, rosewood bridge with white pins, 3-per-side chrome diecast tuners, available in Natural finish, current mfg.

MSR	$319	$225	$150	$95

S-38 S - similar to the S-38, except features solid spruce top, available in Natural finish, current mfg.

MSR	$389	$275	$175	$125

S-40 - dreadnought style, round soundhole, black pickguard, 3-stripe bound body/rosette, nato neck, 14/20-fret bound rosewood fingerboard with pearl dot inlay, rosewood bridge with white black dot pins, bound peghead, 3-per-side chrome diecast tuners, available in Natural finish, disc. 1992.

	N/A	$175	$115

Last MSR was $350.

S-41 - dreadnought style, spruce top, round soundhole, black pickguard with white outline, 3-stripe bound body/rosette, daowood back/sides, nato neck, 14/20-fret bound rosewood fingerboard with pearl dot inlay, rosewood bridge with white black dot pins, 3-per-side chrome diecast tuners, available in Black finish, disc. 1994.

	N/A	$175	$115

Last MSR was $360.

S-46 - dreadnought style, spruce top, round soundhole, black pickguard with white outline, 3-stripe bound body/rosette, daowood back/sides, nato neck, 14/20-fret bound rosewood fingerboard with pearl dot inlay, rosewood bridge with white black dot pins, 3-per-side chrome diecast tuners, available in White finish, disc. 1992.

	N/A	$200	$125

Last MSR was $360.

S-49 - dreadnought style, mahogany top, round soundhole, black pickguard, 3-stripe bound body/rosette, mahogany back/sides, nato neck, 14/20-fret bound rosewood fingerboard with pearl dot inlay, rosewood bridge with white black dot pins, bound peghead, 3-per-side chrome diecast tuners, available in Natural finish, disc. 1992.

	N/A	$175	$115

Last MSR was $360.

S-60 - dreadnought style, spruce top, round soundhole, black pickguard, 3-stripe bound body/rosette, rosewood back/sides, nato neck, 14/20-fret fingerboard with pearl dot inlay, rosewood bridge with white black dot pins, 3-per-side chrome diecast tuners, available in Natural finish, disc. 1992.

	N/A	$200	$125

Last MSR was $390.

S-70 - dreadnought style, spruce top, round soundhole, black pickguard, 3-stripe bound body/rosette, Hawaiian koa back/sides, nato neck, 14/20-fret rosewood fingerboard with pearl dot inlay, rosewood bridge with white black dot pins, 3-per-side chrome diecast tuners, available in Natural finish, disc. 1994.

	N/A	$215	$135

Last MSR was $400.

S-80 S - dreadnought style, solid spruce top, round soundhole, black pickguard, 3-stripe bound body/rosette, jacaranda back/sides, nato neck, 14/20-fret bound rosewood fingerboard with pearl dot inlay, rosewood bridge with white black dot pins, bound peghead, 3-per-side gold diecast tuners, available in Natural finish, disc. 1998.

	N/A	$300	$175

Last MSR was $630.

GRADING	100%	EXCELLENT	AVERAGE

ACOUSTIC: STUDIO SERIES

Studio models are correctly proportioned sized classical models, and are available in 1/4 size, 1/2 size, 3/4 size, and full sized scale lengths. Studio Series models come equipped with a quality gig bag and shoulder strap.

STUDIO - classical style, spruce top, round soundhole, mahogany back/sides, nato neck, 12/19-fret rosewood fingerboard, rosewood tied bridge, slotted peghead, 3-per-side chrome tuners, available in Natural finish, current mfg.

	100%	EXCELLENT	AVERAGE
	$110	$75	$50

Retail prices were the following: JS141 1/4 size, 22 1/2" scale, $159; JS241 1/2 size, 23 5/16" scale, $159; JS341 3/4 size, 24 3/4" scale, $169; JS441 Full size, 25 11/16" scale, $179.

ACOUSTIC ELECTRIC: ES SERIES

All models in this series have the following features: single round cutaway folk-style, round soundhole, 3-stripe bound body/rosette, 21-fret bound rosewood fingerboard with pearl dot inlay, rosewood bridge with white black dot pins, body matching bound peghead, 3-per-side chrome die cast tuners, crystal bridge pickups, 3-band EQ, unless otherwise listed.

ES-31 C - single rounded cutaway dreadnought style body, spruce top, round soundhole, black pickguard, 3-stripe bound body/rosette, nato back/sides/neck, 14/20-fret rosewood fingerboard with pearl dot inlay, rosewood bridge with white pins, 3-per-side chrome tuners. piezo bridge pickup, DJ-2 2-band EQ, available in Black finish, mfg. 1994-current.

MSR	$350	$240	$175	$115

ES-32 C - single rounded cutaway dreadnought style, spruce top, round soundhole, black pickguard, 5-stripe bound body/rosette, mahogany back/sides, nato neck, 14/20-fret rosewood fingerboard with pearl dot inlay, rosewood bridge with white black dot pins, 3-per-side chrome tuners, piezo bridge pickup, DJ-2 2-band EQ, available in Natural finish, mfg. 1994-current.

MSR	$369	$275	$175	$125

ES-312 12-String - similar to the ES-32 C, except features non-cutaway body, nato back and sides, 12-string dreadnought style, 6-per-side tuners, available in Natural finish, mfg. 1994-current.

MSR	$369	$275	$175	$125

ES-33 C - single round cutaway dreadnought style, spruce top, round soundhole, black pickguard, stripe bound body/rosette, mahogany back/sides, nato neck, 14/20-fret rosewood fingerboard with pearl dot inlay, rosewood bridge with white black dot pins, 3-per-side chrome diecast tuners, piezo bridge pickup, 3-band EQ control, available in Natural finish, disc. 1998.

	N/A	$225	$150

Last MSR was $480.

**Jasmine ES-33 C-TOB
courtesy Kaman Music Corp.**

ES-33 C-TOB - similar to ES-33 C, except has single round cutaway, 6 crystal bridge pickups, 2-band EQ control, available in Trans. Orangeburst finish, disc. 1998.

	N/A	$225	$125

Last MSR was $490.

ES-40 C - single round cutaway dreadnought style, round soundhole, black pickguard, 3-stripe bound body/rosette, nato neck, 14/20-fret bound rosewood fingerboard with pearl dot inlay, rosewood bridge with white black dot pins, bound peghead, 3-per-side chrome diecast tuners, piezo bridge pickup, 2-band EQ control, available in Natural finish, disc. 1994.

	N/A	$200	$125

Last MSR was $390.

ES-45C - dreadnought style single cutaway nato body, spruce top, mahogany neck, 14/21-fret rosewood fingerboard with dot inlay, 2-band EQ electronics, 3-per-side-tuners, rosewood bridge, chrome hardware, available in Natural finish, mfg. 2001-current.

MSR	$370	$190	$140	$85

ACOUSTIC ELECTRIC: TC SERIES

TC-28 C - single round cutaway classic style, spruce top, round soundhole, 3-stripe bound body, wood inlay rosette, rosewood back/sides, nato neck, 12/19-fret rosewood fingerboard, tied rosewood bridge, 3-per-side gold tuners with pearloid buttons, piezo bridge pickup, 4-band EQ, available in Natural finish, current mfg.

MSR	$629	$375	$225	$175

TC-30 C - similar to the TC-28 C, except has walnut back/sides, available in Amber finish, current mfg.

MSR	$629	$395	$225	$175

**Jasmine TS-26 C
courtesy Kaman Music Corp.**

J

GRADING		100%	EXCELLENT	AVERAGE

TC-48 MC - single round cutaway classic style, figured maple top, round soundhole, 3-stripe bound body, wood inlay rosette, figured maple back/sides, nato neck, 12/19-fret rosewood fingerboard, tied rosewood bridge, figured maple veneered peghead, 3-per-side gold tuners with pearloid buttons, piezo bridge pickup, 4-band EQ, available in Natural finish, mfg. 1994-98.

		N/A	$325	$175

Last MSR was $650.

ACOUSTIC ELECTRIC: TS SERIES

TS-26 C - mahogany top/back/sides, abalone body purfling, nato neck, pearl diamond fingerboard inlay, black white dot bridge pins, gold diecast tuners, available in White/Black finish, mfg. 1994-98.

		N/A	$325	$200

Last MSR was $650.

TS-33 C - single rounded cutaway body, spruce top, mahogany back/sides, nato neck, rosewood fingerboard, rosewood bridge with black pins, gold diecast tuners, available in Natural finish, current mfg.

MSR	$569	$380	$275	$195

TS-38 C - single rounded cutaway dreadnought body, spruce top, round soundhole, rosewood back/sides, nato neck, 14/20-fret rosewood fingerboard with pearl dot inlay, rosewood bridge with white bridgepins, chrome diecast tuners, available in Natural finish, current mfg.

MSR	$559	$375	$275	$195

TS-41 C - single round cutaway dreadnought style, spruce top, round soundhole, black pickguard with white outline, 3-stripe bound body/rosette, daowood back/sides, nato neck, 14/20-fret bound rosewood fingerboard with pearl dot inlay, rosewood bridge with white black dot pins, 3-per-side chrome diecast tuners, bridge pickup, 4-band EQ control, available in Black finish, disc 1994.

		N/A	$225	$125

Last MSR was $450.

TS-46 C - single round cutaway dreadnought style, spruce top, round soundhole, black pickguard with white outline, 3-stripe bound body/rosette, daowood back/sides, nato neck, 14/20-fret bound rosewood fingerboard with pearl dot inlay, rosewood bridge with white black dot pins, 3-per-side chrome diecast tuners, bridge pickup, 4-band EQ control, available in White finish, disc. 1992.

		N/A	$225	$125

Last MSR was $450.

TS-49 C - single round cutaway dreadnought style, mahogany top, round soundhole, black pickguard, 3-stripe bound body/rosette, mahogany back/sides, nato neck, 14/20-fret bound rosewood fingerboard with pearl dot inlay, rosewood bridge with white black dot pins, bound peghead, 3-per-side chrome diecast tuners, bridge pickup, 4-band EQ control, available in Natural finish, disc. 1992.

		N/A	$225	$125

Last MSR was $450.

TS-50 C - rounded cutaway dreadnought style, spruce top, round soundhole, black pickguard, 3-stripe bound body/rosette, flame maple back/sides, maple neck, 20-fret bound rosewood fingerboard with pearl dot inlay, rosewood bridge with white black dot pins, body matching peghead, 3-per-side chrome diecast tuners, bridge pickup, 4-band volume/EQ control, available in Blue Stain, Ebony Stain, or Red Stain finishes, disc. 1994.

		N/A	$300	$175

Last MSR was $600.

TS-52 C MR - single round cutaway dreadnought style, ash top, round soundhole, black trilamated pickguard, ash back/sides, nato neck, 20-fret bound rosewood fingerboard with pearl dot inlay, rosewood bridge with white black dot pins, body matching bound peghead with screened logo, 3-per-side chrome die cast tuners, piezo bridge pickup, 4-band EQ, available in a Red Stain finishes, mfg. 1994-98.

		N/A	$300	$200

Last MSR was $700.

TS-52 C ME - similar to the TS-52 CMR, except in an Ebony Stain finish, mfg. 1994-98.

		N/A	$300	$200

Last MSR was $700.

TS-58 - jumbo style, cedar top, round soundhole, tortoise pickguard, 3-stripe bound body, wood inlay rosette, daowood back/sides, nato neck, 14/20-fret bound rosewood fingerboard with pearl diamond dot inlay, rosewood bridge with white black dot pins, bound peghead, 3-per-side gold diecast tuners, piezo bridge pickup, 4-band EQ control, available in Natural finish, disc. 1998.

		N/A	$325	$200

Last MSR was $650.

TS-60 - dreadnought style, spruce top, round soundhole, black pickguard, 3-stripe bound body/rosette, rosewood back/sides, nato neck, 14/20-fret fingerboard with pearl dot inlay, rosewood bridge with white black dot pins, 3-per-side chrome diecast tuners, piezo bridge pickup, 4-band EQ, available in Natural finish, disc. 1994.

		N/A	$250	$150

Last MSR was $500.

TS-60 C - similar to TS-60, except has single round cutaway, disc. 1994.

		N/A	$275	$175

Last MSR was $550.

GRADING		100%	EXCELLENT	AVERAGE

TS-612 - dreadnought style, spruce top, round soundhole, black pickguard, 3-stripe bound body/rosette, rosewood back/sides, nato neck, 14/20-fret bound rosewood fingerboard with pearl dot inlay, rosewood bridge with white black dot pins, 6-per-side chrome diecast tuners, piezo bridge pickup, 4-band EQ, available in Natural finish, disc. 1994.

N/A $275 $175
Last MSR was $560.

TS-612 C - similar to 612-TS, except has single round cutaway, mfg. 1994-98.

N/A $350 $200
Last MSR was $720.

TS-74 C - single round cutaway dreadnought style, cedar top, round soundhole, tortoise pickguard, 5-stripe bound body, wood inlay rosette, daowood back/sides, nato neck, 20-fret bound rosewood fingerboard with pearl diamond inlay, rosewood bridge with white black dot pins, bound blackface peghead with screened logo, 3-per-side gold diecast tuners, piezo bridge pickup, 4-band EQ, available in Natural finish, mfg. 1994-98.

N/A $375 $200
Last MSR was $700.

TS-91 C - similar to TS-74 C, except features daowood top/back/sides, nato neck, available in Black finish, current mfg.

MSR $629 $450 $275 $195

TS-92 C - similar to the TS-91 C, except features flame maple top/back/sides, maple neck, available in Red Stain finish, disc. 1994.

N/A $250 $150
Last MSR was $520.

TS-95 C - similar to the TS-91 C, except features flame maple top/back/sides, maple neck, available in Ebony Stain finish, disc. 1994.

N/A $275 $175
Last MSR was $520.

TS-96 C - similar to the TS-91 C, except features daowood top/back/sides, nato neck, black white dot bridge pins, available in White finish, disc. 1994.

N/A $250 $150
Last MSR was $480.

TS-97 C - similar to the TS-91 C, except features cedar top, daowood back/sides, nato neck, pearl diamond fingerboard inlay, gold diecast tuners, available in Natural finish, disc. 1998.

N/A $300 $195
Last MSR was $600.

TS-99 C - similar to the TS-91 C, except features daowood top/back/sides, nato neck, available in Walnut Sunburst finish, disc. 1994.

N/A $250 $150
Last MSR was $480.

Jasmine TS-90 C-LW
courtesy Kaman Music Corp.

J

ACOUSTIC ELECTRIC: ARTIST SERIES

Artist series models feature the design of a slim body and a single cutaway.

TC-29 C - single round cutaway classic style, cedar top, round soundhole, 3-stripe bound body, wood inlay rosette, rosewood back/sides, nato neck, 19-fret rosewood fingerboard, tied rosewood bridge with wood marquetry inlay, 3-per-side gold tuners with pearloid tuners, piezo bridge pickup, 3-band EQ, available in Natural finish, mfg. 1994-98.

N/A $375 $215
Last MSR was $650.

TS-90 C-DW (DARK WALNUT) - burled mahogany top/back/sides, nato neck, available in a Dark Walnut Stain finish, mfg. 1994-current.

MSR $699 $475 $250 $200

TS-90 C-LW - similar to the TS-90 C-DW (Dark Walnut), except finished in a Light Walnut Stain, mfg. 1994-98.

N/A $350 $225
Last MSR was $740.

TS-93 C-A - similar to TS-90 C-DW, except features silky oak top/back/sides, maple neck, available in Amber finish, mfg. 1994-98.

N/A $300 $195
Last MSR was $680.

Jasmine TS-93 C
courtesy Kaman Music Corp.

TS-98 C-FM - similar to TS-93 C-A, except features flame maple top/back/sides, maple neck, available in Cherry Sunburst or Blue Stain finishes, mfg. 1994-98.

	N/A	$325	$205

Last MSR was $680.

ACOUSTIC ELECTRIC BASS

ES-100 C - single rounded cutaway body, round soundhole, black pickguard, nato neck, 14/20-fret bound rosewood fingerboard with dot inlay, rosewood bridge with white black dot pins, bound peghead, 2-per-side chrome diecast tuners, piezo bridge pickup, 2-band EQ control, available in Maple (ES-100 C-M), Natural (ES-100 C-4), or Sunburst (ES-100 C-1) finishes, mfg. 1994-current.

MSR	$739	$550	$325	$250

JAX

Instruments previously produced in Taiwan during the early 1980s.

These solid body guitars consist of entry level designs based on classic American models, (Source: Tony Bacon and Paul Day, *The Guru's Guitar Guide*).

JAY G

See chapter on House Brands.

This trademark has been identified as a sub-brand from the budget line of Chris guitars by the Jackson-Guldan company of Columbus, Ohio, (Source: Willie G. Moseley, *Stellas & Stratocasters*).

JAY TURSER

Instruments currently produced in Asia. Distributed by Music Industries Corporation of Floral Park, New York.

Music Industries is currently offering a wide range of Jay Turser acoustic instruments. These instruments are student and entry level instruments with fairly good quality necks and electronics, and are offered in a good number of finishes.

ACOUSTIC ELECTRIC

JTA-40CEQ - single cutaway thinline acoustic, select spruce top, mahogany back and sides, rosewood fingerboard with dot position markers, 3-per-side tuners, rosewood bridge, 4-band EQ, volume control, available in Natural, Transparent Blue, Transparent Red and Black finishes, mfg. 2001-current.

MSR	$300	$210	$170	$140	$110	$85	$65	$45

JTA-40-12CEQ - single cutaway thinline acoustic, 12-string, select spruce top, mahogany back and sides, 4-band EQ, available in Black finish, mfg. 2001-current.

MSR	$330	$250	$215	$175	$150	$125	$95	$70

JTAC-66T - thinline cutaway acoustic, spruce top, nato neck, nato back and sides, rosewood fingerboard with dot position markers, 3-per-side tuners, 1 Volume/1 Tone control, available in Trans. Black, Trans. Blue, or Trans. Red finishes, mfg. 2001-current.

MSR	$200	$139	$119	$89	$69	$49	$29	$20

JTAC-66T-LH - similar to Model JTAC-66T except, in a left-hand configuration, available in Trans. Black, Trans. Blue, or Trans. Red finishes, mfg. 2001-current.

MSR	$210	$149	$129	$110	$85	$65	$45	$25

JTA-67/NG - dreadnought size acoustic, Canadian spruce top, Honduras mahogany neck, Honduras mahogany back and sides, rosewood bridge, black pickguard, dot position markers, available in Natural finish, mfg. 2001-current.

MSR	$200	$139	$119	$99	$79	$59	$39	$20

Add $20 for left-handed configuration. Add $40 for solid spruce top (JTA-67S).

JTA-68NM - dreadnought size acoustic, Canadian Spruce top, mahogany back and sides, herringbone binding, Honduras Mahogany neck, bound neck and headstock, 3-per-side die-cast tuners, rosewood bridge, available in Natural Matte finish, mfg. 2001-current.

MSR	$230	$159	$135	$110	$85	$65	$45	$25

JTA-69EQ/NM - dreadnought size cutaway acoustic, Canadian spruce top, Honduras mahogany back and sides, rosewood fingerboard with dot position markers, herringbone binding, rosewood bridge, 3-per-side die-cast tuners, bound neck and headstock, 4-band EQ, available in Natural Matte finish, mfg. 2001-current.

MSR	$320	$225	$195	$175	$150	$125	$95	$65

JTA-600CE - single cutaway full body acoustic, flame maple top, die-cast tuners, 3-band EQ, available in Tobacco Sunburst finish, mfg. 2001-02.

	$245	$199	$175	$150	$125	$95	$65

Last MSR was $349.

JTNC-EQ - cutaway classical acoustic electric, spruce top, mahogany back and sides, 4-band EQ, rosewood fingerboard, rosewood bridge, inlaid wood rosette, available in Natural finish, mfg. 2001-02.

	$209	$175	$150	$125	$99	$75	$50

Last MSR was $299.

JISHENG
Instruments currently produced in China.

Jisheng Musical Instruments Manufacturing Ltd. is currently offering a wide range of classical and dreadnought acoustic guitar models, as well as some acoustic/electric dreadnought models (some with single cutaway bodies). The company also produces violin models, and numerous gig bag/carrying bags for guitars, drums, and other musical instruments. For more information contact the company directly (see Trademark Index).

JOHN PEARSE
Instruments previously built in Center Valley, Pennsylvania from 1996 to 1998. Distributed by Breezy Ridge Instruments, Inc. of Center Valley, Pennsylvania.

Starting with Herman Weissenborn's unusual styling, Breezy Ridge Instruments modified the design specifications and created a unique new generation of slide guitars. The John Pearse Vintage Acoustic Steel Guitars were available in 4 different models for the time span of about two years.

ACOUSTIC

All models are 37 7/8" in length, 2 7/8" deep, 10 1/4" wide at treble bout, and 15 3/8" wide at bass bout. The **#100 ACJ** (retail list $1,695) has a solid acajoux top/back/sides/fingerboard, rosewood bridge, orange wood binding, and a vintage satin finish. The **#200 APM** (list $1,795) has an Engelmann spruce top, maple back and sides, rosewood fingerboard/bridge/binding, and vintage satinized Gold varnish; while the **#300 BW** has figured manzoniza walnut back/sides/fingerboard, rosewood and orange wood rope binding (list $1,995). Pearse's **#400 BAF** has highly figured afromosia top/back/sides/fingerboard, rosewood bridge, rosewood and orange wood rope binding, and a vintage satin finish for a retail price of $1,995. If the company name seems familiar, it's because Breezy Ridge is connected with John Pearse Strings – and John Pearse Strings has been producing some pretty fine guitar strings for quite some time.

JOHNSON
Instruments currently produced in Asia. Distributed by the Music Link of Brisbane, California.

The Music Link's Johnson guitars offers a wide range of acoustic and electric guitars, with prices aimed at the entry level and student guitarists. Please contact Music Link directly for more information (see Trademark Index). There are also 8 different practice amps in the Johnson line, as well as numerous accessories like cases, Quartz tuners, and tuning machines.

**Jon Kammerer Cypress
Model 13 Clasical
courtesy Jon Kammerer**

ACOUSTIC: DREADNOUGHTS & JUMBOS

Johnson has greatly expanded their line in recent years. They now offer a full range of dreadnought guitars as well as other sizes. They have the 610, 620, and 620 cutaway Player series. These guitars start at $89 and range up to around $250. They feature many different sizes, features, and color options. There are also acoustic/electric models available. Other series include the Songwriter series and the 000 size series.

The Jumbo Cutaway model **JG-740** has a laminated flame maple top veneer, and are available in Blue, Green, Red, and Sunburst ($199). Some models were also available with a piezo bridge pickup and onboard preamps. All Johnson acoustic guitars are typically available in heavy quantities and sell typically about 30-50% off of retail, depending upon the guitar and how many someone wants to get rid of!

ACOUSTIC: METAL BODY & RESONATORS

Resonator models feature chrome-plated bell brass bodies, mahogany necks, 14/19-fret rosewood fingerboards, and 3-per-side Gotoh tuners. The **JM-998-C Style O-Cutaway** has a single rounded cutaway body ($1,650). It is also available with a biscuit pickup as the **JM-998-CE** ($1,850). Other Sterling Style O models include the full body **JM-998-D Style O** is the same as the cutaway model ($895); the **JM-998-R Style O** full body model has a different pattern on the resonator plate ($895).

Johnson Tricone resonator guitars are modeled after the original, pre-World War II guitars. Models included chrome-plated bell brass bodies, mahogany necks, 12/19-fret rosewood fingerboards, and 3-per-side Gotoh tuners. The **JM-991 Style I** plain body (no design) model lists at $1,650. The **JM-992 Style II** ($2,295) has the Wild Rose engraved design; the **JM-993 Style III** ($2,995) has the engraved Lily of the Valley design; and the **JM-993 Style IV** ($3,595) has the engraved Chrysanthemum design. There is also painted resonators available, model **JM-996**.

Johnson wood body resonators typically have spruce or mahogany bodies with different types of resonators. The **JR-200 Chicago Blues** has a diecast Spider Bridge, is available with a roundneck or squareneck, comes in Blueburst or Sunburst finishes and retails for $299. The **JR-400 Nashville Slide Model** has a Sandcast Spider Bridge and is meant for slide guitar. This guitar comes with Natural, Mahogany, Sunburst, or Cherryburst finishes and retails for $499. The **JR-440 Bass** is the equivilent to the JR-400 and retails for $595 ($675 with a pickup). The **JR-500 Classic Trolian** has M.O.P. position markers, a hard maple biscuit bridge, and retails for $495. The **JR-520-EM Electric Thinbody Triolian** is like the JR-500 except has a single cutaway and a built in humbucking pickup with a spun aluminum resonator. The retail is $625.

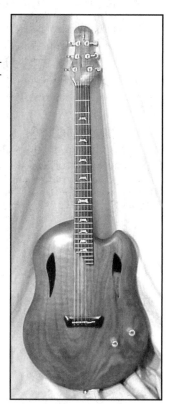

**Jon Kammerer Walnut
Model 8
courtesy Jon Kammerer**

JOHNSON GUITARS
Instruments previously built in Talkkeetna, Alaska.

Luthier Johnson started building guitars in 1981. Originally working out of a gutted R.V. trailer, Johnson operated a one-man shop located in his home in rural Alaska, located at the base of Mt. McKinley (North America's tallest mountain). Johnson narrowed down his line of guitar models to a few select models; and as the single builder gave close attention to each commissioned guitar during construction. Johnson offered such custom options as a custom size or design, Englemann spruce or cedar tops, flame walnut back and sides, and onboard electronics. A standard hard shell case was included in the retail prices.

ACOUSTIC

Johnson offered 5 acoustic models and one archtop model. All models featured a Sitka spruce top, East Indian rosewood back and sides, 25.5" scale ebony fingerboard. The **Size A** Concert listed at $2,000, and was also available in a Classical version at $2,500. The **Size C** Grand Auditorium listed at $2,000, as well as the **Size D** Dreadnought and the **Size E** Jumbo.

The single cutaway **American Archtop** model had a hand carved Sitka or Engelmann spruce top, flame maple back, sides, and neck, 2 f-holes, and an ebony fingerboard, tailpiece, and bridge (last list price was $4,000).

JON KAMMERER GUITARS
Instruments currently manufactured by Jon Kammerer Guitars located in Keokuk, IA, beginning 2000.

Luthier Jon Kammerer originally started manufacturing his unique acoustic instruments because of a 1995 thesis project for industrial design school. After much research, it was determined that up to 2/3 of the sound waves in an acoustic guitar bounce into a corner and directly back onto themselves, canceling each other. Also, the standard boxy appearance of an acoustic guitar had not been changed for a long time. This led to his experimentation with both ceramic and fiberglass guitar bodies. Utilizing state-of-the-art CAD/CAM software and computer controlled milling machines, every wood part in a Kammerer guitar is machine made to high tolerances. The unique contoured body is cut out of two blanks, then precisely glued at the center. All Kammerer instruments include a dual action truss rod, 4-screw neck, Gotoh tuning machines, cast acrylic saddle and nut, strap mounting buttons, and a hard shell case. In 2002 Jon started producing electric guitars as well.

Jon Kammerer makes both acoustics and acoustic electrics, with or without cutaway, and in various colors/finishes. A standard satin acoustic guitar is ($995 MSR), gloss acoustic guitar ($1,250 MSR), single cutaway satin ($1,085), and a single cutaway gloss ($1,430). Options include one flame color inlay ($200 MSR), multi color flame inlay ($300), etched flame inlay ($50 MSR), L.R. Baggs pickup with preamp ($200+ MSR), single cutaway body ($180 MSR), deep body ($100), translucent color finish ($200 MSR), or solid primary color ($200). Please contact Jon Kammerer directly for more information (see Trademark Index).

JOSHUA GUITARS
Instruments currently manufactured in Northridge, CA.

Joshua guitars feature quality woods with neat designs on the side of the body.

ACOUSTIC ELECTRIC

Joshua Guitars utilize maple tops (available in 4 different Sunburst colors), and a glass fiber deep back body with onboard 4-band EQ Peizo pickup system. Current models include the JAE-750F ($375 retail), the JAE-850F ($389 retail), and the JAE-900 ($399 retail).

New models have been released including the JSP-1000, and the JSP-2000 AE.

JUDD GUITARS
Instruments previously built in Cranbrook (British Columbia), Canada.

Judd custom instruments were produced in Cranbrook, British Columbia. Very little information is known about the company and what kind of guitars they produced.

JUNIOR
See chapter on House Brands.

This trademark has been identified as a Gibson built budget line available from 1919 through 1926. The pegheads carry no logo, and essentially are no-frills versions of low end Gibsons. They will have a label different from the standard Gibson label of the time, but still credit Gibson as the manufacturer. As a Gibson-built budget line instrument these guitars do not possess an adjustable truss rod in the neck, (Source: Walter Carter, *Gibson Guitars: 100 Years of an American Icon*).

Section K

K & S

Instruments previously built in Mexico. Previously distributed by K & S Guitars of Berkeley, California.

George Katechis and Marc Silber (K & S), two noted guitar experts, have re-introduced the Acoustic Hawaiian Slide Guitar. Born in the 1920s, this guitar design enjoyed moderate success before being overtaken by the louder resonator-driven National-style guitars of the early 1930s. The new instruments are modeled after designs by Weissenborn, Hilo, and Knutsen.

Prices start at $700 for these solid wood acoustic Hawaiian Slide Guitars. Wood options include Canadian cedar top and Spanish Cedar body; Sitka Spruce top and Spanish cedar, Honduras mahogany, maple, or California koa (acacia) body, or all California koa. Instruments are bound and feature Van Gent tuners.

K.D. DAVIS GUITARS

Instruments currently built in Sonoma, California.

Luthier Kevin D. Davis is currently building handcrafted custom guitars. For further information concerning model specification and pricing, please contact luthier Kevin Davis directly (see Trademark Index).

KAKOS, STEPHEN

Instruments currently built in Mound, Minnesota since 1975.

Luthier Stephen Kakos began building classical guitars in 1972, and turned to full time building in 1975. Kakos concentrates specifically on classical acoustics, although he has built a few flamenco guitars on request. His Standard Model has Indian Rosewood back and sides, Engelmann spruce or cedar top, mahogany or Spanish Cedar neck, Sloan cast bronze tuners, French Polish finish (Retail $4,900). In addition to guitar building, Kakos also performs some repairs. For further information on models and pricing, please contact luthier Kakos directly (see Trademark Index).

KALAMAZOO

See chapter on House Brands.

In the late 1930s, the Gibson guitar company decided to offer their own entry level guitars. While similar to models built for other distributors (Cromwell, Fascinator, or Capital) in construction, the Kalamazoo line was originally only offered for about five years. Models included flattop and archtop acoustics, lap steels (and amps), and mandolins.

Pre-war Kalamazoo instruments, like other Gibson budget instruments, do not have an adjustable truss rod (a key difference), different construction techniques, and no identifying Gibson logo.

In the mid 1960s, Gibson again released an entry level series of guitars under the Kalamazoo trademark, except all models were electric solid body guitars (except a flattop acoustic) that had a double offset cutaway body, bolt-on necks, six on a side headstock, and 1 or 2 pickups. The body profile of late 1960s models then switched to even dual cut-a-ways. The second run of Kalamazoo models came to an end in the early 1970s. These Post-war models do feature an adjustable truss rod.

Kalamazoo serial numbers are impressed into the back of the headstock, and feature six digits like the regular Gibson line. However, the Kalamazoo numbers do not match or correspond with the Gibson serialization (in the back of this book). Further information regarding Kalamazoo serialization will appear in future editions of the *Blue Book of Acoustic Guitars*, (Source: Walter Carter, Gibson Guitars: *100 Years of an American Icon*).

KALIL

Instruments currently built in McComb, Mississippi.

Luthier Edward E. Kalil builds instruments to custom order. Kalil currently offers acoustic steel and nylon models, as well as solid body electrics. Costs will vary due to complexity of the design and appointments.

Kalil began building guitars after attending a class at Guitar Research and Design (GRD) run by Charles Fox in South Strafford, Vermont. Kalil's class instructor was George Morris. Kalil has been a member of the Guild of American Luthiers (G.A.L.) since 1981, and a member of A.S.I.A. (Association of Stringed Instrument Artisans) since 1988.

Kalil instruments can be easily identified by the 'Kalil' headstock logo. Kalil also offers the Lick En Stik travel guitar, a full scale instrument with a compact body and built in amp (with variable distortion). For further information, contact luthier Edward E. Kalil directly (see Trademark Index).

KAMICO

See chapter on House Brands.

This trademark has been identified as the House Brand of the Kay Guitar company. As one of the leading suppliers of House Brand guitars, Kay also supplied an entry level budget line of guitars to various musical instrument distributors, (Source: Willie G. Moseley, *Stellas & Stratocasters*).

**Kalamzoo KG 22
courtesy Guitar Emporium**

K

**Kalamzoo Sport Model
courtesy Rod & Hank's
Vintage Guitar Co.**

KANSAS

Instruments previously built near Lawrence, Kansas.

The Kansas guitar company, located outside of Lawrence, Kansas built acoustic guitars from circa 1910 to World War II. During the war, the company switched over to producing gun stocks. After the war (circa 1946 to 1948) the company was sold to the employees, then went out of business.

A Kansas trademark later showed up on guitars featured by the Sears, Roebuck catalog until the catalog folded in 1991. It is unknown whether or not the two Kansas trademarks were related. Further information will be updated in future editions of the *Blue Book of Acoustic Guitars*.

KAY

See chapter on House Brands. Instruments previously built between the 1930s and the late 1960s. Kay stringed instruments were manufactured and distributed by the Kay Musical Instrument Company of Chicago, Illinois. Kay, along with Harmony, were the two larger suppliers of House Brand instruments for distributors and retailers. The Kay trademark returned in the 1970s. Currently the instruments are produced in Asia, and are distributed by A.R. Musical Enterprises, Inc. of Fishers, Indiana.

The roots of the Kay Musical Instruments company begin back in 1890, when the Groeschel Company of Chicago, Illinois first began building bowl-back (or potato bug) mandolins. In 1918 Groeschel was changed to the Stromberg-Voisenet Company, and incorporated in 1921. Vice-president C.G. Stromberg directed production of guitars and banjos under the Mayflower trademark (See Mayflower). This Stromberg is not to be confused with luthier Charles Stromberg (and son Elmer) of Boston, Massachusetts. Stromberg-Voisenet introduced the process of laminating wood tops and backs in 1924, and also began arching instruments tops and backs. Henry Kay Kuhrmeyer, who later became company president, offered use of his middle name on the more popular Kay-Kraft series of Stromberg-Voisenet's guitars, mandolins and banjos.

The Kay era began when Henry Kay Kuhrmeyer bought the Stromberg-Voisenet company in 1928. Kuhrmeyer renamed the company Kay Musical Instruments in 1931, and began mass-producing stringed instruments in large volume. Kay, like Washburn at the turn of the century, claimed production of almost 100,000 instruments a year by the mid 1930s. Kay instruments were both marketed by the company themselves, or produced for jobbers (distributors) and retail houses under various names. Rather than produce a list here, the *Blue Book of Acoustic Guitars* has attempted to identify Kay-produced House Brands throughout the alphabetical listing in this text. Many of these instruments were entry level or students instruments then, and should be considered entry level even now. But as Jay Scott (author of *50's Cool: Kay Guitars*) points out, "True, the vast majority of Kay's student-grade and intermediate guitars were awful. But the top of each line – banjo, guitar and mandolin (especially the acoustic and electric jazz guitars and flattop acoustics) – were meritorious pieces of postwar musical art."

Kay introduced upright basses in 1937, and marketed them under both the Kay trademark and K. Meyer (a clever abbreviation of Kuhrmeyer?). After Leo Fender debuted his Precision electric bass at the 1951 NAMM trade show, Kay was the first company to join Fender in the electric bass market as they introduced their K-162 model in 1952. Kay also went on to produce some of the coolest mixtures of classic archtop design and '50s modern acrylic headstocks on the "Gold K" line that debuted in 1957.

The Kay Musical Instrument company was sold to an investment group headed by Sydney Katz in 1955. Katz, a former manager of Harmony's service department, was more aggressive and competitive in the guitar market. Kay's production facilities expanded to try to meet the demand of the guitar market in the late 1950s and early 1960s. A large number of guitars were produced for Sears under their Silvertone trademark. At the peak of the guitar boom in 1964, Kay moved into a new million dollar facility located near Chicago's O'Hare Airport.

Unfortunately, by 1965 the guitar market was oversaturated as retail demand fell off. While Kay was still financially sound, Katz sold the company to Seeburg. Seeburg, a large jukebox manufacturer based in Chicago, owned Kay for a period of two years. At this time, the whole guitar industry was feeling the pinch of economics. Seeburg wanted to maintain their niche in the industry by acquiring Valco Guitars, Inc. (See National or Dobro) and producing their own amplifiers to go with the electric Kay guitars. Bob Keyworth, the executive vice-president in charge of Kay, suggested the opposite: Seeburg should sell Kay to Valco.

Robert Engelhardt, who succeeded Louis Dopyera in Valco's ownership in 1962, bought Kay from Seeburg in June 1967. Valco moved into the Kay facilities, but Engelhardt's company was under financed from the beginning. Engelhardt did make some deal with an investment group or financial company, but after two years the bills couldn't be paid. The investment group just showed up one day, and changed the plant locks. By 1969 or 1970, both Valco Guitars Inc., and the Kay trademark were out of business.

The rights to the Kay name were acquired by Sol Weindling and Barry Hornstein, who were importing Teisco Del Rey (Kawai) guitars to the U.S. market with their W.M.I. importing company. W.M.I. begins putting the Kay name on the Teisco products beginning in 1973, and continued on through the 1970s. In 1980, Tony Blair of A.R. Enterprises purchased the Kay trademark. The Kay trademark is now on entry level/beginner guitars built in Asia, (1950s/1960s company history courtesy Jay Scott, *50's Cool: Kay Guitars*; contemporary history courtesy Michael Wright, *Vintage Guitar Magazine*).

KAY KRAFT

Sometimes hyphenated as Kay-kraft. See Kay. Instruments produced in Chicago, Illinois from the mid 1920s to the mid 1950s.

Henry Kay Kuhrmeyer, who worked his was up from company secretary, treasurer, and later president of Stromberg-Voisenet, lent his middle name to a popular selling line of guitars, mandolins, and banjos. When Kuhrmeyer gained control of Stromberg-Voisenet and changed the name to Kay Musical Instruments, he continued to use the Kay Kraft trademark. Instruments using this trademark could thus be either Stromberg-Voisenet or Kay (depending on the label) but was still produced by the *same* company in the *same* facilities.

KEL KROYDEN

See chapter on House Brands.

Faced with the severe American Depression of the 1930s, Gibson general manager Guy Hart converted most of company production to toy manufacturing as a means to keep his workforce employed. Kalamazoo Playthings produced wood blocks and wooden pull-toys from 1931 to 1933, while the Kel Kroyden offshoot built toy sailboats. Wood bodies, strings...and masts!

Kel Kroyden brand guitars seem to appear at the same time period that Kel Kroyden Toys were introduced. The "Kel" lettering is horizontal on the headstock, while "Kroyden" is lettered vertically, (Source: Walter Carter, *Gibson Guitars: 100 Years of an American Icon*).

KELLER, MICHAEL L.

Instruments currently built in Rochester, Minnesota.

Michael Keller currently builds world class instruments using the finest tonewoods in the heart of Southern Minnesota. He uses extreme precision when building guitars and no shortcuts are used. Michael's guitars have even impressed the likes of the famous guitar builder, James Olsen (also of Minnesota)! Contact Keller for any information and any custom work you may be interested in (see Trademark Index).

KELLISON, T. R.

Instruments currently built in Billings, Montana since 1978.

Luthier T.R. Kellison has been handcrafting custom instruments since 1978.

KEMPF, DAVID GUITARS

Instruments currently produced in Bivins, Texas.

David Kempf guitars feature solid wood construction, wood bindings and bound fretboards, and every model is a concert sized (000) fingerstyle guitar. Call Kempf for more information and a price quote (see Trademark Index).

KEN BEBENSEE GUITARS AND BASSES

Instruments currently built in Nevada City, California. Previously built in San Luis Obispo, California.

Luthier Ken Bebensee began building basses and guitars in high school as a musician trying to develop his own style. While studying engineering and industrial technology at Cal Poly State University (San Luis Obispo), Bebensee continued to refine and improve on his designs.

In 1983, Bebensee began offering custom built instruments. Bebensee works out of an old wooden shop in San Luis Obispo, and custom creates a handful of instruments per year. Bebensee's instruments are custom built from the highest grade of sustained yield, exotic woods. For further information (the full color brochure is breathtaking!), please contact luthier Bebensee directly (see Trademark Index).

Bebensee estimates that he has created over 80 instruments since 1983. Bebensee has finished 20 basses and guitars since his color brochure of 1997, most of them custom orders from professional musicians for recording and live performance. The headstock reads a "KB." In 2001/02, KB Guitars and Basses was relocated to Nevada City, California.

**Kay Sherwood Stanard
courtesy Dave Rogers
Dave's Guitar Shop**

ACOUSTIC & ACOUSTIC BASS

The flattop acoustic/electric guitar retails for $2,420. The archtop acoustic guitar retails for $4,420. The acoustic/electric bass retails for $2,650, and in five-string configuration is $2,790. The archtop acoustic bass (how many of these do you see?), retails for $4,680.

KENT

Instruments previously produced in Korea and Japan circa 1960s. Distributed in the U.S. by Buegeleisen & Jacobson of New York, New York; Maxwell Meyers in Texas; Southland Musical Merchandise Corporation in North Carolina; and Harris Fandel Corporation in Massachusetts.

The Kent trademark was used on a full line of acoustic and solid body electric guitars, banjos, and mandolins imported into the U.S. market during the 1960s. Some of the earlier Kent guitars were built in Japan by either the Teisco company or Guyatone, but the quality level at this time is down at the entry or student level. The majority of the models were built in Korea. The address for Kent Guitars (as distributed by Buegeleisen & Jacobson) during the 1960s was 5 Union Square, New York, New York 10003,(Source: Walter Murray, Frankenstein Fretworks; and Michael Wright, *Guitar Stories*, Volume One).

ACOUSTIC

Many of the Kent models were patterned after Gibson models. For example, the Kent **KF-340** is roughly a Gibson Dove knock-off, as it includes the dove motif pickguard, double parallelogram pearl fingerboard inlay, and moustache bridge assembly with pearl dove inlay. Notable design differences include the **KF-340**'s zero fret (which the Dove does not), chrome tuners instead of gold, and an obvious quality level. The **KF-340** was available in Natural and Black finishes. A Kent KF-340 in average condition brings around $100 in value.

KEYSTONE STATE

See Weymann & Sons.

**Kel Kroydon
courtesy Dave Rogers
Dave's Guitar Shop**

KIMAXE

Instruments currently produced in Korea and China. Distributed by Kenny & Michael's Co., Inc. of Los Angeles, California.

Kimaxe guitars are manufactured by Sang Jin Industrial Company, Ltd., which has a head office in Seoul, Korea and manufacturing facilities in four different places (Inchon, Bupyong, and Kongju, Korea; Tien Jin, China). Sang Jin Industrial Company, Ltd. is better known as a main supplier of guitars to world famous companies such as Fender, Hohner, and other buyers' own brand names for the past ten years. Sang Jin builds almost 10,000 guitars for these accounts each month. In 1994, Sang Jin established its own subsidiary (Kenny and Michael's Company) in Los Angeles in order to distribute their own lines of Kimaxe electric guitars and Corina acoustic guitars.

KIMBARA

Instruments previously produced in Japan from the late 1960s to 1990. Trademark re-introduced to British marketplace in 1995. Instruments currently produced in China. Distributed in the U.K. by FCN Music.

The Kimbara trademark was a brand name used by a UK importer on these Japanese-produced budget level instruments. Kimbara acoustics were first introduced in England in the late 1960s. During the 1970s, the Kimbara trademark was also applied to a number of solid body guitars based on classic American designs as well. Kimbara instruments are generally mid to good quality budget models, and a mainstay in the British market through 1990.

In 1995, FCN Music began importing Chinese-built classical and dreadnought acoustic guitars into England. Retail price-wise, the reborn line is back in its traditional niche, (Source: Jerry Uwins, Guitar Magazine [UK]).

KIMBERLY

Instruments currently produced in Seoul, Korea. Distributed by the Kimex Trading Co., Ltd. of Seoul, Korea. Instruments produced in Japan, circa 1960s to early 1970s. Previously distributed by Lafayette Company catalog sales.

According to initial research by Michael Wright in his book *Guitar Stories*, Volume One, Kimberly-branded guitars produced in Japan were sold through the Lafayette company catalog. The U.S. importer during this time period has yet to be pinpointed. Recent evidence that arose indicates that the Teisco company was one of the production companies for this trademark. Photographic evidence of a Kimberly-branded *May Queen* (yes, that infamous Teisco model!) recently arrived at the offices of the *Blue Book of Acoustic Guitars*. Fellow book enthusiasts are invited to send in photographs and information regarding their Kimberly guitars as well.

Current production of guitars under the Kimberly trademark is the Kimex Trading Co., Ltd. of Seoul, Korea. Kimex produces a number of guitar and bass models that favor classic American designs, and are designed with the entry level guitarist and student in mind.

KINGSTON

Instruments previously produced in Japan from 1958 to 1967, and distributed in the U.S. by Westheimer Importing Corporation of Chicago, Illinois.

The Kingston brand name was used by U.S. importer Westheimer Importing Corporation of Chicago, Illinois. Jack Westheimer, who was one of the original guitar importers and distributors, is currently president of Cort Musical Instruments of Northbrook, Illinois. The Kingston trademark was used on a product line of acoustic and solid body electric guitars, electric bass guitars, banjos, and mandolins imported into the U.S. market during the 1960s. It has been estimated that 150,000 guitars were sold in the U.S. during the 1960s. Some of the earlier Kingston guitars were built in Japan by either the Teisco company or Guyatone, (Source: Michael Wright, *Guitar Stories*, Volume One).

KING'S STONE

Instruments previously produced in Japan.

The King's Stone trademark was a brand name used by U.S. importers Elger/Hoshino of Ardmore, Pennsylvania. King's Stone, along with others like Goldentone, Jamboree, and Elger were all used on Japanese guitars imported to the U.S. Elger/Hoshino evolved into Hoshino USA, distributor of Ibanez guitars, (Source: Michael Wright, *Guitar Stories*, Volume One).

KINSCHERFF

Instruments currently built in Texas Hill Country, Texas.

Luthier Jamie Kinscherff has been hand crafting fine acoustic guitars for over many years. His first guitar was built in 1978 and the first guitar with the Kinscherff name on it was in 1990. He produced guitars in Austin, Texas for the most time. While Kinscherff has performed some repair work in the past (and accepts some currently), his main focus has been on building guitars. In 2003 Kingscherff was relocated to the Briarwood Ranch, which is east of Wimberly in the Texas Hill Country. Jamie estimates that he builds 18-20 guitars a year. The base price for guitars, including the hardshell case, is $4,200. For further information regarding his acoustic guitars, please contact luthier Kinscherff directly (see Trademark Index).

KISO GUITARS

Instruments currently produced in Glen Ellen, CA.

The Kiso name comes from the Kiso Valley of Japan where woodworking was of some of the finest. They have teamed up with Steve Klein to produced the KisoKlein guitar, which has several features. Retail prices for the dreadnought and fingerstyle guitars are $3,300. For more information refer to their web site (see Trademark Index).

KLEIN, STEVE
Instruments currently produced in Sonoma, California since 1976.

Steve Klein first began building electric guitars in Berkeley, California in 1967. A year later, Klein's grandfather introduced him to Dr. Michael Kasha at the University of California in Berkeley. Klein built his first acoustic after that meeting. He briefly attended the California College of Arts and Crafts in 1969, but left to continue building guitars.

In 1970, Klein built his second acoustic guitar. He moved to Colorado in the winter of 1970-1971; later that summer he was offered, but did not accept a job at The American Dream guitar shop back in San Diego (this shop was later bought by Bob Taylor and Kurt Listug, and grew into Taylor Guitars).

The third guitar Steve Klein built also had Kasha-inspired designs. Klein travelled to Detroit via Colorado, and met Richard Schneider. Schneider was building Kasha-style classical guitars at the time, and Klein thought that he was going to stay and apprentice with Schneider. Schneider looked at Klein's current guitar and said "Congratulations, You're a guitar builder," and sent Klein back home.

In the fall of 1972 Klein received his business license. He designed the current acoustic body shape and flying brace, and started work on the Electric Bird guitar. Later the next summer, Klein had finished the first L-457 acoustic; and by 1974 had finished three more acoustics, his first 12-string guitar, and the first small (39.6) body. Klein made a deal with Clayton Johnson (staff member of 'Bill Gramm Presents') to be able to get into concerts to show guitars to professional musicians. Klein got to meet such notables as Stills, Crosby, Young, David Lindly, Doc Watson, Roy Buchanan, John Sebastion (Loving Spoonful), and others. In the summer of 1975, Klein went to Los Angeles with guitars and met J.D. Souther; he also received a commission from Joni Mitchell, and set up shop in Oakland.

In 1976, Klein finally settled into his current shop space in Sonoma. He continued building and designing guitars while doing some repair work. Two years later he finished Joni Mitchell's guitar, and the Electric Bird as well. In 1979, Klein met Steve Kauffman at a G.A.L. convention in Boston. That same year, Klein and Carl Margolis began developing a small electric model that was nicknamed Lumpy by David Lindly. Klein also did a side project of antique repair, furniture, and chairs for George Lucas at the Skywalker Ranch. On a more personal note, Klein married Lin Marie DeVincent in the spring of 1985, and Michael Hedges played at their wedding.

The MK Electric model was designed in conjunction with Ronnie Montrose in 1986. By 1988 the small Klein electric design was finished, and was debuted at a trade show in 1989. Klein Electric Division was later started that same year, and Steve Klein began designing an acoustic Harp guitar for Michael Hedges. A year later the acoustic Harp project was dropped in favor of an electrical Harp design instead (Hedges and guitar appeared on the cover of the October 1990 issue of *Guitar Player* magazine).

In the early 1990s, Klein began designing an acoustic bass guitar *for and with* Bob Taylor of Taylor Guitars. The first prototypes were assembled by Steve Kauffman in 1993. A large acoustic guitar order came in from Japan a year later, and the shipment was sent in 1995. In order to concentrate on the acoustic guitar production, Klein sold his Electric Division to Lorenzo German that same year, and the Electric Division still operates out of the original Klein Sonoma facilities. The Taylor/Klein acoustic bass went into production in 1995, and currently there is a waiting period on acoustic models.

In 1997, Klein went into business with Ed Dufault and opened Klein's Sonoma Music. Located on Broadway in Sonoma, California, the music shop services the local community as well as offering acoustic guitars built by Klein and other high grade builders like Michael Lewis. There is an available video "Music That Sings" available from Klein's Sonomo Music.

ACOUSTIC

Klein currently focuses his attention on acoustic guitar building. His **Basic Klein Acoustic Guitar** features Indian Rosewood or walnut back and sides, a spruce top, rosewood neck, ebony bridge and fretboard, and gold plated tuners with Ebony buttons. The **M-43** starts at $6,500 without oval hole, and $7,500 without the oval hole. The model **S-39.6** carries a list price of $11,500; and the **L-45.7** is $12,000. The N-36.5 is also available. Klein offers a fairly fancy ornamentation package including mother-of-pearl snowflake inlays on the guitars. Optional custom features included a 12-string configuration, Florentine cutaway with hidden heel, and use of Brazilian rosewood.

KNIGHT
Instruments previously made in England during the 1970s and 1980s. Instruments currently built in Surrey, England.

Luthier Dick Knight (1907-1996) was a well respected British guitar maker, and examples of his work were collected world-wide. Knight (born Stanley Charles Knight) specialized in archtop guitar construction, notably the Imperial model. While Knight began building his first guitars in the 1930s, he became more prominent in the 1970s (and 1980s), and featured such clients as Dave Gilmour, Paul McCartney, Pete Townshend, and Mike Rutherford (among others).

During Knight's formative years in the 1930s he worked for Lagonda, the motor vehicle manufacturer. After work, Knight would construct wood items at home, and lost the tips of his fingers in an accident. As this accident prevented him from playing guitar, he turned to making instruments as a hobby.

At the outbreak of World War II Knight met Ben and Lew Davis (the owners of Selmers music shop in London), as well as Joe Van Straten (Selmers' shop manager). In addition to instrument repair, Van Straten suggested the two work on producing a quality English archtop. When finances would not permit the business to carry on, Selmers asked Knight to produce some guitars.

Later, when Knight's wife became ill, he left his work at Selmers and professional guitar making for seventeen years. During this time period, he did produce a number of instruments under the 'Knight' logo. Some of his earliest models do not have a name on the headstock. In addition to his archtop models, Knight produced flattop acoustic, solid body and *335*-style guitars. All Knight's instruments were produced with the same high degree of quality.

Recently, Knight's son-in-law Gordon Wells has been continuing to produce guitars and keep the Knight name alive in the guitar-building world, (Source: Keith Smart, *The Zemaitis Guitar Owners Club*).

KNUTSEN
Instruments previously built by Christopher J. Knutsen in Los Angeles, CA circa WWI-1930.

While Weissenborn has become the prestige, and at the same time generic, name for wooden hollow-neck Hawaiian guitars, nevertheless the innovator of this design may well have been Christopher J. Knutsen (1856-1930), also a pioneer of harp-guitar designs (which were later licensed by the estimable Larson Brothers). And Knutsen often combined these two seemingly disparate concepts.

He also made harp-ukuleles, harp mandolins and even the occasional standard instrument, but even a plain roundneck guitar might bear some charming feature testifying to his eccentricity-like an angled metal bracket fixed to neck and body with wing nuts which took the place of the neck's heel. Knutsen was granted a U.S. design patent on the harp guitar in 1898 (he also had Canadian patents in which he attempted to sell a percentage).

He spent most of his life in Seattle and environs, moving to Los Angeles around 1916, interestingly close to the beginnings of the Hawaiian music phenomenon which swept through the mainland after the Panama Pacific Exposition held in San Francisco in 1915. Knutsen aficionados have been trying to determine whether he might have made any Hawaiian guitars during his residency in Washington. If so, such a hypothetical guitar could be a historical Holy Grail, especially if it pre-dated the Exposition.

While some instruments from Washington bear the paper label reading "Harp Guitar Factory," there's little to suggest that his Los Angeles operation was any more than a one-man shop. And while there is an unmistakable exchange of design ideas going back and forth between Weissenborn and Knutsen, there is no concrete evidence that the two ever worked together or one for the other.

Early Hawaiian guitar designs showed a variety of neck joints-from slight extensions of the body up to true hollow necks. While Weissenborn also made some square, solid-neck Hawaiians, Knutsen made several instruments with partial hollow necks; in other words, the headstock joints might be somewhere between the third and 12th frets. One headstock sports original six-on-a-side tuners, perhaps 30 years before Merle Travis's Bigsby or the Fender Broadcaster.

The closest semblance to sales literature for Knutsen's offerings are the picture labels showing examples of his work found in some instruments.

(Many labels have name, business and address information only.) Unlike Weissenborn styles 1 through 4, Knutsen's instruments are not so conveniently identified and have to be considered individually. Some are very plain, while others are extraordinarily elaborate.

Koa and mahogany bodies (sometimes with spruce tops) are the most common woods for body construction. Familiar Knutsen design touches include rope binding (usually larger than Weissenborn's), harp sub-bass and treble strings, a fretboard inlays often mixing shapes, angled back braces and minimal top bracing. Some instruments feature dramatically figured one-piece backs with the grain pattern running at an angle somewhere between crossways or lengthwise. Seeing the variety and ambition of Knutsen's optimistic designs can't help but make the observer think this builder was a colorful benign eccentric.

Knutsen has been disparaged widely in vintage-instrument circles (his instruments are for the most part, woefully under built), but when they hold-or have been patched back-together, they usually sound great. Builder and author Rick Turner said it best when he proclaimed Knutsen "a brilliant hack." His Hawaiian harp guitars are warm, resonant and responsive, but not as haunting and bright as most Weissenborns.

Perhaps the only way to identify an unlabeled Knutsen is to compare other Knutsen instruments. While codifying his designs flies in the face of organization and logic, seeing a few of his creations conveys the notion that Knutsen is better understood by feel and experience than by facts and statistics.

Because there are no standard models of Knutsen instruments, establishing prices becomes largely a matter of finding common ground between selling and buying parties. Weissenborn and other similar instruments can be a guide, with the most important factors being sound, condition and playability. The latter two can be a sticking point for Knutsen instruments, because they are so fragile. Some types of Knutsen instruments lend themselves to functional restoration better than others-e.g., Hawaiian guitars better than harp-guitars with many sub-bass and treble strings. Some guitars that began as Spanish guitars might better be considered as Hawaiians after three generations of cracking and warping.

For Knutsen & Hawaiian guitars, prices can run from $700-$1,000 for a plain, much-repaired example, to the $3,000+ range for a pristine specimen (it does happen). Harp instruments tend to fetch similar prices, with the more elaborate harp guitars running to $4,000 and beyond, (The publisher wishes to express his thanks to Mr. Ben Elder for making this information available).

KNUTSON LUTHIERY
Instruments currently built in Forrestville, California.

Luthier John Knutson has been building and repairing stringed instruments in and around the San Francisco Bay area since 1978. As a custom builder of acoustic, archtop, and electric instruments, Knutson has produced hundreds of guitars, mandolins, dulcimers, and basses (including custom double-and triple-neck combinations). Knutson is currently producing the **Songbird** Archtop guitar (list $5,500), the **Songbird** Archtop mandolin (list $3,750), the Flattop acoustic (list $2,750), and the **Nightlife** Archtop Guitar (list $7,500). All instruments are limited edition, numbered, signed, and handcrafted by the luthier. John Knutson holds the exclusive rights to the Songbird, Messenger, and Ecotone trademarks. For further information contact luthier John Knutson directly (see Trademark Index).

KOHNO
Instruments currently built in Japan since the mid 1960s.

Luthier Masaru Kohno was noted as being the leading Japanese classical-style guitar maker in author Tony Bacon's *Ultimate Guitar Book* (1991). Kohno studied under luthier Arcangel Fernandez in his Madrid workshop, and later opened his own operation in Tokyo during the late 1960s.

Masaru Kohno died of cancer in 1998. Pricing is unsure on these guitars as even the web site states that they cannot estimate guitars. For more information refer to the web site (see Trademark Index).

KONA
Instruments currently produced in Asia. Distributed by M&M Merchandisers of Ft. Worth, Texas.

M&M Merchandisers has owned pawn shops since 1976 and done a lot of buying and selling of instruments as well as other products. In July, 2001, they introduced a line of guitars built overseas. There are acoustics, electrics, and guitar amplifiers. Kona guitars are quality instruments at affordable prices. Most retail prices are between $200 and $250. For more information contact M&M Merchandisers (see Trademark Index).

KOONTZ
See also Standel and Harptone. Instruments previously built in Linden, New Jersey.

Luthier Stan Koontz designed several different models of acoustic and electric guitars and basses for Bob Crooks' Standel company. The instruments were built in Harptone's New Jersey facilities, and have the Standel logo on the peghead. Koontz also built his own custom guitars that featured striking innovations as side-mounted electronics and a hinged internal f-hole cover, (Source: Tom Wheeler, *American Guitars*).

KRAMER
Kramer (the original BKL company) previously located in Neptune, New Jersey since its inception in 1975 to the late 1980s. Production of Kramer (KMI) instruments was at facilities in Eatontown, New Jersey. The Kramer trademark is currently held by the Gibson Guitar Corporation of Nashville, Tennessee. Currently distributed by MusicYo.

Gary Kramer and Dennis Berardi founded the firm in October of 1975 to produce guitars. Kramer, one of the ex-partners of Travis Bean, brought in his guitar building know-how to Berardi's previous retail experience. In the following April, Peter J. LaPlaca joined the two. LaPlaca had worked his way up through Norlin to vice presidency before joining Kramer and Berardi. The original company is named after their three initials: B, K, and L.

Kramer (BKL) opened the Neptune factory on July 1, 1976. The first Kramer guitar was co-designed by luthier Phil Petillo, Berardi, and Kramer. Once the prototypes were completed and the factory tooled up, the first production run was completed on November 15, 1976. The first solid body guitars featured an original body design, and a bolt-on aluminum neck with rear wood inlays.

One month after the first production run was finished, Gary Kramer left the BKL company. Guitar production under the Kramer trademark continued. By the early 1980s, the company line consisted of 14 different guitar and bass designs with a price range of $649 to $1,418. Kramer's high profile continued to rise, thanks to an exclusive endorsement deal with Edward Van Halen. In the mid 1980s, the company flourished as they had the sole license to market the Floyd Rose tremolo system.

In 1985, Berardi bought the Spector company; production and distribution of Spector basses then originated from Kramer's facilities in New Jersey. Throughout the late 1980s, Kramer was one of the guitar companies favored by the hard rock/heavy metal bands (along with Charvel/Jackson). However, the company went into bankruptcy in 1989, attempted refinancing several times, and was purchased at auction by a group that incorporated the holdings under the company name of Kramer Musical Instruments in 1995. The newly-reformed Kramer (KMI) company had also acquired the rights to the Spector trademark and Spector instruments designs. Kramer (KMI) was located in Eatontown, New Jersey.

Kramer (KMI) re-introduced several new models at industry trade shows in 1995, again sporting an aluminum neck design. However, the company never did directly bring any large amount of products to the musical instrument market.

In 1997, the Gibson corporation acquired the Kramer trademark. By 1998, Gibson was displaying Kramer trademarked models at the Summer NAMM industry show, ads in the print media followed a month later.

ACOUSTIC ELECTRIC

In 1988, Kramer offered several models designed by luthier Danny Ferrington. The Kramer Ferringtons were thinline, hollowbody acoustics with bridge mounted piezo pickup systems, volume and tone controls. The six on a side headstocks and slimmer profile necks felt more like an electric guitar, and the instruments could be used in performances with minimal feedback problems.

Currently Kramer has a few acoustic and acoustic/electric models are available. Most of them are priced between $100-$250. For more information on these guitars refer to MusicYo's web site (see Trademark Index).

FERRINGTON II KFS2 - offset double cutaway acoustic body, round soundhole, six on a side pointy headstock, chrome tuners, rosewood bridge, volume/2 tone knobs, available in Black, Red, or White finishes, mfg. 1986-1991.

N/A $350 $200

Last MSR was $550.

GRADING	100%	EXCELLENT	AVERAGE

FERRINGTON II KFT2 - single cutaway acoustic body, round soundhole, six on a side pointy headstock, chrome tuners, rosewood bridge, volume/2 tone knobs, available in Black, Red, or White finishes, mfg. 1986-1991.

	N/A	$350	$200

Last MSR was $550.

KREMONA
Instruments currently produced in Kazanlak, Bulgaria. Distributed by Kremona USA Inc. in Monroe, MI.

Kremona was established in 1924 and produces and distributes stringed musical instruments. Instruments are distributed in the U.S., Russia, and Germany. They produce acoustic guitars along with violins, violas, cellos, and other stringed instruments. All acoustic guitars are classical nylon stringed models and retail prices are typically between $200-$400. Contact the company for more information (see Trademark Index).

KYLE, DOUG
Instruments currently built in Hampstead (Devon), England.

Doug Kyle is currently offering handcrafted guitars. For additional information regarding models, pricing, and specifications, please contact luthier Kyle directly (see Trademark Index).

K is for Krazed! Ryan Triggs (left, Lil' Wilbur), subway fugitive Nelson Ferrer (center), and master luthier James Triggs (Wilbur) are caught having way too much fun in Nashville. Teddy Krause from D'Aquisto Strings Inc. feels sorry for them and regularly gives them booth space. Where are the aliens when you need them?

Section L

LA CADIE

Instruments currently built in Vancouver, B.C., Canada.

Luthier Rod Hannah hand builds both dreadnought and 000 12-Fret acoustic guitars in "short lot" sizes (approximately 4 instruments at a time). Retail list prices start at $3,000 (and up).

LA JOLLA LUTHIERS

Instruments previously built in San Diego, California.

Luthier Wayne Harris and his shop produced both steel-string and classical guitar models. Both models feature the unusual "Bi-Level" design (developed by Roger Pytlewski), in which the guitar's top is bent into two levels; the levels connect in a 10 degree "ramp" where the bridge is located. The purpose of this design (as addressed in their advertising) was "to increase the instrument's high overtones and overall perceived brilliancy and volume." Readers of the *Blue Book of Acoustic Guitars* are encouraged to locate one of these guitars for testing purposes and send said results and photos for upcoming editions.

It is estimated that Harris built about 100 instruments a year. **The Collector's Series Bi Level** steel string model is a dreadnought-sized guitar with a Sitka spruce top, Brazilian rosewood body, fan bracing, adjustable truss rod, and mahogany neck (retail list was $2,167).

LA MANCHA

Instruments currently built in Paracho (Michoacan) Mexico. Distributed by La Mancha Guitars of Nashville, Tennessee.

Jerry Roberts has been providing fine classical guitars for over a quarter century. In 1996, Roberts debuted the La Mancha line, which offers handcrafted guitars inspired by Fleta, Friederick, Gilbert, Hauser, Ramierez, Romanillos, Ruck, and other legendary makers. La Mancha guitars are handmade by a team of highly skilled Mexican luthiers who are supervised by California luthiers Kenny Hill and Gil Carnal. Current models, information and prices can be found on the web site (see Trademark Index).

LA PATRIE

Instruments currently built in La Patrie, Quebec, Canada since 1982. Distributed by La Si Do, Inc. of St. Laurent, Quebec.

The village of La Patrie, Quebec has long been associated with Robert Godin as far back as the introduction of the Norman Guitar Company in 1972. Other Godin trademark instruments have been built there for years, so it was fitting that the line of classical guitars introduced in 1982 should bear the name of the La Patrie village. For full overall company history, see Godin.

L

GRADING		100%	EXCELLENT	AVERAGE

ACOUSTIC

All instruments in this series have the following features, unless otherwise listed: classic style, round soundhole, bound body, wood marquetry rosette, Honduras mahogany neck, 12/19-fret rosewood fingerboard, slotted peghead, 3-per-side gold tuners with pearloid buttons. Available in a Natural finish of special alcohol lacquer (Mfg. 1982 to date). All models may be optionally equipped in a hardshell case.

COLLECTION (MODEL 0463) - solid spruce top, solid rosewood back/sides, ebony tied bridge, high gloss lacquer finish.

MSR	$625		$500	$350	$225

Add $135 for EPM electronics (Model 0470).

CONCERT (MODEL 0425) - solid cedar top, mahogany back/sides, rosewood tied bridge, high gloss lacquer finish.

MSR	$392		$325	$200	$125

Add $40 for a left-handed configuration (Model 0449). Add $135 for EPM electronics (Model 0432). Add $175 for a left-handed configuration with EPM electronics (Model 0456).

ETUDE (MODEL 0340) - solid cedar top, mahogany back/sides, rosewood tied bridge, lacquer satin finish.

MSR	$325		$250	$150	$100

Add $35 for a left-handed configuration (Model 0364). Add $135 for EPM electronics (Model 0357). Add $170 for a left-handed configuration with EPM electronics (Model 0371).

MOTIF (MODEL 8841) - similar to the Etude, except features a more compact body, available in semi-gloss lacquer finish, mfg. 1998-current.

MSR	$309		$225	$150	$100

Add $135 for EPM electronics (Model 8858).

GRADING		100%	EXCELLENT	AVERAGE

PRESENTATION (MODEL 0388) - solid spruce top, rosewood back/sides, rosewood tied bridge, semi-gloss lacquer finish.

MSR	$475		$375	$250	$175

Add $135 for EPM electronics (Model 0395).

LACOTE

Instruments previously built in Paris, France during the early to mid 1800s.

Luthier Rene Lacote was hand building acoustic guitars during the first half of the nineteenth century. According to author Tony Bacon, Lacote is sometimes credited with the invention of the scalloped fingerboard. Many of Lacote's guitars featured relatively small bodies braced with "transverse" strutting inside the top.

During the late 18th century, the European guitar was moving away from earlier designs containing 5 or 6 "courses" (a "course" was a pair of strings) to the simple six single string design. This design is closer to what the modern "classical" guitar looks like today. Lacote's designs in the 1830s followed the six-string models, (Source: Tony Bacon, *The Ultimate Guitar Book*).

LACEY GUITARS

Instruments currently built in Nashville, Tennessee.

Luthier Mark Lacey studied formal training in musical instrument technology at the London School of Design. Lacey has been repairing and building fine instruments since 1974. During that time, he spent two years affiliated at Gruhn Guitars in Nashville, Tennessee where he gained insight from noted vintage guitar expert George Gruhn. Lacey's guitars start at $6,000 and go up to $20,000+ with options. For more information or to order visit Lacey's web site (see Trademark Index).

LADY LUCK

Instruments currently produced in Korea since 1986. Distributed in the U.S., Europe, and South America by Lady Luck Industries, Inc. of Cary, Illinois.

President Terresa Miller has been offering a wide range of imported, affordable guitars that are designed for beginning students up to working professionals. Lady Luck guitar models are designed in the U.S. (specifications and colors). Lady Luck also offers several models of electric bass guitars along with the line of acoustic and electric guitars.

In addition to the Lady Luck and Nouveau brands, Lady Luck Industries also distributes Adder Plus pickups and EV Star Cables.

ACOUSTIC

Lady Luck acoustics feature dreadnought style models with bound tops, mahogany back and sides, rosewood fingerboards and bridges, and 3-on-a-side diecast tuners. The **LLAC1** has a Honeyburst satin finish; the **LLAC2** features a high gloss Tobacco Sunburst finish. The acoustic/electric **LLACE** model has a single rounded cutaway, and bound spruce top. Acoustic electrics have retail list prices that range from $310 to $378.

LAFAYETTE (KOREA MFG.)

Instruments currently built in Korea. Distributed by the More Company of Pooler, Georgia.

The More Company, distributors of Synsonic instruments, is also offering a wide range of acoustic and acoustic/electric guitars; and solid body electric guitars and basses. Acoustic models like the SW 690 have a retail list price of $460; acoustic/electrics start at $500. Solid body electric models range from $350 up to $625, and basses run from $575 to $650. For additional information regarding models, specifications, and pricing, please contact Lafayette (a More Company) directly (see Trademark Index).

LAGARDE

See Cosi.

LAKEWOOD

Instruments currently built in Germany since 1985. Represented in North America by Bill Dixon located in Booth Bay Harbor, ME.

Luthier Martin Seeliger founded Lakewood Guitars in 1985. Seeliger apprenticed for three years with luthier Manfred Pletz, and then worked as a repairman for local music shops. His experience restoring and repairing different types and brands of acoustic guitars was utilized when he began designing his own style of acoustic steel string instruments.

MODEL STYLE APPOINTMENTS

Style 14 to 18: All solid woods, wood binding, rosewood fingerboard, mother-of-pearl Lakewood peghead logo, bone nut, angled bridge saddle, and Schaller machine heads.

Style 22 to 32: All solid woods, wood binding, ebony fingerboard, mother-of-pearl Lakewood peghead logo, bone nut, angled bridge saddle, and Schaller machine heads.

Style 46 to 50: All solid woods, wood binding, ebony fingerboard, abalone Lakewood peghead logo on Brazilian rosewood veneer, bone nut, angled bridge saddle, and gold Schaller machine heads.

Style 54: All solid woods, wood binding, abalone top purfling, ebony fingerboard, abalone Lakewood peghead logo on Brazilian rosewood veneer, bone nut, angled bridge saddle, and gold Schaller machine heads with ebony buttons.

All prices include a deluxe hardshell case. Lakewood offers two different neck widths (the Ragtime and the Medium), and a number of inlay options as well. **Deluxe** models have ebony fingerboards, custom abalone and wood soundhole rosettes, and peghead binding. The following price options are quoted at their suggested retail prices.

Add $130 for a left-handed cutaway body style. Add $200 for Fishman Powerjack. Add $300 for L.R. Baggs ribbon transducer and remote control. Add $490 for a cutaway body style. Add $300 for 12-String configuration.

ACOUSTIC: AUDITORIUM SERIES

Auditorium series guitars feature small bodies coupled with wider necks joined at the body at the twelfth fret.

The **A-14 DELUXE** has a solid spruce top, round soundhole, bound body, inlaid rosette, mahogany back/sides/neck, 12/19-fret rosewood fingerboard with pearl dot inlay, rosewood bridge with black white dot pins, chrome tuning pegs, mother-of-pearl Lakewood logo headstock inlay, 3-per-side slotted headstock, available in Natural gloss finish. disc, and last MSR was $2,799.

The **A-32 DELUXE** has a solid Sitka spruce top, round soundhole, bound body, inlaid rosette, East Indian rosewood back and sides, mahogany neck, 12/19-fret ebony fingerboard with pearl dot inlay, rosewood bridge with black white dot pins, chrome tuning pegs, abalone pearl Lakewood logo headstock inlay, 3-per-side slotted headstock, available in Natural gloss finish, current mfg., and retail of $2,413.

The **A-50 DELUXE** has a solid Sitka spruce top, round soundhole, bound body, inlaid rosette, flamed maple back and sides, mahogany neck, 12/19-fret ebony fingerboard with pearl dot inlay, rosewood bridge with black white dot pins, chrome tuning pegs, abalone pearl Lakewood logo headstock inlay, 3-per-side slotted headstock., available in Natural gloss finish, disc., last MSR was $4,399.

The **A-54 DELUXE** has a solid European spruce top, round soundhole, abalone pearl bound body, abalone pearl rosette, Brazilian rosewood back and sides, mahogany neck, 12/19-fret ebony fingerboard with pearl dot inlay, rosewood bridge with black white dot pins, gold tuning machines with ebony buttons, abalone pearl Lakewood logo headstock inlay, 3-per-side slotted headstock. Available in Natural gloss finish, disc., last MSR was $5,399.

ACOUSTIC: DREADNOUGHT SERIES

Lakewood's dreadnought series guitars feature arched tops and backs for improved dynamic response.

Add $300 for a 12-string configuration.

The **D-14** has a solid spruce top, round soundhole, wood binding, inlaid rosette, mahogany back/sides/neck, 14/20-fret rosewood fingerboard with pearl dot inlay, rosewood bridge with black white dot pins, 3-per-side chrome tuners, white mother-of-pearl Lakewood logo headstock inlay, available in Natural satin finish, current mfg., MSR or $1,929. The **D-14 Deluxe** is similar to the D-14, except features an ebony fingerboard, available in Natural gloss finish, disc. last MSR was $2,299.

The **D-18** has a Sitka spruce top, round soundhole, wood binding, inlaid rosette, ovankol back and sides, mahogany neck, 14/20-fret rosewood fingerboard with pearl dot inlay, rosewood bridge with black white dot pins, 3-per-side chrome tuners, white mother-of-pearl Lakewood logo headstock inlay. Available in Natural satin finish, disc., last MSR was $2,099. The **D-18 Deluxe** is similar to the D-18, except features an ebony fingerboard, available in Natural gloss finish, disc., last MSR was $2,399.

The **D-22** has a Sitka spruce top, round soundhole, wood binding, inlaid rosette, solid walnut back and sides, mahogany neck, 14/20-fret rosewood fingerboard with pearl dot inlay, rosewood bridge with black white dot pins, 3-per-side chrome tuners, white mother-of-pearl Lakewood logo headstock inlay, available in Natural satin finish, disc., last MSR was $2,199. The **D-22 Deluxe** is similar to the D-22, except features an ebony fingerboard, available in Natural gloss finish., disc., last MSR was $2,599.

The **D-32** has a Sitka spruce top, round soundhole, wood binding, inlaid rosette, solid East Indian rosewood back and sides, mahogany neck, 14/20-fret ebony fingerboard with pearl dot inlay, rosewood bridge with black white dot pins, 3-per-side chrome tuners, abalone pearl Lakewood logo headstock inlay, available in Natural satin finish, disc., last MSR was $2,399. The **D-32 Deluxe** is similar to the D-32, available in Natural gloss finish, disc., last MSR was $2,799.

The **D-46 DELUXE** has a European spruce top, round soundhole, wood binding, abalone pearl inlaid rosette, solid East Indian rosewood back and sides, mahogany neck, 14/20-fret ebony fingerboard with pearl dot inlay, bound peghead, rosewood bridge with black white dot pins, 3-per-side gold-plated tuners, abalone pearl Lakewood logo headstock inlay, available in Natural gloss finish, disc., last MSR was $3,699.

The **D-50 DELUXE** has a European spruce top, round soundhole, wood binding, abalone pearl inlaid rosette, solid flame maple back and sides, mahogany neck, 14/20-fret ebony fingerboard with pearl dot inlay, bound peghead, rosewood bridge with black white dot pins, 3-per-side gold-plated tuners, abalone pearl Lakewood logo headstock inlay, available in Natural gloss finish, disc., last MSR was $3,999.

The **D-54 DELUXE** has a European spruce top, round soundhole, abalone pearl top binding, abalone pearl inlaid rosette, solid Brazilian rosewood back and sides, mahogany neck, 14/20-fret ebony fingerboard with pearl dot inlay, rosewood bridge with black white dot pins, 3-per-side gold-plated tuners with ebony buttons, abalone pearl Lakewood logo headstock inlay, available in Natural gloss finish, current mfg., MSR is $4,711.

ACOUSTIC: GRAND CONCERT SERIES

Grand Concert series guitars are slightly smaller and have a narrower waist than their counterpart dreadnought series models.

The **M-14** has a grand concert style body, solid spruce top, round soundhole, wood binding, inlaid rosette, solid mahogany back and sides, mahogany neck, 14/20-fret rosewood fingerboard with pearl dot inlay, rosewood bridge with black white dot pins, 3-per-side chrome tuners, white mother-of-pearl Lakewood logo headstock inlay, available in Natural satin finish, current mfg., MSR is $1,929. The **M-14 Deluxe** is similar to the M-14, except features an ebony fingerboard, available in Natural gloss finish, disc., last MSR was $2,299.

The **M-18** has a grand concert style body, Sitka spruce top, round soundhole, wood binding, inlaid rosette, solid ovankol back and sides, mahogany neck, 14/20-fret rosewood fingerboard with pearl dot inlay, rosewood bridge with black white dot pins, 3-per-side chrome tuners, white mother-of-pearl Lakewood logo headstock inlay, available in Natural satin finish,

**Lakewood A-32
courtesy Lakewood**

**Lakewood D-14
courtesy Lakewood**

disc., last MSR was $2,099. The **M-18 Deluxe** is similar to the M-18, except features an ebony fingerboard, available in Natural gloss finish, disc., last MSR was $2,399.

The **M-22** has a grand concert style body, Sitka spruce top, round soundhole, wood binding, inlaid rosette, solid walnut back and sides, mahogany neck, 14/20-fret rosewood fingerboard with pearl dot inlay, rosewood bridge with black white dot pins, 3-per-side chrome tuners, white mother-of-pearl Lakewood logo headstock inlay, available in Natural satin finish, disc., last MSR was $2,199. The **M-22 Deluxe** is similar to the M-22, except features an ebony fingerboard, available in Natural gloss finish, disc., last MSR was $2,599.

The **M-32** has a grand concert style body, Sitka spruce top, round soundhole, wood binding, inlaid rosette, solid East Indian rosewood back and sides, mahogany neck, 14/20-fret ebony fingerboard with pearl dot inlay, rosewood bridge with black white dot pins, 3-per-side chrome tuners, abalone pearl Lakewood logo headstock inlay, available in Natural satin finish, current mfg., MSR is $2,292. The **M-32 Deluxe** is similar to the M-32, except features an ebony fingerboard, available in Natural gloss finish., disc., last MSR was $2,799.

The **M-46 DELUXE** has a grand concert style body, European spruce top, round soundhole, wood binding, custom abalone rosette, solid East Indian rosewood back and sides, mahogany neck, 14/20-fret ebony fingerboard with pearl dot inlay, bound peghead, rosewood bridge with black white dot pins, 3-per-side gold-plated tuners, abalone pearl Lakewood logo headstock inlay, available in Natural gloss finish, disc., last MSR was $3,699.

The **M-50 DELUXE** has a grand concert style body, European spruce top, round soundhole, wood binding, custom abalone rosette, solid flamed maple back and sides, mahogany neck, 14/20-fret ebony fingerboard with pearl dot inlay, bound peghead, rosewood bridge with black white dot pins, 3-per-side gold-plated tuners, abalone pearl Lakewood logo headstock inlay, available in Natural gloss finish, disc., last MSR was $3,999.

The **M-54 DELUXE** has a grand concert style body, European spruce top, round soundhole, abalone pearl top binding, abalone pearl rosette, solid Brazilian rosewood back and sides, mahogany neck, 14/20-fret ebony fingerboard with pearl dot inlay, rosewood bridge with black white dot pins, 3-per-side gold-plated tuners with ebony buttons, abalone pearl Lakewood logo headstock inlay, available in Natural gloss finish, current mfg., MSR is $4,711.

ACOUSTIC: JUMBO SERIES

The **J-14 DELUXE** has a jumbo style body, solid spruce top, round soundhole, wood binding, inlaid rosette, solid mahogany back and sides, mahogany neck, 14/20-fret ebony fingerboard with pearl dot inlay, rosewood bridge with black white dot pins, 3-per-side chrome tuners, white mother-of-pearl Lakewood logo headstock inlay, available in Natural gloss finish, disc., last MSR was $2,799.

The **J-32** has a solid spruce top, solid rosewood back and sides, mahogany neck, ebony fingerboard and bridge, soundhole rosette with abalone, gold hardware, 3-per-side tuners, available in Natural gloss finish, current mfg. MSR is $2,534.

The **J-46 DELUXE** has a jumbo style body, European spruce top, round soundhole, wood binding, custom abalone rosette, solid Indian rosewood back and sides, mahogany neck, 14/20-fret ebony fingerboard with pearl dot inlay, bound peghead, rosewood bridge with black white dot pins, 3-per-side gold-plated tuners, abalone pearl Lakewood logo headstock inlay, available in Natural gloss finish, disc., last MSR was $4,099.

LANDOLA
Instruments currently built in Pietarsaari, Finland.

Landola has a tradition of guitar building that stretches back to 1942. In the late 1980s, Landola entered into a contract with Peavey to produce acoustic guitars for the U.S. company. Unfortunately, the company was not geared up for the production numbers that Peavey had projected, and this particular agreement had near disastrous results for the company.

However, Landola bounced back, and is currently offering a number of good quality acoustic guitar models. For further information regarding specific models and pricing, contact Landola Guitars directly or visist their web site (see Trademark Index).

ACOUSTIC

Landola offers several models of quality acoustic guitars. Models are constructed with spruce or cedar tops, mahogany or rosewood back/sides, arctic birch or mahogany necks. Landola offers classical models like the **C-75 GL**, 7/8th size **C-21**, and cutaway body **CCE-110**; the **LR** series is a small bodied steel string **L**andola **R**agtime model. Both the **J** Series and the **JCE** Series models feature jumbo style bodies (the JCE models have a cutaway body). Landola **D** Series dreadnought features a solid spruce top, birch (or maple or mahogany) back and sides, and a mahogany neck.

LANGE
See Paramount & Orpheum.

In the late 1890s, William L. Lange was a partner in Rettberg & Lange, a major East coast banjo producer and distributor. Lange expanded the company into the William L. Lange Company in the early 1920s, and supplied the C. Bruno & Son distributor with both **Paramount** and **Orpheum** banjo lines. In 1934, Lange debuted the Paramount guitar series – and some of the models were built by the C.F. Martin guitar company. Lange was quick to add Orpheum-branded guitars, and some of those models were built by Chicago's Kay company.

Lange's company went out of business in the early 1940s, but New York distributor Maurice Lipsky resumed distribution of Orpheum guitars in 1944. By the late 1940s, the Paramount guitar line was distributed by Gretsch & Brenner. Future model designations/identifications will appear in updated editions of the *Blue Book of Acoustic Guitars*, (Source: Tom Wheeler, *American Guitars*).

LANGEJANS GUITARS
Instruments currently built in Holland, Michigan.

Delwyn (Del) Langejans started Del's Guitar Gallery in 1970 and a year later was building his own guitar with the name "Del's" on the headstock. Del is now up to serial number 1,100 and is dedicated full time to building and reparing guitars. He is a warranty service for several brands and he also warranties any Langejans guitar for life to the original owner. Del makes nylon and steel guitars in a variety of configurations and prices start at $3,495 for most models. For information refer to Del's web site (see Trademark Index).

LARK IN THE MORNING
Instruments currently distributed by Lark In The Morning of Mendocino, California.

Lark In The Morning specializes in unusual instruments. Their production includes harp guitars, Cuban tres, Puerto Rican quatro, travel guitars, citterns, bajo sexto, vihuela, guitarrone, octave mandolins, steel guitars, and many others. For more information on their numerous stringed instruments and pricing, please contact the Lark In The Morning directly (see Trademark Index).

LARRIVEE

Instruments currently produced in Vancouver, British Columbia (Canada). Distributed by Larrivee Guitars, Ltd. of Vancouver (British Columbia), Canada; also by Jean Larrivee Guitars Ltd. of Scottsdale, Arizona.

In 1967, luthier Jean Larrivee met and began studying under Edgar Munch. Larrivee guitars was founded in 1968, and guitar building was centered on classical models. The first steel string was introduced in 1971. Larrivee's attention to detail not only in guitar building but special inlay work soon made a Larrivee acoustic the sought after guitar to find.

NUMERICAL SUFFIXES & MODEL OPTIONS

Numerical suffixes listed below indicate individualized features per model suffix.

05 Mahogany Standard (mahogany back/sides). 09 Standard (pearl logo peghead inlay). 10 Deluxe (abalone purfling on top, abalone/pearl fingerboard inlay, peghead bordered by inlaid silver, hand-engraved Eagle, Gryphon, Pelican or Seahorse on headstock). 19 Special (abalone/pearl fingerboard inlay, hand-engraved Eagle, Gryphon, Pelican or Seahorse on headstock). 50 Standard (ebony fingerboard [pearl dot inlay available on request], pearl logo peghead inlay). 60 Special (Eagle [with feather fingerboard inlay], Stallion and Tiger peghead inlay).

70 DeLuxe (abalone purfled body/rosette, Eagle [with feather fingerboard inlay], Stallion and Tiger peghead inlay). 72 Presentation (abalone purfling on all bound edges, abalone rosette, abalone/pearl fingerboard inlay, peghead bordered by inlaid silver, hand-engraved Dancing Ladies, Genies, Jester, Mermaid on Seahorse or Tamborine Lady inlay on headstock, bridge wing inlays). All instruments are available in left-handed versions at no additional charge. All instruments are also available with following options:

A 12-string variation is available in the following models for an additional $190: Cutaway, Cutaway Jumbo, Dreadnought, Jumbo, Larrivee and Larrivee Jumbo Series. Add $140 for Fishman Matrix pickup. Add $280 for Fishman pickup with preamp. Add $1,000 for Brazilian rosewood (when available).

Unless otherwise noted, all Larrivee models are constructed with the same standard materials: spruce top, round soundhole, wood body binding, wooden inlay rosette, transparent pickguard, rosewood or figured maple back/sides, mahogany neck, bound ebony fingerboard, ebony bridge with black pearl dot pins, and 3-per-side chrome tuners.

**Larrivee L-19
California Anniversary
courtesy Larrivee**

ACOUSTIC: CALIFORNIA ANNIVERSARY SERIES

L-19 CALIFORNIA ANNIVERSARY - Larrivee body style, Indian rosewood back and sides, solid Sitka spruce top, mahogany neck, African ebony fingerboard and bridge, multi-layer rosewood body binding, soundhole with abalone rosette, headstock volute, palm tree with logo headstock and 12th fret California inlays, transparent pickguard, gloss finish, new 2003.

| MSR | $2,598 | $1,950 | $1,350 | $925 |

Add $225 for a Venetian cutaway (Model LV-19 CA).
This model is also available as an Orchestra body shape (Model OM-19 CA).

ACOUSTIC: CLASSIC SERIES

Specifications: 66 mm Scale, 15" Lower Bout.

L-30 STANDARD - classic style, unbound fingerboard, tied bridge, 3-per-side gold tuners with pearl buttons, disc.

$1,800	$1,175	$795
	Last MSR was $2,395.	

C-30 Cutaway - similar to the L-30, except features single Florentine cutaway body, disc.

$2,000	$1,350	$1,000
	Last MSR was $2,695.	

ACOUSTIC: CUTAWAY SERIES

The instruments in this series have the Larrivee body style with a single sharp cutaway, specifications: 25 1/2" scale, 20 1/4" length, 16" lower bout, 4" max depth.

C-03 RE ROSEWOOD STANDARD - features a Fishman Prefix+ pickup, disc.

$1,125	$725	$495
	Last MSR was $1,495.	

C-05 MAHOGANY STANDARD - disc.

$1,425	$925	$625
	Last MSR was $1,895.	

C-09 ROSEWOOD STANDARD - disc.

$1,725	$1,130	$750
	Last MSR was $2,295.	

**Larrivee LV-19
California Anniversary
courtesy Larrivee**

GRADING	100%	EXCELLENT	AVERAGE

C-10 ROSEWOOD DELUXE - disc.

	$2,100	$1,375	$925

Last MSR was $2,795.

ACOUSTIC: CUTAWAY JUMBO SERIES

All the instruments in this series have jumbo Larrivee body styles with a single sharp cutaway.

LCJ-05 MAHOGANY STANDARD - disc.

	$1,500	$975	$660

Last MSR was $1,995.

LCJ-09 ROSEWOOD STANDARD - disc.

	$1,875	$1,225	$830

Last MSR was $2,495.

LCJ-10 ROREWOOD DELUXE - disc.

	$2,250	$1,500	$1,000

Last MSR was $2,995.

LCJ-72 PRESENTATION - disc.

	$4,500	$3,000	$2,000

Last MSR was $5,995.

ACOUSTIC: CUTAWAY SMALL BODY SERIES

Fashioned after the Larrivee small body style, these instruments have a single sharp cutaway.

CS-05 MAHOGANY STANDARD - disc.

	$1,425	$925	$625

Last MSR was $1,895.

CS-09 ROSEWOOD STANDARD - disc.

	$1,725	$1,130	$750

Last MSR was $2,295.

CS-10 ROSEWOOD DELUXE - disc.

	$2,100	$1,375	$925

Last MSR was $2,795.

CS-72 PRESENTATION - disc.

	$4,500	$3,000	$2,000

Last MSR was $5,995.

ACOUSTIC: D-LITE SERIES

All instruments in this series have slightly smaller dreadnought style bodies, and are have an optional gig bag. Specifications: 24 1/2" Scale, 19" Length, 15" Lower Bout, 4 1/2" Max Depth.

D-LITE - dreadnought style, solid spruce top, wood fiber body binding, round soundhole, mahogany back/sides, mahogany neck, 14/20-fret ebony fingerboard, 3-per-side chrome tuners, ebony bridge with white bridgepins, (satin) pickguard, available in Natural satin finish, mfg. 1997-99.

	$550	$350	$225

Last MSR was $749.

L-LITE - similar to the D-Lite, except features Larrivee body (Larrivee Series) design, available in Natural satin finish, mfg. 1997-99.

	$550	$350	$225

Last MSR was $749.

ACOUSTIC: DREADNOUGHT SERIES

All instruments in this series have dreadnought style bodies. Specifications: 25 1/2" Scale, 19 3/4" Length, 16" Lower Bout, 4 1/2" Max Depth.

D-02 MAHOGANY STANDARD - disc 2001.

	$524	$325	$210

Last MSR was $699.

Add $100 for Fishman Deluxe SC pickup (Model D02E).

D-03 MAHOGANY STANDARD - current mfg.

MSR	$1,098	$825	$550	$350

D-03E Mahogany Standard - similar to the D-03, except features a Fishman Prefix+ pickup, current mfg.

MSR	$1,249	$950	$675	$425

D-03R Rosewood Standard - similar to the D-03, except features rosewood back/sides, disc. 1999, 2001-current.

MSR	$1,349	$1,025	$700	$450

GRADING		100%	EXCELLENT	AVERAGE

D-03RE Mahogany Standard - similar to the D-03R, except features a Fishman Prefix+ pickup, current mfg.

MSR	$1,499	$1,125	$750	$475

D-03W Walnut Standard - similar to the D-03, except features walnut back/sides, disc. 1999.

		$675	$450	$300

Last MSR was $899.

DV-03 Mahogany Standard - similar to D-03, except has Venetian cutaway, disc.

		$895	$565	$365

Last MSR was $1,199.

Add $200 for Fishman Prefix Plus pickup (Model DV-03E).

D-04 MAHOGANY STANDARD - disc.

		$1,200	$775	$495

Last MSR was $1,599.

Add $100 for Fishman Deluxe SC pickup (Model D-04E), disc. 2000. Add $200 for Fishman Prefix Plus pickup (Model D-04E), new 2001 Add $300 for Venetian cutaway (Model DV-04).

D-05 MAHOGANY STANDARD - current mfg.

MSR	$1,749	$1,325	$875	$575

Add $225 for electronics and a pickup (Models D-05E & DV-05E). Add $250 for Venetian cutaway (Model DV-05). This model is also available with a mahogany top (Model D-05MT).

D-09 ROSEWOOD ARTIST - current mfg.

MSR	$2,298	$1,725	$1,150	$750

Add $225 for electronics and a pickup (Models D-09E & DV-09E). Add $250 for Venetian cutaway (Model DV-09).

D-10 ROSEWOOD DELUXE - current mfg.

MSR	$2,898	$2,175	$1,450	$950

Add $225 for electronics and a pickup (Models D-10E & DV-10E). Add $225 for Venetian cutaway (Model DV-10).

D-72 PRESENTATION - disc.

		$4,125	$2,695	$1,800

Last MSR was $5,495.

Add $225 for Fishman Prefix Pro Blender pickup (Model D-72E).

Larrivee D-03
Mahogany Standard
courtesy Larrivee

ACOUSTIC: KOA SERIES

All instruments in this series have single sharp cutaway style bodies, koa top/back/sides, seashell fingerboard/bridge wing inlay, dolphin peghead inlay, disc. 1994.

C-20 - Larrivee style body.

		N/A	$1,100	$725

Last MSR was $2,110.

CJ-20 - Larrivee jumbo style body.

		N/A	$1,150	$750

Last MSR was $2,210.

CS-20 - Larrivee small style body.

		N/A	$1,100	$725

Last MSR was $2,110.

ACOUSTIC: LARRIVEE SERIES

All instruments in this series have Larrivee style bodies. Specifications: 25 1/2" scale, 20 1/4" length, 16" lower bout, 4" max depth.

L-02 MAHOGANY STANDARD - disc.

		$525	$325	$195

Last MSR was $699.

Add $100 for Fishman Deluxe SC pickup (L-02E).

L-03 MAHOGANY STANDARD - current mfg.

MSR	$1,098	$825	$550	$350

L-03E Mahogany Standard - similar to the L-03, except features a electronics and a pickup, current mfg.

MSR	$1,249	$950	$675	$425

L-03R Rosewood Standard - similar to the L-03, except features rosewood back/sides, disc. 1999, 2001-current.

MSR	$1,349	$1,025	$700	$450

Larrivee L-03E
Mahogany Standard
courtesy Larrivee

GRADING	100%	EXCELLENT	AVERAGE

L-03RE Rosewood Standard - similar to the L-03R, except features a electronics and a pickup, current mfg.

MSR	$1,499	$1,125	$750	$475

L-03W Walnut Standard - similar to the L-03, except features walnut back/sides, disc. 1999.

	$675	$450	$300
	Last MSR was $899.		

L-03-12E - similar to the L-03E except in 12-string configuration, current mfg.

MSR	$1,499	$1,125	$750	$475

LV-03E Mahogany Standard - similar to L-03E except has single Venetian cutaway body, current mfg.

MSR	$1,549	$1,175	$775	$550

LV-03RE - similar to the LV-03, except has rosewood back and sides, current mfg.

MSR	$1,799	$1,350	$950	$700

L-04 MAHOGANY STANDARD - disc. 2001.

	$975	$595	$225
	Last MSR was $1,299.		

Add $100 for Fishman Deluxe SC pickup (Model L-04E). Disc. 2000. Add $200 for Fishman Prefix Pro pickup (Model L-04E). New 2001 Add $300 for Venetian cutaway (Model LV-04). Add $400 for Venetian cutaway and Fishman Deluxe SC pickup (Model LV-04E).

L-05 MAHOGANY STANDARD - current mfg.

MSR	$1,749	$1,325	$925	$650

Add $225 for electronics and a pickup (Models L-05E & LV-05E). Add $225 for Venetian cutaway (Model LV-05). Add $150 for 12-String configuration (Model L-05-12).

Also available with a mahogany top (Model L-05-MT).

L-09 ROSEWOOD ARTIST - current mfg.

MSR	$2,298	$1,725	$1,200	$800

Add $225 for electronics and a pickup (Models L-09E & LV-09E). Add $225 for Venetian cutaway (Model LV 09). Add $150 for 12-String configuration (Model L-09-12).

L-10 ROSEWOOD DELUXE - current mfg.

MSR	$2,898	$2,175	$1,500	$975

Add $225 for electronics and a pickup (Models L-10E & LV-10E). Add $225 for Venetian cutaway (Model LV-10). Add $150 for 12-String configuration (Model L-10-12).

L-72 PRESENTATION - disc.

	$4,125	$2,695	$1,800
	Last MSR was $5,495.		

Add $225 for Fishman Prefix Pro Blender pickup (Model L-72E).

ACOUSTIC: LARRIVEE JUMBO SERIES

All instruments in this series have Larrivee Jumbo style bodies.

LJ-05 MAHOGANY STANDARD - disc.

	$1,195	$775	$500
	Last MSR was $1,599.		

LJ-09 ROSEWOOD STANDARD - disc.

	$1,575	$1,025	$695
	Last MSR was $2,099.		

LJ-10 ROSEWOOD DELUXE - disc.

	$2,065	$1,350	$925
	Last MSR was $2,749.		

LJ-72 PRESENTATION - disc.

	$4,275	$2,795	$1,875
	Last MSR was $5,695.		

ACOUSTIC: LARRIVEE OM SERIES

All instruments in this series have Larrivee OM style bodies. Specifications: 25 1/2" scale, 20 1/4" length, 16" lower bout, 4" max depth.

OM-02 MAHOGANY STANDARD - disc.

	$525	$325	$195
	Last MSR was $699.		

OM-2E - similar to OM-02, except has Fishman Deluxe SC pickup, current mfg.

	$595	$375	$250
	Last MSR was $799.		

GRADING		100%	EXCELLENT	AVERAGE

OM-03 MAHOGANY STANDARD - current mfg.

MSR	$1,098	$825	$550	$350

OM-03E Mahogany Standard - similar to the OM-03, except features electronics and a pickup, current mfg.

MSR	$1,249	$950	$675	$425

OM-03R Rosewood Standard - similar to the OM-03, except features rosewood back/sides, disc. 1999, 2001-current.

MSR	$1,349	$1,025	$700	$450

OM-03RE Rosewood Standard - similar to the OM-03R, except features electronics and a pickup, current mfg.

MSR	$1,499	$1,125	$750	$475

OM-03W Walnut Standard - similar to the OM-03, except features walnut back/sides, disc. 1999.

	$675	$450	$300

Last MSR was $899.

OM-04 STANDARD MAHOGANY - disc.

$975	$625	$395

Last MSR was $1,299.

OM-04E - similar to OM-04, except has Fishman Deluxe SC pickup, current mfg.

$1,125	$695	$450

Last MSR was $1,499.

OM-05 MAHOGANY STANDARD - current mfg.

MSR	$1,749	$1,325	$925	$650

Add $225 for Fishman Prefix Pro Blender pickup(Model OM-05E). Add $225 for Venetian cutaway. This model is also available with a mahogany top (Models OM-05MT, OMV-05MT).

OM-09 ROSEWOOD ARTIST - current mfg.

MSR	$2,298	$1,725	$1,200	$800

Add $225 for electronics and a pickup (Model OM-09E). Add $225 for Venetian cutaway (Model OMV-09).

OM-10 ROSEWOOD DELUXE - current mfg.

MSR	$2,898	$2,175	$1,500	$975

Add $225 for electronics and a pickup (Model OM-10E). Add $225 for Venetian cutaway (Model OMV-10).

OM-72 PRESENTATION - disc.

$4,125	$2,695	$1,800

Last MSR was $5,495.

Add $225 for Fishman Prefix Pro Blender pickup (Model OM-72E).

ACOUSTIC: LARRIVEE SMALL SERIES

All instruments in this series have Larrivee Small style bodies.

LS-05 MAHOGANY STANDARD - disc.

$1,200	$775	$525

Last MSR was $1,595.

LS-09 ROSEWOOD STANDARD - disc.

$1,500	$975	$660

Last MSR was $1,995.

LS-10 ROSEWOOD DELUXE - disc.

$1,875	$1,225	$830

Last MSR was $2,495.

LS-72 PRESENTATION - disc.

$4,125	$2,695	$1,800

Last MSR was $5,495.

ACOUSTIC: LARRIVEE OO SERIES

All instruments in this series have Larrivee OO style bodies.

00-05 MAHOGANY STANDARD - disc.

$1,200	$775	$525

Last MSR was $1,595.

00-09 ROSEWOOD STANDARD - disc.

$1,500	$975	$660

Last MSR was $1,995.

Larrivee L-10
Rosewood Deluxe
courtesy Larrivee

L

Larrivee OM-10
Rosewood Deluxe
courtesy Dave Roger
Dave's Guitar Shop

GRADING	100%	EXCELLENT	AVERAGE

00-10 ROSEWOOD DELUXE - disc.

	$1,875	$1,225	$830

Last MSR was $2,495.

00-72 PRESENTATION - disc.

	$4,125	$2,695	$1,800

Last MSR was $5,495.

ACOUSTIC: JUMBO SERIES

All instruments in this series have Jumbo style bodies. Specifications: 25 1/2" scale, 20 5/8" length, 17" lower bout, 4 3/4" max depth.

J-05 MAHOGANY STANDARD - current mfg.

MSR	$1,899	$1,425	$975	$650

Add $225 for electronics and a pickup (Model J-05E). Add $225 for a Veneitian cutaway (Model JV-05).

J-09 ROSEWOOD STANDARD - current mfg.

MSR	$2,448	$1,850	$1,300	$875

Add $225 for electronics and a pickup (Model J-09E). Add $225 for a Venetian cutaway (Model JV-09).

J-10 ROSEWOOD DELUXE - current mfg.

MSR	$3,048	$2,295	$1,550	$1,025

Add $225 for electronics and a pickup (Model J-10E). Add $225 for a Venetian cutaway (Model JV-10).

J-72 PRESENTATION - disc.

	$4,275	$2,795	$1,875

Last MSR was $5,695.

ACOUSTIC: PARLOR SERIES

O-01 MH PARLOR GUITAR - parlor sized body 13.25" width, South American mahogany back/sides, solid Sitka spruce top, mahogany neck, ebony fingerboard and bridge, transparent pickguard, satin finish, mfg. 2002-current.

MSR	$729	$550	$395	$275

Add $95 for Indian rosewood back and sides (Model O-01 RW). Add $75 for Canadian flamed maple back and side (Model O-01 FM). Add $115 for Hawaiian koa back and sides (Model O-01 KA).

ACOUSTIC: TRADITIONAL SERIES

D-50 TRADITIONAL - dreadnought body style, South American mahogany back and sides, solid Sitka spruce top, mahogany neck, African ebony fingerboard and bridge, Canadian flamed maple body binding, enlarged soundhole with abalone rosette, headstock volute, MOP headstock and fingerboard inlays, tortoise shell pickguard, gloss finish, new 2003.

MSR	$2,249	$1,695	$1,200	$800

Add $225 for a Venetian cutaway (Model DV-50).

This model is also available as an Orchestra body shape (Model OM-50).

D-60 TRADITIONAL - similar to the D-50, except has Indian rosewood back and sides, new 2003.

MSR	$2,799	$2,100	$1,450	$950

Add $225 for a Venetian cutaway (Model DV-60).

This model is also available as an Orchestra body shape (Model OM-60).

LARSON BROTHERS
Instruments previously manufactured by Larson Brothers of Maurer & Co. 1900-1944.

Carl Larson immigrated from Sweden during the 1880s and began working in the musical instrument trade in the Chicago area. He soon sent for younger brother August who also had a great aptitude for woodworking. In 1900 August and other investors bought out Robert Maurer's Chicago-based business of manufacturing guitars and mandolins. August and Carl ran the business and maintained the Maurer & Co. name throughout their careers which ended with the death of August in 1944. During that period they produced a vast array of stringed instruments including guitars, harp guitars, mandolin orchestra pieces and harp mandolin orchestra pieces, and a few ukes, taro-patches, tiples, and mandolinettos. Through the years the styles changed and also the basic sizes of guitars and mandolins. They were built larger starting in the mid 1930s to accommodate the demand from players for more volume.

The Larson brothers house brand was the Maurer up to the transition period of the larger body instruments when the Euphonon brand was initiated for guitars and mandolins. The Maurer brand was used on guitars and mandolin orchestra pieces of many designs during that approximate 35-year period. The guitars ranged from oak body small guitars to pearl and abalone trimmed guitars and mandolins having Tree-of - Life inlays on the fingerboards. These are beautifully made instruments of the highest quality, but even the less fancy models are well made in the tradition of the Larson brothers' craftsmanship. The guitars with the 12-fret-to-the-body neck sizes came in widths of 12-3/4", 13-1/2", 14" and 15".

The Larson brothers also built guitars, harp guitars, and mandolin orchestra pieces for Wm. C. Stahl of Milwaukee and W.J. Dyer of St. Paul, as well as other assorted suppliers who put their own name on the Larsons' products. Stahl and Dyer claimed to be the makers – a common practice during those "progressive years."

The Prairie State brand was added in the mid 1920s for guitars only. These followed the styles of the better and best grade Maurer models but incorporated one of three main systems of steel rods running the length of the guitar body. August was awarded three patents for these ideas which included side items such as adjustable bridges, fingerboards and necks.

The Prairie State guitars and the better and best grade Maurers and Stahls had a system of laminated top braces. August patented this idea in 1904 making the Larsons pioneers in designing the first guitars made for steel strings which are the only kind they ever made. The laminated braces were continued in the larger Prairie States and the better and best grade models of the Euphonon brand. An occasional Maurer brand instrument may be found in the larger size bodies which I attribute to those sold by Wack Sales Co. of Milwaukee during this later period. This outlet was not offered the Euphonon brand, so they sold them under the Maurer name.

The Larson brothers sold their wares to many prominent players from the radio stations in Chicago, mainly WLS and WJJD. These stations put on country music shows with live performances and became very popular. The Larsons also built three guitars for Les Paul, one of which was a step in developing the solid body guitar. A Larson fingerboard can be seen on what Les called "The Log" which he submitted to Gibson to sell his solid body idea. Gene Autry and Patsy Montana bought Euphonon guitars from the Larsons' shop in 1937.

The main brands produced by the Larsons were Maurer, Prairie State, Euphonon, W.J. Dyer, and Wm. C. Stahl. J.F. Stetson was Dyer's brand for their regular flattop guitar, while the Dyer label was used for the "Symphony" series of harp-guitars and harp-mandolin family instruments.

The Larson brands were burned into the center inside back strip below the soundhole. Typically, if an instrument was altered from standard, it was not branded. This led to many not having any markings. All of the instruments built by the Larsons were handmade. Their degree of craftsmanship made them wonderful instruments to play and ensured that they would become highly collectible. Many people believe that the Larsons' products are as good as Martins and Gibsons, and some believe that they are better. The Larson-built Dyer brand harp guitars are considered the best harp guitars ever made!

More information regarding the individual brands can be found under their brand names: Maurer, Prairie State, Euphonon, Wm. C. Stahl and W.J. Dyer.

For more information regarding Maurer & Co. and the Larson Brothers, a Maurer/Prairie State catalog, Wm. C. Stahl catalog, the Larson patents, and a CD by Muriel Anderson which demonstrates the different sounds built into many styles of Larson-made guitars, see The Larsons' Creations, Guitars and Mandolins, by Robert Carl Hartman, Centerstream Publishing, P.O. Box 17878, Anaheim Hills CA 92807, phone/fax (714) 779-9390.

**Larrivee O-01 MH
Parlor Guitar
courtesy Larrivee**

LASKIN, GRIT (WILLIAM)
Instruments currently built in Toronto, Canada.

Luthier Grit Laskin has been building high quality acoustic guitars for a number of years, and is well-known for his inlay work. Laskin's workload keeps him slightly backlogged (a custom order from Laskin may require several years wait) but is well worth waiting for in terms of playability, construction, and any custom inlay work specified. For information regarding models and pricing, please contact Grit Laskin directly (see Trademark Index).

LAUNHARDT & KOBS
Instruments currently produced in Wetslar, Germany.

Launhardt & Kobs specialize in high quality acoustic guitar models. Their classical series feature models like the **Prelude, Sarabande, Bourree,** and **Romantika** with slotted headstocks and traditional Spanish-style bodies. The jumbo-style models include the 6-string **Jack D.** and the 12-string **William D.** guitars.

Launhardt & Kobs also produces five Jazz Guitar (archtop) models, all with a 650 mm scale and choice of Attila Zoller or EMG pickups. In addition to the archtop models, Launhardt & Kobs also offers a Strat-style solid body **Model 1** and Tele-ish **Model 2** models under the LUK trademark.

The **Averell D.** akustik (acoustic bass) model has a single rounded cutaway body, and a 865 mm scale length. Both the **Model 3** and **Model 4** solid body electric basses have Jazz bass-stylings.

LEACH, H.G.
Instruments currently built in Cedar Ridge, California.

Harvey G. Leach has been building acoustic guitars for over 25 years. Leach, a former furniture maker from Vermont, began building banjos and mandolins early on in his musical instrument career. In 1979, he built his first guitar, and then gave it to his wife as a wedding present. All H.G. Leach guitars are individually handcrafted, and built to the owner's specifications. He estimates that 20 to 25 guitars are built each year; a basic model may take a week's worth of work (spread out over a three week time), and a fancier model with mother-of-pearl inlays may take five times more time.

Leach decided that he wanted to focus more time on his inlay work and started the company Cutting Edge Inlays. This means that he is building only about 12 guitars instead of 30 a year.

Leach is also committed to environmental concerns, and produces his guitars with domestic or foreign sustainable yield mahogany and Brazilian (or Bolivian) rosewood. Leach also uses a water-based lacquer finish (a nitrocellulose finish is available on request).

**Larson 12" Maurer Guitar
courtesy Robert Carl Hartman**

Luthier Leach offers a wide range of inlay, abalone trim, wood appointments, and other options to all of his creations (the list is two columns long!). As a result, the custom-ordered guitar is a custom-built guitar, right to the customer's specifications. All list prices include a hardshell case.

ACOUSTIC ARCHTOP

Leach offers an archtop design in two appointment styles, and three body sizes (16", 17", and 18") – as well as a 19" body archtop bass.

The **Excelsior** features a choice of maple, mahogany, sycamore, claro walnut, spruce, western red cedar, incense cedar, and redwood; single rounded cutaway body, black (or white or cream or ivoroid) celluloid binding, graphite-reinforced neck, 25.375" scale, 20-fret rosewood or ebony fingerboard with 'zero' fret and abalone or pearl dot inlay, rosewood or ebony bridge, 2 f-holes, 3-per-side goldplated Grover tuners, raised pickguard, and last retailed at $3,295 for a 16", $3,495 for a 17", and $3,695 for an 18."

The **Elite** has a highly figured back and side woods, single rounded cutaway body, multi-ply binding, graphite-reinforced neck, 25.375" scale, 20-fret rosewood or ebony fingerboard with 'zero' fret and split-block fretboard inlays, brass and pearl peghead inlay, brass or ebony tailpiece, 2 f-holes, 3-per-side goldplated Grover Imperial tuners, raised pickguard, and retails at $8,000 for a 16", $8,500 for a 17", and $9,000 for the monster 18".

ACOUSTIC FLATTOP

The standard appointment for the Flattop models is as follows: choice of maple, mahogany, sycamore, claro walnut, spruce, western red cedar, incense cedar, and redwood; dreadnought style body, black (or white or cream or ivoroid) celluloid binding, graphite-reinforced neck, 25.375" scale, 14/20-fret rosewood or ebony fingerboard with 'zero' fret and abalone or pearl dot inlay, rosewood or ebony bridge, Southwest or herringbone rosette, 3-per-side goldplated Grover tuners, raised pickguard. Numerous options are available.

The **Franconia** is a standard dreadnought size and retails for $4,200. The **Nylon** has a slotted open headstock and is designed for nylon string use. This model is discontinued and the last price on it was $2,495. The **Saratoga** is built in the Grand size, and has a bassy and loud voicing that is geared towards finger picking, retail is $4,900. The **Cremona** has a body size is smaller than the Saratoga model (OOO), but the same shape (has more balance than the Saratoga as well), and retail is $4,700. The **Kirby** has a smaller body, neck joins at the twelfth fret, and retails for $4,700. The **Rachel** has a dreadnought body shape, but 20% smaller body; 15-fret neck, standard scale, and retails for $4,500. The **Sierra** has a retail price for $4,800.

ACOUSTIC: SPECIAL/LIMITED EDITION SERIES

Leach offers the Motherlode option on any guitar model. The Motherlode option has special gold-in-quartz block inlays for the fingerboard (call for pricing and availability).

The **25th Anniversary Model** has a single 'Willoughby' cutaway Cremona-style body, abalone trim on top of body/soundhole/fretboard/peghead/truss rod cover, mother-of-pearl label with Leach family crest and serial number, abalone (or toroise or wood veneer) tuner buttons, disc. and production was limited to 25 guitars. Last retail was $2,500.

The **Roy Rogers Bluesman** is a dreadnought style body, special Roy Rogers fretboard inlays, Roy Rogers Signature label, abalone trim on top of body/soundhole/fretboard/peghead/truss rod cover, choice of abalone (or tortoise or wood veneer) tuner buttons, retail is $4,295.

Thom Bresh is the son of legendary guitarist Merle Travis. The **Thom Bresh Legacy** is a dreadnought style body, spruce top, herringbone trim, round soundhole, bird's-eye maple neck, rosewood back/sides, 14/20 rosewood fretboard with Merle Travis inlays, 6 on a side Merle Travis design scroll peghead, Merle Travis design pickguard, special pearl label (caricature of Thom drawn by Travis), vintage style tuning machines, and retails for $3,795. Brazillian rosewood is available at a price of $5,795. The **Thom Bresh Spirit** is similar to the Thom Bresh Legacy model, with the addition of abalone trim on top of body/soundhole/fretboard/peghead/truss rod cover, and choice of abalone or tortoise or wood veneer tuner buttons, and a retail of $4,795 or with Brazillian rosewood $6,795.

There are other guitars including the **Eddie Pennington**, which retails at $1,997 and the **Eddie Pennington Special** for $5,500. The **Presentation**, which is an upscale guitar with many options, starts at $7,600..

ACOUSTIC ELECTRIC

Leach has offered an electric/acoustic model called the **Cremona/Willoughby/RMC** that is based on the Cremona. This model incorporates a smaller bodied acoustic with a slim, fast neck, a body cutaway that offers access to all 24 frets, and on-board electronics. Besides this model, which is meant especially for an acoustic/electric, all other models have available electronics available. A Baggs Dual Source is an addtional $289. A Highlander IP1 is $185, and the Highlander IP2 is $225. An RMC pickup is also available for $250 with no preamp, $350 for a mono preamp, $425 with an active 4 band EQ, and $650 for either an onboard or rack mount Polydrive system.

ACOUSTIC BASS

The Leach **Acoustic Bass** has a Saratoga body shape and fretless neck, however a fretted neck is optional. Retail is $5,300. The **Excelsior Bass** is now discontinued and has a 19" wide body, patterned after the Excelsior archtop model. Last retail was $3,795. The **Elite Bass** has a 19" wide body, patterned after the Elite archtop model, and retails for a measely $9,500.

LEVIN

Instruments currently built in Sweden. Instruments were previously built in Sweden from 1900-1977. In the early 1970s, Levin was purchased by the Martin Guitar Company of Nazareth, Pennsylvania.

The Levin company of Sweden was founded by luthier Herman Carlson Levin in 1900, and the first guitar and mandolin factory was set up in Goteburg, Sweden. Prior to establishing his factory, luthier Levin had a shop in Manhattan.

Levin was purchased in the early 1970s by the Martin Guitar company. While early Levin models had some "Martin-esque" qualities prior to the sale, they definitely showed Martin influence afterwards. Production focused on flat-tops after the company changed hands. The last Levin guitars were built in 1977, (Source: Aad Overseem, The Netherlands).

Levin guitars was purchased by Bertil Josefson and they are now producing guitars again. They make small wood classic guitars, but no longer make dreadnoughts.

ACOUSTIC

Levin built very good quality single cutaway one (or two) pickup archtops between the 1930s to the 1960s, as well as flattop guitars, banjos, mandolins, lutes, and other stringed instruments. It is estimated that the company built more than 560,000 total instruments while in business. The Model 119 was one guitar to be made by Levin and it featured a small, narrow-waisted, folk 6-string, solid spruce top, 12/18 neck with dot position markers, 3-per-side tuners, no pickguar, red and green rosette. Price is still unknown on used Levin instruments.

LEVITCH
Levitch Guitar Works. Instruments currently built in Scotch Plains, New Jersey.

Luthier Richard Levitch has been offering custom handmade acoustic and electric guitars for the past 12 years. Levitch apprenticed to luthier Sam Koontz in Linden, New Jersey for five years. In addition to his acoustic guitar models, Levitch offers electric guitars with a retail price starting at $950 (call for options).

ACOUSTIC

The Basic **Artisan** model (list $950) features a dreadnought or 15 1/2" round body, Sitka spruce top, mahogany (or maple or Indian rosewood) back and sides, maple or mahogany neck, ebony or rosewood fingerboard and bridge, black headpiece with mother-of-pearl or abalone inlay, gold or nickel plated tuners, plastic or wood binding, and an oval or round soundhole. The Artisan is finished with gloss or satin lacquer, and the price includes a hardshell case.

Options include an Engelmann spruce top (add $125), rounded or sharp cutaway (add $150), Fishman bridge pickup (add $200), and others. Levitch optionally offers the following tonewoods for the back and sides of his Artisan model: figured bubinga, quilted and flame maple, Eucalyptus, Australian figured lacewood, figured paduak, figured walnut, and figured myrtle (add $150), flamed koa (add $200), Brazilian rosewood and quilted mahogany (call for prices).

LEWIS, MICHAEL A.
Instruments currently built in Grass Valley, California.

Luthier Michael A. Lewis has been offering handcrafted banjos and mandolins since 1981. Lewis, a stringed instrument repairman since the early 1980s, began building the archtop and flattop models in 1993.

Lewis offers steel string flat top guitars inspired by those famous pre-war herringbone models. Soundboards are fashioned from either Sitka or Englemann spruce, Western red cedar, or coastal redwood (sequoia sempervirens).

Lewis' archtop models include the **Standard** and less ornate **Studio** models. Both models feature a rounded single cutaway body, raised pickguard, 2 original style f-holes, and bridge/trapeze tailpiece. Prices start at $7,000 and climb up to over $20,000, but are determined by selection of materials, intricacy of inlay, and other appointments. The overall design is strongly influenced by D'Aquisto and D'Angelico's work, but has other concepts and considerations factored in. Built as acoustic instruments, the models are offered with the option of a floating Bartolini hum canceling jazz pickup (controls mounted on the pickguard). For more information refer to the Michael A. Lewis web site (see Trademark Index).

LIIKANEN
Instruments currently built in Helsinki, Finland.

Liikanen Musical Instruments is a company formed by three experienced luthiers to construct high class concert acoustic guitars. The company was founded by Kauko Liikanen in 1986, who has been building guitars for more than 20 years. Keijo Liikanen joined the company in 1990, and in addition to his guitar building also manages the raw material supplies as well as the administrative duties. The company's youngest artisan, Kirsi Vaisanen, graduated from the Lutherie Department of Ikaalinen Institute of Arts and Crafts.

Liikanen guitars are crafted in their workshop in downtown Helsinki. Most models are built after commissioning, and delivery time is usually 6 months. Liikanen Musical Instruments offers both classical and flamenco guitar models, as well as other stringed instruments. For further information regarding specifications and pricing, contact Liikanen Musical Instruments directly (see Trademark Index).

LINCOLN
Instruments previously produced in Japan between the late 1970s and the early 1980s.

Lincoln instruments featured both original designs and designs based on classic American favorites; most guitars considered good quality, (Source: Tony Bacon and Paul Day, *The Guru's Guitar Guide*).

LINDELL
Instruments previously produced in Japan during the mid 1960s.

Research continues into the Lindell trademark, as the producing company in Japan and the American distributor have yet to be identified. Further information will be reported in future editions of the *Blue Book of Acoustic Guitars*.

LIPTON, WALTER
Instruments currently built in Orford, New Hampshire.

Luthier Walter Lipton builds an estimated 10 handcrafted acoustic guitars each year. Lipton's retail list prices start around $3,000, and he offers both steel-string and classical style guitars. Lipton specializes in aged woods (10 to 20 years) and engraved mother-of-pearl inlays. Lipton also operates the Euphonon Co., a parts supply house that offers woods, luthier tools, strings, and fretted instrument parts.

LONE STAR
Instruments currently made in Paracho, Mexico. Distributed by LPD Music International.

Lone Star guitars are produced in the mountain village of Paracho, Mexico, which has a 200-year heritage of guitar building. Lone Star guitars are available with laminate, solid cedar, or solid spruce tops and are designed for the beginner to intermediate student. Retail list prices run from $170 up to $550; most instruments are priced around $150 to $450. For further information contact LPD Music International directly (see Trademark Index).

LOPRINZI

Instruments previously built in Rosemont, Hopeville, and Plainsboro, New Jersey from 1972 to 1980.

Thomas R. LoPrinzi, along with his brother Augustino, originally founded LoPrinzi guitars in New Jersey in early 1972. The business grew from a two- and three-man operation into a staff of 18 employees. Modern production techniques enabled the LoPrinzi brothers to pare the number of employees back to 7 while still producing 60 to 80 guitars a month in the late 1970s. Augustino LoPrinzi, tired of overseeing production, sold the business to Maark Corporation (a subsidiary of AMF). His brother Thomas was then named president of LoPrinzi Guitars. The AMF-owned company continued producing guitars for a number of years, and finally closed the doors in 1980. Years later, Augustino called AMF to request his old trademark back. Working with vice president Dick Hargraves, Augustino officially had the trademark transferred back, and has combined it to form the current "Augustino LoPrinzi" line of classical guitars, (Source: Hal Hammer).

LoPrinzi guitars were available in three styles: Standard, Folk, and 12-String. Early designs featured German silver Spruce tops and Brazilian rosewood; later models had tops built out of Canadian and Alaskan spruce, and bodies constructed with Indian rosewood, flamed maple, and Honduran mahogany. All models have an adjustable truss rod, ebony fingerboard, pearl or abalone inlays, and a rosewood bridge.

LOPRINZI, AUGUSTINO

Instruments currently built in Florida.

Luthier Augustino LoPrinzi originally was trained by his father to be a barber. A self-taught guitar builder, LoPrinzi's original Flemmington, New Jersey barbershop also had a guitar workshop in the back. After ten years dividing his interests, LoPrinzi (and his brother Thomas) founded LoPrinzi guitars in New Jersey in 1972. The business grew from a two- and three-man operation into a staff of 18 employees. Modern production techniques enabled the LoPrinzi brothers to pare the number of employees back to 7 while still producing 60 to 80 guitars a month in 1975. LoPrinzi, tired of overseeing production, sold the business to Maark Corporation (a subsidiary of AMF). Refusing to sign a "Non-compete" clause, LoPrinzi opened "Augustino Guitars" two weeks later – and literally right next door to his original plant! He continued to produce guitars there until 1978, and then moved to Florida. The AMF-owned LoPrinzi company continued producing guitars for a number of years, and finally closed the doors in 1980. Years later, Augustino called AMF to request his old trademark back. Working with vice president Dick Hargraves, Augustino officially had the trademark transferred back, and has combined it to form the current "Augustino LoPrinzi" line of classical guitars. LoPrinzi still builds classical guitars full time (about 8 guitars a month), and is assisted by his daughter, Donna Chavis, and woodworker Bill Kreutzer, (Source: Hal Hammer).

Through the years, Augustino LoPrinzi has consulted or designed instruments for many companies including Guild, Martin, Kramer, Fender, and others. His high quality limited production classical guitars feature quality tonewoods, and range in price from $3,000 to $8,500. LoPrinzi also builds several flamenco models, and a smaller number of steel string acoustics. For further information regarding models, availability, and pricing, please contact luthier LoPrinzi directly (see Trademark Index).

LORCA, ANTONIO

Instruments currently built in Spain. Distributed in the U.S. market by David Perry Guitar Imports.

Antonio Lorca Guitars are known as "A Work of Art." They feature solid cedar tops on flamenco style acoustics. The most current retail list is from 1996 and the prices are: Student models begin at $369, recital models begin at $529, and concert level guitars begin at $599. For additional information, please contact David Perry Guitar Imports directly (see Trademark Index).

LORD

Instruments previously built in Japan.

Guitars with the Lord trademark originated in Japan, and were distributed in the U.S. by the Halifax company, (Source: Michael Wright, *Guitar Stories*, Volume One).

LOTUS

Instruments currently produced in Korea, China, and India. Distributed by Midco International of Effingham, Illinois.

Lotus guitars are designed for the student or entry level guitarist. Lotus offers a wide range of acoustic and electric guitar models (a little something for everyone!).

In addition to the Electric guitar models, Lotus also offers 4 dreadnought acoustics, 2 banjo models, and 4 mandolins. Lotus Electric Basses are offered in a Precision-style L760, as well as a Jazz-style model L750JSB and two modern design basses (L770 4-string and L780 5-string).

LOWDEN

Currently manufactured by hand since 1973 in Newtownards, Northern Ireland. Currently distributed in North American by Lowden Guitars, located in Ft. Worth, TX.

In 1973, luthier George Lowden began designing and manufacturing hand built guitars in Ireland. Demand outgrew the one-person effort and the production of some models were farmed out to luthiers in Japan in 1981. However, full production was returned to Ireland in 1985.

ACOUSTIC: D SERIES

D Series guitars maintain the classic deadnought design with a narrow neck for ease of playing.

D-10 - classic dreadnought style guitar, same specifications as the O-10, disc.

	$1,875	$1,125	$775

Last MSR was $2,500.

Add $400 for single cutaway body.

D-12 - classic dreadnought style guitar, same specifications as the O-12, disc.

	$1,875	$1,125	$775

Last MSR was $2,500.

Add $400 for single cutaway body.

GRADING	100%	EXCELLENT	AVERAGE

D12-12 - similar to the D-12, except has 12-string configuration, 6-per-side tuners, disc.

	$2,100	$1,290	$900

Last MSR was $2,800.

D-22 - dreadnought style, cedar top, round soundhole, wood bound body, abalone rosette, mahogany back/sides, mahogany/sycamore 5-piece neck, 14/20-fret ebony fingerboard with pearl dot inlay, rosewood bridge, rosewood veneered peghead with pearl logo inlay, 3-per-side gold tuners with amber buttons, available in Natural finish, mfg. 1993-95.

	N/A	$1,075	$720

Last MSR was $2,390.

D-23 - classic dreadnought style guitar, same specifications as the O-23, disc..

	$1,875	$1,125	$775

Last MSR was $2,500.

Add $400 for single cutaway body.

D-25 - classic dreadnought style guitar, same specifications as the O-25, disc.

	$2,225	$1,335	$950

Last MSR was $2,950.

Add $450 for single cutaway body.

D-32 - classic dreadnought style guitar, same specifications as the O-32, current mfg.

MSR	$2,990	$2,250	$1,350	$950

Add $450 for single cutaway body.

D32-12 - similar to the D-32, except has 12-string configuration, 6-per-side tuners, current mfg.

MSR	$3,600	$2,700	$1,650	$1,100

Lowden D-10
courtesy Lowden Guitars

ACOUSTIC: F SERIES

The F Series guitars are a mini-jumbo folk style with the standard Lowden neck.

F-10 - mini-jumbo folk guitar, same specifications as the O-10, current mfg.

MSR	$2,950	$2,225	$1,450	$950

Add $400 for single cutaway body.

F-12 - mini-jumbo folk guitar, same specifications as the O-12, current mfg.

MSR	$2,950	$2,225	$1,450	$950

Add $400 for single cutaway body.

F12-12 - similar to the F-12, except has 12-string configuration, 6-per-side tuners, current mfg.

MSR	$3,400	$2,550	$1,700	$1,100

F-22 - folk style, cedar top, round soundhole, wood bound body, wood inlay rosette, mahogany back/sides, mahogany/rosewood 5-piece neck, 14/20-fret ebony fingerboard with pearl dot inlay, rosewood bridge, pearl logo inlay and rosewood veneer on peghead, 3-per-side gold tuners with pearl buttons, available in Natural finish, disc. 1994.

	N/A	$990	$660

Last MSR was $2,145.

F-23 - mini-jumbo folk guitar, same specifications as the O-23, current mfg.

MSR	$2,990	$2,250	$1,350	$950

Add $400 for single cutaway body.

F-24 - similar to F-22, except has spruce top, maple back/sides, mfg. 1994-95.

	N/A	$1,260	$840

Last MSR was $2,790.

F-25 - mini-jumbo folk guitar, same specifications as the O-25, current mfg.

MSR	$2,990	$2,250	$1,350	$950

Add $450 for single cutaway body.

F-32 - mini-jumbo folk guitar, same specifications as the O-32, current mfg.

MSR	$2,990	$2,250	$1,350	$950

Add $450 for single cutaway body.

F32-12 - similar to the F-32, except has 12-string configuration, 6-per-side tuners, current mfg.

MSR	$3,600	$2,700	$1,650	$1,100

F-34 - similar to F-22, except has spruce top, koa back/sides, mfg. 1994-95.

	N/A	$1,440	$960

Last MSR was $3,190.

Lowden F-32
courtesy Lowden Guitars

GRADING	100%	EXCELLENT	AVERAGE

ACOUSTIC: O SERIES

O-10 - jumbo style, cedar top, round soundhole, wood bound body, wood inlay rosette, mahogany back/sides, 5-piece mahogany/rosewood neck, 14/20-fret ebony fingerboard, rosewood bridge, rosewood veneered peghead with pearl logo inlay, 3-per-side custom gold tuners with amber buttons, available in Natural finish, current mfg.

MSR	$2,950		$2,225	$1,450	$950

Add $400 for single cutaway body.

O-12 - similar to O-10, except has spruce top, current mfg.

MSR	$2,950		$2,225	$1,450	$950

Add $400 for single cutaway body.

O12-12 - similar to O-10, except has spruce top, 12-string configuration, 6-per-side tuners, current mfg.

MSR	$3,400		$2,550	$1,700	$1,100

O-22 - jumbo style, cedar top, round soundhole, wood bound body, wood inlay rosette, mahogany back/sides, mahogany/sycamore 5-piece neck, 14/20-fret ebony fingerboard, rosewood bridge, rosewood veneered peghead with pearl logo inlay, 3-per-side gold tuners with amber buttons, available in Natural finish, disc. 1994.

			N/A	$990	$660

Last MSR was $2,145.

O-22/12 - similar to O-22, except has 12-strings configuration, 6-per-side tuners, disc. 1994.

			N/A	$1,100	$735

Last MSR was $2,445.

O-23 - jumbo style, cedar top, round soundhole, wood bound body, abalone/wood inlay rosette, walnut back/sides, mahogany/sycamore 5-piece neck, 14/20-fret ebony fingerboard, rosewood bridge, rosewood veneered peghead with pearl logo inlay, 3-per-side gold tuners with amber buttons, available in Natural finish, current mfg.

MSR	$2,990		$2,250	$1,350	$950

Add $400 for single cutaway body.

O-25 - jumbo style, cedar top, round soundhole, wood bound body, wood inlay rosette, Indian rosewood back/sides, mahogany/rosewood 5-piece neck, 14/20-fret ebony fingerboard, rosewood bridge, pearl logo inlay and rosewood veneer on peghead, 3-per-side gold tuners with amber buttons, available in Natural finish, current mfg.

MSR	$2,990		$2,250	$1,350	$950

Add $400 for single cutaway body.

O25-12 - similar to O-25, except has 12-string configuration, 6-per-side tuners, disc. 1994.

			N/A	$1,240	$825

Last MSR was $2,750.

O-32 - similar to O-25, except has spruce top, pearl tuner buttons, current mfg.

MSR	$2,990		$2,250	$1,350	$950

Add $450 for single cutaway body.

O32-12 - similar to O-32, except has 12-string configuration, 6-per-side tuners with pearl buttons, mfg. 1993-current.

MSR	$3,600		$2,700	$1,650	$1,100

ACOUSTIC: S SERIES

S Series models feature a small compact body with a standard Lowden neck.

S-10 - small bodied folk guitar, same specifications as the O-10, current mfg.

MSR	$2,950		$2,225	$1,450	$950

Add $400 for single cutaway body.

S-12 - small bodied folk guitar, same specifications as the O-12, current mfg.

MSR	$2,950		$2,225	$1,450	$950

Add $400 for single cutaway body.

S12-12 - similar to the S-12, except has 12-string configuration, 6-per-side tuners, current mfg.

MSR	$3,400		$2,550	$1,700	$1,100

S-23 - small bodied folk guitar, same specifications as the O-23, current mfg.

MSR	$2,990		$2,250	$1,350	$950

Add $400 for single cutaway body.

S-23S - folk style, German spruce top, round soundhole, wood bound body, abalone/wood inlay rosette, walnut back/sides, mahogany/sycamore 5-piece neck, 14/20-fret ebony fingerboard, rosewood bridge, rosewood veneered peghead with pearl logo inlay, 3-per-side gold tuners with ebony buttons, available in Natural finish, mfg. 1994-95.

			N/A	$1,075	$720

Last MSR was $2,390.

GRADING		100%	EXCELLENT	AVERAGE

S-25 - small bodied folk guitar, same specifications as the O-25, current mfg.

MSR	$2,990	$2,250	$1,350	$950

Add $450 for single cutaway body.

S-32 - small bodied folk guitar, same specifications as the O-32, current mfg.

MSR	$2,990	$2,250	$1,350	$950

Add $450 for single cutaway body.

S32-12 - similar to the S-32, except has 12-string configuration, 6-per-side tuners, current mfg.

MSR	$3,600	$2,700	$1,650	$1,100

ACOUSTIC: PREMIER 35 & 38 SERIES

All Premier Guitars are available in the four distinctive Lowden body configurations (O, F, D, S). The 35 Series model features a choice of cedar or spruce top, wood bindings/purfling, round soundhole, abalone rosette, maple or mahogany neck, 14/20-fret ebony fingerboard, rosewood bridge, matching veneered peghead with pearl logo inlay, 3-per-side custom gold tuners with amber buttons, available in a Natural finish since 1996.

The 35 Series model is available in Indian rosewood, Claro walnut, or flamed maple at a suggested retail price of $3,9250; and koa, Australian blackwood, quilted maple, or myrtle at $4,125. A Brazilian rosewood model has the suggested list price of $6,200.

The 38 Series is the top of the range Brazilian Rosewood Lowden Guitar. This model features black cedar top, abalone rosette, abalone/wood bound soundboard inlay, mahogany/rosewood 5-piece neck, 14/20-fret ebony fingerboard with leaf inlay, Brazilian rosewood bridge, Brazilian rosewood veneered peghead with pearl logo inlay, and 3-per-side custom gold tuners with amber buttons, available in a Natural finish. The suggested retail price is $8,000.

ACOUSTIC ELECTRIC: STAGE & JAZZ SERIES

LS – 1 (LSE-I) - Venetian cutaway folk style, spruce top, round soundhole, wood bound body, wood inlay rosette, mahogany 2 piece neck, 20-fret ebony fingerboard, rosewood bridge, pearl logo inlay and rosewood veneer on peghead, 3-per-side gold tuners with pearl buttons, transducer bridge pickup, available in Natural finish, current mfg.

MSR	$3,550	$2,675	$1,600	$1,100

LS – 11 (LSE-II) - similar to LSE-I, except has Indian rosewood back/sides, current mfg.

MSR	$3,550	$2,675	$1,600	$1,100

S25 JAZZ - nylon string configuration, small body with cutaway, same specifications as the O-25, except features slotted peghead, 3-per-side tuners with pearloid buttons, transducer bridge pickup, preamp, mfg. 1993-current.

MSR	$3,550	$2,675	$1,600	$1,100

Lowden 0-23
courtesy Lowden Guitars

LUCENA

Instruments currently distributed by Music Imports of San Diego, California.

Music Imports offers a number of quality Lucena guitar models. For further information regarding model specifications and pricing, please contact Music Imports directly.

LUCIDA

See Johnson. Instruments currently produced in Asia. Distributed by the Music Link of Brisbane, California.

The Music Link is the distributor of Lucida classical acoustic guitars with prices aimed at the entry level and student guitarists (prices range from $79.95 to $189). For further information regarding the Lucida models, contact the Music Link directly (see Trademark Index).

LUTHIER

Instruments currently built in Spain. Distributed by Luthier Music Corporation of New York, New York.

The Luthier Music Corporation is importing classical and flamenco guitars from Spain to the U.S. market. Models range from Student and Advanced Student up to Concert level acoustics. Luthier Music Corporation also distributes the Luthier brand nylon strings. Prices range anywhere from $350-$2,695. For further information regarding models and pricing, contact the Luthier Music Corporation directly (see Trademark Index).

LYLE

Instruments previously built in Japan from 1969 to 1980. Distributed by the L.D. Heater company of Portland, Oregon.

The Lyle product line consisted of acoustic and acoustic/electric archtop guitars, as well as solid body electric guitars and basses. These entry level to intermediate quality guitars featured designs based on popular

Lowden S-25
courtesy Lowden Guitars

American models. These instruments were manufactured by the Matsumoku company, who supplied models for both the Arai (Aria, Aria Pro II) company and the early 1970s Epiphone models, (Source: Michael Wright, *Vintage Guitar Magazine*).

G.W. LYON
Currently trademark of instruments built in Korea since the early 1990s. Distributed in the U.S. by Washburn International of Vernon Hills, Illinois.

G.W. Lyon offers a range of instruments designed for the student or beginner guitarist at affordable prices and decent entry level quality.

LYS
Instruments previously built in Canada circa late 1970s.

The *Blue Book of Acoustic Guitars* received some information through the Internet that offered a connection between Lys acoustic guitars and the La Si Do company, makers of Godin and other fine acoustics and electrics. Further research continues into this trademark listing.

L is for Larrivee. Jean Larrivee (l) has been making high quality guitars in Vancouver, British Columbia since 1968. Pictured here with fellow exhibitor Cheryl Erikson at the recent Anaheim NAMM Show.

Section M

MAD ARCHTOP GUITARS
Instruments currently built in Geneva, Switzerland.

Luthier David Marioni is hand crafting Virtuoso model archtop guitars. This classic archtop design features a hand carved Swiss spruce top, flamed maple back and sides, laminated flame maple neck, and ebony fingerboard. The Virtuoso is available in a 16", 17", and 18" body widths.

MTD
Instruments currently built in Kingston, New York since 1994.

Luthier Michael Tobias has been handcrafting guitars and basses since 1977. The forerunner of MTD, Tobias Guitars was started in Orlando, Florida in April 1977. Tobias' first shop name was the Guitar Shop, and he sold that business in 1980 and moved to San Francisco to be partners in a short lived manufacturing business called Sierra Guitars. The business made about 50 instruments and then Tobias left San Francisco in May of 1981 to start a repair shop in Costa Mesa, California.

Several months later, Tobias left Costa Mesa and moved to Hollywood. Tobias Guitars continued to repair instruments and build custom basses for the next several years with the help of Bob Lee, and Kevin Almieda (Kevin went on to work for Music Man). The company moved into 1623 Cahuenga Boulevard in Hollywood and after a year quit the repair business. Tobias Guitars added Bob McDonald, lost Kevin to Music Man, and then got Makoto Onishi. The business grew in leaps and bounds. In June of 1988 the company had so many back orders, it did not accept any new orders until the January NAMM show in 1990.

After several attempts to move the business to larger, better equipped facilities, Michael Tobias sold Tobias Guitars to Gibson on 1/1/90. Late in 1992, it was decided that in the best corporate interests, Tobias Guitars would move to Nashville. Michael Tobias left the company in December 1992, and was a consultant for Gibson as they set up operations in Nashville.

By contractual agreement, after Tobias' consulting agreement with Gibson was up, he had a 1 year non competition term. That ended in December 1993. During that time, Tobias moved to The Catskills in upstate New York and set up a small custom shop. Tobias started designing new instruments and building prototypes in preparation for his new venture. The first instruments were named Eclipse. There are 50 of them and most all of them are 35" bolt-ons. There are three neck-throughs. Tobias finally settled on MTD as the company name and trademark. As of this writing (10/1/97) he has delivered 250 MTD instruments delivered, including bolt-on basses, guitars, neck-through basses, and acoustic bass guitars.

Michael Tobias is currently building nearly 100 instruments per year, with the help of Chris Hofschneider (who works two days per week). Chris has at least 15 years experience, having worked for Sam Koontz, Spector Guitars, Kramer, and being on the road with bands like Bon Jovi and other New Jersey-based bands. Michael Tobias is also doing design and development work for other companies, such as Alvarez, Brian Moore Guitars, Modulus Guitars, Lakland, American Showster (with Chris Hofschneider) and the new Czech-built Grendel basses, (Source: Michael Tobias, MTD fine handmade guitars and basses).

GRADING	100%	EXCELLENT	AVERAGE

ACOUSTIC BASS

All MTD instruments are delivered with a wenge neck/wenge fingerboard, or maple neck/rosewood fingerboard; 21 frets plus a "Zero" fret, 35" scale length. Prices include plush hard shell cases. The standard finish for body and neck is a satin catalyzed urethene. Wood choices for bodies: swamp ash, poplar, and alder. Other woods, upon request, may require up charges. Exotic tops are subject to availability. Beginning 2000, all MTD Basses come equipped with the Buzz Feiten Tuning System. Models can be ordered in 34" or 35" scale. MTD basses are all electric as of 2002.

> Add $100 for a lined fretless neck. Add $150 for a hand rubbed oil stain. Add $300 for wenge. Add $200 for satin epoxy coating on lined or unlined fretless fingerboard. Add $200 for epoxy/oil urethane finished maple fingerboard. Add $200 for a 24-fret fingerboard. Add $400 for Lacquer finish: Sunburst (Amber or Brown), See-Throughs (Transparency) of Red, Coral Blue, or Honey Gold. Add $300 for a korina, African satinwood (Avadore), or lacewood body. Add $500 for a 10 Top of burl, flamed, or quilted maple, myrtle, or mahogany. Add $150 for Highlander system. Add $175 for Fishman Transducer.

ABG 4 - 4-string acoustic bass, flamed myrtle back and sides, spruce top, mfg. 1994-2001.

	$2,200	**$1,800**	**$1,300**
		Last MSR was $2,750.	

ABG 5 - 5-string acoustic bass, flamed myrtle back and sides, spruce top, mfg. 1994-current.

	$2,350	**$1,900**	**$1,300**
		Last MSR was $2,900.	

McCURDY, RIC
Instruments currently built in New York City, New York.

Luthier Ric McCurdy has been producing custom guitars since 1983. Originally based in Santa Barbara, California, he moved to New York City in 1991 where he studied archtop guitar building with Bob Benedetto. Since then, he has been concentrating on building archtops and one-off custom guitars.

Currently using McCurdy guitars are ECM recording artist John Abercrombie and studio ace Joe Beck. All archtops feature the Kent Armstrong adjustable pole piece pickup which can be used with steel or bronze strings.

ACOUSTIC

The Moderna (list price $5,000) is a single cutaway archtop guitar, 16" wide at lower bout. This model features flame maple back and sides with a Sitka spruce top, multi-fine line binding on body head and pickguard, graphite reinforced maple neck with 25.5" scale, and abalone or pearl block inlays on a 22-fret ebony fingerboard. The finish is Nitrocellulose Lacquer.

The vintage styled Kenmare archtop is 17" across the lower bout, and has AAAA flame maple back and sides, and a Sitka spruce top. Other aspects of this model include bound f-holes, multi-ply fine line binding, 25.5" scale, graphite reinforced maple neck, split block inlay on 22-fret ebony fingerboard, vintage peg-head inlay, and Cremona Amber Nitrocellulose finish (list price $7,500).

McELROY GUITARS
Instruments currently built in Seattle, Washington.

Brent McElroy has been building guitars since circa 1995. McElroy's guitars are hand built and supervised by his cat named Picasso. Guitars are based on traditional designs with McElroy's own twist on things. Prices start at $2,200 and there are several options available. For more information on McElroy's guitars refer to his web site or get a hold of him directly (see Trademark Index).

McGILL GUITARS
Instruments currently built in Nashville, TN.

Paul McGill's classical guitars are well-known, and his resonator instruments are similar in design to the old DelVecchio guitar made in Brazil. Prices range from $2,500-$4,500, and waiting time is currently 9 months to a year. For current information and a custom quotation, please contact the company directly (see Trademark Index).

McKERRIHAN
Instruments previously built in Phoenix, Arizona.

Luthier Glen E. McKerrihan handcrafted four different archtop guitar models that featured classic styling and single rounded cutaway bodies. All four models were available in 16" or 17" body widths. Models included the Anastasia (last retail price $3,250), the Finger Style (last retail price $3,750), the Keenan (last retail price $3,000), and Monk's Model (last retail price $3,000). All models had hand carved aged solid tone woods, 25" scale length, ebony fingerboards, and 5-ply body binding.

McNALLY
Instruments currently distributed our of Hibernia, New Jersey.

Bob McNally designed the Strumstick, as well as the backpacker by Martin. The Strumstick is a guitar with 3-strings on it and no matter where you place your fingers, it creates a chord. This is achieved by making the entire fret-board a major scale, so there are no flats or sharps. It is intended for someone who does not know much about instruments, but is versatile enough for professionals to get a lot of use out of it. Prices are also very reasonable between $110-$150. For more information contact the company directly (see Trademark Index).

MACCAFERRI
Instruments previously produced in Italy circa 1923. Instruments designed for the Selmer company in France date between 1931 to 1932. Maccaferri instruments produced in America began circa the early 1950s-early 1990s.

Italian-born luthier Mario Maccaferri (1900-1993) was a former classical guitarist turned guitar designer and builder. Born in Bologna, Italy in 1900, Maccaferri began his apprenticeship to luthier/guitarist Luigi Mozzani in 1911. At age 16 Maccaferri began classical guitar studies at the Academy in Siena, and graduated with highest possible honors in 1926.

Between 1931 and 1932, Maccaferri designed and built a series of instruments for the French Selmer company. Although they were used by such notables as Django Reinhardt, a dispute between the company and Maccaferri led to a short production run. In the two years (1931-1932) that Maccaferri was with Selmer, he estimated that perhaps 200 guitars were built.

In 1936 Maccaferri moved to New York. He founded Mastro Industries, which became a leading producer of plastic products such as clothespins (which he invented during World War II), acoustical tiles, and eventually Arthur Godfrey ukuleles.

In 1953, Maccaferri introduced another innovative guitar made out of plastic. This archtop guitar featured a through-neck design, 3 tuners per side headstock, and two f-holes. Despite the material involved, Maccaferri did not consider them to be a toy. Along with the archtop model Maccaferri produced a flattop version. But the 1953 market was not quite prepared for this new design, and Maccaferri took the product off the market and stored them until around 1980 (then released them again).

In the mid 1950s, Maccaferri was on friendly terms with Nat Daniels of Danelectro fame. As contemporaries, they would gather to discuss amplification in regards to guitar design, but nothing came of their talks. Maccaferri stayed busy with his plastics company and was approached by Ibanez in the early 1980s to endorse a guitar model. As part of the endorsement, Maccaferri was personally signing all the labels for the production run.

The Maccaferri-designed instruments were produced by the atelier of Henri Selmer and Co. of Paris, France between 1931 to 1932 as the Selmer model Concert. However, due to the dispute between the company and Maccaferri, experts estimate that less than 300 were made (note Maccaferri's estimate, above), (Source: George Gruhn and Dan Forte, *Guitar Player* magazine, February 1986; and Paul Hostetter, Guitares Maurice Dupont).

MACDONALD, S.B. CUSTOM INSTRUMENTS

Instruments currently built in Huntington (Long Island), New York.

Luthier Scott.B. MacDonald has been building and restoring stringed instruments for over 20 years. His instruments are built by special order and designed around the needs of each customer. MacDonald offers acoustic, electric, and resophonic instruments. He is also a columnist for *20th Century Guitar*.

One of MacDonald's custom instruments is the Resonator Electric, a vintage-style semi-hollowbody guitar with a resonator cone. For further information on this model and others, contact luthier S.B. MacDonald directly (see Trademark Index).

MAC YASUDA GUITARS

Also Masterbilt Guitars. Instruments currently built in Old Hickory, Tennessee; final production (inlays) is set in California. Distributed by Mac Yasuda Enterprises of Irvine, California.

Mac Yasuda is internationally recognized as a vintage guitar authority and collector, and has been writing on the topic of vintage instruments for well over two decades. Many may not realize that Yasuda is also a first-rate musician who has appeared on stage at the WSM Grand Ole Opry. Yasuda began performing country music on a local radio show in Kobe, Japan at the age of 17, and joined the "Rodeo Rangers" as a singer a year later. This group gained popularity on radio and in nightclubs in western Japan.

In 1970, Yasuda arrived in the U.S. to study at Michigan Technological University. He traveled to Nashville, and later purchased his first vintage guitar from a Denver pawnshop. Since then, virtually thousands of vintage instruments have passed through his hands.

In the late 1980s, Yasuda met Greg Rich. Rich was then acquiring a reputation for his custom musical instruments created for a major guitar producer (located in Nashville). These specialized custom instruments had immediate appeal in the collectibles market. In 1992, Rich collaborated with Mark Taylor (see Tut Taylor, Crafters Of Tennessee) to create a company to produce his latest custom designs. Mac Yasuda currently contracts Rich and Taylor to produce his namesake high quality, custom guitars. In 1997, Rich left the Masterbilt company.

**Maccaferri Plastic Guitar
courtesy The Music Shoppe**

To show his appreciation for country music and the Grand Ole Opry, Yasuda decided to present custom guitars to several of the legendary Opry artists. Yasuda then contacted Rich and Taylor to produce the first of the Mac Yasuda guitars. In early 1995, these custom guitars were presented to Porter Wagoner, Billy Walker, and Jack Greene. Later presentations were made to Hank Snow, Del Reeves, and Jimmy C. Newman. As the gifts were presented, many other Grand Ole Opry stars became interested in the Mac Yasuda guitars.

In 1996, Yasuda and Rich decided to produce a line of guitars. The company was based in California, and debuted at the winter NAMM show in 1997 under the **Masterbilt** trademark. The company currently offers three models, as well as numerous custom options (finishes, custom inlay, hand engraving, binding, etc.). Contact Mac Yasuda for current prices.

The **MYD-42** is a dreadnought sized model with either rosewood or maple back and sides. It features 42-style abalone on the top, tortoise style pickguard, ebony fingerboard with an intricate tree of life inlay, nickel Grover Imperial tuners, and a Nitrocellulose finish.

The **MYD-45** (Mac Yasuda D-45) is also dreadnought sized, and has a selected spruce top with rosewood back and sides. This model features 45-style abalone trim on the top, back, and sides. Other features include a custom pearl inlaid pickguard, bridge, fingerboard, and peghead; ebony overlay on the front and back of the peghead; gold Grover Imperial tuners, and a Nitrocellulose finish.

The jumbo size **MYJ-1000** model has rosewood or curly maple back and sides. The select spruce top has 42-style abalone on the top, combined with multi-layered binding on the back and sides. The pickguard, fingerboard, and peghead are inlaid with custom pearl. The tuning keys are gold Grover Imperial tuners, and is finished in either Natural or Sunburst Nitrocellulose finish.

The **Art Deco Catalina** model has Sitka spruce top, selected curly maple back and sides, ebony fingerboard, and one-piece mahogany neck. This model features mother-of-pearl and abalone inlays depicting palm trees, moons, pyramids in an Art Deco motif; available in Antique Natural, Opaque Black, Pearl White, Translucent Blue, Translucent Green, and Translucent Red finishes.

MADEIRA

See Guild. Instruments previously built in Japan during the early 1970s to late 1980s.

The Madeira line was imported in to augment Guild sales in the U.S. between 1973 and 1974. The first run of solid body electrics consisted of entry level reproductions of classic Fender, Gibson, and even Guild designs (such as the S-100). The electric models were phased out in a year (1973 to 1974), but the acoustics were continued.

The solid body electrics were reintroduced briefly in the early 1980s, and then introduced again in 1990. The line consisted of three guitar models (ME-200, ME-300, ME-500) and one bass model (MBE-100). All shared similar design accoutrements such as bolt-on necks and various pickup configurations, (Source: Michael Wright, *Vintage Guitar Magazine*).

**MacDonald Cedar Top Acoustic
courtesy S.B. McDonald**

M

MAIZE, DAVE
Instruments currently built in Cave Junction, Oregon.

Luthier Dave Maze handbuilds acoustic bass guitars with environmentally-friendly woods (either woods certified by SmartWood or non-endangered species).

Dave Maize instruments typically have spruce, redwood or cedar tops and bodies of figured claro walnut, bigleaf maple, myrtlewood, or other select woods. Standard features include solid wood construction (including binding), Sperzel locking tuners, double action truss rod, bolt-on walnut neck, and a beautiful peghead inlay. Maize offers several custom options (cutaway body, electronics, etc.). Prices for both acoustic guitars and acoustic bass guitars start at $2,750. Players currently using Maize instruments include: Jack Casady, Phil Lesh, Adam Clayton and Jeff Ament. Maize's location used to be Talent, Oregon. For more information on Maize refer to his web site (see Trademark Index).

MANEA CUSTOM GUITARS
Instruments currently built in Nashville, Tennessee.

Luthier Dumitru Manea's goal is to make high quality affordable guitars for the beginner as well as professional recording artists. Manea has thirty years experience in woodworking and manufacturing techniques Manea guitars were previously made in Goodlettsville, Tennessee.

ACOUSTIC

Manea's new **Scodie** model is a 4-in-1 acoustic with a patented method to change from a 12-string configuration to 6-string, 9-string, or Nashville tuning in a matter of seconds.

Both the steel string model **M-2000** and classical model **AV-1** feature hand-carved spruce or cedar tops, mahogany or cedar necks and Indian rosewood back and sides. Both models feature ebony fingerboards and bridges, and a number of additionally priced design options. In addition to the AV-1, Manea also offers a Kid's Classical model (**CJ-11**) and two student models (**MP-14 Steel String and ME-14 Classical**).

MANSON
A.B. Manson & Company. Instruments currently built in Devon, England from the late 1970s. Distributed in the U.S. by S.A. Music of Santa Barbara, California.

Stringed instruments bearing the Manson name come from two separate operations. Acoustic guitars, mandolins, bouzoukis (and even triplenecks!) are built by Andrew Manson at A.B. Manson & Company. Electric guitars and electric basses are built by Hugh Manson at Manson Handmade Instruments. Andrew and Hugh Manson have been plying their luthier skills for over twenty five years. Both Mansons draw on a wealth of luthier knowledge as they tailor the instrument directly to the player commissioning the work.

Hand sizing (for neck dimensions), custom wiring, or custom choice of wood – it's all done in house. Both facilities are located in Devon, and both Mansons build high quality instruments respective of their particular genre. U.S. retail prices range around $3,275 for various models like the **Dove, Heron**, and **Sandpiper**. For further information regarding model specifications, pricing, and availability, please contact either Andrew or Hugh Manson directly (see Trademark Index).

According to authors Tony Bacon and Paul Day (*The Guru's Guitar Guide*), Manson instruments can be dated by the first two digits of the respective instrument's serial number.

MANZANITA GUITARS
Instruments currently built in Rosdorf, Germany.

Manzanita Guitars was founded in 1993 by Moritz Sattler and Manfred Pietrzok. However, Manfred put the first label for a Manzanita in a guitar in 1985. During their first year of cooperation, they concentrated on building acoustic steel string guitars, blending traditional shapes with design and construction ideas that soon became accepted as typical for Manzanita Guitars.

Today they offer a wide variety of custom-made flattop, hollow neck and resophonic guitars. Outstanding musicians using Manzanita Guitars include David Lindley, Ron Wood and Gero Drnek (Fury in the Slaughterhouse). Prices vary since each instrument is "one of a kind" in every way. For more information refer to their web site (see Trademark Index).

MANZER
Instruments currently built in Toronto, Canada since 1974.

Luthier Linda Manzer was first inspired to build stringed instruments after seeing Joni Mitchell perform on a dulcimer in 1969. Manzer began building full time in 1974, and apprenticed under Jean Claude Larrivee until 1978. In 1983, Manzer spent several months with James D'Aquisto while learning the art of archtop guitar building. Manzer gained some industry attention after she completed Pat Metheny's "Pikasso" multi-necked guitar (the model has four necks sharing one common body and 42-strings). In 1990, Manzer was commissioned by the Canadian Museum of Civilization to create a guitar for one of their displays. In addition to building the high quality guitar that she is known for, Manzer included inlay designs in the shape of one of Canada's endangered species on the neck. The extra ornamentation served as a reminder for environmental concerns. Noted players using Manzer guitars include Pat Metheny, Bruce Cockburn, and Carlos Santana.

ACOUSTIC: ARCHTOP SERIES

All Manzer archtops use only highest grade aged spruce tops and curly maple back, sides, and neck. Other features include an ebony fingerboard, bridge, and floating pickguard, as well as a gold plated height adjustment for the ebony tailpiece, and Schaller machine heads. Body depth is 3" at the side and 5" at the middle, a scale length of 25 1/4" (64 cm), and an overall length of 41" (104.5 cm) - except the Absynthe, which is 43" long (109 cm).

The **Studio** (list $13,900) is offered in either 16 1/2" or 17" lower bout width, and has ivoroid binding, dot inlay on fingerboard, Manzer signature inlay, and is available in a Blonde finish. The **Au Naturel** is 17" wide across the lower bout, and features all wood binding, highest grade woods, Orchid inlay and signature on the peghead, plain fingerboard, and art deco f-holes. This model is available in a Blonde finish, and has a retail list of $17,900.

The **Blue Note** model has a 5-ply maple/mahogany top and back, with curly maple sides and a body width of 16". Other features include an "In body" custom made PAF pickup that delivers rich warm tone with on-board volume and tone controls. Finished in a Light Tangerine Honey Burst, with all ebony appointments (list $9,500). The **JazzCAT** (list $17,900) is a 17" all wood model with contemporary *A* soundholes, bevelled veneered peghead, and Manzer signature inlay. This model is equipped with a Manzer JazzCAT pickup with adjustable pole pieces, and is finished in Honey Tangerine. The 18" **Absynthe** has deluxe binding, highest grade woods, ebony bound fingerboard with split block inlay, and Orchid with engraved mother-of-pearl scroll inlay of peghead. This model is available in Blonde or custom colors, and has a list price of $20,900.

ACOUSTIC: FLATTOP SERIES

There are several Manzer flattop models, each with their own "personality." Again, construction features aged spruce or Western cedar, Indian rosewood, and ebony. Manzer's most popular model, the **Manzer Steel String** ($6,500) has a 25 1/2" scale, rosewood back and sides, and an ebony fingerboard. The **Baritone** ($7,000) was designed in conjunction with Craig Snyder, and features a longer 29" scale. The longer scale supports the lower tuning (either low B to B, or low A to A) thus giving guitars access to a fuller voice. Back and sides are constructed of curly koa, and the fingerboard and bridge are ebony. The **Cowpoke** ($6,500) shares construction similarities with the standard Manzer, but features a larger and deeper body. Original inspiration was derived from a tall guy who wanted a Manzer, only bigger! The **Classical** ($7,500) offers a design that accommodates both traditional classical playing and modern jazz styles. A **12-string** configuration flattop is also offered (add $600). The **Little Manzer Steel** and the **Little Manzer Classical** are discontinued.

MAPSON, JAMES L.
Instruments currently built in Santa Ana, California.

Luthier James L. Mapson individually tailors both acoustic and electro-coustic archtop guitars by commission, balancing both design and construction to achieve performance goals for the professional musician. Beginning his career in 1995, James is largely self-taught. After considerable study of construction theory, he settled upon pursuing the D'Angelico approach, passed down and further developed by James L. D'Aquisto and subsequently by John Monteleone. Today Jim continues this approach to acoustic design, as well as his own designs to improve the electric archtop for performance and recording-minded clientele. Noted players using Mapson's instruments include Mundell Lowe, Ron Eschete, Frank Potenza and John Abercrombie.

Prices vary with each design, with base models starting at $4,500. Models include the Solo ($7,500), Lusso ($12,500), and the limited edition (only two built per year!) Avante ($18,500). The Bopcity lists for $5,550 and the Jazz Standard for $4,500. Contact luthier/designer James L. Mapson directly or visit Mapson's web site (see Trademark Index).

MARATHON
See chapter on House Brands.

This trademark had been identified as a House Brand previously used by Abercrombie & Fitch during the 1960s by author/researcher Willie G. Moseley. However, a number of newer guitars sporting the same trademark have been recently spotted. These guitars are built in Korea by the Samick company, and serve as an entry level instrument for the novice guitarist.

**Manzer Blue Absynthe
courtesy Scott Chinery**

MARCHIONE
Instruments currently handcrafted in Houston, Texas. Perviously built in New York (Manhattan), New York.

Stephen Marchione builds recording quality archtop and special commission guitars. Marchione's clientele primarily consists of New York's top studio and stage players, and he has received commissions from the likes of Mark Whitfield, John Abercrombie, Vernon Reed, and Mark Knofler. Other notables playing Marchione's guitars are George Wadenius (Steely Dan's *Alive in America* CD), Mark Stewart (Bang on a Can's *Music for Airports* CD), and Kenny Brescia and Ira Seigel (sound track for the Broadway smash *Rent*).

Marchione approaches his craft from many different angles. He understands players' sound and comfort needs as a guitar player himself. Marchione also seriously studies the great guitar and violin instruments in order to build archtop guitars that function as pinnacle pieces. When a player brings in a D'Aquisto or D'Angelico to Marchione's Manhattan shop, Marchione scrutinizes the instrument's construction, draws blueprints, and then quizzes the player about the instrument's best qualities. These important elements are then incorporated into his own designs.

The violin tradition has also figured prominently in Marchione's building. A hands-on understanding of cello arching is crucial to Marchione's ability to recreate the arching subtleties that imbue his archtop guitars with full acoustic volume and tambour. Marchione's friendship with violin maker Guy Rabut has impressed upon Marchione the importance of incorporating centuries of stringed instrument knowledge. Their friendship has also given Marchione the opportunity to measure and draw plans from Guarnieri cellows as well as Rabut's renowned instruments.

Personal musicianship, an exacting approach to guitar making, and the experience of hand building almost three hundred acoustic archtops, neck-throughs, and electric guitars are the groundwork for each and every Marchione guitar. (Company information courtesy Stephanie Green.)

ACOUSTIC ARCHTOP MODELS

There are several construction features that make Marchione's acoustic Archtops unique. Marchione chalk fits the neck dovetail joint to get a full contact suction fit – this provides the guitar with its long ringing sustain. Final top tuning is performed with the guitar strung up to pitch; thus, he can fine tune the tambour and volume of the guitar while it is being played (no guessing allowed!). Marchione also hand carves the soundboard recurve all the way around the perimeter of the soundboard, including the cutaway, making the whole instrument acoustically useful. In order to maximize the instrument's sound, Marchione suspends the pickguard, the entire fingerboard extension, the tailpiece, and the pickup over the top. Marchione has noticed from studying cellos and other acoustic guitars that as soon as anything touches the top, the instrument's sound is decreased by up to one-third.

Archtop guitars are available as Steel String or Nylon String models. All instruments feature loft-dried cello grade tonewoods including High Alpine Engelmann spruce (tops) and highly figured maple (back, sides, and necks). Other features

**Marchione Archtop
courtesy Marchione**

include an ebony fingerboard, pickguard, tailpiece, and bridge. Instruments are constructed with all wood binding and purfling, and have mother-of-pearl inlay. The **Acoustic Archtop** model was featured in 16", 17", and 18" body widths, and are available with or without electronics. Currently the acoustic archtop is available as a 16" built for Mark Whitfield, and retails for $18,500.

MARCO POLO

Instruments previously built in Japan circa early 1960s. Distributed by the Marco Polo Company of Santa Ana, California.

The Marco Polo product line offered acoustic flattops, thinline hollowbody acoustic/electric guitars, and solid body electric guitars and basses. These inexpensive Japanese-built instruments were the first to be advertised by its U.S. distributors, Harry Stewart and the Marco Polo company. While the manufacturers are currently unknown, it is estimated that some of the acoustics were built by Suzuki, and some electric models were produced by Guyatone, (Source: Michael Wright, *Vintage Guitar Magazine*).

MARK WESCOTT GUITARS

Instruments currently built in Somers Point, New Jersey.

Mark Wescott's approach to guitar building is one of innovative design that is based on the importance of sound and the interaction between the guitar and the player. Wescott is one of the growing number of modern builders who are systematically re-examining the mechanics of how a guitar produces sound.

Wescott's background in music began early as he grew up in a musical family where violins, violas, and cellos were always present. While Wescott first trained as an apprentice in cabinet making and furniture restoration, his musical background led him back to creating high quality acoustic guitars.

In 1980, Wescott built his first guitar under the guidance of George Morris, while attending the Charles Fox Guitar Research and Design School (GRD). Several years later, Wescott attended Richard Schneider's Kasha Design Seminar. Wescott continued on as resident luthier for three years at Schneider's Lost Mountain Center for the Guitar; it was there that he acquired a solid background in the Kasha method of radial soundboard bracing. This method was first invented by Dr. Michael Kasha, and pioneered by Master Luthier Richard Schneider.

ACOUSTIC

Wescott designs his guitars (including the most recent **Intrepid** model) using the Kasha system of soundboard design. Asymmetrical radial soundboard bracing in conjunction with the impedance matching bridge enables Wescott to tailor the tonal response of the instrument. The **Intrepid** model is available in 6 - and 7-string configurations, and features a Sitka spruce top, East Indian rosewood back and sides, Honduran mahogany neck, 24-fret ebony fingerboard, Kasha-type bridge, 3-per-side Schaller mini tuners, graphite soundboard braces, Wechter-style access panel (trap door) tail block. Commissioned retail price is $8,000, and comes complete with deluxe hardshell case.

MARLING

Instruments previously produced in Japan during the mid 1970s.

As the Italian-based EKO guitar company was winding down, they were marketing an EKO guitar copies built in Japan (although they may have been built by EKO). EKO offered a number of Marling acoustic models, as well as electric guitars. These guitar models were poor quality compared to the 1960s Italian EKOs, (Source: Michael Wright, *Guitar Stories*, Volume One).

MARONI

Instruments previously produced in Italy in the mid 1960s.

Reader Gene Van Alstyne of Cushing, Oklahoma called in this classical-styled guitar, built by luthier Farfisa. The guitar has a zero fret, a split saddle, 38mm tuning pegs, and a "Made in Italy" label in the soundhole. When the Farfisa name was uttered, the immediate talk turned to those 1960s organs. A connection, perhaps? Further research is underway.

MARTELLE

See chapter on House Brands.

The distributor of this Gibson-built budget line of guitars has not yet been identified. Built to the same standards as other Gibson guitars, they lack the one true Gibson touch: an adjustable truss rod. House Brand Gibsons were available to musical instrument distributors in the late 1930s and early 1940s, (Source: Walter Carter, *Gibson Guitars: 100 Years of an American Icon*).

MARTIN

Currently manufactured by The Martin Guitar Co., using the "C.F. Martin & Co. Est. 1833" trademark, with headquarters and plant located in Nazareth, PA since 1839. C.F. Martin & Company was originally founded in New York in 1833.

The Martin Guitar company has the unique position of being the only company that has always been helmed by a Martin family member. Christian Frederick Martin, Sr. (1796-1873) came from a woodworking (cabinet making) family background. He learned guitar building as an employee for Johann Stauffer, and worked his way up to Stauffer's foreman in Vienna (Austria). Martin left Stauffer in 1825, and returned to his birthplace in Markneukirchen (Germany). Martin got caught up in an on-going dispute between the violin makers guild and the cabinet makers guild. Martin and his family emigrated to America in the fall of 1833, and by the end of the year set up a full line music store. The Martin store dealt in all types of musical instruments, sheet music, and repairs – as well as Martin's Stauffer-style guitars.

After six years, the Martin family moved to Nazareth, Pennsylvania. C.A. Zoebich & Sons, their New York sales agency, continued to hold "exclusive" rights to sell Martin guitars; so the Martin guitars retained their New York labels until a business falling-out occurred in 1898. The Martin family settled outside of town, and continued producing guitars that began to reflect less of a European design in favor of a more straightforward design. Christian Martin favored a deeper lower bout, Brazilian rosewood for the back and sides, cedar for necks, and a squared-off slotted peghead (with 3 tuners per side). Martin's scalloped X-bracing was developed and used beginning in 1850 instead of the traditional "fan" bracing favored by Spanish luthiers (fan bracing is favored on classical guitars today).

In 1852, Martin standardized his body sizes, with "1" the largest and "3" the smallest (size 2 and 2 1/2 were also included). Two years later, a larger "0" and smaller "5" sizes were added as well. Martin also standardized his style (or design) distinctions in the mid 1850s, with the introduction of Style 17 in 1856 and Styles 18 and 27 a year later. Thus, every Martin guitar has a two-part name: size number and style number. Martin moved into town in 1857 (a few blocks north of town square), and built his guitar building factory right next door within two years.

C.F. Martin & Company was announced in 1867, and in three years a wide range of styles were available. A larger body size, the **00** debuted in 1877. Under the direction of C.F. Martin, Jr. (1825-1888), the company decided to begin producing mandolins – which caused the business split with their New York sales agency. Martin bowl-back mandolins were offered beginning in 1895, three years before the snowflake inlay Style 42 became available. Also as important, Martin began serializing their guitars in 1898. The company estimated that 8,000 guitars had been built between 1833 to 1898; and so started the serialization with number 8,000. This serialization line is still intact today (!), and functions as a useful tool in dating the vintage models. The 15" wide body Size 000, as well as more pearl inlay on Martin guitars were introduced in 1902, which led to the fancier **Style 45** two years later.

A major materials change occurred in 1916, as mahogany replaced cedar as the chosen wood for neck building. White celluloid (ivoroid) became the new binding material in 1918. The Martin company also took a big technological leap in 1922, as they adapted the Model 2 - 17 for steel strings instead of gut strings (all models would switch to steel string configuration by 1929). To help stabilize the new amount of stress in the necks, an ebony bar was embedded in the neck (the ebony bar was replaced by a steel T-Bar in 1934). Martin briefly built banjos in the early to mid 1920s, and also built a fair share of good quality ukuleles and tiples.

In 1929, Martin was contacted by Perry Bechtel who was looking for a flattop guitar with 14-frets clear of the body (Martin's models all joined at the 12th fret). The company responded by building a 000 model with a slimmed down 14/20-fret neck – announced in the 1930 catalog as the OM (Orchestra Model) (the 14/20-fret neck was adopted by almost all models in the production line by 1934). Martin also began stamping the model name into the neck block of every guitar in 1931.

While the Jazz Age was raising a hubaloo, Martin was building archtop guitars. The three C models were introduced in 1931, the R-18 two years later, and the F-7 (the shape that eventually became the profile of the M, 0000, and J models) in 1935. Martin archtop production lasted until 1942. The archtops of 1931 have since been overshadowed by another model that debuted that year – Martin's 16" wide dreadnought size. Guitar players were asking for more volume, but instead of making a bigger "0000" body, Martin chose to design a new type of acoustic guitar. Martin was already building a similar type of guitar originally as a model for the Oliver Ditson company in 1916; they just waited for the market to catch up to them!

Martin D-45VR
courtesy Martin Guitar

The Dreadnought acoustic (so named after large World War I battleships) with X-bracing is probably the most widely copied acoustic guitar design in the world today. A look at today's music market could confirm a large number of companies building a similar design, and the name "Dreadnought" has become an industry standard. Back in the 1930s, a singing cowboy of some repute decided to order a Dreadnought size guitar in the Style 45. Gene Autry became the first owner of Martin's D-45.

In 1938, the X-bracing (on Dreadnought models only) was shifted back to approximately 2 inches from soundhole, presumably to strengthen the top. In 1939, the neck was narrowed slightly. In mid 1944, the Martin company stopped the practice of "scalloping" (shaving a concave surface) the braces on their guitar tops. 1947 saw the end of herringbone trim on the guitar tops, due to a lack of consistent sources (either German or American). The first two dozen (or so) 1947 D-28 models did have herringbone trim. Some thirty years later, Martin's HD-28 model debuted with the "restored" scalloped bracing and herringbone trim (this model is still in production today).

The folk boom of the late 1950s increased the demand for Martin guitars. The original factory produced around 6,000 guitars a year, but that wasn't enough. Martin began construction on a new facility in 1964, and when the new plant opened a year later, production began to go over 10,000 guitars a year. While expansion of the market is generally a good thing, the limited supply of raw materials is detrimental (to say the least!). In 1969, Brazil put an embargo on rosewood logs exported from their country. To solve this problem, Martin switched over to Indian rosewood in 1969. Brazilian rosewood from legal sources does show up on certain limited edition models from time to time.

The 1970s was a period of fluctuation for the Martin company. Many aggressive foreign companies began importing products into the U.S. market, and were rarely challenged by complacent U.S. manufacturers. To combat the loss of sales in the entry level market, Martin started the Sigma line of overseas-produced guitars for dealers. Martin also bought Levin, the Swedish guitar company, in 1973. The Size M, developed in part by Mark Silber, Matt Umanov, and Dave Bromberg, debuted in 1977. E Series electric guitars were briefly offered beginning in 1979 (up until 1983). A failed attempt at union organization at the Martin plant also occurred in the late 1970s. Martin's Custom Shop was formally opened in 1979, and set the tone for other manufacturers' custom shop concepts.

The late C.F. Martin III, who had steered the company through the Great Depression, said that 1982 was the most devastating year in the company's history. The balance of the 1980s produced some innovations and radical changes at the Martin company. It was 1985 when current CEO and Chairman of the Board Chris F. Martin IV assumed his duties at the youthful age of 28. The Martin Guitar of the Month program, a limited production/custom guitar offering was introduced in 1984 (and continued through 1994, prior to the adoption of the Limited Edition series) as well as the new Jumbo J Series. The most mind-boggling event occurred the next year: The Martin Company adopted the adjustable truss rod in 1985! Martin always

Martin D-28
courtesy Martin Guitar

maintained the point of view that a properly built guitar wouldn't need one. The Korean-built Stinger line of solid body electrics was offered the same year as the Shenandoah line of Japanese-produced parts/U.S. assembly.

The Martin company continues producing guitars only in Pennsylvania. The recent Road Series models, with their CNC-carved necks and laminated back and sides are being built in the same facilities producing the solid wood bodies and custom shop models.

The X Series was introduced in 1998, and features HPL (high pressure laminate) constructed components, decal rosette, screened headstock logo, and patented neck mortise. Martin has brought all model production (figuratively and literally) under one roof. During 1999, Martin proudly opened up its new 85,000 square foot addition, making this facility one of the most state of the art guitar plants on the planet. Production has risen to 225 guitars per day. This new efficient technology also has enabled Martin to keep consistent high quality production within the U.S., while actually lowering consumer costs.

With the recent additions of the unique DXM (released 1998, with composite body and top), and Alternative X (released 2001, solid aluminum top with composite body) models, Martin's ongoing commitment to product research using other tone woods and alternative materials ensures a future when confronted with dwindling supplies of traditional woods and related building materials. Martin also adheres to the guidelines and conservation efforts set by such organizations as the Forest Stewardship Council (FSC), Rainforest Foundation International, and SmartWood Certified Forestry (Certified Wood products).

At the 2001 summer NAMM Show in Nashville, TN, Martin showcased yet another milestone in its company's history – instrument number 750,000. This Peacock Deluxe flattop is the most elaborate and ornate Martin guitar ever manufactured, with over 2,000 handcut pieces of shell inlayed on the back, sides, pickguard, and neck. Also new for 2001 was the introduction of the D-50 Deluxe Edition and SP+ extended life strings.

During 2002, Martin continued to expand its line of regular models, with prices ranging from $619 to $25,000! Additionally, Martin released 18 new special/limited editions at the winter NAMM Show, and 11 new special/limited editions at the Nashville Summer NAMM Show. With this new lineup, Martin continues to be the leader in acoustic instruments, covering a wide variety of price points, building materials, and both vintage and high tech guitar construction techniques.

Serial number 800,000 (a CFM3 Commemorative) was announced at the Anaheim winter NAMM in Jan., 2003. During mid-2003, the first Martin resonator guitar was introduced (Alternative II resonator), in addition to the X Series "Little Martin," which is the least expensive of the Martin full size models. Martin guitar price points currently range from $274-$45,000, ensuring that everyone can own a Martin guitar, regardless of income.

Sources: Mike Longworth, *Martin Guitars: A History*; Walter Carter, *The Martin Book: A Complete History of Martin Guitars*; and Tom Wheeler, American Guitars. Information and pricing on Martin's more recent Custom Shop production, including both Limited and Special Editions can be found in its magazine, *The Sounding Board*, published in Jan. and July. It is highly recommended that you get these informative newsletters to keep abreast on what's happening with Martin's Custom Shop and regular production. Additionally, Martin's web site: www.cfmartin.com, is one of the most up-to-date and complete in the industry.

VISUAL IDENTIFICATION FEATURES

Martin has been in the same small town for 160 years and serialization has remained intact and consistent since their first instrument. When trying to determine the year of an instrument's construction, some quick notes about features can be helpful. The few notes contained herein are for readily identifying the instrument upon sight and are by no means meant to be used for truly accurate dating of an instrument. All items discussed are for flattop steel string guitars and involve instruments that are standard production models.

The earliest dreadnoughts, and indeed just about all instruments produced with a neck that joins the body at the 12th fret, have bodies that are bell shaped on the top, as opposed to the more square shouldered styles of most dreadnoughts. Between 1929 to 1934, Martin began placing 14-fret necks on most of their instruments and this brought about the square shouldered body style. A few models maintained 12-fret necks into the late 1940s and several had a 12-fret neck until the late 1980s.

Turn of the century instruments have square slotted pegheads with the higher end models (models 42 and 45) displaying an intricate pearl fern inlay that runs vertically up the peghead. This was replaced by a vertical inlay known as the flowerpot or the torch inlay, in approximately 1905. In 1932, the "C.F. Martin & Co. Est. 1833" scroll logo began appearing on certain models' pegheads. By approximately 1934, a solid peghead with a vertical pearl "C.F. Martin" inlay had replaced the former peghead design.

Bridges from the 1900s are rectangular with pyramid wings. In approximately 1929, the belly bridge replaced the rectangle bridge. This bridge has a straight slot cut across the entire length of the center section of the bridge. In 1965, the straight cut saddle slot was changed to a routed slot. It was in approximately 1936, that Martin began using the tied bridge on their classical instruments.

Pickguards were not standard features on instruments until 1931 (1930 on some OM models) when tortoise pickguards were introduced. In 1967, black pickguards became standard. In 1969, Martin stopped using Brazilian rosewood for its regular production instruments, ending with serial number 254498. As a result, premiums are being asked for instruments manufactured from this exotic wood. After 1969, Martin began to use East Indian rosewood backs and sides on standard production instruments in Style 21 or higher (D-21, D-28, etc.); and mahogany backs and sides on Style 20 or lower (D-18, D-1220, etc.) production models.

INSTRUMENTS BUILT FOR OTHER TRADEMARKS (BRAND NAMES)

Martin did build guitars for other retailers, teachers, and musical instrument distributors; unlike Harmony's or Kay's house brands, though, "retitled" Martins were the exception and not the rule. If any of these trademarks are spotted, here's a partial hint to origin:

Bacon Banjo Company: Around 1924, Martin supplied a number of guitars without Martin stamps or labels. However, most of the Bacon-trademarked guitars were built by Regal (Chicago, Illinois).

Belltone: Only a few Style 3K guitars, mandolins, and ukuleles were built for the Perlburg and Halpin company of New York City, New York.

Bitting Special: Both guitars and mandolins were built for this well-known music teacher in Bethlehem, Pennsylvania between 1916 to 1919.

Briggs Special: 65 specially trimmed mandolin models were built for the Briggs Music shop in Utica, New York circa 1914 to 1919.

C. Bruno: Long before they were acquired by Kaman Music, C. Bruno was associated with C.F. Martin in 1838. Guitars carry a paper label that says "C.F. Martin & Bruno." Later C. Bruno & Sons guitars were not built by Martin.

Oliver Ditson & Co.: Ditson had stores in Boston, New York, and Philadelphia. Martin built guitars, bowl-back and flat mandolins, ukuleles, tiples, and taro patch stringed instruments for their stores. Martin built a dreadnought-style guitar for them in 1916, long before Martin offered it under their own trademark in 1931. Another Ditson branch in Chicago went on to fame producing and marketing Washburn guitars in the 1900s.

Carl Fischer: The Carl Fisher firm of New York City, New York ordered a number of special O-18T (tenor) guitars in 1929.

William Foden: Concert guitarist and teacher William Foden had his own series of Foden Specials built by Martin. These models were primarily sold to his students between 1900 to 1920. Foden's insistence on a twenty fret fingerboard is now a standard feature on Martin guitars.

J.A. Handley: J.A. Handley was an instructor in Lowell, Massachusetts. He is credited with the developement of the Style 6A mandolin.

Jenkins: This dealer in Kansas City, Missouri sold Martin ukuleles, renumbered #35 (Style 1) and #40 (Style 2).

Montgomery Ward: Martin had a short term deal with the Montgomery Ward company circa 1932. Martin supplied mahogany guitars, flat mandolins, and ukuleles.

Vahdah Olcott-Bickford: Vahdah Olcott-Bickford was a well-known concert artist and teacher. Guitars built to her specifications were called a Style 44, or Soloist.

Paramount: Paramount ordered about 30 special resonator models under the Paramount logo. Paramount was well-known for their banjo models, which were not Martin instruments.

Rolando: The Rolando trademark shows up on a series of Martin-built koa Hawaiian-style guitars ordered by the Southern California Music Company (circa 1917-1920). Records also show a direct sale to J.J. Milligan Music.

Rudick's: The Rudick's firm of Akron, Ohio ordered a number of OO-17 guitars with the number O-55 stamped inside (circa 1935).

William J. Smith: The William J. Smith firm of New York City, New York had Martin-built ukuleles, taro patches and tiples in stock circa 1917.

Stetson: W.J. Dyer & Bro., known for their association with Larson Brothers acoustics, also specified 3 guitars for their Stetson trademark circa 1922.

S.S. Stewart: Distributors Buegeleisen and Jacobson of New York City, New York ordered ukuleles and other stringed instruments with their S.S. Stewart label circa 1923 to 1925.

John Wanamaker: The Wanamaker department store in Philadelphia, Pennsylvania ordered special models circa 1909.

H.A. Weymann & Son: The Weymann firm of Philadelphia, Pennsylvania was known for their banjos; Martin built a number of ukuleles and taro patches models around 1925.

Wolverine: The Wolverine trademark was applied to Martin-built guitars and mandolins for the Grinnell Brothers of Detroit, Michigan. Wolverine instruments carry the regular Martin serial numbers.

Rudolph Wurlitzer: The Wurlitzer music store chain ordered special model guitars between 1922 to 1924.

(Information on "Retitled" Martin instruments courtesy: Mike Longworth, *Martin Guitars: A History*; Walter Carter, *The Martin Book: A Complete History of Martin Guitars*; and Tom Wheeler, *American Guitars*).

**Martin D-50 Deluxe
courtesy Martin Guitar**

CURRENT MODEL DESIGNATIONS

The Martin model series listing follows the model nomenclature. Additional information within the following parentheses lists the Martin company's current Series designation. To avoid any potential confusion, current models are listed just as their model name is stamped on their neck block (Martin began stamping model designations on the neck block in 1930).

For example, Martin's Road Series models feature common construction design (models have solid spruce tops, and laminated back/sides). However, the models in the Road Series include both dreadnought size and 000 auditorium size models (The DM, DR, and 000M).

GUITARS OF THE MONTH/CUSTOM SHOP MODELS

Martin's Guitars of the Month were manufactured from Oct. 1984-1995. The Custom Shop was established circa 1979, and both series of instruments are fancier or slightly different takes on established models. They are usually identified with a suffix, and are listed in this text in chronological sequence with the year in parentheses after the model name (some have unusual prefixes.) It is not our intention to list every variation but the reader should be aware that these instruments do exist. Custom Shop guitars are stamped "Custom" on the neck block. Custom Shop instruments can only be valued on an individual basis. Please refer to the categories Guitar of the Month/Year and Special/Limited Editions in the back of this section for detailed listings, model descriptions and pricing guidelines.

MARTIN GUITARS MADE BEFORE 1898

Any Martin guitar made before 1898 almost has to be dealt with on an individual basis – nearly all of them were rosewood construction; they featured different amounts of trim. From Style 17 at the low end (at the time a rosewood and spruce guitar with relatively plain trim) to Style 42 at the high end, the largest of these instruments would be considered small by today's standards. Martin guitars from before the turn of the century seem to start at about $1,500 for something in average condition (and not fancy), and go up in excess of $35,000 for the fanciest guitars.

In 1898 Martin started serially numbering their guitars. They estimated that they'd made about 8,000 guitars up to that time; that's when they started their numbering system. Some models with low production totals (10 or less, usually) may be ignored here.

**Martin 00-17
courtesy Dave Hull**

GRADING	100%	EXCELLENT	AVERAGE

COMMON MARTIN ABBREVIATIONS

A - Ash

AE - Acoustic/Electric

B - Acoustic Bass or Brazilian

BK - Black

BR - Brazilian Rosewood

C - Classic or Classical

C - Cutaway

CEO – Chief Executive Officer

C.I.T.E.S. – Convention for International Trade of Endangered Species (July 1, 1975)

D - Dreadnought

DB - Deep Body

E - Designates Onboard Electronics (various configurations)

EMP - Employee

FMG - Figured Mahogany

G - Gut (later nylon) String

GE - Golden Era

GM - Grand Marquis

GOM - Guitar of the Month

GT - Gloss Top

H - Herringbone or Hawaiian

HP - Herringbone Pearl

HPL - High Pressure Laminate

J - Jumbo

K - Koa (back & sides)

K2 - Koa (top, back & sides)

L - Left-Hand

LE - Limited Edition

LS (LSH) - Large Soundhole

M - Mahogany

MB - Maple binding

MP - Morado Rosewood

N - Martin Classical Shape (non low profile neck)

O - Concert

OO - Grand Concert

000 - Auditorium

0000 - Grand Auditorium

OM - Orchestra Model

P - Plectrum or Low Profile

Q - Old Style non adj. neck (1985-current)

R - Rosewood

2R - 2 Soundhole Rings

S - Special or Special Order (pre 1995)

S - 12-Fret Slotted Neck

SE - Signature Edition

SP - Special (post 1995) or Special Appointments

SW - Smart Wood Certified

T - Tenor

V - Vintage (suffix for models after 1983)

VS – Vintage Sunburst

W - Walnut

ACOUSTIC GUITARS: GENERAL INFORMATION & PRICING OPTIONS

The following layout has been used in this section for convenience and speed. Initial series start (i.e., D Series, J Series, M Series, O Series, OM Series, and X Series), followed by numerical body sizes (0000, 000, 00, 0, 1/4, 1/2, 1, 2, 21/2, 3, 31/2, 4, 5, and 7), followed by alpabetical configurations (Archtop, Backpacker, & Classical).

Left-handed models are available at no extra charge.

Retail list prices on currently manufactured guitars includes a hardshell case, except for the X Series.

> Add 20%-30% for Sunburst finish (over Natural finish).
>
> Add 20% for first year of manufacture for most models mfg. before WWII.
>
> Add $228 for new Sunburst, "Vintage" toner, or "Aging" toner finishes on recently manufactured instruments.
>
> Add $258 for new High Gloss finish on recently manufactured instruments.
>
> Add $239 for Prefix (Fishman). Add $269 for Prefix Pro (Fishman). Add $309 for Prefix Pro Blend (new mid -2001). Add $169 for Classic IV Sonicore (Fishman). Add $279 for Prefix Plus (Fishman). Add $339 for Prefix Onboard Blender (Fishman). Add $215 for Pro EQ (outboard preamp only). Add $149 for Porta-Con outboard preamp (new 2000). Add $299 for SLI Matrix EQ (Martin/Fishman, disc. mid -2002). Add $219 for L.R. Baggs RT System (disc. 1998). Add $335 for L.R. Baggs Dual Source System (disc. 1998). Add $150 for System 1 Fishman (disc. 2000). Add $200 for single coil Rare Earth soundhole pickup (disc. 2000). Add $250 for humbucker Rare Earth soundhole pickup (disc. 2000). Add $450 for Blender model Rare Earth soundhole pickup (disc. 2000). Add $113 for Martin Second Generation Thinline 332. Add $189 for Martin Thinline 332+Plus with Active Jack. Add $223 for Martin Thinline Gold+Plus (Natural or Maximum).

ACOUSTIC ELECTRIC GUITARS

Rather than include all of the Martin acoustic electric models with descriptions in this section again, these acoustic electric models have been listed together within their individual series. Please refer to the individual acoustic electric models listed within their categorized sections for more information and current pricing. All Martin acoustic electric instruments have the definitive E suffix.

ACOUSTIC: D (DREADNOUGHT) SERIES

Size D (dreadnought) guitars feature a lower bout width of 15 5/8 inches, 4 7/8 (14-fret) or 4¾ (12-fret) in. depth, 20 (14-fret) or 20 15/16 (12-fret) in. length, and 25.4 in. scale.

DM (ROAD SERIES) - solid spruce top, round soundhole, black body binding, laminated mahogany back/sides, mahogany neck, 14/20-fret rosewood fingerboard with white dot inlay, single band herringbone rosette, tortoise pickguard, 3-per-side chrome tuners, available in Natural Satin finish, new 1996.

MSR	$949	$670	$485	$380

DCM (Road Series) - similar to DM, except features rounded Venetian cutaway, Custom Shop Mfg. 1996-98.

	$795	$575	$475

Last MSR was $1,150.

DCME (Road Series) - similar to DCM, except has onboard electronics, new 1999.

MSR	$1,419	$995	$725	$530

GRADING	100%	EXCELLENT	AVERAGE

DCRE (Road Series) - similar to DCME, except has rosewood back/sides. Custom Shop Mfg. 1999 only.

	$1,050	**$750**	**$575**

Last MSR was $1,500.

DM-12 (Road Series) - similar to DM, except has 12-string configuration, 6-per-side tuners, new 1996.

MSR	$1,199	$850	$625	$475

DR (Road Series) - similar to DM, except features laminated rosewood back/sides, available in Natural Satin finish, new 1996.

MSR	$1,149	$795	$600	$455

D-1 (1 SERIES) - solid Sitka spruce top, round soundhole, tortoise bound body, 3-stripe rosette, solid mahogany back, laminated mahogany sides, mahogany neck, 14/20-fret rosewood fingerboard with dot inlay, rosewood bridge with white black dot pins, tortoise pickguard, 3-per-side chrome tuners, available in Natural Satin finish, new 1993.

MSR	$1,129	$790	$600	$445

D-1R - similar to D-1, except has rosewood back/sides, mfg. 1994-late 2002.

	$875	**$660**	**$480**

Last MSR was $1,329.

DC-1 - similar to D-1, except features a rounded Venetian cutaway, Custom Shop mfg. 1996-99.

	$850	**$650**	**$475**

Last MSR was $1,300.

DC-1R - similar to D-1, except features a rounded Venetian cutaway, rosewood back/sides, Custom Shop mfg. 1998-99.

	$975	**$750**	**$575**

Last MSR was $1,499.

Martin D-M
courtesy Martin Guitar

DC-1E - similar to D-1, except features a rounded Venetian cutaway, Martin Gold+Plus bridge pickup, Martin/Fishman Prefix preamp/EQ system, current mfg.

MSR	$1,569	$1,100	$775	$600

D12-1 - similar to D-1, except has a 12-string configuration, 6-per-side headstock. Mfg. 1996-2001.

	$850	**$650**	**$475**

Last MSR was $1,300.

D-2R (1 SERIES) - solid spruce top, round soundhole, ivoroid bound body, 3-stripe rosette, laminated East Indian rosewood back/sides, mahogany neck, 14/20-fret rosewood fingerboard with dot inlay, rosewood bridge with white black dot pins, black pickguard, 3-per-side chrome tuners, available in Natural Satin finish, mfg. 1996-late 2002.

	$910	**$675**	**$500**

Last MSR was $1,399.

This model features appointments that pay tribute to the appearance of the D-28 model.

D-3R (1 SERIES) - similar to D-2R, except features bound fingerboard, 3-piece back of laminated East Indian rosewood, available in Natural Satin finish, mfg. 1996-late 2002.

	$965	**$695**	**$515**

Last MSR was $1,479.

This model features appointments that pay tribute to the appearance of the D-35 model.

D-15 (15 SERIES) - solid mahogany top, round soundhole, single band gold herringbone decal rosette, solid mahogany back/sides, mahogany neck, no body binding, 14/20-fret rosewood fingerboard with white dot inlay, rosewood bridge with white pins, tortoise pickguard, 3-per-side chrome tuners, current mfg.

MSR	$979	$695	$525	$375

DC-15E - similar to D-15, except features a single rounded cutaway body, bridge pickup, onboard electronics, available in Natural Satin finish, new 1998.

MSR	$1,499	$1,050	$775	$625

D-15S - similar to D-15, except features 12/20-fret rosewood fingerboard and sapele/mahogany top, back/sides, D-1 style bracing, new mid 2001.

MSR	$1,219	$850	$625	$425

J12-15 - similar to D-15, except is 12-string, new 2000.

MSR	$1,139	$800	$575	$395

Martin D-15
courtesy Martin Guitar

D-16T (16 SERIES) - spruce top, round soundhole, black pickguard, tortoise bound body, herringbone rosette, solid mahogany back/sides, mahogany neck, 14/20-fret rosewood fingerboard with pearl dot inlay, rosewood bridge with black pins, tortoise pickguard, 3-per-side chrome tuners, available in Natural Satin finish, mfg. 1986-1998.

| | $1,050 | $825 | $625 |

Last MSR was $1,650.

D-16A - similar to the D-16, except features ash back/sides, mfg. 1987-1988, 1990.

| | N/A | $1,000 | $750 |

D-16K - similar to the D-16, except features koa back/sides, mfg. 1986.

| | N/A | $1,200 | $850 |

D-16W - similar to the D-16, except features walnut back/sides, mfg. 1987, 1990.

| | N/A | $1,200 | $850 |

D-16TR - similar to the D-16T, except has solid rosewood back/sides, available in Natural Satin finish, mfg. 1996-98.

| | $1,195 | $925 | $675 |

Last MSR was $1,850.

D-16 LYPTUS (16 SERIES) - solid Sitka spruce top with Lyptus back/sides, Spanish cedar neck with 14/20-fret rosewood fingerboard, polish gloss/maple stain finish, new mid 2003.

| MSR | $1,849 | $1,295 | $975 | $750 |

D-16GT (16 SERIES) - solid spruce top, solid mahogany back/sides/neck, gloss top, satin back and sides, new 1999.

| MSR | $1,279 | $895 | $650 | $450 |

D-16RGT - similar to the D-16GT, except has rosewood back/sides, new 2001.

| MSR | $1,479 | $1,050 | $750 | $575 |

DC-16E - similar to the D-16GT, except is cutaway and sides/back are sapele, Spanish cedar neck with 14/20-fret black Micarta fingerboard, paua rosette, tortoise colored bindings, Schertler Blue Stick electronics, new 2003.

| MSR | $2,199 | $1,525 | $1,175 | $875 |

DC-16GTE - similar to the D-16GT, except has cutaway body and onboard electronics including co-polymer pickup and Fishman Prefix Pro electronics, new 1999.

| MSR | $1,699 | $1,195 | $825 | $600 |

DC-16GTE Premium - similar to the D-16GTE, except has Spanish Cedar neck and Fishman Prefix Premium Onboard blender electronics, new 2003.

| MSR | $1,749 | $1,225 | $850 | $625 |

DC-16RGTE - similar to the D-16GTE, except has solid Indian rosewood body/sides, new 2000.

| MSR | $1,939 | $1,350 | $975 | $715 |

DC-16RGTE Premium - similar to the D-16RGTE, except has Spanish Cedar neck and Fishman Prefix Premium Onboard blender electronics, gloss finished top, semi-gloss neck, new 2003.

| MSR | $1,989 | $1,395 | $1,025 | $750 |

J12-16GT - similar to D-16GT, except is 12-string, new 2000.

| MSR | $1,499 | $1,060 | $750 | $575 |

DC-16RE - similar to DC-16GTE, except has solid Sitka spruce top, single ring blue paua pearl with white/black inlay, hybrid scalloped bracing with quarter inch tone bars, polished gloss finish and Bluestick electronics from Schertler, new mid 2002.

| MSR | $2,399 | $1,675 | $1,225 | $875 |

D-17 - solid mahogany top, back and sides, 2-piece back, 14/20-fret ebony or black Micarta fingerboard, polished gloss finish with dark mahogany stain, new 2000.

| MSR | $1,650 | $1,150 | $850 | $575 |

DC-17E - similar to the D-17, except has single cutaway and Fishman Prefix Stereo onboard blender electronics, mfg. 2002 only.

| | $1,450 | $995 | $725 |

Last MSR was $2,199.

D-17GT - similar to the D-17, except has satin finished sides and gloss top, mfg. 2002 only.

| | $995 | $750 | $550 |

Last MSR was $1,499.

GRADING	100%	EXCELLENT	AVERAGE

D-18 - solid spruce top, round soundhole, tortoise bound body, 3-stripe purfling/rosette, mahogany back/sides/neck, 12/19-fret ebony fingerboard with pearl dot inlay, ebony bridge with black white dot pins, 3-per-side chrome tuners, available in Natural finish, mfg. 1932-current.

1932-1933	N/A	N/A	$18,000
1934-1938	N/A	$20,000	$12,000
1939-1944	N/A	$10,000	$6,000
1944-1946 (not scalloped)	N/A	$9,000	$5,000
1947-1950	N/A	$5,000	$4,000
1951-1959	N/A	$3,500	$2,500
1960-1967	N/A	$2,500	$1,800
1968-present	N/A	$1,500	$1,000

Add 25% for Sunburst finish mfg. in 1930s mfg.

In 1934, 14/20-fret fingerboard replaced the 12/19-fret fingerboard. Some early D-18 models have sold as high as $30,000. In 1932, pickguard became an option. By 1946, rosewood fingerboard/bridges replaced original ebony parts.

D-18 (Standard Series)

MSR	$2,159	$1,500	$1,100	$795

D-18E - similar to D-18, except has 2 single coil exposed DeArmond pickups, mixing switch, 1 volume and 2 tone controls. Mfg. 1959-1965.

N/A	$1,650	$1,200

D-18S - similar to D-18, except has prewar dreadnought style body, 12/20-fret fingerboard, Custom Shop mfg. 1967-1993.

1967-1969	N/A	$2,000	$1,500
1970-1993	N/A	$1,800	$1,200

Last MSR was $2,330.

D12-18 - similar to D-18, except has 12-strings, 6-per-side tuners, Custom Shop mfg. 1973-1996.

$1,495	$1,175	$750

Last MSR was $2,350.

**Martin D-18
courtesy Martin Guitar**

D-18V (VINTAGE SERIES) - solid spruce top, round soundhole, tortoise bound body, special design striped rosette, solid mahogany back/sides, mahogany neck, 14/20-fret ebony fingerboard with abalone dot inlay, ebony bridge with white black dot pins, beveled tortoise pickguard, (old style) squared off headstock, 3-per-side open gear chrome tuners with "butterbean" knobs, available in Aging Toner Lacquer finish, new 1996.

MSR	$2,849	$1,995	$1,475	$1,025

D-18VS - similar to the D-18V, except features a 12/19-fret fingerboard, slotted headstock, new 1996.

MSR	$3,249	$2,275	$1,650	$1,150

D-19 - spruce top, round soundhole, black pickguard, 3-stripe bound body/rosette, mahogany back/sides/neck, 14/20-fret rosewood fingerboard with pearl dot inlay, rosewood bridge with white black dot pins, rosewood peghead veneer with logo decal, 3-per-side chrome tuners. Available in Dark Brown finish, mfg. 1976-1988.

N/A	$1,200	$850

D-19M - similar to the D-19, except has mahogany top, mfg. 1980 & 1982.

N/A	$1,200	$850

D12-20 - solid spruce top, round soundhole, black pickguard, 3-stripe bound body/rosette, mahogany back/sides/neck, 12/20-fret rosewood fingerboard with pearl dot inlay, rosewood bridge with black white dot pins, 6-per-side chrome tuners, available in Natural finish. Custom Shop mfg. 1964-1991.

N/A	$1,100	$800

Last MSR was $2,480.

D-21 - spruce top, round soundhole, tortoise bound body, herringbone rosette, Brazilian rosewood back/sides, mahogany neck, 14/20-fret Brazilian rosewood fingerboard with pearl dot inlay, Brazilian rosewood bridge with black white dot bridgepins, 3-per-side chrome tuners, mfg. 1955-1969.

1956-1960	N/A	$4,500	$3,000
1961-1967	N/A	$3,200	$2,500
1967-1969	N/A	$2,500	$1,900

D-25K - spruce top, round soundhole, black pickguard, bound body, 4-stripe purfling, 5-stripe rosette, koa back/sides, mahogany neck, 14/20-fret rosewood fingerboard with pearl dot inlay, rosewood bridge with black white pins, rosewood veneered peghead with screened logo, 3-per-side chrome tuners, available in Natural finish, mfg. 1980-89.

N/A	$1,100	$750

Last MSR was $1,610.

**Martin D-21
courtesy Martin Guitar**

M

GRADING	100%	EXCELLENT	AVERAGE

D-25K2 - similar to D-25 K, except has koa top, available in Natural finish, mfg. 1980-89.

	N/A	$1,200	$750

Last MSR was $1,735.

D-28 - solid spruce top, round soundhole, black pickguard, bound body, herringbone purfling standard until approx. 1946, 5-stripe rosette, rosewood 2-piece back/sides, 14/20-fret ebony fingerboard with pearl diamond inlay, ebony bridge with white black dot pins, 3-per-side chrome tuners. finish, mfg. 1931-current.

1931-1933 Herringbone	N/A	$50,000+	$35,000+
1935-1938 Herringbone	N/A	$40,000	$30,000
1939-1944 Herringbone	N/A	$30,000	$20,000
1944-1946 (non-scalloped)	N/A	$25,000	$15,000
1947-1949	N/A	$8,000	$6,000
1950-1959	N/A	$6,000	$4,000
1960-1969	N/A	$4,500	$2,500
1970-1996 (Indian rosewood)	N/A	$1,800	$1,100

Subtract 10% for black finish.

1946 was the last year that the herringbone trim around the top was offered (although the last batch was in early 1947). By 1935, Shaded top finish became an option. 1933 was the last year for the 12-fret model. These models may command a higher premium. In 1944, scalloped bracing was discontinued, and pearl dot fingerboard inlay replaced the split diamond inlays. In 1969, Indian rosewood replaced Brazilian rosewood.

D-28 (STANDARD SERIES)

MSR	$2,469	$1,725	$1,275	$995

D-28E - dreadnought style, spruce top, round soundhole, black pickguard, 3-stripe bound body/rosette, rosewood back/sides, 14/20-fret ebony fingerboard with pearl dot inlay, ebony bridge with white black dot pins, 3-per-side tuners, gold hardware, 2 single coil exposed gold DeArmond pickups, 2 volume/2 tone controls, 3 position switch, available in Natural finish, mfg. 1959-1965.

	N/A	$1,800	$1,200

D-28S - similar to D-28, except has a 12-fret dreadnought style body, 12/20-fret fingerboard, slotted headstock, mfg. 1964-1993.

1964-1969	N/A	$4,800	$3,800
1970-1993	N/A	$1,800	$1,200

Last MSR was $2,620.

D12-28 (Standard Series) - similar to D-28, except has 12-strings, mfg. 1970-current.

1970-1996	N/A	$1,200	$900
MSR	$2,689	$1,875	$1,350	$995

D-28V (Vintage Series) - similar to D-28, fashioned after the original dreadnought design, herringbone bound body, square headstock, available in Antique Top finish, mfg. 1983-85.

	N/A	$4,500	$3,000

Last MSR was $2,600.

DC-28 - similar to D-28, except has single round cutaway, 14/22-fret fingerboard, mfg. 1981-1996.

1981-1989	N/A	$1,600	$1,200
1990-1996	N/A	$1,200	$925

Last MSR was $2,810.

HD-28 (STANDARD SERIES) - solid spruce top, round soundhole, black pickguard, herringbone bound body/rosette, rosewood 2-piece back/sides, 14/20-fret ebony fingerboard with pearl dot inlay, ebony bridge with white black dot pins, 3-per-side chrome tuners, available in Natural finish, mfg. 1976-current.

1976-1997	N/A	$1,800	$1,200
MSR	$2,959	$2,050	$1,500	$1,175

This model is also available with solid red cedar top (CHD-28) or a larchtop (LHD-28). The larchtop was discontinued in 1994.

HD-28 2R - similar to HD-28, except has larger soundhole, 2 rows of herringbone purfling.

	N/A	$1,450	$925

Last MSR was $2,900.

CUSTOM 15 - similar to HD-28, except features tortoise pickguard, unbound ebony fingerboard, slotted-diamond inlay, chrome tuners, available in Natural finish, mfg. 1980-1995.

	$2,300	$1,600	$1,175

Last MSR was $3,070.

The Custom 15 was named after the 15th custom-ordered guitar of 1980. This model is similar to the HD-28, with added features.

HD-28V (VINTAGE SERIES) - solid spruce top, round soundhole, grained ivoroid body binding, 5-stripe rosette, solid rosewood back/sides, mahogany neck, 14/20-fret ebony fingerboard with pearl diamonds and squares inlay, ebony bridge with white black dot pins, beveled tortoise pickguard, (old style) squared headstock, 3-per-side chrome tuners with "butterbean" buttons, available in Natural Gloss finish, current mfg.

MSR	$3,479	$2,425	$1,750	$1,395

GRADING		100%	EXCELLENT	AVERAGE

HD-28VS - similar to the HD-28VR, except features 12/19-fret fingerboard, slotted headstock, available in Natural Gloss and Aging Toner finishes, current mfg.

MSR	$3,879		$2,700	$1,900	$1,475

HD-28LSV LARGE SOUNDHOLE (VINTAGE SERIES) - Adirondack spruce top, oversized round soundhole, ivoroid body binding, 5-stripe rosette, rosewood back/sides, mahogany neck, 14/20-fret ivoroid bound rosewood fingerboard with pearl diamonds and squares inlay/side dot position markers, ebony bridge with white black dot pins, beveled tortoise pickguard, (old style) squared headstock, 3-per-side Waverly tuners with ivoroid buttons, available in Natural Gloss finish, mfg. 1998-current.

MSR	$3,799		$2,650	$1,875	$1,450

This model is based on a 1934 D-28 once owned by Clarence White (Kentucky Colonels).

D-35 - solid spruce top, round soundhole, tortoise pickguard, 5-stripe bound body/rosette, rosewood 3-piece back/sides, mahogany neck, 14/20-fret bound ebony fingerboard with pearl dot inlay, ebony bridge with white black dot pins, 3-per-side chrome tuners, available in Natural finish, mfg. 1965-current.

1965-1970		N/A	$3,500	$2,500
1970-1997		N/A	$1,500	$1,100

In 1967, black pickguard replaced original parts/design.

D-35 (Standard Series)

MSR	$2,599		$1,800	$1,295	$925

D-35S - similar to D-35, except has a 12-fret dreadnought style body, 12/20-fret fingerboard, slotted headstock, mfg. 1966-1993.

1966-1969		N/A	$4,500	$3,500
1970-1993		N/A	$1,800	$1,200

Last MSR was $2,760.

D12-35 - similar to D-35 S, except has 12-string configuration, mfg. 1965-1993.

1965-1969		N/A	$1,900	$1,500
1970-1993		N/A	$1,200	$900

Last MSR was $2,760.

**Martin D-28
courtesy Willie's
American Guitar**

HD-35 (STANDARD SERIES) - solid spruce top, round soundhole, black pickguard, herringbone bound body/rosette, rosewood 3-piece back/sides, 14/20-fret bound ebony fingerboard with pearl dot inlay, ebony bridge with white black dot pins, 3-per-side chrome tuners, available in Natural finish, mfg. 1978-current.

1978-1997		N/A	$1,800	$1,375
MSR	$3,349	$2,325	$1,675	$1,300

Also available with solid red cedar top (CHD-35).

D-37K - spruce top, round soundhole, tortoise pickguard, 5-stripe bound body, abalone rosette, figured koa 2-piece back/sides, mahogany neck, 14/20-fret ebony fingerboard with pearl inlay, ebony bridge with white black dot pins, koa peghead veneer with logo decal, 3-per-side chrome tuners, available in Amber Stain finish, mfg. 1980-1995.

		N/A	$1,900	$1,300

Last MSR was $2,740.

D-37K2 - similar to D-37K, except has figured koa top, black pickguard.

		N/A	$1,800	$1,300

Last MSR was $2,920.

D-40 (STANDARD SERIES) - solid spruce top, round soundhole, solid rosewood back/sides, abalone rosette, mahogany neck, 14/20-fret bound ebony fingerboard with abalone hexagon position markers, bound headstock with (style 45) abalone pearl logo, 3-per-side gold enclosed tuning machines, available in Natural Gloss finish, current mfg.

MSR	$3,489		$2,425	$1,750	$1,375

D-41 - solid spruce top, round soundhole, black pickguard, bound body, abalone purfling/rosette, rosewood back/sides, mahogany neck, 14/20-fret bound ebony fingerboard with abalone hexagon inlay, ebony bridge with white abalone dot pins, rosewood veneer on bound peghead with white pearl vertical logo inlay, 3-per-side gold tuners, available in Natural finish, mfg. 1969-current.

1969 (Brazilian rosewood)		N/A	$8,000	$6,000
1970-1997		N/A	$2,500	$1,800

D-41 (Standard Series)

MSR	$4,199		$2,925	$2,150	$1,525

In 1987, tortoise pickguard, smaller abalone hexagon fingerboard inlay, abalone logo peghead inlay replaced original parts/designs.

**Martin HD-28
courtesy Martin Guitar**

D12-41 - similar to D-41, except has 12-strings, 12/20-fret fingerboard, 6-per-side tuners, mfg. 1988-1994.

		N/A	$2,600	$2,200

Last MSR was $3,860.

D-41S - similar to D-41, except has a prewar dreadnought style body, 12/20-fret fingerboard, slotted headstock, mfg. 1970-1993.

		N/A	$2,600	$2,200

Last MSR was $3,720.

HPD-41 - similar to D-41, except has herringbone trimmed rosette, top binding and back seam, pearl fingerboard inlays, mfg. 1999-2001.

		$3,495	$2,700	$2,150

Last MSR was $5,399.

D-42 (STANDARD SERIES) - solid spruce top, round soundhole, abalone/grained ivoroid body binding, abalone rosette, solid rosewood back/sides, mahogany neck, 14/20-fret bound ebony fingerboard with pearl snowflake inlay, ebony bridge with white black dot pins, tortoise pickguard, 3-per-side gold tuners, available in Natural Gloss finish, new 1996.

MSR	$5,179	$3,625	$2,650	$2,075

D-42K - similar to D-42, except has highly flamed Hawaiian koa sides/back, new 2000.

MSR	$5,579	$3,900	$2,825	$2,200

D-42K2 - similar to D-42K, except also has solid flamed Hawaiian koa top, new 2000.

MSR	$5,779	$4,000	$2,950	$2,325

D-45 (PRE-WWII MFG.) - solid spruce top, round soundhole, bound body, abalone purfling back/top, abalone rosette, rosewood back/sides, mahogany neck, 14/20-fret bound ebony fingerboard with snowflake inlay until 1937 then switched to hexagonal inlay, ebony bridge with white abalone dot pins, rosewood veneer on bound peghead with abalone vertical logo inlay, 3-per-side chrome tuners, available in Natural finish, mfg. 1933-1942.

The prices of Prewar D-45s are constantly increasing. According to Martin production records, only 91 instruments were produced between 1933 and 1942. Currently, the market has only accounted for 72 of the 91. Furthermore, 25 of the 72 have been refinished or oversprayed. Depending on the original condition, prewar D-45s are currently priced in the $125,000+ range. The *Blue Book of Acoustic Guitars* highly recommends that several professional appraisals be secured before buying/selling/trading any pre-war Martin D-45.

D-45 (1968-Current Mfg.) - production resumed in 1968, and continues to date, current manufacture uses Indian rosewood.

1968-1969 (Brazilian rosewood)		N/A	$22,000	$18,000
1970-1996 (Indian rosewood)		N/A	$5,500	$4,000
MSR	$7,979	$5,550	$3,950	$3,075

1968 and 1969 were the last full production models to be constructed with Brazilian rosewood back and sides. The 1968 models command a slightly higher premium over the 1969 models.

D-45S - similar to D-45, except has a 12-fret dreadnought style body, 12/20-fret fingerboard, slotted headstock, mfg. 1970-1993.

		N/A	$6,000	$4,000

Last MSR was $6,860.

The few Brazilian rosewood examples command a higher premium.

D-45V (Vintage Series) - similar to D-45, except features highly colored abalone border around top/fingerboard perimeter/rosette, grained ivoroid binding, diamond and snowflake fingerboard inlay, gold Gotoh tuners, current mfg.

MSR	$9,099	$6,325	$4,575	$3,125

D12-45 - similar to D-45S, except has 12-strings, 6-per-side tuners with pearl buttons, mfg. 1969-1994.

		N/A	$4,000	$3,000

Last MSR was $7,020.

For Brazilian rosewood (rare), use the 6-String pricing listed above as a guideline.

D-50 DELUXE/D-50 DELUXE KOA - please refer to listings under the Special/Limited Editions category.

D-60 - solid spruce top, round soundhole, tortoise pickguard, 3-stripe bound body/rosette, bird's-eye maple back/sides, maple neck, 14/20-fret ebony fingerboard with pearl snowflake inlay, ebony bridge with white red dot pins, bird's-eye maple veneer on ebony bound peghead, 3-per-side gold tuners with ebony buttons, available in Natural finish, mfg. 1989-1995.

		$2,300	$1,600	$1,150

Last MSR was $3,060.

D-62 - similar to D-60, except has figured maple back/sides, mahogany neck, figured maple peghead veneer, gold tuners with pearl buttons, mfg. 1987-1995.

		$1,825	$1,225	$875

Last MSR was $2,420.

D-76 (BICENTENNIAL LIMITED EDITION) - solid spruce top, round soundhole, black pickguard, herringbone bound body/rosette, Indian rosewood 3-piece back/sides, mahogany neck, 14/20-fret ebony fingerboard with 13 pearl star inlays, ebony bridge with white black dot pins, rosewood peghead veneer with pearl eagle/logo inlay, 3-per-side gold tuners, available in Natural finish, mfg. 1975-76.

		N/A	$3,000	$2,350

There were 1,976 models constructed, with an additional 98 (D-76 E) built exclusively for employees.

GRADING	100%	EXCELLENT	AVERAGE

ACOUSTIC: D-16 SPECIAL (SP) LIMITED EDITION SERIES

The D-16 Series Special (SP) edition models feature scalloped "X"-bracing, a (style 45) multi-colored back inlay strip, and compensated saddle. These models were introduced in 1996. While originally designated with a T (for example: SP D-16T), the T designation was dropped in 1998.

SPD-16 (SPD-16T) - spruce top, round soundhole, black pickguard, tortoise bound body, abalone pearl rosette, solid mahogany back/sides, mahogany neck, 14/20-fret rosewood fingerboard with abalone fingerboard inlays, rosewood bridge with abalone snowflake inlay and black pins, tortoise pickguard, 3-per-side chrome tuners, available in Natural Gloss finish. Custom Shop mfg. 1996-2000.

	$1,175	$900	$650
	Last MSR was $1,800.		

SPD-16E - similar to SPD-16, except has onboard electronics, Custom Shop mfg. 1999 only.

	$1,575	$1,225	$700
	Last MSR was $1,950.		

SPD-16B - similar to the SP D-16, available in Black Gloss finish, mfg. 1998-2000.

	$1,475	$1,125	$875
	Last MSR was $2,250.		

SPD-16M - similar to the SP D-16, except features solid maple back/sides, mfg. 1998-2000.

	$1,275	$975	$725
	Last MSR was $1,950.		

SPD-16R (SP D-16TR) - similar to the SP D-16, except features solid East Indian rosewood back/sides, mfg. 1996-2000.

	$1,350	$1,025	$825
	Last MSR was $2,050.		

SPD12-16R - similar to the SPD-16R, except has 12-strings. Mfg. 1999-2002.

	$1,525	$1,150	$890
	Last MSR was $2,319.		

Martin D-42
courtesy Martin Guitar

SPD-16K - similar to the SP D-16, except features solid koa back/sides, new 2000.

MSR	$2,319	$1,625	$1,175	$895

SPD-16K2 - similar to the SP D-16, except features solid koa top/back/sides, new 2000.

MSR	$2,519	$1,750	$1,300	$975

SPD-16W - similar to the SP D-16, except features solid walnut back/sides, mfg.1998-2000.

	$1,275	$975	$725
	Last MSR was $1,950.		

SPDC-16R (SP DC-16TR) - similar to the SP D-16R, except features rounded Venetian cutaway, Custom Shop mfg. 1996-2000.

	$1,495	$1,150	$875
	Last MSR was $2,100.		

SP0M-16 - spruce top, solid mahogany back/sides, OM style body, mfg. 1999-2000.

	$1,195	$925	$675
	Last MSR was $1,950.		

SP00-16RST - solid spruce top, Indian rosewood back/sides, 00 style body, 12-fret, satin top, mfg. 1999-2000.

	$1,675	$1,275	$925
	Last MSR was $2,550.		

SP000-16 (SP 000-16T) - similar to SP D-16, except in 000 body size, available in Natural Gloss finish, Custom Shop mfg. 1997-2000.

	$1,175	$900	$650
	Last MSR was $1,800.		

SP000C-16 - similar to SP000-16, except has cutaway body. Custom Shop mfg. 1999 only.

	$1,375	$1,050	$875
	Last MSR was $2,100.		

SP000C-16E - similar to SP000-16, except has onboard electronics. Custom Shop mfg. 1999-2000.

	$1,475	$1,125	$750
	Last MSR was $2,250.		

SP000-16R (SP 000-16TR) - similar to SP 000-16, except features solid East Indian rosewood back and sides. Custom Shop Mfg. 1997-2000.

	$1,300	$1,000	$675
	Last MSR was $2,000.		

Martin SPDC-16TR
courtesy Martin Guitar

M

GRADING	100%	EXCELLENT	AVERAGE

SP000C-16R (SP 000C-16TR) - similar to the SP 000-16R, except features a rounded Venetian cutaway. Custom Shop mfg. 1997-2000.

	$1,550	$1,150	$775

Last MSR was $2,300.

ACOUSTIC: J (JUMBO) SERIES

Size J (Jumbo) guitars feature a lower bout width of 16 inches, a body depth of 4 7/8 inches, 20 1/8 length, and 25.4 in. scale. J Series models had the "M" suffix as part of the model designation until 1990. All J Series models have scalloped braces.

JM (ROAD SERIES) - solid spruce top, round soundhole, black body binding, laminated mahogany back/sides, mahogany neck, 14/20 rosewood fingerboard with white dot inlay, single band herringbone rosette, tortoise pickguard, 3-per-side chrome tuners, available in Natural Satin finish, mfg. 1998-late 2002.

	$615	$585	$330

Last MSR was $949.

J-1 (1 SERIES) - solid Sitka spruce top, round soundhole, tortoise bound body, 3-stripe rosette, solid mahogany back, laminated mahogany sides, mahogany neck, 14/20-fret rosewood fingerboard with dot inlay, rosewood bridge with white black dot pins, tortoise pickguard, 3-per-side chrome tuners, available in Natural Satin finish, Custom Shop mfg, disc. 2001.

	$725	$550	$400

Last MSR was $1,099.

JC-1E (1 SERIES) - similar to J-1, except has cutaway body, and onboard electronics, Custom Shop mfg. 1999-2001.

	$975	$750	$575

Last MSR was $1,499.

J-15 (15 SERIES) - mahogany top/sides, new 1999.

MSR	$979	$675	$550	$375

JC-15E - similar to J-15, except has Venetian cutaway and Fishman Sonicore pickup with Classic 4 onboard preamp, satin finished body, mfg. 2001 only.

	$875	$675	$475

Last MSR was $1,349.

JC-16GTE - features Jumbo cutaway body (16 Series), solid spruce top with solid mahogany back/sides, multi-colored wooden mosaic rosette, Madagascar ebony fingerboard and bridge, gloss top, includes Fishman co-polymer pickup with Prefix Pro electronics, new 2000.

MSR	$1,739	$1,200	$875	$650

JC-16RGTE - similar to JC-16GTE, except has rosewood back/sides, new 2000.

MSR	$1,939	$1,350	$950	$695

JC-16WE - similar to JC-16GTE, except has solid Sitka spruce top, solid walnut sides/two-piece back, single ring rosette with blue paua pearl and white/black inlay, polished gloss finish, Bluestick electronics from Schertler, new mid 2002.

MSR	$2,249	$1,550	$1,175	$850

SPJC-16E - similar to JC-16GTE, except has abalone pearl rosette and tortoise colored pickguard, mfg. 2000-late 2002.

	$1,675	$1,225	$875

Last MSR was $2,459.

SPJC-16RE - similar to SPJC-16E, except has rosewood back/sides, new 2000.

MSR	$2,659	$1,850	$1,375	$925

J-18 (J-18M) - solid spruce top, round soundhole, tortoise pickguard, 5-stripe bound body/rosette, mahogany back/sides/neck, 14/20-fret rosewood fingerboard with pearl dot inlay, rosewood bridge with black white dot pins, rosewood peghead veneer, 3-per-side chrome tuners with ebony buttons, available in Natural finish, mfg. 1987-1996.

	N/A	$1,250	$700

Last MSR was $2,300.

J-21 (J-21M) - spruce top, round soundhole, tortoise pickguard, 5-stripe bound body/rosette, rosewood back/sides, mahogany neck, 14/20-fret rosewood fingerboard with pearl dot inlay, rosewood bridge with black white dot pins, rosewood veneer peghead, 3-per-side chrome tuners, available in Natural finish, mfg. 1985-1996.

	N/A	$1,400	$1,150

Last MSR was $2,520.

J-21MC - similar to J-21 M, except has single round cutaway, oval soundhole, 5-stripe rosette, ebony buttoned tuners, mfg. 1987 only.

	N/A	$1,400	$1,150

Last MSR was $1,750.

GRADING			100%	EXCELLENT	AVERAGE

J-40 STANDARD SERIES (J-40M) - solid spruce top, round soundhole, black pickguard, 5-stripe bound body/rosette, Indian rosewood back/sides, mahogany neck, 14/20-fret bound ebony fingerboard with abalone hexagon inlay, ebony bridge with white abalone dot pins, rosewood peghead veneer, 3-per-side chrome tuners, available in Natural finish, new 1985.

1985-1997			N/A	$1,800	$1,250
MSR	$3,489		$2,425	$1,775	$1,375

J-40BK (J-40MBK) - similar to J-40, except has Black finish, disc. 1996.

			N/A	$1,800	$1,250

Last MSR was $3,470.

JC-40 (J-40MC) - similar to J-40, except has single round cutaway, mfg. 1987-1996.

			N/A	$1,900	$1,500

Last MSR was $3,390.

J12-40 (J12-40M) - similar to J-40, except has 12-strings, 6-per-side gold tuners with ebony buttons, mfg. 1987-1996.

			N/A	$1,400	$1,150

Last MSR was $3,350.

J-65 (J-65M) - solid spruce top, round soundhole, tortoise pickguard, tortoise bound body, 3-stripe rosette, figured maple back/sides, maple neck, 14/20-fret bound ebony fingerboard with pearl dot inlay, ebony bridge with white red dot pins, rosewood peghead veneer with logo decal, 3-per-side gold tuners with pearl buttons, available in Natural finish, mfg. 1985-1995.

			N/A	$1,500	$1,000

Last MSR was $2,520.

J12-65 (J12-65M) - similar to J-65, except has 12-strings, 6-per-side tuners, mfg. 1985-1994.

			N/A	$1,400	$1,000

Last MSR was $2,610.

Martin JC-16GTE
courtesy Martin Guitar

Custom J-65 (CMJ-65) - solid spruce top, round soundhole, tortoise pickguard, white body binding, herringbone purfling, 3-stripe rosette, figured maple back/sides, maple neck, 14/20-fret bound ebony fingerboard with pearl dot inlay, ebony bridge with white red dot pins, rosewood peghead veneer with logo decal, 3-per-side gold tuners with pearl buttons, available in Natural finish, mfg. 1993-96.

			N/A	$1,750	$1,100

Last MSR was $2,900.

Custom J-65 Electric - similar to Custom J-65, except has MEQ-932 acoustic amplification system, mfg. 1993-96.

			N/A	$1,750	$1,100

Last MSR was $3,070.

HJ-28 (STANDARD SERIES) - solid spruce top, round soundhole, grained ivoroid body binding, 5-stripe rosette, solid rosewood back/sides, mahogany neck, 14/20-fret ebony fingerboard with pearl diamonds and squares inlay, ebony bridge with white black dot pins, beveled tortoise pickguard, (old style) squared headstock, 3-per-side chrome tuners with "butterbean" knobs, available in Natural Gloss finish, Custom Shop mfg. 1996-2001.

			$1,850	$1,425	$1,100

Last MSR was $2,850.

ACOUSTIC: M SERIES

Size M guitars feature a lower bout width of 16 inches, a body depth of 4 1/8 inches, 20 1/8 in. length, and 25.4 in. scale.

CM-0089 - spruce top, round soundhole, tortoise pickguard, bound body, herringbone purfling, pearl rosette, rosewood back/sides, mahogany neck, 14/20-fret ebony fingerboard with pearl dot inlay, rosewood bridge with white black dot pins, 3-per-side chrome tuners, available in Natural finish, mfg. 1979 only.

There has not been sufficient quantity traded to quote prices. Only 25 of these instruments were produced.

M-16GT - solid Sitka spruce top, round soundhole, solid mahogany back/sides/neck, 0000 M body style, 14/20-fret black Micarta fingerboard, hybrid scalloped bracing, bold herringbone rosette with D-18 rings on each side of herringbone, gloss top with Satin back/sides, mfg. 2002 only.

			$850	$675	$475

Last MSR was $1,279.

MC-16GTE - similar to M-16GT, except has single cutaway body and Fishman Prefix Stereo onboard blender electronics, new 2002.

MSR	$1,699		$1,175	$875	$625

Martin J-40
courtesy Martin Guitar

GRADING	100%	EXCELLENT	AVERAGE

M-18 - spruce top, round soundhole, black pickguard, bound body, 3-stripe purfling/rosette, mahogany back/sides/neck, 14/20-fret rosewood fingerboard with pearl dot inlay, rosewood bridge with black white dot pins, 3-per-side chrome tuners, available in Natural finish, mfg. 1984-88.

	N/A	$1,450	$1,000

Last MSR was $1,550.

The first instruments of this line had ebony fingerboards/bridges. Three have a Blue/Red/White finish.

M-36 (M-35) - solid spruce top, round soundhole, tortoise pickguard, 5-stripe bound body/rosette, rosewood back/sides, mahogany neck, 14/20-fret bound ebony fingerboard with pearl dot inlay, rosewood bridge with white black dot pins, rosewood veneer on bound peghead, 3-per-side chrome tuners, available in Natural finish, mfg. 1978-1996.

	$1,900	$1,400	$975

Last MSR was $2,540.

Early production models came with an unbound peghead. This instrument began production as the M-35. After 26 were manufactured, the model was renamed the M - 36.

M-38 STANDARD SERIES (0000-38) - solid spruce top, round soundhole, 5-stripe bound body, abalone rosette, solid rosewood back/sides, mahogany neck, 14/20-fret bound ebony fingerboard with pearl dot inlay, rosewood bridge with white black dot pins, rosewood veneer on bound peghead, tortoise pickguard, 3-per-side chrome tuners, available in Natural finish, mfg. 1977-1998.

		N/A	$1,750	$1,300
1977-1997		N/A	$1,750	$1,300
1998		$2,050	$1,600	$1,200

Last MSR was $3,150.

In 1996, the M-38 model was redesignated the 0000-38.

M-64 - similar to M-36, except has figured maple back/sides/neck, unbound fingerboard/peghead, mfg. 1985-1995.

	N/A	$1,600	$1,250

Last MSR was $2,520.

MC-28 - single round cutaway body, solid spruce top, oval soundhole, black pickguard, 3-stripe bound body/rosette, rosewood back/sides, mahogany neck, 22-fret ebony fingerboard with pearl dot inlay, ebony bridge with white black dot pins, rosewood peghead veneer, 3-per-side chrome tuners, available in Natural finish, mfg. 1981-1996.

	$2,100	$1,575	$1,025

Last MSR was $2,810.

MC-37K - single round cutaway body, spruce top, oval soundhole, tortoise pickguard, bound body, pearl rosette, figured koa back/sides, mahogany neck, 22-fret ebony fingerboard with abalone flake inlay, ebony bridge with white black dot pins, 3-per-side chrome tuners, available in Amber Stain finish, mfg. 1981-82, and 1988.

	$3,000	$2,000	$1,600

Last MSR was $2,000.

18 of these instruments were produced.

MC-68 - single round cutaway body, solid spruce top, oval soundhole, tortoise pickguard, 5-stripe bound body/rosette, figured maple back/sides, maple neck, 22-fret bound ebony fingerboard with abalone dot inlay, ebony bridge with white abalone dot pins, rosewood veneer on white bound peghead with vertical CF Martin abalone inlay, 3-per-side gold tuners, available in Natural or Sunburst finishes, mfg. 1985-1995.

	$2,225	$1,675	$1,250

Last MSR was $2,930.

ACOUSTIC: N SERIES

Size N (Classical) guitars feature a lower bout width of 14 7/16 inches, 4 1/8 in. depth, 19 1/8 length, and 26 3/8 or 25.4 (early Mfg.) in. scale.

N-10 - wooden inlay rosette, mahogany back/sides, rosewood fingerboard/bridge, mfg. 1968-1993, 1995.

	N/A	$1,100	$850

Last MSR was $2,620.

N-20 - wooden inlay rosette, rosewood back/sides, ebony fingerboard/bridge, mfg. 1968-1995.

1968-1969		N/A	$2,200	$1,850
1970-1995		N/A	$1,350	$1,000

Last MSR was $3,190.

ACOUSTIC: OM (ORCHESTRA MODEL) SERIES

Size OM (Orchestra Model) guitars feature a lower bout width of 15 inches, 4 1/8 in. depth, 19 3/8 in. length, and 25.4 in. scale.

OM-1 - solid spruce top, mahogany sides/back, Satin finish, mfg. 1999-2001.

	$715	$550	$400

Last MSR was $1,099.

OMM (ROAD SERIES) - solid spruce top, laminated mahogany back/sides, 2-piece back, bold herringbone rosette, Satin finish. Mfg. 2000-late 2002.

	$650	$485	$350

Last MSR was $949.

GRADING		100%	EXCELLENT	AVERAGE

OM-15 - solid mahogany top, sides/back, gold and black herringbone decal rosette, Satin finish, Indian rosewood fingerboard, mfg. 2001-late 2002.

MSR	$979	$675	$500	$345

OMC-15E - similar to OM-15, except has solid sapele/mahogany top, sides/back, single cutaway body, satin finish, A-frame bracing, and Fishman Prefix Plus electronics, new 2001.

MSR	$1,499	$1,050	$775	$575

OM-16GT - solid Sitka spruce top, mahogany sides/back, 2-piece back, bold herringbone rosette, D-1 hybrid scalloped bracing, gloss top with light red mahogany toner, new 2001.

MSR	$1,279	$895	$675	$475

OMC-16WE - solid Sitka spruce top, walnut sides/back, single cutaway, single ring rosette, black micarta fingerboard/bridge, solid Spanish cedar neck, hybrid scalloped bracing, Gloss finish, includes Fishman Gold Plus Natural I electronics, new 2002.

MSR	$2,199	$1,525	$1,125	$775

OMC-16E - similar to OMC-16WE, except has solid sapele back/sides, new 2003.

MSR	$2,199	$1,525	$1,125	$775

OMC-16RE - similar to OMC-16E, except is rosewood, new 2003.

MSR	$2,399	$1,675	$1,250	$850

SPOM-16 - please refer to the individual listing under D-16 Series Special (SP) Limited Editions subsection.

OM-18 - spruce top, tortoise pickguard, round soundhole, wooden bound body, rope pattern rosette, mahogany back/sides/neck, 14/20-fret ebony fingerboard with pearl dot inlay, ebony bridge with black pearl dot pins, 3-per-side tuners with ivoroid buttons, available in Natural or Sunburst finishes, mfg. 1929-1933.

1929-1931		N/A	$15,000	$9,000
1932-1933		N/A	$9,000	$7,000

Add a premium for 1929 models with no pickguard. Add a premium for 1929-1931 models with banjo tuners, small pickguard, and rosewood binding. Add 25% for Sunburst finish.

This model had banjo style tuners from 1929 to 1931, then standard tuners from then on. From 1929 to 1930, this model had no pickguard. From 1930 to 1931, this model had a small pickguard. Beginning mid-1931, this model was produced with a standard size pickguard.

OM-18V (Vintage Series) - solid spruce top, patterned after the vintage OM-18s of the early 1930s, solid mahogany back/sides, mfg. 1999 - current.

MSR	$2,849	$1,995	$1,450	$975

OM-18GE (Golden Era) - solid Adirondack spruce top, 000 body size, mahogany back/sides/neck with Brazilian rosewood strip top/back binding, 14/20-fret ebony fingerboard, banjo tuners, gloss top with Mahogany Stain and Aging Toner, optional electronics, new 2003.

MSR	$4,199	$2,925	$2,175	$1,675

OM-21 (STANDARD SERIES) - solid spruce top, round soundhole, tortoise pickguard, bound body, herringbone rosette, Indian rosewood back/sides, mahogany neck, 14/20-fret rosewood fingerboard with pearl dot inlay, rosewood bridge with black dot pins, 3-per-side chrome tuners, available in Natural finish, mfg. 1992 - current.

1992-1997		N/A	$1,200	$1,000
MSR	$2,299	$1,595	$1,175	$925

OM-28 - spruce top, round soundhole, black pickguard, 5-stripe bound body/rosette, rosewood back/sides, mahogany neck, 14/20-fret ebony fingerboard with pearl dot inlay, ebony bridge with white black dot pins, rosewood peghead veneer, 3-per-side chrome tuners, available in Natural finish, mfg. 1929-1933.

1929-1931		N/A	$30,000	$20,000
1932-1933		N/A	$25,000	$18,000

Add a premium for 1929 models with no pickguard. Add a premium for 1929-1931 models with banjo tuners, small pickguard, and rosewood binding.

This model had banjo style tuners from 1929 to 1931, then standard tuners from then on. From 1929 to 1930, this model had no pickguard. From 1930 to 1931, this model had a small pickguard. Beginning mid-1931, this model was produced with a standard size pickguard.

OM-28V (Vintage Series) - solid spruce top, round soundhole, 5-stripe rosette, grained ivoroid binding/herringbone purfling, rosewood back/sides, mahogany neck, 14/20-fret ebony fingerboard with pearl snowflake inlay, ebony bridge with white black dot pins, rosewood peghead veneer, squared off headstock, tortoise pickguard, 3-per-side chrome tuners, available in Natural Gloss finish, mfg. 1990 - current.

1990-1997		N/A	$1,750	$1,350
MSR	$3,479	$2,400	$1,775	$1,375

Martin OM-15
courtesy Martin Guitar

M

Martin OM-28V
courtesy Martin Guitar

GRADING		100%	EXCELLENT	AVERAGE

OM-35 - 000-size body, solid Sitka spruce top, solid Indian rosewood back (three piece) and sides, mahogany neck with 14/20-fret ebony fingerboard, wide 1 3/4 in. neck, gloss finish, new 2003.

MSR	$2,999		$2,095	$1,575	$1,250

OM-42 - solid spruce top, solid Indian rosewood back/sides, bound top, back, fingerboard, and peghead, features wide neck and long scale format, new 1999.

MSR	$5,179		$3,625	$2,650	$1,625

OM-45 (1930-32 MFG.) - solid spruce top, round soundhole, black pickguard, abalone bound body/rosette, rosewood back/sides, mahogany neck, 14/20-fret bound ebony fingerboard with abalone snowflake inlay, ebony bridge with white abalone dot pins, bound rosewood veneered peghead with abalone logo inlay, 3-per-side gold banjo style tuners with ivoroid buttons, available in Natural finish, mfg. 1930-32.

		N/A	N/A	$40,000-50,000

The OM-45 is a very rare instrument, and original finish and parts are everything, and make a huge difference in value. The *Blue Book of Acoustic Guitars* highly recommends a competent appraisal(s) be obtained before buying, selling, or trading this model.

OM-45 (1977-1994 Mfg.) - similar to OM-45, except has abalone hexagon fingerboard inlay, gold enclosed tuners, mfg. 1977 - 1994.

		N/A	$5,000	$4,000
			Last MSR was $6,530.	

OM-45 Deluxe - similar to OM-45, except has abalone vine pickguard inlay, abalone snowflake bridge wings inlay, mfg. 1930.

		N/A	N/A	$125,000+

Only 14 instruments were built. The OM-45 Deluxe is a very rare instrument, and original finish and parts are everything, and make a huge difference in value. The *Blue Book of Acoustic Guitars* highly recommends a competent appraisal(s) be obtained before buying, selling, or trading this model.

ACOUSTIC: X SERIES

X Series instruments have a lower bout width of 16 inches. Martin debuted the X Series in 1998. The top, back, and sides of this model are constructed of a wood fiber derivative material that is laminated under high pressure with a wood grain image photographically reproduced. The resulting material is a pre-finished laminate that is shaped into the construction parts for the guitar building.

DXM - laminated top with spruce grain, round soundhole, black body binding, laminated back/sides with mahogany grain, solid mahogany neck, 14/20-fret morado fingerboard with white dot inlay, mahogany grained peghead veneer with gold silk-screen logo, applied gold/black herringbone decal rosette, morado bridge with white bridgepins, tortoise pickguard, 3-per-side chrome tuners, available in Natural Semi-Gloss finish, new 1998.

MSR	$619		$425	$335	$250

D12X1/D12XM - 12-string variation of the DXM, D12X1 has solid spruce top and was introduced in 2001, D12XM disc. 2000, new 1999.

MSR	$769		$535	$400	$300

DXME - similar to the DXM, except features bridge pickup, on-board electronics, A frame X bracing, available in Natural Semi-gloss finish, new 1998.

MSR	$789		$550	$415	$310

DCXME - similar to the DXME, except has cutaway body, Classic 4 Sonicore electronics, herringbone decal rosette, mfg. 1999-2001.

		$550	$425	$325
			Last MSR was $849.	

DCX1E - solid spruce top, similar to the DCXME, except has inlaid Boltron with red fiber, black Micarta fingerboard and bridge, D-1 style bracing, new 2001.

MSR	$949		$660	$495	$375

DCXE-BLACK - solid spruce top, similar to the DCX1E, except has black back/sides, new mid-2001.

MSR	$949		$660	$495	$375

DXR - similar to DXM, except has laminated rosewood sides/back, mfg. 1999 only.

		$425	$325	$250
			Last MSR was $649.	

DX1 - similar to DXM, except has solid spruce top, no body finish, new 2000.

MSR	$669		$465	$350	$275

DX1R - similar to DX1, except has rosewood wood grain image reproduced on wood fiber composite laminate sides/back, new 2000.

MSR	$669		$465	$350	$275

DXK2 - similar to DX1R, except has koa wood grain image on top and sides, no pickguard, gold and black herringbone decal rosette, new mid 2002.

MSR	$619		$430	$315	$235

DXB - similar to DXM, except has black sides/back, mfg. 1999 only.

		$535	$400	$295
			Last MSR was $649.	

GRADING	100%	EXCELLENT	AVERAGE

DXBR - similar to DXB, except has Brazilian rosewood grained sides/back, mfg. 1999 only.

	$525	$425	$300

Last MSR was $749.

LXM/LXME LITTLE MARTIN - uses a modified 0-14 fret tenor Martin shape with a 23 in. scale, mahogany patterned HPL back/sides, top is spurce patterned HPL, rust stratabond neck with black micarta fingerboard/bridge, with (LXME) or w/o (LXM) mini-Q Fishman transducer, incudes gig bag. New mid 2003.

MSR	$349	$245	$185	$125

Add $75 for onboard Fishman mini-electronics (Model LXME).

ACOUSTIC: 0000 GRAND AUDITORIUM SERIES

Size 0000 (Grand Auditorium) guitars feature a lower bout width of 16 inches.

0000-1 (1 SERIES) - solid spruce top, round soundhole, tortoise body binding, solid mahogany back, laminated mahogany sides, mahogany neck, 3-stripe rosette, 14/20-fret rosewood fingerboard with dot inlay, rosewood bridge, chrome hardware, 3-per-side tuners, disc. 2000.

	$715	$550	$375

Last MSR was $1,099.

0000-28H (STANDARD SERIES) - solid spruce top, round soundhole, ivoroid body binding, solid rosewood back/sides, mahogany neck, 5-stripe rosette, 14/20-fret rosewood fingerboard with pearl dot inlay, rosewood bridge with white black dot pins, chrome hardware, 3-per-side tuners. Custom Shop mfg, disc. 2000.

	$1,800	$1,400	$1,150

Last MSR was $2,770.

**Martin DCXE-Black
courtesy John Beeson
The Music Shoppe**

ACOUSTIC: 000 GRAND AUDITORIUM SERIES

Size 000 (Auditorium) guitars feature a lower bout width of 15 inches, 4 1/8 (14-fret) or 4 1/16 (12-fret) in. depth, 19 3/8 (14-fret) or 20 7/16) in. length, and 24.9 (most common) or 25.4 (1924-1934 Mfg., 12-fret only) in. scale.

000M (ROAD SERIES) - solid spruce top, round soundhole, black body binding, laminated mahogany back/sides, mahogany neck, 14/20 rosewood fingerboard with white dot inlay, single band herringbone rosette, tortoise pickguard, 3-per-side chrome tuners, available in Natural Satin finish, current mfg.

MSR	$949	$650	$485	$365

OOO-R - similar to the OOO-M, except features laminated rosewood back sides, available in Natural Satin finish, Custom Shop mfg. 1998-2000.

	$725	$550	$400

Last MSR was $1,099.

OOO-CME - similar to the 000-M, except has cutaway body and onboard electronics. Custom Shop mfg, 1999-2000.

	$850	$625	$450

Last MSR was $1,300.

000X1/000XM (X SERIES) - mahogany grained composite fiber laminate sides/back, DX (000XM - disc.) or 000-1 style A frame (000X1) bracing, solid wood mortised neck, solid spruce top (000X1), herringbone decal (000XM) or inlaid Boltaron with red fiber rosette, 000-X1 introduced 2001, OOOXM disc. 2001.

MSR	$669	$465	$355	$265

000XE BLACK (X SERIES) - similar to 000X1, except has black sides/back, and Fishman Prefix Pro electronics, new 2001.

MSR	$929	$650	$485	$385

000CXE BLACK (X SERIES) - similar to 000XE, except has single cutaway body, new 2002.

MSR	$949	$665	$500	$395

000CX1E (X SERIES) - similar to 000X1, except has cutaway body, single ring rosette, hand rubbed urethane finish, and Fishman Pro Prefix electronics, mfg. 2002 only.

	$750	$575	$450

Last MSR was $1,049.

000-1 (1 SERIES) - solid Sitka spruce top, round soundhole, mahogany neck, solid mahogany back, 3-ply mahogany sides, 25.4" scale, 14/20 rosewood fingerboard with dot inlay, rosewood bridge, tortoise pickguard, 3-per-side tuners, chrome hardware, available in Natural Satin finish, new 1996.

MSR	$1,129	$790	$595	$450

**Martin 000XE Black
courtesy Dave Rogers
Dave's Guitar Shop**

GRADING	100%	EXCELLENT	AVERAGE

000-1R - similar to the 000-1, except features 3-ply laminated Indian rosewood back and sides, mfg. 1996-2002.

	$875	$665	$480

Last MSR was $1,329.

000C-1 - similar to the 000-1, except features a rounded Venetian cutaway. Custom Shop mfg, disc. 1998.

	N/A	$850	$550

Last MSR was $1,300.

000C-1E - similar to the 000-1, except features a rounded Venetian cutaway, Martin Gold+Plus bridge mounted pickup, Martin/Fishman Prefix preamp/EQ system. Custom Shop Mfg, disc. 2000.

	$975	$750	$600

Last MSR was $1,499.

000-15 (15 SERIES) - solid mahogany top, round soundhole, single band gold herringbone decal rosette, solid mahogany back/sides, mahogany neck, no body binding, 14/20-fret rosewood fingerboard with white dot inlay, rosewood bridge with white pins, tortoise pickguard, 3-per-side chrome tuners, new 1998.

MSR	$979	$675	$495	$375

000C-15E - similar to the 000-15, except has cutaway body and onboard electronics, mfg. 1999-late 2002.

	$1,000	$740	$560

Last MSR was $1,499.

000-15S - similar to the 000-15, except has 12/20-fret fingerboard, and 000-1 style A bracing, new 2000.

MSR	$1,219	$850	$625	$425

000-16GT/000-16T (16 SERIES) - solid spruce top, round soundhole, tortoise bound body, herringbone rosette, solid mahogany back/sides, mahogany neck, 14/20-fret rosewood fingerboard with abalone diamonds/squares inlay, rosewood bridge with black white dot pins, tortoise pickguard, 3-per-side chrome tuners, available in Natural Aging Toner top/Satin body finish (Model 000-16T, disc. 1999) or gloss top (000-16GT, new 2000), new 1989.

1989-1999		$1,075	$825	$600
MSR	$1,279	$895	$650	$495

000-16SGT - similar to the 000-16GT, except has 12/20-fret fingerboard, and hybrid 12-fret A-frame bracing, new 2000.

MSR	$1,469	$1,025	$775	$595

000-16SRGT - similar to the 000-16SGT, except has rosewood sides/back. Mfg. 2002 only.

	$1,160	$875	$625

Last MSR was $1,669.

000-16RGT - similar to the 000-16GT, except has rosewood sides/back, new 2001.

MSR	$1,479	$1,035	$775	$575

000-16TR - similar to the 000-16T, except features solid rosewood back and sides, mfg. 1996-99.

	$1,195	$925	$675

Last MSR was $1,850.

000C-16T - similar to OOO-16, except has single rounded Venetian cutaway, disc. 1999.

	$1,195	$925	$675

Last MSR was $1,850.

OOOC-16 - similar to the OOO-16, except features an oval soundhole and single rounded Venetian cutaway, mfg. 1990-95.

	N/A	$1,100	$800

OOOC-16T - similar to the OOO-16, except features a single rounded Venetian cutaway, mfg. 1990-95.

	N/A	$900	$750

The OOOC-16T is similar to the OOOC-16, except has a round soundhole.

OOOC-16GTE - similar to the 000-16, except has gloss top and onboard electronics, new 1999.

MSR	$1,699	$1,175	$875	$650

000C-16GTE Premium - similar to the 000C-16GTE, except has Spanish cedar neck and Fishman Prefix Premium Onboard blender electronics, new 2003.

MSR	$1,749	$1,225	$850	$625

000C-16RGTE - similar to the 000C-16GTE, except has rosewood sides/back, new 2001.

MSR	$1,939	$1,350	$975	$675

000C-16RGTE Premium - similar to the 000C-16RGTE, except has Spanish cedar neck and Fishman Prefix Premium Onboard blender electronics, new 2003.

MSR	$1,989	$1,385	$995	$700

000C-16SGTNE - western red cedar top, single ring rosette with blue paua pearl and white/black inlay, no pickguard, solid mahogany back/sides/neck, rosewood fingerboard, nylon strings, A-frame X bracing, Gloss finish, Fishman Prefix Pro-Blend with sound board transducer electronics, new mid 2002.

MSR	$1,899	$1,325	$975	$675

GRADING		100%	EXCELLENT	AVERAGE

000C-16SRNE - similar to 000C-16SGTNE, except has East Indian rosewood sides, back, and fingerboard, Spanish cedar neck, polished gloss finish, special X bracing, new 2003.

MSR	$2,399		$1,675	$1,275	$995

000-17 - mahogany top/back/sides, round soundhole, 3-stripe rosette, rosewood fingerboard with dot inlay, tortoise pickguard, available in Natural finish, approx. 25 mfg. 1952 only.

			N/A	$1,650	$1,275

000-17S - solid mahogany top, sides/back/neck, 12/20-fret black Micarta fingerboard, single ring rosette, slotted headstock, hybrid scalloped bracing, Polish Gloss finish with Dark Stain, new 2002.

MSR	$1,899		$1,325	$975	$675

000-18 - solid spruce top, round soundhole, black pickguard, wood bound body, rope rosette, rosewood back/sides, cedar neck, 12/19-fret ebony fingerboard, ebony pyramid bridge with black pearl dot pins, 3-per-side brass tuners with ivory buttons, available in Natural finish, mfg. 1911-current.

		EXCELLENT	AVERAGE
1911-1926	N/A	$6,000	$4,500
1927-1930	N/A	$6,500	$5,000
1931-1933	N/A	$7,500	$5,500
1934-1938	N/A	$8,000	$5,500
1939-1944	N/A	$6,500	$3,500
1945-1946	N/A	$3,400	$2,500
1947-1959	N/A	$3,000	$2,000
1960-1969	N/A	$2,000	$1,200
1970-1997	N/A	$1,400	$900

Add 25% for 1930's Mfg. models with Sunburst finish.

In 1917, mahogany back/sides/neck replaced original parts/designs. In 1920, 12/20-fret fingerboard became standard. In 1929, straight bridge replaced original parts/design. In 1930, belly bridge replaced original parts/design. In 1932, pickguard became an option. In 1934, black body binding, all metal tuners replaced original parts/designs. In 1934, 14/20-fret fingerboard replaced the 12/19-fret fingerboard (the first half production in 1934 featured an OM scale). These guitars had an ebony fingerboard and bridge until 1945, except for some models made between 1935-36, which were rosewood. In 1945, rosewood fingerboard and bridge replaced ebony fingerboard and bridge.

Martin 000-18
courtesy Guitar Emporium

000-18 (Standard Series)

MSR	$2,289		$1,595	$1,175	$795

000-21 - solid spruce top, round soundhole, wood bound body, herringbone rosette, rosewood back/sides, cedar neck, 12/19-fret ebony fingerboard with pearl dot inlay, ebony pyramid bridge with black pearl dot pins, 3-per-side brass tuners with ivory buttons, available in Natural finish, mfg. 1902-1959.

	100%	EXCELLENT	AVERAGE
1902-1937 (rare)	N/A	N/A	N/A
1938-1944	N/A	$10,000	$8,000
1945-1947 (non-scalloped braces)	N/A	$7,000	$5,000
1948-1959	N/A	$5,500	$4,500

In 1923, mahogany neck, 12/20-fret fingerboard replaced original parts. In 1930, belly bridge replaced original parts. In 1932, pickguard became an option. In 1938, 14/20-fret fingerboard replaced original parts. In 1947, rosewood fingerboard/bridge replaced original parts.

000-28 - solid spruce top, round soundhole, ivory bound body, herringbone purfling, 5-stripe rosette, rosewood back/sides, cedar neck, 12/19-fret ebony fingerboard, ebony pyramid bridge with black pearl dot pins, 3-per-side brass tuners with ivory buttons, available in Natural finish, mfg. 1902-current.

	100%	EXCELLENT	AVERAGE
1902-1924 (rare)	N/A	N/A	N/A
1925-1933 (12-frets)	N/A	$18,000	$12,000
1934-1938	N/A	$25,000	$15,000
1939-1944	N/A	$18,000	$12,000
1945-1946	N/A	$12,000	$8,000
1947-1959	N/A	$6,500	$4,500
1960-1969	N/A	$5,000	$3,500
1970-1997	N/A	$1,600	$1,200

000-28 (Standard Series)

MSR	$2,599		$1,795	$1,350	$895

In 1901, pearl diamond fingerboard inlay was introduced. In 1917, 12/20-fret fingerboard replaced original parts, mahogany neck replaced original parts. In 1929, belly bridge replaced original parts. In 1932, pickguard became an option. In 1934, pickguard became standard, 14/20-fret fingerboard replaced original parts. In 1944, pearl dot fingerboard inlay replaced original parts. In 1947, 5-stripe purfling replaced original parts.

Martin 000-28
Blue Book Publications

GRADING	100%	EXCELLENT	AVERAGE

000-28C - similar to OOO-28, except has classical style body, mfg. 1962-69.

	N/A	$2,000	$1,500

000-28H - similar to OOO-28, except has herringbone back inlay strip, mfg. 2000-01.

	$1,875	$1,425	$1,000

Last MSR was $2,850.

000-28EC ERIC CLAPTON SIGNATURE (VINTAGE SERIES) - solid Sitka spruce top, round soundhole, ivoroid body binding/herringbone purfling, herringbone rosette, solid East Indian rosewood back/sides, mahogany neck, 14/20-fret ebony fingerboard with abalone (pre-war style 28) snowflake inlay/mother-of-pearl Eric Clapton signature at 20th fret, rosewood bridge with white black dot pins, chrome hardware, 3-per-side tuners, available in Natural Gloss finish, new 1996.

MSR	$3,719	$2,595	$1,925	$1,400

000-28VS (VINTAGE SERIES) - solid spruce top, solid East Indian rosewood back/sides, square tapered slotted headstock, 12-fret, long scale 000, new 1999.

MSR	$3,879	$2,700	$1,975	$1,400

000-42 - solid spruce top, round soundhole, ivory bound body, pearl purfling/rosette, rosewood back/sides, cedar neck, 12/19-fret ivory bound ebony fingerboard with pearl diamond/snowflakes inlay, ivory bridge with black pearl dot pins, 3-per-side silver tuners with pearl buttons, available in Natural finish, mfg. 1918-1942.

	N/A	$45,000+	$35,000

The OOO-42 is the rarest OOO model. In 1919, plastic body binding, ebony bridge replaced original parts. In 1923, mahogany neck, 12/20-fret fingerboard, nickel tuners replaced original parts. In 1929, belly bridge replaced original parts. In 1932, pickguard became an option. In 1938, 14/20-fret fingerboard replaced original parts.

000-45 - solid spruce top, round soundhole, ivory bound body, pearl purfling top/back/sides, pearl rosette, rosewood back/sides, cedar neck, 12/19-fret ivory bound ebony fingerboard with pearl diamond/snowflakes inlay, ivory bridge with black pearl dot pins, pearl bound slotted peghead with pearl torch inlay, 3-per-side silver tuners with pearl buttons, available in Natural finish, mfg. 1907-1942, 1970-1985.

1907-1933	N/A	$45,000	$35,000
1934-1942	N/A	$55,000+	$40,000
1970-1985	N/A	$5,000	$4,000

Last MSR was $6,530.

In 1917, 12/20-fret fingerboard replaced original parts/design. In 1919, ebony bridge replaced original parts/design. In 1923, plastic binding replaced original parts/design. In 1929, belly bridge replaced original parts/design. In 1932, pickguard became an option. In 1934, pearl peghead logo inlay was introduced, 14/20-fret fingerboard replaced original parts/design. In 1936, chrome tuners replaced original parts/design. In 1939, gold tuners replaced original parts/design.

ACOUSTIC: 00 GRAND CONCERT SERIES

Size 00 (Grand Concert) guitars feature a lower bout width of 14 5/16 (14-fret) or 14 1/8 (12-fret) inches, 4 1/8 (14-fret) or 4 1/16 (12-fret) in. depth, 18 7/8 (14-fret) or 19 5/8 (12-fret) in. length, and 24.9 in. scale.

00CXAE (X SERIES) - 00 (grand concert) thin body with cutaway, choice of red (disc. 2001), black (00CXAE Black), navy matrix (disc. 2001) colors or mahogany or rosewood wood grain image on wood fiber composite laminate top, laminate sides/back, DX bracing, black Micarta fingerboard and bridge, Fishman Sonicore pickup with Classic 4 onboard preamp, new 2000.

MSR	$849	$595	$440	$315

Add $150 for spruce top (new 2003, Model 00CX1AE Black.)

00M (ROAD SERIES) - 00 (Grand Concert) body similar to OM-1, except has mahogany laminate back/sides, mfg. 2001 only.

	$625	$475	$325

Last MSR was $925.

00-1 (1 SERIES) - solid Sitka spruce top, round soundhole, mahogany neck, solid mahogany back, 3-ply mahogany sides, 14/20 rosewood fingerboard with dot inlay, rosewood bridge, tortoise pickguard, 3-per-side tuners, chrome hardware, available in Natural Satin finish, Custom Shop mfg. 1996-2000.

	$825	$625	$475

Last MSR was $1,250.

00-1R - similar to the 00-1, except features 3-ply laminated Indian rosewood back/sides, Custom Shop mfg. 1996-98.

	$950	$725	$575

Last MSR was $1,450.

00C-MAE (Road Series) - similar to the 00-1, except features single rounded cutaway body, laminated mahogany back/sides, bridge pickup, onboard electronics, Custom Shop mfg. 1998-2000.

	$925	$700	$475

Last MSR was $1,450.

00-15 (15 SERIES) - solid mahogany top, round soundhole, single band gold herringbone decal rosette, solid mahogany back/sides, mahogany neck, no body binding, 14/20-fret rosewood fingerboard with white dot inlay, rosewood bridge with white pins, tortoise pickguard, 3-per-side chrome tuners, new 1998.

MSR	$979	$685	$495	$375

GRADING	100%	EXCELLENT	AVERAGE

00C-15AE - features thin body cutaway design, solid mahogany top/back/sides, includes Fishman Soni-core pickup with Classic 4 onboard preamp, mfg. 2000-01.

	$895	$675	$475

Last MSR was $1,349.

00C-16DB (16 SERIES) - single rounded cutaway body, spruce top, round soundhole, black pickguard, tortoise bound body, abalone pearl rosette, solid mahogany back/sides, mahogany neck, 14/20-fret rosewood fingerboard with abalone fingerboard inlays, rosewood bridge with abalone snowflake inlay and black pins, tortoise pickguard, 3-per-side chrome tuners, available in Black Gloss finish, mfg. 1998-2000.

	$1,500	$1,150	$875

Last MSR was $1,450.

00C-16GTAE - thin body grand concert cutaway with solid Sitka spruce top and solid mahogany back/sides/neck, black Micarta 14/20-fret fingerboard, triple ring rosette, hybrid scalloped bracing, gloss top with satin sides/back, includes Fishman Prefix Pro electronics, mfg. 2002.

	$1,150	$875	$625

Last MSR was $1,649.

00C-16FMBUAE - solid flame maple top/back/sides with two-piece maple neck and black micarta fingerboard, Translucent Blue finish, hybrid scalloped bracing, 14/20-fret, Gloss finish, new 2003.

MSR	$3,299	$2,300	$1,650	$1,275

00-16DBM - similar to the 00C-16 DB, except does not have cutaway body, new 1999.

MSR	$1,649	$1,150	$875	$625

00-16DBFM - please refer to listing under Guitar of the Month/Year, Limited, and Special Editions category name.

00-16C - solid spruce top, round soundhole, bound body, 3-stripe rosette, mahogany back/sides/neck, 12/19-fret rosewood fingerboard, tied rosewood bridge, slotted peghead, 3-per-side tuners with pearl buttons, available in Natural finish, Custom Shop mfg. 1962-1994.

1962-1982	N/A	$900	$550
1983-1994	N/A	$1,625	$995

Last MSR was $2,330.

The 00-16 C is a classical model (nylon string).

00-17 (1908-1917 MFG.) - spruce top, round soundhole, 3-stripe bound body/rosette, mahogany back/sides/neck, 14/20-fret rosewood fingerboard, rosewood bridge with black pins, 3-per-side tuners, available in Dark Natural finish, mfg. 1908-1917.

	N/A	$3,000	$2,200

00-17 (1930-1960 Mfg.) - mahogany top, no body binding, rosewood fingerboard, mfg. 1930 - 1960.

1930-1945	N/A	$1,900	$1,500
1946-1960	N/A	$1,500	$1,200

00-17 (2000-Current Mfg.) - mahogany top/sides/back, ebony fingerboard and bridge, style 17 3-ring rosette, Polish Lacquer finish, electronics available at additional cost, new 2000.

MSR	$1,650	$1,150	$875	$575

00-18 - 3-stripe rosette, rosewood or mahogany back/sides, fingerboard/bridge, mfg. 1898-1994.

1898-1917 (rosewood back/sides)	N/A	$4,000	$3,200
1918-1933 (mahogany back/sides)	N/A	$3,800	$2,800
1934-1944	N/A	$4,000	$3,000
1945-1946	N/A	$2,800	$2,200
1947-1959	N/A	$2,200	$1,800
1960-1969	N/A	$1,500	$1,000
1970-1994	N/A	$1,100	$750

Last MSR was $2,480.

Add 25% for 1930s mfg. models with Sunburst finish.

These guitars had an ebony fingerboard and bridge until 1945, except for some models made between 1935-36, which were rosewood.

00-18C (Classical) - similar to the 00-18, mfg. 1959-1992.

1959-1965	N/A	$1,200	$900
1966-1992	N/A	$800	$500

The 00-18 C was a classical model (nylon string).

00-18E - similar to 00-18, except has 1 neck position pickup, 1 volume and 1 tone control knob, mfg. 1959-1965.

	N/A	$2,000	$1,400

**Martin 000-45
courtesy Michael Jones**

**Martin 00-18
courtesy Fred Oster**

GRADING		100%	EXCELLENT	AVERAGE

00-18G - mahogany back/sides, ebony fingerboard/bridge, available in Polished Lacquer finish, mfg. 1936-1962.

1936-1946		N/A	$1,200	$900
1947-1962		N/A	$900	$600

The 00-18 G was a classical model (nylon string). The first models produced had pin bridges. After the 1940s, these models came with a rosewood fingerboard/bridge.

00-18H - similar to the 00-18, except features Hawaiian configuration (raised nut, flat fingerboard, flush frets, non-slanted saddle), mfg. 1935-1941.

		N/A	$3,200	$2,600

Most of the 0O-18 H models were in a Sunburst finish.

00-18K - similar to the 00-18, except features koa top/back/sides, mfg. 1918-1934.

		N/A	$3,200	$2,600

00-18V (Vintage Series) - features solid Sitka spruce top, mahogany back/sides/neck with 14/20-fret ebony fingerboard, 1/4 in. scalloped bracing, tortoise colored bindings and beveled pickguard, Gloss finish with stain/aging toner. New 2003.

MSR	$2,849	$1,995	$1,450	$1,100

00-21 - spruce top, round soundhole, black pickguard, multi-bound body, 3-stripe rosette, rosewood back/sides, mahogany neck, 12/19-fret rosewood fingerboard with pearl dot inlay, rosewood bridge with black white dot pins, rosewood veneered solid peghead with screened logo, 3-per-side chrome tuners, available in Natural finish, mfg. 1898-1995.

1898-1925		N/A	$4,000	$3,200
1926-1930		N/A	$4,400	$3,400
1931-1944 (w/belly bridge)		N/A	$5,500	$4,000
1945-1946		N/A	$5,000	$4,000
1947-1959		N/A	$3,500	$3,000
1960-1969		N/A	$3,000	$2,500
1970-1995		N/A	$1,600	$1,200

Last MSR was $2,730.

00-21NY - similar to the 00-21, except has no pickguard, available in Natural finish, mfg. 1961-65.

		N/A	$2,500	$2,000

00-28 - herringbone bound body, 3-stripe rosette, rosewood back/sides ebony fingerboard/bridge, mfg. 1898-1941.

1898-1930		N/A	$6,000	$4,500
1931-1941		N/A	$8,000	$5,000

00-28C - 3-stripe rosette, rosewood back/sides, ebony fingerboard/bridge, mfg. 1966-1994.

1966-1969		N/A	$1,600	$1,400
1970-1994		N/A	$1,000	$800

Last MSR was $2,760.

The 00-28 C was a classical model (nylon string).

00-28G - rosewood back/sides, 12/20-fret ebony fingerboard, mfg. 1936-1962.

1936-1946		N/A	$2,200	$1,700
1947-1962		N/A	$1,600	$1,300

The 00-28 G was a classical model (nylon string).

00-28K - similar to the 00-28, except features koa back/sides, raised nut, non-slanted saddle, mfg. 1919-1933.

		N/A	$6,000	$4,000

00-30 - rosewood back/sides/fingerboard/bridge, mfg. 1899-1921.

		N/A	$5,000	$3,000

00-42 - pearl bound body/rosette, rosewood back/sides/fingerboard/bridge, mfg. 1898-1942.

1898-1930		N/A	$12,000	$9,000
1931-1942		N/A	$18,000	$12,000

00-45 - pearl bound body/rosette/fingerboard/peghead, rosewood back/sides/fingerboard/bridge, mfg. 1904-1938.

		N/A	$22,500+	$19,000

ACOUSTIC: 0 (CONCERT) SERIES

Size 0 (Concert) guitars feature a lower bout width of 13 1/2 inches, 4 1/4 (14-fret) or 4 3/16 (12-fret) in. depth, 18 3/8 (14-fret) or 19 1/8 (12-fret) in. length, and 24.9 in. scale.

0-15 - mahogany top, round soundhole, 2-stripe rosette, tortoise pickguard, mahogany back/sides/neck, 14/20-fret rosewood fingerboard with white dot inlay, rosewood bridge with white pins, black face peghead with logo decal, 3-per-side nickel tuners with plastic buttons, available in Natural finish, mfg. 1935 (2 specimens only) and 1940-1961.

1940-1945		N/A	$1,200	$900
1946-1961		N/A	$900	$750

0-15T - similar to the 0-15, except has tenor neck, mfg. 1960-63.

		N/A	$600	$500

GRADING	100%	EXCELLENT	AVERAGE

0-16NY - spruce top, round soundhole, 3-stripe bound body/rosette, mahogany back/sides/neck, 12/19-fret rosewood fingerboard, rosewood bridge with black white dot pins, slotted peghead 3-per-side tuners with plastic buttons, available in Natural finish, mfg. 1961-1995.

1961-1969	N/A	$1,200	$900
1970-1995	N/A	$900	$700

0-16 - similar to the 0-16NY, except has tortoise pickguard, available in Natural satin finish, mfg. 1961.

	N/A	$1,200	$900

0-17 (1906-1917 MFG.) - spruce top, round soundhole, mahogany back/sides, cedar neck, 12/20-fret ebony fingerboard with pearl dot inlay, ebony bridge with black pins, slotted peghead, 3-per-side nickel tuners with plastic buttons, available in Natural finish, mfg. 1906-1917.

	N/A	$2,500	$2,000

In 1914, rosewood bound body, 3-stripe rosette was introduced.

0-17 (1929-1948, 1966-68 Mfg.) - mahogany top/back/sides, round soundhole, cedar neck, 12/20-fret rosewood fingerboard with pearl dot inlay, rosewood bridge with black pins, slotted peghead, 3-per-side nickel tuners with plastic buttons, available in Natural finish, mfg. 1929-1948, 1966-68.

1929-1948	N/A	$1,500	$1,100
1966-1968	N/A	$900	$750

In 1929, rosewood bound body was discontinued. In 1931, pickguard became an option. In 1934, solid peghead and 14/20-fret fingerboard replaced original parts/design.

0-17H - similar to the 0-17, except features flat fingerboard/flush frets, high nut, and non-slanted saddle, mfg. 1930-39.

	N/A	$1,500	$1,000

0-17T - similar to the 0-17, except has tenor neck, mfg. 1932-1963.

1932-1945	N/A	$800	$500
1946-1960	N/A	$600	$400

0-18 - solid spruce top, round soundhole, wood bound body, rope rosette, rosewood back/sides, cedar neck, 12/19-fret ebony fingerboard, pyramid ebony bridge with black pearl dot pins, 3-per-side brass tuners with ivory buttons, available in Natural finish, mfg. 1898-1995.

1898-1917	N/A	$2,500	$2,000
1918-1931	N/A	$2,000	$1,500
1932-1946	N/A	$2,500	$1,800
1947-1959	N/A	$1,600	$1,250
1960-1969	N/A	$1,200	$1,000
1970-1995	N/A	$900	$700

Add 25% for Sunburst finish on 1930s mfg. instruments.

In 1909, pearl dot fingerboard inlay was introduced. In 1917, mahogany back/sides/neck replaced original parts/designs. In 1919, rosewood bound body was introduced. In 1920, 12/20-fret fingerboard became standard. In 1921, straight bridge replaced original parts/design. In 1923, belly bridge replaced original parts/design. In 1932, pickguard became an option. In 1934, black body binding replaced original parts/design. By 1932, 14/20-fret fingerboard became standard item. By 1945, rosewood fingerboard/bridge replaced original parts/design.

0-18K - similar to the 0-18, except has koa top/back/sides, mfg. 1918-1935.

	N/A	$2,200	$1,500

0-18T - similar to the 0-18, except has tenor neck, mfg. 1929-1994.

1929-1931 (small pickguard, banjo tuners)	N/A	$1,200	$900
1932-1945	N/A	$1,000	$700
1946-1994	N/A	$800	$500

0-21 - solid spruce top, round soundhole, wood bound body, herringbone rosette, rosewood back/sides, cedar neck, 12/19-fret ebony fingerboard with pearl dot inlay, pyramid ebony bridge with ebony pearl dot pins, 3-per-side brass tuners with ivory buttons, available in Natural finish, mfg. 1898-1948.

1898-1929	N/A	$3,000	$2,500
1930-1948	N/A	$2,500	$2,000

In 1917, mahogany neck replaced original parts/design. In 1923, 12/20-fret fingerboard became standard item. In 1927, belly bridge replaced original parts/design. In 1932, pickguard became an option.

0-21H - similar to the 0-21, except features flat fingerboard/flush frets, high nut, and non-slanted saddle, mfg. 1918 only.

The O-21H model is very rare. Too few of these exist for accurate statistical representation.

0-21K - similar to the 0-21, except has koa top/back/sides, mfg. 1919-1929.

	N/A	$3,200	$2,200

Martin 0-15
courtesy Dale Hanson

Martin 0-21
courtesy Killer Vintage

M

GRADING	100%	EXCELLENT	AVERAGE

0-28 - solid spruce top, round soundhole, ivory bound body, herringbone rosette, rosewood back/sides, cedar neck, 12/19-fret ebony fingerboard, pyramid ebony bridge with ebony pearl dot pins, 3-per-side brass tuners with ivory buttons, available in Natural finish, mfg. 1898-1931, 1937.

1898-1929	N/A	$3,500	$3,000
1930-1937	N/A	$5,500	$4,000

> **Models with belly bridge will bring a higher premium.**

In 1901, pearl dot fingerboard inlay was introduced. In 1917, 12/20-fret fingerboard replaced original parts/design, mahogany neck replaced original parts/design. In 1929, belly bridge replaced original parts/design. In 1937, pickguard became standard item, 14/20-fret fingerboard replaced original parts/design.

0-28K - similar to the 0-28, except has koa top/back/sides, mfg. 1917-1935.

	N/A	$4,500	$3,500

0-28T (1930-31 Mfg.) - similar to the 0-28, except has tenor neck, mfg. 1930-31.

	N/A	$1,800	$1,200

0-30 - solid spruce top, round soundhole, ivory bound body/colored purfling, pearl rosette, Brazilian rosewood back/sides, cedar neck, 12/19-fret ivory bound ebony fingerboard with pearl dot inlay, pyramid ebony bridge with ebony pearl dot pins, 3-per-side silver brass tuners, available in Natural finish, mfg. 1899-1921.

	N/A	$4,000	$3,000

Between 1917 to 1923, mahogany neck replaced the cedar neck.

0-34 - solid spruce top, round soundhole, ivory bound body/colored purfling, pearl rosette, Brazilian rosewood back/sides, cedar neck, 12/19-fret ivory bound ebony fingerboard with pearl slotted diamond inlay, pyramid ivory bridge with ebony pearl dot pins, 3-per-side silver brass tuners, available in Natural finish, mfg. 1898-99, 1907.

	N/A	$4,500	$3,500

0-40 - solid spruce top, round soundhole, ivory bound body, pearl rosette, Brazilian rosewood back/sides, cedar neck, 12/19-fret ebony fingerboard with pearl snowflake inlay, pyramid ivory bridge with ebony pearl dot pins, 3-per-side silver brass tuners, available in Natural finish, mfg. 1912-13.

The O-40 model is very rare. Too few of these exist for accurate statistical representation.

0-42 - solid spruce top, round soundhole, ivory bound body, pearl purfling/rosette, rosewood back/sides, cedar neck, 12/19-fret ivory bound ebony fingerboard with pearl diamond/snowflake inlay, pyramid ivory bridge with ebony pearl dot pins, 3-per-side silver tuners with pearl buttons, available in Natural finish, mfg. 1898-1942.

	N/A	$9,000	$6,000

In 1914, ivory peghead pegs were an option. In 1919, plastic binding, ebony bridge replaced original parts/designs. In 1923, mahogany neck, 12/20-fret fingerboard, nickel tuners replaced original parts/designs. In 1929, belly bridge replaced original parts/design.

0-45 - solid spruce top, round soundhole, ivory bound body, pearl purfling/rosette, Brazilian rosewood back/sides, cedar neck, 12/19-fret ivory bound ebony fingerboard with pearl snowflake/diamond inlay, pyramid ivory bridge with ebony pearl dot pins, ivory/pearl bound peghead with pearl torch inlay, 3-per-side brass tuners with ivory buttons, available in Natural finish, mfg. 1904-1939.

	N/A	$20,000	$14,000

In 1917, mahogany neck replaced the cedar neck, 12/20-fret fingerboard replaced the 12/19-fret fingerboard. In 1919, plastic binding, ebony bridge replaced original parts/designs. In 1929, belly bridge replaced original parts/design.

ACOUSTIC: SMALLER SIZED MARTINS: 1/4, 1/2, 1, 2, 2 1/2, 3, & 3 1/2 MFG. 1898-1938

Between 1898 and 1938, Martin made guitars in these other small bodied sizes.

Martin made a few unusual sized guitars in its history. Generally these guitars are too rare to price; you simply won't find them. Between 1918 and 1931 Martin made 22 quarter-sized guitars with the designation 1/4-18. In 1918, they made 6 1/4 12-strings. No mention is made of the woods used for the back and sides on these. In 1918 and 1919 they made 18 half-sized guitars designated 1/2-18. In 1919, they made a 1/2-21. In 1921, they made four 3/4-18s and one 3/4-21. It would be easy to say that these should price out about the same as Martin's other small guitars from the same period, but in reality they never show up. Because of their rarity the price really needs to be negotiated on an individual guitar basis. In 1975, they made two 1/4-28s. One was used by then-customer-relations-guru Mike Longworth to carry on airplanes so he'd have something to play on the road. In 1981, another dozen of these were made, but the model never caught on. You'd expect to pay about as much as a 5-28 from the same period for one of these later guitars. Martin also made a very few other unusual guitars. The Schuyler Model America, essentially a guitar with two bodies, one on top of the other, the tops connected by wooden dowels was made in 1907 and again in 1909, for a total of two. This is truly a seller's market. In 1909, they made a harp guitar, and in 1912 they made another called a Dubetz. In 1916 they listed a guitar with an extra-long 17" body. For more information on these unusual guitars check out Mike Longworth's excellent book, *Martin Guitars, A History*. Before Martin started serializing their guitars in 1898, there are no production totals to go by. Any pre-1898 guitar needs to be taken on its own merits—they are so rare and unusual that it's nearly impossible to price them.

Early **Size 1/4** instruments had a lower bout width of 6 3/16 in., 2 7/8 in. depth, 12 in. length, and 17 in. scale. Late **Size 1/4** body width was 8 5/16 in., 3 9/16 in. depth, 12 1/16 in. length, and a 17 in. scale. The **Size 1/2** had a body width of 10 1/8 in., 3 3/8 in. depth, 15 1/16 in. length, and 20 7/8 in. scale. The **Size 1** had a lower bout width of 12 3/4 in., 4 3/16 in. depth, 18 7/8 in. length, and 24.9 in. scale. The **Size 2** body width was 12 in., 4 in. depth, 18 1/4 in. length, and 24.5 in. scale. The **Size 2 1/2** body width was 11 5/8 in., 3 7/8 in. depth, 17 7/8 in. length, and 24.5 in. scale. The **Size 3** had a body width of 11 1/4 in., 3 3/16 in. depth, 17 3/8 in. length, and 23 7/8 in. scale. The **Size 3 1/2** had a body width of 10 11/16 in., 3 7/8 in. depth, 16 7/8 in. length, and 22 in. scale. Models can be cross-referenced in regards to styles by hyphenated description (for example, a 2-**17** or a 1-**45**).

Small body Martin models tend to trade for close to the values of their single 0 stylistic counterparts (for example, a 1-18K would sell for a little less than an 0-18K).

GRADING	100%	EXCELLENT	AVERAGE

ACOUSTIC: 5 SERIES

Size 5 guitars feature a lower bout width of 11 1/4 inches, 3 7/8 in. depth, 16 in. length, and 23 (after 1930) in. scale, except the 5-15, which is 21.38 in.

5-15 (15 SERIES) - solid mahogany top, round soundhole with gold and black herringbone decal, mahogany back/sides/neck, 12/18-fret rosewood fingerboard and bridge, 3 per side tuners, 21.38 in. scale, Satin finish, new mid 2002.

MSR	$979		$675	$500	$350

5-16 - spruce top, round soundhole, 3-stripe bound body/rosette, mahogany back/sides/neck, 12/19-fret rosewood fingerboard, rosewood bridge with black white dot pins, 3-per-side chrome tuners, available in Natural finish, mfg. 1962-63.

		N/A	$1,000	$800

5-16GT - similar to older 5-18, except that spruce top is bound in black Boltron, High Gloss top finish, mahogany back/neck/sides have satin lacquer, 12/18-fret black micarta fingerboard, new 2003.

MSR	$1,279		$895	$675	$525

5-17 (1912-16 MFG.) - spruce top, round soundhole, 3 black soundhole rings, mahogany back/sides/neck, 12/19-fret unbound ebony fingerboard, rosewood bridge with black pins, 3-per-side die cast tuners with nickel buttons, available in Dark finish, mfg. 1912-16.

The 5-17 model is very rare. Too few of these exist for accurate statistical representation.

5-17 (1927-1943 Mfg.) - similar to the 5-17 (1912 to 1916 Mfg.), except features mahogany top, rosewood fingerboard with dot inlay, 3-stripe top binding/rosette, mfg. 1927-1943.

		N/A	$1,400	$1,000

5-17T - similar to the 5-17 (1927-1943 mfg.), except has tenor neck, 22" scale, mfg. 1927-1949.

		N/A	$800	$500

Martin 5-15
courtesy Martin Guitar

5-18 - rosewood back and sides, 5-stripe body binding, colored wood "rope" pattern soundhole, rectangular bridge, unbound ebony fingerboard, 3-per-side tuners, mfg. 1898-1989.

1898-1931	N/A	$1,800	$1,500
1932-1946	N/A	$1,600	$1,300
1947-1959	N/A	$1,500	$1,000
1960-1969	N/A	$1,400	$900
1970-1989	N/A	$1,200	$900

5-21 - rosewood back and sides, herringbone soundhole ring, 5-stripe body binding, unbound ebony fingerboard with slotted diamond inlay, 3-per-side tuners, mfg. 1902-1927. (Extremely rare.)

	N/A	$2,800	$2,400

5-28 - Brazilian rosewood back and sides, ivory bound top, herringbone top purfling, unbound ebony fingerboard with slotted diamond inlay, 3-per-side tuners, mfg. 1901-1939, 1968-1981.

1901-1939 (rare)	N/A	$2,500	$1,800
1968-1969	N/A	$2,000	$1,500
1970-1981	N/A	$1,100	$800

MINI-MARTIN (SPECIAL EDITION) - patterned after the vintage 5-28, solid Sitka spruce top, East Indian rosewood back/sides, mahogany neck with ebony fingerboard, hand carved volute, 21 3/8 in. scale length, ornate pearl rosette and top binding, herringbone top trim, lacquered and polished High Gloss finish, new 1999.

MSR	$3,449		$2,415	$1,825	$1,450

ACOUSTIC: 7 SERIES

Size 7 guitars are designed to be a 7/8 size dreadnought (scaled down body size). Lower bout width is 13 11/16 in., 14 3/8 in. depth, 171/2 in. length, and 23 in. scale.

7-28 - Indian rosewood back and sides, round soundhole, bound body, black pickguard, unbound ebony fingerboard, 3-per-side tuners, mfg. 1980-87.

		N/A	$1,600	$1,100

7-37K - similar to the 7-28, except features koa back and sides, pearl soundhole ring, tortoise pickguard, slotted diamond fingerboard inlay, mfg. 1980-87.

		N/A	$1,600	$1,100

ACOUSTIC: ARCHTOP C, F, & R SERIES

Tailpiece variations were common on all arch and carved top instruments. Size C guitars feature a lower bout width of 15 inches, 4 3/16 in. depth, 19 3/8 in. length, and 24.9 in. scale. Size F guitars feature a lower bout width of 16 inches,

Martin 5-17T
courtesy Martin Guitar

4 1/8 in. depth, 20 1/8 in. length, and 24.9 in. scale. Size R guitars had a body width of 14 5/8 in., 4 1/4 in. depth, 18 7/8 in. length, and 24.9 in. scale.

Archtop series models with round soundholes tend to command a slightly higher premium.

C-1 - carved spruce top, round soundhole, raised black pickguard, bound top/rosette, mahogany back/sides/neck, 14/20-fret rosewood fingerboard with white dot inlay, rosewood bridge/trapeze tailpiece, vertical pearl logo inlay on headstock, 3-per-side nickel tuners, available in Sunburst finish, mfg. 1931-1942.

| | N/A | $1,600 | $1,250 |

In 1934, f-holes replaced original parts/design.

C-2 - similar to C-1, except has stripe bound body/rosette, rosewood back/sides, ebony fingerboard with pearl snowflake inlay, ebony bridge, available in Dark Lacquer finish, mfg. 1931-1942.

| | N/A | $2,350 | $1,650 |

In 1934, f-holes replaced original parts/design, Golden Brown top finish became standard. In 1935, bound fingerboard, pickguard were introduced. In 1939, hexagon fingerboard inlay was introduced.

C-3 - similar to C-1, except has 2-stripe bound body/rosette, pearl bound pickguard, rosewood back/sides, bound ebony fingerboard with pearl snowflake inlay, ebony bridge, gold tailpiece, bound peghead, gold single unit tuners, available in Lacquer finish, mfg. 1932-35.

| | N/A | $4,000 | $3,000 |

In 1934, Stained top finish was introduced, bound pickguard, f-holes replaced original parts/designs.

F-1 - carved spruce top, f-holes, raised black pickguard, stripe bound top, mahogany back/sides/neck, 14/20-fret ebony fingerboard with white dot inlay, adjustable ebony bridge/trapeze tailpiece, logo decal on headstock, 3-per-side nickel tuners, available in Sunburst finish, mfg. 1940-42.

| | N/A | $1,750 | $1,125 |

F-2 - similar to F-1, except has rosewood back/sides, very few mfg.

| | N/A | $3,850 | $2,750 |

F-5 - similar to F-1, except features maple back/sides/neck, mfg. 1940 only.

Only 2 instruments were produced. While pricing is an irrelevant issue with this model, it is significant more for what it is (a maple bodied archtop) than for how much it is. It is interesting that Martin saw a market for such a guitar, yet decided not to pursue it.

F-7 - similar to F-1, except has bound pickguard, rosewood back/sides, bound fingerboard with ivoroid hexagon inlay, bound peghead with pearl vertical logo inlay, chrome hardware, available in Sunburst finish, mfg. 1935-1942.

| | N/A | $4,500+ | $3,500 |

In 1937, pearloid fingerboard inlay replaced original parts/design.

F-9 - similar to F-1, except has stripe bound pickguard, Brazilian rosewood back/sides, bound fingerboard with pearl hexagon inlay, bound peghead with pearl vertical logo inlay, gold hardware, available in Golden Brown Sunburst finish, mfg. 1935-1942.

| | N/A | $13,000 | $7,500 |

The F-9 is Martin's finest archtop instrument, one of rarest and fanciest guitars that Martin ever made. The *Blue Book of Acoustic Guitars* highly recommends obtaining competent appraisals before buying/selling/trading this model.

R-17 - arched mahogany top, f-holes, raised black (or tortoiseshell) pickguard, black or tortoise body binding, mahogany back/sides/neck, 14/20-fret rosewood fingerboard, rosewood bridge/trapeze tailpiece, logo decal on peghead, 3-per-side nickel single unit tuners, available in Sunburst finish, mfg. 1934-1942.

| | N/A | $975 | $700 |

Body binding and pickguard color always match on the R-17 and R-18 acoustic archtop models (black binding with black pickguard, tortoise binding with tortoise pickguard).

R-18 - similar to R-17, except has arched spruce top, 3-stripe bound body/rosette, white dot fingerboard inlay, mfg. 1932-1941.

| | N/A | $1,250 | $850 |

In 1933, f-holes replaced original parts/design.

ACOUSTIC: BACKPAKCER SERIES

The Backpacker Travel Guitar was developed by luthier/designer Bob McNally in 1994. Backpackers have shown up in the most unusual of places, from the Space Shuttle to the Himalayas! Models are currently produced in Martin's Mexican facility located in Navojoa, Sonora, Mexico.

Add $135 for factory installed Martin 332 Thinline bridge pickup. Add $160 for factory installed System 1 pickup (Classical Backpacker only).

BACKPACKER - travel style "paddle"-shaped body, solid spruce top, round soundhole, one-piece mahogany body/neck with hollowed out sound cavity, 15-fret hardwood fingerboard with white dot inlay, hardwood bridge with white black dot pins, 3-per-side chrome mini tuners, available in Natural finish, new 1994.

| MSR | $274 | | $185 | $145 | $95 |

Backpacker Classical - similar to Backpacker, except is designed for nylon strings, current mfg.

| MSR | $274 | | $185 | $145 | $95 |

GRADING	100%	EXCELLENT	AVERAGE

ACOUSTIC: CLASSICAL SERIES

MARTIN/HUMPHREY C-TSH CLASSICAL (STANDARD SERIES) - solid Englemann spruce top, round soundhole, rose-patterned mosaic rosette, solid East Indian 2-piece back with (style 45) mosaic inlay strip, solid East Indian rosewood sides, rosewood/black/white body binding, classic neck shape incorporates neck to body shape and sound board arching, mahogany neck, 12/19 "elevated" ebony fingerboard, slotted headstock, 3-per-side gold tuners with white buttons, available in Natural Gloss finish, mfg. 1996-mid 2002.

$2,525   **$1,925**   **$1,450**

Last MSR was $3,850.

In 1996, luthier Thomas Humphrey contracted a standardized design of his Millennium design to the C.F. Martin Guitar company (see Thomas Humphrey).

Martin/Humphrey C-1R Classical (1 Series) - similar to the C-TSH Classical, except features a solid western red cedar top, laminated rosewood back/sides, black body binding, rosewood fingerboard and bridge, available in Natural Satin finish, mfg. 1996 -mid-2002.

$1,050   **$800**   **$575**

Last MSR was $1,575.

GUITAR OF THE MONTH/YEAR SERIES

Wherever possible, both pricing and the amount of instruments made are provided in the individual listings. Where N/As appear, accurate secondary marketplace pricing cannot be provided, since these instruments do not trade sufficiently enough to list pricing.

The models listed below are in chronological sequence (the original year of manufacture appears after the model name). The D-16 SP Special Editions appear under their own subcategory heading at the end of this section.

As customer demand opened up for specified, limited edition models, Martin announced the Guitar of the Month program in October, 1984. This ambitious plan to offer an announced custom-built limited edition model every month was scaled back to four or five models per year. This program continued through 1994, when Martin switched to annual offerings of limited/special editions. Between 1984 to 1985, Guitar of the Month models have special paper labels signed by C.F. Martin III and C.F. Martin IV. Special/limited editions after 1986 are signed by C.F. Martin IV (unless otherwise listed below).

Some Guitar of the Month models are built in a "fixed," predetermined production amount; while others may be "open - ended" and are limited to the number sold (or ordered) through the calender year.

Prior to 1995, these Limited Edition models were labelled separately for Domestic (US) and Foreign markets: a model may be #1 of 100 in the US, while the next model may be numbered #1 of 12 (Overseas). Thus, the total production may be 112 for this model (and not the number given on the US label). Separate Foreign label editions are marked with a (*). In 1995, Martin began to issue one label worldwide.

Martin special editions are typically commemorative models which pay tribute to those Martin models which have been historically significant – these include the Golden Era Series, certified wood models, and other special editions. Special editions do not have a total quantity assigned to each variation, and are made as demand dictates. Limited editions are usually associated with a particular artist or event, and the quantity of each variation is usually determined at the time of release. In many cases, a portion of the sales go to charities of the artist's choice. Limited editions are usually made for a limited time, and are available until the variation sells out. Sometimes, a sellout can occur in weeks (i.e., Jimmy Buffett Signature HD-18JB mfg. 1998), while others may take considerably.

Whenever possible, the year a special/limited edition was introduced is listed after the model name in parentheses. In many cases, these instruments will continue to be listed on Martin's price sheets until they are sold out. On recently manufactured special and limited editions, unless the model is marked special edition in parentheses after the model name, you can assume that the model is a limited edition.

Guitar of the Month models are usually identified with a suffix. For example, a HD-28BLE (1990) is an HD-28 with Brazilian rosewood back and sides. Due to the limited production amounts (and fierce loyalty of Martin guitar owners), these specialty guitars rarely trade only infrequently in the acoustic vintage market. Most models encountered are in Excellent to Mint condition (i.e. well cared for).

For readers new to Martin products, please note: Aging Toner finish, or a " Toned Top" model refers to the golden-toned lacquer that is shot on the top (soundboard) of the guitar. The following models are listed as to the features that differ from similarly designated stock models (for that year).

A special note from Martin: "As a general rule, Martin has produced two prototypes of each limited edition in order to develop model specifications and help determine production costs. Generally these prototypes are not for sale. However, due to factory space constrictions, many prototypes have already or eventually may be sold." When buying/selling/trading these rare Martin factory prototype, it is recommended to get as much original paperwork as possible to establish provenance, as well as documenting legal ownership.

The source material for Martin's Guitar of the Month series courtesy Dick Boak, Martin Guitar Company. Additional detailed information can be found in Jim Washburn and Richard Johnson's *Martin Guitars: An Illustrated Celebration of America's Premier Guitarmaker*, Rodale Books, 1997; or Walter Carter's *The Martin Book: A Complete History of Martin Guitars*, GPI Books, 1995).

Martin C-2
courtesy Fly By Night

M

Martin R-18
courtesy Austin Vintage

GRADING	100%	EXCELLENT	AVERAGE

GUITAR OF THE MONTH/YEAR AND SPECIAL/LIMITED EDITION PRICING

Whenever possible, prices are listed for the following models, whether they are guitars of the month, special or limited editions. N/As indicate that the rarity factor and lack of activity in the secondary marketplace (especially those older models with high demand) precludes accurate pricing.

As a rule of thumb, many instruments listed in this section that are 5 years or older are typically worth at least 65%-75% value at the time of production, but there are exceptions (i.e. Eric Clapton, etc.). It is recommended that you follow this niche marketplace by studying dealer listings and the Internet/Ebay for possible listings and current prices. Remember, even though some of these special models are relatively rare and now almost 20 years old, it doesn't necessarily mean that they are valued higher than a similar current production model with the same appointments and features. One exception is any model made with Brazilian rosewood, as values for this South American tone wood have skyrocketed in recent years.

OO-18V (OCTOBER, 1984) - prewar OO-18 style, 25.4" scale, tortoise binding, ebony fingerboard, gold tuners, tortoise shell pickguard, ebony bridge, available in Aging Toner finish.

	N/A	$2,250	$1,250

Last MSR was $1,520.

Only 9 instruments were manufactured.

D-28 CUSTOM (NOVEMBER, 1984) - D-28 style, Indian rosewood back/sides, ebony fingerboard with snowflake inlay, unbound peghead with torch inlay, scalloped braces, stamped logo on back of peghead.

	N/A	$3,000	$1,750

Last MSR was $2,000.

Only 43 instruments were manufactured.

M-21 CUSTOM (DECEMBER, 1984) - Indian rosewood back/sides, tortoise binding, (Style 28) rosette, unbound rosewood fingerboard with slotted diamond inlay, tortoise shell pickguard, black bridgepins with white dots, available in Aging Toner finish.

	N/A	$2,750	$1,750

Last MSR was $1,600.

Only 16 instruments were manufactured.

D-18V (SEPTEMBER 1985) - prewar D-18 style, tortoise binding, ebony fingerboard, tortoise shell pickguard, ebony bridge.

	N/A	$2,750	$1,750

Last MSR was $1,640.

Only 56 instruments were manufactured.

OM-28LE (OCTOBER 1985) - OM-28 style, ivoroid binding, diamonds and squares fingerboard inlay, tortoise shell pickguard under finish, available in Aging Toner finish.

	N/A	$3,000	$1,750

Last MSR was $2,180.

Only 41 instruments were sold (39 Domestic, 2 Foreign).

D-21LE (NOVEMBER 1985) - D-21 style, Indian rosewood back/sides, rosewood fingerboard, herringbone rosette, rosewood bridge, tortoise binding, tortoise shell pickguard under finish.

	N/A	$2,600	$1,550

Last MSR was $1,550.

Only 75 instruments were manufactured.

HD-28LE (DECEMBER, 1985) - HD-28 style, scalloped bracing, herringbone top purfling/ivoroid binding, diamonds and squares fingerboard inlay, square peghead, tortoise shell pickguard under finish, white bridgepins with red dots, available in Aging Toner finish.

	N/A	$4,500	$3,000

Last MSR was $2,100.

Only 87 instruments were manufactured.

J-21MC (1986) - J-21 style, cutaway body design, black binding, 9-ply rosette, tortoise shell pickguard, chrome tuners with ebony buttons.

	N/A	$2,500	$1,450

Last MSR was $1,750.

Only 56 instruments were sold (55 Domestic, 1 Foreign). This model was the first J-style with a cutaway body shape.

HD-28SE (SEPTEMBER, 1986) - HD-28 style, herringbone top purfling/ivoroid binding, diamonds and squares fingerboard inlay, tortoise shell pickguard under finish, ebony tuner buttons, available in Toned Top finish.

	N/A	$4,500	$3,000

Last MSR was $2,300.

Only 138 instruments were sold (130 Domestic, 8 Foreign). The underside of these tops are signed by C.F. Martin III, C.F. Martin IV, and company foremen.

D-62LE (OCTOBER, 1986) - D-62 style, flamed maple back/sides, tortoise binding, snowflake fingerboard inlay, tortoise shell pickguard, white bridgepins with tortoise shell dots.

	N/A	$2,250	$1,550

Last MSR was $2,100.

Only 48 instruments were sold (46 Domestic, 2 Foreign).

GRADING	100%	EXCELLENT	AVERAGE

CUSTOM J-45M DELUXE (DECEMBER, 1986) - J-45 style, Englemann or European spruce top, Indian rosewood back/sides, pearl rosette, pearl bordering/tortoise binding, pearl bound ebony fingerboard with hexagonal inlay, pearl bound tortoise pickguard, pearl hexagon outline inlay on bridge tips, gold tuners with small ebony buttons, black bridgepins with pearl dots.

	N/A	$5,500	$3,250
		Last MSR was $6,900.	

Only 17 instruments were sold (16 Domestic, 1 Foreign).

D-18LE (1986-1987, LIMITED EDITION) - D-18V style, quilted mahogany back/sides, herringbone backstrip, tortoise shell pickguard, available in Natural finish. Approx. 30 mfg. 1986-87.

	N/A	$2,000	$1,450

D-45LE (SEPTEMBER, 1987) - D-45 style, Brazilian rosewood back/sides, pearl bound fingerboard, hexagon outline fingerboard inlays, hexagon outline at bridge ends, pearl bound headstock, tortoise shell pickguard, gold tuners with ebony buttons.

	N/A	$23,500	$19,000
		Last MSR was $7,500.	

Only 50 instruments were sold (44 Domestic, 6 Foreign).

OO-21LE (SEPTEMBER, 1987) - OO-21 style, 24.9" scale, scalloped braces, herringbone rosette, tortoise binding, slotted peghead, 14-fret ebony fingerboard, tortoise shell pickguard, rectangular ebony bridge, black bridgepins with white dots, 3-per-side tuners with pearloid buttons, available in Aging Toner finish.

	N/A	$1,850	$1,200
		Last MSR was $2,350.	

Only 19 instruments were sold (18 Domestic, 1 Foreign). This model was available without the optional tortoise pickguard.

**1934 Martin D-28
courtesy Mass Street Music**

HD-18LE (OCTOBER, 1987) - D-18V style, scalloped braces, herringbone top trim/tortoise binding, tortoise pickguard, diamonds and squares inlay, ebony tuner buttons, black bridgepins with white dots, available in Aging Toner finish.

	N/A	$2,000	$1,450
		Last MSR was $2,250.	

Only 51 instruments were sold (50 Domestic, 1 Foreign).

J-40MBLE (NOVEMBER, 1987) - J-40 style, Brazilian rosewood back/sides, tortoise pickguard, snowflake fingerboard inlay, gold tuners w/large pearloid buttons, available in Aging Toner finish.

	N/A	$6,000	$4,000
		Last MSR was $3,000.	

Only 17 instruments were sold (16 Domestic, 1 Foreign).

HD-28BSE (1987) - D-28 style, Brazilian rosewood back/sides, ivoroid binding, tortoise pickguard, (Style 42) fingerboard inlay, gold tuners with ebony buttons, available in Aging Toner finish.

	N/A	$4,950	$3,000
		Last MSR was $3,300.	

Only 93 instruments were sold (88 Domestic, 5 Foreign). The underside of these tops are signed by C.F. Martin IV and company supervisors.

D-42LE (1988) - D-42 style, scalloped braces, low profile neck, white binding, small hexagonal fingerboard inlay, gold tuners with large ebony buttons, tortoise pickguard.

	N/A	$2,400	$1,550
		Last MSR was $3,300.	

Only 75 instruments were sold (69 Domestic, 6 Foreign). The underside of the top is signed by the C.F. Martin IV and company foremen.

HD-28M (1988) - HD-28 style, mahogany back/sides, scalloped braces, herringbone top purfling, diamonds and squares inlay, gold tuners with large pearloid buttons, tortoise pickguard, white bridgepins with tortoise dots, available in Aging Toner finish.

	N/A	$1,750	$1,250
		Last MSR was $2,170.	

Only 81 instruments were sold (77 Domestic, 4 Foreign).

HD-28PSE (1988) - HD-28 style, scalloped braces, low profile (P) neck, squared off peghead, herringbone top purfling/ivoroid binding, snowflake fingerboard inlay, 3-per-side chrome tuners with ebony tuner buttons, tortoise pickguard, white bridgepins with tortoise dots, available in Aging Toner finish.

	N/A	$2,250	$1,500
		Last MSR was $2,750.	

Only 96 instruments were sold (93 Domestic, 3 Foreign). The underside of the top is signed by the C.F. Martin IV and company supervisors.

**Martin D-28
courtesy Vintage Instruments**

GRADING	100%	EXCELLENT	AVERAGE

M2C-28 (1988) - MC-28 style, double cutaway design, pearl single ring rosette, gold self-locking tuners with small ebony buttons, white bridgepins with pearl dots.

N/A $2,000 $1,375
Last MSR was $2,700.

Only 22 instruments were sold (20 Domestic, 2 Foreign). This model was available without the optional pickguard, or Thinline pickup.

D-18 SPECIAL (D-18 GOM, 1989) - D-18 style, scalloped braces, low profile neck, rosewood binding, diamonds and squares fingerboard inlay, tortoise pickguard, black bridgepins with pearl dots, 3-per-side Grover tuners.

N/A $1,800 $1,200
Last MSR was $1,950.

Only 28 instruments were sold (15 Domestic, 13 Foreign).

D-41BLE (1989) - D-41 style, Engelmann spruce top, Brazilian rosewood back/sides, scalloped braces, low profile neck, pearl bound headstock, pearl bound fingerboard with hexagon inlays, gold tuners with large ebony buttons, tortoise pickguard, available in Aging Toner finish.

N/A $4,950 $3,250
Last MSR was $4,800.

Only 39 instruments were sold (31 Domestic, 8 Foreign). The underside of the top is signed by the C.F. Martin IV and company foremen.

HD-28GM GRAND MARQUIS (1989) - HD-28 style, Indian rosewood back/sides, scalloped braces, herringbone top purfling/tortoise binding, herringbone rosette, snowflake fingerboard inlay, snowflake inlay on bridge ends, "Grand Marquis" decal on back of peghead, gold tuners with embossed "M" on buttons, tortoise shell pickguard, black bridgepins with abalone dots.

N/A $3,750 $2,500
Last MSR was $3,198.

Only 120 instruments were sold (112 Domestic, 8 Foreign).

HOM-35 (1989) - OM-35 style, Brazilian rosewood sides/3-piece back, herringbone trim/top purfling, ivoroid binding top/back, ivoroid-bound ebony fingerboard with diamonds and squares inlay, gold tuners, tortoise shell OM-style pickguard, white bridgepins with red dots, Martin stamp on back of peghead, available in Aging Toner finish.

N/A $6,000 $4,250
Last MSR was $4,000.

Only 60 instruments were sold (53 Domestic, 7 Foreign).

D-18MB (1990) - D-18 style, Engelmann spruce top, "X"-bracing, flamed maple binding/backstrip/peghead veneer, white bridgepins with red dots, available in Aging Toner finish.

N/A $2,000 $1,350
Last MSR was $2,300.

Only 99 instruments were sold (96 Domestic, 3 Foreign). The underside of the top is signed by the company foremen.

D-40BLE (1990) - D-40 style, Engelmann spruce top, Brazilian rosewood back/sides, bound top/back, pearl rosette, bound ebony fingerboard with snowflake inlay, two 6-point snowflake inlay on bridge, bound peghead, engraved gold tuners with "M" buttons, tortoise pickguard, white bridgepins with pearl dots.

N/A $9,250 $5,500
Last MSR was $5,598.

Only 58 instruments were sold (50 Domestic, 8 Foreign). This model has a special label signed by C.F. Martin IV and Mike Longworth. Models came with a Mark Leaf hardshell case.

HD-28BLE (1990) - HD-28 style, Brazilian rosewood back/sides, low profile neck, herringbone top trim/ivoroid binding, herringbone rosette, ivoroid bound headstock, diamonds and squares fingerboard inlay, 3-per-side chrome tuners, tortoise pickguard, white bridgepins with red dots, available in Aging Toner finish.

N/A $5,250 $3,250
Last MSR was $3,900.

Only 108 instruments were sold (100 Domestic, 8 Foreign).

OMC-28 (1990) - OM-28 style, rounded cutaway design, scalloped bracing, oval soundhole, low profile neck, C.F. Martin in mother-of-pearl headstock inlay, gold tuners with small pearloid buttons, tortoise pickguard, white bridgepins with red dots.

N/A $2,500 $1,650
Last MSR was $3,148.

Only 76 instruments were sold (74 Domestic, 2 Foreign).

D3-18 (1991) - Vintage D-18 style, 3-piece back, white purfling, tortoise-bound ebony fingerboard with mother-of-pearl diamonds and squares inlay, diamond inlays on bridge ends, tortoise pickguard, chrome tuners with embossed "M" on buttons, black bridgepins with white dots, available in Aging Toner finish.

N/A $2,000 $1,300
Last MSR was $2,398.

Only 80 instruments were sold (72 Domestic, 8 Foreign).

GRADING	100%	EXCELLENT	AVERAGE

D-28LSH (1991) - D-28 style, Indian roswood back/sides, large soundhole (LSH) with 2 pearl soundhole rings, ivoroid binding, herringbone top trim, 22-fret fingerboard with snowflake inlay, snowflake inlay on bridge ends, tortoise pickguard, gold tuners, ebony tuner buttons with snowflake inlay, available in Aging Toner finish.

	N/A	$2,150	$1,500
		Last MSR was $4,398.	

Only 211 instruments were sold (200 Domestic, 11 Foreign). The underside of the top is signed by C.F. Martin IV and company employees. The label is signed by Les Wagner, who retired in 1991 after 47 years service with Martin guitar company.

D-45KLE (1991) - D-45 style, Engelmann spruce top, flamed koa back/sides, ivoroid binding, pearl bound Brazilian rosewood peghead veneer, snowflake fingerboard inlay, tortoise pickguard, snowflake bridge inlays, gold tuners with embossed "M" on buttons, available in Aging Toner finish.

	N/A	$7,250	$4,750
		Last MSR was $7,800.	

Only 54 instruments were sold (50 Domestic, 4 Foreign). The underside of the top is signed by company employees. This model came with a Mark Leaf hardshell case.

OM-21 SPECIAL (1991) - OM-21 style, tortoise binding, striped Macassar ebony fingerboard with mother-of-pearl diamonds and squares inlay, striped ebony bridge, herringbone rosette, tortoise-bound peghead with mother-of-pearl Martin logo inlay, gold tuners with pearloid buttons, OM-style tortoise pickguard, white bridgepins with red dots, available in Aging Toner finish.

	N/A	$1,650	$1,000
		Last MSR was $3,998.	

Only 36 instruments were sold (32 Domestic, 4 Foreign).

D-18 VINTAGE (1992) - D-18 style, scalloped braces, tortoise binding, ebony fingerboard, ebony bridge with saddle slot, tortoiseshell pickguard, 3-per-side Grover tuners black bridgepins with white dots, available in Aging Toner finish.

	N/A	$1,650	$1,100
		Last MSR was $1,998.	

Only 218 instruments were sold (215 Domestic, 3 Foreign).

Martin D-45
courtesy Greg Rich

D-45S DELUXE (1992) - D-45 style, Brazilian rosewood back/sides, calloped braces, ivoroid binding, neck joins at 12th fret, solid peghead with pearl borders, snowflake fingerboard inlay, snowflake inlay at bridge ends, pearl border on fingerboard, gold tuners with ebony buttons and pearl "M" inlay, tortoise pickguard, available in Aging Toner finish.

	N/A	$10,000	$6,250
		Last MSR was $9,760.	

Only 60 instruments were sold (50 Domestic, 10 Foreign). This modified version was based on a 1937 D-45S (12-fret version with solid peghead).

HD-28 C.T.B. (1992, CUSTOM TORTOISE BOUND) - D-28 style, tortoise binding, slotted peghead with torch pattern inlay, mother-of-pearl diamonds and squares fingerboard inlay with CFM script at 12th fret, gold tuners with embossed "M" on buttons, tortoise shell pickguard, white bridgepins with red dots, available in Aging Toner finish.

	N/A	$2,950	$2,000
		Last MSR was $3,800.	

Only 97 instruments were sold (89 Domestic, 8 Foreign).

HJ-28 (1992) - J-28 style, Indian rosewood back/sides, herringbone top purfling, ivoroid binding, unbound ebony fingerboard with diamonds and squares inlay, chrome tuners with embossed "M" on buttons, tortoiseshell pickguard, white bridgepins with red dots, available in Aging Toner finish.

	N/A	$1,850	$1,125
		Last MSR was $3,050.	

Only 69 instruments were sold (56 Domestic, 13 Foreign).

D-28 1935 SPECIAL (1993) - D-28 style (more similar to the HD-28 VR), Indian rosewood back/sides, scalloped bracing, ivoroid binding, square tapered peghead with Brazilian rosewood veneer, tortoise shell pickguard.

	$2,650	$1,900	$1,450
		Last MSR was $3,800.	

Only 237 instruments were sold (217 Domestic, 20 Foreign). This model is based on the D-28 with features available back in 1935. This model had an optional Dark Sunburst finish.

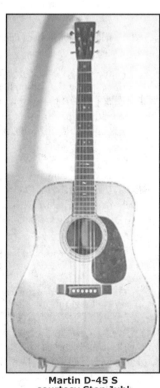

Martin D-45 S
courtesy Sten Juhl

GRADING   **100%   EXCELLENT   AVERAGE**

D-45 DELUXE (1993) - D-45 style, bear claw figured spruce top, Brazilian rosewood back/sides, ivoroid binding, bridge/pickguard inlay, highly figured pearl Tree of Life fingerboard inlay, peghead/fingerboard pearl borders, gold tuners with large gold buttons embossed with "M," fossilized ivory bridgepins with pearl dots, black pickguard, available in Aging Toner finish.

                            $22,500 $18,500 $13,000
                                    Last MSR was $18,200.

Only 60 instruments were sold (50 Domestic, 10 Foreign).

D-93 (1993) - dreadnought style, mahogany back/sides, white binding, herringbone rosette, bound Brazilian rosewood veneer peghead, bound ebony fingerboard with diamonds and squares inlay/"CFM" script inlay at 3rd fret, diamond inlay at bridge ends, gold tuners with ebony buttons, tortoise shell pickguard, white bridgepins with red dots, available in Aging Toner finish.

                            $3,000 $2,350 $1,800
                                    Last MSR was $3,000.

Only 165 instruments were sold (148 Domestic, 17 Foreign). This model commemorates Martin's 160 years of guitar building (1833 to 1993).

HD-28C LSH (1993) - HD-28 style, cutaway design, scalloped braces, herringbone top purfling, large soundhole, rosewood peghead veneer, tortoise shell pickguard, white bridgepins with red dots, built-in pickup, available in Sunburst finish.

                            $2,450 $1,850 $1,250

Production amount unknown.

OM-28 PERRY BECHTEL (1993) - OM-28 (VR) style, herringbone top trim, ivoroid binding, wood purfling in rosette, diamonds and squares fingerboard inlay, Brazilian rosewood headstock veneer, pyramid bridge, chrome tuners with embossed "M" on buttons, tortoise shell pickguard, available in Aging Toner finish.

                            $2,450 $1,650 $1,250
                                    Last MSR was $4,000.

Only 94 instruments were sold (77 Domestic, 17 Foreign). This model features a special label signed by Mrs. Ina Bechtel (Perry Bechtel's widow).

D-45 GENE AUTRY (1994) - D-45 style, scalloped braces, neck joins at 12th fret, "Gene Autry" pearl script fingerboard inlay, torch inlay on peghead, 3-per-side Waverly tuners.

                            $18,500 $14,000 $8,950
                                    Last MSR was $22,000.

Only 66 instruments were sold (50 Domestic, 16 Foreign). This model was also available with snowflake inlay and "Gene Autry" at 19th fret. The interior label is signed by Gene Autry.

HD-28GM LSH GRAND MARQUIS (1994) - HD-28 style, herringbone top purfling, tortoise binding, large soundhole with 2 herringbone soundhole rings, unbound ebony fingerboard with snowflake inlay and "Grand Marquis" in pearl script at 12th fret, "CF Martin" pearl logo inlay on peghead, snowflake inlay on bridge, tortoise pickguard, gold tuners with embossed "M" on buttons, available in Aging Toner or Shaded top finishes.

                            $3,500 $2,950 $1,975

Add 10% for Sunburst finish.

                                    Last MSR for Natural finish was $4,500.
                                    Last MSR for Sunburst finish was $4,830.

Only 151 instruments were sold (115 in Natural finish; 36 in Sunburst finish). Of the 115 in Natural finish, 106 Domestic, 9 Foreign. Of the 36 in Sunburst finish, 30 Domestic, 6 Foreign.

HJ-28M (1994) - jumbo style, mahogany back/sides, herringbone top purfling, ivoroid binding, striped Madagascar ebony fingerboard/bridge, chrome tuners with large ebony buttons and pearl "M" inlay, tortoiseshell pickguard, white bridgepins with tortoise dots, available in Aging Toner finish.

                            $3,250 $2,650 $1,800
                                    Last MSR was $3,900.

Only 72 instruments were sold (60 Domestic, 12 Foreign). This model has HD-28 (Vintage Series) features on a jumbo-style body.

OM-40LE (1994) - OM-40 style, Indian rosewood back/sides, herringbone top purfling, pearl rosette, pearl border on top, unbound ebony fingerboard with snowflake inlay, "CF Martin" pearl logo on unbound peghead, gold tuners with large ebony buttons and pearl 4-point snowflake inlays, white bridgepins with pearl dots, available in Natural and Shaded Top finishes.

                            $3,950 $2,950 $1,950

Add 10% for Sunburst finish.

                                    Last MSR for Natural finish was $7,100
                                    Last MSR for Sunburst finish was $7,430

Only 86 instruments were sold (57 in Natural finish; 29 in Sunburst finish). Of the 57 in Natural finish, 45 Domestic, 12 Foreign. Of the 29 in Sunburst finish, 20 Domestic, 9 Foreign. This model has similar features that are found on current OM (Vintage Series) models.

ACOUSTIC: CUSTOM SHOP SPECIAL/LIMITED SERIES

Martin formally opened its Custom Shop in 1979. As production for the first five years focused on one-of-a-kind custom creations, a catalog for pricing and listed options was never published! Many production runs that feature specialty woods are simply stamped "Custom" on the neck block.

Between 1983 to 1987, some of Martin's rosewood models were built using Brazilian rosewood. These guitars were initially stamped with a V (Vintage) after the model code; after 1985 the guitars were stamped with a B (Brazilian). Some "B" models do not have vintage features; some "V" models do not have Brazilian rosewood, but have vintage features.

GRADING	100%	EXCELLENT	AVERAGE

Beginning in 1995, Martin discontinued the Guitar of the Month/Year program, and introduced their Limited/Special Editions. The following models are listed in chronological sequence. For information on the D-16 Series Special (SP) Limited Editions, please refer to the subcategory located after the D (Dreadnought) Series.

The source material for Martin's older Custom Shop and Limited Edition models can be found in Jim Washburn and Richard Johnson's *Martin Guitars: An Illustrated Celebration of America's Premier Guitarmaker,* Rodale Books, 1997. Information and pricing on Martin's more recent Custom Shop production, including both Limited and Special Editions can be found in its magazine, *The Sounding Board*, published in Jan. and July. It is highly recommended that you get these informative newsletters to keep abreast on what's happening with Martin's Custom Shop and regular production.

ERIC CLAPTON SIGNATURE 000-42 EC (1995)
- solid Sitka spruce top, 24.9" scale length, ivoroid body binding/herringbone purfling, herringbone rosette, solid East Indian rosewood back/sides, mahogany neck, 14/20-fret ebony fingerboard with special abalone inlay/mother-of-pearl Eric Clapton signature inlay, snowflake inlay on bridge, 3-per-side tuners with "butterbean" buttons, available in Natural gloss and Shaded Top finishes.

	$9,250	$8,000	$4,950

Add 10%-15% for Sunburst finish.
Last MSR for Natural finish was $8,100. Last MSR was for Sunburst finish was $8,320.
Only 461 instruments were sold (433 in Natural finish; 28 in Sunburst finish).

D-18 GOLDEN ERA (1995)
- D-18 style, abalone dot pattern on neck, Brazilian rosewood peghead veneer, old style logo, available in Natural and Shaded Top (Sunburst) finishes.

	$3,000	$2,450	$1,500

Add 10% for Sunburst finish.
Last MSR for Natural finish was $3,100. Last MSR was Sunburst finish was $3,320.
Only 320 instruments were sold (272 in Natural finish; 48 in Sunburst finish). This model was based on a 1937 D-18, and in addition to late 1930s styling also has similar features that are found on the current D-18VM (Vintage Series) models.

Martin HD-28
courtesy Martin Guitar

D-35 30TH ANNIVERSARY (1995)
- D-35 style, Brazilian rosewood center wedge (3 pc. back)/peghead veneer, ivoroid binding, mitered fingerboard binding, "1965-1995" logo inlaid at 20th fret, tortoise pickguard, 3-per-side gold tuners with "M" buttons, available in Natural finish.

	$3,000	$2,450	$1,500
		Last MSR was $4,000.	

Only 207 instruments were manufactured.

HD-28 SO (1995)
- HD-28 style, ivoroid binding, 12/19-fret fingerboard with mother-of-pearl *Sing Out!* logo inlay, slotted peghead, available in Natural finish.

	$3,250	$2,650	$1,850
		Last MSR was $4,500.	

Only 45 instruments were manufactured. This model celebrates the 45th Anniversary of *Sing Out!* magazine. The inside label is signed by Pete Seeger. The HD-28 SO has similar features that are found on current HD-28VS (Vintage Series) models.

000-28 12-FRET GOLDEN ERA (1996)
- bookmatched Sitka spruce top, round soundhole, wood rosette, 2-piece East Indian rosewood back, East Indian rosewood sides, herringbone marquetry/ivoroid body binding, 12/19-fret ebony fingerboard with abalone diamonds and squares inlay, ebony pyramid bridge, 3-per-side Waverly-Sloane tuners, available in Aging Toner lacquer finish.

	$3,500	$2,800	$1,975
		Last MSR was $4,000.	

Only 367 instruments were manufactured. The edition run was limited to those guitars ordered in 1996. The pickguard was optional on this edition.

C.F. MARTIN SR. DELUXE D-45 (1996)
- Sitka spruce top, Brazilian rosewood back/sides/headstock veneer, abalone/grained ivoroid body binding, abalone rosette, bound ebony fingerboard with abalone (style 45) snowflake inlay, abalone snowflake bridge inlay, 3-per-side gold open geared tuners with "butterbean" knobs.

	$16,500	$13,750	$8,500
		Last MSR was $19,500.	

Only 91 instruments were manufactured.

C.F. Martin Sr. Commemorative D-45 (1996)
- similar to the C.F. Martin Sr. Deluxe, except features East Indian rosewood back and sides, and standard Style 45 abalone body decoration.

	$8,500	$6,750	$4,250
		Last MSR was $11,000.	

Only 114 instruments were manufactured. This model commemorates the 200 years since the birth of company founded C.F. Martin, Sr. (1796).

Martin D-18
Blue Book Publications

M

GRADING	100%	EXCELLENT	AVERAGE

MARTY STUART HD-40MS (1996) - solid Sitka spruce top, round soundhole, pearl rosette, East Indian rosewood back/sides, grained ivoroid body/fingerboard/headstock binding, 103-piece pearl/abalone/recomposite stone fingerboard inlay (steer horns, horseshoes, dice, hearts, and flowers), 3-per-side gold open geared tuners with "butterbean" knobs.

	$3,950	$3,250	$2,250

Last MSR was $5,400.

Only 250 instruments were manufactured.

MTV 1 "MTV UNPLUGGED" DREADNOUGHT (1996) - solid Sitka spruce top, round soundhole, pearl rosette, East Indian rosewood bass (or top) side of guitar, mahogany treble (or lower) side of body, mahogany neck, 14/20-fret ebony fingerboard with paua shell "Unplugged" inlay, "MTV" pearl headstock inlay, ebony bridge, available in Natural Gloss or Natural Satin finishes.

	$1,995	$1,550	$900

Add 10% for Gloss finish.

Last MSR for Satin finish was $2,200.
Last MSR for Gloss finish was $2,450.

Only 697 instruments were manufactured.

MTV 2/MTV 2G "MTV UNPLUGGED" - 000 body size, solid Sitka spruce top, features unusual split back with flame maple on one side and solid Inadian rosewood on the other, "Unplugged" in single letters inlaid in blue paua on ebony fingerboard, clear pickguard, Satin or optional Gloss Lacquer finish, includes Thinline 332 electronics. New 2003.

MSR	$2,749		$1,925	$1,425	$1,150

Add $250 for gloss finish (MTV 2G.)
200 models are scheduled for production in both versions.

00-45 ST STAUFFER LIMITED EDITION (1997) - Brazilian rosewood top/back/sides, abalone rosette/body binding, "ice cream cone" shaped neck heel, grained ivoroid bindings, Stauffer-style curved headstock, belly bridge with pyramid wings, black ebonized neck finish, Martin mother-of-pearl headstock inlay.

	$25,000	$18,500	$11,750

Last MSR was $20,000.

Only 25 instruments were manufactured.

00-40 ST Stauffer Limited Edition (1997) - similar to the 00-45, except features East Indian rosewood back and sides.

	$6,000	$5,000	$3,500

Last MSR was $7,900.

Only 75 instruments were manufactured.

JIMMIE RODGERS 000-45 JR "BLUE YODEL" (1997) - bookmatched Adirondack spruce top, round soundhole, Brazilian rosewood back/sides, (style 45) pearl body inlay/ivoroid body binding, 12/19-fret bound ebony fingerboard with pearl "Jimmy Rodgers" inlay, pearl "Blue Yodel" peghead inlay, slotted headstock, snowflake inlay on bridge tips.

	$17,500	$13,000	$8,250

Last MSR was $25,000.

Only 100 instruments were manufactured. This model is the replica of Jimmie Rodgers' 1928 000-45. The limited editions are available with the optional "THANKS" printing on back.

ARLO GUTHRIE 0000-28H AG (1997) - M-38 style, Sitka spruce top, round soundhole, 3-piece abalone pearl rosette, East Indian rosewood back/sides, mahogany neck, herringbone body trim/ivoroid binding, ebony fingerboard with circles and arrows/ "Alice's Restaurant 30th"/Arlo Guthrie signature inlay, Martin raised gold logo/engraved pearl representation of Alice's restaurant peghead inlay.

	$4,150	$3,650	$2,725

Last MSR was $4,750.

Only 30 instruments were manufactured. This model comes with a denim covered hardshell case.

Arlo Guthrie 000012-28H AG (1997) - similar to the Arlo Guthrie 0000-28H, except in a 12-string configuration, 6-per-side tuners. Available in Natural finish.

	$3,995	$3,500	$2,600

Last MSR was $4,950.

Only 30 instruments were manufactured. This model comes with a denim covered hardshell case.

PAUL SIMON OM-42 PS (1997) - solid Sitka spruce top, round soundhole, tortoise body binding, East Indian rosewood back/sides, 25.4" scale, 14/20-fret tortoise bound ebony fingerboard with (style 42) abalone pearl snowflake inlay/mother-of-pearl Paul Simon signature inlay, OM-style pickguard, snowflake inlay on bridge, nickel Waverly open geared tuners with ivoroid buttons.

	$5,500	$4,650	$3,300

Last MSR was $8,000.

Only 500 instruments were manufactured. The interior label of the instruments is signed by both Paul Simon and C.F. Martin IV.

M

GRADING	100%	EXCELLENT	AVERAGE

CEO'S CHOICE LIMITED EDITION (CEO-1) (1997) - SP D-16T style, spruce top, round soundhole, abalone rosette, herringbone top trim, solid mahogany back/sides, ebony fingerboard with "hexagon outline"/mother-of-pearl C.F. Martin IV signature inlays, hexagon outline on bridge, tortoise pickguard, 3-per-side gold tuners with ebony buttons.

	$2,150	$1,850	$1,000

Last MSR was $2,600.

Only 128 instruments were manufactured. Model design and appointments were chosen by CEO and Chairman of the Board, C.F. Martin IV. This model comes with an interior label signed by C.F. Martin IV, and a vintage "tweed" case.

CEO-1 R Limited Edition (1997) - similar to the CEO's Choice, except features solid East Indian rosewood back/sides.

	$2,400	$2,000	$1,250

Last MSR was $2,800.

Only 191 instruments were manufactured.

JOHNNY CASH SIGNATURE D-42 JC (1997) - D-42 style, spruce top, round soundhole, pearl border/ivoroid body binding, 3-piece East Indian rosewood back, East Indian rosewood sides, 14/20-fret bound ebony fingerboard with abalone star inlay/Johnny Cash signature pearl inlay, abalone rosette, 3-per-side vintage-style tuners, available in Gloss Black lacquer finish.

	$6,250	$5,000	$3,250

Last MSR was $8,200.

Only 200 instruments were manufactured. This model is the first limited edition model to be finished in Black.

KINGSTON TRIO SET: D-28, 0-18T, VEGA BANJO (1997) - All three models feature special mother-of-pearl "The Kingston Trio"/1957 - 1997 fingerboard inlay. The special D-28 model features a solid spruce top, East Indian back and sides, ebony fingerboard and bridge, and a Brazilian rosewood peghead veneer. The 0-18T tenor features a similar solid spruce top, ebony fingerboard and bridge, and mahogany back and sides.

	$8,500	$6,750	$5,000

Last MSR was $12,500.

Martin Jimmie Rodgers
000-45 Jr "Blue Yodel"
courtesy Martin Guitar

There are 40 limited edition sets were manufactured. In 1997, Martin noted that "Additional Kingston Trio D-28 models (D-28KT) will be offered after the limited edition sets are ordered." However, these models were not issued, nor were any additional prototypes constructed.

00-16DB (1997, WOMEN AND MUSIC SERIES) - 00 style body with extra deep mahogany sides, spruce top, black binding, round soundhole, classical-style wood mosaic rosette, OM-style black pickguard, mahogany back, 14/19-fret ebony fretboard with diamonds and squares inlay, slotted peghead, 3-per-side tuners, available in Natural finish, mfg. 1997 only.

	$1,950	$1,575	$850

Last MSR was $2,100.

Only 97 instruments were manufactured. In 1997, the Martin Guitar company specifically designed a guitar model for women. Martin's own Women and Music Program was responsible for initiating the first limited edition model.

00-16BR (1998, WOMEN AND MUSIC SERIES) - spruce top, black binding, round soundhole, mosaic soundhole rosette, solid Brazilian rosewood sides, 25 1/2" scale, ebony fingerboard with pearl diamonds and squares inlay, slotted peghead, 3-per-side Waverly tuners, available in Natural finish, mfg. 1998 only.

	$4,000	$3,250	$2,400

Last MSR was $2,400.

In 1997, the Martin Guitar company specifically designed a guitar model for women. Martin's own Women and Music Program was responsible for initiating the first limited edition model.

JOAN BAEZ SIGNATURE 0-45 JB (1998, WOMEN AND MUSIC SERIES) - 0-45 style, Sitka spruce top, abalone pearl rosette, abalone pearl/grained ivoroid binding, East Indian rosewood back/sides, 2-piece back, ebony fingerboard with style 45 abalone snowflake inlay.

	N/A	N/A	$2,750

Last MSR was $9,850.

Only 59 instruments were manufactured. This model is the first "Woman and Music" program Artist's Signature edition.

00-21GE GOLDEN ERA (1998) - 00-21 style, 12/19-fret fingerboard, slotted peghead.

	$2,795	$2,200	$1,450

Last MSR was $3,950.

Martin CEO-1
courtesy Martin Guitar

GRADING	100%	EXCELLENT	AVERAGE

OM-45GE GOLDEN ERA (1998) - OM-45 style, Adirondack spruce top, Brazilian rosewood back/sides, tortoise teardrop-shaped pickguard with abalone inlay, 3-per-side banjo tuners with mother-of-pearl buttons.

	N/A	$25,000	$18,500

Last MSR was $27,500.

Only 14 instruments were manufactured. This model is a reproduction of the 1930 OM-45 (only 14 were originally made).

HANK WILLIAMS SR. COMMEMORATIVE D-28 HW (1998) - D-28 style, bookmatched spruce top, grained ivoroid binding, mahogany neck, 2-piece Brazilian rosewood back, ebony fingerboard with diamonds and squares inlay, available in Natural finish.

	N/A	$6,750	$3,750

Last MSR was $9,000.

Only 150 instruments were manufactured.

LESTER FLATT D-28 LF (1998) - D-28 style, grained ivoroid body binding, Brazilian rosewood back/sides, ebony fingerboard with special Mike Longworth custom inlay reproduction, ebony bridge, enlarged tortoise pickguard.

	$7,500	$6,250	$4,300

Last MSR was $8,500.

Only 50 instruments were manufactured. Interior label in signed by C.F. Martin IV. Model includes a Geib Vintage Style deluxe hardshell case.

DON MCLEAN D-40 DM (1998) - D-40 style, Engelmann spruce top, abalone pearl rosette, East Indian rosewood back/sides, mahogany neck, ebony fingerboard with custom hexagon inlay, bound ebony headplate, white body binding, tortoise pickguard, available in Aging Toner finish, mfg. 1998-2000.

	$3,995	$3,250	$2,150

Last MSR was $5,750.

Only 71 instruments were manufactured. The interior label is signed by Don McLean and C.F. Martin IV, and features McLean's hand colored Thumb's Up logo.

STEPHEN STILLS D-45 SS (1998) - D-45 style, European Alpine spruce top, abalone pearl top/rosette/back/sides/endpiece/neck joint binding, pre-CITES Brazilian rosewood back and sides, tortoise pickguard with abalone Southern Cross 5 star inlay.

	$17,500	$13,000	$7,500

Last MSR was $19,000.

Only 91 instruments were manufactured. The interior label is signed by Stephen Stills and C.F. Martin IV.

JIMMY BUFFET SIGNATURE HD-18 JB (1998) - vintage D-28 appointments, bookmatched spruce top, grained ivoroid binding, abalone rosette, selected mahogany back/sides, Palm Tree headstock inlay, tortoise pickguard.

	N/A	$3,750	$2,600

Last MSR was $3,650.

Only 424 instruments were manufactured. The interior label is signed by both Jimmy Buffet and C.F. Martin IV.

WILLIE NELSON N-20 WN (1998) - N-20 style, Sitka spruce top, 25.4" scale, ebony fingerboard, square (non-tapered) slotted headstock, 3-per-side Walverly Sloane tuners, Fishman transducer, available in Aging Toner finish, mfg. 1998-99.

	$4,125	$3,500	$2,400

Last MSR was $5,500.

Only 100 total instruments were manufactured, between the N-20 WN and N-20 WN B. This model is a reproduction of Nelson's guitar, nicknamed "Trigger." The interior label is signed by Willie Nelson and C.F. Martin IV. This model was equipped with a Geib Deluxe hardshell case.

Willie Nelson N-20 WN B (1998) - similar to the Willie Nelson N-20 WN, except features Brazilian rosewood back/sides, mfg. 1998-99.

	N/A	$8,750	$4,950

Last MSR was $9,800.

Only 30 of the 100 total instruments were manufactured with Brazilian rosewood back and sides.

STING CLASSICAL SIGNATURE CMSH (1998) - Martin/Humphrey classical style, Western red cedar top, solid quilted mahogany back/sides, tortoise body binding, mahogany neck, ebony fingerboard with inset abalone pearl bordering, Martin/Fishman Thinline Goldplus system, available in Aging Toner finish.

	$3,150	$2,650	$1,850

Last MSR was $4,450.

Only 250 instruments were manufactured.

CEO'S CHOICE CEO-2 (1998) - abalone pearl rosette, black body binding, laminated Macassar striped ebony back/sides, ebony fingerboard, with hollow hexagon inlay, ebony bridge with hollow hexagon inlay, 3-per-side gold enclosed tuners with ebony buttons, tortoise pickguard.

	$2,175	$1,750	$1,200

Last MSR was $2,900.

The interior label is signed by C.F. Martin IV.

GRADING	100%	EXCELLENT	AVERAGE

EMPLOYEE MODEL EMP-1 (1998) - 000 style, single rounded cutaway body, wooden rosette, solid ovankol 3-piece back with rosewood center wedge, solid ovankol sides, abalone pearl peghead logo, available in Natural finish.

	$1,995	$1,625	$1,100

Last MSR was $2,450.

Only 262 instruments were manufactured.

CONCEPT J CUTAWAY (1998) - solid spruce top, solid maple back/sides, abalone rosette, unbound body edges, ebony fingerboard with hollow hexagon inlay, ebony bridge with hollow hexagon inlay, active electronics, available in "Holographic" finish (made with suspended metallic particles), mfg. 1998-99.

	$3,075	$2,050	$1,500

Last MSR was $4,100.

CERTIFIED WOOD SWD (1998, SPECIAL EDITION) - cherry back/sides/neck (and interior blocks), katalox fingerboard and bridge, basswood interior lining, available in Natural finish, mfg. 1998-2000.

	$1,050	$700	$500

Last MSR was $1,399.

This instrument featured construction of woods certified by the Rainforest Alliance's "SmartWood" plan.

CERTIFIED SWD RED BIRCH (2003, SPECIAL EDITION) - SWD red birch, solid Sitka rescued spruce, Old Style 18 rosette, certified solid red birch back and sides, certified cherry neck, 14/20-fret certified Katalox fingerboard, polish gloss, Autumn Maple Toner finish, new 2003.

MSR	$1,749	$1,225	$875	$675

**Martin SWD Red Birch
courtesy Martin Guitar**

DAVE MATTHEWS SIGNATURE DM3MD (1999) - Engelmann spruce top, solid East Indian rosewood back/sides with African padauk center wedge, abalone rosette, unusual 3-piece headstock utilizing rosewood and padauk, distinctive antique half-herringbone wood binding bordered in red and grained ivoroid, high gloss finish, ebony fingerboard, Dave Matthews signature inlaid in pearl between 19th & 20th fret, mfg. 1999 only.

	$2,450	$1,625	$1,200

Last MSR was $3,250.

Only 262 instruments were manufactured.

EMPLOYEE MODEL EMP-2 (1999) - 000 style, single rounded cutaway body, arrow pattern rosette featuring turquoise inlays, sides/back are certified Tzalam SmartWood, abalone pearl peghead logo, flying saucer paua shell inlays, available in Natural finish, mfg. 1999 only.

	$2,025	$1,350	$975

Last MSR was $2,700.

CEO'S CHOICE CEO-3 (1999) - features hollow hexagon fingerboard and bridge inlays, unique gold top, and veneered Brazilian rosewood back/sides, mfg. 1999-2000.

	$2,625	$1,750	$1,300

Last MSR was $3,500.

150 were manufactured. The interior label is signed by C.F. Martin IV.

ROGER MCGUINN D12-42RM (1999) - 12-string, 14-fret dreadnought, bookmatched Sitka spruce top, abalone pearl rosette, solid Indian rosewood back/sides, mahogany neck with ebony fingerboard, ivoroid binding, Roger McGuinn's signature pearl inlaid between 19th & 20th frets, mfg. 1999 only.

	$5,175	$3,450	$2,500

Last MSR was $6,900.

D18-GE GOLDEN ERA (1999, SPECIAL EDITION) - replica of circa 1934 D-18, with Adirondack red spruce top and interior bracing, new 1999.

MSR	$3,729	$2,595	$1,895	$1,350

ANDY GRIFFITH D18 (2003, SPECIAL EDITION) - bearclaw Sitka spruce top, solid quilted mahogany back/sides, mahogany neck, 14/20-fret solid Brazilian rosewood fingerboard and bridge, Andy Griffith signature inlaid between 19th and 20th frets, "Lonesome Rhodes" laser etched on front block, polished gloss, dark mahogany stain with aging toner, signed and numbered by CFM IV and Andy Griffith. New 2003.

MSR	$3,699	$2,575	$1,875	$1,325

D28-GE GOLDEN ERA (1999, SPECIAL EDITION) - replica of pre-war D-28 herringbone, Adirondack red spruce top, pre-CITES certified Brazilian rosewood back/sides, with adjustable truss rod, new 1999.

MSR	$9,529	$6,675	$4,800	$3,225

**Martin Andy Griffith D18
courtesy Martin Guitar**

GRADING	100%	EXCELLENT	AVERAGE

D-35 ERNEST TUBB (2003, LIMITED EDITION) - solid Italian Alpine spruce, solid East Indian rosewood three piece back with Brazilian rosewood center wedge, solid East Indian rosewood sides, mahogany neck, longhorn cattle skull inlaid in headstock, 14/20-fret ebony fingerboard with State of Texas silhouette at 5th fret, Style 42 at 7th, Lone Star at 9th, Style 42 Pearl at 12th & 15th, Style 45 rosette, polished gloss top with Vintage toner, Fishman Gold Plus Natural II electronics, signed by CFM IV and Talmadge Tubb, new 2003.

	MSR	$4,499		$3,150	$2,300	$1,675

90 instruments are scheduled to be produced.

D-37W LUCINDA WILLIAMS (2003, LIMITED EDITION) - solid Engelmann spruce top, solid flamed claro walnut back/sides, mahogany neck, 14/20-fret ebony fingerboard, Style 45 rosette, Aztec two-headed multi-color serpent inlaid on headstock, polished gloss top with Vintage Sunburst finish, signed by Lucinda Williams and CFM IV, new 2003.

	MSR	$4,999		$3,500	$2,650	$1,850

OM-28 GOLDEN ERA (2003, SPECIAL EDITION) - 000 body, solid Adirondack spruce top, solid Brazilian rosewood back/sides, mahogany neck, 14/20-fret solid ebony fingerboard, 1930s style belly bridge, ivroid binding, herringbone neck inlays, polished gloss top, aging toner, new 2003.

	MSR	$9,529		$6,675	$4,800	$3,250

STEVE HOWE 00-18 SH (1999) - Englemann spruce top, solid mahogany back/sides, old style rosette, tortoise colored bindings and pickguard, unbound ebony fingerboard with vintage abalone position dots, nickel plated Kluson "oil-hole" tuners, tinted "vintage toner" soundboard, mfg. 1999-2000.

	$2,075	$1,500	$1,250
		Last MSR was $2,950.	

Only 250 instruments were manufactured.

WOODY GUTHRIE 000-18 WG (1999, SPECIAL EDITION) - 000 style, 14-fret, spruce top, bookmatched mahogany back/sides, vintage style rosette, V-shaped mahogany neck, tapered headstock, old style Martin decal logo, mfg. 1999-2000.

	$2,375	$1,575	$1,300
		Last MSR was $3,150.	

MARTIN CARTHY 000-18 MC (2003, SPECIAL EDITION) - 000 style body, features zero fret, ebony fingerboard, solid Sitka spruce top, signed by CFM IV and Martin Carthy, new 2003.

	MSR	$3,199		$2,250	$1,650	$1,375

88 instruments were manufactured.

GRAHAM NASH 000-40Q2GN (2003, SPECIAL EDITION) - 000 style body, features quilted mahogany top/back/sides, herringbone top binding with style 45 paua shell inlaid rosette, headstock has red heart with mother-of-pearl wings, ebony fingerboard and bridge, signed by Graham Nash and CFM IV, gloss finish, includes Geib style hardshell case, new 2003.

	MSR	$4,699		$3,500	$2,650	$1,950

147 instruments were manufactured.

JIMMY BUFFETT 000-JBP/000-JBS (2003, SPECIAL EDITION) - 000 style body, features solid Sitka spruce (000-JBP Pollywog) or mahogany (000-JBS Shellback) top, solid mahogany back/sides/neck with 12/20-fret ebony fingerboard and bridge, Jimmy Buffet signature inlaid between 19th and 20th frets, special headstock inlay featuring round ship's porthole with palm tree on inside, signed by Jimmy Buffett and CFM IV, new 2003.

	MSR	$3,699		$2,575	$1,875	$1,500

CONCEPT II (1999, SPECIAL EDITION) - 000 style with cutaway, spruce top, curly maple back/sides, features contiguous holographic opalescent gloss lacquer finish, on-board EQ or Gold+Plus electronics, mfg. 1999-2000.

	$2,750	$2,100	$1,500
		Last MSR was $4,199.	

CONCEPT III (2003, SPECIAL EDITION) - 000 style with cutaway, features solid Sitka spruce top with single blue paua/pearl rosette, curly red maple sides/back and two piece neck, 14/20-fret black micarta fingerboard, bindingless body, special high gloss gold flake pigment finish. New 2003.

	MSR	$3,299		$2,300	$1,700	$1,275

SWB (1999, SPECIAL EDITION) - 4-string bass, bookmatched solid Sitka spruce top, certified cherry back/sides/neck, katalox fingerboard and bridge, Gold+Plus active pickup, Sting signature pearl inlaid above last fret, mfg. 1999-2000.

	$2,095	$1,600	$1,200
		Last MSR was $2,950.	

SWC (1999) - 6-string, 12-fret classical, solid Sitka spruce top, features patented Humphrey elevated fingerboard design and classical body shape, certified Machiche back/sides, certified cherry neck, katalox fingerboard and bridge, Gold+Plus active pickup, mfg. 1999-2000.

	$2,275	$1,750	$1,325
		Last MSR was $3,500.	

GRADING	100%	EXCELLENT	AVERAGE

EMPLOYEE MODEL EMP-NS (2000) - features dreadnought style body, solid spruce top and solid flamed maple back/sides, ebony fingerboard and bridge, abalone pearl rosette, gloss transparent black body finish, mfg. 2000.

	$1,500	$1,150	$800

Last MSR was $2,299.

Only 199 instruments were produced.

JIM CROCE D-21JC (2000) - dreadnought body with solid Sitka spruce top and solid Indian rosewood back/sides, 2-piece back, gloss body finish, style 18 rosette, mfg. 2000 only.

	$2,250	$1,725	$1,300

Last MSR was $3,450.

Only 73 instruments were manufactured.

JIM CROCE D-21JCB (2000) - dreadnought body with solid Sitka spruce top and solid Brazilian rosewood back/sides, 2-piece back, gloss body finish, style 18 rosette, features unique dime inlaid in 3rd fret, mfg. 2000.

	$7,500	$6,250	$3,750

Last MSR was $8,745.

Only 73 instruments were manufactured.

GRAND OLE OPRY HD0 (2000) - dreadnought body with solid Sitka spruce top with solid Indian rosewood back/sides, WSM Grand Ole Opry 1925-2000 inlaid in cream Micarta pickboard. Mfg. 2000-mid. 2003.

	$2,345	$1,700	$1,300

Last MSR was $3,350.

Only 650 instruments were manufactured.

GEORGE NAKASHIMA NWD (2000) - dreadnought body with solid Italian alpine spruce top and claro walnut back/sides, ebony fingerboard and bridge, back panels are joined with dovetailed butterflies, abalone/pearl rosette, mfg. 2000.

	$3,100	$2,375	$1,850

Last MSR was $4,750.

Only 100 instruments were manufactured.

JONNY LANG JLJCR (2000) - jumbo cutaway body, solid Sitka spruce top with laminated Indian rosewood back/sides, one piece back, double black rosette with white center rings, onboard electronics, Jonny Lang signature between 17th & 20th fret, mfg. 2000.

	$1,800	$1,375	$975

Last MSR was $2,750.

Only 111 instruments were produced.

BABYFACE 000C-16RV (2000) - 000 body with cutaway, solid alpine spruce top, with solid Indian rosewood back/sides, abalone/pearl rosette, 2-piece back, zig zag (HD) back inlay, gloss body finish, mfg. 2000.

	$2,000	$1,500	$995

Last MSR was $2,850.

Only 100 instruments were produced.

ERIC CLAPTON 000-42ECB (2000) - 000 body with solid Engelmann spruce top, solid Brazilian rosewood back/sides, 2-piece back, style 45 abalone/pearl rosette, signed by Eric Clapton & C.F. Martin IV, mfg. 2000.

	$15,000	$13,500	$8,250

Last MSR was $15,000.

Only 200 instruments were produced.

00-17SO SINGOUT (2000) - 00 grand concert body, solid mahogany top/back/sides, 2-piece back, single ring rosette (old style), ebony pickguard/bridge, mfg. 2000.

	$1,575	$1,200	$825

Last MSR was $2,399.

Only 50 instruments were produced.

SWOM CERTIFIED WOOD (2000, SPECIAL EDITION) - OM style body, solid spruce (reclaimed pulpwood) top with certified cherry back/sides, 2-piece back, certified Katalox fingerboard and bridge, A frame X bracing, mfg. 2000 only.

	$950	$725	$500

Last MSR was $1,450.

**Martin D-35 Ernest Tubb
courtesy Martin Guitar**

**Martin Jimmy Buffett 00-JBP
courtesy Martin Guitar**

M

GRADING		100%	EXCELLENT	AVERAGE

COWBOY X (2000) - 000 body with Robert Armstrong HPL photo laminate cowboy night/campfire scene on top, high pressure laminate top/sides, black Micarta fingerboard and bridge, introduced at summer NAMM, July 2000, mfg. 2000 only.

		$995	$795	$550

Last MSR was $999.

COWBOY II (2001) - 000 body with Robert Armstrong HPL photo laminate cowboy morning chuckwagon scene on top, high pressure laminate top/sides, black Micarta fingerboard and bridge, mfg. 2001.

		$650	$450	$350

Last MSR was $999.

Only 500 instruments were produced.

COWBOY III (2002) - 000 body with Robert Armstrong HPL photo laminate cowboy corral scene on top, 750 mfg. 2002 only.

		$550	$400	$325

Last MSR was $1,099.

COWBOY IV (2003) - 000 body with Robert Armstrong HPL photo laminate cowboy scene featuring CFM IV with cattle brand branding a Cowboy IV guitar on top, cattle brand on back, 250 mfg. beginning 2003.

MSR	$1,199	$795	$450	$325

CEO-IV (2001, SPECIAL EDITION) - dreadnought body with sloped shoulder, solid Adirondack spruce top with solid mahogany back/sides, black Micarta 14/20-fret fingerboard and bridge with white Boltaron binding, black pickguard, single black & white rosette band, polished lacquer with Dark Sunburst finish, new 2001.

MSR	$2,500	$1,750	$1,300	$875

CLARENCE WHITE D-18CW (2001) - dreadnought body with solid Adirondack spruce top, solid quilted mahogany back/sides, ebony fingerboard and bridge, single abalone/pearl rosette, old style D-18 tortoise pickguard, Clarence White signature on 19th fret, electronics optional, mfg. 2001.

		$2,600	$2,000	$1,650

Last MSR was $3,999.

Only 292 instruments were produced.

KEB' MO' HD-28KM (2001) - dreadnought body with solid Englemann spruce top and Hawaiian flamed koa back/sides, ebony fingerboard and bridge, 3-piece abalone pearl rosette, Gloss Lacquer body finish, mfg. 2001.

		$2,950	$2,250	$1,750

Last MSR was $3,999.

Only 250 instruments were produced.

SWDGT CERTIFIED WOOD (2001, SPECIAL EDITION) - similar to SWD (1st Certified Wood Special Edition), except has D-1 style bracing and ivoroid and black back inlays, Gloss Top finish, new 2001.

MSR	$1,550	$1,075	$795	$600

SWOMGT CERTIFIED WOOD (2001, SPECIAL EDITION) - similar to SWOM, except has gloss top, new 2001.

MSR	$1,550	$1,075	$795	$600

ALTERNATIVE X (2001, SPECIAL EDITION) - 00 (grand concert) thin body with cutaway, solid aluminum top with gray & white grafitti patterns, jet black HPL back/sides with no finish, black Micarta 14/20-fret fingerboard and bridge, 25.4 in. scale, includes Fishman Prefix Pro electronics, new 2001.

MSR	$1,199	$840	$650	$475

00-16DBFM (2001, SPECIAL EDITION) - 00 (grand concert) deep body with solid Sitka spruce top and flamed maple back/sides, ebony fingerboard and bridge, mahogany body binding, Women & Music wooden mosaic rosette, black OM teardrop pickguard, slotted headstock, Gloss body finish, new 2001.

MSR	$2,839	$2,050	$1,500	$1,025

KENNY WAYNE SHEPARD JC-16KWS (2001) - jumbo cutaway body, solid Sitka spruce blue top with solid Sapele black back/sides, 3-piece rosette with blue fiber inlays, gloss lacquer with translucent blue toner top, includes Martin Thinline Gold Plus+ onboard electronics, mfg. 2001.

		$2,075	$1,600	$1,200

Last MSR was $3,179.

Only 198 instruments were produced.

ELIZABETH COTTEN 0018-CTN (2001) - 00 body (grand concert) with solid Sitka spruce top and mahogany back/sides, ebony fingerboard and bridge, old style 18 rosette, old style tortoise color pickguard, scalloped bacing with 1/4 in. braces, 2-piece back, Gloss body finish, signed by Larry Ellis, Sr. (her grandson) and C.F. Martin IV, electronics optional, mfg. 2001.

		$2,300	$1,750	$1,250

Last MSR was $3,299.

Only 76 instruments were produced.

GRADING	100%	EXCELLENT	AVERAGE

MERLE HAGGARD 000C-28SMH (2001) - 000 body (auditorium) with cutaway, solid Sitka spruce top with solid Indian rosewood back/sides, ebony fingerboard and bridge with Merle Haggard signature on lower fretboard, slotted headstock with "Blue Yodel" inlay, style 45 abalone/pearl (3-piece) rosette, Gloss Lacquer finish, electronics optional, mfg. 2001.

	$3,125	$2,400	$1,850
		Last MSR was $4,799.	

Only 122 instruments were produced.

NAMM 100TH ANNIVESARY SPNAMM100 (2001) - 000 body (auditorium) with cutaway, solid Sitka spruce top with solid mahogany back/sides, striped ebony fingerboard with snowflake inlays, 45 style rosette, polished gloss lacquer with 35 style sunburst top, tortoise pickguard, includes onboard Fishman blender electronics, mfg. 2001.

	$1,950	$1,350	$925
		Last MSR was $2,499.	

Only 100 instruments were manufactured.

D-45GE GOLDEN ERA (2001, SPECIAL EDITION) - dreadnought body, D-45 features select Adirondack spruce top, solid Brazilian rosewood (D-4 grade) back/sides, ebony fingerboard and bridge, style 45 heart abalone/pearl rosette and vintage pickguard, 2-piece back, polished lacquer finish, new 2001.

MSR	$18,500	$12,950	$9,650	$6,500

OM45GE GOLDEN ERA (2001, SPECIAL EDITION) - OM body, similar to D-45GE, except has style 45 high color pearl rosette with maple and black fiber inlays, new 2001.

MSR	$18,500	$12,950	$9,650	$6,500

D-50 DELUXE (2001) - dreadnought body, most elaborate custom shop Martin ever produced, C.I.T.I.E.S. certified Brazilian select rosewood back/sides, with extensive abalone and pearl inlays on fretboard, headstock, pickguard, bridge, sides, and back, tree of life inlay, engraved gold butterbean tuners, special leather hardshell case with onboard humidity/temparture gauge, signed by C.F. Martin IV, mfg. 2001.

	$37,500	$25,000	$19,500
		Last MSR was $50,000.	

**Martin D-45GE Golden Era
courtesy Martin Guitar**

Only 50 instruments were produced.

D-50 KOA DELUXE (2003, LIMITED EDITION) - similar to D-50 Deluxe, except has solid Sitka spruce top with heavy bearclaw, solid highly flamed koa back/sides, mahogany neck, 14/19-fret ebony fingerboard, tree of life inlay on headstock/pickguard/fingerboard/bridge, herringbone pearl bordered by heart pearl back binding, polished gloss top with aging toner, label signed by CFM IV, new 2003.

MSR	$45,000	$33,750	$21,000	$17,000

Only 50 instruments are scheduled to be produced.

BECK D-16BH (2001, LIMITED EDITION) - dreadnought body with shallow 000 depth, solid Sitka spruce top with rosewood two piece back/sides, 14/20 African ebony fingerboard, Style 45 green abalone/pearl rosette, polished gloss finish with vintage toner on top, includes Fishman Gold Plus II Natural System, mfg. 2001 only.

	$1,975	$1,450	$1,000
		Last MSR was $2,950.	

Only 99 instruments were produced.

DAN FOGELBERG D-41DF (2001, LIMITED EDITION) - dreadnought body style with solid Sitka spruce top and Indian rosewood two piece back/sides, block inlays in black African ebony fingerboard, non-scalloped bracing, ivoroid bound fingerboard and binding, black pickguard, Polished Gloss finish with aging toner on top, mfg. 2001 only.

	$3,450	$2,600	$1,875
		Last MSR was $4,750.	

Only 141 instruments were produced.

MARK KNOPFLER HD-40MK (2001, LIMITED EDITION) - dreadnought body with solid Alpine spruce top and Indian rosewood two piece back/sides, special diamond shaped rosette, ivoroid bound fingerboard and binding, mfg. 2001 only.

	$3,350	$2,525	$1,925
		Last MSR was $4,999.	

Only 251 instruments were produced.

**Martin D-50 Koa Deluxe
courtesy Martin Guitar**

GRADING	100%	EXCELLENT	AVERAGE

PETER ROWAN 000-40 SPR (2001, LIMITED EDITION) - 000 body with Sitka spruce top and mahogany two piece back/sides, scalloped bracing with tone bars, tortoise color pickguard and binding, Style 45 blue paua shell rosette, slotted headstock, Polished Gloss finish with aging toner on top, disc. 2001.

		$3,150	**$2,525**	**$1,925**

Last MSR was $4,999.

Only 87 instruments were produced.

CEO-4R (2002, SPECIAL EDITION) - similar to CEO-IV, except has solid East Indian rosewood back and sides and gold color frets, new 2002.

MSR	$2,699	**$1,895**	**$1,400**	**$975**

CEO-5 (2002, SPECIAL EDITION) - dreadnought body, solid Sitka spruce top with solid sapele back/sides, 12/20-fret ebony fingerboard with gold color frets, herringbone pearl rosette, hybrid scalloped bracing, grained ivoroid binding, Polished Gloss with aging toner on top, new summer 2002.

MSR	$2,649	**$1,850**	**$1,375**	**$925**

ALTERNATIVE II 000C (2002, SPECIAL EDITION) - similar to Alternative X, except has 000C cutaway body, new 2002.

MSR	$1,199	**$840**	**$625**	**$475**

ALTERNATIVE II RESONATOR (2003, SPECIAL EDITION) - similar to Alternative II, except is resonator, new 2003.

MSR	$1,399	**$975**	**$725**	**$550**

ALTERNATIVE III DC (2002, SPECIAL EDITION) - similar to Alternative II, except has dreadought cutaway body, new 2002.

MSR	$1,199	**$840**	**$625**	**$475**

DVM VETERAN'S MODEL (2002, SPECIAL EDITION) - dreadnought body with solid Sitka spruce top, East Indian rosewood back/sides, 14/20-fret ebony fingerboard and bridge, headstock includes the 5 Armed Forces emblems, triple ring rosette, polished gloss finish with aging toner on top, supplied with 2 genuine steel dog tags with serial number, new 2002.

MSR	$3,199	**$2,225**	**$1,650**	**$1,250**

NED STEINBERGER DCRNS (2002, LIMITED EDITION) - dreadnought cutaway body with solid Sitka spruce top, solid East Indian rosewood two piece sides/back, patented Transaction System allows the player to adjust the neck angle without loosening the strings, triple ring rosette with blue paua shell and black and white inlays, black pickguard, modified hybrid X-bracing, black micarta 14/20-fret fingerboard and bridge, polished gloss finish, Martin/Fishman prefix stereo with onboard blender installed, new 2002.

MSR	$3,649	**$2,550**	**$1,900**	**$1,375**

100 instruments are scheduled to be produced.

KITTY WELLS HTA (2002, LIMITED EDITION) - dreadnought body with 000 depth, solid Englemann spruce top, solid Indian rosewood back/sides/neck, polished black headstock w/o Martin trademark and angel inlaid in green ripple abalone pearl, Polished Gloss finish with vintage toner on top, mfg.mid 2002-mid 2003.

		$2,300	**$1,750**	**$1,275**

Last MSR was $3,299.

No set quantity, but had limited ordering period until Sept. 18, 2002.

NEGATIVE HDN (2002, LIMITED EDITION) - dreadnought body, solid Englemann spruce top, solid Indian rosewood back/sides, polished black lacquer body with Style 45 rosette and white Micarta bridge/fingerboard, white pickguard, white headstock overlay, black reverse label inside, vintage Geib case included, mfg. mid 2002-mid 2003.

		$2,575	**$1,925**	**$1,350**

Last MSR was $3,699.

No set quantitiy, but had limited ordering period until Sept. 18, 2002.

DEL McCOURY D-28DM (2002, LIMITED EDITION) - dreadnought style, solid Adirondack red spruce top, solid Indian rosewood back/sides/neck, triple ring rosette with blue paua pear inlay middle ring, polished and beveled tortoise colored pickguard, forward shifted bracing, Polished Gloss finish with aging toner on top, mfg. mid 2002-mid 2003.

		$3,425	**$2,500**	**$1,995**

Last MSR was $4,899.

No set quantity, but had limited ordering period until Sept. 18, 2002.

DAVID CROSBY D-18DC (2002, LIMITED EDITION) - dreadnought body with solid Engelmann spruce top and solid quilted mahogany back/sides, 14/20-fret ebony fingerboard and bridge, triple ring rosette with blue paua pearl and black/white inlay, tortoise color binding, polished gloss body with vintage toner on top, mfg. 2002 only.

		$2,850	**$2,150**	**$1,550**

Last MSR was $3,799.

250 instruments were produced.

GRADING	100%	EXCELLENT	AVERAGE

JUDY COLLINS HD35SJC (2002, LIMITED EDITION) - dreadnought body with solid Sitka spruce top, solid East Indian rosewood sides, East Indian rosewood with Pacific Big Leaf flamed maple wedge, triple ring select abalone rosette with black/white inlays, 12/19-fret ebony fingerboard, grained ivoroid binding, polished gloss with vintage toner on top, mfg. 2002 only.

	$3,750	$2,900	$2,100
	Last MSR was $5,149.		

50 instruments were produced.

JUDY COLLINS HD1235SJC (2002, LIMITED EDITION) - similar to Judy Collins Model HD35SJC, except is 12 string, mfg. 2002 only.

	$3,850	$3,000	$2,200
	Last MSR was $5,349.		

33 instruments were produced.

SHAWN COLVIN M3SC (2002, LIMITED EDITION) - 0000 M (grand auditorium) body, solid Engelmann spruce top with solid mahogany sides, solid mahogany back with East Indian rosewood wedge, single ring select abalone rosette with wood fiber inlays, 14/20-fret 16 in. radius ebony fingerboard, tortoise color pickguard, hybrid scalloped bracing, tortoise color binding, Polished Gloss with vintage toner on top, includes Fishman Gold Plus Natural I electronics, mfg. 2002 only.

	$2,225	$1,675	$1,225
	Last MSR was $3,199.		

120 instruments were produced.

**Martin Alternative II
courtesy Martin Guitar**

PHILLY FOLK FESTIVAL MPFF (2002, LIMITED EDITION) - 0000 M (grand auditorium) body, solid Engelmann spruce with solid East Indian rosewood two piece back/sides, 14/20-fret ebony fingerboard with Brazilian rosewood bridge, ivoroid binding and bound fingerboard, A frame hybrid scalloped X bracing, Style 45 highly colorful abalone pearl rosette, polished gloss finish with vintage toner on top, mfg. 2002 only.

	$2,395	$1,775	$1,325
	Last MSR was $3,449.		

85 instruments were produced.

HAWAIIAN X (2002, LIMITED EDITION) - 000 auditorium body with custom HPL texture finish top, back and sides, 14/20-fret black micarta 16 in. radius fingerboard and bridge, top has Hawaiian luau scene artwork by R. Armstrong, new 2002.

MSR	$1,099		$750	$575	$425

500 instruments are scheduled to be produced.

GODFREY DANIELS 00016RGD (2002, LIMITED EDITION) - 000 auditorium body with solid Sitka spruce top, solid Indian rosewood two piece back/sides, 14/20-fret black micarta fingerboard, tortoise color binding, triple ring rosette with select abalone inlays, hybrid scalloped bracing, Polish Gloss finish with aging toner on top, mfg. 2002-mid 2003.

	$1,995	$1,475	$1,025
	Last MSR was $2,849.		

100 instruments were produced.

DION 000CBD (2002, LIMITED EDITION) - 000 cutaway body, solid Sitka spruce top, solid mahogany back/sides, single ring rosette inlayed with blue paua pearl, black beveled and polished pickguard, scalloped bracing with hybrid A-frame, black binding, 14/20-fret ebony fingerboard and bridge, Black Polished Gloss finish, includes Fishman Gold Plus Natural II pickup, mfg. 2002 only.

	$2,300	$1,750	$1,275
	Last MSR was $3,299.		

57 instruments are scheduled to be produced.

LONNIE DONEGAN 000-28LD (2002, LIMITED EDITION) - 000 Auditorium body, solid Sitka spruce top, solid East Indian rosewood sides/back, 14/20-fret ebony fingerboard with 16 in. radius, grained ivoroid binding, triple ring rosette with blue paua pearl inlay, polished gloss sunburst finish, includes Fishman Gold Plus Natural II pickup, mfg. 2002 only.

	$2,850	$2,150	$1,725
	Last MSR was $4,099.		

LONNIE DONEGAN 000-28LDB (2002, LIMITED EDITION) - similar to Lonnie Donegan Model 00028LD, except has solid Brazilian rosewood sides/back, mfg. 2002-mid 2003.

	$7,500	$6,150	$3,750
	Last MSR was $8,219.		

75 instruments were produced.

**Martin David Crosby D-18DC
courtesy Martin Guitar**

GRADING	100%	EXCELLENT	AVERAGE

PAUL SIMON PS2 (2002, LIMITED EDITION) - 000 body, solid Sitka spruce top with solid Indian rosewood sides/back, mahogany neck with traditional diamond volute, square tapered headstock is faced with polished African ebony white "whirl" inlay centered under Martin script logo, Paul Simon signature in white pearl between the 19th & 20th frets, polished gloss finish with aging toner on top, mfg. mid 2002-mid 2003.

	$2,450	$1,875	$1,325

Last MSR was $3,499.

ERIC CLAPTON 000-28ECB (2002, LIMITED EDITION) - 000 auditorium body, solid Sitka spruce top, solid Brazilian rosewood back/sides, 14/20-fret ebony fingerboard and bridge, triple ring rosette with herringbone pearl and black/white inlay, tortoise color pickguard, grained ivoroid binding, Natural or Sunburst polished gloss/vintage toner finish, new 2002.

MSR	$9,999	$6,995	$5,150	$3,425

500 instruments are scheduled to be produced.

LAURENCE JUBER OMC18 VLJ (2002, LIMITED EDITION) - OMC cutaway body, solid Adirondack spruce, solid mahogany back/sides, triple ring, old Style 18 rosette with black/white inlays, 14/20-fret ebony fingerboard with 16 in. radius, tortoise color binding, scalloped 14 in. Adirondack spruce binding, no pickguard, Polished Gloss finish with aging toner on top, mfg. 2002 only.

	$3,100	$2,275	$1,775

Last MSR was $4,449.

133 instruments were produced.

0045S (2002, SPECIAL EDITION) - 00 grand concert body, solid Adirondack spruce, solid Brazilian rosewood two piece back/sides, triple ring rosette with select abalone inlays, scalloped bracing, tortoise butterfly patterned pickguard with select abalone inlays placed between soundhole and bridge, tree of life abalone inlays on neck, 14/19-fret ebony fingerboard with white micarta bridge, grained ivoroid binding, slotted peghead, polished gloss finish with vintage toner on top, patterned after the 1902 style 45, includes special coffin case, new 2002.

MSR	$25,000	$17,500	$13,750	$9,250

100 instruments are scheduled to be produced.

ALTERNATIVE XT (2002, SPECIAL EDITION) - 00CX thin body acoustical electric with cutaway, patterned solid aluminum top, jet black HPL back/sides with no finish, black Micarta fingerboard with tune-o-matic bridge and Bigsby tremolo, 25.4 in. scale, includes Dimarzio Fast Track 2 humbucker pickups with coil tap switch, new mid 2002.

MSR	$1,469	$1,025	$775	$575

ALTERNATIVE XMIDI (2003, SPECIAL EDITION) - 00CX thin body, acoustical electric with cutaway, patterned solid aluminum top, jet black HPL back/sides with no finish, black Micarta fingerboard and bridge, features Roland GK divided Midi pickup (interface with any 13 pin device), can simulatneously blend Fishman Prefix Pro onboard pickup with Midi, provides a variety of different sounds, new mid 2003.

MSR	$1,599	$1,100	$850	$650

GRAPHITE X (2002, SPECIAL EDITION) - DC dreadnought body with cutaway, graphite/polycarbonate top with jet black HPL back/sides with no finish, black Micarta fingerboard, 25.4 in. scale, includes Fishman Prefix Pro electronics, new mid 2002.

MSR	$1,349	$950	$700	$500

GRAPHITE II (2003, SPECIAL EDITION) - 00 thin body with cutaway, graphite/polycarbonate top with jet black HPL back/sides with no finish, black Micarta fingerboard and bridge, includes Fishman Prefix Pro electronics, new 2003.

MSR	$1,349	$950	$700	$500

CLARENCE WHITE D-28CW (2002, SPECIAL EDITION) - patterned after Clarence White's 1935 D-28, Adirondak spruce top, solid Indian rosewood sides/two-piece back/neck, authentic tortoise patterned pickguard, grained ivroid binding, scalloped Golden Era style bracing, Polished Gloss finish with aging toner on top, new mid 2002.

MSR	$4,899	$3,425	$2,475	$1,975

CLARENCE WHITE BRAZILIAN D-28CWB (2002, LIMITED EDITION) - similar to D-28CW, except has Brazilian rosewood back/sides, new mid 2002.

MSR	$9,999	$6,995	$5,100	$3,450

150 instruments are scheduled to be produced.

SWMGT CERTIFIED WOOD (2002, SPECIAL EDITION) - 0000-M body style, reclaimed solid Sitka spruce pulp wood top, certified solid cherry back/sides/neck, D-1 style bracing, certified Katalox 14/20-fret fingerboard and bridge, tortoise color binding, tortoise color pickguard, gloss top with aging toner, satin finished back and sides, new mid 2002.

MSR	$1,550	$1,075	$795	$595

SWJGT CERTIFIED WOOD (2002, SPECIAL EDITION) - jumbo body, reclaimed solid Sitka spruce pulp wood top, certified solid cherry back/sides/neck, D-1 style bracing, certified Katalox 14/20-fret fingerboard and bridge, tortoise color binding, tortoise color pickguard, gloss top with aging toner, satin finished back and sides, new mid 2002.

MSR	$1,550	$1,075	$795	$595

GRADING	100%	EXCELLENT	AVERAGE

SUGAR RAY DSR (2002, LIMITED EDITION) - dreadnought body with rounded contiguous edges, solid mahogany top/sides/two-piece back/neck, triple ring rosette with center ring of green ripple pearl, black pickguard, 14/20-fret ebony fingerboard and bridge, polished gloss with Translucent Burgundy finish, mfg. mid 2002-mid 2003.

$1,750 $1,275 $875
Last MSR was $2,499.

No set quantity, but had limited ordering period until Sept. 18, 2002.

BOB SHANE D-28KTBS (2003, LIMITED EDITION) - features premium Sitka spruce top with scalloped 5/16 in. X top bracing, Indian rosewood back/sides with mahogany neck and 14/20-fret ebony fingerboard (the Kingston Trio logo inlaid between 11th-13th frets, Bob Shane signature between 19th-20th frets), signed by Bob Shane and CFM IV, new 2003.

MSR $3,799 $2,650 $1,975 $1,550

Add $200 for double black pickguards (Model D-28KTBSDG.)

DIANE PONZIO JDP (2003, LIMITED EDITION) - features jumbo body, Sunburst solid spruce top, Style 45 headstock, three piece Indian rosewood back with herringbone back strips, 14/20-fret ebony fingerboard, abalone rosette/fretboard inlays, Gloss finish, new 2003.

MSR $3,999 $2,795 $2,100 $1,650

101 instruments were manufactured.

ERIC JOHNSON MC-40 (2003, LIMITED EDITION) - 0000 M (grand auditorium) body, solid Engelmann spruce, solid East Indian rosewood back/sides, mahogany neck, Southwestern marquetry (brown and blue arrows) back purfling, 14/20-fret ebony fingerboard with planetary inlays at 1st, 3rd, 5th, 7th, 9th, 12th, 17th, and 19th frets, ebony belly bridge, mother-of-pearl angel inlaid on headstock, grained ivroid binding, polished gloss top with sand adobe toner, signed and numbered by Eric Johnson and CFM IV, new 2003.

MSR $4,999 $3,500 $2,650 $1,850

JOHN MAYER OM-28 (2003, LIMITED EDITION) - solid Engelmann spruce top, solid East Indian rosewood back/side, mahogany neck, 14/20-fret ebony fingerboard, herringbone bound top, ebony belly bridge, triangle with dots at 12th fret, John Mayer signature between 19th fret and 20th fret, polished gloss top with vintage toner, signed and numbered by John Mayer and CFM IV, Fishman Gold Plus Natural I electronics, new 2003.

MSR $4,499 $3,150 $2,300 $1,800

404 instruments are scheduled to be produced.

**Martin Eric Clapton
000-28ECB
courtesy Martin Guitar**

ACOUSTIC BASS/ACOUSTIC ELECTRIC BASS

Unless otherwise listed, all models have jumbo style bodies, and are available with fretless fingerboard at no additional charge.

Add $325 to all models for acoustic bridge pickup with active preamp, volume/tone control.

BM (ROAD SERIES) - solid spruce top, round soundhole, black body binding, laminated mahogany back/sides, mahogany neck, 14/20 rosewood fingerboard with white dot inlay, single band herringbone rosette, tortoise pickguard, 2-per-side chrome tuners, available in Natural Satin finish, mfg. 1998-2001.

$850 $650 $475
Last MSR was $1,299.

B-1 (1 SERIES) - solid Sitka spruce top, round soundhole, mahogany neck, solid mahogany back, 3-ply mahogany sides, 34" scale, 17/23 rosewood fingerboard with dot inlay, rosewood bridge, tortoise pickguard, 2-per-side tuners, chrome hardware, available in Natural satin finish, current mfg.

MSR $1,499 $1,050 $795 $595

B-1E - similar to B-1, except has Fishman Prefix Plus Bass System electronics, new mid 2002.

MSR $1,819 $1,275 $900 $700

BC-15E (15 SERIES) - solid mahogany top/back/sides, cutaway body with onboard Gold Plus electronics, herringbone decal rosette, 2-piece back, rosewood fingerboard and bridge, new 1999.

MSR $1,699 $1,195 $850 $675

B-40 - jumbo style, solid spruce top, round soundhole, black pickguard, 5-stripe bound body/rosette, rosewood back/sides, mahogany neck, 17/23-fret ebony fingerboard, ebony bridge with white black dot pins, rosewood peghead veneer, 2-per-side chrome tuners, available in Natural finish, mfg. 1988-1996.

$2,175 $1,450 $950
Last MSR was $2,900.

**Martin Graphite II
courtesy Martin Guitar**

BC-40 - similar to B-40, except has single round cutaway, oval soundhole, mfg. 1990-96.

| | $2,350 | $1,550 | $995 |

Last MSR was $3,120.

B-540 - similar to B-40, except has 5-strings, striped ebony fingerboard/bridge, 5/2-per-side tuners, mfg. 1992-95.

| | $2,450 | $1,550 | $995 |

Last MSR was $2,790.

B-65 - similar to B-40, except has tortoise pickguard, figured maple back/sides, mfg. 1987-1995.

| | $1,950 | $1,450 | $950 |

Last MSR was $2,610.

MASTER
Instruments currently built in Los Angeles, California.

Luthier George Gorodnitski has been building fine handcrafted acoustic and semi-hollowbody electric guitars for a number of years. For further information, please contact luthier Gorodnitski directly (see Trademark Index).

MASTERBILT
See Mac Yasuda Guitars.

MASTERTONE
See chapter on House Brands.

While the Mastertone designation was applied to high end Gibson banjos in the 1920s, the Mastertone trademark was used on a Gibson-produced budget line of electric guitars beginning in 1941. Some acoustic "Hawaiian" guitars from the 1930s by Gibson also carried the Mastertone label. While built to the same standards as other Gibson guitars, they lack the one "true" Gibson touch: an adjustable truss rod. House Brand Gibsons were available to musical instrument distributors in the late 1930s and early 1940s, (Source: Walter Carter, *Gibson Guitars: 100 Years of an American Icon*).

MATES, TOM
Instruments currently built in England.

Luthier Tom Mates produces handcrafted acoustic guitars. One notable player using a rather ornately inlaid version is Dave Pegg (of Jethro Tull), (Source: Tony Bacon, *The Ultimate Guitar Book*).

MATON
Instruments currently produced in Australia since 1946.

Maton is Australia's longest established guitar manufacturer. The Maton trademark was established in 1946 by British emigre Bill May, a former woodworking teacher. His trademark name was a combination of his last name, and tone – just what every luthier seeks.

In the 1940s, it was a commonly held belief among Australian guitarists and musical instrument retailers that American guitars were the best in the world. While Bill May may have subscribed to that general idea, it didn't stop him from questioning why Australians shouldn't build their own guitars. As May related in a 1985 interview, "I wanted to make better guitars, beyond what people thought you had the ability to do. People asked 'How do you think you can do it, you've never been to see how it's done and what do you know about it? And it's Australia. You don't know anything here. If you want good instruments, you have to wait and get them from America.' But I didn't believe that."

May was raised with craftsman skills and a positive attitude, both for his own self esteem and for his country. Bill May originally completed his apprenticeship in cabinet making, and later an honors course in art and graphic design before he spent ten years as a woodwork teacher. When May couldn't find a decent sounding guitar in a reasonable price range, he began building guitars in the garage of his Thornbury home. While there was no wealth of guitar building information back in the 1940s, May learned from the various guitars that passed through his hands. Production tools for the time period were the same sort used by furniture craftsmen, like chisels, planes, or the occasional belt-sander or bench saw. Rather than knock out copies of American models, May produced designs that were distinctive in appearance and sound – and featured Australian woods and distinctly Australian names. After the humble beginnings in his garage, a factory was established outside of Melbourne in 1951. Maton guitars began to be offered through local stores; by the mid 1960s Maton instruments had established a solid reputation throughout Australia.

May passed away on his 75th birthday in 1993, but the company continues to produce quality acoustic guitars. The modern factory located in Bayswater is certainly different from Maton's original site in Canterbury, but the traditional use of hand craftsmanship still co-exists with the new CNC router at the plant. While the focus of current production has been on acoustic guitars, the company also promises that there will be a return of production electrics later on, (Company history courtesy John Stephenson, *The Maton Book* (1997); additional model descriptions courtesy Linda Kitchen (Bill May's daughter) and Haidin Demaj, Maton Guitars).

Maton estimates that 80,000 guitars were sold in the past forty years. The current company builds over 400 acoustics per month.

ACOUSTIC

Maton has been focused on producing quality acoustic guitar for the past several years. Current models feature Canadian Sitka spruce tops, Queensland maple and walnut as well as Tasmanian and Victorian blackwood in the back and sides. Other timbers include Brazilian and Indian rosewood, and rock maple. Most models feature solid wood back and sides. the acoustic/electric models feature an installed AP5 pickup and on-board preamp built by Australian piezo manufacturer GEC-Marconi. Maton's guitars retail starting at $799 and climb up to $4,200. For more information refer to their web site (see Trademark Index).

M

MATSUOKA, R.

Instruments previously produced in Japan circa late 1970s. Distributed by Unicord of Westbury, New York.

Luthier R. Matsuoka offered these good quality classical guitars that featured ebony fingerboards, select hardwoods, and a hand-rubbed finish. Suggested list prices as well as used prices are still unknown at this time.

MAURER & CO.

See Larson Brothers (1900-1944).

The Maurer brand was used by Robert Maurer prior to 1900 and by the Larson brothers, Carl and August, starting in 1900. The Larsons produced guitars, ukes, and mandolin family instruments under this brand until the mid -1930s when they, and the rest of the industry, changed designs from the small body guitars with slot pegheads and 12-frets-to-the-body necks to larger bodies with necks becoming narrower but extending the fingerboard to now have 14-frets-to-the-body.

The most commonly found Maurer instrument is the flattop guitar having either X-bracing or straight, ladder-type bracing. Some of the X-braced instruments have the laminated X-braces which were patented by August in 1904. The Maurers were offered in student grade, intermediate grade and best grade. The Maurer brand was also used on the harp guitar, uke, taro-patch, mandolinetto, mandola, octave mandolin, mando-cello, and mando-bass.

The style of the Maurers was carried through in the instruments sold to Wm. C. Stahl and the Prairie State brand. They ranged from the very plain to the pearl and abalone trimmed with the fanciest having a beautiful tree of life fingerboard. The Maurers are high quality instruments and are more commonly found than the other Larson brands.

For more detailed information regarding all the Larson brands, the Larson patents, and a Maurer/Prairie State catalog reprint, see The Larsons' Creations, Guitars and Mandolins, by Robert Carl Hartman, Centerstream Publishing, P.O. Box 17878, Anaheim Hills CA 92807, phone/fax (714) 779-9390.

MAXINE

Instruments currently produced in China. Distributed by Bejing Eternal Musical Instrument Corp. Ltd.

Maxine is a company that makes an endless amount of guitars. Pretty much any color, design, and configuration is available. They are mainlyl entry level guitars and don't sell for much. It is unknown if a U.S. distributor has been established yet. For more information refer to their web site and good luck reading it (see Trademark Index).

MAXTONE

Instruments currently produced in Taiwan, and distributed by the Ta Feng Long Enterprises Company, Ltd. of Tai Chung, Taiwan. Distributed in Singapore by the Renner Piano Company.

Maxtone instruments are designed with the entry level to student quality guitars. They produce a whole slug of guitars and prices are mainly between $100-$200. For further information, contact Maxtone directly (see Trademark Index).

MAYFAIR

Instruments previously produced in Japan, circa 1960s.

Research continues on the Mayfair trademark.

MAYFLOWER

Instruments previously built in Chicago, Illinois from 1918 to 1928.

The Groeschel Company of Chicago, Illinois first began building bowl-back (or "potato bug") mandolins in 1890. Guitars were also manufactured under the Flower & Grochsl trademark. In 1918 Groeschel was changed to the Stromberg-Voisenet Company, who produced guitars and banjos under the Mayflower trademark. This Stromberg company is not to be confused with luthier Charles Stromberg (and son Elmer) of Boston, Massachusetts.

Henry Kay Kuhrmeyer bought the Stromberg-Voisenet company in 1928, and renamed it Kay Musical Instruments in 1931 (See Kay).

MEGAS, TED

Instruments currently built in San Francisco, California since 1989.

Luthier Ted Megas has been building guitars since 1975, and in 1989 began building archtop guitars, which represented the best combination of his musical interests and his knowledge and skills as a woodworker. For more information, please contact luthier Megas directly (see Trademark Index).

ACOUSTIC

Megas currently builds three archtop models. All his guitars have hand carved Spruce tops, hand carved, highly figured maple backs with matching sides, solid ebony fingerboard, bridge, pickguard, and peg overlay, figured hard maple neck and adjustable truss rod, high gloss Nitro-cellulose lacquer finish, and come with a 5-ply hardshell case. All models are made in 16", 17", and 18" bodies.

Megas Archtop
Blue Book Publications

Add $250 for a floating Kent Armstrong pickup. Add $300 for custom shading or Sunburst finish. Add $400 for left-handed configuration. Add $500 for a 7-string configuration.

The **Athena** is classically styled with multi-lined plastic bindings throughout; split block MOP inlays on fingerboard; abalone dot side position markers; X-bracing; MOP nut; precision machined brass tailpiece construction with ebony overlay; and Schaller tuning machines with ebony buttons. List prices range from the 16" body width ($6,200), 17" width ($6,500), and the 18" width ($7,100).

The **Apollo** features wood bindings; abalone, dot side position makers; X-bracing; cello style f-holes; MOP nut; precision machined brass tailpiece construction with ebony overlay; and Schaller tuning machines with ebony buttons. List prices range from the 16" body width ($5,400), 17" width ($5,700), and the 18" width ($6,200).

The **Spartan** has a single bound body, neck, and peg head; parallel bracing; bone nut; ebony tailpiece with brass anchor; gold Gotoh tuning machines. List prices range from the 16" body width ($4,500), 17" width ($4,800), and the 18" width ($5,200).

MELLO, JOHN F.
Instruments currently built in Kensington, California.

Since 1973, John Mello has been building classical and small-bodied steel-string guitars, with an emphasis on clarity, projection, and providing the player with a wide dynamic range and broad palette of colors to interpret his/her music. His building is informed by extensive experience in restoring master instruments by both historic and contemporary makers, and his guitars have been exhibited at the Renwick Gallery of the Smithsonian Institution, played on recordings by Douglas Woodful Harris and Alex Degrassi, and gained him mention as one of America's 17 best classical guitar makers by *Musician Magazine*.

MELO GUITARS
Instruments currently built in Sabadell, Spain. Distributed in the USA by Golden Age Fretted Instruments L.L.C.

Josep Melo has a family backround that allows him to combine intellectual work with craftsmanship. He has studied with L. D'Aquisto, as well as a number of other people. Melo produces fine acoustic guitars with all different types of designs and patterns. Retail prices start around $2,000 and can climb to almost $10,000 with options. For more information refer to their web site (see Trademark Index).

MELPHONIC
Instruments previously built by Valco of Chicago, Illinois circa mid 1960s.

Melphonic resonator guitars were built by Valco (see Valco or Dobro), (Source: Michael Wright, *Vintage Guitar Magazine*).

MENKEVICH GUITARS
Instruments currently built in Philadelphia, Pennsylvania.

Luthier Michael Menkevich has been handcrafting quality guitars for a number of years. He builds classical guitars from original designs to reproductions of popular models. For more information concerning model specifications and pricing, please contact luthier Menkevich directly (see Trademark Index).

MERRILL
Instruments previously produced in New York, New York circa late 1880s.

Company president Neil Merrill began experimenting with aluminum in the mid -1880s. He debuted his aluminum bodied guitars in 1894 and offered a wide range of stringed instruments based on this design, (Source: Tom Wheeler, *American Guitars*).

MERMER
Instruments currently built in Sebastian, Florida.

Luthier Richard Mermer, Jr. is producing concert quality, handcrafted instruments designed and built for the individual. Steel string, nylon string, electric-acoustic instruments, and acoustic Hawaiian steel guitars are offered.

All Mermer guitars feature: solid wood construction, choice of select tone woods, decorative wood binding, custom wood and stone inlay, custom scale lengths, fully compensated saddles and precision intonation, adjustable truss rod, choice of hardware and accessories, and optional pickup and microphone installation. For a list of options and additional information refer to their web site (see Trademark Index).

MESROBIAN
Instruments previously built in Salem, Massachusetts.

Luthier Carl Mesrobian offered a high quality, 17-inch archtop model that featured a hand-graduated Sitka or European spruce top and figured maple back and sides.

MICHAEL DOLAN CUSTOM GUITARS
Instruments currently built in Santa Rosa, Sonoma County, California since 1977.

Luthier Michael Dolan has been handcrafting quality guitars for over twenty years. After Dolan graduated from Sonoma State University with a Bachelor of Arts degree in Fine Arts, he went to work for a prestigious bass and guitar manufacturer.

Dolan's full service shop offers custom built guitars and basses (solid body, arch-top, acoustic, neck-through, bolt-on, set-neck, and headless) as well as repairs and custom painting. He and his staff work in domestic and exotic woods, and use hardware and electronics from all well-known manufacturers. Finishes include their standard acrylic top coat/polyester base, nitrocellulose, and hand rubbed oil.

As luthier Dolan likes to point out, a "Custom Guitar is a unique expression of the vision of a particular individual. Because there are so many options and variables, offering a price list has proven to be impractical." However, Dolan's prices generally start at $1,250 and the average cost may run between $1,500 to $2,500. Prices are determined by the nature of the project, and the costs of components and building materials.

Working with their custom guitar order form, Michael Dolan can provide a firm up-front price quote. All custom guitars are guaranteed for tone, playability, and overall quality.

MIRAGE
Instruments previously produced in Taiwan during the late 1980s.

Entry level to intermediate quality guitars based on classic American designs, (Source: Tony Bacon and Paul Day, *The Guru's Guitar Guide*).

MITCHELL, BILL GUITARS
Instruments currently built in Wall, New Jersey.

Bill Mitchell has been building and designing guitars since 1979. After attending the Timberline school of Lutherie, Mitchell began focusing on acoustic guitars; in 1985 he began to pursue crafting guitars full time. Mitchell offers both one-of-a-kind and production guitars in a variety of models. For further information, contact Bill Mitchell directly (see Trademark Index).

The retail prices on Mitchell guitars run from $1,999 (MJ-10) up to $2,795 (MS-Manitou). Mitchell offers different body styles in his production series. 10 Series models feature solid Sitka spruce top, mahogany back/sides/neck, rosewood fingerboard and bridge; while the 15 Series (retail list $2,295) models have flame maple back and sides, and a maple neck. The 20 Series (retail list $2,395) features rosewood back and sides, and a mahogany neck. Mitchell's MS - Manitou Series has a single cutaway body, flame maple neck/back/sides, ebony fingerboard and bridge, and a Fishman Matrix pickup. All models are offered with a wide range of options in wood choices, bindings, and inlays.

MOLL CUSTOM INSTRUMENTS
Instruments currently built in Springfield, Missouri.

Luthier Bill Moll is currently offering custom crafted archtop guitars and solid body bass models which feature premium materials, as well as restoration services for all stringed instruments. At Moll Custom Instruments, much of the training has been in applied acoustical physics, so instruments are built to perform acoustically before electronics are applied.

Moll Custom Instruments offer four archtop models in either a 16", 17," or 18" body width (a 19" body width is an option for an additional $500). The Classic (list $3,000) has a solid carved X-braced spruce top, solid carved maple back/sides/neck, ebony fingerboard, solid brass tailpiece, and Gotoh tuners. The Express (list $5,000) is a modern design archtop with teardrop-shaped soundholes. The D'Angelico-derived New Yorker has the fancy inlays and stairstep bridge and pickguard that most jazz players lust after (list $6,500). A John Pizzarelli model is available for $4,000.

Moll custom basses feature laminated figured maple and American walnut in their through-body neck designs, and use active Seymour Duncan Basslines soapbar pickups. Prices run from $2,800 (4-string), to $3,000 (5-string), and up to $3,250 (6-string) base list prices.

Moll also offers a custom shop where just about anything can be made. All you have to do is ask. For more information refer to their web site (see Trademark Index).

Mesrobian Archtop
Blue Book Publications

MONTALVO
Instruments currently built Mexico. Distributed by Berkeley Music in Berkeley, California.

Montalvo guitars are the result of a collaboration between George Katechis-Montalvo (a highly skilled craftsman) and Marc Silber (a noted guitar historian, restorer and designer). Montalvo had already been importing guitars from Mexico since 1987. Silber joined him in 1990 to found the K & S Guitar Company. K & S introduced higher quality woods, glues, finishes and American builders' knowledge to the Mexican luthiers for actual production in Mexico. The resulting K & S guitars are set up and inspected at their Berkeley, California shop.

ACOUSTIC

Montalvo classical and flamenco acoustic guitars are constructed of Engelmann spruce or Canadian red cedar tops, mahogany or Spanish cedar necks, and rosewood or ebony fingerboards. Retail prices range from $825 up to $1,850. For more information refer to Berkeley's web site (see Trademark Index).

MONTANA
Instruments currently produced in Korea and previously distributed by the Kaman Music Corporation of Bloomfield, Connecticut.

Montana produces a range of acoustic and acoustic/electric guitars priced for the novice and intermediate players.

MONTCLAIR
See chapter on House brands.

This trademark has been identified as a House Brand of Montgomery Wards, (Source: Willie G. Moseley, *Stellas & Stratocasters*).

Moll Archtop
courtesy Mol Guitars

MONTELEONE, JOHN
Instruments currently built in Islip, New York.

Luthier John Monteleone has been building guitars and mandolins for almost three decades. A contemporary of James D'Aquisto, Monteleone performed repair and restoration work for a number of years while formulating his own archtop designs. Monteleone's archtop guitars feature such unique ideas as a flush-set truss rod cover, recessed tuning machine retainers, and a convex radius headstock. Prices start at $10,000. For further information, please contact luthier John Monteleone directly (see Trademark Index).

MOON GUITARS LTD.
Instruments currently built in Glasgow, Scotland.

Moon Guitars was established by Jimmy Moon in 1979, and the Moon Guitars name has become synonymous with custom built instruments of very high quality as they are producing modern instruments with strong traditional roots. Originally, Moon Guitars produced acoustic guitars, mandolins, mandolas, and dulcimers. Moon moved into the electric market during the eighties, producing for an impressive client list of famous names. A shift in the market pre-emptied a return to building acoustics and mandolins (while continuing with custom built electrics, basses, and electric mandolins).

Moon Guitars' latest successful development is the Moon electro acoustic mandolin, which comes in various body shapes with a piezo-based pickup system. For further information, please contact Moon Guitars Ltd. directly (see Trademark Index).

MOONSTONE
Instruments currently built in Eureka, California (Guitar production has been in different locations in California since 1972). Distributed directly by Moonstone Guitars of Eureka, California.

In 1972, self-taught luthier Steve Helgeson began building acoustic instruments in an old shingle mill located in Moonstone Heights, California. By 1974, Helgeson moved to Arcata, California, and began producing electric Earth Axe guitars. By 1976, Helgeson had moved to a larger shop and increased his model line and production. Helgeson hit boom sales in the early 1980s, but tapered off production after the market shifted in 1985. Rather than shift with the trends, Helgeson preferred to maintain his own designs. In 1988, a major disaster in the form of a deliberately set fire damaged some of his machinery. Steve's highly figured wood supply survived only a minor scorching. Helgeson moved and reopened his workshop in 1990 at the current location in Eureka, California, where he now offers a wide range of acoustic and electric guitars and basses. In addition to the standard models, Moonstone also offers custom guitars designed in accordance with the customer's request. All current prices include a hardshell case.

All Moonstone instruments are constructed from highly figured woods. Where burl wood was not used in the construction, the wood used is highly figured. Almost all necks are reinforced with veneers, or stringers. Bass necks are reinforced with through body graphite stringers. Moonstone has always utilized exotic woods such as African purpleheart, paduak, wenge, koa, mahogany, Sitka and Engelmann spruce, Myrtlewood, and black burl walnut.

Some older models can also be found with necks entirely made of graphite composite with phenolic fingerboards. Helgeson commissioned Modulus Graphite to produce these necks, and used them on models like the Eclipse Standard, Deluxe Basses, Vulcan Standard and Deluxe guitars, the M-80, D-81 Eagle 6 - and 12-string models, as well as the D-81 Standard and the Moondolin (mandolin). In 1981, most wood necks were reinforced with a Graphite Aluminum Honeycomb Composite (G.A.H.C.) beam with stainless steel adjustment rod.

M

ACOUSTIC

All necks currently are reinforced with 3/8" by 1/2" *U* channel graphite beam with a 3/16" adjustment rod.

Moonstone has guitars that are based off of traditional popular designs. The 000-42 features Brazillian rosewood and retails for $8,180. The 000-45 has 50-year old Brazillian rosewood and retails for $10,180. The OM-45 has koa wood and lists for $7830.

D-81 EAGLE 6 - spruce top, round soundhole, black pickguard, bound body, wood inlay rosette, quilted maple back/sides, graphite neck, 14/20-fret bound phenolic fingerboard with abalone vine inlay, eagle shape ebony bridge with black pins, walnut burl peghead veneer with abalone halfmoon/logo inlay, 3-per-side gold tuners, available in Natural finish, mfg. 1981-84.

	N/A	$1,200	$750

Last MSR was $2,075.

D-81 Eagle 12 - similar to D-81 Eagle 6, except has 12-strings, 6-per-side tuners.

	N/A	$1,250	$750

Last MSR was $2,255.

J-90 - Sitka spruce top, round soundhole, bound body, rifling twist rosette, wenge back/sides/neck, 14/20-fret bound ebony fingerboard with abalone/pearl flower/vine inlay, ebony bridge with pearl flower wing inlay, black pearl dot bridge pins, ebony peghead veneer with abalone halfmoon/logo inlay, 3-per-side gold tuners, available in Natural finish, mfg. 1992-current.

MSR $3,400

Add $650 for J-90 Eagle Makassar ebony with top rim inlay and full vine inlay.

J-90 EAGLE - similar to the J-90, except features carved eagle bridge, bird fingerboard inlays, current mfg.

MSR $3,600

This model is an option with quilted Pacific or Canadian flame maple, rosewood, curly koa, or paduak back and sides (Call for prices); cutaway body design, abalone top purfling, Engelmann spruce top.

J-90 Eagle Macassar Ebony - similar to the J-90 Eagle, except has Makassar ebony back and sides, current mfg.

MSR $5,050

J-90 Eagle Koa - similar to the J-90 Eagle, except has koa back and sides, current mfg.

MSR $7,295

J-90 Eagle Brazillian Rosewood - similar to the J-90 Eagle, except has Brazillian rosewood back and sides, current mfg.

    MSR   **$12,620**

J-99 - slope shouldered jumbo body, 17" width, Asian rosewood back and sides, 12/19 fret fingerboard with bird inlay, 3-per-side gold tuners, available in Natural finish, current mfg.

    MSR   **$3,450**

ACOUSTIC BASS

B-95 - Englemann spruce top, round soundhole, 35" scale, wenge (or rosewood or curly koa or paduak or burl maple) back/sides/neck, ebony fingerboard with abalone filled mother-of-pearl inlays, 2-per-side tuners, available in Natural finish, current mfg.

    MSR   **$3,900**

B-95 Five-String - similar to the B-95, except in five-string configuration, 3/2-per-side tuners, current mfg.

    MSR   **$4,100**

MORGAN
Instruments currently built in North Vancouver (British Columbia), Canada.

Morgan acoustic guitars are hand crafted by luthier David Iannone, and feature premier woods and construction techniques. Iannone began building guitars in 1981. His apprenticeship carried on a guitar lineage that dates back to the very birth of the modern classic guitar. Morgan Guitars, named after his first son, is Welsh for "working by the sea" (which he does).

ACOUSTIC

Morgan guitars all share the following features: high grade spruce or cedar top, rosewood (or mahogany or maple) back and sides, one piece mahogany neck, bound ebony fingerboard, wood binding and purfling, wood marquetry or abalone rosette, transparent or tortoise shell pickguard, and Morgan engraved machine heads.

Morgan Rosewood model guitars are offered in configurations like the **Concert, OM, Dreadnought**, and **OO** models (list $2,565 each); **Florentine Cutaway** ($3,000); **Venetian Cutaway** ($2,890). **Classic** (list $2,510); **Traditional Jumbo** ($2,675), **Jumbo 12 String** ($2,890), and the **Concert 12 String** ($2,780).

Morgan Mahogany model guitars are offered in configurations like the **Concert, OM, Dreadnought**, and **OO** models (list $1,965 each); **Venetian Cutaway** ($2,290), **Traditional Jumbo** ($1,800), **Jumbo 12-String** ($2,290), and the **Concert 12-String** ($2,180).

Options include a figured maple back and sides, koa back and sides, Brazilian rosewood back and sides (call for quote), and other custom options.

**Moonstone J-90 Eagle
courtesy Steve Helgeson**

MORIDAIRA
See also Morris. Instruments currently produced in Japan.

The Moridaira company is an OEM manufacturer of guitars for other companies, under different trademark names. The company has produced a wide range of entry level to very good quality guitars through the years, depending on the outside company's specifications. Further research continues for upcoming editions of the *Blue Book of Acoustic Guitars.*

MORRELL
Instruments currently built in Tennessee. Distributed by the Joe Morrell Music Distributing Company of Bristol, Tennessee.

The Joe Morrell Music Distributing company sells products wholesale to music dealers, instrument repair personnel, and instrument builders. Their current catalog offers a wide range of Morrell stringed instruments all built in the U.S., such as resonator guitars, lap steel guitars, dulcimers, and flaptop mandolins. In addition, the Morrell company also lists music songbooks, instructional videos, guitar cases, name brand guitar strings and accessories, guitar/banjo/violin parts, drum heads and drum parts, and other music store accessories. Besides their own U.S. built Morrell instruments, the Morrell company offers low cost, quality acoustic and electric instruments from overseas manufacturers.

ACOUSTIC

Additional Morrell stringed instruments include their Tennessee Mountain dulcimer (list $119.95), Tennessee Flattop Mandolin (list $299.95), and Lap Steel guitars. A two octave student model in natural finish has a retail price of $219.95 (black or red sparkle finish is $50 extra), and the three octave Professional model Joe Morrell Pro 6 or Little Roy Wiggins 8 string have a retail price of $399.95 each.

Morrell is currently offering the **FlintHill** series of resonator guitars, available in roundneck and square neck models. These resonator models feature a maple top, walnut back and sides, walnut neck, ebony fingerboard, and 3-per-side closed tuners. Models are available in Natural (**Model MDR-1/MDS-1**) and Tobacco Sunburst (**Model MDR-2/MDS-2**) finishes. All resonator models have a retail list price of $799. Morrell also stocks replacement parts for performing repairs on other resonator models.

**Moonstone B-95
courtesy Steve Helgeson**

MORRIS

Instruments currently produced in Korea. Distributed in the USA by Moridaria USA Inc, in Suisun City, California.

The Moridaira company offers a wide range of acoustic and solid body electric guitars designed for the beginning student up to the intermediate player under the Morris trademark. Morris guitars are advertised as "Made for Fingerpickers;" hope they are not talking about the nose. Moridaira has also built guitars (OEM) under other trademarks for a number of other guitar companies.

MORSE, JOHN DAVID

Instruments currently built in Santa Cruz, California since 1978. Luthier Morse is currently concentrating on violin making.

Luthier John David Morse combined his artistic backgrounds in music, sculpture, and woodcarving with the practical scientific knowledge of stress points and construction techniques to produce a superior modern archtop guitar. Morse, a descendant of Samuel Morse (the telegraph and Morse code), studied under fine violin makers Henry Lannini and Arthur Conner to learn the wood carving craft. Morse still combines scientific processes in his building, and has identified means to recreate his hand graduated tops.

Morse is currently making high quality violins. A number of his violins are currently in use with the San Francisco Symphony, and he is building models for concertmaster Ramond Kobler and conductor Herbert Blomstedt. Any potential commissions for archtop guitar models should be discussed directly with luthier Morse.

MORTORO, GARY

Instruments currently built in Miami, Florida since 1991.

Luthier Gary Mortoro has been building handcrafted instruments since 1991, under the guidance and direction of Master Luthier and Archtop Builder Robert Benedetto. Gary's dedication to the crafting of his guitars combined with his playing ability has resulted in an instrument not only of fine detail and craftsmanship, but of exquisite sound and beauty. Some of the players who own a Mortoro guitar are George Benson, Tony Mottola, Jimmy Vivino, Rodney Jones, Gene Bertoncini, Joe Cinderella, and Jimmy Buffet.

Mortoro currently offers six different models that are available in carved or laminate versions. For further information, please contact Gary Mortoro directly (see Trademark Index).

ACOUSTIC

Carved models have select tops and backs with matching sides and neck. **Laminate** models feature laminated tops and backs, with necks and sides of flamed maple. All models feature a single cutaway and come in 14", 16", or 17" bodies. Body thickness is up to the player's choice. Motoro guitars feature ebony for the fingerboard, pickguard, bridge, and tailpiece, Pearl inlay, Schaller tuners, and a floating Mortoro pickup by Kent Armstrong. Models come with a hard shell case and warranty. A number of options; custom colors, custom inlays, 7 string models, etc. are also available.

The **Free Flight** (Volo Libero) has no body (or neck) binding, narrow or traditional pickguard. The Carved Solid Top/Back version retails for $5,000 and the laminated body version retails for $3,000.

The **Songbird** (L'uccello Cantante) black/white body binding, narrow or traditional pickguard with inlay, inlaid tailpiece. The Carved solid top and back version retails for $5,700 and the laminated version retails for $3,700.

The **Starling** (Il Storno) has multiple "bird" soundholes in upper and lower bout, "bird" cutout on side of upper bout, no body/neck binding, 12th fret pearl inlay, narrow pickguard. The Carved solid top and back version retails for $6,000 and the laminated version is $4,000. Mortoro's non-traditional "bird" soundholes in place of f-holes sets the Starling (Il Storno) into a new area where form and function cross into a nicely voiced, pleasant to the eye archtop design.

The **Free Bird** (Uccello Libero) has 2 "bird" soundholes (instead of 2 f-holes), "bird" cutout on side of upper bout, no body/neck binding, 12th fret pearl inlay, narrow pickguard. The Carved solid top and back version retails for $5,300 and the laminated version is $3,300.

MOSRITE

Instruments previously produced in Bakersfield, California during the 1960s; earlier models built in Los Angeles, California during the mid to late 1950s. Distribution in the 1990s was handled by Unified Sound Association, Inc. Production of Mosrite guitars ceased in 1994.

There were other factory sites around the U.S. during the 1970s and 1980s: other notable locations include Carson City, Nevada; Jonas Ridge, North Carolina; and Booneville, Arkansas (previous home of Baldwin-operated Gretsch production during the 1970s).

Luthier/designer Semie Moseley (1935-1992) was born in Durant, Oklahoma. The family moved to Bakersfield, California when Moseley was 9 years old, and Semie left school in the seventh grade to travel with an evangelistic group playing guitar.

Moseley, 18, was hired by Paul Barth to work at Rickenbacker in 1953. While at Rickenbacker, Moseley worked with Roger Rossmeisl. Rossmeisel's "German carve" technique was later featured on Moseley's guitar models as well. Moseley was later fired from Rickenbacker in 1955 for building his own guitar at their facilities. In the later years, Moseley always credited Barth and Rossmeisl (and the Rickenbacker company) for his beginning knowledge in guitar building.

With the help of Reverend Ray Boatright, who co-signed for guitar building tools at Sears, Moseley began building his original designs. The Mosrite trademark is named after **Mos**eley and Boat**right** ("-rite"). After leaving Rickenbacker, Moseley built custom instruments for various people around southern California, most notably Joe Maphis (of "Town Hall Party" fame). Moseley freelanced some work with Paul Barth's "Barth" guitars, as well as some neck work for Paul Bigsby.

After traveling for several months with another gospel group, Moseley returned to Bakersfield and again set up shop. Moseley built around 20 guitars for Bob Crooks (Standel). When Crooks asked for a Fender-styled guitar model, Moseley flipped a Stratocaster over, traced the rough outline, and built the forerunner to the "Ventures" model!

After Nokie Edwards (Ventures) borrowed a guitar for a recording session, Stan Wagner (Ventures Manager) called Moseley to propose a business collaboration. Mosrite would produce the instruments, and use the Venture's organization as the main distributor. The heyday of the Mosrite company was the years between 1963 and 1969. When the demand set in, the company went from producing 35 guitars a month to 50 and later 300. The Mosrite facility had 105 employees at one point, and offered several different models in addition to the Ventures model (such as the semi-hollowbody Celebrity series, the Combo, and the Joe Maphis series).

In 1963, investors sold the Dobro trademark to Moseley, who built the first 100 or 150 out of parts left over from the Dobro plant in Gardenia. Later Bakersfield Dobros can be identified by the serial number imprinted on the end of the fingerboard. The Mosrite company did not build the amplifiers which bear the Mosrite trademark; another facility built the Mosrite amplifiers and fuzz pedals, and paid for the rights to use the Mosrite name.

The amplifier line proved to be the undoing of Mosrite. While some of the larger amplifiers are fine, one entry level model featured a poor design and a high failure rate. While covering for returns, the Ventures organization used up their line of credit at their bank, and the bank shut down the organization. In doing so, the Mosrite distribution was shut down as well. Moseley tried a deal with Vox (Thomas Organ) but the company was shut down in 1969. Moseley returned to the Gospel music circuit, and transferred the Dobro name to OMI in a series of negotiations.

Between the mid 1970s and the late 1980s, Moseley continued to find backers and sporadically build guitars. In 1972, *Guitar Player* magazine reported, "Semie Moseley is now working with Reinhold Plastics, Inc. to produce Mosrite of California guitars." Later that year, Moseley set up a tentative deal with Bud Ross at Kustom (Kustom Amplifiers) in Chanute, Kansas. Moseley was going to build a projected 200 guitars a month at his 1424 P Street location, and Ross' Kustom Electronics was going to be the distributor. This deal fell through, leaving Moseley free to strike up another deal in April of 1974 with Pacific Music Supply Company of Los Angeles, California. Pacific Music Supply Company had recently lost their Guild account, and was looking for another guitar line to distribute. One primary model in 1974 was the solid body Model 350 Stereo. The **Brass Rail** model was developed around 1976/1977. While shopping around his new model with "massive sustain," Moseley met a dealer in Hollywood Music in Los Angeles. This dealer had connections in Japan, and requested that Moseley begin recreating the original-style Ventures models. Moseley set out to build 35 to 50 of these reproductions per month for a number of months. Several years after Moseley recovered from an illness in 1983, he began rebuilding his dealer network with a number of models like the **V-88, M-88**, and **Ventures 1960's Reissues**. These models were built at his Jonas Ridge location.

Moseley's final guitar production was located in Booneville, Arkansas. The Unified Sound Association was located in a converted Walmart building, and an estimated 90% to 95% of production was earmarked for the Japanese market.

Moseley passed away in 1992. His two biggest loves were Gospel music, and building quality guitars. Throughout his nearly forty year career, he continued to persevere in his guitar building. Unified Sound Association stayed open through 1994 under the direction of Loretta Moseley, and then later closed its doors as well, (Information courtesy of Andy Moseley and Hal Hammer [1996]; additional information courtesy Willie G. Moseley, *Stellas and Stratocasters*, and Tom Wheeler, *American Guitars*, Mosrite catalogs and file information courtesy John Kinnemeyer, JK Lutherie; model dating estimations courtesy Carlos Juan, *Collectables & Vintage '95*, Stuttgart, Germany).

**Mortoro Starling
courtesy Gary Mortoro**

MODEL IDENTIFICATION

Mosrite guitars are easily identifiable by the "M" notch in the top of the headstock. Mosrite models produced in the 1960s have a "M" initial in a edged circle, and "Mosrite" (in block letters) "of California" (in smaller script) logo.

Contrary to vintage guitar show information in the current "Age of Fender mania", Mosrite instruments were not available in those (rare) Fender finishes like "Candy Apple Red" and "Lake Placid Blue." Catalog colors were identified as Blue or Red. Mosrite did offer option colored finishes like Metallic Blue and Metallic Red.

Semie's designs offered numerous innovations, most notable being the Vibra-Mute vibrato. This item was designed for the Ventures models and can be used to help identify early Mosrite instruments. The early vibratos (pre-1977) have Vibra-Mute and Mosrite on them, while later vibratos have Mosrite alone on them. More distinction can be made among the earliest instruments with Vibra-Mutes by observing the casting technique used. While the early vibratos were sandcast, later units were diecast (once funding was available).

During the heyday of Mosrite production in Bakersfield, model designations in the catalog would list a **Mark I** to designate a 6-string model, **Mark XII** to indicate the 12-string version, and **Mark X** to designate the bass model within a series. These Mark designations are a forerunner to – but not the same usage as – the later **1967-1969 Mark** "No Logo" series.

PRODUCTION DATES

Mosrite models in this edition of the *Blue Book of Acoustic Guitars* feature estimated dates of production for each model. Just as it is easy to take for granted a sunny day in the Summer until it rains, most dealers and collectors take a Mosrite model as "Just a Mosrite" without really double checking the true nature of **which** model it really is. Of course, the corollary of this way of thinking is to assume that the Mosrite in question is going to end up in the Far East with the rest of them! Is Johnny Ramone the only current American guitar player to use these guitars? Are there no mega-Mosrite collectors? Ventures fans unite!

The *Blue Book of Acoustic Guitars* is actively seeking additional input on Mosrite models, specifications, date of production, and any serialization information. This year's section is the official "Line Drawn in the Sand" for Mosrite fans – assume that this is the drawing board, or the foundation to build upon. Any extra information gathered on Mosrite will be updated in future editions of the *Blue Book of Acoustic Guitars*. For the time being, assume that **all Production Dates are either CIRCA and/or ESTIMATED**.

For further information regarding Mosrite electric models, please refer to the *Blue Book of Electric Guitars*.

**Mortoro Small Starling
courtesy Gary Mortoro**

GRADING	100%	EXCELLENT	AVERAGE

ACOUSTIC: BALLADERE & SERENADE MODELS

The D-8 Memphis 5-string banjo was built between 1966 to 1969, and featured a maple top/back/sides, single body binding, 26" scale, East Indian rosewood fingerboard, Type C resonator and cover plate, 12 round mini-soundholes arranged around the resonator, bridge/metal tailpiece. The D-8 Memphis was available in a Blonde finish, and had a new retail list price of $229.00 (in 1966).

BALLADERE I (MODE 401) - dreadnought style, 3 1/4" body depth, bound spruce top, round soundhole, mahogany back/sides, 24 1/2" scale, 14/20-fret Indian rosewood fingerboard, rosewood bridge with white bridgepins, 3-per-side chrome enclosed tuners, available Natural or Transparent Sunburst finishes, mfg. 1966-69.

N/A   **$550**   **$275**
Last MSR was $198.

Balladere II (Model 402) - similar to the Balladere I, except features rosewood back/sides, 2 color laminated line purfling (top and back), bound fingerboard, available Natural or Transparent Sunburst finishes, body thickness 5", mfg. 1968-69.

N/A   **$600**   **$350**
Last MSR was $398.

SERENADE - Dreadnought style, spruce top, round soundhole, mahogany back/sides, mahogany neck, celluloid double binding on body, 14/20-fret rosewood fingerboard with dot inlay, rosewood bridge with white bridgepins, black celluloid batwing pickguard, 3-per-side Kluson tuners, available in Natural Spruce Top/Shaded Burgundy high gloss finish, mfg. 1965-69.

N/A   **$500**   **$250**
Last MSR was $198.

A similar model, the Seranade I (Model 401) featured maple back and sides, and was available in Natural Spruce Top, Transparent Cherry Red and Transparent Sunburst finishes.

ACOUSTIC: DOBRO/MOSRITE RESONATOR MODELS

In addition to the acoustic and electric guitars and basses, Semie Moseley and Mosrite produced **Dobro by Mosrite** between 1965 to 1969. "Dobro Goes Mod!," proclaimed the catalogs, "The In Sound". Many of these models (C-3, D-12, D-50, D-100 Californian kept the Dobro logo on the headstock, but added creme colored single coil pickups and a different soundhole mesh design.

C-3 MONTEREY (3/4 SIZE) - Dobro/Resonator style, 3 5/16" body depth, maple top, mahogany back/sides, 23 1/4" scale, 20-fret fingerboard, Type C resonator, bridge/metal tailpiece, solid peghead, 3-per-side tuners, available in Cherryburst, Deep Black, Metallic Blue, Metallic Red, Pearl White, or Sunburst finishes, mfg. 1966-69.

N/A   **$450**   **$175**
Last MSR was $239.

C-3 E Monterey - similar to the C-3 Monterey, except features one single coil pickup, available in Natural finish, mfg. 1966-69.

N/A   **$525**   **$200**
Last MSR was $264.

D-12 COLUMBIA 12-STRING - Dobro/resonator style, 3 5/16" body depth, mahogany or maple body, 24 5/8" scale, 14/20-fret fingerboard, Type D resonator, bridge/metal tailpiece, 6-per-side tuners, available in Cherryburst, Deep Black, Metallic Blue, Metallic Red, Pearl White, or Sunburst finishes, mfg. 1966-69.

N/A   **$600**   **$350**
Last MSR was $349.

D-12 E Columbia 12-String - similar to the D-12 Columbia, except features one single coil pickup, available in Natural finish, mfg. 1966-69.

N/A   **$650**   **$350**
Last MSR was $379.

D-50 RICHMOND - Dobro/resonator style, 3 5/8" body depth, mahogany or maple body, 2 small mesh-covered soundholes in upper bouts, Type D resonator, 24 5/8" scale, 14/20-fret rosewood fingerboard with dot inlay, bridge/metal tailpiece, solid peghead, 3-per-side tuners, available in Cherryburst, Deep Black, Metallic Blue, Metallic Red, Pearl White, or Sunburst finishes, mfg. 1966-69.

N/A   **$575**   **$350**
Last MSR was $298.

D-50 E Richmond - similar to the D-50 Richmond, except features one single coil pickup, available in Natural finish, mfg. 1966-69.

N/A   **$650**   **$350**
Last MSR was $349.

D-50 S UNCLE JOSH - Dobro/resonator style, 3 5/16" body depth, mahogany or maple body, 2 small mesh-covered soundholes in upper bouts, Type D resonator, 24 5/8" scale, 14/20-fret rosewood fingerboard with dot inlay, bridge/metal tailpiece, slotted peghead, 3-per-side tuners, available in Cherryburst, Deep Black, Metallic Blue, Metallic Red, Pearl White, or Sunburst finishes, mfg. 1966-69.

N/A   **$575**   **$350**
Last MSR was $298.

D-50 SE Uncle Josh - similar to the D-50 S Uncle Josh, except has one single coil pickup, available in Natural finish, mfg. 1966-69.

N/A   **$575**   **$350**
Last MSR was $349.

ACOUSTIC: MOBRO MODELS

The "Mobro" name is derived from "Mosrite Dobro"; in other words, Dobro models built by the Mosrite company.

MOBRO STANDARD - resonator style, hollow wood body, 2 mesh covered mini-soundholes in upper bouts, 14/20-fret fingerboard, chrome resonator, bridge/metal tailpiece, Mosrite-style headstock, "Mosrite/Mobro" headstock logos, 3-per-side chrome tuners, available in Natural finish, mfg. 1972-73.

	N/A	$550	$300

Last MSR was $349.

Mobro Standard E - similar to the Mobro Standard, except features one single coil pickup, available in Natural finish, mfg. 1972-73.

	N/A	$650	$350

Last MSR was $429.

MOBRO STEEL - similar to Mobro Standard, except features a metal body, available in chrome finish, mfg. 1972-73.

	N/A	$550	$300

Last MSR was $349.

Mobro Steel E - similar to the Mobro Steel, except features one single coil pickup, available in chrome finish, mfg. 1972-73.

	N/A	$650	$350

Last MSR was $429.

ACOUSTIC ELECTRIC

D-100 CALIFORNIAN (MARK I) - slim line semi-hollow dual cutaway bound body, maple neck, Type D resonator, 24 5/8" scale, 22-fret rosewood fingerboard with dot inlay, adjustable bridge/metal tailpiece, chrome hardware, 3-per-side tuners, 2 exposed pole piece single coil pickups, volume/tone controls, 3 way selector toggle switch (controls plus a 1/4" jack mounted to celluloid controls plate), available in Cherry and Cherry Sunburst finishes, length 41 1/2", body width 16 1/8", body thickness 3 1/2," mfg. 1966-69.

	N/A	$1,000	$600

Last MSR was $359.

In 1968, Deep Black, Metallic Blue, Metallic Red, Pearl White, and Transparent Sunburst finishes were introduced.

D-100 Californian 12-String (MARK XII) - similar to the D-100 Californian, except features 12-string configuration, 6-per-side tuners, Length 41 1/2", Body Width 16 1/8", Body Thickness 3 1/2," mfg. 1966-69.

	N/A	$950	$500

Last MSR was $398.

ACOUSTIC ELECTRIC BASS

D-100 CALIFORNIAN BASS (MARK X) - slim line semi-hollow dual cutaway bound body, maple neck, Type D resonator, 30 1/4" scale, 20-fret rosewood fingerboard with dot inlay, adjustable bridge/metal tailpiece, chrome hardware, 2-per-side tuners, 2 exposed pole piece pickups, volume/tone controls, 3 way selector toggle switch (controls plus a 1/4" jack mounted to celluloid controls plate), available in Cherry, Cherry Sunburst, or Natural finishes, mfg. 1966-69.

	N/A	$800	$500

Last MSR was $349.

MOSSMAN

Instruments previously built in Winfield, Kansas from 1969 to 1977. Some models were available from Mossman's private shop after 1977. Current production of Mossman guitars has been centered in Sulphur Springs, Texas since 1989.

Luthier Stuart Mossman originally built acoustic guitars in his garage in 1969. Mossman then founded the S. L. Mossman Company, and set up a factory to produce guitars. Mossman inspected each finished guitar before shipping; the scale of the Mossman factory was to build eight to ten guitars a day (at the most). Actually, when discussing acoustic guitars, it is probably proper to say complete eight to ten guitars a day, as the actual construction would take longer to complete (gluing the bodies, neck/body joint assembly and set up, etc.). It is estimated that around 1,400 guitars had been built between 1970 and 1975, when a fire struck the factory in February. With the support of local businessmen, Mossman returned to production. However, due to a disagreement with his distributors, the Mossman company closed shop in August of 1977. Stuart Mossman then opened a private shop, and offered a number of instruments privately.

M

GRADING	100%	EXCELLENT	AVERAGE

In 1989, John Kinsey of Dallas, Texas resurrected the Mossman trademark. In mid 1990, Bob Casey joined the company as a part owner. The company operated in a suburb of Dallas until August of 1991 when it was moved to an old dairy barn in Sulpher Springs, Texas. The company has operated in Sulphur Springs since then. The Mossman line of acoustic guitars is still regarded as one of the finest handmade instruments in the country, (Company history courtesy John Kinsey, Mossman Guitars).

Mossman Guitars manufactures basically the same models as Stuart Mossman manufactured in Winfield, Kansas. Some of the lower line models have been discontinued, but the mainstream line (Texas Plains, Winter Wheat, South Wind, and Golden Era) continue to be produced. Several improvements have been made to the standard models, such as scalloped bracing being made a standard feature. Mossman Guitars, Inc. has also developed the "next step in the evolution of X-bracing," they refer to it as Suspension Bracing. This modification helps projection as well as producing a clear, clean punch on the lower end. For further information on Texas-made or Kansas-made Mossman instruments, please contact Mossman Guitars, Inc. directly (see Trademark Index).

ACOUSTIC

In 1975, a fire started in the finishing area at Mossman Guitars. While no employees were hurt and the machinery suffered minor losses, the company's supply of Brazilian rosewood was depleted. Models that featured Brazilian rosewood before the fire were converted to Indian rosewood after the fire (a minor instrument dating tip).

FLINT HILLS - dreadnought style, 25 3/4" scale, sitka spruce top, round soundhole, East Indian rosewood back/sides, 20-fret ebony fingerboard, ebony pin bridge, 3-per-side Grover (or Schaller) tuners, available in Natural finish, mfg. 1969-1977.

N/A $1,300 $750

Last MSR was $350.

This model was an option with abalone top and soundhole inlay as the Flint Hills Custom (retail list $525).

GOLDEN ERA - dreadnought style, 25 3/4" scale, German spruce top with abalone inlay, round soundhole, abalone trim, Brazilian rosewood back/sides, 20-fret ebony fingerboard, black pickguard, adjustable ebony bridge with white pins, 3-per-side gold Grover (or Schaller) tuners, available in Natural finish, mfg. 1969-1977.

N/A $1,700 $950

Last MSR was $750.

This model was an option with abalone tree-of-life floral inlay as the Golden Era Custom (retail list price $900).

GREAT PLAINS - dreadnought style, 25 3/4" scale, German spruce top, round soundhole, herringbone inlay, Brazilian rosewood back/sides, 20-fret ebony fingerboard, ebony pin bridge, 3-per-side Grover (or Schaller) tuners, available in Natural finish, mfg. 1969-1977.

N/A $1,500 $800

Last MSR was $425.

TENNESSEE FLATTOP - dreadnought style, 25 3/4" scale, sitka spruce top, round soundhole, black plastic body binding, Honduran mahogany back/sides, 20-fret rosewood fingerboard, adjustable bridge, 3-per-side Grover (or Schaller) tuners, available in Natural finish, mfg. 1969-1977

N/A $1,350 $750

Last MSR was $350.

M

Section N

NAPOLITANO, ARTHUR
Instruments currently built in Allentown, New Jersey.

Luthier Arthur Napolitano began building electric guitars in 1967, and offered repair services on instruments in 1978 in Watchung, New Jersey. Napolitano moved to Allentown in 1992, and began building archtop guitars in 1993. Napolitano currently offers several different archtop models like the **Primavera, Acoustic, Philadelphian, Jazz Box,** and a **Seven-String** model. Prices range from $4,900 to $9,800. For more information refer to Napolitano's web site (see Trademark Index).

NASH
Instruments previously built in Markneukirchen, Germany 1996-2000. Previously distributed in the U.S. by Musima North America of Tampa, Florida.

Nash acoustics guitars debuted in the United States, Canada, and South American markets in 1996. The guitars were built by Musima, Germany's largest acoustic guitar manufacturer (the company headquarters in Markneukirchen, Germany are near the Czech border). In 1991, Musima was purchased by industry veteran Helmet Stumpf. The Musima facilities currently employs 130 workers, and continue to produce Musima stringed instruments.

NASHVILLE GUITAR COMPANY
Instruments currently built in Nashville, Tennessee.

Luthier/musician Marty Lanham began working on stringed instruments in San Francisco during the late 1960s, and moved to Nashville in 1972. He accepted a job at Gruhn Guitar's repair shop, and spent eight years gaining knowledge and lutherie insight. In 1985, Lanham went into business custom building his own acoustic guitars.

Nashville Guitar's custom steel string acoustic models feature German or sitka spruce tops; mahogany, koa, Indian or Brazilian rosewood, Tasmanian blackwood, and Malagasy kingwood back and sides; mahogany neck, and an ebony or rosewood fingerboard. Contact the company for more information (see Trademark Index).

National Triolian
courtesy Dave Hull

NATIONAL
Instruments previously produced in Los Angeles, California during the mid 1920s to the mid 1930s.

Instruments produced in Chicago, Illinois from mid 1930s to 1969. After National moved production to Chicago in mid the 1930s, they formally changed the company name to Valco (but still produced National brand guitars).

Instruments produced in Japan circa 1970s. Distributed by Strum'N Drum of Chicago, Illinois. When Valco went out of business in 1969, the National trademark was acquired by Strum'N Drum, who then used the trademark on a series of Japanese built guitars.

The Dopyera family emigrated from the Austro-Hungary area to Southern California in 1908. In the early 1920s, John and Rudy Dopyera began producing banjos in Southern California. They were approached by guitarist George Beauchamp to help solve his "volume" (or lack thereof) problem with other instruments in the vaudeville orchestra. In the course of their conversation, the idea of placing aluminum resonators in a guitar body for amplification purposes was developed. John Dopyera and his four brothers (plus some associates like George Beauchamp) formed National in 1925.

The initial partnership between Dopyera and Beauchamp lasted for about two years, and then John Dopyera left National to form the Dobro company. National's corporate officers in 1929 consisted of Ted E. Kleinmeyer (pres.), George Beauchamp (sec./gen. mgr.), Adolph Rickenbacker (engineer), and Paul Barth (vice pres.). In late 1929, Beauchamp left National, and joined up with Adolph Rickenbacker to form Ro-Pat-In (later Electro String/Rickenbacker).

At the onset of the American Depression, National was having financial difficulties. Louis Dopyera bought out the National company; and as he owned more than 50% of the stock in Dobro, "merged" the two companies back together (as National Dobro). In 1936, the decision was made to move the company to Chicago, Illinois. Chicago was a veritable hotbed of mass produced musical instruments during the early to pre-World War II 1900s. Manufacturers like Washburn and Regal had facilities, and major wholesalers and retailers like the Tonk Bros. and Lyon & Healy were based there. Victor Smith, Al Frost, and Louis Dopyera moved their operation to Chicago, and in 1943 formally announced the change to Valco (The initials of their three first names: Victor-Al-Louis Company). Valco worked on war materials during World War II, and returned to instrument production afterwards. Valco produced the National/Supro/Airline fiberglass body guitars in the 1950s and 1960s, as well as wood-bodied models.

In 1969 or 1970, Valco Guitars, Inc. went out of business. The assets of Valco/Kay were auctioned off, and the rights to the National trademark were bought by the Chicago, Illinois-based importers Strum'N Drum. Strum'N Drum, which had been importing Japanese guitars under the Norma trademark, were quick to

National Style 1 Tricone
courtesy Dave Rogers
Dave's Guitar Shop

N

GRADING	100%	EXCELLENT	AVERAGE

introduce National on a line of Japanese produced guitars that were distributed in the U.S. market. Author/researcher Michael Wright points out that the National "Big Daddy170 bolt-neck black LP copy was one of the first models that launched the Japanese "Copy Era" of the 1970s. Early company history courtesy Bob Brozman, *The History and Artistry of National Resonator Instruments*; model descriptions compiled by Dave Hull, "Copy Era" National information courtesy Michael Wright.

ACOUSTIC: SINGLE CONE MODELS

STYLE O - nickel plated bell brass body, 2 f-holes, maple neck, 12/19-fret ebonized maple fingerboard with pearl dot inlay, 3-per-side tuners, available with Sandblasted Hawaiian Scene on body, mfg. 1930-1941.

Spanish 12-fret	N/A	$3,500	$2,500
Spanish 14-fret	N/A	$2,800	$2,200
Hawaiian	N/A	$2,300	$2,000

The 12-fret guitars with rolled in f-holes command a premium (produced for about one year).

The first few hundred Style O models featured steel bodies. The Hawaiian Style O has a wooden neck. Some 14-fret models may have parallelogram fingerboard inlays. Until 1933, the f-holes were flat cut. After 1933, the f-holes were rolled in (these are the rarest and most expensive Style 0 models). In late 1934, 14-fret fingerboard replaced 12-fret fingerboard.

STYLE N - German silver body, 12/19-fret fingerboard, square headstock with pearloid overlay (no sandblasting or etching design), mfg. 1930-34.

Spanish 12-fret	N/A	$4,200	$3,500

THE DON #1 - German silver body, 14/20-fret fingerboard with dot inlay, available with plain body with engraved edged borders.

Spanish 14-fret	N/A	$3,000	$2,500

The Don guitar models are fairly rare and are rarely traded in the vintage market.

The Don #2 - similar to The Don #1, except features pearloid headstock overlay, pearl square fingerboard inlay, available with geometric engraving.

Spanish 14-fret	N/A	$3,300	$2,800

The Don #3 - similar to The Don #1, except features pearloid headstock overlay, pearl square fingerboard inlay, available with Floral Pattern engraving.

Spanish 14-fret	N/A	$3,500	$3,000

DUOLIAN - thinner gauge steel body, 2 flat cut f-holes, mahogany or maple neck, 12/19-fret dyed maple fingerboard with pearl or ivoroid dot inlay, mfg. 1931-1940.

Spanish 12-fret	N/A	$2,000	$1,500
Spanish 14-fret	N/A	$1,600	$1,300

After 1933, rolled in f-holes replaced flat cut f-holes. In 1935 a 14/20-fret fingerboard was introduced with a basswood neck. Before 1938, Duolian models featured a crystalline paint finish.

TRIOLIAN - wooden body, 2 flat cut f-holes, 12/19-fret fingerboard, available in Light Green finish with a light overspray of several colors; neck, fingerboard, and peghead featured matching finish, decals were then placed on the body; early models feature a bouquet design, later models feature a hula girl design, mfg. 1928-1941.

1928 (Tricone)			
1928-1929 wood body	N/A	$2,000	$1,500
1929-1934	N/A	$2,400	$1,800
1935-1941	N/A	$1,800	$1,500

Only 12 of the 1928 Tricone Triolian models exist, making this an extremely rare model. Rarity and lack of activity in the secondary marketplace precludes accurate pricing on this model. In 1929, steel body replaced wooden bodies. In 1933, rolled in f-holes replaced flat cut fholes. In 1935, 14/20-fret fingerboard replaced 12/19-fret fingerboards. The first Triolians were an attempt to make a budget tricone. National then almost immediately switched to a single resonator cone on the wooden body; a steel body was later adopted.

ACOUSTIC: TRICONE MODELS

The Tricone Nationals came in two configurations: round neck (**Spanish**) and square neck (**Hawaiian**). The round neck was basically a "German Silver" body with an attached wooden neck, while the square neck was a hollow extension of the body (all the way up to the attached wooden headstock). The tenor and plectrum instruments were built on a smaller triangular shaped body and only came in the Spanish style.

Generally speaking, the plectrum instruments will command a premium over the tenors. All of these instruments feature minor (and sometimes not so minor) changes through the years; a good place to research those would be Bob Brozman's fine work: "National Resonator Instruments" (published by Center stream Publications).

STYLE 1 - German silver body, mahogany neck, ebony fingerboard with pearl dot inlay, National logo decal on headstock, available in Plain (no engraving) body, mfg. 1928-1941.

Spanish	N/A	$6,000	$4,500
Hawaiian	N/A	$2,500	$1,500

Style 1 models below serial number 380 have a rosewood fingerboard instead of ebony.

	N/A	$1,500	$1,000

Tenor and plectrum models feature maple necks.

GRADING	100%	EXCELLENT	AVERAGE

STYLE 2 - German silver body, mahogany neck, ebony fingerboard with pearl dot inlay, National logo decal on headstock, available in a Wild Rose engraving pattern, mfg. 1927-1939.

Spanish	N/A	$7,000	$5,500
Hawaiian	N/A	$3,000	$2,500

Tenor and plectrum models feature maple necks.

	N/A	$2,000	$1,500

Style 2 models below serial number 400 have a rosewood fingerboard instead of ebony.

STYLE 3 - German silver body, mahogany neck, ebony fingerboard with pearl square inlay, engraved National logo inlay on ebony peghead overlay (some models feature a pearloid engraved overlay), available in a Lily of the Valley engraving pattern, mfg. 1928-1941.

Spanish	N/A	$12,000	$8,000
Hawaiian	N/A	$5,000	$4,000

Tenor and plectrum models feature maple necks.

	N/A	$2,500	$1,800

STYLE 4 - German silver body, mahogany neck, ebony fingerboard with pearl square inlay, engraved National logo inlay on pearloid peghead overlay, available in a Chrysanthemum engraving pattern, mfg. 1928-1941.

Spanish	N/A	$15,000	$10,000
Hawaiian	N/A	$3,500	$2,500

STYLE 35 - nickel plated brass body, mahogany neck (Spanish) or integral neck (Hawaiian), ebony fingerboard with pearl dot inlay, black and white celluloid peghead overlay, available in a Sandblasted Scene of a minstrel, colored with airbrushed enamel, mfg. 1936-1940.

Spanish	N/A	$6,000	$5,000
Hawaiian	N/A	$3,000	$2,500

The Style 35 is extremely rare. The Hawaiian featured an ebonoid fingerboard.

STYLE 97 - nickel plated brass body, mahogany neck (maple neck on Hawaiian), ebony fingerboard with pearl dot inlay, black and white celluloid peghead overlay, available in a Sandblasted Scene of a female surfer, colored with airbrushed enamel, mfg. 1936-1940.

Spanish	N/A	$6,000	$5,000
Hawaiian	N/A	$5,000	$4,000

Tenor and plectrum models feature maple necks, single resonator cone.

	N/A	$1,500	$1,000

The Style 97 is extremely rare. The Hawaiian featured an ebonoid fingerboard. The Hawaiian models tend to price closer to their Spanish sisters, because they are convertible.

ACOUSTIC: WOODEN BODY MODELS

Wooden body Nationals have a single resonator cone.

ARAGON - 18" body width, spruce top, maple back and sides, 14-fret fingerboard with parallelogram inlays, mfg. circa 1938-1941.

	N/A	$6,000	$4,000

Bodies for the Aragon model were produced by Harmony or Kay.

HAVANA - spruce top, 14-fret fingerboard, mfg. circa 1938-1941.

	N/A	$1,500	$1,000

Not much is known about this guitar. The Havana was apparently introduced around the same time as the Aragon, and featured a Kay-built body.

EL TROVADOR - laminated mahogany body, mahogany neck, 12-fret fingerboard with pearl dot inlay, slotted peghead, mfg. 1932-33.

	N/A	$1,600	$1,200

The El Trovador model featured a Kay-built body.

ESTRALIA, ROSITA, TROJAN - wooden body, mfg. circa 1930s to 1940s.

	N/A	$1,200	$800

Most of the wooden body Nationals (Estralia, Rosita, and Trojan) seen today are one of these models. These guitars feature Harmony bodies, usually of birch or basswood. In the words of National expert Bob Brozman, they produce a "mushy sound."

NATIONAL RESO-PHONIC GUITARS

Instruments currently built in San Luis Obispo, California since 1988.

Founders Don Young and McGregor Gaines met in 1981. Young had been employed on and off at OMI (building Dobro-style guitars) since the early 1970s. After their first meeting, Young got Gaines a job at OMI, where he was exposed to guitar production techniques. In the mid to late 1980s, both Young and Gaines had

National Style 1
courtesy Dave Hull

National Style 97
courtesy Dave Hull

N

disagreements with the management at OMI over production and quality, and the two soon left to form the National Reso-Phonic Guitars company in 1988.

The company has been producing several models of resonator acoustic guitars in the last ten years. The most recent model the company has devised is the single cutaway resonator **Bendaway Radio Tone model.** For additional information concerning specifications and availability, contact National Reso-Phonic directly (see Trademark Index), (Early company history courtesy Bob Brozman, *The History and Artistry of National Resonator Instruments*).

ACOUSTIC

National Reso-Phonic offers additional nickel-finished brass body models, such as the mirror finish Style "1" (retail list $2,750), hand-engraved Style "2" Wild Rose (list $3,600), and hand-engraved Style "4" Chrysanthemum (list $6,000). These three models are available in either single cone or tri-cone configurations. In addition to their guitar models, National Reso-Phonic also offers the Style "N" Ukulele and Steel Ukulele models. National Reso-Phonic has several new models out as well. Look for more information in futher editions.

BENDAWAY RADIO TONE - single rounded cutaway body, maple top/back/sides, slotted upper bout ports, maple neck, single cone resonator, 12/19-fret rosewood fingerboard with pearl dot inlay, biscuit bridge/trapeze tailpiece, chrome hardware, blackface peghead with logo/art deco design, 3-per-side tuners, available in Light Amber finish, current mfg.

MSR $1,680

DELPHI - hollow steel body, 2 f-holes, mahogany neck, 12/19-fret ivoroid bound rosewood fingerboard with pearl dot inlay, single cone resonator, spider bridge/chrome trapeze tailpiece, slotted headstock with logo, 3-per-side chrome tuners, available in Baked Wrinkle finish in a variety of colors, current mfg.

MSR $1,850

This model is available in a squareneck configuration.

ESTRALITA - hollowbody, maple top/back/sides, 2 f-holes, maple neck, single cone resonator, 12/19-fret ivoroid bound rosewood fingerboard with pearl dot inlay, biscuit bridge/trapeze tailpiece, chrome hardware, ivoroid peghead overlay with logo, slotted peghead, 3-per-side tuners, available in Dark Walnut Burst finish, current mfg.

MSR $1,500

This model is available in a squareneck configuration.

POLYCHROME TRICONE - hollow steel body, "louver" upper bout soundports, maple neck, 12/19-fret bound rosewood fingerboard with pearl dot inlay, tri-cone resonator, bridge/chrome trapeze tailpiece, blackface headstock with logo/art deco design, 3-per-side chrome tuners, available in Baked Wrinkle finish in a variety of colors, current mfg.

MSR $2,150

RESOLECTRIC - single rounded cutaway solid maple body, maple neck, single cone resonator, 14/21-fret rosewood fingerboard with pearl dot inlay, biscuit bridge/trapeze tailpiece, chrome hardware, natural peghead with logo, 3-per-side tuners, creme colored pickguard, creme colored Seymour Duncan P-90 single coil pickup, Highlander pickup, magnetic volume/Highlander volume/tone chickenhead knob controls, 3-way selector toggle switch, available in Amber and Dark Walnut finishes, current mfg.

MSR $2,040

Earlier models may have a lipstick tube single coil pickup instead of the creme colored P-90 single coil pickup.

STYLE "0" - hollow nickel-plated brass body, 2 f-holes, maple neck, 12/19-fret bound ebony fingerboard with mother-of-pearl dot inlay, single cone resonator, spider bridge/chrome trapeze tailpiece, slotted peghead, blackface headstock with logo, 3-per-side chrome tuners, available in engraved Hawaiian finish (front and back), current mfg.

MSR $2,400

This model is available without etching for a plain mirror finish (Style "N").

STYLE "1" - hollow nickel-plated brass body, crossed sound holes, mahogany neck, 12/19-fret bound ebony fingerboard with mother-of-pearl dot inlay, tri-cone resonator, spider bridge/chrome trapeze tailpiece, slotted peghead, blackface headstock with logo, 3-per-side chrome tuners, available in chrome finish, current mfg.

MSR $2,990

Style "1" Baritone - similar to the Style "1," except in Baritone configuration, current mfg.

MSR $3,360

Style "1-E" Etched - similar to the Style "1," except has an etched body, current mfg.

MSR $3,200

STYLE "3" TRICONE - hollow nickel-plated brass body, "louver" upper bout soundports, mahogany neck, 12/19-fret bound ebony fingerboard with mother-of-pearl dot inlay, tri-cone resonator, bridge/chrome trapeze tailpiece, slotted peghead, ivoroid headstock overlay with logo, 3-per-side chrome tuners, available in hand-engraved Lily of the Valley finish, current mfg.

MSR $5,900

Style "3" Single Resonator - similar to the Style "3" Tricone, except has a single cone resonator, 2 f-holes, current mfg.

MSR $5,720

STYLE "4" - similar to the Style "3," except has more elaborate engraving on body, current mfg.

MSR $6,500

NEW WORLD GUITAR COMPANY
Instruments currently built in Ben Lomond, California.

New World Guitar Company was established in 1995 by American luthier Kenny Hill, in association with Swiss luthier Gil Carnal and guitar dealer Jerry Roberts. They specialize in the manufacture of high quality nylon string guitars directed at the wholesale market. They currently produce several models based on classical and flamenco guitars of recognized masters in the history of guitar building, such as Hauser, Fleta, Ramirez, Santos, and Panormo. The instruments are all handmade of the highest quality materials. They are concert quality instruments at very reasonable prices.

New World Guitar products are currently being marketed under the names La Mancha by Jerry Roberts (800-775-0650) and Hill/Carnal. Retail list prices are from $1,750 to $3,500 and dealer inquiries are encouraged.

NICKERSON
Instruments currently built in Northampton, Massachusetts since the early 1980s.

Luthier Brad Nickerson, born and raised on Cape Cod, Massachusetts, has been building archtop guitars since 1982. Nickerson attended the Berklee College of Music, and worked in the graphic arts field for a number of years. While continuing his interest in music, Nickerson received valuable advice from New York luthier Carlo Greco, as well as Cape Cod violin builder Donald MacKenzie. Nickerson also gained experience doing repair work for Bay State Vintage Guitars (Boston), and The Fretted Instrument Workshop (Amherst, Massachusetts).

With his partner Lyn Hardy, Nickerson builds archtop, flattop, and electric guitars on a custom order basis. Nickerson is also available for restorations and repair work. For further information regarding specifications and availability, please contact Nickerson Guitars directly (see Trademark Index).

ACOUSTIC

Nickerson's instruments are constructed out of Sitka or European spruce tops, European cello or figured maple back and sides, and ebony tailpiece, bridge, and compound radius fingerboard.

Add $200 for pickup with endpin jack. Add $400 for left-handed configuration. Add $500 for 7-string configuration.

CORONA - Sitka or European spruce top, figured maple back/sides, multiple-ply body binding, bound fingerboard/peghead/finger rest, macassar ebony tailpiece/finger rest/peghead, gold Schaller M6 tuners with ebony buttons, available in Blonde, Cherry Sunburst, Brown Sunburst, or custom color nitrocellulose finishes, body width 17", body depth 3" (or 3 1/8"), current mfg.

MSR	$6,500

EQUINOX - European spruce top, European cello maple back/sides, all wood binding, macassar ebony tailpiece/finger rest/peghead veneer, gold Schaller M6 tuners with ebony buttons or Waverly gold tuners, available in Blonde finish, Body Width 18", current mfg.

MSR	$8,000

F C 3 - flattop model, single rounded cutaway, Sitka or European spruce top, wood purfling, cherry binding, Indian rosewood back/sides, laminated walnut neck, 25 1/4" scale, 20-fret fingerboard with pearl diamond inlays, macassar ebony peghead veneer, Schaller M6 mini tuners, available in Natural finish, body width 16", body depth 3 3/8" (or 4 3/8"), current mfg.

MSR	$2,800

This model is also offered in a non-cutaway body version as the Model F 3.

F C 3 S - similar to the F C 3, body width 15", body depth 3 3/8" (or 4 3/8"), available in Natural finish, current mfg.

MSR	$2,800

This model is also offered in a non-cutaway body version as the Model F 3 S.

SOLSTICE (L'ANIMA) - Sitka spruce top, maple back/sides, rock maple neck, body binding, macassar ebony tailpiece/finger rest, macassar ebony or figured maple or burl peghead veneer, Schaller M tuners, available in Shaded Brown, Reddish Brown, and Burnt Tangerine nitrocellulose finishes, body width 15 1/2", body depth 3" (or 2 7/8"), current mfg.

MSR	$3,800

SKYLARK - semi-hollow mahogany body, carved spruce top, ivoroid body binding, macassar ebony tailpiece/finger rest/peghead veneer, Schaller M6 mini tuners, available in custom color nitrocellulose finish, body width 14 3/8", body depth 1 3/4", current mfg.

MSR	$2,700

VIRTUOSO - European spruce top, European maple back/sides, all wood binding, macassar ebony tailpiece/finger rest, macassar ebony or figured maple or burl peghead veneer, gold Schaller M6 tuners with ebony buttons, available in Shaded Brown, Reddish Brown, and Burnt Tangerine nitrocellulose finishes, body width 17", body depth 3" (or 3 1/8"), current mfg.

MSR	$5,700

**Nickerson Equinox
courtesy Brad Nickerson**

**Nickerson Skylark
courtesy Brad Nickerson**

NOBLE

Instruments previously produced in Italy circa 1950s to 1964. Production models were then built in Japan circa 1965 to 1969. Distributed by Don Noble and Company of Chicago, Illinois.

Don E. Noble, accordionist and owner of Don Noble and Company (importers), began business importing Italian accordions. By 1950, Noble was also importing and distributing guitars (manufacturer unknown). In 1962 the company began distributing EKO and Oliviero Pigini guitars, and added Wandre instruments the following year.

In the mid 1960s, the Noble trademark was owned by importer/distributor Strum'N Drum of Chicago. The Noble brand was then used on Japanese-built solid body electrics (made by Tombo) through the late 1960s.

When the Valco/Kay holdings were auctioned off in 1969, Strum'N Drum bought the rights to the National trademark. Strum'N Drum began importing Japanese-built versions of popular American designs under the National logo, and discontinued the Noble trademark during the same time period, (Source: Michael Wright, *Vintage Guitar Magazine*).

NOBLE, ROY

Instruments currently built in California. Distributed by the Stringed Instument Division of Missoula, Montana.

Luthier Roy Noble has been handcrafting acoustic guitars for over 37 years. Noble has been plying his guitar building skills since the 1950s, when he first began building classical instruments after studying the construction of Jose Ramirez' Concert models. Noble later moved to a dreadnought steel string acoustic design in the late 1950s and early 1960s as he practiced his craft repairing vintage instruments, and has produced anywhere from two to twenty guitars a year since then. Noble constantly experimented with the traditional uses of tonewoods, and his designs reflect the innovative use of coco bolo in bridges, and western red cedar for tops.

In 1964/1965, Noble replaced the top and neck on Clarence White's pre-war Martin D-28 when it came in for repairs (this instrument is currently owned by Tony Rice). White so enjoyed the sound that he later recorded with two Noble acoustics in many of his studio recordings, (Source: Michael R. Stanger and Greg Boyd, Stringed Instrument Division).

Noble currently offers two models: an orchestra-sized acoustic or a dreadnought-sized acoustic. Models are built in one of three configurations. The Standard features mahogany and Indian rosewood construction, while the Deluxe features mahogany, Indian rosewood, koa, pau ferro, or coco bolo. The Custom offers construction with koa, pau ferro, coco bolo or CITES certified Brazilian rosewood. For further information regarding models, specifications, and pricing please contact the Stringed Instrument Division directly (see Trademark Index).

NORMA

Instruments previously built in Japan between 1965 to 1970 by the Tombo company. Distributed by Strum'N Drum, Inc., of Chicago, Illinois.

These Japanese built guitars were distributed in the U.S. market by Strum'N Drum, Inc. of Chicago, Illinois. Strum'N Drum also distributed the Japanese-built Noble guitars of the mid to late 1960s, and National solid body guitars in the early 1970s, (Source: Michael Wright, *Guitar Stories*, Volume One).

NORMAN

Instruments currently built in La Patrie, Quebec, Canada since 1972. Norman Guitars are distributed by La Si Do, Inc., of St. Laurent, Canada.

In 1968, Robert Godin set up a custom guitar shop in Montreal called Harmonilab. Harmonilab quickly became known for its excellent work and musicians were coming from as far away as Quebec City to have their guitars adjusted. Harmonilab was the first guitar shop in Quebec to use professional strobe tuners for intonating guitars.

Although Harmonilab's business was flourishing, Robert was full of ideas for the design and construction of acoustic guitars. So, in 1972 the Norman Guitar Company was born. From the beginning the Norman guitars showed signs of the innovations that Godin would eventually bring to the guitar market. By 1978 Norman guitars had become quite successful in Canada and France, and continued expansion into the U.S. market. Today, Norman guitars and other members of the La Si Do guitar family are available all over the world.

For full company history, see Godin. Early models may be optionally equipped with L.R. Baggs electronics.

ACOUSTIC: B15 SERIES

B-15 (MODEL 0579) - dreadnought style, wild cherry top, round soundhole, black pickguard, bound body, black ring rosette, wild cherry back/sides, mahogany neck, 14/21-fret rosewood fingerboard with pearl dot inlay, rosewood bridge with white black dot pins, 3-per-side chrome tuners, available in Natural semi-gloss finish, current mfg.

	MSR	$350		$275	$150	$115

Add $154 for Fishman Basic EQ electronics (Model 7981). Add $35 for a left-handed configuration (Model 0715). Add $189 for a left-handed configuration and Fishman Basic EQ electronics (Model 8025).

B-15 COLORED (MODEL 0586) - similar to B-15, available in Burgundy (0586), Brown (0593), or TobaccoBurst (0609) semi-gloss finishes, current mfg.

	MSR	$369		$295	$175	$115

Add $154 for Fishman Basic EQ electronics.

B-15 (12) (MODEL 0685) - similar to B-15, except has 12 strings, 6-per-side tuners, current mfg.

	MSR	$436		$350	$195	$150

Add $153 for Fishman Basic EQ electronics (Model 8081). Add $44 for a left-handed configuration (Model 0807). Add $198 for a left-handed configuration and Fishman Basic EQ electronics (Model 8032).

GRADING	100%	EXCELLENT	AVERAGE

ACOUSTIC: B20 SERIES

B-20 (MODEL 0890) - dreadnought style, solid spruce top, round soundhole, black pickguard, bound body, one ring rosette, cherry back/sides, mahogany neck, 14/21-fret rosewood fingerboard with pearl dot inlay, rosewood bridge with white black dot pins, 3-per-side chrome tuners, available in Natural semi-gloss finish, current mfg.

MSR	$399		$325	$175	$125

Add $154 for Fishman Basic EQ electronics (Model 8087). Add $265 for Fishman Prefix EQ electronics (Model 8094). Add $41 for a left-handed configuration (Model 0951). Add $195 for a left-handed configuration and Fishman Basic EQ electronics (Model 8124). Add $306 for a left-handed configuration and Fishman Prefix EQ electronics (Model 8131).

B-20 HG (Model 1019) - similar to B-20, available in Natural high gloss lacquer finish, current mfg.

MSR	$477		$375	$250	$150

Add $376 for Fishman Blender EQ electronics (Model 8179). Add $265 for Fishman Prefix EQ electronics (Model 8162). Add $49 for a left-handed configuration (Model 1040). Add $425 for a left-handed configuration and Fishman Blender EQ electronics (Model 8193). Add $314 for a left-handed configuration and Fishman Prefix EQ electronics (Model 8186).

B-20 (12) (MODEL 0920) - similar to B-20, except has 12 string configuration, 6-per-side tuners., available in Natural semi-gloss finish, current mfg.

MSR	$515		$395	$195	$150

Add $375 for Fishman Blender EQ electronics (Model 8117). Add $265 for Fishman Prefix EQ electronics (Model 8100). Add $50 for a left-handed configuration (Model 0982). Add $425 for a left-handed configuration and Fishman Blender EQ electronics (Model 8155). Add $315 for a left-handed configuration and Fishman Prefix EQ electronics (Model 8148).

B-20 CW (MODEL 0517) - similar to B-20, except has single rounded cutaway body, available in Natural semi-gloss finish, current mfg.

MSR	$525		$395	$200	$150

Add $375 for Fishman Blender EQ electronics (Model 7943). Add $265 for Fishman Prefix EQ electronics (Model 7936).

B-20 CW HG (Model 0548) - similar to B-20, except has single rounded cutaway body. Available in Natural high gloss finish, current mfg.

MSR	$592		$475	$295	$195

Add $376 for Fishman Blender EQ electronics (Model 7967). Add $265 for Fishman Prefix EQ electronics (Model 7950).

B-20 FOLK (MODEL 0838) - similar to B-20, except has folk-style body, available in Natural semi-gloss finish, current mfg.

MSR	$399		$325	$175	$125

Add $154 for Fishman Basic EQ electronics (Model 8049). Add $265 for Fishman Prefix EQ electronics (Model 8056). Add $41 for a left-handed configuration (Model 0869). Add $195 for a left-handed configuration and Fishman Basic EQ electronics (Model 8063). Add $306 for a left-handed configuration and Fishman Prefix EQ electronics (Model 8070).

ACOUSTIC: B50 SERIES

B-50 (MODEL 1132) - dreadnought style, solid spruce top, round soundhole, black pickguard, bound body, 3-ring wooden inlay rosette, maple back/sides, mahogany neck, 14/21-fret rosewood fingerboard with pearl dot inlay, rosewood bridge with white black dot pins, 3-per-side chrome tuners, available in Natural high gloss finish, current mfg.

MSR	$745		$595	$300	$225

Add $375 for Fishman Blender EQ electronics (Model 8230). Add $265 for Fishman Prefix EQ electronics (Model 8223).

B-50 (12) (MODEL 1163) - similar to B-50, except has 12-strings, 6-per-side tuners, available in Natural high gloss finish, current mfg.

MSR	$850		$695	$350	$275

Add $375 for Fishman Blender EQ electronics (Model 8254). Add $265 for Fishman Prefix EQ electronics (Model 8247).

ACOUSTIC: ST SERIES

ST-40 (MODEL 1071) - dreadnought style, solid cedar top, round soundhole, black pickguard, bound body, 3-stripe rosette, mahogany back/sides/neck, 14/21-fret rosewood fingerboard with pearl dot inlay, rosewood bridge with white black dot pins, 3-per-side chrome tuners, available in Natural semi-gloss finish, current mfg.

MSR	$450		$350	$195	$150

Add $375 for Fishman Blender EQ electronics (Model 8216). Add $265 for Fishman Prefix EQ electronics (Model 8209).

N

GRADING	100%	EXCELLENT	AVERAGE

ST-68 (MODEL 1255) - dreadnought style, solid spruce top, round soundhole, black pickguard, bound body, 3-ring wooden inlay rosette, solid rosewood back, rosewood sides, mahogany neck, 14/21-fret ebony fingerboard with pearl dot inlay, ebony bridge with white black dot pins, 3-per-side chrome tuners, available in Natural high gloss finish, current mfg.

MSR	$1,000		$825	$450	$350

> Add $375 for Fishman Blender EQ electronics (Model 8292). Add $265 for Fishman Prefix EQ electronics (Model 8285). Add $100 for a left-handed configuration (Model 1286). Add $475 for a left-handed configuration and Fishman Blender EQ electronics (Model 8315). Add $365 for a left-handed configuration and Fishman Prefix EQ electronics (Model 8308).

ST-68 CW (MODEL 8346) - similar to ST-68, except has a single rounded cutaway body, available in Natural high gloss finish, mfg. 1998-current.

MSR	$1,227

> Add $376 for Fishman Blender EQ electronics (Model 8339). Add $265 for Fishman Prefix EQ electronics (Model 8322).

NORTHWOOD GUITARS
Instruments currently built in Langley, British Columbia, Canada.

John McQuarrie is the president of Northwood Guitars, and they currently offers 5 models of acoustic guitars that feature solid tonewood tops, flamed or quilted maple and Indian rosewood back and sides, ebony fingerboards, and other wood appointments. They also make solid-body electric guitars. For more information refer to their web site (see Trademark Index).

NORTHWORTHY
Instruments currently built in England since 1987.

Northworthy currently offers hand crafted acoustic guitars, and well as custom and left-handed models. Previous original design solid body guitars are generally of very good quality, and feature such model designations as the **Dovedale, Edale**, and **Milldale**. Models include classical and dreadnought styles (also a few others), as well as a range of manddolins, mandolas, octave mandolins, bozoukis, and electric instruments. Interested persons are urged to contact Alan Marshall at Northworthy directly (see Trademark Index).

N

Section O

OAHU

Previous trademark of instruments distributed by the Oahu Publishing Company of Cleveland, Ohio.

The Oahu Publishing Company offered Hawaiian and Spanish style acoustic guitars, lap steels, sheet music, and a wide range of accessories during the Hawaiian music craze of pre-war America. Catalogs stress the fact that the company is a major music distributor (thus the question of who built the guitars is still unanswered). Oahu production totals are still unknown.

OAKLAND

Instruments previously produced in Japan from the late 1970s through the early 1980s.

These good quality solid body guitars featured both original designs and designs based on classic American favorites, (Source: Tony Bacon and Paul Day, *The Guru's Guitar Guide*).

ODELL

Previous trademark of instrument (possibly produced by the Vega Guitar Company of Boston, Massachusetts), and dstributed through the Vega Guitar catalog circa early 1930s to the early 1950s.

Odell acoustic guitars with slotted headstocks were offered through early Vega Guitar catalogs in the early 1930s. In the 1932 catalog, the four Odell models were priced above Harmony guitars, but were not as pricey as the Vega models.

Other Odell mystery guitars appear at guitar shows from time to time. David Pavlick is the current owner of an interesting archtop model. The 3 tuners per side headstock features a decal which reads "Odell - Vega Co., - Boston," and features a 16 1/2" archtop body, one Duo-Tron pickup, 20-fret neck, volume/tone controls mounted on the trapeze tailpiece. Inside one f-hole there is "828H1325" stamped into the back wood. Any readers with further information are invited to write to the *Blue Book of Acoustic Guitars,* (Source: David J. Pavlick, Woodbury, Connecticut).

ACOUSTIC

The four Odell acoustic models featured in the 1932 catalog have a round soundhole, 3-per-side brass or nickel-plated tuners, slotted headstock, pearl position dots, and are described as full standard size or concert size. The **Model A** had a white spruce top, mahogany body/neck, black and white purfling, blackwood fingerboard/bridge, and a 1930s list price of $15! The **Model B** featured a mahogany top/body/neck, and rosewood fingerboard/bridge (new list $20). The professional **Model C** had a black and white pyralin bound white spruce top, mahogany body, and a new price of $25. The quartet was rounded out by a 4-string **Tenor Guitar** ($15) with mahogany top/body/neck, with the neck joining the body at the 15th fret. Used prices at this point are still unknown.

OLD KRAFTSMAN

See chapter on House Brands.

This trademark has been identified as a House Brand of Speigel, and was sold through the Speigel catalogs. The Old Kraftsman brand was used on a full line of acoustic, thinline acoustic/electric, and solid body guitars from circa 1930s to the 1960s. Old Kraftsman instruments were probably built by various companies in Chicago, including Kay and some models by Gibson, (Source: Michael Wright, *Vintage Guitar Magazine*).

OLSEN AUDIO

Instruments currently built in Saskatoon (Saskatchewan), Canada.

Luthier Bryan Olsen has been building guitars and performing repairs for a number of years. His new project features a metal bodied tricone-style resonator guitar with a single cutaway. The body shape has been designed from the ground up, and has an innovative stacked cone tray assembly.

OLSON, JAMES A.

Instruments currently built in Circle Pines, Minnesota.

Luthier James A. Olson began building acoustic guitars full time in 1977. Olson had previous backgrounds in woodworking and guitar playing, and combined his past favorites into his current occupation. Olson's creations have been used by James Taylor (since 1989), Phil Keaggy, Sting, Leo Kottke, Justin Hayward (Moody Blues), and Kathy Mattea.

Olson handcrafts 60 guitars a year, and currently has a waiting list. All models are custom made with a wide variety of options to choose from. Olson builds in either the **SJ** (Small Jumbo) or **Dreadnought** configuration, and features East Indian rosewood back and sides, a Sitka spruce or western red cedar top, and a five piece laminated neck (rosewood center, maple, and mahogany outer sections). Either configuration also offers an ebony fingerboard, bridge, and peghead overlay, tortoise shell bound body, bound headstock and side purfling, herringbone top purfling, mother-of-pearl fingerboard position dots, a carved volute on back of the headstock, chrome Schaller tuners, and gloss nitro-cellulose lacquer finish. Prices range from $5,000-$25,000. For a complete listing of available options, or for further information please contact luthier Olson.

**Oahu Lap Guitar
courtesy John Beeson
The Music Shoppe**

**Olympia OD11TAM
courtesy Olympia**

OLYMPIA

Instruments currently produced in Korea. Distributed by Tacoma Guitars USA of Tacoma, Washington.

Olympia instruments are engineered and set up in the U.S., and feature a number of dreadnought and jumbo body style models with designs based on the U.S.-produced Tacoma acoustic guitars. New retail prices run from $179 up to $529.

OMEGA INSTRUMENTS

Instruments currently built in Saylorsburg, Pennsylvania. Distributed by Kevin Gallagher Guitars, Inc. of Saylorsburg, Pennsylvania.

Luthier Kevin Gallagher is currently offering a range of quality, handcrafted acoustic guitars from his shop in Saylorsburg. Gallagher's Omega Instruments are offered in dreadnought, jumbo (and mini-jumbo), grand concert, and "000" style guitar models. In addition to a well built, good sounding instrument, Gallagher also offers high quality inlay work that ranges from simple dots to a full fingerboard vine inlay. Current retail prices range from $1,850 to $2,200; 000 models run at $3,000. For further information, please contact Kevin Gallagher directly (see Trademark Index).

OPUS

Instruments currently produced in Japan.

The Opus trademark is a brand name of U.S. importers Ampeg/Selmer, (Source: Michael Wright, *Guitar Stories,* Volume One).

ORBIT

See Teisco Del Rey. Instruments previously built in Japan during the mid to late 1960s.

The Orbit trademark is the brand name of a UK importer. Orbit guitars were produced by the same folks who built Teisco guitars in Japan; so while there is the relative coolness of the original Teisco design, the entry level quality is the drawback, (Source: Tony Bacon and Paul Day, *The Guru's Guitar Guide*).

ORIGINAL MUSIC INSTRUMENT COMPANY, INC.

Instruments currently produced in Nashville, Tennessee (previous production was located in Long Beach, California through December, 1996). Distributed by Gibson Guitar Corporation of Nashville, Tennessee.

In 1960, Emil Dopyera and brothers Rudy and John founded the Original Music Instrument company to build resonator guitars. They soon resumed production on models based on their wood-body Dobros. In the late 1960s, OMI also began production of metal-bodied resonators roughly similar to their old National designs. Ron Lazar, a Dopyera nephew, took over the business in the early 1970s. In 1993, OMI was sold to the Gibson Guitar Corporation, although production is still centered in California. For further information on OMI/Dobro, see current model listings under Dobro, (Early company history courtesy Bob Brozman, *The History and Artistry of National Resonator Instruments*).

ORPHEUM

See also Lange. Instruments previously manufactured in Chicago, Illinois circa 1930s to 1940s. Distributed by William L. Lange Company of New York, New York, and by C. Bruno & Son. Instruments later manufactured in Japan circa 1960s. Distributed by Maurice Lipsky Music Company, Inc., of New York, New York.

Orpheum guitars were first introduced by distributor William L. Lange Company of New York in the mid 1930s. The Orpheum brand instruments were also distributed by C. Bruno & Son during this early period. It is estimated that some of the Orpheum models were built in Chicago, Illinois by the Kay company.

Lange's company went out of business in the early 1940s, but New York distributor Maurice Lipsky resumed distribution of Orpheum guitars circa 1944. The Maurice Lipsky Music Company continued distributing Orpheum guitars, through to the 1960s (See also Domino), (Source: Tom Wheeler, *American Guitars*; Orpheum Manufacturing Company catalog courtesy John Kinnemeyer, JK Lutherie).

Until more research is done in the Orpheum area, prices will continue to fluctuate. Be very cautious in the distinction between the American models and the later overseas models produced in Japan. "What the market will bear" remains the watchword for Orpheums.

OSCAR SCHMIDT

Current trademark manufactured in Korea, and distributed by Oscar Schmidt International of Mundelein, Illinois.

The original Oscar Schmidt company was based in Jersey City, New Jersey, and was established in the late 1800s by Oscar Schmidt and his son, Walter. The Oscar Schmidt company produced a wide range of stringed instruments and some of the trade names utilized were Stella, Sovereign, and LaScala among others. The company later changed its name to Oscar Schmidt International, and in 1935 or 1936 followed with the Fretted Instrument Manufacturers. After the company went bankrupt, the Harmony Company of Chicago, Illinois purchased rights to use Oscar Schmidt's trademarks in 1939.

In the late 1900s, the Oscar Schmidt trademark was revived by the Washburn International Company of Illinois. Oscar Schmidt currently offers both acoustic guitars and other stringed instruments for the beginning student up to the intermediate player, (Source: Tom Wheeler, *American Guitars*).

ACOUSTIC: CLASSICAL

OC1 - classical body, agathis top, mahogany back and sides, nylon strings, available in Natural Satin finish, current mfg.

MSR	$120	$75	$50	$35

OC9 - classical body, mahogany top, back and sides, nylon strings, available in Natural finish, current mfg.

MSR	$160	$150	$110	$75

OC11 - classical body, select spruce top, mahogany back and sides, available in Natural finish, current mfg.

MSR	$200	$225	$130	$90

ACOUSTIC: DREADNOUGHT

OG2M - dreadnought body, mahogany top, back and sides, available in Natural finish, current mfg.

MSR	$269	N/A	$200	$130

Add $10 for Transparent Red and Transparent finishes.

GRADING		100%	EXCELLENT	AVERAGE

OG2N - dreadnought body, select spruce top, mahogany back and sides, available in Natural finish, current mfg.

	MSR	$279	N/A	$209	$135

Add $30 for left-hand model (OG2NLH).

OG3S - dreadnought body, solid spruce top, mahogany back and sides, Schaller tuners, available in High Gloss Natural finish, new 2001.

	MSR	$369	$275	$165	$105

OG240 - dreadnought body, select spruce top, mahogany back and sides, 3-per-side tuners, black pickguard, available in Natural finish, current mfg.

	MSR	$199	$149	$90	$60

OG260 - similar to Model OG240, except has basswood top, back and sides, available in Semi-Satin finish, current mfg.

	MSR	$249	$185	$110	$70

Oscar Schmidt Model 6240 FWR
courtesy Dave Rogers
Dave's Guitar Shop

ACOUSTIC ELECTRIC

OG11CE - dreadnought body with single cutaway, select spruce top, rosewood fingerboard, dot position markers, 3-per-side tuners, passive pickups, available in Natural finish, current mfg.

	MSR	$399	$299	$175	$115

Add $70 for Ash top. Available in Antique Natural and Transparent Red finishes.

OG20CE - dreadnought body, ash top, active pickups, rosewood fingerboard with dot position markers, available in Trans Red, Trans Blue, Black Pearl, or Metallic Apple finishes, current mfg.

	MSR	$449	$335	$198	$130

OUTBOUND

Instruments previously built in Boulder, Colorado.

Outbound produced a scaled down travel guitar that maintains the look of a regular acoustic.

OVATION

Instruments currently built in New Hartford, Connecticut since 1967. Distribution is handled by the Kaman Music Corporation of Bloomfield, Connecticut.

The Ovation guitar company, and the nature of the Ovation guitar's synthetic back are directly attributed to founder Charles H. Kaman's experiments in helicopter aviation. Kaman, who began playing guitar back in high school, trained in the field of aeronautics and graduated from the Catholic University in Washington, D.C. His first job in 1940 was with a division of United Aircraft, home of aircraft inventor Igor Sikorsky. In 1945, Kaman formed the Kaman Aircraft Corporation to pursue his helicopter-related inventions.

As the company began to grow, the decision was made around 1957 to diversify into manufacturing products in different fields. Kaman initially made overtures to the Martin company, as well as exploring both Harmony and Ludwig drums. Finally, the decision was made to start fresh. Due to research in vibrations and resonances in the materials used to build helicopter blades, guitar development began in 1964 with employees John Ringso and Jim Rickard. In fact, it was Rickard's pre-war Martin D-45 that was used as the "test standard." In 1967, the Ovation company name was chosen, incorporated, and settled into its "new facilities" in New Hartford, Connecticut. The first model named that year was the Balladeer.

Ovation guitars were debuted at the 1967 NAMM show. Early players and endorsers included Josh White, Charlie Byrd, and Glen Campbell. Piezo pickup equipped models were introduced in 1972, as well as other models. During the early 1970s, Kaman Music (Ovation's parent company) acquired the well-known music distributors Coast, and also part of the Takamine guitar company. By 1975, Ovation decided to release an entry level instrument, and the original Applause/Medallion/Matrix designs were first built in the U.S. before production moved into Korea.

In 1986, Kaman's oldest son became president of Kaman Music. Charles William Bill Kaman II had begun working in the Ovation factory at age 14. After graduating college in 1974, Bill was made Director of Development at the Moosup, Connecticut plant. A noted Travis Bean guitar collector (see Kaman's Travis Bean history later in this book), Bill Kaman remained active in the research and development aspect of model design. Kaman helped design the Viper III, and the UK II solid bodies.

Bill Kaman gathered all branches of the company *under one roof* as the Kaman Music Corporation (KMC) in 1986. As the Ovation branch was now concentrating on acoustic and acoustic/electric models, the corporation bought the independent Hamer company in 1988 as the means to re-enter the solid body guitar market. Furthermore, KMC began distributing Trace-Elliot amplifiers the same year, and bought the company in 1992. The Kaman Music Corporation acts as the parent company, and has expanded to cover just about all areas of the music business. As a result, the Ovation branch now concentrates specifically on producing the best acoustic guitars, with the same attention to detail that the company was founded on, (Source: Walter Carter, *The History of the Ovation Guitar*).

Ovation Adamas 1687
courtesy Ovation

FOUR DIGIT MODEL CODES

Ovation instruments are identified by a four digit model code. The individual numbers within the code will indicate production information about that model.

The first digit is (generally) 1.

GRADING	100%	EXCELLENT	AVERAGE

The second digit describes the type of guitar:

1	**Acoustic Roundbacks or Semi-hollow electrics**
2	**Solid Body or Semi-hollowbody electrics**
3	**Ultra acoustics**
4	**Solid body**
5	**Acoustic/Electric cutaway Adamas and II/Elite/Ultra electric**
6	**Acoustic/Electric Roundbacks**
7	**Deep**
8	**Shallow**

The third digit indicates the depth of the guitar's bowl:

1	**Standard (5 1/2 13/16" deep)**
2	**Artist (5 1/2 1/8" deep)**
3	**Elite/Matrix electric deep bowl**
4	**Matrix shallow bowl**
5	**Custom Balladeer/Legend/Legend 12/Custom Legend 12/Anniversary**
6	**Cutaway electric, deep bowl**
7	**Cutaway electric, shallow bowl**
8	**Adamas (6 1/2 1/16" deep)**

The fourth digit indicates the model (for the first 8 acoustics):

1	**Balladeer**
2	**Deluxe Balladeer**
3	**Classic**
4	**Josh White**
5	**12 String**
6	**Contemporary Folk Classic**
7	**Glen Campbell Artist Balladeer**
8	**Glen Campbell 12 String**

The color code follows the hyphen after the four digit model number. Colors available on Ovation guitars are Sunburst (1), Red (2), Natural (4), Black (5), White (6), LTD Nutmeg/Anniversary Brown/Beige/Tan (7), Blue (8), Brown (9), Barnwood [a grey to black sunburst] (B), and Honeyburst (H). Other specialty colors may have a 2-or 3-letter abbreviation, (Information collected in Mr. Carter's Ovation Appendices was researched and compiled by Paul Bechtoldt).

ACOUSTIC: GENERAL INFORMATION

Ovation is currently offering a 8-string Mandolin (**Model MM68**) and 8-string Mandocello (**Model MC868**). Both models feature a solid Sitka spruce top, 21-fret ebony fingerboard, gold hardware, and onboard preamp. The Mandolin has a list price of $1,499, and the Mandocello is $2,199.

Select Ovation acoustic/electric models can be ordered with a factory installed **Roland GK-2** synthesizer interface as an option. This option includes a magnetic hex pickup, synth/guitar mix controls, and a controller output jack.

All Ovation acoustic and acoustic/electric instruments have a synthetic rounded back/sides construction. The model number in parenthesis following the name is the current assigned **Model Number**.

In 1976/1977, Ovation debuted the Medallion series guitars – which was later renamed the Matrix series. These models were produced in the U.S., and featured a wood top, synthetic bowl back, and plastic headstock overlay. The original list price was $249.

Ovation has released several Anniversary models over the years as many guitar companies do, to commemorate how many years they have been in business. Several of these models haven't been circulated in the secondary market and little is known about them.

ACOUSTIC: ADAMAS SERIES

All Adamas models have a composite top consisting of 2 carbon-graphite layers around a birch core, and carved fiberglass body binding. There are also 11 various sized soundholes with leaf pattern maple veneer around them, situated around the upper bouts on both sides of the fingerboard. All models have 6 piezo bridge pickups, volume/3-band EQ controls, and an active OP-24 preamp. The Adamas model was introduced in 1976, and discontinued in 1999.

ADAMAS 6 (MODEL 1687) - composite top, mahogany neck, 14/24-fret walnut extended fingerboard with maple/ebony inlay, walnut bridge with carved flower designs, carved flower design on peghead, 3-per-side gold tuners, available in Blue finish, mfg.1977-1998.

$2,150	$1,700	$1,100

Last MSR was $3,099.

Earlier models may have Beige, Black, Brown, or Red finishes.

Adamas 6 Cutaway (Model 1587) - similar to Adamas 6, except has venetian cutaway, no soundholes on cutaway side, available in Black finish, mfg. 1979-1998.

$2,200	$1,800	$1,150

Last MSR was $3,199.

ADAMAS 12 (MODEL 1688) - similar to Adamas 6, except has 12 strings, available in Black finish, disc. 1998.

$2,300	$1,900	$1,200

Last MSR was $3,299.

ADAMAS (MODEL 6581) - deep lyrachord bowl, carbon graphite/birch composite top, mahogany neck, 14/24-fret ebony extended fingerboard, ebony bridge, natural peghead with Adamas logo, 3-per-side gold tuners, Optima pickup system, available in High Gloss Black and Opaque Burgundy finishes, mfg. 1998.

$1,925	$1,150	$800

Last MSR was $2,499.

Also available with round soundhole rather than multiple soundholes for last MSR $1,749 (Model 6591).

GRADING	100%	EXCELLENT	AVERAGE

ADAMAS SMT (MODEL 1597) - mid depth Lyrachord bowl, carbon graphite/birch composite top, mahogany neck, 14/24-fret ebony extended fingerboard, ebony bridge, blackface peghead with Adamas logo, 3-per-side gold tuners, CP-100 pickup, Optima pickup system, available in Natural Graphite finish, mfg. 1998-99.

	$1,500	**$900**	**$630**

Last MSR was $1,899.

Can also be ordered with round soundhole rather than multiple soundholes for $1,749 (Model 6591).

Adamas SMT 12-String (Model 1598) - similar to Model 1597, except in a 12-string version, available in Natural Graphite and Red Graphite finishes, mfg. 1999 only.

	$1,550	**$930**	**$650**

Last MSR was $1,999.

ADAMAS Q (MODEL Q181) - deep carbon graphite bowl, carbon graphite top, through body graphite neck, 14/24-fret ebony extended fingerboard, ebony bridge, blackface peghead with Adamas logo, 3-per-side gold tuners, available in Natural Graphite finish, mfg. 1998 only.

	$4,600	**$2,750**	**$1,895**

Last MSR was $5,999.

Ovation Adamas II 1581
courtesy Ovation

ACOUSTIC: ADAMAS II SERIES

Similar to the original Adamas series, the Adamas II featured the standard Ovation headstock and bridge instead of the carved walnut, and a five piece mahogany and maple laminate neck instead of the solid walnut neck. The Adamas II model was introduced in early 1982; the series was discontinued in 1998.

ADAMAS II (MODEL 1681) - composite top, mahogany/maple 5-piece neck, 14/24-fret walnut extended fingerboard with maple/ebony triangle inlay, walnut bridge, walnut veneer on peghead, 3-per-side gold tuners, available in Black, Blue, or Blue Green finishes, disc. 1998.

	$1,650	**$1,375**	**$795**

Last MSR was $2,399.

ADAMAS II CUTAWAY (MODEL 1581) - similar to Adamas II, except has venetian cutaway, no soundholes on cutaway side, available in Blue finish, disc. 1998.

	$1,750	**$1,400**	**$850**

Last MSR was $2,499.

In 1994, soundholes on cutaway side were introduced.

ADAMAS II 12 (MODEL 1685) - similar to Adamas II, except has 12 strings, 6-per-side tuners, available in Black finish, disc. 1998.

	$1,850	**$1,475**	**$850**

Last MSR was $2,599.

ADAMAS II CUTAWAY SHALLOW (MODEL 1881) - similar to Adamas II, except has shallow bowl body, venetian cutaway, available in Black or Blue Green finishes, mfg. 1994-98.

	$1,750	**$1,400**	**$850**

Last MSR was $2,499.

ADAMAS II 12 SHALLOW (MODEL 1885) - similar to Adamas II, except has shallow bowl body, 12 strings, 6-per-side tuners, available in Black finish, mfg. 1994-98.

	$1,850	**$1,450**	**$850**

Last MSR was $2,699.

ACOUSTIC: BALLADEER SERIES

The Balladeer was the first model introduced by the Ovation company in 1967.

CUSTOM BALLADEER (MODEL 1712) - spruce top, round soundhole, 5-stripe bound body, leaf pattern rosette, 5-piece mahogany/maple neck, 14/20-fret ebony fingerboard, 12th fret pearl diamond/dot inlay, walnut strings through bridge with pearl dot inlay, 3-per-side nickel tuners, 6 piezo bridge pickups, volume control, 3-band EQ, FET preamp, available in Black, Natural, Sunburst, or White finishes, disc. 1996.

	$650	**$475**	**$350**

Last MSR was $995.

This model has cedar top as an option. In 1994, the pearl dot bridge inlay was discontinued.

Custom Balladeer Cutaway (Model 1860) - similar to Custom Balladeer, except has single round cutaway, shallow bowl body, disc. 1996.

	$750	**$575**	**$375**

Last MSR was $1,095.

Custom Balladeer 12 - similar to Custom Balladeer, except has 12 strings, 6-per-side chrome tuners with pearloid buttons, disc. 1994.

	N/A	**$625**	**$425**

Last MSR was $1,250.

Ovation Standard Balladeer
Cutaway 1861
courtesy Ovation

GRADING	100%	EXCELLENT	AVERAGE

STANDARD BALLADEER (MODEL 1111) - folk-style, solid Sitka spruce top, round soundhole, 5-stripe bound body, leaf pattern rosette, cedro neck, 14/20-fret rosewood fingerboard with pearl dot inlay, rosewood strings through bridge with pearl dot inlay, 3-per-side chrome tuners, available in Natural finish, mfg. 1967-2001.

	100%	EXCELLENT	AVERAGE
1967-1979	N/A	$600	$400
1980-1993	N/A	$500	$350
1994-2001	$650	$425	$300

Last MSR was $849.

Standard Balladeer 12-String (Model 1151) - similar to the Balladeer, except in 12-string configuration, disc. 1999.

	$700	$475	$325

Last MSR was $899.

STANDARD BALLADEER ELECTRIC (MODEL 1711) - similar to Standard Balladeer, except has piezo bridge pickups, 4-band EQ, available in Natural, Cadillac Green, or Cherry Cherryburst finishes, disc. 2000.

	$750	$475	$325

Last MSR was $949.

Standard Balladeer Electric 12-String (Model 1751) - similar to the Balladeer, except in 12-string configuration, disc. 1998.

	$800	$500	$350

Last MSR was $1,149.

STANDARD BALLADEER CUTAWAY (MODEL 1761) - similar to Standard Balladeer, except has single round cutaway, deep bowl, piezo bridge pickups, 4-band EQ, available in Black, Natural, Cadillac Green, or Cherry Cherryburst finishes, disc. 2000.

	$825	$525	$350

Last MSR was $1,049.

Standard Balladeer Cutaway Mid-Depth (Model 1771) - similar to Standard Balladeer except has a Mid-Depth bowl body, available in Natural, Black, or Cherry Cherryburst, current mfg.

MSR	$999	$700	$500	$325

STANDARD BALLADEER CUTAWAY (MODEL 1861) - similar to Standard Balladeer, except has single round cutaway, super shallow bowl, piezo bridge pickups, 4-band EQ, available in Black, Natural, Cadillac Green, or Cherry Cherryburst finishes, current mfg.

MSR	$999	$700	$500	$325

Standard Balladeer Cutaway 12-String (Model 6751) - similar to the Standard Balladeer, except in 12-string configuration, available in Black, Natural, or Cherry Cherryburst finishes, current mfg.

MSR	$1,129	$795	$550	$350

BALLADEER (MODEL 4861) - solid spruce top, super shallow cutaway body, satin finish mahogany neck with 20-frets, rosewood fingerboards-100 Thinline pickup, OP24 Plus Preamp and electronics, available in Sunburst, Natural, or Black finishes, disc. 2000.

	$575	$400	$265

Last MSR was $799.

BALLADEER SPECIAL (MODEL S771) - similar to Standard Balladeer except has Mid-Depth bowl body, available in Natural, Sundance, or Teardrop Burst finishes, current mfg.

MSR	$929	$650	$475	$350

Balladeer Special Super Shallow (Model S861) - similar to Balladeer Special except has a Super Shallow bowl body, available in Natural, Sundance, or Teardrop Burst, current mfg.

MSR	$929	$650	$475	$350

ACOUSTIC: CELEBRITY SERIES

The Celebrity series is Ovation's entry level introduction to the product line.

CELEBRITY (MODEL CC-01) - deep bowl, spruce top, round soundhole, bound body, leaf pattern rosette, 2-piece mahogany neck, 14/20-fret bound rosewood fingerboard with dot inlay, walnut bridge with pearloid dot inlays, rosewood veneer on peghead, 3-per-side chrome tuners, piezo bridge pickup, DJ-4 preamp/electronics, available in Natural or Mahogany finishes, current mfg.

MSR	$420	$295	$210	$120

Celebrity Shallow (Model CC-057) - similar to Celebrity, except features a super shallow cutaway bowl, available in Natural, Black, Mahogany, or Ruby Red finishes, current mfg.

MSR	$600	$420	$275	$150

Celebrity Mid-Depth (Model CC-047) - similar to the Celebrity except has a mid-depth cutaway bowl, available in Natural finish, disc. 1999.

	$500	$350	$200

Last MSR was $700.

CELEBRITY (MODEL CC-11) - spruce top, round soundhole, 5-stripe bound body, leaf pattern rosette, mahogany neck, 14/20-fret bound rosewood fingerboard with pearl dot inlay, walnut bridge with pearloid dot inlays, rosewood veneer on peghead, 3-per-side chrome tuners, available in Barn board, Brownburst, Natural, or Sunburst finishes, disc. 1996.

	$275	$200	$125

Last MSR was $400.

Add $100 for 12-string configuration (Model CC-15, Disc.). Add $200 for 12-string configuration, piezo bridge pickups, 4-band EQ (Model CC-65, Disc.). Available in Natural finish.

GRADING	100%	EXCELLENT	AVERAGE

CELEBRITY CUTAWAY (MODEL CC026) - similar to the Celebrity, except has a mid-depth body, available in Natural finish, mfg. 2000-current.

MSR	$440		$305	$225	$125

CELEBRITY CUTAWAY COLOR (MODEL CK057) - similar to the Celebrity Cutaway except is available in Dark Blue Pearl, Silver Satin Pearl, or Deep Purple Quilted finishes, mfg. 2002-current.

MSR	$620		$440	$310	$175

Add $35 for Deep Purple Quilted finish.

CELEBRITY NYLON STRING (MODEL CC059) - similar to the Celebrity, except in nylon string configuration with open tuners, available in Natural Cedar finish, mfg. 2002-current.

MSR	$630		$445	$315	$180

CELEBRITY TREKKER (MODEL TC-012) - compact mini body, spruce top, round soundhole, bound body, leaf pattern rosette, 2-piece mahogany neck, short scale 14/20-fret bound rosewood fingerboard with dot inlay, walnut bridge with pearloid dot inlays, rosewood veneer on peghead, 3-per-side chrome tuners, piezo bridge pickup, available in Black or Natural finishes, mfg. 1998-99.

MSR	$400		$295	$200	$130

Celebrity Trekker (Model CS-212) - similar to Trekker Model CC-012 except has a mutli-soundholes, available in Natural finish, current mfg.

MSR	$470		$330	$250	$150

Celebrity Electric (Model CC-67) - similar to Celebrity, except has piezo bridge pickups, 4-band EQ, available in Barn board, Brownburst, or Natural finishes, mfg. 1994-96.

			$350	$250	$150

Last MSR was $500.

CELEBRITY CLASSIC (MODEL 1113) - classical style, spruce top, round soundhole, 5-stripe bound body, leaf pattern rosette, mahogany neck, 12/19-fret bound rosewood fingerboard, walnut bridge, 3-per-side gold tuners with pearloid buttons, available in Natural finish, disc. 1996.

			$275	$200	$125

Last MSR was $400.

Add $100 for piezo bridge pickups, 4-band EQ (Model 1613). Available in Natural finish (Mfg. 1994 to 1996). Add $200 for venetian cutaway, piezo bridge pickups, volume/tone control (Model 1663).

CELEBRITY CUTAWAY - single round cutaway, spruce top, round soundhole, 5-stripe bound body, leaf pattern rosette, mahogany neck, 20-fret bound rosewood fingerboard with pearloid diamond/dot inlay, walnut bridge with pearloid dot inlay, walnut veneer on peghead, 3-per-side chrome tuners, 6 piezo bridge pickups, volume/tone control, available in Barn board, Brownburst, Natural, or Sunburst finishes, mfg. 1991-96.

			$385	$275	$150

Last MSR was $550.

Add $50 for shallow bowl body (Celebrity Cutaway Shallow).

**Ovation Celebrity CK 057
courtesy Dave Rogers
Dave's Guitar Shop**

ACOUSTIC: CELEBRITY DELUXE SERIES

The Celebrity Deluxe series features the same multiple soundholes of the Adamas and Elite designs on a laminated spruce or cedar top.

CELEBRITY DELUXE (MODEL CS-247) - mid depth Lyrachord bowl, solid spruce top, multi-sized soundholes with leaf pattern maple veneer, 5-stripe bound body, 2-piece nato neck, 14/23 fret bound rosewood extended fingerboard with pearl diamond/dot inlay, rosewood strings through bridge, rosewood veneered peghead with logo decal, 3-per-side gold tuners, piezo bridge pickups, OP-24+ system, available in Natural finish, mfg. 1998-current.

MSR	$830		$585	$415	$250

Celebrity Deluxe Left-Hand (Model LCS-247) - similar to the Celebrity Deluxe, except in left-handed configuration, available in Black finish, mfg. 2002-current.

MSR	$850		$595	$425	$250

Celebrity Deluxe 12-String (Model CS-245) - similar to the Celebrity Deluxe, except in 12-String configuration, mfg. 1998-current.

MSR	$900		$630	$450	$275

CELEBRITY DELUXE (MODEL CC-267) - cedar top, multi-sized soundholes with leaf pattern maple veneer, 5-stripe bound body, mahogany neck, 14/23 fret bound rosewood extended fingerboard with pearl diamond/dot inlay, rosewood strings through bridge, rosewood veneered peghead with logo decal, 3-per-side gold tuners, piezo bridge pickups, 4-band EQ, available in Antique Sunburst or Natural finishes, disc. 1996.

			$450	$325	$200

Last MSR was $650.

This model has spruce and sycamore tops as an option.

**Ovation Celebrity
Deluxe CS-247
courtesy Ovation**

GRADING	100%	EXCELLENT	AVERAGE

Celebrity Deluxe Cutaway (Model CC-268) - similar to Celebrity Deluxe, except has single round cutaway, available in Black, Natural, or Wineburst finishes, disc. 1996.

	$500	$350	$225

Last MSR was $700.

CELEBRITY DELUXE CUTAWAY SHALLOW (MODEL CS-257) - similar to Celebrity Deluxe, except has spruce top, single round cutaway, shallow bowl body, OP-24 Plus preamp, available in Black, Natural, Blue Transparent, or Ruby Redburst finishes, current mfg.

MSR	$750	$525	$330	$225

Add $60 for Cherry Cherryburst Quilted Maple or Vintage Flame finishes.

Autumn Burst finish added in 1999.

Celebrity Deluxe Cutaway Shallow 12-String (Model CS255) - similar to the Celebrity Deluxe Cutaway Shallow, except has 12-String configuration, available in Honey Burst finish, current mfg.

MSR	$900	$630	$450	$275

Celebrity Deluxe Cutaway Shallow Doubleneck (Model CSD255) - similar to the Celebrity Deluxe Cutaway Shallow, except has 2 necks with a 6-and 12-String configurations, available in Black Cherryburst finish, current mfg.

MSR	$1,600	$1,150	$800	$450

ACOUSTIC: CLASSIC SERIES

CLASSIC (MODEL 1613) - classical style, cedar top, round soundhole, 5-stripe bound body, leaf pattern rosette, 5-piece mahogany/maple neck, 12/19-fret extended ebony fingerboard, walnut bridge, walnut veneer on peghead, 3-per-side gold tuners, piezo bridge pickup, volume/3-band EQ control, active preamp, available in Natural finish, disc. 1994.

	N/A	$800	$450

Last MSR was $1,420.

Classic Cutaway (Model 1663) - similar to Classic, except has venetian cutaway, available in Natural and White finishes, disc. 1994.

	N/A	$850	$500

Last MSR was $1,520.

This model had shallow bowl as an option.

ACOUSTIC: COLLECTOR'S SERIES

The Collector's Series offers limited edition guitars. Beginning in 1982, a different model is featured each year, and production of that model is limited to that year only. The following descriptions list the number of instruments built per model, and also the listed retail price, (Information compiled by Paul Bechtoldt, and featured in Walter Carter's *The History of the Ovation Guitar* book.).

1982 COLLECTOR'S (MODEL 1982-8) - bowl back acoustic guitar, round soundhole, mfg. 1982 only.

	N/A	$750	$450

Last MSR was $995.

A total of 1,908 guitars were produced.

1983 COLLECTOR'S (MODEL 1983-B) - super shallow bowl, single cutaway, round soundhole, available in Barn board (exaggerated grain) finish, mfg. 1983 only.

	N/A	$750	$450

Last MSR was $995.

A total of 2,754 guitars were produced.

1984 COLLECTOR'S (MODEL 1984-5) - Elite model design, Super shallow bowl, single cutaway, available in Ebony stain finish, mfg. 1984 only.

	N/A	$750	$450

Last MSR was $995.

A total of 2,637 guitars were produced.

1985 COLLECTOR'S (MODEL 1985-1) - Elite model design, Super shallow bowl, single cutaway, available in Autumnburst finish, mfg. 1985 only.

	N/A	$800	$475

Last MSR was $1,095.

A total of 2,198 guitars were produced.

1985 Collector's (Model 2985-1) - similar to the 1985 Collector's model, except offered in limited quantities as a 12-string model, available in Autumnburst finish, mfg. 1985 only.

	N/A	$825	$475

Last MSR was $1,195.

A total of 715 guitars were produced.

1986 COLLECTOR'S (MODEL 1986-6) - super shallow bowl, single cutaway, round soundhole, available in Pearl White finish, mfg. 1986 only.

	N/A	$800	$475

Last MSR was $1,095.

A total of 1,858 guitars were produced.

GRADING	100%	EXCELLENT	AVERAGE

1986 Collector's (Model 2986-6) - similar to the 1986 Collector's model, except offered in limited quantities as a 12-string model, available in Pearl White finish, mfg. 1986 only.

	N/A	$825	$475

Last MSR was $1,195.

A total of 392 guitars were produced.

1987 COLLECTOR'S (MODEL 1987-7) - Elite model design, deep bowl, single cutaway, available in Nutmeg stain finish, mfg. 1987 only.

	N/A	$1,200	$700

Last MSR was $1,800.

A total of 820 guitars were produced.

1987 Collector's (Model 1987-5) - similar to the 1987 Collector's model, except offered in limited quantities in a Black finish, mfg. 1987 only.

	N/A	$1,300	$750

Last MSR was $1,800.

A total of 108 guitars were produced.

1988 COLLECTOR'S (MODEL 1988-P) - Elite model design, Super shallow bowl, single cutaway, available in a Pewter finish, mfg. 1988 only.

	N/A	$900	$525

Last MSR was $1,195.

A total of 1,177 guitars were produced.

1989 COLLECTOR'S (MODEL 1989-8) - super shallow bowl, single cutaway, round soundhole, available in Blue Pearl finish, mfg. 1989 only.

	N/A	$900	$525

Last MSR was $1,299.

A total of 981 guitars were produced.

1990 COLLECTOR'S (MODEL 1990-7) - Elite model design, bird's-eye maple top, deep bowl, single cutaway, available in Nutmeg finish, mfg. 1990 only.

	N/A	$1,000	$600

Last MSR was $1,599.

Ovation Collector 2001 FR
courtesy Ovation

A total of 500 guitars were produced.

1990 Collector's (Model 1990-1) - similar to the 1990 Collector's model (1990-7), except offered in extremely limited quantities in a Sunburst finish, mfg. 1990 only.

	N/A	$1,000	$600

Last MSR was $1,599.

A total of 50 guitars were produced.

1990 Collector's (Model 199S-7) - similar to the 1990 Collector's model (1990-7), except offered in limited quantities with a Super shallow bowl and Nutmeg finish, mfg. 1990 only.

	N/A	$1,000	$600

Last MSR was $1,599.

A total of 750 guitars were produced.

1990 Collector's (Model 199S-1) - similar to the 1990 Collector's model (1990-7), except offered in limited quantities with a Super shallow bowl and a Sunburst finish, mfg. 1990 only.

	N/A	$1,000	$600

Last MSR was $1,599.

A total of 100 guitars were produced.

1991 COLLECTOR'S (MODEL 1991-4) - deep bowl, single cutaway, round soundhole, available in Natural finish, mfg. 1991 only.

	N/A	$850	$500

Last MSR was $1,159.

A total of 1,464 guitars were produced.

1991 Collector's (Model 1991-5) - deep bowl, single cutaway, round soundhole, available in Black Metallic finish, mfg. 1991 only.

	N/A	$850	$500

Last MSR was $1,159.

A total of 292 guitars were produced.

1992 COLLECTOR'S (MODEL 1992-H) - Elite model design, quilted ash top, super shallow bowl, single cutaway, available in Honeyburst finish, mfg. 1992 only.

	N/A	$1,100	$650

Last MSR was $1,699.

A total of 1,995 guitars were produced.

Ovation Collector 2003-VN
courtesy Ovation

GRADING	100%	EXCELLENT	AVERAGE

1993 COLLECTOR'S (MODEL 1993-4) - single round cutaway folk-style, solid spruce top, multi upper bout soundholes, 5-stripe bound body, multiple woods veneer around soundholes, medium bowl body, mahogany/padauk/ebony 5-piece neck, 22-fret ebony fingerboard with 12th fret banner inlay, strings through walnut bridge, maple logo inlay on peghead, 3-per-side gold Schaller tuners with ebony buttons, piezo bridge pickup, volume/3-band EQ control, active preamp, available in Natural finish, mfg. 1993 only.

	N/A	$950	$625

Last MSR was $1,499.

A total of 1,537 guitars were produced.

1994 COLLECTOR'S (MODEL 1994-7) - single round cutaway folk style, solid spruce top, round soundhole, bound body, multi wood purfling, ash/ebony/pearl rosette, medium bowl body, mahogany/ebony/purpleheart 5-piece neck, 21-fret ebony extended fingerboard with 12th fret banner inlay, strings through ebony bridge, ebony veneered peghead with screened logo, 3-per-side gold tuners with ebony buttons, piezo bridge pickup, Optima EQ system, available in Nutmeg finish, mfg. 1994 only.

	N/A	$1,100	$650

Last MSR was $1,695.

A total of 1,763 guitars were produced.

1995 COLLECTOR'S (MODEL 1995-7) - new mid-depth bowl, single cutaway, round soundhole, available in Nutmeg finish, mfg. 1995 only.

$1,400	$1,000	$550

Last MSR was $1,899.

A total of 1,502 guitars were produced.

1996 COLLECTOR'S (MODEL 1996-TPB) - solid Sitka spruce top, mid-depth bowl, single cutaway, five piece mahogany/maple/ebony neck, bound ebony fingerboard with mother-of-pearl inlay, Stereo HexFX piezo pickup system, 3+3 headstock, round soundhole, available in a Trans. Burgundy finish, mfg. 1996 only.

$1,450	$1,125	$700

Last MSR was $2,199.

A total of 1,280 guitars were produced.

1997 COLLECTOR'S (MODEL 1997-7N) - narrow waist ("salon style") walnut-bound body, solid Sitka spruce top, round soundhole, maple leaf rosette, unbound 14/20-fret fingerboard, CP 100 piezo pickup system, 3-per-side slotted headstock with walnut veneer, onboard Stealth TS preamp, available in Nutmeg Stain finish, mfg. 1997 only.

$1,300	$1,000	$600

Last MSR was $1,799.

This model is also available with a wider neck as Model 1997-7W. Every 1997 Collector's Series instrument is accompanied by a copy of Walter Carter's *The History of the Ovation Guitar* book. Although this is the 1997 Collector's model, it is assumed that there may be a few still available among Ovation dealers (thus the retail list price is still listed).

1998 COLLECTOR'S (MODEL 1998) - single round cutaway style, figured maple top, laser cut leaf epaulets shaped with a cluster of 15 smaller soundholes, bound body, mid depth bowl body, 5-piece maple/mahogany neck, 22-fret rosewood fingerboard with 12th fret inlay, strings through rosewood bridge, 3-per-side tuners, piezo bridge pickup, OP-24E system, available in New England Burst finish, mfg. 1998 only.

$1,200	$900	$550

Last MSR was $1,649.

1999 COLLECTOR'S (MODEL 1999) - single cutaway style, laser cut leaf epaulets with a cluster of 15 soundholes, red waterfall bubinga top, Optima preamp with tuner, 5-piece maple/mahogany neck, 22-fret ebony fingerboard, mid depth bowl body with light bracing, 3-per-side tuners, mfg. 1999 only.

$1,250	$950	$575

Last MSR was $1,749.

2000 COLLECTOR'S (MODEL 2000-THA) - single cutaway style, laser cut leaf epaulets with a cluster of 15 soundholes, figured lacewood top, 5-piece mahogany/maple neck, "V" shaped neck, Optima preamp, Tru-Balance pickup, built in chromatic tuner, mid-depth body, 3-per-side tuners, gold Ovation tuners, available in Transparent Honey finish, mfg. 2000 only.

$1,150	$865	$525

Last MSR was $1,599.

2001 COLLECTOR'S (MODEL 2001-FRA) - single cutaway style, laser cut leaf epaulets with a cluster of 15 soundholes, figured solid Redwood top, 5-piece mahogany/maple neck, Ovation Tru-Balance pickup, OP-24+C preamp, 3-band EQ, 2 mid frequencies, built in chromatic tuner, gold Ovation tuners, 3-per-side tuners, available in Figured Redwood Natural Gloss finish, mfg. 2001 only.

$1,350	$1,100	$700

Last MSR was $1,899.

2002 COLLECTOR'S (MODEL 2002-AC) - mid depth single cutaway style, multi soundhole 5-piece epaulet, figured figured African Cherry top, ebony fingerboard and bridge, 12th fret MOP inlay, Ovation Tru-Balance pickup, OP-40 preamp, 3-band EQ, volume, built in chromatic tuner, gold Ovation tuners, 3-per-side tuners, available in African Cherry finish, mfg. 2002 only.

$1,400	$1,150	$700

Last MSR was $1,999.

2003 COLLECTOR'S (MODEL 2003-VN) - mid depth single cutaway style, multi soundhole 5-piece epaulet, solid Sitka spruce top, ebony fingerboard and bridge, 12th fret LE inlay, Ovation Hi-Output pickup, OP-40 preamp, 3-band EQ, volume, built in chromatic tuner, gold Ovation tuners, 3-per-side tuners, available in Vintage Natural finish, mfg. 2003 only.

MSR	$2,159	$1,550	$1,150	$700

GRADING	100%	EXCELLENT	AVERAGE

ACOUSTIC: ELITE SERIES

The Elite Series design is similar to the Adamas models, but substitutes a solid Spruce or solid cedar top in place of the composite materials. Standard models feature 22 soundholes of varying sizes, while the cutaway models only have 15 soundholes.

ELITE (MODEL 1718) - spruce top, 5-stripe bound body, 5-piece mahogany/maple neck, 14/22-fret extended rosewood fingerboard with maple triangle inlay, walnut bridge, 3-per-side gold tuners, 6 piezo bridge pickups, volume control, 3-band EQ, active OP-24 preamp, available in Black, Natural, Natural Cedar, Sunburst, or White finishes, mfg. 1982-1997.

	$975	$850	$550

Last MSR was $1,395.

Elite Deep Cutaway (Model 1768) - similar to Elite, except has single cutaway body, available in Sunburst finish, disc 1999.

	$1,200	$825	$550

Last MSR was $1,699.

Elite Mid-Depth Model (Model 1778) - similar to Elite Model 1768 except has a mid-depth bowl body, available in Natural, Black, or Black Cherryburst, current mfg. (3 months delivery time in 2001).

MSR	$1,499	$1,050	$750	$475

Elite Left-Handed Mid-Depth Model (Model L778) - similar to the Elite mid-depth, except in left-handed configuration, available in Natural or Black Cherryburst finishes, current mfg.

MSR	$1,799	$1,275	$900	$550

Elite Shallow (Model 1868) - similar to Elite, except has super shallow bowl body, single rounded cutaway, available in Black, Black Cherryburst, Natural, or Sunburst finishes, current mfg.

MSR	$1,499	$1,050	$750	$475

Elite Shallow 12 (Model 1858) - similar to Elite Shallow, except in 12-string configuration, available in Black Cherryburst or Sunburst finishes, mfg. 1994-current.

MSR	$1,589	$1,12S5	$800	$500

CUSTOM ELITE (MODEL CE-768) - spruce top, single cutaway body, deep bowl, 5-piece mahogany/maple neck, 22-fret extended rosewood fingerboard with maple triangle inlay, walnut bridge, 3-per-side gold tuners, piezo bridge pickup, volume control, 3-band EQ, active OP-X preamp, available in Black Cherryburst finish, disc.

	$1,500	$1,000	$650

Last MSR was $1,999.

Custom Elite Mid-Depth (Model CE-778) - similar to Elite, except has Mid-Depth bowl body, available in Black Cherryburst finish, current mfg.

MSR	$1,999	$1,400	$975	$650

Custom Elite Shallow (Model CE-868) - similar to Elite, except has super shallow bowl body, available in Black Cherryburst finish, current mfg.

MSR	$1,999	$1,400	$975	$650

ELITE SPECIAL (MODEL S778) - single cutaway mid-depth bowl, A Grade spruce top, rosewood slanted end fingerboard, walnut bridge, multi-soundhole 5-piece epaulet, Thinline under-saddle pickup, OP30 preamp, 3-per-side Ovation chrome tuners, available in Natural or Autumn Burst finishes, mfg. 2000-current.

MSR	$1,099	$775	$550	$350

Elite Special (Model S868) - similar to the Elite Special, except has a shallow body, available in Natural finish, mfg. 2000-current.

MSR	$1,099	$775	$550	$350

ELITE STANDARD (MODEL 6718) - spruce top, 5-stripe bound body, mahogany neck, 14/22-fret extended rosewood fingerboard, strings through rosewood bridge with pearl dot inlay, rosewood veneered peghead with ebony/maple logo inlay, 3-per-side chrome tuners, piezo bridge pickups, volume control, 3-band EQ, active preamp, available in Cherry Sunburst, Root Beer, or Vintage finishes, mfg. 1993-96.

	$775	$575	$350

Last MSR was $1,095.

Elite Standard Cutaway (Model 6778) - similar to Elite Standard, except has single round cutaway, available in Black, Black Cherryburst, Cadillac Greenburst, or Natural finishes, disc.

	$1,000	$650	$450

Last MSR was $1,349.

Elite Standard 12-String (Model 6758) - similar to Elite Standard Cutaway, except in a 12-string variation, available in Natural and Black Cherryburst finishes, disc.

	$1,100	$700	$475

Last MSR was $1,449.

Ovation Elite Mid-Depth Model 1778 courtesy Ovation

Ovation Custom Elite CE-778 courtesy Ovation

GRADING	100%	EXCELLENT	AVERAGE

Elite Standard Cutaway Shallow (Model 6868) - similar to Elite Standard Cutaway, except has a super shallow bowl body, available in Black, Black Cherry, or Natural finishes, disc.

	$1,000	**$650**	**$450**
		Last MSR was $1,349.	

In 1998, Aspen Blue finish was introduced.

ELITE T (MODEL 1778T) - single cutaway mid depth body, solid spruce top, ebony fingerboard and bridge, multi 11-hole soundhole on bass side only, Ovation thinline pickup, OP-30 preamp, 3-per-side black tuners, available in Black or Pewter finishes, mfg. 2002-current.

MSR	**$999**	**$700**	**$500**	**$325**

Elite T Shallow (Model 1868T) - similar to the Elite T, except has a super shallow body, mfg. 2002-current.

MSR	**$999**	**$700**	**$500**	**$325**

ACOUSTIC: FOLKLORE SERIES

The Folklore series was introduced in 1979. Current listings feature the new updated versions that have been re-introduced to the Ovation line.

FOLKLORE (MODEL 6774) - single cutaway solid Sitka spruce top, round soundhole, mid-depth bowl back, inlaid rosette, 5-piece mahogany/ maple neck, 21-fret ebony fingerboard, walnut bridge, 3-per-side slotted headstock, OP-X preamp, available in a Natural finish, mfg. 1979-current.

MSR	**$1,799**	**$1,275**	**$900**	**$600**

Country Artist (Model 6773) - similar to Folklore model, except is designed for nylon string use, available in Natural finish, current mfg.

MSR	**$1,799**	**$1,275**	**$900**	**$600**

PARLOR (MODEL 5741) - narrow waist ("salon style") body, mid-depth bowl back, solid Sitka spruce top, round soundhole, inlaid rosette, 5-piece mahogany/maple neck, unbound 14/21-fret ebony fingerboard, 3-per-side headstock with walnut veneer, walnut bridge, CP 100 piezo pickup system, OP-X preamp, available in Brown Sunburst finish, mfg. 1998 only.

	$1,100	**$750**	**$495**
		Last MSR was $1,499.	

ACOUSTIC: GLEN CAMPBELL SERIES

GLEN CAMPBELL BALLADEER (MODEL 1127) - Balladeer style, shallow bowl, diamond inlays, gold tuners, mfg. 1968-1990.

	N/A	**$500**	**$350**

GLEN CAMPBELL 12-STRING (MODEL 1118) - Legend style body, 12-string configuration, shallow bowl, diamond inlays, gold tuners, mfg. 1968-1982.

	N/A	**$700**	**$450**

ACOUSTIC: LEGEND SERIES

The Legend series shares similar design patterns with the Custom Legend models, except a less ornate rosette and a standard Ovation bridge instead of the custom carved walnut version. Outside of the all acoustic Model 1117, Legend series models feature the active OP-24 preamp electronics.

LEGEND (MODEL 1117) - spruce top, round soundhole, 5-stripe bound body, leaf pattern rosette, 5-piece mahogany/maple neck, 14/20-fret bound rosewood fingerboard with pearl diamond/dot inlay, walnut bridge, walnut veneer on peghead, 3-per-side gold tuners, available in Black, Natural, Sunburst, or White finishes, disc. 1999.

	$725	**$500**	**$325**
		Last MSR was $999.	

In 1994, Cherry Cherryburst and Tobacco Sunburst finishes were introduced, bound ebony fingerboard replaced original parts/design, Sunburst and White finishes were discontinued.

Legend Electric (Model 1717) - similar to Legend, except has piezo bridge pickup, volume control, 3-band EQ, OP-X active preamp, available in Cherry Cherryburst or Natural finishes, mfg. 1994-98.

	$950	**$700**	**$450**
		Last MSR was $1,349.	

Legend 12 Electric - similar to Legend, except has 12-string configuration, 6-per-side tuners, volume/3-band EQ controls, active preamp, disc. 1994.

	N/A	**$725**	**$475**
		Last MSR was $1,450.	

LEGEND CUTAWAY ELECTRIC (MODEL 1777) - similar to Legend, except has single round cutaway, mid-depth bowl, volume control, 3-band EQ, OP-X active preamp, available in Black, Cherry Cherryburst, Natural, or Red Stain finishes, current mfg.

MSR	**$1,359**	**$950**	**$675**	**$425**

Add $100 for Recording Model Telex mic/OptiMax preamp system (Model 1777-4RM).

Legend Cutaway Electric Super Shallow 12 String (Model 1866-4HFXb) - similar to Legend except is in 12-string configuration and has a super shallow bowl body, HexFX electronics, 6-per-side tuners, available in Natural finish, disc 2001.

	$1,000	**$725**	**$450**
		Last MSR was $1,399.	

GRADING		100%	EXCELLENT	AVERAGE

Legend Cutaway Electric Shallow (Model 1867) - similar to Legend Cutaway Electric, except has a super shallow bowl body, available in Black, Cherry Cherryburst, Natural, or Red Stain finishes, current mfg.

MSR	$1,359	$950	$675	$425

HexFX electronics system can be special ordered at no additional cost (Model 1867-HexFX, 3 months delivery time in 2000)

Legend 12 Cutaway Electric (Model 1866) - similar to Legend Cutaway electric, except has 12-string configuration, available in Black, Cherry Cherryburst, or Natural finishes, current mfg.

MSR	$1,459	$1,025	$750	$450

HexFX electronics system can be special ordered at no additional cost.

Legend Special Order Left Hand Model (Model L777) - similar to Legend except in a left hand configuration, mid-depth bowl body, available in Natural, Black, or Cherry Cherryburst finishes, current mfg. (3 months delivery time).

MSR	$1,699	$1,195	$850	$550

NYLON STRING LEGEND (MODEL 1763, NYLON STRING CLASSIC BALLADEER)

- single round cutaway, AAA cedar top, round soundhole, 5-stripe bound body, leaf pattern rosette, 5-piece mahogany/maple neck, 19-fret ebony fingerboard, rosewood bridge, 3-per-side gold tuners with pearloid buttons, piezo bridge pickup, volume/3-band EQ control, OP-X preamp, available in Natural finish, mfg. 1994-99.

		$1,325	$800	$550

Last MSR was $1,649.

Add $100 for Recording Model with OptiMax preamp (Model 1763-4RM).

Nylon String Legend Shallow (Model 1863) - similar to the Nylon String Legend, except has a super shallow bowl, Natural finish, current mfg.

MSR	$1,649	$1,150	$825	$550

This model is also available with a mid-depth bowl (Model 1773), and has a 3 month special order.

Ovation Legend 12 Electric courtesy Dave Rogers Dave's Guitar Shop

ACOUSTIC: CUSTOM LEGEND SERIES

Custom Legend models have an AAA grade solid Sitka spruce top, spruce struts, custom bracing, and the active OP-24 piezo electronics package.

CUSTOM LEGEND (MODEL 1719)

- spruce top, round soundhole, abalone bound body, abalone leaf pattern rosette, 5-piece mahogany/maple neck, 14/20-fret bound ebony fingerboard with abalone diamond/dot inlay, strings through walnut bridge with carved flower design/pearl dot inlay, walnut veneered peghead with abalone logo inlay, 3-per-side gold tuners with pearloid buttons, piezo bridge pickups, volume control, 3-band EQ, active preamp, available in Black, Natural, Sunburst, or White finishes, disc. 1996.

		$1,125	$825	$525

Last MSR was $1,595.

Custom Legend Cutaway (Model 1769) - similar to Custom Legend, except has single rounded cutaway, available in Cherry Cherryburst, Cadillac Greenburst, and Sunburst finishes, disc.

		$1,400	$975	$650

Last MSR was $1,999.

Al Dimeola Signature Model available for $2,199. Black finish only. (Model 1769-AD5). Still in mfg. Even though base model is disc. (2000).

Custom Legend Shallow Cutaway (Model 1869) - similar to Custom Legend, except has single round cutaway body, super shallow bowl, available in Black, Cherry Cherryburst, Natural, or Sunburst finishes, current mfg.

MSR	$1,999	$1,400	$975	$650

Custom Legend 12 (Model 1759) - similar to Custom Legend, except in 12-string configuration, 6-per-side tuners, available in Black and Natural finishes, disc.

		$1,675	$1,050	$695

Last MSR was $2,099.

Custom Legend Special Order (Model 1779) - similar to Custom Legend except has mid-depth bowl body, available in Sunburst or Cherry Cherryburst finishes, current mfg. (3 months delivery time).

MSR	$1,999	$1,500	$1,050	$650

Custom Legend Special Order USA (Model 1779-USA) - similar to the Custom Legend special order, except has custom American Flag graphics, mfg. 2002-current.

MSR	$3,299	$2,500	$1,800	$1,200

Custom Legend Special Order 12 String (Model 6759) - similar to Custom Legend Special Order except in a 12-string configuration, available in Natural or Black finishes, current mfg. (3 months delivery time).

MSR	$2,099	$1,600	$1,100	$700

Ovation Legend Shallow Cutaway Model 1869 courtesy Ovation

GRADING	100%	EXCELLENT	AVERAGE

CUSTOM LEGEND WITH ROLAND GR SYNTH (MODEL R 869) - similar to the Custom Legend, except has a factory installed Roland GR Series synthesizer interface, available in Natural finish, mfg. 1998 only.

	$1,750	$1,250	$825

Last MSR was $2,499.

CUSTOM LEGEND AL DI MEOLA SIGNATURE (MODEL 1769-AD5) - Custom Legend style body, AAA Sitka spruce top, hand inlaid abalone purfling, ebony fingerboard and bridge, abalone inlays, Ovation piezoelectric pickup, OP-50 preamp, mfg. 1999-current.

MSR	$2,199		$1,650	$1,150	$725

ACOUSTIC: LONGNECK SERIES

LONGNECK (MODEL DS 768) - similar to the Elite model six string, except has a scale length of 28 1/3 " and is tuned one full step lower than a standard guitar. Five piece maple and mahogany neck, gold-plated hardware, and OP-X preamp, available in Natural or Cherry Cherryburst finishes, mfg. 1995-99.

	$1,350	$950	$625

Last MSR was $1,899.

LONGNECK (MODEL DS 778) - similar to Model 768, mid-depth acoustic electric, available in Natural finish, current mfg.

MSR	$1,899	$1,350	$950	$625

LONGNECK (MODEL DCS-247S) - similar to the longneck style, except has a solid spruce top, rosewood fingerboard, MOP inlays, Thinline pickup, OP-24+ preamp, gold hardware, available in Natural or Black finishes, mfg. 2000-02.

	$575	$400	$250

Last MSR was $800.

ACOUSTIC: PINNACLE SERIES

PINNACLE - folk-style, spruce top, 5-stripe bound body, leaf pattern rosette, mahogany neck, 14/20-fret rosewood fingerboard with white dot inlay, rosewood bridge with white dot inlay, rosewood veneer on peghead, 3-per-side chrome tuners, 6 piezo bridge pickups, volume control, 3-band EQ, FET preamp, available in Barn board, Black, Ebony Stain, Natural, Opaque Blue, Sunburst, Trans. Blue Stain and White finishes, mfg. 1991-92.

	N/A	$600	$350

Last MSR was $900.

Pinnacle Shallow Cutaway - similar to Pinnacle, except has single round cutaway, shallow bowl body, mfg. 1991-94.

	N/A	$700	$400

Last MSR was $1,000.

PINNACLE (MODEL CU147) - single cutaway mid-depth body, AA grade solid Sitka spruce top, round soundhole with abalone rosette, two piece mahogany neck, rosewood fingerboard with abalone dot inlays, walnut bridge, 3-per-side gold tuners, Ovation Thinline pickup, OP-30 preamp, available in Honey Burst finish, mfg. 2002-current.

MSR	$750	$525	$375	$225

PINNACLE DELUXE (MODEL CU247) - similar to the Pinnacle, except has quintad bracing, and mulit-soundholes with 5-piece epaulet, available in Ruby Redburst finish, mfg. 2002-current.

MSR	$900	$630	$450	$275

ACOUSTIC: TANGENT SERIES

TANGENT (MODEL T257) - single cutaway super shallow body, spruce top, multi soundhole balck epaulet, nato neck, dark rosewood fingerboard with abalone diamond inlay, Thin-line pickup, 2/4-per-side gunmetal gray tuners, available in Black finish, mfg. 2002-current.

MSR	$780	$550	$390	$240

TANGENT (MODEL 357) - similar to the Tangent, except has no Epaulet soundhole inlays, available in Black Pearl or White Pearl, mfg. 2002-current.

MSR	$780	$550	$390	$240

TANGENT (MOB47) - similar to the Tangent design, except has a "surf" inspired design and surf board shaped soundholes, mid-depth body, nick named "My Other Board," available in Blue Surf Burst, new 2003.

MSR	$800	$560	$400	$250

TANGENT (MOB57) - similar to the Tangent MOB47, except has a shallow body, new 2003.

MSR	$800	$560	$400	$250

ACOUSTIC: ULTRA DELUXE SERIES

The Ultra Deluxe models feature a solid spruce top, two piece mahogany neck, on-board OP-24Plus electronics, and a 20-fret bound rosewood fingerboard.

ULTRA DELUXE (MODEL 1312-D) - spruce top, round soundhole, 5-stripe bound body, leaf pattern rosette, 14/20-fret bound rosewood fingerboard with abalone diamond/dot inlay, walnut bridge with white dot inlay, rosewood veneer on peghead, 3-per-side gold tuners, available in Barn board, Black, Brownburst, Natural, or Sunburst finishes, disc. 1996.

	$350	$225	$150

Last MSR was $500.

This model has flame maple top with Brownburst finish as an option.

Ultra Deluxe Electric (Model 1517-D) - similar to Ultra Deluxe, except has piezo bridge pickup, 4-band EQ, FET preamp, available in Black or Natural finishes, mfg. 1994-96.

$425 $300 $195

Last MSR was $600.

This model has flame maple top with Brownburst finish as an option.

ULTRA DELUXE 12 (MODEL 1515-D) - similar to Ultra Deluxe, except has 12-strings, 6-per-side tuners, disc. 1994.

$375 $275 $175

Last MSR was $530.

Ultra Deluxe 12 Electric - similar to Ultra Deluxe, except has 12-strings, 6-per-side tuners, piezo bridge pickups, 4-band EQ, preamp, available in Black or Natural finishes, mfg. 1994-96.

$495 $350 $225

Last MSR was $700.

ULTRA DELUXE CUTAWAY (MODEL 1528-D) - similar to Ultra Deluxe, except has single round cutaway, piezo bridge pickup, volume/tone control, FET preamp, available in Barn board, Brownburst, or Sunburst finishes, disc. 1994.

$525 $375 $225

Last MSR was $730.

Ultra Deluxe Shallow Cutaway - similar to Ultra Deluxe, except has single round cutaway, shallow bowl body, piezo bridge pickups, volume/tone control, FET preamp, available in Barn board, Black, Brownburst, Natural, Redburst, Sunburst, or White finishes, disc. 1994.

$495 $350 $250

Last MSR was $700.

This model has flame maple top with Brownburst finish as an option.

ACOUSTIC ELECTRIC: VIPER SERIES

The Viper name is back! Originally a solid body guitar from the mid 1970s to the early 1980s, the Viper name has now been affixed to a new, 1990s acoustic/electric slim body design. The Viper model has a solid Spruce top, and a mahogany body with acoustic chambers. An onboard active electronics package (volume and three band EQ) allows control over feedback.

VIPER (MODEL EA68) - single cutaway mahogany body with routed sound chamber, bound spruce top, 14 multi-size soundholes with various leaf wood overlay, 5-piece mahogany/maple neck, 24-fret bound ebony fingerboard, strings through rosewood bridge, rosewood veneered peghead with screened logo, 3-per-side gold tuners, 6 piezo bridge pickups, volume/3-band EQ controls, available in Black or Natural finishes (3 months delivery time for Natural finish), mfg. 1994-current.

MSR $1,999 $1,500 $1,050 $650

VIPER 12 (MODEL EA 58) - similar to the Viper, except in 12-string variation, available in Black and Natural finishes, disc. 1999.

$1,550 $1,075 $825

Last MSR was $2,099.

VIPER (MODEL CV68) - similar to the Viper, except has a rosewood fingerboard, walnut bridge, and has a Viper Thinline Graphic preamp, available in Black or Honey Burst finishes, mfg. 2000-current.

MSR $830 $585 $415 $250

VIPER (MODEL EA68) - similar to the Viper except has a solid spruce top, available in Natural finish, current mfg.

MSR $1,999 $1,500 $1,050 $650

VIPER NYLON SPECIAL ORDER (MODEL EA63) - similar to the Viper, except in 6-string nylon variation, available in Black or Natural finishes (Black disc. 2000), current mfg. (3 months delivery time for Natural finish).

MSR $1,999 $1,500 $1,050 $650

ACOUSTIC ELECTRIC BASS

B778 BASS - single cutaway mid-depth cutaway body, solid spruce top, ebony fingerboard with MOP inlay, walnut bridge, multi soundhole 5-piece epaulet, tru-balance pickup, OP-40 preamp, gold hardware, available in Black or Natural finishes, mfg. 2000-current.

MSR $2,199 $1,550 $1,100 $700

CELEBRITY (MODEL CC-074) - single round cutaway, spruce top, round soundhole, 5-stripe bound body, leaf pattern rosette, mahogany neck, 20-fret bound rosewood fingerboard with pearloid diamond/dot inlay, walnut bridge with pearloid dot inlay, walnut veneer on peghead, 2 per side chrome tuners, piezo bridge pickups, volume/tone control, FET preamp, available in Ebony Stain, Natural, or Sunburst finishes, mfg. 1993-96, 1998-current.

MSR $830 $585 $415 $250

Ovation Tangetn Model T257
courtesy Ovation

Ovation Viper EA68
courtesy Dave Rogers
Dave's Guitar Shop

Celebrity Deluxe (Model CC-274) - similar to the Celebrity, except features cedar top, multi-sized soundholes with leaf pattern maple veneers, 22-fret rosewood extended fingerboard with pearl dot inlay, rosewood strings through bridge, rosewood veneered peghead with logo decal, 2 per side gold tuner, piezo bridge pickup, 4-band EQ, available in Antique Sunburst, Black, Natural, or Sunburst finishes, mfg. 1994-96.

$575   **$400**   **$275**

Last MSR was $800.

This model has spruce and sycamore tops as an option.

Celebrity Deluxe 5 (Model CC-275) - similar to Celebrity Deluxe, except has 5 strings, 19-fret fingerboard, 3/2 per side chrome tuners, available in Black finish, mfg. 1994-96.

$600   **$425**   **$275**

Last MSR was $850.

ELITE (MODEL B-768) - single round cutaway, spruce top, 5-stripe bound body, multiple soundholes around the top bouts with leaf pattern veneer, 5-piece mahogany/maple neck, 22-fret extended rosewood fingerboard with maple triangle inlay, walnut bridge, 2 per side gold tuners, piezo bridge pickup, volume/3-band EQ control, active preamp, available in Black, Natural, or Sunburst finishes, mfg. 1992-99.

$1,550   **$1,075**   **$725**

Last MSR was $2,199.

In 1994, bound fingerboard was introduced, Sunburst finish was discontinued.

Elite 5 (Model B-5768) - similar to the Elite bass, except has five strings and a 2/3 headstock design, available in Black or Natural finishes, mfg. 1995-98.

$1,650   **$1,375**   **$795**

Last MSR was $2,399.

VIPER BASS (MODEL EAB68) - single cutaway mahogany body with routed sound chamber, bound spruce top, 14 multi-size soundholes with various leaf wood overlay, 5-piece mahogany/maple neck, 24-fret bound ebony fingerboard, strings through rosewood bridge, rosewood veneered peghead with screened logo, 2 per side gold tuners, 4 piezo bridge pickups, volume/3-band EQ controls, available in Black, Cherry Cherryburst, or Natural finishes, mfg. 1994-98.

$1,700   **$1,250**   **$800**

Last MSR was $2,399.

OZARK

Instruments currently produced in Korea. Distributed in the United Kingdom by Senator Music Co. LTD.

Ozark guitars have been produced since the early 1980s. These guitars represent "excellent value at a modest price." They offer several different acoustic models as well as resonators, banjos, mandolins, and basses. For more information contact Senator Music directly (see Trademark Index).

O

Section P

PMC GUITARS

Instruments currently built in Asia. Distributed by Sound Trek Distributors of Tampa, Florida.

PMC guitars are good quality acoustics designed for the entry or student level up to the medium grade player.

PACE

Instruments previously produced in Korea, circa early 1970s.

Pace brand guitars were moderate quality acoustics imported to the U.S. market.

The Pace model **F-200** featured a spruce top, round soundhole, mahogany back and sides, black pickguard, 14/20-fret rosewood fingerboard, rosewood bridge with black bridge pins, 3-per-side closed chrome tuners. Pace acoustic guitars in average condition range in price between $100 to $150, (Source: Walter Murray, *Frankenstein Fretworks*).

PALMER

Instruments currently produced in Asia from the late 1980s. Distributed by Chesbro Music Company of Idaho Falls, Idaho, and Tropical Music Corporation of Miami, Florida.

Both the Chesbro Music Company and Tropical Music Corporation are distributing Palmer brand acoustic and classical models. These models are geared towards the entry level or student guitarist.

During the late 1980s, Palmer offered instruments were entry level solid body guitars that feature designs based on traditional American designs. Solid body models were marketed under the trademark (or model designation) of Biscayne, Growler, Baby, and Six. The Biscayne trademark is still distributed by Tropical Music Corporation. Palmer acoustic guitars are usually priced in the used market between $85 and $250.

PANORMO

Instruments previously built in London, England during the early nineteenth century.

During the early 1800s, luthier Louis Panormo ran a productive workshop in London. Panormo, the son of an Italian violin-maker, was one of the few outside of Spain that braced the tops of his acoustics with "fan - strutting," and advertised himself as the "only maker of guitars in the Spanish style," (Source: Tony Bacon, *The Ultimate Guitar Book*).

PAO CHIA

Instruments currently produced in China. Distributed by the Guangzhou Bourgade Musical Instruments Factory Co. Ltd.

Pao Chia instruments have been produced since 1988. They produce an entire line of acoustic guitars, as well as classical guitars, and electric guitars and basses. These instruments are mainly entry level models at entry level prices. For more information in Chinese, refer to their web site (see Trademark Index).

PARAMOUNT

See Lange. Instruments previously produced in America during the 1930s and 1940s.

In 1934, the William L. Lange Company (New York) debuted the Paramount guitar series – and some of the models were built by the C.F. Martin guitar company. However, Lange's company went out of business in the early 1940s. In the late 1940s, the Paramount guitar line was re-introduced and distributed by Gretsch & Brenner, (Source: Tom Wheeler, *American Guitars*).

PARKSONS

Instruments currently produced in Korea. Distributed by Paxphil in Korea.

Parksons produces an entire line of acoustic guitars as well as electrics, basses, banjos, mandolins, and resonators. These guitars are mainly entry level instruments that retail for under $200. Refer to their web site for more information and a full listing of every guitar that they produce (see Trademark Index).

PATRICK EGGLE GUITARS

Instruments currently built in England. Imported and distributed into the U.S. by Maverick Sales, Inc., located in South Miami, FL. Distributed in the U.K. by John Montague.

Patrick James Eggle is an English luthier who builds high quality archtop instruments. Models include a Barle with 17 in. lower bout and 3 in. depth, and features carved tailpiece, "partridge profile" f-holes, and carved spruce top. Current MSR is $6,500. Almost all of Patrick Eggle guitars are electric models. Please contact the importer directly for more information (see Trademark Index).

PAUL REED SMITH GUITARS (PRS)

Acoustic instruments were previously produced in Annapolis, Maryland. PRS Guitars was originally located in Annapolis, Maryland from 1985 to 1996. In 1996, PRS Guitars completed the move to newer and larger facilities in Stevensville, Maryland.

Combining the best aspects of vintage design traditions in modern instruments, luthier Paul Reed Smith devised a guitar that became very influential during the late 1980s. With meticulous attention to detail, design, and production combined with the concept of "graded" figured wood tops, PRS guitars became touchstone to today's high end guitar market. The concept of a ten top (denoting the flame in the maple figuring) began at PRS Guitars, and to hear the slang phrase "It's a ten top with birds" is magic at guitar shows nowadays.

Paul Reed Smith built his first guitar for a college music class. Drawing on his high school shop classes and his musical experiences, his first attempt gained him an *A.* Working out of his home attic in the mid 1970s, Smith began designing and revising his guitar models while involved with the guitar repair trade. He continued to work out of a small repair shop for the better part of eight years, and was selling a number of hand crafted guitars between 1976 through 1984 without major advertising. By 1982 he had finished designing and building a guitar that combined his original ideas with traditional ones.

In 1985, Smith received some major financial backing and was able to start limited handmade production of the PRS Custom model. Part of the new finances guaranteed his high quality products would finally see advertising in the major magazines. One major difference between PRS and other guitar companies of the 1980s is Smith made – or had exclusively made – all of his own components for his own guitars. Of course, choosing highly figured woods for construction wasn't a bad choice either! Through the years, Paul Reed Smith has continued to experiment with pickup design, body and neck variations, and even amplification and speaker systems.

ACOUSTIC

This series of instruments was designed and built by Dana Bourgeois and Paul Reed Smith. Since only 11 were manufactured, prices can vary significantly due to almost no supply and significant demand. Due to the rarity factor and the current popularity of PRS acoustic instruments, pricing for these models is extremely hard to evaluate.

CUSTOM CUTAWAY - single flat cutaway dreadnought style, spruce top, round soundhole, abalone bound body and rosette, figured maple back/sides, mahogany neck, 20-fret Brazilian rosewood fingerboard with abalone bird inlay, Brazilian rosewood bridge with ebony pearl dot pins, 3-per-side chrome locking PRS tuners, volume/tone control, preamp system, available in Amber Sunburst, Antique Natural, Black Cherry, Gray black, or Walnut Sunburst finishes, disc. 1992.

	N/A	N/A	N/A

Last MSR was $2,590.

MAHOGANY CUTAWAY - single flat cutaway dreadnought style, spruce top, round soundhole, wood bound body and rosette, mahogany back/sides/neck, 20-fret rosewood fingerboard, rosewood bridge with ebony pearl dot pins, rosewood veneer on peghead, 3-per-side chrome locking PRS tuners, volume/tone control, preamp system, available in Antique Natural, Black, or Natural finishes, disc. 1992.

	N/A	N/A	N/A

Last MSR was $1,970.

ROSEWOOD SIGNATURE - dreadnought style, spruce top, round soundhole, abalone bound body and rosette, rosewood back/sides, mahogany neck, 20-fret Brazilian rosewood fingerboard with abalone bird inlay, Brazilian rosewood bridge with ebony pearl dot pins, 3-per-side gold locking PRS tuners, gold endpin, volume/tone control, preamp system, available in Antique Natural or Rosewood Sunburst finishes, disc. 1992.

	N/A	N/A	N/A

Last MSR was $3,190.

PEAL
Instruments currently produced in Korea. Distributed by the Ye-Il International Company.

Peal produces a line of acoustic, electric, bass, and round back guitars that are mainly entry level instruments. For more information refer to their web site (see Trademark Index).

PEARL RIVER
Instruments currently produced in China.

Pearl River produces an entire line of acoustic guitars, as well as electric guitars. Pearl River guitars is a derivative of the Pearl River Guitar Company. They are mainly entry level instruments at an entry level prices. For more information refer to their web site (see Trademark Index).

PEAVEY
Instruments currently built in Meridian and Leaksville, Mississippi. Distributed by Peavey Electronics Corporation of Meridian, Mississippi since 1965. Peavey also has a factory and distribution center in Corby, England to help serve and service the overseas market.

Peavey Electronics is one of the very few major American musical instrument manufacturers still run by the original founding member and owner. Hartley Peavey grew up in Meridian, Mississippi and spent some time working in his father's music store repairing record players. He gained some recognition locally for the guitar amplifiers he built by hand while he was still in school, and decided months prior to college graduation to go into business for himself. In 1965 Peavey Electronics was started out of the basement of Peavey's parents home. Due to the saturated guitar amp market of the late 1960s, Peavey switched to building P.A. systems and components. By 1968, the product demand was great enough to warrant building a small cement block factory on rented land and hire another staff member.

The demand for Peavey products continued to grow, and by the early 1970s the company's roster had expanded to 150 employees. Emphasis was still placed on P.A. construction, although both guitar and bass amps were doing well. The Peavey company continued to diversify and produce all the components needed to build the finished product. After twelve years of manufacturing, the first series of Peavey guitars was begun in 1977, and introduced at the 1978 NAMM show. An advertising circular used by Peavey in the late '70s compared the price of an American built T-60 (plus case) for $350 versus the Fender Stratocaster's list price of $790 or a Gibson Les Paul for $998.50 (list). In light of those list prices, it's also easy to see where the Japanese guitar makers had plenty of maneuvering room during their "copy" era.

GRADING	100%	EXCELLENT	AVERAGE

The "T-Series" guitars were introduced in 1978, and the line expanded from three models up to a total of seven in five years. In 1983, the product line changed, and introduced both the mildly wacky Mystic and Razer original designs (the Mantis was added in 1984) and the more conservative Patriot, Horizon, and Milestone guitars. The Fury and Foundation basses were also added at this time. After five years of stop tailpieces, the first Peavey "Octave Plus" vibratos were offered (later superseded by the Power bend model). Pickup designs also shifted from the humbuckers to single or double "blade" pickups.

Models that debuted in 1985 included the vaguely stratish Predator, and the first doubleneck (!), the Hydra. In response to the guitar industry shifting to "superstrat" models, the Impact was introduced in 1986. Guitars also had the option of a Kahler locking tremolo, and two offsprings of the '84 Mantis were released: The Vortex I or Vortex II. The Nitro series of guitars were available in 1987, as well as the Falcon, Unity, and Dyna-Bass. Finally, to answer companies like Kramer or Charvel, the Tracer series and the Vandenberg model(s) debuted in 1988.

As the U.S. guitar market grew more conservative, models like the Generation S-1 and Destiny guitars showed up in guitar shops. Peavey basses continued to evolve into sleeker and more solid instruments like the Palaedium, TL series or B Ninety. 1994 saw the release of the Midibase (later the Cyberbass) that combined magnetic pickups with a MIDI-controller section.

One of Peavey's biggest breakthroughs in recent years was the development of the Peavey EVH amplifier, developed in conjunction with Edward Van Halen. Due to the success and acceptance of the EVH 5150 amplifier, Van Halen withdrew his connection with his signature Ernie Ball model (which is still in production as the Axis model), and designed a "new" **Wolfgang** model with Peavey. This new model had a one year "waiting period" from when it was announced at the NAMM industry trade show to actual production. Many Peavey dealers who did receive early models generally sold them at new retail (no discount) for a number of months due to slow supply and re-supply.

Rather than stay stuck in a design "holding pattern," Peavey continues to change and revise guitar and bass designs, and they continue the almost twenty year tradition of American built electric guitars and basses, (Model History, nomenclature, and description courtesy Grant Brown, Peavey Repair section).

Information on virtually any Peavey product, or a product's schematic is available through Peavey Repair. Grant Brown, the head of the Repair section, has been with Peavey Electronics for over eighteen years.

In 1994, a series of Peavey acoustic guitars was announced. Although some models were shipped in quantity, the acoustic line was not as wide spread as other guitar models that were introduced. Peavey acoustics have a solid Alpine Spruce top, and either laminated or solid rosewood sides, and a mahogany neck. So, if some Peavey acoustics are encountered, the following list will at least indicate the range envisioned.

ACOUSTIC: COMPACT CUTAWAY, DREADNOUGHT & JUMBO SERIES

Compact Cutaway Series: Two models comprise the Compact body design that featured a single cutaway: the **CC-37PE** ($1,099) had a five piece mahogany/rosewood neck, piezo pickup system, and Schaller hardware; the **CC-3712PE** ($1,149) was the accompanying 12-string model.

Dreadnought Series: The **SD-9P** ($499) was the only model to feature a solid cedar top in the Dreadnought design. The **SD-11P** ($599) featured the same body design with a Spruce top and laminated mahogany sides and back, and the **DD-21P** ($699) substitutes laminated rosewood in place of the mahogany. The **SD-11PCE** ($759) featured a single cutaway and piezo under-the-bridge pickup system with 3-band EQ and volume control.

Jumbo Series: The **CJ-33PE** ($1,049) featured the Jumbo body design and a piezo system; the **CJ-3312PE** ($1,099) was the accompanying 12-string model.

The Briarwood was released as a series in 2003. This series features models from basic dreadnoughts to acoustic/electrics and cutaways. Retail prices start at $170 and go to $500. Look for more information in further editions.

ACOUSTIC: DELTA SERIES

BRIARWOOD - dreadnought style body, spruce top, mahogany back and sides, 20-fret rosewood fingerboard, compensated bridge saddles, 3-per-side tuners, chrome hardware, pickguard, Natural finish, disc. 2002.

$175	$115	$70

Last MSR was $230.

CLARKSDALE - dreadnought body style, 25 1/2" scale, traditional X-bracing, spruce top, nato back, neck, and sides, bound body, rosewood fingerboard, 20-fret, sealed die-cast tuners, compensated bridge saddle, Satin finish on neck, gloss finish on body, chrome hardware, Natural finish, mfg. 1999-2000.

$155	$95	$65

Last MSR was $209.

GLENDORA - western body style, solid spruce top, mahogany back and sides, traditional X-bracing, cream bound rosewood fingerboard, 20 frets, sealed die-cast tuners, chrome hardware, compensated bridge saddles, Satin finish on neck and headstock, Gloss finish on body, mfg. 2001-02.

$375	$275	$185

Last MSR was $500.

GRADING	100%	EXCELLENT	AVERAGE

Glendora 12 - similar to Glendora, except in a 12-string configuration, mfg. 2001 only.

	$550	$400	$275

Last MSR was $675.

INDIANOLA ER - western body style, 25 1/2" scale, traditional X-bracing, spruce top, mahogany back, sides, and neck, bound body, rosewood fretboard, 20 frets, sealed die-cast tuners, chrome hardware, compensated bridge saddle, Satin finish on neck, Gloss finish on body, available in Natural finish, mfg. 1999-2002.

	$250	$175	$125

Last MSR was $310.

McCOMB - 25 1/2" scale, solid cedar top, mahogany back and sides, cream bound rosewood fingerboard, sealed die-cast tuners, compensated bridge saddles, inlaid rosette, available in Satin finish, mfg. 2001-02.

	$375	$225	$150

Last MSR was $500.

TUPELO ER - western body style, 25 1/2" scale, traditional X-bracing, spruce top, mahogany back, neck, and sides, bound body, rosewood fingerboard, 20 frets, sealed die-cast tuners, chrome hardware, compensated bridge saddle, Satin finish, available in Natural finish, mfg. 1999-2002

	$195	$135	$95

Last MSR was $260.

ACOUSTIC ELECTRIC

ECOUSTIC - single rounded cutaway dreadnought style, cedar top, oval soundhole, bound body, 5-stripe rosette, mahogany back/sides, maple neck, 22-fret rosewood fingerboard with white dot inlay, rosewood bridge with white pins, 3-per-side gold tuners, piezo bridge pickup, 3-band EQ, available in Black, Natural, or Trans. Red finishes, disc. 1999.

	$750	$475	$325

Last MSR was $959.

ECOUSTICATS - single rounded cutaway dreadnought style, maple top, oval soundhole, bound body, 5-stripe rosette, poplar back/sides, rock maple neck, 22-fret rosewood fingerboard with white dot inlay, rosewood ATS Tremolo bridge with white pins, 3-per-side chrome tuners, piezo bridge pickup, 3-band EQ, available in Black, Natural, or Trans. Red finishes, mfg. 1995-99.

	$775	$500	$335

Last MSR was $999.

ABERDEEN - 25" scale, single cutaway body, ash top, mahogany back and sides, cream bound rosewood fingerboard, sealed die-cast tuners, compensated bridge saddles, piezo pickup with 4-band preamp. Satin finished neck and headstock, high gloss body, mfg. 2001-02.

	$470	$350	$250

Last MSR was $600.

INDIANOLA AE - Western body style, 25 1/2" scale, traditional X-bracing, spruce top, mahogany back, neck, and sides, bound body, rosewood fingerboard, 20 frets, sealed die-cast tuners, compensated bridge saddle, chrome hardware, gloss finish on body, satin finish on neck, piezo under saddle bridge, preamp with 3-band EQ, rotary volume control, battery check LED and test button, switching jack, available in Natural finish, mfg. 1999-2002.

	$275	$185	$125

Last MSR was $360.

ROUTE 61 - 25" scale, solid spruce top, rosewood sides and back, single cutaway body, cream bound rosewood fingerboard, sealed die-cast tuners, piezo pickup with preamp, compensated bridge saddles, Satin finished neck and headstock, Gloss finished body, mfg. 2001-02.

	$525	$395	$250

Last MSR was $700.

TUPELO AE - western body style, 25 1/2" scale, spruce top, mahogany back, neck, and sides, bound body, rosewood fretboard, 20 frets, sealed die-cast tuners, chrome hardware, compensated bridge saddle, piezo under saddle bridge, 3-band EQ, rotary volume control, battery check LED and test button, switching jack, available in Natural Satin finish, mfg. 1999-2001.

	$329	$200	$135

Last MSR was $440.

PEDERSON, CRAIG

Instruments currently built in Brooklyn, New York. Distributed by Rudy's Music Shop of New York City, New York.

Luthier Craig Pederson has been building guitars for the past 27 years. While currently based in New York (on the fourth floor of the Gretsch building!), Pederson has had workshops in Minneapolis, Minnesota as well as Albuquerque, New Mexico. Throughout his luthier career, Pederson has produced various acoustic guitar models, semi-hollowbody guitars, and archtop guitars.

In addition to his various guitar models, Pederson also produces mandolins, mandolas, and mandocellos. Flat top models start at $1,300 (add $200 for wood binding), and caved top models start at $3,200 (add $300 for wood binding). Call for a price quote for custom options on any Pederson stringed instrument.

ACOUSTIC

All prices include a Harptone hardshell case. Pederson's **Archtop** guitars have a list price beginning at $4,000. Add $500 for wood binding on all guitar models (the following model prices quoted are for plastic body binding).

The **Pederson Nylon String** has a rounded body with venetian cutaway, round soundhole, set-in neck, rosette, 20-fret fingerboard, 3-per-side tuners. Retail pricing is $2,370 for both the cypress flamenco and rosewood classic versions.

The **Pederson Resonator** has a rounded body with florentine cutaway, set-in neck, 20-fret fingerboard, 3-per-side tuners, resonator, round covered soundhole on bass bout. Retail prices are $2,670 for either rosewood or curly maple, and $2,470 for mahogany.

The **Pederson Steel String** has a rounded body with florentine cutaway, round soundhole, set-in neck, rosette, 20-fret fingerboard, 3-per-side tuners. Retail pricing is $2,170 for the mahogany and $2,370 for rosewood or curly maple.

Pederson Archtop
courtesy Craig Pederson

PEERLESS
Instruments currently produced in Korea.

Peerless is another Korean guitar manufacture that produces entrly level instruments. Their lineup consists of acoustic and electric guitars. Refer to their web site if you can understand Korean (or whatever it is, see Trademark Index).

PENNCO
Instruments previously produced in Japan circa 1970s. Distributed by the Philadelphia Music Company of Philadelphia, Pennsylvania.

This trademark has been identified as a House Brand of the Philadelphia Music Company of Philadelphia, Pennsylvania, the U.S. distributor of these Japanese-built instruments. The Pennco (sometimes misspelled Penco) brand name was applied to a full range of acoustic and solid body electric guitars, many entry level to intermediate quality versions of popular American designs, (Source: Michael Wright, *Vintage Guitar Magazine*).

PENNCREST
See chapter on House Brands.

This trademark has been identified as a House Brand of J.C. Penneys, (Source: Willie G. Moseley, *Stellas & Stratocasters*).

PETE BACK GUITARS
Instruments currently built in Richmond (North Yorkshire), England since 1975.

Luthier Pete Back is noted for his custom handcrafted guitars of the highest quality. His electric, folk, and classical guitar construction uses the finest woods available. Pete has his own original designs, but will make whatever the guitarist requires. He also offers repairs (refretting, set-ups, and resprays). For more information on Pete Back Guitars refer to their web site (see Trademark Index).

PETILLO, PHILLIP J.
Instruments currently manufactured in Ocean, NJ. Petillo Masterpiece Guitars and Accessories was founded in 1968.

Luthier Phillip J. Petillo has been creating custom handcrafted instruments, repairing and restoring guitars and other instruments for over thirty years. Petillo was one of the original co-designers of the Kramer aluminum neck guitar in 1976, and built the four prototypes for Kramer (BKL). Later, he severed his connections with the company.

Currently, Petillo makes acoustic carved top and back guitars, flattop acoustics, semi-hollowbody guitars, and solid body guitars and basses. Petillo also makes and repairs the bowed instruments. Petillo, a holder of a BS, MS, and PHD in Engineering, also offers his talents in Engineering for product development, research and development, engineering, and prototype building for the musical instruments industry.

Phillip and Lucille Petillo are the founders and officers of a research corporation that develops devices and technology for the medical industry. While seeming unrelated to the music industry, the Phil-Lu Incorporated company illustrates Petillo's problem-solving skills applied in different fields of study.

Petillo estimates that he hand builds between 8 to 20 guitars a year on his current schedule. Prices begin at $1,200 and are priced by nature of design and materials utilized. Custom Marquetry Inlay and other ornamental work is priced by the square inch. Petillo offers 170 different choices of lumbers, veneers, and mother-of-pearl.

Restoration, alteration and repair work are price quoted upon inspection of the instrument. In addition, he markets his patented products such as Petillo Frets, the Acoustic Tonal Sensor, Petillo Strings and Polish, and a fret micro-polishing system.

Some of his clients include: Tal Farlow, Chuck Wayne, Jim Croce, Elvis Presley, James Taylor, Tom Petty, Howie Epstein, Dave Mason, The Blues Brothers, Bruce Springsteen, Gary Talent, Steve Van Zant, Southside Johnny, and many others.

Petillo MP Bass 1BB
courtesy Petillo

PETROS
Instruments currently built in Kaukauna, Wisconsin since 1972.

Luthier Bruce Petros has been handcrafting guitars for overthirty years. Petros currently offers handmade acoustic dreadnought and finger style guitars as well as a classical model and a 4-string solid body electric bass.

In addition to his guitars, Petros is a complete repair shop and authorized repair center for Martin and other companies. The address was previously in Holland Wisconsin. For more information and pricing refer to the web site (see Trademark Index).

Petros is also the manufacturer/distributor of Petros guitar care products that include: Professional Fingerboard Oil, Miracle Finish Restorer, and Professional Guitar Polish.

ACOUSTIC

All Petros guitars feature an arched Sitka spruce top, spruce/ebony bridgeplate, ebony fingerboard/bridge, wood binding and purfling, Gotoh tuners, and a enviro-friendly Gloss finish.

The **D** body size is a dreadnought style guitar with a tighter "waist," and the **FS** body style has a smaller body/wider neck more suited for finger style playing.

The **Apple Creek** model features black walnut back/sides, abalone dot fingerboard markers, and abalone rosette and prices start at $5,300. The **Holland Rose** is a walnut guitar with a Rose fingerboard inlay from the 12th to 17th fret; while the **Jordan** features a Dove fingerboard inlay. Both of these guitars have a base price of $5,800. The **High Cliff** model features a unique fingerboard/rosette inlay, curly maple binding, bound fingerboard, and a set of gold Grover tuners. Petros' limited edition **The Rite of Spring** has a unique Tulip Headstock, curly maple binding, abalone purfling, gold Grover tuners, and Tulip rosette/fingerboard inlays. The Prarire is the top of the line model and starts at $7,400.

PHIL
Instruments currently produced in South Korea by the Myung Sung Music Ind. Co.

The Myung Sung Music Ind. Co., Ltd. is currently offering a wide range of well constructed acoustic and acoustic electric guitar models. There is a large variety of styles, configurations, colors, and affordable price points. Construction utilizes top quality laminates, rosewood, spruce, mahogany, and build quality is top shelf. Acoustic electric models have onboard equalization. For more information on the current model availability and pricing, please contact Myung Sung Music Ind. Co. directly, (see Trademark Index).

ACOUSTIC

The **MD 58CE-12** is a 12-string, single cutaway hollowbody, spruce top, mahogany back and sides, nato neck, rosewood fingerboard with dot inlays, 6-per-side tuners, 20 frets, rosewood bridge, 4-band EQ pickup, chrome hardware, available in Natural finish only.

The **MD 79CE** is a single cutaway hollowbody, solid spruce top, rosewood back and sides, abalone pearl top binding, nato neck, rosewood fingerboard with pearl block inlays, 3-per-side tuners, 20 frets, rosewood bridge, 5-band EQ pickup, round soundhole, gold hardware, available in Natural finish only.

The **MD 86CE** is a single cutaway hollowbody, sycamore top, back and sides, round soundhole, maple neck, rosewood fingerboard, 20 frets, 3-per-side tuners, rosewood bridge, 5-band EQ pickup, gold hardware, available in Amber Satin finish only.

The **MDS 85CE** is a single cutaway hollowbody, sycamore top, back, and sides, round soundhole, nato neck, rosewood fingerboard with Blue Pearl dot inlays, 3-per-side tuners, 20 frets, rosewood bridge, 4-band EQ pickup, gold hardware, available in Transparent Black finish only.

The **MJ 66** is a super jumbo, Bird's-eye maple top, mahogany back and sides, nato neck, rosewood fingerboard with dot inlays, 3-per-side tuners, 20 frets, rosewood bridge, chrome hardware, available in Brown Burst finish only.

The **MS 95CE** is a single cutaway hollowbody, solid spruce top, sycamore back and sides, abalone pearl top binding, nato neck with rosewood fingerboard, 20 frets, rosewood bridge, offset fot inlays, 3-per-side tuners, round soundhole, 4-band EQ pickup, gold hardware, available in Natural finish only.

The **MS 96CE** is a single cutaway hollowbody, solid spruce top, rosewood back and sides, nato neck, rosewood fingerboard with dot inlays, 20 frets, 3-per-side tuners, round soundhole, abalone pearl top binding, 5-band EQ pickup, Tortoise Gold hardware, available in Natural finish only.

The **MS 97CE** is a single cutaway hollowbody, sycamore double archtop, sycamore back and sides, nato neck, rosewood fingerboard with pearl snowflake inlays, 20 frets, 3-per-side tuners, f-holes, rosewood and casino bridge, 4-band EQ pickup, lyre tailpiece, gold hardware, available in Brown Burst finish only.

The **MS 99CE** is a single cutaway hollowbody, sycamore double arch top, sycamore sides, nato neck, rosewood fingerboard with pearl block inlays, 20 frets, 3-per-side tuners, abalone pearl top binding, rosewood bridge, round soundhole, 4-band EQ pickup, gold hardware, available in Old Black Brown Burst finish.

The **MSD 69** is a single cutaway hollowbody, sycamore top, mahogany back and sides, round soundhole, nato neck, rosewood fingerboard with dot inlays, 21 frets, rosewood bridge, 5-band EQ pickup, gold hardware, available in Tobacco Sunburst finish only.

The **MSD 93CE** is a single cutaway hollowbody, sycamore top, back, and sides, round soundhole, nato neck with rosewood fingerboard, peal snowflake inlays, 20 frets, 3-per-side tuners, rosewood bridge, 4-band EQ pickup, chrome hardware, available in Blue Burst finish only.

The **MSS 87CE** is a single cutaway hollowbody, spruce top, mahogany back and sides, nato neck, rosewood fingerboard with pearl snowflake inlays, 3-per-side tuners, 20 frets, Florentine cutaway, rosewood bridge, 4-band EQ pickup, gold hardware, available in Natural finish only.

The **MSS 87-7** is a 7 string, single cutaway hollowbody, solid spruce top, mahogany back and sides, nato neck, rosewood fingerboard with pearl snowflake inlays, 20 frets, rosewood bridge, gold hardware, available in Tobacco Sunburst finish only.

ACOUSTIC BASS

The **MB 36CE** is a single cutaway hollowbody, cedar top, mahogany back and sides, nato neck, rosewood fingerboard with dot inlays, 2 per side tuners, round soundhole, 20 frets, rosewood bridge, 5-band EQ pickup, chrome hardware.

The **MB 38C**E is a single Florentine cutaway hollowbody, sycamore top, back, and sides, arched back, nato neck, rosewood fingerboard with dot inlays, 20 frets, 2 per side tuners, rosewood bridge, 4-band EQ pickup, chrome hardware, available in 3-Tone Sunburst finish only.

PHOENIX GUITAR COMPANY
Instruments previously produced in Phoenix, Arizona.

George Leach produced guitars in the late 1980s and early 1990s. He produced both acoustic and electric models. In 1995, the original staff at Phoenix was hired by the Gibson Guitar Company, and Phoenix shut down. Look for more information in further editions.

PIGNOSE
Instruments currently produced overseas.

Pignose amplifiers have been around since 1972. A kid went to a distributor in Oakland with this prototype amp that was built in a wooden box. The idea of a portable, battery operated amp wasn't taken by storm from the distributor in Oakland. He later gave a prototype to Terry Kath of Chicago who took interest in the idea. The volume knob kept coming loose and he brought it his tech. The rubber knob was melted and when it was fixed, Terry said that it looked like a pig's nose. Some of the first models were produced with these "pignose" knobs, and there only two of them known in existence. It's funny how names sometimes come about.

This amp was one of the first that was completely portable amplifier. Now Pignose offers amps that are run strictly on DC battery power along with a rechargeable model. Not only are these amps novel ideas, they are also fairly cheap. They currently offer a wide range of products, including some tube models. They have also introduced an acoustic Dreadnought model, which retails for under $100.

PIMENTEL & SONS
Instruments currently built in Albuquerque, New Mexico since 1951.

Luthier Lorenzo Pimentel builds high quality classical and steel string acoustic guitars and requintos. Pimentel, originally born in Durango, Mexico, learned guitar making from his older brothers. Though trained as a baker, Pimentel moved to El Paso, Texas, in 1948 to work for master violin maker Nagoles. A few years later, Pimentel moved to Albuquerque, and began building guitars as his livelihood. Today, Lorenzo Pimentel and his sons handcraft perhaps 40 to 80 guitars a month, and the entire family is involved in some aspect of the business.

List prices start at $1,000 depending on the model and woods used in the construction, and can go up to over $15,000 for some Brazillian rosewood work. Only Lorenzo Pimentel builds the top-of-the-line **Grand Concert** model, while his sons professionally build other models in the line. For more information refer to their web site (see Trademark Index).

PINKHAM, RONALD
Instruments currently built in Glen Cove, Maine. Distributed by Woodsound Studio of Glen Cove, Maine.

Luthier Ronald Pinkham currently offers high quality concert-grade classic and steel-string acoustic guitars, as well as cellos. Pinkham also has one of the largest orchestral and fretted instrument repair facilities in New England. For further information, please contact luthier Pinkham directly (see Trademark Index).

PRAIRIE STATE
See Larson Brothers (1900-1944).

The Larson brothers added the Prairie State brand to Maurer & Co. in the mid 1920s. This brand was used exclusively for guitars. The main difference between the Maurer and the Prairie State was the use of a support rod and an adjustable rod running the length of the guitar body from end block to neck block. These 12-fret-to-the-body guitars have the double rod system, which may vary according to the period it was made because August Larson was awarded three patents for these ideas. The rod closest to the soundhole is larger than the lower one, and, in some cases, is capable of making adjustments to the fingerboard height. The function of the lower rod is to change the angle of the neck. Most all Prairie States have laminated top braces and laminated necks. They were built in the lower bout widths of 13-1/2", 14", and 15" for the standard models, but special order guitars were built up to 21" wide. In the mid -1930s, the Prairie State guitars were built in the larger 14-fret-to-the-body sizes, all now sporting the large rod only. The common body widths of these are 15", 16", 17", 19", and a rare 21". The single cutaway style was used on one known 19" f-hole and one 21" guitar. The Prairie State guitar is rarer than the other Larson brands. They are of very high quality and are sought by players and collectors. The rigid body produces great sustain and a somewhat different sound from the Maurers and Euphonon guitars. Almost all the Prairie State guitars were made with beautiful rosewood back and sides except the f-hole models which were commonly made with maple bodies, all having select spruce tops.

For more information regarding other Larson-made brands, see Maurer, Euphonon, Wm. C. Stahl, W.j. Dyer, and The Larson Brothers.

For more detailed information regarding all the Larson brands and a Maurer/Prairie State catalog reprint, see The Larsons' Creations, Guitars and Mandolins, by Robert Carl Hartman, Center stream Publishing, P.O. Box 17878, Anaheim Hills CA 92807, phone/fax (714) 779-9390.

PRAIRIE VOICE
See chapter on House Brands.

This trademark has been identified as a Harmony-built "Roy Rodgers" style guitar built specifically for the yearly Canadian "Calgary Stampede." The *Blue Book of Acoustic Guitars* is interested in more information on either the guitars produced for this celebration, or the celebration itself! (Source: Willie G. Moseley, *Stellas & Stratocasters*).

PREMIER
Instruments currently produced in Korea. Distributed in the U.S. market by Entertainment Music Marketing Corporation (EMMC) of Deer Park, New York. Instruments produced in New York during the 1950s and 1960s. Later models manufactured in Japan.

**Phil MF-807N
courtesy Kelsey Fjestad**

**Praire State
courtesy Robert Carl Hartmen**

P

Premier was the brand name of the Peter Sorkin Music Company. Premier-branded solid body guitars were built at the Multivox company of New York, and distribution of those and the later Japanese built Premiers was handled by the Sorkin company of New York City, New York. Other guitars built and distributed (possibly as rebrands) were Royce, Strad-o-lin, Belltone, and Marvel.

Current Premier models are built in Korea, and feature a slimmed (or sleek) strat-style guitar body and P-style bass body. New list prices range are around $200-$300.

Premier solid body guitars featured a double offset cutaway body, and the upper bout had a "carved scroll" design, bolt-on necks, a bound rosewood fingerboard, 3+3 headstocks (initially; later models featured 6-on-a-side), and single coil pickups. Later models of the mid to late 1960s featured wood bodies covered in sparkly plastic.

Towards the end of the U.S. production in the mid 1960s, the **Custom** line of guitars featured numerous body/neck/electronics/hardware parts from overseas manufacturers like Italy and Japan. The guitars were then assembled in the U.S, and available through the early 1970s.

Some models, like the acoustic line, were completely made in Japan during the early 1970s. Some Japanese-built versions of popular American designs were introduced in 1974, but were discontinued two years later. By the mid 1970s, both the Sorkin company and Premier guitars had ceased. Multivox continued importing and distributing Hofner instruments as well as Multivox amplifiers through the early 1980s. Hofners are currently distributed by the Entertainment Music Marketing Corporation of New York, as well as the current line of Premier solid body electric guitars and basses, (Source: Michael Wright, *Guitar Stories,* Volume One).

PRENKERT, RICHARD
Instruments currently built in the U.S. Distributed by Kirkpatrick Guitar Studios of Baltimore, Maryland.

Luthier Richard Prenkert is currently building high quality classical guitars. Guitar prices start at $2,500 and waiting time is about 3 months for delivery of a guitar.

PRUDENCIO SAEZ
Instruments currently produced in Spain. Distributed by Saga Musical Instruments of San Francisco, California.

Prudencio Saez classical acoustics are designed for the beginning to advancing player. Handmade in Spain, these guitars feature a solid cedar top, mahogany neck, rosewood fingerboard and bridge, an inlaid marquetry rosette, Clear High Gloss finish, and a slotted 3-per-side headstock. Some models feature mahogany back and sides (like the **PS-4A** and **PS-6A**) while others have walnut backs and sides (**PS-8A**). Prices are right around $400 for guitars. For more information refer to Saga's web site (see Trademark Index).

PURE-TONE
See chapter on House Brands.

This trademark has been identified as a House Brand of Selmer (UK), (Source: Willie G. Moseley, *Stellas & Stratocasters*).

P

Section R

RAIMUNDO

Instruments currently distributed by Luthier Music Corporation of New York, New York, and Music Imports of San Diego, California.

Raimundo offers a wide range of classical and flamenco-style acoustic guitars.

RAINSONG

Instruments currently produced in Maui, Hawaii since 1994. Distributed by Kuau Technology, Ltd. since 1985. Previous instrument production was a joint effort between facilities in Hawaii and Albuquerque, New Mexico.

Kuau Technology, Ltd. was initially founded in 1982 by Dr. John A. Decker, Jr. to research and provide development on optical instrumentation and marine navigation. Decker, a physicist with degrees in engineering, also enjoys playing classical guitar. Since 1985, the company began concentrating on developing and manufacturing graphite/epoxy Classical and Steel String guitars. Members of the design team included Dr. Decker, as well as noted luthier Lorenzo Pimentel and composite materials expert George M. Clayton. In the company's beginning, the R & D facility was in Maui, Hawaii; and manufacturing was split between Escondido, California and Pimentel and Sons guitar makers of Albuquerque, New Mexico. The California facility handled the work on the composite materials, and the Pimentels in New Mexico supplied the lutherie and finishing work (Pimentel and Sons themselves build quality wooden guitars). The Rainsong All-Graphite acoustic guitar has been commercially available since 1992.

In December 1994, full production facilities were opened in Maui, Hawaii. George Clayton of Bi-Mar Productions assisted in development of the factory and manufacturing processes, then returned to the mainland to continue his own work. The product line has expanded to include classical models, steel string acoustic guitars and basses, acoustic/electric models, and hollowbody electric guitars and basses. Kuau Technologies, Ltd. currently employs ten people on their production staff.

Rainsong guitars and basses feature Rainsong's proprietary graphite/epoxy technology, Schaller tuning machines, optional Fishman transducers, and EMG pickups (on applicable models). Models also available with a single cutaway, in left-handed configurations, a choice of three peghead inlay designs, side-dot fret markers, and wood marquetry rosette. Instruments shipped in a hardshell case.

Rainsong WS1000
courtesy Rainsong

ACOUSTIC

The Rainsong **Limited Edition** model features a Fishman Prefix Pro pickup system, and an abalone inlay on the 12th fret. They are available in Burgundy, Platinum, and Sapphire finishes. Only 300 models are scheduled in the Edition (list $1,995).

The **Russ Freeman Signature Jazz** model is available in 6-string (list $2,995) and 12-string ($3,295) configurations.

RainSong guitars are optional with peghead inlay like the **Maui Girl**, **Modest Maui Girl**, and a **Whale** design. Prices range from $100 to $150 for peghead inlay.

Circa 2000, Rainsong decided to go ahead and rename/overhaul there complete line. They still make the same type of guitars but all the names and some configurations are now different. Retail prices start at $1,995 on current models. Look for more information in further editions.

CLASSICAL - black unidirectional-graphite soundboard, 650 mm scale, 2" width at nut, slotted (open) peghead with 3-per-side tuners, gold Schaller tuners with ebony buttons, and abalone rosette, current mfg.

> **MSR $2,195**
>
> The Classical model is patterned after Pimentel & Sons Grand Concert model.

FLAMENCO - similar to the Classical, except has solid headstock, current mfg.

> **MSR $2,195**

6-STRING DREADNOUGHT - dreadnought size body, choice of 14/20 or 12/20-fret fingerboard, solid peghead, Schaller black tuning pegs, shark inlay design on the twelfth fret, side dot markers, Fishman Prefix transducer, volume/tone controls, current mfg.

> **MSR $2,195**
>
> *12-String Dreadnought* - similar to the 6-String dreadnought, except features 12-string configuration, 6-per-side tuners, mfg. 1997-current.
>
> **MSR $2,195**

12-FRET WINDSONG - jumbo size single cutaway body, 12/20-fret fingerboard, solid peghead, Fishman Prefix transducer, Schaller black tuning pegs, shark inlay design on the twelfth fret, and side dot markers, current mfg.

> **MSR $2,195**

Rainsong JM-1000
courtesy Rainsong

R

14-Fret WindSong - similar to the 12-Fret WindSong, except the neck joins the body at the 14th fret, 14/20 fingerboard, current mfg.

MSR $2,195

12-String WindSong - similar to the 14-Fret WindSong, except has 12-string configuration, 6-per-side tuners, mfg. 1997-current.

MSR $2,195

ACOUSTIC BASS

ACOUSTIC BASS - body patterned similar to the Windsong guitar, 844 mm scale, 4-string configuration, 2-per-side tuners, solid headstock, abalone rosette, side dot fret markers, Fishman Prefix transducer/preamp, volume/tone controls, current mfg.

MSR $2,195

Add $250 for fretless fingerboard (Model Fretless Bass).

ACOUSTIC ELECTRIC

6-STRING JAZZ GUITAR - single cutaway body, f-holes, 648 mm scale, 3+3 headstock, black Schaller tuning machines, graphite tailpiece, EMG 91 Custom pickup, Mike Christian tune-o-matic acoustic piezo bridge, volume/tone controls, 3-way pickup selector, current mfg.

MSR $2,495

12-String Jazz Guitar (StormSong) - similar to the 6-String Jazz Guitar, except features a 12-string configuration, 6-per-side tuners, EMG 89R humbucker pickups, 5-way pickup selector, mfg. 1997-current.

MSR $2,495

WINDSONG ACOUSTIC/ELECTRIC - similar to the Windsong acoustic model, except has thinner body, oval soundhole, Fishman Axis-M transducer/preamp, and oval abalone rosette, current mfg.

MSR $4,000

STAGESONG - similar to the Windsong Acoustic/Electric model, except has no soundhole in the top soundboard, current mfg.

MSR $2,195

12-String StageSong - similar to the StageSong, except features 12-string configuration, 6-per-side tuners, mfg. 1997-current.

MSR $2,195

Stagesong Classical - similar to the StageSong, except has classical stylings, current mfg.

MSR $2,195

ACOUSTIC ELECTRIC BASS

STAGESONG BASS - similar to the Acoustic Bass, except has no soundhole in the top soundboard, current mfg.

MSR $2,195

RALEIGH

Instruments previously built in Chicago, Illinois. Distributed by the Aloha Publishing and Musical Instrument Company of Chicago, Illinois.

The Aloha company was founded in 1935 by J.M. Raleigh. True to the nature of a House Brand distributor, Raleigh's company distributed both Aloha instruments and amplifiers and Raleigh brand instruments through his Chicago office. Acoustic guitars were supplied by Harmony, and initial amplifiers and guitars for the Aloha trademark were supplied by the Alamo company of San Antonio, Texas. By the mid 1950s, Aloha was producing their own amps, but continued using Alamo products, (Source: Michael Wright, *Vintage Guitar Magazine*).

RAMIREZ, JOSE

Instruments currently built in Madrid, Spain for four generations. Distributed in the U.S. exclusively by Guitar Salon International of Santa Monica, California.

Jose' Ramirez (1858-1923), originally apprenticed with luthier Francisco Gonzalez, began the family business in 1882. Many well known players, such as Segovia, Tarrega, Sabicas, Llobet, Yepes, and others had used Ramirez guitars during the course of their careers. The Madrid-based family business then passed to Jose' II (1885-1957), and then to Jose' III (born 1922-1994).

The acoustic guitars today are built in the workshop that is supervised by Jose' Ramirez IV. Ramirez IV, born in 1953, apprenticed in the family workshop when he was eighteen years old. By 1976, he had approached journeyman status, and within three years was working in maestro status. His sister, Amalia Ramirez, oversees the business side of the company.

In the early 1980s, the family workshop employed 17 workers and was producing 1,000 guitars a year. In the mid 1990s, the Ramirez workshop cut back production numbers to the amount the workshop could build without sub-contracting to outside builders. This level of supervision aids in maintaining the high quality of the guitars that carry the Ramirez name.

ACOUSTIC

The Madrid workshop continues to produce a full line of classical and flamenco guitars, lauds, bandurrias, and even cutaway guitar models with installed pickups. Ramirez continues to offer the two top of the line models, the **Tradicional** and the **Especial**.

RANGE RIDER

See chapter on House Brands.

This trademark has been identified as a House Brand of the Monroe Catalog House, (Source: Willie G. Moseley, *Stellas & Stratocasters*).

RECORDING KING

See chapter on House Brands.

The Recording King trademark was the House Brand of Montgomery Wards, and was used on a full range of acoustic flattops, electric lap steels, acoustic and electric archtop guitars, mandolins, and banjos. Instruments were built by a number of American manufacturers such as Gibson, Gretsch, and Kay between the 1930s through the early 1940s.

The high end models of the Recording King line were built by Gibson, but the low end models were built by other Chicago-based manufacturers. Recording King models built by Gibson will not have an adjustable truss rod (like other budget brands Gibson produced). Chances are that the low end, Chicago-built models do not either. Recording King had a number of endorsers, such as singing cowboy movie star Ray Whitley, country singer/songwriter Carson Robison, and multi-instrumental virtuoso Roy Smeck, (Source: Walter Carter, *Gibson Guitars: 100 Years of an American Icon*).

Recording King models have become very collectible and the right models are asking quite a bit of money.

Recording King M-5
courtesy Marvin G Mahler

REDGATE, J.K.

Instruments currently built in Adelaide, Australia. Distributed exclusively in the U.S by Classic Guitars International of Westlake Village, California.

Luthier Jim Redgate was born in London, England in 1963. His family emigrated to Australia in 1966. Redgate left school at age 15 to pursue a trade in plumbing. After his apprenticeship, Redgate began pursuing a career in music. Disappointed in a music shop's lackluster repair of his guitar, Redgate decided to fix the guitar himself (a neck reset performed on the kitchen table!).

Redgate has been building guitars since 1984. An accomplished player himself, Redgate holds a Bachelor of Music Performance in Classical Guitar from the Elder Conservatories. Although not formally trained in guitar building, his background in guitar playing comes to bear in his guitar design.

In 1992, Redgate became a full time luthier – and began marketing worldwide by 1995. Redgate is well-known for his classical concert guitars with carbon fibre reinforced lattice bracing and arched backs. His high grade construction materials include Brazilian rosewood, W.R. cedar, German spruce, black ebony, and Honduras mahogany.

Redgate builds about fifteen or so guitars a year, with minimal use of power tools. This limited number of instruments are available from Jim Redgate direct, and custom requirements can be catered for. Retail list price in the U.S. is $5,200 as of 1996s price list. For further information, please contact Jim Redgate directly (see Trademark Index).

REDONDO

See chapter on House Brands.

This trademark has been identified as a House Brand of the Tosca Company, (Source: Willie G. Moseley, *Stellas & Stratocasters*).

REEDMAN

Instruments currently built in Korea. Distributed by Reedman America of Whittier, California.

The Reedman Musical Instrument company is currently offering a wide range of good quality acoustic, acoustic/electric, and solid body electric guitars. For further information, please contact Reedman America directly (see Trademark Index).

REGAL

Instruments currently produced in Korea. Distributed by Saga Musical Instruments of San Francisco, California. Original Regal instruments produced beginning 1896 in Indianapolis, Indiana. Regal reappeared in Chicago, Illinois in 1908, possibly tied to Lyon and Healy (Washburn). U.S. production was centered in Chicago from 1908 through the late 1960s. Models from the mid 1950s to the late 1960s produced in Chicago, Illinois by the Harmony company. Some Regal models licensed to Fender, and some appear with Fender logo during the late 1950s to mid 1960s (prior to Fender's own flattop and Coronado series).

Emil Wulschner was a retailer and wholesaler in Indianapolis, Indiana during the 1880s. In the early 1890s he added his stepson to the company, and changed the name to "Wulschner and Son." They opened a factory around 1896 to build guitars and mandolins under three different trademarks: Regal, University, and 20th Century. Though Wulschner passed away in 1900, the factory continued on through 1902 or 1903 under control of a larger corporation. The business end of the company let it go when the economy faltered during those final years. This is the end of the original Regal trademarked instruments.

In 1904 Lyon & Healy (Washburn) purchased the rights to the Regal trademark, thousands of completed and works in progress instruments, and the company stockpile of raw materials. A new Regal company debuted in Chicago, Illinois in 1908 (it is not certain what happened during those four years) and it is supposed that they were tied to Lyon & Healy. The new company marketed ukuleles and tenor guitars, but not 6-string guitars.

However, experts have agreed that Regal built guitar models for other labels (Bruno, Weyman, Stahl, and Lyon & Healy) during the 1910-1920 era. Regal eventually announced that their six string models would be distributed through a number of wholesalers.

Regal Big Boy
courtesy Rod & Hank's
Vintage Guitar

R

In 1930, the Tonk Bros. Company acquired the rights to the Washburn trademark when the then-current holder (J.R. Stewart Co.) went bankrupt. Regal bought the rights to the **Stewart** and **LeDomino** names from Tonk Bros., and was making fretted instruments for all three trademarks. Also in the early 1930s, Regal had licensed the use of Dobro resonators in a series of guitars. In 1934 they acquired the rights to manufacture Dobro brand instruments when National-Dobro moved to Chicago from California. Regal then announced that they would be joining the name brand guitar producers that sold direct to dealers in 1938. Regal was, in effect, another producer of House Brand guitars prior to World War II.

It has been estimated by one source that Regal-built Dobros stopped in 1940, and were not built from then on. During World War II, guitar production lines were converted to the war effort. After the war, the Regal Musical Instrument company's production was not as great as the pre-war production amounts. In 1954 the trademark and company fixtures were sold to Harmony. Harmony and Kay, were the other major producers of House Brand instruments. Regal guitars were licensed to Fender in the late 1950s, and some of the Harmony built "Regals" were rebranded with the Fender logo. This agreement continued up until the mid 1960s, when Fender introduced their own flattop guitars.

In 1987, Saga Musical Instruments reintroduced the Regal trademark to the U.S. market. Regal now offers a traditional resonator guitar in both a roundneck and squareneck versions. Saga, located in San Francisco, also offers the **Blueridge** line of acoustic instruments, as well as mandolins, and stringed instrument parts and replacement pieces.

Early Regal history courtesy John Teagle, *Washburn: Over One Hundred Years of Fine Stringed Instruments*. This noteworthy book brilliantly unravels core histories of Washburn, Regal, and Lyon & Healy and is a recommended must read to guitar collectors.

ACOUSTIC

All of the new Regal RD-45 resonator guitar models feature a mahogany body and neck, multi-ply white body binding, a bound rosewood fingerboard with mother-of-pearl position dots, chrome hardware, and a 10 1/2" spun aluminum cone with the traditional spider bridge.

The **RD-45** roundneck resonator has a spruce top, solid 3+3 peghead, a 21-fret neck that joins at the 14th fret, and an adjustable truss rod. Available in Black, Cherryburst, Natural, and Sunburst. The all-mahogany version (**RD-45 M**) has a Gloss finish.

The **RD-45S** squareneck resonator model also has a spruce top, and a more traditional slotted 3+3 peghead, as well as the 14/21-fret neck. The RD-45 S models are also available in Black, Cherryburst, Natural, and Sunburst. The all-mahogany version (**RD-45S M**) has a Gloss finish.

Regal briefly offered the **RD-65** resonator guitar. This roundneck model features all maple body construction, a mahogany neck, bound 14/21-fret rosewood fingerboard with mother-of-pearl position dots, solid 3+3 peghead, and a 7-ply white/black/white body binding. The **RD-65S** squareneck model is similar in construction, except has a slotted 3+3 headstock, 12th fret neck joint, and all white body binding. Both models have a Sunburst finish. Regal's **RD-65M** has a body constructed out of mahogany with the same specifications as the RD-65. The RD-65M has a dark-stained high gloss finish. All three of the **RD-65** series resonators are now discontinued.

ACOUSTIC BASS

Regal has recently introduced the **RD-05** resonator bass guitar. Similar to the RD-45 resonator guitar models, the RD-05 has 23-fret neck that joins the body at the 17th fret, a 2+2 solid headstock, and a spruce top. The RD-05 is currently available in a Sunburst finish only.

REGENT
Instruments previously produced in Ottawa, Canada.

Regent produced guitars circa 1940s-1960s. The headstock features the name Regent in distinctive block lettering with one leg of the R extended to underline the rest of the word. They made both archtop and flattop models. More information will be in upcoming editions.

RENAISSANCE GUITAR COMPANY
Instruments currently manufactured in Santa Cruz, CA. Sales and marketing are done by John Connolly & Co. in Northport, New York.

Renaissance currently manufactures a variety of acoustic electric "Ampli-Coustic" models, including an acoustic electric bass. Please refer to the *Blue Book of Electric Guitars* for more information and current pricing on these models.

REX
See chapter on House Brands.

In the early 1900s, the Rex models were Kay-built student quality guitars distributed by the Fred Gretsch Manufacturing Company. By 1920 the Fred Gretsch Mfg. Co. had settled into its new ten story building in Brooklyn, New York, and was offering music dealers a very large line of instruments that included banjos, mandolins, guitars, violins, drums, and other band instruments. Gretsch distributed both the 20th Century and Rex trademarks prior to introduction of the Gretsch trademark in 1933.

Another Rex trademark has also been identified as a House Brand of the Great West Music Wholesalers of Canada by author/researcher Willie G. Moseley.

RIBBECKE, TOM
Instruments currently built in the San Francisco bay area in California since 1973.

Luthier Tom Ribbecke has been building and repairing guitars and basses for over twenty three years in the San Francsico bay area. Ribbecke's first lutherie business opened in 1975 in San Francisco's Mission District, and remained open and busy for ten years. In 1985, Ribbecke closed down the storefront in order to focus directly on client commissions.

Ribbecke guitars are entirely hand built by the luthier himself, while working directly with the customer. Beyond his signature and serial number of the piece, Ribbecke also offers a history of the origin of all materials involved in construction.

All prices quoted are the base price new, and does not reflect additions to the commissioned piece. For further information, please contact luthier Tom Ribbecke directly (see Trademark Index).

ACOUSTIC

16" 17" OR 18" ARCH TOP STANDARD - construction material as quoted in the base price is good quality domestic figured maple back and sides, Sitka spruce top, ebony fingerboard, ebony pickguard, gold hardware, and solid ebony tailpiece, available in 25.4", 25", or 24.75" scale length, current mfg.

> **MSR** **$15,000**
>
>> Add $300 for mother-of-pearl block inlay. Add $300 for pickup and volume control. Add $400 for Sunburst finish. Add $800 for wood body binding. Add $1,000 for 18" body width (Call for specifics). Add $1,000 for 7-string configuration. Add $1,500 for 8-string configuration (Call for specifics).
>
> Earlier models were designated either a Monterey or Homage model; the Monterey features a cascade type peghead design, while the Homage features a peghead design reminiscent of a D'Angelico.

ACOUSTIC STEEL STRING - first quality spruce top, Indian rosewood back and sides, ebony fingerboard, ebony Bridge, and dot inlays, current mfg.

> **MSR** **$4,500**
>
>> Add $300 for wood body binding.

SOUND BUBBLE STEEL STRING - solid carved top, first quality Indian rosewood back and sides, ebony fingerboard, ebony bridge, and dot inlays, current mfg.

> **MSR** **$6,000**
>
>> Add $300 for wood body binding.
>
> The Sound Bubble, a slightly domed area on the bass side of the lower bout, increases the guitar's ability to translate the energy of the strings into sound. Patented in 1981 by artisan Charles Kelly and luthier Tom Ribbecke.

ACOUSTIC BASS

CARVED TOP ACOUSTIC BASS - solid carved spruce top with elliptical soundhole, maple back and sides, ebony fingerboard, 34" scale, chrome hardware, and dot inlays, available in Natural finish only, current mfg.

> **MSR** **$6,000**

Ribbecke Archtop courtesy Scott Chinery

RICHTER
See chapter on House Brands.

This trademark has been identified as a House Brand of Montgomery Wards. Judging from the impressed stamp on the back of the headstock, instruments built by the Richter Manufacturing Company were produced in Chicago, Illinois. The production date is still unknown, but the instruments seem to have a pre-World War II aura about them – 1930s to 1940s, (Information courtesy Bob Smith, Cassville, Wisconsin).

One example was found by Earl Oliver. He claims that the guitar was built using cheap materials, but the craftsmanship is excellent throughout the instrument. Dating is very precise as there is a physical date stamped in the guitar but no evidence of a serial number. More information and accurate pricing are being researched.

RICKENBACKER
Instruments currently produced in Santa Ana, California. Distributed by Rickenbacker International Corporation of Santa Ana, California. Rickenbacker instruments have been produced in California since 1931.

In 1925, John Dopyera (and brothers) joined up with George Beauchamp and Adolph Rickenbacker and formed National to build resonator guitars. Beauchamp's attitudes over spending money caused John Dopyera to leave National and start the Dobro company. While at National, Beauchamp, Rickenbacker and Dopyera's nephew, Paul Barth, designed the *Frying Pan* electric lap steel. In 1929 or 1930, Beauchamp was either forced out or fired from National – and so allied himself with Adolph Rickenbacker (National's tool and die man) and Barth to form Ro-Pat-In.

In the summer of 1931, Ro-Pat-In started building aluminum versions of the Frying Pan prototype. Early models have "Electro" on the headstock. Two years later, Rickenbacker (or sometimes Rickenbacher) was added to the headstock, and Ro-Pat-In was formally changed to the Electro String Instrument Corporation. Beauchamp left Electro sometime in 1940, and Barth left in 1956 to form his own company.

In December of 1953, F.C. Hall bought out the interests of Rickenbacker and his two partners. The agreement stated that the purchase was complete, and Electro could "continue indefinitely to use the trade name Rickenbacker." Hall, founder of Radio-Tel and the exclusive Fender distributor, had his Fender distributorship bought out by Leo Fender and Don Randall. The Rickenbacker company was formed in 1965 as an organizational change (Electro is still the manufacturer, and Rickenbacker is the sales company). Rickenbacker instruments gained popularity as the Beatles relied on a number of their guitars in the 1960s. One slight area of confusion: the model names and numbers differ from the U.S. market to models imported in to the U.K.

Ribbecke 17" Archtop courtesy Tom Ribbecke

R

market during the short period in the 1960s when Rose Morris represented Rickenbacker in the U.K (at all other times, the model numbers worldwide have been identical to the U.S. market).

In 1984 John Hall (F.C. Hall's son) officially took control by purchasing his father's interests in both the Rickenbacker, Inc. and Electro String companies. Hall formed the Rickenbacker International Corporation (RIC) to combine both interests, (Source: John C. Hall, Chief Executive Officer, Rickenbacker International Corporation; and Tom Wheeler, *American Guitar*).

For further information regarding Rickenbacker electric models, please refer to the *Blue Book of Electric Guitars*.

ACOUSTIC ARCHTOP

Rickenbacker currently offers the 5002V58 Mandolin, a vintage-style solid body electric mandolin based on a similar model issued in 1958. The current reproduction has a maple and walnut laminated body, 8-string configuration, and single coil pickups. Available in Fireglo or Mapleglo finishes (retail list is $1,489).

760J JAZZ-BO - single rounded cutaway hollowbody, bound carved spruce top, set-in neck, solid maple sides, carved maple back, 2 bound cat's-eye f-holes, 14/21-fret rosewood fingerboard with pearl triangle inlay, adjustable rosewood bridge/metal trapeze tailpiece, 3-per-side tuners, gold hardware, available in Natural or Sunburst finishes, current mfg.

MSR	$4,898	$3,925	$2,375	$1,750

ACOUSTIC

385 - dreadnought style, maple top, round soundhole, pickguard, checkered body/rosette, maple back/sides/neck, 21-fret rosewood fingerboard with pearl triangle inlay, rosewood bridge with white pins, available in Burst finishes, mfg. 1958-1972.

1958-1965	N/A	$2,000	$1,300
1966-1972	N/A	$1,250	$850

This model was also available in a classic style body (Model 385-S).

385-J - similar to 385, except has jumbo style body.

N/A	$2,150	$1,400

390 - a few prototypes were made (circa 1957), but this model was never put into production.

700 COMSTOCK (MODEL 700C) - jumbo style, bound spruce top, round soundhole, solid maple back/sides, 14/21-fret rosewood fingerboard with pearl triangle inlay, rosewood bridge, 3-per-side tuners, chrome hardware, available in Natural finish, current mfg.

MSR	$2,438	$1,950	$1,275	$925

700 Comstock 12 String (Model 700C/12) - similar to the 700 Comstock, except has a 12-string configuration, 6-per-side tuners, current mfg.

MSR	$2,538	$2,025	$1,325	$950

700 SHASTA (MODEL 700S) - similar to the 700 Comstock, except features solid rosewood back/sides, current mfg.

MSR	$2,538	$2,025	$1,350	$950

700 Shasta 12 String (Model 700S/12) - similar to the 700 Shasta, except has a 12-string configuration, 6-per-side tuners, current mfg.

MSR	$2,638	$2,100	$1,375	$975

730 LARAMIE (MODEL 730L) - dreadnought style, bound spruce top, round soundhole, solid maple back/sides, 14/21-fret rosewood fingerboard with pearl triangle inlay, rosewood bridge, 3-per-side tuners, chrome hardware, available in Natural finish, current mfg.

MSR	$2,198	$1,750	$1,175	$850

730 Laramie 12 String (Model 730L/12) - similar to the 730 Laramie, except has a 12-string configuration, 6-per-side tuners, current mfg.

MSR	$2,298	$1,850	$1,200	$875

730 SHILOH (MODEL 730S) - similar to the 730 Laramie, except features solid rosewood back/sides, current mfg.

MSR	$2,298	$1,850	$1,200	$875

730 Shiloh 12 (Model 730S/12) - similar to the 730 Shiloh, except has a 12-string configuration, 6-per-side tuners, current mfg.

MSR	$2,398	$1,925	$1,250	$925

RICKMANN

Instruments previously in Japan during the late 1970s.

The Rickmann trademark was a brand name used by a UK importer. Instruments are generally intermediate quality copies of classic American designs, (Source: Tony Bacon and Paul Day, *The Guru's Guitar Guide*).

RICO

See B.C. Rich

RIEGER-KLOSS

See BD Dey.

RJS

Instruments currently built in Fort Worth, Texas.

Luthier R.Jeffrey Smith has been building guitars since 1994 and established the company with Steve Carson. His works of art are all natural with no inlays and he is obviously inspired by Jimmy D'Aquisto. He began building solid body guitars and progressed to stunning archtop acoustics. We recently had the opportunity to photograph his guitars at the Arlington Vintage Guitar Show and we found them to be among the most beautiful guitars we have observed. He is currently producing one model, the Modena. Contact RJS' web site for more information (see Trademark Index).

RIPLEY, STEVE

Instruments previously built in Tulsa, Oklahoma.

Luthier Steve Ripley had established a reputation as both a guitarist and recording engineer prior to debuting his Stereo Guitar models at the 1983 NAMM show. Ripley's designs were later licensed by Kramer (BKL). In 1986, Ripley moved to Tulsa, Oklahoma and two years later severed his relationship with Kramer, (Source: Tom Wheeler, *American Guitars*).

ROBERT GUITARS

Instruments currently built in British Columbia, Canada.

Luthier Mikhail Robert was born in Moldavia, USSR in 1960. He moved to Canada and studied math, physics, and guitars. In 1981 he built his first guitars. By 1987 he had recieved international recognition and has been consistently producing high quality classical guitars since. For more information refer to Robert Guitars web site (see Trademark Index).

RODIER

Instruments previously built in Kansas City, Kansas circa 1900s.

While not much information is known about the Rodier instruments, Mr. Jim Reynolds of Independence, Missouri is currently researching materials for an upcoming book. It is unknown if this book was ever completed (or started) and there is no information to contact Mr. Reynolds.

RODRIGUEZ, MANUEL AND SONS

Instruments currently built in Madrid, Spain. Distributed in the U.S. market by Fender Musical Instruments Corporation of Scottsdale, Arizona.

Luthier Manuel Rodriguez, grandson of noted flamenco guitarist Manuel Rodriguez Marequi, has been building classical style guitars for a number of years. He began learning guitar construction at the age of 13 in Madrid and apprenticed in several shops before opening his own. Rodriguez emigrated to Los Angeles in 1959 and professionally built guitars for nearly 15 years. In 1973, Rodriguez returned to Spain and currently builds high quality instruments. Distribution is handled by Fender now (FMIC).

RJS Modena
courtesy R.J. Smith

ACOUSTIC MODELS

A (MODEL 094-9100) - classical style, solid Canadian red cedar top, round soundhole, Indian rosewood back/sides, sapele neck, rosewood fingerboard, 3-per-side goldplated standard tuners, available in Natural Gloss finish, current mfg.

MSR	$720	$540	$375	$250

B (MODEL 094-9140) - classical style, solid Canadian red cedar top, round soundhole, Indian rosewood back/sides, sapele neck, ebony fingerboard, 3-per-side goldplated standard tuners, available in Natural Gloss finish, current mfg.

MSR	$840	$630	$425	$275

C (MODEL 094-9180) - classical style, solid Canadian red cedar top, round soundhole, Indian rosewood back/sides, cedar neck with ebony reinforcement, ebony fingerboard, 3-per-side goldplated standard tuners, available in Natural Gloss finish, current mfg.

MSR	$980	$735	$495	$325

C-1 (MODEL 094-9030) - classical style, solid Canadian red cedar top, round soundhole, Indian rosewood back/sides, sapele neck, rosewood fingerboard, 3-per-side nickelplated tuners, available in Natural Gloss finish, current mfg.

MSR	$550	$415	$275	$190

C-1 M (Model 094-9015) - similar to the C-1, except features Natural Satin finish, current mfg.

MSR	$500	$375	$250	$175

C-3 (MODEL 094-9080) - classical style, solid Canadian red cedar top, round soundhole, Indian rosewood back/sides, sapele neck, rosewood fingerboard, 3-per-side nickelplated tuners, available in Natural Gloss finish, current mfg.

MSR	$630	$475	$325	$225

R

GRADING		100%	EXCELLENT	AVERAGE

C-3 F (Model 094-9082) - flamenco style, solid German spruce top, round soundhole, sycamore back/sides, sapele neck, rosewood fingerboard, 3-per-side nickelplated tuners, available in Natural Gloss finish, current mfg.

MSR	$630	$475	$325	$225

D (MODEL 094-9240) - classical style, solid Canadian red cedar top, round soundhole, Indian rosewood back/sides, Honduran cedar neck with ebony reinforcement, ebony fingerboard, 3-per-side goldplated standard tuners, available in Natural Gloss finish, current mfg.

MSR	$1,250	$940	$650	$450

D Rio (Model 094-9260) - similar to the D, except has Brazillian rosewood back and sides, current mfg.

MSR	$1,660	$1,250	$850	$600

E (MODEL 094-9300) - classical style, solid Canadian red cedar top, round soundhole, solid Indian rosewood back/sides, Honduran cedar neck with ebony reinforcement, ebony fingerboard, 3-per-side goldplated standard tuners, available in Natural Gloss finish, current mfg.

MSR	$1,860	$1,395	$950	$650

FC (MODEL 094-9360) - classical style, solid Canadian red cedar top, round soundhole, solid Indian rosewood back/sides, Honduran cedar neck with ebony reinforcement, ebony fingerboard, 3-per-side goldplated standard tuners, available in Natural Gloss finish, current mfg.

MSR	$2,220	$1,675	$1,100	$750

FF (MODEL 094-9280) - flamenco style, solid German cedar top, round soundhole, solid cypress back/sides, Honduran cedar neck with ebony reinforcement, ebony fingerboard, 3-per-side goldplated standard tuners, available in Natural Gloss finish, current mfg.

MSR	$1,400	$1,050	$700	$475

FG (MODEL 094-9400) - classical style, solid Canadian red cedar top, round soundhole, solid Indian rosewood back/sides, Honduran cedar neck with ebony reinforcement, ebony fingerboard, 3-per-side goldplated deluxe tuners, available in Natural Gloss finish, current mfg.

MSR	$2,800	$2,100	$1,400	$950

ACOUSTIC: HAND-MADE CLASSICAL GUITARS

The following four models are completely handmade. The Brazilian rosewood used in Rodriguez guitars has been aged for over twenty five years. CITES Treaty documentation is available upon request. List prices include a hardshell case.

NORMAN RODRIGUEZ (MODEL 094-9420) - classical style, solid Canadian red cedar top, round soundhole, solid Brazilian rosewood back/sides, Honduran cedar neck with ebony reinforcement, ebony fingerboard, 3-per-side goldplated deluxe tuners, available in Natural Gloss finish, current mfg.

MSR	$4,600	$3,695	$2,400	$1,600

MANUEL RODRIGUEZ JR. (MODEL 094-9440) - classical style, solid Canadian red cedar top, round soundhole, solid Indian rosewood back/sides, Honduran cedar neck with ebony reinforcement, ebony fingerboard, 3-per-side goldplated deluxe tuners, available in Natural Gloss finish, current mfg.

MSR	$5,600	$4,495	$2,900	$1,900

MANUEL RODRIGUEZ JR. (MODEL 094-9480) - classical style, solid Canadian red cedar top, round soundhole, solid Brazilian rosewood back/sides, Honduran cedar neck with ebony reinforcement, ebony fingerboard, 3-per-side goldplated deluxe tuners, available in Natural Gloss finish, current mfg.

MSR	$7,600	$6,095	$3,950	$2,600

MANUEL RODRIGUEZ SR. (MODEL 094-9451) - classical style, solid Canadian red cedar top, round soundhole, solid Brazilian rosewood back/sides, Honduran cedar neck with ebony reinforcement, ebony fingerboard, 3-per-side goldplated deluxe tuners, available in Natural Gloss finish, current mfg.

MSR	$19,000	$15,250	N/A	N/A

ACOUSTIC ELECTRIC

Rodriguez Nylon String Acoustic Electrics feature a cutaway design and built-in electronics.

B CUTAWAY (MODEL 094-9150) - classical style with cutaway design, solid Canadian red cedar top, round soundhole, Indian rosewood back/sides, sapele neck, ebony fingerboard, 3-per-side goldplated standard tuners, L.R. Baggs pickup, onboard preamp, volume/3-band EQ/mid-sweep controls, available in Natural Gloss finish, current mfg.

MSR	$1,480	$1,125	$750	$500

C CUTAWAY (MODEL 094-9190) - classical style with cutaway design, solid Canadian red cedar top, round soundhole, Indian rosewood back/sides, cedar neck with ebony reinforcement, ebony fingerboard, 3-per-side goldplated standard tuners, L.R. Baggs pickup, on-board preamp, volume/3-band EQ/mid-sweep controls, available in Natural Gloss finish, current mfg.

MSR	$1,680	$1,275	$850	$575

F CUTAWAY (MODEL 094-9290) - classical style with single cutaway, solid German Spruce top, solid cypress back & sides, Honduran Cedar neck with ebony reinforcement, ebony fingerboard, goldplated 3-per-side tuners, Fishman Pro Blend Pickup system, gloss Natural finish, mfg. 2002-current.

	MSR	$2,600		$1,950	$1,300	$850

ROGER

Instruments previously built in West Germany from the late 1950s to mid 1960s.

Luthier Wenzel Rossmeisl built very good to high quality archtop guitars as well as a semi-solid body guitar called "Model 54." Rossmeisl derived the trademark name in honor of his son, Roger Rossmeisl.

Roger Rossmeisl (1927-1979) was raised in Germany and learned luthier skills from his father, Wenzel. One particular feature was the "German Carve," a feature used by Wenzel to carve an indented plane around the body outline on the guitar's top. Roger Rossmeisl then travelled to America, where he briefly worked for Gibson in Kalamazoo, Michigan (in a climate not unlike his native Germany). Shortly thereafter he moved to California, and was employed at the Rickenbacker company. During his tenure at Rickenbacker, Rossmeisl was responsible for the design of the Capri and Combo guitars, and custom designs. His apprentice was a young Semie Moseley, who later introduced the "German Carve" on his own Mosrite brand guitars. Rossmeisl left Rickenbacker in 1962 to help Fender develop their own line of acoustic guitars (Fender had been licensing Harmony-made Regals up till then), and later introduced the Montego and LTD archtop electrics.

ROGERS

See chapter on House Brands.

This trademark has been identified as a House Brand of Selmer (UK), (Source: Willie G. Moseley, *Stellas & Stratocasters*).

ROGUE

Instruments currently produced in Korea. Distributed by Musician's Friend (catalog house), located in Medford, Oregon.

Musician's Friend distributes a line of good quality student and entry level instruments through their mail order catalog. Musician's Friend now offers a wide range of good quality guitars at an affordable price. For further information, contact Musician's Friend directly (see Trademark Index).

ROK AXE

Instruments currently produced in Korea. Distributed by Muse of Inchon, Korea.

The Muse company is currently offering a wide range of electric guitar and bass models, as well as a number of acoustic guitar models. Rok Axe models are generally fine entry level to student quality instruments.

ROSE, JONATHAN W.

Instruments currently built in Strasburg, Virginia.

Luthier Jonathan W. Rose creates one-of-a-kind guitars, specializing in archtops. His aim is to push current design and tonal parameters. Rose's goal is to work closely with each client, giving them exactly what they want – a very personal instrument. For further information, contact Jonathan W. Rose directly (see Trademark Index).

ROYALIST

See chapter on House Brands.

This trademark has been identified as a House Brand of the RCA Victor Records Store, (Source: Willie G. Moseley, *Stellas & Stratocasters*).

RUBIO

Instruments previously built in England. Previously built in Spain & America.

English Master Luthier David Rubio apprenticed in Madrid, Spain at the workshop of Domingo Esteso (which was maintained by Esteso's nephews). In 1961 Rubio built guitars in New York City, New York. Returning to England in 1967, he set up a workshop and continued his guitar building. One of Rubio's apprentices was Paul Fischer, who has gone on to gain respect for his own creations. David died of cancer on October 21st, 2000.

RUBEN FLORES GUITARS

Instruments currently built in Seal Beach, California. Ruben Flores is the exclusive worldwide distributor of Ruben Flores Guitars.

Ruben Flores Classical and Flamenco guitars are handcrafted in Spain's foremost lutherie workshops employing the finest materials and workmanship. The Flores Classical guitars are constructed in scales of 48, 49, 54.4, 58, 63.6, and 65 centimeters. These guitars are designed to be played by children, young adults and professionals. Many of the models are available with cutaways, regular or thin bodies, with onboard pickups. As with the classical guitars, Ruben Flores Flamenco Guitars come in a various models, some with cutaways,

R

suitable for entry level, intermediate and professional guitarists. Some Flamenco models are available with rosewood back and sides. For further information regarding pricing and model specifications, please contact luthier Flores directly (see Trademark Index).

Classical models include the Model 600 with rosewood back and sides and solid spruce top ($1,190), the Model 700 with solid rosewood back and sides and solid spruce top ($1,500), the Model 900 with solid rosewood back and sides and solid spruce top ($2,070), and the Model 910 with solid rosewood back and sides and solid spruce top ($2,770). Flamenco models include the 700 with solid cypress or roseood back and sides, solid spruce top and ebony fingerboard ($1,930), the Model 900 with solid cypress or rosewood back and sides, solid spruce top and ebony fingerboard ($2,770), and the Professional with solid spruce top, solid cypress or rosewood back and sides ($3,990). There are several other models available and the web site lists all the prices for the models (see Trademark Index).

RUCK, ROBERT
Instruments currently built in Kauai, Hawaii, and previously in Florida, Georgia, Wisconsin and Washington since 1966.

Luthier Robert Ruck has been building high quality classical guitars since 1966. Ruck handcrafts between 25-30 guitars a year, and estimates that he has produced around 770 instruments altogether. Ruck's guitars are sought after by classical guitarists, and do not surface too often on the collectible market. In 2002, Ruck relocated to Hawaii. For further information as to models, specifications, and availability, please contact luthier Ruck directly (see Trademark Index).

R is for Really Beautiful! C.F. Martin IV shows off Martin ser. no. 750,000 - the most elaborate and ornate Martin guitar ever built - a custom shop D-45 Peacock (back of guitar showcases inlaid large peacock), featuring over 2,000 hand cut pieces of shell, green abalone, paua, and mother-of-pearl.

Section S

S-101

Instruments currently produced in China. Distributed by American Sejung Corporation in Walnut, California.

The Sejung Musical Instrument Corporation produces the S-101 line of guitars and was introduced in 2002. They have a 600,000 square foot manufacturing facility and produce a wide variety of fretted instruments, guitar amplifiers, and pianos. Currently they have over 50 different acoustic models being produced. For more information visit their web site (see Trademark Index).

SAEHAN

Instruments currently built in Korea. Distributed by the Saehan International Co., Ltd. of Seoul, Korea.

The Saehan International company offers a wide range of acoustic guitars from standard to cutaway model dreadnoughts, jumbo style body designs, and acoustic/electric models. For further information, please contact the Saehan International company directly (see Trademark Index).

T. SAKASHTA GUITARS

Instruments currently built in Van Nuys, California. Distribution is directly handled by T. Sakashta Guitars of Van Nuys, California.

Luthier Taku Sakashta builds high quality acoustic archtop and steel string guitars. All are offered with custom options per model.

ACOUSTIC: ARCHTOP SERIES

Because the following archtop models are available with numerous custom body wood choices, hardware wood choices, and finishes, The *Blue Book of Acoustic Guitars* recommends contacting luthier Sakashta in regards to exact pricing. The following information is offered as a guideline to the available models produced by luthier Sakashta.

The **Avalon** features a 17" single cutaway body constructed of AAA quarter-sawn Sitka spruce top and AA Eastern rock maple sides and matching back. The neck is one piece Honduran mahogany neck with an East Indian rosewood fingerboard and pearl inlays. The Avalon also has either an ebony or rosewood tailpiece, and a rosewood bridge, pickguard, and peghead overlay.

The **Karizma** also features 17" single cutaway body. The top is built of AAA quarter-sawn Englemann spruce, and has sides and matching back of AA Eastern rock maple. The neck again is one piece Honduran mahogany, with East Indian rosewood fingerboard with pearl inlays. The Karizma has either an ebony or rosewood tailpiece, rosewood bridge, pickguard, and peghead overlay.

ACOUSTIC: STEEL STRING SERIES

The following steel string models are available with numerous custom wood options for tops, backs and sides. Addition of custom choices will add to the base price quoted. All Steel String Acoustic guitar models are equipped with a deluxe hardshell case as part of the asking price.

The **Auditorium** model features a top of Sitka or Englemann spruce, or Western red cedar. The back and matching sides are constructed of East Indian rosewood; and the bound Honduras mahogany one piece neck has a Gaboon ebony fingerboard and peghead with diamond or dot position markers. The Auditorium also has a Brazilian rosewood bridge, Abalone soundhole ring decoration, three on a side Schaller tuning machines, and a nitrocellulose natural lacquer finish. The **S 0** model is similar to the Auditorium model, except the design is slightly modified.

The **Dreadnought** model features the same construction materials, but designed along the lines of a dreadnought style guitar. Though similar, the **S D** model is a modified version of the Dreadnought.

The **Jumbo** model features the same construction materials as well, and is a full sized acoustic guitar design. The modified version **S J** model is similar in base design to the Jumbo.

SAMICK

Instruments currently produced in Korea since 1965. Current production of instruments is in Korea and City of Industry, California. Distributed in the U.S. market by Samick Music Corporation of City of Industry, California.

For a number of years, the Samick corporation was the "phantom builder" of instruments for a number of other trademarks. In fact, when the Samick trademark was finally introduced to the U.S. guitar market, a number of consumers thought that the company was brand new! However, Samick has been producing both upright and grand pianos, as well as stringed instruments for nearly forty years.

The Samick Piano Co. was established in Korea in 1958. By January of 1960 they had started to produce upright pianos, and within four years became the first Korean piano exporter. One year later in 1965, the company began manufacturing guitars, and by the early 1970s expanded to produce grand pianos and harmonicas as well. In 1973 the company incorporated as the Samick Musical Instruments Mfg. Co., Ltd. to

S

reflect the diversity it encompassed. Samick continued to expand into guitar production. They opened a branch office in Los Angeles in 1978, a brand new guitar factory in 1979, and a branch office in West Germany one month before 1981.

Throughout the 1980s Samick continued to grow, prosper, and win awards for quality products and company productivity. The Samick Products Co. was established in 1986 as an affiliate producer of other products, and the company was listed on the Korean Stock Exchange in September of 1988. With their size of production facilities (the company claims to be cranking out over a million guitars a year, according to a recent brochure), Samick could be referred to as modern day producer of House Brand guitars as well as their own brand. In the past couple of years Samick acquired Valley Arts, a guitar company known for its one-of-a-kind instruments and custom guitars. This merger stabilized Valley Arts as the custom shop wing of Samick, as well as supplying Samick with quality American designed guitars.

Samick continues to expand their line of guitar models through the use of innovative designs, partnerships with high exposure endorsees (like Blues Saraceno and Ray Benson), and new projects such as the Robert Johnson Commemorative and the D'Leco Charlie Christian Commemorative guitars. Currently, it is guesstimated that Samick builds 50% of the world's guitar production, (Samick Company History courtesy Rick Clapper; Model Specifications courtesy Dee Hoyt).

In 1998, Samick decided to overhaul their entire line. They brought in Greg Bennett, who has been in the guitar industry for over 20 years, to create a sense of continuity throughout the entire line of guitars. In 2001, they stopped their previous line of guitars. In 2002, they introduced an entirely new line of guitars with Greg Bennett on every headstock, which is smaller as well. By combining Samick and Bennett, there is over 70 years of experience in guitars.

In addition to their acoustic and electric guitars and basses, Samick offers a wide range of other stringed instruments such as autoharps, banjos, mandolins, and violins.

ACOUSTIC: AMERICAN CLASSIC SERIES

SC-330 S - classical style, solid spruce top, rosewood back and sides, gloss finish, mahogany set neck, rosewood fingerboard and bridge, 19-frets, gold standard tuners, disc 2001.

	100%	Excellent	Average
	$450	$300	$195

Last MSR was $600.

SC-430 S N (LE GRANDE) - classical style, solid spruce top, round soundhole, bound body, wooden inlay rosette, rosewood back/sides, nato neck, 12/19-fret rosewood fingerboard, rosewood bridge, 3-per-side gold tuners, available in Natural finish, disc. 1999.

	$340	$225	$150

Last MSR was $450.

SC-433 - similar to the SC-430 S N, except features solid cedar top, laser-cut soundhole mosaic, mfg. 1997-2000.

	$340	$225	$150

Last MSR was $450.

SC-438 ES FS - classical style, solid cedar top, round soundhole, bound body, laser-cut sunflower mosaic, rosewood back/sides, nato neck, 12/19-fret rosewood fingerboard, rosewood bridge, 3-per-side gold tuners, piezo pickup, volume/3-band EQ slider controls, available in Natural finish, disc. 1999.

	$475	$325	$215

Last MSR was $650.

SR-100 - folk (wide shoulder/narrow waist) style, solid spruce top, round soundhole, bound body, multi stripe purfling/rosette, sapele back/sides, 14/20-fret rosewood fingerboard with dot inlay, rosewood bridge with black white dot pins, slotted headstock, 3-per-side chrome die-cast tuners, available in Natural finish, disc. 2000.

	$355	$235	$160

Last MSR was $470.

SR-200 - similar to the SR-100, except features jacaranda back/sides, snowflake fingerboard inlay, available in Natural finish, disc. 2000.

	$520	$365	$255

Last MSR was $690.

SW-790 S - dreadnought style, handmade, solid spruce top, round soundhole, bound body, multi stripe purfling/rosette, solid jacaranda back/sides, 14/20-fret ebony fingerboard with ornate abalone inlay, rosewood bridge with black white dot pins, tortoise shell pickguard, 3-per-side chrome tuners, available in Natural finish, disc 2001.

	$640	$420	$285

Last MSR was $850.

SJ-210 (MAGNOLIA) - jumbo style, sycamore top, round soundhole, black pickguard, 5-stripe bound body/rosette, nato back/sides/neck, 14/20-fret bound rosewood fingerboard with pearl dot inlay, rosewood bridge with white black dot pins, 3-per-side black chrome tuners, available in Black or White finishes, disc. 1994.

	N/A	$150	$100

Last MSR was $330.

SJD-210 - jumbo style body, spruce top, metal resonator/2 screened soundholes, bound body, mahogany back/sides/neck, 14/20-fret bound rosewood fingerboard with pearl dot inlay, covered bridge/metal trapeze tailpiece, 3-per-side chrome die-cast tuners, available in Natural finish, current mfg.

	$550	$325	$225

Last MSR was $750.

GRADING	100%	EXCELLENT	AVERAGE

SJ-218 CE - jumbo style body with single rounded cutaway, spruce top, round soundhole, black pickguard, bound body, abalone rosette, nato back/sides/neck, 14/20-fret rosewood fingerboard with abalone dot inlay, rosewood bridge with white black dot pins, 3-per-side Gotoh tuners, piezo pickup, volume/3-band EQ slider controls, available in Natural finish, disc. 2000.

$450 $295 $200
Last MSR was $600.

AMCT-CE - thin line depth dreadnought body with single florentine cutaway, solid spruce top, bound body, rosewood back/sides, mahogany neck, 14/20-fret bound extended rosewood fingerboard with abalone diamond inlay, ebony bridge and pins, 6-on-a-side chrome die-cast tuners, piezo bridge pickup, volume/3-band EQ slider controls, available in Natural (N), Transparent Purple (TP), and Vintage Sunburst (VSB), current mfg.

MSR $855 $640 $375 $250

AMCT-CE/PBE - similar to AMCT-CE, except has Pink Bird's-Eye top, back, and sides. Current Mfg.

MSR $855 $650 $375 $250

SW-218 CE TT - dreadnought style with single rounded cutaway, spruce top, laser cut round soundhole design, bound body, mahogany back/sides/neck, 14/20-fret rosewood fingerboard with white dot inlay, rosewood bridge with black white dot pins, 3-per-side die-cast tuners. piezo bridge pickup, volume/3-band EQ slider controls, XLR jack, available in Natural finish, disc. 2000.

$425 $280 $190
Last MSR was $570.

EAG-88 (BLUE RIDGE) - single round cutaway flat-top body, spruce top, oval soundhole, bound body, wood purfling, abalone rosette, maple back/sides, mahogany neck, 24-fret bound extended rosewood fingerboard with pearl dot inlay, rosewood bridge, bound peghead with screened logo, 6-on-a-side black chrome tuners, piezo bridge pickup, volume/tone controls, available in Natural finish, disc. 1995.

N/A $225 $150
Last MSR was $500.

**Samick EAG-89
courtesy Samick**

Earlier models had a figured maple top, 22-fret bound rosewood fingerboard, and were available in Blue Burst, Natural, and Tobacco Sunburst finishes.

EAG-89 - similar to the EAG-88, except features a figured maple top, rosewood back/sides, gold tuners, available in Natural, Red Stain, or Sunburst finishes, disc. 1995.

N/A $270 $180
Last MSR was $600.

EAG-93 - thin line depth dreadnought body with single rounded cutaway, solid spruce top, oval soundhole, bound body, abalone purfling/rosette, rosewood back/sides, mahogany neck, 24-fret bound extended ebony fingerboard with pearl eagle inlay, rosewood bridge, abalone bound peghead with screened logo, 6-on-side tuners, black hardware, piezo bridge pickup, volume/3-band EQ slider controls, available in Natural finish, mfg. 1994-2001.

$1,050 $685 $465
Last MSR was $1,400.

EAG-98 BLS - single cutaway design with flamed maple top, maple back and sides with sandstone finish, oval raised wood bound soundhole, rosewood fingerboard with dot inlays, 23 frets, rosewood bridge, black diecast tuners, EQ-700 System electronics, available in high gloss Trans. Blue finish, disc 2001.

$775 $460 $299
Last MSR was $1,035.

ACOUSTIC: ARTIST SERIES

EJ-1 - dreadnought style, spruce top, round soundhole, mahogany back/sides, 9-string configuration, rosewood bridge with black pins, chrome tuners, built-in guitar slide holder, available in Natural finish, mfg. 1997-2001.

$450 $265 $175
Last MSR was $597.

ACOUSTIC: ARTIST CLASSICAL SERIES

Instruments in this series have a classical style body, round soundhole, bound body, wooden inlay rosette, 12/19-fret fingerboard, slotted peghead, tied bridge, 3-per-side chrome tuners as following features (unless otherwise listed).

**Samick SC-450
courtesy Samick**

S

GRADING	100%	EXCELLENT	AVERAGE

SC-310 (SEVILLE) - select spruce top, mahogany back/sides/neck, rosewood fingerboard/bridge, available in Pumpkin finish, disc. 2001.

	$279	$165	$110

Last MSR was $375.

SC-330 (DEL REY) - select spruce top, rosewood back/sides, mahogany neck, rosewood fingerboard/bridge, available in Pumpkin finish, disc 2001.

	$415	$250	$160

Last MSR was $555.

SC-410 S - solid cedar top, sapele back/sides, mahogany neck, rosewood fingerboard/bridge, available in Pumpkin finish, mfg. 1997-2001.

	$395	$235	$150

Last MSR was $525.

SC-450 (LA TOUR) - select spruce top, sapele back/sides, nato neck, rosewood fingerboard/bridge, available in Pumpkin finish, disc 2001.

	$315	$185	$125

Last MSR was $420.

SC-450 S (SC-430) - similar to the SC-450, except features solid spruce top, available in Pumpkin finish, disc.

	$265	$175	$120

Last MSR was $350.

SCT-450 CE (GRANADA) - single round cutaway classical style, select spruce top, round soundhole, bound body, wooden inlay rosette, rosewood back/sides, nato neck, 12/19-fret rosewood fingerboard, rosewood bridge, rosewood peghead veneer, 3-per-side chrome tuners, active piezo pickup, volume/tone slider controls, available in Natural finish, disc.

	$495	$295	$195

Last MSR was $660.

ACOUSTIC: ARTIST CONCERT FOLK SERIES

Instruments in this series have a wide shoulder/narrow waist *folk*-style body, round soundhole, bound body, multi stripe purfling/rosette, 14/20-fret rosewood fingerboard with dot inlay, rosewood bridge with black white dot pins, 3-per-side chrome tuners as following features (unless otherwise listed).

SF-115 - select natural spruce top, mahogany back/sides/neck, chrome tuners, available in Natural finish, disc.

	$275	$165	$110

Last MSR was $375.

SF-210 (SF-210 M SWEETWATER) - select natural spruce top, mahogany back/sides/neck, die-cast chrome tuners, available in Natural finish, disc.

	$210	$140	$95

Last MSR was $280.

SF-291 (CHEYENNE) - solid spruce top, solid rosewood back/sides, nato neck, rosewood veneer on peghead, gold plated die-cast tuners, available in Natural finish, disc.

	$330	$220	$145

Last MSR was $440.

ACOUSTIC: ARTIST DREADNOUGHT SERIES

SW-21 NM - dreadnought style, select natural spruce top, round soundhole, black pickguard, ivory body binding, multi stripe rosette, nato back/sides/neck, 14/20-fret rosewood fingerboard with white dot inlay, rosewood bridge with black pins, 3-per-side die-cast tuners, available in Natural finishes, mfg. 1997-2000.

	$144	$70	$60

Last MSR was $238.

SW-015 D (SANTA FE) - dreadnought style, mahogany top, round soundhole, black pickguard, bound body, multi stripe rosette, mahogany back/sides/neck, 14/20-fret rosewood fingerboard with white dot inlay, rosewood bridge with white black dot pins, 3-per-side die-cast tuners, available in Black, Natural, or White gloss finishes, mfg. 1994-2001.

	$295	$175	$115

Last MSR was $390.

Add $15 for Black (BK) and White (WH) finishes.

SW-115-12 - dreadnought style, 12-string configuration, select natural spruce top, round soundhole, black pickguard, bound body, multi stripe rosette, mahogany back/sides/neck, 14/20-fret rosewood fingerboard with white dot inlay, rosewood bridge with white black dot pins, 6-per-side standard tuners, available in Natural finish, disc 2001.

	$295	$175	$120

Last MSR was $405.

SW-115 DE - dreadnought style, select natural spruce top, round soundhole, black pickguard, bound body, multi stripe rosette, mahogany back/sides/neck, 14/20-fret rosewood fingerboard with white dot inlay, rosewood bridge with white black dot pins, 3-per-side die-cast tuners, neck pickup, volume/tone controls, available in Black, Natural, or White gloss finishes, mfg. 1994-2001.

	$325	**$195**	**$125**

Last MSR was $435.

Add $15 for Black (BK) and White (WH) finishes.

SW-210 (GREENBRIAR) - dreadnought style, select natural spruce top, round soundhole, black pickguard, bound body, multi stripe rosette, mahogany back/sides/neck, 14/20-fret rosewood fingerboard with white dot inlay, rosewood bridge black pins, 3-per-side die-cast tuners, available in Natural finish, disc 2001.

	$335	**$199**	**$130**

Last MSR was $450.

SW-210 LH (Beaumont) - similar to the SW-210, except in a left-handed configuration, disc 2001.

	$350	**$205**	**$135**

Last MSR was $465.

SW-210 BB 1 - similar to the SW-210, except features select natural bamboo top/back/sides, available in Natural finish, mfg. 1997-99.

	$355	**$235**	**$160**

Last MSR was $470.

SW-210 S (Bluebird) - similar to the SW-210, except features a solid spruce top, disc 2001.

	$450	**$265**	**$175**

Last MSR was $600.

SW-210-12 (Savannah) - similar to the SW-210, except in a 12-String configuration, 6-per-side tuners, disc 2001.

	$395	**$235**	**$150**

Last MSR was $525.

**Samick SW-210 LH
courtesy Samick**

SW-210 CE (LAREDO) - dreadnought style with single rounded cutaway, select natural spruce top, round soundhole, black pickguard, bound body, multi stripe rosette, mahogany back/sides/neck, 14/20-fret rosewood fingerboard with white dot inlay, rosewood bridge with white black dot pins, 3-per-side die-cast tuners. piezo bridge pickup, volume/3-band EQ slider controls, available in Natural finish, disc 2001.

	$495	**$285**	**$190**

Last MSR was $645.

SW-220 HS CE (AUSTIN) - dreadnought style with single rounded cutaway, solid cedar top, oval soundhole, 5-stripe bound body/rosette, cedar back/sides, maple neck, 14/20-fret bound rosewood fingerboard with pearl dot inlay, stylized pearl inlay at 12th fret, rosewood bridge with white black dot pins, cedar veneer on bound peghead, 3-per-side gold tuners, piezo pickup, volume/tone slider control, available in Natural finish, disc. 1994.

	$325	**$205**	**$135**

Last MSR was $450.

SW-230-12 HS (VICKSBURG) - dreadnought style, 12-String configuration, solid spruce top, round soundhole, black pickguard, bound body, herringbone purfling/rosette, rosewood back/sides, mahogany neck, 14/20-fret rosewood fingerboard with pearl dot inlay, rosewood bridge with black white dot pins, 6-per-side tuners gold die cast tuners, available in Natural finish, disc 2001.

	$585	**$345**	**$225**

Last MSR was $780.

SW-250 (ASPEN) - dreadnought style, spruce top, round soundhole, black pickguard, 3-stripe bound body/rosette, sapele back/sides, nato neck, 14/20-fret rosewood fingerboard, rosewood bridge with white black dot pins, rosewood veneer on peghead, 3-per-side chrome tuners, available in Natural finish, disc. 1994.

	N/A	**$115**	**$75**

Last MSR was $250.

SW-260-12 B (NIGHTINGALE 12) - dreadnought style, 12-string configuration, maple top, round soundhole, black pickguard, bound body, multi stripe purfling/rosette, mahogany back/sides/neck, 14/20-fret rosewood fingerboard with pearl dot inlay, rosewood bridge with black pins, 6-per-side chrome die-cast tuners, available in Black gloss finish, disc 2001.

	$425	**$250**	**$165**

Last MSR was $570.

**Samick SW-630 HS
courtesy Samick**

S

GRADING	100%	EXCELLENT	AVERAGE

SW-260 CE N (GALLOWAY) - single rounded cutaway dreadnought style, maple top, round soundhole, tortoise pickguard, bound body, multi stripe purfling/rosette, maple back/sides/neck, 14/20-fret bound rosewood fingerboard with pearl diamond/dot inlay, rosewood bridge with white black dot pins, bound peghead with pearl logo inlay, 3-per-side die-cast chrome tuners, piezo bridge pickup, volume/3-band EQ slider controls, available in Natural finish, disc 2001.

	$550	$320	$195

Last MSR was $720.

Black finish added in 1999 at no additional charge.

SW-270 HS NM (JASMINE) - dreadnought style, cedar top, round soundhole, black pickguard, bound body, herringbone purfling/rosette, walnut back/sides, mahogany neck, 14/20-fret bound rosewood fingerboard with pearl block inlay, bound peghead with pearl logo inlay, rosewood bridge with white black dot pins, 3-per-side chrome die-cast tuners, available in Natural finish, disc 2001.

	$460	$275	$175

Last MSR was $615.

SW-292 S (NIGHTINGALE) - dreadnought style, solid spruce top, round soundhole, black pickguard, 3-stripe bound body/rosette, mock birdseye maple back/sides, nato neck, 14/20-fret bound rosewood fingerboard with pearl dot inlay, rosewood bridge with white black dot pins, bound headstock, 3-per-side chrome tuners, available in Trans. Black finish, disc. 1994.

	N/A	$160	$105

Last MSR was $350.

SW-630 HS (LAUREL) - dreadnought style, solid spruce top, round soundhole, black pickguard, bound body, herringbone purfling/rosette, rosewood back/sides, mahogany neck, 14/20-fret bound rosewood fingerboard with pearl tree of life inlay, rosewood bridge with white black dot pins, bound peghead with pearl logo inlay, 3-per-side gold die-cast tuners, available in Natural finish, disc 2001.

	$425	$250	$165

Last MSR was $750.

SW-730 SP - dreadnought style, solid spruce top, round soundhole, black pickguard, bound body, multi stripe purfling/rosette, rosewood back/sides, mahogany neck, 14/20-fret ebony fingerboard with abalone dot inlay, ebony bridge with black white dot pins, bound peghead with abalone logo inlay, 3-per-side chrome tuners, available in Natural finish, mfg. 1994-96.

	$500	$380	$250

Last MSR was $840.

SW-790 SP - similar to the SW-730 SP, except features jacaranda back/sides, bound fingerboard, available in Natural finish, mfg. 1994-96.

	N/A	$325	$220

Last MSR was $720.

SWT-210 CE - thin line depth dreadnought style with single rounded cutaway, spruce top, round soundhole, mahogany back/sides/neck, 14/20-fret rosewood fingerboard, rosewood bridge with white black dot pins, 3-per-side chrome tuners, piezo bridge pickup, volume/tone controls, available in Natural finish, disc 2001.

	$525	$299	$199

Last MSR was $705.

SWT-217 CE ASHTR - thin line depth dreadnought style with single rounded cutaway, ash top, round soundhole, mahogany back/sides/neck, 14/20-fret bound rosewood fingerboard with pearl diamond inlay, rosewood bridge with white black dot pins, 3-per-side die-cast chrome tuners, piezo bridge pickup, volume/3-band EQ slider controls, available in Trans. Red finish, disc 2001.

	$615	$365	$240

Last MSR was $825.

SDT-110 CE OSM - thin line depth dreadnought style with single rounded cutaway, kusu top/back/sides/headstock, round soundhole, tortoise pickguard, bound body, multi stripe purfling/rosette, 14/20-fret bound rosewood fingerboard with pearl diamond/dot inlay, rosewood bridge with white black dot pins, bound peghead with pearl logo inlay, 3-per-side die-cast chrome tuners, piezo bridge pickup, volume/3-band EQ slider controls, available in Cherry Sunburst finish, disc. 2000.

	$430	$280	$190

Last MSR was $570.

ACOUSTIC: BEAUMONT SERIES

D 7 - dreadnought style body, solid cedar top, rosewood sides and back, 8-ply white binding, tortise pickguard, 3-per-side Grover tuners, chrome hardware, available in Natural finish, mfg. 2001-current.

MSR	$285		$215	$145	$80

D 7 CE - similar to the D 7, except has a single cutaway with an active EQ and built in tuner, mfg. 2001-current.

MSR	$385		$290	$195	$115

D 7 12 - similar to the D 7, except has in 12-string configuration, mfg. 2001-current.

MSR	$335		$255	$170	$95

GRADING		100%	EXCELLENT	AVERAGE

OM 7 - orchestra model style body, solid cedar top, rosewood sides and back, 8-ply white binding, tortise pickguard, 3-per-side Grover tuners, chrome hardware, available in Natural finish, mfg. 2001-current.

MSR	$285		$215	$145	$80

ACOUSTIC: BLACKBIRD SERIES

TMJ 17 CE - single sharp thin medium jumbo body, solid spruce top, maple sides and back, rosewood fingerboard with block inlays, abalone and black binding, 3-per-side black Grover tuners, Fishman Classic 4-Band EQ, available in Black finish, mfg. 2000-current.

MSR	$525		$395	$270	$180

ACOUSTIC: CAROLINA SERIES

SJ 14 - southern jumbo body, solid cedar top, rosewood back and sides, herringbone trim, tortoise pickguard, 3-per-side chrome Grover tuners, available in Natural finish, mfg. 2000-current.

MSR	$360		$270	$180	$105

SJ 14 CE - similar to the SJ 14, except has a Fishman Classic 4-Band EQ, mfg. 2000-current.

MSR	$480		$360	$240	$150

D 14 - dreadnought single cutaway body, solid cedar top, rosewood back and sides, herringbone trim, tortoise pickguard, 3-per-side chrome Grover tuners, available in Natural finish, mfg. 2000-current.

MSR	$480		$360	$240	$150

ACOUSTIC: CHEYENNE SERIES

D 10 CE - dreadnought single cutaway style body, solid spruce top, mahogany sides and back, 8-ply white binding, tortoise pickguard, 3-per-side Grover tuners, chrome hardware, Fishman Classic 4-Band EQ, available in Natural, Wine Red, or Black finishes, mfg. 2000-current.

MSR	$455		$345	$230	$140

MJ 10 CE - medium jumbo single cutaway style body, solid spruce top, mahogany sides and back, 8-ply white binding, tortoise pickguard, 3-per-side Grover tuners, chrome hardware, Fishman Classic 4-Band EQ, available in Wine Red or Black finishes, mfg. 2000-current.

MSR	$455		$345	$230	$140

SMJ 10 CE - similar to the MJ 10 CE, except has a small body cutaway and a L.R. Baggs EQ, mfg. 2000-current.

MSR	$575		$435	$280	$190

ACOUSTIC: CONTINENTAL SERIES

D 8 - dreadnought style body, solid cedar top, rosewood sides and back, abalone trim, tortoise pickguard, 3-per-side Grover tuners, gold hardware, available in Natural finish, mfg. 2001-current.

MSR	$360		$270	$180	$105

D 8 CE - similar to the D 8, except has a single cutaway with a Fishman classic 4-band EQ, mfg. 2001-current.

MSR	$480		$360	$240	$150

J 8 CE - jumbo style body, solid cedar top, rosewood sides and back, abalone trim, tortoise pickguard, 3-per-side Grover tuners, Fishman classic 4-band EQ, gold hardware, available in Natural finish, new 2003.

MSR	$480		$360	$240	$150

OM 8 CE - orchestra model style body, solid cedar top, rosewood sides and back, abalone trim, tortoise pickguard, 3-per-side Grover tuners, Fishman classic 4-band EQ, gold hardware, available in Natural finish, new 2003.

MSR	$480		$360	$240	$150

ACOUSTIC: EDEN PLAINS SERIES

D 4 - dreadnought style body, solid spruce top, ash sides and back, 6-ply reverse binding, black pickguard, 3-per-side Grover tuners, chrome hardware, available in Trans. Red, Trans. Blue, Amber, Trans. Black finishes, mfg. 2001-current.

MSR	$225		$170	$115	$65

D 4 CE - similar to the D 4, except has an Active EQ with built in tuner, mfg. 2001-current.

MSR	$325		$245	$165	$90

**Samick SD-50
courtesy Samick**

S

GRADING		100%	EXCELLENT	AVERAGE

ACOUSTIC: ELAN SERIES

TMJ 11 CE - single cutaway thin medium jumbo body, quilted maple top, sides, and back, rosewood fingerboard with offset inlays, 3-per-side Grover tuners, Fishman Classic 4-band EQ, chrome hardware, available in Trans. Red, Trans. Blue, Trans. Violet, or Trans. Black, mfg. 2000-current.

MSR	$550	$415	$275	$190

ACOUSTIC: EXOTIC WOOD SERIES

SD-50 - dreadnought style, spruce top, round soundhole, black pickguard, bound body, multi stripe purfling/rosette, maple back/sides, mahogany neck, 14/20-fret rosewood fingerboard with pearl diamond/dot inlay, maple veneered peghead with pearl split diamond/logo inlay, rosewood bridge with white black dot pins, 3-per-side chrome tuners, available in Natural finish, mfg. 1994-95.

		N/A	$150	$100

Last MSR was $300.

SD-60 S - dreadnought style, solid spruce top, round soundhole, black pickguard, bound body, multi stripe purfling/rosette, bubinga back/sides, mahogany neck, 14/20-fret rosewood fingerboard with abalone diamond/dot inlay, rosewood bridge with white black dot pins, bubinga veneered peghead with abalone split diamond/logo inlay, 3-per-side chrome tuners, available in Natural finish, mfg. 1994-95.

		N/A	$225	$150

Last MSR was $450.

SD-80 CS - dreadnought style, figured maple top, round soundhole, black pickguard, bound body, multi stripe purfling/rosette, maple back/sides, mahogany neck, 14/20-fret bound rosewood fingerboard with abalone pearl diamond/dot inlay, bound peghead with abalone split diamond/logo inlay, rosewood bridge with white black dot pins, 3-per-side chrome tuners, available in Sunburst finish, mfg. 1994-95.

		N/A	$175	$115

Last MSR was $350.

ACOUSTIC: GOLD RUSH SERIES

D1 - dreadnought body style, nato top, back, and sides, black binding, nato neck, 14/20 fret rosewood fingerboard with pearl dot inlays, rosewood bridge, abalone type rosette, 3-per-side tuners, black pickguard, Natural finish, mfg. 2001-current.

MSR	$142	$110	$75	$45

Add $10 for Natural, White, Black, Brown Sunburst, or Wine Red finishes. Add $25 for left-handed configuration.

D1E - similar to the D1, except has PS-2000 passive electronics, Natural finish, mfg. 2001-current.

MSR	$185	$140	$95	$60

Add $20 for cutaway (D1CE).

ST6 1 - 36" student folk style body, nato top, back, and sides, nato neck, rosewood fingerboard, 3-per-side tuners, Natural finish, mfg. 2001-current.

MSR	$115	$90	$60	$30

Add $10 for Black finish.

ST9 1 - 39" student folk style body, nato top, back, and sides, nato neck, rosewood fingerboard, 3-per-side tuners, Natural finish, mfg. 2001-current.

MSR	$120	$95	$65	$30

Add $10 for Black finish.

ACOUSTIC: IMPERIAL SERIES

D 9 - dreadnought style body, solid spruce top, maple sides and back, abalone trim, black reverse binding, pickguard, 3-per-side Grover tuners, chrome hardware, available in Natural finish, mfg. 2001-current.

MSR	$360	$270	$180	$105

D 9 CE - similar to the D 9, except has a single cutaway with a Fishman classic 4-band EQ, available in Natural or Black finishes, mfg. 2001-current.

MSR	$480	$360	$240	$150

D 9 12 CE - similar to the D 9 CE, except in 12-string configuration, available in Black finish, mfg. 2001-current.

MSR	$525	$395	$270	$180

J 9 CE - jumbo style sharp cutaway body, solid spruce top, maple sides and back, abalone trim, black reverse binding, pickguard, 3-per-side Grover tuners, chrome hardware, available in Natural or Black finishes, mfg. 2001-current.

MSR	$480	$360	$240	$150

S

GRADING	100%	EXCELLENT	AVERAGE

ACOUSTIC: KENSINGTON SERIES

D 3 - dreadnought style body, striped mahogany back, top, and sides, 6-ply reverse binding, 14/20-fret rosewood fingerboard with dot inlays, pickguard, 3-per-side tuners, available in Natural or Wine Red finishes, mfg. 2001-current.

MSR	$205		$155	$105	$60

D 3 CE - similar to the D 3, except has an AS-3000 active 2-band EQ, Natural finish, mfg. 2001-current.

MSR	$300		$225	$150	$95

OM 3 - dreadnought style body, striped mahogany back, top, and sides, 6-ply reverse binding, 14/20-fret rosewood fingerboard with dot inlays, pickguard, 3-per-side tuners, Natural finish, mfg. 2001-current.

MSR	$205		$155	$105	$60

ACOUSTIC: LAREDO SERIES

D 16 CE - dreadnought single cutaway body, solid cedar top, ovangkol sides and back, 6-ply maple binding, 3-per-side gold Grover tuners, Fishman Classic 4-Band EQ, available in Natural finish, mfg. 2000-current.

MSR	$525		$395	$270	$180

SJ 16 CE - southern jumbo single cutaway body, solid cedar top, ovangkol sides and back, 6-ply maple binding, 3-per-side gold Grover tuners, Fishman Classic 4-Band EQ, available in Natural finish, mfg. 2000-current.

MSR	$525		$395	$270	$180

ACOUSTIC: PRO SERIES

All instruments in this series are handmade. This series was also known as the **Handcrafted Series**.

S-7 - concert style, spruce top, round soundhole, rosewood pickguard, bound body, multi stripe wood purfling/rosette, rosewood back/sides, mahogany neck, 14/20-fret bound ebony fingerboard with pearl dot inlay, ebony bridge with black white dot pins, pearl peghead logo inlay, 3-per-side chrome tuners, available in Natural finish, mfg. 1994-95.

			N/A	$350	$230
				Last MSR was $700.	

SK-5 (MARSEILLES) - folk style, solid spruce top, round soundhole, tortoise shell pickguard, wooden bound body, wooden inlay rosette, ovankol back/sides, nato neck, 14/20-fret bound rosewood fingerboard with pearl dot inlay, ebony bridge with white black dot pins, ovankol veneer on peghead with pearl logo inlay, 3-per-side chrome tuners, available in Natural finish, disc. 1994.

			N/A	$230	$150
				Last MSR was $460.	

SK-7 (VERSAILLES) - similar to Marseilles, except has solid cedar top, rosewood back/sides, brown white dot bridge pins, disc. 1994.

			N/A	$350	$230
				Last MSR was $700.	

S-7 EC (CHAMBRAY) - single round cutaway folk style, solid cedar top, round soundhole, rosewood pickguard, wooden bound body, wooden inlay rosette, rosewood back/sides, nato neck, 14/20-fret ebony fingerboard with pearl dot inlay, ebony bridge with black white dot pins, rosewood veneer on peghead with pearl logo inlay, 3-per-side Schaller gold tuners with pearl buttons, acoustic pickup, volume/tone control, preamp, available in Natural finish, disc. 1995.

			N/A	$550	$365
				Last MSR was $1,100.	

SDT-10 CE - single round cutaway dreadnought style, ash top, round soundhole, tortoise pickguard, bound body, multi stripe purfling/rosette, ash back/sides, maple neck, 14/20-fret bound rosewood fingerboard with pearl diamond/dot inlay, rosewood bridge with white black dot pins, bound peghead with pearl logo inlay, 3-per-side chrome tuners, piezo bridge pickup, 4-band EQ, available in Natural finish, mfg. 1994-95.

			N/A	$225	$150
				Last MSR was $450.	

S

GRADING		100%	EXCELLENT	AVERAGE

ACOUSTIC: REGENCY SERIES

ST6 2 - 36" student folk style guitar, nato sides and back, select spruce top, rosewood fingerboard, Natural finish, mfg. 2001-current.

	MSR	$140	$105	$70	$35

ST9 2 - similar to the ST6 2, except is 39" body, mfg. 2001-current.

	MSR	$160	$120	$80	$40

D2 - dreadnought style, nato sides and back, select spruce top, rosewood fingerboard with dot inlay, 3-per-side tuners, single-ply cream binding, Natural finish, mfg. 2001-current.

	MSR	$180	$135	$90	$50

D2-12 - similar to the D2, except is in 12-string configuration, mfg. 2001-current.

	MSR	$225	$170	$110	$65

D2CE - similar to the D2, except has a single cutaway and PS-2000 passive electronics, mfg. 2001-current.

	MSR	$275	$210	$135	$75

J2 - jumbo style, nato sides and back, select spruce top, rosewood fingerboard with dot inlay, 3-per-side tuners, single-ply cream binding, Natural finish, mfg. 2001-current.

	MSR	$190	$140	$95	$55

OM2 - orchestra body style, nato sides and back, select spruce top, rosewood fingerboard with dot inlay, 3-per-side tuners, single-ply cream binding, Natural finish, mfg. 2001-current.

	MSR	$180	$135	$90	$50

ACOUSTIC: REMINGTON SERIES

MJ 13 CE - single cutaway medium jumbo body, solid cedar top, striped mahogany back and sides, 6-ply reverse black binding, 3-per-side Grover chrome tuners, Fishman Classic 4-band EQ, available in Natural finish, mfg. 2000-current.

	MSR	$480	$360	$240	$150

OM 13 CE - single cutaway orchestra model body, solid cedar top, striped mahogany back and sides, 6-ply reverse black binding, 3-per-side Grover chrome tuners, Fishman Classic 4-band EQ, available in Natural finish, mfg. 2000-current.

	MSR	$480	$360	$240	$150

SMJ 13 CE - similar to the MJ13 CE, except has a solid body with a L.R. Baggs EQ, mfg. 2000-current.

	MSR	$625	$470	$310	$200

C SMJ 13 CE - similar to the SMJ 13 CE, except is a Classic, mfg. 2000-current.

	MSR	$790	$595	$390	$250

ACOUSTIC: RIO GRANDE SERIES

D 15 E - dreadnought body, solid cedar top, ovangkol sides and back, turquoise dyed maple trim, maple binding, 3-per-side gold Grover tuners, Fishman Classic 4-Band EQ, available in Natural finish, mfg. 2000-current.

	MSR	$480	$360	$240	$150

OM 15 CE - Orchestra Model single cutaway body, solid cedar top, ovangkol sides and back, turquoise dyed maple trim, maple binding, 3-per-side gold Grover tuners, Fishman Classic 4-Band EQ, available in Natural finish, mfg. 2000-current.

	MSR	$480	$360	$240	$150

ACOUSTIC: STANDARD DREADNOUGHT SERIES

C-41 - dreadnought style, mahogany top, round soundhole, black pickguard, bound body, multi stripe rosette, mahogany back/sides/neck, 14/20-fret rosewood fingerboard with dot inlay, rosewood bridge with black pins, 3-per-side chrome tuners, available in Black satin, Natural, or White satin finishes, disc. 1995.

		N/A	$75	$50

Last MSR was $160.

LF-006 - smaller scale (36" length) folk style, nato top/back/sides/neck, bound body, round soundhole, rosewood fingerboard with dot inlay, rosewood bridge with black pins, 3-per-side chrome tuners, available in Natural satin finish, disc 2001.

		$140	$82	$55

Last MSR was $186.

Tobacco Sunburst finish added in 1999 for an additional $20 (LF-006G TS). Jewel Mist and Mint Juilep added in 2000 for an additional $30 (LF-006G).

LF-009 - smaller scale (39" length) folk style, nato top/back/sides/neck, bound body, round soundhole, rosewood fingerboard with dot inlay, rosewood bridge with black pins, 3-per-side chrome tuners, available in Natural satin finish, disc 2001.

		$145	$85	$55

Last MSR was $192.

Tobacco Sunburst finish added in 1999 for an additional $20 (LF-009G TS). Arizona Blue and Grape Mist finishes added in 2000 for an additional $20 (LF-009G).

LF-015 - (full scale) folk style, nato top/back/sides/neck, bound body, round soundhole, rosewood fingerboard with dot inlay, rosewood bridge with black pins, 3-per-side chrome tuners, available in Natural satin finish, disc 2001.

           $175 $105 $70
           Last MSR was $234.

LW-005 - dreadnought style, spruce top, nato back and sides, nato bolt-on neck, rosewood fingerboard and bridge, 20 frets, chrome enclosed gears, available in Natural Satin finish, mfg. 1999-2001.

           $165 $95 $65
           Last MSR was $222.

Add $18 for gloss finish (LW-005G). Add $48 for Black, Original Sunburst, Trans. Vintage, Trans. Blue and Vintage Sunburst finishes (LW-005G).

LW-005G VS - similar to LW-005, except has Vintage Sunburst gloss finish, mfg. 1999-2000.

           $110 $65 $50
           Last MSR was $148.

LW-015 - dreadnought style, nato top, round soundhole, black pickguard, bound body, multi stripe rosette, nato back/sides/neck, 14/20-fret rosewood fingerboard with dot inlay, rosewood bridge with black pins, 3-per-side chrome tuners, available in Natural satin finish, mfg. 1994-2001.

           $165 $98 $65
           Last MSR was $223.

LW-015 LH - similar to the LW-015, except in a left-handed configuration, available in Natural satin finish, disc 2001.

           $195 $115 $75
           Last MSR was $255.

LW-015 G - similar to the LW-015, available in Black, Sunburst, or White gloss finishes, disc 2001.

           $189 $110 $75
           Last MSR was $252.

Samick LC-015G
courtesy Samick

LW-015 E - dreadnought style, nato top, round soundhole, black pickguard, bound body, multi stripe rosette, nato back/sides/neck, 14/20-fret rosewood fingerboard with dot inlay, rosewood bridge with black pins, 3-per-side chrome tuners, piezo bridge pickup, volume/tone controls, available in Natural Satin finish, disc 2001.

           $225 $130 $85
           Last MSR was $300.

LWO-15 E LH - similar to the LW-015, except in a left-handed configuration, available in Natural Satin finish, disc 2001.

           $235 $139 $90
           Last MSR was $315.

LW-020 G - similar to the LW-015, except features solid natural Agathis top, 3-per-side enclosed tuners, available in Blonde (top only) finish, disc 2001.

           $200 $120 $80
           Last MSR was $270.

LW-025 G - dreadnought style, spruce top, round soundhole, black pickguard, bound body, multi stripe rosette, nato back/sides, mahogany neck, 14/20-fret rosewood fingerboard with dot inlay, rosewood bridge with white black dot pins, 3-per-side chrome die-cast tuners, available in Natural gloss finish, mfg. 1994-2001.

           $235 $140 $90
           Last MSR was $315.

LW-025 G CEQ - dreadnought style with single rounded cutaway, spruce top, round soundhole, black pickguard, bound body, multi stripe rosette, nato back/sides, mahogany neck, 14/20-fret rosewood fingerboard with dot inlay, rosewood bridge with white black dot pins, 3-per-side chrome die-cast tuners, piezo pickup, volume/EQ slider controls, available in Natural Gloss finish, mfg. 1997-2001.

           $325 $190 $125
           Last MSR was $435.

For an additional $45, Transparent Green, Transparent Blue, & Transparent Red finishes are available.

LW-027 G - similar to the LW-025 G, except features ovankol back/sides, available in Natural gloss finish, disc 2001.

           $280 $165 $110
           Last MSR was $375.

Samick HFB-590 N
courtesy Samick

S

GRADING	100%	EXCELLENT	AVERAGE

LW-028 A NEW - similar to the LW-025 G, except features ivory body binding, 3-per-side Grover tuners, available in Natural satin finish, mfg. 1997-2001.

	$225	$130	$85

Last MSR was $300.

LW-028 SA - similar to LW-028, except has solid spruce top, Natural satin finish, disc 2001.

	$245	$145	$95

Last MSR was $324.

Gloss finish available at no additional charge (LW-028 GSA).

LW-044 G CEQ NEW - similar to the LW-025 G CEQ, except features ovankol back/sides, ABS body binding, available in Natural Gloss finish, mfg. 1997-current.

	$350	$195	$135

Last MSR was $465.

LW-060 GA - full size dreadnought, spruce top, rosewood back and sides, abalone inlay, mahogany set neck, rosewood fingerboard and bridge, 20 frets, gold Grover tuners, gloss Natural finish, mfg. 1999-2001.

	$369	$215	$140

Last MSR was $493.

Vintage Sunburst finish available at no extra charge (LW-060 GA VS).

ACOUSTIC: STANDARD CLASSICAL SERIES

Instruments in this series have a classical style body, round soundhole, bound body, marquetry rosette, 12/19-fret fingerboard, slotted peghead, tied bridge, 3-per-side tuners as following features (unless otherwise listed).

LC-006 - smaller scale (36" length) classical style, nato top/back/sides/neck, rosewood fingerboard/bridge, chrome tuners, available in Natural satin finish, mfg. 1997-2001.

	$135	$80	$50

Last MSR was $180.

LC-009 - smaller scale (39" length) classical style, nato top/back/sides/neck, rosewood fingerboard/bridge, chrome tuners, available in Natural satin finish, mfg. 1997-2001.

	$139	$80	$55

Last MSR was $186.

LC-015 G - nato mahogany top/back/sides/neck, rosewood fingerboard/bridge, chrome tuners, available in Natural gloss finish, mfg. 1994-2001.

	$170	$99	$65

Last MSR was $225.

Available in Black finish for an additional $10 (LC-015 G BK).

LC-025 G - natural spruce top, mahogany back/sides/neck, rosewood fingerboard/bridge, chrome tuners, available in Natural finish, mfg. 1994-2001.

	$200	$120	$80

Last MSR was $276.

LC-034 G (NEW) - solid spruce top, ovankol back/sides, mahogany neck, rosewood fingerboard/bridge, gold plated tuners, available in Natural finish, mfg. 1997-2001.

	$235	$140	$90

Last MSR was $315.

ACOUSTIC: WINDSOR SERIES

D 6 - dreadnought style, solid spruce top, ovankol back and sides, rosewood fingerboard, 3-per-side Grover tuners, pickguard, chrome hardware, available in Natural finish, mfg. 2001-current.

MSR	$275	$205	$140	$80

D 6 CE - similar to the D 6, except has a single cutaway and an active EQ with built in tuner, available in Natural finish, mfg. 2001-current.

MSR	$375	$285	$190	$120

ACOUSTIC: WORTHINGTON SERIES

D 5 - dreadnought style, solid spruce top, striped mahogany back and sides, rosewood fingerboard, 3-per-side Grover tuners, pickguard, chrome hardware, available in Natural finish, mfg. 2001-current.

MSR	$225	$170	$115	$65

Add $15 for left-handed configuration (D 5 LH).

D 5 12 - similar to the D 5, except in 12-string configuration, mfg. 2001-current.

MSR	$275	$205	$140	$80

GRADING		100%	EXCELLENT	AVERAGE

D 5 CE - similar to the D 5, except has a single cutaway and an active EQ with built in tuner, available in Natural or Wine Red finishes, mfg. 2001-current.

MSR	$325		$245	$165	$95

TD 5 CE - similar to the D 5, except has a thin body, available in Natural finish, mfg. 2001-current.

MSR	$325		$245	$165	$95

SJ 5 - Southern Jumbo style, solid spruce top, striped mahogany back and sides, rosewood fingerboard, 3-per-side Grover tuners, pickguard, chrome hardware, available in Natural finish, mfg. 2001-current.

MSR	$225		$170	$115	$65

TMJ 5 CE - similar to the SJ 5, except has a thin medium body with a single cutaway and an active EQ with built in tuner, available in Natural, Black, or Wine Red finishes, mfg. 2001-current.

MSR	$325		$245	$165	$95

OM 5 - orchestra model style, solid spruce top, striped mahogany back and sides, rosewood fingerboard, 3-per-side Grover tuners, pickguard, chrome hardware, available in Natural finish, mfg. 2001-current.

MSR	$225		$170	$115	$65

OM 5 CE - similar to the OM 5, except has a single cutaway and an active EQ with built in tuner, available in Natural finish, mfg. 2001-current.

MSR	$325		$245	$165	$95

ACOUSTIC ELECTRIC BASS: AMERICAN CLASSIC SERIES

HFB-590 N (KINGSTON) - single round cutaway flattop body, maple top, bound body, bound f-holes, maple back/sides/neck, 21-fret bound rosewood fingerboard with pearl dot inlay, strings through rosewood bridge, blackface peghead with pearl logo inlay, 2-per-side black chrome tuners, piezo bridge pickup, 4-band EQ, available in Natural finish, disc. 2000.

		$640	$420	$285
		Last MSR was $850.		

**Samick HFB-60 RB FL N
courtesy Samick**

Earlier models were also available in Black, Pearl White, and Tobacco Sunburst finishes.

HFB-690 RB TBK - similar to HF590, except has 5 strings, arched quilted maple top, 3/2-per-side tuners, available in Trans. Black finish, mfg. 1994-95 & 1999-2000.

		$900	$630	$445
		Last MSR was $1,200.		

This model is also available with a bird's-eye maple top, maple satin neck, fretless fingerboard and Natural finish at no additional cost. (Model HFB5-690 RB FL N).

ACOUSTIC ELECTRIC BASS: CURRENT MFG. SERIES

ELAN AB 11 CE - single sharp cutaway thin medium jumbo body, quilted maple top, back, and sides, 8-ply binding, rosewood fingerboard, 2-per-side chrome tuners, Fishman Classic 4-Band EQ, available in Amber finish, current mfg.

MSR	$790		$595	$400	$250

REGENCY AB 2 - single cutaway medium jumbo body, select spruce top, nato sides and back, 2-per-side chrome tuners, available in Natural finish, current mfg.

MSR	$335		$250	$170	$110

REMINGTON SOLID BODY SAB 13 - single cutaway body, cedar top, mahogany back, ablone dot inlays and rosette, rosewood fingerboard, 2-per-side tuners, L.R. Baggs EQ system, available in Natural finish, current mfg.

MSR	$910		$685	$460	$290

SAND, KIRK
Instruments currently built in Laguna Beach, California.

Luthier Kirk Sand began playing guitar at six years old and played professionally and taught until the age of nineteen when he moved from his hometown of Springfield, Illinois to Southern California to study classical guitar.

His love of the instrument led him to co-establish the Guitar Shoppe in 1972 with Jim Matthews in Laguna Beach, California, which produces some of the finest custom instruments built today as well as being one of the premier repair facilities on the West Coast. The head of the repair section is Mark Angus (see Angus Guitars) who works full-time as well as building his custom acoustics throughout the year.

By 1979, Kirk's twenty years of dedicated experience with guitars, guitar repair and restoration inspired him to begin building guitars of his own design. Sand guitars feature Sitka or Englemann spruce tops, Brazilian or Indian rosewood backs and sides, ebony fingerboards, and custom designed active electronics. For further information, contact Sand Guitars directly (see Trademark Index).

**Santa Cruz Archtop
courtesy Santa Cruz**

S

GRADING		100%	EXCELLENT	AVERAGE

SANDNER

Instruments previously produced between 1947 to 1958.

The Sandner trademark can be found on a series of acoustic archtops. These models may have "Alosa" or "Standard" on the headstock (or tailpiece). Company was founded by Alois Sandner in Egerland, Germany (now part of the Czech Republic) and initially operated as a cottage industry. Since 1953, factory is located in Bubenreuth, Germany and had three employees until 1958. They offered approximately twenty models with a total production of less than 500 pieces. The company still manufactures stringed instruments, but no longer produces guitars.

SANOX

Instruments previously produced in Japan from the late 1970s through the mid 1980s.

Intermediate to good quality guitars featuring some original designs and some designs based on American classics, (Source: Tony Bacon and Paul Day, *The Guru's Guitar Guide*).

SANTA CRUZ

Instruments currently built in Santa Cruz, California since 1976. Distributed by the Santa Cruz Guitar Company (SCGC) located in Santa Cruz, California.

The Santa Cruz Guitar company has been creating high quality acoustic guitars since 1976. Founded by Richard Hoover, who first became interested in guitar building around 1969, and moved to Santa Cruz in 1972 where he studied once a week under a classical guitar builder. Hoover continued honing his skills through daily on-the-job training and talking with other builders. While he was learning the guitar building trade, Hoover was still playing guitar professionally. Hoover ran his own shop for a number of years, producing guitars under the "Rodeo" trademark.

The Santa Cruz Guitar Company was formed by Richard Hoover and two partners in 1976. Their objective was to build acoustic guitars with consistent quality. By drawing on building traditions of the classical guitar and violin builders, Hoover based the new company's building concept on wood choice, voicing the tops, and tuning the guitar bodies. The company's production of individually-built guitars has expanded by working with a group of established luthiers. Santa Cruz now offers fifteen different guitar models with a wide variety of custom options. It is estimated that over half of the guitars are made to order to customer's specifications.

ACOUSTIC ARCHTOP

ARCHTOP 16" - single rounded 16" cutaway, bound carved Engelmann or Sitka spruce top, raised bound ebony pickguard, bound f-holes, multi-wood purfling, German maple back/sides/neck, 21-fret bound ebony fingerboard with abalone fan inlay, adjustable ebony bridge/fingers tailpiece, ebony veneered bound peghead with abalone logo inlay, 3-per-side tuners, gold hardware, pickups are an option, available in Natural finish, current mfg.

MSR	$10,500	$8,500	$5,500	$3,600

Archtop 17 Inch - similar to the Archtop, except has a 17" bout, current mfg.

MSR	$10,950	$8,800	$5,725	$3,775

Archtop 18 Inch - similar to the Archtop, except has an 18" bout, current mfg.

MSR	$14,000	$11,200	$7,400	$4,800

ACOUSTIC

Santa Cruz offers a wide range of custom options on their guitar models. These options include different wood for tops, back/sides, tinted and Sunburst finishes, abalone, wood, or herringbone binding, and 12-string configurations. For current option pricing, availability, or further information, please contact the Santa Cruz Guitar Company directly (see Trademark Index).

All models have round soundholes with wood inlay rosettes, ivoroid body binding with wood purfling, and Natural finish (unless otherwise listed). The options are literally endless.

Add $315 for German Spruce top. Add $525 for German maple back and sides. Add $1,315 for koa back and sides. Add $500 for Adirondack spruce top. Add $190 for cedar top. Add $365 for Sunburst finish top. Add $280 for Tinted top. Add $295 for abalone rosette. Add $520 for Cutaway. Add $340 for left-hand Models.

MODEL D - dreadnought style, Sitka spruce top, Indian rosewood back/sides, mahogany neck, 14/20-fret bound ebony fingerboard, ebony bridge with black pearl dot pins, ebony veneer on bound peghead with pearl logo inlay, 3-per-side chrome Scaller tuners, current mfg.

MSR	$3,100	$2,400	$1,600	$1,025

Model D Pre-War - similar to Model D, except has advanced pre-war style X-bracing, enhanced bass response, available in Natural finish, current mfg.

MSR	$2,500	$1,950	$1,250	$800

12-Fret D Model - Sitka spruce top, herringbone purfling/rosette, tortoise pickguard, mahogany back/sides, 12/20-fret ebony fingerboard with pearl diamond inlay, ebony bridge with pearl dot pins, ebony veneer on slotted peghead with pearl logo inlay, 3-per-side Waverly tuners, current mfg.

MSR	$3,450	$2,675	$1,750	$1,150

MODEL F - Sitka spruce top, Indian rosewood back/sides, mahogany neck, 14/21-fret bound ebony fingerboard with abalone fan inlay, ebony bridge with black pearl dot pins, ebony veneer on bound peghead with pearl logo inlay, 3-per-side chrome Schaller tuners, current mfg.

MSR	$3,350	$2,625	$1,700	$1,100

GRADING		100%	EXCELLENT	AVERAGE

MODEL FS - single rounded cutaway, red cedar top, Indian rosewood back/sides, mahogany neck, 21-fret ebony fingerboard, Brazilian rosewood binding, ebony bridge with black pearl dot pins, 3-per-side gold Schaller tuners with ebony buttons, current mfg.

MSR	$3,995		$3,400	$2,200	$1,450

MODEL H - Sitka spruce top, Indian rosewood back/sides, mahogany neck, 14/20-fret bound ebony fingerboard, ebony bridge with black pearl pins, ebony veneer on bound peghead, 3-per-side chrome Schaller tuners with ebony buttons, current mfg.

MSR	$3,100		$2,425	$1,600	$1,025

Santa Cruz Model D
courtesy Santa Cruz

Model H A/E - spruce top, mahogany back/sides/neck, abalone top border and rosette, 21-fret ebony fingerboard with pearl/gold ring inlay, ebony bridge with black pearl dot pins, 3-per-side gold Schaller tuners with ebony buttons, bridge pickup with micro drive preamp, current mfg.

MSR	$5,000		$3,950	$2,600	$1,650

MODEL PJ - parlour-size, Sitka spruce top, Indian rosewood back/sides, mahogany neck, herringbone border, 14/20-fret bound ebony fingerboard with diamond and squares inlay, ebony bridge with pearl dot bridgepins, 3-per-side chrome Waverly tuners with ebony buttons, current mfg.

MSR	$3,325		$2,595	$1,700	$1,075

MODEL OO - OO 14.5" body, solid sitka spruce top, Indian rosewood back/sides, mahogany neck, herringbone border, 12/21 fret ebony fingerboard, slotted headstock, 3-per-side tuners, Natural finish, current mfg.

MSR	$3,595		$3,050	$1,975	$1,295

MODEL OOO-12 - Sitka spruce top, tortoise pickguard, Indian rosewood back/sides, mahogany neck, 25.375" scale, 12/19-fret bound ebony fingerboard with pearl diamond and squares inlay, slotted headstock, ebony bridge with ebony mother-of-pearl dot pins, ebony peghead veneer, 3-per-side Waverly W-16 tuners. Mfg. 1995 to date.

MSR	$3,595		$3,050	$1,975	$1,295

MODEL OM - Sitka spruce top, tortoise pickguard, Indian rosewood back/sides, mahogany neck, 14/20-fret bound ebony fingerboard with pearl dot inlay, ebony bridge with black pearl dot pins, ebony peghead veneer, 3-per-side chrome Waverly tuners, current mfg.

MSR	$3,450		$2,675	$1,750	$1,150

Model OM-Prewar - similar to Model OM, except has advanced X-bracing, enhanced bass response. Available in Natural finish. Current Mfg.

MSR	$2,500		$1,950	$1,250	$750

BOB BROZMAN BARITONE - German spruce top, mahogany back and sides (figured koa back and sides optional), 3-per-side Waverly tuners, 27" scale, 12-frets to the body, no pickguard, available in Natural finish, current mfg.

MSR	$4,310		$3,250	$2,100	$1,375

JANIS IAN MODEL - parlour-size with single rounded cutaway, Sitka spruce top, abalone rosette, Indian rosewood back/sides, mahogany neck, 14/20-fret bound ebony fingerboard with gold ring inlay/rude girl logo, ebony bridge with pearl dot bridgepins, 3-per-side black Schaller tuners, L.R. Baggs pickup system, available in all Black finish, current mfg.

MSR	$4,220		$2,950	$1,925	$1,250

TONY RICE MODEL - dreadnought style, Sitka spruce top, tortoise pickguard, herringbone bound body/rosette, Indian rosewood back/sides, mahogany neck, 14/20-fret bound ebony fingerboard with pearl logo inlay at 12th fret, Tony Rice signature on label, ebony bridge with black pearl dot pins, ebony peghead veneer, 3-per-side chrome Waverly tuners, current mfg.

MSR	$3,450		$2,650	$1,725	$1,125

This model was designed in conjunction with guitarist Tony Rice.

TONY RICE PROFESSIONAL - similar to Tony Rice Model, except has German spruce top, Brazilian rosewood back and sides, 25 1/4" scale, enlarged soundhole, ivoroid/black/ivoroid binding on the fingerboard and peghead, gold Waverly tuners, available in Natural finish, current mfg.

MSR	$7,500		$5,600	$3,750	$2,400

VINTAGE JUMBO - jumbo style, inspired by round-shouldered dreadnoughts of the 1940s, Sitka spruce top, mahogany back and sides, 14-frets to the body, round soundhole, 3-per-side Waverly tuners, available in Sunburst finish, current mfg.

MSR	$3,450		$2,600	$1,750	$1,150

Schaefer Archtop
courtesy Schaefer Guitars

S

GRADING		100%	EXCELLENT	AVERAGE

VINTAGE ARTIST - dreadnought style, Sitka spruce top, tortoise pickguard, herringbone body trim, mahogany back/sides/neck, 14/21-fret bound ebony fingerboard with pearl dot inlay, ebony bridge with black pearl dot pins, Brazilian rosewood veneer on bound peghead with pearl logo inlay, 3-per-side Waverly tuners, current mfg.

MSR	$3,350		$2,625	$1,700	$1,100

SANTA ROSA
Instruments currently built in Asia. Distributed by AR Musical Enterprises of Fishers, Indiana.

Santa Rosa acoustic guitars are geared more towards the entry level or student guitarist.

SCHAEFER GUITARS
Instruments currently built in Duluth, Minnesota beginning mid-2003. Previously built in Fort Worth, Texas until 2003 and Hillsboro, Texas.

Luthier Ed Schaefer studied classical guitar in college while working as a guitar tech at R.B.I. The Rhythm Band Instrument Company was a sister company of I.M.C. (International Music Corporation – See Hondo or Charvel/Jackson). Schaefer's main job was fret re-surfacing and set-ups on imported guitars that sat out on ships for too long! Schaefer's first lutherie attempt was building a classical guitar (with the guidance of Irving Sloan's guitar construction book). In 2003, Schaefer relocated to the Land of 10,000 Lakes (MN).

ACOUSTIC

Schaefer's archtop models feature AAA Sitka or Englemann spruce tops, American sycamore backs and sides, and 3-piece sycamore necks. Schaefer's professional painting background has led him to the opinion that "Nitrocellulose lacquer – the only way" to finish guitars. Schaefer is currently constructing his archtop guitars on a custom order, commission basis. For model listing please refer to the *Blue Book of Electric Guitars*. For further information regarding specifications and pricing, please contact Ed Schaefer directly (see Trademark Index).

SCHARPACH GUITARS
Instruments currently built in the Netherlands since 1979.

Guitarmaker Theo Scharpach was born near Vienna, Austria. He has been working in Bergeyk, the Netherlands for more than 20 years and exports his guitars to Spain, Germany, Austria, Turkey, New Zealand and the USA as well as other countries. Only 10-12 exclusive handmade guitars are produced each year. Guitars are built only on commission. Prices begin at $4,500.

ACOUSTIC

The **Classical Concert Model** has a two soundhole design with raised fingerboard, using only 1st quality, 100-year-old Brazilian rosewood with either spruce or cedar top. Standard is a unique semi-cutaway which, in combination with the raised fingerboard, allows you to play in the highest registers, up to the 24th fret very easily. Construction techniques result in extremely long sustain with a well balanced mellow sound, current mfg, and MSR $7,400.

The **Blue Vienna Jazz Acoustic Archtop** is built using only the finest European cello-woods, and is available in Blue, Honey, and other finishes available, current mfg, and is MSR $8,500.

The **Original Selmer Design** is built in the style of Marrio Maccaferry, "Gypsy" style. Used by Tolga Emilio and Raphael Fays, current mfg. and MSR is $6,800.

The **Steel String Jumbo** is available with or without cutaway, and is also available are 8-string, 12-string, and baritone models. The Model SKD was custom built for Steve Howe.

The **Arch** is a small, semi-acoustic model, nylon strings. Used by Al di Meola, current mfg.

The **Teardrop** is a jazz oriented style instrument, current mfg.

SCHECTER
Instruments currently produced in Los Angeles, California. Production of high quality replacement parts and guitars began in Van Nuys, California in 1976.

The Schecter company, named after David Schecter, began as a repair/modification shop that also did some customizing. Schecter began making high quality replacement parts (such as Solid Brass Hardware, Bridges, Tuners, and the MonsterTone and SuperRock II pickups) and build-your-own instrument kits. This led to the company offering of quality replacement necks and bodies, and eventually to their own line of finished instruments. Schecter is recognized as one of the first companies to market tapped pickup assemblies (coil tapping can offer a wider range of sound from an existing pickup configuration). Other designers associated with Schecter were Dan Armstrong and Tom Anderson.

In 1994, Michael Ciravolo took over as the new director for Schecter Guitar Research. Ciravolo introduced new guitar designs the same year, and continues to expand the Schecter line with new innovations and designs.

In 1998, Schecter and Maestro Alex Gregory teamed up to offer the 7-String Limited Edition Signature model based on the patented specifications and neck profile of Gregory's original 1989 model. This signature model will be individually numbered, and comes with a signed Certificate of Authenticity (list $2,595), (Source: Tom Wheeler, *American Guitars*).

By the mid 1980s, Schecter was offering designs based on early Fender-style guitars in models such as the Mercury, Saturn, Hendrix, and Dream Machine. In the late 1980s Schecter also had the U.S. built Californian series as well as the Japan-made Schecter East models Recently they introduced an Acoustic line as well.

ACOUSTIC

DIAMOND ACOUSTIC - single cutaway body, figured maple top over composite oval back (like Ovation), mahogany set-neck, 20-fret rosewood fingerboard with diamond inlays, body and neck binding, 3-per-side Grover tuners, Diamond Piezo pickup, active 4-band EQ, chrome or gold hardware, available in Trans. Amber, Trans. Black, or Red Sunburst, current mfg.

MSR	$399		$280	$200	$125

GRADING		100%	EXCELLENT	AVERAGE

Diamond Acoustic Elite - similar to the Diamond Acoustic, except has a quilted maple top and abalone binding, available in Trans. Blue or Antique Brown Sunburst finishes, current mfg.

MSR	$499		$350	$250	$150

SW 3500 ACOUSTIC - single cutaway body, quilted maple top, South American Rosewood sides and back, mahogany set-neck, 22-fret rosewood fingerboard with dot inlays, body and neck binding, 3-per-side Grover tuners, Fishman Piezo pickup & active 4-band EQ, chrome hardware, available in Trans. Amber, or Vintage Natural Gloss, current mfg.

MSR	$599		$425	$300	$195

Schecter Diamond Acoustic
courtesy Schecter

SCHEERHORN CUSTOM RESONATOR GUITARS

Instruments currently built in Kentwood, Michigan since 1989. Instruments are available through Scheerhorn or Elderly Instruments of Lansing, Michigan.

Luthier Tim Scheerhorn has background training as a tool and die maker, a tool engineer, and is a specialist in process automation for manufacturing. In the past, his hobbies generally involved rebuilding something – either boats or classic cars. But in 1986, Scheerhorn picked up a resonator guitar and later found himself immersed in the world of custom guitar building.

Although Scheerhorn did have prior experience setting up banjos and resonator guitars for other players, he had never built a musical instrument from scratch. He did possess a new OMI Dobro, and a Regal from the 1930s. In February of 1989, Scheerhorn began building guitars based on the Regal model and his own innovations. In the summer of 1989 the guitar was tested by Mike Auldridge (Seldom Scene) at the Winterhawk festival in New York. Encouraged by Auldridge's enthusiasm, Scheerhorn returned to his workshop and continued building.

Scheerhorn limits production to 3 or 4 instruments a month. All guitars are hand built by Scheerhorn.

ACOUSTIC

Both Scheerhorn models share the same revised resonator design. The resonators are built of bright chrome plated brass, Spun Quarterman cone, and a spider bridge of aluminum. The bridge insert is made of hard maple with ebony tops. Both models also feature chrome Schaller M-6 tuning machines.

The **Curly Maple Regal Body** model has a bookmatched solid curly maple top, with matching sides and back. The three piece neck consists of curly maple and walnut, and has a 19-fret ebony fingerboard. The body and neck are bound in either an ivoroid or dark tortoise (Natural Blond finish), and finished in hand-rubbed lacquer. The **Curly Maple Large Body** model has similar specifications, but with a larger body size (longer, deeper, wider) for additional volume and projection.

The **Mahogany/Spruce Regal Body** model has a book-matched quartersawn Sitka spruce top, solid mahogany back and sides, and a two piece mahogany neck. The **Mahogany/Spruce Large Body** model has similar specifications, but with a larger body size for additional volume and projection.

Scheerhorn also builds a Weissenborn Style Reissue dubbed the "**Scheerhorn Hawaiian**." The body is constructed out of solid Figured Koa (top, back, and sides), and the peghead has a Curly Maple overlay. The bridge is cocobolo with a bone saddle, and the cocobolo fingerboard has Curly Maple binding and abalone inlays. This model also features Kluson style tuners, a built in McIntyre pickup, and a hand-rubbed lacquer finish.

Scheerhorn's newest model in the **Acoustic/Electric**, which features solid curly maple top/back/sides and neck, ebony fingerboard with flush frets, a 9" Quarterman cone and National-style coverplate, a Seymour Duncan mini-humbucker/McIntyre transducer pickups (with volume and tone for each system) and a 3-way selector switch. This model is wired for stereo.

SCHNEIDER, RICHARD

Instruments previously built in Washington State, and other locations. Distributed by the Lost Mountain Center for the Guitar of Carlsborg, Washington.

In 1996, when luthier/designer Richard Schneider was asked what he considered his occupation, he simply replied, "I don't make guitars, I make guitar makers." While known for his Kasha-inspired acoustic guitar designs, Schneider also trained and encouraged younger builders to continue crafting guitars. At last count, some 21 full term apprentices had been taught in the craft of classical guitar design. Schneider is best known for his over 25 year collaboration with Dr. Michael Kasha, in their advanced design for the classical guitar. Kasha, the Director of Institute of Molecular Biophysics at Florida State University, worked with Schneider to pioneer an entirely new and scientific way of designing and constructing classical guitars. This advanced design has been the topic of controversy for a number of years in the classical guitar community.

Schneider first apprenticed with Juan Pimentel in Mexico City, Mexico from 1963 to 1965. Schneider served as proprietor of **Estudio be las Guitarra** from 1965 to 1972, which housed a guitar making workshop, retail store and music instruction studio. It was during this time period that Schneider began his collaboration with Dr. Kasha. In 1973, Schneider became the director and owner of the Studio of Richard Schneider in Kalamazoo, Michigan. This studio was devoted solely to classical guitar design and fine construction using the Kasha/Schneider design. Schneider was a consultant to the Gibson Guitar company between 1973 to 1978.

S

His duties included design, engineering, and production procedures for the **Mark** series guitars, which was based on the Kasha/Schneider design. He also designed the **The Les Paul** electric guitar model. In 1983, Schneider also engineered and built five **Taxi** prototypes for Silver Street, Inc. of Elkhart, Indiana.

In 1984, Schneider moved his family and workshop to Sequim, Washington. The Lost Mountain Center for the Guitar was founded in 1986 as a non-profit organization whose purposes include research, development, and information disseminating about improvements in guitar design. Schneider continued to make improvements to his Kasha/Schneider design, which made significant improvements to the tonal functions and playability. Luthier Richard Schneider passed away on January 31st, 1997, (Biography courtesy Bob Fischer, Lost Mountain Center).

Schneider estimated that he constructed over 200 guitars by 1996. Approximately 60 were handcrafted traditional concert guitars, while 50 models were the advanced Schneider/Kasha design. Rather than assign a serial number to his guitars, Schneider used to name them instead.

In addition to his own guitar designs, Schneider estimated that he had built over 100 prototypes for the Gibson Guitar company, and Baldwin-era Gretsches.

Schneider met with Maestro Andres Segovia on 18 separate occasions, and auditioned new instruments with Segovia on 6 of these visits for purposes of critique and analysis. After Segovia passed away, Schneider then consulted with guitarist Kurt Rodarmer, whose new CD The Goldberg Variations features two of Schneider's guitars.

SCHOENBERG, ERIC
Instruments currently built in Tiburon, California. Previous production was in Massachusetts. Nazareth, Pennsylvania from 1985 to 1996. Schoenberg Guitars set up a new, separate production facility in Massachusetts in 1997.

Eric Schoenberg is regarded as one of the finest ragtime and finger style guitarists of the last twenty years. While operating out of the Music Emporium in Massachusetts, Schoenberg released a number of high quality acoustic guitars that were built in conjunction with the C.F. Martin company of Nazareth, Pennsylvania, and individually finished by either Schoenberg or luthier Dana Bourgeois. The Martin facilities assembled the bodies, then final touches were controlled by Schoenberg and Bourgeois. Luthier Bourgeois was involved in the project from 1986 to mid 1990. Luthier T.J. Thompson worked with Schoenberg from the mid 1990s until 1995. Beginning 1997, Schoenberg Guitars are individually handmade by several independent luthiers, including Bruce Sexauer of Petaluna, CA, & Robert Anderson of Victoria, British Columbia. For more information refer to their web site (see Trademark Index).

ACOUSTIC

Schoenberg debuted the **Soloist** model in the late 1980s. The Soloist was a modern version of a Martin OM-style acoustic, and featured top grade woods originally overseen by Bourgeois. The Soloist model featured a European spruce top, Brazilian back and sides, a one piece mahogany neck, 20-fret ebony fingerboard with diamond shaped pearl inlays, and Kluson-styled Grover tuning machines. Retail list price back in the late 1980s was $2,850 (which seems more than reasonable now!). Current price is $4,250 for the Soloist.

SCHWARTZ, SHELDON
Instruments currently built in Toronto (Ontario), Canada.

Luthier Sheldon Schwartz currently offers high quality handcrafted acoustic guitars that are immaculately constructed. Schwartz began working on guitars at fifteen, and has had lutherie associations with such builders as Grit Laskin and Linda Manzer. In 1992, Schwartz began building full time, and attended vintage guitar shows to display his work.

ACOUSTIC

Schwartz prefers working with the top quality, master grade woods that generally don't show up in the large production factories, and matches back, sides, tops, and necks for both appearance and tonal qualities. Depending on the commission, Schwartz also works in other woods such as Engelmann spruce, Bear claw Sitka spruce, and Brazilian rosewood; and will negotiate rates on custom inlay work.

Add $300 for curly maple back and sides. Add $450 for Venetian (rounded) cutaway. Add $650 for curly koa back and sides. Add $550 for 12-string configuration.

ADVANCED AUDITORIUM CUSTOM (BASIC MODEL SIX STRING) - dreadnought style, Sitka spruce top, dovetail mahogany neck, 25 1/2" scale, bound ebony fingerboard with two abalone dots at 12th fret, East Indian back and sides, abalone rosette, rosewood binding/heelcap/headstock veneer, mitered top/back purfling, ebony bridge, solid Spanish cedar lining, bone nut and saddle, brass dot side position markers, 3-per-side Schaller M6 tuning machines, available in Natural high gloss nitrocellulose finish, current mfg.

MSR   **$3,100**

Price includes hardshell case. This model has a 16 1/8" lower bout. A clear Mylar pickguard is available on request.

ADVANCED AUDITORIUM ELITE (BASIC MODEL PLUS) - similar to the Basic Model Six String, except usesd all master-grade materials and features handpicked, color matched abalone top purfling, current mfg.

MSR   **$3,900**

LIMITED EDITION MODEL - similar to the Basic Model Six string, except has 130-year-old birdseye maple back and sides, reclaimed salmon trap soundboard, Brazilian rosewood fingerboard, bridge, binding, and front and back headstock veneers, gold tuners, gold mother-of-pearl 12-fret position marker, current mfg.

MSR   **$4,900**

SCHWARTZ MAPLE SERIES - single cutaway, curly or bird's-eye maple body, Brazillian rosewood fingerboard, bridges, and bindings, current mfg.

CURLY MSR   **$3,400**
BIRD'S MSR   **$3,700**

SEAGULL GUITARS

Instruments currently built in La Patrie, Quebec, Canada since 1980. Seagull Acoustic Guitars are distributed by the La Si Do, Inc. of St. Laurent, Canada.

In 1968 Robert Godin set up a custom guitar shop in Montreal called Harmonilab. Harmonilab quickly became known for its excellent work and musicians were coming from as far away as Quebec City to have their guitars adjusted.

Although Harmonilab's business was flourishing, Robert was full of ideas for the design and construction of acoustic guitars. So in 1972 the Norman Guitar Company was born. From the beginning the Norman guitars showed signs of the innovations that Godin would eventually bring to the guitar market. By 1978, Norman guitars had become quite successful in Canada and France.

In 1980, Godin introduced the Seagull guitar. With many innovations like a bolt-on neck (for consistent neck pitch), pointed headstock (straight string pull) and a handmade solid top, the Seagull was designed for an ease of play for the entry level to intermediate guitar player. Most striking was the satin lacquer finish. Godin borrowed the finishing idea that was used on fine violins, and applied it to the acoustic guitar. When the final version of the Seagull guitar went into production, Godin went about the business of finding a sales force to help introduce the Seagull into the U.S. market. Several independent U.S. sales agents jumped at the chance to get involved with this new guitar, and armed with samples, off they went into the market. A couple of months passed, and not one guitar was sold. Rather than retreat back to Harmonilab, Godin decided that he would have to get out there himself and explain the Seagull guitar concept. So he bought himself an old Ford Econoline van and stuffed it full of about 85 guitars, and started driving through New England visiting guitar shops and introducing the Seagull guitar. Acceptance of this new guitar spread, and by 1985 La Si Do was incorporated and the factory in La Patrie expanded to meet the growing demand. For full company history, see Godin.

Schwartz Advance Auditorium courtesy Schwartz Guitar

ACOUSTIC: ARTIST SERIES

CAMEO CW (MODEL 21758) - full sized single cutaway body, solid spruce top, solid flame maple back and sides, mahogany neck, 14/21 fret rosewood fingerboard with dove inlay, rosewood bridge, high gloss natural lacquer, case included, new 2003.

MSR	$995	$750	$500	$295

Add $100 for Element electronics (Model 22632). Add $110 for Quantum II EQ electronics (Model 22649). Add $250 for I-Beam Duet electronics (Model 21895).

GRAND ARTIST (MODEL 10561) - solid spruce top, black pickguard, round soundhole, multi-stripe rosette, solid rosewood back, laminated rosewood sides, Honduran mahogany neck, 25 11/32" scale, 14/21-fret rosewood fingerboard with pearl dot inlay, bound headstock, rosewood bridge with white bridgepins, 3-per-side chrome tuners, available in Natural high gloss finish, mfg. 1993-99.

	$795	$525	$350

Last MSR was $995.

This model is designed to be a modern version of a "turn of the century" parlor guitar.

MOSAIC (MODEL 21802) - full sized body, solid cedar top, solid mahogany back and sides, mahogany neck, 14/21 fret rosewood fingerboard with dove inlay, rosewood bridge, hand polished natural lacquer, case included, new 2003.

MSR	$795	$595	$400	$250

Add $100 for Element electronics (Model 22571). Add $110 for Quantum II EQ electronics (Model 22588). Add $250 for I-Beam Duet electronics (Model 21949).

Mosaic CW (Model 21765) - similar to the Mosaic, except has a single cutaway, new 2003.

MSR	$895	$675	$450	$275

Add $100 for Element electronics (Model 22670). Add $110 for Quantum II EQ electronics (Model 22656). Add $250 for I-Beam Duet electronics (Model 21901).

PEPPINO MODEL CW - full sized single cutaway body, solid spruce top, solid rosewood back and sides, mahogany neck, 14/21 fret rosewood fingerboard with dove inlay, rosewood bridge, signature on headstock, high gloss Natural lacquer finish, new 2003.

MSR	$1,755	$1,325	$900	$550

PORTRAIT CW (MODEL 21772) - full sized single cutaway body, solid spruce top, solid mahogany back and sides, mahogany neck, 14/21 fret rosewood fingerboard with dove inlay, rosewood bridge, high gloss Natural lacquer, case included, new 2003.

MSR	$995	$750	$500	$295

Add $100 for Element electronics (Model 22618). Add $110 for Quantum II EQ electronics (Model 22625). Add $250 for I-Beam Duet electronics (Model 21918).

S

GRADING		100%	EXCELLENT	AVERAGE

STUDIO (MODEL 21819) - full sized body, solid spruce top, solid rosewood back and sides, mahogany neck, 14/21 fret rosewood fingerboard with dove inlay, rosewood bridge, hand polished natural lacquer, case included, new 2003.

MSR	$1,095		$825	$550	$350

Add $125 for Element electronics (Model 22557). Add $130 for Quantum II EQ electronics (Model 22564). Add $250 for I-Beam Duet electronics (Model 21956).

Studio CW (Model 21796) - similar to the Studio, except has a single cutaway, new 2003.

MSR	$1,195		$900	$600	$375

Add $125 for Element electronics (Model 22595). Add $130 for Quantum II EQ electronics (Model 22601). Add $250 for I-Beam Duet electronics (Model 21932).

ACOUSTIC: M SERIES

M6 CEDAR GT (MODEL 22342) - full sized body, solid cedar top, mahogany back and sides, 14/21 fret fingerboard with dot inlay, tortoise pickguard, 3-per-side chrome tuners, laquer finished Natural gloss top, new 2003.

MSR	$489		$370	$245	$160

Add $100 for Quantum EQ electronics (Model 22359). Add $135 for Element electronics (Model 22366).

M6 GLOSS (MODEL 22373) - full sized body, solid cedar top, mahogany back and sides, 14/21 fret fingerboard with dot inlay, tortoise pickguard, 3-per-side chrome tuners, high gloss laquer Natural finish, current mfg.

MSR	$559		$420	$280	$190

Add $100 for Quantum EQ electronics (Model 22380). Add $135 for Element electronics (Model 22397).

M6 Gloss Left (Model 22434) - similar to the M6 Gloss, except in left-handed configuration, current mfg.

MSR	$615		$465	$310	$205

Add $100 for Quantum EQ electronics (Model 22441). Add $135 for Element electronics (Model 22458).

M6 SPRUCE (MODEL 1842) - similar to M6 Gloss, except has a semi-gloss lacquer finish, disc 2001.

			$350	$225	$149

Last MSR was $469.

M12 GLOSS (MODEL 22403) - similar to the M6 Gloss, except in 12-string configuration, current mfg.

MSR	$639		$480	$320	$210

Add $100 for Quantum EQ electronics (Model 22410). Add $135 for Element electronics (Model 22427).

ACOUSTIC: S SERIES

S 6 (MODEL 22229) - dreadnought style bound body, solid cedar top, black pickguard, round soundhole, multi stripe rosette, wild cherry back/sides, mahogany neck, 14/21-fret rosewood fingerboard with pearl dot inlay, rosewood bridge with white black dot pins, blackface peghead with screened logo, 3-per-side chrome tuners, available in Natural finish, mfg. 1993-current.

MSR	$419		$315	$205	$135

Add $100 for Quantum EQ electronics. Add $135 for Element electronics.

This model was previously known as the 10257.

S 6 Left (Model 22250) - similar to the S 6, except in left-handed configuration, current mfg.

MSR	$459		$345	$220	$145

Add $100 for Quantum EQ electronics. Add $135 for Element electronics.

S6+ CEDAR (MODEL 10318) - similar to S6, except has a solid Cedar top. "+ version" uses a special staining process that results in a rich Violin Brown finish, disc 2002.

			$315	$195	$125

Last MSR was $417.

S6+ Spruce (Model 10370) - similar to S6, except has solid Spruce top, disc 2002.

			$325	$215	$135

Last MSR was $435.

S6+ Burst (Model 1323) - similar to S6, except has Sunburst finish, disc 2002.

			$365	$235	$150

Last MSR was $485.

S6 + Cutaway Burst (Model 2160) - similar to S6 + Burst, except has a single cutaway, available in Sunburst finish, disc 2002.

			$435	$285	$185

Last MSR was $580.

S 12 - similar to S 6, except has 12-strings, 6-per-side tuners, disc. 1998.

			N/A	$240	$125

Last MSR was $450.

S6+ CEDAR GT (MODEL 22281) - similar to the S6+, except has a laquer finish with a gloss top, new 2003.

MSR	$479		$360	$240	$160

Add $100 for Quantum EQ electronics. Add $135 for Element electronics.

GRADING		100%	EXCELLENT	AVERAGE

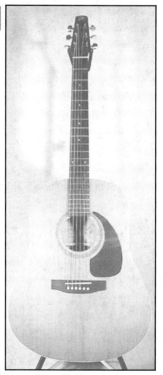

S6+ Cedar GT Left (Model 22311) - similar to the S6+ Cedar GT, except in left-handed configuration, new 2003.

MSR	$516		$390	$260	$175

Add $100 for Quantum EQ electronics. Add $135 for Element electronics.

S6+ BURST GT - similar to the S6+, except has a Sunburst finish, new 2003.

MSR	$489		$370	$245	$160

Add $100 for Quantum EQ electronics. Add $135 for Element electronics.

S6+ CUTAWAY CEDAR (MODEL 22465) - similar to S6, except has a single cutaway, current mfg.

MSR	$529		$400	$265	$175

Add $100 for Quantum EQ electronics. Add $135 for Element electronics. Add $150 for Quantum II electronics.
This model was previously known as the Model 2214.

S6+ Cutaway Cedar Left (Model 22502) - similar to the S6+ Cutaway Cedar, except in left-handed configuration, current mfg.

MSR	$579		$435	$290	$185

Add $100 for Quantum EQ electronics. Add $135 for Element electronics. Add $150 for Quantum II electronics.

S6+ Cutaway Cedar GT (Model 22540) - similar to the S6+ Cutaway Cedar except has a gloss top and Quantum II electronics, new 2003.

MSR	$799		$599	$400	$250

S 6 DELUXE - dreadnought style bound body, solid spruce top, black pickguard, round soundhole, multi stripe rosette, wild cherry back/sides, mahogany neck, 14/21-fret rosewood fingerboard with pearl dot inlay, rosewood bridge with white black dot pins, blackface peghead with screened logo, 3-per-side chrome tuners, available in Honeyburst or Natural finishes, disc. 1998.

		N/A	$225	$125

Last MSR was $435.

Seagull S6 + Cedar courtesy Gordo and Betty Orth

This model has single round cutaway or left-hand version as an option.

S 12 Deluxe - similar to S 6 Deluxe, except has 12-strings, 6-per-side tuners, disc. 1998.

		N/A	$225	$150

Last MSR was $495.

S 12+ (MODEL 22106) - similar to S6+, except in 12-string configuration, current mfg.

MSR	$489		$370	$245	$160

Add $100 for Quantum EQ electronics. Add $135 for Element electronics.

S6+ Folk Left (Model 22137) - similar to the S12+, except in left-handed configuration, mfg. 1999-current.

MSR	$539		$405	$270	$175

Add $100 for Quantum EQ electronics. Add $135 for Element electronics.

S6+ FOLK (MODEL 2474) - Folk style body, solid cedar top, 3-layer wild cherry back, wild cherry sides, silver leaf maple neck, 14/21 fret fingerboard with dot inlay, 3-per-side chrome tuners, available in Natural semi-gloss lacquer finish, mfg. 1999-current.

MSR	$429		$325	$215	$140

Add $100 for Quantum EQ electronics. Add $135 for Element electronics.

S6+ Folk Left (Model 2511) - similar to the S6+ Folk, except in left-handed configuration, mfg. 1999-current.

MSR	$469		$350	$235	$150

Add $100 for Quantum EQ electronics. Add $135 for Element electronics.

S GRAND (MODEL 8728) - grand sized body, solid cedar top, 3-layer wild cherry back, wild cherry sides, silver leaf maple neck, 14/21 fret fingerboard with dot inlay, 3-per-side chrome tuners, available in Natural semi-gloss lacquer finish, mfg. 2002-current.

MSR	$419		$315	$205	$135

Add $100 for Quantum EQ electronics. Add $135 for Element electronics.

S 6 MAHOGANY (MODEL 1767) - dreadnought style bound body, solid cedar top, black pickguard, round soundhole, multi stripe rosette, mahogany back/sides/neck, 14/21-fret rosewood fingerboard with pearl dot inlay, rosewood bridge with white black dot pins, blackface peghead with screened logo, 3-per-side chrome tuners, available in Natural finish, disc.

		$350	$175	$125

Last MSR was $450.

This model has left-handed version as an option (Model 1804).

S

GRADING	100%	EXCELLENT	AVERAGE

S6+ SPRUCE (MODEL 22199) - similar to the S6+, except has a solid spruce top, current mfg.

	MSR	$449		$340	$225	$145

Add $100 for Quantum EQ electronics. Add $135 for Element electronics.

S 6 FLAME MAPLE CUTAWAY (MODEL 2375) - round cutaway dreadnought style bound body, solid spruce top, round soundhole, herringbone rosette, maple back/sides, mahogany neck, 21-fret ebony fingerboard with offset dot inlay, ebony bridge with white black dot pins, bound flame maple veneered peghead with screened logo, 3-per-side gold tuners, available in Blackburst or Natural finishes, disc.

$695	$375	$275

Last MSR was $895.

S 6 *Flame Maple Micro EQ* (Model 2399) - similar to S 6 Flame Maple, except features piezo bridge pickup, onboard EQ, disc.

$795	$550	$425

Last MSR was $1,084.

SM6 (M6 Gloss) (MODEL 1927) - round cutaway dreadnought style bound body, solid spruce top, black pickguard, round soundhole, multi stripe rosette, mahogany back/sides/neck, 14/21-fret rosewood fingerboard with pearl dot inlay, rosewood bridge with white black dot pins, blackface peghead with screened logo, 3-per-side chrome tuners, available in Natural finish, disc.

$425	$250	$175

Last MSR was $537.

SM 12 (M12 Spruce) (Model 1972) - similar to SM 6, 12-strings, 6-per-side tuners, disc.

$495	$250	$200

Last MSR was $620.

SEBRING
Instruments currently built in Korea. Distributed by V.M.I. Industries of Brea, California.

Sebring instruments are designed towards the intermediate level guitar student.

SEDONA
Instruments currently built in Asia. Distributed by V.M.I. Industries of Brea, California.

Sedona offers a range of instruments that appeal to the beginning guitarist and entry level player.

SEGOVIA
Instruments currently produced in Asia. Distributed by the L.A. Guitar Works of Reseda, California.

Segovia acoustic dreadnought guitars are offered with solid headstocks, spruce tops, and 3-per-side chrome tuning machines.

SEKOVA
Instruments previously produced in Japan.

Sekova brand instruments were distributed in the U.S. market by the U.S. Musical Merchandise Corporation of New York, New York, (Source: Michael Wright, *Guitar Stories,* Volume One).

HENRI SELMER & CO.
Instruments previously built in Paris, France between 1931 to 1952.

Between 1931 and 1932, Mario Maccaferri designed and built a series of instruments for the French Selmer company. They were originally referred to as the "modele Concert," and featured a "D" shaped soundhole. Although they were used by such notables as Django Reinhardt, a dispute between the company and Maccaferri led to a short production run. In the two years (1931-1932) that Maccaferri was with Selmer, he estimated that perhaps 200 guitars were built. After Macaferri left the business arrangement, the Selmer company continued to produce acoustic guitar models that featured an oval soundhole and a longer scale. All in all, an estimated 950 guitars were built, (Source: Paul Hostetter, Guitares Maurice Dupont).

SEXAUER
Instruments currently hand built in Petaluma, CA. Previously built in Sausalito, CA 1979-1999, and in Vancouver (British Columbia), Canada from 1967 through 1977.

Luthier Bruce Sexauer has been handcrafting contemporary flattop acoustic guitars since 1967. For the last several years, Sexauer has become increasingly interested in Archtop guitars, and in addition to his quality carved tops has become well-known for his highly innovative **Coo'stik Dominator** (a successful interpretation of the Selmer/Macaferri concept).

S

ACOUSTIC

While Sexauer continues to build true custom guitars, he also offers several standard models. The noted prices represent the simplest trim level, and most customers choose to indulge themselves somewhat more. The FT-15 ($6,100) is a concert sized flattop model, while the FT-16 ($6,000) is full sized. Sexauer offers a jazz-style hand carved archtop model in both a 16" body width, and 17" body width (JZ-17), and the prices range from $6,000-$10,000 for most models. For $12,500 it will build an instrument that "would intimidate almost anybody. His Coo'stik Dominator and the Blu'stik Harmonizer are also available.

GRADING	100%	EXCELLENT	AVERAGE

SHANTI
Instruments currently built in Avery, California.

Luthier Michael Hornick has been handcrafting acoustic guitars under the Shanti trademark for the past several years. All guitars are designed with input from the commissioning player, so specifications on woods and inlay work will vary. Contact Michael Hornick for further details.

Hornick produces about 9 or 10 guitars a year. In addition, Hornick hosts a mandolin-building course each year at the RockyGrass Festival in Lyons, Colorado; and has been affiliated with the Troubadour singer/songwriter competition in Telluride, Colorado for a good number of years.

SHENANDOAH
Instruments previously assembled from imported Japanese components in Nazareth, Pennsylvania between 1983 to 1996. Distributed by the C.F. Martin Guitar Company of Nazarath, Pennsylvania.

Shenandoah production began in 1983. Initially viewed as a way to offer entry level models for Martin dealers, Shenandoah models featured Japanese-built unfinished body and neck kits imported to the Martin plant for final assembly and finishing. However, Shenandoah guitars are not as ornate, and may feature different construction methods than the Martin models.

While this may have been cost effective to some degree, the labor intensive work of assembly and finishing at the Martin plant led Martin to considering producing the whole guitar in Nazareth – which led to the introduction of Martin's U.S.-built **Road** and **1** Series.

Instruments were produced in Japan and assembled in the U.S. between 1983 to 1993; full Japanese production was featured between 1994 to 1996. Shenandoah model codes add a -32 suffix after a Martin-style model designation. Thus, a D-1832 is Shenandoah's version of a D-18. Models carrying a CS prefix designation indicate a custom model, usually fancier than the standard version (custom models were built in limited runs of 25 instruments).

ACOUSTIC

Some models have a factory installed thinline bridge pickup. Most models feature a tortoise shell pickguard, and laminated back/sides.

C-20 - classic style, solid spruce top, round soundhole, wooden bound body, wooden inlay rosette, rosewood back/sides, nato neck, 12/19-fret ebonized rosewood fingerboard, ebonized rosewood tied bridge, rosewood peghead veneer, 3-per-side gold tuners with pearl buttons, available in Natural or Yellow Stained Top finishes.

	N/A	$535	$370
		Last MSR was $1,280.	

This model had no factory installed pickup.

D-1832 - dreadnought style, solid spruce top, round soundhole, tortoise pickguard, 3-stripe bound body/rosette, mahogany back/sides, nato neck, 14/20-fret rosewood fingerboard with pearl dot inlay, rosewood bridge with black pins, rosewood peghead veneer, 3-per-side chrome tuners, available in Natural finish.

	N/A	$450	$250
		Last MSR was $1,075.	

D-1932 - similar to D-1832, except has quilted mahogany veneer back/sides.

	N/A	$625	$425

Add $20 for 12-string version (D12-1932).

		Last MSR was $1,320.	

D-2832 - dreadnought style, solid spruce top, round soundhole, tortoise pickguard, 3-stripe bound body/rosette, rosewood back/sides, nato neck, 14/20-fret ebonized rosewood fingerboard with pearl dot inlay, ebonized rosewood bridge with white black dot pins, rosewood peghead veneer, 3-per-side chrome tuners, available in Natural finish.

	N/A	$550	$350

Add $75 for 12-string version of this model (D12-2832).

		Last MSR was $1,125.	

HD-2832 - similar to D-2832, except has herringbone purfling.

	N/A	$600	$400

D-3532 - similar to D-2832, except has bound fingerboard.

	N/A	$550	$400
		Last MSR was $1,175.	

D-4132 - similar to D-2832, except has abalone bound body/rosette, bound fingerboard with abalone hexagon inlay, white abalone dot bridge pins, bound peghead, gold tuners.

	N/A	$800	$575
		Last MSR was $1,750.	

S

GRADING	100%	EXCELLENT	AVERAGE

D-6032 - similar to D-2832, tortoise binding, except has bird's-eye maple back/sides.

N/A $550 $375
Last MSR was $1,320.

D-6732 - dreadnought style body, solid spruce top, round soundhole, tortoise pickguard, tortoise binding, 3-stripe rosette, quilted ash back/sides, nato neck, 14/20-fret bound ebonized rosewood neck with pearl dot inlay, pearl vine/diamond inlay at 12th fret, ebonized rosewood bridge with white black dot pins, bound peghead with quilted ash veneer, 3-per-side gold tuners with ebony buttons, available in Natural finish.

N/A $625 $475
Last MSR was $1,490.

SE-2832 - single round cutaway folk style, solid spruce top, round soundhole, 3-stripe bound body/rosette, rosewood back/sides, nato neck, 14/21-fret bound ebonized rosewood fingerboard with pearl diamond inlay, ebonized rosewood bridge with white black dot pins, rosewood veneer peghead, 3-per-side chrome tuners, active EQ with volume/treble/mid/bass slider control, available in Natural or Sunburst Top finishes.

N/A $600 $450
Last MSR was $1,470.

SE-6032 - similar to SE-2832, except has tortoise binding, bird's-eye maple back/sides/peghead veneer, pearl tuner buttons, available in Burgundy Burst, Dark Sunburst, or Natural finishes.

N/A $675 $525
Last MSR was $1,540.

000-2832 - folk style, solid spruce top, round soundhole, tortoise shell pickguard, 3-stripe bound body/rosette, rosewood back/sides, nato neck, 14/20-fret ebonized rosewood fingerboard with pearl dot inlay, ebonized rosewood bridge with white black dot pins, rosewood peghead veneer with abalone torch inlay, 3-per-side chrome tuners, available in Natural finish.

N/A $550 $350
Last MSR was $1,210.

SHERWOOD
See chapter on House Brands.

This trademark has been identified as a House Brand of Montgomery Wards, (Source: Willie G. Moseley, *Stellas & Stratocasters*).

SHO-BUD
Also Sho-Bro. Instruments previously built in the U.S. during circa early 1970s. Distributed through the Gretsch Guitar company catalog between 1972 to 1975; possibly as late as 1979.

While this company is best known for their pedal steel guitars, the company did produce a number of acoustic guitars. Sho-Bud and Sho-Bro guitars were designed by Shot Jackson (known for his Sho-Bud pedal steel guitars). Two models appear in the Gretsch catalogs of the early 1970s: The **Sho Bro**, a resonator with a single cutaway body and dot fingerboard inlays; and the **Sho Bud**, a non-cutaway model with inlays similar to the Sho-Bud lap steels (the four suits of the card deck), (Information courtesy John Brinkmann, Waco Vintage Instruments; and John Sheridan).

ACOUSTIC

Sho-Bro resonator guitars in the early 1970s featured a 17" body (4 5/8" body depth) with maple back and sides, bound rosewood fingerboard, 3-per-side polished plated geared tuners, metal resonator, 2 grill covered soundholes. The **Model 6031 Hawaiian** model has a squared neck, and playing card suites fingerboard inlays; the **Model 6030 Spanish** model has a rounded neck and "thumbprint" fingerboard inlays.

Later Sho-Bud acoustics have spruce tops and mahogany necks. The **Club (Model 7720)** features mahogany sides, and a 2-piece back; the **Diamond (Model 7722)** features rosewood sides and the 2-piece back. The **Heart (Model 7724)** has rosewood back and sides, mother-of-pearl inlays, and abalone purfling; the **Spade (Model 7726)** features a rosewood fingerboard, ebony bridge, and abalone bridge pins. The aptly named **Grand Slam (Model 7728)** has jacaranda back and sides, and an inlaid heel plate.

Sho-Bud and Sho-Bro acoustic guitars turn up infrequently at guitar shows. Average prices run from $800 to $1,200; buyers in the market have more control in the buy/sell arena by choking up on their wallets similar to big league baseball players choking up on their bats during a big ball game!

SHUTT
Instruments previously built in Topeka, Kansas circa 1900s.

While not much information is known about the Shutt instruments, Mr. Jim Reynolds of Independence, Missouri is currently researching materials for an upcoming book.

SIGMA
Instruments previously assembled in Asia, with final finishing/inspection in Nazareth, Pennsylvania. Distributed by the C.F. Martin Guitar Company of Nazareth, Pennsylvania.

In 1970, the Martin Guitar Company expanded its product line by introducing the Sigma line. The instruments begin their assembly in Japan, and then are shipped in to Pennsylvania where the Martin company can oversee the final finishing and setup. Sigma guitars are great introductory models to the classic Martin design, (Source: Michael Wright, *Guitar Stories*, Volume One).

GRADING	100%	EXCELLENT	AVERAGE

ACOUSTIC: CLASSICAL MODELS

CS-1 - classic style, spruce top, round soundhole, bound body, wooden inlay rosette, mahogany back/sides/neck, 20/19-fret ebonized fingerboard/tied bridge, 3-per-side chrome tuners, available in Antique Stain finish, disc. 1996.

	N/A	$80	$50

Last MSR was $210.

CS-1 ST - classic style, solid spruce top, round soundhole, bound body, wood inlay rosette, mahogany back/sides/neck, 14/19-fret ebonized fingerboard, ebonized tied bridge, 3-per-side chrome tuners with nylon buttons, available in Natural finish, mfg. 1994-96.

	N/A	$145	$85

Last MSR was $335.

CS-2 - classic style, spruce top, round soundhole, bound body, wooden inlay rosette, mahogany back/sides/neck, 20/19-fret ebonized fingerboard/tied bridge, 3-per-side chrome tuners, available in Natural finish, disc. 1994.

	N/A	$130	$80

Last MSR was $295.

CS-4 - classic style, spruce top, round soundhole, bound body, wooden inlay rosette, mahogany back/sides/neck, 12/19-fret rosewood fingerboard, rosewood tied bridge, rosewood peghead veneer, 3-per-side chrome tuners with pearl buttons, available in Antique finish, disc. 1996.

	N/A	$140	$85

Last MSR was $340.

CR-8 - classic style, solid spruce top, round soundhole, bound body, wooden inlay rosette, rosewood back/sides, mahogany neck, 12/19-fret ebonized fingerboard/tied bridge, 3-per-side gold tuners with pearl buttons, available in Natural finish, disc. 1996.

	N/A	$225	$150

Last MSR was $570.

**Sho-Bud The Club Model
courtesy The Music Shoppe**

ACOUSTIC: DREADNOUGHT (DM) MODELS

DM-1 - dreadnought style, spruce top, round soundhole, black pickguard, bound body, 3-stripe rosette, mahogany back/sides/neck, 14/20-fret ebonized fingerboard with pearl dot inlay, ebonized bridge with black pins, 3-per-side chrome tuners, available in Natural or Black finishes, disc. 1996.

	N/A	$100	$65

Last MSR was $260.

Add $25 for 12-string version (DM12-1).

DM-1 ST - dreadnought style, solid spruce top, round soundhole, tortoise pickguard, 3-stripe bound body/rosette, mahogany back/sides/neck, 14/20-fret ebonized fingerboard with pearl dot inlay, ebonized bridge with black white dot pins, abalone logo peghead inlay, 3-per-side chrome tuners, available in Natural finish, mfg. 1994-96.

	N/A	$150	$85

Last MSR was $345.

DR-1 ST - similar to DM-1 ST, except has rosewood back/sides, mfg. 1994-96.

	N/A	$140	$85

Last MSR was $375.

DM12-1 ST - similar to DM-1 ST, except has 12-strings, 6-per-side tuners, mfg. 1994-96.

	N/A	$185	$135

Last MSR was $410.

DM-2 - dreadnought style, spruce top, round soundhole, tortoise shell pickguard, 3-stripe bound body/rosette, mahogany back/sides/neck, 14/20-fret rosewood fingerboard with pearl dot inlay, rosewood bridge with black white dot pins, 3-per-side chrome tuners, available in Natural finish, disc. 1994.

	N/A	$150	$100

Add $45 for 12-string version (DM12-2).

Last MSR was $375.

DM-2E/WH - similar to DM-2, except has ebonized fingerboard/bridge, acoustic pickup, 3-band EQ with volume control, available in White finish, disc. 1994.

	N/A	$275	$175

Add $25 for single round cutaway, white black dot bridge pins. Available in Black finish (DM-2CE/B).

Last MSR was $630.

**Sigma CS-1st
courtesy Martin Guitar**

GRADING	100%	EXCELLENT	AVERAGE

DM-4 - dreadnought style, spruce top, round soundhole, black pickguard, 3-stripe bound body/rosette, mahogany back/sides/neck, 14/20-fret ebonized fingerboard with pearl dot inlay, pearl horizontal teardrop inlay at 12th fret, ebonized bridge with black white dot pins, rosewood peghead veneer, 3-per-side chrome tuners, available in Black or Natural finishes, disc. 1996.

	N/A	$170	$115

Last MSR was $430.

Add $30 for Black finish. Add $40 for 12-string version (DM12-4). Add $40 for left handed version (DM-4L). Subtract $20 for stained mahogany top (DM-4M). Add $45 for herringbone bound body/rosette (DM-4H). Add $45 for Antique and Tobacco Sunburst finishes (DM-4Y and DM-4S).

In 1994, Antique finish (DM-4Y) was discontinued.

DM-4C - similar to DM-4, except has single round cutaway, mfg. 1994-96.

	N/A	$200	$140

Last MSR was $505.

Add $45 for Black finish.

DM-4CV - similar to DM-4, except has venetian cutaway, available in Violin finish.

	N/A	$185	$120

Last MSR was $560.

DM-4C/3B - similar to DM-4, except has single round cutaway, acoustic pickup, 3-band EQ with volume control, available in Natural finish, disc. 1994.

	N/A	$300	$235

Last MSR was $715.

DM12-4 - similar to DM-4, except has 12-strings, 6-per-side tuners, mfg. 1994-96.

	N/A	$185	$120

Last MSR was $470.

DM-18 - dreadnought style, solid spruce top, round soundhole, tortoise pickguard, 3-stripe bound body/rosette, mahogany back/sides/neck, 14/20-fret ebonized fingerboard with pearl dot inlay, ebonized bridge with black white dot pins, abalone logo peghead inlay, 3-per-side chrome tuners, available in Natural finish, disc. 1996.

	N/A	$225	$150

Last MSR was $525.

ACOUSTIC: DREADNOUGHT (DR, DT, & DV) MODELS

DR-2 - similar to DM-2, except has rosewood back/sides, ebonized fingerboard/bridge, disc. 1994.

	N/A	$250	$150

Last MSR was $510.

DR-4H - similar to DM-4, except has tortoise pickguard, herringbone bound body/rosette, rosewood back/sides, available in Natural finish.

	N/A	$250	$150

Last MSR was $510.

DR-28 - dreadnought style, solid spruce top, round soundhole, tortoise shell pickguard, 3-stripe bound body/rosette, rosewood back/sides, mahogany neck, 14/20-fret ebonized fingerboard with pearl dot inlay, ebonized bridge with white abalone dot pins, rosewood veneered peghead with abalone logo inlay, 3-per-side chrome tuners, available in Natural finish, disc. 1996.

	N/A	$350	$225

Last MSR was $620.

DR-28H - similar to DR-28, except has herringbone bound body, pearl diamond fingerboard inlay.

	N/A	$400	$250

Last MSR was $670.

Add $35 for 12-string version (DR12-28H), mfg. 1993-96.

DR-35 - dreadnought style, solid spruce top, round soundhole, tortoise shell pickguard, 5-stripe bound body/rosette, rosewood back/sides, mahogany neck, 14/20-fret bound ebonized fingerboard with pearl dot inlay, ebonized bridge with white abalone dot pins, bound rosewood veneered peghead with abalone logo inlay, 3-per-side chrome tuners, available in Natural finish, disc. 1996.

	N/A	$325	$215

Last MSR was $655.

DR-41 - dreadnought style, solid spruce top, round soundhole, tortoise shell pickguard, abalone bound body/rosette, rosewood back/sides, mahogany neck, 14/20-fret bound ebonized fingerboard with abalone hexagon inlay, ebonized bridge with white abalone dot pins, bound rosewood veneered peghead with abalone logo inlay, 3-per-side chrome tuners, available in Natural finish, disc. 1996.

	N/A	$425	$250

Last MSR was $725.

DR-45 - dreadnought style, solid spruce top, round soundhole, tortoise shell pickguard, abalone bound body/rosette, rosewood back/sides, mahogany neck, 14/20-fret abalone bound rosewood fingerboard with abalone hexagon inlay, rosewood bridge with white abalone dot pins, abalone bound rosewood veneered peghead with abalone logo inlay, 3-per-side gold tuners, available in Natural finish, mfg. 1994-96.

	N/A	$850	$600

Last MSR was $1,745.

GRADING	100%	EXCELLENT	AVERAGE

DT-4N - similar to DM-4, except has chestnut back/sides/peghead veneer, available in Violin finish.

	N/A	$250	$150

Last MSR was $495.

Add $35 for Violin finish (DT-4). Add $75 for 12-string version (DT12-4).

DV-4 - similar to DM-4, except has ovankol back/sides, available in Antique finish, disc. 1994.

	N/A	$275	$160

Last MSR was $595.

ACOUSTIC: MISC. MODELS

**Sigma GCS-1
courtesy Martin Guitar**

FD-16M - folk style, spruce top, round soundhole, black pickguard, bound body, 3-stripe rosette, mahogany back/sides/neck, 14/20-fret ebonized fingerboard with pearl dot inlay, ebonized bridge with black pins, 3-per-side chrome tuners, available in Natural finish, mfg. 1994-96.

	N/A	$225	$125

Last MSR was $460.

FDM-1 - similar to DM-1, except has folk style body, mfg. 1994-96.

	N/A	$100	$60

Last MSR was $255.

GCS-1 - similar to DM-1, except has grand concert style body, disc. 1996.

	N/A	$100	$65

Last MSR was $260.

GCS-2 - similar to DM-2, except has grand concert style body, disc. 1994.

	N/A	$175	$100

Last MSR was $420.

GCS-4 - grand concert style, spruce top, round soundhole, black pickguard, 5-stripe bound body/rosette, mahogany back/sides/neck, 14/20-fret ebonized fingerboard with pearl dot inlay, horizontal teardrop inlay at 12th fret, ebonized bridge with black white dot pins, rosewood peghead veneer, 3-per-side chrome tuners, available in Natural finish, disc. 1996.

	N/A	$200	$125

Last MSR was $395.

GCS-4C - similar to GCS-4, except has single round cutaway, disc. 1994.

	N/A	$250	$150

Last MSR was $550.

GCS-4C/3B - similar to GCS-4, except has single round cutaway, acoustic pickup, 3-band EQ with volume control, disc. 1994.

	N/A	$350	$225

Last MSR was $715.

000-18M - auditorium style, solid spruce top, round soundhole, tortoise pickguard, 3-stripe bound body, 5-stripe rosette, mahogany back/sides/neck, 14/20-fret ebonized fingerboard with pearl dot inlay, ebonized bridge with black white dot pins, rosewood peghead veneer with abalone logo inlay, 3-per-side chrome tuners, available in Antique finish, mfg. 1993-96.

	N/A	$250	$140

Last MSR was $525.

000-18MC/3B - similar to 000-18M, except has venetian cutaway, acoustic pickup, 3-band EQ with volume control, disc. 1994.

	N/A	$450	$250

Last MSR was $940.

SE-1 - single round cutaway folk style, spruce top, round soundhole, 3-stripe bound body/rosette, mahogany back/sides/neck, 22-fret bound ebonized fingerboard with pearl dot inlay, ebonized bridge with white black dot pins, rosewood peghead veneer with abalone logo inlay, 3-per-side chrome tuners, acoustic pickup, volume/2-band EQ control, available in Black or Natural finishes, mfg. 1994-96.

	N/A	$275	$185

Last MSR was $565.

SE-18/2BC - single round cutaway folk style, spruce top, round soundhole, 3-stripe bound body/rosette, mahogany back/sides/neck, 22-fret bound ebonized fingerboard with pearl dot inlay, ebonized bridge with white black dot pins, rosewood peghead veneer with abalone logo inlay, 3-per-side chrome tuners, acoustic pickup, 2-band EQ with chorus effect, volume control, available in Black, Natural, Red, or Tobacco Sunburst finishes, mfg. 1993-94.

	N/A	$425	$225

Last MSR was $905.

S

GRADING	100%	EXCELLENT	AVERAGE

SE-18/3B - similar to SE-18/2BC, except has 3-band EQ with volume control, available in Natural or Tobacco Sunburst finishes, mfg. 1993-94.

	N/A	$375	$200

Last MSR was $860.

ACOUSTIC BASS

STB-M/E - jumbo style, spruce top, round soundhole, tortoise pickguard, 5-stripe bound body/rosette, maple back/sides/neck, 15/21-fret ebonized fingerboard with pearl dot inlay, ebonized strings through bridge with pearl dot inlay, maple peghead veneer, 2-per-side chrome tuners, acoustic pickup, 3-band EQ with volume control, available in Natural finish, mfg. 1993-96.

	N/A	$575	$375

Last MSR was $1,145.

STB-R/E - similar to STB-M, except has black pickguard, rosewood back/sides.

	N/A	$600	$400

Last MSR was $1,160.

STB-M - similar to STB-M/E, except has no acoustic pickup, 3-band EQ with volume control, mfg. 1994-96.

	N/A	$375	$250

Last MSR was $785.

Add $15 for black pickguard, rosewood back/sides.

SIGNET
Instruments previously produced in Japan circa early 1970s.

The Signet trademark was a brand name used by U.S. importers Ampeg/Selmer, (Source: Michael Wright, *Guitar Storie,s* Volume One).

SILVERTONE
See chapter on House Brands. Instruments currently produced in Asia and distributed by Samick.

This trademark has been identified as a House Brand owned and used by Sears and Roebuck between 1941 to 1970. There was no company or factory; Sears owned the name and applied it to various products from such manufacturers as Harmony, Valco, Danelectro, and Kay. Sears and Roebuck acquired Harmony in 1916 to control its respectable ukulele production. Harmony generally sold around 40 percent of its guitar production to Sears. The following is a word of caution: Just because it says Silvertone, do not automatically assume it is a Danelectro! In fact, study the guitar to determine possible origin (Harmony, Valco and Kay were originally built in Illinois, Danelectro in New Jersey; so all were U.S. However, mid 1960s models were built in Japan by Teisco, as well!). Best of all, play it! If it looks good, and sounds okay – it was meant to be played. As most Silvertones were sold either through the catalog or in a store, they will generally be entry level quality instruments.

Certain Silvertone models have garnered some notoriety, such as the Danelectro-produced combination of guitar and amp-in-case. Sears also marketed the Teisco company's TRG-1 (or TRE-100) electric guitar with amp built in! This guitar has a six-on-a-side "Silvertone" headstock, and a single cutaway pregnant Telecaster body design (the small built-in speaker is in the tummy). Harmony produced a number of electric hollowbody guitars (like the Sovereign) for the Silvertone label; Kay also offered a version of their Thin Twin model as well as arch top models.

Today, Silvertone guitars are being produced by Samick. They have a wide variety of acoustic models form dreadnoughts to classicals. Prices are targeted to those who are entry to mid level guitar players. Paul Stanley of Kiss is an endorser of Silvertone now (c. 2002), and has an entire line of guitars including an acoustic model.

SIMON & PATRICK
Instruments currently built in La Patrie, Quebec, Canada since 1985. Simon & Patrick Acoustic Guitars are distributed by La Si Do, Inc., of St. Laurent, Canada.

Robert Godin set up a custom guitar shop in Montreal called Harmonilab in 1968. Harmonilab quickly became known for its excellent work and musicians were coming from as far away as Quebec City to have their guitars adjusted.

Although Harmonilab's business was flourishing, Robert was full of ideas for the design and construction of acoustic guitars. So in 1972 the Norman Guitar Company was born. From the beginning the Norman guitars showed signs of the innovations that Godin would eventually bring to the guitar market.

By 1978 Norman guitars had become quite successful in Canada and France. In 1980 Godin introduced the Seagull guitar. With many innovations like a bolt-on neck, pointed headstock and a handmade solid top, the Seagull was designed for an ease of play for the entry level to intermediate guitar player. Godin borrowed the finishing idea that was used on fine violins (a satin-finish lacquer), and applied it to the acoustic guitar.

Acceptance of this new guitar spread, and by 1985 La Si Do was incorporated and the factory in La Patrie expanded to meet the growing demand. In 1985 Godin introduced the Simon & Patrick line (named after his two sons) for people interested in a more traditional instrument. Simon & Patrick guitars still maintained a number of Seagull innovations. For full company history, see GODIN.

ACOUSTIC: S&P SERIES

S&P 6 CEDAR (MODEL 2719) - solid cedar top, wild cherry back and sides, rosewood fingerboard and bridge, 3-per-side headstock, lacquer finish, current mfg.

MSR	$395		$300	$180	$125

Add $150 for B-Band NF-1 EQ electronics (Model 15276). Add $250 for B-Band NF-2 EQ electronics (Model 15283).

S&P 6 Cedar Left (Model 2757) - similar to the S&P, except in left-handed configuration, current mfg.

MSR	$435		$325	$200	$135

Add $150 for B-Band NF-1 EQ electronics (Model 15375). Add $250 for B-Band NF-2 EQ electronics (Model 15382).

GRADING		100%	EXCELLENT	AVERAGE

S&P 6 Cedar Tobaccoburst (Model 13616) - similar to the S&P, except has a Tobaccoburst finish, current mfg.

MSR	$485		$370	$225	$150

Add $150 for B-Band NF-1 EQ electronics (Model 15290). Add $250 for B-Band NF-2 EQ electronics (Model 15306).

S&P 6 Cedar Cutaway (Model 2559) - similar to S&P 6, except has a single cutaway, current mfg.

MSR	$520		$390	$250	$175

Add $150 for B-Band NF-1 EQ electronics (Model 15177). Add $250 for B-Band NF-2 EQ electronics (Model 15283).

S&P 12 CEDAR (MODEL 2733) - similar to S&P 6, except as a 12-string model with 6-on-a-side tuners, current mfg.

MSR	$462		$350	$225	$150

Add $150 for B-Band NF-1 EQ electronics (Model 15351). Add $250 for B-Band NF-2 EQ electronics (Model 15368). Add $40 for left-handed configuration (Model 2771).

S&P 6 CEDAR MAHOGANY (MODEL 2870) - similar to the S&P 6, only has mahogany back and sides instead of wild-cherry, and has a satin lacquer finish, current mfg.

MSR	$450		$395	$300	$225

Add $150 for B-Band NF-1 EQ electronics (Model 15450). Add $250 for B-Band NF-2 EQ electronics (Model 15467). Add $40 for left-handed configuration (Model 2894).

S&P 6 SPRUCE (MODEL 2795) - similar to the S&P, except has a solid spruce top, current mfg.

MSR	$414		$315	$190	$130

Add $150 for B-Band NF-1 EQ electronics (Model 15375). Add $250 for B-Band NF-2 EQ electronics (Model 15184).

S&P 6 Spruce Cutaway (Model 2580) - similar to S&P Spruce 6, except has a single cutaway, current mfg.

MSR	$545		$410	$260	$180

Add $150 for B-Band NF-1 EQ electronics (Model 15191). Add $250 for B-Band NF-2 EQ electronics (Model 15207).

S&P 12 SPRUCE (MODEL 2733) - similar to S&P Spruce 6, except as a 12-string model with 6-on-a-side tuners, current mfg.

MSR	$483		$365	$225	$150

Add $150 for B-Band NF-1 EQ electronics (Model 15436). Add $250 for B-Band NF-2 EQ electronics (Model 15443).

S&P 6 SPRUCE MAHOGANY (MODEL 2917) - similar to the S&P Spruce 6, only has mahogany back and sides instead of wild-cherry, and has a satin lacquer finish, current mfg.

MSR	$469		$350	$220	$145

Add $150 for B-Band NF-1 EQ electronics (Model 15498). Add $250 for B-Band NF-2 EQ electronics (Model 15504). Add $40 for left-handed configuration (Model 2931).

ACOUSTIC: PRO SERIES

S&P 6 PRO MAHOGANY (MODEL 2955) - similar to the S&P 6, except has a solid spruce top, mahogany back and sides, mahogany neck, and high gloss lacquer finish, current mfg.

MSR	$685		$525	$350	$225

Add $125 for B-Band NF-1 EQ electronics (Model 15535). Add $200 for B-Band NF-2 EQ electronics (Model 15542). Add $40 for left-handed configuration (Model 3006).

S&P 6 PRO FLAME MAPLE (MODEL 3051) - similar to the S&P Pro Mahogany, except has flame maple sides and solid back, current mfg.

MSR	$765		$575	$395	$250

Add $125 for B-Band NF-1 EQ electronics (Model 15573). Add $200 for B-Band NF-2 EQ electronics (Model 15580). Add $40 for left-handed configuration (Model 3105).

S&P 6 Pro Flame Maple Cutaway (Model 2665) - similar to S&P 6 Pro Flame Maple, but body is in the cutaway configuration, current mfg.

MSR	$895		$675	$450	$300

Add $125 for B-Band NF-1 EQ electronics (Model 15238). Add $200 for B-Band NF-2 EQ electronics (Model 15245).

S&P 6 PRO ROSEWOOD (MODEL 3150) - similar to the S & P Pro Mahogany, except has Indian rosewood back and sides, current mfg.

MSR	$895		$675	$450	$300

Add $125 for B-Band NF-1 EQ electronics (Model 15610). Add $200 for B-Band NF-2 EQ electronics (Model 15627). Add $40 for left-handed configuration (Model 3204).

S&P 6 Pro Rosewood Cutaway (Model 2603) - similar to S&P 6 Pro Rosewood, except features cutaway configuration, current mfg.

MSR	$1,055		$795	$530	$325

Add $125 for B-Band NF-1 EQ electronics (Model 15214). Add $200 for B-Band NF-2 EQ electronics (Model 15221).

Silvertone S-40
courtesy Ted Kornblum

S

GRADING		100%	EXCELLENT	AVERAGE

S&P 6 PRO QUILTED MAPLE (MODEL 3259) - similar to the S&P Pro Mahogany, except the back and sides are solid quilted maple, current mfg.

MSR	$1,165		$875	$595	$375

Add $125 for B-Band NF-1 EQ electronics (Model 15658). Add $200 for B-Band NF-2 EQ electronics (Model 15665). Add $40 for left-handed configuration (Model 3303).

SLAMAN GUITARS

Instruments currently built in Den Haag, Netherlands since 1978. Distributed through Luthier Slaman's workshop, Casa Benelly in Den Haag, and La Guitarra Buena in Amsterdam.

Luthier Daniel Slaman began building classical guitars in 1978. Slaman participated in a guitar making Masterclass hosted by Jose L. Romanillos in 1988, and professes a strong design influence by Romanillos. In 1997, Slaman and Robert Benedetto presented guitar making workshops at the Instrument Museum in Berlin during the *History of the Guitar in Rock and Jazz* exhibition.

Slaman introduced a number of new acoustic models in 1996 as well. By slightly offsetting the body contour, Slaman produced a cutaway on his classical model (which allows access to all 20 frets); this model has been named the **Classic Access** (list price $3,000). A variation named the **Flamenco Access** (list $2,500) is in the works. Another model is a European jazz guitar inspired by the Selmer models built in France from 1932 to 1952. Slaman's **Modele Jazz** is offered as brand new, or with antique parts and distressing as the **Modele Jazz Patina** (prices start at $2,500). List prices include a Hiscox case.

The majority of Slaman's instruments were built after 1992. Slaman currently produces between ten and fifteen handcrafted instruments a year, although archtop building is more time consuming and thus tends to slow down the building schedule.

ACOUSTIC

Luthier Slaman uses European spruce for his classical guitar tops, and either Brazilian or Indian rosewood, cocobolo or maple for the back and sides. When building **flamenco instruments**, Slaman offers soundboards of either European spruce or Western red cedar, and bodies of Spanish cypress or rosewood. Prices on classical models start at $3,000; and flamenco models begin at $2,500.

The **North Sea Standard** 17" has a carved Sitka spruce top, two piece flamed maple back with matching sides/neck, ebony fingerboard with mother-of-pearl/ Mexican green abalone inlays, ebony tailpiece/pickguard, Brazilian rosewood bridge/headplate, 3-per-side Schaller gold tuning machines. Available in hand-applied nitrocellulose finish, and the MSR is $6,342, add $250 for 18" or 18 1/2" wide body. List price includes a Calton DeLuxe fiberglass case. This model is available with an optional Benedetto S-6 suspended pickup. This model is available with select aged European Cello grade flamed maple back and sides as the North Sea Cello 17". This model is available with special Thuya wood headplate/pickguard/bridge wings/tailpiece as the North Sea Special 17".

The **North Sea Natural 17"** is similar to the North Sea Standard, except features all wood binding (no plastic), no pearl inlay, and MSR is $4,500.

The **North Sea 7-String Swing** is similar to the North Sea, except in a 7-string configuration, 4/3-per-side headstock, and MSR is $4,500.

The **North Sea Orchestra** is similar to the North Sea, except has non-cutaway body style, 18" width (across lower bout), European spruce top, European flamed maple back/sides/neck and the MSR is $4,750.

SLINGERLAND

Instruments previously built in Chicago, Illinois from the mid 1930s to circa mid 1940s.

Slingerland is perhaps better known for the drums the company produced. The Slingerland Banjo and Drum Company was established in 1916 in Chicago. In terms of construction, a banjo and drum do have several similarities (the soundhead stretched over a circular frame and held by a retaining ring). The company introduced the Marvel line of carved top guitars in 1936. A catalog of the time shows that Slingerland guitars were also sold under various brand names such as Songster, College Pal, and May-Bell, as well as the Slingerland trademark, (Source: Tom Wheeler, *American Guitars*).

SMALLMAN GUITARS

Instruments currently built in New South Wales, Australia since the early 1980s.

Luthier Greg Smallman continues to push the mechanical limits on the classical guitar form. Though the instruments look conventional, Smallman utilizes a flexible criss-cross lattice-like internal strutting composed of balsawood reinforced by carbon fiber under a thin top to increase the volume of the guitar. Backs and sides are constructed from laminated rosewood, which reduces the amount of energy that they might absorb from the top, which also enhances the guitar's projection. Smallman favors cedar for his guitar tops, (Source: Tony Bacon, *The Ultimate Guitar Book*).

Luthier Smallman makes a small number of guitars each year, has a moderately high asking price, and has a long waiting list. 'Used' Smallman guitars rarely turn up on the secondary market.

SOBELL, STEFAN

Instruments currently built in England. Distributed in the U.S. by Dream Guitars.

Luthier Stefan Sobell was a pioneer in the development of the "cittern" (similar to a long necked mandolin) in the early 1970s (the cittern proved popular in the British Celtic music revival). Sobell then changed to building acoustic guitars in the early 1980s. Currently he produces about 35 guitars a year, "bent" or carved top "flat tops" (the top and back feature a cylindrical arch). Sobell also builds citterns, mandolins, and Irish bouzoukis. Contact Dream guitars for more information and for ordering (see Trademark Index).

SONNET

Instruments previously produced in Japan.

Sonnet guitars were distributed in the U.S. by the Daimaru New York Corporation of New York, New York, (Source: Michael Wright, *Guitar Stories*, Volume One).

SORRENTINO

Instruments previously built by Epiphone in New York, New York circa mid 1930s. Distributed by C.M.I. (Chicago Musical Instruments).

In the book, *Epiphone: The House of Stathopoulo*, authors Jim Fisch and L.B. Fred indicate that Sorrentino instruments were built by Epaminondas Stathopoulos' Epiphone company during the mid 1930s. Unlike other 1930s budget lines, the Sorrentinos are similar in quality and prices to Epiphones during this time period. Of the six models (Luxor, Premier, Artist, Avon, Lido, and Arcadia), two models were even higher priced than their Epiphone counterpart!

Sorrentinos share construction designs and serialization similar to same-period Epiphones, and headstock designs similar to the Epiphone-built Howard brand models. Sorrentinos, like budget line Gibsons, do not have a truss rod in the neck. Labels inside the body read: *Sorrentino Mfg. Co., USA*, (Source: Jim Fisch and L.B. Fred, *Epiphone: The House of Stathopoulo*).

**Slingerland Songster
courtesy Dale Hanson**

SQUIRE

Instruments currently produced in Mexico, Korea, and China. Distributed by the Fender Musical Instrument Corporation in Scottsdale, Arizona. Previously produced in Japan.

In 1982, the Fender division of CBS established Fender Japan in conjunction with Kanda Shokai and Yamano music. Production of the Squire instruments began in 1983 at the Fugi Gen Gakki facilities in Matsumoto, Japan. The Squire trademark was based on the V.C. Squire string making company that produced strings for Fender in the 1950s, and was later aquired by Fender in 1965. Originally, the Squire trademark was intended for European distribution, but soon became a way for Fender to provide entry level instruments to its customers. Squire instruments are typically based off of the popular Fender designs. The Squire II series was introduced in 1986. In 1996 Fender greatly expanded its line with several models available at competitive prices.

ACOUSTIC

MC-1 (NO. 092-0100-021) - 3/4 scale mini-classical body, laminated agathis top, back, and sides, nato neck with rosewood fingerboard, 18 frets, 23.3" scale, nylon strings, open-gear tuners, available in Natural finish, current mfg.

	MSR	$150	$105	$75	$50

MA-1 (NO. 094-0100-021) - 3/4 scale mini-acoustic, laminated agathis top, back, and sides, nato neck with rosewood fingerboard, chrome, open-gear tuners, 18 frets, 23.3" scale, available in Natural finish, current mfg.

	MSR	$160	$115	$80	$55

SD-6 (DG-6, NO. 095-0600-021) - dreadnought style, laminated agathis top, back and sides, nato neck with rosewood fingerboard, dot inlays, rosewood bridge, compensated Urea saddle, 25.3" scale, chrome tuners, black pickguard, available in Natural satin (- 021) finish, mfg. 2001-current.

	MSR	$200	$140	$95	$65

SD-6 G (No. 095-0600-XXX) - similar to the SD-6 except is available in Candy Apple Red, White, or Metallic Blue, mfg. 2001-current.

	MSR	$233	$165	$110	$75

STEINEGGER, ROBERT

Instruments currently produced in Portland, OR, since 1976.

Robert Steinegger developed an interest in guitars while in high school. Arthur Overholtzer coached him on classical guitar construction, and while attending school in Utah, he met Phil Everly of the Everly Brothers. In 1981, he was commissioned by Phil Everly to build an updated, improved version of the now highly collectible Gibson Everly Brothers Model. The "Ike Everly Model" was the result, and was built until 2001, when production was suspended. Robert Steinegger also builds numerous other acoustic configurations, built per individual customer order. Current standard models include the Style 18 ($3,915), Style 21 ($3,985), Style 28 ($4,570), Style 42 ($5,440), Style 45 ($8,225), and the Oregon Grand ($4,570). Additionally, Brazilian rosewood is available as a $1,250 surcharge.

S.S. STEWART

Instruments also produced as Stewart & Bauer. Instruments previously produced in Philadelphia, Pennsylvania, during the late 1800s.

S.S. Stewart was a major banjo producer of the late 1800s, and was one of the first to apply mass production techniques to instrument building with good consequences. Stewart became partners with well-known guitar builder George Bauer, and issued guitars under the Stewart & Bauer trademark from Philadelphia.

After the company was dissolved, Stewart's family put out guitars under the **S.S.** Stewart's Sons trademark. The Stewart name also appears on a series of entry level to medium grade guitars built by Harmony (circa 1950s); and others for Weymann. These later models are not at the same level of quality as the Philadelphia-era models, (Source: Tom Wheeler, *American Guitars*).

**Squire MC-1
courtesy Fender**

S

STAHL, WILLIAM C.
See Larson Brothers (1900-1944).

William C. Stahl was a prominent music publisher and teacher of guitar, mandolin, and banjo in Milwaukee from the turn of the century to the early 1940s. He sold instruments to his students but also advertised heavily in the trade papers. The Larson brothers of Maurer & Co. in Chicago supplied most of his guitar and mandolin family instruments, the remainder being made by Washburn, Regal, or others.

The Larson-made Stahl guitars followed the designs of the Maurer and Prairie State brands also built by the Larsons. The difference in the Stahl labeled guitars is that maple is used for bracing rather than spruce. Some of the top-of-the-line Stahl guitars have the Prairie State system of steel rods which strengthen the body and add sustain as well as help to produce a somewhat different sound from other Larson brands. The Larson-made Stahl instruments have a Stahl logo burned or stamped on the inside center strip. Author Robert Hartman believes that Stahl's paper label was also used on some Larsons, as well as the ones made by other builders. Stahl offered guitars and mandolins ranging in quality from student grade to the highest degree of presentation grade instruments.

For more information regarding other Larson-made brands, see Maurer, Prairie State, Euphonon, W.j. Dyer, and The Larson Brothers. For more detailed information regarding all the Larson brands and a Stahl catalog reprint, see The Larsons' Creations, Guitars and Mandolins, by Robert Carl Hartman, Centerstream Publishing, P.O. Box 17878, Anaheim Hills CA 92807, phone/fax (714) 779-9390.

STELLA
See Harmony. See Oscar Schmidt.

STEVENS CUSTOM GUITARS
Instruments currently built in Munchen (Munich), Germany.

Werner Kozlik, Stefan Zirnbauer, and the other guitar builders at Stevens Custom Guitars are crafting high quality acoustic models. For additional information regarding models and specifications, please contact Stevens Custom Guitars directly (see Trademark Index).

STILES, GILBERT L.
Instruments previously built in Independence, West Virginia and Hialeah, Florida between 1960 to 1994.

Luthier/designer Gilbert L. Stiles (1914-1994) had a background of working with wood, be it millwork, logging or house building. In 1960, he set his mind to building a solid body guitar, and continued building instruments for over the next thirty years. In 1963, Stiles moved to Hialeah, Florida. Later on in his career, Stiles also taught for the Augusta Heritage Program at the Davis and Elkins College in Elkins, West Virginia.

Stiles built solid body electrics, archtops, flattop guitars, mandolins, and other stringed instruments. It has been estimated that Stiles had produced over 1,000 solid body electric guitars and 500 acoustics during his career. His archtop and mandolins are still held in high esteem, as well as his banjos.

Stiles guitars generally have Stiles or G.L Stiles on the headstock, or Lee Stiles engraved on a plate at the neck/body joint of a bolt-on designed solid body. Dating a Stiles instrument is difficult, given that only the electric solids were given serial numbers consecutively, and would only indicate which number guitar it was, not when built, (Source: Michael Wright, *Guitar Stories,* Volume One).

STOLL
Instruments currently built in Taunusstein, Germany since 1983. Distributed in the U.S. by Salwender International of Trabuco Canyon, California.

Christian Stoll began his lutherie career in the mid 1970s as an apprentice at Hopf guitars, then left to study under Dragan Musulin. Stoll finished his period of apprenticeship with Andreas Wahl, and founded the Stoll Guitar Company in 1983.

Between 1983 to 1985, Stoll produced custom orders for classical and steel string models (and some electric guitars and basses), and began to work on developing an acoustic bass guitar. In 1988, Stoll began adding other luthiers to his workshop, and currently has three on staff.

Stoll also offers the McLoud acoustic pickup system on a number of his acoustic models. This internal system features a piezo pickup, endpin jack, and a battery clip for 9-volt batteries.

ACOUSTIC

Stoll offers handcrafted steel string acoustic guitar and acoustic bass models. The models are built from quality wood, and inlays and trim are used sparingly as the emphasis is on tone and craftsmanship. Guitars are then finished in nitrocellulose lacquer or Shellac (French polish method).

Classical models feature solid cedar or spruce tops, rosewood or ovankol sides and backs, 20-fret ebony fingerboards, and Schaller tuners. The Steel String acoustics have solid spruce tops, maple or rosewood backs and sides, cedro necks, 21-fret rosewood or ebony fingerboards and chrome or gold Schaller tuners. All models are available with options like cutaways, left-handed configurations, and more.

SPEXX acoustic basses feature a wider cutaway body design, solid spruce top, maple back and sides, a 21-fret ebony fingerboard, and gold Schaller tuners. Basses are available in fretless, left-handed, 5- and 6-string configurations.

STRADIVARI
Instruments previously built in Italy during the late 1600s.

While this reknowned builder is revered for his violins, luthier Antonio Stradivari (1644-1737) did build a few guitars; a handful survive today. The overall design and appearance is reminiscent of the elegant yet simple violins that command such interest today, (Source: Tony Bacon, *The Ultimate Guitar Book*).

STRAD-O-LIN
Instruments previously produced in New York during the 1950s and 1960s. Later models manufactured in Japan.

Strad-O-Lin was a brand name of the Peter Sorkin Music Company. A number of solid body guitars were built at the Multivox company of New York, and distribution of those and the later Japanese built models were handled by the Sorkin company of New York City, New York. Other guitars built and distributed (possibly as rebrands) were Royce, Premier, Belltone, and Marvel.

STROMBERG

Instruments previously built in Boston, Massachusetts between 1906 and the mid 1950s.

The Stromberg business was started in Boston, Massachusetts in 1906 by Charles Stromberg (born in Sweden 1866) who immigrated to Boston in April 1886. Charles Stromberg was a master luthier. He specialized in banjo, drum, mandolin, and guitars after working for several years at Thompson and Odell (est. 1874), a Boston based firm that manufactured brass instruments, percussion instruments, fretted instruments, music publications, stringed instruments, and accessories. Thompson & Odell sold the manufacturing of the fretted instrument business to the Vega Company in Boston in 1905. Stromberg was one of the country's leading repairers of harps with his masterful ability in carving headstocks, replacing sound boards, and making new machine mechanisms. His reputation among Boston's early engravers, violin, drum, banjo, and piano makers was very high. Charles, in addition, repaired violins, cellos, and basses. Repairs were a steady source of income for the Stromberg business. His oldest son, Harry (born in Chelsea, Massachusetts 1890), worked with Charles from 1907 on and his youngest son, Elmer (born in Chelsea in 1895), apprenticed at the shop with older brother Harry from July 1910 until March 1917, when Elmer left the business to serve in World War I. He returned to the business in March 1919 after serving his country for two years in France.

**Stromberg G3
courtesy Tom Van Hoose**

At that time, the shop was located at 40 Sudbury Street and later moved to 19 Washington Street in early 1920s. Shop locations were in an area based in the heart of Boston's famous Scollay Square with burlesque and theater establishments. The Strombergs produced drums, mandolins, guitars, and banjos during the early 1920s from the 19 Washington Street location.

Throughout the 1920s (the Jazz Age of banjo music), the Strombergs produced custom tenor banjos. They competed with other banjo manufacturers, and were part of the eastern corridor in banjo manufacturing. The Stromberg reputation was very strong in Boston and the New England area. Banjoists who often desired a custom-made instrument chose the Stromberg banjo as it was highly decorative and the sound would carry for the player in large dance halls. In October of 1926, Elmer Stromberg applied for a patent for a series of tubes around the tone chamber of the banjo just under the head. This created a new sustaining sound and more volume and was called the "Cupperphone." The Stromberg Cupperphone banjo consisted of 41 hollow, perforated metal tubes -13/16 inches high and -13/16 inches in diameter fitted to the wooden rim to produce a louder and clearer tone. This was an option for the banjos, and this Cupperphone feature made the Stromberg banjo one of the loudest and heaviest built in the country. The two models offered at this time were the Deluxe, and Marimba models. The patent was granted in June of 1928.

Harry Stromberg left the business in 1927. By the late 1920s, banjo players were beginning to switch from banjo to guitar to create deeper sounding rhythm sections in orchestras. As the style of music changed, the guitar needed to be heard better. While musicians' needs focused towards the guitar, the banjo's popularity declined and Elmer began producing archtop guitars for Boston musicians.

In June of 1927, the shop relocated to 40 Hanover Street where they began producing archtop guitars. By the early 1930s, banjo players began ordering guitars. As early as 1927, Elmer began taking guitar orders, and offered several types based on a 16 inch body, called the G series. The models G1, G2, and Deluxe models were offered featuring a small headstock, with laminated body and segmented f-holes.

During the American Depression of the 1930s, Elmer wanted as many musicians as possible to enjoy his instruments and kept the cost of the instrument affordable. After the Depression, the guitars began to change in looks and construction. By the mid 1930s (1935-37), musicians requested fancier models with larger bodies that could produce more volume. The Stromberg guitar went through at least two major headstock dimension sizes and designs and body specifications between 1936 and 1940. Elmer's response to players' needs (and the competition) was to widen the body on the G series guitars to 17-3/8 inches, and add two more models: the 19 inch **Master 400** model was introduced around 1937/38, and the Master 300 was introduced in the same time period. The larger body dimensions of the Master 300 and 400 made them the largest guitars offered from any maker.

Elmer's top-of-the-line model was the Master 400. This guitar would set the Stromberg guitar apart from other rhythm acoustic archtop guitars, especially during the swing era: Elmer added decorative pearl inlay to the headstock, additional binding, and a fine graduated top carving that would carry its sound volume across the brass sections of a large orchestra. By 1940, a new, longer headstock style and the single diagonal brace was added to Master series guitars, switching from a traditional parallel bracing to a single brace for yet more carrying power. The graduation of the tops also changed during this period. By 1940 to '41, a single tension rod adjustment was added to the Master series (and was later added to the Deluxe and G series). By 1941, the G1 and G3 series body dimensions increased to 17-3/8 inches, and featured a new tailpiece design that was "Y" shaped in design. The f-holes became non-segmented and followed the graceful design of the Deluxe model.

Elmer Stromberg built all of the guitars and the majority of banjos. His name never appeared on an instrument, with the exception of a Deluxe Cutaway (serial number 634, a short scale made for guitarist Hank Garland). Every label read Charles A. Stromberg and Son with a lifetime guarantee to the original purchaser. Elmer is described by many players who knew him as a gentle man with a heart of gold. He wanted to please his family of guitarists with the best instrument he could make.

Stromberg history and model specifications courtesy Jim Speros. Speros is currently compiling a Stromberg text, portions of which were supplied to this edition of the *Blue Book of Acoustic Guitars*. Interested parties can contact Speros through Stromberg Research, P.O. Box 51, Lincoln, Massachusetts 01773.

The apparent rarity of the individual guitars (it is estimated that only 640 guitars were produced), like D'Angelicos, combined with condition and demand, makes it difficult to set a selling price in the vintage

S

market. The *Blue Book of Acoustic Guitars* recommends at least two or three professional appraisals or estimates before buying/selling/trading any Stromberg guitar (or any other Stromberg instrument, especially the banjos).

STROMBERG GUITAR IDENTIFICATION

Early G series (G1, G2, G3, Deluxe) from 1927-1930 has a 16 inch body and a label reading "40 Hanover Street, Tel Bowdoin 1228R-1728-M" (Stromberg's current business card). Narrow banjo-style headstock, Stromberg logo, Victorian-style, hand-painted with floral accents. Fingerboard (G1, G2, G3) mother-of-pearl inlays, diamond shape, oval at 14th fret. The Deluxe model featured solid pearl blocks position markers on an ebony fingerboard. The headstock was Victorian-style, engraved, hand-painted. Pressed back Indian rosewood or maple, carved spruce top, segmented f-holes. Trapeze-style tailpiece brass with chrome plating on models G1, G2, and G3 (gold plated on the Deluxe model). All shared rosewood bridge with adjustments for bridge height, top location thumb adjustments. Bracing: two parallel braces, 3 ladder type braces.

Mid to late 1930s (1935-37), the **G-100, G1, G3, Deluxe, Ultra Deluxe**, 17-3/8 inch body. Blonde finish guitars began appearing during the late 1930s. Construction featured a pressed back, carved spruce top, Grover tailpiece (chrome plated). Blue shipping labels inside guitar body read "Charles A. Stromberg & Son" in the late 1930s was typewritten or handwritten. The headstock shape changed to a larger bout and from the early 1930s had a laminated, embossed, plastic engraved Stromberg logo characterizing the new style. Bracing: dual parallel bracing top. The Master 400 had a "stubby" style headstock, parallel braced top, inlaid mother-of-pearl or Victorian laminated style.

1940'S STYLE GUITARS

Master 400: body size 19 inches wide x 21-3/4 inch length. Top: carved and graduated spruce -7/8 inch thickness. F-holes bound white/black, neck was a 5 piece rock maple with Ivoroid binding (black and white) on fingerboard. The bridge was adjustable compensating rosewood and pickguard was imitation tortoise shell that was inlaid with white and black Ivoroid borders. Available in Natural or Sunburst finishes. Ebony fingerboard, position markers were three segmented pearl blocks. Bracing: single diagonal brace from upper bout to lower bout (began about 1940). Tailpiece: 5 Cutout "Y" shaped with Stromberg engraving (gold plated).

Master 300: body size 19 inches wide x 21-3/4 inch length. Top: carved and graduated spruce -7/8 inch thickness. F-holes bound white. Neck: rock maple with ebony fingerboard, position markers solid pearl block. Ivoroid binding on fingerboard (black and white). Bridge: adjustable compensating rosewood. The pickguard was imitation tortoise shell inlaid with white and black Ivoroid borders. Available in Natural or Sunburst finishes. Bracing: single diagonal brace from upper bout to lower bout (began about 1940). Tailpiece: 5 Cutout "Y" shaped with Stromberg engraving (gold plated).

Deluxe: body size 17-3/8 inches wide x 20-3/4 inch length. Top: graduated and carved spruce -7/8 inch thickness. F-holes Ivoroid bound (white/black). Bridge: adjustable compensating rosewood. The pickguard was imitation tortoise shell inlaid with white and black Ivoroid borders. Available in Natural or Sunburst finishes. The ebony fingerboard had position markers solid pearl blocks. Bracing: single diagonal brace from upper bout to lower bout (1940-41). Tailpiece: 5 Cutout "Y" shaped (gold plated).

G-3: body size 17-3/8 inches wide x 20-3/4 inch length. Top: graduated and carved spruce -7/8 inch thickness. F-holes not bound. Bridge: adjustable compensating rosewood. The pickguard was imitation tortoise shell inlaid with white and black Ivoroid borders. Available in Natural or Sunburst finishes. The rosewood fingerboard had position markers of two segmented pearl blocks. Bracing: single diagonal brace from upper bout to lower bout (mid to late 1940s). Tailpiece: 3 Cutout "Y" shaped (gold plated).

G-1: body size 17-3/8 inches wide 20-3/4 inch length. Top: graduated and carved spruce -7/8 inch thickness. F-hole not bound. Bridge: adjustable compensating rosewood. The pickguard was imitation tortoise shell inlaid with white and black Ivoroid borders. Available in Natural or Sunburst finishes. The rosewood fingerboard had position markers of diamond shaped pearl with four indented circle cutouts in inner corners. Bracing: single diagonal brace from upper bout to lower bout (mid to late '40s). Tailpiece: 3 Cutout "Y" shaped (chrome plated).

CUTAWAYS: INTRODUCED IN 1949

Master 400: body size 18-3/8 inches wide x 21-3/4 inch length. Top: carved and graduated spruce 7/8 inch thickness. F-holes bound white/black. Neck: 5-piece rock maple. Ivoroid binding on fingerboard (black and white). Bridge: adjustable compensating rosewood. The pickguard was imitation tortoise shell inlaid with white and black Ivoroid borders. Available in Natural or Sunburst finishes. Ebony fingerboard had position markers of three segmented pearl blocks or solid pearl blocks. Bracing: single diagonal brace from upper bout to lower bout. Tailpiece: 5 Cutout "Y" shaped with the new Stromberg Logo engraved and gold plated.

Deluxe Cutaway: body size 17-3/8 inches wide x 20-3/4 inch length. Top: graduated and carved spruce 7/8 inch thickness. F-holes Ivoroid bound white/black. Bridge: adjustable compensating rosewood. The pickguard was imitation tortoise shell inlaid with white and black Ivoroid borders. Available in Natural or Sunburst finishes. Position markers were solid pearl blocks. Bracing: single diagonal brace from upper bout to lower bout. Tailpiece: 5 Cutout "Y" shaped with Stromberg engraving (gold plated).

G-5 Cutaway (introduced 1950): body size 17-3/8 inches wide x 20-3/4 inch length. Top: graduated and carved spruce 7/8 thickness. F-holes Ivoroid bound white. Bridge: adjustable compensating rosewood. Pickguard was imitation tortoise shell inlaid with white and black Ivoroid borders. Available in Natural or Sunburst finishes. Ebony fingerboard had position markers of solid pearl blocks. Bracing: single diagonal brace from upper bout to lower bout. Tailpiece: 3 Cutout "Y" shaped with Stromberg engraving (gold plated).

G-3 Cutaway: body size 17-3/8 inches wide x 20-3/4 inch length. Top: graduated and carved spruce 7/8 thickness. F-hole unbound. Bridge: adjustable compensating rosewood. The pickguard was imitation tortoise shell inlaid with white and black Ivoroid borders. Available in Natural or Sunburst finishes. Rosewood fingerboard had position markers of split pearl blocks. Bracing: single diagonal brace from upper bout to lower bout. Tailpiece: 3 Cutout "Y" shaped (gold plated).

STUDIO KING
See chapter on House Brands.

While this trademark has been identified as a House Brand, the distributor is currently unknown at this time. As information is uncovered, future listings in the *Blue Book of Acoustic Guitars* will be updated, (Source: Willie G. Moseley, *Stellas & Stratocasters*).

SUNGEUM
Instruments currently produced in Korea.

Sungeum is a guitar brand that was associated with Crafter guitars.

SUPERIOR

See chapter on House Brands.

While this trademark has been identified as a House Brand, the distributor is currently unknown. As information is uncovered, future editions of the *Blue Book of Acoustic Guitars* will be updated, (Source: Willie G. Moseley, *Stellas & Stratocasters*).

SUPERTONE

See chapter on House Brands.

This trademark has been identified as a House Brand of Sears, Roebuck and Company between 1914 to 1941. Instruments produced by various (probably) Chicago-based manufacturers, especially Harmony (then a Sears subsidiary). Sears used the Supertone trademark on a full range of guitars, lap steels, banjos, mandolins, ukuleles, and amplifiers.

In 1940, then-company president Jay Krause bought Harmony from Sears by acquiring the controlling stock, and continued to expand the company's production. By 1941, Sears had retired the Supertone trademark in favor of the new Silvertone name. Harmony, though a separate business entity, still sold guitars to Sears for sale under this new brand name, (Source: Michael Wright, *Vintage Guitar Magazine*).

SUPRO

See chapter on House Brands.

The Supro trademark was the budget brand of the National Dobro company (See National or Valco), who also supplied Montgomery Wards with Supro models under the Airline trademark. National offered budget versions of their designs under the Supro brand name beginning in 1935.

When National moved to Chicago in 1936, the Supro name was on wood-bodied lap steels, amplifiers, and electric Spanish arch top guitars. The first solid body Supro electrics were introduced in 1952, and the fiberglass models began in 1962 (there's almost thirty years of conventionally built guitars in the Supro history).

In 1962, Valco Manufacturing Company name was changed to Valco Guitars, Inc. (the same year that fiberglass models debuted). Kay purchased Valco in 1967, so there are some Kay-built guitars under the Supro brand name. Kay went bankrupt in 1968, and both the Supro and National trademarks were acquired by Chicago's own Strum 'N Drum company. The National name was used on a number of Japanese-built imports, but not the Supro name.

Archer's Music of Fresno, California bought the rights to the Supro name in the early 1980s. They marketed a number of Supro guitars constructed from new old stock (N.O.S.) parts for a limited period of time, (Source: Michael Wright, *Vintage Guitar Magazine*).

SUZUKI

Instruments currently built in Korea. Currently distributed in the U.S. market by Suzuki Guitars of San Diego, California.

Suzuki, noted for their quality pianos, offered a range of acoustic and electric guitars designed for the beginning student to intermediate player. In 1996, the company discontinued the guitar line completely. Suzuki guitars are similar to other trademarked models from Korea at comparable prices. There are now guitars and amplifiers again available by Suzuki.

SWARTELE GUITARS

Instruments currently manufactured in Rushville, NY by luthier Arthur Swartele.

Mr. Swartele worked for 21 years as a pattern maker before he began building guitars. He builds Model "D" guitars in small production lots of 40 instruments and finalizes production in groups of 5-6 pieces. He uses Honduras mahogany for the back, sides and necks and European and Engelmann spruce for the tops as well as Northwestern red cedar. He has also used Sitka spruce. Necks are graphite reinforced and graphite is also used for the nut and saddle. Swartele guitars are known for their sustain and tonal balance. Instruments are finished in a Natural oil finish. Distributed by Sphere Sound in Rochester, New York.

S

NOTES

S is for Saga Musical Instruments. Richard Keldsen, President of Saga, takes a little time to fingerpick at a recent trade show. We know what you're thinking, and no, there are no plans for a *Blue Book of Banjos* (at least not this year!)

Section T

T. SAKASHTA GUITARS
Please refer to the S section in this text.

20TH CENTURY
Instruments previously produced by Regal (original company of Wulschner & Son) in the late 1890s through the mid 1900s.

Indianapolis retailer/wholesaler Emil Wulschner introduced the Regal line in the 1880s, and in 1896 opened a factory to build guitars and mandolins under the following three trademarks: Regal, 20th Century, and University. In the early 1900s the 20th Century trademark was a sub-brand distributed by the Fred Gretsch Manufacturing Company. By 1920 the Fred Gretsch Mfg. Co. had settled into its new ten story building in Brooklyn, New York, and was offering music dealers a very large line of instruments that included banjos, mandolins, guitars, violins, drums, and other band instruments. Gretsch used both the 20th Century and Rex trademarks prior to introduction of the Gretsch trademark in 1933.

TACOMA GUITARS CO.
Instruments currently produced in Tacoma, Washington since 1995. Distributed by Tacoma Guitars direct sales force.

Tacoma Guitars is the newest USA-produced acoustic guitar line. The company estimates that 55 to 70 guitars are produced a day, and all models feature a unique bracing pattern that is called the Voice Support Bracing. Almost all models are available with electronics. For more information on the availability of electronics refer to their web site. Electronics typically add $100-$200 onto the price.

GRADING	100%	EXCELLENT	AVERAGE

Tacoma C1
courtesy Tacoma

ACOUSTIC: CHIEF SERIES

C1 - similar to the Papoose, except has full sized body/neck, single rounded cutaway, cedar top, mahogany back and sides, rosewood fingerboard and bridge, unbound body, mfg. 1997-current.

	MSR	$979		$785	$490	$310

    Add $250 for Fishman Prefix piezo pickup system (Model Chief C1CE).

CKK9C - similar to the P1, except has a figured Koa body and tortise bound top, satin finish, current mfg.

	MSR	$1,279		$1,025	$640	$400

CF26C - similar to the P1, except has a sitka spruce top, figured maple back and sides, and tortoise bound top, Satin finish, current mfg.

	MSR	$1,499		$1,200	$750	$475

CM28C - similar to the P1, except has mahogany back and sides, and an ebony fingerboard and bridge, Gloss finish, current mfg.

	MSR	$1,449		$1,160	$725	$450

ACOUSTIC: DREADNOUGHT SERIES

DM9 - dreadnought style, solid mahogany back and sides, solid Sitka spruce top, rosewood fingerboard with abalone dot position markers, 3-per-side tuners, tortoise bound top, clear pickguard, herringbone rosette, branded logo on headstock, available in Light Satin finish, mfg. 2000-current.

	MSR	$899		$725	$450	$275

    DM9-C - similar to DM9, except has a single cutaway, mfg. 2000-current.

	MSR	$1,099		$875	$550	$325

    DM912 - similar to DM9, except in 12-string configuration, mfg. 2000-current.

	MSR	$1,049		$840	$525	$300

DM10 - dreadnought style, solid Sitka spruce top, round soundhole with abalone trim, mahogany back/sides, tortoise body binding, mahogany neck, 14/20-fret rosewood fingerboard with white dot inlay, rosewood bridge, 3-per-side headstock, chrome hardware, available in Natural satin finish, mfg. 1997-current.

	MSR	$1,049		$840	$525	$300

    Add $250 for Fishman piezo pickup and active EQ (Model DM10E).

DR12 - dreadnought style body, solid Sitka spruce top, solid rosewood back and sides, one piece mahogany neck, rosewood fingerboard with abalone dot position markers, abalone rosette, rosewood bridge, chrome hardware, clear pickguard, Ivoroid bound body and neck, Ivoroid logo inlaid on headstock, available in Natural Gloss top with Satin back and sides, mfg. 2000-02.

				$925	$575	$325

             Last MSR was $1,149.

Tacoma DM10
courtesy Tacoma

T

GRADING		100%	EXCELLENT	AVERAGE

DM14C - similar to the DR14, except has a single cutaway, mahogany back and sides, and ebony fingerboard and bridge, new 2003.

MSR	$1,249	$999	$625	$400

DR14 - similar to the DR12, except has an ebony fingerboard and bridge, mfg. 2002-current.

MSR	$1,199	$960	$600	$375

DK14 - similar to the DR14, except has figured koa back and sides, mfg. 2002-current.

MSR	$1,299	$1,040	$650	$425

DM16-C - dreadnought style with single cutaway, solid Sitka spruce top, solid mahogany back, solid sides, rosewood fingerboard with abalone dot position markers, abalone rosette, torrtoise bound body, inlaid ivoroid logo on headstock, rosewood bridge, available in Gloss Natural finish, current mfg.

MSR	$1,349	$1,080	$675	$450

DR16-R - similar to DM16-C, except has solid rosewood back. Natural Gloss finish, current mfg.

MSR	$1,449	$1,160	$725	$475

DM18 - dreadnought style body, solid Sitka spruce top, solid mahogany back and sides, rosewood fingerboard with abalone "Gingko" position markers, rosewood bridge, abalone rosette, tortoise bound body, 4-color top purfle, clear pickguard, inlaid ivoroid logo on headstock, available in Natural Gloss finish, current mfg.

MSR	$1,239	$995	$625	$395

DM1812 - similar to DM18, except in a 12-string configuration, Natural Gloss finish, mfg 2000-current.

MSR	$1,389	$1,115	$695	$475

DR20 - similar to the DM10, except features rosewood back/sides, herringbone pufling/ivoroid body binding, available in Natural gloss finish, mfg. 1997-current.

MSR	$1,299	$1,040	$650	$425

Add $150 for Fishman Basic piezo pickup and active EQ (Model DR20E).

DF21 - dreadnought style Sitka spruce top, figured maple back and sides, rosewood fingerboard and bridge, tortise binding, pearl inlays, herringbone purfle, available in Gloss finish, mfg. 2001-current.

MSR	$1,599	$1,275	$800	$525

DR38 - dreadnought style body, solid Sitka spruce top, solid Rosewood back and sides, ebony fingerboard with abalone "Gingko" position markers, abalone top purfle, abalone rosette, ebony bridge, ivoroid bound body and neck, inlaid ivoroid logo on headstock, chrome hardware, clear pickguard, available in Natural Gloss finish, current mfg.

MSR	$1,899	$1,525	$950	$600

DK40 - dreadnought style Sitka spruce top, figured koa back and sides, ebony fingerboard and bridge, tortise binding, rosette & neck inlays, abalone purfle, available in Gloss finish, mfg. 2002-current.

MSR	$1,999	$1,600	$1,000	$625

DR55 - dreadnought style, red spruce body, Brazillian ebony fingerboard, ebony bridge, maple binding, abalone purfle and neck inlay, available in Gloss finish, mfg. 2002-current.

MSR	$2,349	$1,875	$1,175	$675

DR55 - dreadnought style, sitka spruce top, 3-piece rosewood back and sides, ebony fingerboard and bridge, herringbone purfle and rosette, available in Gloss finish, mfg. 2002-current.

MSR	$3,099	$2,475	$1,600	$1,000

ACOUSTIC: JUMBO SERIES

JM9 - jumbo body, Sitka spruce top mahogany back and sides, rosewood fingerboard and bridge, tortise top binding, herringbone rosette, available in Light Satin finish, current mfg.

MSR	$999	$800	$500	$300

JM16 - jumbo body, 25 1/2" scale, solid Sitka spruce top, solid mahogany back and sides, rosewood fingerboard with abalone dot position markers, rosewood bridge, ivoroid bound body, neck and headstock, ivoroid logo inlaid in the headstock, abalone rosette, chrome hardware, available in Gloss Natural finish, disc 2001.

		$1,150	$720	$475

Last MSR was $1,429.

JM16C - similar to JM16, except has a single cutaway, available in Gloss Sunburst finish, disc 2002.

		$1,200	$750	$475

Last MSR was $1,499.

JM1612C - similar to JM16C, except in a 12-string configuration, available in Natural Gloss finish, mfg. 2000-02.

		$1,325	$825	$550

Last MSR was $1,649.

JF1912 - jumbo body, Sitka spruce top, figured maple back and sides, tortoise binding, 12-string configuration, Gloss finish, mfg. 2002-current

MSR	$1,749	$1,400	$875	$600

GRADING		100%	EXCELLENT	AVERAGE

JF21 - jumbo body, Sitka spruce top, figured maple back and sides, tortise binding, herringbone purfle, Pearl Wave inlays, Gloss finish, current mfg.

MSR	$1,699	$1,375	$850	$575

JK50C - rounded lower bout/slim waist style with single rounded cutaway, solid Sitka spruce top, round soundhole with abalone trim, koa back/sides, herringbone purfling/ivoroid body binding, mahogany neck, 14/20-fret bound rosewood fingerboard with abalone inlay, bound flamed koa peghead with maple logo inlay, rosewood bridge, 3-per-side headstock, chrome hardware, available in Natural satin finish, mfg. 1997-current.

MSR	$1,899	$1,525	$950	$625

JR55 - jumbo body, Sitka spruce top, rosewood 3-piece back and sides, maple binding, abalone purfle, rosette & neck inlays, Gloss finish, current mfg.

MSR	$2,449	$1,975	$1,225	$750

**Tacoma JR55
courtesy Dave Rogers
Dave's Guitar Shop**

ACOUSTIC: LITTLE JUMBO SERIES

Lawrence Juber (LJ) Little Jumbo Series designed in conjunction with guitarist Lawrence Juber.

EM9 - small body jumbo, solid Sitka spruce top, solid mahogany back and sides, rosewood fingerboard with abalone dot position markers, rosewood bridge, Tortoise bound top, clear pickguard, herringbone rosette, logo branded on headstock, available in Light Satin Natural finish, current mfg.

MSR	$999	$800	$500	$300

EM9C - similar to EM9, except has a single cutaway, Light Satin Natural finish, mfg 2000-current.

MSR	$1,199	$960	$600	$350

EM19 - similar to EM9, except has black hardware, inlaid Ivoroid logo on headstock, ebony fingerboard, ebony bridge, ivoroid bound body, available in Gloss finish, disc 2001.

		$925	$575	$325

Last MSR was $1,149.

EM19C - similar to EM19, except has a single cutaway, available in Gloss finish, disc 2002.

		$1,200	$750	$475

Last MSR was $1,499.

EKK19C - similar to EM19, except has a cutaway figured koa body, ebony fingerboard and bridge, and herringbone rosette, available in Gloss finish, new 2003.

MSR	$1,599	$1,275	$800	$525

ER19C - similar to EM19, except has rosewood back and sides, new 2003.

MSR	$1,599	$1,275	$800	$525

ER22C - similar to EM19C, except has solid cedar top, solid rosewood back and sides, available in Gloss Natural finish, current mfg.

MSR	$1,599	$1,275	$800	$525

ECR38C - single cutaway body, cedar top, rosewood back and sides, ebony fingerboard and bridge, avalone purfle & neck inlay, gloss finish, mfg. 2002-current.

MSR	$2,199	$1,775	$1,100	$700

ECR52C - single cutaway body, Englemann spruce top, rosewood back and sides, koa binding, ebony fingerboard and bridge, abalone purfle & neck inlay, gloss finish, new 2003.

MSR	$2,399	$1,925	$1,200	$750

EBZ24 - single cutaway body, sitka spruce top, Brazillian rosewood back and sides, ivoroid binding, ebony fingerboard and bridge, abalone purfle & neck inlay, gloss finish, new 2003.

MSR	$2,649	$2,125	$1,325	$950

ECR15NC - nylon single cutaway body, cedar top, rosewood back and sides, ivoroid binding, rosewood fingerboard and bridge, inlaid rosewood rosette, gloss finish, mfg. 2002-current.

MSR	$1,199	$960	$600	$350

ER64NC - similar to the ECR15NC, except has an Englemann spruce top, ebony fingerboard and bridge, and abalone prufle inlaid rosewood rosette, mfg. 2002-current.

MSR	$1,899	$1,525	$950	$600

ACOUSTIC: PAPOOSE SERIES

P1 - travel sized solid mahogany body and sides, cedar top, mahogany neck, 15/21-fret rosewood fingerboard with white dot inlay, quotation mark soundhole in bass bout, pinless bridge, 3-per-side headstock, chrome hardware, available in Natural satin finish, mfg. 1995-current.

MSR	$579	$465	$290	$175

Add $100 for piezo pickup and endpin jack (Model Papoose P1E).

This model is voiced as a tenor-style guitar (up a fourth) from a standard acoustic guitar.

T

GRADING	100%	EXCELLENT	AVERAGE

P2 - similar to the P1, except has rosewood back, sides, and fingerboard, and a bound body, disc 2002.

	$625	**$390**	**$250**

Last MSR was $779.

P4KN - Papoose sized figured koa body, nylon string configuration, Ivoroid bound top, current mfg.

MSR	$949	**$760**	**$475**	**$300**

P6K - Papoose sized figured koa body, ebony fingerboard and bridge, gold hardware, Ivoroid bound top, available in Gloss Natural finish, current mfg.

MSR	$1,399	**$1,125**	**$700**	**$450**

ACOUSTIC: PARLOR SERIES

PM9 - parlor style body, Sitka spruce top, mahogany back and sides, rosewood fingerboard and bridge, tortoise bound top, herringbone purfle, light satin finish, current mfg.

MSR	$999	**$800**	**$500**	**$300**

PR12 - parlor style body, Sitka spruce top, rosewood back and sides, rosewood fingerboard and bridge, ivoroid binding, gloss top and satin back and sides finish, mfg. 2002-current

MSR	$1,149	**$925**	**$575**	**$350**

PM20 - rounded lower bout/slim waist style, solid Sitka spruce top, round soundhole with abalone trim, mahogany back/sides, herringbone purfling/ivoroid body binding, 25.5" scale, mahogany neck, 14/20-fret bound rosewood fingerboard with white dot inlay, rosewood bridge, 3-per-side headstock, chrome hardware, available in Natural gloss finish, mfg. 1997-current.

MSR	$1,249	**$999**	**$625**	**$375**

Add $250 for Fishman Prefix piezo pickup and active EQ (Model PM20E).

PK30 - similar to the PM20, except features koa back/sides, bound flamed koa peghead with maple logo inlay, abalone position markers, available in Natural gloss finish, mfg. 1997-current.

MSR	$1,999	**$1,600**	**$1,000**	**$650**

Add $250 for Fishman Prefix piezo pickup and active EQ (Model PK30E).

PKK40 - parlor style body, figured koa body, ebony fingerboard and bridge, abalone purfle & floral neck inlay, gloss finish, current mfg.

MSR	$3,399	**$2,725**	**$1,750**	**$1,250**

ACOUSTIC: ROADKING DREADNOUGHT SERIES

RM6 - dreadnought style body, same design as the Chief, Sitka spruce top, mahogany back and sides, sound hole on bass bout, rosewood fingerboard and bridge, unbound body, available in light satin finish, mfg. 2002-current.

MSR	$799	**$640**	**$400**	**$250**

RM6C - similar to the RM6, except has a single cutaway, mfg. 2002-current.

MSR	$929	**$745**	**$465**	**$290**

RR8 - dreadnought style body, same design as the Chief, Sitka spruce top, rosewood back and sides, sound hole on bass bout, rosewood fingerboard and bridge, tortise bound top, inlaid logo, available in satin finish, mfg. 2002-current.

MSR	$999	**$800**	**$500**	**$300**

RR8C - similar to the RR8, except has a single cutaway, mfg. 2002-current.

MSR	$1,129	**$905**	**$565**	**$350**

RMM9C - dreadnought style single cutaway body, same design as the Chief, mahogany body, sound hole on bass bout, rosewood fingerboard and bridge, tortoise bound top, available in light satin finish, mfg. 2002-current.

MSR	$999	**$800**	**$500**	**$300**

RM26C - dreadnought style single cutaway body, same design as the Chief, Sitka spruce top, mahogany back and sides, sound hole on bass bout, rosewood fingerboard and bridge, tortoise bound top, available in gloss finish, mfg. 2002-current.

MSR	$1,279	**$1,025**	**$640**	**$375**

ACOUSTIC ELECTRIC

EM10CE2 - single Florentine cutaway hollowbody, 3 1/4" deep, solid Sitka spruce top, solid mahogany back and sides, rosewood fingerboard with abalone dot position markers, rosewood bridge, tortoise bound neck and body, inlaid ivoroid logo on headstock, abalone rosette, Tacoma E2 Preamp system, available in Satin Natural finish, disc.

	$950	**$550**	**$375**

Last MSR was $1,189.

EM16CE4 - similar to EM10CE2, except has abalone "wave" position markers, available in Gloss Sunburst finish, disc.

	$1,195	**$695**	**$465**

Last MSR was $1,489.

GRADING	100%	EXCELLENT	AVERAGE

JK50CE - rounded lower bout/slim waist style with single rounded cutaway, solid Sitka spruce top, round soundhole with abalone trim, koa back/sides, herringbone purfling/ivoroid body binding, mahogany neck, 14/20-fret bound rosewood fingerboard with abalone inlay, bound flamed koa peghead with maple logo inlay, rosewood bridge, 3-per-side headstock, chrome hardware, Fishman Prefix system, available in Natural satin finish, mfg. 1997-2000.

$1,150 $685 $450
Last MSR was $1,449.

ACOUSTIC BASS: THUNDERCHIEF SERIES

The Thunderchief Bass series is just what it sounds. It is a bass version of the Chief series. All of these models have the soundhole in the upper bass bout. All models are available in fretless configuration for no additional cost (suffix F).

CB10C - single cutaway chief style body, Sitka spruce top, mahogany back and sides, rosewood fingerboard, unbound body, 2-per-side tuners, light satin finish, current mfg.

MSR	$1,099		$875	$550	$325

  CB105C - similar to the CB10C, except in five-string configuration, 3/2-per-side tuners, current mfg.

MSR	$1,289		$1,035	$645	$375

CB28C - single cutaway chief style body, Sitka spruce top, figured maple back and sides, ebony fingerboard, tortoise binding, pearl inlay, 2-per-side tuners, gloss finish, current mfg.

MSR	$1,699		$1,375	$850	$500

  CB285C - similar to the CB28C, except in five-string configuration, 3/2-per-side tuners, current mfg.

MSR	$1,899		$1,525	$950	$550

TAKAMINE

Instruments currently manufactured in Japan. Distributed by the Kaman Music Corporation of Bloomfield, Connecticut.

The Takamine brand was originally set up to be Martin's Sigma series with the help of Coast distributors. However, when the Kaman Music Corporation (Ovation) bought Coast, Martin had to contract Sigma production elsewhere. Ovation encouraged Takamine to enter the market under their own trademark, and have since distributed the guitars in the U.S. market, (Source: Michael Wright, *Guitar Stories,* Volume One).

During the 1980s, Takamine offered an acoustic model with a V-shaped body. Originally dubbed the "Acoustic Flying V," the name was later changed to the "Flying A." This model was available in Natural, Metallic Red, and Metallic Blue finishes.

Takamine uses certain designation to indicate aspects of the model: The E prefix indicates an acoustic/electric model, the C prefix indicates a cutaway body, and the -12 indicates as 12-string configuration.

ACOUSTIC: G-10-240 SERIES

G-10 - dreadnought style, cedar top, round soundhole, bound body, multi stripe purfling/rosette, mahogany back/sides/neck, 14/20-fret rosewood fingerboard, rosewood bridge with white black dot pins, 3-per-side gold tuners, available in Natural finish, mfg. 1994-99.

$360 $180 $150
Last MSR was $499.

  EG-10C - similar to G-10, except has single round cutaway, crystal bridge pickups, 4-band EQ, available in Natural finish, mfg. 1994-current.

MSR	$860		$625	$450	$275

EG-15C - similar to G-10, except has a gloss finish, current mfg.

MSR	$1,000		$700	$500	$300

EG-40C - NEX single cutaway body, solid cedar top, Sepele mahogany with solid back, rosewood fingerboard, N4B electronics, available in Gloss Natural finishes, current mfg.

MSR	$900		$630	$450	$275

EG-45SC - small body acoustic electric with cutaway, solid spruce top, rosewood back and sides, N4B preamp system, gold tuners, Sante Fe position marker at the 12th fret, available in Natural finish, current mfg.

MSR	$1,000		$700	$500	$300

G-116 - classical body style, spruce top, nato back and sides, rosewood fingerboard, available in Gloss Natural finish, current mfg.

MSR	$220		$155	$110	$75

  EG-116 - similar to the G-116, except has DJ2 electronics, current mfg.

MSR	$350		$245	$175	$115

**Tacoma RM20
courtesy Sid Harper**

**Tacoma CB10C
courtesy Dave Rogers
Dave's Guitar Shop**

T

GRADING	100%	EXCELLENT	AVERAGE

G-124 - classical style, spruce top, round soundhole, bound body, wood marquetry rosette, nato back/sides, mahogany neck, 12/19-fret rosewood fingerboard, tied rosewood bridge, 3-per-side chrome tuners with plastic buttons, available in Natural finish, mfg. 1994-2001.

	$295	$135	$115

Last MSR was $389.

G-124S - similar to the G-124, except has a solid spruce top, mfg. 1994-current.

MSR	$500	$350	$250	$175

EG-124C - similar to G-124, except has single round cutaway, crystal bridge pickups, 4-band EQ, available in Natural finish, mfg. 1994-current.

MSR	$730	$525	$315	$225

EG-140SRC - small body acoustic electric with cutaway, solid spruce top, rosewood back and sides, gold tuners, N4B preamp system, available in Red Stain finish, disc.

MSR	$949	$711	$340	$265

EG-141SC - similar to EG-140SRC except, has spruce top, nato back and sides, available in Black Gloss finish, current mfg.

MSR	$850	$595	$425	$275

G-240 - dreadnought body style, spruce top, nato back and sides, rosewood fingerboard, available in Natural or Red Stain finishes, current mfg.

MSR	$250	$175	$125	$75

Add $35 for Gloss Black finish (Model G241).

EG-240 - dreadnought body style, spruce top, nato back and sides, rosewood fingerboard, available in Natural or Red Stain finishes, DJ2 electronics, current mfg.

MSR	$360	$250	$180	$115

Add $35 for Gloss Black finish (Model G241).

ACOUSTIC: G-300 SERIES

G-330 - dreadnought style, spruce top, round soundhole, black pickguard, 3-stripe bound body and rosette, mahogany back/sides/neck, 14/20-fret rosewood fingerboard with white dot inlay, rosewood bridge with white pins, 3-per-side chrome tuners, available in Natural finish, disc.

	$280	$140	$115

Last MSR was $399.

Add $40 for Black finish (Model G-330B).

In 1993, Red Stain finish was introduced (discontinued 1994).

G-330S - similar to the G-330, except has a solid spruce top, current mfg.

MSR	$430	$305	$215	$135

Add $50 for Gloss Black finish (Model G-330SB).

GS-330S - similar to the G-330, except has a solid cedar top, current mfg.

MSR	$400	$280	$200	$125

EG-330SC - similar to G-330S, except has single round cutaway, crystal bridge pickups, 4-band EQ, available in Natural finish, mfg. 1994-current.

MSR	$730	$525	$375	$225

Add $50 for left-hand model (Model EG-330SLH). Add $35 for Red Stain finish (Model EG-330RC). Add $35 for Ocean Blue Burst finish (Model EG330OBB). This model is also available with a solid cedar top and a satin finish (Model EGS330SC).

G-332 S - dreadnought style, solid spruce top, round soundhole, black pickguard, 3-stripe bound body and rosette, mahogany back/sides/neck, 14/20-fret rosewood fingerboard with white dot inlay, rosewood bridge with white pins, 3-per-side chrome tuners, available in Natural finish, current mfg.

MSR	$580	$410	$290	$175

EG-332C - similar to G-332, except has single round cutaway, crystal bridge pickups, 4-band EQ, available in Natural finish, mfg. 1994-current.

MSR	$800	$560	$400	$240

G-334 - dreadnought style, spruce top, round soundhole, black pickguard, wood bound body and rosette, rosewood back/sides, mahogany neck, 14/20-fret bound rosewood fingerboard with pearl dot inlay, rosewood bridge with white black dot pins, 3-per-side gold tuners, available in Natural or Black finishes, disc. 1994.

	N/A	$250	$165

Last MSR was $500.

EG-334SC - similar to G-334, except has single rounded cutaway, ovangkol back and sides, crystal bridge pickups, 4-band EQ, available in Natural finish, mfg. 1994-current.

MSR	$850	$595	$425	$275

EG-334SBC (EG-334RC) - similar to G-334, except has single rounded cutaway, crystal bridge pickups, 4-band EQ. Available in Black (B) Stain and Red (R) Stain finishes, mfg. 1994-current.

MSR	$900	$630	$450	$300

GRADING	100%	EXCELLENT	AVERAGE

G-335 12-STRING - dreadnought style, spruce top, round soundhole, black pickguard, 3-stripe bound body and rosette, mahogany back/sides/neck, 14/20-fret rosewood fingerboard with white dot inlay, rosewood bridge with white pins, 6-per-side chrome tuners, available in Natural finish, disc. 1999.

	$460	$200	$165

Last MSR was $599.

Add $75 for Acoustic/Electric version with N4B preamp system (Model EG-335).

EG-335SC-12 - similar to the G-335, except has a single cutaway, solid spruce top and nato back and sides, mfg. 2000-current.

MSR	$740	$525	$375	$250

ACOUSTIC: G-400 & G-500 SERIES

EGS430SC - NEX single cutaway body, solid cedar top, nato back and sides, rosewood fingerboard, N4B electronics, available in Satin Natural finish, current mfg.

MSR	$730	$525	$365	$240

G-501S - OM style body, solid spruce top, Bolivian rosewood back and sides, rosewood fingerboard, available in Gloss Natural finish, current mfg.

MSR	$500	$350	$250	$175

EG-501S - similar to the EG-501S, except has TK4NT electronics, current mfg.

MSR	$700	$495	$350	$225

EG-522 - classical style single cutaway body, spruce top, nato back and sides, rosewood fingerboard, TK4NT electronics, available in Gloss Natural finish, current mfg.

MSR	$600	$420	$300	$175

EG-523SC - jumbo style single cutaway body, solid spruce top, flamed maple back and sides, rosewood fingerboard, TK4NT electronics, available in Gloss Natural finish, current mfg.

MSR	$730	$525	$365	$240

EG-523SC-12 - similar to the EG-523SC, except in 12-string configuration, current mfg.

MSR	$830	$585	$415	$275

Takamine G-334
courtesy Takamine

G-530S - dreadnought style body, spruce top, nato back and sides, rosewood fingerboard, Natural finish, current mfg.

MSR	$400	$280	$200	$125

EG-530SC - dreadnought body with cutaway, spruce top, nato back and sides, TK-4N preamp system, available in Natural Gloss finish, current mfg.

MSR	$650	$455	$325	$175

Also available in Red Stain finish (Model EG-530C-RS) and Black finish (Model EG-531C).

EG-535C-12 - similar to the EG-530SC, except in 12-string configuration, current mfg.

MSR	$650	$455	$325	$175

EG-540SC - mini jumbo body with cutaway, spruce top, nato back and sides, TK-4N preamp system, chrome hardware, available in Natural, Red Stain, or Cherry Burst finishes, current mfg.

MSR	$650	$455	$325	$175

Also available in Black finish (Model EG-541C).

EG-560CBS - similar to EG-540C model except in Blue Sunburst finish, current mfg.

MSR	$650	$455	$325	$175

EG-561 - similar to the EG-560CBS, except has Gloss Black finish, current mfg.

MSR	$600	$420	$300	$150

EG-562C - classical style body, spruce top, nato back and sides, rosewood fingerboard, TV3 electronics, available in Gloss Natural finish, current mfg.

MSR	$700	$495	$350	$175

EG-568C - thinline FXC body, spruce top, nato back and sides, rosewood fingerboard, TV3 electronics, available in Gloss Natural, Gloss Black, or Cherry Burst finish, current mfg.

MSR	$700	$495	$350	$175

The Cherry Burst finish has a flamed maple top.

ACOUSTIC: TRADITIONAL (F) SERIES

EF-261SAN/SBL - Artist/FXC cutaway body, solid cedar top, mahogany back & sides, dot position inlays, Graph EX preamp system, available in Antique Stain Gloss or Gloss Black finishes, current mfg.

MSR	$880	$620	$440	$275

Takamine EF-350MC
courtesy Takamine

T

GRADING		100%	EXCELLENT	AVERAGE

EF-325SRC - dreadnought style, single rounded cutaway, solid spruce top, round soundhole, black pickguard, 5-stripe bound body/rosette, bubinga back/sides, mahogany neck, 14/20-fret bound rosewood fingerboard with pearl dot inlay, rosewood bridge with white black dot pins, 3-per-side chrome tuners, crystal bridge pickups, 3-band EQ, available in Clear Red finish, current mfg.

MSR	$1,400	$980	$700	$425

F-340 - dreadnought style, spruce top, round soundhole, black pickguard, 3-stripe bound body and rosette, mahogany back/sides/neck, 14/20-fret rosewood fingerboard with pearl dot inlay, rosewood bridge with black white dot pins, 3-per-side chrome tuners, available in Natural finish, disc. 1999.

		$580	$260	$215

Last MSR was $769.

EF-340SC - dreadnought body with cutaway, spruce top, mahogany back and sides, rosewood fingerboard, 3-per-side tuners, piezo pickups, Graph EX preamp, 3-band EQ, Exciter control, volume, battery check, available in Natural finish, current mfg.

MSR	$1,000	$700	$500	$300

Add $75 for left-hand model (EF-340C-LH).

F-340S - similar to F-340, except has solid spruce top, disc. 1999.

		$645	$315	$260

Last MSR was $899.

FD-340SC - similar to EF340C model except, has solid spruce top, DSP preamp, chromatic tuner, 10 factory presets, 10 write-your-own settings, dual digital reverb, bass, treble and parametric EQ, feedback absorber, available in Natural finish, disc.

		$1,025	$495	$375

Last MSR was $1,369.

F-341 - dreadnought style, spruce top, round soundhole, black pickguard, 5-stripe bound body and rosette, campnosparma back/sides, mahogany neck, 14/20-fret bound rosewood fingerboard with pearl dot inlay, rosewood bridge with white black dot pins, bound peghead, 3-per-side chrome tuners, available in Black finish, disc. 1996.

		$525	$390	$260

Last MSR was $780.

EF-341 - similar to F-341, except has crystal bridge pickups, 3-band EQ, disc. 1999.

		$835	$490	$325

Last MSR was $1,129.

EF-341SC - similar to F-341, except has single rounded cutaway, crystal bridge pickups, 3-band EQ, current mfg.

MSR	$1,000	$700	$500	$300

EF-350MHC - dreadnought body with cutaway, spruce top, maple back and sides, rosewood fingerboard, 3-per-side tuners, Graph EX preamp, 3-band EQ, volume, exciter control, available in Vintage Satin finish, disc.

		$975	$465	$350

Last MSR was $1,299.

EF-350SMC-SB - similar to EF-350MHC except, has solid spruce top, flamed maple back and sides, dot position markers, DSP preamp system. Available in Sunburst finish. Current Mfg.

MSR	$1,300	$910	$650	$450

F-360S - dreadnought style, solid spruce top, round soundhole, black pickguard, 5-stripe bound body/rosette, rosewood back/sides, 14/20-fret bound rosewood fingerboard with pearl dot inlay, rosewood bridge with white black dot pins, 3-per-side chrome tuners, available in Natural finish, disc. 1999.

		$775	$575	$350

Last MSR was $1,089.

EF-360S - similar to the F-360S, except has electronics, disc.

		$800	$600	$350

Add $130 for left-handed version of this model (F-360SLH).

EF-360SC - dreadnought body with cutaway, solid spruce top, rosewood back and sides, rosewood fingerboard, CT4B preamp system, available in Natural finish, current mfg.

MSR	$1,400	$980	$700	$450

FD-360SC - dreadnought body with cutaway, solid spruce top, rosewood back and sides, rosewood fingerboard, DSP preamp system, available in Natural finish, disc.

		$1,185	$565	$425

Last MSR was $1,579.

EF-381C - dreadnought style, single rounded cutaway, 12-string configuration, spruce top, round soundhole, black pickguard, 5-stripe bound body/rosette, campnosparma back/sides, mahogany neck, 14/20-fret rosewood fingerboard with pearl diamond/dot inlay, rosewood bridge w/white black dot pins, 6-per-side chrome tuners, crystal bridge pickup, 3-band EQ, available in Black finish, current mfg.

MSR	$1,100	$770	$550	$325

GRADING		100%	EXCELLENT	AVERAGE

F-385 - dreadnought style, spruce top, round soundhole, black pickguard, 5-stripe bound body/rosette, mahogany back/sides/neck, 14/20-fret rosewood fingerboard with pearl dot inlay, rosewood bridge with black white dot pins, 6-per-side chrome tuners, available in Natural finish, disc. 1999.

		$700	**$400**	**$245**
			Last MSR was $859.	

EF-385 - similar to F-385, except has crystal bridge pickup, 3-band EQ, current mfg.

MSR	**$1,100**	**$770**	**$550**	**$325**

EF-400SC 12-STRING - dreadnought body with cutaway, 12-string, solid spruce top, rosewood back and sides, rosewood fingerboard, DSP preamp system, available in Natural finish, current mfg.

MSR	**$1,600**	**$1,125**	**$800**	**$500**

JJ-325SRC JOHN JORGENSON SIGNATURE MODEL - dreadnought body with cutaway, solid spruce top, bubinga back and sides, rosewood fingerboard, DSP preamp system, available in Red Stain finish, current mfg.

MSR	**$1,600**	**$1,125**	**$800**	**$500**

Add $75 for 12-string configuration (JJ-325SRC-12). Available in Red Stain finish

ACOUSTIC: CLASSICAL SERIES

C-128 - classical style, spruce top, round soundhole, 5-stripe bound body, wooden rosette, rosewood back/sides, mahogany neck, 12/19-fret rosewood fingerboard, rosewood bridge, 3-per-side gold tuners with nylon buttons, available in Natural finish, current mfg.

MSR	**$700**	**$495**	**$350**	**$225**

EC-128 - similar to C-128, except has mahogany back/sides, crystal bridge pickups, 3-band EQ, disc. 1999.

		$700	**$480**	**$245**
			Last MSR was $869.	

C-132S - classical style, solid cedar top, round soundhole, 5-stripe bound body, wooden rosette, rosewood back/sides, mahogany neck, 12/19-fret rosewood fingerboard, rosewood bridge, 3-per-side gold tuners with nylon buttons, available in Natural finish, current mfg.

MSR	**$880**	**$625**	**$440**	**$250**

EC-132C - similar to C-132S, except has single rounded cutaway, spruce top, crystal bridge pickups, 3-band EQ, current mfg.

MSR	**$1,000**	**$700**	**$500**	**$300**

EC-132SC - similar to EC-132C except, has solid cedar top, DSP preamp system, available in Natural finish, current mfg.

MSR	**$1,230**	**$865**	**$615**	**$375**

Add $150 for Gloss Black finish (Model EC-132SC-BL).

CP-132SC - similar to C-132S, except single rounded cutaway, crystal bridge pickup, parametric EQ, disc. 1999.

		$985	**$560**	**$380**
			Last MSR was $1,249.	

ACOUSTIC: HIRADE CLASSICAL SERIES

This series was designed by Mass Hirade, Takamine founder.

H-5 - classical style, solid cedar top, round soundhole, 5-stripe wood bound body, wooden rosette, rosewood back/sides, mahogany neck, 12/19-fret ebony fingerboard, ebony bridge, 3-per-side gold tuners with pearl buttons, available in Natural finish, current mfg.

MSR	**$1,700**	**$1,195**	**$850**	**$500**

This model is also available with CT4B electronics.

HE-5C - similar to H-5 model except, has classical body with cutaway and electronics, available in Natural finish, current mfg.

MSR	**$1,800**	**$1,275**	**$900**	**$550**

H-8 - similar to H-5, except features a solid spruce top, disc. 1999.

		$1,500	**$720**	**$595**
			Last MSR was $2,199.	

H-8SS - similar to H-8 except, has solid spruce top, solid rosewood back and sides, no electronics, available in Natural finish, current mfg.

MSR	**$2,800**	**$1,975**	**$1,400**	**$850**

HE-8SS - similar to H-8SS, except CT4B electronics, current mfg.

MSR	**$2,940**	**$2,075**	**$1,475**	**$900**

Takamine EF-381C
courtesy Takamine

Takamine C-132S
courtesy Takamine

T

GRADING	100%	EXCELLENT	AVERAGE

H-15 - classical style, solid spruce top, round soundhole, wood bound body, wooden rosette, rosewood back/sides, mahogany neck, 12/19-fret ebony fingerboard, ebony bridge with rosette matching inlay, 3-per-side gold tuners with pearl buttons, available in Natural finish, disc. 1999.

	$2,760	$1,350	$1,100

Last MSR was $3,899.

HP-7 - classical style, solid cedar top, round soundhole, 5-stripe wood bound body, wooden rosette, rosewood back/sides, mahogany neck, 12/19-fret ebony fingerboard, ebony bridge, 3-per-side gold tuners with pearl buttons, crystal bridge pickups, parametric EQ, available in Natural finish, disc. 1999.

	$1,675	$780	$645

Last MSR was $2,349.

HE-90 - classical body with cutaway, solid spruce top, rosewood back and sides, DSP preamp system, available in Natural finish, current mfg.

MSR	$2,700	$1,895	$1,350	$800

ACOUSTIC: LIMTED EDITION SERIES

Since 1997, Takamine has been producing a limited edition every year. Each year the guitar has a different theme to it. Look for more information in upcoming editions of the *Blue Book of Acoustic Guitars*.

ACOUSTIC: NATURAL & SUPER NATURAL SERIES

AN10S - dreadnought body style, solid cedar top, solid mahogany back and sides, rosewood fingerboard, available in Satin Natural, current mfg.

MSR	$900	$630	$450	$300

Add $75 for left-handed configuration.

N-10 - dreadnought style, solid cedar top, round soundhole, 3-stripe bound body, 5-stripe rosette, mahogany back/sides/neck, 14/20-fret rosewood fingerboard, rosewood strings through bridge, 3-per-side gold tuners w/amber buttons, available in Natural finish, disc. 1999.

	$660	$325	$275

Last MSR was $949.

EN-10 - similar to N-10, except has crystal bridge pickup, 3-band EQ, disc. 1999.

	$980	$500	$375

Last MSR was $1,239.

EAN-10C - similar to N-10, except has single rounded cutaway, crystal bridge pickup, 3-band EQ, current mfg.

MSR	$1,200	$850	$600	$350

Add $50 for left-handed configuration (Model EAN10C-LH).

EN-12C-12 - dreadnought body with cutaway, 12-string, solid cedar top, Silky Oak back and sides, rosewood fingerboard, Graph EX preamp system, available in Natural finish, disc.

	$1,185	$565	$450

Last MSR was $1,579.

N-15 - dreadnought style, solid cedar top, round soundhole, 3-stripe bound body, 5-stripe rosette, rosewood back/sides, mahogany neck, 14/20-fret rosewood fingerboard, rosewood strings through bridge, 3-per-side gold tuners with amber buttons, available in Natural finish, disc. 1999.

	$800	$570	$350

Last MSR was $1,139.

NP-15C - similar to N-15, except has single round cutaway, crystal bridge pickups, parametric EQ, disc. 1999.

	$1,175	$730	$535

Last MSR was $1,579.

EAN-15C - similar to N-15 model except, has single cutaway dreadnought body, DSP preamp system, padauk, ebony and maple rosette, available in Natural finish, current mfg.

MSR	$1,570	$1,100	$785	$450

AN16S - dreadnought body style, solid spruce top, solid Indian rosewood back and sides, rosewood fingerboard, available in Gloss Natural, current mfg.

MSR	$1,500	$1,050	$750	$450

Add $50 for left-handed configuration.

EAN-16S - similar to the AN16S, except has CT4B electronics, current mfg.

MSR	$1,700	$1,195	$850	$550

Add $15 for left-handed configuration (Model EAN-16S-LH).

NP-18C - dreadnought style, single rounded cutaway, solid spruce top, round soundhole, abalone bound body/rosette, rosewood back/sides, mahogany neck, 14/20-fret ebony fingerboard, ebony strings through bridge, abalone logo peghead inlay, 3-per-side gold tuners with amber buttons, crystal bridge pickup, parametric EQ, available in Natural finish, disc. 1999.

	$1,650	$875	$555

Last MSR was $2,199.

GRADING		100%	EXCELLENT	AVERAGE

N-20 - jumbo style, solid cedar top, round soundhole, 3-stripe bound body, 5-stripe rosette, mahogany back/sides/neck, 14/20-fret rosewood fingerboard, rosewood strings through bridge, 3-per-side gold tuners with amber buttons, available in Natural finish, disc. 1996.

	$650	**$470**	**$310**

Last MSR was $940.

EN-20 - similar to N-20, except has crystal bridge pickup, 3-band EQ, disc. 1999.

	$1,080	**$740**	**$465**

Last MSR was $1,389.

EAN-20C - similar to N-20, except has CT4B electronics, current mfg.

MSR	**$1,200**	**$850**	**$600**	**$375**

NP-25C - jumbo style, single rounded cutaway, solid cedar top, round soundhole, 3-stripe bound body, 5-stripe rosette, mahogany back/sides/neck, 14/20-fret rosewood fingerboard, rosewood strings through bridge, 3-per-side gold tuners, crystal bridge pickups, parametric EQ, available in Natural finish, mfg. 1994-99.

	$1,200	**$850**	**$550**

Last MSR was $1,679.

ND-25C - similar to NP-25C model except, has rosewood back sides and fingerboard, DSP preamp system, available in Natural finish, disc.

	$1,295	**$625**	**$495**

Last MSR was $1,729.

EAN-30C-FXC/Aritist single cutaway body, solid cedar top, mahogany with solid back, rosewood fingerboard, CT4B electronics, Satin Natural finish, current mfg.

MSR	**$1,200**	**$850**	**$600**	**$375**

**Takamine EAN-40C
courtesy Takamine**

N-40 - dreadnought style, solid red cedar top, round soundhole, 3-stripe bound body, 5-stripe rosette, mahogany back/sides/neck, 14/20-fret rosewood fingerboard, rosewood strings through bridge, 3-per-side gold tuners, available in Natural finish, mfg. 1994-99.

	$755	**$325**	**$270**

Last MSR was $949.

EAN-40C - similar to N-40, except has single round cutaway, crystal bridge pickups, 3-band EQ, mfg. 1994-current.

MSR	**$1,200**	**$850**	**$600**	**$375**

Add $75 for 12-String configuration (Model EAN-40C12). Add $150 for 12-String left-handed configuration (Model EAN-40C12-LH).

NP-45C - dreadnought style, single rounded cutaway, red cedar top, round soundhole, 3-stripe bound body, 5-stripe rosette, rosewood back/sides, mahogany neck, 14/20-fret rosewood fingerboard, rosewood strings through bridge, 3-per-side gold tuners, crystal bridge pickups, parametric EQ, available in Natural finish, mfg. 1994-99.

	$1,075	**$635**	**$440**

Last MSR was $1,489.

EAN-45C - similar to the NP-45C, except has CT4B electronics, current mfg.

MSR	**$1,600**	**$1,125**	**$800**	**$475**

EAN-46C - similar to the EAN-45C, except has a solid spruce top, current mfg.

MSR	**$1,700**	**$1,195**	**$850**	**$525**

EAN-60C - FXC nylon string single cutaway body, solid cedar top, mahogany back and sides, rosewood fingerboard, CT4B electronics, Satin Natural finish, current mfg.

MSR	**$1,200**	**$850**	**$600**	**$375**

NP-65C - "country classic" body style, single rounded cutaway, solid cedar top, round soundhole, 3-stripe bound body, wooden rosette, rosewood back/sides, mahogany neck, 20-fret ebony fingerboard, classic style ebony bridge, classic style peghead, 3-per-side gold tuners with amber buttons, crystal bridge pickups, parametric EQ, available in Natural finish, disc. 1999.

	$1,050	**$615**	**$425**

Last MSR was $1,499.

ND-65C - similar to NP-65C except, has rosewood fingerboard, DSP preamp system, available in Natural finish, disc.

	$1,225	**$585**	**$450**

Last MSR was $1,629.

ACOUSTIC: SANTA FE & NOVEAU SERIES

Santa Fe series instruments feature turquoise or abalone inlays and rosette designs with a Southwestern flavor.

T

GRADING		100%	EXCELLENT	AVERAGE

ESF-93 - folk style, single rounded cutaway, solid cedar top, round soundhole, multi bound, wood inlay rosette, silky oak back/sides, mahogany neck, 21-fret ebony fingerboard with turquoise eagle inlay, ebony bridge with white black dot pins, silky oak peghead veneer with turquoise dot/abalone logo inlay, 3-per-side gold tuners with amber buttons, piezo bridge pickups, parametric EQ, active electronics. Available in Natural finish, mfg. 1993 only.

		N/A	$750	$495

Last MSR was $1,500.

PSF-15C - dreadnought style, single rounded cutaway, solid cedar top, round soundhole, 3-stripe bound body/black crow rosette, rosewood sides, bookmatched rosewood back, mahogany neck, 21-fret rosewood fingerboard with turquoise dot inlay, turquoise eagle inlay at 12th fret, black headstock, rosewood bridge, 3-per-side gold tuners, bridge pickup, preamp and parametric EQ, available in Natural finish, mfg. 1993-99.

		$900	$540	$450

Last MSR was $1,699.

DSF-15C - similar to PSF-15C model except, has DSP preamp system, available in Natural Gloss finish, current mfg.

MSR	$1,749	$1,325	$625	$495

PSF-35C - folk style, single rounded cutaway, solid cedar top, round soundhole, 3-stripe bound body/black crow rosette, rosewood back/sides, mahogany neck, 21-fret rosewood fingerboard with turquoise dot inlay, turquoise eagle inlay at 12th fret, open classical-style headstock, rosewood bridge, 3-per-side gold tuners with amber buttons, bridge pickup, preamp and parametric EQ, available in Natural finish, mfg. 1993-95.

		N/A	$750	$495

Last MSR was $1,700.

PSF-48C - folk style, single rounded cutaway, solid spruce top, round soundhole, multi-bound body, wood inlay rosette, rosewood back/sides, mahogany neck, 21-fret ebony fingerboard with green abalone eagle inlay, strings through ebony bridge, rosewood peghead veneer with abalone dot/logo inlay, 3-per-side gold tuners with amber buttons, piezo bridge pickups, parametric EQ, active electronics, available in Natural finish, mfg. 1993-99.

		$1,440	$720	$595

Last MSR was $1,999.

ESF-48C - similar to PSF-48C except, has electronics, available in Natural Gloss finish, current mfg.

MSR	$2,000	$1,600	$1,000	$650

PSF-65C - folk style, single rounded cutaway, solid cedar top, round soundhole, 3-stripe bound body/black crow rosette, rosewood back/sides, mahogany neck, 21-fret rosewood fingerboard with turquoise dot inlay, turquoise eagle inlay at 12th fret, open classical-style headstock, rosewood bridge, 3-per-side gold tuners, bridge pickup, preamp and parametric EQ, available in Natural finish, mfg. 1993-99.

		$1,200	$600	$495

Last MSR was $1,699.

The PSF-65C was designed for nylon string use.

PSF-94 - folk style, single rounded cutaway, solid cedar top, round soundhole, multi-layer binding, wood inlay rosette, koa back/sides, mahogany neck, 20-fret rosewood fingerboard with abalone eagle inlay, rosewood strings through bridge, koa peghead veneer with abalone logo inlay, 3-per-side gold tuners with brown pearl buttons, piezo bridge pickups, parametric EQ, available in Natural finish, mfg. 1994 only.

		$1,295	$925	$610

Last MSR was $1,850.

ACOUSTIC ELECTRIC BASS

B-10 - 34" scale, single cutaway all maple body, spruce top, f-holes, Striped Ebony fretless fingerboard, DSP preamp system, 2 per side tuners, available in Red Stain finish, current mfg.

MSR	$3,500	$2,450	$1,750	$1,200

EG512C - jumbo style single cutaway body, spruce top, rosewood back and sides, rosewood fingerboard, TK4NT electronics, available in Gloss Natural finish, current mfg.

MSR	$730	$515	$365	$250

TAMA
Instruments previously produced in Japan from 1975 through 1979 by Ibanez. Distributed in the U.S. by the Chesbro Music Company of Idaho Falls, Idaho.

The Tama trademark is better known on the Hoshino-produced quality drum sets. Never the less, the Tama trademark was used on 2 series of acoustic guitars offered during the mid to late 1970s. The first series introduced was entry level to good quality D-45 shaped acoustics that featured a laminated top. However, the quality level jumped on the second series. The second series featured a solid top, mahogany neck, and East Indian and Brazilian rosewoods, as well as a light oil finish.

One way to determine a solid top acoustic from a ply or laminated top is to check the cross section of the wood on the edge of the soundhole. If the wood seems continuous, it's probably a solid top. If you can see layers, or if the inside of the edge is painted (check the wood inside the top – if it is different in appearance from the outside it's probably laminated), then the top is plywood. No, it's not the sheets that you build houses with! A plywood top is several layers of wood glued and pressed together. However, a solid top guitar will resonate better (because it's one piece of wood) and the tone will get better as the wood ages, (Tama Guitars overview courtesy Michael R. Stanger, Stringed Instrument Division of Missoula, Montana).

GRADING	100%	EXCELLENT	AVERAGE

TANARA

Instruments currently built in Korea and Indonesia. Distributed by the Chesbro Music Company of Idaho Falls, Idaho.

Tanara offers a range of acoustic and electric guitars designed for the entry level to student guitarist.

ACOUSTIC: ACOUSTIC SERIES

All Tanara guitar models feature a round soundhole, 3-per-side headstock, chrome hardware, and a Natural finish (unless otherwise specified).

SC26 - concert size steel string, pacific spruce top, mahogany back/sides, current mfg.

	MSR	$219		$165	$110	$75

SD24 - dreadnought size, pacific spruce top, mahogany back/sides, available in Natural gloss finish, current mfg.

	MSR	$219		$165	$110	$75

SD26 - dreadnought size, natural spruce top, mahogany back/sides, adjustable neck, 3-per-side machine heads, available in Black, Brown Sunburst, and Natural gloss finish, current mfg.

	MSR	$239		$180	$120	$80

SD30 - dreadnought size, spruce top, mahogany back/sides, rosewood fingerboard/bridge, scalloped 'X-bracing', 3-per-side die-cast tuners, available in Natural satin finish, current mfg.

	MSR	$339		$255	$170	$115

SD32 - similar to the SD30, except in a 12-string configuration, 6-per-side tuners, covered tuning gears, current mfg.

	MSR	$379		$285	$185	$125

ACOUSTIC: CLASSICAL SERIES

TC26 - concert size, spruce top, mahogany back/sides, adjustable neck, 3-per-side butterfly knobs, available in Pumpkin Amber finish, current mfg.

	MSR	$189		$140	$90	$65

TC46 - similar to the TC26, except features ovankol back/sides, multiple binding, available in Pumpkin Amber finish, current mfg.

	MSR	$259		$195	$130	$90

ACOUSTIC ELECTRIC

TSF1 - grand concert size with single cutaway, spruce top, mahogany back/sides, bound body/headstock, bound rosewood fingerboard with offset pearl position markers, rosewood bridge, 3-per-side chrome tuners, piezo pickup, volume/3-band EQ controls, current mfg.

	MSR	$569		$425	$280	$190

TSJ5 - solid spruce top, mahogany back/sides/neck, rosewood fingerboard, 3-per-side gold tuners, Fishman pickup, volume/EQ controls, current mfg.

	MSR	$669		$500	$330	$225

ACOUSTIC ELECTRIC BASS

TR720BF - select maple top, maple back/sides/neck, die-cast tuners, available in Natural finish, current mfg.

	MSR	$779		$585	$385	$260

Takamine ESF-48C courtesy Takamine

TANGLEWOOD

Instruments currently produced in Korea and Indonesia. Distributed by the European Music Company, Ltd. of Kent, England.

The European Music Company, Ltd. is currently offering a wide range of acoustic and electric guitar models under the **Tanglewood** trademark. These solidly built instruments offer the beginning and intermediate player a quality guitar for the price. For further information regarding model specification and pricing, contact the European Music Company, Ltd. directly (see Trademark Index).

TAYLOR

Instruments currently built in El Cajon, California. Distributed by Taylor Guitars of El Cajon, California. Previous production was based in Lemon Grove, California from 1974 through 1987.

Founding partners Bob Taylor, Steve Schemmer, and Kurt Listug were all working at the American Dream guitar repair shop in Lemon Grove, California, in the early 1970s. In 1974, the trio bought the shop and converted it into a guitar building factory. The company went through early growing pains throughout the late 1970s, but slowly and

T

GRADING		100%	EXCELLENT	AVERAGE

surely the guitars began catching on. In 1983, Listug and Taylor bought out Schemmer's share of the company, and re-incorporated. Fueled by sales of models such as the **Grand Concert** in 1984, the company expanded into new facilities in Santee, California (near El Cajon) three years later. Taylor and Listug continue to experiment with guitar construction and models – a good example would be the **Baby Taylor** model (list $299) which is a 3/4 size guitar with a solid top and laminated back and sides.

TAYLOR MODEL DESIGNATIONS AND BODY DIMENSIONS

Taylor Retail list prices do not include a case. Cases carry an additional cost. TC Series hardshell cases retail at $299, and SC Series SKB/Taylor cases retail at $199. Taylor acoustics are available with a wide range of custom options., including Engelmann spruce tops or Fishman transducer systems. There is not charge for a left-handed configuration (not available on all models).

Each Taylor model number also describes the particular guitar in relationship to the overall product line. The first of three numbers denotes the series (Taylor series comprise a specific combination of woods, bindings, inlays, etc.). The second number indicates whether it is a six string (1), or a 12-string (5). The exception to this rule is the 400 series, which include models 420 and 422. Finally, the third number indicates the body size: Dreadnought (0), Grand Concert (2), and Jumbo (5). The Grand Auditorium size models carry a prefix of **GA**. Any upper case letters that follow the three digit designation may indicate a cutaway (**C**) or a left-handed model (**L**).

Dreadnought: Body Width 16", Body Length 20", Body Depth 4 5/8".

Grand Auditorium: Body Width 16", Body Length 20", Body Depth 4 5/8".

Grand Concert: Body Width 15", Body Length 19 1/2", Body Depth 4 1/8".

Jumbo: Body Width 17", Body Length 21", Body Depth 4 5/8".

Add $240 for Sunburst finish.

ACOUSTIC: BABY TAYLOR SERIES

The Baby Taylor series is currently produced in Mexico. The Baby Taylor and Taylor Mahogany have the same price points. The Baby bubinga, koa, maple, and the rosewood all have the same price points.

BABY TAYLOR - 3/4 size, dreadnought body, solid Sitka spruce top, round soundhole, laser-etched rosette, mahogany veneer back/sides, mahogany neck, 14/19-fret ebony fingerboard with pearloid dot inlay, ebony bridge, Lexan peghead veneer, 3-per-side chrome diecast tuners, available in Natural satin finish, mfg. 1997-current.

MSR	$348		$250	$175	$115

BABY TAYLOR (MAPLE, BUB, KOA, AND RW) - similar to the Baby Taylor, except features respective wood type top, available in Natural satin finish, current mfg.

MSR	$428		$300	$215	$150

BIG BABY - similar to the Baby Taylor, except has a 15/16" sized body, available in Natural satin finish, current mfg.

MSR	$478		$340	$240	$175

ACOUSTIC: 300 SERIES

The 300 series models each feature a solid Sitka spruce top, sapele mahogany back and sides, 3-ply black plastic body binding, plastic ring inlay rosette, mahogany neck, 25 1/2" scale, 20-fret ebony fingerboard with pearl dot inlay, Indian rosewood peghead veneer, ebony bridge, Tusq nut and saddle.

310 - dreadnought body, tortoise shell pickguard, 6-string configuration, 3-per-side chrome Grover tuners, available in Natural satin finish with gloss top, mfg. 1998-current.

MSR	$1,348		$950	$675	$450

310 CE - similar to the 310, except features a single Venetian cutaway dreadnought body, Fishman Prefix electronics, available in Natural satin finish with gloss top, mfg. 1998-current.

MSR	$1,798		$1,275	$900	$575

312 CE - grand concert body with single Venetian cutaway, tortoise shell pickguard, 6-string configuration, 3-per-side chrome Grover tuners, Fishman Prefix electronics, available in Natural satin finish with gloss top, mfg. 1998-current.

MSR	$1,868		$1,325	$935	$600

314 - grand auditorium body, tortoise shell pickguard, 6-string configuration, 3-per-side chrome Grover tuners, available in Natural satin finish with gloss top, mfg. 1998-current.

MSR	$1,478		$1,050	$750	$475

314 CE - similar to the 314, except features a single Venetian cutaway dreadnought body, Fishman Prefix electronics, available in Natural satin finish with gloss top, mfg. 2000-current.

MSR	$1,938		$1,375	$975	$625

315 CE - jumbo body, tortoise shell pickguard, 6-string configuration, 3-per-side chrome Grover tuners, available in Natural satin finish with gloss top, mfg. 1998-current.

MSR	$1,938		$1,375	$975	$625

355 - jumbo cutaway body, tortoise shell pickguard, 12-string configuration, 6-per-side chrome Grover tuners, available in Natural satin finish with gloss top, mfg. 1998-current.

MSR	$1,678		$1,175	$850	$550

355 CE - similar to the 355, except has a single cutaway and electronics, mfg. 2000-current.

MSR	$2,088		$1,475	$1,050	$675

GRADING		100%	EXCELLENT	AVERAGE

ACOUSTIC: 400 SERIES

In 1998, Taylor changed the 400 series' mahogany or maple back and sides in favor of solid ovankol (also spelled ovangkol). All 6-string models feature scalloped bracing. Earlier acoustic/electric models may be equipped with an optional Acoustic Matrix pickup system.

410 - dreadnought body, solid Sitka spruce top, round soundhole, tortoise shell pickguard, white plastic body binding, 3-ply body, 3-ring inlay rosette, solid mahogany back/sides, mahogany neck, 14/20-fret rosewood fingerboard with pearl dot inlay, rosewood bridge, rosewood veneer on peghead, 3-per-side chrome Grover tuners, available in Natural satin finish with gloss top, current mfg.

MSR	$1,598	$1,125	$800	$525

In 1994, pearl peghead logo inlay was introduced. In 1998, ovankol back/sides replaced mahogany back/sides; ebony fingerboard replaced the rosewood fingerboard; ebony bridge replaced the rosewood bridge.

410 CE - similar to 410, except has an single Venetian cutaway body, Fishman Prefix system, available in Natural satin finish with gloss top, current mfg.

MSR	$2,048	$1,450	$1,025	$650

412 - grand concert body, solid spruce top, round soundhole, tortoise shell pickguard, white plastic body binding, 3-ply body, 3-ring inlay rosette, solid mahogany back/sides, mahogany neck, 14/20-fret rosewood fingerboard with pearl dot inlay, rosewood bridge, rosewood veneer on peghead, 3-per-side chrome Grover tuners, available in Natural satin finish with gloss top, disc. 1998.

$825	$625	$375

Last MSR was $998.

412 CE - similar to the 412, except features single Venetian cutaway body, ovankol back/sides, ebony fingerboard, ebony bridge, Fishman Prefix electronics, available in Natural satin finish with gloss top, mfg. 1998-current.

MSR	$2,128	$1,495	$1,075	$725

414 - grand auditorium body, solid Sitka spruce top, round soundhole, tortoise shell pickguard, white plastic body binding, 3-ply body, 3-ring inlay rosette, solid ovankol back/sides, mahogany neck, 14/20-fret ebony fingerboard with pearl dot inlay, ebony bridge, rosewood veneer on peghead, 3-per-side chrome Grover tuners, available in Natural satin finish with gloss top, mfg. 1998-current.

MSR	$1,758	$1,475	$900	$575

414 CE - similar to 414, except has a single Venetian cutaway body, Fishman Prefix system, available in Natural satin finish with gloss top, current mfg.

MSR	$2,208	$1,550	$1,125	$700

415 - jumbo body, solid Sitka spruce top, round soundhole, tortoise shell pickguard, white plastic body binding, 3-ply body, 3-ring inlay rosette, solid ovankol back/sides, mahogany neck, 14/20-fret ebony fingerboard with pearl dot inlay, ebony bridge, rosewood veneer on peghead, 3-per-side chrome Grover tuners, available in Natural satin finish with gloss top, mfg. 1998-current.

MSR	$1,758	$1,250	$900	$575

420 - similar to 410, except has maple back and sides, available in Natural finish, disc. 1997.

$850	$750	$425

Last MSR was $1,198.

420 PF Limited Edition - similar to 420, except has solid pau ferro back and sides, disc. 1997.

$1,100	$650	$425

Last MSR was $1,400.

422 - similar to 412, except has maple back and sides, disc. 1998.

$900	$750	$425

Last MSR was $1,198.

450 - similar to 410, except has 12-string configuration, 6-per-side tuners, disc. 1997.

$975	$800	$475

Last MSR was $1,298.

455 - jumbo body, solid Sitka spruce top, round soundhole, tortoise shell pickguard, 12-string configuration, white plastic body binding, 3-ply body, 3-ring inlay rosette, solid ovankol back/sides, mahogany neck, 14/20-fret ebony fingerboard with pearl dot inlay, ebony bridge, rosewood veneer on peghead, 6-per-side chrome Grover tuners, available in Natural satin finish with gloss top, mfg. 2000-current.

MSR	$1,958	$1,395	$1,000	$625

455 CE - similar to the 455, except has a cutaway with electronics, mfg. 2000-current.

MSR	$2,358	$1,650	$1,200	$750

ACOUSTIC: 500 SERIES

The 500 series models feature solid mahogany backs and sides; current fancy appointments include abalone inlay on the soundhole rosettes and pearl diamond inlays on the fingerboard.

T

510 - dreadnought body, solid Engelmann spruce top, round soundhole, tortoise shell pickguard, 3-stripe bound body/rosette, solid mahogany back/sides/neck, 14/20-fret ebony fingerboard with pearl dot inlay, ebony bridge with black pins, rosewood veneer on peghead, 3-per-side gold tuners, available in Natural gloss finish, current mfg.

MSR	$2,348		$1,650	$1,175	$725

In 1994, pearl peghead logo inlay, abalone rosette, abalone slotted diamond fingerboard inlay, black abalone dot bridgepins replaced original items. In 1998, chrome Grover tuners replaced the gold-plated tuners.

510 CE - similar to 510, except has a single Venetian cutaway body, Fishman Onboard Blender system, available in Natural gloss finish, mfg. 1998-current.

MSR	$2,948		$2,075	$1,500	$975

512 - grand concert body, solid Engelmann spruce top, round soundhole, tortoise shell pickguard, 3-stripe bound body/rosette, solid mahogany back/sides/neck, 14/20-fret ebony fingerboard with pearl dot inlay, ebony bridge with black pins, rosewood veneer on peghead, 3-per-side gold tuners, available in Natural gloss finish, disc. 2000.

	$2,375	$1,375	$925

Last MSR was $2,868.

In 1994, pearl peghead logo inlay, abalone rosette, abalone slotted diamond fingerboard inlay, black abalone dot bridgepins replaced original items. In 1998, chrome Grover tuners replaced the gold-plated tuners.

512 CE - similar to 512, except has a single Venetian cutaway body, Fishman Onboard Blender system, available in Natural gloss finish, mfg. 2001-current.

MSR	$3,068		$2,150	$1,550	$1,000

514 C - grand auditorium body with single Venetian cutaway, solid Western red cedar top, round soundhole, tortoise shell pickguard, 3-stripe bound body/rosette, solid mahogany back/sides/neck, 14/20-fret ebony fingerboard with pearl dot inlay, ebony bridge with black pins, rosewood veneer on peghead, 3-per-side gold tuners, available in Natural gloss finish, disc. 1998.

	$1,750	$1,350	$795

Last MSR was $2,198.

In 1994, pearl peghead logo inlay, abalone rosette, abalone slotted diamond fingerboard inlay, black abalone dot bridgepins replaced original items. In 1998, chrome Grover tuners replaced the gold-plated tuners.

514 CE - similar to 514 C, except has a Fishman Onboard Blender system, available in Natural gloss finish, mfg. 1998-current.

MSR	$3,188		$2,250	$1,600	$1,025

555 - jumbo body, 12-string configuration, solid Sitka spruce top, round soundhole, tortoise shell pickguard, 3-stripe bound body/rosette, solid mahogany back/sides/neck, 14/20-fret ebony fingerboard with pearl dot inlay, ebony bridge with black pins, rosewood veneer on peghead, 6-per-side gold tuners, available in Natural gloss finish, current mfg.

MSR	$2,778		$1,950	$1,400	$900

In 1994, pearl peghead logo inlay, abalone rosette, abalone slotted diamond fingerboard inlay, black abalone dot bridgepins replaced original items. In 1998, chrome Grover tuners replaced the gold-plated tuners.

555 CE - similar to 555, except has Fishman Onboard Blender system, available in Natural gloss finish, mfg. 1998-current.

MSR	$3,388		$2,375	$1,700	$1,100

ACOUSTIC: 600 SERIES

The 600 series features curly maple back and side, scalloped bracing (on the 6-string models), an abalone soundhole rosette, and pearl "Leaf Pattern" inlays.

The models originally featured Amber-stained back and sides and gloss finish. In 1998, when 5 acoustic/electric models debuted, the stain colors expanded to Amber, Black, Blue, Green, Natural, and Red (and gloss finish).

610 - dreadnought body, solid spruce top, round soundhole, tortoise shell pickguard, white plastic body binding, ring design rosette, solid maple back/sides, mahogany neck, 14/20-fret bound rosewood fingerboard with pearl dot inlay, rosewood bridge with black pins, rosewood veneer on peghead, 3-per-side gold Grover tuners, available in Amber Stain finish, disc.

	$1,500	$1,150	$675

Last MSR was $1,898.

In 1994, the abalone rosette, bound ebony fingerboard with pearl leaf inlay, ebony bridge with black abalone dot bridge pins, ebony peghead veneer with pearl logo inlay replaced original items.

610 CE - similar to 610, except has an single Venetian cutaway body, Sitka spruce top, Big leaf maple back/sides, Fishman Onboard Blender system, available in Amber, Black, Blue, Green, Natural, or Red gloss finishes, mfg. 1998-current.

MSR	$3,348		$2,350	$1,675	$1,075

612 - grand concert body, solid spruce top, round soundhole, tortoise shell pickguard, 3-stripe bound body/rosette, solid maple back/sides, mahogany neck, 14/20-fret bound rosewood fingerboard with pearl dot inlay, rosewood bridge with black pins, rosewood veneer on peghead, 3-per-side gold tuners, available in Natural finish, disc. 1992.

	N/A	$950	$650

Last MSR was $1,840.

612 C - similar to 612, except has single Venetian cutaway body, mfg. 1993-98.

	N/A	$1,500	$800

Last MSR was $2,198.

In 1994, single round cutaway, abalone rosette, bound ebony fingerboard with pearl leaf inlay, ebony bridge with black abalone dot bridge pins, ebony peghead veneer with pearl logo inlay replaced original items.

GRADING		100%	EXCELLENT	AVERAGE

612 CE - similar to 612, except has an single Venetian cutaway body, Sitka spruce top, Big leaf maple back/sides, Fishman Onboard Blender system, available in Amber, Black, Blue, Green, Natural, or Red gloss finishes, mfg. 1998-current.

MSR	$3,488	$2,450	$1,595	$1,050

614 C - grand auditorium body, with single Venetian cutaway, solid spruce top, round soundhole, tortoise shell pickguard, 3-stripe bound body/rosette, solid maple back/sides, mahogany neck, 14/20-fret bound rosewood fingerboard with pearl dot inlay, rosewood bridge with black pins, rosewood veneer on peghead, 3-per-side gold tuners, available in Natural finish, disc. 1998.

		$1,875	$1,400	$895

Last MSR was $2,298.

614 CE - similar to 614, except has an single Venetian cutaway body, Sitka spruce top, Big leaf maple back/sides, Fishman Onboard Blender system, available in Amber, Black, Blue, Green, Natural, and Red gloss finishes, mfg. 1998-current.

MSR	$3,628	$2,550	$1,850	$1,250

615 - jumbo body, solid spruce top, round soundhole, tortoise pickguard, 3-stripe bound body/rosette, solid maple back/sides, mahogany neck, 14/20-fret bound rosewood fingerboard with pearl dot inlay, rosewood bridge with black pins, rosewood veneer on peghead, 3-per-side gold tuners, available in Natural finish, disc. 1998.

		$1,700	$1,350	$775

Last MSR was $2,198.

In 1994, abalone rosette, bound ebony fingerboard with pearl leaf inlay, ebony bridge with black abalone dot bridge pins, ebony peghead veneer with pearl logo inlay replaced original items.

615 CE - similar to 615, except has an single Venetian cutaway body, Sitka spruce top, Big leaf maple back/sides, Fishman Onboard Blender system, available in Amber, Black, Blue, Green, Natural, or Red gloss finishes, mfg. 1998-current.

MSR	$3,628	$3,550	$1,850	$1,250

655 - jumbo body, 12-string configuration, solid spruce top, round soundhole, tortoise pickguard, 3-stripe bound body/rosette, solid maple back/sides, mahogany neck, 14/20-fret bound rosewood fingerboard with pearl dot inlay, rosewood bridge with black pins, rosewood veneer on peghead, 6-per-side gold tuners, available in Natural finish, disc. 1998, reintroduced 2001-current.

MSR	$3,218	$2,275	$1,625	$1,100

655 CE - similar to 655, except has an single Venetian cutaway body, Sitka spruce top, Big leaf maple back/sides, Fishman Onboard Blender system, available in Amber, Black, Blue, Green, Natural, or Red gloss finishes, mfg. 1998-current.

MSR	$3,828	$2,695	$1,925	$1,300

**Taylor 615 CE
courtesy Dave Rogers
Dave's Guitar Shop**

ACOUSTIC: 700 SERIES

The 700 Series models feature Indian rosewood back and sides, abalone soundhole rosette and neck dot inlays. Models prior to 1998 have solid spruce tops; models after 1998 now feature Western red cedar tops.

710 - dreadnought body, solid spruce top, round soundhole, tortoise shell pickguard, 3-stripe bound body/rosette, rosewood back/sides, mahogany neck, 14/20-fret ebony fingerboard with pearl dot inlay, ebony bridge with black pins, rosewood veneer on peghead, 3-per-side gold tuners, available in Natural finish, current mfg.

MSR	$2,548	$1,795	$1,275	$825

In 1994, abalone rosette, abalone dot fingerboard inlay, black abalone dot bridge pins, pearl logo peghead inlay replaced original items. In 1998, a Western Red cedar top replaced spruce top.

710 CE - similar to 710, except has a single Venetian cutaway body, Fishman Onboard Blender system, available in Natural gloss finish, mfg. 1998-current.

MSR	$3,148	$2,225	$1,575	$1,050

712 - grand concert body, solid spruce top, round soundhole, tortoise shell pickguard, 3-stripe bound body and rosette, rosewood back/sides, mahogany neck, 14/20-fret ebony fingerboard with pearl dot inlay, ebony bridge with black pins, rosewood veneer on peghead, 3-per-side gold tuners, available in Natural finish, current mfg.

MSR	$2,668	$1,875	$1,350	$900

In 1994, abalone rosette, abalone dot fingerboard inlay, black abalone dot bridge pins, pearl logo peghead inlay replaced original items. In 1998, a Western Red cedar top replaced spruce top.

712 CE - similar to 712, except has a single Venetian cutaway body, Fishman Onboard Blender system, available in Natural gloss finish, mfg. 2000-current.

MSR	$3,278	$2,295	$1,650	$1,100

**Taylor 712
courtesy Taylor**

T

GRADING		100%	EXCELLENT	AVERAGE

714 - grand auditorium body, solid spruce top, round soundhole, tortoise shell pickguard, 3-stripe bound body and rosette, rosewood back/sides, mahogany neck, 14/20-fret ebony fingerboard with pearl dot inlay, ebony bridge with black pins, rosewood veneer on peghead, 3-per-side gold tuners, available in Natural finish, current mfg.

MSR	$2,798	$1,975	$1,400	$925

In 1998, a Western Red cedar top replaced spruce top.

714 CE - similar to 714, except has a single Venetian cutaway body, Fishman Onboard Blender system, available in Natural gloss finish, mfg. 1998-current.

MSR	$3,408	$2,395	$1,725	$1,175

750 - similar to 710, except has 12-string configuration, 6-per-side tuners, disc. 1998.

		$1,575	$1,150	$675

Last MSR was $1,898.

ACOUSTIC: 800 SERIES

The Taylor 800 series are referred to as "the descendants of Bob Taylor's original design." These deluxe models feature Indian rosewood back and sides, scalloped bracing (on 6-string models), abalone soundhole rosette, and pearl "Progressive Diamond" fretboard inlay.

810 - dreadnought body, solid Sitka spruce top, round soundhole, tortoise shell pickguard, 3-stripe bound body, abalone rosette, Indian rosewood back/sides, mahogany neck, 14/20-fret bound rosewood fingerboard with pearl snowflake inlay, rosewood bridge with black abalone dot pins, rosewood veneer on bound peghead w/pearl logo inlay, 3-per-side gold tuners, available in Natural finish, current mfg.

MSR	$2,848	$1,995	$1,450	$925

In 1994, pearl progressive diamond fingerboard inlay replaced the snowflake inlay. In 1998, ebony fingerboard replaced rosewood fingerboard; ebony bridge replaced the rosewood bridge.

810 CE - similar to 810, except has a single Florentine or Venetian cutaway body, Fishman Onboard Blender system, available in Natural gloss finish, mfg. 1998-current.

MSR	$3,448	$2,425	$1,725	$1,200

812 - grand concert body, solid (Sitka) spruce top, round soundhole, tortoise shell pickguard, 3-stripe bound body, abalone rosette, rosewood back/sides, mahogany neck, 14/20-fret bound rosewood fingerboard with pearl snowflake inlay, rosewood bridge with black abalone dot pins, rosewood veneer on bound peghead with pearl logo inlay, 3-per-side gold tuners, available in Natural finish, disc. 1992.

		N/A	$1,200	$750

Last MSR was $1,960.

812 C - similar to 812, except has single sharp cutaway, mfg. 1993-98.

		$1,800	$1,350	$800

Last MSR was $2,298.

In 1994, single round cutaway, pearl progressive diamond fingerboard inlay replaced original items.

812 CE - similar to 812, except has a single Florentine or Venetian cutaway body, Fishman Onboard Blender system, available in Natural gloss finish, mfg. 1998-current.

MSR	$3,598	$2,525	$1,800	$1,250

814 C - grand auditorium body with single rounded cutaway, solid Sitka spruce top, round soundhole, tortoise pickguard, 3-stripe bound body, abalone rosette, rosewood back/sides, mahogany neck, 14/20-fret bound rosewood fingerboard with pearl snowflake inlay, rosewood bridge with black abalone dot pins, rosewood veneer on bound peghead with pearl logo inlay, 3-per-side gold tuners, disc. 1998.

		$1,995	$1,450	$825

Last MSR was $2,398.

814 CE - similar to 814 C, except has a Fishman Onboard Blender system, available in Natural gloss finish, mfg. 1998-current.

MSR	$3,738	$2,625	$1,875	$1,275

815 C - jumbo body with single sharp cutaway, solid (Sitka) spruce top, round soundhole, tortoise pickguard, 3-stripe bound body, abalone rosette, rosewood back/sides, mahogany neck, 14/20-fret bound rosewood fingerboard with pearl snowflake inlay, rosewood bridge with black abalone dot pins, rosewood veneer on bound peghead with pearl logo inlay, 3-per-side gold tuners, mfg. 1993-98.

		N/A	$1,450	$825

Last MSR was $2,398.

In 1994, pearl progressive diamond fingerboard inlay replaced original item.

815 CE - similar to 815 C, except has a Fishman Onboard Blender system, available in Natural gloss finish, mfg. 1998-current.

MSR	$3,738	$2,625	$1,875	$1,275

855 - jumbo body, 12-string configuration, solid (Sitka) spruce top, round soundhole, tortoise shell pickguard, 3-stripe bound body, abalone rosette, rosewood back/sides, mahogany neck, 14/20-fret bound rosewood fingerboard with pearl snowflake inlay, rosewood bridge with black abalone dot pins, rosewood veneer on bound peghead with pearl logo inlay, 6-per-side gold tuners, available in Natural finish, current mfg.

MSR	$3,328	$2,350	$1,675	$1,125

In 1994, pearl progressive diamond fingerboard inlay replaced original item.

855 CE - similar to 855, except has a Fishman Onboard Blender system, available in Natural gloss finish, mfg. 2000-current.

MSR	$3,938	$2,775	$1,975	$1,350

T

GRADING	100%	EXCELLENT	AVERAGE

ACOUSTIC: 900 SERIES

The deluxe 900 series models feature Engelmann spruce tops, Indian rosewood back and sides, scalloped bracing (on the 6-string models), abalone top edging combined with rosewood binding, distinct abalone soundhole rosette, and the abalone and pearl "Cindy" design fingerboard inlays.

910 - dreadnought body, solid Engelmann spruce top, round soundhole, tortoise shell pickguard, abalone edge inlay/rosewood body binding, abalone rosette, maple back/sides/neck, 14/20-fret ebony fingerboard with abalone stylized inlay, ebony bridge with black abalone dot pins, rosewood peghead veneer with abalone stylized T/logo inlay, 3-per-side gold tuners, available in Natural finish, current mfg.

MSR	$3,998		$2,795	$2,000	$1,400

In 1993, rosewood back/sides, mahogany neck were optional. In 1994, abalone purfling, abalone flower fingerboard inlay replaced original items, abalone stylized T peghead inlay was discontinued.

910 CE - similar to 910, except has single Florentine or Venetian cutaway body and Fishman Onboard Blender system, available in Natural Gloss finish, mfg. 1998-current.

MSR	$4,598		$3,225	$2,300	$1,500

912 - grand concert body, solid (Engelmann) spruce top, round soundhole, tortoise shell pickguard, wood bound body, abalone rosette, maple back/sides/neck, 14/20-fret ebony fingerboard with abalone stylized inlay, ebony bridge with black abalone dot pins, rosewood veneer with abalone stylized T/logo inlay on peghead, 3-per-side gold tuners, available in Natural finish, disc. 1992.

	N/A		$1,450	$950

Last MSR was $2,715.

912 CE - similar to 912, except has single Florentine or Venetian cutaway body, and Fishman Onboard Blender system, mfg. 1993-current.

MSR	$4,798		$3,375	$2,400	$1,600

In 1994, abalone purfling, abalone flower fingerboard inlay replaced original items, abalone stylized T peghead inlay was discontinued.

914 CE - similar to the 912, except features a grand auditorium body with a single Florentine or Venetian cutaway, and Fishman Onboard Blender system, current mfg.

MSR	$4,998		$3,500	$2,500	$1,700

915 - jumbo body, solid spruce top, round soundhole, tortoise pickguard, wood bound body, abalone rosette, maple back/sides/neck, 14/20-fret ebony fingerboard with abalone stylized inlay, ebony bridge with black abalone dot pins, rosewood veneer with abalone stylized T/logo inlay on peghead, 3-per-side gold tuners, available in Natural finish, disc. 1992.

	N/A		$1,500	$950

Last MSR was $2,815.

915 CE - similar to 915, except has single Florentine or Venetian cutaway body, mfg. 1998-current.

MSR	$4,998		$3,500	$2,500	$1,700

955 - jumbo body, 12-string configuration, solid spruce top, round soundhole, tortoise shell pickguard, wood bound body, abalone rosette, maple back/sides/neck, 14/20-fret ebony fingerboard with abalone stylized inlay, ebony bridge with black abalone dot pins, rosewood veneer with abalone stylized T/logo inlay on peghead, 6-per-side gold tuners, Natural finish, current mfg.

MSR	$4,598		$3,225	$2,300	$1,500

ACOUSTIC: KOA SERIES

Different Koa Series models feature Engelmann spruce, western red cedar, or Hawaiian koa tops. Each model features Hawaiian koa back and sides, tortoise shell body binding, abalone rosette, mahogany neck, 20-fret ebony fingerboard with a special 1995 Limited Edition pattern, ebony bridge with black bridgepins, ebony peghead veneer, gold plated Grover tuners. In 2000, all models that had cutaways had electronics put in them.

K 10 - dreadnought body, Engelmann spruce top, 6-string configuration, 3-per-side tuners, available in Natural gloss finish, mfg. 1998-current.

MSR	$3,698		$2,595	$1,850	$1,250

K 12 - grand concert body, Engelmann spruce top, 6-string configuration, 3-per-side tuners, available in Natural gloss finish, mfg. 1998-current.

MSR	$3,878		$2,725	$1,950	$1,300

K 14 CE - grand auditorium body with single Venetian cutaway, Fishman Onboard Blender system, western red cedar top, available in Natural gloss finish, mfg. 1998-current.

MSR	$4,668		$3,275	$2,350	$1,500

Taylor 815 L
courtesy Dave Rogers
Dave's Guitar Shop

T

GRADING		100%	EXCELLENT	AVERAGE

K 20 - dreadnought body, koa top/back/sides/neck, round soundhole, tortoise pickguard, 3-stripe bound body, abalone rosette, 14/20-fret rosewood fingerboard with pearl diamond inlay, rosewood bridge with black abalone dot pins, ebony veneer with abalone logo inlay on peghead, 3-per-side gold tuners, available in Natural finish, disc. 1992.

		N/A	$1,750	$1,150

Last MSR was $2,115.

This model had solid spruce top as an option.

K 20 C - similar to the K 20, except features single Venetian cutaway body, Hawaiian koa top, mahogany neck, ebony fingerboard with 1995 Limited Edition pattern inlay, ebony bridge, tortoise body binding, available in Natural gloss finish, mfg. 1998-2000.

		$3,225	$1,900	$1,150

Last MSR was $3,896.

K 20 CE - similar to the K 20C, except has Fishman onboard Blender system, mfg. 2001-current.

MSR	$4,498	$3,150	$2,250	$1,500

K 22 (VERSION I) - grand concert body, koa top/back/sides/neck, round soundhole, tortoise pickguard, 3-stripe bound body, abalone rosette, 14/20-fret rosewood fingerboard with pearl diamond inlay, rosewood bridge with black abalone dot pins, ebony veneer with abalone logo inlay on peghead, 3-per-side gold tuners, available in Natural finish, disc. 1992.

		N/A	$1,500	$900

Last MSR was $2,190.

K 22 (VERSION II) - similar to the K 22 (Version I), except features a Hawaiian koa top, mahogany neck, tortoise body binding, 14/20-fret ebony fingerboard with the 1995 Limited Edition pattern inlay, ebony bridge, mfg. 1998-2000.

		$3,210	$1,895	$1,250

Last MSR was $3,872.

K 22CE - similar to the K 22, except has a single cutaway and Fishman onboard Blender system, mfg. 2000-current.

MSR	$4,668	$3,275	$2,350	$1,450

K 55 - jumbo koa body, 12-string configuration, available in Natural finish, mfg. 2000-current.

MSR	$4,268	$2,995	$2,150	$1,350

K 65 - jumbo body, Hawaiian koa top, 12-string configuration, 6-per-side tuners, available in Natural gloss finish, mfg. 1998-99.

MSR	$4,246	$2,975	$2,075	$1,375

K 65CE - similar to the K 65, except has a single cutaway and Fishman onboard Blender system, mfg. 2000-current.

MSR	$5,068	$3,550	$2,550	$1,600

ACOUSTIC: NYLON SERIES

NS32CE - deep grand concert nylon body, Sitka spruce top, sapele back and sides, ebony fingerboard and bridge, 3-per-side open tuners, available in Natural finish, Fishman Prefix Pro electronics, new 2003.

MSR	$1,698	$1,195	$850	$525

NS42CE - deep grand concert nylon body, Sitka spruce top, ovangkol back and sides, ebony fingerboard and bridge, 3-per-side open tuners, available in Natural finish, Fishman Prefix Pro electronics, new 2003.

MSR	$1,898	$1,350	$950	$575

NS52CE - deep grand concert nylon body, Sitka spruce top, mahogany back and sides, ebony fingerboard and bridge, 3-per-side open tuners, available in Natural finish, Fishman Prefix Pro electronics, new 2003.

MSR	$2,498	$1,750	$1,250	$750

NS62CE - deep grand concert nylon body, Sitka spruce top, maple back and sides, ebony fingerboard and bridge, 3-per-side open tuners, available in Natural finish, Fishman Prefix Pro electronics, new 2003.

MSR	$2,798	$1,975	$1,400	$850

NS72CE - deep grand concert nylon body, Sitka spruce top, rosewood back and sides, ebony fingerboard and bridge, 3-per-side open tuners, available in Natural finish, Fishman Prefix Pro electronics, new 2003.

MSR	$3,198	$2,250	$1,600	$975

ACOUSTIC: PRESENTATION SERIES

The Taylor **Presentation Series** guitar models each feature a solid Engelmann spruce top, scalloped X-bracing (tapered on the PS 55), ivoroid body binding with abalone edging, solid Hawaiian koa back and sides, abalone soundhole rosette, mahogany neck, 25 1/2" scale, 20-fret ebony fingerboard with "Byzantine" fretboard inlays, ebony bridge, ebony peghead veneer, Tusq nut and saddle, and gold Schaller tuners with ebony buttons.

PS 10 - dreadnought body, 6-string configuration, 3-per-side tuners, available in Natural gloss finish, current mfg.

MSR	$9,498	$6,700	$4,750	$3,100

PS 12 C - grand concert body with single Venetian cutaway, 6-string configuration, 3-per-side tuners, available in Natural gloss finish, current mfg.

MSR	$10,168	$7,150	$5,100	$3,300

PS 14 C - grand auditorium body with single Venetian cutaway, 6-string configuration, 3-per-side tuners, available in Natural gloss finish, current mfg.

MSR	$10,648	$7,500	$5,325	$3,500

GRADING		100%	EXCELLENT	AVERAGE

PS 15 - jumbo body, 6-string configuration, 3-per-side tuners, available in Natural gloss finish, current mfg.

MSR	$10,448		$7,350	$5,225	$3,400

PS 55 - jumbo body, 12-string configuration, 6-per-side tuners, available in Natural gloss finish, current mfg.

MSR	$10,648		$7,500	$5,325	$3,500

ACOUSTIC: SIGNATURE SERIES

DCSM DAN CRARY SIGNATURE - single rounded cutaway dreadnought body, Sitka spruce top, round soundhole, tortoise pickguard, 5-stripe white plastic body binding, abalone rosette, Indian rosewood back/sides, mahogany neck, 25 1/2" scale, 14/20-fret bound ebony fingerboard with pearl diamond inlay, ebony bridge with black abalone dot pins, bound rosewood peghead veneer w/pearl logo inlay, 3-per-side gold tuners, body width 16", body length 20", body depth 4 5/8", available in Natural gloss finish, disc. 2000.

		$2,290	$1,475	$975

Last MSR was $2,798.

This model was designed in conjunction with guitarist Dan Crary.

DDSM DOYLE DYKES SIGNATURE - single sharp cutaway dreadnought body, Sitka spruce top, round soundhole, 5-stripe white plastic body binding, abalone rosette, big leaf maple back/sides, mahogany neck, 25 1/2" scale, 14/20-fret bound ebony fingerboard, available in Black or Natural finishes, mfg. 2000-current.

MSR	$4,998		$3,500	$2,500	$1,700

LKSM12 LEO KOTTKE SIGNATURE - 12-string configuration, jumbo body, spruce top, round soundhole, rosewood body binding, rosette, American mahogany back/sides, mahogany neck, 14/20-fret ebony fingerboard, ebony bridge with black pins, rosewood peghead veneer with pearl logo inlay, 6-per-side gold tuners, body width 17", body length 21", body depth 4 5/8", available in Natural finish, current mfg.

MSR	$3,298		$2,325	$1,625	$1,050

In 1994, 12th fret fingerboard inlay was discontinued. This model was designed in conjunction with guitarist Leo Kottke.

LKSM-6 Leo Kottke Signature - similar to the LKSM, except in a 6-string configuration, 3-per-side tuners, available in Natural gloss finish, body width 17", body length 21", body fepth 4 5/8", mfg. 1997-current.

MSR	$3,098		$2,175	$1,500	$1,000

ACOUSTIC: WALNUT SERIES

Different Walnut Series models feature Sitka spruce, Western red cedar, or Claro walnut tops. Each Walnut Series guitar models feature scalloped X-bracing (tapered on the W 65), ivoroid body binding with abalone edging, solid Claro walnut back and sides, abalone soundhole rosette, mahogany neck, 25 1/2" scale, 20-fret ebony fingerboard with Original 900 Series inlay pattern, ebony bridge, ebony peghead veneer, Tusq nut and saddle, and gold Grover tuners. Taylor's Walnut Series was introduced in 1998.

W 10 - dreadnought body, Sitka spruce top, 6-string configuration, 3-per-side tuners, available in Natural gloss finish, mfg. 1998-current.

MSR	$2,798		$1,975	$1,400	$925

W 10CE - similar to the W10, except has a single cutaway and Fishman onboard Blender system, current mfg.

MSR	$3,398		$2,395	$1,700	$1,150

W 12 C - grand concert body with single Venetian cutaway, Western red cedar top, 6-string configuration, 3-per-side tuners, available in Natural gloss finish, mfg. 1998-2000.

		$3,375	$1,995	$1,325

Last MSR was $4,070.

W 12CE - similar to the W12C, except has a single cutaway and Fishman onboard Blender system, mfg. 2000-current.

MSR	$3,538		$2,495	$1,775	$1,200

W 14 C - grand auditorium body with single Venetian cutaway, Western red cedar top, 6-string configuration, 3-per-side tuners, available in Natural gloss finish, mfg. 1998-2000.

		$3,525	$2,095	$1,375

Last MSR was $4,256.

W 14CE - similar to the W14C, except has a Fishman onboard Blender system, mfg. 2000-current.

MSR	$3,678		$2,575	$1,850	$1,250

Taylor K-20
courtesy Taylor

T

GRADING		100%	EXCELLENT	AVERAGE

W 15 - jumbo body, Sitka spruce top, 6-string configuration, 3-per-side tuners, available in Natural gloss finish, mfg. 1998-current.

MSR	$3,078		$2,175	$1,550	$1,025

W 55 - jumbo body, Sitka spruce top, 12-string configuration, 6-per-side tuners, available in Natural gloss finish, mfg. 2000-current.

MSR	$3,278		$2,295	$1,650	$1,075

W 65 - jumbo body, Claro walnut top, 12-string configuration, 6-per-side tuners, available in Natural gloss finish, current mfg.

			$3,625	$2,125	$1,395

Last MSR was $4,356.

W 65CE - similar to the W65, except has a single cutaway and Fishman onboard Blender system, mfg. 2000-current.

MSR	$4,078		$2,875	$2,050	$1,350

ACOUSTIC BASS: AB SERIES

Bob Taylor and Steve Klein collaborated on an acoustic bass design in a 34" scale with a Fishman pickup system. The rugged padded gig bag for the AB Series basses lists at $155.

AB 1 - single rounded cutaway body, Sitka spruce top, round soundhole offset to the treble bout, tuned Imbuia ring rosette, Imbuia Brazilian Walnut back/sides, mahogany neck/Imbuia peghead, 24-fret ebony fingerboard with pearl Steve Klein signature inlay, ebony bridge, Imbuia peghead veneer, 2-per-side chrome Grover tuners, available in Natural satin finish, current mfg.

MSR	$2,750		$1,925	$1,350	$895

AB 2 - similar to the AB 1, except features Imbuia top. Available in Natural satin finish, current mfg.

MSR	$2,850		$1,995	$1,350	$900

AB 3 - similar to the AB 1, except features big leaf maple back/sides, tuned ebony ring rosette, maple neck, ebony peghead veneer, white plastic body binding, available in Amber, Black, Blue, Green, Natural, or Red gloss finishes, current mfg.

MSR	$2,950		$2,075	$1,450	$950

AB 4 - similar to the AB 3, except features a maple top, available in Amber, Black, Blue, Green, Natural, or Red gloss finishes, current mfg.

MSR	$3,150		$2,225	$1,575	$1,050

TEISCO

See Teisco Del Rey. Instruments previously produced in Japan. Distributed in the U.S. by Westheimer Musical Instruments of Evanston, Illinois.

One of the original Teisco importers was George Rose of Los Angeles, California. Some instruments may bear the shortened "Teisco" logo, many others were shipped in unlabeled. Please: no jokes about Teisco "no-casters," (Source: Michael Wright, *Guitar Stories,* Volume One).

TEISCO DEL REY

Instruments previously produced in Japan from 1956 to 1973. Distributed in the U.S. by Westheimer Musical Instruments of Evanston, Illinois.

In 1946, Mr. Atswo Kaneko and Mr. Doryu Matsuda founded the Aoi Onpa Kenkyujo company, makers of the guitars bearing the Teisco and other trademarks (the company name roughly translates to the **Hollyhock Soundwave or Electricity Laboratories**). The Teisco name was chosen by Mr. Kaneko, and was used primarily in domestic markets. Early models include lap steel and electric-Spanish guitars. By the 1950s, the company was producing slab-bodied designs with bolt-on necks. In 1956, the company name was changed to the Nippon Onpa Kogyo Co., Ltd. – but the guitars still stayed Teisco!

As the demand for guitars in the U.S. market began to expand, Mr. Jack Westheimer of WMI Corporation of Evanston, Illinois started to import Japanese guitars in the late 1950s, perhaps circa 1958. WMI began importing the Teisco-built Kingston guitars in 1961, and also used the Teisco Del Rey trademark extensively beginning in 1964. Other Teisco-built guitars had different trademarks (a rebranding technique), and the different brand names will generally indicate the U.S. importer/distributor. The Japanese company again changed names, this time to the Teisco Co. Ltd. The Teisco line included all manners of solid body and semi-hollowbody guitars, and their niche in the American guitar market (as entry level or beginner's guitars) assured steady sales.

In 1967, the Kawai Corporation purchased the Teisco company. Not one to ruin a good thing, Kawai continued exporting the Teisco line to the U.S. (although they did change some designs through the years) until 1973. Due to the recent popularity in the Teisco name, Kawai actually produced some limited edition Teisco Spectrum Five models lately in Japan, although they were not made available to the U.S. market, (Source: Michael Wright, *Vintage Guitar Magazine*).

One dating method for identifying Teisco guitars (serial numbers are non-existent, and some electronic parts may not conform to the U.S. EIA code) is the change in pickguards that occurred in 1965. Pre-1965 pickguards are plastic construction, while 1965 and post-1965 pickguards are striped metal. Pricing on Teisco Del Rey models and other Teiscos remains a bit strange. Most models that hang on walls are tagged at $99 (and sometimes lower), but clean cool shaped models sometimes command the $200 to $300 range.

TELE-STAR

Instruments previously produced in Japan circa late 1960s to 1983.

The Tele-Star trademark was distributed in the U.S. by the Tele-Star Musical Instrument Corporation of New York, New York. Tele-Star offered a full range of acoustic, thinline acoustic/electric hollow body, and solid body electric guitars and basses. Many built by Kawai of Japan, and some models feature sparkle finishes, (Source: Michael Wright, *Vintage Guitar Magazine*).

TEXARKANA

Instruments currently built in Korea. Distributed by the V. J. Rendano Music Company, Inc. of Youngstown, Ohio.

Texarkana offers a number of acoustic guitar models designed for the entry level or beginning guitar student. Suggested new retail prices range from $129 (dreadnought style) up to $379 (cutaway dreadnought with piezo pickup system).

THOMAS
Instruments previously produced in Italy from the late 1960s through the early 1970s.

Thomas semi-hollowbodies are medium quality guitars that feature original designs, (Source: Tony Bacon and Paul Day, *The Guru's Guitar Guide*).

THOS SHA CZAR
Instruments previously built in Valley Stream, New York circa late 1970s through 1980s.

Luthier/designer Tom Leiberman of "The Woodshop" in Valley Stream, New York built a number of acoustic bowl-back basses for the past number of years. In addition to a custom bass built several years ago for Jack Cassidy (Hot Tuna), Leiberman also built the **Stanley Clarke Bass** back in the 1970s. Leiberman current focuses his talents on furniture, but may accept custom commissions, (Preliminary information courtesy Jeff Meyer). In the late 1970s, Leiberman's Thos Sha Czar bowl-backed basses had a list price of $4,000.

THREET GUITARS
Instruments currently built in Calgary (Alberta), Canada since 1990.

Always interested in music, luthier Judy Threet had been playing guitar both semi-professionally and for pleasure for many years. Initially pursuing an academic career, she earned her Ph.D in Philosophy at Stanford (Palo Alto, California) in 1986; she then taught for a few years at the University of Calgary (Alberta, Canada). While teaching in Calgary, Threet met luthier Michael Heiden (see Heiden Stringed Instruments) and learned the art of inlay ("as a diversion," she claims).

Living in Calgary at the time, Heiden was gaining a reputation as a highly gifted luthier – and as a result was becoming increasingly busy. Heiden needed some help at his shop (especially doing inlay work), and Threet's Fine Arts background from her early university days served her well as she offered to help. Over the next year and a half, Threet spent time away from her teaching career working with Heiden on inlays, and in the process began to learn the rudiments of guitar building.

In 1990, Threet decided to switch careers and become a luthier. She asked Heiden to teach her how to build and repair guitars, and it was agreed that under his careful supervision she would build a guitar from start to finish. When Heiden subsequently moved to British Columbia, Threet opened her own shop in 1991. Initially concentrating on guitar repair, Threet's focus shifted to building acoustic guitars. She designed and completed eight guitars by the end of 1994.

In her current location (a warehouse loft in one of Calgary's oldest areas), Threet individually handcrafts acoustic guitars and often customizes them to her client's wishes. Custom inlays are a specialty and are highly encouraged. Threet guitars are relatively small-bodied instruments, usually with Sitka spruce tops and mahogany backs and sides. Lightweight but strong, they are especially well-suited to finger style playing. Threet estimates that she produces 10 to 12 instruments on a yearly basis.

**Threet Acoustic
courtesy Judy Threet**

ACOUSTIC

Threet individually handcrafts each guitar, and takes great care in choosing the tonewoods and in voicing the tops. Necks are entirely handcarved and are joined in the traditional dove-tail joint. Each instrument is monitored throughout the building process to optimize its tone. Many *Custom Options*, such as a left-handed configuration, or an Englemann spruce top, or koa or walnut back and sides are available; most at an additional cost.

All 4 Threet models are available in 2 set styles: **Standard** and **Deluxe**. Customers can also design their own guitar as a **Custom** model. The **Standard** configuration includes a Sitka spruce top, Honduran mahogany back and sides, tortoise shell plastic body binding, cocobola fingerboard/bridge/faceplate, wood purfling rosette, a 14/20-fret fingerboard with pearl dot inlay, and a natural nitrocellulose lacquer finish. The **Deluxe** configuration differs with an ebony with holly purfling body/fingerboard/headstock binding, Indian rosewood fingerboard/bridge, ebony faceplate, abalone rosette, pearl snowflake position markers/small asymmetrical "torch," and a rosewood/ebony/holly backstrip.

The four Threet acoustic models correspond roughly to the traditional sizes of *0, 00, 000*, and *dreadnought*. Threet's **Model A** is practically a parlor sized guitar, with dimensions: Body Length - 18 3/8", Width - 13 3/4", and Depth - 3 1/2" tapering to 4 1/4". The **Model B** is a slightly larger parlor sized guitar: Body Length - 18 7/8", Width - 14 1/8", and Depth - 3 1/2" tapering to 4 1/8". The **Model C** is larger still, with dimensions: Body Length - 19 3/8", Width - 14 1/2", and Depth - 3 1/2" tapering to 4 1/8". The **Model D** is a hybrid size best described as a cross between a *Model C* and a *Dreadnought*: Body Length - 20", Width - 15 1/4", and Depth - 3 1/2" tapering to 4 1/2". Models A, B, and C have a 24 27/32" scale, while the Model D has a 25 11/32" scale. The price for a Deluxe guitar is $4,500.

For further information regarding Custom pricing, inlay work, and additional model specifications, please contact luthier Judy Threet directly (see Trademark Index).

TILTON
Instruments previously manufactured in Boston, Massachusetts from 1865 to the early 1900s.

The Oliver Ditson Company, Inc. was formed in 1835 by music publisher Oliver Ditson (1811-1888). Ditson was a primary force in music merchandising, distribution, and retail sales on the East Coast. He also helped establish two musical instrument manufacturers: The John Church Company of Cincinnati, Ohio, and Lyon & Healy (Washburn) in Chicago, Illinois.

In 1865 Ditson established a manufacturing branch of his company under the supervision of John Haynes, called the John C. Haynes Company. This branch built guitars for a number of trademarks, such as **Bay State**, **Tilton**, and **Haynes Excelsior**, (Source: Tom Wheeler, *American Guitars*).

T

**Triggs New Yorker
courtesy Scott Chinery**

TIMELESS INSTRUMENTS
Instruments currently built in Tugaske (Saskatchewan), Canada.

Since 1980, Luthier David Freeman has specialized in custom-built classical and steel string guitars, bouzoukis, mandolins, and harps with ornate inlays or special woods. Prices vary wth materials. In addition to his custom instruments, luthier Freeman also offers acoustic guitar luthier training and luthurie supplies. For further information, please contact him directly (see Trademark Index).

TIPPIN GUITAR COMPANY
Instruments currently built in Marblehead, Massachusetts.

Luthier Bill Tippin started building guitars in 1978 on a part time basis for his friends. In 1992, the "part time" became full time when he founded his Tippin Guitar Company. Tippin and his craftsmen are now creating a range of acoustic guitar and acoustic bass models. For further information, contact Bill Tippin directly (see Trademark Index).

TIPS MCGEE GUITARWORKS
Instruments currently built Fort Tilden, NY.

Please contact the company directly (see Trademark Index listing) for current model availability and pricing.

TOMMYHAWK
Instruments currently built in New Jersey. Distributed by Tom Barth's Music Box of Succasuanna, New Jersey.

Designer Tom Barth offers a 24" travel-style guitar that is a one-piece carved mahogany body (back, sides, neck, and bracing). The solid spruce top, bridge, and top bracing are then glued on – forming a solid, tone projecting little guitar! In 1997, the soundhole was redesigned into a more elliptical shape. Barth's full size (25 1/2" scale) electric/acoustic has a double cutaway body, Tele-style neck with a 21-fret rosewood or maple fingerboard, and a Seymour Duncan Duckbucker pickup. For more information refer to the Tommyhawk web site (see Trademark Index).

TONEMASTER
See chapter on House Brands.

This trademark has been identified as a House Brand ascribed to several distributors such as Harris-Teller of Illinois, Schmidt of Minnesota, and Squire of Michigan. While one recognized source has claimed that instruments under this trademark were built by Harmony, author/researcher Willie G. Moseley has also seen this brand on a Valco-made lap steel, (Source: Willie G. Moseley, *Stellas & Stratocasters*).

TORRES
Instruments previously built in Spain.

Noted luthier Don Antonio de Torres Jurado (1817-1892) has been identified as the leading craftsman of what scholars have termed the "third renaissance" of the guitar, and developed the guitar to its current classical configuration.

Before the early 1800s, the European guitar featured five courses, which could be a single string or a pair of strings. Torres' new design focused on the five individual strings, and also added the low 'E' string for a total of six individual strings. Torres developed a larger bodied guitar design, and fan-bracing to support a thinner, more resonant top. The new design offered a larger tonal range (especially in the bass response), and was widely adopted both in Spain and throughout Europe.

Torres had two workshops during his career. He produced guitars both in Seville (1852-1869), and his place of birth, Almeria (1875-1892). It has been estimated that Torres built about 320 guitars during his two workshop period. Only 66 instruments have been identified as his work, (Source: Tony Bacon, *The Ultimate Guitar Book*).

TOYOTA
Instruments previously produced in Japan circa early 1970s.

Toyota guitars were distributed in the U.S. by the Hershman company of New York, New York. The Toyota trademark was applied to a full range of acoustic, thinline acoustic/electric hollowbody, and solid body electric guitars and basses, (Source: Michael Wright, *Guitar Stories,* Volume One).

TRAUGOTT, JEFF
Instruments currently built in Santa Cruz, California since 1991.

Luthier Jeff Traugott builds a line of high-end acoustic steel string guitars and produces 15-20 guitars per year. He focuses on high-level craftsmanship, as well as a clean, sophisticated sense of design. Jeff Traugott's Guitars hve a reputation for excellent projection and clear, bell-like tones up and down the neck. Traugott guitars come in four basic models and a variety of woods but Traugott is especially known for using old growth, high grade Brazilian Rosewood back and sides and German spruce tops on his instruments. For more information on model specification, pricing, and availability, please contact Jeff Traugott directly (see Trademark Index). Don't get your hopes up though, Traugott's current waiting list extends into 2011!

ACOUSTIC

The **Model BK** has a 25.375" scale, and has an MSR of $8,950. The **Model 00** has a 24.9" scale and has an MSR of $8,950. The **Model R** has an 25.375" scale has an MSR of $8,950. The **Model RE** is an acoustic-electric cutaway with German spruce top, 25.375" scale and MSR is $10,450.

TRIGGS, JAMES W.
Instruments currently hand built in Kansas City, KS. Previously manufactured in Nashville, Tennessee.

Luthier Jim Triggs has been building instruments since the mid -1970s. While at Gibson during 1986-1992, Jim wore many hats, including Artist Relations, Custom Shop Manager, Archtop Guitar Supervisor, Custom Mandolin Builder, and Art Guitar Designer. Jim left Gisbon in March of 1992, and has been custom building ever since, including many stars. His more famous clients have included: Alan Jackson, Steve Miller, Elliot Easton, Pat Martino, Mundell Lowe, Vince Gill, and Marty Stuart.

Jim's son Ryan is currently working with him in the shop, and this "team," maybe the only father & son duo currently working on archtops together. The Triggs Boys keep busy with a constant back order of flattops, archtops, and F-5 style mandolins. Much of Jim's time in the shop is spent on design work for other companies. Several models are in Cort Guitars line already, and 4 new Triggs designed "Tradition Guitars" will debuted at the Nashville Summer NAMM Show in July, 2001.

The sky's the limit with a Triggs guitar. Flattop prices start at $3,000, archtops around $4,000, and F-5s for around $6,000. Please contact Triggs directly for more information and a personal price quotation (see Trademark Index), if the aliens haven't abducted him (again!).

Section U

UNGER, DALE
See American Archtop. Instruments currently built in Stroudsburg, Pennsylvania since 1996.

Dale Unger was an apprentice to Bob Benedetto for four years, and has since opened up his own shop. For further information, see the American Archtop listing earlier in this text.

UNICORD
See Univox. Instruments previously produced in Japan.

The Merson Musical Supply Company of Westbury, New York was the primary importer of Univox guitars. Merson evolved into Unicord, and also became a distributor for Westbury brand guitars, (Source: Michael Wright, *Guitar Stories,* Volume One).

UNITY
Instruments currently built by the Unity Guitar Company of Vicksburg and Kalamazoo, Michigan since 1994.

The Unity Guitar Company was founded by Aaron Cowles and Kevin Moats in 1994. Cowles, a former Gibson employee (from 1961 to 1983) opened his own music and repair shop after the Kalamazoo plant was closed down. Moats, son of Heritage Guitar's J.P. Moats, comes from a family background of musical instrument building.

In 1994, Unity offered a limited edition of the **100th Anniversary Model** arch top guitar, which celebrates the 100 years of musical instrument building in Kalamazoo, Michigan. The inlay work was done by Maudie Moore (Moore's Engraving), who has over thirty years' experience. Unity was scheduled to begin offering their Custom Carved series of archtop guitars in 1995. It is unknown if they are still producing guitars today or not.

UNIVERSITY
Instruments previously produced by Regal (original company of Wulschner & Son) in the late 1890s.

Indianapolis retailer/wholesaler Emil Wulschner introduced the Regal line in the 1880s, and in 1896 opened a factory to build guitars and mandolins under the following three trademarks: Regal, 20th Century, And University. After Wulschner's death in 1900, the factory became part of a larger corporation, (Source: John Teagle, *Washburn: Over One Hundred Years of Fine Stringed Instruments*).

UNIVOX
Instruments previously built in Japan circa 1969 to 1978, and imported into the U.S. by the Merson Musical Supply Company of Westbury, New York.

Merson Musical Supply later evolved into the Unicord company. The Univox trademark was offered on a full range of acoustic, thinline acoustic/electric hollow body, and solid body electric guitars and basses. The majority of the Univox guitars produced were built by Arai of Japan (See Aria), and are entry level to intermediate quality for players, (Source: Michael Wright, *Guitar Stories,* Volume One). Most Univox acoustic guitars can be found priced under $250.

U

NOTES

U is for ultra-rare and ultra-expensive. Well-known vintage guitar dealer, collector, and author, Dr. Tom Van Hoose shows off one of Jimmy D'Aquisto's rarest and most expensive instruments, the Solo model.

1994 D'AQUISTO SOLO the last solo made by Jimmy D. This is the "Big Time!!" $96,000 ⁰⁰

Section V

VAGABOND

Instruments currently built in Albany, New York.

Luthier Kevin Smith's Vagabond Travel Guitar has been "defining the acoustic travel guitar since 1981." Smith says that his design is the perfect balance of playability, portability, and sound in an attractive shape.

The Vagabond Travel Guitar has a solid spruce top, mahogany integral neck, adjustable truss rod, 24.5" scale with 21 full frets. The **Standard** model (list $295) has laminated maple back and sides, black and white binding, Gotoh open tuners, and a deluxe travel bag. The **Deluxe** (last MSR was $499) is similar, but has purpleheart and herringbone custom bindings, a tortoise shell pickguard, and Schaller mini tuners. Both models are available with a Fishman transducer or Fishman Matrix active system at an additional cost. Occasionally, there are factory seconds available at a lower cost. Visit the Vagabond web site for more information (see Trademark Index).

VALCO

See National.

Louis Dopyera bought out the National company, and as he owned more than 50% of the stock in Dobro, "merged" the two companies back together (as National Dobro). In 1936, the decision was made to move the company to Chicago, Illinois. Chicago was a veritable hotbed of mass produced musical instruments during the early to pre-World War II 1900s. Manufacturers like Washburn and Regal had facilities, and major wholesalers and retailers like the Tonk Bros. and Lyon & Healy were based there. Victor Smith, Al Frost, and Louis Dopyera moved their operation to Chicago, and in 1943 formally announced the change to Valco (the initials of their three first names: V-A-L company). Valco worked on war materials during World War II, and returned to instrument production afterwards. Valco produced the National/Supro/Airline fiberglass body guitars in the 1950s and 1960s, as well as wood-bodied models. In the late 1960s, Valco was absorbed by the Kay company (See Kay). In 1968, Kay/Valco Guitars, Inc. went out of business. Both the National and the Supro trademarks were purchased at the 1969 liquidation auction by Chicago's Strum 'N Drum Music Company, (Source: Tom Wheeler, *American Guitars*).

VALLEY ARTS

Instruments currently produced in Nashville, Tennessee. Currently distributed by Gibson. Previously produced in City of Industry, California, and distributed by the Samick Music Corp from 1993-2002. Previous production was based in North Hollywood, California from 1979 to 1993.

Valley Arts originally began as a North Hollywood teaching studio in 1963. The facilities relocated to Studio City, California and through the years became known as a respected retail store that specialized in professional quality music gear. Production moved back to North Hollywood and into larger facilities in 1989, and luthier/co-owner Michael McGuire directed a staff of 15 employees.

In 1992, the Samick corporation became involved in a joint venture with Valley Arts, and by June of 1993 had acquired full ownership of the company. Samick operated Valley Arts as the custom shop wing for the company, as well as utilizing Valley Arts designs for their Samick production guitars built overseas.

In 2002, Mike McGuire and Al Carness, who both founded Valley Arts in the beginning, became part of the company again when Gibson acquired the company. Al is now the manager of the Valley Arts retail Store and Mike is the operations manager for the Gibson Custom Shop. Valley Arts is currently a custom order only guitar manufacturer. There are online order forms to select what you want. They are also a repair shop for guitars. Visit their web site for more information (see Trademark Index).

GRADING	100%	EXCELLENT	AVERAGE

ACOUSTIC: GRAND SERIES

VALLEY ARTS GRAND (MODEL VAGD-1) - dreadnought style, solid AAA spruce top, herringbone binding, round soundhole, mahogany neck, 25 1/2" scale, ebony fingerboard/bridge, rosewood back/sides, tortoise pickguard, 3-per-side tuners, gold hardware, available in Natural finish, disc 2002.

	$1,150	$775	$525

Last MSR was $1,580.

VALLEY ARTS GRAND CONCERT (MODEL VAGC-1) - 'OOO' style, solid AAA spruce top, herringbone binding, round soundhole, mahogany neck, 25" scale, ebony fingerboard/bridge, rosewood back/sides, tortoise pickguard, 3-per-side tuners, gold hardware, available in Natural finish, disc 2002.

	$1,150	$775	$525

Last MSR was $1,580.

GRADING	100%	EXCELLENT	AVERAGE

ACOUSTIC: ROBERT JOHNSON ESTATE SERIES

RJ 1935 N - jumbo style body, solid spruce top, round soundhole, maple back/sides, 12/19-fret rosewood fingerboard with pearl dot inlay, rosewood bridge, 3-per-side deluxe Kluson tuners, engraved plate on headstock, available in Natural (N) or Vintage Black Burst (B) finishes, mfg. 1994-96.

> Model has not traded sufficiently to quote pricing.

ACOUSTIC ELECTRIC

VALLEY ARTS GRAND ELECTRIC (MODEL VAGD-1E) - dreadnought style, solid AAA spruce top, herringbone binding, round soundhole, mahogany neck, 25 1/2" scale, ebony fingerboard/bridge, rosewood back/sides, tortoise pickguard, 3-per-side tuners, gold hardware, piezo bridge pickup, volume/3-band active EQ, available in Natural finish, disc 2002.

$1,290   **$845**   **$570**
Last MSR was $1,720.

VALLEY ARTS GRAND CONCERT ELECTRIC (MODEL VAGD-1E) - 'OOO' style, solid AAA spruce top, herringbone binding, round soundhole, mahogany neck, 25" scale, ebony fingerboard/bridge, rosewood back/sides, tortoise pickguard, 3-per-side tuners, gold hardware, piezo bridge pickup, volume/3-band active EQ, available in Natural finish, disc. 2002.

$1,290   **$845**   **$570**
Last MSR was $1,720.

VANTAGE

Instruments currently produced in Korea. Original production was based in Japan from 1977 to 1990. Distributed by Music Industries Corporation of Floral Park, New York, since 1987.

This trademark was established in Matsumoto, Japan, around 1977. Instruments have been manufactured in Korea since 1990. Vantage offers a wide range of guitars designed for the beginning student to the intermediate player.

ACOUSTIC: CLASSICAL SERIES

VC-10 - classical style, spruce top, round soundhole, bound body, wooden inlay rosette, nato back/sides/neck, 12/19-fret rosewood fingerboard/tied bridge, rosewood peghead veneer, 3-per-side chrome tuners with plastic buttons, available in Light Pumpkin finish, disc.

N/A   **$100**   **$65**
Last MSR was $200.

VC-20 - classic style, cedar top, round soundhole, bound body, wooden inlay rosette, ovankol back/sides, nato neck, 12/19-fret rosewood fingerboard/tied bridge, ovankol peghead veneer, 3-per-side gold tuners with plastic buttons, available in Natural finish, current mfg.

MSR	$339		$255	$165	$115

VC-20CE - similar to VSC-20, except has single round cutaway, piezo bridge pickup, 3-band EQ with volume slide control.

MSR	$439		$325	$215	$145

VSC-30 - similar to VSC-20, except has rosewood back/sides, available in Light Pumpkin finish.

MSR	$429		$320	$200	$135

ACOUSTIC: DREADNOUGHT SERIES

VS-5 - dreadnought style, spruce top, round soundhole, black pickguard, bound body, 3-stripe rosette, nato back/sides/neck, 14/20-fret nato fingerboard with white dot inlay, ebonized maple bridge with white black dot pins, 3-per-side chrome tuners, available in Natural finish, current mfg.

MSR	$319		$240	$150	$100

> Add $10 for left-handed version (Model VS-5/LH).

VS-10 - similar to VS-5, except has 3-stripe bound body.

MSR	$329		$235	$140	$90

VS-12 - similar to VS-10, except has 12 strings, 6-per-side tuners.

MSR	$329		$235	$140	$90

> Add $10 for Black finish (Model VS-12B).

VS-15 - dreadnought style, spruce top, round soundhole, black pickguard, 3-stripe bound body/rosette, nato back/sides/neck, 14/20-fret rosewood fingerboard with white dot inlay, rosewood bridge with black white dot pins, 3-per-side chrome tuners, available in Natural finish, current mfg.

MSR	$309		$225	$120	$80

GRADING		100%	EXCELLENT	AVERAGE

VS-20 - dreadnought style, nato top, round soundhole, black pickguard, 3-stripe bound body/rosette, nato back/sides/neck, 14/20-fret bound rosewood fingerboard with white dot inlay, rosewood bridge with white black dot pins, bound peghead, 3-per-side chrome tuners, available in Black, Natural, or Tobacco Sunburst finishes, current. mfg.

MSR	$369		$275	$185	$125

VS-25 - dreadnought style, cedar top, round soundhole, black pickguard, herringbone bound body/rosette, ovankol back/sides, mahogany neck, 14/20-fret rosewood fingerboard with white dot inlay, rosewood bridge with white black dot pins, 3-per-side tuners, available in Natural finish, current mfg.

MSR	$379		$255	$165	$115

Add $50 for solid cedar top (Model VS-25S). Add $60 for left-handed version with solid cedar top (Model VS-25S/LH).

VS-25SCE - similar to VS-25, except has single sharp cutaway, solid cedar top, piezo bridge pickup, 3-band EQ with volume slide control.

MSR	$459		$345	$225	$150

VS-25SCE-12 - similar to VS-25SCE, except has 12 strings, 6-per-side tuners.

MSR	$629		$475	$300	$215

VS-30 - dreadnought style, maple top, round soundhole, black pickguard, 3-stripe bound body/rosette, maple back/sides/neck, 14/20-fret bound rosewood fingerboard w/white dot inlay, rosewood bridge w/white black dot pins, bound peghead, 3-per-side chrome tuners, available in Natural finish, current mfg.

MSR	$379		$285	$190	$125

VS-33 - dreadnought style, spruce top, round soundhole, black pickguard, 5-stripe bound body/rosette, oak back/sides, mahogany neck, 14/20-fret bound rosewood fingerboard, rosewood bridge with white black dot pins, bound peghead, 3-per-side chrome tuners, available in Trans. Black, Trans. Blue, or Trans. Red finishes, current mfg.

MSR	$399		$295	$200	$125

Vantage VCT-20CE
courtesy Vantage

VS-35CE - single sharp cutaway dreadnought style, nato top, oval soundhole, 3-stripe bound body/rosette, nato back/sides/neck, 20-fret bound rosewood fingerboard with white dot inlay, rosewood bridge with white black dot pins, bound peghead, 3-per-side chrome tuners, piezo bridge pickup, 3-band EQ with volume slide control, available in Black or Tobacco Sunburst finishes, disc. 1997.

			N/A	$225	$150

Last MSR was $430.

Add $10 for left-handed version of this model (Model VS-35CE/LH).

VS-50S - dreadnought style, solid spruce top, round soundhole, black pickguard, herringbone bound body/rosette, nato back/sides/neck, 14/20-fret rosewood fingerboard with white dot inlay, rosewood bridge with white black dot pins, bound peghead, 3-per-side gold tuners, available in Natural finish, current mfg.

MSR	$449		$335	$220	$150

Add $10 for left-handed version of this model (Model VS-50S/LH).

ACOUSTIC ELECTRIC

VS-40CE - single sharp cutaway dreadnought style, nato top, oval soundhole, 3-stripe bound body/rosette, nato back/sides/neck, 20-fret bound rosewood fingerboard with white dot inlay, rosewood bridge with white black dot pins, bound peghead, 3-per-side chrome tuners, piezo bridge pickup, 3-band EQ with volume slide control, available in Black or White finishes, current mfg.

MSR	$499		$375	$245	$165

VS-40CE/M - similar to VS-40CE, except has maple back/sides.

MSR	$519		$390	$250	$170

Add $10 for left-handed version of this model (Model VS-40CE/MLH). Add $10 for 12-string version of this model (VS-40CEM-12).

VST-40SCE - single sharp cutaway dreadnought style, solid spruce top, round soundhole, 3-stripe bound body, herringbone rosette, nato back/sides/neck, 20-fret rosewood fingerboard with white dot inlay, rosewood bridge with white black dot pins, bound peghead, 3-per-side gold tuners, piezo bridge pickup, 3-band EQ with volume slide control, available in Natural finish, current mfg.

			N/A	$250	$165

Last MSR was $500.

Vantage VS-33CE
courtesy Vantage

VANTEK

Instruments curently produced in Korea, and distributed by Music Industries Corporation of Floral Park, New York.

These instruments are built with the entry level player or beginning student in mind by Vantage in Korea.

VARSITY

See Weymann & Sons.

VEGA

Instruments currently built in Korea, and distributed by Antares. Originally, Vega guitars were produced in Boston, Massachusetts.

The predessor company to Vega was founded in 1881 by Swedish immigrant Julius Nelson, C.F. Sunderberg, Mr. Swenson, and several other men. Nelson was the foreman of a 20-odd man workforce (which later rose to 130 employees during the 1920s banjo boom). Nelson, and his brother Carl, gradually bought out the other partners, and incorporated in 1903 as Vega (which means 'star'). In 1904, Vega acquired banjo maker A.C. Fairbanks & Company after Fairbanks suffered a fire, and Fairbank's David L. Day became Vega's general manager.

Vega built banjos under the Bacon trademark, named after popular banjo artist Frederick J. Bacon. Bacon set up his own production facility in Connecticut in 1921, and a year later wooed Day away from Vega to become the vice president in the newly reformed **Bacon & Day** company. While this company marketed several models of guitars, they had no facility for building them. It is speculated that the Bacon & Day guitars were built by the Regal company of Chicago, Illinois.

In the mid 1920s Vega began marketing a guitar called the **Vegaphone**. By the early 1930s, Vega started concentrating more on guitar production, and less on banjo making. Vega debuted its Electrovox electric guitar and amplifier in 1936, and a electric volume control footpedal in 1937. Vega is reported to have built over 40,000 guitars during the 1930s.

In the 1940s, Vega continued to introduce models such as the Duo-Tron and the Supertron; and by 1949 had become both a guitar producer and a guitar wholesaler as it bought bodies built by Harmony. In 1970 Vega was acquired by the C.F. Martin company for its banjo operations. Martin soon folded Vega's guitar production, and applied the trademark to a line of imported guitars. Ten years later, Martin sold the Vega trademark rights to a Korean guitar production company, (Source: Tom Wheeler, *American Guitars*).

Vega guitars are becomin increasingly collectible and can bring some good money for the right model. Look for more information in further editions of the *Blue Book of Acoustic Guitars*.

VEILLETTE GUITARS

Instruments currently produced in Woodstock, NY.

Veillette Guitars are individually handmade by well known luthier Joe Veillette. Veillette offers a wide range of quality acoustic electric instruments in various configurations, including the world's first baritone 12-string acoustic electric guitar. Prices start at $1,950. For more information regarding these instruments, please contact the company directly (see Trademark Index).

VENSON

Instruments currently produced in Seoul, Korea. Distributed by Sungbo Industrial Co., Ltd.

Sungbo Industrial Co., Ltd. is currently offering a wide range of acoustic guitars and acoustic basses under the **Venson** trademark. The acoustic guitar line contains a number of dreadnought, jumbo, and classical models. For further information, please contact Sungbo Industrial Co., Ltd. directly (see Trademark Index).

VENTURA

Instruments previously produced in Japan circa 1970s.

Ventura guitars were distributed in the U.S. market by C. Bruno & Company of New York, New York. Ventura models were both full body and thinline hollow body electric archtop guitars, and generally medium to good quality versions of popular American models, (Source: Michael Wright, *Guitar Stories,* Volume One; and Sam Maggio).

During the 1970s, a "Barney Kessel Custom"-style copy (the model is a V-1400, by the way) had a suggested retail price of $199.50. If one of these guitars gets sold at a big guitar show for $200 to $250, does this mean that the guitar "has appreciated in value" or the retail price of today's Korean semi-hollow body guitars has risen over the past twenty five years? Traditionally, there is a ceiling to how high a price can raise on imported laminate wood semi-hollowbody guitars – but who can put a price tag on that intangible "funkiness" factor?

VERSOUL

Instruments currently built in Helsinki, Finland since 1994.

Versoul Ltd. was founded in 1994 by Kari Nieminen, who has over 20 years background in guitar making and design. Nieminen combines concern for the acoustic tone of his instruments with his innovative designs to produce a masterful instrument. Nieminen's production is on a limited basis (he estimates about one guitar a week) in his humidity controlled workshop.

Both the handcrafted **Zoel** and **Touco** acoustic models reflect his commitment to excellence. Models are available in Silver label (mahogany body), Gold label (Indian rosewood body), and Platinum label (Honduran rosewood body) configurations. The Zoel model has a squared-shoulder design, with spruce top and reverse headstock. Nieminen is also offering an **Acoustic Sitar Guitar**, which provides instant exotic sitar sound with adjustable bridge piece for each string (and 13 sympathetic strings). The fingerboard is scalloped, and the guitar has an extra long scale length for twanging sound. The Buxom is a jumbo model also available.

There are other models available such as resonators electric guitars, bass guitars, sitars, and bariton guitars For further information, please contact luthier Nieminen directly (see Trademark Index).

VESTAX

Instruments currently built in Japan. Distributed by the Vestax Corporation of Fairfield, California.

Vestax offers high quality guitars including one model that echos the classic designs of the 1940s and 1950s, as well as a semi-hollow electric model. The D'Angelico-Vestax **Phil Upchurch** model is a single cutaway New Yorker-style acoustic with bound body, 2 bound f-holes, bound headstock, 3-per-side gold tuners, 22-fret bound ebony fingerboard with pearl block inlay, raised rosewood pickguard, adjustable rosewood bridge/ stairstep rosewood tailpiece, floating humbucker pickup. Vestax's **Superior Limited Series** semi-hollow **GV-98** looks like a double cutaway Strat or PRS design, but features hollowed out tone chambers under the flamed maple top. The **GV-98** has a Wilkinson VSVG (GG) tremolo bridge, 2 single coil/humbucker pickups, and 22-fret fingerboard.

VICTOR

See chapter on House Brands.

This trademark has been identified as a House Brand of the RCA Victor Record Stores, (Source: Willie G. Moseley, *Stellas & Stratocasters*).

VINTAGE

Instruments currently produced in Asia. Distributed by John Hornby Skewes & Co., Ltd. of Garforth (Leeds), England.

The **Vintage** trademark is the brand name of U.K. distributor John Hornby Skewes & Co., Ltd.

ACOUSTIC

Vintage acoustic model MSRs are typically in the $225-$550 price range. For more information, including current models and pricing, please contacting the distributor directly (see Trademark Index).

ACOUSTIC ELECTRIC

Vintage acoustic electric model MSRs are typicallyin the $225-$550 price range. For more information, including current models and pricing, please contacting the distributor directly (see Trademark Index).

Vega C-71
courtesy Killer Vintage

VIVI-TONE

Instruments previously built in Kalamazoo, Michigan circa early 1930s.

After pioneering such high quality instruments for Gibson in the 1920s (such as the F-5 Mandolin), Designer/ engineer/builder Lloyd Loar founded the Vivi-Tone company to continue exploring designs too radical for Gibson. It is rumored that Loar designed a form of stand-up bass that was amplified while at Gibson, but this prototype was never developed into a production model.

Loar, along with partners Lewis A. Williams and Walter Moon started Vivi-Tone in 1933. Loar continued building his pioneering designs, such as an acoustic guitar with sound holes in the rear, but failed to find commercial success. However, it is because of his early successes at Gibson that researchers approach the Vivi - tone designs with some wonderment instead of discounting the radical ideas altogether, (Source: Tom Wheeler, *American Guitars*).

VOX

Instruments previously built in England from 1961 to 1964; production was then moved to Italy for the mid 1960s up to the early 1970s. After Italian production ceased, some solid body models were built in Japan during the 1980s.

The Vox company, perhaps better known for its amplifier design, also built fashionable and functional guitars and basses during the 1960s. While the early guitar models produced tended to be entry level instruments based on popular Fender designs, later models expressed an originality that fit in well with the 1960s British "Pop" music explosion.

Thomas Walter Jennings was born in London, England on February 28, 1917. During World War II he saw action with the English Royal Engineers, and received a medical discharge in 1941. By 1944 Jennings had a part-time business dealing in secondhand accordians and other musical instruments, and by 1946 had set up shop. Along with fellow musical acquaintance Derek Underdown, Jennings produced the Univox organ in 1951 and formed the Jennings Organ Company not long after. Based on the success of his organs for several years, Jennings teamed up with engineer Dick Denney to build amplifiers under the Vox trademark. In mid 1958, Jennings reincorporated the company as Jennings Musical Instruments (JMI). When rock 'n roll hit Britain, Vox amps were there.

The first Vox guitars were introduced in 1961. Early models like the **Stroller** or **Clubman** were entry level instruments based on Fender designs. Quality improved a great deal when Vox brought in necks built by EKO in Recanati, Italy. Tom Jennings then assembled a three engineer design team of Bob Pearson (quality and materials control), Mike Bennett (prototypes), and Ken Wilson (styling design) to develop a more original-looking instrument. The resulting 5-sided **Phantom** in late 1962 featured a Strat-ish three single coil pickup selection and a Bigsby-derived tremolo. Further Phantom models were developed in 1963, as well as the **Mark VI** series ("teardrop" body shapes). When production moved to Italy in 1964, Vox guitars were built by EKO. Vox also offered a 12-string **Mandoguitar**, and a double cutaway 12-string called the **Bouzouki**. A number of

Vox Rio Grande
courtesy John Beeson
The Music Shoppe

hollowbody models such as the **Lynx**, **Bobcat**, and **Cougar** were made by Crucianelli in Italy during the mid 1960s.

In order to generate funds for the company, Jennings sold a substantial amount of shares to the Royston group in 1964, and later that same year the entire shareholding was acquired. JMI was officially renamed Vox Sound Ltd. Thomas Organs was already supplying JMI for organs in the British market, and was looking for a reciprocal agreement to import Vox amps to the U.S. market. However, Joe Benaron (president of Thomas Organs) was really into transistors, and began supplementing the British tube models with solid-state amps developed at Thomas laboratories at Sepulveda, California. To clearly illustrate this sorry state of affairs, compare a U.S. **Super Beatle** amp against a British **AC-100**.

The Vox line began the slump that befell other corporate-run music instrument producers during the late 1960s and 1970s. Soon Japanese-built models appeared on the market with Vox on their headstock, including a Les Paul-derived issued in 1970. Later, the Vox name appeared on a series of original design solid body guitars (**24** series, **25** series, **White Shadows**) during the early to mid 1980s. Distribution in the U.S. during this time period was through the Pennino Music Company of Westminster, California; and Allstate Music Supply Corporation of Greensboro, North Carolina.

The Vox trademark was later purchased by the Korg company (Korg USA in the American Market). Korg USA distributes Korg synthesizers, Marshall Amplifiers, Parker guitars, and the new line of Vox amplifiers in the U.S. market. In 1998, Korg/Vox debuted 5 "new" electric guitar models which feature designs based on previous Vox models.

Vox's new models include the Mark III model VM3B with Bigsby tremolo (list $1,400), the Mark III model VM3F with fixed tailpiece (list $1,200), the Mark III model VM3CFWD with fixed tailpiece, chrome pickguard, and matching finish headstock (list $1,300), the Mark VI model VM6V with Bigsby tremolo (list $1,400), and the Mark XII model VMXII 12-string guitar (list $1,400).

MODEL NAME IDENTIFICATION

Identification of Vox instruments is fairly easy, as the model names generally appear on the pickguards. However, there are models and configurations that do need to be doublechecked! Collectible Vox guitars seem to be the models built between 1962 and 1969, and solid body models are favored over the hollowbody ones.

ACOUSTIC

In the mid to late 1960s, Thomas Organ distributed a number of Vox acoustic guitars. Steel-string models such as the **Country Western**, **Folk XII**, and **Folk Twelve Electro** had a simple horizontal Vox logo on the peghead. The **Rio Grande**, **Shenandoah** (12-string), and **Silver Sage** (12-string) had more ornate inlay decorations around the logo, and the horizontal Vox lettering was thicker.

Section W

W & S
See Weymann & Sons.

WABASH
See chapter on House Brands.

This trademark has been identified as a House Brand of Wexler, (Source: Willie G. Moseley, *Stellas & Stratocasters*).

WALKER GUITARS
Instruments currently built in North Stonington, Connecticut since 1984.

Luthier Kim Walker was involved in the musical instrument making business since 1973, and began building F-5 style mandolins in 1982. Walker worked for a number of years at George Gruhn's repair and restoration workshop, were hew was able to work in close association with other fine instrument builders such as Mark Lacey, Paul McGill, and Steven Gilchrist. Walker later served as both a prototype builder and R&D/Custom shop supervisor at Guild beginning in 1986.

Walker currently offers three different archtop models, and his combination of premier woods and over twenty years experience make for a truly solid, high quality guitar. Models like the **Black Tie, Excel,** and **Classic** are traditional style archtops with different appointments and body binding styles, while the top-of-the-line **Empress** is a limited edition custom model. Walker as builds flattop acoustic guitars that feature pre-war style scalloped bracing, and are finished in a gloss varnish. For further information on model specifications, pricing, and availability please contact luthier Walker (see Trademark Index).

WARWICK
Instruments currently produced in Markneukirchen, Germany by Warwick Gmbh & Co., Musicequipment KG since 1982. Distributed exclusively in the U.S. by Dana B. Goods of Santa Barbara, California.

Hans Peter Wilfer, son of Framus' Frederick Wilfer, established the Warwick trademark in 1982 in Erlangen (Bavaria). Wilfer literally grew up in the Framus factories of his father, and learned all aspects of construction and production right at the source. The high quality of Warwick basses quickly gained notice with bass players worldwide.

In 1995, Warwick moved to Markneukirchen (in the Saxon Vogtland) to take advantage of the centuries of instrument-making traditions. Construction of the new plant provided the opportunity to install new state-of-the-art machinery to go with the skilled craftsmen. The Warwick company continues to focus on producing high quality bass guitars; and since 1993, Warwick also offers a full range of bass amplification systems and speaker cabinets.

**Walker Archtop
courtesy Kim Walker**

GRADING		100%	EXCELLENT	AVERAGE

ACOUSTIC BASS

ALIEN - single sharp cutaway concert style, spruce top, asymmetrical soundhole located in upper bout, rosewood thumb rest, wood bound body, ovankol soundhole cap, ovankol back/sides, 2-piece mahogany neck with wenge center strip, 24-fret wenge fingerboard, wenge/metal bridge, ebony peghead veneer with pearl W inlay, 2-per-side chrome tuners, piezo pickup, 4-band EQ, active electronics, available in Natural finish, disc. 1994.

N/A   **$1,700**   **$1,100**
Last MSR was $3,300.

WASHBURN
Instruments currently produced both in Chicago, Illinois and Korea. Distributed by Washburn International, located in Vernon Hills, Illinois. Washburn is currently a division of U.S. Music Corporation.

Historically, Washburn instruments were produced in the Chicago, Illinois area from numerous sources from the late 1800s to 1940s. When the trademark was revived in the 1960s, instruments were produced first in Japan, and then later in Korea.

The Washburn trademark was originated by the Lyon & Healy company of Chicago, Illinois. George Washburn Lyon and Patrick Joseph Healy were chosen by Oliver Ditson, who had formed the Oliver Ditson Company, Inc. in 1835 as a musical publisher. Ditson was a primary force in music merchandising, distribution, and retail sales on the East Coast. In 1864 the Lyon & Healy music store opened for business. The late 1800s found the company ever expanding from retail, to producer, and finally distributor. The Washburn trademark was formally filed for in 1887, and the name applied to quality stringed instruments produced by a manufacturing department of Lyon & Healy.

Lyon & Healy were part of the Chicago musical instrument production conglomerate that produced musical instruments throughout the early and mid 1900s. As in business, if there is demand, a successful business will supply. Due to their early pioneering of mass production, the Washburn facility averaged up to one hundred

**Warwick Alien Acoustic Bass
courtesy Warwick**

instruments a day! Lyon & Healy/Washburn were eventually overtaken by the Tonk Bros. company, and the Washburn trademark was eventually discarded.

When the trademark was revived in 1964, the initial production of acoustic guitars came from Japan. Washburn electric guitars were re-introduced to the American market in 1979, and featured U.S. designs on Japanese-built instruments. Production of the entry level models was switched to Korea during the mid to late 1980s. As the company gained a larger foothold in the guitar market, American production was reintroduced in the late 1980s as well. Grover Jackson (ex-Jackson/Charvel) was instrumental in introducing new designs for Washburn for the Chicago series in 1993.

In 1998, Washburn adopted the Buzz Feiten Tuning System on the American-produced models. The Buzz Feiten Tuning System is a new tempered tuning system that produces a more "in-tune" guitar.

Early company history courtesy of John Teagle in his book *Washburn: Over One Hundred Years of Fine Stringed Instruments*. The actual history is a lot more involved and convoluted than the above outline suggests, and Teagle's book does a fine job of unravelling the narrative.

ACOUSTIC: CLASSIC GUITAR SERIES

C20 - classic style, spruce top, round soundhole, 3-stripe bound body, wooden inlay rosette, mahogany back/sides/neck, 12/19-fret rosewood fingerboard, tied rosewood bridge, 3-per-side nylon head chrome tuners, available in Natural finish, mfg. 1994-96.

| | N/A | $100 | $65 |

Last MSR was $180.

C40 - classic style, spruce top, round soundhole, 3-stripe bound body, wooden inlay rosette, mahogany back/sides, mahogany neck, 12/19-fret rosewood fingerboard, tied rosewood bridge, 3-per-side nylon head chrome tuners, available in Natural finish, current mfg.

| MSR | $280 | $199 | $140 | $85 |

C60 ZARAZOGA - classic style, spruce top, round soundhole, 3-stripe bound body, wooden inlay rosette, rosewood back/sides, mahogany neck, 12/19-fret rosewood fingerboard, tied rosewood bridge, rosewood peghead veneer, 3-per-side nylon head gold tuners, available in Natural finish, disc. 1994.

| | N/A | $190 | $125 |

Last MSR was $370.

C80 S - classic style, solid cedar top, round soundhole, 3-stripe bound body, wooden inlay rosette, rosewood back/sides, mahogany neck, 12/19-fret rosewood fingerboard, tied rosewood bridge, rosewood peghead veneer, 3-per-side nylon head gold tuners, available in Natural finish, current mfg.

| MSR | $480 | $350 | $240 | $150 |

C100 S W VALENCIA - classic style, solid cedar top, round soundhole, 3-stripe bound body, wood marquetry rosette, rosewood back/sides, mahogany neck, 12/19-fret ebony fingerboard, jacaranda bridge with bone saddle, rosewood peghead veneer, 3-per-side pearl head gold tuners, available in Natural finish, disc. 1991.

| | N/A | $750 | $450 |

Last MSR was $1,500.

C200 S W SEVILLA - similar to C100 S W, except has ebony reinforcement in the neck, disc. 1991.

| | N/A | $850 | $500 |

Last MSR was $1,900.

ACOUSTIC: DREADNOUGHT SERIES

D8 - dreadnought style, spruce top, round soundhole, black pickguard, bound body, 3-stripe purfling/rosette, mahogany back/sides/neck, 14/20-fret rosewood fingerboard with pearl dot inlay, rosewood bridge with black white dot pins, rosewood peghead veneer with screened logo, 3-per-side chrome tuners, available in Natural finish, mfg. 1994-96.

| | N/A | $105 | $65 |

Last MSR was $200.

D8 M - similar to D8, except has mahogany top, mfg. 1994-96.

| | N/A | $100 | $65 |

Last MSR was $190.

D10S - dreadnought style, select spruce top, round soundhole, black pickguard, 3-stripe bound body and rosette, mahogany back/sides/neck, 14/20-fret rosewood fingerboard with pearl dot inlay, rosewood bridge with pearl dot black pins, 3-per-side chrome Grover tuners, available in Natural or Sunburst finishes, current mfg.

| MSR | $350 | $225 | $150 | $100 |

Black, Trans. Red, and Blueburst finishes are available for an additional $20. Trans. Red and Blueburst finishes discontinued in 1999.

D10S12 - similar to D10S, except in 12-string configuration, 6-per-side tuners, available in Natural finish, current mfg.

| MSR | $420 | $295 | $210 | $130 |

D10SLH - similar to D10S, except in left-hand configuration, available in Natural finish, current mfg.

| MSR | $400 | $280 | $200 | $125 |

D10 M - similar to D10, except has mahogany top, available in Caribbean Blue, Mahogany, or Trans. Wine Red finishes, disc 2000.

| | $230 | $150 | $100 |

Last MSR was $329.

Caribbean Blue finish discontinued in 1999. Trans. Blue finish introduced in 2000.

D10 Q - similar to D10, except has a quilted maple top, available in Sunburst finish, current mfg.

| MSR | $400 | $280 | $200 | $140 |

GRADING		100%	EXCELLENT	AVERAGE

D11 - similar to D10, except has a mountain ash top, mountain ash back/sides, available in Antique Natural, Brown, Trans. Red, or Trans. Blue finishes, current mfg.

    MSR $390 $275 $180 $130

    Natural finish introduced in 2000.

D12 - dreadnought style, spruce top, round soundhole, black pickguard, 3-stripe bound body and rosette, mahogany back/sides/neck, 14/20-fret rosewood fingerboard with pearl dot inlay, rosewood bridge with pearl dot black pins, 3-per-side chrome diecast tuners, available in Black, Brown, Natural, or White finishes, disc. 1994.

                      N/A $175 $100

                      Last MSR was $350.

    D12 LH - similar to D12, except in left-handed configuration, available in Natural finish, disc. 1996.

                      N/A $195 $100

                      Last MSR was $380.

    D1212 - similar to D12, except features 12-string configuration, 6-per-side chrome diecast tuners, available in Black, Brown, Natural, Tobacco Sunburst, or White finishes, disc. 1996.

                      N/A $195 $125

                      Last MSR was $400.

D12 S - similar to D12, except has a solid spruce top, available in Black or Natural finishes, mfg. 1994-2000.

                  $325 $225 $150

                      Last MSR was $449.

    D12 S LH - similar to D12 S, except in left-handed configuration, available in Natural finish, disc 2000.

                  $350 $235 $150

                      Last MSR was $499.

    D12 S 12 - similar to D12 S, except features 12-string configuration, 6-per-side chrome diecast tuners, available in Natural finish, disc 2000.

                  $350 $250 $150

                      Last MSR was $499.

D13 - dreadnought style, spruce top, round soundhole, black pickguard, 3-stripe bound body and rosette, ovankol back/sides, mahogany neck, 14/20-fret rosewood fingerboard with pearl dot inlay, rosewood bridge w/white black dot pins, 3-per-side chrome diecast tuners, available in Natural finish, disc. 1994.

                      N/A $200 $125

                      Last MSR was $390.

    D1312 12-String - similar to D13, except has 12-string configuration, 6-per-side tuners, disc. 1994.

                      N/A $225 $125

                      Last MSR was $450.

    D13 S - similar to D13, except has solid spruce top, mfg. 1994-96, 1998-current.

    MSR $500 $350 $250 $150

    D1312S 12-String - similar to D13, except has 12-string configuration, solid spruce top, 6-per-side tuners, mfg. 1994-96.

                      N/A $250 $150

                      Last MSR was $500.

D14 - dreadnought style, spruce top, round soundhole, tortoise pickguard, 3-stripe bound body and rosette, rosewood back/sides, mahogany neck, 14/20-fret rosewood fingerboard with pearl dot inlay, rosewood bridge with pearl dot white pins, 3-per-side chrome diecast tuners, available in Natural or Tobacco finishes, disc. 1992.

                      N/A $175 $100

                      Last MSR was $350.

D15S - dreadnought style, solid spruce top, mahogany back and sides, mahogany neck, 14/20-fret rosewood fingerboard with pearl dot inlays, 3-per-side tuners, abalone top binding, tortoise pickguard, available in Natural finish, mfg. 1999-2000.

                  $450 $350 $250

                      Last MSR was $599.

D20 - dreadnought style, Hawaiian koa top, round soundhole, 3-stripe bound body/rosette, Hawaiian koa back/sides, mahogany neck, 14/20-fret rosewood fingerboard with pearl dot inlay, rosewood bridge with white bridgepins, 3-per-side gold diecast tuners, available in Natural finish, disc. 1999.

                  $600 $400 $275

                      Last MSR was $799.

D20 S - dreadnought style, solid spruce top, round soundhole, tortoise shell pickguard, 3-stripe bound body and rosette, flame maple back/sides, mahogany neck, 14/20-fret rosewood fingerboard with pearl diamond/12th fret W inlay, rosewood bridge with pearl dot white pins, rosewood veneer on peghead, 3-per-side chrome diecast tuners, available in Natural finish, disc. 1994.

                      N/A $275 $175

                      Last MSR was $530.

Washburn D-12
courtesy Dave Rogers
Dave's Guitar Shop

W

D21 S - dreadnought style, solid spruce top, round soundhole, tortoise shell pickguard, 3-stripe bound body/rosette, rosewood back/sides, mahogany neck, 14/20-fret rosewood fingerboard with pearl diamond/12th fret W inlay, rosewood bridge with pearl dot white pins, rosewood peghead veneer, 3-per-side gold diecast tuners, available in Natural or Tobacco Sunburst finishes, disc 2000.

	$450	$295	$195

Last MSR was $599.

In 1994, Tobacco Sunburst finish was discontinued.

D21 S LH - similar to D21S, except is left-handed, available in Natural finish, disc. 1992.

	N/A	$250	$150

Last MSR was $510.

D28 S - dreadnought style, solid spruce top, round soundhole, black pickguard, 3-stripe bound body and rosette, 3-piece rosewood back/sides, mahogany neck, 14/20-fret bound rosewood fingerboard with snowflake inlay, rosewood bridge with pearl dot white pins, bound peghead, 3-per-side gold diecast tuners, available in Natural finish, disc. 1996.

	N/A	$325	$200

Last MSR was $600.

D28 S LH - similar to D28 S, except has left-handed configuration, disc. 1992.

	N/A	$275	$175

Last MSR was $580.

D28 S 12 - similar to D28 S, except has 12-string configuration, 6-per-side tuners, disc. 1994.

	N/A	$325	$200

Last MSR was $650.

D28 12 LH - similar to D28 S, except is select spruce top, left-handed configuration, 12-string configuration, 6-per-side tuners, disc. 1992.

	N/A	$300	$175

Last MSR was $620.

D29 S (ORIGINAL VERSION) - dreadnought style, solid cedar top, round soundhole, tortoise shell pickguard, 3-stripe bound body and rosette, rosewood back/sides, 5-piece mahogany/rosewood neck, 14/20-fret rosewood fingerboard with diamond/12th fret W inlay, rosewood bridge with pearl dot white pins, 3-per-side gold diecast tuners, available in Natural finish, disc. 1994.

	N/A	$300	$175

Last MSR was $550.

D29 S (2nd Version) - similar to the D29 S (Original Version), except features a solid spruce top, jacaranda back/sides, available in Natural finish, disc. 1999.

	$675	$425	$275

Last MSR was $899.

D31S - dreadnought style, solid spruce top, round soundhole, tortoise shell pickguard, 3-stripe bound body/rosette, flamed maple back/sides, mahogany neck, 14/20-fret rosewood fingerboard with pearl dot inlay, rosewood bridge with white bridgepins, 3-per-side gold diecast tuners, available in Natural finish, mfg. 1998-99.

	$750	$450	$325

Last MSR was $999.

D33S - similar to the D31 S, except features rosewood back/sides, available in Natural finish, mfg. 1998-99.

	$825	$525	$350

Last MSR was $1,099.

D34S (AUGUSTA) - dreadnought style, solid spruce top, quilted maple back and sides, maple neck, bound body, rosewood finberboard and butterfly bridge, diamond inlays, 3-per-side tuners, crown style headstock, Buzz Feiten Tuning System, available in Natural finish, mfg. 2002-current.

MSR	$850	$595	$425	$275

D36S (TAHOE) - dreadnought style, solid spruce top, rosewood back and sides, mahogany neck, bound body, ebony finberboard and butterfly bridge, arrowhead inlays, 3-per-side tuners, crown style headstock, Buzz Feiten Tuning System, available in Natural finish, mfg. 2002-current.

MSR	$900	$650	$450	$300

D36SDL - similar to the D36S, except has MOP tree of life inlay, mfg. 2002-current.

MSR	$1,000	$700	$500	$325

D42 S (SOUTHWEST) - dreadnought style, solid North American spruce top, Honduran mahogany back and sides, mahogany neck, bound top, offset position markers, rosewood fingerboard, 3-per-side tuners, available in Natural finish, mfg. 2000-02.

	$375	$250	$175

Last MSR was $500.

D46 S (SOUTHWEST) - dreadnought style, Alaskan close grained spruce top, Macasssar rosewood back and sides, rosewood fingerboard, offset position markers, bound top, 3-per-side tuners, available in Natural finish, mfg. 2000-current.

MSR	$550	$395	$275	$175

D46S12 - similar to the D46S, except in 12-string configuration, 6-per-side tuners, mfg. 2000-current.

MSR	$600	$425	$300	$200

W

GRADING	100%	EXCELLENT	AVERAGE

D61 S W PRAIRIE SONG - dreadnought style, solid spruce top, round soundhole, rosewood pickguard, 3-stripe bound body, 5-stripe rosette, rosewood back/sides, mahogany neck, 14/20-fret rosewood fingerboard with pearl dot inlay, rosewood bridge with pearl dot black pins, rosewood veneer on peghead, 3-per-side chrome diecast tuners, available in Natural finish, disc. 1994.

	N/A	$650	$375

Last MSR was $1,200.

In 1993, ovankol back/sides replaced original item.

D61 S W 12 - similar to D61 S W, except has 12-string configuration, 6-per-side tuners, disc. 1992.

	N/A	$500	$300

Last MSR was $940.

D68 S W HARVEST - dreadnought style, solid spruce top, round soundhole, rosewood pickguard, maple/rosewood binding and rosette, rosewood back/sides, 5-piece mahogany/rosewood neck, 14/20-fret rosewood fingerboard with pearl dot inlay, ebony bridge with pearl dot black pins, rosewood veneered maple bound peghead with abalone Washburn inlay, 3-per-side chrome diecast tuners with pearloid buttons, available in Natural finish, disc. 1994.

	N/A	$800	$500

Last MSR was $1,500.

D70 S W HARVEST DELUXE - dreadnought style, solid spruce top, round soundhole, rosewood pickguard, maple/rosewood bound body, abalone inlay rosette, 3-piece rosewood back/sides, 5-piece mahogany/rosewood neck, 14/20-fret ebony fingerboard with abalone eye inlay, ebony bridge with abalone box inlay and Washburn inlay, 3-per-side chrome diecast tuners with pearloid buttons, available in Natural finish, mfg. 1990-94.

	N/A	$1,200	$750

Last MSR was $2,000.

**Washburn D-48S
courtesy Washburn**

D80SW (HIGHLAND USA) - dreadnought style, AAA solid spruce top, solid figured maple back and sides, one piece mahogany neck, rosewood fingerboard with small pearl dots, tortoise shell pickguard, roman style headstock, 3-per-side tuners, abalone rosette, Buzz Feiten tuning system, Natural finish, mfg. 2002-current.

MSR	$1,900	$1,350	$950	$600

D82SW (HIGHLAND USA) - dreadnought style, AAA solid spruce top, solid Indian Rosewood back and sides, one piece mahogany neck, rosewood fingerboard with small pearl dots, tortoise shell pickguard, roman style headstock, figured maple body binding, 3-per-side tuners, abalone rosette, Buzz Feiten tuning system, Natural finish, mfg. 2002-current.

MSR	$2,000	$1,400	$1,000	$650

D84SW (HIGHLAND USA) - dreadnought style, AAA solid spruce top, solid Hawaiian Koa back and sides, one piece mahogany neck, rosewood fingerboard with small pearl dots, tortoise shell pickguard, figured maple body binding, roman style headstock, 3-per-side tuners, abalone rosette, Buzz Feiten tuning system, Natural finish, mfg. 2002-current.

MSR	$2,300	$1,625	$1,150	$750

D90 S W GOLDEN HARVEST - similar to D70 S W, except has abalone bound body, tree of life abalone inlay on fingerboard, unbound peghead and pearloid head gold diecast tuners, disc. 1994.

	N/A	$2,500	$1,250

Last MSR was $4,000.

D200 S K - dreadnought style, solid spruce top, round soundhole, tortoise shell pickguard, bound body, 3-stripe rosette, flamed maple back/sides, mahogany neck, 14/20-fret bound rosewood fingerboard with pearl dot inlay, rosewood bridge with white bridgepins, 3-per-side gold diecast tuners, Buzz Feiten tuning system, available in Natural finish, mfg. 1998-99.

	$1,350	$875	$615

Last MSR was $1,799.

D250 S K - similar to the D200 S K, except features rosewood back/sides, Buzz Feiten tuning system, available in Natural finish, mfg. 1998-99.

	$1,425	$925	$650

Last MSR was $1,899.

ACOUSTIC: FOLK SERIES

F1 SK (JOEY) - smaller travel guitar, solid spruce top, round soundhole, ovankol back/sides, mahogany neck, rosewood fingerboard with pearl dot inlay, rosewood bridge with white bridgepins, 3-per-side chrome Grover tuners, available in Natural finish, mfg. 1998-2000.

	$225	$145	$100

Last MSR was $299.

**Washburn D-55 SW
courtesy Washburn**

GRADING		100%	EXCELLENT	AVERAGE

F10S - folk style, solid spruce top, mahogany back/sides, mahogany neck, 14/20-fret bound rosewood fingerboard with pearl dot inlay, rosewood bridge with black bridgepins, 3-per-side tuners, available in Natural finish, mfg. 2002-current.

MSR	$340	$240	$170	$125

F11 - folk style, mountain ash top, round soundhole, bound body, 3-stripe purfling/rosette, mountain ash back/sides, mahogany neck, 14/20-fret bound rosewood fingerboard with pearl dot inlay, rosewood bridge with black bridgepins, 3-per-side chrome Grover tuners, available in Antique Natural, Brown, or Natural finishes, disc 2002.

		$275	$180	$130

Last MSR was $380.

Natural finish discontinued in 1999.

ACOUSTIC: JUMBO SERIES

D24 S 12 12-STRING - jumbo style, solid spruce top, round soundhole, tortoise pickguard, bound body, 3-stripe purfling/rosette, mahogany back/sides/neck, 14/20-fret rosewood fingerboard with pearl dot inlay, rosewood bridge with white black dot pins, 6-per-side chrome Grover tuners, available in Natural finish, mfg. 1994-99.

		$575	$375	$250

Last MSR was $799.

D25 S - jumbo style, solid spruce top, round soundhole, tortoise pickguard, bound body 3-stripe purfling/rosette, mahogany back/sides/neck, 14/20-fret rosewood fingerboard with pearl diamond/12th fret 'W' inlay, rosewood bridge with pearl dot white pins, 3-per-side gold diecast tuners, available in Natural or Tobacco Sunburst finishes, mfg. 1993-2000.

		$475	$315	$200

Last MSR was $630.

In 1994, bound fingerboard/peghead, Tobacco Sunburst finish were introduced; 12th fret inlay was discontinued. In 1999 Tobacco Sunburst finish was discontinued.

D25 S 12 - similar to D25 S, except has 12-string configuration, 6-per-side tuners, disc. 1994.

		N/A	$275	$150

Last MSR was $500.

D30 S - jumbo style, solid cedar top, round soundhole, tortoise pickguard, bound body, 3-stripe purfling, 5-stripe rosette, bird's-eye maple back/sides, mahogany neck, 14/20-fret rosewood fingerboard with pearl dot inlay, rosewood bridge with pearl dot white pins and bone saddle, bird's-eye maple peghead veneer, 3-per-side chrome diecast tuners, available in Natural finish, disc. 1994.

		N/A	$375	$250

Last MSR was $750.

D32 S - similar to D30S, except has Makassar back/sides, bound fingerboard/peghead, Makassar veneer on peghead, disc. 1994.

		N/A	$400	$275

Last MSR was $800.

D32 S 12 12-String - similar to D32S, except has 12-string configuration, 6-per-side tuners, disc. 1992.

		N/A	$375	$250

Last MSR was $780.

D34 S - jumbo style, solid spruce top, round soundhole, bound body 3-stripe purfling/rosette, mahogany back/sides, mahogany neck, 14/20-fret rosewood fingerboard with pearl dot inlay, rosewood bridge with white bridgepins, 3-per-side gold diecast tuners, available in Natural finish, disc. 1999.

		$550	$350	$225

Last MSR was $729.

J20 S - jumbo style, solid cedar top, oval soundhole, bound body, 5-stripe rosette, walnut back/sides, mahogany neck, 21-fret rosewood fingerboard with pearl snowflake inlay at 12th fret, rosewood bridge with pearl dot white pins and bone saddle, walnut veneer on peghead, 3-per-side chrome diecast tuners, available in Natural finish, disc. 1994.

		N/A	$500	$300

Last MSR was $900.

J28SDL - jumbo style, AAA solid spruce top, quilted maple back/sides, maple neck with truss-rod, rosewood fingerobard and butterfly bridge, tortoise shell pickguard, black and white top binding, crown style headstock, 3-per-side tuners, available in Natural finish, mfg. 2000-current.

MSR	$900	$650	$450	$300

J28S12DL - similar to the J28SDL, except in 12-string configuration, 6-per-side tuners, mfg. 2000-current.

MSR	$950	$675	$475	$325

J50 S - similar to J20 S, except features a solid spruce top, birdseye maple back/sides, 21-fret bound rosewood fingerboard with pearl snowflake inlay at the 12th fret, birds eye maple veneer on bound peghead, 3-per-side pearl button gold diecast tuners, available in Natural finish, disc. 1994.

		N/A	$600	$375

Last MSR was $1,150.

ACOUSTIC: PR (PRAIRIE STATE) SERIES

The Prairie State series features guitars that have a unique body shape to them. They are based on a type of 1920s body styling where the body looks like it has been squashed on the top to make it wider and shorter.

GRADING		100%	EXCELLENT	AVERAGE

PR100S - 1920s body style, solid cedar top, mahogany back and sides with inlay strip, rosewood finger-board with dot inlay, rosewood "bass balanced" bridge, roman style headstock, 3-per-side tuners, Buzz Feiten tuning system, available in Sunburst finish, mfg. 2002-current.

	MSR	$1,400		$995	$700	$450

PR200S - 1920s body style, solid cedar top, rosewood back and sides with inlay strip, rosewood fingerboard with dot inlay, rosewood "bass balanced" bridge, roman style headstock, 3-per-side tuners, Buzz Feiten tuning system, available in Sunburst finish, mfg. 2002-current.

	MSR	$1,500		$1,050	$750	$475

ACOUSTIC: R SERIES (1896 REISSUE) SERIES

R301 - concert style, solid spruce top, round soundhole, bound body, 3-stripe purfling/rosette, mahogany back/sides/neck, 12/18-fret rosewood fingerboard with pearl dot inlay, rosewood bridge with black white dot pins, rosewood veneered slotted peghead, 3-per-side diecast chrome tuners, available in Natural finish, mfg. 1994-96.

		N/A	$325	$200
			Last MSR was $600.	

This instrument is a reissue of a model available in 1896.

R306 - similar to R301, except features solid cedar top, rosewood back/sides, mahogany neck, 12/18-fret rosewood fingerboard with pearl multi symbol inlay, rosewood bridge with carved fans/pearl dot inlay, white abalone dot bridge pins, rosewood veneered slotted peghead with pearl fan/diamond inlay, 3-per-side diecast chrome tuners with pearl buttons, available in Natural finish, mfg. 1993-96.

		N/A	$425	$275
			Last MSR was $800.	

This instrument is a reissue of a model available in 1896.

R310 - parlor (concert) style, solid spruce top, round soundhole, bound body, 3-stripe purfling/rosette, rosewood back/sides, mahogany neck, 12/18-fret rosewood fingerboard with pearl dot inlay, rosewood bridge with black bridgepins, rosewood veneered slotted peghead, 3-per-side diecast chrome tuners, available in Natural finish, disc. 1998.

		N/A	$750	$475
			Last MSR was $1,499.	

Washburn WD20 S
courtesy Washburn

ACOUSTIC: STEPHEN'S EXTENDED CUTAWAY SERIES

This series has a patented neck to body joint called the Stephen's Extended Cutaway (designed by Stephen Davies) that allows full access to all 24-frets.

DC60 LEXINGTON - single round cutaway dreadnought style, solid spruce top, oval soundhole, bound body, 3-stripe purfling/rosette, ovankol back/sides, mahogany neck, 24-fret bound rosewood fingerboard with pearl dot inlay, rosewood bridge with black dot pins, 3-per-side pearloid chrome diecast tuners, available in Natural finish, disc. 1992.

		N/A	$425	$275
			Last MSR was $830.	

DC80 CHARLESTON - similar to DC60 Lexington, except features a solid cedar top, rosewood back/sides, mahogany neck, 24-fret bound rosewood fingerboard with diamond inlay, rosewood bridge with pearl dot white pins, rosewood veneer on bound peghead, 3-per-side pearloid head gold diecast tuners, available in Natural finish, disc. 1992.

		N/A	$450	$300
			Last MSR was $900.	

ACOUSTIC: WC SERIES

WD20 S - dreadnought style, solid spruce top, round soundhole, black pickguard, bound body, 3-stripe rosette, mahogany back/sides/neck, 14/20-fret rosewood fingerboard with pearl dot inlay, rosewood bridge with black white dot pins, rosewood peghead veneer with screened logo, 3-per-side chrome tuners, available in Natural finish, mfg. 1993-99.

		$475	$300	$200
			Last MSR was $629.	

WD32 S - dreadnought style, solid spruce top, round soundhole, bound body, mahogany back/sides/neck, 14/20-fret rosewood fingerboard with pearl slash inlay, rosewood butterfly bridge with black white dot pins, crown headstock, 3-per-side chrome tuners, available in Natural finish, mfg. 2000-current.

		$475	$300	$200

WD40 S - similar to WD20 S, except features a solid cedar top, rosewood back/sides, mahogany neck, available in Natural finish, mfg. 1993-96.

		N/A	$265	$175
			Last MSR was $530.	

GRADING		100%	EXCELLENT	AVERAGE

ACOUSTIC ELECTRIC: CLASSIC SERIES

C64 CE - single rounded cutaway classical body, spruce top, round soundhole, bound body, wood marquetry rosette, ovankol back/sides, mahogany neck, 19-fret rosewood fingerboard, tied rosewood bridge, 3-per-side gold tuners with nylon buttons, acoustic bridge pickup, volume/tone controls, Equis Standard preamp, available in Natural finish, mfg. 1994-current.

MSR	$500		$350	$250	$175

C84 CE - single rounded cutaway body, solid spruce top, round soundhole, 3-stripe bound body, wood marquetry rosette, rosewood back/sides, mahogany neck, 12/19-fret rosewood fingerboard, tied rosewood bridge, rosewood peghead veneer, 3-per-side nylon head gold tuners, acoustic bridge pickup, 4-band EQ, available in Natural finish, disc. 1996.

			N/A	$350	$225

Last MSR was $650.

In 1994, solid cedar top replaced original item.

C94 S CE - similar to the C84CE, except features solid cedar top, wooden inlay rosette, jacaranda back/sides, 19-fret rosewood fingerboard, volume/tone control, 3-band EQ, available in Natural finish, mfg. 1994-96.

			N/A	$450	$275

Last MSR was $900.

C104 S CE - single rounded cutaway classical body, solid cedar top, round soundhole, bound body, wood marquetry rosette, rosewood back/sides, mahogany neck, 19-fret rosewood fingerboard, tied rosewood bridge, 3-per-side gold tuners with nylon buttons, acoustic bridge pickup, volume/tone controls, Equis Silver preamp, available in Natural finish, mfg. 1997-current.

MSR	$750		$525	$375	$225

EC41 TANGLEWOOD - classical style, spruce top, oval soundhole, 5-stripe bound body/rosette, ovankol back/sides, mahogany neck, 21-fret bound rosewood fingerboard with pearl dot inlay, rosewood bridge, ovankol veneer on bound peghead, 3-per-side pearl button gold tuners, EQUIS II preamp system, available in Natural finish, disc 1992.

			N/A	$350	$225

Last MSR was $700.

ACOUSTIC ELECTRIC: DREADNOUGHT SERIES

D10 E - dreadnought style, select spruce top, round soundhole, black pickguard, 3-stripe bound body/rosette, mahogany back/sides/neck, 14/20-fret rosewood fingerboard with pearl dot inlay, rosewood bridge with pearl dot black pins, 3-per-side chrome Grover tuners, piezo bridge pickup, volume/tone controls, passive preamp, available Natural finish, disc 2000.

			$305	$200	$130

Last MSR was $420.

Black finish available for an additional $10.

D10SCE - single rounded cutaway dreadnought style, select spruce top, round soundhole, black pickguard, 3-stripe bound body and rosette, mahogany back/sides/neck, 14/20-fret rosewood fingerboard with pearl dot inlay, rosewood bridge with pearl dot black pins, 3-per-side chrome Grover tuners, piezo bridge pickup, volume/tone controls, 3-band EQ, Equis Standard preamp, available in Black or Natural finishes, mfg. 1993-current.

MSR	$450		$325	$225	$150

D10SCE LH - similar to the D12 CE, except features a left-handed configuration, available in Natural finish, current mfg.

MSR	$550		$395	$275	$165

D10 CE M - similar to the D10 CE, except features a mahogany top (and mahogany back/sides), available in Trans. Wine Red, or Caribbean Blue finishes, disc 2000.

			$350	$220	$145

Last MSR was $499.

Caribbean Blue finish discontinued in 1999. Trans. Blue finish was introduced in 2000.

D10 CE Q - similar to the D10 CE, except features a quilted maple top, available in Sunburst finish, current mfg.

MSR	$480		$350	$240	$165

D12 CE - single rounded cutaway dreadnought style, spruce top, round soundhole, black pickguard, 3-stripe bound body and rosette, mahogany back/sides/neck, 14/20-fret rosewood fingerboard with pearl dot inlay/pearl W inlay at 12th fret, rosewood bridge with pearl dot black pins, 3-per-side chrome diecast tuners, piezo bridge pickup, volume/tone control, 3-band EQ, Equis Standard preamp, available in Black, Natural, Tobacco Sunburst, White, or Woodstone Brown finishes, mfg. 1993-94.

			N/A	$325	$200

Last MSR was $600.

D12 S CE - similar to the D12 CE, except features a solid spruce top, available in Black and Natural finishes, mfg. 1994-2000.

			$460	$300	$200

Last MSR was $629.

D1212 CE - similar to D12 CE, except has 12-string configuration, 6-per-side tuners, available in Natural or Tobacco Sunburst finishes, disc. 1994.

			N/A	$350	$225

Last MSR was $680.

GRADING	100%	EXCELLENT	AVERAGE

D1212 E - similar to D12 CE, except has non-cutaway body, 12-string configuration, 6-per-side tuners. Available in Natural finish, mfg. 1994-96.

	N/A	$275	$175

Last MSR was $530.

D17 S CE - single rounded cutaway dreadnought style, solid spruce top, round soundhole, black pickguard, 3-stripe bound body/rosette, mahogany back/sides/neck, 20-fret bound rosewood fingerboard with pearl diamond inlay, stylized W inlay at 12th fret, rosewood bridge with black white dot pins, pearl diamond inlay on bridge wings, bound peghead, 3-per-side gold tuners with pearl buttons, acoustic bridge pickup, volume/tone control, 3-band EQ, 1/4/XLR output jack, available in Black or Natural finishes, disc. 1996.

	N/A	$425	$250

Last MSR was $800.

Add $50 for 12-string configuration of this model (D17 S CE 12). Available in Natural finish only.

D17 CE - similar to D17 S CE, except has flamed sycamore top/back/sides, available in Brown or Wine Red finishes, disc. 1998.

	N/A	$575	$325

Last MSR was $999.

D17 CE 12 12-String - similar to D17 S CE, except has 12-string configuration, 6-per-side tuners, flamed sycamore top/back/sides, disc. 1994.

	N/A	$450	$295

Last MSR was $880.

D21 SE - dreadnought style, solid spruce top, round soundhole, tortoise shell pickguard, 3-stripe bound body and rosette, flame maple back/sides, mahogany neck, 14/20-fret rosewood fingerboard with pearl diamond/12th fret W inlay, rosewood bridge with pearl dot white pins, rosewood veneer on peghead, 3-per-side chrome diecast tuners, acoustic bridge pickup, volume/tone control, 3-band EQ, available in Natural finish, disc. 1992.

	N/A	$300	$175

Last MSR was $570.

**Washburn C104 S CE
courtesy Washburn**

D34SCE (AUGUSTA) - dreadnought style, solid spruce top, quilted maple back and sides, maple neck, bound body, rosewood finberboard and butterfly bridge, diamond inlays, 3-per-side tuners, crown style headstock, Buzz Feiten Tuning System and B Band electronics, available in Natural or Tobacco Sunburst finishes, mfg. 2002-current.

MSR	$1,000	$700	$500	$325

D42SC E - dreadnought style, single cutaway design, solid spruce top, mahogany back and sides, rosewood fingerboard, offset position markers, 3-per-side tuners, Equis Extra preamp, 3-band EQ, presence and volume, available in Natural finish, mfg. 2000-02.

	$525	$400	$250

Last MSR was $699.

D46SC E (SOUTHWEST) - dreadnought style, single cutaway design, solid spruce top, Makassar Rosewood back and sides, rosewood fingerboard, offset position markers, 3-per-side tuners, Equis Plus preamp, 3-band EQ with mid-sweep and presence, feedback elimination filter, bypass switch, available in Natural finish, mfg. 2000-current.

MSR	$650	$475	$325	$200

D46SC E 12 - similar to Model D46SC E except in a 12-string configuration, 6-per-side tuners, available in Natural finish, mfg. 2000-current.

MSR	$800	$575	$400	$250

D61 S CE - single round cutaway dreadnought style, solid spruce top, round soundhole, wood bound body, 3-stripe wood purfling, 5-stripe rosette, ovankol back/sides, mahogany neck, 14/20-fret rosewood fingerboard with pearl dot inlay, rosewood bridge with pearl dot black pins, rosewood peghead veneer, 3-per-side chrome diecast tuners, available in Natural finish, mfg. 1993-96.

	N/A	$750	$500

Last MSR was $1,500.

D68 S CE - single rounded cutaway dreadnought style, solid spruce top, round soundhole, wood body binding, 5-stripe wood purfling/rosette, rosewood back/sides, 5-piece mahogany/rosewood neck, 14/20-fret rosewood fingerboard w/pearl dot inlay, rosewood bridge with black pearl dot pins, rosewood veneered maple bound peghead w/abalone Washburn inlay, 3-per-side pearloid head chrome diecast tuners, rosewood pickguard, acoustic bridge pickup, 4-band EQ, available in Natural finish, mfg. 1993-96.

	N/A	$900	$600

Last MSR was $1,800.

**Washburn D17 CE
courtesy Washburn**

GRADING	100%	EXCELLENT	AVERAGE

ACOUSTIC ELECTRIC: FESTIVAL (EA) SERIES

Washburn's Festival Series models are equipped with Equis preamp systems and Fishman USA pickups.

EA10 - deep single sharp cutaway jumbo body, spruce top, oval soundhole, bound body, 3-stripe purfling/rosette, mahogany back/sides/neck, 21-fret bound rosewood fingerboard with pearl dot inlay, rosewood bridge with white black dot pins, bound peghead with screened logo, 3-per-side chrome Grover tuners, acoustic bridge pickup, Equis Standard preamp, available in Black or Natural finishes, mfg. 1994-current.

	MSR	$730	$525	$365	$225

Circa 2000, Buzz Reiten Tuning System was introduced.

EA16 - similar to the EA10, except features a thin single sharp cutaway folk body, ash top, ash back/sides, available in Metallic Blue or Pearl Black finishes, mfg. 2000-current.

	MSR	$600	$420	$300	$175

EA18 - similar to the EA10, except features a thin single sharp cutaway folk body, maple top, maple back/sides, available in Trans. Red or Tobacco Sunburst finishes, mfg. 1997-current.

	MSR	$750	$525	$375	$225

EA20SDL NEWPORT - thin single sharp cutaway jumbo body, select spruce or mahogany top, oval soundhole, bound body, 3-stripe rosette, mahogany back/sides/neck, 21-fret rosewood fingerboard with pearl dot inlay, rosewood bridge with pearl dot white pins, 3-per-side Grover diecast tuners, acoustic bridge pickup, Equis Gold preamp, available in Black or Tobacco Sunburst finishes, mfg. 1979-current.

	MSR	$900	$650	$450	$300

In 1994, Natural finish was introduced.

EA2012 - similar to EA20, except has 12-strings, 6-per-side tuners, available in Black or Natural finishes, disc. 1994.

			N/A	$450	$300

Last MSR was $900.

EA20 X Melissa - similar to EA20, except has special Melissa fingerboard inlay, available in Black finish, mfg. 1995 only.

			N/A	$575	$350

Last MSR was $949.

This model was designed in conjunction with Greg Allman (Allman Brothers). It is estimated that only 500 instruments were built.

EA22 NUNO BETTENCOURT LIMITED EDITION - single sharp cutaway folk style, spruce top, oval soundhole, bound body, 5-stripe purfling, 9-stripe rosette, mahogany back/sides/neck, 21-fret bound rosewood fingerboard with pearl wings inlay, rosewood bridge with white black dot pins, bound blackface peghead with screened signature/logo, 3-per-side chrome Grover tuners, acoustic bridge pickup, volume/tone control, 3-band EQ, numbered commemorative metal plate inside body, available in Black finish, mfg. 1994-96.

			N/A	$550	$350

Last MSR was $1,000.

EA26 CRAIG CHACQUICO SIGNATURE - thin single sharp cutaway jumbo body, select spruce top, oval soundhole, bound body, abalone rosette, mahogany back/sides/neck, 21-fret rosewood fingerboard with special abalone position markers, rosewood bridge with pearl dot white pins, 3-per-side Grover diecast tuners, gold hardware, acoustic bridge pickup, volume/tone controls, Equis Gold preamp, available in Black, Natural, or White finishes, disc 2000.

		$950	$575	$375

Last MSR was $1,199.

Black finish discontinued in 1999.

EA27 K - similar to the EA26, except features chrome hardware, Equis Silver preamp, available in Natural finish, mfg. 1997-99.

		$850	$550	$350

Last MSR was $1,159.

EA30 MONTEREY - single sharp cutaway dreadnought style, spruce top, oval soundhole, bound body, 3-stripe purfling, 5-stripe rosette, flame maple back/sides, mahogany neck, 21-fret rosewood fingerboard, rosewood bridge with white pearl dot pins, 3-per-side chrome diecast tuners, acoustic bridge pickup, volume/tone control, 3-band EQ, available in Natural, Trans. Red, Trans. Blue, or Trans. Black finishes, disc. 1992.

		N/A	$375	$225

Last MSR was $730.

Add $40 for 12-string configuration of this model (Model EA3012), available in Natural finish. Add $100 for left-handed configuration of this model (Model EA30 LH).

EA33 S K - deep single sharp cutaway jumbo body, solid spruce top, oval soundhole, bound body, 3-stripe rosette, flamed maple back/sides, mahogany neck, 21-fret rosewood fingerboard with pearl dot inlay, rosewood bridge with pearl dot white pins, 3-per-side Grover diecast tuners, gold hardware, acoustic bridge pickup, volume/tone controls, Equis Gold preamp, available in Natural finish, disc. 1999.

		$1,200	$850	$550

Last MSR was $1,699.

This model features the Buzz Feiten Tuning System.

W

GRADING	100%	EXCELLENT	AVERAGE

EA36 MARQUEE (EA46) - single cutaway dreadnought style, figured maple top, 3-stripe bound body, diagonal sound channels, figured maple back/sides, mahogany neck, 23-fret rosewood bound fingerboard with pearl diamond inlay, rosewood bridge with pearl dot black pins, flame maple veneer on bound peghead, 3-per-side pearl button gold diecast tuners, acoustic bridge pickup, Equis Gold preamp, available in Natural or Tobacco Sunburst finishes, disc. 1998.

	N/A	$600	$375

Last MSR was $1,199.

EA3612 - similar to EA36, except has 12-strings, 6-per-side tuners, disc. 1994.

	N/A	$525	$350

Last MSR was $1,050.

EA40 WOODSTOCK - single sharp cutaway dreadnought style, mahogany top, oval soundhole, bound body, abalone purfling/rosette, mahogany back/sides/neck, 21-fret bound rosewood fingerboard, rosewood bridge with pearl dot black pins, 3-per-side chrome diecast tuners, Equis II preamp system, available in Black or White finishes, disc. 1992.

	N/A	$550	$350

Last MSR was $1,100.

Add $40 for string version of this model (Model EA4012), disc. 1992.
This model had birdseye maple back/sides with Natural finish as an option.

EA44 - single sharp cutaway dreadnought style, solid cedar top, oval soundhole, bound body, 3-stripe purfling/rosette, rosewood back/sides, mahogany neck, 20-fret bound rosewood fingerboard with pearl diamond inlay, rosewood bridge with white black pins, bound peghead with rosewood veneer, 3-per-side chrome tuners with pearl buttons, acoustic bridge pickup, volume/tone control, 3-band EQ, available in Black, Natural, or Tobacco Sunburst finishes, disc. 1994.

	N/A	$550	$350

Last MSR was $1,100.

EA45 - similar to EA44, available in Natural or Tobacco Sunburst finishes, disc. 1996

	N/A	$575	$375

Last MSR was $1,150.

EA45S - similar to the EA45, except has a solid cedar top, koa back and sides, and B Band electronics, available in Natural finish, mfg. 2000-current.

MSR	$1,000	$700	$500	$325

EA220 DOUBLENECK - deep single sharp cutaway jumbo body, select spruce top, oval soundhole, bound body, 3-stripe rosette, mahogany back/sides/neck, 21-fret rosewood fingerboard with pearl dot inlay, rosewood bridge with pearl dot white pins, 12-string configuration neck (6-per-side Grover diecast tuners), 6-string configuration neck (3-per-side Grover diecast tuners), chrome hardware, acoustic bridge pickups, volume/tone controls, neck selector toggle switch, Equis Gold preamp, available in Black or Natural finishes, disc 2000.

$1,470	$970	$640

Last MSR was $2,100.

Black finish discontinued in 1999.

ACOUSTIC ELECTRIC: JUMBO SERIES

J21 CE - single rounded cutaway jumbo body, spruce top, oval soundhole, bound body, 3-stripe purfling, 5-stripe rosette, mahogany back/sides/neck, 21-fret bound rosewood fingerboard, pearl diamond inlay at 12th fret, rosewood bridge with white black dot pins, bound rosewood veneered peghead with screened logo, 3-per-side chrome tuners, acoustic bridge pickup, 4-band EQ, available in Black, Natural, or Tobacco Sunburst finishes, mfg. 1994-96.

	N/A	$325	$225

Last MSR was $650.

J28 S CE(DL) - single rounded cutaway jumbo body, solid spruce top, round soundhole, bound body, inlaid rosette, mahogany back/sides/neck, 14/20-fret bound rosewood fingerboard with pearl 'crown' inlay, rosewood bridge with white bridgepins, 3-per-side chrome Grover tuners, piezo bridge pickup, volume/3-band EQ controls, Equis Gold preamp, available in Tobacco Sunburst or Natural finishes, current mfg.

MSR	$1,100	$805	$530	$350

Natural finish was introduced in 2000.

J30 S CE - similar to J28 S CE, available in Black, Trans. Wine Red, or Natural finishes, mfg. 1998-99.

$1,300	$925	$600

Last MSR was $1,849.

This model features the Buzz Feiten Tuning System.

**Washburn EA 20
courtesy Washburn**

**Washburn EA 220 Doubleneck
courtesy Washburn**

W

GRADING	100%	EXCELLENT	AVERAGE

J61 S CE K - similar to J28 S CE, except features flamed maple back/sides, available in Natural or Tobacco Sunburst finishes, disc. 1999.

	$1,300	$925	$600

Last MSR was $1,849.

ACOUSTIC ELECTRIC: NV (ELECTRO-ACOUSTIC) SERIES

NV100 - adjustable pitch single cutaway style, solid spruce top, 1-piece mahogany back, mahogany neck, roman style headstock, 3-per-side tuners, ebony fingerboard and bridge, bound body, B-Band electronics, available in Natural, Black, or Vintage Sunburst finishes, mfg. 2002-current.

MSR	$1,700	$1,200	$850	$550

Add $75 for padauk back and sides with Padauk Natural Matte finish.

NV100C - classic single cutaway style, solid spruce top, 1-piece mahogany back, mahogany neck, roman style headstock, 3-per-side tuners, ebony fingerboard and bridge, bound body, B-Band electronics, available in Natural, Black, or Natural Matte finishes, mfg. 2002-current.

MSR	$2,000	$1,400	$1,000	$650

NY300 - similar to the NV100, except has Fishman piezo and electronics, available in Natural, Vintage Sunburst, Black, or Natural Matte finishes, mfg. 2002-current.

MSR	$1,900	$1,350	$950	$600

Add $75 for padauk back and sides with Padauk Natural Matte finish.

ACOUSTIC ELECTRIC: RED ROCKER SERIES

These models were designed in conjunction with guitarist Sammy Hagar.

RR150 - single Florentine cutaway semi-hollow alder body, bound quilted maple top, mahogany neck, 22-fret rosewood fingerboard with pearl dot inlay, blackface peghead, rosewood bridge, 3-per-side Grover tuners, chrome hardware, 2 exposed coil humbucker pickups/ acoustic piezo pickup, 2 volume/tone controls, 3-position toggle switch, available in Black or Trans. Red finishes, mfg. 1997-99.

	$900	$550	$395

Last MSR was $1,199.

RR300 (U.S. MFG.) - similar to the MR250, except features a mahogany body, bound spruce top, P-90-style single coil pickup/Fishman bridge transducer, available in Trans. Red or Vintage Sunburst finishes, mfg. 1997-99.

	$1,500	$950	$650

Last MSR was $1,999.

This model features the Buzz Feiten Tuning System.

ACOUSTIC ELECTRIC: SOLID BODY SERIES

CB400 - solid body acoustic single cutaway, solid spruce/maple top, 1 piece mahogany back, mahogany neck, rosewood fingerboard with pearl slash inlays, rosewood bridge, B Band electronics and pickup, three knobs on face of guitar, available in Vintage Sunburst, Quilted Cherry Gloss, or FCRB finishes, mfg. 2002-current.

MSR	$2,000	$1,400	$1,000	$650

SBC20 - single rounded cutaway classic style, spruce top, round soundhole, bound body, wooden inlay rosette, routed out mahogany body, mahogany neck, 22-fret rosewood fingerboard with pearl dot inlay, rosewood bridge, 3-per-side chrome diecast tuners, Sensor pickups, volume/tone control, available in Natural finish, disc. 1992.

	N/A	$275	$175

Last MSR was $550.

SBC70 - single cutaway classic style routed out mahogany body, multi-bound spruce top, mahogany neck, 22-fret bound rosewood fingerboard, tied rosewood bridge, rosewood veneered slotted peghead, 3-per-side chrome tuners with pearloid buttons, acoustic bridge pickup, volume/tone controls, available in Natural finish, mfg. 1994-96.

	N/A	$350	$225

Last MSR was $700.

SBF24 - single round cutaway dreadnought style, spruce top, round soundhole, bound body, wooden inlay rosette, routed out mahogany body, mahogany neck, 22-fret rosewood fingerboard with pearl dot inlay, rosewood bridge with white pearl dot pins, 3-per-side chrome diecast tuners, Sensor pickups, volume/tone control, active electronics, available in Natural, Pearl White, or Black finishes, disc. 1992.

	N/A	$275	$175

Last MSR was $570.

SBF80 - single cutaway dreadnought style routed out mahogany body, multi-bound figured maple top, mahogany neck, 22-fret bound rosewood fingerboard with pearl slotted diamond inlay, rosewood bridge with white abalone dot pins, bound figured maple peghead with screened logo, 3-per-side chrome Grover tuners with pearloid buttons, acoustic bridge pickup, volume/treble/bass controls, active electronics, available in Cherry Sunburst finish, mfg. 1993-96.

	N/A	$375	$250

Last MSR was $750.

GRADING	100%	EXCELLENT	AVERAGE

ACOUSTIC ELECTRIC: STEPHEN'S EXTENDED CUTAWAY SERIES

DC60 E - single round cutaway dreadnought style, solid spruce top, oval soundhole, bound body, 3-stripe purfling/rosette, ovankol back/sides, mahogany neck, 24-fret bound rosewood fingerboard with pearl dot inlay, rosewood bridge with black dot pins, 3-per-side pearloid chrome diecast tuners, acoustic bridge pickup, 4-band EQ, disc. 1994.

	N/A	$700	$450

Last MSR was $1,400.

DC80 E - similar to DC60 E, except features a solid cedar top, rosewood back/sides, mahogany neck, 24-fret bound rosewood fingerboard with diamond inlay, rosewood bridge with pearl dot white pins, rosewood veneer on bound peghead, 3-per-side pearloid head gold diecast tuners, acoustic bridge pickup, 4-band EQ, disc. 1994.

	N/A	$750	$495

Last MSR was $1,500.

ACOUSTIC ELECTRIC: WD SERIES

WD20SCE - single rounded cutaway dreadnought style, solid spruce top, round soundhole, black pickguard, bound body, 3-stripe rosette, mahogany back/sides/neck, 14/20-fret rosewood fingerboard with pearl dot inlay, rosewood bridge with black white dot pins, rosewood peghead veneer with screened logo, 3-per-side chrome tuners, acoustic bridge pickup, volume/tone control, 3-band EQ, available in Natural finish, mfg. 1994-96.

	N/A	$375	$225

Last MSR was $700.

WD32SCE - dreadnought with a venetian cutaway style, solid spruce top, round soundhole, bound body, mahogany back/sides/neck, 14/20-fret rosewood fingerboard with pearl slash inlay, rosewood butterfly bridge with black white dot pins, crown headstock, 3-per-side chrome tuners, B-Band electronics, available in Natural finish, mfg. 2000-current.

MSR	$660	$470	$330	$200

Washburn AB30
courtesy Washburn

ACOUSTIC ELECTRIC BASS: AB SERIES

AB10 - single sharp cutaway thin jumbo body, select spruce top, diagonal slotted sound channels (soundhole), bound body, mahogany back/sides, maple neck, 23-fret rosewood fingerboard with pearl dot inlay, rosewood bridge with brass insert, 2-per-side tuners, chrome hardware, Equis Silver bass preamp system, available in Black or Natural finishes, mfg. 1997-current.

MSR	$900	$650	$450	$300

AB20 - single sharp cutaway thin jumbo body, mahogany top, diagonal sound channels, bound body, mahogany back/sides, maple neck, 23-fret rosewood fingerboard with pearl dot inlay, rosewood bridge with brass insert, 2-per-side tuners, chrome hardware, Equis Gold bass preamp system, available in Black, Natural, or Tobacco Sunburst finishes, disc. 1999.

	$900	$550	$395

Last MSR was $1,199.

This model was available with a fretless fingerboard (this option discontinued in 1996). In 1997, Natural finish was discontinued.

AB25 - similar to AB20, except has 5 strings, available in Black or Tobacco Sunburst finishes, disc. 1996.

	$725	$500	$325

Last MSR was $1,049.

AB30 - similar to the AB32 except has diagonal sound channels, disc. 1999.

	$825	$525	$350

AB32 similar to AB20, except has single rounded cutaway deep dreadnought body, select spruce top, oval soundhole, Equis Silver bass preamp system, available in Natural or Tobacco Sunburst finishes, disc. 1999.

	$825	$525	$350

Last MSR was $1,099.

AB34 - single round cutaway jumbo style, select spruce top, round soundhole, bound body, mahogany back/sides, rosewood fingerboard with graphic inlay, ebonized rosewood bridge, 2-per-side tuners, chrome hardware, Equis Extra bass preamp system, available in Natural finish, current mfg.

	$1,575	$1,100	$750

W

AB40 - single round cutaway jumbo style, arched spruce top, diagonal sound channels, bound body, quilted ash back/sides, multi layer maple neck, 24-fret bound ebony fingerboard with pearl dot inlay, ebonized rosewood bridge with brass insert, bound peghead with pearl Washburn logo and stylized inlay, 2-per-side tuners, gold hardware, active electronics, volume/2 tone controls, Equis II bass preamp system, available in Natural or Tobacco Sunburst finishes, disc. 1996

| | $1,575 | $1,100 | $750 |

Last MSR was $2,250.

Subtract $150 for fretless fingerboard (Model AB40 FL).

AB42 - similar to AB40, except has humbucker pickup, available in Tobacco Sunburst finish, disc. 1996.

| | $1,750 | $1,150 | $825 |

Last MSR was $2,500.

AB45 - similar to AB40, except has 5-string configuration, 3/2-per-side tuners, available in Tobacco Sunburst finish, disc. 1991.

| | $1,600 | $1,150 | $825 |

Last MSR was $2,300.

WEBBER GUITARS
Instruments currently built in North Vancouver, Canada.

Luthier David Webber and his "small factory" build high quality acoustic guitars. He has currently built close to 700 guitars. For further information regarding model pricing and specification, please contact David Webber directly (see Trademark Index).

WECHTER GUITARS
Instruments curently built in Paw Paw, Michigan. Distributed by Wechter Guitars of Paw Paw, Michigan. Distributed in Japan by Okada International, Inc. of Tokyo, Japan.

Luthier Abraham Wechter began his guitar building career in the early 1970s by making dulcimers and repairing guitars in Seattle, Washington. Shortly thereafter he started looking for a mentor to apprentice with. In December of 1974, he moved to Detroit to begin an apprenticeship with Richard Schneider. He was captivated by Schneider's art, along with the scientific work Schneider was doing with Dr. Kasha.

Wechter worked with Schneider developing prototypes for what later became the "Mark" project at Gibson Guitars. Schneider was working regularly for Gibson developing prototypes, and as a result Wechter started working for Gibson as a model (prototype) builder. Schneider and Wechter moved to Kalamazoo in December 1976. After a few years, Wechter was given the opportunity to work as an independent consultant to Gibson. He continued on until June of 1984, performing prototype work on many of the guitars Gibson produced during that time period.

While at Gibson, Wechter continued his apprenticeship with Schneider, building handmade, world-class guitars. He actually rented space from Schneider during this time and started building his own models. In 1984, when Gibson moved to Nashville, Wechter decided to remain in Michigan. Wechter moved to Paw Paw, Michigan, a rural town about 20 miles west of Kalamazoo, where he set up shop and started designing and building his own guitars.

Wechter built handmade classical, jazz-nylon, bass, and steel-string acoustic guitars. He did a tremendous amount of research into how and why guitars perform. As a result, he became sought after by many high profile people in the industry. Between 1985 and 1995, Wechter designed and hand built guitars for artists like John McLaughlin, Steve Howe, Al DiMeola, Giovanni, John Denver, Earl Klugh, and Jonas Hellborg. During this time period he developed a reputation as one of the world's finest craftsman and guitar designers.

In November of 1994, Wechter built a prototype of an innovative new design, and realized that it would have applications far beyond the high price range he was working in. This was the birth of the Pathmaker guitar. The Pathmaker model is a revolutionary acoustic guitar. The double cutaway construction (patent pending) provides a full 19-frets clear of the body in a design that is both inherently stable and visually striking.

Wechter is currently laying the groundwork for mass production and distribution of the Pathmaker – the first production models were scheduled for January, 1997. A limited number of handmade premier models are being built, along with a small number of classical and jazz-nylon guitars.

For more information on availability and pricing, contact Wechter Guitars directly (see Trademark Index), (Biography courtesy Abraham Wechter and Michael Davidson, August 2, 1996).

ACOUSTIC

In November of 1994, Wechter built a prototype of an innovative new design that led to the introduction of the Pathmaker. The unique double cutaway body design features a neck with 19-frets clear of the body.

Earlier model may be equipped with either a Fishman Axis system or Axis+ or Axis-M. The **Pathmaker** "Recessed Tailblock" has a Fishman Matrix transducer mounted on the tailblock of the instrument.

Wechter has expanded their line immensely. They now have guitars from their high quality ones that they have always produced to models that are retail priced at $280! These guitars (1000 Series) have their final set-up in the Wechter shop but are built elsewhere. There is also the 3000 series, which is also produced elsewhere but set up in the Wechter shop. These guitars start at $400 and have several options.

Add $50 for a Fishman Onboard Blender. Add $150 for an Engelmann spruce top. Add $200 for Fishman Prefix Plus/Natural One pickup.

The **PATHMAKER STANDARD** has a dual cutaway acoustic body, solid Sitka spruce top, solid mahogany or rosewood back/sides, round soundhole, abalone rosette, wood binding, mahogany neck, 19/22-fret rosewood fingerboard with offset abalone dot inlay, 3-per-side tuners, rosewood peghead veneer with mother-of-pearl logo inlay, rosewood bridge with white bridgepins, tortoise pickguard, Fishman Prefix + system, available in Natural gloss finish. With mahogany back and sides MSR is $1,899. With rosewood back and sides MSR is $1,999. This model is also available in a Satin gloss finish. List price includes a hardshell case.

The **Pathmaker Elite Nylon String** is similar to the Pathmaker Standard, except features a nylon string configuration, available in Natural gloss finish With mahogany back and sides MSR is $2,049. With rosewood back and sides MSR is $2,149. This model is also available in a Satin gloss finish. List price includes a hardshell case.

The **Pathmaker Starburst** is similar to the Pathmaker Standard, except features white ABS body binding, available in Tobacco Brown Starburst finish With mahogany back and sides MSR is $2,099. With rosewood back and sidesMSR is $2,199. For more information on Wechter guitars refer to their web site (see Trademark Index).

WEISSENBORN
Instruments previously built in California during the 1920s and early 1930s.

H. Weissenborn instruments were favorites of slide guitar players in Hawaii and the West Coast in the early 1900s. All four models featured koa construction, and different binding packages per model. Further model specifications and information updates will be contained in future editions of the *Blue Book of Acoustic Guitars*.

Perhaps not since Stratmania of the eighties has an instrument increased in price as quickly as Weissenborn acoustic Hawaiian lap steels have in the last ten years. After the advent of resonator and electric instruments in the thirties, these odd koa instruments were seemingly appreciated only by a handful of players like David Lindley, Ry Cooder and John Fahey. More recently, Weissenborns have been made popular by Ben Harper, and used by steel and resonator-guitar players like Jerry Douglas, Mike Auldridge, Greg Leisz, Sally Van Meter and Cindy Cashdollar.

As prices of Weissenborns have multiplied, new enthusiasts have discovered in these guitars a mysterious sound adaptable to many musical styles and the first instrument specifically made for Hawaiian playing. More than just a Spanish guitar laid flat on the lap, Weissenborns were made with a high nut and inlaid flush fret markers. Credit for the hollow-neck design might belong to Christopher J. Knutsen (also a harp-guitar pioneer), but Weissenborn enjoyed more success, both structurally and commercially.

Weissenborn's guitars also directly influenced the instruments of his undoing – National and Dobro resophonics. Hermann C. Weissenborn (often confused with and likely not related to Herman W. Weissenborn, a mid -1800s partner of Charles Bruno in New York City) was born in Hanover, Germany in 1863. He took up musical instrument-making around 1879, later emigrating to New York City around 1900, moving to Los Angeles around 1910. He emphasized violin building, instrument repair and piano tuning even after the Hawaiian music craze was in full swing. All dates pertaining to Weissenborn instruments are approximate, because his instruments are not dated or serial numbered, but a general range would be 1920 up until his death in 1937. There does seem to be a progression of features that suggest an evolution of these instruments and a means of distinguishing relative age.

Confusion exists as to which instruments are Weissenborn-made and which aren't. It's not precisely true that anything that looks like a Weissenborn (hollow neck, koa wood, rope-marquetry binding) probably was made by him. The most often-encountered Weissenborn-made brand is the Kona Hawaiian guitar, marketed by Los Angeles teacher and publisher C.S. DeLano. Although Konas and Weissenborns initially appear identical (a vintage-instrument calendar made this mistake, despite a visible Kona label), Konas are narrower across the lower bout (13-1/4 in. vs.15-1/4 in.) and deeper (4 in. vs. 3 in.) than most Weissenborns. Konas have solid round necks that join the body at the seventh fret with an angled joint. Konas have wire frets rather than flush markers. The sound of Konas is generally regarded as equivalent to (though deeper than) Weissenborns. The most-often encountered marking is a 1 in. shield enclosing H. WEISSENBORN, LOS ANGELES, CAL and burned into the backstrip inside the soundhole. Some instruments have an additional brand of Henry STADLMAIR, NEW YORK, SOLE EASTERN DISTRIBUTOR.

Brands that, despite appearances, are not Weissenborn-made include Knutsen (see separate entry), Hilo and brands of Los Angelesí Schireson Brothers, including Lyric and Mai Kai. The principal feature that distinguishes Weissenborns from these other brands is Weissenborn's use of X-bracing on the tops. Hilo and the Schireson brands (more similar to each other than to Weissenborns), are ladder-braced. The difference is even more audible than visible. Hilos generally fall far short of Weissenborns in volume and tone. The manufacturer of these instruments was probably one of the large Chicago factories of the period, while some theories say Oscar Schmidt.

**Weissenborn Style 1
courtesy Dave Hull**

MODEL & STYLE INFORMATION

Most Weissenborn Hawaiians are three inches deep, although there are early Examples ranging from 2 to 2-1/2" and some little more than 1 in. deep. In general, Weissenborns were made in four styles:

Style 1: No body binding, three light-colored rings around the soundhole, single pearl-dot fret markers. Catalogs mention optional spruce top on Styles 1 and 2, but these are seen more often on early instruments.

Style 2: Black body binding, rope marquetry around soundhole, French curve on end of fingerboard (unique to Style 2), light wood binding on fretboard, fancier fret marker pattern.

Style 3: Rope (alternating angled light and dark wood marquetry) binding around top, soundhole and fretboard. Fretmarkers include double dots at 5 and 9, diamond or parallelogram at 12.

Style 4: Like Style 3, but with rope binding around back and headstock.

Additional pearl triangle marker lies with long side flush against nut.

Konas seem to follow this general scheme, except a Style 2 with black body binding has never been reported. There are Konas with variations on Style 1: some examples have no body binding; others have white plastic binding around the top. Experts including George Gruhn tend to regard these white-bound examples as Style 1 variants rather than as a separate style. Several Style 1 Konas have spruce tops–bound and unbound. Weissenborn also made Spanish guitars and other instruments, although the Hawaiians seem to be the most numerous extant today. A handful of examples of mandolins, tenor and plectrum guitars have been seen and several uke models appear in Tonk Bros. catalogs. The curious paucity of ukuleles encountered so far makes valuation speculative at best.

Spanish guitar models (and plectrum instruments; tenor bodies are smaller) are similar in dimension to a 12-fret Martin "0" size. Their bodies are also exactly the same dimensions as Kona Hawaiians, except for the Konasí unique 7th-fret neck joint. Weissenborn Spanish instruments are designated Styles A, B, C, and D, which parallel the Hawaiians 1, 2, 3, and 4. Weissenborn Spanish guitars feature X-bracing, and necks without truss rods. Spanish-neck Weissenborns tend to need neck re-sets (Weissenborn used a dovetail neck joint). Weissenborn Spanish guitars don't sound as distinctively different from other round-necks as do the Weissenborn Hawaiians from other steels. However, because of their rarity, Weissenborn Spanish guitar prices run close to those of their corresponding Hawaiian models and not much less than the more numerous Martin koa Spanish models like the 0-18K and 0-28K.

**Weissenborn Style 4
courtesy Dave Hull**

Note: Konas (because of they are less familiar among players, collectors and experts) and Spanish guitars with features equivalent to the Hawaiian models above may bring slightly lower prices.

The publisher wishes to express his thanks to Mr. Ben Elder for the above information.

RANGE PRICES OF WEISSENBORN HAWAIIANS

Style 1–$1,500 - $3,000
Style 2–$1,800 - $3,500
Style 3–$2,100 - $4,500
Style 4–$2,500 - $5,000

RANGE PRICES OF KONA HAWAIIANS

Style 1–$1,500 - $3,000
Style 2–$1,800 - $3,500
Style 3–$2,100 - $4,500
Style 4–$2,000 - $4,500

RANGE PRICES OF WEISSENBORN SPANISH GUITARS

Style A–$1,400 - $2,700
Style B–$1,800 - $3,000
Style C–$2,000 - $4,000
Style D–$2,000 - $4,500

WEYMANN & SON

Instruments previously built in Philadelphia, Pennsylvania from 1864 to the early part of the 1900s. Some models under the Weymann & Son trademark were built by Regal (Chicago, Illinois), and Vega (Boston, Massachusetts).

H.A. Weymann & Son, Incorporated was established in 1864 in Philadelphia. Later, it incorporated as the Weymann Company in 1904, and distributed numerous guitar models that ranged from entry level student up to fine quality. Other trademarks may include Weymann, Keystone State, W & S, and Varsity. Some of the guitars were actually produced by Vega or Regal, and share similarities to the company of origin's production instruments.

WHITEBROOK, MARK

Instruments previously built in California during the 1970s.

Mark Whitebrook was an apprentice to luthier Roy Noble for a number of years. Whitebrook built high quality acoustic guitars, and was luthier to James Taylor for a number of years. Further information will be updated in future editions of the *Blue Book of Acoustic Guitars*.

WINDSOR

See chapter on House Brands.

The Windsor trademark was a House Brand for Montgomery Wards around the turn of the century (circa 1890s to mid 1910s). These beginner's grade acoustic flattop guitars and mandolins were built by various American manufacturers such as Lyon & Healy (and possibly Harmony), (Source: Michael Wright, *Vintage Guitar Magazine*).

WINGERT, KATHY

Instruments currently produced in Rancho Palos Verdes, California.

Luthier Kathy Wingert is currently offering a number of handcrafted acoustic guitars. Guitars start at $5,600. For more information regarding model specifications and pricing options, contact Kathy Wingert (see Trademark Index).

WINSTON

Instruments previously produced in Japan circa early 1960s to late 1960s. Distributed in the U.S. by Buegeleisen & Jacobson of New York, New York.

The Winston trademark was a brand name used by U.S. importers Buegeleisen & Jacobson of New York, New York. The Winston brand appeared on a full range of acoustic guitars, thinline acoustic/electric archtops, and solid body electric guitars and basses. Winston instruments are generally the shorter scale beginner's guitar. Although the manufacturers are unknown, some models appear to be built by Guyatone, (Source: Michael Wright, *Vintage Guitar Magazine*).

WOOD, RANDY

Instruments currently built in Savannah, Georgia, since 1978.

Luthier Randy Wood was one of three partners who formed GTR, Inc. in Nashville in 1970. Wood left GTR to form the Old Time Picking Parlor in 1972, a combination custom instrument shop and nightclub that featured Bluegrass music. In 1978, he sold the Parlor and moved to Savannah, Georgia to concentrate on instruments building. Since then, he has produced over 1,500 stringed instruments from guitars to mandolins, dobros, violins, and banjos. For more information refer to their web site (see Trademark Index).

Section Y

YAMAHA

Instruments currently produced in U.S., Taiwan, and Indonesia. Distributed in the U.S. by the Yamaha Corporation of America, located in Buena Park, California.

Instruments previously produced in Japan. Yamaha company headquarters is located in Hamamatsu, Japan.

Yamaha has a tradition of building musical instruments for over 100 years. The first Yamaha solid body electric guitars were introduced to the American market in 1966. While the first series relied on designs based on classic American favorites, the second series developed more original designs. In the mid 1970s, Yamaha was recognized as the first Oriental brand to emerge as a prominent force equal to the big-name U.S. builders.

Production shifted to Taiwan in the early 1980s as Yamaha built its own facility to maintain quality. In 1990, the Yamaha Corporation of America (located in Buena Park, California) opened the Yamaha Guitar Development (YGD) center in North Hollywood, California. The Yamaha Guitar Development center focuses on design, prototyping, and customizing both current and new models. The YGD also custom-builds and maintains many of the Yamaha artist's instruments. The center's address on Weddington Street probably was the namesake of the Weddington series instruments of the early 1990s.

The Yamaha company produces a full range of musical instruments, including pianos, band instruments, stringed instruments, amplifiers, and sound reinforcement equipment.

GRADING		100%	EXCELLENT	AVERAGE

ACOUSTIC: CLASSICAL SERIES

C40 - classical style, spruce top, round soundhole, Indonesian mahogany back/sides, Nato neck, 14/19-fret Javanese rosewood fingerboard, tied Javanese rosewood bridge, 3-per-side chrome tuners, available in Natural finish, current mfg.

	MSR	$200		$150	$100	$75

CG40 A - classical style, spruce top, round soundhole, bound body, wooden inlay rosette, jetulong back/sides, Nato neck, 12/19-fret sonokeling fingerboard, bridge, 3-per-side chrome tuners, available in Natural finish, disc. 1996.

			$120	$95	$50

Last MSR was $170.

CS40 - 7/8 scale entry level classical guitar, spruce top, meranti sides and back, rosewood fingerboard and bridge, chrome tuners, available in Natural finish, current mfg.

	MSR	$170		$125	$85	$65

G50 A - similar to the CG40 A, except has judaswood back/sides, bubinga fretboard, red/black rosette, pearl tuner buttons, mfg. 1970-73.

			N/A	$95	$50

This model was also available with a pine top.

CG90 M A - classical style, spruce top, round soundhole, bound body, wooden inlay rosette, nato back/sides/neck, 12/19-fret bubinga fingerboard, Indian rosewood bridge, 3-per-side chrome tuners, available in Natural finish, disc.

			$195	$130	$85

Last MSR was $259.

CG90 S A - similar to CG90 M A, except has solid spruce top, rosewood fingerboard, available in Natural satin finish, disc.

			$235	$150	$100

Last MSR was $299.

CG100 A - classical style, spruce top, round soundhole, bound body, wooden inlay rosette, nato back/sides/neck, 12/19-fret bubinga fingerboard, rosewood bridge, 3-per-side chrome tuners, available in Natural finish, disc.

			$215	$135	$95

Last MSR was $279.

CG100 S A - similar to CG100 A, except has Solid spruce top, rosewood fingerboard and bridge, available in Natural finish, disc.

			$240	$150	$100

Last MSR was $309.

CS100 A - similar to CG100 A, except has 7/8 size body, mfg. 1994-96.

			$215	$145	$90

Last MSR was $310.

GRADING	100%	EXCELLENT	AVERAGE

CG101 - concert size guitar, spruce top, nato back and sides, nato neck, rosewood fingerboard, nylon strings, rosewood bridge, available in Natural Satin finish, disc 2002.

		$175	$115	$75

Last MSR was $249.

CG101M - similar to the CG101, except has a Natural Matte finish, current mfg.

MSR	$270		$190	$135	$80

Add $50 for Natural finish (Model CG101).

CG101MS - similar to Model CG101M except, has a solid spruce top, available in Natural Matte finish, current mfg.

MSR	$300		$210	$135	$90

CS101C - ¾ scale guitar, beginner series, nylon strings, solid cedar top, nato back, sides and neck, rosewood fingerboard, rosewood bridge, chrome plated tuners, available in Natural Gloss finish, disc. 2002.

MSR	$319		$225	$145	$95

Last MSR was $319.

CG110 A - classical style, spruce top, round soundhole, bound body, wooden inlay rosette, nato back/sides/neck, 12/19-fret rosewood fingerboard & bridge, 3-per-side chrome tuners, available in Natural finish, disc.

		$225	$110	$90

Last MSR was $319.

CG110 S A - similar to CG110 A, except has solid spruce top, mfg. 1994-99.

		$295	$175	$125

Last MSR was $379.

CG111S - similar to Model CG101 except, has solid spruce top, nato back and sides, nato neck, nylon strings, rosewood fingerboard, rosewood bridge, chrome plated tuners, available in Natural finish, current mfg.

MSR	$330		$225	$160	$110

Also available with solid cedar top (Model CG111C), available in Natural finish, current mfg.

CG120 A - similar to CG110 A, except has different rosette, rosewood fingerboard and bridge, disc.

		$275	$175	$125

Last MSR was $359.

CG130 A - classical style, spruce top, round soundhole, bound body, wooden inlay rosette, rosewood back/sides, nato neck, 12/19-fret bubinga fingerboard, rosewood bridge, 3-per-side gold tuners, disc. 1996.

		$275	$175	$100

Last MSR was $390.

CG130 S A - similar to CG110 S A, except has solid spruce top, nato back/sides, Indian rosewood fingerboard, available in Natural finish, mfg. 1998-2000.

		$300	$195	$130

Last MSR was $409.

CG131S - similar to Model CG111S except, has solid Sitka spruce top with multi-binding, available in Natural finish, current mfg.

MSR	$400		$279	$185	$120

CG150 S A - classical style, solid spruce top, round soundhole, bound body, wooden inlay rosette, ovankol back/sides, nato neck, 12/19-fret rosewood fingerboard, rosewood bridge, rosewood veneer on peghead, 3-per-side gold tuners, available in Natural finish, disc.

		$350	$225	$150

Last MSR was $469.

This model is an option with a solid cedar top (Model CG150 CA).

CG151S - similar to CG131S except, has ovankol back and sides, ebony fingerboard, gold plated tuners, available in Natural finish, current mfg.

MSR	$500		$350	$225	$150

Also available with Solid American Cedar top (Model CG151C), available in Natural finish, current mfg.

CG170 S A - classical style, solid spruce top, round soundhole, wooden inlay bound body and rosette, rosewood back/sides, nato neck, 12/19-fret rosewood fingerboard, rosewood bridge, rosewood veneer on peghead, 3-per-side gold tuners, available in Natural finish, disc.

		$450	$295	$195

Last MSR was $609.

This model is optional with a solid cedar top (Model CG170 CA).

CG171S - similar to Model CG151S except, has rosewood back and sides, available in Natural finish, current mfg.

MSR	$650		$450	$295	$195

Also available with solid American Cedar top (Model CG171C), available in Natural finish, current mfg.

CG171SF (Flamenco) - similar to the CG171S, except has cypress back and sides, current mfg.

MSR	$500		$350	$250	$150

CG180 S A - similar to 170 S A, except has solid white spruce top, different binding/rosette, ebony fingerboard, disc.

		$550	$350	$250

Last MSR was $739.

GRADING	100%	EXCELLENT	AVERAGE

Y

CG201S - solid European Spruce top, solid mahogany back and sides, nato neck, ebony fingerboard, rosewood bridge, gold plated tuners, nylon strings, available in Natural finish, current mfg.

	MSR	$850		$595	$385	$250

ACOUSTIC: DREADNOUGHT (DW) SERIES

DW4 S - dreadnought style, solid spruce top, round soundhole, nato back/sides/neck, 14/20-fret rosewood fingerboard, rosewood bridge, 3-per-side gold tuners, available in Natural finish, disc. 1999.

	$450	$295	$195

Last MSR was $599.

Add $50 for 12-string configuration (Model DW4 S-12).
This model is also available left-handed with electronics (Model SW4 S LE) and with a cutaway body/electronics (Model DW4 S C).

DW5 S - similar to the DW4 S, available in Natural and Tobacco Sunburst finishes, disc. 1999.

	$475	$295	$195

Last MSR was $649.

DW6 - dreadnought style, solid Sitka spruce top, nato sides, back, and neck, rosewood fingerboard and bridge, chrome hardware, available in Natural gloss finish, disc.

	$410	$280	$185

Last MSR was $549.

DW8 - similar to DW6, except has gold hardware, available in Natural, Brown Sunburst, or Black finishes, disc 2002.

	$450	$300	$200

Last MSR was $599.

Also available in LH configuration (DW8 L). Add $50 for 12-string configuration with chrome hardware (DW8-12).

DWX8 C - cutaway dreadnought, solid Sitka spruce top, nato back, neck, and sides, rosewood fingerboard and bridge, gold hardware, System 39 pickup, 3-band EQ with adjustable mid-range and volume, battery light, mute, available in Natural, Oriental Blue Burst, or Black finishes, mfg. 1999-2002.

	$635	$430	$285

Last MSR was $849.

DW10 - dreadnought style, solid Sitka spruce top, rosewood back and sides, nato neck with rosewood fingerboard, rosewood bridge, die-cast gold hardware, available in Natural gloss finish, disc.

	$525	$350	$230

Last MSR was $699.

DW20 - dreadnought style body, solid Sitka spruce top, rosewood back and sides, nato neck with rosewood fingerboard, snowflake inlays, rosewood bridge, gold hardware, abalone soundhole rosette and binding, available in Natural gloss finish, disc.

	$685	$475	$300

Last MSR was $949.

DW105 - dreadnought style, solid spruce top, round soundhole, nato back/sides/neck, 14/20-fret rosewood fingerboard, rosewood bridge, 3-per-side chrome tuners, available in Natural satin finish, disc. 1999.

	$450	$295	$195

Last MSR was $599.

ACOUSTIC: FG SERIES

Yamaha has produced several different models of the FG series over the years. Because there were so many and information is scarce on them now it is difficult to put them into individual model listings. Hopefully the following information will be of some help. The **FG-140**, **FG-180**, and the **FG-300** were the original 6-string jumbo guitars introduced in 1969. Also released that year was the 12-string **FG-230**, Spanish **FG-75**, and the folk body **FG-110** and **FG-150** models. Guitars from this era have a red label, and early models have wide heads.

In 1971 some higher end models were introduced (and these may be some of the only models that are worth a few coins). The **FG-580**, **FG-630**, **FG-700S**, **FG-1000J**, **FG-1200J**, **FG-1500**, **FG-2000**, and the **FG-2500** were all introduced. By now you should be able to tell that the higher the number on the guitar is, decides how much value it holds.

In 1972 the FG-140, FG-300, FG-230, and FG170 were discontinued as a whole new line of models were introduced. In the six string series the **FG-160**, **FG-210**, **FG-280**, **FG-165S**, and the **FG-295S** were introduced. The 12-String model was now the **FG-260**. A 3/4 sized model was introduced as the **FG-45**. The folk series gained the **FG-170**. The first acoustic/electrics debuted this year as well with the **FG-100E** and the **FG-160E**. Guitars now feature a green label, and should all have the narrow headstock.

In 1974, all the models have an I suffix. I'm not sure what that means because all the guitars models are the same. The only thing that was changed was that the labels were now black and the necks were made out of Toog.

In 1977, they pretty much brought in a new line of guitars. The only models to survive the switch were the acoustic electric models (these would get the axe in 1981), and the high-end models. Eight new models were introduced in 1977 for the 6-strings and they included the **FG-335**, **FG-340**, **FG-345**, **FG-350W**, **FG-365S**, **FG-375S**, **FG-336SG**, and the **FG-351SB**. The S suffix now stood for solid top instead of Sunburst, which was now SB. The 12-String series welcomed the **FG-312**, **FG-412SB**, and the **FG-512**. The Spanish body was now the FG-325. The Folk Guitar series introduced the **FG-300** and the **FG-331**. This era of guitars featured orange oval labels and a nato neck.

In 1978, the high-end series became the LL series. In 1979 a mid-range series was introduced featuring the FG-750S and FG-770S models. Between 1978 and 1980, a transition of moving the tension rod adjustment from the head to the body occurred. By 1981, the tension rod was in the body.

In 1981, the FG-350W, FG-336SB, and the FG-351SB were all discontinued. In the same series the **FG-340T** and **355SB** were introduced. It appears that this year a prefix was added to all the models, but what happen is unknown. The 12-String series gained the model **FG-612S**. The Folk guitar series became the Semi-Jumbo series and brought in the models **SJ-180** and **SJ-400S**. The acoustic/electric series was overhauled with new models **FG-335E** and **FG-365SE** replacing the old ones. In 1982 the **FG-332** was added to the six-string line. In 1984 the FG-335SB and the FG-346SB were introduced for one year only into the six-string line. Also in 1984, the first cutaway acoustics were introduced with the models CW-350E, CW-370SE, and non-electric models CW-350 and the CW-370 were introduced.

In 1985, the entire line of FG acoustic guitars was overhauled. No models retained there same model designation. The six-string jumbo models were now the **FG-400, FG-405, FG-410, FG-420, FG-430, FG-440, FG-450S, FG-460S, FG-470S**, and the **FG-480S** (essentially a model for EVERYONE!). The 12-String series switched to the FG-420-12, FG-440-12, and the FG-460S-12. The Folk series was the only series to retain the 300 series but introduced a new prefix with the **FS-310** and **FS-350S**. The new cutaways introduced in 1984 were simply switched over to the **FG-420EC, FG-450CE**, and non-electric **FG-420C** and **FG-450C**. The C stands for cutaway.

Model remained unchanged until 1989 when all models earned an A suffix. The FG-405, FG-440, and the FG-480 were all discontinued. The FS-350S, and the cutaway FG-420C and FG-450C models were discontinued. 1989 marked the first year for Yamaha left-handed acoustic instruments. These new models were the **FG-420LA** and **FG-450LA** (the L suffix stands for left-hand). The leaf logo was now on the headstock.

In 1995, they discontinued many of the models and changed the last 0 to a one, so an FG-400A became the FG-401, etc. In 1999 the dropped the 1 in favor of a 2 and introduced some new models. Then in 2001, they dropped the 2 for the 3. Most models are listed individually from 1989 on, which brings us up to where we are now. As more information and pricing becomes available, it will be published in upcoming editions.

Pricing is all across the board for these models. There are a good 50 different models, and each one has a different feature. These guitars never sold for too much money, and because of this aren't very collectible today. Most of these gutiars were played on because they may have been a guitarists first instrument. Most guitars are worth between $50-$250 depending on the condition and features. Some of the higher end models may command a higher premium

JR1 (FG JUNIOR) - (travel guitar) 3/4 size dreadnought body, spruce top, round soundhole, teardrop-shaped tortoise pickguard, black body binding, 2-stripe rosette, Indonesian mahogany back/sides, nato neck, 14/20-fret Javanese rosewood fingerboard with pearl dot inlay, rosewood bridge with white bridgepins, 3-per-side chrome tuners, available in Natural satin finish, mfg. 1998-current.

| | MSR | $200 | | $145 | $95 | $60 |

FFG300 A - dreadnought style, spruce top, round soundhole, bound body, 3-stripe rosette, black pickguard, jetulong back/sides, nato neck, 14/20-fret sonokeling fingerboard with pearl dot inlay, sonokeling bridge with white pins, 3-per-side chrome tuners with plastic buttons, available in Natural finish, disc. 1996.

| | | | N/A | $100 | $65 |
| | | | | *Last MSR was $230.* |

FG400 A - dreadnought style, spruce top, round soundhole, bound body, 3-stripe rosette, black pickguard, nato back/sides/neck, 14/20-fret bubinga fingerboard with pearl dot inlay, nato bridge with white pins, 3-per-side chrome tuners with plastic buttons, available in Natural finish, mfg. 1989-1994.

| | | | N/A | $125 | $80 |
| | | | | *Last MSR was $260.* |

FG401 - similar to FG400A, except has jumbo style body, available in Natural finish, mfg. 1994-97.

| | | | N/A | $175 | $85 |
| | | | | *Last MSR was $319.* |

FG402 - dreadnought style, spruce top, round soundhole, black pickguard, bound body, 5-stripe rosette, nato back/sides/neck, 14/20-fret Indian Rosewood fingerboard with pearl dot inlay, nato bridge with white bridgepins, 3-per-side diecast chrome tuners, available in Natural finish, mfg. 1999-2002.

| | | | $250 | $170 | $115 |
| | | | | *Last MSR was $339.* |

FG402 MS - similar to FG402 except, has solid spruce top and Matte finish, mfg. 1999-2002.

| | | | $250 | $170 | $115 |
| | | | | *Last MSR was $349.* |

FG403S - dreadnought style, spruce top, round soundhole, black pickguard, bound body, 5-stripe rosette, nato back/sides/neck, 14/20-fret Indian rosewood fingerboard with pearl dot inlay, nato bridge with white bridgepins, 3-per-side diecast chrome tuners, available in Natural finish, new 2003.

| | MSR | $300 | | $210 | $150 | $80 |

FG410 A - dreadnought style, spruce top, round soundhole, bound body, 5-stripe rosette, black pickguard, nato back/sides/neck, 14/20-fret bubinga fingerboard with pearl dot inlay, nato bridge with white pearl dot pins, 3-per-side chrome tuners with plastic buttons, available in Natural finish, mfg. 1989-1994.

| | | | N/A | $190 | $100 |
| | | | | *Last MSR was $330.* |

FG410-12 A - similar to FG410 A, except has 12-strings, 6-per-side tuners, mfg. 1989-1994.

| | | | N/A | $220 | $125 |
| | | | | *Last MSR was $360.* |

FG410 E A - similar to FG410 A, except has piezo pickups and volume/2 tone controls, mfg. 1989-1994.

| | | | N/A | $250 | $150 |
| | | | | *Last MSR was $520.* |

FG411 - dreadnought style, spruce top, round soundhole, black pickguard, bound body, 5-stripe rosette, nato back/sides/neck, 14/20-fret rosewood fingerboard with pearl dot inlay, nato bridge with white black dot pins, 3-per-side diecast chrome tuners, available in Natural or Violin Sunburst finishes, mfg. 1995-98.

	N/A	$200	$125
		Last MSR was $399.	

Add $50 for left-handed configuration (Model FG411 L).
This model had agathis back/sides/neck with Black finish as an option.

FG411-12 - similar to FG411, except has 12-strings, bubinga fingerboard, 6-per-side tuners, mfg. 1995-98.

	N/A	$225	$150
		Last MSR was $449.	

FG411 C - similar to FG411, except has single round cutaway body, available in Natural finish, mfg. 1995-96.

	N/A	$300	$175
		Last MSR was $600.	

This model has agathis back/sides as an option.

FG411 C-12 - similar to FG411, except has 12-strings, single round cutaway, 6-per-side tuners, piezo bridge pickup, volume/treble/bass controls, mfg. 1995-98.

	N/A	$325	$200
		Last MSR was $750.	

This model has agathis back/sides with Black finish as an option.

FG411 S - dreadnought style, solid spruce top, round soundhole, black pickguard, bound body, 5-stripe rosette, nato back/sides/neck, 14/20-fret rosewood fingerboard with pearl dot inlay, nato bridge with white black dot pins, 3-per-side diecast tuners, available in Violin Sunburst finish, mfg. 1995-98.

	N/A	$225	$125
		Last MSR was $449.	

Add $50 for left-handed configuration (Model FG411 S L).

FG411 S C - similar to FG411S, except has single round cutaway, solid spruce top, piezo bridge pickup, volume/treble/bass controls, available in Natural or Violin Sunburst finishes, mfg. 1995-96.

	N/A	$330	$200
		Last MSR was $660.	

FG411 S-12 - similar to FG411S, except has 12-strings, 6-per-side tuners, mfg. 1994-96.

	N/A	$250	$175
		Last MSR was $490.	

FG412 - dreadnought style, spruce top, round soundhole, black pickguard, bound body, 5-stripe rosette, nato back/sides/neck, 14/20-fret rosewood fingerboard with pearl dot inlay, nato bridge with white bridgepins, 3-per-side chrome diecast tuners, available in Black, Natural, or Violin Sunburst finishes, mfg. 1998-2001.

$299	$205	$135
	Last MSR was $399.	

Add $100 for left-handed configuration (Model FG412 L). Available in Natural finish only.

FG412-12 - similar to FG412, except has 12-string configuration, 6-per-side tuners, available in Natural finish, mfg. 1998-2001.

$335	$230	$150
	Last MSR was $449.	

FG412 S - similar to FG412, except has a solid spruce top, available in Natural finish, mfg. 1998-2001.

$335	$230	$150
	Last MSR was $449.	

FG413S - dreadnought style, spruce top, round soundhole, black pickguard, bound body, 5-stripe rosette, nato back/sides/neck, 14/20-fret rosewood fingerboard with pearl dot inlay, nato bridge with white bridgepins, 3-per-side chrome diecast tuners, available in Natural or Sandburst finishes, mfg. 2002-current.

MSR	$370	$260	$185	$105

Add $60 for left-handed configuration. Add $60 for 12-String configuration.
This model is available as a student model in 7/8 size.

FG420 A - dreadnought style, spruce top, round soundhole, black pickguard, 3-stripe bound body, abalone rosette, nato back/sides/neck, 14/20-fret bound bubinga fingerboard with pearl dot inlay, rosewood bridge with white pearl dot pins, 3-per-side chrome tuners, available in Natural finish, mfg. 1989-1994.

$265	$175	$100
	Last MSR was $380.	

This model was also available in a left-handed version (Model FG420 L A).

GRADING	100%	EXCELLENT	AVERAGE

FG420-12 A - similar to FG420A, except has 12-strings, 6-per-side tuners, mfg. 1989-1994

	$295	**$200**	**$125**

Last MSR was $420.

FG420 E-12 A - similar to FG420A, except has 12-strings, piezo electric pickups and volume/treble/bass controls, mfg. 1995-98.

	$375	**$225**	**$150**

Last MSR was $530.

FG421 - dreadnought style, spruce top, black pickguard, round soundhole, 5-stripe bound body/rosette, nato back/sides/neck, 14/20-fret bound rosewood fingerboard with pearl dot inlay, rosewood bridge with white black dot pins, 3-per-side diecast chrome tuners, available in Natural finish, mfg. 1994-96.

	$300	**$225**	**$125**

Last MSR was $430.

FG422 - dreadnought style, spruce top, round soundhole, black pickguard, bound body, 5-stripe rosette, nato back/sides/neck, 14/20-fret bound rosewood fingerboard with pearl dot inlay, nato bridge with white bridgepins, 3-per-side diecast chrome tuners, available in Natural, Oriental Blue Burst, or Tobacco Sunburst finishes, mfg. 1998-2001.

	$330	**$230**	**$150**

Last MSR was $469.

FG423S - dreadnought style, spruce top, round soundhole, black pickguard, bound body, 5-stripe rosette, nato back/sides/neck, 14/20-fret bound rosewood fingerboard with pearl dot inlay, nato bridge with white bridgepins, 3-per-side diecast chrome tuners, available in Natural, Oriental Blue Burst, Dark Sun Red, or Tobacco Brown finishes, mfg. 2002-current.

MSR	**$450**	**$315**	**$225**	**$150**

FG430 A - dreadnought style, spruce top, round soundhole, black pickguard, 3-stripe bound body, abalone rosette, nato back/sides/neck, 14/20-fret bound rosewood fingerboard with pearl dot inlay, rosewood bridge with white pearl dot pins, bound peghead, 3-per-side chrome tuners, available in Natural finish, mfg. 1989-1994.

	N/A	**$225**	**$125**

Last MSR was $430.

FG432 - dreadnought style, spruce top, round soundhole, black pickguard, bound body, 5-stripe rosette, nato back/sides/neck, 14/20-fret bound rosewood fingerboard with pearl dot inlay, bound headstock, nato bridge with white bridgepins, 3-per-side diecast chrome tuners, available in Natural finish, mfg. 1998-2000.

	$360	**$245**	**$160**

Last MSR was $479.

FG432 S - similar to FG432, except features a solid spruce top, available in Natural finish, mfg. 1998-2001.

	$410	**$275**	**$180**

Last MSR was $549.

FG433S - dreadnought style, spruce top, round soundhole, black pickguard, bound body, 5-stripe rosette, nato back/sides/neck, 14/20-fret bound rosewood fingerboard with pearl dot inlay, bound headstock, nato bridge with white bridgepins, 3-per-side diecast chrome tuners, available in Natural finish, mfg. 2001-current.

MSR	**$530**	**$375**	**$265**	**$165**

FG435 A - dreadnought style, spruce top, round soundhole, black pickguard, agathis back/sides, nato neck, 14/20 bound bubinga fingerboard with pearl snowflake inlay, rosewood bridge with white pearl dot pins, bound peghead, 3-per-side chrome tuners, available in Black, Marine Blue, Oriental Blue, Tinted, or Tobacco Brown Sunburst finishes, disc. 1994.

	N/A	**$200**	**$125**

Last MSR was $420.

FG441 - dreadnought style, spruce top, round soundhole, black pickguard, 3-stripe bound body, abalone rosette, ovankol back/sides, nato neck, 14/20-fret bound rosewood fingerboard with pearl dot inlay, rosewood bridge with black white dot pins, bound blackface peghead with pearl leaf/logo inlay, 3-per-side chrome tuners, available in Natural or Tobacco Brown Sunburst finishes, mfg. 1994-97.

	N/A	**$225**	**$150**

Last MSR was $460.

Add $70 for left-handed configuration (Model FG441 L).
This model had agathis back/sides with Black finish as an option.

FG441 C - similar to FG441, except has single round cutaway, piezo bridge pickup, volume/treble/bass controls, available in Natural and Tobacco Brown Sunburst finishes, mfg. 1994-96.

	N/A	**$375**	**$250**

Last MSR was $750.

This model had agathis back/sides with Black and Marine Blue finish as an option.

FG441 S - similar to FG441, except has solid spruce top, available in Natural finish, mfg. 1994-97.

	N/A	**$275**	**$150**

Last MSR was $529.

FG441 S-12 - similar to FG44 1, except has 12-strings, solid spruce top, 6-per-side tuners, available in Natural finish, mfg. 1994-96.

	N/A	**$300**	**$175**

Last MSR was $580.

GRADING		100%	EXCELLENT	AVERAGE

G450 S A - dreadnought style, solid spruce top, round soundhole, black pickguard, bound body, abalone rosette, ovankol back/sides, nato neck, 14/20-fret bound rosewood fingerboard with pearl snowflake inlay, rosewood bridge with black pearl dot pins, bound peghead with rosewood veneer, 3-per-side chrome tuners, available in Natural finish, mfg. 1989-1994.

		N/A	$250	$150

Last MSR was $500.

This model had left-handed configuration (Model FG450 S L A) as an option.

G460 S A - similar to 450S A, except has rosewood back/sides, gold hardware, disc 1994.

		N/A	$300	$175

Last MSR was $590.

FG460 S-12 A - similar to FG450SA, except has 12-strings, rosewood back/sides, 6-per-side tuners, gold hardware, disc 1994.

		N/A	$325	$200

Last MSR was $620.

G461 S - dreadnought style, solid spruce top, round soundhole, black pickguard, bound body, abalone purfling/rosette, rosewood back/sides, nato neck, 14/20-fret bound rosewood fingerboard with pearl cross inlay, rosewood bridge with black pearl dot inlay, bound blackface peghead with pearl leaf/logo inlay, 3-per-side diecast gold tuners, available in Natural finish, mfg. 1994-97.

		N/A	$350	$225

Last MSR was $679.

G470 S A - dreadnought style, solid spruce top, round soundhole, black pickguard, bound body, abalone rosette, rosewood back/sides, nato neck, 14/20-fret bound rosewood fingerboard with pearl snowflake inlay, rosewood bridge with black pearl dot pins, bound peghead with rosewood veneer, 3-per-side gold tuners, available in Natural finish, disc 1994.

		N/A	$350	$225

Last MSR was $660.

FG502 - folk model, solid spruce top, solid mahogany back and sides, nato neck, rosewood fingerboard with dot position markers, 3-per-side Kluson tuners, rosewood bridge, available in natural Matte finish, mfg. 2001-current.

MSR	$799	$560	$400	$250

FG502 M - similar to FG502 except has a solid mahogany top, available in Natural Matte finish, mfg. 2001-current.

MSR	$799	$560	$400	$250

Yamaha FG222 OBB
courtesy Sid Harper

ACOUSTIC: CJ, F, & FJ SERIES

CJ12 - country jumbo style, spruce top, round soundhole, bound body, 3-stripe rosette, black pickguard, Agathis back/sides, mahogany neck, 14/20-fret Indian Rosewood fingerboard with pearl dot inlay, rosewood bridge with white pins, 3-per-side gold tuners with plastic buttons, available in Natural finish, current mfg.

MSR	$700	$525	$325	$225

CJ32 (HANDCRAFTED) - handcrafted country jumbo body, solid spruce top, mahogany back and sides, maple neck, ebony fingerboard, available in Cherry Sunburst finish, mfg. 2001-current.

MSR	$2,500	$1,750	$1,150	$850

F310 - dreadnought style, spruce top, round soundhole, bound body, 3-stripe rosette, black pickguard, jetu-long back/sides, nato neck, 14/20-fret sonokeling fingerboard with pearl dot inlay, sonokeling bridge with white pins, 3-per-side chrome tuners, available in Natural finish, current mfg.

MSR	$230	$165	$115	$65

This model is also available in the Yamaha Gig Maker package, along with a case, digital tuner, strings, string winder, polish and cloth, picks, a strap, and a video (retail list $330).

F340 - dreadnought style, spruce top, meranti back and sides, nato neck with rosewood fingerboard, rosewood bridge, 3-per-side chrome tuners, available in Natural and Black finishes, current mfg.

MSR	$299	$225	$135	$90

F380 - dreadnought style, spruce top, meranti back and sides, nato neck with rosewood fingerboard, rosewood bridge, 3-per-side chrome tuners, available in Natural and Black finishes, current mfg.

MSR	$299	$225	$135	$90

FJ645 A - jumbo style, spruce top, round soundhole, black pickguard, bound body, abalone rosette, agathis back/sides, nato neck, 14/20-fret bound rosewood fingerboard with pearl pyramid inlay, nato bridge with white pearl dot pins, bound peghead, 3-per-side chrome tuners, available in Black Burst finish, mfg. 1989-1994.

		N/A	$275	$175

Last MSR was $550.

Y

GRADING	100%	EXCELLENT	AVERAGE

FJ651 - jumbo style, spruce top, round soundhole, black pickguard, 5-stripe bound body/rosette, agathis back/sides, mahogany neck, 14/20-fret bound rosewood fingerboard with pearl pentagon inlay, rosewood bridge with white black dot inlay, bound blackface peghead with pearl leaves/logo inlay, 3-per-side diecast gold tuners, available in Violin Sunburst finish, mfg. 1994-97.

	N/A	$275	$175

Last MSR was $560.

ACOUSTIC: FS SERIES

FS310 A - parlor style, spruce top, round soundhole, black pickguard, bound body, 5-stripe rosette, nato back/sides/neck, 14/20-fret bubinga fingerboard with pearl dot inlay, nato bridge with white pins, 3-per-side chrome tuners, available in Natural finish, disc. 1995.

	N/A	$170	$95

Last MSR was $330.

FS311 - 7/8 scale dreadnought body, spruce top, round soundhole, bound body, 3-stripe rosette, black pickguard, nato back/sides/neck, 14/20-fret rosewood fingerboard with pearl dot inlay, rosewood bridge with white pins, 3-per-side chrome tuners, available in Natural finish, current mfg.

MSR	$399	$225	$125	$90

FS340 - 7/8 scale semi-jumbo, spruce top, meranti back and sides, nato neck with rosewood fingerboard, rosewood bridge, chrome hardware, 3-per-side tuners, available in Natural finish, current mfg.

MSR	$299	$225	$150	$100

ACOUSTIC: HANDCRAFTED CLASSICAL (GC) SERIES

GC21 - handcrafted classical body, solid top, available in Natural finish, current mfg.

MSR	$1,600	$1,125	$785	$495

Also available with solid cedar top, available in Natural finish, current mfg.

GC30 - classic style, solid white spruce top, round soundhole, bound body, wooden inlay rosette, rosewood back/sides, mahogany neck, 12/19-fret ebony fingerboard, jacaranda bridge, rosewood peghead veneer, 3-per-side gold tuners, available in Natural finish, disc.

	$1,035	$600	$425

Last MSR was $1,379.

This model has solid cedar top (Model GC30C) as an option.

GC31 - handcrafted classical body, solid top, solid rosewood back and sides, available in Natural finish, current mfg.

MSR	$2,300	$1,599	$1,050	$735

Also available with solid cedar top (Model GC31C). Available in Natural finish. Current Mfg.

GC40 - classic style, solid white spruce top, round soundhole, bound body, wooden inlay rosette, jacaranda back/sides, mahogany neck, 12/19-fret ebony fingerboard, jacaranda bridge, jacaranda peghead veneer, 3-per-side gold tuners, available in Natural finish, disc, 1998.

	N/A	$950	$625

Last MSR was $2,000.

This model is also available with solid cedar top (Model GC40C).

GC41 - handcrafted classical body, solid top, solid rosewood back and sides, available in Natural finish, current mfg.

MSR	$2,600	$1,825	$1,195	$925

Also available with solid cedar top (Model GC41C). Available in natural finish. Current Mfg.

GC50 - classic style, solid White Spruce top, round soundhole, bound body, wooden inlay rosette, selected solid rosewood back/sides, Honduras mahogany neck, 12/19-fret ebony fingerboard, select rosewood bridge, jacaranda peghead veneer with stylized Y groove, 3-per-side gold tuners, available in Lacquer finish, disc.

	$2,850	$1,550	$1,000

Last MSR was $3,799.

This model is also available with solid cedar top (Model GC50C).

GC60 - classic style, solid German spruce top, round soundhole, bound body, wooden inlay rosette, selected solid rosewood back/sides, Honduras mahogany neck, 12/19-fret ebony fingerboard, select rosewood bridge, jacaranda peghead veneer with stylized Y groove, 3-per-side gold tuners, available in Lacquer finish, disc.

	$3,750	$2,850	$1,650

Last MSR was $4,999.

This model is also available with solid cedar top (Model GC60C) optionally.

GC70 - classic style, solid German Spruce top (Rumanian Spruce 2001), round soundhole, bound body, wooden inlay rosette, Selected Solid Rosewood back/sides, Honduras mahogany neck, 12/19-fret ebony fingerboard, select rosewood bridge, jacaranda peghead veneer with stylized Y groove, 3-per-side gold tuners, available in Shellac finish, current mfg.

MSR	$12,000	$8,995	$6,750	$3,950

This model is available with solid cedar top (Model GC70C), and is also available with no peghead groove (Model GC71), add $200.

GC71 - handcrafted classical style body, solid German spruce top, selected solid rosewood back and sides, Segovia design, special order only, available in Natural finish, current mfg.

MSR	$12,000	$8,995	$6,750	$3,950

GRADING	100%	EXCELLENT	AVERAGE

GD10 - classic style, solid white spruce top, round soundhole, wooden inlay rosette, Indian rosewood back/sides, African mahogany neck, 12/19-fret ebony fingerboard, Indian rosewood bridge, rosewood peghead veneer, 3-per-side gold tuners, Natural finish, disc.

	$630	$430	$280

Last MSR was $839.

This model is also available with solid cedar top (Model GD10C).

GD20 - classic style, solid spruce top, round soundhole, wooden inlay rosette, rosewood back/sides, mahogany neck, 12/19-fret ebony fingerboard, rosewood bridge, rosewood peghead veneer, 3-per-side gold tuners, available in Natural finish, disc. 1996.

	N/A	$475	$300

Last MSR was $950.

This model had solid cedar top (Model GD20C) as an option.

ACOUSTIC: L SERIES

LA8 - dreadnought style, solid spruce top, round soundhole, 3-stripe bound body, abalone rosette, rosewood back/sides, mahogany neck, 14/20-fret bound ebony fingerboard with pearl snowflake/cross inlay, ebony bridge with white black dot pins, bound rosewood veneered peghead with pearl logo inlay, 3-per-side gold tuners, available in Natural finish, mfg. 1993-98.

	N/A	$450	$300

Last MSR was $949.

LA18 - mid-size dreadnought style, solid spruce top, round soundhole, bound body, abalone rosette, mahogany back/sides, mahogany neck, 14/20-fret bound ebony fingerboard with pearl dot inlay, ebony bridge with white pearl dot pins, bound peghead with rosewood veneer and pearl/abalone double L inlay, 3-per-side gold tuners, available in Natural finish, mfg. 1990-96.

	N/A	$575	$350

Last MSR was $1,130.

LA28 - similar to LA18, except has rosewood back/sides and pearl diamond inlay, mfg. 1990-96.

	N/A	$800	$450

Last MSR was $1,600.

LD10 - dreadnought style, solid white spruce top, round soundhole, black pickguard, abalone bound body and rosette, rosewood back/sides, mahogany neck, 14/20-fret bound rosewood fingerboard with pearl dot inlay, rosewood bridge with black pearl dot pins, bound peghead with rosewood veneer, 3-per-side gold tuners, available in Natural finish, mfg. 1990-96.

	N/A	$375	$225

Last MSR was $760.

LD10E - similar to LD10, except has piezo electric pickups and pop up volume/2 tone and mix controls, mfg. 1990-96.

	N/A	$475	$275

Last MSR was $950.

LL11 - full size acoustic with scalloped bracing and L-block heel joint, solid white spruce top, rosewood sides and back, African mahogany neck with rosewood fingerboard, rosewood bridge, gold hardware, available in Natural finish, mfg. 1995-current.

	$570	$390	$250

Last MSR was $759.

LL11 E - similar to LL11, except has Indian rosewood back and sides, Indian rosewood fingerboard and bridge, external acoustic preamp system and 2-way piezo pickup system, 3-Band EQ with adjustable midrange, volume, battery light, EQ bypass, available in Natural finish, mfg. 1995-current.

	$900	$600	$400

LL15 - dreadnought style, solid spruce top, round soundhole, black pickguard, 5-stripe bound body and rosette, mahogany back/sides/neck, 14/20-fret ebony fingerboard with pearl dot inlay, ebony bridge with black pearl dot pins, rosewood veneer on peghead, 3-per-side gold tuners, available in Natural finish, mfg. 1984-1996.

	N/A	$575	$350

Last MSR was $1,130.

LL35 - dreadnought style, solid white spruce top, round soundhole, black pickguard, 3-stripe bound body, abalone rosette, jacaranda back/sides, mahogany neck, 14/20-fret bound ebony fingerboard with pearl snowflake inlay, ebony bridge with black pearl dot pins, bound peghead with rosewood veneer and pearl/abalone double L inlay, 3-per-side gold tuners, available in Natural finish, mfg. 1984-1996.

	N/A	$875	$575

Last MSR was $1,900.

**Yamaha FS340
courtesy Sid Harper**

Y

LL400 - handcrafted acoustic, LL body style, solid Sitka spruce top, solid mahogany back and sides, mahogany neck with rosewood finger-board, mother-of-pearl snowflake inlays, rosewood bridge, abalone rosette, ivory cell binding, gold tuners, available in Natural gloss finish, mfg. 1999-current.

	MSR	$1,499		$1,095	$695	$450

LL500 - similar to LL400, except has solid rosewood back/sides, available in Natural finish, mfg. 1999-current.

	MSR	$1,799		$1,325	$865	$550

LS400 - handcrafted acoustic, LS body style, solid Sitka spruce top, solid mahogany back and sides, rosewood fingerboard and bridge, MOP snowflake inlays, abalone rosette, gold tuners, Ivory cell binding, available in Natural, Black, or Vintage Tint finishes, mfg. 1999-current.

	MSR	$1,499		$1,095	$695	$450

LS500 - similar to LS400, except has solid rosewood back and sides, available in Natural gloss finish, mfg. 1999-current.

	MSR	$1,799		$1,325	$865	$550

LW15 - dreadnought style, solid spruce top, round soundhole, black pickguard, 5-stripe bound body/rosette, mahogany back/sides/neck, 14/20-fret bound rosewood fingerboard with pearl flower inlay, rosewood bridge with black white dot pins, bound rosewood veneered peghead with pearl logo inlay, 3-per-side chrome tuners, available in Natural finish, mfg. 1994-96.

			N/A	$350	$225

Last MSR was $700.

LW25 - dreadnought style, solid spruce top, round soundhole, black pickguard, 5-stripe bound body/rosette, rosewood back/sides, mahogany neck, 14/20-fret bound ebony fingerboard with pearl flower inlay, ebony bridge with black white dot pins, bound rosewood veneered peghead with pearl logo inlay, 3-per-side gold tuners, available in Natural finish, mfg. 1994-96.

			N/A	$400	$250

Last MSR was $800.

ACOUSTIC ELECTRIC: APX SERIES

APX T1 (TRAVEL SERIES) - single rounded cutaway body, spruce top, oval soundhole, bound body, 3-stripe rosette, agathis/alder back/sides, maple neck, 23 5/8" scale, 22-fret rosewood fingerboard with pearl dot inlay, string-through rosewood bridge, blackface peghead with screened flowers/logo, 3-per-side chrome tuners, piezo bridge pickup, volume/tone controls, available in BlueBurst or Violin Sunburst finishes, mfg. 1998-current.

	MSR	$469		$325	$225	$150

This model is available in a nylon string configuration (Model APX T1 N).

APX 4 A - single round cutaway dreadnought style, spruce top, oval soundhole, 5-stripe bound body and rosette, nato back/sides, nato neck, 25 1/2" scale, 22-fret rosewood fingerboard with pearl dot inlay, rosewood bridge with white bridgepins, blackface peghead with screened flowers/logo, 3-per-side chrome tuners, piezo bridge pickup, volume/treble/bass controls, available in Black, Natural, or Violin Sunburst finishes, disc.

			$495	$295	$195

Last MSR was $649.

APX 4 A Special - similar to APX 4 A, except has flamed sycamore top, volume/mute/3-band EQ controls, available in Marine BlueBurst and Tobacco Brown Sunburst finishes, disc 1998.

			$560	$380	$250

Last MSR was $749.

APX 4-12 A - similar to APX4, except has 12-strings, 6-per-side tuners, available in Natural or Violin Sunburst finishes, mfg. 1994-98.

			$500	$300	$225

Last MSR was $679.

APX 5A - single cutaway thinline body design, spruce top, nato back and sides, rosewood fingerboard with dot position markers, rosewood bridge, 3-per-side die-cast chrome plated tuners, System 46 preamp, piezo pickup mounted under the saddle, 3-band EQ, adjustable midrange, available in Natural, Black, Sand Burst, or Trans. Blue Burst finishes, mfg. 2001-current.

	MSR	$730		$525	$365	$195

Also available in a nylon string configuration with Natural finish (Model APX 5NA). New 2001.

Add $50 for 12-string variation (Model APX 5A12). Available in Black and Sandburst finishes. New 2001. Add $100 for left-hand model (Model APX 5LA). Available in Sandburst finish. New 2001.

APX 6 - single round cutaway dreadnought style, spruce top, oval soundhole, 5-stripe bound body, wooden inlay rosette cap, nato back/sides, nato neck, 24-fret extended rosewood fingerboard with pearl dot inlay, rosewood bridge with white pearl dot pins, 3-per-sides chrome tuners, bridge/body piezo pickups, pop up volume/treble/bass/mix controls, available in Black, Cherry Sunburst, or Cream White finishes, disc. 1994.

			N/A	$375	$225

Last MSR was $730.

APX 6 A - similar to APX 6, except has volume/tone controls, 3-band EQ, available in Natural, Brown Sunburst, Trans. Green Burst, or Trans. Blue Burst, disc. 1994.

			$625	$375	$275

Last MSR was $819.

Add $180 for left-handed configuration (Model APX 6 L A).

APX 6 N A - classical style, spruce top, oval soundhole, 5-stripe bound body, wooden inlay rosette, ovankol back/sides, nato neck, 14/22-fret rosewood fingerboard, rosewood bridge, 3-per-side gold tuners, bridge/body piezo pickups, volume/treble/bass/mix controls, available in Natural finish, disc.

$600 $375 $250

Last MSR was $799.

APX 7 - single round cutaway dreadnought style, spruce top, oval soundhole, 5-stripe bound body, wooden inlay rosette cap, agathis back/sides, mahogany neck, 24-fret extended bound rosewood fingerboard with pearl dot inlay, rosewood bridge with white pearl dot pins, bound peghead, 3-per-side gold tuners, 2 bridge/body piezo pickups, volume/treble/bass/mix controls, available in Black, Blue Burst, or Light Brown Sunburst finishes, disc. 1996.

N/A $425 $275

Last MSR was $850.

This model was optional with ovankol back/sides (Model APX 7 CT).

APX 7A - similar to APX 5A except, has solid spruce top, 3-per-side die-cast gold plated tuners and System 44 pre amp, available in Natural, Oriental Blue Burst, Amber or Trans. Green Burst finishes, mfg. 2001-current.

MSR $900 $629 $399 $265

APX 7 CN - single round cutaway classic style, spruce top, oval soundhole, 5-stripe bound body, rosette decal, ovankol back/sides, nato neck, 24-fret extended rosewood fingerboard, rosewood tied bridge, rosewood veneered peghead, 3-per-side gold tuners with paroled buttons, piezo bridge pickup, volume/tone controls, 3-band EQ, available in Natural finish, mfg. 1994-96.

N/A $450 $300

Last MSR was $900.

APX 8 A - similar to APX 7, except has bridge piezo pickup, mode switch, available in Gray Burst or Light Brown Sunburst finishes, disc.

$825 $525 $350

Last MSR wa $1,099.

Add $100 for 12-string configuration (Model APX 8-12 A). In 1999, Natural finish was added and Grey Burst finish discontinued.

APX 8 C - single round cutaway folk style, spruce top, oval soundhole, 5-stripe bound body, wooden abalone inlay rosette cap, agathis back/sides, mahogany neck, 24-fret bound extended fingerboard with pearl dot inlay, rosewood bridge with white black dot pins, bound blackface peghead with screened leaves/logo, 3-per-side gold tuners, piezo bridge pickups, volume/tone/mix controls, 3-band EQ, available in Blackburst, Brownburst, or Trans. Blueburst finishes, mfg. 1994-96.

N/A $625 $375

Last MSR was $1,100.

APX 8 C-12 - similar to APX 8 C, except has 12-strings, 6-per-side tuners, mfg. 1994-96.

N/A $650 $375

Last MSR was $1,190.

APX 8 D - similar to APX8C, except has solid spruce top, mfg. 1994-96.

N/A $650 $375

Last MSR was $1,200.

APX 9C - similar to APX 7A except, has sycamore back and sides, ebony fingerboard with dot position markers, System 45 2-way preamp, piezo pickup mounted under the saddle and also a condenser microphone mounted inside the body, 3-band EQ, adjustable Midrange Frenquency control, phase reverse switch, master volume, mike volume, available in Black Cherry, Yellow Natural Satin, or Dusk Sun Red finishes, mfg. 2001-current.

MSR $1,200 $839 $550 $350

Also available in a nylon string variation (Model APX 9NA).

APX 9-12 - single round cutaway dreadnought style, spruce top, oval soundhole, 5-stripe bound body, wooden inlay rosette cap, agathis back/sides, mahogany neck, 24-fret extended bound rosewood fingerboard with pearl dot inlay, rosewood bridge with white pearl dot pins, bound peghead, 6-per-side chrome tuners, 2 bridge/body piezo pickups, volume/treble/bass/mix controls, mode switch, available in Black, Blue Burst, or Light Brown Sunburst finishes, disc. 1994.

N/A $575 $350

Last MSR was $1,150.

Y

GRADING	100%	EXCELLENT	AVERAGE

APX 10 A - single round cutaway dreadnought style, spruce top, oval soundhole, 5-stripe bound body, abalone rosette cap, ovankol back/sides, mahogany neck, 24-fret extended bound ebony fingerboard with pearl diamond inlay, ebony bridge with white pearl dot pins, bound peghead, 3-per-side gold tuners, bridge/body piezo pickups, volume/treble/bass/mix controls, mode switch, available in Antique Stain Sunburst, Black Burst, or Burgundy Red finishes, mfg. 1993-2000.

	$1,125	$695	$475

Last MSR was $1,499.

Add $60 for left-handed configuration (Model APX 10 L A).

In 1994, Antique Brown Sunburst finish was introduced, Burgundy Red finish was discontinued. In 1999, Natural Satin and Black Cherry finishes were introduced & Black Burst & Antique Satin Sunburst finishes were discontinued.

APX 10 NA - single round cutaway classic style, spruce top, oval soundhole, 5-stripe bound body, wooden inlay rosette, rosewood back/sides, mahogany neck, 24-fret ebony fingerboard, rosewood bridge, rosewood veneer on peghead, 3-per-side gold tuners, bridge/body piezo pickups, volume/treble/bass/mix controls, mode switch, available in Natural finish, disc.

	$975	$600	$425

Last MSR was $1,299.

APX 10 CT - similar to APX 10 C, except has rosewood back/sides, Natural finish, mfg. 1994-96.

	N/A	$750	$500

Last MSR was $1,500.

APX 20 C - single round cutaway dreadnought style, spruce top, oval soundhole, abalone bound body, abalone rosette cap, sycamore back/sides, mahogany neck, 24-fret extended bound ebony fingerboard with abalone/pearl pentagon inlay, ebony bridge with white pearl dot pins, bound peghead, 3-per-side gold tuners, bridge/body piezo pickups, volume/treble/bass/mix controls, mode switch, available in Cream White or Light Brown Sunburst finishes, disc. 1996.

	N/A	$800	$530

Last MSR was $1,600.

In 1994, volume/tone/mix controls, 3-band EQ replaced original item.

ACOUSTIC ELECTRIC: CLASSIC SERIES

CGX101A - classical body, spruce top, nato back and sides, nato neck, rosewood fingerboard and bridge, chrome tuners, nylon strings, System 33 1-way preamp, 3-band EQ, Variable Midrange frequency control, volume, mute, available in Natural finish, current mfg.

MSR	$550	$385	$250	$165

CG110 CE - single rounded cutaway classical body, spruce top, round soundhole, bound body, wooden inlay rosette, nato back/sides/neck, 12/19-fret rosewood fingerboard, rosewood bridge, 3-per-side chrome tuners, piezo bridge pickup, volume/3-band EQ controls, available in Natural finish, disc.

	$475	$295	$195

Last MSR was $629.

CGX111SC - similar to CGX101 except, has single cutaway classical body, solid spruce top, System 42 preamp, EMF high-response B-Band pickup mounted under the saddle, volume, high and low tone controls, available in Natural finish, current mfg.

MSR	$700	$489	$315	$195

CG150 CCE - similar to the CG110 CE, except features a cedar top, ovankol back/sides, gold hardware, available in Natural finish, disc.

	$550	$325	$250

Last MSR was $729.

CGX171CC - similar to Model CGX111SC except, has solid American cedar top, rosewood back and sides, ebony fingerboard, System 43 preamp, B-Band pickup mounted under the saddle in addition to a condenser microphone mounted inside the body, high and low tone controls, volume and mike-mix switch, available in Natural finish, current mfg.

MSR	$1,000	$700	$450	$295

ACOUSTIC ELECTRIC: COMPASS SERIES

Compass Series (CPX) models have bodies which are larger than the APX Series models.

CPX 5 - single rounded cutaway design, spruce top, nato back and sides, rosewood fingerboard with dot position markers, rosewood bridge, die-cast chrome plated 3-per-side tuners, System 39 pickup system, 3-band EQ, AMF (Adjustable Midrange Frequency), Mid Shape Switch, available in Yellow Natural, Black, Trans. Blue Burst, or Violin Sunburst finishes, current mfg.

MSR	$700	$489	$315	$195

Add $70 for solid spruce top (CPX 5S).

CPX 7 - single rounded cutaway jumbo style, spruce top, round soundhole, bound body, inlaid rosette, mahogany back/sides, mahogany neck, 25 1/2" scale, 14/20-fret bound Indian rosewood fingerboard with offset pearl triangle inlay, Indian rosewood bridge with black pearl dot pins, 3-per-side chrome tuners, piezo bridge pickups, volume/mid-shape/3-band EQ controls, available in Natural finish, mfg. 1998-2000.

	$675	$460	$300

Last MSR was $899.

GRADING	100%	EXCELLENT	AVERAGE

CPX 8M - single cutaway body design, solid cedar top, mahogany back and sides, nato neck, rosewood fingerboard with dot position markers, rosewood bridge, die-cast gold plated 3-per-side tuners, System 45 2-way pre-amp, piezo pickup mounted in the bridge, condenser microphone inside the body, 3-band EQ, available in Natural finish, current mfg.

MSR	$1,200		$850	$600	$375

CPX 8SY - similar to Model CPX 8M except, available in Dusk Sun Red and Lagoon Green finishes, mfg. 2001-current.

MSR	$1,200		$850	$600	$375

CPX8-12 - similar to Model CPX 8M except, in 12-string configuration with solid spruce top, Natural finish, mfg. 2001-current.

MSR	$1,300		$900	$650	$425

CPX 10 - similar to the CPX 7, except features solid spruce top, rosewood back/sides, ebony fingerboard/bridge, gold hardware, available in Natural finish, mfg. 1998-2000.

		$1,050	$715	$470
		Last MSR was $1,399.		

CPX 15 - single cutaway, handcrafted nautical theme, solid spruce top, rosewood sides/back, mahogany neck w/ebony fingerboard, wood flags soundhole inlay, 25 1/2" scale, ebony bridge, L.R. Baggs pickup system, gold hardware, available in Natural finish, current mfg.

MSR	$1,900		$1,425	$975	$650

CPX 15 E - similar to CPX 15, except has handcrafted Egyptian theme, quilted mahogany back and sides, rosewood neck, wood Egyptian symbols soundhole inlay, available in Egyptian Sunburst finish, mfg. 1999-current.

MSR	$1,900		$1,425	$975	$650

CPX 15 N - similar to CPX 15 except has handcrafted Artic theme, solid spruce top, sycamore back and sides, available in Snowburst finish, current mfg.

MSR	$1,900		$1,425	$975	$650

CPX 15 S - similar to CPX 15, except has handcrafted Caribbean theme, White Sycamore back and sides, wood palm trees soundhole inlay, available in Miami Ocean Burst finish, current mfg.

MSR	$1,900		$1,425	$975	$650

CPX 15 W - similar to CPX 15, except has handcrafted western theme, walnut back and sides, wood buffalo horn soundhole inlay, available in Antique Violin Sunburst finish, current mfg.

MSR	$1,900		$1,425	$975	$650

CJX32 (HANDCRAFTED) - similar to Model CJ32 Acoustic guitar except, has piezo pickup mounted under the saddle and a condenser microphone mounted inside the body, 3-band EQ, volume, midrange controls, available in Natural finish, mfg. 2001-current.

MSR	$2,900		$2,025	$1,325	$850

CPX 50 - single cutaway, handcrafted acoustic/electric, deluxe nautical theme, solid Sitka spruce top, solid rosewood back, rosewood sides, mahogany neck with ebony fingerboard, wood deluxe flags soundhole inlay, ebony bridge, 25 1/2" scale, L.R. Baggs pickup system, gold hardware, available in Natural finish, current mfg.

MSR	$7,999		$5,995	$4,500	$2,500

Yuriy Archtop
courtesy Yuriy

ACOUSTIC ELECTRIC: FGX SERIES

FGX 412 - dreadnought style, spruce top, round soundhole, black pickguard, bound body, 5-stripe rosette, nato back/sides/neck, 14/20-fret rosewood fingerboard with pearl dot inlay, nato bridge with white bridgepins, 3-per-side chrome diecast tuners, piezo bridge pickup, volume/mute. 3-band EQ controls, available in Natural finish, mfg. 1998-2001.

		$395	$265	$175
		Last MSR was $529.		

FGX 412 C - similar to FGX 412, except has a single rounded cutaway body, available in Natural, Marine BlueBurst, or Violin Sunburst finishes, mfg. 1998-2001.

		$490	$330	$220
		Last MSR was $649.		

FGX 412 C-12 - similar to FGX 412, except has a single rounded cutaway body, 12-string configuration, 6-per-side tuners, available in Black, Natural, or Violin Sunburst finishes, mfg. 1998-2001.

		$525	$360	$235
		Last MSR was $699.		

FGX 412 S C - similar to FGX 412, except has a solid spruce top, available in Natural or Tobacco Sunburst finishes, mfg. 1998-2001.

		$520	$350	$230
		Last MSR was $699.		

GRADING		100%	EXCELLENT	AVERAGE

ACOUSTIC ELECTRIC: FINGERSTYLE SERIES

FPX 300 - folk size guitar, solid cedar top, ovankol back and sides, nato neck, rosewood fingerboard slightly wider than normal for finger picking, rosewood bridge, gold plated classical style tuners, System 45 2-way preamp, piezo pickup in the bridge, condenser microphone mounted inside the body, 3-band EQ, Adjustable Midrange Frequency, Phase Reverse, available in Natural finish, mfg. 2001-current.

MSR	$999	$699	$465	$295

FPX 300N - similar to Model FPX 300 except, in a nylon string variation, available in Natural finish, mfg. 2001-current.

MSR	$999	$699	$65	$295

LSX400 - similar to Model LS400 Acoustic guitar except, has 2-way pickup system, ribbon transducer pickup under the saddle and a condenser microphone mounted inside the body, 3-band EQ, volume, blend and midrange controls, soundhole cover included, available in Natural finish, current mfg.

MSR	$1,899	$1,325	$865	$565

LLX400 - similar to Model LL400 Acoustic guitar except, has 2-way pickup system, ribbon transducer pickup under the saddle and a condenser microphone mounted inside the body, 3-band EQ, volume, blend, and midrange controls, soundhole cover included, available in Natural finish, current mfg.

MSR	$1,899	$1,325	$865	$565

LLX500C (HANDCRAFTED) - similar to Model LL500 Acoustic guitar except, has 2-way pickup system, ribbon transducer pickup under the saddle and a condenser microphone mounted inside the body, 3-band EQ, volume, blend and midrange controls, available in Natural finish, mfg. 2001-current.

MSR	$2,399	$1,675	$1,095	$725

ACOUSTIC ELECTRIC: SILENT GUITAR SERIES

The Silent Guitar by Yamaha is a guitar designed to travel and be a silent instrument that you can plug headphones in directly to hear. There are onboard effects yet the guitar can be plugged in to external equipment to be amplified. The body is also very light with only the outline of the body making up the majority of the guitar.

SLG100N - single cutaway maple body, mahogany neck, rosewood fingerboard with dot inlays, 2-per-side tuners, nylon string, B-Band electronics, available in Natural finish, mfg. 2002-current.

MSR	$850	$595	$425	$275

SLG100S - similar to the SLG100N, except in steel string configuration, L.R. Baggs electronics, and a finger rest, new 2003.

MSR	$900	$630	$450	$295

YAMAKI
See Daion. Instruments previously produced in Japan during the late 1970s through the 1980s.

YAMATO
Instruments previously produced in Japan during the late 1970s to the early 1980s.

Yamato guitars are medium quality instruments that feature both original and designs based on classic American favorites (Source: Tony Bacon and Paul Day, *The Guru's Guitar Guide*).

YURIY
Instruments previously built in Wheeling, Illinois since 1990.

Luthier Yuriy Shishkov was born in 1964 in St. Petersburg. As with many other guitar makers, Shishkov began his career from discovering a big personal attraction to music. After spending 10 years playing guitars that he found unsatisfactory, Yuriy attempted to build his own instrument in 1986. The results amazed everyone who played the instrument, including Yuriy himself! From this initial bit of success, Yuriy gained a reputation as a luthier as well as several orders for guitars.

In 1990, Yuriy moved to Chicago, Illinois. A year later, he secured a job at Washburn International, a major guitar company based in Chicago. His experience with personal guitar building lead him to a position of handling the difficult repairs, restorations, intricate inlay work, company prototypes, and the custom-built instruments for the artist endorsees.

Luthier Yuriy Shishkov is currently offering custom designed and construction of instruments from solid body guitars to his current passion of archtop acoustics and hollowbody electrics. Yuriy is no longer producing guitars. He is currently the Senior Master builder at the Fender Custom Shop. You can still reach luthier Yuriy (see Trademark Index).

ACOUSTIC

Yuriy had a number of Jazz-style archtop guitars. Models include the 16" **Minuet** (list $3,700) or Soprano ($3,900), 17" **Capitol** ($4,300), **Sunset** ($4,600), and **Concerto** ($4,900), and 18" **Imperial** ($5,400) and **Triumph** ($5,900). Archtop models include features like hand carved spruce tops, figured maple back and sides, rock maple necks, and rosewood fingerboard. Models are finished in Nitrocellulose Lacquer finishes. All prices are the last retail listed.

Section Z

**Zeidler Jazz Deluxe
courtesy Scott Shinery**

ZEIDLER
Instruments previously built in Philadelphia, Pennsylvania.

Luthier John R. Zeidler built quality custom instruments for twenty years between 1982-2002. Zeidler's background encompasses woodworking, metalsmithing, tool making and music. Zeidler built high quality archtop and flattop guitars, as well as mandolins. John passed away in May, 2002.

GRADING	100%	EXCELLENT	AVERAGE

ACOUSTIC

AUDITORIUM - tight waist/rounded lower bout design, hand split select Sitka spruce top, East Indian rosewood back and sides, 5-piece laminated mahogany/maple/rosewood neck, round soundhole, 20-fret ebony fingerboard, ebony head veneer/bridge, mother-of-pearl truss rod cover, tortoise shell pickguard, black/white body binding, 3-per-side gold-plated Schaller tuners, available in high gloss nitrocellulose finish, disc 2002.

	$4,700	$4,000	$2,500
		Last MSR was $4,700.	

Add $500 for cutaway body design.

EXCALIBUR - sloped shoulder design, hand split select Sitka spruce top, East Indian rosewood back and sides, 5-piece laminated mahogany/maple/rosewood neck, round soundhole, 20-fret ebony fingerboard, ebony head veneer/bridge, mother-of-pearl truss rod cover, tortoise shell pickguard, black/white body binding, 3-per-side gold-plated Schaller tuners, available in high gloss nitrocellulose finish, disc 2002.

	$4,700	$4,000	$2,500
		Last MSR was $4,700.	

Add $500 for cutaway body design.

ACOUSTIC ARCHTOP

ARCH TOP - select Sitka spruce top, curly maple back and sides, 5-piece laminated mahogany/maple/rosewood neck, 2 f-holes, 22-fret bound ebony fingerboard, ebony head veneer/bridge, ebony/gold-plated brass hinged tailpiece, mother-of-pearl truss rod cover, black/white body binding, 3-per-side gold-plated Schaller tuners, available in high gloss nitrocellulose finish, current mfg.

	$8,200	$7,500	$5,000
		Last MSR was $8,200.	

JAZZ (16" OR 17" BODY) - hand graduated Sitka spruce top, curly maple back and sides, 2-piece laminated curly maple neck, 2 f-holes, 22-fret bound ebony fingerboard with pearl diamond inlay, ebony head veneer/bridge, ebony/gold-plated brass hinged tailpiece, mother-of-pearl truss rod cover, black/white body binding, 3-per-side gold-plated Schaller tuners, available in high gloss nitrocellulose finish, current mfg.

	$9,000	$8,000	$6,000
		Last MSR was $9,000.	

Add $1,000 for 18" body width (Model Jazz 18").

JAZZ DELUXE (16" OR 17" BODY) - hand split select Adirondack spruce top, highly figured curly maple back and sides, 2-piece laminated curly maple neck, 2 f-holes, 22-fret bound ebony fingerboard, ebony head veneer/bridge, ebony/gold-plated brass hinged tailpiece, mother-of-pearl truss rod cover, celluloid body binding, 3-per-side gold-plated Schaller tuners, available in high gloss spirit varnish finish, current mfg.

	$11,000	$9,500	$7,000
		Last MSR was $11,000.	

Add $1,000 for 18" body width (Model Jazz Deluxe 18").

ZEMAITIS
Instruments previously hand built in England 1957-2001.

Tony Zemaitis was born Antanus (Anthony) Casimere (Charles) Zemaitis in 1935. While his grandparents were Lithuanian, both Tony and his parents were born in the UK. At age 16 he left college to be an apprentice at cabinet making. As part of a hobby, he refashioned an old damaged guitar found in the family attic. In 1955, the first turning point to luthiery: Zemaitis built his first half decent guitar, a classical, nylon string with peghead. In the mid to late 1950s, Zemaitis served for two years in Britian's National Service.

Upon his return to civilian life, Zemaitis continued his guitar building hobby, only now a number of the guitars began turning up onto the folk scene. By 1960 he was selling guitars for the price of the materials, and a number of the originals that Zemaitis calls **Oldies** still exist. Early users include Spencer Davis, Long John Baldry, and Jimi Hendrix.

**Zemaitis Acoustic
courtesy Zemaitis**

In 1965, Zemaitis' hobby had acquired enough interest that he was able to become self employed. By the late 1960s, the orders were coming in from a number of top players such as Ron Wood, Eric Clapton, and George Harrison. The house and shop all moved lock, stock, and barrel to Kent in 1972. A **Student** model was introduced in 1980, but proved to be too popular and time consuming to produce the number of orders, so it was discontinued. In 1995, Zemaitis celebrated the 40th Anniversary of the first classical guitar he built in 1955. Guitar production was limited to 10 guitars a year. In 2001, Tony Zemaitis finally decided to retire and enjoy himself.

Sadly, in 2002, Tony passed away. His family and friends commented that despite his retirement, he couldn't stay out of the workshop!

Several years ago, George Harrison lent 3 of his Zemaitis acoustic models to an exhibition in the U.K. organized by Viscount Linley (Princess Margaret's son). Source: Tony Zemaitis, March 1996, Keith Smart 2001, Information courtesy Keith Smart and Keith Rogers, The Z Gazette: magazine of the Zemaitis Guitar Owners Club based in England.

AUTHENTICITY

In the late 1980s, Zemaitis was surprised to see that his guitars were even more valuable in the secondhand market than originally priced. As his relative output was limited, an alarming trend of forgeries has emerged in England, Japan, and the U.S. Serial number identification and dating on guitars will continue to be unreported in this edition, due to the number of forgeries that keep turning up (and we're not going to add tips to the "help-yourself merchants" as Tony liked to call them). To clarify matters simply: **Tony Zemaitis granted NO ONE permission to build reproductions and NO licensing deals were made to any company**.

POINTS TO CONSIDER WHEN BUYING A ZEMAITIS

Prior to spending a large amount of money on what may very well turn out to be a copy of a Zemaitis, it is always best to ask for advice.

There are German, Japanese, and English copies. At first glance they may look a little like a Zemaitis, but they will not sound like one due to the use of second-rate materials. Because of the mass produced nature of these fakes, the intonation and general finish will be inferior to the genuine article. Even more alarming, what starts out as a cheap copy changes hands once or twice and eventually ends up being advertised as the real thing without proper research.

The more difficult fakes to spot are the genuine Zemaitis guitars that started life as a cheaper version (Student or Test model), and has been unofficially upgraded. In other words, a plain front guitar suddenly becomes a Pearl Front guitar. While parts and pieces will be genuine, the newer finish and general appearance are nothing like the real thing.

Always ask for a receipt, even if you are not buying from a shop. Always check the spelling of "Zemaitis." Look at the engraving, and make sure that it is engraved by hand (not photo etching – it is too clean and has not been worked on by hand, (Reprinted courtesy Keith Smart, The Z Gazette).

The *Blue Book of Acoustic Guitars* strongly recommends two or three written estimates of any Zemaitis instrument from accredited sources. If possible, ask to see the original paperwork. Here are two more serious tips: Usually the person who commissioned the guitar has their initials on the truss rod cover. Additionally, some of Zemaitis' acoustic models do not have truss rods. Also, review the printed label and logo (there's only one correct spelling for Mr. Zemaitis' name - and contrary to word of mouth, he does not intentionally misspell it on his guitars. Prices on models in excellent condition easily start at $10,000 and can go to and above $25,000.

MODEL DESCRIPTIONS

Here is a brief overview of model histories and designations. During the late 1950s, a few basic acoustic models were built to learn about sizes, shapes, wood response, and soundholes. From 1960 to 1964, guitar building was still a hobby, so there was no particular standard; also, the paper labels inside are hand labeled. In 1965, Zemaitis turned pro and introduced the **Standard**, **Superior**, and **Custom** models of acoustic guitars. These terms are relative, not definitive as there is some overlapping from piece to piece. While some soundholes are round, there are a number of acoustic guitars built with the heart-shaped sound hole.

ZIMNICKI
Instruments currently built in Allen Park, Michigan.

Luthier Gary Zimnicki has been developing his guitar building skills since 1978, and is currently focusing on building quality archtop and flattop guitars. For further information, please call Gary Zimnicki directly (see Trademark Index).

ACOUSTIC/ACOUSTIC ELECTRIC

Zimnicki uses aged tonewoods for his carved graduated tops, and wood bindings. Due to the nature of these commissioned pieces, the customer determines the body size, neck scale, types of wood/fingerboard inlays/pickups, and finish. All prices include a hardshell case.

Add $150 for European maple back on the archtop models. Add $200 for Sunburst finish. Add $250 for seven string configuration

ACOUSTIC ARCHTOP - single cutaway bound body, carved arched top, 2 f-holes, ebony tailpiece/full contact bridge/fingerboard, 3-per-side Schaller gold tuners, available in Natural or Trans. high gloss nitrocellulose lacquer finishes, current mfg.

    MSR   **$7,500**

CLASSICAL - classical style, round soundhole with rosette, 14/20-fret unbound fingerboard, 3-per-side headstock, classical style tied bridge, current mfg.

    MSR   **$3,350**

FLATTOP STEEL STRING - exaggerated waist dreadnought style, single rounded cutaway, round soundhole with rosette, 12/20 or 14/20-fret unbound fingerboard, 3-per-side headstock, conventional style bridge, current mfg.

    MSR   **$2,900**

    This model is available in a non-cutaway configuration.

ELECTRIC ARCHTOP - similar in construction to the Acoustic Archtop, except has gold-plated harp tailpiece, footed ebony bridge, pickup and volume/tone controls mounted on soundboard, current mfg.

    MSR   **$6,500**

SERIALIZATION

AMERICAN ARCHTOP SERIALIZATION

According to luthier Dale Unger, the digits after the dash in the serial number are the year the guitar was completed.

BENEDETTO SERIAL NUMBERS

To date, Robert Benedetto has completed over 750 musical instruments. 466 are archtop guitars, with the remainder comprising of 51 violins, 5 violas, 1 classical guitar, 2 mandolins, 11 semi-hollow electrics, 209 electric solid body electric guitars and basses, and one cello.

The 11 semi-hollow electrics include six unique carved top, semi-hollow electrics made between 1982 and 1986. The other five include three prototypes for, and two finished examples of, his new "benny" semi-hollow electric line introduced in 1998.

The 209 electric solid bodies include 157 electric guitars and 52 electric basses. Benedetto began making them in 1986 with John Buscarino. He stopped making them in the Spring of 1987.

The 11 semi-hollow electrics and the 1 classical guitar are included in the archtop guitar serial numbering system. The two mandolins have no serial numbers. The violins, violas and cello have their own serial number system (starting with #101) as do the electric solid body guitars and basses (starting with #1001).

Serial Numbers:

All Benedetto archtop guitars (except his first two) are numbered in one series, Electric solidbodies and basses each have their own separate series, as do the violins, violas and cello.

Archtop guitars have a 4- or 5- digit serial number with configuration ##(#)yy.

2 (or 3) digits ##(#)=ranking, beginning with #1 in 1968.

Last 2 digits yy=year.

Example:

43599 was made in 1999 and is the 435th archtop made since 1968.

From Robert Benedetto's Archtop Guitar Serial Number Logbook
(Note: year listed on the right indicates date shipped, not made).

Serial	Year
0168 (#1)*	1968
0270 (#2)*	1970
0372	1972
0473	1973
0575 through 0676	1976
0777 through 1177	1977
1277 through 2778	1978
2879 through 4279	1979
4380 through 5580	1980
5681 through 7381	1981
7482 through 9582	1982
9682 through 10983	1983
11084 through 11984	1984
12085 through 12885	1985
12986 through 13586	1986
13686 through 13987-A	1987
14087 through 16488	1988
16588 through 19189	1989
19289 through 22490-A	1990
22591 through 25091	1991
25192 through 28092	1992
28193 through 30293	1993
30393 through 32994	1994
33095 through 36595	1995
36696 through 39496	1996
39597 through 40697	1997
40798 through 4349	1998
43599 through 45199	1999
45200 through 46200	2000
46301 through 46601	2001

Note: Benedetto models made at the Guild Custom Shop in Nashville have a separate serial number system beginning with the letter N.

*Actual number in log: Benedetto did not adopt his current serial number system until his third guitar, serial #0372.

Seven guitar serial numbers are follwed by the letter "A". Example: archtop guitar #23891 and #23891-A are two separate instruments even though both are numbered the "238th".

Further information and a full serial number list can be found in Robert Benedetto's book, Making an Archtop Guitar (Centerstream Publishing/Hal Leonard, 1994).

BREEDLOVE SERIALIZATION

Breedlove serial numbers can be found on the guitar's label inside the guitar (look through the soundhole). The first two digits of the serial number are the year (last two digits of the year; i.e., "19XX") the guitar was built.

BUSCARINO SERIAL NUMBERS

Luthier John Buscarino had the priviledge of apprenticing with not one but two Master Builders, Augustino LoPrinzi and Robert Benedetto. Buscarino formed his first company, **Nova U.S.A.** in 1981; he changed the company to **Buscarino Guitars** in 1990.

The last two digits of the Buscarino serial number are the year the guitar was completed.

COLLINGS SERIALIZATION

Collings guitar serial numbers are expressed as the date, which is written on the label on the inside of the guitar. However, here is a more expanded view on Collings serialization:

Flattop Serialization

1975-1987: Guitars do not posses a serial number. Most are marked with a handwritten date on the underside of the top. Some guitars from 1987 may have a serial number.

1988 to date: Guitars began a consecutive numbering series that began with number 175. The serial number is stamped on the neck block.

Archtop Serialization

Before 1991: Archtops before 1991 had their own separate serialization.

1991 to date: Archtops are now numbered with a two part serial number. The first number indicates the archtop as part of the general company serialization; and the second number indicates the ranking in the archtop series list.

(Serialization information courtesy Collings Guitars, Inc.)

D'ANGELICO SERIAL NUMBERS

Master Luthier John D'Angelico (1905-1964) opened his own shop at age 27, and every guitar was hand built - many to the specifications or nuances of the customer commissioning the instrument. In the course of his brief lifetime, he created 1,164 numbered guitars, as well as unnumbered mandolins, novelty instruments, and the necks for the plywood semi-hollowbody electrics. The nature of this list is to help identify the numbered guitars as to the date produced.

D'Angelico kept a pair of ledger books and some loose sheets of paper as a log of the guitars created, models, date of completion (or possibly the date of shipping), the person or business to whom the guitar was sold, and the date. The following list is a rough approximation of the ledgers and records.

First *Loose Sheets*

1002 through 1073	1932 to 1934

Ledger Book One

1169 through 1456	1936 to 1939
1457 through 1831	1940 to 1949
1832 through 1849	1950

Ledger Book Two

1850 through 2098	1950 to 1959
2099 through 2122	1960
2123	1961

Second *Loose Sheets*

2124 through 2164	Dates not recorded

Again, we must stress that the above system is a guide only. In 1991, author Paul William Schmidt published a book entitled *Acquired of the Angels: The lives and works of Master Guitar Makers John D'Angelico and James L. D'Aquisto* (The Scarecrow Press, Inc.; Metuchen, N.J. & London). In appendix 1 the entire ledger information is reprinted save information on persons or businesses to whom the guitar was sold. This book is fully recommended to anyone seeking information on luthiers John D'Angelico and James L. D'Aquisto.

D'AQUISTO SERIAL NUMBERS

Master Luthier James L. D'Aquisto (1935-1995) met John D'Angelico around 1953. At the early age of 17 D'Aquisto became D'Angelico's apprentice, and by 1959 was handling the decorative procedures and other lutherie jobs.

D'Aquisto, like his mentor before him, kept ledger books as a log of the guitars created, models, date of completion (or possibly the date of shipping), the person or business to whom the guitar was sold, and the date. The following list is a rough approximation of the ledger. As the original pages contain some idiosyncrasies, the following list will by nature be inaccurate as well - and should only be used as a guide for dating individual instruments. The nature of this list is only to help identify the numbered guitars as to the date produced.

The D'Aquisto Ledger

1001 through 1035	1965 to 1969
1036 through 1084	1970 to 1974
1085 through 1133	1975 to 1979
1134 through 1175	1980 to 1984
1176 through 1228	1985 to 1990

Beginning in 1988, serial number was 1230. 1257 was D'Aquisto's last serial number on non-futuristic models.

Other guitars that D'Aquisto built had their own serial numbers. For example, solid body and semi-hollow body guitars from 1976 to 1987 had an *E* before the three digit number. D'Aquisto also built some classical models, some flat-top acoustics, and some hollow body electric models (hollowbody guitars run from #1 to #30, 1976 to 1980; and #101 to #118, 1982 to 1988).

In 1991, author Paul William Schmidt published a book entitled *Acquired of the Angels: The Lives and Works of Master Guitar Makers John D'Angelico and James L. D'Aquisto* (The Scarecrow Press, Inc.; Metuchen, N.J. & London). In appendix 2 the entire ledger information is reprinted up to the year 1988 except for information on persons or businesses to whom the guitar was sold. This book is fully recommended to anyone seeking information on luthiers John D'Angelico and James L. D'Aquisto.

DOBRO SERIAL NUMBERS

The convoluted history of the Dopyera brothers (Dobro, National Dobro, Valco, Original Music Instrument Company) has been dis-cussed in a number of wonderful guitar texts. Serialization of Dobro instruments is far less tangled, but there are different forms of the numbers to contend with. Dobro serial numbers should always be used in conjunction with other identifying features for dating purposes.

Dobro was founded in Los Angeles in 1929, and production continued until the outbreak of World War II in 1942 (resonator guitar production ends). The numbers listed by year are the serialization ranges, not production amounts.

# 900 - 2999	1928-1930
# 3000 - 3999	1930-1931

Between 1931 to 1932, the *cyclops* models carried a serial number code of B XXX.

# 5000 - 5599	1932-1933
# 5700 - 7699	1934-1936
# 8000 - 9999	1937-1942

In the mid 1950s, Rudy and Ed Dopyera return to building wood bodied Dobros from pre-war parts under the trademark of **DB Original**. The serialization of these models is still unknown.

In 1961, Louis Dopyera of Valco transfers the **Dobro** trademark to Rudy and Ed. These models are distinguished by a serialization code of D plus three digits.

After Semie Moseley gained the rights to the Dobro trademark, the Original Music Instrument Company was founded in 1967 by Ed, Rudy, and Gabriela Lazar. OMI regained the Dobro name in 1970, and instituted a new coding on the instruments. The code had a prefix of D (Wood body) or B (Metal body), followed by three or four digits (production ranking) and a single digit to indicate the year, thus:

D XXXX Y	OMI Dobro coding 1970 - 1979

The code reversed itself in 1980. The single digit prefix indicated the year/decade, then three or four digits (production ranking), another single digit to indicate the year, then the body material designation (D or B), like:

8 XXXX YD	OMI Dobro coding 1980 - 1987

In 1988, the code became a little more specialized, and shared more information. The prefix consisted of a letter and number that indicated the model style, three or four digits for production ranking, another letter for neck style, 2 digits for year of production, and the body material designation (D or B):

AX XXXX NYYD	OMI Dobro coding 1988 - 1992

In 1993, Gibson bought OMI/Dobro. Production was maintained at the California location from 1993 to 1996, and the serialization stayed similar to the 1988 - 1992 style coding. In 1997, Gibson moved Dobro to Nashville.

EPIPHONE SERIAL NUMBERS

In 1917, Epaminondas *Epi* Stathopoulos began using the **House of Stathopoulo** brand on the family's luthiery business. By 1923 the business was incorporated, and a year later the new trademark was unveiled on a line of banjos. Stathopoulos combined his nickname *Epi* with the Greek word for sound, *phone*. When the company was recapitalized in 1928, it became the **Epiphone Banjo Company**.

Guitars were introduced in 1930, and were built in New York City, New York through 1953. Company manufacturing was moved to Philadelphia due to union harrassment in New York, and Epiphone continued on through 1957. Serial numbers on original Epiphones can be found on the label.

Epiphone **Electar** electric instruments were numbered consecutively, using a die stamped number on the back of the headstock. The numbering system began at 000 in 1935, terminating at about 9000 in 1944. Between about 1944 and 1950, the two number prefixes 15, 25, 26, 60, 75, or 85 were assigned to specific models. These were followed by three digits which were the actual "serial" number. In 1951, electric instruments were brought under the same numbering system as acoustics, and serial numbers were relocated to a paper label in the instrument's interior. Some transitional instruments bear both impressed numbers and a paper label with differing numbers. The latter are the more accurate for use in dating.

Number	Year
1000 - 3000 [electrics only]	1937-1938
4000 - 5000 [electrics only]	1939-1941
5000 [acoustics]	1932
6000	1933
7000	1934
8000 - 9000	1935
10000	1930-1932, 1936
11000	1937
12000	1938
13000	1939-1940
14000 - 15000	1941-1942
16000 - 18000	1943
19000	1944

In 1944, a change was made in the numbering sequence.

51000 - 52000	1944
52000 - 54000	1945
54000 - 55000	1946
56000	1947
57000	1948
58000	1949
59000	1950
60000 - 63000	1951
64000	1952
64000 - 66000	1953
68000	1954
69000	1955-1957

ELECTRIC INSTRUMENTS (Numbers are approximate):

1935	000 to 249
1936	250 to 749
1937	750 to 1499
1938	1500 to 2499
1939	2500 to 3499
1940	3500 to 4999
1941	5000 to 6499
1942	6500 to 7499
1943	7500 to 8299
1944	8300 to 9000

In May of 1957, Epiphone was purchased by CMI and became a division of Gibson. Parts and materials were shipped to the new home in Kalamazoo, Michigan. Ex-Epiphone workers in New Berlin, New York "celebrated" by hosting a bonfire behind the plant with available lumber (finished and unfinished!).

Gibson built Epiphone guitars in Kalamazoo from 1958 to 1969. Hollow body guitars had the serial number on the label inside, and prefixed with a "A-" plus four digits for the first three years. Electric solid body guitars had the serial number inked on the back of the headstock, and the first number indicates the year: "8" (1958), "9" (1959), and "0" (1960).

In 1960, the numbering scheme changed as all models had the serial number pressed into the back on the headstock. There were numerous examples of duplication of serial numbers, so when dating a Epiphone from this time period consideration of parts/configuration and other details is equally important.

Number	Year
100 - 41199	1961
41200 - 61180	1962

61450 - 64222	1963
64240 - 70501	1964
71180 - 95846	1962* *(Numerical sequence may not coincide to year sequence)
95849 - 99999	1963*
000001 - 099999	1967*
100000 - 106099	1963 or 1967*
106100 - 108999	1963
109000 - 109999	1963 or 1967*
110000 - 111549	1963
111550 - 115799	1963 or 1967*
115800 - 118299	1963
118300 - 120999	1963 or 1967*
121000 - 139999	1963
140000 - 140100	1963 or 1967*
140101 - 144304	1963
144305 - 144380	1963 or 1964
144381 - 145000	1963
147001 - 149891	1963 or 1964
149892 - 152989	1963
152990 - 174222	1964
174223 - 179098	1964 or 1965
179099 - 199999	1964
200000 - 250199	1964
250540 - 290998	1965
300000 - 305999	1965
306000 - 306099	1965 or 1967*
307000 - 307984	1965
309653 - 310999	1965 or 1967*
311000 - 320149	1965
320150 - 320699	1967*
320700 - 325999	1967*
325000 - 326999	1965 or 1966
327000 - 329999	1965
330000 - 330999	1965 or 1967 or 1968*
331000 - 346119	1965
346120 - 347099	1965 or 1966
348000 - 349100	1966
349101 - 368639	1965
368640 - 369890	1966
370000 - 370999	1967
380000 - 380999	1966 to 1968*
381000 - 385309	1966
390000 - 390998	1967
400001 - 400999	1965 to 1968*
401000 - 408699	1966
408800 - 409250	1966 or 1967
420000 - 438922	1966
500000 - 500999	1965 to 1966, or 1968 to 1969*
501009 - 501600	1965
501601 - 501702	1968
501703 - 502706	1965 or 1968*
503010 - 503109	1968
503405 - 520955	1965 or 1968*
520956 - 530056	1968
530061 - 530850	1966 or 1968 or 1969*
530851 - 530993	1968 or 1969
530994 - 539999	1969
540000 - 540795	1966 or 1969*
540796 - 545009	1969
555000 - 556909	1966*

558012 - 567400	1969
570099 - 570755	1966*
580000 - 580999	1969
600000 - 600999	1966 to 1969*
601000 - 606090	1969
700000 - 700799	1966 or 1967*
750000 - 750999	1968 or 1969
800000 - 800999	1966 to 1969*
801000 - 812838	1966 or 1969*
812900 - 819999	1969
820000 - 820087	1966 or 1969*
820088 - 823830	1966*
824000 - 824999	1969
828002 - 847488	1966 or 1969*
847499 - 858999	1966 or 1969*
859001 - 895038	1967*
895039 - 896999	1968*
897000 - 898999	1967 or 1969*
899000 - 972864	1968*

In 1970, production of Epiphone instruments moved to Japan. Japanese Epiphones were manufactured between 1970 to 1983. According to author/researcher Walter Carter, the serial numbers on these are unreliable as a usable tool for dating models. Comparison to catalogs is one of the few means available. Earlier Kalamazoo labels were generally orange with black printing and said "Made in Kalamazoo", while the Japanese instruments featured blue labels which read "Epiphone of Kalamazoo, Michigan" (note that it doesn't say made in Kalamazoo, nor does it say Made in Japan). While not a solid rule of thumb, research of the model should be more thorough than just glancing at the label.

During the early 1980s, the Japanese production costs became pricey due to the changing ratio of the dollar/yen. Production moved to Korea, and again the serial numbers are not an exact science as a dating mechanism. In 1993, a structure was developed where the number (or pair of numbers) following the initial letter indicates the year of production (i.e. "3" indicates 1993, or a "93" would indicate the same).

Some top of the line Epiphones were produced in the U.S. at either Gibson's Nashville or Montana facilities in the 1990s. These instruments are the only ones that correspond to the standard post-1977 Gibson serialization. Like Gibson numbers, there are 8 digits in the complete number, and follows the code of YDDDYNNN. The YY (first and fifth) indicate the year built. DDD indicates the day of the year (so DDD can't be above 365), and the NNN indicates the instrument's production ranking for that day (NNN = 021 = 21st guitar built). The Nashville facility begins each day at number 501, and the Montana workshop begins at number 101. **However**, in 1994, the Nashville-produced Epiphones were configured as YYNNNNNN: YY = 94 (the year) and NNNNNN is the ranking for the entire year.

Information for this chart of Epiphone serial numbers can be found in Walter Carter's book Epiphone: The Complete History (Hal Leonard, 1995). Not only a fascinating story and chronology of the original Epiphone company and its continuation, but also an overview of product catalogs as well as serial numbers. Walter Carter serves as the Gibson Historian as well as being a noted songwriter and author. He also wrote The Martin Book, and co-authored several with expert George Gruhn including Gruhn's Guide to Vintage Guitars, Acoustic Guitars and Other Fretted Instruments, and Electric Guitars and Basses: A Photographic History (All are available through GPI/Miller-Freeman books).

FENDER SERIALIZATION

Serial numbers, in general, are found on the bridgeplate, the neckplate, the backplate or the peghead. From 1950-1954, serial numbers are found on the bridgeplate or vibrato backplate. From 1954-1976, the serial numbers are found on the neckplate, both top or bottom of

the plate. From 1976 to date, the serial number appears with the peghead decal. Vintage Reissues have their serial numbers on the neckplate and have been in use since 1982.

The Fender company also stamped (or handwrote) the production date on the heel of the neck, in the body routs, on the pickups, and near the wiring harness (the body, pickup, and wiring dating was only done sporadically, during certain time periods). However, the neck date (and body date) indicate when the neck (or body) part was completed! Fender produces necks and guitar bodies separately, and bolts the two together during final production. Therefore, the date on the neck will generally be weeks or months before the actual production date.

When trying to determine the manufacturing date of an instrument by serialization, it is best to keep in mind that there are no clear cut boundaries between where the numbers began and where they ended. There were constant overlapping of serial numbers between years and models. The following are approximate numbers and dates.

1950	0001-0750
1951	0200-1900
1952	0400-4900
1953	2020-5030
1954	2780-7340
1955	6600-12800
1956	7800-16000
1957	14900-025200
1958	022700-38200
1959	31400-60600
1960	44200-58600
1961	55500-81700
1962	71600-99800
1963	81600-99200

In 1962, as the serialization count neared 100000, for one reason or another, the transition did not occur. Instead, an L preceded a 5 digit sequence. It ran this way from 1962 to 1965.

1962	L00400-L13200
1963	L00200-L40300
1964	L20600-L76200
1965	L34980-L69900

In 1965, when CBS bought Fender Musical Instruments, Inc., the serialization has come to be known as the F Series, due to an "F" being stamped onto the neckplate. This series of numbers went from 1965 to 1973. The approximate numbers and years are as follows:

1965	100001-147400
1966	112170-600200
1967	162165-602550
1968	211480-627740
1969	238945-290835
1970	278910-305415
1971	272500-380020
1972	301395-412360
1973	359415-418360

In early 1973, Fender stopped the practice of writing/stamping the production date on the heel of the neck (through 1982). The following are rough approximations for the years 1973 to 1976:

Early 1973 to Late 1976:	400000 series
Late 1973 to Late 1976:	500000 series
Mid 1974 to Mid 1976:	600000 series
Mid 1976 to Late 1976:	700000 series

In late 1976, Fender decided to move to a new numbering scheme for their serialization. The numbers appeared on the pegheads and for the remainder of 1976 they had a prefix of 76 or S6 preceding a 5 digit sequence. In 1977, the serialization went to a letter for the decade, followed by a single digit for the year and then 5 to 6 digits. Examples of the letter/digit code follow like this: S for the '70s, E for the '80s, N for the '90s, etc.

1970s	S	(example) S8 - 1978
1980s	E	(example) E1 - 1981
1990s	N	(example) N2 - 1992

While the idea was fine, the actuality was a different matter. Instrument production did not meet the levels for which decals had been produced, so there are several overlapping years. **Sometimes several prefixes found within a single year's production**. Here is the revised table of letter/digit year codes:

1976	S6 (also 76)
1977	S7 and S8
1978	S7, S8, and S9
1979	S9 and E0
1980-1981	S9, E0, and E1
1982	E1, E2, and E3
1984-1985	E3 and E4
1985-1986	*No U.S. Production
1987	E4
1988	E4 and E8
1989	E8 and E9
1990	E9, N9 (by accident), and N0
1991	N0 (plus 6 digits)
1992	N2
1993	N3
1994	N4
1995	N5
1996	N6
1997	N7
1998	N8
1999	N9
2000	Z0
2001	Z1
2002	Z2
2003	Z3

Serialization on Fender Japan Models

Fender Japan was established in March, 1982, in a negotiation between CBS/Fender, Kanda Shokai, and Yamano Music. Instruments were built by Fuji Gen Gakki, initially for the European market. When the Vintage/Reissues models were offered in the early 1980s, a *V* in the serial number indicated U.S. production, while a *JV* stood for Fender Japan-built models. For the first two years of Japanese production, serial numbers consisted of a 2 letter prefix to indicate the year, followed by five digits. In late 1984, this code was changed to a single letter prefix and six digits. Note the overlapping year/multi-prefix letter codes:

1982-1984	JV
1983-1984	SQ
1984-1987	E (plus 6 digits)
1985-1986	A, B, and C
1986-1987	F
1987-1988+	G
1988-1989	H
1989-1990	I and J
1990-1991	K
1991-1992	L
1992-1993	M
1993-1994	N
1994-1995	O
1995-1996	P

Dating a Fender instrument by serialization alone can get you within

an approximate range of years, but should not be used as a definitive means to determine the year of actual production.

(Fender Serialization overview courtesy A.R. Duchossoir; Later year production codes courtesy Michael Wright, Vintage Guitar Magazine)

FRAMUS SERIAL NUMBERS

Framus serial numbers were generally placed on the back of the peghead or on a label inside the body. The main body of the serial number is followed by an additional pair of digits and a letter. This additional pair of numbers indicate the production year.

For example:

51334 63L =	1963
65939 70L =	1970

(Serial number information courtesy Tony Bacon and Barry Moorehouse, The Bass Book, GPI Books, 1995)

GIBSON SERIALIZATION

Identifying Gibson instruments by serial number is tricky at best and downright impossible in some cases. The best methods of identifying them is by using a combination of the serial number, the factory order number and any features that are particular to a specific time that changes may have occurred in instrument design (i.e. logo design change, headstock volutes, etc). There have been 6 different serial number styles used to date on Gibson instruments.

The first serialization started in 1902 and ran until 1947. The serial numbers started with number 100 and go to 99999. All numbers are approximates. In most cases, only the upper end instruments were assigned identification numbers.

YEAR	LAST #
1903	1150
1904	1850
1905	2550
1906	3350
1907	4250
1908	5450
1909	6950
1910	8750
1911	10850
1912	13350
1913	16100
1914	20150
1915	25150
1916	32000
1917	39500
1918	47900
1919	53800
1920	62200
1921	69300
1922	71400
1923	74900
1924	80300
1925	82700
1926	83600
1927	85400
1928	87300
1929	89750
1930	90200
1931	90450
1932	90700
1933	91400
1934	92300
1935	92800
1936	94100
1937	95200

YEAR	APPROXIMATE SERIAL RANGE
1938	95750
1939	96050
1940	96600
1941	97400
1942	97700
1943	97850
1944	98250
1945	98650
1946	99300
1947	99999

White oval labels were used on instruments from 1902 to 1954, at which time the oval label was changed to an orange color. On instruments with round soundholes, this label is visible directly below it. On f-hole instruments, it is visible through the upper f-hole. The second type of serial numbers used started with an *A* prefix and ran from 1947 to 1961. The first number is A 100.

YEAR	LAST #
1947	A 1305
1948	A 2665
1949	A 4410
1950	A 6595
1951	A 9420
1952	A 12460
1953	A 17435
1954	A 18665
1955	A 21910
1956	A 24755
1957	A 26820
1958	A 28880
1959	A 32285
1960	A 35645
1961	A 36150

When production of solid body guitars began, an entirely new serial number system was developed. Though not used on the earliest instruments produced (those done in 1952), a few of these instruments have 3 digits stamped on the headstock top. Some time in 1953, instruments were ink stamped on the headstock back with 5 or 6 digit numbers, the first indicating the year, the following numbers are production numbers. The production numbers run in a consecutive order and, aside from a few oddities in the change over years (1961-1962), it is fairly accurate to use them when identifying solid body instruments produced between 1953 and 1961. Examples of this system:

4 2205 = 1954
614562 = 1956

In 1961 Gibson started a new serial number system that covered all instrument lines. It consisted of numbers that are impressed into the wood. It is also generally known to be the most frustrating and hard to understand system that Gibson has employed. The numbers were used between the years 1961-1969. There are several instances where batches of numbers are switched in order, duplicated, not just once, but up to four times, and seem to be randomly assigned, throughout the decade. In general though, the numbers are approximately as follows:

YEAR	APPROXIMATE SERIAL RANGE
1961	100-42440
1962	42441-61180
1963	61450-64220
1964	64240-70500
1962	71180-96600
1963	96601-99999

YEAR	APPROXIMATE SERIAL RANGE
1967	000001-008010
1967	010000-042900
1967	044000-044100
1967	050000-054400
1967	055000-063999
1967	064000-066010
1967	067000-070910
1967	090000-099999
1963, 1967	100000-106099
1963	106100-108900
1963, 1967	109000-109999
1963	110000-111549
1963, 1967	111550-115799
1963	115800-118299
1963, 1967	118300-120999
1963	121000-139999
1963, 1967	140000-140100
1963	140101-144304
1964	144305-144380
1963	144381-145000
1963	147009-149864
1964	149865-149891
1963	149892-152989
1964	152990-174222
1964, 1965	174223-176643
1964	176644-199999
1964	200000-250335
1965	250336-291000
1965	301755-302100
1965	302754-305983
1965, 1967	306000-306100
1965, 1967	307000-307985
1965, 1967	309848-310999
1965	311000-320149
1967	320150-320699
1965	320700-321100
1965	322000-326600
1965	328000-328500
1965	328700-329179
1965, 1967	329180-330199
1965, 1967, 1968	330200-332240
1965	332241-347090
1965	348000-348092
1966	348093-349100
1965	349121-368638
1966	368640-369890
1967	370000-370999
1966	380000-385309
1967	390000-390998
1965, 1966, 1967, 1968	400001-400999
1966	401000-407985
1966	408000-408690
1966	408800-409250
1966	420000-426090
1966	427000-429180
1966	430005-438530
1966	438800-438925
1965, 1966, 1968, 1969	500000-500999
1965	501010-501600
1968	501601-501702
1965, 1968	501703-502706

YEAR	APPROXIMATE SERIAL RANGE
1968	503010-503110
1965, 1968	503405-520955
1968	520956-530056
1966, 1968, 1969	530061-530850
1968, 1969	530851-530993
1969	530994-539999
1966, 1969	540000-540795
1969	540796-545009
1966	550000-556910
1969	558012-567400
1966	570099-570755
1969	580000-580999
1966, 1967, 1968, 1969	600000-600999
1969	601000-601090
1969	605901-606090
1966, 1967	700000-700799
1968, 1969	750000-750999
1966, 1967, 1968, 1969	800000-800999
1966, 1969	801000-812838
1969	812900-814999
1969	817000-819999
1966, 1969	820000-820087
1966	820088-823830
1969	824000-824999
1966, 1969	828002-847488
1966	847499-858999
1967	859001-880089
1967	893401-895038
1968	895039-896999
1967	897000-898999
1968	899000-899999
1968	900000-902250
1968	903000-920899
1968	940000-941009
1968	942001-943000
1968	945000-945450
1968	947415-956000
1968	959000-960909
1968	970000-972864

GIBSON'S F O N SYSTEM

In addition to the above serial number information, Gibson also used **Factory Order Numbers (F O N) to track batches of instruments being produced at the time. In the earlier years at Gibson, guitars were normally built in batches of 40 instruments. Gibson's Factory Order Numbers were an internal coding that followed the group of instruments through the factory. Thus, the older Gibson guitars may have a serial number and a F O N. The F O N may indicate the year, batch number, and the ranking (order of production within the batch of 40).**

This system is useful in helping to date and authenticate instruments. There are three separate groupings of numbers that have been identified and are used for their accuracy. The numbers are usually stamped or written on the instrument's back and seen through the lower F hole or round soundhole, or maybe impressed on the back of the headstock.

1908-1923 Approximate #s

YEAR	F O N
1908	259
1909	309
1910	545, 927
1911	1260, 1295
1912	1408, 1593
1913	1811, 1902
1914	1936, 2152
1915	2209, 3207
1916	2667, 3508
1917	3246, 11010
1918	9839, 11159
1919	11146, 11212
1920	11329, 11367
1921	11375, 11527
1922	11565, 11729
1923	11973

F O Ns for the years 1935-1941 usually consisted of the batch number, a letter for the year and the instrument number. Examples are as follows:

722 A 23

465 D 58

863 E 02.

Code Letter and Year

A	1935
B	1936
C	1937
D	1938
E	1939
F	1940
G	1941

Code Letter F O Ns were discontinued after 1941, and any instruments made during or right after World War II do not bear an F O N codes. In 1949, a four digit F O N was used, but not in conjunction with any code letter indicating the year.

From 1952-1961, the F O N scheme followed the pattern of a letter, the batch number and an instrument ranking number (when the guitar was built in the run of 40). The F O N is the only identification number on Gibson's lower grade models (like the ES-125, ES-140, J-160E, etc.) which do not feature a paper label. Higher grade models (such as the Super 400, L-5, J-200, etc.) feature both a serial number **and** a F O N. When both numbers are present on a higher grade model, remember that the F O N was assigned at the beginning of the production run, while the serial number was recorded later (before shipping). The serial number would properly indicate the actual date of the guitar. F O N examples run thus:

Y 2230 21

V 4867 8

R 6785 15

Code Letter and Year

Z	1952
Y	1953
X	1954
W	1955
V	1956
U	1957
T	1958
S	1959
R	1960
Q	1961

After 1961 the use of FONs was discontinued at Gibson.

When the Nashville Gibson plant was opened in 1974, it was decided that the bulk of the production of products would be run in the South; the Kalamazoo plant would produce the higher end (fancier) models in the North. Of course, many of the older guitar builders and craftsmen were still in Kalamazoo; and if they weren't ready to change how they built guitars, then they may not have been ready to change how they numbered them! Certain guitar models built in the late 1970s can be used to demonstrate the old-style 6 digit serial numbers. **It is estimated that Gibson's Kalamazoo plant continued to use the 6 digit serial numbers through 1978 and 1979.** So double check the serial numbers on those 1970s L-5s, Super 400s, and Super 5 BJBs! It has come to light recently that the Kalamazoo plant did not directly switch over to the "new" 8 digit serialization method in 1977.

From 1970-1975 the method of serializing instruments at Gibson became even more randomized. All numbers were impressed into the wood and a six digit number assigned, though no particular order was given and some instruments had a letter prefix. The orange labels inside hollow bodied instruments were discontinued in 1970 and were replaced by white and orange rectangle labels on the acoustics, and small black, purple and white rectangle labels were placed on electric models.

In 1970, the words **MADE IN USA** was impressed into the back of instrument headstocks (although a few instruments from the 1950s also had *MADE IN USA* impressed into their headstocks as well).

Year(s)	Approximate Series Manufacture
1970, 1971, and 1972	100000s, 600000s, 700000s 900000s
1973	000001s, 100000s, 200000s, 800000s and a few "A" + 6 digit numbers
1974 and 1975	100000s, 200000s, 300000s, 400000s, 500000s, 600000s, 800000s and a few *A-B-C-D-E-F* + 6 digit numbers

During the period from 1975-1977 Gibson used a transfer that had eight digit numbers, the first two indicate the year, 99=1975, 00=1976 and 06=1977, the following six digits are in the 100000 to 200000 range. *MADE IN USA* was also included on the transfer and some models had *LIMITED EDITION* also applied. A few bolt-on neck instruments had a date ink stamped on the heel area.

In 1977, Gibson first introduced the serialization method that is in practice today. This updated system utilizes an impressed eight digit numbering scheme that covers both serializing and dating functions. The pattern is as follows:

YDDDYPPP

YY is the production year
DDD is the day of the year
PPP is the plant designation and/or instrument rank.

The numbers 001-499 show Kalamazoo production, 500-999 show Nashville production. The Kalamazoo numbers were discontinued in 1984.

When acoustic production began at the plant built in Bozeman, Montana (in 1989), the series' numbers were reorganized. Bozeman instruments began using 001-299 designations and, in 1990, Nashville instruments began using 300-999 designations. It should also be noted that the Nashville plant has not reached the 900s since 1977, so these numbers have been reserved for prototypes. On Gibson acoustic serialization between 1989-2000, more research is under way regarding the format used.

In 1994, for Gibson's Centennial, they used a new serialization for that one year. Every serial number started with 94 followed by 6 digits which were the production dates and number.

70108276 means the instrument was produced on Jan.10, 1978, in Kalamazoo and was the 276th instrument stamped that day.

82765501 means the instrument was produced on Oct. 3, 1985, in Nashville and was the 1st instrument stamped that day.

There are still some variances that Gibson uses on some instruments produced today, but for the most part the above can be used for identifying most instruments.

On Custom Shop Signature models, the serialization is the initials of the artist guitar it is and the number in sequence following.

GRETSCH SERIALIZATION

Before World War II, serial numbers were penciled onto the inside backs of Gretsch's higher end instruments. By 1949, small labels bearing *Fred Gretsch Mfg. Co.*, serial and model number replaced the penciled numbers inside the instruments. This label was replaced by a different style label, an orange and grey one, sometime in 1957. A few variations of this scheme occurred throughout the company's history, the most common being the use of impressed numbers in the headstock of instruments, beginning about 1949. Serial numbers were also stamped into the headstock nameplate of a few models. The numbers remain consecutive throughout and the following chart gives approximations of the years they occurred.

APPROXIMATE SERIALIZATION RANGE	YEARS
001 - 1000	1939-1945
1001 - 2000	1946-1949
2001 - 3000	1950
3001 - 5000	1951
5001 - 6000	1952
6001 - 8000	1953
8001 - 12000	1954
12001 - 16000	1955
16001 - 21000	1956
21001 - 26000	1957
26001 - 30000	1958
30001 - 34000	1959
34001 - 39000	1960
39001 - 45000	1961
45001 - 52000	1962
52001 - 63000	1963
63001 - 78000	1964
78001 - 85000	1965

In the latter part of 1965, Gretsch decided to begin using a date coded system of serialization. It consists of the first digit (sometimes two) that identified the month; the second or third identifying the year, and the remaining digit (or digits) represented the number of the instrument in production for that month. Some examples of this system would be:

997	September, 1969 (7th instrument produced)
11255	November, 1972 (55th instrument produced)

On solid body instruments, impressed headstock numbers were used. In 1967, *Made in USA* was added. Hollow body instruments still made use of a label placed on the inside back of the instrument.

Around circa 1973, the label style changed once again, becoming a black and white rectangle with *Gretsch Guitars* and the date coded serialization on it. A hyphen was also added between the month and the year to help avoid confusion, thus:

12-4387	December, 1974 (387th instrument produced)
3-745	March, 1977 (45th instrument produced)

Contemporary Gretsch serialization beginning in 1989 utilizes 9 digits in a YYMMmmm(m)xxx format. YY indicates the last 2 digits of the year (i.e., 01 = 2001). M or MM indicates the month of the year (1-12). mmm(m) references the model number with either 3 or 4 digits (i.e., a 6136 reads 136). x(xx) refers to a 1-3 digit production count.

GUILD SERIALIZATION

Guild Serialization went through three distinct phases, and can be both a helpful guide as well as confusing when trying to determine the manufacturing date of a guitar. The primary idea to realize is that most Guild models use a <u>separate serial numbering system for each guitar model</u> - there is no "overall system" to plug a number into! While serial numbers are sometimes a helpful tool, other dating devices like potentiomter codes or dating by hardware may be more exact.

1952-1965: Between the inception of the Guild company in 1952 to 1965, the serialization was sequential for all models.

APPROXIMATE LAST NUMBER	YEAR
350	1952
840	1953
1526	1954
2468	1955
3830	1956
5712	1957
8348	1958
12035	1959
14713	1960
18419	1961
22722	1962
28943	1963
38636	1964
46606	1965

1966-1969: While some models retained the serialization from the original series, many models were designated with a 2 letter prefix and an independent numbering series for each individual model between 1966 to 1969.

Continued Original Serialization Series

APPROXIMATE LAST NUMBER	YEAR
46608	1966
46637	1967
46656	1968
46695	1969

The models that were numbered with the new 2 letter prefix started each separate serial number series with 101.

1970-1979: The following chart details the serial numbers as produced through the 1970s. There are no corresponding model names or numbers for this time period.

APPROXIMATE LAST NUMBER	YEAR
50978	1970
61463	1971
75602	1972
95496	1973
112803	1974
130304	1975
149625	1976
169867	1977
190567	1978
211877	1979

1979-1989: In 1979, Guild returned to the separate prefix/serial number system. Serial numbers after the 2 letter prefix in each separate system began with 100001 (thus, you would need a serialization table for each model/by year to date by serialization alone). In 1987, a third

system was devised. In some cases, the **Model Designation** became the *prefix* for the serial number. For example:

D300041   D-30, #0041 (41st D-30 instrument produced)

With acoustic models, you can cross-reference the model name to the serial number to judge the rest of the serialization; the resulting serial number must still be checked in the serialization table.

1990-Date: Guild continued with the separate prefix/serialization system. In 1994, only the Model Prefix and last serial numbers for each model were recorded; better records continued in 1995.

Serialization on currently manufactured Guilds (non-custom shop) through 2000 typically utilize a 2 character alphabetical prefix (denoting specific models), followed by 6 digits. Current alphabetical prefixes include: AA, AB, AD, AE, AF, AG, AK, CL, FB, and FC. Please check Guild's web site (www.guildguitars.com) for a cross reference listing of models and their assigned alphabetical prefixes.

Guild Custom Shop: The three Guild Custom Shop models (**45th Anniversary, Deco,** and **Finesse**) all use a completely different serial numbering system. Each instrument has a serial number on the back of the headstock that indicates the "which number out of the complete series". Inside the guitar there is a seven digit code: The first three numbers (starting with #500) indicate the production sequence, while the last four digits indicate the date of production (the 4th and 7th digit **in reverse** indicate the year, the 5th and 6th digits are the month). Note: Benedetto models made at the Guild Custom Shop in Nashville have a separate serial number system beginning with the letter N.

Guild has a series of charts available on their website (www.guildguitars.com - Ask Mr. Gearhead) to help date a Guild model during its different manufacturing periods. It is recommended that you refer to this information, as there are many charts neede for the individual model serialization. Through the years (and different owners of the company), some of the historical documentation has been lost or destroyed. However, these tables are some of the most comprehensive available to the public. They are up to date through Dec. of 1997.

(Serialization reference source: Hans Moust, The Guild Guitar Book; and Jay Pilzer, Guild authority; additional company information courtesy Bill Acton, Guild Guitars)

IBANEZ MODEL NOMENLCATURE & SERIALIZATION

IBANEZ MODEL NUMBERING SYSTEM

Ibanez offers a wide selection of models with a corresponding wide range of features. This means there are a lot of models and, of course, a lot of different model numbers to try and keep track of. Ibanez serial numbers never indicated the model number, and still don't. Most solid body Ibanez guiatrs and basses didn't feature model numbers until recently, and even then, only on Korean made instruments. On some semi-hollow models, some model numbers will appear on the label visible through the f-hole.

Here's how the Ibanez model numbers work (most of the time, of course, there are always exceptions - but for the Ibanez models commonly encountered, this system applies pretty consistently).

SERIES: the first in the model number designate the series: RG550BK, RG Series; SR800BK is a Soundgear, etc. Also, in the Artstar lines, AS indicates (A)rtstar (S)emihollow, AF indicates (A)rtstar (F)ull hollow.

FINISH: the last 2 letters designate the finish: RG550BK, Black finish; RX240CA, Candy Apple. **Exceptions**: finishes such as Amber Pearl and Stained Oil Finish use 3 letters: AMP, SOL, etc. (having offered so many finishes, Ibanez is running out of traditional 2 letter cominations!)

The numbers following the Series letters indicate 2 items:

1. Point of Manufacture

On solid body guitars and basses, the numbers 500 and above indicate

Japanese manufacture: RG550BK, SR800BK, BL850VB, the numbers 400 and below indicate Korean manufacture: SR400BK, RX240MG, etc.

This system doesn't apply to hollow bodies, and many signature guitars. J of White Zombie's signature model, the IJ100WZ is made in Japan, as is the JPM100.

2. Pickup Configuration

On solid body guitars only, the last 2 numbers indicate pickup configuration:

20= two humbucking pickups with or w/o pickguard (ex: TC420MD)

30 = three single coils with or w/o pickguard (no current models)

40 = sin/sin/hum with a pickguard (ex: TC740MN)

50 = hum/sin/hum with a pickguard (ex: RG550BK)

60 = sin/sin/hum with no pickguard (no current models)

70 = hum/sin/hum with no pickguard (ex: RG570FBL)

Exceptions: Of course! For example, TC825 (which has 2 humbuckers and a pickguard). BL1025 (hum/sin/hum with a pickguard), etc.

IBANEZ SERIALIZATION

Author/researcher Michael Wright successfully discussed the Ibanez/Hoshino history in his book, *Guitar Stories Volume One* (Vintage Guitar Books, 1995). Early serial numbers and foreign-built potentiometer codes on Japanese guitars aren't much help in the way of clues, but Ibanez did institute a meaningful numbering system as part of their warranty program in 1975.

Before 1987: In general, Ibanez serial numbers between 1975 to 1987 had seven digits, arranged XYYZZZZ. The letter prefix "X" stands for the month (January = A, February = B, etc. on to L); the next following two digits "YY" are the year. The last four digits indicate the number of instruments built per month through a particular production date.

An outside source indicated that the month/letter code prefix was discontined in 1988, and the previous dating code was discontinued in 1990. However (or whatever), in 1987 the XYYZZZZ still appeared the same, but the new listing shifted to XYZZZZZ.

1987 and later: The opening alphabetical prefix "X" now indicates production **location** instead of month: **F** (Fuji, Japan), or **C** (Cort, Korea). The first digit "Y" indicates the year: As in 198Y - and as in 199Y. Bright-eyed serialization students will have already noticed that while the year is obtainable, the decade isn't! Because of this, it is good to have a working knowledge of which models were available approx. which time periods. All following numbers again are the production ranking code (ZZZZZ).

Mid 1997: Ibanez changed the format, and the second two digit after the alphabetical prefix indicate the last 2 digits of the actual year of production (i.e, F0003680 indicates guitar built in Fuji during 2000).

CE Designation: In late 1996, in addition to the serial number on the back of the headstock, Ibanez electric guitars and basses added the "CE" designation. This indicates that the product meets the electronic standards of the European Common Market, similar to our UL approval.

(Source: Michael Wright, Guitar Stories Volume One, Jim Donahue, Ibanez Guitars)

MARTIN GUITAR SERIAL NUMBERS

YEAR	LAST #
1898	8348
1899	8716
1900	9128
1901	9310
1902	9528
1903	9810
1904	9988
1905	10120
1906	10329
1907	10727
1908	10883
1909	11018
1910	11203
1911	11413
1912	11565
1913	11821
1914	12047
1915	12209
1916	12390
1917	12988
1918	13450
1919	14512
1920	15848
1921	16758
1922	17839
1923	19891
1924	22008
1925	24116
1926	28689
1927	34435
1928	37568
1929	40843
1930	45317
1931	49589
1932	52590
1933	55084
1934	58679
1935	61947
1936	65176
1937	68865
1938	71866
1939	74061
1940	76734
1941	80013
1942	83107
1943	86724
1944	90149
1945	93623
1946	98158
1947	103468
1948	108269
1949	112961
1950	117961
1951	122799
1952	128436
1953	134501
1954	141345
1955	147328
1956	152775
1957	159061
1958	165576
1959	171047
1960	175689
1961	181297
1962	187384
1963	193327
1964	199626
1965	207030
1966	217215
1967	230095

YEAR	LAST #
1968	241925
1969	256003
1970	271633
1971	294270
1972	313302
1973	333873
1974	353387
1975	371828
1976	388800
1977	399625
1978	407800
1979	419900
1980	430300
1981	436474
1982	439627
1983	446101
1984	453300
1985	460575
1986	468175
1987	476216
1988	483952
1989	493279
1990	503309
1991	512487
1992	522655
1993	535223
1994	551696
1995	570434
1996	592930
1997	624799
1998	668796
1999	724077
2000	780500
2001	845644
2002	916759

(Source: Lon Werner, The Martin Guitar Company)

MOONSTONE SERIALIZATION

The most important factor in determining the year of manufacture for Moonstone instruments is that each model had its own set of serial numbers. There is no grouping of models by year of manufacture.

D-81 EAGLE

L001-L004	1981
L005-L011	1982

EAGLE (Electrics)

52950-52952	1980
52953-52954	1981
52955-52959	1982
52960	1983

EARTHAXE

(26 total instruments made)

0001-0013	1975
0014-0026	1976

ECLIPSE Guitar models

(81 total instruments made)

79001-79003	1979
8004-8036	1980
8037-8040	1981
1041-1052	1981
1053-1075	1982
1076-1081	1983

ECLIPSE Bass models

(124 total instruments made)

3801-3821	1980
3822-3828	1981
3029-3062	1981
3063-3109	1982
3110-3118	1983
3119-3123	1984

EXPLODER Guitar models

(65 total instruments made)

7801-7806	1980
7007-7020	1981
7021-7052	1982
7053-7065	1983

EXPLODER Bass models

(35 total instruments made)

6801-6803	1980
6004-6013	1981
6014-6031	1982
6032-6035	1983

FLYING V Guitar models

(52 total instruments made)

5801-5812	1980
5013-5028	1981
5029-5045	1982
5046-5048	1983
5049-5052	1984

FLYING V Bass models

(6 total instruments made)

9001-9006	1981

M-80

(64 total instruments made)

4801-4808	1980
4809-4816	1981
4017-4031	1981
4032-4052	1982
4053-4064	1983

MOONDOLINS

T001-T002	1981
T003-T006	1983
T007	1984

VULCAN Guitar models

(162 total instruments made)

5027	1977
5028-5034	1978
107835-107838	1978
17939-179115	1979
179116-179120	1980
80121-80129	1980
80130-80134	1981
8135-8167	1981
8168-8185	1982
8186-8191	1983
7988-7991	1984

VULCAN Bass models

(19 total instruments made)

V001-V002	1982
V003-V016	1983

V017-V019	1984

OVATION SERIALIZATION

Three Digit numbers (no letter prefix)

006-319	1966
320-999	1967 (February - November)

Four Digit numbers (no letter prefix)

1000-	1967 (November) to 1968 (July)

Five Digit numbers (no letter prefix)

10000-	1970 (February) to 1972 (May)

Six Digit numbers (1971 to Present, except Adamas models)

000001-007000	1972 (May - December)
007001-020000	1973
020001-039000	1974
039001-067000	1975
067001-086000	1976
086001-103000	1977 (January - September)
103001-126000	1977 (September) to 1978 (April)
126001-157000	1978 (April - December)
157001-203000	1979
211011-214933	1980
214934-263633	1981
263634-291456	1982
291457-302669	1983
302670-303319	1984 [Elite models only]
315001-331879	1984 (May - December) [Balladeer models only]
303320-356000	1985 to 1986
357000-367999	1987
368000-382106	1988
382107-392900	1989
403760-420400	1990
421000-430680	1991
402700-406000	1992
446001-457810	1992
457811-470769	1993
470770-484400	1994
484401-501470	1995
501470-507000	1996
PENDING	1997
PENDING	1998

Adamas Models Serialization

Serialization for the Adamas models begins with number 0077 on September, 1977.

0077-0099	1977
0100-0608	1978
0609-1058	1979
1059-1670	1980
1671-2668	1981
2669-3242	1982
3243-3859	1983
3860-4109	1984
4110-4251	1985
4252-4283	1986
4284-4427	1987
4428-4696	1988
4697-4974	1989
4975-5541	1990
5542-6278	1991
6279-7088	1992
7089-8159	1993
8160-9778	1994

9779-11213	1995
11214-12000	1996
PENDING	1997
PENDING	1998
PENDING	1999
PENDING	2000
PENDING	2001
PENDING	2002
PENDING	2003

Letter Prefix plus digits

A + 3 digits	1968 (July - November)
B + 3 digits	1968 (November) to 1969 (February)
B + 5 digits	1974 to 1979 [Magnum solid body basses]
C + 3 digits	1969 (February - September)
D + 3 digits	1969 (September) to 1970 (February)
E + 4 digits	1973 (January) to 1975 (February) [solid bodies]
E + 5 digits	1975 (February) to 1980 [solid bodies]
E + 6 digits	1980 (late) to 1981 [UK II guitars]
F Prefix	1968 (July) to 1970 (February)
G Prefix	1968 (July) to 1970 (February)
H Prefix	1970 to 1973 [Electric Storm series]
I Prefix	1970 to 1973 [Electric Storm series]
J Prefix	1970 to 1973 [Electric Storm series]
L Prefix	1970 to 1973 [Electric Storm series]

(Source: Walter Carter, The History of the Ovation Guitar. Information collected in Mr. Carter's Ovation Appendices was researched and compiled by Paul Bechtoldt)

RICKENBACKER SERIAL NUMBERS

Rickenbacker offered a number of guitar models as well as lap steels prior to World War II, such as the **Ken Roberts Spanish** electric f-hole flattop (mid 1930s to 1940) and the **559** model archtop in the early 1940s. The company put production on hold during the war; in 1946, began producing an **Electric Spanish** archtop. Serialization on early Rickenbacker models from 1931 to 1953 is unreliable, but models may be dated by patent information. This method should be used in conjunction with comparisons of parts, and design changes.

In 1953, Rickenbacker/Electro was purchased by Francis C. Hall. The **Combo 600** and **Combo 800** models debuted in 1954. From 1954 on, the serial number appears on the bridge or jackplate of the instrument. The Rickenbacker serial numbers during the 1950s have four to seven digits. The letter within the code indicates the type of instrument (Combo/guitar, bass, mandolin, etc), and the number after the letter indicates the year of production:

Example: X(X)B7XX   (A bass from 1957)

1961 to 1986: In 1961, the serialization scheme changes. The new code has **two letter** prefixes, followed by digits. The first letter prefix indicates the year; the second digit indicates the month of production.

PREFIX	YEAR
A	1961
B	1962
C	1963
D	1964
E	1965
F	1966
G	1967
H	1968
I	1969
J	1970

PREFIX	YEAR
K	1971
L	1972
M	1973
N	1974
O	1975
P	1976
Q	1977
R	1978
S	1979
T	1980
U	1981
V	1982
W	1983
X	1984
Y	1985
Z	1986
A	January
B	February
C	March
D	April
E	May
F	June
G	July
H	August
I	September
J	October
K	November
L	December

In 1987, the serialization was revised, again. The updated serial number code has letter prefix (A to L) that still indicates month; the following digit that indicates the year:

DIGIT	YEAR
0	1987
1	1988
2	1989
3	1990
4	1991
5	1992
6	1993
7	1994
8	1995
9	1996

The following digits after the month/year digits are production (for example, *L2XXXX* would be an instrument built in December, 1989).

Rickenbacker is currently not disclosing the current system of serialization. If a collector or dealer needs a recent instrument dated, Rickenbacker invites individuals to contact the company through the Customer Service department.

STROMBERG SERIALIZATION

This Boston-based instrument shop was founded by Charles Stromberg, a Swedish immigrant, in 1906. Stromberg generally concentrated on banjo and drum building, leaving the guitar lutherie to his son Elmer. Elmer joined the family business in 1910, and began building guitars in the late 1920s.

Total production of guitars reached about 640. The labels on the guitars were business cards, so the instruments can be dated (roughly) by the telephone number on the cards.

Bowdoin 1228R-1728-M	1920-1927
Bowdoin 1242 W	1927-1929
Bowdoin 1878 R	1929-1932
CA 3174	1932-1945 (In the late 1930s,
CA 7-3174	1949-1955

the Blue shipping labels inside the guitar body were either typ written or handwritten)

(Source: Jim Speros, Stromberg research)

TAKAMINE SERIALIZATION

The eight digit serial number on Takamine instruments can be deciphered by breaking down the number into 4 groups of two digits, thus:

YYMMDDXX   = (YY)(MM)(DD)(XX)

The first two digits (YY) indicate the year; the next two digits (MM) indicate the month; the third group of digits (DD) indicates the day of production; and the remaining two digits indicates the ranking in the number of instruments produced that day. If a nine digit serial number is encountered, assume that the last three digits indicate the production ranking.

Example: 91060979 indicates an instrument manufactured June 9th of 1991, and was the 79th instuments manufactured that day.

TAYLOR SERIAL NUMBERS

Taylor did not introduce serialization until 1975 and used the first two numbers as the year (10 was 1975, 20 was 1976, and 30 was 1977) and the next three numbers were production numbers. In 1977 they started with a new system that was strictly numeric and ran until 1992. In 1993 they started a serialization system that can pinpoint when the guitar was made down to the day and month. Between 1993 and 1999 they used a nine-digit number system. The first two digits indicate the year. The next two are the month. The third two indicate the exact day production was started on the guitar, the seventh digit is either a 1 or 0 and 300 and 400 series instruments get the 0 and 500 or higher recieve the 1 designation. The final two digits indicate the production number that day. In 2000 they expanded to an 11-digit system where the only difference is there is now a four digit year to accomodate to Y2K worries. For example: serial number 980626109 indicates a 500 series or higher guitar built (started) on June 26, 1998 and was the ninth instrument of the day. Another example of the 11 digit system would be 20010402012 indicating a 300 or 400 series built on April 2, 2001 and was the 12th instrument produced that day.

Year	Serial Number Range
1974	Didn't Use Serial Numbers
1975	10109-10146
1976	20147-20315
1977	30316-30XXX
1977	001-450
1978	541-900
1979	901-1300
1980	1301-1400
1981	1401-1670
1982	1671-1951
1983	1952-2445
1984	2446-3206
1985	3207-3888
1986	3889-4778
1987	4779-5981
1988	5982-7831
1989	7832-10070
1990	10071-12497
1991	12498-15249
1992	15250-17947
1993-current	See Above

Source: www.taylorguitars.com

THREET GUITARS SERIALIZATION

The serial number on Threet acoustic guitars consists of a letter followed by three (sometimes four) numbers. The letter indicates the model:

A   Parlor-size (similar to a traditional Model O)
B   A "large person's" Parlor-size (similar to a Model OO)
C   Larger, balanced sound Parlor-size
     (similar to a Model OOO)
D   Cross between a Model C and a Dreadnaught

The first two numbers indicate the year the guitar was started (and, hopefully, completed). The third (and occasionally fourth) number indicate the guitar's "rank" in that year's production. For example:

C 964 =   Model C   built in 1996   4th Guitar Produced

Keep in mind, Threet guitars are offered in both a *Standard* and *Deluxe* versions. Review the appointments to determine the level of construction, and watch for *Custom* level inlays as well.

(Source: Judy Threet, Threet Guitars)

WASHBURN SERIALIZATION

The Washburn trademark was introduced by the Lyon & Healy company of Chicago, Illinois in 1864. While this trademark has changed hands a number of times, the historical records have not! Washburn suffered a fire in the 1920s that destoyed all records and paperwork that was on file; in the 1950s, another fire destroyed the accumulated files yet again.

When the trademark was revived yet again in 1964, the first production of Washburn acoustic guitars was in Japan. Washburn electric guitars debuted in 1979, and featured U.S. designs and Japanese production.

Production of Washburn guitars changed to Korea in the mid to late 1980s; a number of U.S.-produced **Chicago Series** models were introduced in the late 1980s as well. Serial numbers from 1988 on use the first two digits of the instrument's serial number to indicate the year the instrument was produced (1988 = 88XXX). This process works for most, but not all, of the instruments since then.

Washburn Limited Editions feature the year in the model name. For example, **D-95** LTD is a Limited Edition introduced in 1995. No corresponding serialization information is available at this time.

(Washburn information courtesy Dr. Duck's AxWax)

YAMAHA SERIAL NUMBERS

Yamaha instruments were originally produced in Japan; production switched to Taiwan in the early 1980s. Instruments are currently produced in the U.S., Taiwan, and Indonesia. It is important to recognize that Yamaha uses two different serialization systems.

Yamaha electric guitars and basses have a letter/number (2 letters followed by 5 numbers) code that indicates production date. The first two letters of the serial number indicate the year and month of production (the first letter indicates the year, the second letter indicates the month). Yamaha's coding system substitutes a letter for a number indicating year and month, thus:

CODE LETTER	MONTH or YEAR NUMBER
H	1
I	2
J	3
K	4
L	5
M	6
N	7
O	8
P	9
X	10
Y	11
Z	12

For example, an "H" in the first of two letters would be a "1", indicating the last digit of the year (1981 or 1991). An "H" in the second of two letters would also be a "1", indicating the first month (January). Like Hamer, the digits will cycle around every 10 years.

After the two letter prefixes, 5 digits follow. The first two digits represent the day of the month, and the three digits indicate the production ranking for that day. For example:

NZ19218   December 19, 1987
                 (or 1997); #218.

The example's code should be properly broken down as N - Z - 27 - 428. The "N" in the first of the two letters would be a "7", indicating the last digit of the year (1987 or 1997). The "Z" in the second of the two letters would be a "12", indicating the 12th month (December). The two digit pair after the letters is the day of the month, the 19th. The final three digits indicate production ranking, therefore this imaginary guitar is the 218th instrument built that day.

Yamaha Acoustics and Acoustic Electrics contain 8 digit serial numbers. In this coding scheme, the first digit represents the last digit of the year (for example, 1987 = 7); the second and third numbers indicate the month (numbers 01 through 12); the fourth and fifth numbers will indicate the day of the month, and the final three digits will indicate the production ranking of the instrument.

This system works for most (but not all) of Yamaha products. If a serial number doesn't fit the coding system, Yamaha offers internal research via their website (www.yamahaguitars.com) - just email your request in.

GUITAR REFERENCES

Maybe the best advice any guitar player/collector will ever get is "For every guitar you purchase, buy 5 guitar books". It's still a good rule of thumb. The guitar industry has been very fortunate in that many good reference works have been published within the last several decades. In terms of the major trademarks, it's pretty much over – most of the good books are already out there. All you have to do is buy 'em and read 'em. Some are even out of print, and have already become very collectible (expensive).

If you're a player, collector, or just kind of an all-around average guitar pervert, you gotta do your homework. And there have never been more ways to bone up on your chosen homework assignments. Even though the web does a good job of performing many basic guitar information services, it's still not a book. It's also necessary that you subscribe to a few good magazines within your area (please refer to Periodicals listing).

The following titles represent a good cross sectional cut of those reference that are outstanding in their field(s). Spending $300 annually to have these valuable books at your fingertips is the cheapest insurance policy you'll every buy. If you're serious about your guitars, this information could also save you thousands of dollars and a lot of bad attitude. So bone up or bail out! No whining either – it's a pretty cool homework assignment.

Most of the books listed below can be obtained through:

JK Lutherie
11115 Sand Run
Harrison, OH 45030
Phone: 800.344.8880
www.jklutherie.com
Guitar@jklutherie.com

JK Lutherie also attends many major guitar shows annually, and you may want to stop by the booth to either purchase or inquire about any new releases. Many video releases are also available, and can be found on his web site.

Achard, Ken,
The Fender Guitar, The Bold Strummer, Ltd., Westport CT, 1990

Achard, Ken,
The History and Development of the American Guitar, The Bold Strummer, Ltd., Westport CT, 1990

Bacon, Tony (Editor), et al
Classic Guitars of the 50s, Miller Freeman, San Francisco, CA, 1996

Bacon, Tony (Editor), et al
Classic Guitars of the 60s, Miller Freeman, San Francisco, CA, 1997

Bacon, Tony
The History of the American Guitar, Friedman/Fairfax Publishers, New York, NY, 2001

Bacon, Tony, et al
The Classical Guitar - A Complete History, Outline Press Ltd./Miller Freeman, San Francisco, CA, 1997

Bacon, Tony
Electric Guitars - The Illustrated Encyclopedia, Thunder Bay Press/Advantage Publishers Group, San Diego, CA, 2000

Bacon, Tony,
The Ultimate Guitar Book, Alfred A. Knopf, Inc., New York NY, 1991

Bacon, Tony
50 Years of the Gibson Les Paul, Backbear Books, San Francisco, CA, 2002

Bacon, Tony and Day, Paul, et al (Editors)
Guitar - A Complete Guide for the Player, Thunder Bay Press, San Diego, CA, 2002

Bacon, Tony and Day, Paul,
The Fender Book, GPI/Miller Freeman Inc., San Francisco CA, 1992

Bacon, Tony and Day, Paul
50 Years of Fender, Balafon Books, London, England, 2000

Bacon, Tony and Day, Paul,
The Gibson Les Paul Book, GPI/Miller Freeman Inc., San Francisco CA, 1993

Bacon, Tony and Day, Paul,
The Gretsch Book, GPI/Miller Freeman Inc., San Francisco CA, 1996

Bacon, Tony and Day, Paul,
The Guru's Guitar Guide, Track Record Publishing, London England, 1990

Bacon, Tony and Day, Paul,
The Rickenbacker Book, GPI/Miller Freeman Inc., San Francisco CA, 1994

Bacon, Tony and Moorhouse, Barry,
The Bass Book, GPI/Miller Freeman Inc., San Francisco CA, 1995

Bechtoldt, Paul,
G&L: Leo's Legacy, Woof Associates, 1994

Bechtoldt, Paul and Tulloch, Doug,
Guitars from Neptune - A Definitive Journey Into Danelectro Mania, JK Lutherie, Harrison OH, 1996

Benedetto, Robert,
Making an Archtop Guitar - The Definitive Work on the Design and Construction of an Acoustic Archtop Guitar, Centerstream Publishing/Hal Leonard Corp, Anaheim Hills, CA, 1996

Bishop, Ian C.,
The Gibson Guitar, The Bold Strummer, Ltd., Westport CT, 1990

Bishop, Ian C.,
The Gibson Guitar From 1950 Vol. 2, The Bold Strummer, Ltd., Westport NY 1990

Blasquiz, Klaus,
The Fender Bass, Hal Leonard Publishing Corp., Milwaukee WI, 1990

Briggs, Brinkman and Crocker,
Guitars, Guitars, Guitars, All American Music Publishers, Neosho MO, 1988

Brozeman, Bob,
The History and Artistry of National Resonator Instruments, Centerstream Publishing, Anaheim Hills CA, 1993

Burrluck, Dave
The PRS Guitar Book, Backbeat Books, San Francisco, CA, 2002

Carter, Walter,
Epiphone, The Complete History, Hal Leonard Corporation, Milwaukee WI, 1995

Carter, Walter,
Gibson Guitars, 100 Years of an American Icon, General Publishing, Inc., New York NY, 1994

Carter, Walter,
The History of the Ovation Guitar, Hal Leonard Corporation, Milwaukee WI, 1996

Carter, Walter,
The Martin Book, GPI/Miller Freeman Inc., San Francisco CA, 1995

Chapman, Richard.
The Complete Guitarist, (Foreword by Les Paul), DK Publishing, New York, NY, 1993

Chapman, Richard
Guitar - Music, History, Players (Foreword by Eric Clapton), DK Publishing, New York, NY, 2000

Charle, Francois
The Story of Selmer Maccaferri Guitars, published by the author, Paris, France, 1999

Day, Paul,
The Burns Book, The Bold Strummer, Ltd., Westport Connecticut, 1990

Denyer, Ralph,
The Guitar Handbook, Alfred A. Knopf Inc., New York NY, 1982

Duchossoir, A.R.,
Gibson Electrics, Hal Leonard Publishing Corp., Milwaukee WI, 1981

Duchossoir, A.R.,
Gibson Electrics - The Classic Years, Hal Leonard Publishing Corp., Milwaukee WI, 1994

Duchossoir, A.R.,
Guitar Identification, Hal Leonard Publishing Corp., Milwaukee WI, 1983

Duchossoir, A.R.,
The Fender Stratocaster, Hal Leonard Publishing Corp., Milwaukee WI, 1989

Duchossoir, A.R.,
The Fender Telecaster, Hal Leonard Publishing Corp., Milwaukee WI, 1991

Erlewine, Vinolpal and Whitford,
Gibson's Fabulous Flat-Top Guitars, Miller Freeman Books, San Francisco CA, 1994

Evans, Tom and Mary Anne,
Guitars from the Renaissance to Rock, Facts on File, New York NY, 1977

Fisch, Jim, and Fred, L.B.
Epiphone: The House of Stathopoulo, Amsco Publications (Music Sales Corporation), New York NY, 1996

Freeth, Nick and Alexander, Charles
The Acoustic Guitar, Courage Books, Philadelphia, PA, 1999

Freeth, Nick and Alexander, Charles
The Electric Guitar, Courage Books, Philadelphia, PA, 1999

Freeth, Nick and Alexander, Charles
The Guitar, Salamander Books, London, England, 2002

Fullerton, George,
Guitar Legends, Centerstream Publishing, Fullerton CA, 1993

Giel, Kate, et al,
Ferrington Guitars, HarperCollins, New York NY, 1992

Giltrap, Gordon and Marten, Neville,
The Hofner Guitar - A History, International Music Publications Limited, Essex England, 1993

Gjörde, Per
Pearls and Crazy Diamonds - Fifty Years of Burns Guitars 1952-2002, Addit Information AB, Göteborg, Sweden, 2001

Goudy, Rob
Electric Guitars, Schiffer Publishing, Atglen, PA, 1999

Green, Frank Wm.
The Custom Guitar Shop and Wayne Richard Charvel (What's In a Name?), Working Musician Publications, Sierra Madre, CA, 1999

Gruhn, George, and Carter, Walter,
Acoustic Guitars and Other Fretted Instruments, Miller Freeman Inc., San Francisco CA, 1993

Gruhn, George, and Carter, Walter,
Electric Guitars and Basses, GPI/Miller Freeman Inc., San Francisco CA, 1994

Gruhn, George, and Carter, Walter,
Gruhn's Guide to Vintage Guitars, GPI/Miller Freeman Inc., San Francisco CA, 1991

Gruhn, George, and Carter, Walter,
Gruhn's Guide to Vintage Guitars, GPI/Miller Freeman Inc., San Francisco CA, 1999

Hartman, Robert Carl,
The Larsons' Creations, Guitars and Mandolins, Centerstream Publishing, Fullerton CA, 1995

Howe, Steve,
The Steve Howe Guitar Collection, GPI/Miller Freeman, Inc., San Francisco CA, 1993

Huber, John
The Development of the Modern Guitar, The Bold Strummer, Ltd., Westport, CT, 1994

Ingram, Adrian
A Concise History of the Electric Guitar, Mel Bay Publications, Pacific, MO, 2001

Ingram, Adrian
The Gibson L5, Centerstram Publishing, Anaheim Hills, CA, 1997

Ingram, Adrian
The Gibson ES175, Music Maker Books, Cambs, England, 1994

Iwanade, Yasuhiko,
The Beauty of the 'Burst, Rittor Music, Tokyo Japan, 1997

Iwanade, Yasuhiko,
The Galaxy of Strats, Rittor Music, Tokyo Japan, 1998

Juan, Carlos,
Collectables and Vintage, American Guitar Center, Stuttgart Germany, 1995

Longworth, Mike,
Martin Guitars, a History, 4 Maples Press Inc., Minisink Hills PA, 1987

Meiners, Larry
Gibson Shipment Totals 1937-1979, Flying Vintage Publications, 2001

Meiners, Larry
Flying V - The Illustrated History of this Modernistic Guitar, Flying Vintage Publications, 2001

Minhinnett, Ray and Young, Bob
The Story of the Fender Stratocaster, Miller Freeman Books, San Francisco, CA, 1995

Moseley, Willie G.,
Classic Guitars U.S.A., Centerstream Publishing, Fullerton CA, 1992

Moseley, Willie G.,
Stellas and Stratocasters, Vintage Guitar Books, Bismarck ND, 1994

Moseley, Willie G.,
Guitar People, Vintage Guitar Books, Bismarck ND, 1997

Moseley, Willie G. and Carson, Bill
Bill Carson - My Life and Times with Fender Musical Instruments, Hal Leonard Corp., Milwaukee, WI, 1998

Moust, Hans,
The Guild Guitar Book, The Company and the Instruments, 1952-1977, Guitar Archives Publications, The Netherlands, 1995

Production, Maurice
Burst Gang, 1G Inc., Tokyo, Japan, 1999

Rich, Bill and Nielsen, Rick,
Guitars of the Stars, Volume 1: Rick Nielsen, Gots Publishing Ltd., A Division of Rich Specialties, Inc., Rockford IL, 1993

Rittor Music,
Bizarre Guitars, Vol. 2, Japan, 1993

Rittor Music,
Guitar Graphic, Vol. 1, Tokyo Japan, 1994

Rittor Music,
Guitar Graphic, Vol. 2, Tokyo Japan, 1995

Rittor Music,
Guitar Graphic, Vol. 3, Tokyo Japan, 1995

Rittor Music,
Guitar Graphic, Vol. 4, Tokyo Japan, 1996

Rittor Music,
Guitar Graphic, Vol. 5, Tokyo Japan, 1996

Rittor Music,
Guitar Graphic, Vol. 6, Tokyo Japan, 1997

Rittor Music,
Guitar Graphic, Vol. 7, Tokyo Japan, 1997

Rittor Music,
Guitar Graphic, Vol. 8, Tokyo Japan, 1998

Roberts, Jim
How the Fender Bass Changed the World, Backbeat Books, San Francisco, CA, 2001

Sandberg, Larry
The Acoustic Guitar Guide, a cappella books, Pennington, NJ, 1991

Schmidt, Paul William,
Acquired of the Angels: The lives and works of master guitar makers John D'Angelico and James L. D'Aquisto, The Scarecrow Press, Inc., Metuchen, NJ, 1991

Scott, Jay,
'50s Cool: Kay Guitars, Seventh String Press, Hauppauge NY, 1992

Scott, Jay,
The Guitars of the Fred Gretsch Company, Centerstream Publishing, Fullerton CA, 1992

Scott, Jay and Da Pra, Vic,
'Burst 1958-'60 Sunburst Les Paul, Seventh String Press, Hauppauge NY, 1994

Smith, Richard R.,
Fender - The Sound Heard 'Round the World, Garfish Publishing Company, Fullerton CA, 1995

Smith, Richard R.,
Fender Custom Shop Guitar Gallery, Hal Leonard Corporation, Milwaukee WI, 1996

Smith, Richard R.,
The History of Rickenbacker Guitars, Centerstream Publishing, Fullerton CA, 1989

Teagle, John,
Washburn: Over One Hundred Years of Find Stringed Instruments, Music Sales Corp, New York NY, 1996

Teeter, Don E.
The Acoustic Guitar, University of Oklahoma Press, Oklahoma City, OK

Trynka, Paul (Editor)
The Electric Guitar - An Illustrated History, Chronicle Books, San Francisco, CA, 1993

Van Hoose, Thomas A.,
The Gibson Super 400, Miller Freeman, Inc., San Francisco, 1991

Vose, Ken,
Blue Guitar, Chronicle Books, San Francisco, CA, 1998

Wade, Graham
A Concise History of the Classic Guitar, Mel Bay Publications, Pacific, MO, 2001

Washburn, Jim and Johnston, Richard
Martin Guitars, Rodale Press, Emmaus, PA, 1997

Wheeler, Tom,
American Guitars, HarperCollins Publishers, New York NY, 1990

Wheeler, Tom,
The Guitar Book, A Handbook for Electric and Acoustic Guitarists, Harper and Row, New York NY, 1974

White, Forrest, Fender: *The Inside Story*, GPI/Miller Freeman Books, San Francisco CA, 1994

Wright, Michael,
Guitar Stories, Volume One, Vintage Guitar Books, Bismarck ND, 1995

Wright, Michael,
Guitar Stories, Volume Two, Vintage Guitar Books, Bismarck, ND, 2000

PERIODICALS LISTINGS

You've bought this book so you're obviously interested in stringed instruments. Being knowledgeable about any subject is a good idea and having the up-to-the-minute news is the best form of knowledge. We recommend the following publications for instrument information, collecting news, updates and show announcements, luthier and artist insights, and loads of other information that might interest you.

20th Century Guitar
135 Oser Avenue
Hauppauge, New York 11788
Phone number: 631-273-1674
Fax: 631-435-9057
Web site: www.tcguitar.com
Email: tcguitar@tcguitar.com
Published monthly. 12 month subscription is $15.00 in the USA.

Acoustic Guitar
String Letter Publishing, Inc.
255 W. End Ave.
San Rafael, California 94901
Phone number: 415-485-6946
Fax: 415-485-0831
Web site: www.acousticguitar.com
Published monthly. 12 month subscription is $29.95 in the USA.

Bass Guitar
Harris Publications, Inc.
1115 Broadway, 8th Flr.
New York, New York 10010
Phone number: 800-866-2886
http://www.guitarworld.com
Published monthly. 6 month subscription is $16.97 in the USA.

Bass Player
Music Player Group
2800 Campus Drive,
San Mateo, California 94403
Phone number: 650-513-4400
Web site: www.bassplayer.com
Published monthly. 12 month subscription is $29.95, 2 years is $45.95 in the USA.

Bassics
MI Media, LLC
22760 Hawthorne Blvd., Suite 208
Torrance, California 90505
Phone: 310-370-1695, Fax: 310-465-1788
Email: bassicRG@aol.com, or lynngarant@aol.com
Web site: www.bassics.com
Published bimonthly. 6 issues/year subscription is $29.95

Downbeat
102 N. Haven Road
Elmhurst, Illinois 60126-3379
Phone: 630-941-2030 Fax: 630-941-3210
Published monthly, $34.95 for 12 issues

EQ
Michele Fonville
Phone: 212.378.0449, Fax: 212.378.2160
Web site: www.eqmag.com
Email: mfonville@uemedia.com

Gitarre & Bass (Germany)
MM-Musik-Media-Verlag GmbH,
An Der Wachsfabrik 8, Koln, 50996 Germany
Phone number: 011-39-2236-96217
Fax: 011-39-2236-96217-5

Web site: www1.gitarrebass.de/magazine/index.htm
Published monthly.

Guitar Club (Italy)
Il Volo Srl
Via Brazzini 14
Milano, Italy

Guitar Digest
P.O. Box 66
The Plains, Ohio 45780
Phone number: 740-797-3351 or 740-592-4614
Web site: www.guitardigest.com
Published 6 times a year. A six issue subscription is $10.00 in the USA.

Guitar One
Cherry Lane Magazines, LLC
Six East 32nd St., 11th Flr.
New York, NY 10016
Phone number: 212-561-3000
Fax: 212-251-0840
www.cherrylane.com
Published monthly. 12 month subscription is $19.95 in the USA, and a two year subscription is $34.95 in the USA.

Guitar Player
411 Borel Avenue #100
San Mateo, California 94402
Phone number: 800-289-9939
Web site: www.guitarplayer.com
Email: guitarplayer@neodata.com
Published monthly. 12 month subscription is $24.00 in the USA.

Guitar World
Harris Publications, Inc.
1115 Broadway, 8th Flr.
New York, New York 10010
Phone number: 800-866-2886
Email: guitarworld@neodata.com
Web site: www.guitarworld.com
Published monthly. 12 month subscription is $23.94 in the USA.

Guitar World Acoustic
Harris Publications, Inc.
1115 Broadway, 8th Flr.
New York, New York 10010
Phone number: 800-866-2886
Web site: www.guitarworld.com
Email: gwa@harris-custsvc.com
Published monthly. 6 month subscription is $21.97 in the USA.

Guitarist UK
Future Publishing
Published monthly. 13 month subscription is 84 euros in the USA
Web site: www.futurenet.com or www.guitarist.co.uk

JazzTimes
8737 Colesville Rd., 9th Floor,
Silver Spring, MD 20910-3921
Phone: 301.588.4114 Fax: 301.588.5531
Web site: www.jazztimes.com
Email: info@jazztimes.com
Published 10 times/year. A one year subscription is $23.95 in the USA.

Just Jazz Guitar
P.O. Box 76053
Atlanta, Georgia 30358-1053
Phone number: 404-250-9298
Fax: 404-250-9298
Web site: www.justjazzguitar.com
Published 4 times a year. A one year subscription is $40 in the USA.

Musician's Hotline
Published by Heartland Communications Group
Phone number: 888-247-2009
Web site: www.musicianshotline.com
Published monthly. One year subscription is $16.95

Musico Pro
Music Maker Publications, Inc.
5412 Idylwild Trail, Suite 100
Boulder, Colorado 80301
Phone number: 303-516-9118,
Fax: 303-516-9119
A music/gear magazine is published in Spanish (available in U.S., Argentine, Chile, Mexico, and Spain).
Published 9 times a year. Subscription is $19.95 in the USA.

Vintage Guitar Magazine
P.O. Box 7301
Bismarck, North Dakota 58507
Phone number: 701-255-1197
Fax: 701-255-0250
Web site: www.vintageguitar.com
Published monthly. 12 month subscription is $24.95 in the USA.

Women Who Rock Magazine
Cherry Lane Magazines, LLC
Six East 32nd St., 11th Flr.
New York, NY 10016
Phone number: 212-561-3000 Fax: 212-251-0840
Web site: www.womewhorockmag.org
Published monthly. 12 month subscription is $17.95 (USA)

In addition to the regular publications put out by these publishers, most offer Special Edition (i.e., yearly buyers' guides, new product reviews, market overviews, etc.) magazines that are released annually, or bi-annually. Please contact them directly for more information.

STRINGS/LUTHIER ORGANIZATIONS

Another aspect of tone generation is Strings. How strings interact with the instrument and the player is another crucial portion of the overall "chain" of the sound produced.

The following is a brief review of String Companies.

ADAMAS
Distributed by Kaman Music (OVATION)
P.O. Box 507
Bloomfield CT 06002-0507
860.509.8888
www.kamanmusic.com

CHARLIE STRINGER
SNARLING DOGS STRINGS
Dept. GW
P.O. Box 4241
Warren NJ 07059
908.469.2828
Fax: 908.469.2882

CONCERTISTE
Picato Musician Strings
Unit 24, Treorchy Ind. Est.
Treorchy Mid Glamorgan
United Kingdom CF42 6EJ
44.144.343.7928
Fax: 44.144.343.3624

J. D'ADDARIO
J. D'Addario & Co.
595 Smith Street
Farmingdale NY 11735
800.323.2746
631.439.3300
Fax: 631.439.3333
strings@daddario.com
www.daddario.com

D'AQUISTO
20 E. Industry Court
P.O. Box 569
Deer Park NY 11729
631.586.4426
Fax: 631.586.4472

DEAN MARKLEY
3350 Scott Blvd. #45
Santa Clara CA 95054
408.988.2456
Fax: 408.988.0441
www.deanmarkley.com

DR STRINGS
7 Palisades Avenue
Emerson NJ 07630
201.599.0100
Fax: 201.599.0404
www.drstrings.com
email: DRStaff@aol.com

ELIXIR STRINGS
W. L. Gore & Associates
201 Airport Rd.
Elkton, MD 21921
888.367.5533
email: mail@goremusic.com
www.goremusic.com

ERNIE BALL
P.O. Box 4117
San Luis Obispo CA 93401
805.544.7726
Fax: 805.544.7275
www.ernieball.com

EVERLY
Everly Music Company
2305 West Victory Blvd.
Burbank, CA 91506
888.4EVERLY
www.everlymusic.com

FENDER
Fender Musical Instruments Corp.
7975 N Hayden Road
Scottsdale AZ 85258
480.596.9690
Fax: 480.596.1385
www.fender.com

GHS
G.H.S. Corporation
P.O. Box 136
2813 Wilber Avenue
Battle Creek MI 49016
800.388.4447
616.968.3351
Fax: 616.968.6913
Strings@GHStrings.com
www.ghsstrings.com

GIBSON
Gibson Strings & Accessories
A Manufacturing Division of Gibson Guitar
Corp.
1150 Bave Rd.
Elgin IL 60123
800.544.2766
Fax: 847.741.4644
www.gibson.com

JOHN PEARSE STRINGS
Breezy Ridge Instruments
P.O. Box 295
Center Valley PA 18034
610.691.3302
Fax: 610.691.3304
www.johnpearsestrings.com
jpinfo@aol.com

LABELLA
256 Broadway
Newburg NY 12550
845.562.4400
Fax: 845.562.4491
www.labella.com
bellaon@msn.com

MARI
14 W. 71st Street
New York NY 10023-4209
212.799.6781
Fax: 212.721.3932

MARTIN STRINGS
C.F.Martin & Co.
510 Sycamore Street
Nazareth PA 18064
800.633.2060
610.759.5757
info@mguitar.com
www.mguitar.com

MAXIMA
57 Crooks Avenue
Clifton NJ 07011
garpc@ix.netcom.com

PHANTOM STRINGS
80353 Qunicy Mayger Rd.
Clatskanie, OR 97016
503.728.4825
Fax: 503.728.4979
www.phantomguitars.com

SABINE
NitroStasis Strings
13301 Highway 441
Alachua FL 32615-8544
904.418.2000
Fax: 904.418.2001
sabine@sabineinc.com
www.sabineinc.com

S.I.T. STRINGS
815 S. Broadway
Akron OH 44311
330.434.8010
email: sinfositstrings@aol.com

THOMASTIK-INFELD
P.O. Box 93
Northport NY 11768
800.644.5268
www.thomastik-infeld.com
info@connollyandco.com

YAMAHA STRINGS
6600 Orangethorpe Avenue
Buena Park CA 90620
714.522.9011
Fax: 714.739.2680

LUTHER ORGANIZATIONS

Association of Stringed Instrument Artisans (ASIA)
c/o David Vinopal
P.O. Box 341
Paul Smiths, NY 12970
518-891-5379
(GUITARMAKER is the quarterly newsletter/publication of ASIA)

Guild of American Luthiers (GAL)
8222 South Park Avenue
Tacoma, WA 98408
206-472-7853
(AMERICAN LUTHIERS is the quarterly journal of GAL)

Fretted Instrument Guild of America
c/o Glen Lemmer, Editor
2344 S. Oakley Avenue
Chicago, IL 60608
(FIGA, official publication)

IDENTIFYING HOUSE BRANDS MUSICAL INSTRUMENTS

The phenomenon of large production companies producing House Brand instruments dates back to the late 1800s and early 1900s. A House Brand is defined as a trademark used by distributors, wholesalers, and retailers to represent their respective company instead of the manufacturer. These brands are found (for the most part) on budget instruments, although some models are currently sought after by players and collectors on the basis of playability, tone, or relative degree of "coolness" they project.

In the 1800s, many guitar manufacturers were located in New York and Philadelphia; by the early 1900s large guitar factories were centered in Chicago. The "Big Three" that evolved out of the early 1930s were Harmony, Kay, and Valco. Valco, producer of National and Supro instruments, produced the Airline House Brand as well as bodies and resonator parts that were sold to Harmony and Kay. However, the majority of House Brand instruments found today probably originated at either Harmony or Kay. On the East Coast, Danelectro was a large builder/supplier to Sears & Roebuck under Sears' Silvertone label (sometimes up to 85 percent of Danelectro's output).

Prior to World War II, Harmony and Kay sold straight to wholesalers like catalog houses and large distributors. In turn, these wholesalers would send their salesmen and "reps" out on the road to generate sales – no territories, no music store chains – just straight sales. Business was fierce, and companies used their own private labels to denote "their" product. House Brands were typically used as a marketing tool for distributors, wholesalers, and/or retailers to try to eliminate consumer shopping for the best price on popular makes and models of the time. How could you shop a trademark that didn't exist anywhere else? Tom Wheeler, in his book, *American Guitars*, quoted former Harmony president Charles A. Rubovits' recollection that the company built 57 private brands for the wholesalers – and sold over five million guitars.

An informative essay about House Brands and their place in the vintage guitar spectrum can be found in Stellas & Stratocasters (Vintage Guitar Books) by Willie G. Moseley, feature writer/columnist for *Vintage Guitar Magazine*. Moseley's commentary includes a listing of thirty-eight brands and their retailers/distributors, brief anecdotes about the major American manufacturers of budget instruments (Harmony, Kay, etc.) and photos of twenty-five American-made House Brand instruments.

Since writing that article, Moseley has advised the *Blue Book of Acoustic Guitars*: "I've come across a couple of other house brands in my travels; one example was a low-end, Stella-type variant with `Superior' sloppily screen-printed on its headstock. It was one of those cheap, beginner's instruments that were and still are at the nadir of American-made guitars, but so far I haven't been able to determine anything about its brand name...not that it matters too much!"

"It's my opinion, and I dare say the opinion of most vintage guitar enthusiasts, that a good rule of thumb concerning the collectibility of House Brands would be something along the lines of 'If it was a budget instrument then, it's proportionally a budget instrument now.' Regrettably, as the interest in vintage guitars continues to grow, some individuals and/or businesses tend to assume that simply because an instrument is 'old' and/or 'discontinued' and/or 'American-made', that automatically makes it a 'collector's item' and/or 'valuable.' That's certainly not the case, especially with House Brands. It's disheartening to walk into a pawn shop and see a Kay-made Silvertone archtop electric from the Sixties labeled as an 'antique' and priced at $499, when the instrument is worth no more than $100 in the vintage guitar market, and such incidents are apparently on the increase. And that's unfortunate for everybody."

The *Blue Book of Acoustic Guitars* is continuing to collect data and evaluate the collectibility and pricing on these House Brand instruments. Condition is a large factor in the pricing, as a thirty-to-forty year old guitar ordered from a catalog may have been used/abused by younger members of a household (to the detriment of the instrument). House Brand guitars may be antiques, they may be somewhat collectible, and they may be "classic pieces of Americana" (as one antique shop's sign declared), but they should still be relatively inexpensive when compared to the rest of the vintage guitar market. We believe Mr. Moseley to be correct in his C-note assessment of this aspect of the vintage market (at 80% to 90% condition); other music markets that service players and students may find pricing at a slightly wider range of $75 to $150 depending on other factors (playability, possessing an adjustable truss rod, appearance/"coolness" factor, a solid wood top versus plywood, veneer sides, additional parts, etc.) This is the bottom line: this book should help identify the brand/original company, give a few hints as to the quality and desirability, and a price range. The rest is up to you! We will continue to survey the market for pricing trends and "hot" models – further information will be included in upcoming editions of the *Blue Book of Acoustic Guitars*.

Blue Book of Acoustic Guitars

TRADEMARK INDEX

A. FULLER SOUND
2224 Coloma Street
Oakland, CA 946602
phone: 510-482-1996
warren@afullersound.com
www.afullersound.com

A.C.E. GUITARS
A division of The Poly-Tech Company
113 Crosby Rd. Unit 13
Dover, NH 03820
phone: 603-742-1160
ppak@rcn.com
www.ace-guitars.com

ABILENE
Distributed by Samick
18521 Railroad St.
City of Industry, CA 91748
phone: 626-964-4700
fax: 626-965-5224
guitars@samickmusicusa.com

ADAMAS
Distributed by Kaman Music Corp.
P.O. Box 507
Bloomfield, CT 06002
www.adamasguitars.com

ADLER CUSTOM GUITARS
P.O. Box 553
Calimesa, CA 92320
phone: 909-203-6549
www.adlerguitars.com

ALBERICO, FABRIZIO
14566 Creditview Road
Cheltenham, Ontario L0P 1C0
Canada
phone: 905-838-5016
alberico@DIRECT.CA
www.albericoguitar.com

ALLAIN, DON
366 Lakeshore Drive
Hewitt, NJ 07421
phone: 973-853-4000
fretwork@warwick.net

ALLEN GUITARS
P.O. Box 1883
Colfax, CA 95713
phone: 530-346-6590
fax: 530-346-6590
all@allenguitar.com
www.allenguitar.com

ALVAREZ
Distributed by St. Louis Music
www.alvarezgtr.com

ALVAREZ YAIRI
Distributed by St. Louis Music
www.alvarezgtr.com

AMALIO BURGUET
Distributed by Saga Music
www.sagamusic.com

AMERICAN ARCHTOP
RR#6 Box 6379B
Stroudsburg, PA 18360
phone: 570-992-4956
dale@americanarchtop.com
www.americanarchtop.com/
home.htm

AMOUR, DAVID
802 Carmen Drive Apt B
Mount Shasta, CA 96067
phone: 530-926-2208

ANDERSEN STRINGED INSTRUMENTS
7811 Greenwood Ave. N.
Seattle, WA 98103
phone: 206-782-8630
steve@AndersenGuitars.com
www.andersenguitars.com

ANDREW SACCO GUITARS
1715 Matthew Lane
Santa Cruz, CA 95062
phone: 831-566-5666
andrew@andrewsaccoguitars.com
www.andrewsaccoguitars.com

ANDREWS GUITARS
5306 Roosevelt Way NE
Seattle, WA 98105
phone: 206-295-4821
andrewsguitars@yahoo.com

ANGELLA GUITAR CO.
1644 American Beauty Drive
Oakland, CA 94609
phone: 925-680-1287
randangella@aol.com

ANTONIO KROGER GUITARS
612 Griegos Road N.W.
Albuquerque, NM 87107
phone: 505-341-3723
toniokroger@cybermesa.com

ANTONIO LORCA
Distributed by David Perry Guitar Imports
14519 Woodstar Court
Leesburg, VA 22075-6055 USA
800-593-1331
phone: 703-771-1331
fax: 703-771-8170

APPLAUSE
Distributed by Kaman Music
www.kamanmusic.com

APPLEGATE GUITARS
16615 81st Avenue North
Maple Grove, MN 55311
phone: 952-250-7063
brian@applegateguitars.com
www.applegateguitars.com

ARCHER GUITARS
Dynamic Music Distributing Inc
P.O. Box 27655
Milwaukee, WI 53227
800-343-3003
fax: 800-211-5570

ARIA
A division of N.H.F. Musical Merchandise Inc.
9244 Commerce Highway
Pennsauken, NJ 08110
800-524-0441
fax: 888-401-3051
www.ariausa.com

ART & LUTHERIE
Distributed by La Si Do, Inc.
info@artandlutherieguitars.com
www.artandlutherieguitars.com

ARTISTA
Distributed by Musicorp/MBT
Hondo Guitar Company
P. O. Box 30819
Charleston, SC 29417
800-845-1922
phone: 843-763-9083
fax: 843-763-9096

ASTURIAS
Distributed by J.T.G. of NASHVILLE
5350 Hillsboro Road
Nashville, TN 37215
phone: 615-665-8384
fax: 615-665-9468

ATTUNEABLE WOOD
27 C Jordan Street
San Rafael, CA 94901
phone: 415-458-8622

AUSTIN
A Division of St. Louis Music, Inc.
1400 Ferguson Ave.
St. Louis, MO 63133
phone: 314-727-4512
fax: 314-727-8929
www.austingtr.com

AXL
Distributed by The Music Link
www.themusiclink.net

AYERS
chris@ayersmusic.com
www.ayersmusic.com

AZOLA BASSES
P.O.Box 1519
Ramona, CA 92065 USA
phone: 760-789-8581
steve@azola.com
www.azola.com

B.C. RICH
A division of HHI
4940 Delhi Pike
Cincinnati, OH 45238
saleswest@bcrich.com
www.bcrich.com

BACORN CUSTOM GUITARS & MANDOLINS
2230 River Rd.
Nichols, NY 13812
phone: 607-699-3094
reb@clarityconnect.com
www.bacornguitars.com

BARANIK GUITARS
1300 E 8th Street #102
Tempe, AZ 85281
phone: 480-894-3448
info@baranikguitars.com
www.baranikguitars.com

BARNEY, CARL
P.O. Box 128
Southbury, CT 06488
phone: 203-264-9207
fax: 203-267-5857
barneys@wtco.net

BARTHELL, JOHN PETER
1883 Doe Run Road
Sequim, WA 98382
phone: 360-683-1665
barbnpete@msn.com
www.barthellguitars.com

BEAR CREEK GUITARS
29 Palena Place
Kula, HI 96790
877-622-8216
bcguitar@bcguitar.com
www.bcguitars.com

BEAUREGARD, MARIO
118 Yamaska Street
Denise-sur-Richelieu, Quebec J0H 1K0 Canada
phone: 450-787-2555
mariocbeauregard@videotron.ca

BELTONA
SM21691@IHUG.co.nz
www.beltona.net

BENEDETTO, ROBERT
A Division of Fender Musical Instrument Corporation
Guild Guitars
www.guildguitars.com
www.benedetto-guitars.com

BENETEAU GUITARS
109 Forest Avenue
St Thomas, Ontario N5R 2J8
Canada
phone: 519-633-6994
beneteauguitars@sympatico.ca
www.beneteauguitars.com

BERKOWITZ GUITARS
121 13th Street NE #G1
Washington, DC 20002
phone: 202-543-1806
ddb@berkowitzguitars.com
www.berkowitzguitars.com

BERTONCINI STRINGED INSTRUMENTS
3700 14th Ave S. E. #53
Olympia, WA 98501
phone: 360-491-5051
www.bertoncini.com

BEYOND THE TREES
2026 Back Ranch Raod
Santa Cruz, CA 95060
phone: 831-423-9264
wildols@beyondthetrees.com
www.beyondthetrees.com

BIG HEART
Distributed by the Big Heart Slide Company
937 Rashford Drive
Placentia , CA 92870
phone: 714-993-1573
fax: 714-579-3019
shelly@bigheartslide.com
www.bigheartslide.com

BLANCHARD GUITARS
1745 Koocanuse Estates
Eureka, MT 59917
phone: 406-889-3003
markath@eurekadsl.net
www.blanchardguitars.com

BLUERIDGE
Distributed by Saga Music
www.sagamusic.com

BOAZ ELKAYAM GUITARS
800-394-4747
rglick@fineguitarconsultants.com

BORGES GUITAR
401 Great Road A-2
Littleton, MA 01460
phone: 978-486-9077
julius.borges@verizon.net
www.borgesguitars.com

BOURGEOIS
2 Cedar Street
Lewiston, ME 04240
phone: 207-786-0385
info@pantheonguitars.com
www.pantheonguitars.com

BOZO
1817 Elmwood Drive
Lindenhurst, IL 60046
phone: 847-356-3685
fax: 847-356-6715
www.guitars.net/bozo.htm

BREEDLOVE
19885 8th Street
Tumalo, OR 97701
phone: 541-385-8339
fax: 541-385-8183
info@breedloveguitars.com
www.breedloveguitars.com

BROOKS, RICHARD ALLEN
9699 Pebble Brook Drive
Moreno Valley, CA 92557
phone: 909-247-5882

BURRELL GUITARS
1919 Madison Avenue
Huntington, WV 25704 USA
phone: 304-429-4848
billyjonesiii@burrellguitars.com
www.burrellguitars.com

BUSCARINO, JOHN
2348 Wide Horizon Drive
Franklin , NC 28734
phone: 828-349-9867
fax: 828-349-4668
John@Buscarino.com
www.buscarino.com

CA GUITARS
P.O. Box 3100
Lafayette, LA 70502
phone: 337-291-2642
fax: 337-235-1067
www.caguitars.com

C.B. ALYN GUITARWORKS
www.promediamarketing.net/cba-lyn/cbalyn.htm

CAMPELLONE, M., GUITARS
5 Mapleville Road
Smithfield, RI 02828
phone: 401-949-3716
mcgtr@att.net
www.campelloneguitars.com

CARRUTH, ALAN
51 Camel Hump Road
Newport, NH 03773
phone: 603-863-7064
akcarrytg@aol.com
www.alcarruthluthier.com

CARTER, WILLIE
294 Park Avenue
Long Beach, CA 90803
phone: 831-402-0648

CARVIN
12340 World Trade Drive
San Diego, CA 92128
phone: 858-487-1600
www.carvin.com

CASSOTTA, DAVE
4930 Pacific Street
Rocklin, CA 95677
phone: 916-624-3794
dave@sonfatherguitars.com
sonfatherguitars.com

CHAPIN
1709 Little Orchard Street Unit D
San Jose, CA 95125
phone: 408-295-6252
fax: 408-295-6252
shades@chapinguitars.com
www.chapinguitars.com

CHAPPELL GUITARS
2619 Columbia Avenue
Richmond, CA 94804
phone: 510-528-2904
fax: 510-528-8310
sean@east-bay.com

CHARLES FOX GUITARS
2745 S.W. Scenic Drive
Portland, OR 97225
phone: 503-292-2385
cfox@charlesfoxguitars.com
www.charlesfoxguitars.com

CHRIS LARKIN CUSTOM GUITARS
Castlegregory
Castlegregory, County Kerry Ireland
fax: +353 (0) 66 713 9330
chris@ChrisLarkinGuitars.com
www.chrislarkinguitars.com

CIMARRON GUITARS
538 Sherman Box 511
Ridgway, CO 81432
phone: 970-626-4464
cimgit@cimarronguitars.com
www.cimarronguitars.com

CITRON
282 Chestnut Hill Road
Woodstock, NY 12498
phone: 914-679-7138
fax: 914-679-3221
harvey@citron-guitars.com
www.citron-guitars.com

CLINESMITH INSTRUMENTS
P.O. Box 31
Redcrest, CA 95569
phone: 707-725-0600
www.clinesmithinstruments.com

COLLINGS GUTIARS
11025 Signal Hill Drive
Austin, TX 78737
phone: 512-288-7776
fax: 512-288-6045
sales@collingsguitars.com
www.collingsguitars.com

COMINS GUITARS

P.O. Box 611
Willow Grove, PA 19090
phone: 215-376-0595
20bill@cominsguitars.com
www.cominsguitars.com

CONDE HERMANOS

Distributed by Luthier Music Corporation
Calle Felipe V, 2 Corner Arrieta,3
Madrid, 28013 Spain
phone: 915470612
fax: 915590985
condehermanos@condeher-manos.com
www.condehermanos.com

COOG INSTRUMENTS

147 Sacramento Ave
Santa Cruz, CA
phone: 831-425-4933
ron@cooginstruments.com
www.coog.com

CORT

3451 W. Commercial Ave.
Northbrook, IL 60062
phone: 847-498-6491
fax: 847-498-5370
www.cort.com

COSI

phone: 33 (0)4 94 87 98 78
fax: 33 (0)4 94 06 09 15
jclagarde@cosi-lagarde.com
www.cosi-lagarde.com

CRAFTER

Distributed by HSS, A Division of Hohner
1000 Technology Park Drive
Glen Allen, VA 223059-4500
phone: 804-515-1900
fax: 804-515-0347
info@crafterguitars.com
www.crafterguitars.com

CRAFTERS OF TENNESSEE

14919 Lebanon Rd
Old Hickory, TN 37138
888-773-7311
phone: 615-773-7200
fax: 615-773-7201
charlie@crafterstn.com
www.crafterstn.com

CROUCH STRINGED INSTRUMENTS

4539 Market Road
Mechanicsville, VA 23111
phone: 804-781-0812
guitarjwc@comcast.net

CUMPIANO, WILLIAM R.

8 Easthampton Road PO Box 854
Northampton, MA 01027
phone: 413-586-3730
william@cumpiano.com
www.cumpiano.com

CURBOW

PO Box 309 24 Allen Lane
Morganton, GA 30560
phone: 706-374-2873
fax: 706-374-2530
greg@curbow.com
www.curbow.com

D.C. HILDER BUILDER

2 Yorkshire Street N.
Guelph, Ontario N1H 5A5 Canada
phone: 519 821-6030
fax: 519 837-2268

D'ANGELICO

P.O. Box 627
Westfield, NJ 07090
phone: 732-380-0995
fax: 732-380-1303
dangelicoguitars@aol.com
www.dangelicoguitars.com

D'ANGELICO

1-18-6 Wakabayashi
Tokyo, Setagaya-ku 154-0023
Japan
phone: 81-3-3412-7011
fax: 81-3-3412-7013
info@vestax.co.jp
www.dangelicoguitars.com

D'ANGELICO REPLICA

Working Musician
1760 Claridge Street
Arcadia, CA 91006
phone: 626-355-5554

DAISY ROCK

Distributed by Alfred Publishing
16320 Roscoe Blvd Ste #100
Van Nuys, CA 91410-0003
877-693-2479
fax: 800-632-1928
info@daisyrock.com
www.daisyrock.com

DALACK, TED

8940 Bay Drive
Gainesville, GA 30506
phone: 770-889-1104

DANA BOURGEOIS GUITARS

2 Cedar Street
Lewiston, ME 04240
phone: 207-786-0385
fax: 207-786-2104
dana@danabourgeois.com

DAVID DAILY GUITARS

phone: 775-359-6370
fax: 775-359-2047

DAVID HAXTON GUITARS

5321 S Grattan Street
Seattle, WA 98118
phone: 206-723-9328
david@davidhaxtonguitars.com
www.davidhaxtonguitars.com

DAVIS, J. THOMAS

fax: 614-447-0174
www.jthomasdavis.com

DAVIS, WILLIAM

57 Main Street
Boxford, MA 01921
phone: 508-887-0282
fax: 508-887-7214

DE JONGE GUITAR COMPANY

883 Robson Street
Oshawa, Ontario L1H 4C6 Canada
phone: 905-576-2255
info@dejongeguitars.com
www.dejongeguitars.com

DE JONGE, JOSHIA

500 Rue Villeray
Montreal, Quebec H2R 1H4
Canada
phone: 514-271-8238
info@joshiadejonge.com
www.joshiadejonge.com

DEAN

15251 Roosevelt Blvd. Suite 206
Clearwater, FL 33760
phone: 727-519-9669
www.deanguitars.com

DECAVA

369 Nichols Ave.
Stratford, CT 06614
phone: 203-377-0096
fax: 203-377-0096
Admin@decava.com
www.decava.com

DEERING BANJO COMPANY

3733 Kenora Drive
Spring Valley, CA 91977-1829
phone: 619-464-8252
fax: 619-464-0833
info@deeringbanjos.com
www.deeringbanjos.com

DELL' ARTE INSTRUMENTS

10050 Prospect Avenue Suite P
Santee, CA 92071
phone: 619-596-7739
fax: 619-698-2237
www.dellarteinstruments.com

DICARLO, R.J.

Classical Guitar Maker
141 Roosevelt Avenue
Massapequa Park, NY 11762
phone: 516-795-3941

DILLON GUITARS

phone: 570-784-7552
artranch@aol.com
www.artranch.net/dillonguitars/
dg.html

DINOSAUR

21088 Commerce Pointe Drive
Walnut, CA 91789
phone: 909-468-1382
fax: 909-468-1652
info@eleca.com
www.dinosauramps.com

DOBRO

A Division of Gibson
www.gibson.com/products/oai

DOMINIC'S MUSIC

fax: 978-525-2916
www.dominicsmusic.com

DRAGONY, JOE

P.O. Box 2177
Carmichael, CA 95609
phone: 916-482-5060
dragony@pacbell.net

DREAM GUITARS

P.O. Box 323
Perrineville, NJ 08535
phone: 609-208-1531
fax: 609-208-1953
paul@dreamguitars.com
www.dreamguitars.com

DUNN, MICHAEL

708 3rd Ave.
New Westminster, British Columbia
V3M 1N7 Canada
phone: 604-524-1943
guitarbuilder@telus.net
www.michaeldunnguitars.com

DUNWELL GUITAR

1891 CR 68-J Magnolia Star Route
Nederland, CO 80466
phone: 303-939-8870
alan@dunwellguitar.com
dunwellguitar.com

DURANGO

Distributed by Saga Music
www.sagamusic.com

EDWARD ALAN MORENO MOORE

Av. Los Leones 2900
Nunoa, Santiago Chile
phone: 56-2-225-24-98
fax: 56-2-225-24-98
rmorenom@ctcreuna.cl

EDWINSON GUITARS

5306 Roosevelt Way N.E.
Seattle, WA 98105
phone: 206-729-6745
edwinsongtr@yahoo.com

EGGLE, PATRICK JAMES

sales@patrickeggleguitars.com
www.patrickeggleguitars.com

EHLERS GUITARS

35003 Washburn Heights Drive
Brownsville, OR 97327
phone: 541-466-3355
www.buffalobros.com

EICHELBAUM CUSTOM GUITARS

304 South Blanch Street
Ojai, CA 93023
800-451-9811
david@eichelbaumguitars.com
www.eichelbaumguitars.com

EISELE

923 Mokapu Blvd.
Kailua, HI 96734
phone: 808-254-6679
eiselegtr@aol.com

ELLIOT, JEFFREY R.

2812 S. E. 37th Ave.
Portland, Oregon 97202
phone: 503-233-0836
jeff@elliotguitars.com

EMERALD

Cavanacaw St. Johnston Co.
Donegal, Ireland
phone: 353 74 48019
fax: 353 74 48070
emeraldguitars@yahoo.com
www.emeraldguitars.com

ENCORE

Distributed by John Hornby Skewes
& Co. Ltd.
Salem House Parkinson Approach
Garforth
Leeds , Leeds United Kingdom
phone: (+44) (0) 113 286 5381
fax: (+44) (0) 113 286 8515
webinfo@jhs.co.uk
www.jhs.co.uk

ESTEVE

Distributed by Fernandez Music
Box 5153
Irvine, CA 92616
phone: 949-856-1537
fax: 949-856-1529
ron@fernandezmusic.com
www.fernandezmusic.com

EUPHONON COMPANY

P.O. Box 100
Orford, NH 03777
888-517-4678
phone: 603-353-4882

EVERETT, KENT

2338 Johnson Ferry Road
Atlanta, GA 30341
phone: 770-454-6618
everett@mindspring.com
www.everettguitars.com

EVERGREE MOUNTAIN INSTRUMENTS

1608 Jasper
Cove, OR 97824
phone: 541-568-4687
emi@eoni.com
www.eoni.com/~emi

EVERGREEN MOUNTAIN INSTRUMENTS

1608 Jasper
Cove, OR 97824
phone: 541-568-4687
emi@eoni.com
www.eoni.com/~emi

FENDER

Fender Musical Instrument Corporation
8860 Chapparal Road Suite 100
Scottsdale, AZ 85250-2618
phone: 480-596-9690
fax: 480-367-5262
custserv@fenderusa.com
www.fender.com

FERNANDES

www.fernandesguitars.com

FERRINGTON, DANNY

P.O. Box 923
Pacific Palisades, CA 90272
phone: 310-454-0692

FINOCCHIO GUITAR WORKS

20 South Maple Street
Easton, PA 18042
phone: 610-258-5154
www.finocchioguitar.com

FITZPATRICK JAZZ GUITARS GUITARS

54 Enfield Avenue
Wickford, RI 02852
phone: 401-294-4801

FLANDERS CUSTOM GUITARS

520 Hawkins Ave.
Lake Ronkonkoma, NY 11779
phone: 516-588-4167

FLEISHMAN

guitars@fleishmaninstruments.com
www.fleishmaninstruments.com

FLETCHER BROCK STRINGED INSTRUMENTS

1417 Boat Street
Seattle, WA 98105
phone: 206-547-2279
tofletcher@yahoo.com

FLORES, RUBEN

USA Distributor
P.O. Box 2746
Seal Beach, CA 90740
phone: 562-598-9800
fax: 562-598-2459
rubenflores@msn.com
www.rubenflores.com

FOLEY GUITARS

221 Brighton Road. P.O. Box 646
Andover, NJ 07821
phone: 973-786-6077
fax: 973-786-5627

FONTANILLA, ALAN

P.O. Box 31423
San Francisco, CA 94131
phone: 415-642-9375

FORBIDDEN FRUIT GUITARS

32 Locke Street
Cambridge, MA 02140
phone: 617-661-3086
pnorman@forbiddenguitars.com
www.forbiddenguitars.com

FROGGY BOTTOM GUITARS

198 Timson Hill Road
Newfance, VT 05345
phone: 802-348-6665
fax: 802-348-7445
froggy@sover.net
www.froggybottomguitars.com

GALLAGHER GUITARS

P.O. Box 128
Wartace, TN 37183
phone: 931-389-6455
fax: 931-389-6455
dong@cafes.net
www.gallagherguitar.com

GALLOUP, BRYAN

10804 Northland Drive
Big Rapids, MI 49307
phone: 231-796-5611
bryan@galloupguitars.com
www.galloupguitars.com

GARCIA GUITARS

9432 Feickert Drive
Elk Grove, CA 95624
phone: 916-714-7625
gary@garciaguitars.com
www.garciaguitars.com

GARRISON GUITARS

P.O. Box 13096
St. John's, Newfoundland A1N 3V8
Canada
phone: 709-745-6677
fax: 709-745-6688
info@garrisonguitars.com
www.garrisonguitars.com

GENEVA INTERNATIONAL CORPORATION

29 E. Hintz Road
Wheeling, IL 60090
800-533-2388
phone: 847-520-9970
fax: 847-520-9593
geneva-intl@msn.com

GIBSON

Gibson Musical Instruments
1818 Elm Hill Pike
Nashville, TN 37210-3781
800-846-4376
phone: 615-871-4500
fax: 615-889-5509
www.gibson.com

Gibson Montana
1894 Orville Way
Bozeman, MT 59718
phone: 406-587-4117
fax: 406-587-9109
www.gibson.com/acoustics

GILBERT GUITARS, JOHN AND BILL
phone: 805-239-9080
wgilbert@surfari.net
www.wgilbertguitars.freehomepage.com

GILCHRIST, STEPHEN
Distributed by Carmel Music
P.O. Box 2296
Carmel, CA 93921
phone: 831-624-8078
fax: 831-624-2066
info@carmelmusic.com
www.carmelmusic.com

GIRDIS, ROBERT
8745 Evanston Ave. N.
Seattle, WA 98103
phone: 206-781-2427
www.cybozone.com/fg/girdis.html

GODIN
19420 Avenue Clark-Graham
Baie D Urfe, Quebec H9X 3R8
info@godinguitars.com
www.godinguitars.com

GONSTEAD GUITARS
333-B County Road 550
Marquette, MI 49855
phone: 906-345-0149
sven@lighthouse.net
www.gonsteadguitars.com

GOODALL
P.O. Box 3542
Kailua-Kona, HI 96745-3542
phone: 808-329-8237
fax: 808-329-2708
contact@goodallguitars.com
www.goodallguitars.com

GRACIA GUITARS
Lincoln 32 1875 Wilde
Pcia de Buenos Aires, Argentina
gracia@guitarfcagracia.com.ar

GRAF, OSKAR
Box 2502
Clarendon, Ontario K0H 1J0 Canada
phone: 613-279-2610
grafco@frontenac.net
web.ctsolutions.com/grafguitars

GRAND
info@grandintl.com

GRAZIANO, TONY
www.grazianoukuleles.com

GREEN MOUNTAIN GUITARS
39 Saddleback Road
Bradford, VT 05033
phone: 802-222-9012
wderusha@mail.greenmountainguitar.com
www.greenmountainguitar.com

GREENFIELD, MICHAEL
3899 St-Dominique
Montreal, Quebec H2W 2A2 Canada
phone: 514-499-1352
fax: 514-499-1793
mike@greenfieldguitars.com
www.greenfieldguitars.com

GRETSCH
A division of Fender
8860 East Chaparral Road Suite 100
Scottsdale, AZ 85250
www.gretschguitars.com

GREVEN GUITARS
1906 SE 42nd Ave
Portland, OR 97215
phone: 503-233-8525
fax: 503-233-8525
grevenguitars@msn.com
www.grevenguitars.com

GRIMES GUITARS
1520 Kamehameiki
Kula, HI 96790
phone: 808-878-2076
fax: 808-878-2076
www.grimesguitars.com

GROVES CUSTOM GUITARS
ggroves100@earthlink.net
home.earthlink.net/~ggroves100

GUILD
A Division of Fender Musical Instruments Corporation
www.guildguitars.com

GUITAR FACTORY
2816 Edgewater Drive
Orlando, FL 32804
800-541-1070
phone: 407-425-1070
fax: 407-425-7276

GUITAR SALON INTERNATIONAL
3100 Donald Douglas Loop
Santa Monica, CA 90405
phone: 310-399-2181
fax: 310-396-9283
www.guitarsalon.com

GUITARRAS ALMANSA
Distributed by Ruben Flores
P.O. Box 2746
Seal Beach, CA 90740
phone: 562-598-9800
fax: 562-598-2459
ruben_flores@msn.com
www.rubenflores.com

GUITARRAS LA ESPANOLA
prol. 20 de noviembre no 1513
Parache, Michoacan 60250 Mexico
phone: 423-52-5-10-30
fax: 423-52-5-01-52
guitespa@compusep.com

HAMBLIN GUITARS
P.O. Box 3584
Telluride, CO 81435
phone: 970-708-1741
khamblin@aol.com

HANNAH
hannahguitars@hotmail.com

HEIDEN, MICHAEL
7285 Hinkley Road
Chilliwac, British Columbia V2P
6H3 Canada
phone: 604-794-7261
mheiden@uniserve.com
www.users.uniserve.com/~mheiden

HEMKEN, MICHAEL
1121 Zygmunt Drive
Saint Helena, CA 94574
phone: 707-963-8256
hemken@comcast.com

HEWETT GUITARS
22430 Gail Street
New Caney, TX 77357
phone: 281-354-7894
guitar@wt.net
www.hewettguitars.com

HILL GUITAR COMPANY
5905 Highway 9
Felton, CA 95018
800-262-8858
phone: 831-335-0442
fax: 831-335-3602
khill@hillguitar.com
www.hillguitar.com

HILL, DENNIS
Leitz Music Inc
508 Harrison Avenue
Panama City, FL 32401
phone: 850-769-0111
fax: 850-785-1779

HOFFMAN GUITARS
2219 East Franklin Ave.
Minneapolis, MN 55404
phone: 612-338-1079
choffman@hoffmanguitars.com
www.hoffmanguitars.com

HOFNER
Distributed by The Music Group
10949 Pendleton Street
Sun Valley, CA 91352
phone: 818-252-6305
fax: 818-252-6351
rob.olsen@musicgroup.com
www.musicgroup.com

HOHNER
Distributed by HSS
P.O. Box 15035
Richmond, VA 23227
800-446-6010
info@hohnerusa.com
www.hohnerusa.com

HOLLENBECK, BILL
160 Half Moon Street
Lincoln, IL 62656
phone: 217-732-6933
hollenbeckguitar@yahoo.com
members.cox.net/kwakefield1/hollenbeck/index.html

HOLST, STEPHEN
82722 Bear Creek Road
Creswell, OR 97426
phone: 541-895-2362
sholst@pacinfo.com
www.pacinfo.com/~sholst/index.htm

HONDO GUITAR COMPANY
Distributed by Musicorp/MBT
P.O. Box 30819
Charleston, SC 29417
800-845-1922
phone: 843-763-9083
fax: 843-763-9096
hondoguitars.com

HOPF, DIETER
Distributed by Luthier Music Corporation
341 West 44th Street
New York, NY 10036
phone: 212-397-6038
fax: 212-397-6048
guitar@luthiermusic.com
www.luthiermusic.com

HONDO
Distributed by MBT International
P.O. Box 30819
Charleston, SC 29417
800-641-6931
phone: 843-763-9083
fax: 843-763-9096
sales@mbtinternational.com
www.hondoguitars.com

HOPKINS GUITARS
97 Grandview Street
Penticton, British Columbia V2A
4E5 Canada
phone: 250-493-4318
peter@hopkinsguitars.com
www.hopkinsguitars.com

HOYER
Distributed in Germany by Fa.
Mario Pellarin
phone: 02234 16011
fax: 02234 14042
info@hoyer-guitars.com
www.hoyer-guitars.com

HUIPE, BENITO
Distributed by Casa Talamantes
2424 Candelaria Road NE
Albuquerque, NM 87107
phone: 505-265-2977
casatalamt@aol.com
www.casatalamantes.com/guitar.htm

HUSS & DALTON
420 Bridge Street
Staunton, VA 24401
phone: 540-887-2313
fax: 540-887-2383
hdguitar@cfw.com
www.hussanddalton.com

HUVARD, ANTHONY J.
P.O. Box 130
Sandston, VA 23150
gitarmkr@cybozone.com
www.cybozone.com/luthier

IBANEZ
Distributed by Hoshino, Inc.
1726 Winchester Road
Bensalem, PA 19020
800-669-4226
phone: 215-638-8670
fax: 215-245-8583
www.ibanez.com

ITHACA GUITAR WORKS
215 North Cayuga Street Dewitt
Mall
Ithaca, NY 14850
888-202-5004
phone: 607-272-2602
fax: 607-272-6241
chris@guitarworks.com
www.guitarworks.com

ITHACA STRINGED INSTRUMENTS

6115 Mount Road
Trumansburg, NY 14886
phone: 607-387-3544
fax: 607-387-3544
luthiers@ithacastring.com
www.ithacastring.com

J. RAMSAY FINE GUITARS

2060 Chicago Avenue #C-9
Riverside, CA 92507
phone: 909-784-4040
jbramsay@jramsayfineguitars.com
www.jramsayfineguitars.com

J.B. PLAYER

Distributed by MBT International
P.O. Box 30819
Charleston, SC 29417
800-641-6931
phone: 843-763-9083
fax: 843-763-9096
sales@mbtinternational.com
www.jbplayer.com

J.S. BOGDANOVICH GUITARS

P.O. Box 293 32100 Middle Ridge Road
Albion, CA 95410
phone: 707-937-1855
jsb@mcn.com
www.jsbguitars.com

JACKSON, DOUGLAS R.

175 Stahlman Ave.
Destin, FL 32541
phone: 850-654-1048
fax: 850-654-1048
drjguitars@juno.com

JASMINE

Distributed by Kaman Music
P.O. Box 507
Bloomfield, CT 06002-0507
800-647-2244
phone: 860-243-7105
fax: 860-243-7287
info@kamanmusic.com
www.kamanmusic.com

JENKINS, CHRIS

829 Kingston Drive
Mansfield, TX 76063
phone: 817-472-0404
jcj@cjenkinsluthier.com
www.cjenkinsluthier.com

JISHENG

RM 111 Building 41
Taoyuanst Xihu Rd
Guangzhou, P.R. China
phone: 0086-20-81840008
fax: 0086-20-81845765
gzjsheng@public.guangzhou.gd.cn

JOHNSON

Distributed by The Music Link
P.O. Box 162
Brisbane, CA 94005
1-888-552-5465
phone: 650-615-8991
fax: 650-615-8997
feedback@themusiclink.net
www.themusiclink.com

JON KAMMERER GUITARS

222 Timea Street
Keokuk, IA 52632
phone: 319-526-7651
fax: 319-526-7649
jon@jonkammererguitars.com
www.jonkammererguitars.com

JOSEPH BANDY GUITARS

516 52nd Street
Oakland, CA 94609
phone: 510-652-5123
josephbandy@earthlink.net

JOSHUA GUITARS

phone: 909-464-2304

K&S GUITARS INC

2923 Adeline Street
Berkeley, CA 94703
phone: 510-644-1958
fax: 510-644-1958
bmiex@global.california.com

KAKOS, STEPHEN

1720 Finch Lane
Mound, MN 55364
phone: 952-472-4732
kakosg@aol.com

KALIL

132 S. Front Street
McComb, MS 39648
phone: 601-249-3894
edekalil@aol.com
members.aol.com/edekalil/kalil.html

KATHY WINGERT GUITARS

28364 S. Western Ave. #451
Rancho Palos Verdes, CA 90275
phone: 310-522-9596
kathy@wingertguitars.com
www.kathywingertguitars.com

KAUFFMAN LUTHERIE

phone: 925-283-6520
www.kauffmanguitars.com

KAY

Distributed by A.R. Musical Enterprises, Inc.
9031 Technology Drive
Fishers, IN 46038
800-428-4807
phone: 317-577-6999
fax: 800-933-8207
Info@armusical.com
www.armusical.com

KELLER, MICHAEL L.

2207 30th Avenue S.E.
Rochester, MN 55904
phone: 507-288-9226
michael@kellerguitar.com
www.kellerguitar.com

KEN BEBENSEE GUITARS AND BASSES

18001 Salmon Mine Rd.
Nevada City, CA 95959
phone: 530-292-0156
ken@kbguitars.com
www.kbguitars.com

KEVIN RYAN GUITARS

14082 Willow Lane
Westminster, CA 92683
phone: 800-311-1527
ryanguitar@aol.com
www.ryanguitars.com

KHONO

5-27-20 Nishi-ikebukuro Toshima-ku
Tokyo, Japan
msakurai@kohno-guitar.com
www.kohno-guitar.com/kohno.html

KIMBARA

Distributed by FCN Music
Melody House Wealden Business Park
Farningham Road
Crowborough, E Sussex TN6 2JJ
England
phone: 01892 603730
fax: 01892 613220
purchasing@fcnmusic.co.uk
www.fcnmusic.co.uk

KIMBERLY

Distributed by Kimex Trading
www.kimextrading.co.kr

KINSCHERFF

500 Deer Lake Road
Wimberley, TX 78676
phone: 512-842-3232
jamie@kinscherff.com
www.kinscherff.com

KIRKPATRICK GUITAR STUDIO

4607 Maple Avenue
Baltimore, MD 21227-4023
phone: 410-242-2744
fax: 410-242-0326
info@guitar1stop.com

KISO

P.O. Box 13
Glen Ellen, CA 95442
phone: 707-996-1333
fax: 707-996-1333
mark@goeninternational.com
www.kisoguitars.com

KLEIN, STEVE

521 Broadway
Sonoma, CA 95476
phone: 877-455-3467
steve@kleinguitars.com
www.kleinguitars.com

KNUSTON LUTHIERY

P.O. Box 945
Forestville, CA 95436
phone: 707-887-2709
john@knutsonluthiery.com
www.knutsonluthiery.com

KONA

Distributed by M&M Merchandisers
1923 Bomar Ave.
Ft. Worth, TX 76103
800-687-0203
phone: 817-339-1400
fax: 817-335-2314
www.mmwholesale.com

KRAMER

Distributed by MusicYo.com
Fursdon Moreton
Hampstead
Devon, TQ13 8QT England
phone: 44-647-70394
www.musicyo.com

KREMONA

Distributed by Kremona U.S.A. Inc.
330 Detroit Ave. Suite D
Monroe, MI 48162
phone: 734-243-2903
fax: 734-243-1050

LTD

Distributed by ESP Guitar Company
www.espguitars.com

LA MANCHA

Distributed by La Mancha Guitars
of Nashville, TN
P.O. Box 40223
Nashville, TN 37204
phone: 615-269-3929
fax: 615-832-4010
jroberts@lamancha.com
www.lamancha.com

LACEY GUITARS

P.O. Box 24646
Nashville, TN 37202
phone: 615-952-3045
mark@laceyguitars
www.laceyguitars.com

LAKEWOOD GUITARS

Distributed by Dana B. Goods
35394 Giessen
Zum Bahnhopf 6a, Germany
phone: 0641-43088
fax: 0641-491398
www.lakewoodguitars.com

LakeWood Guitars North American Representative:
Bill Dixon
P.O. Box 552
Booth Bay Harbor, ME 04538
bigartdog@aol.com

LANDOLA

Audiosal Oy Ab Pännäistentie 141
PIETARSAARI, FIN-68600 Finland
phone: +358 (0)6-723-0407
fax: +358 (0)6-723-4564
landola@landola.fi
www.landola.fi

LANGEJANS GUITARS

23 East 8th Street
Holland, MI 49423
phone: 616-396-4597
info@langejansguitars.com
www.langejansguitars.com

LARK IN THE MORNING

P.O. Box 799
Fort Bragg, CA 95437
phone: 707-964-5569
fax: 707-964-1979
larkinam@larkinam.com

LARRIVEE

Factory
780 E. Cordova Street
Vacouver, BC V6A 1M3 Canada
phone: 604-253-7111
fax: 604-253-5447
info@larrivee.com
www.larrivee.com

Larrivee U.S. Distribution
1070 Yarnell Place
Oxnard, CA 93033
phone: 805-487-9980
info@larrivee.com
www.larrivee.com

LASKIN, GRIT (WILLIAM)

26 Noble Street No. 12
Toronto, Ontario M6K 2C9 Canada
phone: 416-536-2135
fax: 416-533-8705
grit@interlog.com
www.williamlaskin.com

LAURIE WILLIAMS GUITARS

Goshen valley Road P.O. Box 130
Mangonui, Far North 0557 New Zealand
phone: 649-405-0559
williams@guitars.co.nz
www.guitars.co.nz

LEACH, H.G.

P.O. Box 1315
Cedar Ridge, CA 95924
phone: 530-477-2938
leagit@netshel.net
www.leachguitars.com

LEHMANN STRINGED INSTRUMENTS

34 Elton Street
Rochester, NY 14607
phone: 585-461-2117
bernie@lehmannstrings.com
www.lehmannstrings.com

LEWIS, MICHAEL A.

20807 E. Spring Ranches Rd.
Grass Valley, CA 95949
phone: 530-272-4124
fax: 818-355-5554
malewis@nccn.net
www.svlg.org/member/lewis/default.htm

LIIKANEN

Kirvesmiehenkatu 10B
Helsinki, 00880 Finland
phone: +358-9-7554642
fax: +358-9-72732801
uwe.florath@liikanenguitars.com
www.liikanenguitars.com

LONE STAR

Distributed by LPD Music International
32575 Industrial Drive
Madison Heights, MI 48071
800-527-5292
phone: 248-585-9630
fax: 248-585-7360
mail@lpdmusic.com
www.lonestarguitars.com

LOPRINZI, AUGUSTINO

1929 Drew Street
Clearwater, FL 33765
phone: 727-447-2276
fax: 727-446-7704
loprinzi@gate.net
www.augustinoloprinzi.com

LORCA, ANTONIO

Distributed by David Perry Guitar Imports
P.O. Box 188
Leesburg, VA 20175
800-593-1331
fax: 703-771-8170
dperry@dpguitars.com
www.dpguitars.com

LOS GATOS

359 Village Lane
Los Gatos, CA 95030 USA
phone: 408-395-4770
jim@lggg.com
www.lggg.com

LOWDEN

8 Glenford Way
Newtownards, BT23 4BX United Kingdom
phone: +44 (0) 28 9182 0542
fax: +44 (0) 28 9182 0650
info@lowdenguitars.com
www.lowdenguitars.com

Lowden U.S.A.
14950 F.A.A Boulevard
Fort Worth, TX 76155
1-800-872-5856
fax: 817-685-5699
info@lowdenguitars.com
www.lowdenguitars.com

LUCIDA

Distributed by The Music Link
www.themusiclink.net

LUTHIER

Distributed by Luthier Music Corporation
341 West 44th Street
New York, NY 10036
phone: 212-397-6038
fax: 212-693-6048
support@luthiermusic.com
www.luthiermusic.com

LUTHIER MUSIC CORP.

341 West 44th Street
New York, NY 10036 USA
phone: 212-397-6038/39
fax: 212-397-6048
guitar@luthiermusic.com
www.luthiermusic.com

LYON, G.W.

Distributed by Washburn International
255 Corporate Woods Parkway
Vernon Hills, IL 60061-3109
800-US-SOUND
phone: 708-913-5511
fax: 708-913-7772
jhawk103@aol.com
www.washburn.com

MCALISTER GUITARS

40 Eucalyptus Drive
Watsonville, CA 95076
phone: 831-761-8393
mcaguitars@aol.com
www.mcalisterguitars.com

MCCOLLUM GUITARS

P.O. Box 806
Colfax, CA 95713
phone: 530-346-7657
mccollum@mccollumguitars.com
www.mccollumguitars.com

MCCURDY, RIC

19 Hudson St.
New York, NY 10013
phone: 212-274-8352
fax: 212-274-8352
info@mccurdyguitars.com
www.mccurdyguitars.com

MCELROY GUITARS
2315 Western Ave #310
Seattle, WA 98121
phone: 206-728-9055
brent@mcelroyguitars.com
mcelroyguitars.com

MCGILL GUITARS
808 Kendall Drive
Nashville, TN 37209
phone: 615-385-9071
fax: 615-352-9876
conecaster@AOL.com

MCHUGH GUITARS
P.O. Box 2216
Northbrook, IL 60065-2216
phone: 847-498-3319

MCNALLY
Box 387
Hibernia , NJ 07842
800-397-6563
fax: 973-625-7794
mcnallyinstruments@strum-
stick.com
www.strumstick.com

MCSPADDEN, ANDREW
440 East Street
Healdsburg, CA 95448
phone: 530-346-7657
mccollum@mccollumguitars.com

M.A. BASHKIN GUITARS
1404 Olive Court
Fort Collins, CO 80524
phone: 970-495-1011
michaelbashkin@hotmail.com
www.bashkinguitars.com

MAC YASUDA GUITARS
Masterbilt Guitar Company
17971 Skypark Circle Suite L
Irvine, CA 92614
phone: 949-474-6020
fax: 949-474-7571

MACDONALD, S.B. CUSTOM INSTRUMENTS
22 Fairmont Street
Huntington, NY 11743
phone: 631-421-9056
guitardoc@customguitars.com
customguitars.com

MAIZE, DAVE
P.O. Box 2129
Cave Junction, OR 97523
phone: 541-592-6217
dave@maizeguitars.com
www.maizeguitars.com

MANEA CUSTOM GUITARS
PO Box 140166
Nashville, TN 37214-0166
877-MANEA13
phone: 615-883-0399
fax: 615-391-0893

MANSON
Andy Manson
The Ark 18 High Street
Crediton, Devon EX17 3AH
England
phone: +44 (0) 1363 773119
fax: +44 (0) 1363 773119
andy@andymanson.fsnet.co.uk
www.andymanson.co.uk

Hugh Manson
phone: 01363 775603
hugh@mansons.co.uk
www.andymanson.co.uk

Manson's Guitar Shop
39 New Bridge Street
Exeter, Devon EX4 3AH England
phone: 01392 496379
fax: 01392 496335
sales@mansons.co.uk
www.andymanson.co.uk

MANUEL RODRIGUEZ AND SONS, S.L.
Distributed by Fender
manuel.jr@guitars-m-r-sons.com
www.guitars-m-r-sons.com

MANZANITA GUITARS
Sellenfried 3 D-37124
Rosdorf, Germany
phone: +49-551-782417
fax: +49-551-782417
info@manzanita.de
www.manzanita.de

MANZER GUITARS
65 Metcalfe Street
Toronto, Ontario M4X 1R9 Canada
phone: 416-927-1539
fax: 416-927-8233
linda@manzer.com
www.manzer.com

MAPSON, JAMES L.
3230 South Susan Street
Santa Ana, CA 92704
phone: 714-754-6566
j.mapson@mapsoneng.com
www.mapsonguitars.com

MARCHIONE
Houston, TX
phone: 713 522 7221
guitar@angel.net
www.marchione.com

MARTIN
C.F. Martin & Co. Inc.
510 Sycamore Street
P.O. Box 329
Nazareth, PA 18064-0329
phone: 610-759-2837
fax: 610-759-5757
www.mguitar.com
info@martinguitar.com

MASTER
info@master-guitars.com
www.master-guitars.com

MATON
6 Clarice Road Box Hill
Victoria, 3128 Australia
phone: 61 3 9896 9500
fax: 61 3 9896 9501
sales@maton.com.au
www.maton.com.au

MATSUDA, MICHIHIRO
2240 Filbert Street Suite C
Oakland, CA 94607
phone: 510-839-0224
matsudaguitars@yahoo.com

MAUEL GUITARS
77 Sylvan Vista Drive
Auburn, CA 95603
phone: 530-885-1265
www.mauelguitars.com

MAXINE
Distributed by the Eternal Musical
Instrument Corp. Ltd.
xsma@embmusic.com
www.embmusic.com

MAXTONE
Distributed by the Renner Piano
Company
No.1 Sophia Road #01-09/10
Peace Centre, Singapore
phone: +65 3370216
fax: +65 3368396
support@renner.com.sg
www.renner.com.sg

MEDEA CORPORATION
fax: 386-672-9214
www.floridafolkmusic.org

MEGAS, TED
601 NE South Shore Road
Portland, OR 97211
phone: 503-289-8788
fax: 503-289-8789
ted@megasguitars.com
www.megasguitars.com

MELLO, JOHN F.
437 Colusa Ave.
Kensington, CA 94707
phone: 510-528-1080
fax: 510-528-1080
jfm@lmi.net
www.johnfmello.com

MELO GUITARS
Distributed by Golden Age Guitars
Pare Sallares 79-81
Sabadell, 08201 Spain
phone: 93 725 03 97
fax: 34 93 725 03 97
josepmelo@cataloniamail.com
www.goldenageguitars.com

Melo Guitars U.S. Distribution
Distributed by Golden Age Guitars
720 Monroe Street Suite E209
Hoboken, NJ 07030
phone: 201-798-1300
fax: 201-798-1326
info@goldenageguitars.com
www.goldenageguitars.com

MELOBAR
Distributed by Smith Family Music
Products
9175 Butte Road
Sweet, ID 83670
800-942-6509
phone: 208-584-3349
fax: 208-584-3312
enhancr@micron.net

MENKEVICH GUITARS
624 Stetson Road
Elkins Park, PA 19027
phone: 215-635-0694
fax: 215-635-0694
michael@menkevich.com
www.menkevich.com

MERMER
P.O. Box 782132
Sebastian, FL 32978
phone: 772-388-0317
mermer@mermerguitars.com
www.mermerguitars.com

MERRILL CUSTOM SHOP
phone: 253-973-8177

MICHAEL DOLAN CUSTOM GUITARS
3222 Airway Drive #4
Santa Rosa, CA 95403
phone: 707-575-0654
mndolan@aol.com
www.dolanguitars.com

MICHAEL KNEPP GUITARS
518 Ninth Street
Davis, CA 95616
phone: 530-758-9783
yukonmike@earthlink.net

MICHELETTI GUITAR CO.
19590 Shafer Ranch Road
Willits, CA 95490
phone: 707-459-0820
rick@michelettiguitars.com
www.michelettiguitars.com

MIDCO INTERNATIONAL
908 W. Fayette Avenue
Effingham, IL 62401
800-356-4326
phone: 800-35-MIDCO
fax: 800-700-7006

MIRANDA GUITARS
P.O. Box 175
Los Altos, CA 94023
phone: 650-948-9454
psgreen@miranda-tech.com
www.miranda-tech.com

MITCHELL, BILL GUITARS
phone: 732-681-3430
www.billmitchell.com

MOLL CUSTOM INSTRUMENTS
2304 E. Cardinal
Springfield, MO 65804
1-877-838-7348
mollinst@earthlink.net
www.mollinst.com

MONTALVO
Distributed by Berkeley Music
2923 Adeline St
Berkeley, CA 94703
866-548-7538
bmie@berkeleymusic.com
www.berkeleymusic.com

MONTELONE, JOHN
P.O. Box 52
Islip, NY 11751
phone: 631-277-3620
john@monteleone.net
www.monteleone.net

MOON GUITARS LTD.
974 Pollokshaws Road
Glasgow, G41 2HA Scotland
phone: 0044(0)141 632 9526
fax: 0044(0)141 632 4928
moonguitars@btinternet.com
www.moonguitars.co.uk

MOONSTONE
P.O. Box 757
Eureka, CA 95502
phone: 707-445-9045
steve@moonstoneguitars.com
www.moonstoneguitars.com

MORGAN
3007 Plymouth Drive
Vancouver, BC V7H 1C6 Canada
phone: 604-929-0292
fax: 604-929-5517
info@morganguitars.com
www.morganguitars.com

MORRELL, JOE
2306 West State Street
Bristol, TN 37620
800-545-5811
phone: 800-545-5811

MORRIS
4476 Green Valley Road
Suisun City, CA 94585
phone: 707-864-1442
fax: 707-864-1209
moridairausa@att.net
www.morris-guitar.com

MORTORO, GARY
P.O. Box 161225
Miami, FL 33116-1225
phone: 305-238-7947
fax: 305-259-8745
mortorogtr@aol.com

MOSSMAN
1813 Main Street
Sulphur Springs, TX 75482
phone: 903-885-4992
tony@mossman-guitars.com
mossman-guitars.com

MUSIC INDUSTRIES CORPORATION
99 Tulip Avenue Suite 101
Floral Park, NY 11001
800-431-6699
phone: 516-352-4110
fax: 516-352-0754
mic@musicindustries.com
www.musicindustries.com

NYS
RR3 Box 84 Hauverville Road
Middleburgh, NY 12122
phone: 518-827-5965
fax: 518-827-5965
NYSBlackcreek@aol.com

NAPOLITANO, ARTHUR
P.O. Box 0294
Allentown, NJ 08501
phone: 609-259-8818
napolitanoguitar.home.att.net/
index.html

NASHVILLE GUITAR COMPANY
P.O. Box 160412
Nashville, TN 37216
phone: 615-262-4891
fax: 615-262-4891
nashgtar@bellsouth.net
www.nashguitar.com

NATIONAL RESO-PHONIC GUITARS
871 Via Esteban #C
San Luis Obispo, CA 93401
phone: 805-546-8442
fax: 805-546-8430
natres@nationalguitars.com
www.nationalguitars.com

NICKERSON
8 Easthampton Rd.
Northampton, MA 01060
phone: 413-586-8521
nickersonguitars@hotmail.com
www.nickersonguitars.com

NOBLE, ROY
8140 East Avenue U
Little Rock, CA 93543
phone: 661-944-5548
royrncg@mac.com
www.roynoble.net

NORMAN
19420 Ave. Clark Graham
Baie d' Urfe, PQ H9X 3R8 Canada
phone: 514-457-7977
fax: 514-457-5774
info@normanguitars.com
www.normanguitars.com

NORTHWOOD GUITARS
20445 62nd Ave #308
Langley, BC V3A 5E6 Canada
phone: 604-514-7576
fax: 604-514-7586
info@northwoodguitars.com
www.northwoodguitars.com

NORTHWORTHY
Main Road Hulland Ward
Ashbourne
Derbyshire, DE6 3EA England
phone: +44 (0)1335 370806
fax: +44 (0)1335 370806
info@northworthy.com
www.northworthy.com

OBERG GUITARS
1312 Cambridge Court
San Marcos, CA 92069
phone: 760-295-4428
sdluthier@yahoo.com
www.newmillguitar.com/
poberg.html

OLSON, JAMES A.
11840 Sunset Ave.
Circle Pines, MN 55014
phone: 763-780-5301
fax: 763-780-8513
www.olsonguitars.com

OLYMPIA
Distributed by Tacoma Guitars
4615 East 192nd Street
Tacoma, WA 98446
www.tacomaguitars.com

OMEGA GUITARS
R.R. 3 Box 3384 410 Shady Oaks
Drive E
Saylorsburg, PA 18353
phone: 610-381-4041
omegaguitars@hotmail.com
www.omegaguitars.com

OSCAR SCHMIDT INTERNATIONAL
Distributed by Washburn International
255 Corporate Woods Parkway
Vernon HIlls, IL 60061
800-877-6863
phone: 847-913-5511
fax: 847-913-7772
washburn@washburn.com
www.washburn.com

OTHON
8838 Greenback Lane
Orangevale, CA 95662-4019
phone: 916-988-8533
fax: 916-988-8533

OVATION
Distributed by Kaman Music Corp.
P.O. Box 507
Bloomfield, CT 06002-0507
phone: 860-243-7105
fax: 860-243-7287
info@ovationguitars.com
www.ovationguitars.com

OZARK

Distributed by Stentor Music Co. Ltd.
Albert North Road
Regiate, Surrey RH2 9EZ
phone: +44 (0) 1737-240226
fax: +44 (0) 1737-242748
info@stentor-music.com
www.stentor-music.com

PMC GUITARS

Distributed by Sound Trek Distributors U.S.A.
2119 W. Hillsborough Avenue
Tampa, FL 33603
888-466-TREK
phone: 888-466-TREK

PALMER

Distributed by Tropical Music Corporation
phone: 305-740-7454
fax: 305-666-7625
www.tropicalmusic.com

PAO CHIA

Distributed by Guangzhou Bourgade Musical Instruments Factory Co. Ltd.
www.paochia.com

PARKSONS

Distribute by Paxphil
#207 HYUNDAI BLDG. 982-4 YANGCHEON-KU
SEOUL, SHINWOL-DONG Korea
phone: 82-2-2607-8283/4
fax: 82-2-2607-8285
biech@paxphil.co.kr
www.paxphil.co.kr

PATRICK EGGLE GUITARS

Distributed by Maverick International Inc
1108 Kirkview Lane #102
Charlotte, NC 28213
phone: 704-599-3700

PAUL FISHER GUITARS

5290 Buckboard Lane
Paradise, CA 95969
phone: 530-876-9900
fisher@fishermodels.com
www.fishermodels.com

PAUL REED SMITH (PRS)

107 Log Canoe Circle
Stevensville, MD 21666
phone: 410-643-9970
fax: 410-643-9980
www.prsguitars.com

PAUL ROBINSON GUITARS

1500 Prairie Dog Drive
Modesto, CA 95355
phone: 209-529-8616
prguitars@sbcglobal.net

PEAL

Distributed by Ye-II International Company
phone: (82-31) 879-3175
fax: (82-31) 879-3389
yeilint@netsgo.com
www.guitar-peal.com

PEARL RIVER

wmk@pearlriverpiano.com
www.pearlriverpiano.com

PEAVEY

Peavey Electronics
711 A Street
Meridian, MS 39301
phone: 601-483-5365
www.peavey.com

PEERLESS

www.peerlessguitar.com

PERLMAN, ALAN

1319 48th Avenue
San Francisco, CA 94122
phone: 415-242-4457
alan@perlmanguitars.com
www.perlmanguitars.com

PETE BACK GUITARS

8 Silver Street Reeth
Richmond, Yorkshire DL11 6SP England
phone: 01748 884887
guitarman@guitarmaker.co.uk
www.guitarmaker.co.uk

PETILLO, PHILLIP J.

1206 Herbert Ave.
Ocean, NJ 07712-4035
phone: 732-531-6338
fax: 732-531-3045
Philluinc@aol.com
www.petilloguitars.com

PETROS

345 Co Rd CE
Kaukauna, WI 54130
phone: 920-766-1295
petros@petrosguitars.com
www.petrosguitars.com

PHIL

#141-3 Deungwon-Ri
Jori-Myun
Paju City, Kyunggi-do Korea
phone: 031 941-5477
fax: 031 941-7938

PICATO

Distributed bt Saga Musical Instruments - see listing

PICHKUR, JOE

Pichkur's Guitar Center
306 Jericho Turnpike
Floral Park, NY 11001
phone: 516-488-5343

PIGNOSE

3430 Precision Drive N.
Las Vegas, NV 89030
800-974-4667
fax: 702-648-3430
www.pignose.com

PIMENTEL & SONS

3316 Lafayette Dr. NE
Albuquerque, NM 87107
phone: 505-884-1669
info@pimentelguitars.com
www.pimentelguitars.com

PINKHAM, RONALD

Distributed by Woodsound Studio
P.O. Box 245
Glen Cove , ME 04846
phone: 207-596-7407

PREMIER

Premier Guitars & Amps Distributed by the Entertainment Music Marketing Corp.
770-9 Grand Blvd.
Deer Park, NY 11729
800-345-6013
phone: 516-243-0600
fax: 516-243-0605

PRENKERT, RICHARD

10992 Peaks Pike
Sebastopol, CA 95472
phone: 707-829-6719
fax: 707-829-6719
prenkertguitars@hotmail.com
www.maui.net/~rtadaki/prenkert.html

PRUDENCIO, SAEZ

Distributed by Saga Musical Instruments
www.sagamusic.com

RJS

Fort Worth, TX 76116
phone: 817-738-5780
modenaman@webtv.net
www.rjsguitars.com

RAIMUNDO

Distributed by Luthier Music Corporation
www.luthiermusic.com
www.raimundoyaparicio.com

RAINSONG

12604 NE 178th Street
Woodinville, WA 98072
phone: 425-485-7551
fax: 425-485-7274
webinquiry@rainsong.com
www.rainsong.com

RALSTON

P.O. Box 138
Grant Town, WV 26574

RANDALL KRAMER GUITARS

phone: 530-587-1757

REDGATE, J.K.

46 Penno Parade North
Belair, 5052 Australia
phone: 61 8 83703198
fax: 61 8 83703198
redgate@ozemail.com.au
www.cybozone.com/fg/redgate2.html

REGAL

Distributed by Saga Musical Instruments

RENAISSANCE GUITAR COMPANY

P.O. Box 93
Northport, NY 11768
800-644-5268
fax: 516-757-0021
chrisr@connollyandco.com

Renaissance Guitar Company Factory

P.O. Box 7440
Santa Cruz, CA 95060-7440

RENDANO, V.J.

V.j. Rendano Music Company Inc
777 E. 82nd St.
Cleveland, OH 44103
800-321-4048
phone: 800-321-4048
fax: 216-432-3642

RIBBECKE, TOM

P.O. Box 2215
Healdsburg, CA 95448
phone: 707-433-3778
ribguitar@aol.com
www.ribbecke.com

RICHTER, SCOTT

457 Scenic Road
Fairfax, CA 94930
phone: 415-453-1424
scott_richter@msn.com
www.richterguitars.com

RICK TURNER GUITARS

815 Almar Avenue
Santa Cruz, CA 95060
phone: 831-460-9144
rturner466@aol.com

RICKENBACKER

3895 S. Main Street
Santa Ana, CA 92707
phone: 714-545-5574
fax: 714-754-0135
sales@rickenbacker.com
www.rickenbacker.com

ROBERT GUITARS

Box 894
Summerland, BC V0H 1Z0
mail@robertguitars.com
www.robertguitars.com

ROBINSONG GUITARS

263 Irish Way
Pismo Beach, CA 93449
phone: 805-773-6698
info@robinsongguitars.com
robinsongguitars.com

RODRIGUEZ, MANUEL AND SONS

Distributed by Fender Musical Instrument Corporation
8860 E. Chaparral Road Suite 100
Scottsdale, AZ 85250-2618
phone: 480-596-9690
fax: 480-596-1384
www.fender.com/rodriguez

ROGUE

Distributed by the Musician's Friend
www.musiciansfriend.com

ROSEWOOD MUSIC

394 Lake Ave S.
Duluth, MN 55802
phone: 218-720-6086

RUBEN FLORES GUITARS

Distributed by Ruben Flores
P.O. Box 2746
Seal Beach, CA 90740-1746
phone: 562-598-9800
fax: 562-598-2459
ruben_flores@email.msn.com

RUCK, ROBERT

3611 Hanapepe Road
Hanapepe, HI 96716
phone: 808-335-6000
ruckguitars@earthlink.com
www.maui.net/~rtadaki/ruck.html

RUNNING DOG GUITARS

1394 Stage Road
Richmond, VA 05477
phone: 802-434-4399
vtguitars@aol.com
www.vtguitars.com

RUSSELL GUITARS

2249 Canal Drive
Redding, CA 96001
phone: 530-241-1921
james@russellguitars.com
www.russellguitars.com

S-101

Distributed by America Sejung Corporation
295 Brea Canyon Road
Walnut, CA 91789
phone: 909-839-0757
fax: 909-839-0713
sales@ascguitars.com
www.ascguitars.com

S3 GUITARS

3098 Country Club Court
Palo Alto, CA 94304
phone: 650-948-6689
steve@s3guitars.com
www.s3guitars.com

SAGA MUSICAL INSTRUMENTS

P.O. Box 2841
South San Francisco , CA 94080
800-BUY-SAGA
phone: 650-588-5558

SAMICK

424 Chongchon Dong
Pupyong-Gu, Inchon Korea
phone: 82-32-453-3361-4
fax: 82-32-453-3376-9
smi23@samick.co.kr
www.samickguitar.com

Samick U.S. Headquarters

18521 Railroad Street
City of Industry, CA 91748
800-592-9393
info@samickguitar.com
www.samickguitar.com

SAND, KIRK

1027 N. Pacific Coast Hwy
Laguna Beach, CA 92651
phone: 949-497-5570
fax: 949-497-5570
ksandca@aol.com
www.sandguitars.com

SANTA CRUZ

151 Harvey West Boulevard
Suite C
Santa Cruz, CA 95060
phone: 831-425-0999
fax: 831-425-3604
scgc@cruzio.com
www.santacruzguitar.com

SANTA FE GUITARS

Santa Fe Guitar Works
1412 Llano St.
Santa Fe, NM 87505
phone: 505-988-4240

SANTA ROSA

Distributed by A R Musical Enterprises
9031 Technology Drive
Fishers, IN 46038
phone: 317-577-6999
fax: 800-933-8207
info@armusical.com
www.armusical.com

SAVAGE

www.savageguitars.com

SCHAEFER GUITARS

4221 W. 4th Street
Duluth, MN 55807
phone: 218-624-7231
ed@schaeferguitars.com
www.schaeferguitars.com

SCHARPACH GUITARS

Kuiperstraat 46
Duiven , 6921GM The Netherlands
phone: +31-316-264512
fax: +31-497-540580
guitars@scharpach.com
www.scharpach.com

SCHECTER

Schecter Guitar Research
1840 Valpreda Street
Burbank, CA 91504
800-660-6621
phone: 818-846-2700
fax: 818-846-2727
www.schecterguitars.com

SCHEERHORN CUSTOM RESONATOR GUITARS

Distributed by Elderly Instruments
1100 North Washington
Lansing, MI 48906
888-473-5810
phone: 517-372-7890
fax: 517-372-5155
web@elderly.com
www.elderly.com

SCHOENBERG, ERIC

106 Main Street
Tiburon, CA 94920
phone: 415-789-0846
eric@om28.com
www.om28.com

SCHWARTZ, SHELDON

2717 Concession Road #5 RR1
Loretto, Ontario L0G 1L0 Canada
phone: 905-729-0024
sheldon@schwartzguitars.com
www.schwartzguitars.com

SEAGULL

Distributed by La Si Do, Inc.
19420 Ave. Clark Graham
Baie d Urfe, PQ H9X 3R8 Canada
phone: 514-457-7977
fax: 514-457-5774
www.seagullguitars.com

SERENO GUITARS

126 Greenbriar Lane
La Puente, CA 91744
phone: 626-336-1931
lynkev@earthlink.net

SEXAUER

724 H Street
Petaluma, CA 94952
phone: 707-782-1044
bruce@sexauerluthier.com
www.sexauerluthier.com

SHANTI GUITARS
P.O. Box 341
Avery, CA 95224
phone: 209-795-5299

SHELLEY D. PARK GUITARS
1755 East 2nd Avenue
Vancouver, BC V5N 1E3 Canada
phone: 604-988-4324
shelley1@attcanada.ca
www.parkguitars.com

SHIFFLETT, CHARLES R.
124 7 Avenue SW
High River , Alberta T1V 1A2
Canada
phone: 403-652-1526

SID JACOBS
3052 Lake Hollywood Drive
Los Angeles, CA 90068
phone: 323-874-4110
fax: 323-874-5408
sidjacobs@sidjacobs.com
sidjacobs.com

SILVERTONE
Distributed by Samick Music Corporation
18251 Railroad Street
City of Industry, CA 91748
phone: 626-964-4700
fax: 626-965-5224
guitars@samickmusic.com
www.samickguitar.com

SIMON & PATRICK
Distributed by La Si Do, Inc.
19420 Ave. Clark Graham
Baie d Urfe, PQ H9X 3R8 Canada
phone: 514-457-7977
fax: 514-457-5774
www.simonandpatrick.ca

SIMPSON GUITARS
www.simpsonguitars.com

SLAMAN GUITARS
Westeinde 58 2512 HE
Den Haag, The Netherlands
phone: 31 (0)70 389 42 32
daniel@slamanguitars.com
www.slamanguitars.com

SMILE MUSICAL INSTRUMENTS
321 Valle Vista
Monrovia, CA 91016
phone: 626-303-6392
wstaffo@cslanet.calstatela.edu

SOBELL, STEFAN
Distributed by Dream Guitars
4 Mountainview Court
Clarksburg, NJ 08510
phone: 609-208-153
info@dreamguitars.com
www.dreamguitars.com

SOMOGYI, ERVIN
516 52nd Street
Oakland, CA 94609
phone: 510-652-5123
esomogyi@aol.com
www.esomogyi.com

SOUND PORT TECHNOLOGY USA
18214 Parthenia St.
Northridge, CA 91324
phone: 909-464-2304

SOUND TREK DISTRIBUTORS U.S.A.
2119 W. Hillsboro Avenue
Tampa, FL 33603
888-466-TREK

SPIRIT GUITARS
1940 E. Sagebrush Street
Gilbert, AZ 85296
phone: 480-216-8298
bobnsg@cox.net

SQUIER
Distributed by Fender Musical
Instrument Corporation
8860 Chapparral Road Suite 100
Scottsdale, AZ 85250-2618
phone: 480-596-9690
fax: 480-367-5262
custserv@fenderusa.com
www.fender.com

ST. LOUIS MUSIC INC
1400 Ferguson Avenue
St. Louis, MO 63133
800-727-4512
phone: 314-727-4512
fax: 314-727-8929

STAGG
www.staggmusic.com

STEINEGGER, ROBERT
P.O. Box 25304
Portland, OR 97225

STEVENS CUSTOM GUITARS
www.guitars.de

STIEFEL GUITARS
P.O. Box 58828
Salt Lake City, UT 84158
phone: 801-914-6940
ssteifel@hsc.utah.edu

STOLL
Distributed by Salwender International
Schwalbacher Str. 18
Waldems-Esch, 65529 Germany
phone: +49 6126 589888
fax: +49 6126 589889
info@Stollguitars.de
www.stollguitars.de

SUZUKI
P.O. Box 261030
San Diego, CA 92196
phone: 858-566-9710
www.suzuki.com

SWARTELE GUITARS
Rushville, NY 14544
phone: 585-554-3573
www.swartele.com

T. CERLETTI GUITARS
Healdsburg, CA
phone: 707-433-4749
t@cerletti.com
www.cerletti.com

TACOMA
4615 East 192nd Street
Tacoma, WA 98446
phone: 253-847-6508
fax: 253-847-1599
www.tacomaguitars.com

TAKAMINE
Distributed by Kaman Music Corporation
P.O. Box 507
Bloomfield, CT 06002-0507
info@takamine.com
www.takamine.com

TAKU SAKASHTA GUITARS
P.O. Box 2403
Sebastopol, CA 95473
phone: 707-823-0284
sakashtaguitars@california.com
www.sakashtaguitars.com

TANARA
Distributed by the Chesbro Music
Company
327 Broadway
Idaho Falls, ID 83402
phone: 208-522-8691
retailsales@chesbromusic.com
www.chesbromusicretail.com

TANGLEWOOD
Unit 6 Concorde Business Centre
Biggin Hill
Kent, TN16 3YN England
fax: 01959 572267
emc@tanglewoodguitars.co.uk
www.tanglewoodguitars.co.uk

TAYLOR
1980 Gillespie Way
El Cajon, CA 92020-1096
800-943-6782
phone: 619-258-6957
www.taylorguitars.com

THREET GUITARS
#212 1215 13th Street S.E.
Calgary, Alberta T2G 3J4 Canada
phone: 403-232-8332

TICE, BOB
Robert Tice Luthier
HCR #1 Box 465
Sciota, PA 18354
phone: 570-992-5695
fax: 570-992-5695
luthier@enter.net

TIMELESS INSTRUMENTS
P.O. Box 51
Tugaske, Saskatchewan S0H 4B0
Canada
1-888-884-2753
fax: 306-759-2729
david@timelessinstruments.com
www.timelessinstruments.com

TIMM, JERRY
4512 47th Street S.E.
Auburn, WA 98092
phone: 253-833-8667
fax: 253-833-1820

TIPPIN GUITAR COMPANY
3 Beacon Street
Marblehead, MA 01945
phone: 781-631-5749
fax: 781-639-0934
bill@tippinguitar.com
www.tippinguitar.com

TOBIAS, MICHAEL
Michael Tobias Design
3 Lauren Court
Kingston, NY 12401
phone: 845-246-0670
fax: 845-246-1670
mike@mtdbass.com
www.mtdbass.com

TOM BILLS CUSTOM GUITARS
9712 Radio Drive
St. Louis, MO 63123
phone: 314-631-1435
tom@tbguitars.com
www.tbguitars.com

TOM BLACKSHEAR
17303 Springhill Drive
San Antonio, TX 78232-1552
phone: 210-494-1141
fax: 210-494-1141
tguitars@texas.net

TOMMYHAWK
19 Rt. 10 Bldg 1
Suite 3
Succasuanna, NJ 07876
phone: 973-927-6711
NJLuck@aol.com
www.tommyhawk.com

TOWNSEND GUITARS
516 52nd Street
Oakland, CA 94609
phone: 510-847-4988

TRAUGOTT, JEFF
2553 B Mission Street
Santa Cruz, CA 95060
phone: 831-426-2313
fax: 831-426-0187
jeff@traugottguitars.com
www.traugottguitars.com

TRIGGS, JAMES W.
phone: 913-962-2254
jim@triggsguitars.com
www.triggsguitars.com

TRUE NORTH GUITARS
175 Perry Lea Side Ride
Waterbury, VT 05676
phone: 802-244-6488
dennis@truenorthguitars.com
www.truenorthguitars.com

US BAND & ORCHESTRA SUPPLIES INC
1933 Woodson Road
St. Louis, MO 63114
800-844-9653
phone: 314-429-3439
fax: 314-429-3255

VAGABOND
P.O. Box 845
Albany, NY 12201
800-801-1341
luthier@stringsmith.com
www.stringsmith.com

VALLEY ARTS
A Division of Gibson
1121 Church Street
Nashville, TN 37203
phone: 615-244-0252
www.valleyartsguitar.com/
index.html

VEILLETTE GUITARS
2628 Route 212
Woodstock, NY 12498
phone: 845-679-6154
joe@veilletteguitars.com
www.veilletteguitars.com

VENSON
Room 605 Dongyang Plaza #152
Gumgok-Dong
Pungdang-Gu
Sungnam-Shi, Kyonggi-Do 463-480
Korea
phone: 82-31-713-3996/7
fax: 82-31-713-5777
venson@unitel.co.kr
www.venson.co.kr

VERSOUL
Kutomotie 13 C
Helsinki, FIN-00380 Finland
phone: + 358 9 565 1876
fax: + 358 9 565 1876
kari.nieminen@versoul.com
www.versoul.com

VINES, TONY
243 E Charlemont Avenue
Kingsport, TN 37660
phone: 423-245-5952
vinesguitars@hotmail.com
www.tonyvinesguitars.com

VINTAGE
Distributed by John Hornby Skewes
Salem House Parkinson Approach
Garforth
Leeds, LS25 2HR United Kingdom
phone: (+44) (0) 113 286 5381
fax: (+44) (0) 113 286 8515
webinfo@jhs.co.uk
www.jhs.co.uk

WALDEN
800-994-4984
www.waldenguitars.com

WALKER GUITARS
314 Pendleton Hill Road
North Stonington, CT 06359
phone: 860-599-1907
WalkerGtrs@aol.com
www.walkerguitars.com

WARWICK
Distributed by Dana B. Goods
4054 Transport St Unit A.
Ventura , CA 93003
800-741-0109
fax: 805-644-6332
www.warwick.de

Warwick Factory
Distributed by Dana B. Goods
Gewerbegebiet Wohlhausen
Markneukirchen, Germany
phone: 0049-037422-555-0
fax: 0049-037422-555-99
info@warwick.sh.cn
www.warwick.de

WASHBURN
A Division of U.S. Music Corporation
444 East Courtland Street
Mundelein, IL 60060
phone: 847-949-0444
fax: 847-949-8444
washburn@washburn.com
www.washburn.com

WEBBER GUITARS
1385A Crown St.
North Vancouver, British Columbia
Canada
phone: 604-980-0315
david@axion.net
www.webberguitar.com

WECHTER GUITARS
phone: 763-537-7374

WILLIE CARTER GUITARS
phone: 831-402-0648
wcarterguitars@earthlink.net

WOOD, RANDY
1304 E. Highway 80
Bloomingdale, GA 31302
phone: 912-748-1930
fax: 912-354-3408
info@randywoodguitars.com
www.randywoodguitars.com

WOODTONE GUITARS
14 Bayley Street
Hamilton, VIC 03300 Australia
phone: 011-61-3-557-11477
woodtoneguitars@bigpond.com

WORLAND GUITARS
810 N. First Street
Rockford, IL 61107
phone: 815-961-8854

YAMAHA
6600 Orangethorpe Ave.
P.O. Box 6600
Buena Park, CA 90622-6600
www.yamaha.com

YURIY
phone: 909-902-1092
yfs64@inreach.com

ZEIDLER
201 W. Rose Valley Road
Wallingford, PA 19086
phone: 610-566-1097
jrzeidler@aol.com
www.zeidler.com

ZIMNICKI
15106 Garfield
Allen Park, MI 48101
phone: 313-381-2817
gzim@flash.net
www.zimnicki.com

INDEX

A

H

PS: ACOUSTIC ALPHABET QUEST

So all you rocket scientists think you know your Trademark logos pretty well, huh? Here is an interactive game to see how smart you really are. There is one letter from each of the 26 in the alphabet, and each of the letters is a letter from a trademark in the guitar industry. See if you can identify what they are by just seeing one letter. Answers are posted on our website at www.bluebookinc.com. Remember, this is meant to be fun, so forget about $E=MC^2$ for awhile!

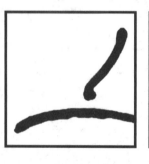    

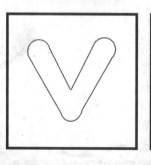